TATTOO TRADITIONS OF ASIA

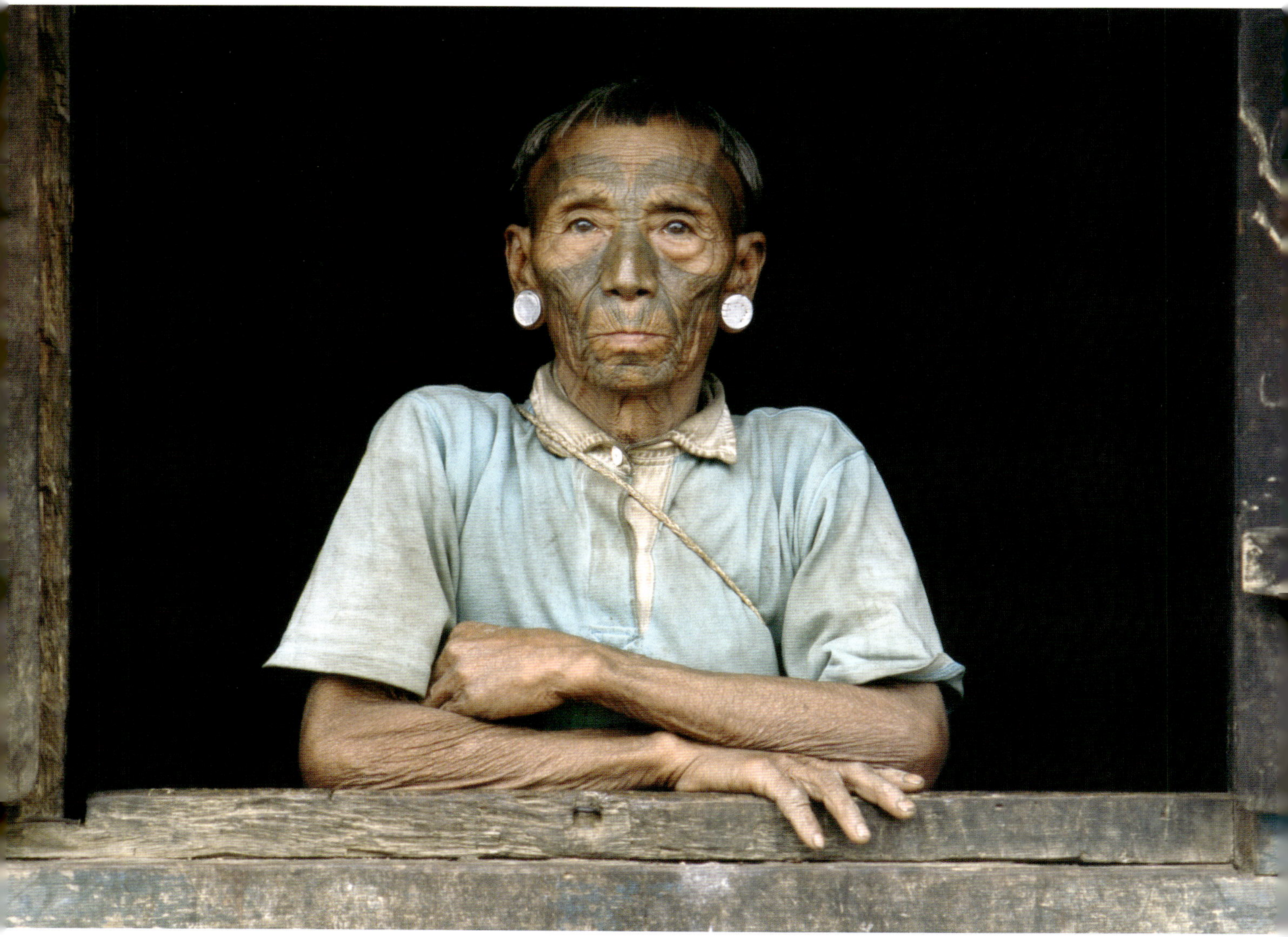

LARS KRUTAK

TATTOO TRADITIONS OF ASIA

ANCIENT AND CONTEMPORARY EXPRESSIONS OF IDENTITY

UNIVERSITY OF HAWAIʻI PRESS
HONOLULU

Printed in China

First printing, 2024

Library of Congress Cataloging-in-Publication Data

Names: Krutak, Lars F., author.
Title: Tattoo traditions of Asia : ancient and contemporary expressions of identity / Lars Krutak.
Description: Honolulu : University of Hawaiʻi Press, [2024] | Includes bibliographical references and index.
Identifiers: LCCN 2023040809 (print) | LCCN 2023040810 (ebook) | ISBN 9780824895709 (hardcover) | ISBN 9780824897956 (pdf) | ISBN 9780824897970 (kindle edition) | ISBN 9780824897963 (epub)
Subjects: LCSH: Tattooing—Asia—History. | Indigenous art—Asia. | Indigenous peoples—Asia—Social life and customs.
Classification: LCC GT2346.A8 K78 2024 (print) | LCC GT2346.A8 (ebook) | DDC 391.6/5095—dc23/eng/20230927
LC record available at https://lccn.loc.gov/2023040809
LC ebook record available at https://lccn.loc.gov/2023040810

Publication of this book has been assisted by grants from

Daniele Agostino Derossi Foundation

Furthermore: a program of the J. M. Kaplan Fund

University of Hawaiʻi Press books are printed on acid-free paper and meet the guidelines for permanence and durability of the Council on Library Resources.

Designed by Mardee Melton

Cover: Posen Mangyut, a Lazu Naga elder, Khonsa, Arunachal Pradesh, India, 2008. Photograph © Lars Krutak. *Frontispiece:* Khohap, a Konyak Naga elder and former warrior of Tang village, Nagaland, 2010. Photograph © Lars Krutak.

Dedication page: Photograph courtesy of Daniele Agostino Derossi

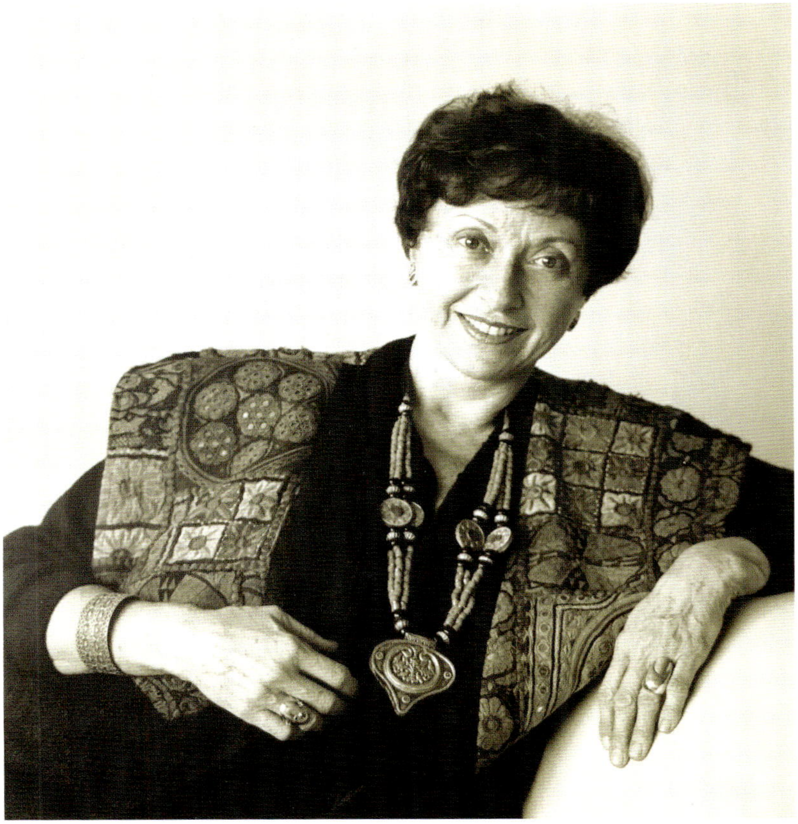

To the memory of

FLAVIA ROBINSON DEROSSI
(1926–2014)

who dedicated her life to supporting Indigenous education, health, nutrition, housing, and socioeconomic development around the world

Contents

Preface

My history of engagement with Indigenous tattoo traditions predates my initial fieldwork experiences in Asia, which began in 2002. As an anthropology graduate student in Alaska (1996–1998), my master's thesis focused on the little-studied tattooing practices of the St. Lawrence Island Yupik people living in the northern Bering Sea. On this windswept and treeless island, I was fortunate to be invited by community leaders to work with the last generation of tattooed female elders and their families. Over pots of coffee, boiled seal meat wrapped in seaweed, and fresh whale meat dipped in butter, together we recorded the biographical and community histories behind these hard-earned markings that encompassed clan and family identities, social achievements, and rites of passage as well as those associated with spiritual beliefs and therapeutic practices. Realizing that this significant Indigenous cultural heritage would likely vanish within the next generation, I began to think and read about other locations in the Indigenous world where remarkable tattooing traditions endured but had yet to be carefully documented through meaningful collaborations with other Indigenous communities.

In turn, I traveled to Bosnia (1998), Kosovo (2000–2001), and northern Greece (2002) to learn about Indigenous tattooing traditions among Catholic, Vlach, and other local populations, and as this preliminary research concluded, I was invited to travel to Borneo (2002) to help photograph and document the tattooing traditions of the Skrang River Iban of Sarawak for a National Geographic International Channel pilot project. I had never visited Asia before this trip.

It was an exceptionally humid September morning when we arrived on the Skrang. At the boat jetty, we learned that the approximately eighty-seven-year-old Iban master tattoo artist and designer Mang anak Jilap of Rumah Entalau, whom we had planned to meet, was deathly ill and about ready to meet his ancestors. Traveling with several of Mang's family friends, including Iban tattoo artist Eddie David, we asked the production team if we could split off from the group after reaching our first destination, Lalang longhouse, which was four hours upriver from our launching point. As our services were not necessary for a couple of days, they agreed, but by the time we reached Lalang darkness was fast approaching. Here we received more information regarding

Mang's deteriorating condition, and we immediately transported our supplies into another dugout and sped off upriver with our headlamps firmly fastened.

For the next several hours our expert Iban boatmen navigated a series of treacherous rapids, pockets of car-size logs speeding downstream, and whirlpools—believed to be haunted by evil spirits—that had claimed countless human lives over the generations. These watery graves were feared and greatly respected, and as we approached each one our voices fell eerily silent.

Exhausted and weary after a long day of dangerous travel on the unpredictable Skrang, we finally arrived at Entalau around 11 p.m. We walked down the long communal *ruai,* or verandah of the longhouse, and entered Mang's *bilik,* or apartment. Here, the old tattoo master was curled up on the floor and covered with a blanket. His eyes were closed, skin pale, and the bones of his emaciated frame seemed to almost pierce his flesh. He was surrounded by a circle of female relatives, some of whom were whispering among themselves or quietly sobbing. One of these women announced our arrival, and Mang's eyes opened and he slowly returned to life. He sat up and recognized Eddie immediately, and a wide grin spread across his wrinkled face. We provided him with a few gifts, and he was extremely happy we had made the long journey; now he wanted to speak with us. And for the next three hours, he entertained us with tales of adventure, war, magic, and tattoo.

Luckily, we had brought a small first-generation HD video camera and captured these incredible moments together, which were later broadcast. Eddie told me that Mang revealed to us many "secrets" he had never shared with them before, including a special charm—a meteorite—he sometimes dipped into the tattooing pigment he made for "protective" purposes. Mang also spoke about his *antu nulong,* or tattoo spirit guide, and about Sebayan, the Iban land of the dead.

Sadly, our time with Mang had come to an end, and as I shook his hand to thank him for an incredible evening, I said we would come back in the morning to say goodbye before our return to Lalang. We then headed to the *bilik* of Eddie's cousin Legan, the former *penghulu,* or headman of the Skrang Iban. We found our beds upon the floor and prepared for a well-deserved rest. For the first thirty minutes I stared at the ceiling, and my mind raced with thoughts of Mang and other tattooed Indigenous elders I had interviewed in the past. So much traditional knowledge associated with Indigenous tattooing culture and practice was becoming lost before it could be properly recorded, and I wished that I had been born one hundred years earlier. So much more could have been done!

At that moment a very loud clap of thunder erupted nearby, signaling a fast-approaching storm. Powerful flashes of lightning began to streak across the dark sky, which I could see through the cracks in the longhouse walls and ceiling. I could feel the force of the lightning as it echoed through the air and seemingly reverberated through the very foundations of the longhouse itself. But just as quickly as it came, the storm disappeared and all was quiet again.

Eddie and I awoke early the next morning. As we sipped hot tea and ate our morning meal, we heard a knock on the door of Legan's *bilik.* A woman I recognized from the night before entered, and she said that Mang had died in his sleep.

This book celebrates Mang's memory and attempts to preserve the stories and biographies of other tattooed Indigenous men and women across Asia who, for two decades, have shared with me their homes, memories, and experiences of tattooing.

Acknowledgments

This book is the result of many unique voices and life experiences that have been, and continue to be, enmeshed in the cultures and landscapes that gave rise to them. Several of my Asian travels and investigations were funded by the Daniele Agostino Derossi Foundation (DADF) and the late Flavia Robinson Derossi through four Special Projects grants (Philippines, Nagaland, Sarawak, and Myanmar). I originally met Flavia, who was a passionate photographer, with my wife, Heidi, during PhD fieldwork on ethnic tourism in the Rarámuri village of Norogachi, Mexico, in 2005. Here, she was reviewing a grant proposal to fund an Indigenous women's health project. She was then in her midseventies, and she and her assistant needed a ride to the nearest bus station in Creel. During our several hours' journey we spoke about our mutual interests and my previous research focusing on Indigenous women, tattooing, and photography. Flavia suggested that if I ever returned to the field to document Indigenous women's tattooing, I should apply for a Special Projects grant in photography, and three years later I did—*thankfully with success!*—to build on my earlier research of Kalinga tattooing traditions in the northern Philippines. The result of this collaboration led to the publication of *Kalinga Tattoo: Ancient and Modern Expressions of the Tribal* (2010), the first single volume on the tattooing traditions of these Cordilleran people of the northern Philippines. Additional DADF support made it possible to travel to Sarawak in 2011, leading to the publication of *Spiritual Skin: Magical Tattoos and Scarification* (2012). Over the years, our conversations continued via email and in person at her home in Torino, Italy, with additional DADF funds supporting two extended trips to the Naga regions of India and Myanmar. Most of this Naga material remained unpublished, but now it has been brought together to form the basis of chapter 6.

Flavia's nephew Daniele Derossi and the board of the DADF have helped us bring this beautiful book to print through a generous subvention grant. In December 2023, *Furthermore*, a program of the J. M. Kaplan Fund provided yet another book subvention grant. These funds have been deployed to make this book the best it can be and to contribute to our understanding of the antiquity, durability, and significance of Indigenous Asian tattooing, illuminating how different societies of the past and present employ(ed) their skins in the construction of their identities.

Moreover, I remain indebted to Vince Hemingson for inviting me to travel to Sarawak in 2002 to take part in the filming of the National Geographic International Channel's pilot *The Vanishing Tattoo*. This was my first trip to Asia, and our experiences on the Skrang River with the intrepid Iban of Entalau and Emperan, not to mention my solo visits to the various Orang Ulu peoples (Kayan, Kejaman, Sihan, Punan Bah, and Lahanan) of the upper Rajang River, will always be remembered and cherished.

Fieldwork was also made possible by Half Yard Productions and the Discovery Channel through their support of my television series *Tattoo Hunter*. During our filming in 2006–2008, I was fortunate enough to travel to several Indigenous Asian communities (Kalinga, Mentawai, Wancho, and Thai) to learn about local tattooing traditions and associated cultural and religious practices.

I extend my gratitude to Apo Whang-Od Oggay and Grace Palicas for being valued friends and collaborators during my stays in Buscalan village (Kalinga Province, Philippines), and to the late Ashok Elwin (d. 2023) of Shillong, Meghalaya, for opening his home and father's Naga archive to me on separate occasions; indeed, Elwin Verrier's meticulous field notebooks from the time of the 1950s shed light on many aspects of Naga tattooing that have largely been forgotten.

With a heavy heart I send my deepest condolences to the family of the charismatic and empathetic *sikerei* (shaman) Aman Lau Lau Manai of the Buttui clan, who passed in February 2023. He was a defender of his people and culture and keeper of the rainforest, and I will always cherish our time together on Siberut and the experiences and laughter we shared, which seem like they were yesterday. May your spirit soar forever.

As noted, I have spent the better part of twenty years assembling the information presented in this book. My journeys have taken me to museum collections and archives on four continents, more than two hundred Indigenous communities, and the homes of hundreds of tattooed elders, Indigenous knowledge experts, and tattoo artists who are named within the pages of *Tattoo Traditions of Asia*. As a collaborative project, this book would never have been possible without their support and tutelage, and I greatly respect, admire, and thank them all for sharing their stories.

Special accolades must be given to author and traveling companion Phejin Konyak, who always infused our journeys across Nagaland with much needed humor, energy, wit, and cultural knowledge of her people. I am eternally grateful to Uipo Naga tattoo artist Mo Naga for our enduring friendship over the years and our wide-ranging conversations in Guwahati and Delhi. I remain indebted to my Chen Naga collaborators and house hosts Chen-o Khuzuthrupa of Hoyang (d. 2023) and Chenngam Khuzuthrulymn Konyak of Chenwetnyu village for sharing their personal experiences and knowledge with me, not to mention the late Tolei Angh (d. 2023), who shared many details about the Chen "tiger-spirit" tattoo over hot tea and biscuits at his family hearth. I would also like to thank Anungla Longkumer, Temsuyanger Longkumer, Arkotong Longkumer, Phorchun Mema, and Khunwang TangJang for providing interview material and other important Naga resources. Additional backing for the Naga chapter was made possible by crowdfunding support for the documentary series *Patterns of Life*, and filmmakers Michael Zomer and Sophie Brouwer. My late friend and traveling partner Neisatuo Keditsu (d. 2017) of Kohima made my first journeys (in 2008 and 2010) into Nagaland possible during the Restricted Area Permit days. I will never forget our expeditions and experiences together "hunting for tattoos."

Other individuals provided guidance, contacts, photography, research materials, tattoo knowledge, humor, and warm meals and coffee when I needed them the most. In this regard, I extend my sincere appreciation and deepest gratitude to Jens Uwe Parkitny; Saw Hla Chit; Stéphane Gros; Chen Wen-Shan (Angusan); Rafe Walters and Yayun Veihui; Ryoichi Keroppy Maeda; Chao-Ling Kuo; Gunther C. O. Deichmann; Weichun Huang; Prof. Yousuke Kaifu; Tzi-Ning Li; Dr. John Ting-Hui Ho; Lin Min-hsuan; Huang Ju-Huang; Hu Yaling; Emily Shen; Thomas Murray and Wenhua Liu; Charles LeNoir; Andy Maluche; Analyn Salvador-Amores; Javier Rodríguez Barrera; Elle Festin; Joe Ash; Mark of the Four Waves Tribe; Missouri Historical Society; Ben Neild; Dan EDan; Ruel Bimuyag; James Mascariñas; Sidney Snoeck; Andrea Malaya M. Ragragio; Jacob Maentz; Monica Freeman; Sonia Solmssen; Simon and Eddie David; Sven Torfinn; Jeroen Franken; Mang anak Jilap; Michael Heppell; Sitty Nurhamiza; Dr. Jérôme Rousseau; Hulo Luhat; Dr. Chris Darling; Valentina Dragotto, Gianluca Lazzerini, and the Associazione Culturale Firenze Indelebile; Matthias Reuss; Anthony Howarth; Sébastien Galliot; Anne and Julien; Sean Mallon; Benoît Robitaille; Aaron Deter-Wolf; Yasmine Bergner; Daniel Levoh; Charles Lindsay; Tomasz Madej; Abel Jaboh; Peter Bos; Dr. Janet Hoskins; Bernadino Soares; Fajar Dhika Vandra; Stacii Samidi; Rachèl Luttikhuisen Tauran; Yves Picq; Wang Qingyuan; Nicholas Haimendorf; Jonathan Derksen; Ruokuonuo Yhome; Michael Laukien; and Peter van Ham.

I would also like to thank Dr. Sinah Kloß (Universität Bonn) and Dr. Jeffrey Schrader (University of Colorado Denver) for inviting me to present preliminary papers at international conferences in Cologne and New York City that have come to inform chapter sections.

Documenting the history and significance of the Indigenous tattoo traditions of Asia would have been quite difficult without the assistance of the following museums, archives, libraries, and other institutions that provided permission to reproduce written documents, drawings, objects of material culture, and photography. They include Sarawak Museum Department, Kuching; National Museum of Natural History and National Anthropological Archives, Smithsonian Institution; Penn Museum and Archives, Philadelphia; Metropolitan Museum of Art, New York; Library of Congress; University Museum, the University of Tokyo; National Taiwan Museum; National Taiwan University, Department of Anthropology; Taiwan Panorama; Laiyi Indigenous Museum; Museo Nacional de Antropología, Madrid; Field Museum; State Library of New South Wales; National Library of Australia; Leiden University Library; Wellcome Library Collection; British Library; Tropenmuseum; Brighton & Hove Museums; Muséum National d'histoire naturelle, Paris; University of London, Special Collections, SOAS Library; National Museum of Ethnology, Leiden; Frobenius-Institut; Kauffmann Nachlass, Institut für Ethnologie, University of Munich; and Pitt Rivers Museum.

I would also like to give special recognition to Stephanie Chun, Gianna Marsella, Ivo Fravashi, Wendy Lawrence, Mardee Melton, and the staff at the University of Hawaiʻi Press and to two anonymous peer reviewers for bringing my dream into reality by assisting with the publication of this work. Numerous others, including my wife Heidi and daughter Neena, also supported me over the course of this long journey, and I thank you all with a warm embrace.

Note on Terms

The terms "Indigenous" and "Native" are capitalized throughout this book because they are used as proper nouns and adjectives describing certain ethnic groups. Furthermore, the terms are capitalized because they articulate and identify one or more groups of sovereign political and historical communities, compared to lowercase "indigenous" or "native," which can refer to anyone. The capitalization of these terms is a rejection of Euro-American society's history of viewing Indigenous Peoples as having no legitimate national identities.

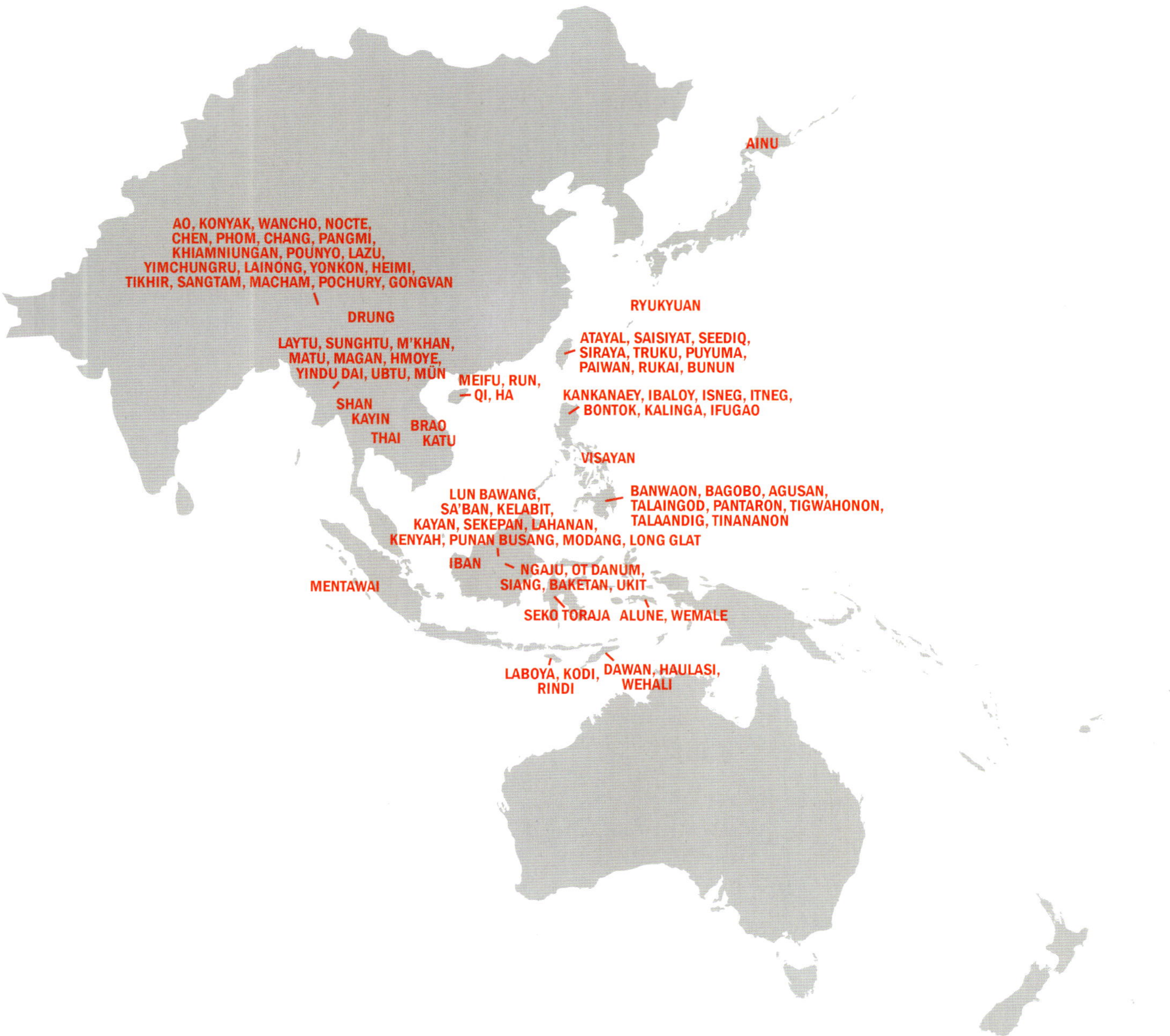

Indigenous societies discussed in the text.

INTRODUCTION

What seems to have been largely forgotten in contemporary conversations concerning the popularity of tattooing, as well as its cultural heritage, is the role that Indigenous Peoples inhabiting Asia played in the invention of some of the world's oldest tattoos. For millennia, the Indigenous tattoos of Asia have documented the history of humanity one painful mark at a time. Although these ancient traditions span numerous countries, ancestral lands, and a multitude of societies, no single volume has been dedicated to the anthropological study of this globally significant Indigenous cultural heritage until now. Indeed, the history of tattooing here remains poorly understood and fragmented. This is due in large part to the geographical expanse of Asia and the suppression of tattooing by colonial, missionary, governmental, and other acculturative agents of change. Moreover, most early ethnographic sources about tattooing appear in obscure journals that for English-language readers have not been translated from Chinese, Japanese, German, Dutch, and other sources. These and other invaluable accounts, including unpublished notebooks, fieldnotes, and manuscript materials, are housed in sometimes distant archival collections that, for the most part, are difficult to access (i.e., do not appear online), remain uncataloged, and are largely unknown to the public.

For the present volume, however, I have stitched together all these fragments of tattoo history, translating numerous foreign language sources into English for the first time. I have also scoured museum, archival, and private collections worldwide to reconnect readers to the intangible cultural heritage of a near universal cultural tradition that in some Indigenous areas of the world has faded from view but in others has been revitalized through the inspirational works of contemporary tattoo practitioners. Apart from this painstaking work, since 2002 I have conducted numerous field research expeditions across mainland and insular Southeast Asia. From Borneo to Taiwan and from Nagaland to Indonesia and points beyond, over a twenty-year period I recorded the voices and captured the portraits of hundreds of Native knowledge experts and tattooed elders, many of whom have since passed away. I deeply treasure the invaluable cultural knowledge that was shared with me, because it helped me to better understand how tattooing operated in local

FIGURE I.1
U Shwe Kyi is an octogenarian from Kankeret village, Myanmar, 2015. "I was tattooed by master U Pan Sein, a Bama, when I was seventeen years old. I still remember the sound the tattoo needle made when penetrating my skin: *tschwa, tschwa, tschwa* . . . and the pain when the knee area was tattooed!" he recalled. "The master gave me a special betel nut to chew so I could bear the pain; it was charged with his spiritual power. When my waist was tattooed, helpers of the master had to hold me down as it was so painful. . . . When I was young," he said, "I performed traditional martial arts and before every match I showed my tattoo. I don't like the contemporary tattoos of young men nowadays. They are of poor design and are not related to our traditions." © Jens Uwe Parkitny.

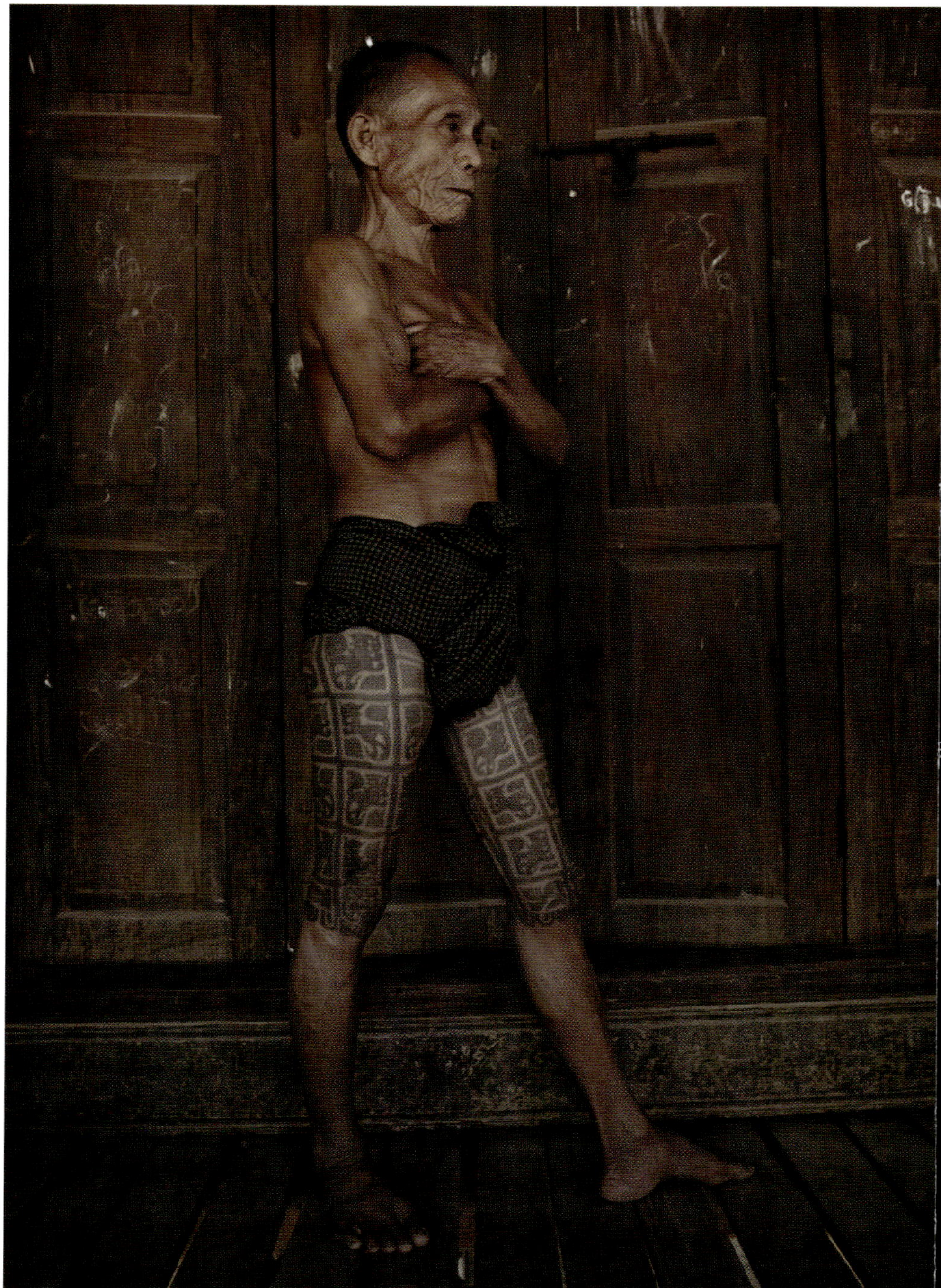

societies through the purview of an Indigenous perspective. This information also allowed me to analyze and critique extant literary sources in order to bring you—the reader—accurate, nuanced, and culturally informed content concerning the scope and diversity of these Indigenous body modification practices.

Notwithstanding, I have also been supported by numerous photographers in these encyclopedic endeavors, and many of their exquisite images appear within the pages of this book. Furthermore, I have invited two of my colleagues, Myanmar-based scholar and image maker Jens Uwe Parkitny and Dr. Stéphane Gros (Centre National de la Recherche Scientifique), to contribute their research to this volume. Their expertise on Indigenous body marking in Myanmar and Southwest China provides new insights into the tattooing traditions of the Chin, Kayin, and Drung people. Parkitny's stunning photography, which focuses on some of the last tattoo bearers of the Kayin and Chin, accentuates this volume in profound ways. His Kayin photos have never appeared in print.

STORIES ON SKIN

For the purposes of this volume, Asia will be defined as comprising China, mainland and insular Southeast Asia, Japan, and Northeast India where related tattooing traditions and technologies endured. Across these regions the practice of Indigenous tattooing, or the process of inserting pigment into the skin to create lasting permanent designs and iconography (see Deter-Wolf and Krutak 2017), served as a powerful visual language of the skin that spoke to the people who witnessed it as well as the person who wore it. As a cultural text, tattoo permanently recorded the memories, life stories, rites of passage, ancestral ties, spiritual values, and communal and personal achievements of its bearers on skin for all to see and read.

In recent decades several authors have described Indigenous forms of tattooing as a process of writing or visual language of the body (e.g., Caplan 2000; Dinter and Khoo 2020; Ellis 2008; Friedman 2015; Schildkrout 2001; Woods 2012, etc.). However, they refrain from explaining what is meant by these broad generalizations. Thus, what does it mean to say that Indigenous tattoos—or any tattoos for that matter—are texts or even a visual language of the skin?

In this volume, I unpack this question by considering how tattooed skin across Asia embodied a powerful narrative function that was fundamental in establishing personal and collective identity, and a person's time and place in the world. For me, Indigenous tattoos, no matter where they were created, represented the individual like a name and transmitted aspects of a person's being beyond their corporeal limits. Because with tattooing "the body multiplies . . . and subsidiary selves are created; spirits, ancestors, and [others] take up residence in an integument which begins to take on a life of its own" (Gell 1993:39). Although the meanings of specific designs may not always be decipherable or easily interpretable today, especially by people who are not equipped to read them, Indigenous tattoo bearers across Asia who were enculturated into these visual worlds of ink were able to retrieve information about others because tattoos made people and their cultural worlds clearly understood. Even though other communication technologies, including material culture, conveyed meanings comparable to tattoos, human beings produced tattoos because there was

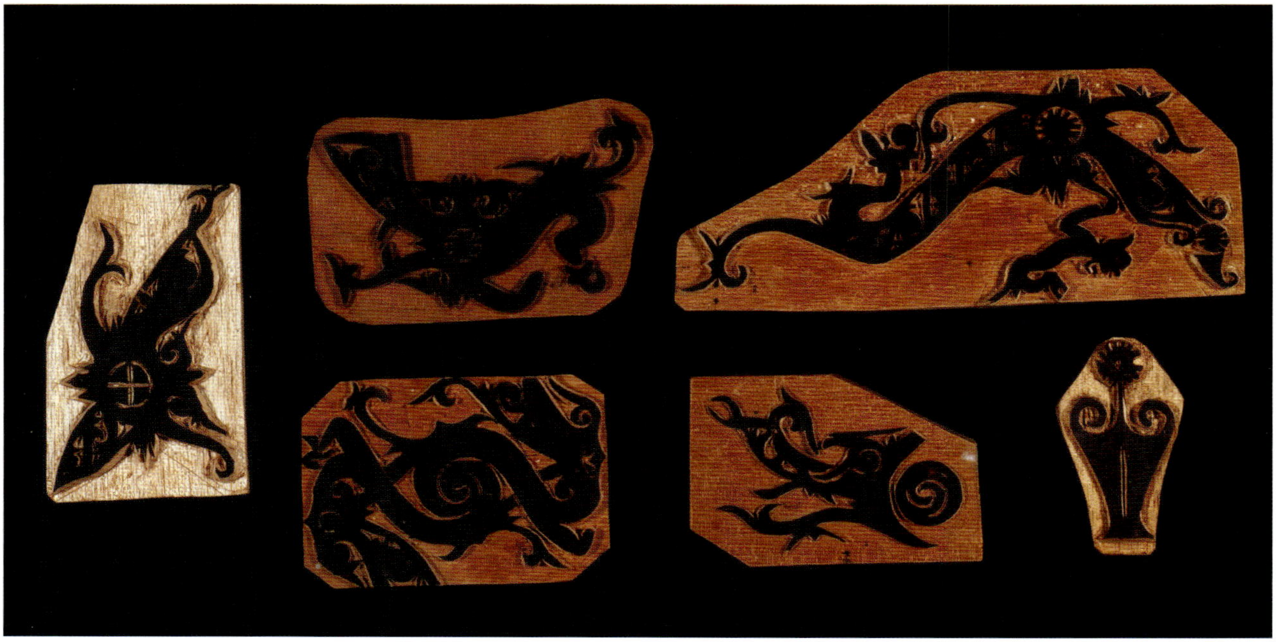

FIGURE I.2
Iban *cuan telingai* (tattoo stencil blocks), ca. 1905. *Left, top row: undai* (prawn), *aso'* (dragon-dog), *kala* (scorpion); *bottom row: naga belanggar* (facing dragons), *naga* (dragon), and *katak* (frog) throat tattoo. Collection of Pitt Rivers Museum, Oxford (1923.86).

something that demanded to be expressed that could not otherwise be articulated via other mediums of communication (cf. Eco 1997). The permanent and personal nature of tattoos made them special, implying an unconditional adhesion to a vision of the world. And it was through these visual cues that societies become conscious of who they are vis-à-vis other beings from the human and even nonhuman worlds. Tattoos transmitted information regarding where a person came from, what territory they belonged to, and who their ancestors were (see Trimble 2018). Tattooed bodies were the containers of personal and collective existence, of experience and personality, and performed a significant role in integrating sociocultural relationships while also (re)producing and organizing world views.

Indigenous tattooing operated like writing. Although some scholars may not agree with this view, tattoos do possess a strong and unambiguous declarative power through which people tell stories. And for millennia these traditions of body marking have been deployed as a system of intercommunication based on the use of conventional visible marks produced on durable surfaces (see von Petzinger 2016), namely human skin. While it is not known who produced the first tattoos, the origins of the practice have been linked to specific named and unnamed deities and spirits through oral histories (Batchelor 1882:213; Galliot 2018:26–27; Horton 1948:281; Light 1972:13; Lowenstein 1993:70; Molnar 2011:99n20; Skinner 1926:267; Te Awekotuku 2007:12–14) and symbols appearing on objects of material culture (Chenciner, Ismailov, and Magomedkhanov 2006:24, 39–40; Papa 2013; Rudenko 1929; Tillema 1930:204), some of which are very ancient.

Notwithstanding these ethnographic insights, independent subjective thought must have played a significant role in the development of tattooing, because the first tattoos were undoubtedly inspired by representations of fundamental images derived from nature (e.g., plant life, animal forms, celestial objects, landmarks, etc.) that humans created for themselves to communicate and to convey specific types of information. This new visual framework offered a method for transferring data to the skin in the form of local iconography specific to local cultures and design elements that eventually came to integrate human activity within an institutionalized and socially agreed on classification system that was patterned, inscribed, and embodied a narrative (cf. Harris 1995; Mignolo 1994). As Indigenous tattoos thus conveyed stories that left behind their traces on the body's surfaces, they operated like texts because they were composed of signs that related to an awareness of things (e.g., identity, genealogy, status, achievement, medicine) and ontological relations (e.g., ancestors, spirits, animals) Other than themselves (Krutak 2007, 2013a, 2019, 2020). Bound to human skin like writing on parchment or paper, tattoos arrested or fixed the world at specific moments in time and, in this way, they preserved ephemeral events in concrete visual detail while at the same time they embodied human emotions, intentions, ancestry, and prayers. As tattooed Māori scholar Ngahuia Te Awekotuku (2006:135) has written, "[Tattoo] inscribes your soul, it uplifts your senses, and it changes you forever. It is the ultimate engagement with one's body, because it cannot be removed."

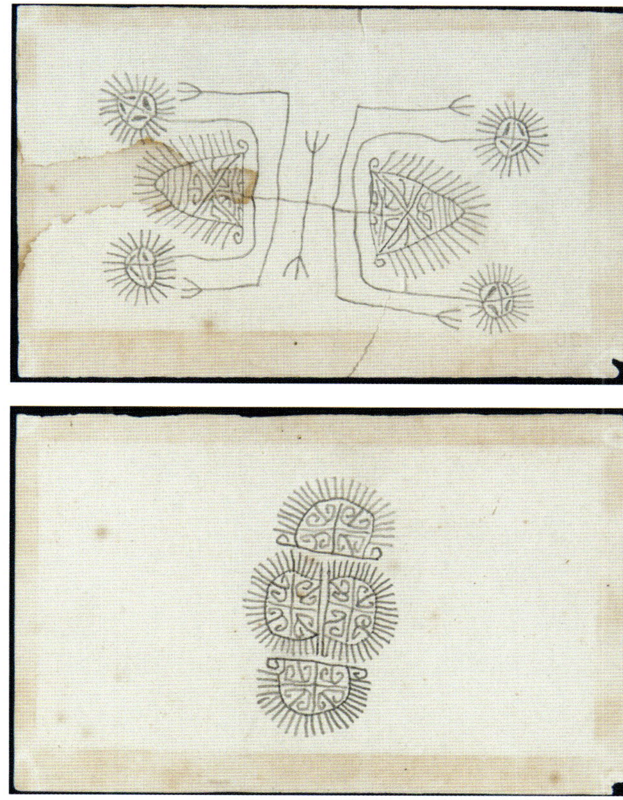

FIGURE I.3
Two motifs drawn (*above*) by Raboe, West Timor, before 1862. Raboe was a female Tetun tattooist who employed a tattoo pattern book containing 388 designs of her work. National Museum of Ethnology, Leiden (inv. 26–37).

Tattooing is often recognized in Indigenous languages as a textual-like activity; such languages have largely been described as "unwritten" in the scientific literature. In the Chinese lexicon, the contemporary term for "tattoo" is based on the ancient approximately first millennium BC Han character *wen* 文, which also means "to write." Today, *wen* embodies literacy, cultural sophistication, and civilization (see Bachner 2014), but the original 文 character is believed to be derived from a tattooed individual, perhaps a northern Indigenous "barbarian" with a marked chest (Reed 2000a:12n27). For the Paiwan of southern Taiwan (see chapter 2, this volume), the term *vecik* is employed for tattooing and "writing" (Ming-Chieh [Taligu] 2013:13). Prior to its virtual abandonment in the mid-twentieth century, Paiwan tattooing was intimately associated with social status, leadership, accomplishment, and ancestral connections to deities and spirits (Ho 1960). Similarly, for "tattooing" the Atayal of northern Taiwan employed the term *patas*, which can refer to "writing words" (Ho 1960:7). Atayal tattoos demarcated ancestral teachings, social status, rites of passage, and spiritual beliefs, among other important facets of culture, including what it meant to be

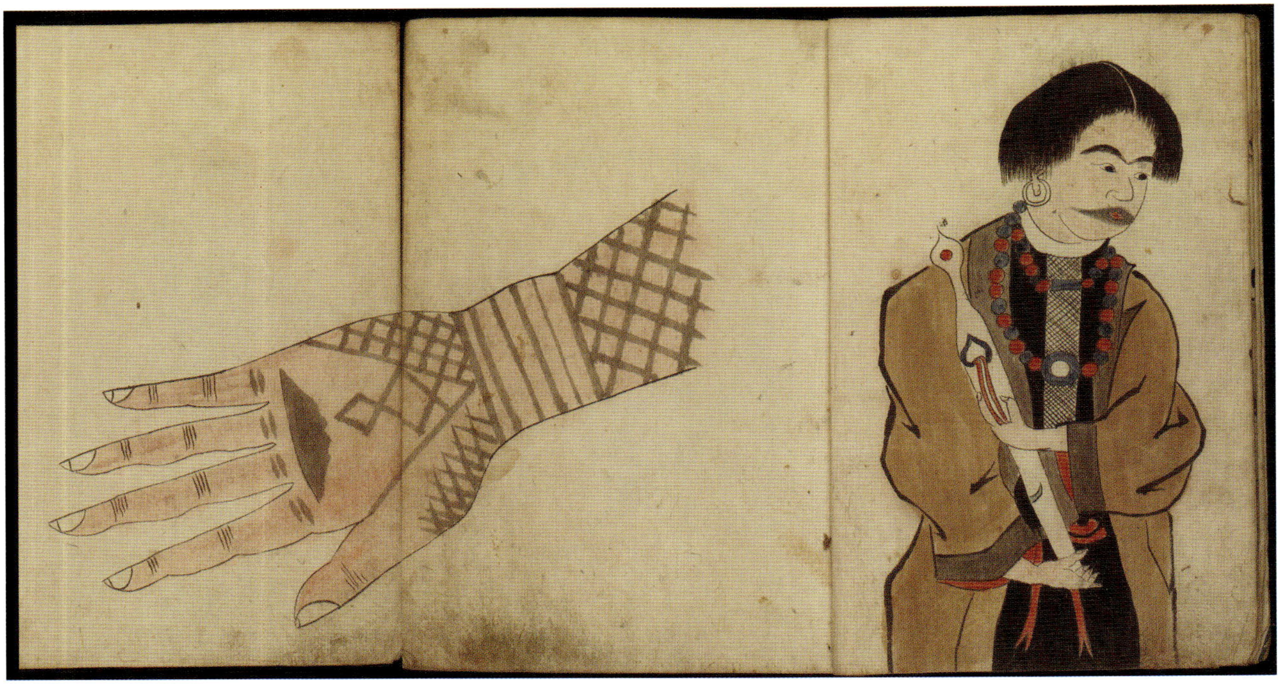

FIGURE I.4
Tattooed Ainu woman portrayed in the book *Ezotō kikan* by Awagimaru Hata (1764–1808), 1799. Japanese Rare Book Collection, Library of Congress. From Hata 1799.

an "ideal" man or woman, a perfectly accomplished human being (Krutak 2007; Ma 1998; Vadan, Dao, and Dada 2008). The Ainu of Japan (see chapter 1, this volume) originally used the term *nuye,* which conveyed several meanings: "to carve," "to tattoo," and "to write" (van Gulik 1982:188). Tattooing here was connected to medicinal treatment, apotropaic power, sympathetic magic, cosmic relations to specific deities, and the afterlife (Batchelor 1901; Hilger 1971; Honda 2000; Krutak 2007; Munro 1963). In Northeast India, the performance of Ao Naga women's tattooing was textual in its syntax (*atep,* "to write") and literally textual as an act of writing "figures or pictures in the skin" (E. W. Clark 1911:167) (see chapter 6, this volume). Permanent body marking with tattoos was intimately connected to complex rites of passage, tribal and clan identity, and concepts regarding the afterlife.

What this brief ethnographic survey reveals is that tattooing practices across the Indigenous Asian world inscribed, documented, and recorded various cultural meanings and concepts to form, in a more or less faithful way, a visual language of the skin. As a form of knowledge transmission, tattooing accounted for ways of being in the world through anchoring significant Indigenous values and ontological concerns on the skin via a visual mosaic rooted in traditional practice (Krutak 2007). The bodily performance of tattooing across Asia, which was almost universally ritualized, reenacted ancestral practices and oral traditions, and as it related these occurrences of the past to the present it bound the tattoo recipient to a deeply felt collective history. In turn, tattooing traced a pathway through the world that individuals navigated in their attempts to acquire new knowledge of themselves and their position in the world while documenting their experiences along the way.

In order to better comprehend these complex realities, this book considers Indigenous tattooing as a form of writing. However, it also looks beyond this corporeal landscape of material signs or symbols to one that is patterned by unwritten narratives and invisible sources that lie in more metaphysical locations. Namely, I will argue, as I have before (Krutak 2019, 2020), that in order to better understand Indigenous tattoos one must acknowledge their ontological associations with nonhuman entities (i.e., spirits, deities, and ancestors) who played an active role in shaping a tattooed person's sense of self, and their attitudes and orientations toward the cultural worlds they lived in. As extensions of the self and Other-than-human self, tattoos embodied aspects of being via textual relations, iconography, and interspecies communication.

This inquiry, at once epistemological and ontological, focuses on how Indigenous Peoples understood themselves with respect to nonhuman Others and how specific forms of tattooing questioned human views about being alive. It is also a metadiscourse about textuality, bodily narratives, and spiritually intertwined subjects within the context of an interspecies world that existed across the Indigenous Asian world.

TATTOO TRADITIONS OF ASIA

Over the past two decades tattooing has become more mainstream and popular than perhaps at any time in human history. Tattooing has gained respectability as a form of fine art and personal expression (Galliot, Bagot, and Anne & Julien 2014; Kakoulas 2009, 2010; Okazaki 2009). In the United States alone, there are some twenty-one thousand tattoo studios serving forty-five million tattooed individuals. Although the range of motivations for becoming tattooed are as varied as the tattoo styles available, tattooing has become not only a celebration of the self and the human body but also a celebration of the global tattoo community and human nature.

Today, tattooing influences contemporary art, film, fashion, product design, and academic research. Regarding the latter, there has been a recent surge in the anthropological and archaeological study of ancient and historic forms of tattooing precisely because they offer proxies from which to reconstruct important aspects of human (pre)history and socioreligious behavior, not to mention patterns of human migration through tattooing technology, associated material culture, and even "tattooed" medicine (Clark and Langley 2020; Krutak 2017a, 2019; Krutak and Deter-Wolf 2017; Piombino-Mascali and Krutak 2020; Robitaille 2007).

Nowadays every style of tattooing in the world is at our fingertips. Since the introduction of the Internet, Facebook, and Instagram, the number of tattooed people has radically increased. Tattoo artists are constantly innovating and exploring what a tattoo can be. What has emerged in the tattooing culture of the twenty-first century is a kaleidoscopic mix of traditional Euro-American and contemporary forms of tattooing practice.

Nevertheless, China and Japan have been home to ancient tattooing traditions and technology for thousands of years. Prehistoric mortuary urns and other ceramic vessels dating to the Majiayao culture (3300–2000 BC) of Northern China feature human heads bearing chin, nose,

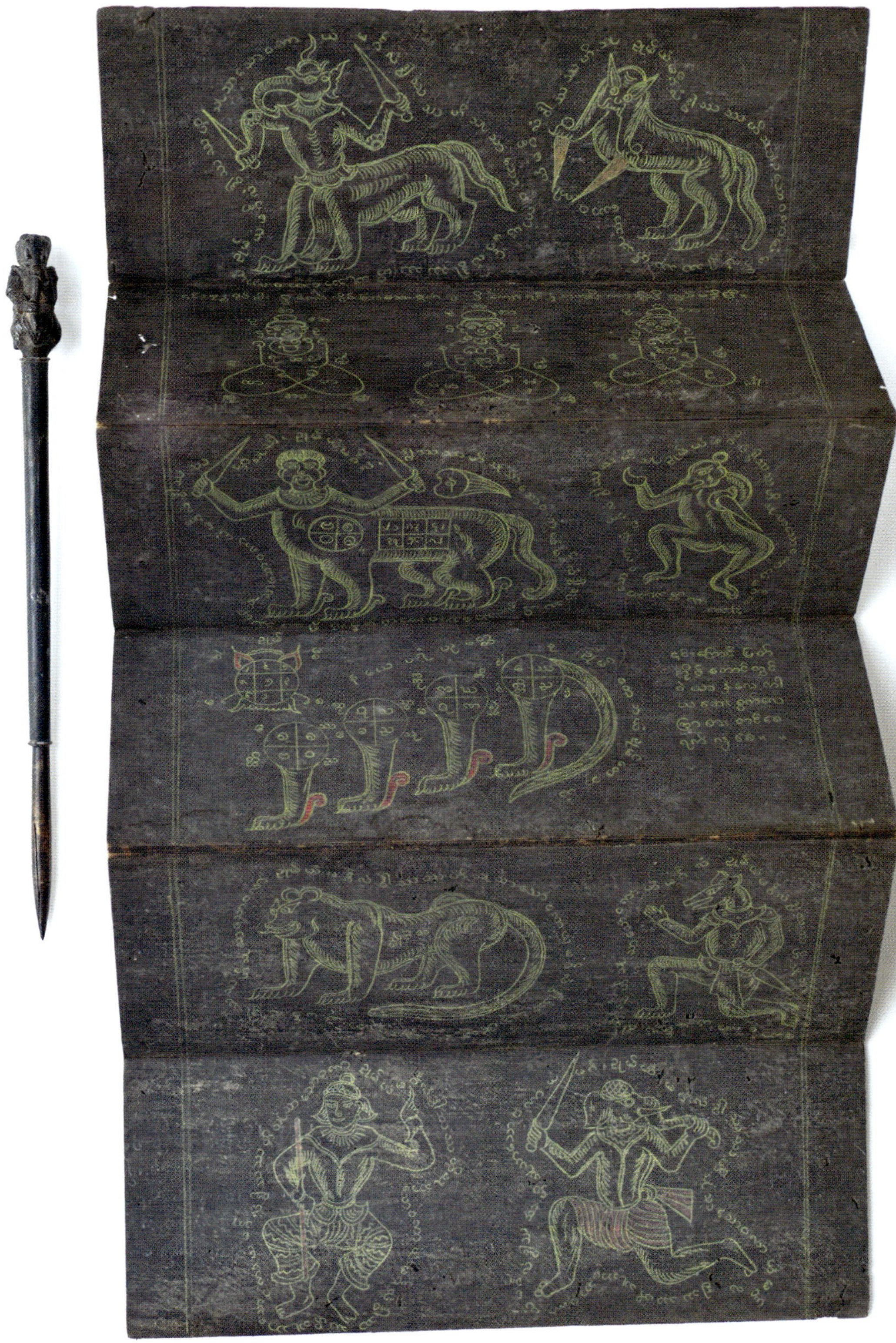

FIGURE I.5

Burmese tattooing tool (late nineteenth century) and *parabaik* (tattoo pattern book) (mid-to-late nineteenth century), 2023. *Parabaik* were the tattooist's "flash sheets" of the historic era. Many of the tattoo motifs possessed supernatural powers, but they were not effected until the tattooist uttered ritual phrases over the magical tattoo pigments he prepared. Brass tattooing rods, tipped with "tattoo weights," helped control the depth of the tattoos, and usually featured mythological animals or beings that added to the magical potential of the tattoos. This example features the Hindu deity Ganesh, a symbol of prosperity and wealth. Collection of the author.

FIGURE I.6

(OPPOSITE PAGE)

Jōmon Tribe Project bodysuit, 2016. The Jōmon were a prehistoric people ancestral to the Ainu of Hokkaido and inhabited Japan as early as sixteen thousand years ago. Jōmon artisans created *dogū* (ceramic figurines) that were probably used for protection against illness, infertility, and spirits. Markings on the faces and bodies of many of these objects likely represented tattooing, a custom also practiced by the Ainu until recently. Tokyo-based tattoo artist Taku Oshima is attempting to breathe life into these extinct practices through contemporary tattoo designs based on timeworn iconography. © Ryoichi Keroppy Maeda.

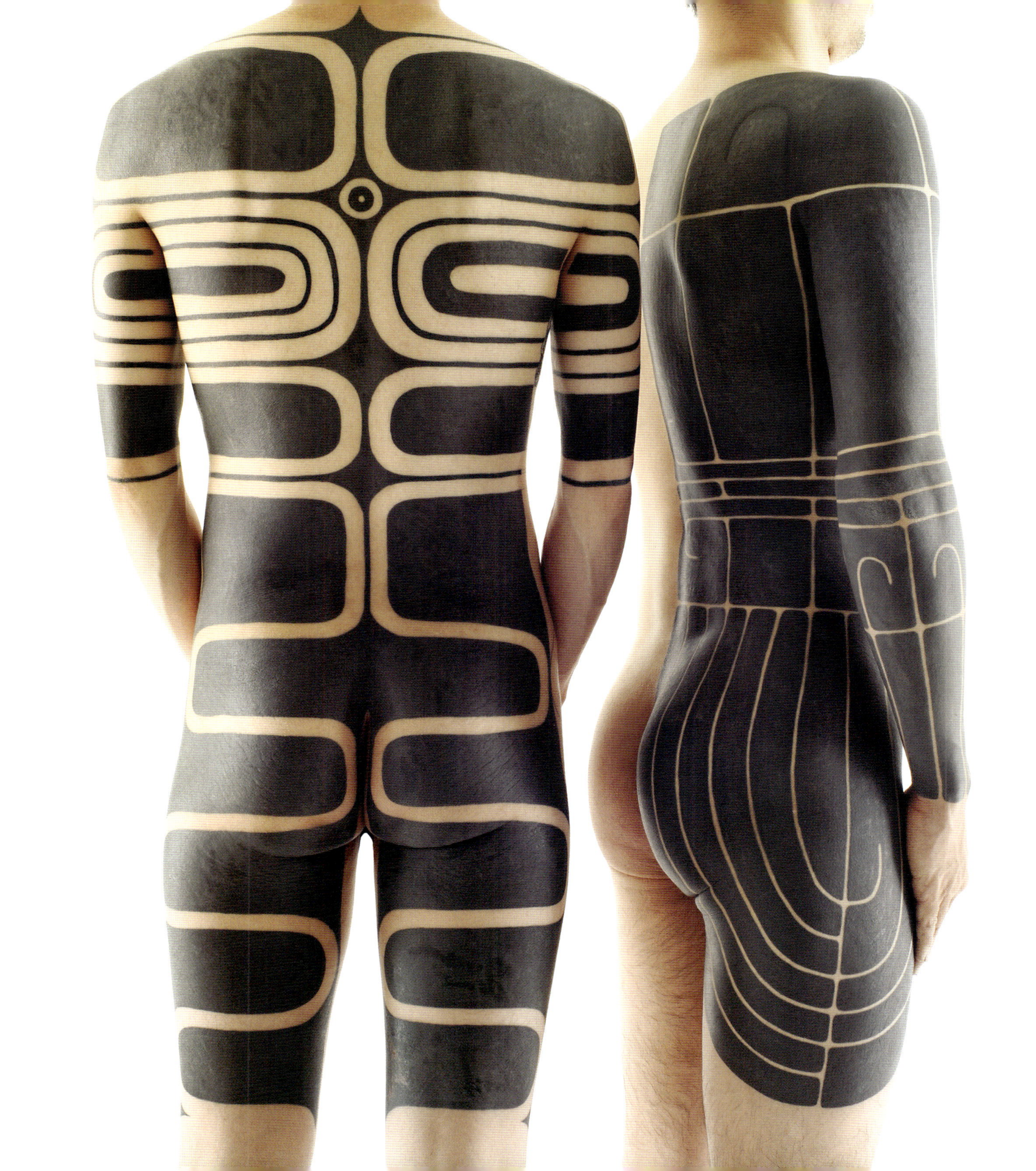

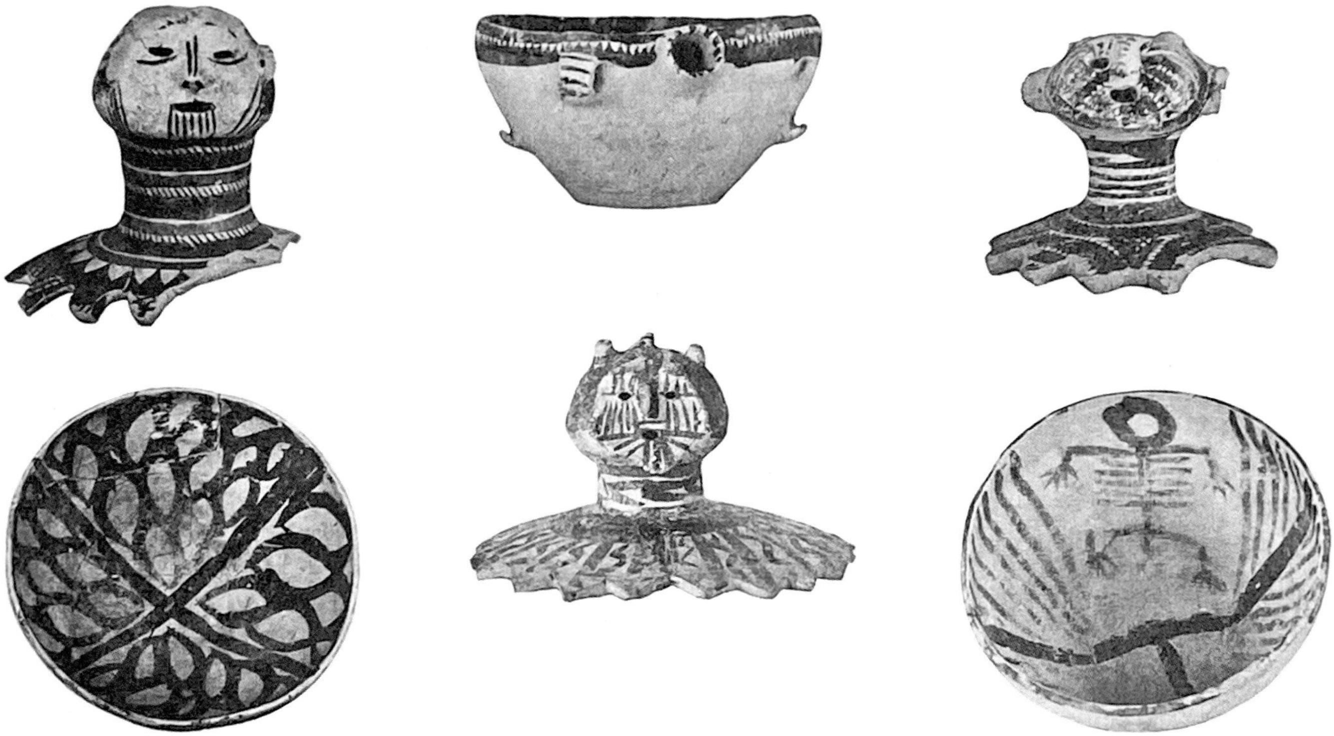

FIGURE I.7
Prehistoric Majiayao culture mortuary urns excavated in Gansu Province, China, some of which bear women's chin, nose, and other facial markings likely representing tattoos, 3300–2000 BC. From Palmgren 1934: pl. 29.

and other facial markings (Palmgren 1934: pl. 19; Priewe 2017). These painted figures closely parallel ethnographic traditions of female facial tattooing still extant in Southwest China, Myanmar, Northwest India, and Siberia (Krutak 2014a, 2017b; see chapters 5–6, this volume). "Tattooed" *dogū* (anthropomorphic ceramic figurines) and human heads adorning vessels dating to the Middle Jōmon culture (2500–1500 BC) of Japan also portray deeply engraved female facial markings (Kaner 2009:106, fig. 13; 130–131, figs. 35–36; 138–139, figs. 41–42; see chapter 1, this volume), which also signal toward much later ethnographic traditions of tattooing (Krutak 2007).

Recent scholarship posits that southern Mainland China was the point of origin for perpendicularly hafted hand-tapping tools prior to 1500 BC (Robitaille 2007:159), an innovation that eventually spread into insular Southeast Asia, the islands of the Pacific Ocean, Melanesia, and northwesterly to Myanmar, Northeast India, and other regions of China (Ambrose 2012; Clark and Langley 2020; Furey 2017). The early origins of hand-tapped tattooing in Asia are possibly supported by archaeological finds in the northern Philippines.

Comblike instruments that may be very early hand-tapping tools, dating from 370 BC to AD 220 (or earlier), were unearthed in a grave at Arku cave, Benguet, Luzon (Bacus 2002; Salvador-Amores 2017; Thiel 1988). The tattooed "fire mummies" of Benguet, Philippines, some

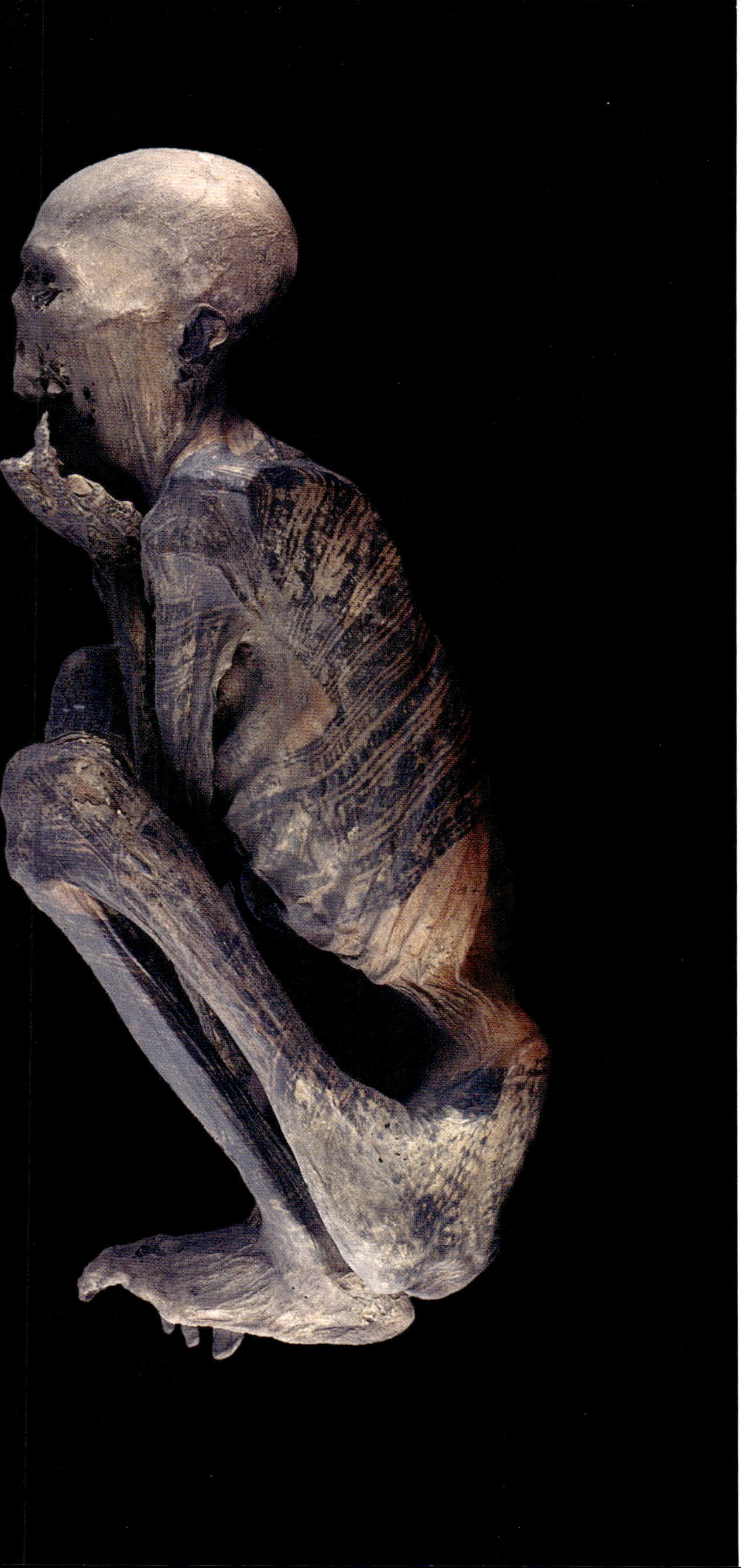

FIGURE I.8

Apo Anno, a mummified warrior and demigod of Natubleng, Benguet, with elaborate tattoos related to his life experiences, Luzon, northern Philippines, AD 1100–1300. © Gunther C. O. Deichmann.

dating to AD 1100–1300, also attest to the long-standing practice of tattooing in Southeast Asia. These fantastically preserved mummies are the ancestors of contemporary Ibaloy and Kankanaey villagers inhabiting the rugged Cordillera region of northern Luzon, and as sacred beings they actively intervene in the world of the living in a variety of ways (Picpican 2003; Piombino-Mascali et al. 2017; Salvador-Amores 2017).

These mummies, and the living Indigenous tattoo practitioners working in the Philippine Cordillera, such as Kalinga hand-tap tattooist Apo Whang-Od Oggay, who may be the world's oldest practitioner, have ignited pan-Filipino, diasporic, and even international interest in the tribal tattooing traditions of the country's First Peoples. Annually, thousands of domestic travelers from all corners of the country descend on Whang-Od's home village of Buscalan to acquire timeless and unique markings based on traditional Kalinga patterns (Almendral 2017).

These "tattoo tourists" desire to root themselves in something larger than themselves and to reaffirm their Filipino roots.[1] The resulting "Tattoo Mania" has also spread to thousands of visiting international tourists, who, spurred by numerous documentary films and online media outlets (CNN Travel, BBC Travel, Great Big Story, DW, YAHOO!, the *New York Times*, etc.), themselves visit Whang-Od and her cadre of female apprentices for unique tattoo iconography and memorable life experiences (see chapter 3, this volume).

Despite this global interest, the Indigenous tattoo traditions of Southeast Asia are grossly underrepresented in the scientific and popular literature. A handful of detailed and thoroughly researched works exist, but these are generally country specific and focus on a single Indigenous society or tradition (Cummings 2012; Franken and Torfinn 1998; Konyak and Bos 2017; Krutak 2007; McCabe 2002; Ming-Chieh [Taligu] 2013; Obara 1962; Parkitny 2007, 2017; Salvador-Amores 2013; Vadan, Dao, and Dada 2008). Other surveys contain dated (Hambly [1925] 2009; Hose and Shelford 1906) or questionable (armchair) scholarship that is not based on actual field studies (Fiksa 2019, 2021; van Dinter 2005), resulting in factual misunderstandings and inaccuracies that continue to be perpetuated via the Internet, popular media, academic conferences, museum exhibitions, publications, and tattoo studios.

TATTOO REVIVALS

For many Indigenous tattoo artists of the postcolonial period, the predicament that underlies their revival efforts is the acquisition of reliable information concerning the meanings, patterns, values, tattoo technologies, and performances of their tradition that were nearly eradicated by Christian missionaries and other external agents of cultural change over centuries of forced assimilation (Carter and Kaszas 2018; Krutak 2010a, 2014a, 2014b, 2020; Mallon, Brunt, and Thomas 2010; Mallon and Galliot 2018; Mangos and Utanga 2011; Te Awekotuku 2007; Thomas, Cole, and Douglas 2005). Their quest is an attempt to reclaim the Indigenous tattoo, which was nearly eradicated, then largely forgotten by younger generations in the twentieth and twenty-first centuries. Their journey is one of self-possession, self-knowledge, and revelation that exposes those indelible elements in their tattooing cultures that, for religious, political, and other reasons, have remained hidden, devalued, and repressed but are now celebrated anew again (see Krutak 2020).

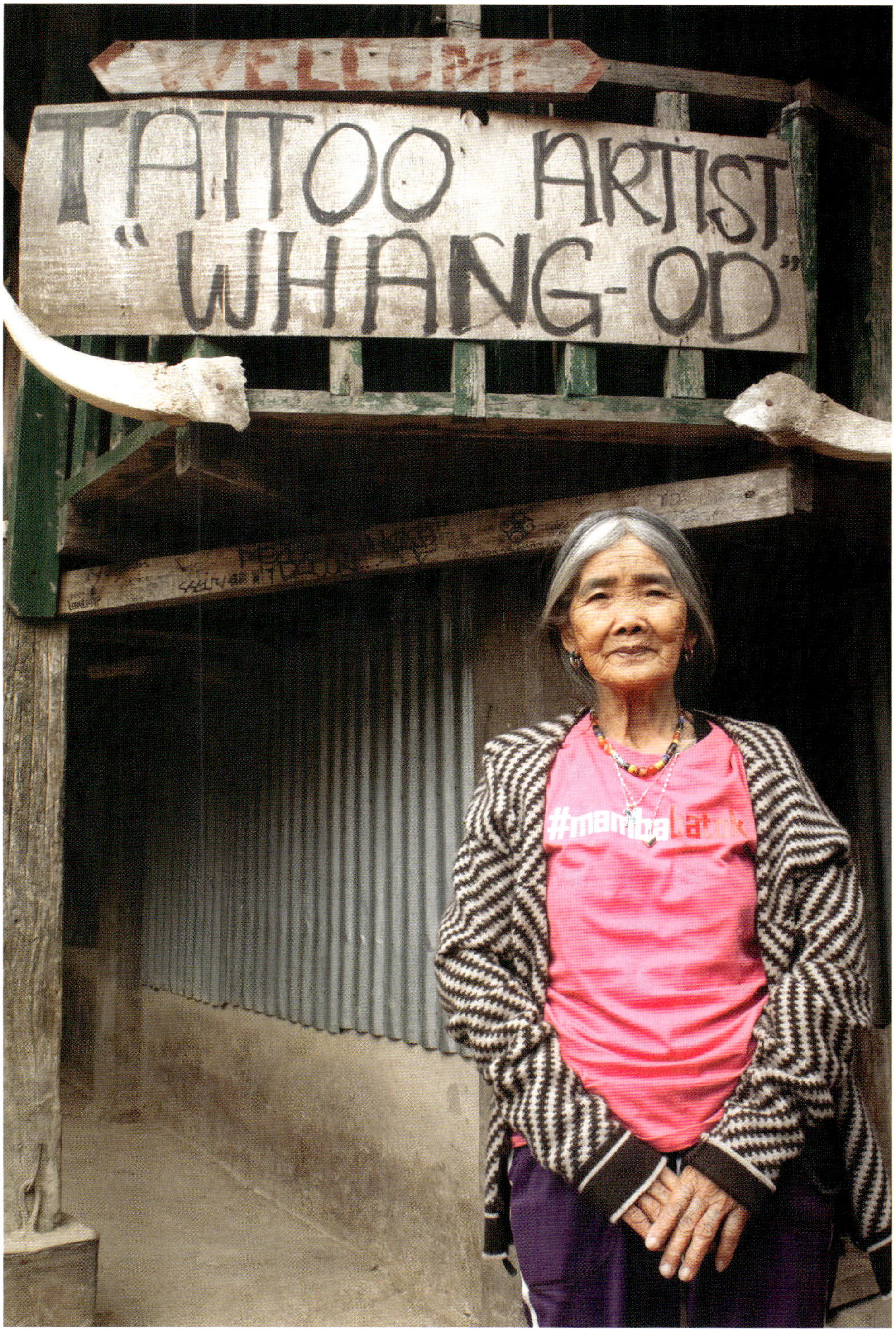

FIGURE I.9
Kalinga *mambababok* (tattoo master) Apo Whang-Od Oggay standing in front of her home in Buscalan village, Kalinga Province, northern Philippines, 2016. © Lars Krutak.

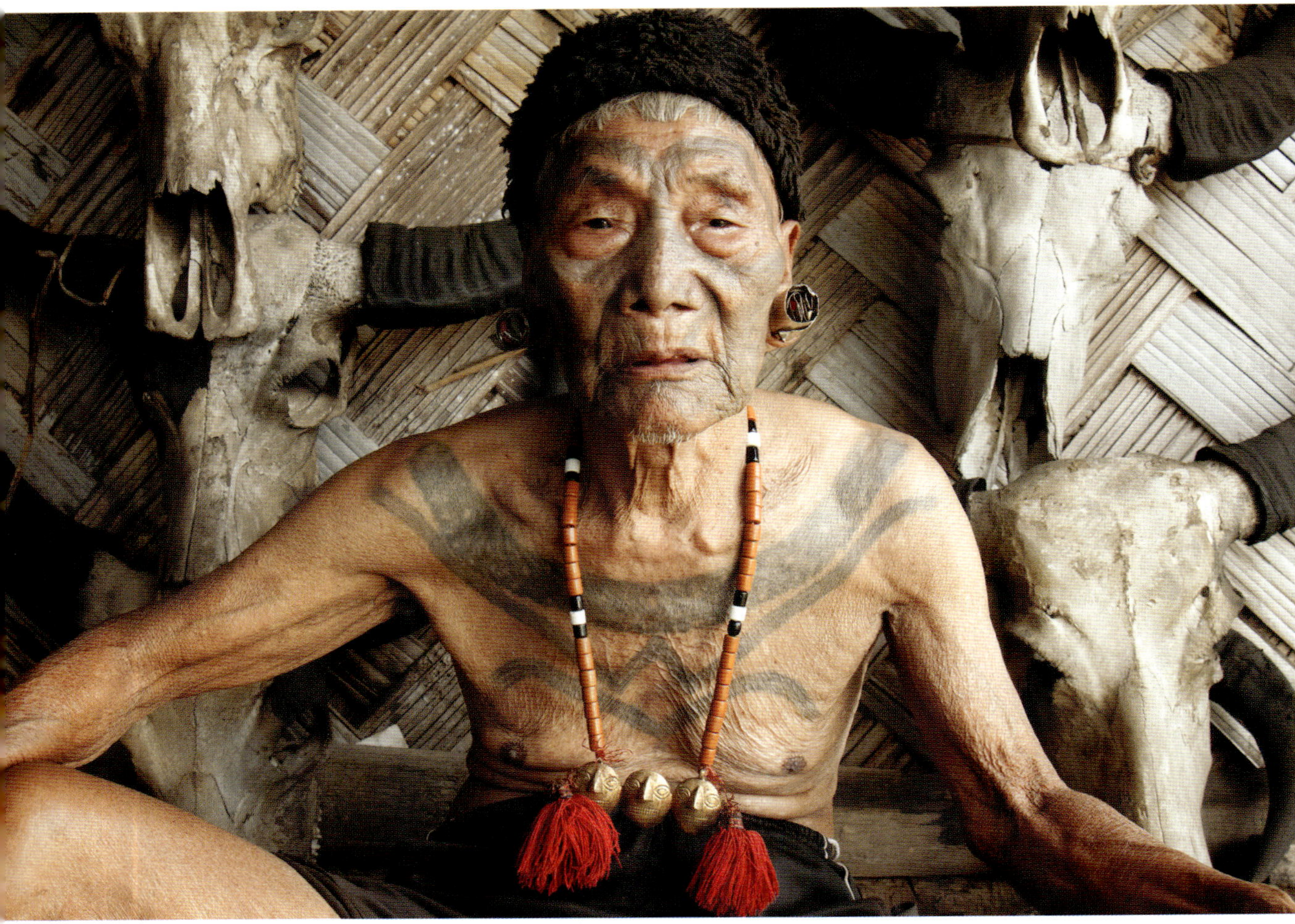

FIGURE I.10
Konyak elder Nokging Wangnao, Hungphoi village, Nagaland, 2018. Due to headhunting bans imposed by the Indian government in the 1950s, the Indigenous Naga people of Northeast India retraditionalized their cultural practices to allow their men to receive the warrior tattoos of their ancestors. Because Wangnao and his age-mates greatly desired these markings, under the guidance of their village leaders they devised a new military tactic to earn their marks. The young men secretly traveled behind the territorial boundary of their sworn enemy and fired their muzzle loaders in the direction of their adversaries' village. This feat, Wangnao said, was equivalent to taking an enemy's head, and on their return home, three days of feasting and dancing commenced as if it had been a real headhunt. Wangnao's tattoos were received shortly thereafter. © Lars Krutak.

Their narratives, many of which are featured throughout this book, speak of the nascent process of Indigenous tattoo decolonization, whereby the practical functions of tattooing (e.g., marks of identity and life achievements) have been restored.

In today's world, identity is a complicated issue for many Indigenous Peoples, especially in regard to contemporary tattoo revivals. Native North American tattoo practitioner Dion Kaszas (2018:9,12) writes, "The revival of Indigenous tattooing is a process of re-indigenization. We are using our traditional tattoo practices in a way that communicates who we are at the core of our being. Our ancestors never had to worry about who they were because they grew up in a community with story, culture and language that affirmed who they were. Today we are fragmented by colonial machinery that has commodified our minds and bodies. When we take on our traditional markings, we are resisting colonialism and affirming who we are in a way that makes us visible as Indigenous people to ourselves and to the world."

For Uipo Naga tattooist Moranngam Khaling (Mo Naga), who is attempting to revive traditional Naga tattoos in Northeast India through new design concepts, his work has not yet been fully embraced by his fellow people (see chapter 6, this volume). He acknowledges that he is attempting to reclaim Naga tattoo culture from the machinations of the colonial-missionary era, but he needs more time for this "movement" to catch on, to move it forward. "I don't look at it *yet* as a form of decolonization *per se* or as a form of cultural healing, like the Native North Americans and other ethnic groups such as the Māori, who have embraced and reclaimed their tattoo cultures for several decades," he says. "I have not had time to think about the movement in this way, but perhaps in the future it will hold these meanings as more people join the movement" (Krutak 2020:203).

For Mo Naga and the other cultural tattoo practitioners featured in this book, however, the tattoo revival movement happening across Asia does involve a process of re-Indigenization. Here, traditional Indigenous beliefs, values, tattooing motifs, and cultural practices have been reconfigured, and unfold through a performative modification and (re)invigoration of an ethnic tattoo complex that, in some cases, died out long ago. This tattoo retraditionalization energizes the character of Indigenous tattoo practices and sign systems through the formation of neotraditional and hybrid forms of tattooing that are exchanged across the local, global, and digital tattoo landscape. The works of Mo Naga and the other cultural tattoo practitioners featured in this volume give new expression to an inerasable and unquestionable mark of ethnic identity and being, and in the process have transformed contemporary perceptions of this now re-emergent cultural tattoo movement.

With these thoughts in mind, my hope is to present the tattooing traditions of Asia not as a dying or vanishing cultural practice but as one that is re-emerging, giving voice to the people and practitioners to whom these traditions belong. Indeed, Indigenous tattoos today are unique expressions of the human experience and not remnants of a lost history. Rather they are a mutable and vibrant part of living cultures, revealing inspirational stories as told in skin and ink.

1

TATTOOS OF JAPAN

Many Islands, Many Tales

The pain when you tattoo me,
I will gladly bear.
So please, please prick me with tattoos,
The best you can.

The money I have,
I cannot take it to the other world [afterlife].
The tattoos on my hands,
follow me there.

—**Okinawan tattoo songs for women** (Obara 1962:9)

Stretching some seventeen hundred miles from Hokkaido in the north to Hateruma in the southern Ryukyu Islands, Japan has an ancient history of tattooing practice that spans thousands of years. Prehistoric artisans of the Jōmon people, who inhabited Japan as early as sixteen thousand years ago, created *dogū* (anthropomorphic figurines) that display facial markings resembling tattoo patterns worn by historic Indigenous Peoples such as the Ainu (Krutak 2007; McCallum 1988:109). Recent DNA evidence, dental morphology, and other biological traits suggest the Ainu of Hokkaido and Ryukyuan peoples of the 南島 Nantō (Southern Islands) are direct descendants of the ancient Jōmon people (Arutiunov 1999:31; Ishida 1999:56; Jinam et al. 2012; Jinam et al. 2015), but exactly when this divergence took place remains a mystery. Until the late nineteenth century, the Ainu and the Ryukyuans each maintained distinctive tattooing traditions, and similarities in their ceremonial beliefs and religious practices, including their former feminocentric tattoo customs, seemingly link them to one another in profound ways.

RYUKYUAN AND AINU TATTOOING

In 1962, Japanese researcher Kazuo Obara's groundbreaking study on Ryukyuan tattooing practices, known as *hajichi* or *pajichi* (tattooing/needle prick), was posthumously published. Based on fieldwork conducted in the summers of 1930–1932, it was the first book to study these ancient tattooing traditions in detail. Several decades would pass before other published works appeared. By this time, however, the remaining tattooed Ryukyuans were very elderly (i.e., born in the 1870s–1890s) and their knowledge associated with the practice was fragmentary (cf. Nakijin Village Board of Education 1983).

Tattooing practices across the Ryukyu archipelago began to fade at the turn of the century. The Japanese government discouraged it around 1879, when it annexed the Ryukyu Islands. In 1899, the empire officially banned tattooing, declaring that anyone caught performing or receiving tattoos could be fined or jailed as criminals (Barske 2013).[1] To further shame practitioners and tattoo recipients, their addresses and names were published in local newspapers. Similarly, among the Ainu, the Ezo Shogunate issued a ban on women's tattoos as early as 1799, and in 1871 the government's Hokkaido Development Mission strictly prohibited the custom (Hilger 1971:150).

Far-flung peoples such as the Ryukyuans and the Ainu were considered "primitive" and "backward," in contrast to modern Japanese society. The State proclaimed a duty to modernize these Indigenous Peoples in order to effectively integrate them through a process of sociocultural assimilation, or *dōka* (making the same) (Edwards 2014:47). Anachronistic customs, such as tattooing and shamanism, and incomprehensible languages and dialects were condemned. More specifically, the Japanese attitude toward tattooing was disapproving because for centuries the act was associated with crime and the punishment of criminal acts,[2] and in the Ryukyus it was a "barbaric custom [and] obstacle to civilized social development" (Nakijin Village Board of Education 1983:42). Ryukyuan women bearing tattoos were made to feel ashamed of them, and photographs from the turn of the twentieth century depict women wearing gloves. In 1898, dozens of female students from an Okinawa high school attempted to remove their *hajichi* with chemicals, and apparently a hospital in Naha specialized in tattoo removal (NSJNJH 1998:349; Yamamoto 1995:42). In turn, Indigenous tattooing praxis was subsequently driven underground, the designs became abbreviated in form, and by 1980 only a few Ryukyuan and Ainu women bore a complete set of tattoos. *Hajichi* faded altogether with the deaths of the last tattoo bearers in the 1990s, and the last Ainu woman with traditional tattooing died in 1998 (Krutak 2007).

Notwithstanding, scholars past and present have neglected to compare Ryukyuan and Ainu cultures through an analysis of their tattooing traditions. Obara (1962:24), for example, felt that the two could not have originated from the same cultural base. He wrote, "Even though Ainu tattooing custom was [largely] limited to women, it should be noted that women of Ryukyu never applied tattoos on their face while for the Ainu facial tattoos were extremely important. This makes one suspect that the origin of tattooing must be different between these two people. For the Ainu, tattooing seems to be used as a sexual symbol."

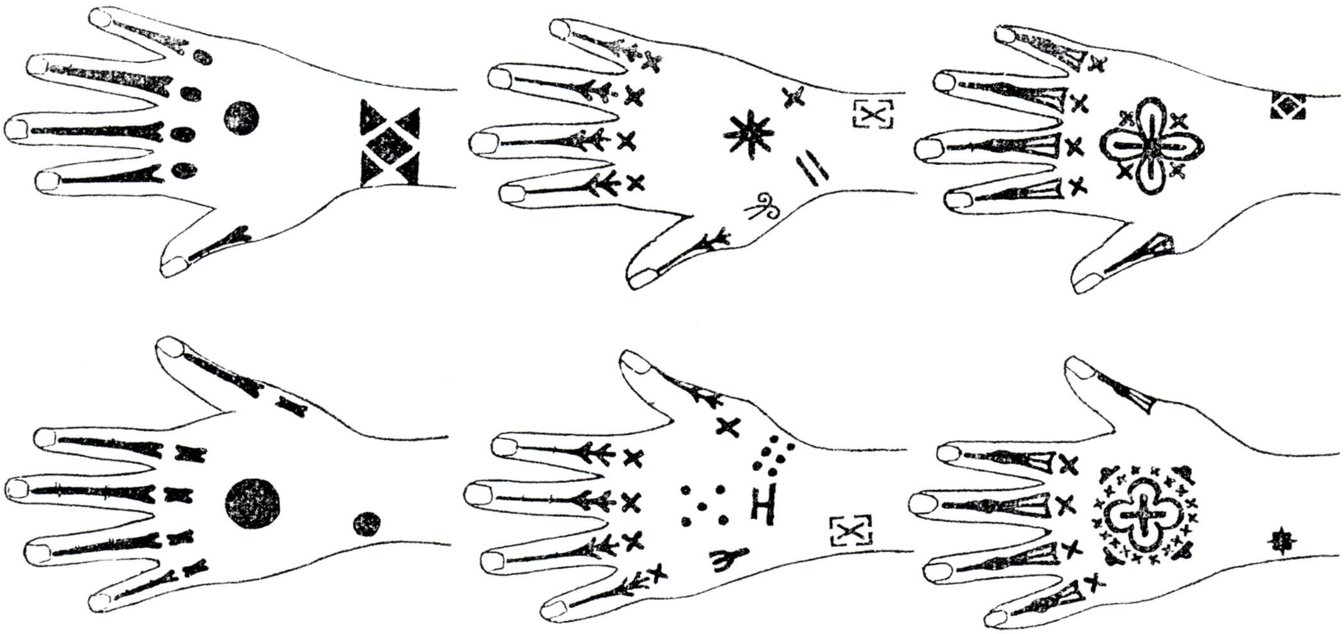

FIGURE 1.1
Hand tattoos of Okinawa (*left column*), Miyako (*center*), and Amami Ōshima Island (*right*). From Furness 1899a: 10, fig. 3.

I firmly disagree that female tattooing among the Ainu was simply a "sexual symbol," because it was much more than that (see Krutak 2007). I also believe that the presence or absence of a cultural trait such as facial tattooing is not a solid baseline from which to help delineate the potentiality for shared cultural origins, especially since genetic evidence now supports ancestral linkages between the Ryukyuans and the Ainu. Moreover, several of the Austronesian-speaking Indigenous groups of Taiwan practiced tattooing on the face (e.g., Atayal, Saisiyat, Truku, and Seediq), while others marked only their arms and hands (e.g., Paiwan and Rukai).[3] Furthermore, the Atayal and the Paiwan share several distinct genetic traits (Wu et al. 2010). And as we will come to see below, I feel there is striking evidence that Ryukyuan and Ainu tattooing traditions are related, but this documentation has been overlooked until now.[4]

RYUKYUAN TATTOO ORIGIN STORIES

Despite the government bans on Ryukyuan tattooing, because the custom was deeply ingrained into local Indigenous culture there were still women who continued the practice as a profession into the early twentieth century. The ancestral tradition had existed for hundreds if not thousands of years. One oral account from the northern islands, which is paraphrased after Obara (1962:12–13) and has numerous variations, speaks about a beautiful princess, Montoku, who was the *kikoe-ōgimi* (high priestess) of the land and sister of the Ryukyuan king Shō En. Approximately five hundred years ago, she made her annual pilgrimage from Shuri Castle

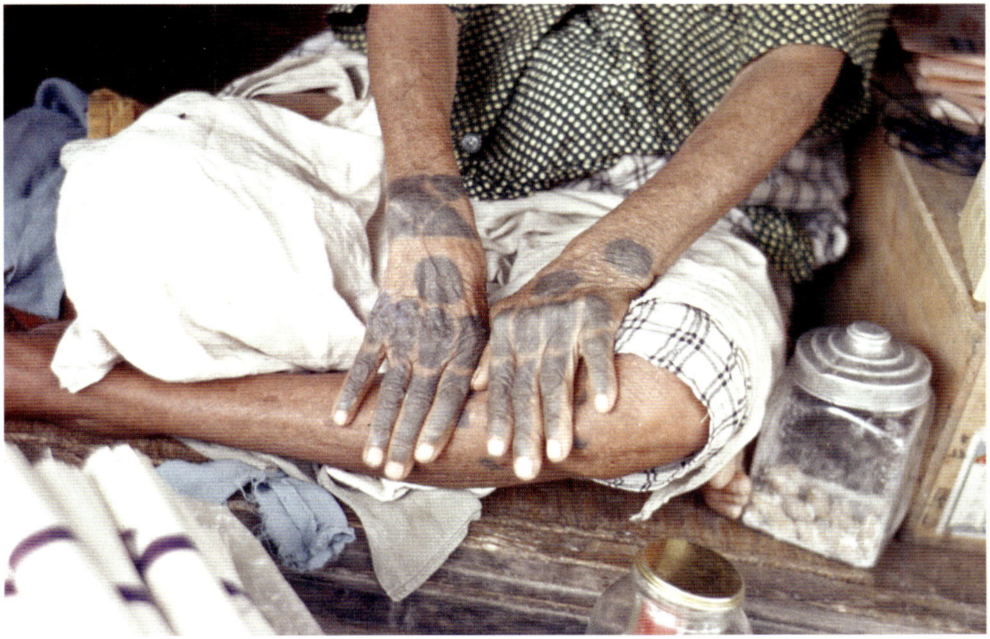

FIGURE 1.2
Tattooed Okinawan elder, Itoman District, ca. 1960s. Therapeutic tattoos appear on her upper shin, beneath her hands. Collection of the author.

on Okinawa to sacred Kudaka Island, where the Ryukyuan Creation goddess Amamikyu first descended to earth to create the Ryukyuan people and introduce foodstuffs essential for human life. On the return voyage to Okinawa, a typhoon carried Montoku and her royal retinue northward to the coast of Satsuma Province on the island of Kyūshū. News of the beautiful princess traveled far and wide, and the lord of the Satsuma clan ordered her to his palace. He was very much impressed with her beauty and charm and was anxious to keep her in his court as long as possible.

Montoku told the high lord that she must return to the kingdom of Okinawa since she was the highest of all *noro*, or Ryukyuan priestesses. The Lord of Satsuma declined to let her go. One day, an envoy of the Okinawan Kingdom arrived and was surprised to find the princess alive; she was presumed to have been lost in the typhoon along with her fellow travelers. The high priestess told the envoy of her wish to return home, but that the Lord of Satsuma continued to decline her repeated requests. The envoy whispered a plan in her ear, to which she consented readily. Soon thereafter, the envoy's messenger arrived and brought a package to the priestess. It contained needles and a blue dye. He commenced to tattoo the back of her hands and then requested an audience with the Lord of Satsuma.

When Montoku appeared before the high lord, he stared at the tattooed marks in horror and disgust, and then left the room without any comment. After a few days, he sent word that the priestess could return to Okinawa with her envoy. After she had returned to her castle, other ladies in the Okinawan court imitated her and had tattoos done on the backs of their hands.

They believed the tattoos would safeguard them from similar misfortunes and protect their chastity until they were married. Afterward, all women of Okinawa had tattoos placed on their hands.

In the Nantō (Southern Islands), specifically in the Yaeyama archipelago, Obara (1962:14–15) documented two variations of a different tattoo origin story. In my opinion, this story is more ancient, and ties tattooing to a female sea deity; Ainu tattooing is also linked to a female deity, the goddess of the hearth.

Once upon a time, a group of people were sailing in the southern islands and lost their way because of a navigating error or a storm. The party sailed to an unknown island that was surrounded by very muddy shoals. The ship began to sink, and its passengers looked into the water and saw two women, one with tattoos on her hands and the other without. The tattooed woman was pushing the boat upward so it would not sink, whereas the other was pulling it down. The fight was fierce, and the people on the boat began praying to their gods that the tattooed woman would win. Because the voyage was long and in their struggle the women were tossing the boat about, the nails on the bottom of the ship came off and the ship nearly fell apart. Suddenly, *Trochus* shells appeared and began filling in the nail holes. The tattooed woman won the battle, and the boat, aided by a strong wind gifted by the deity, was able to safely return to Yaeyama. The passengers realized the deity was the Goddess of Sailing and asked women and girls at home to place tattoos on their hands to honor the goddess.

Comparing these two tattoo origin stories reveals certain characteristics that lead me to believe that the second story appears to predate the first story, which is heavily Japanized in form. The second story contains several traits that appear to be purely local, Indigenous, and animistic and that tie tattooing to a specific deity and her supernatural powers. These elements are hallmarks of traditional Okinawan religion rather than imports from foreign sources such as Shinto, Buddhism, and Confucian traditions that appear in the Princess Montoku story. In these religions, acts of bodily defilement (i.e., tattooing) are unholy because they are considered impure, unclean, and unnatural. In contrast, the anthropologist William Lebra (1966:57), who conducted a detailed study of Okinawan religion in the 1950s, wrote that Okinawans tend to conceive ritual purity more as "freedom from malevolent spirits and things" than as "physical purity" in the Japanese sense. Returning to the Princess Montoku tale, it is clear that the Lord of Satsuma was horrified by her tattoos because her body had been defiled. Moreover, the title (*kikoe-ōgimi*) of the chief princess in this story is Japanized. Lebra (1966:viii) observed that when using this title during interviews with his Okinawan informants, most elicited blank responses because they were accustomed to the Indigenous Okinawan term for "high priestess," *chifijing ganashii mee*. Finally, what this oral account implies is that female disfigurement via tattooing, especially on the body of an exotic Indigenous woman, was a successful method of evading kidnapping. This convenient theme has been documented around the Indigenous world in connection with the origin of female tattooing practices (e.g., Chen, Luo, and Yang 2004; Nisbett 1901; Powers 1877; Wise 1883). However, in nearly every case the connection has been shown to be false (Gros 2012; Krutak 2014a, 2014b, 2014c; Parkitny 2010, 2017; Tian Fu 2010), because these stories fail to account for the deeply engrained spiritual beliefs and rite-of-passage ceremonies embodied in these ancient tattooing traditions.[5] In short, foreigners such as the Japanese who first encountered tattooed peoples in the

Ryukyus could not make sense of their permanent body markings, and it was more convenient to invent a "moral story" told from their cultural perspective to account for the practice than to attempt to grasp its true meanings. Colonial regimes the world over have sought to heighten the aura of exoticism and threatening Otherness posed by "uncivilized" tattooed peoples to justify their control and eventual administration (cf. Krutak 2007).

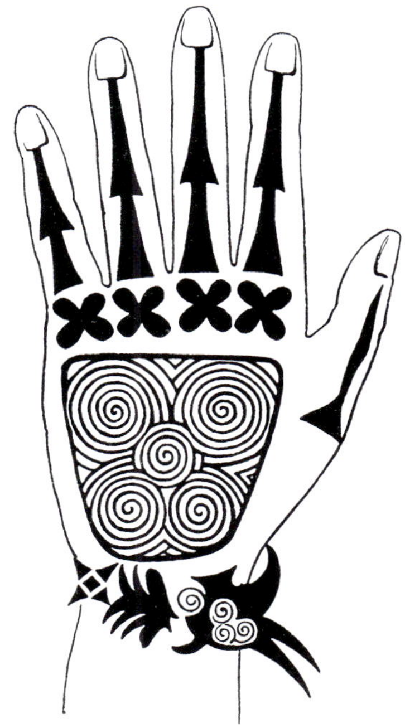

FIGURE 1.3
Intricate hand and wrist tattoo from Amami Ōshima Island. From Simon 1914:146. 1914.

Notwithstanding, tattooed elders interviewed across the Ryukyuan region over the last century stated that the receipt of tattoos was a spiritual experience, because *hajichi* were necessary prerequisites for the afterlife. Several accounts speak about the torments women faced after death if they were not tattooed, specifically performing laborious tasks such as "digging reed potatoes" (Iha [1919] 2000:270 cited by Barske 2013:84). Obara (1962:62) observed, "[You] could not be reborn in paradise after death, and one's soul would be lost" forever if you did not carry *hajichi*. Across Indigenous cultures worldwide, tattooing was needed for this important journey, because the ancestors could recognize you only by the tattoos worn on the body (Codrington 1891; Hose and Shelford 1906; Krutak 2007, 2012, 2014a, 2014c, 2014d, 2017a, 2017b, 2019, 2020; Mallick 2020; Rudolph 2008; Salvador-Amores 2017). In this way, tattoos formed a significant aspect of an individual's physical and spiritual identity, and in the case of the Ryukyuans they would not have been created as a form of disfigurement; that is the ultimate myth.

Obara (1962:16) speculated that Ryukyuan tattooing traditions may have originated in the southern islands and moved north. I would argue instead that the most ancient forms of "traditional" Ryukyuan tattooing would have been *preserved* in the southern islands, especially if the Ainu and the Ryukyuans were descended from the same cultural base in deep antiquity; this implies a north-to-south movement, not one that is south-to-north. I base this on an Arctic analogy, since it has been shown that the earliest forms of Indigenous women's tattooing in the Arctic originated in northwest Alaska more than fifteen hundred years ago. Over the next millennia, prehistoric people called the Thule carried these traditions eastward to Greenland and the Canadian Arctic, where, until very recently, these ancient tattoos continued to be worn by elderly Inuit and Ammassalingmiut women, respectively (Krutak 2007, 2014a, 2019). Moreover, there is a marked diversity of recorded tattooing motifs in the southern islands as compared to the north, and especially on and around Okinawa, where there is a general "commonality" of pattern placement and even "fixed patterns" for specific social classes (Yamamoto 1996). It also seems there was a greater diversity of therapeutic tattoos documented across the southern islands as compared to the northern islands surrounding Okinawa (Yamamoto 1995).

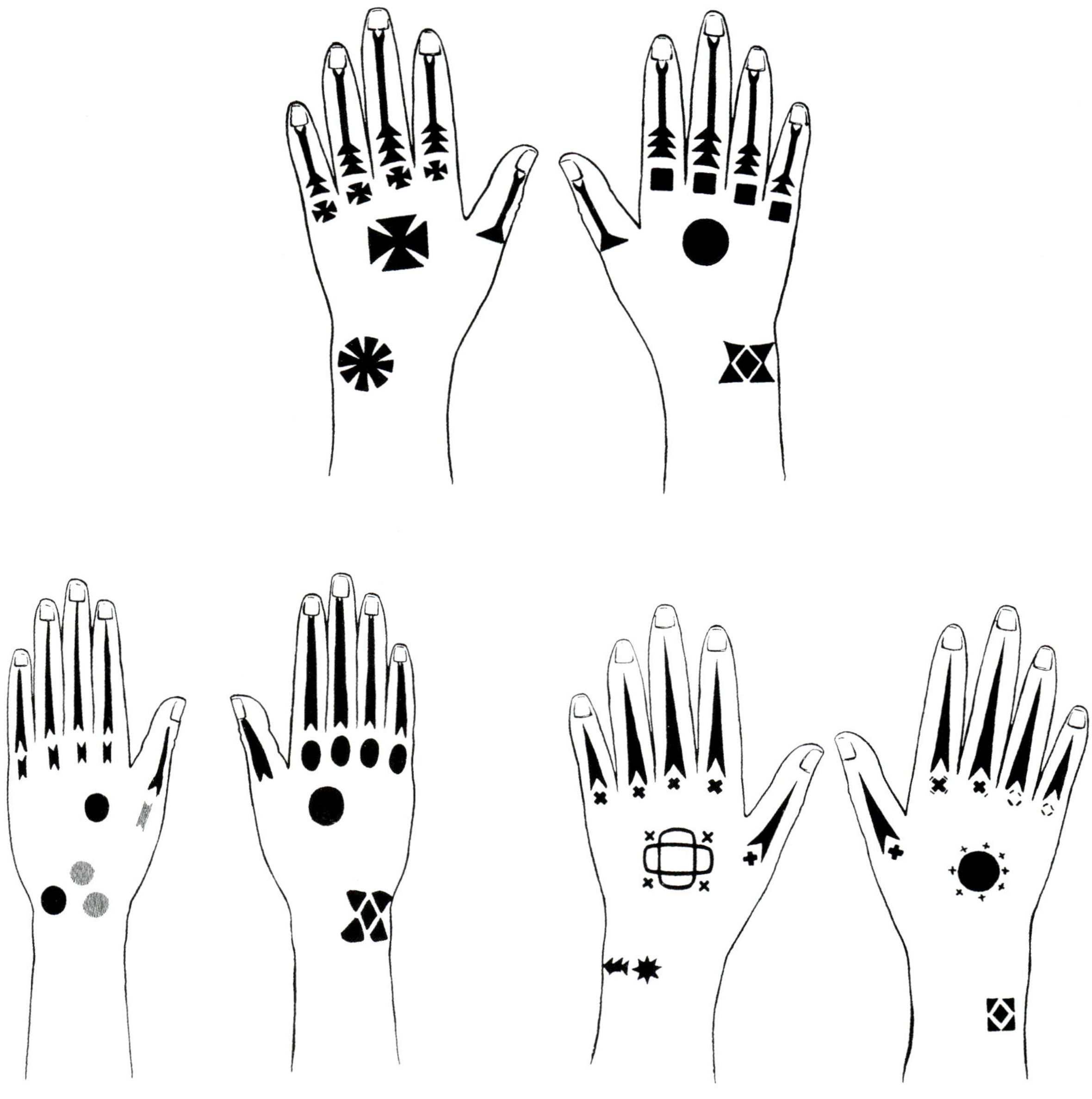

FIGURE 1.4

Tattoos of Yaeyama Island, Shuri District of Okinawa, and Tokunoshima Island. From Simon 1914: 138–139, 141.

MAGICAL AND MEDICINAL MARKS

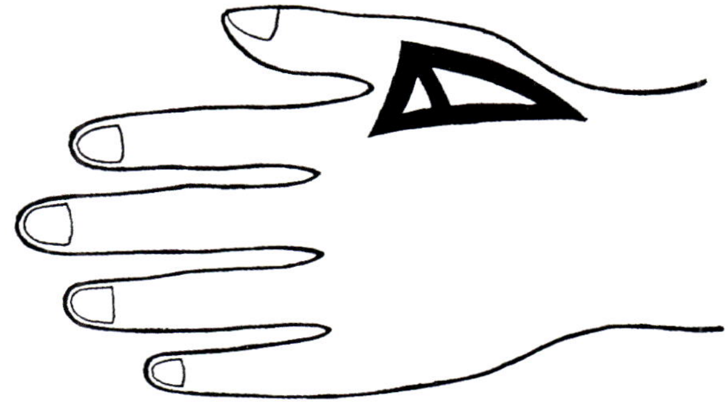

FIGURE 1.5
Ainu man's hand tattoo for enhanced skill in archery, Kussharo village, Kushiro Province. From Kodama 1970:130, fig. 54.

Prior to speaking about the performances of Ryukyuan tattooists, who, like the Ainu, were invariably female, it is important to note additional similarities in the tattooing culture of these peoples. Although tattooing was almost always carried out by women for female clients, there were three types of tattoos produced for men in both regions. These markings were either inserted into the skin as a form of sympathetic magic, for apotropaic means, or as a medicinal treatment.

The Japanese anatomist and anthropologist Sakuzaemon Kodama (1970:130, fig. 54), who conducted extensive research among the Ainu beginning in the 1930s, observed firsthand a long, triangular tattoo placed between the thumb and index finger of an elderly man as a "charm to wish for skill in shooting an arrow [while] hunting." He noted this tattoo could appear on the right or left hand. American travel writer and ethnologist William H. Furness, who also visited Ainu settlements in the late nineteenth century, did not document male tattooing among them. Nevertheless, in the Ryukyuan village of Itoman on Okinawa he observed that fishermen and young boys possessed tattooed images of tridents on their upper right arms, and in other cases, these motifs were replaced with zigzagging lines directed downward like the teeth of a saw (Furness 1899a:11). On questioning his informants, they replied that these tattoos had the effect of repelling the evil spirits they encountered at sea.

Other visitors to Okinawa noted this tattooing tradition among the "fishermen class." Captain Basil Hall (1820:185) of the British Royal Navy observed that "most" of the men he met on Okinawa were tattooed with a three-pronged, barbed trident mark called a "fish spear"; some men displayed the mark on the right arm, and some on the left. Apparently, these customs became extinct sometime in the early twentieth century, according to American geographer Clarence Glacken (1955:238), who reported that by 1950 elders could vaguely remember them.

Another category of Ryukyuan and Ainu male tattooing was therapeutic. Therapeutic tattoos, usually placed over an aching limb or place of injury, were widespread across the genders in the Indigenous world (Krutak 2007, 2013a, 2019:101; Piombino-Mascali and Krutak 2020:122–123; see table 1.1). Until recently, I was uncertain if this treatment existed among male Ainu. I suspected it did, however, because medicinal tattooing has been documented for Ainu women. Through my investigations for this book, I located an obscure 1894 publication in German by Japanese anatomist Yoshikiyo Koganei, who studied the physical anthropology of numerous Ainu of Hokkaido in the late nineteenth century. In Shamani village, Hidaka Province, Koganei met an adult man with a three-centimeter-long blue line along the back of his left thumb. In Kutcharo village, Kushiro Province, he encountered an adult man and a boy with a cross placed in the same location; he noted the cruciform pattern might also appear on the outside of an upper arm. On another rare occasion, he witnessed female forms of "medicinal" tattooing, including a woman from Ishikari Province who possessed

FIGURE 1.6
Men's tattoo marks seen on Okinawa. From Hall 1820.

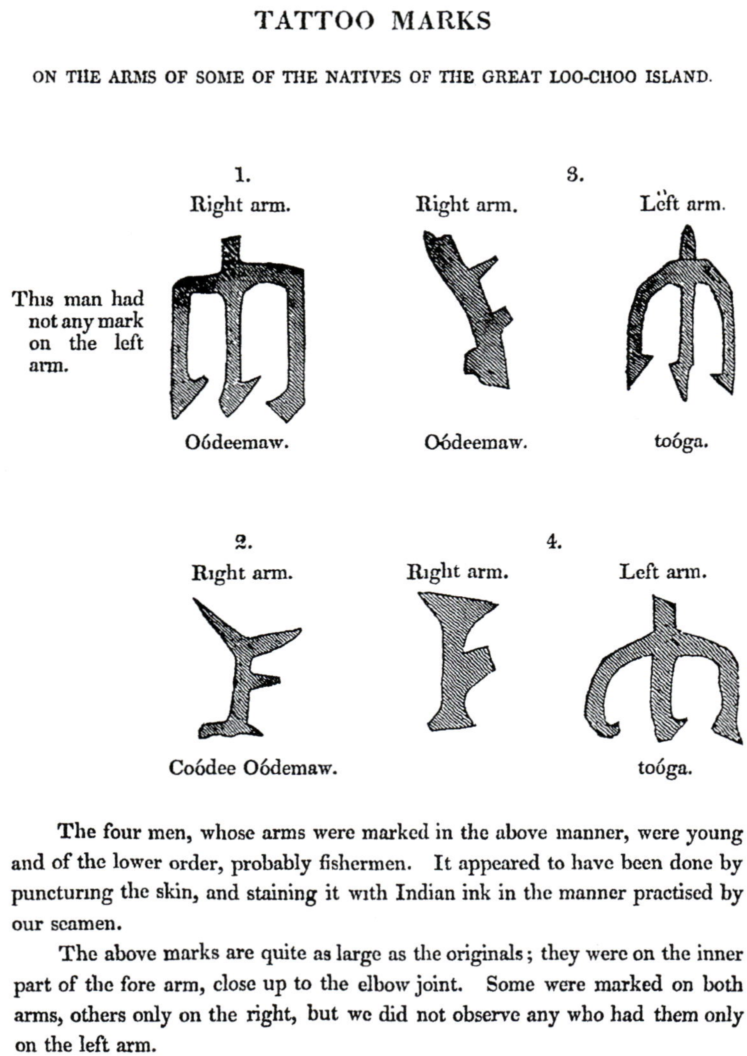

TATTOO MARKS

ON THE ARMS OF SOME OF THE NATIVES OF THE GREAT LOO-CHOO ISLAND.

1. Right arm. — Oódeemaw.
This man had not any mark on the left arm.

Right arm. — Oódeemaw.

3. Left arm. — toóga.

2. Right arm. — Coódee Oódemaw.

4. Right arm. Left arm. — toóga.

The four men, whose arms were marked in the above manner, were young and of the lower order, probably fishermen. It appeared to have been done by puncturing the skin, and staining it with Indian ink in the manner practised by our seamen.

The above marks are quite as large as the originals; they were on the inner part of the fore arm, close up to the elbow joint. Some were marked on both arms, others only on the right, but we did not observe any who had them only on the left arm.

"two blue stripes on the thorax at the level of the third rib and four such stripes on the forehead" (Koganei 1894:264). He continued, "Such abnormally tattooed areas have arisen from the fact that bad blood has been extracted through skin incisions to strengthen the body [or relieve head or joint pain], and afterwards soot has been rubbed in to stop the bleeding. . . . They are therefore not to be regarded as decorations."

The British Anglican missionary John Batchelor (1901:23) documented other instances of Ainu *pashka-oingara* (therapeutic tattooing). He wrote, "When the eyes of old women are

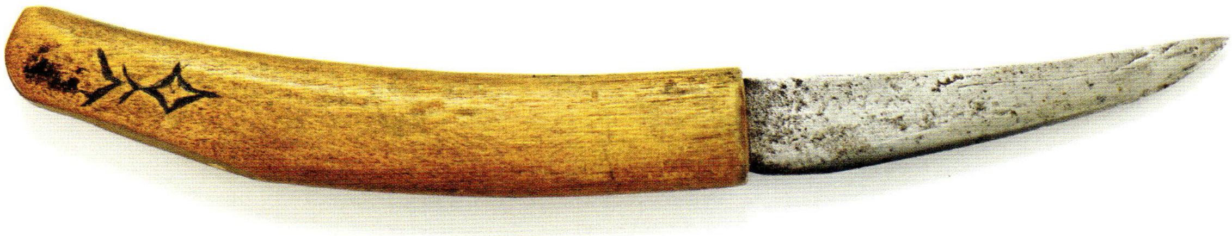

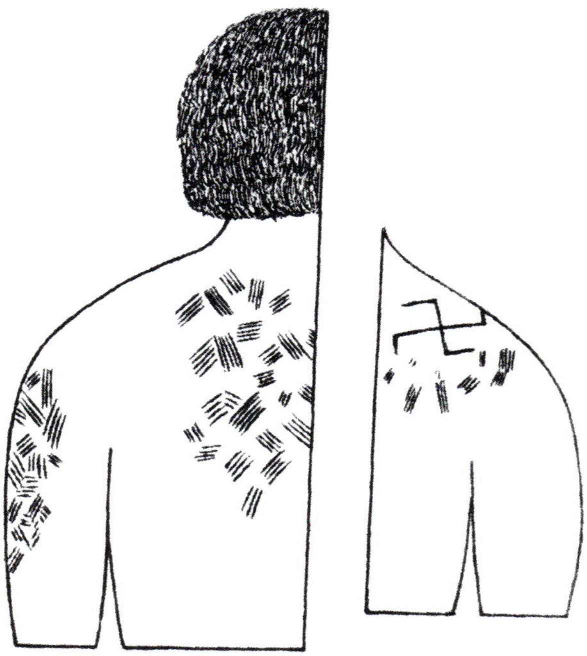

FIGURE 1.7
Ainu *makiri*, or tattoo knife. An apotropaic motif is carved into the handle. Collected by Romyn Hitchcock in 1888 in Piratori village, Hokkaido. National Museum of Natural History, Smithsonian Institution (150715). © Lars Krutak.

FIGURE 1.8
Medicinal Ainu tattooing seen on two women, 1935. Apart from the rows of irregular cuts, which were regarded as a "charm" against ailments such as painful rheumatism, a swastika motif was applied to the upper shoulder. This tattoo pattern was also used by the Ryukyuan people. The women who possessed these tattoos stated they were cured after the tattoo application. At the time of their tattooing (at twenty-four and fourteen years of age), both were residents of villages in the Tokachi Province of Hokkaido. From Kodama 1970:123, fig. 49.

growing dim and they are becoming blind, they should re-tattoo their mouths and hands, that they might see better. . . . I am well acquainted with one old lady who actually tattoos herself quite frequently, in order to strengthen her eyesight."

In the 1930s, Kodama encountered other Ainu women with various forms of medicinal marking. Unlike Ryukyuan hand-poked tattooing, the Ainu applied all forms of tattooing through an incision technique, whereby a *makiri* (lancet) of iron, or obsidian in ancient times, was employed to cut the skin with short strokes. Tattoo pigment (see below) was then rubbed into the wound, making it indelible.

FIGURE 1.9
Women's tattoo patterns of Miyako Island. From Obara 1962:129.

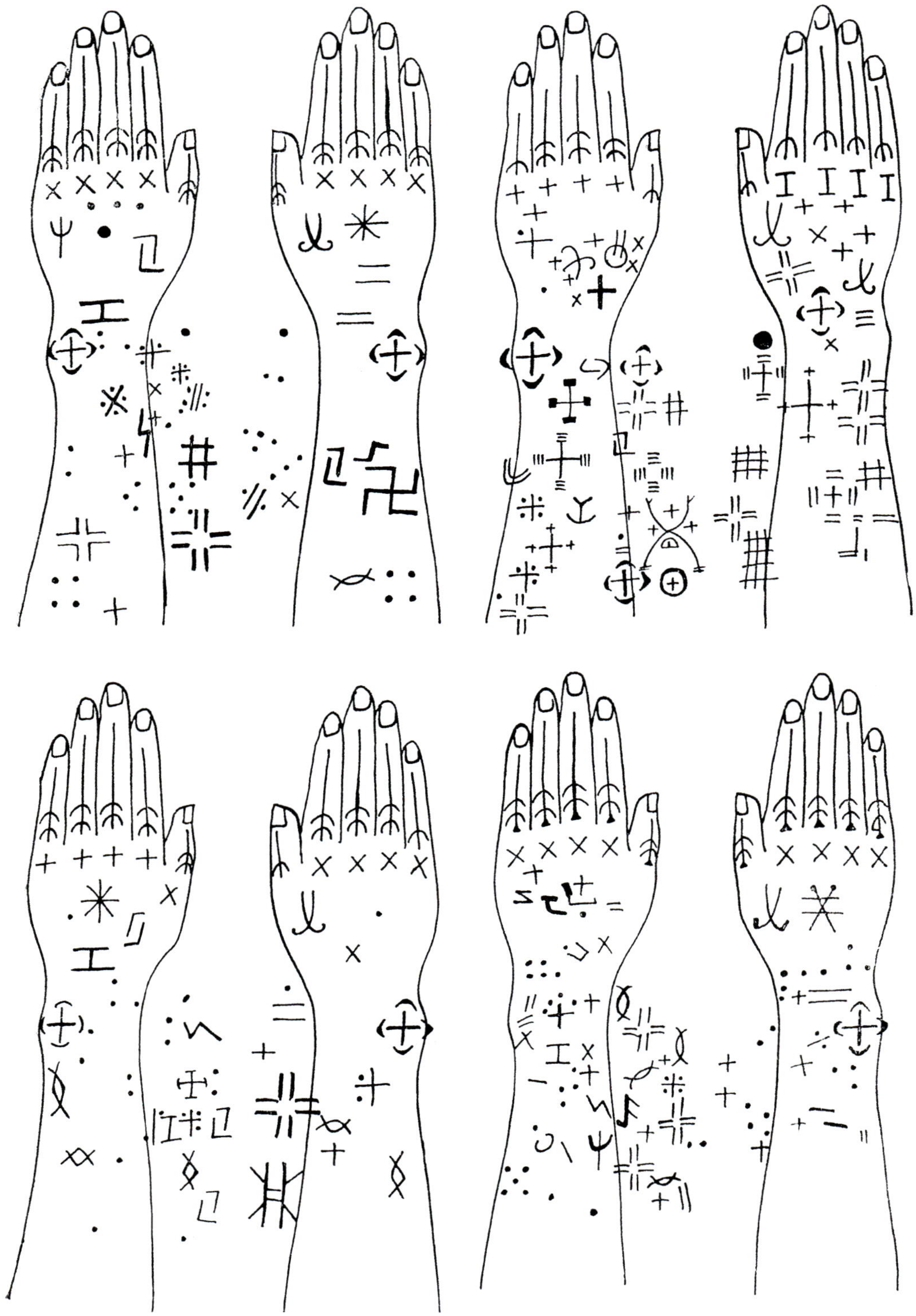

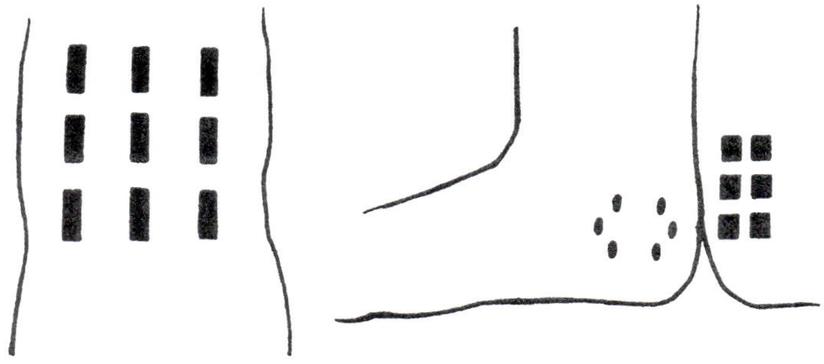

FIGURE 1.10
Medicinal tattooing of Okinawa. From Simon 1914:135.

The Ainu employed the terms *nuye* or *sinuye* for tattooing, meaning "to write," "to carve," or "to carve oneself." Ainu therapeutic tattoos consisted of rows of irregular lines placed on the injured body part (usually the back, upper arms, and shoulders) to cure rheumatism or swelling and pain in the region. One Ainu woman, eighty-seven-year-old Taka Hosoda of Otofuke village, told Kodama she had been thrown from a horse at the age of fourteen. Her aunt had applied a series of incisions to her injured right shoulder, which included a swastika pattern. Soon after the operation, the pain ceased and the "bad blood" was released from her body (Kodama 1970:124).

Similarly, Furness (1899a:11) noted that it was very common to see crisscross markings on the legs, arms, or shoulders of Ryukyuan men and women to cure rheumatism. Women also employed swastika designs in their arm tattoos, but no medicinal value has been attributed to them.

The German anthropologist Edmund Simon (1914:135) witnessed curative tattooing on Okinawa in the early 1900s. One woman possessed three sets of three thick parallel lines tattooed on the posterior side of her knee just above the calf. Another female had two sets of tattoos placed around her right heel; the instep contained six squares arranged in two vertical rows while the outer side displayed six oval tattoos arranged in a circle below the ankle.

Such therapeutic tattooing praxis continued into the twentieth century in the Ryukyus. Glacken wrote that medicinal tattooing on Okinawa was commonly seen on elders in 1951–1952. Sets of blue spots and circles of blue dots made from indigo ink came to rest on the back of the neck, the shoulder, or the upper part of the back. The Japanese anthropologist Yoshimi Yamamoto (1995) reported that *yabuu*, male medicinal practitioners versed in aspects of Chinese medicine, usually applied therapeutic tattoos in the Yaeyema Islands that consisted of Chinese ink mixed with sake or the local spirit *awamori*. Occasionally *yuta* (female shamans) also tattooed clients in this insular region for various injuries. Some of the ailments tattoos relieved included hot flashes, migraines, back pain or sciatica, sprains, and general joint pain. Akin to a form of tattoo-acupuncture (cf. Krutak 1999) practiced in other parts of the world (e.g., Field 1958; Krutak 2013a, 2015a, 2019; Pabst et al. 2010; Piombino-Mascali and Krutak 2020; Samadelli et al. 2015), this treatment was regarded as a universal cure-all. According to Glacken (1955:236), it was considered to be especially effective in remedying neuralgia, inflammation of the joints, neck pain, rheumatism, and general soreness of the back or shoulder.

RYUKYUAN TATTOO PRACTITIONERS: PROCESS, PIGMENTS, AND PAYMENTS

Although Chinese and India inks were used to make tattooing pigment in the Ryukyus, soot from the hearth was used in antiquity as well as in recent times (Nakijin Village Board of Education 1983; Obara 1962). Soot is tied to the *fii nu kami*, or Ryukyuan hearth goddess, who is intimately connected to all women. While there are many *kami* (deities and spirits) in the Ryukyuan universe, the hearth spirit is perhaps the most important because it functions as the messenger to higher *kami* and the spirits of ancestors (Lebra 1966). As it is a female deity, it is almost exclusively prayed to by women because they were believed to be spiritually superior to males. When invoked, this action was for the benefit of the community, kin, or family group, and not individuals themselves.

Apart from tattooing pigment, the ashes of the hearth were used in apotropaic rituals: they were placed at the house gate to prevent attacks by evil spirits, and at the site of a person's death (if it occurred away from the house), as well as in their tomb, to prevent the deceased from becoming a ghost (Lebra 1966).

Similarly, the Ainu hearth is also associated with a female deity, and soot obtained from the sacred fire was used to create women's tattoos, which were believed to be embodied with apotropaic properties. Fuchi, the Ainu fire goddess who was believed to be tattooed, was invoked before all ceremonials because communication with other *kamuy* (deities and spirits) was impossible without her divine intervention (Krutak 2007). Thus, among the Ryukyuans and the Ainu, the goddess of the hearth guarded over families and communities in times of uncertainty and danger and functioned as an important messenger to higher powers. In both cultures, the central hearth was a living microcosm of the universe, because as a ritual space it provided a means by which to actively intervene in the cosmos itself.

The documentary literature on the Ryukyuan tattooing process is sparse and highly fragmentary. So too are the recorded meanings behind many of the tattoo motifs. Through gleaning the available records, however, the process was accompanied by certain rituals, and a few motifs were believed to provide women with spiritual protection from malicious entities.

As noted, Ryukyuan tattooists were almost always female and largely professional practitioners. In remote communities, if there was not a tattooist nearby, the client had to travel to the tattooist, which could entail a somewhat costly, lengthy, and potentially dangerous sailing voyage. Yamamoto (1996:92) recounted late nineteenth-century stories of a client from remote Tonaki Island who made a "once-in-a-lifetime" trip to Naha, Okinawa, for her tattoos. She asked the tattooer "to work carefully" because she might not be able to return. In the southern islands of the Yaeyama archipelago, Yamamoto (1995:4) documented that most tattoo practitioners were centered on Ishigaki Island, and clients living on remoter islands usually traveled there for tattoos unless a tattooist lived nearby.

The tattoo procedure was fairly standard across the Ryukyus, but most documentarians of the last century have failed to record much information concerning its ritualistic associations. I attribute this to Japanese cultural assimilation, the tattooing ban of 1899, and the fragmented memories of many tattooed elders who carried largely incomplete forms of *hajichi* into the twentieth

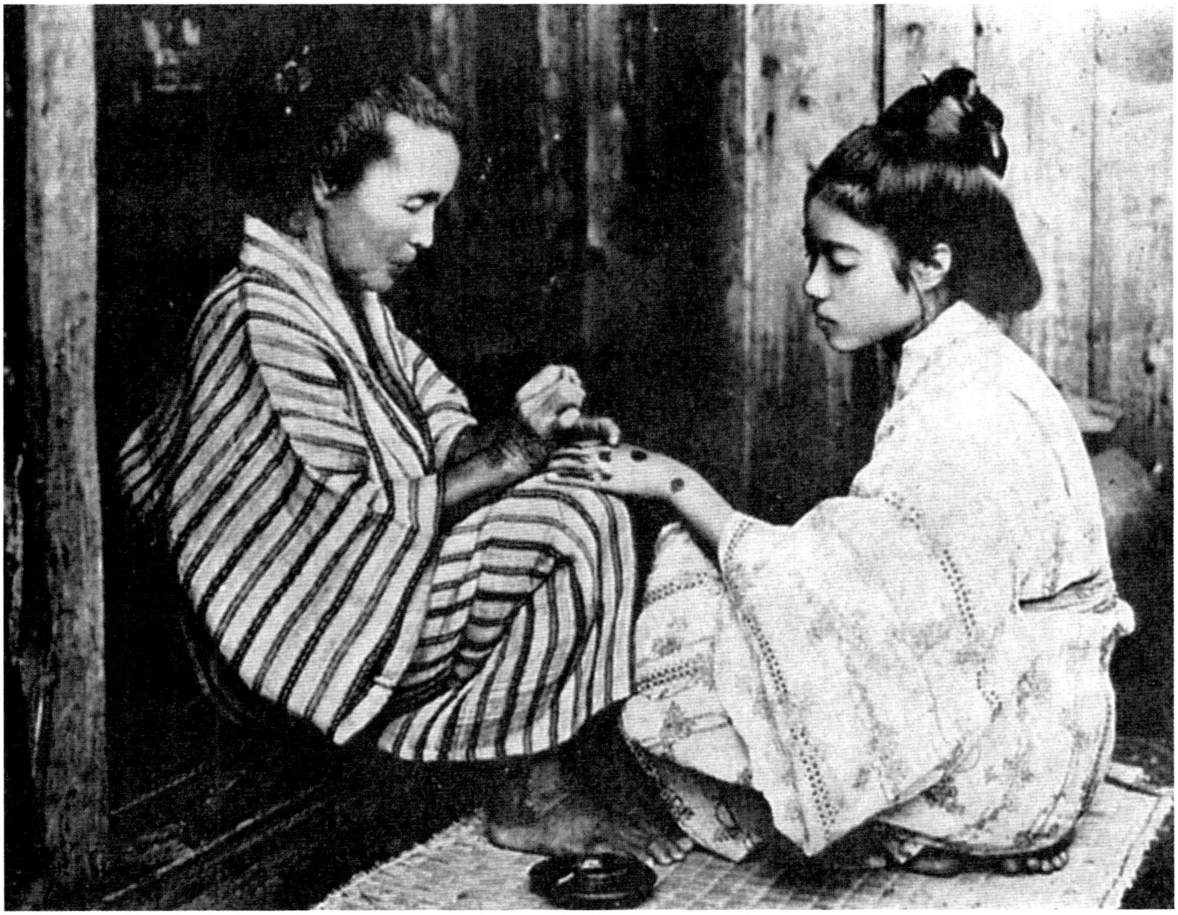

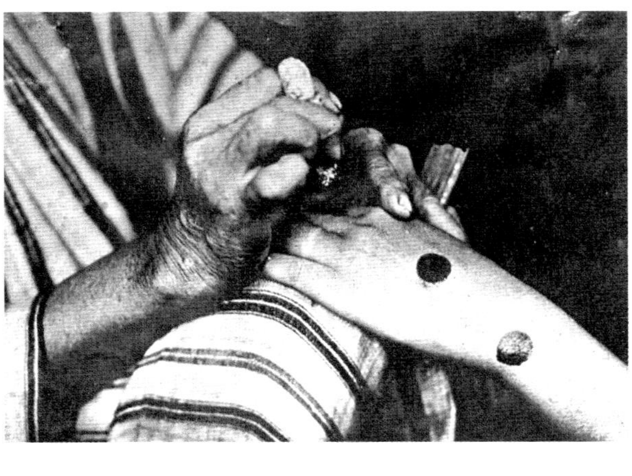

FIGURE 1.11
Ryukyuan tattooing demonstration (*above*), and close-up view (*left*), ca. 1932. From Obara 1962.

century. However, vestiges of the tattoo's spiritual components, which I suspect were commonplace several hundred years ago, survived in the memories of a few women interviewed in the mid- to late twentieth century.

A full set of tattoos took several sessions and years to complete (Nakijin Village Board of Education 1983; Obara 1962). While there are a variety of terms for "tattooist" due to dialectical differences across the islands, I will use the term *hajichyaa* (lit. "person who pokes [with] needles") (Nakijin Village Board of Education 1983:18).[6] A girl's first tattoos were very small, about the size of a kidney bean, and the order of placement depended on the region where the girl was tattooed. Obara (1962:51) stated the general order was as follows: "The order of the tattoo was from the right ring finger, right middle finger, right index finger, and right thumb, followed by the side of the pinky finger, the first knuckle section, and then the stem-shaped protrusions on the side. Once the right hand was finished, the left hand would be tattooed in the same order."

Some authors have stated the process began as early as the age of seven or eight, or even earlier (Nakijin Village Board of Education 1983). Eventually, the tattoos were enlarged when a girl reached puberty (twelve to fifteen years), and again a few years later (seventeen to eighteen years) before she was married (Obara 1962:46; Yamamoto 1996:90). However, Lebra (1966:194) checked village records during his time on Okinawa, and marriages as early as the fourteenth year were common at the end of the nineteenth century. Because it was compulsory for a young woman to receive her tattoos prior to marriage (Nakijin Village Board of Education 1983; Obara 1962),[7] women must have received a full complement of tattoos much earlier than most elders could remember when interviewed in the late twentieth century. Also, Lebra observed that seventy-five years before his fieldwork in the 1950s, the Ryukyuans more strictly observed a lunar calendar, which ran in cycles of twelve years. Calendrical dates and important events occurring on specific years were closely watched by the senior female of the household. He wrote, "The recurrence of one's birth year (*nmari-dushi*) in the thirteenth, twenty-fifth, thirty-seventh . . . sixty-first [etc.] is believed to be a time of danger and susceptibility to misfortune" (Lebra 1966:48).

Reviewing the Japanese tattooing sources cited above, all posit that most girls were tattooed before or after their thirteenth year. Moreover, the Okinawan American writer Akiko Yamagawa Hibbett's (2011:67) partially tattooed Okinawan mother, Hana Yamagawa (b. 1894), whose elder sister was completely tattooed at the age of fourteen in 1891, revealed that, traditionally, "a girl was considered to have reached the age of puberty at the completion of her first zodiacal cycle of twelve years. . . . Often she was tattooed in the twelfth year." These findings suggest that up to and before the late nineteenth century, cosmology was more closely tied to female tattooing traditions, and that calendrical (mis)fortunes were more closely observed before the tattooing ban of 1899.

During their cultural preservation survey of tattooed women in the early 1980s, the Nakijin Village Board of Education (1983) on Okinawa provided a table recording the ages at which women first received a tattoo. Another table documented the tattooing tools and pigments remembered by ninety-six tattooed informants, all now deceased; only two of these women bore a complete set of tattoos. Many of the informants stated that "sumi ink" was used as the pigment mixed with oil, although a few mentioned that tree ash, *nabe* (pan soot), and in one case "indigo juice" was employed; Obara (1962:52) mentioned squid ink as well. From a production standpoint, sumi ink is carbon-based and either made of lamp soot or burnt pine soot. Furness (1899a:11) and others have observed that *shōchū*, a distilled alcoholic beverage, was used to "moisten" the ink; "strong" sake was used too (Yamamoto 1995:5).

The needled tool or bundle could have numerous configurations, anywhere from a single needle to three, five, ten, twenty, or forty-five sewing needles bunched together. Multiple groupings of needles were used to fill in larger patterns on the back of the hand and smaller groupings for finer work on the fingers and arms. In some cases, however, the *hajichyaa* used the needlelike protective barbs from the leaf stems of *Cycas revoluta* (Japanese sago palm) or thorns from *Erythrina variegata* ("tiger's claw" tree).

While traveling on Okinawa and Amami Ōshima Island, Furness collected two tattooing tools, composed of needled bundles, a stick for tracing patterns, an ink slab, and a container for mixing the pigment. The tool from Okinawa held twelve needles, whereas the Amami Ōshima needle contained three needles (Furness 1899b:49). Today, these tools are housed in the collections of the Penn Museum in Philadelphia, Pennsylvania. Furness noted that tattooing usually occurred

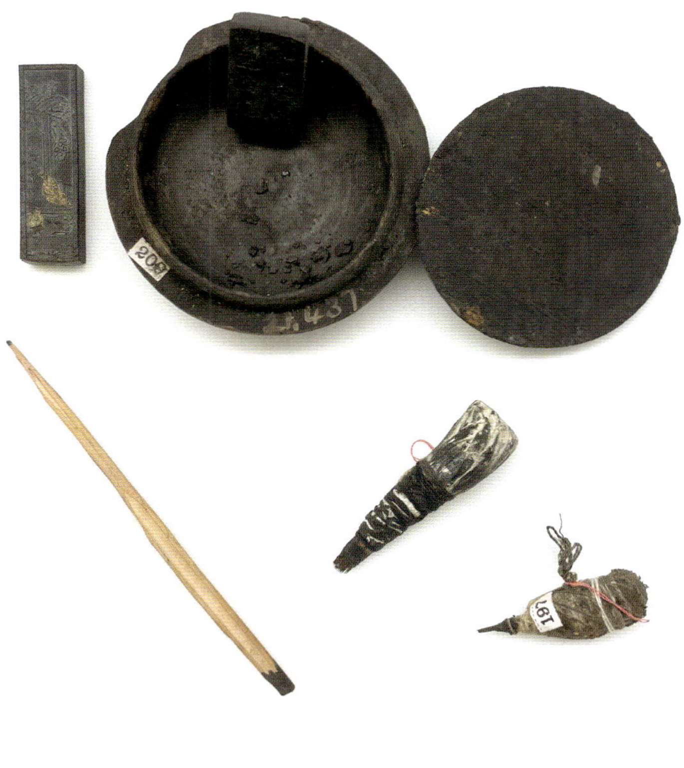

FIGURE 1.12
Ryukyuan tattooing tools from Okinawa and Amami Ōshima (*left*), consisting of two needled implements, a stencil stick, an ink slab, and a ceramic pigment pot, 1896. The twelve-needle tool (*below*) is from Okinawa and the smaller three-needle tool is from Amami Ōshima Island. The needles are cemented together in a row between two strips of bamboo, which are set in a bulbous handle of crumpled paper. Courtesy of the Penn Museum (21436–37).

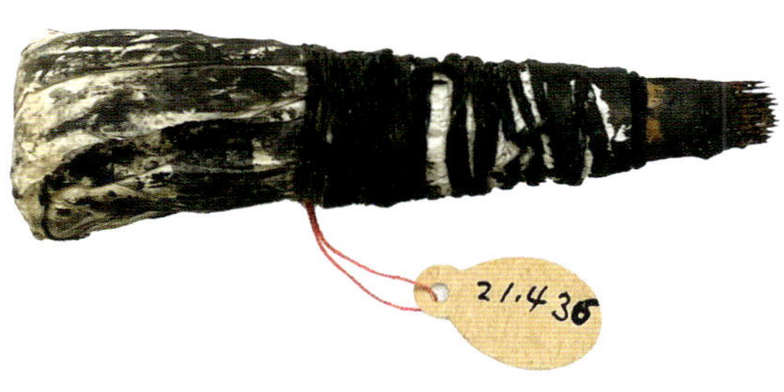

in the winter months of July and August, since work in the agricultural fields had ceased. He also provided a detailed account of the practice: "The design is pricked in with a small sheaf of needles stuck into a piece of soft wood or stiff paper, and then wrapped with cotton thread until a handle of convenient size is obtained. The ink is put on thickly, and the needles jabbed through it into the skin until all of the design has been marked out; the ink is then washed off, and the lighter spots and patches touched up a second time. The whole of the pattern is not done at one sitting, but a part of the hand is tattooed in successive years" (Furness 1899a:11–12). Indeed, the last two completely tattooed women from Nakijin village, Okinawa, indicated that their tattoos were reinked due to fading, a process that occurred "once annually for several years" (Nakijin Village Board of Education 1983:25).

Obara (1962:51) provided further details regarding the tattoo performance: "[T]he tattooist would sit in a one-knee-up stance, placing the hand to be tattooed on that knee, firmly bracing the girl's thumb and forefinger, and placing her middle and ring fingers on a board shaped like a rice paddle."

The tattooing process was extremely painful, and sometimes girls attempted to avoid the pain by chewing on raw rice grains or sesame seeds, cooked soybeans, sugar, and sweets, or they were "soothed" by a song or music from the *sanshin*, a three-stringed musical instrument (Nakijin Village Board of Education 1983; Yamamoto 1996:93). Obara (1962) noted a girl's mother might hold her hand to offer support. The most painful spot was said to be near the fingernails, and if the tattooist punctured her client with the needles held at an angle this was supposedly less painful; tools composed of many needles bundled together were said to be less painful when they hit the skin. Hibbett (2011:200n10) explained "that if a woman could withstand the pain of being tattooed, she would be able to endure the hardships of life as a daughter-in-law."

Once the girl's tattoo was complete, a cloth dampened with distilled spirits was then used to wipe away excess ink and blood because it had disinfecting properties (Obara 1962). In other cases, the tattoos were washed with potato broth. A girl's tattoos might also be rubbed with tofu or covered with the leaves of particular plants, such as *sadifu* (*Crinum asiaticum* L.),[8] to help cool them down (Yamamoto 1996:95), since her raw punctures would have felt very "hot." A white cloth, sometimes of silk, was laid over her hands, then she sat on her knees in the *seiza* position, a common practice in meditation while performing various Japanese traditions (Obara 1962:49n4). The girl was then presented as a woman to her attendant female relatives, as men were not permitted to witness the tattooing, and a congratulatory drinking party was held for the tattooist, who was also paid at this time.

Tattoo work was paid for through various means. Outside of the higher classes, *hajichi* fees could encompass foodstuffs (e.g., liters of rice, millet, or barley, or duck eggs), labor, cash, alcohol, or tobacco, among other items. These payments would have been made at each successive stage of tattooing, although some families might pay the artist in full all at once (i.e., at the beginning) as a way of boasting and indicating their wealth to others (Obara 1962:50). Highly skilled tattoo artists who worked for members of wealthy Ryukyuan families or nobility commanded very high prices. Tattoos for high-class Ryukyuans were refined and slender in form in contrast to the larger and more robust tattoos of commoners. Women admired the fine tattoo work of expert artisans,

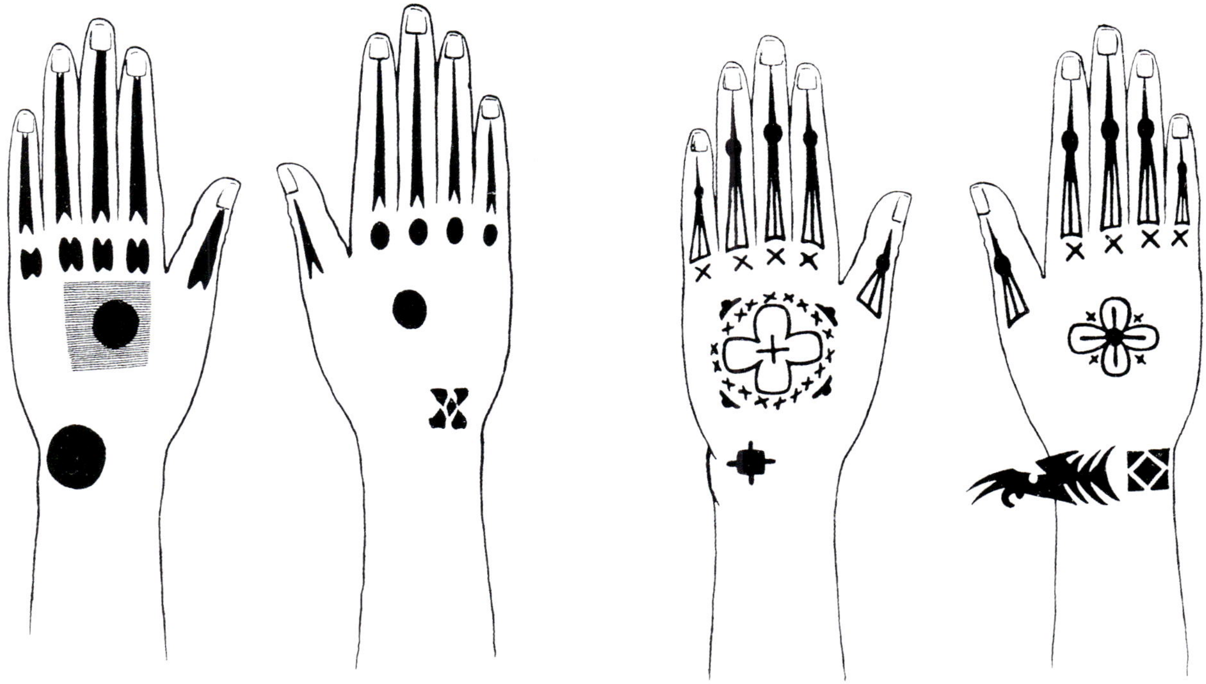

FIGURE 1.13
Women's tattoo patterns of the Naha District of Okinawa and Amami Ōshima Island. From Simon 1914:140, 145.

especially those who tattooed for noble and wealthy families, because they could not afford the high prices charged by these *hajichyaa* experts. In turn, depending on the quality of the completed tattooing, a woman's social status could be read by her tattoos.

Obara (1962) described the costs incurred by a noble Okinawan family in 1892 to celebrate the "coming out" party of their tattooed daughter so that she could join what has been described elsewhere as the "society of women" (Nakijin Village Board of Education 1983:2). Because of the length of Obara's account, I will paraphrase it here. It occurred at Nagasaku Palace, and numerous offerings—a large amount of salt, rice, and dozens of *kammon* (old copper coins)—were presented for use at the tattoo ceremony and eventual ancestor worship that followed. An "inconvenience fee" was presented to the owner of the palace, which included an amount of cut rice, other foodstuffs, and sake to be paid in two installments. Hundreds of cut flowers and a diverse menu of seafood, vegetables, poultry and eggs, fruits, and soups were prepared for the attending guests of the Naha Imperial Court. Another extensive menu was prepared for the grandchildren of the guests, not to mention yet another for additional attendees, consisting of "official assistants, personal suppliers, and calligraphers" (Obara 1962:57). A broth and rice dish were prepared for the maidservants and main cleanup servants, numbering ninety in total.

What can be gleaned from this Okinawan account is that there was a spiritual component of the *hajichi* commemoration ceremony, since offerings were made to the ancestors and the tattooing rite was celebrated with a "formal religious ceremony" (Hibbett 2011:67). Indeed, the date

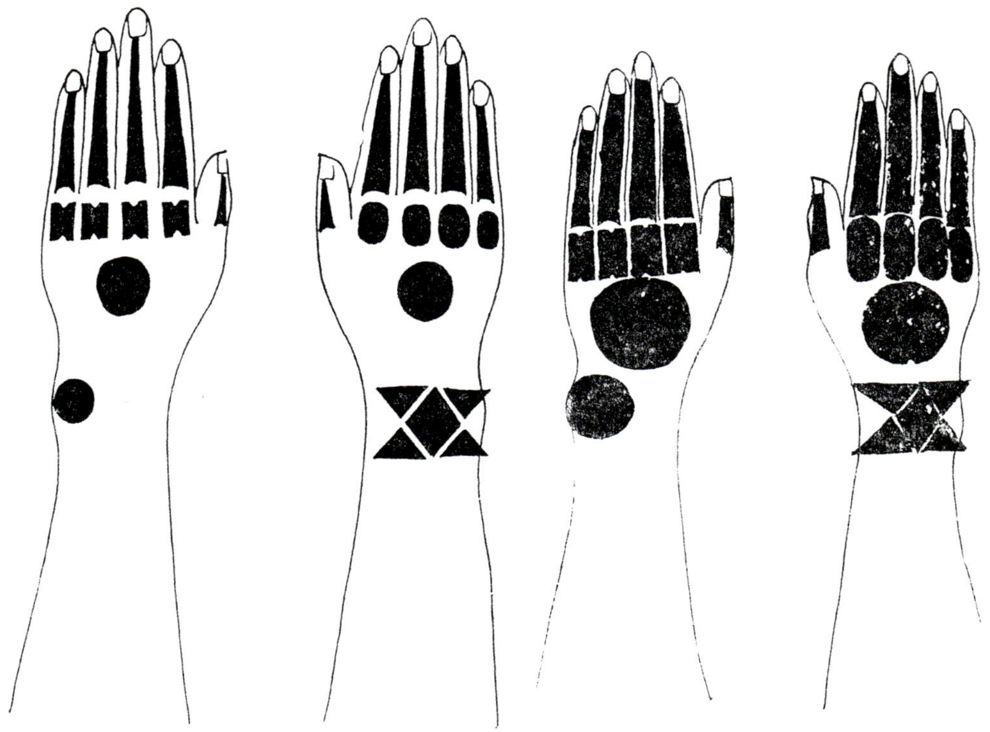

FIGURE 1.14
Women's tattoo patterns of the Naha and Itoman Districts, Okinawa, ca. 1930. From Obara 1962:125.

of the tattooing ceremony was divined through ancestral communications and consultation with the lunar and astrological calendars. Specific days were considered to be fortuitous for tattooing and other activities. On Ishigaki Island, Yamamoto (1995:7) observed that the tattooing day was divined, and close female relatives of the girl to be marked prayed to the goddess of the hearth and to their female ancestors for a successful tattooing session. Generally speaking, Obara (1962:53) noted that the tattooist, before starting the tattoo, "would pray to her own gods [*kami*] that her own tattoo pattern would not fade or change color, making multiple offerings and leaving foods for the gods [and ancestors]." He recorded that tattooists in the Yaeyama archipelago, when working for middle- and lower-class women, provided offerings consisting of sake, flowers piled on a nested box of rice, and *makagu*—a rice ball with miso.

TATTOO TABOOS AND MAGICAL MOTIFS

Various taboos have also been mentioned concerning the Ryukyuan tattooing rite, which provides further evidence of the spiritual nature of this ancient ancestral practice. On Minnajima, Yamamoto (1996:94) wrote that menstruating women could not approach the tattooing site, and that to keep the newly tattooed skin clean a girl would eat only *ochazuke* (comfort foods such as rice, tea, and pickles) and refrain from consuming particular kinds of seafood for one week, especially

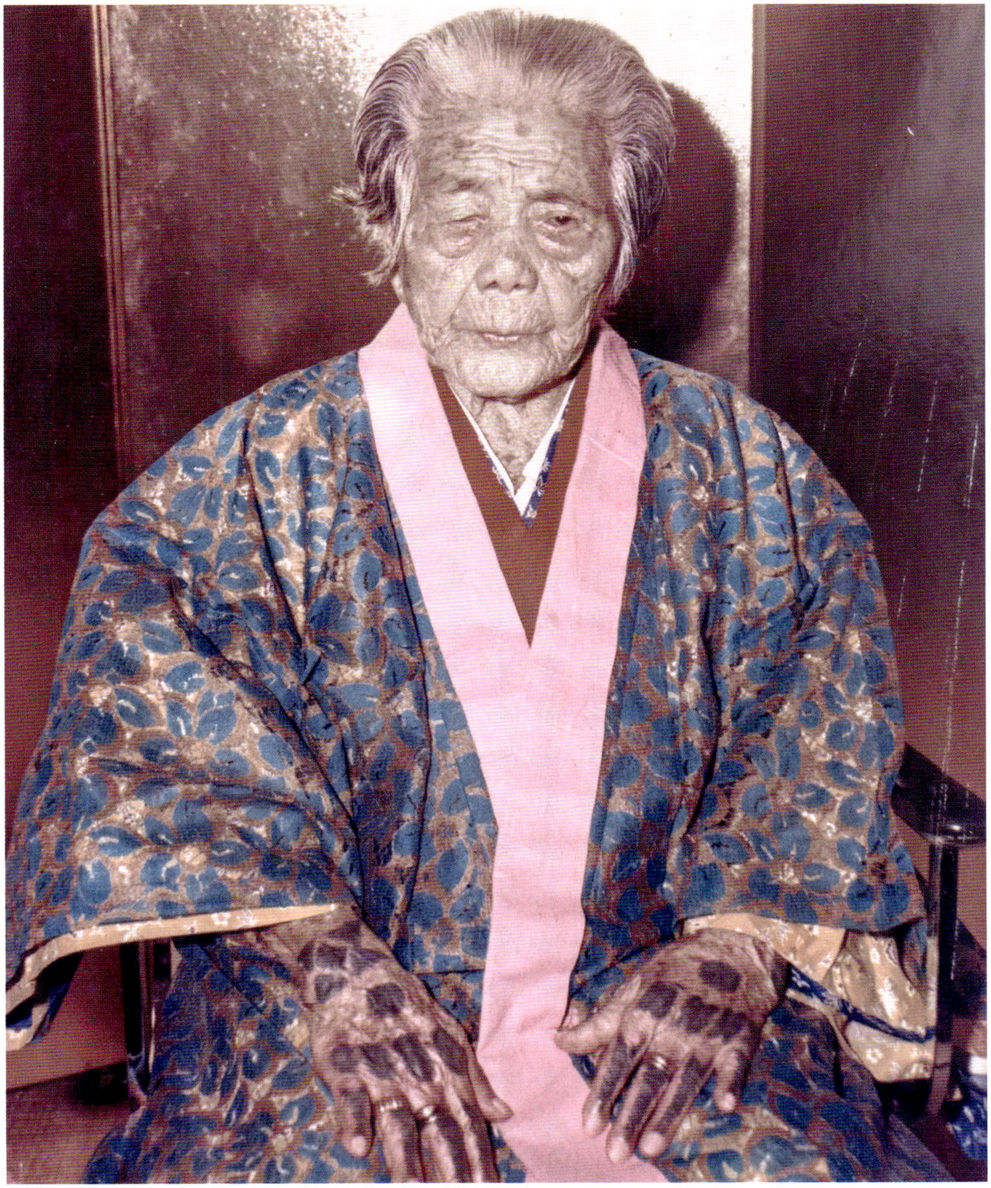

FIGURE 1.15
Women's tattoo patterns of the Kamara District, Okinawa, ca. 2001. © Tube Photo Studio.

octopus, squid, or bonito, which were associated with pus. In another article, she mentioned that women who had recently visited a gravesite or the homes of puerperal women should not attend the tattooing ceremony (Yamamoto 1995:7). Men were also forbidden from witnessing the female tattoo rite.

FIGURE 1.16

Women's tattoo patterns of Amami Ōshima Island, ca. 1930. From Obara 1962:98.

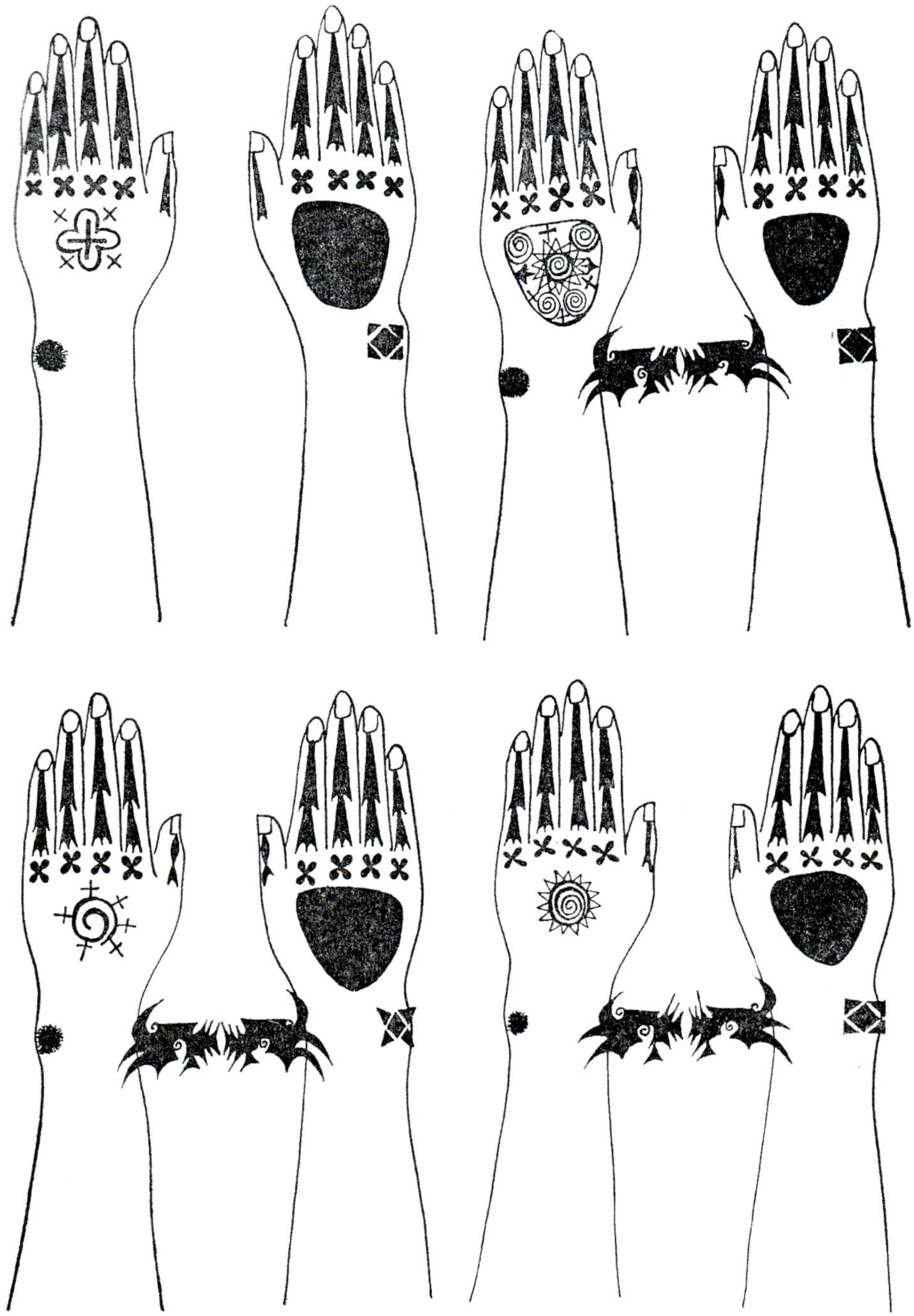

Lebra (1966:49) stated that things or acts that defile or pollute were in themselves considered offensive to *kami* and were termed *chigarimung*. They rendered an individual more susceptible to misfortune because a breach of *chiji* (taboo) impaired the relationship one had with their *kami* and ancestors, since they were no longer under their protection. Although Lebra (1966:50) did not specifically note any taboos associated with newly tattooed women, he did observe that a general taboo period extended to all menstruating women, those who had recently given birth, and women recently widowed because they were sources of pollution. He also commented that these once traditional ritual observations appeared to be in decline, and that young women often ignored them.

Even after the tattooing ban of 1899, many girls continued to be tattooed in secret by practitioners or were marked with small tattoos on their hands by other girls and relatives with sewing needles. Although many motivations compelled them to receive their painful *hajichi* tattoos, some simply wanted to emulate their "glamorous" tattooed elder sisters and "properly bear the symbol[s] of [their] sex and status in accordance with custom" (Hibbett 2011:48). However, *hajichi* were significant from the perspective of traditional spirituality, because nearly every documentarian of the practice has observed that tattoos were necessary vehicles for traveling into the afterlife. As mentioned at the opening of this chapter, Obara (1962) recorded a "tattoo song" relating that tattoos were the only personal possessions a woman could bring with her to the afterworld. Other authors, such as the American missionary Reverend Earl Rankin Bull (1958:64), provided similar poetry detailing these beliefs, such as this poem from Tokunoshima in the Amami Islands: "Marriage is once / Death is once / But I wish to be tattooed for eternal life." In some locales, if a Ryukyuan woman did not receive her tattoos before death, her friends and relatives brushed motifs on her body with ink before the funeral to ensure she was prepared to meet her ancestors (Yomitan-son Kyōiku I'inkai 1982:8). This reminds me of a similar tradition among the Ainu. An informant of the American Benedictine nun and anthropologist M. Inez Hilger attended the wake of an untattooed eighteen-year-old. Her lips were "painted blue . . . with ink," because "even though it was a false [tattoo], the girl would not have been accepted by the Ainu in the other world" (Hilger 1971:46). Indeed, a tattooed Ainu woman "was assured of life after death in the place of her deceased ancestors" (Hilger 1971:151) because tattoos are forever.

As noted above, another spiritual aspect of Ryukyuan tattooing was its apotropaic function. Some motifs worn by women and men appear to have afforded their wearers protection from malevolent spirits of the land or sea. Elderly tattooed women on Yoronjima told Obara (1962:36) in the 1930s that X patterns on knuckles, which were worn by women throughout the Ryukyus, were a "talisman" against evil spirits. He also believed that + patterns of the knuckles were derived from this source. Among the Ainu X motifs appeared on numerous forms of material culture due to their evil-averting powers and crosshatched or netlike tattoo motifs composed of many intersecting X's marked the lower forearms of some women (van Gulik 1982:200–201). As noted, harpoon or barbed "fish-spear" tattoos were worn by Ryukyuan fishermen to repel evil spirits, and women also wore barbed "arrow" tattoos on the backs of their fingers (Obara 1962).[9] The Ainu attributed apotropaic power to bows and arrows, and in some areas "arrow" or "harpoon-head" figures were tattooed on women just above each finger joint (Kodama 1970:129–130; van Gulik 1982:201).

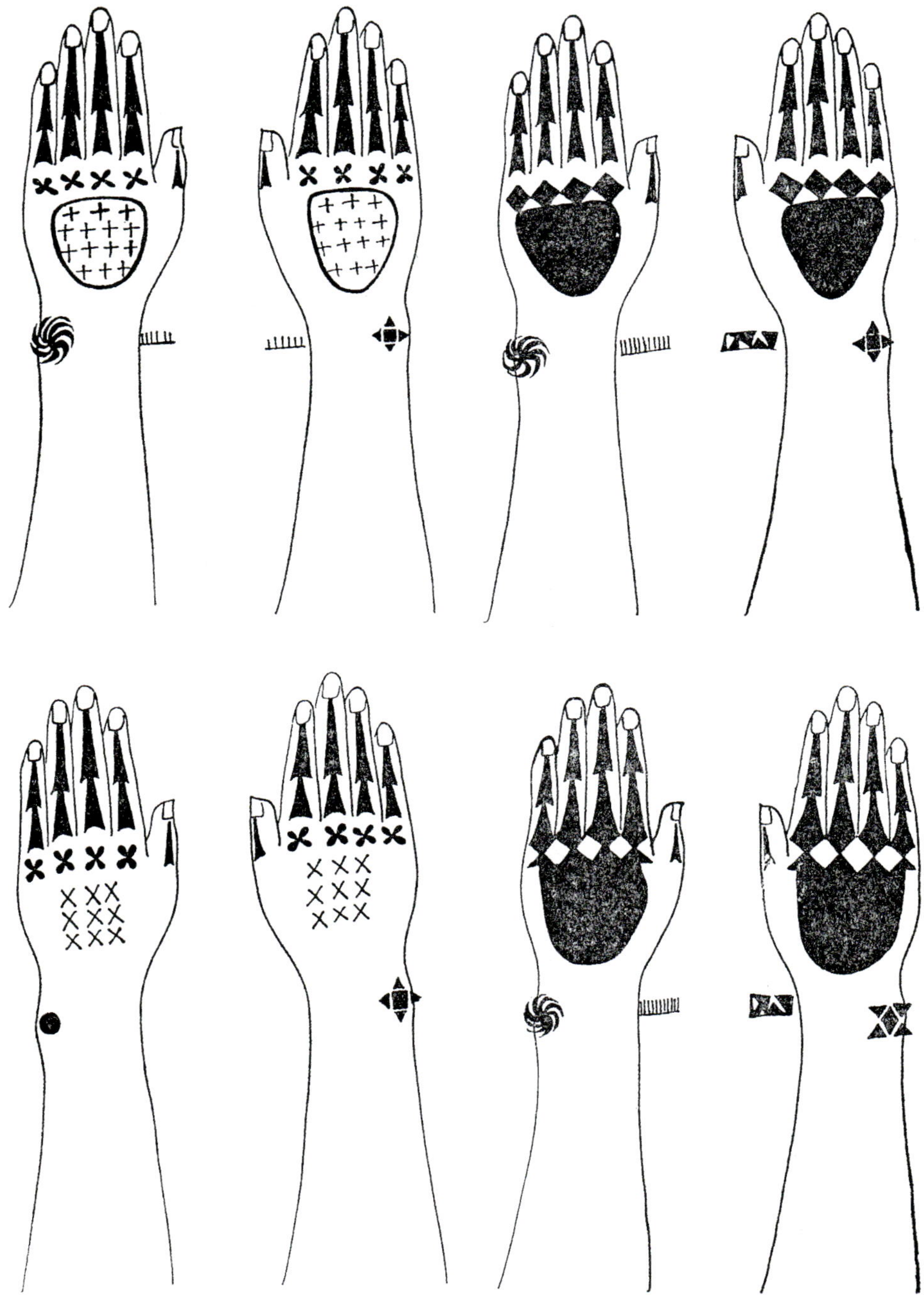

FIGURE 1.17
Women's tattoo patterns of Kikaijima Island, ca. 1930. From Obara 1962:95.

These magical qualities should not be surprising, since globally most Indigenous tattoos were made of soot, ashes, and charcoal, and these carbon-based substances were also widely used in rituals to repel evil entities (Krutak 2007, 2013a, 2014a, 2019). In the Ryukyu Islands, when newborn children were introduced to the hearth goddess, a small mark of ash was placed on the forehead as a means of protection.[10] After a girl married, she sometimes took ashes from her family hearth and transported them to the household of her groom. After a person in a household died, some of the ashes were thrown away, because the deceased no longer needed protection (Furuie 1994). Soot or ash was spiritually potent, and when placed in a tattoo the protective potential of the substance was activated.[11] In this sense every Ryukyuan tattoo, no matter the motif, embodied and transmitted protective power.

Hajichi chroniclers have recorded dozens of traditional tattoo motifs, and completely marked women might bear fifty or more designs on their fingers, hands, and arms. These designs came from nature and included moons, suns, stars, shells, chopsticks, rice, scissors, and bobbins, among many others. Most elders could not remember the particular meanings or functions of the tattoos they bore, although in a few instances some corresponding information was recorded. Insular Yoronjima and Okinoerabujima women wore a *masu*, or blackened square pattern, on the backs of their hands. It was tattooed as a kind of badge of honor because it displayed the woman's "ability to effectively manage a household" (Obara 1962:38). One of the most common tattoos across the Ryukyus was a composite motif consisting of four black triangles circumscribing a diamond. Called "five-star," this motif typically appeared on or near the bony protuberance of the ulnar styloid process of the right wrist. Hibbett (2011:48) wrote about this design on her aunt, which covered three-quarters of her right wrist: "The triangles symbolized the enclosure of the family compound, and the diamond in the middle, herself, daughter-in-law. She was never to abandon the house she was married into. The pattern as a whole symbolized the family ideal of cooperating and working for the goals of the household."

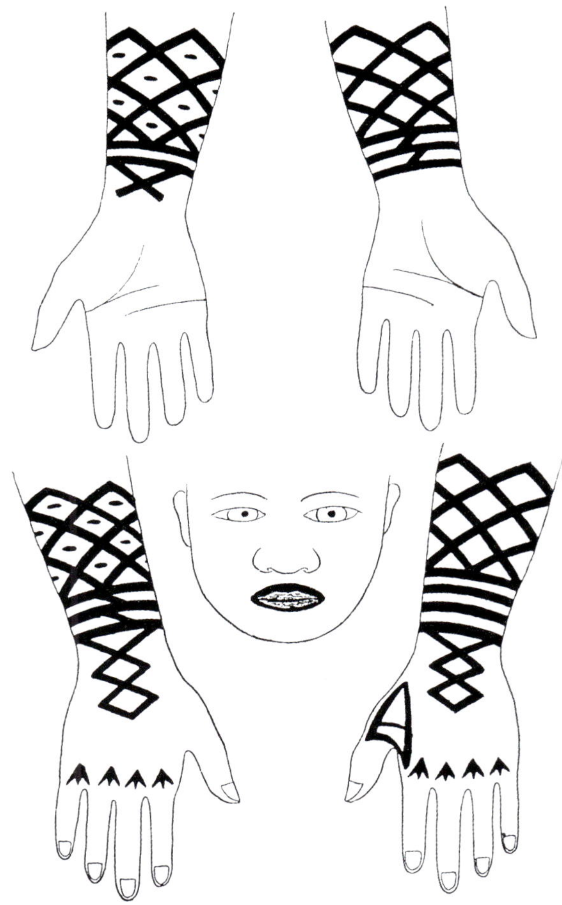

FIGURE 1.18
Tattoo patterns of Kitami, an Ainu woman of Bihoro village, Hokkaido, 1930s. From Kodama 1970:129, fig. 53.

Other tattoo motifs spoke about new family connections and desires, and whether or not they were believed to be forms of sympathetic magic has not been recorded but is perhaps implied. On Miyako Island, one hand was tattooed with a "high table"; one wrist had a "chopsticks" pattern; and the other, a *nigirimeshi* (rice ball). Other motifs adorned the arms and hands of women, but one tattooist told the Japanese writer Shigeharu Ichikawa (1983:114–115) that if a woman was tattooed with the aforementioned motifs she would "become a bride of a rich house, use chopsticks

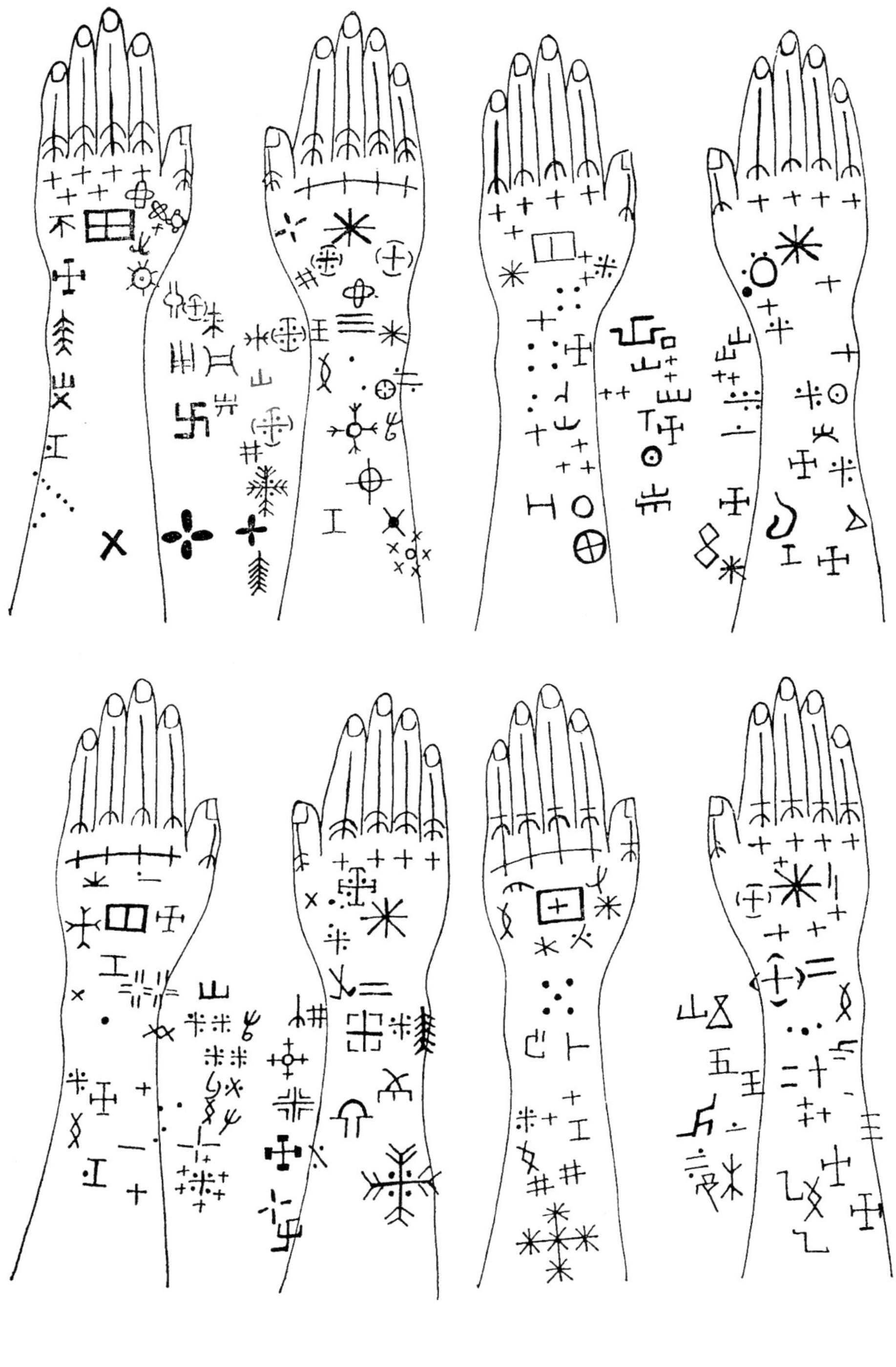

FIGURE 1.19
Women's tattoo patterns of Minnajima Island that include the swastika pattern, ca. 1930. From Obara 1962:147.

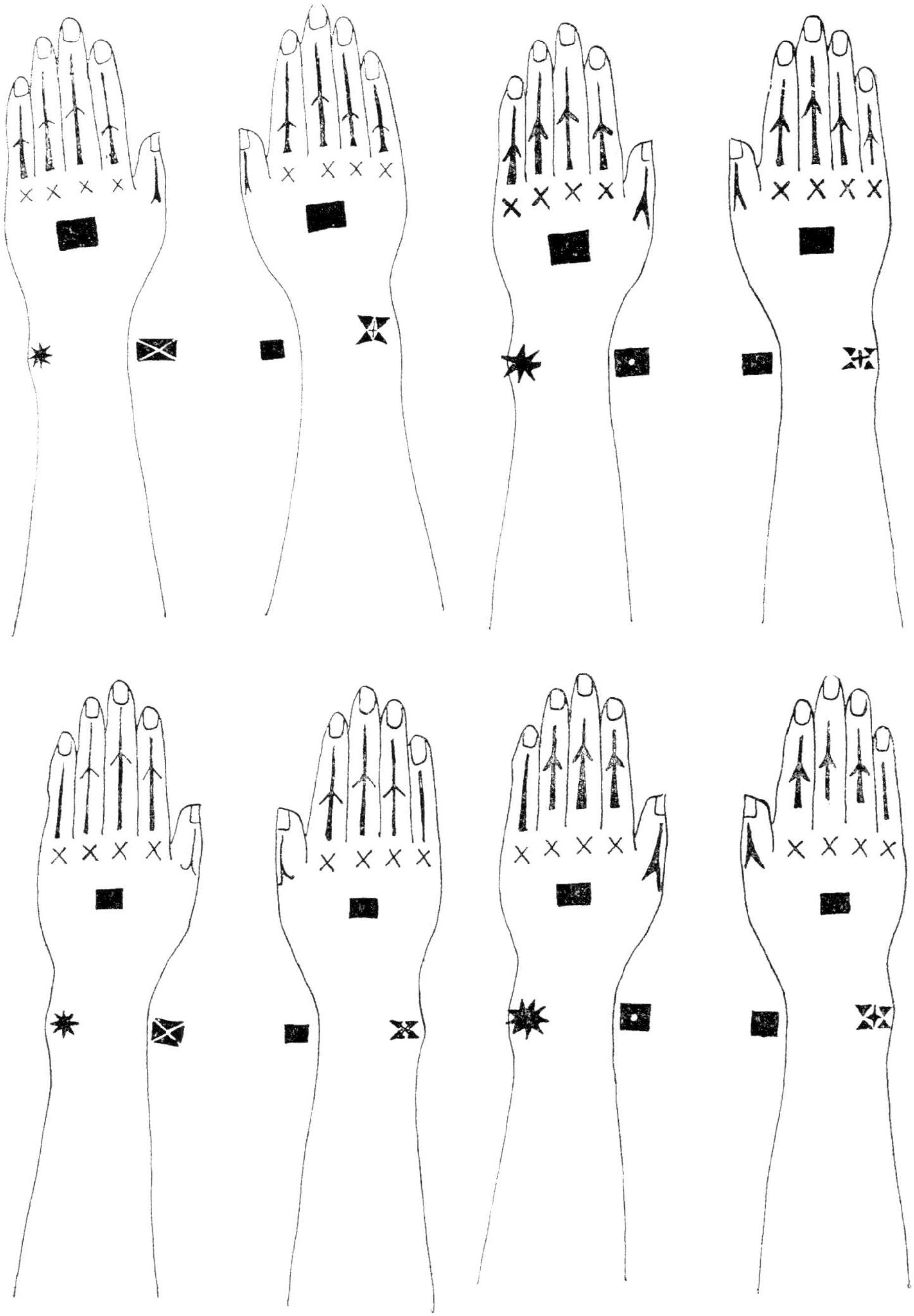

FIGURE 1.20
Women's tattoo patterns of Yoronjima Island, ca. 1930. From Obara 1962:121.

FIGURE 1.21
Women's tattoo patterns of Miyako Island, ca. 1930. Two parallel lines grouped together represent "chopsticks"; six dots, "rice"; and the X motif circumscribed in brackets on or near the wrist, a "high table." From Simon 1914:136–37.

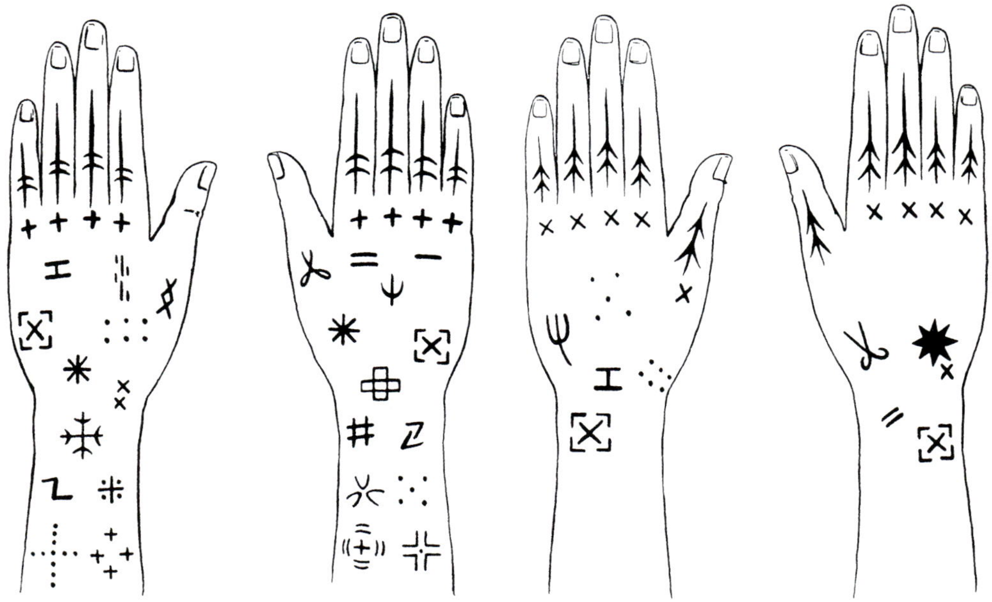

on a high table, and eat rice." Another very important tattoo on Miyako Island was called *umare-ban*, and consisted of one small dot placed on the inside of both wrists. According to Ichikawa, it was a symbol of wealth and well-being, but it too had to be shown to the ancestors and gods to enter the afterlife.

AINU TATTOOS

The Indigenous People of northern Japan call themselves "Ainu," meaning "people" or "humans" in their language (Fitzhugh 1999:9). DNA evidence suggests that the Ainu, who inhabit Hokkaido (and formerly the Kurile Islands, southern Sakhalin Island, and parts of the southern Kamchatka Peninsula of Russia), are the direct descendants of the ancient Jōmon people who inhabited Japan as early as sixteen thousand years ago. The Jōmon existed in Japan for approximately fourteen thousand years, one of the world's longest archaeological periods (Mizoguchi 2017:521), and many Ainu artistic traditions appear to have evolved from the ancestral Jōmon, including tattoo and other body modification practices such as ritual tooth ablation (Inoue and Kochi 1987; Takenaka et al. 2001).

For more than one hundred years, various scholars have argued that engraved *dogū*, or anthropomorphic ceramic figurines, display facial tattooing that closely resembles that of Ainu women (Ryūzō 1919; Takayama 1969). The precise function of these enigmatic objects is not known, but scholars suggest they were deeply embedded in animistic religious traditions associated with the interplay of spiritual, animal, and ancestral forces from which all life was created, proceeded, and on which it depended. It has been posited that *dogū* may have been used for protection against disease-bearing spirits and/or worked as fertility devices, since most examples exhibit one or more female traits, such as breasts, distended abdomens (indicating pregnancy), or sexual organs (McCallum 1988:111). Some figurines were constructed to stand alone or be handled, and many display extremely realistic and detailed facial features. This style of representation suggests that figurines of this type may signify individuals—perhaps ancestors, deities, cultural heroes, or supernatural beings of some sort (Mizoguchi 2017:530).

This artistic tradition continued to some degree into the subsequent Yayoi period (500 BC–250 AD) of Japanese history, when an influx of farming peoples from the Asian mainland arrived in the Japanese archipelago to introduce rice agriculture (Kaner 2009:130). Primarily centered in Kyūshū and extending to northern Honshū, the Yayoi people gradually displaced Indigenous Jōmon hunter-gatherers and eventually gave rise to their descendants—the Japanese people. It has been suggested that the Yayoi practiced tattooing in antiquity. Surviving ceramic vessels detail carefully engraved markings about the mouth that closely resemble those of Ainu women (see McCallum 1988:115, fig. 6).[12] Although it is not known if they were specifically referring to the Yayoi people, early Chinese texts dating to circa AD 300 describe the tattooing practices of the Wa people who inhabited Japan during this time: "As for the men, whether high or low [social class], they all tattoo their faces and bodies . . . in order to ward off harm" from various mythological creatures and animals (van Gulik 1982:24). A later text from circa AD 445 revealed: "[I]t is recorded that the Wa, both men and women, tattoo their faces and decorate their bodies with designs, the size and position of these designs varying according to difference of rank" (van Gulik 1982:24).

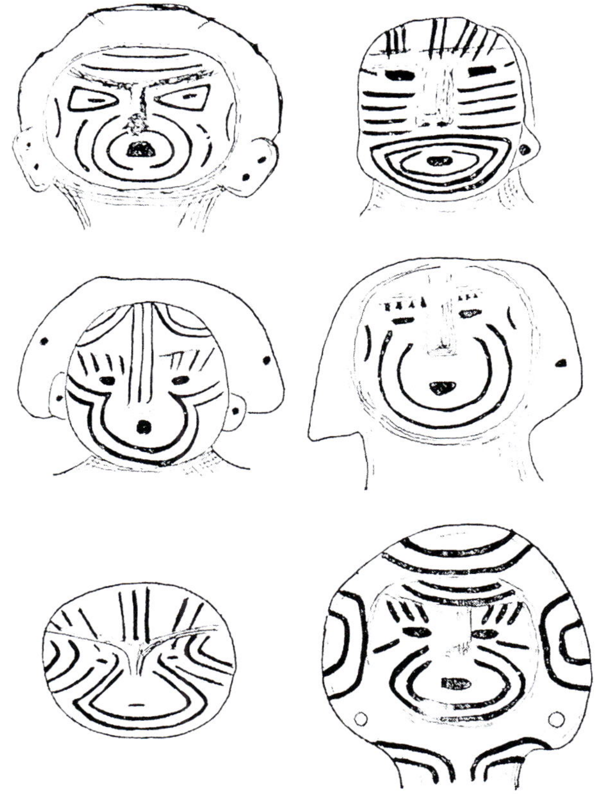

FIGURE 1.22 Facial markings of Jōmon *dogū*. From Esaka 1967:309.

Notwithstanding, the Japanese archaeologist Torii Ryūzō (1919:152) wrote that in all the provinces of the empire, Neolithic and prehistoric statuettes are found with facial markings that represent "tattooed characters"; the tattooing of the mouth was "absolutely identical" to female forms of tattooing. He also mentioned that Ainu men in the Kuriles previously tattooed their lips and, based on historical descriptions of these tattoos, argued that they resembled those seen on some *dogū* figurines, which he offered as comparative illustrative material.

Only a handful of records recount this tattooing tradition among Ainu men, but all traces of it disappeared by the late nineteenth century. During his journeys across the Russian Far East in

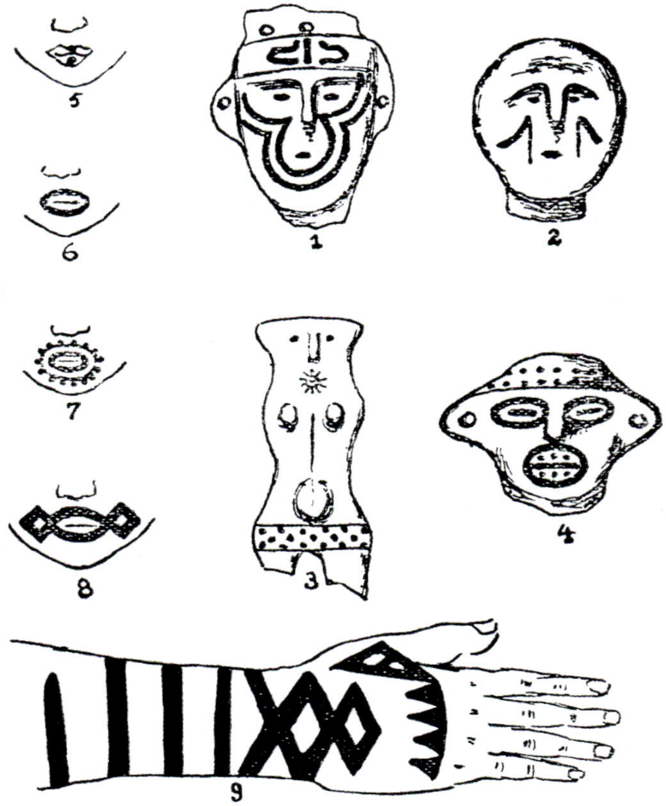

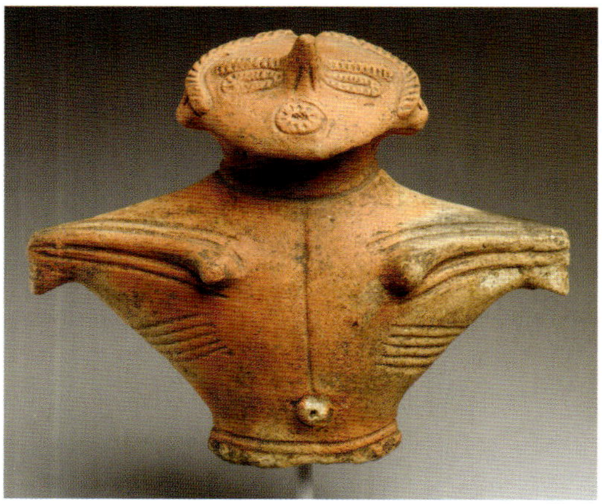

FIGURE 1.23
Jōmon *dogū* (*right*, #1–4), Ainu tattooing motifs of the Kurile Islands (#5–8), Hokkaido woman's arm tattoo (#9), and *dogū* (*below*) dating to the Final Jōmon period (ca. 1000–300 BC). Drawings from Montandon (1937:143, fig. 69). Photograph from Metropolitan Museum of Art, New York (1975.268.193).

the 1760s, the Russian explorer Stepan Krachennikov (1768:165) encountered male tattooing in the Kuriles, writing, "Men only blacken the middle of the lips; but those of the women are all black, and they have spots and borders all around. [Women] still have different figures on their arms, almost to the elbows." Another Russian, the scientist Aleksandr Polonski (1871) cited in Ryūzō (1919:151), observed, "The Natives of the Kuriles, the men as well as the women, tattooed their bodies. However, the men stopped practicing it, but the women continued." As noted previously in this chapter, it is known that Ainu men acquired specific tattoos on their hands to improve their hunting skills. It is also very likely that they practiced medicinal forms of tattooing, as implied by Yoshikiyo Koganei (1894).

Until very recently (the last fully tattooed Ainu woman died in 1998), Ainu women retained a tradition of facial tattooing. The profession of tattooist was exclusive to elder females, and the position of tattooist was customarily performed by grandmothers or maternal aunts who were called "tattoo aunts" or, more simply, "tattoo women" (Honda 2000). According to oral traditions, tattooing was brought to earth by one of two tattooed female deities (Batchelor 1882:213): the sister of the Ainu god and culture hero Ainurakkur (Batchelor 1882:213), who was responsible

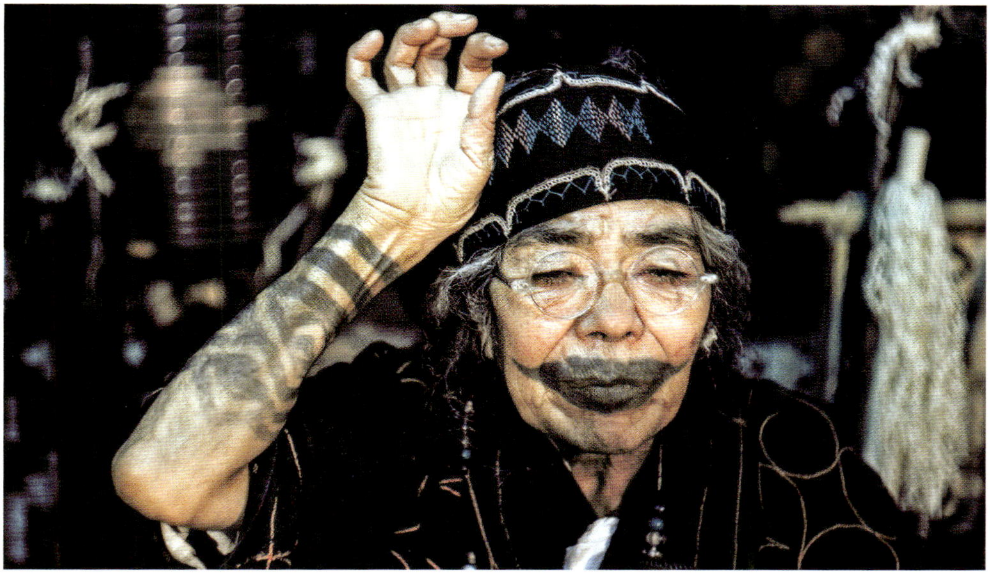

FIGURE 1.24
Ainu woman's facial and arm tattoos, 1962. © Michele and Tom Grimm.

for teaching the people their lifestyle and numerous customs (Ogihara 1999:275) or, as the British physician Neil Gordon Munro (1963:118) noted, the goddess of the hearth, Fuchi.[13] Both of these goddesses also provided instruction, teaching the women the work expected of them. Because Ainu women greatly desired a tattoo like those worn by the goddess, they were taught how to tattoo before the deity returned to the sky (Hilger 1971:151). John Batchelor (1882:213) wrote that Ainu women continued to receive tattoos after the Japanese compelled them to stop, because, as one woman said, "Our ancestral mother . . . commanded us to keep up the practice."[14]

In some mythological traditions, the mother of Ainurakkur's heavenly sister was the deity Chikisani (Irimoto 1997:26), who is associated with fire and elm trees; elm wood was a winter fuel source for the sacred Ainu household hearth. Suffice it to say that these stories connect female tattooing to female Ainu deities, fire, and, as will be discussed below, products derived from the fire itself.

More specifically, the most important female deity in the Ainu pantheon was Fuchi *kamuy*, who was also called Grandmother Hearth (Ohnuki-Tierney 1976:136) or the Great Ancestress (Seligman 1963:13). The Ainu consider themselves to be the "children" of the fire goddess Fuchi, and she was the first *kamuy* to descend from the sky world to the human world when the latter world was created (Tanaka 2000:211–212). Every Ainu home was constructed according to a sacred ancestral plan wherein the central hearth took prominence; it was believed to be the "entrance to the abode of the dead" (Munro 1963:17). Within the hearth was kindled fire, and within the fire was the home of Fuchi, who served as the mediator between all Ainu deities (Krutak 2007). Soot derived from the hearth was used as tattoo pigment, and Fuchi was invoked before all ceremonials because communication with other *kamuy* was impossible without her divine

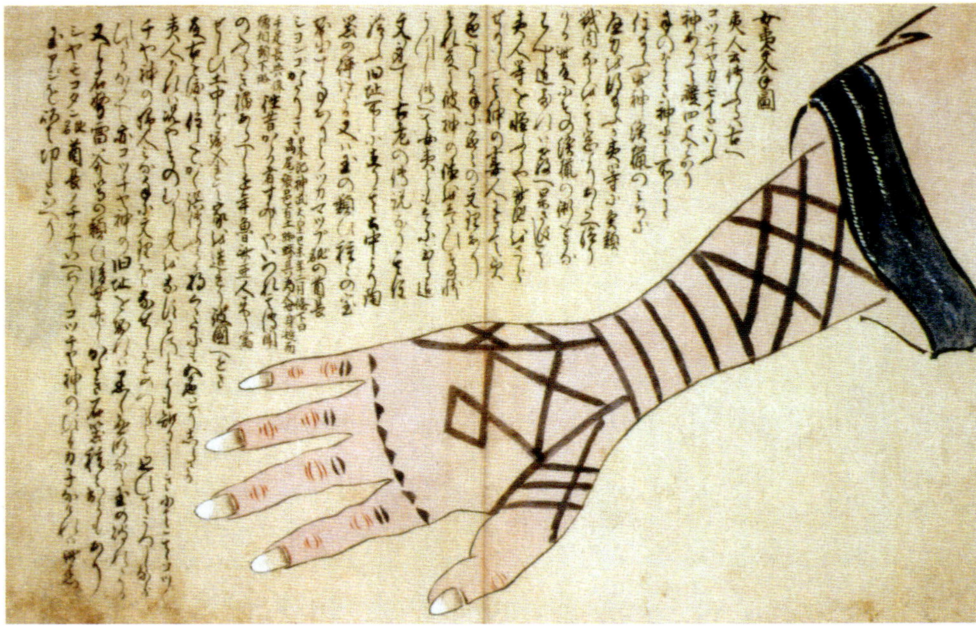

FIGURE 1.25
Ainu woman's hand and arm tattoo, ca. 1790s. From Murikami 1799.

intervention. Fuchi guarded over families and lent her spiritual support in times of trouble, illness, and death (Krutak 2007). However, the hearth was also the space where the Ainu and the gods grew weary of one another, especially if the fire was not always burning. It was never extinguished, and nothing was allowed to contaminate it, because Fuchi never left the hearth. When the hearth fire was covered with ashes at bedtime, Fuchi was "supposed to retire to rest" (Munro 1963:17).

Traditional Ainu tattoo instruments called *makiri* were knifelike in form, and sometimes the sheaths and handles of these tools were carved with zoomorphic or apotropaic motifs (Keira and Keira 1999:235). Before the introduction of iron-tipped *makiri*, or razor blades, razor-sharp obsidian points were used to cut in Ainu tattoos. These tools were wound with fiber near their tips to control the depth of the resulting incisions. Before the skin cutting began, a kind of dark greenish *nire*, or antiseptic liquid, was prepared that helped staunch the flow of blood and perhaps also helped affix the tattoo pigment (Munro 1963:118). A clean pot was strung above the hearth. Depending on local availability, bark from one species of ash tree was first soaked then boiled in the pot; Manchurian ash (*Fraxinus mandschurica*), flowering ash (*Fraxinus sieboldiana*), or Japanese ash (*Fraxinus lanunginosa*, Aodamo) was used (Kodama 1970:117–118; Koganei 1894:263). Sometimes bark of the spindle tree (*Euonymus japonicus*) was employed. These materials, along with *noya*, or mugwort leaves (*Artemisia vulgaris* L. var *yezoana* Kedo), and water were added to the pot. White birch bark was lit under the pot to form a layer of *pash* (soot). The Ainu believed *noya* was efficacious in repelling evil spirits, and white birch is associated with women because its wood was selected to make charms and ritual objects for female deities, including the fire goddess Fuchi (Ohnuki-Tierney 1976:136, 2014:65, 219n9; Philippi 1979:192n3).

After the antiseptic solution and soot were ready, the tattooist took a black cloth and dipped it into the mixture. She carefully wiped down the part of the girl's body to be tattooed. With her fingers, the tattooist took soot from the bottom of the pan and drew the pattern she would soon cut into the flesh. In ancient times, an obsidian projectile point soaked in water was placed in the hearth with charred white birch bark to make pigment. After the birch soot accumulated on its surface, the residue, called *shuma-pashi*, or "stone soot," was used for tattooing (Kodama 1970:119). As the skin cutting began, the flowing blood was wiped away with the cloth at regular intervals. At the same time, the tattooist smeared pot soot on her fingers and vigorously rubbed them into the *makiri* cuts. Female relatives of the tattoo client were on hand to restrain her if she struggled; sometimes the women held the girl's hands behind her back so she could not "fight them" (Hilger 1971:152). While she worked, the tattooer might sing a portion of a *yukar*, or epic poem, to calm her nerves. When tattooing a girl's lips, she sang, "Even without it, she's so beautiful. The tattoo around her lips, how brilliant it is. It can only be wondered at" (Honda 2000:138). The tattooist might also tell a story or fable, including one that spoke about not completing the tattooing: "If you have to quit midway, just because it hurts a bit, you won't be able to withstand childbirth once you've become a bride. And if you go to Kamui Moshir [the afterlife] without a tattoo, they'll tattoo you with a bamboo knife, and that, I tell you, will *really* be painful" (Honda 2000:140). Afterward, the tattooist recited a kind of magic spell as more pigment was laid into the skin: "*Pash ci-yai, roshki, roshki, pash ren-ren*," meaning "Soot enclosed remain, soot sink in, sink in" (Munro 1963:119). This was repeated, usually three times in succession, and perhaps helped activate the tattoos' protective potential as an offering to Fuchi. In Ainu ritual contexts this process is called *ciramatkore*, or "to impart a spirit" (Lewallen 2016:159). Once the cutting ceased, the tattooist rubbed more pan soot into the cuts and cleaned the incised surfaces with the antiseptic solution. But this was not the end of the operation. To complete her tattoos, a girl needed to repeat the process over successive sessions in the coming years. Hilger (1971:152) reported that if the swelling and pain did not dissipate after one week, the cuts were rubbed with mulberry juice because it "ended the pain, but it destroyed the pretty blue color."

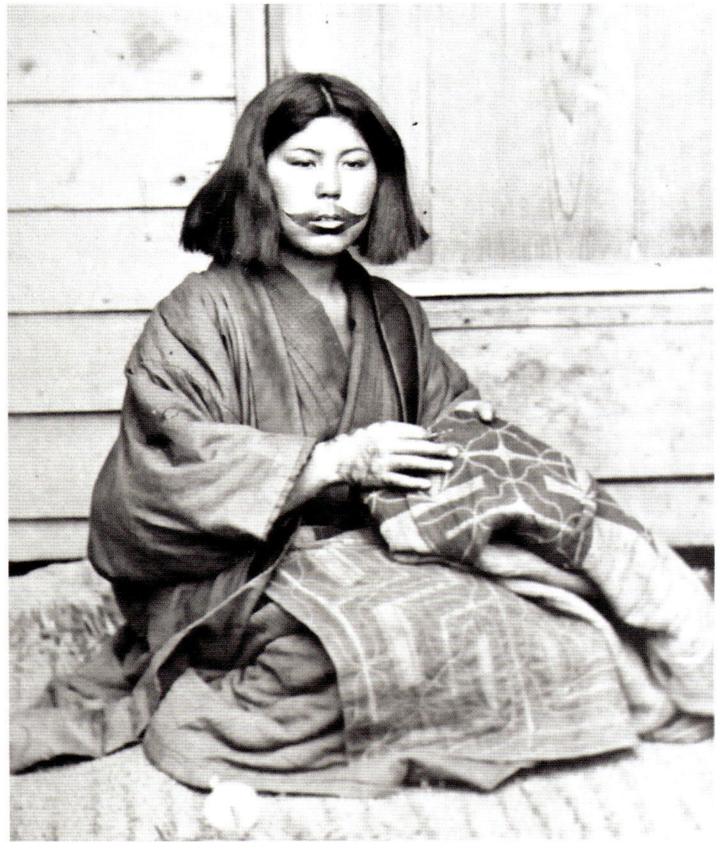

FIGURE 1.26
Young Ainu woman displaying facial and hand tattooing, ca. 1900. Courtesy of Penn Museum Archives (PU-Mu. 1060).

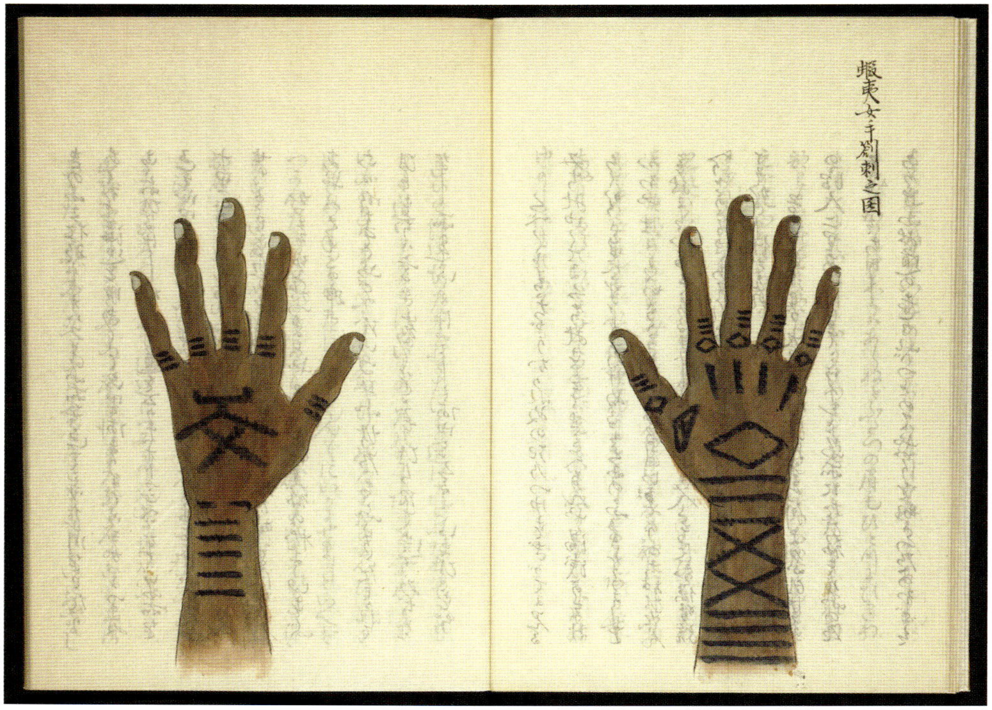

FIGURE 1.27
Ainu woman's hand and arm tattooing, ca. 1810. From Fukui 1814.

Generally speaking, a girl received her first lip cuts at the age of seven or eight, although in some areas tattooing might, in rare cases, first occur at the age of fourteen or fifteen. Once a girl reached eleven or twelve years of age, her hands and arms were tattooed in stages. By the age of seventeen or eighteen, a girl was typically fully tattooed, since it was preferred that her tattooing was completed before she married. Ainu elders told Kodama (1970:119) that tattooing appeared bolder and more beautiful if placed on the "soft" skin of younger girls, although he did note that in some villages the tattoos might not have been completed until after one's marriage.

The first lip cuts were small and placed on the upper lip; when completed they resembled a crescent moon. These were gradually expanded over additional tattoo sessions, usually three, whereupon the tattoo eventually enclosed the entire mouth. Depending on the region where the girl lived, the edges of the lip tattoo might flare upward (central and southern Hokkaido), flare downward (northern Hokkaido), run parallel to the corners of the mouth (Chikabumi Ainu), or not flare in any direction and simply encircle the mouth (Kurile Islands, Sakhalin Island, and parts of northern Hokkaido). There were several other stylistic variations regarding the lip tattoo on Hokkaido, including the addition of two diamond-shaped lozenges at the corners of the mouth, and on the Kurile Islands a series of dots might encircle the lip tattoo.

Although I have not found detailed commentary regarding the stylistic attributes of Ainu facial tattoos in relation to a woman's specific tribal or regional membership, I believe facial tattoos, among other things, operated as a kind of local or regional identity marker because viewers versed in the aesthetic subtleties of a woman's facial tattoo could most likely tell where she came from. Of course, women also carried intricate hand and forearm tattoos that relayed similar identifying information.[15]

A few taboos associated with female tattooing have been recorded. Munro (1963:119) noted several restrictions, most notably that menstruating women were forbidden from being tattooed. After a woman was tattooed about the mouth, she was compelled to observe a strict diet. Perhaps these restrictions were due, in part, to the fact that after receiving the painful tattoo the woman's mouth was swollen and she had difficulty swallowing solid substances or even speaking for some time afterward. Nevertheless, the tattoo recipient abstained from fatty foods and meat and subsisted on water for the first two to three days. When she became thirsty, a piece of cotton grass dipped in water was placed against her lips for sucking (Honda 2000). During the first week she remained at home and eventually began consuming vegetables.

Munro's (1963:119) elderly female informants told him that female tattooing was not only "beautiful" but also emphasized "group solidarity" and "communion with their great spirit ancestress, Kamui Fuchi, whose soot protects them against the evil spirits which, though invisible, are always near." For the Ainu, most sicknesses, diseases, and misfortunes were attributed to the actions and advances of malevolent spirits (Munro 1963:11). Furthermore, a woman's completed tattoos indicated to society that she had reached maturity and was ready for marriage. Indeed, between the intervals of receiving her mouth and arm tattoos (which were gradually enlarged over the

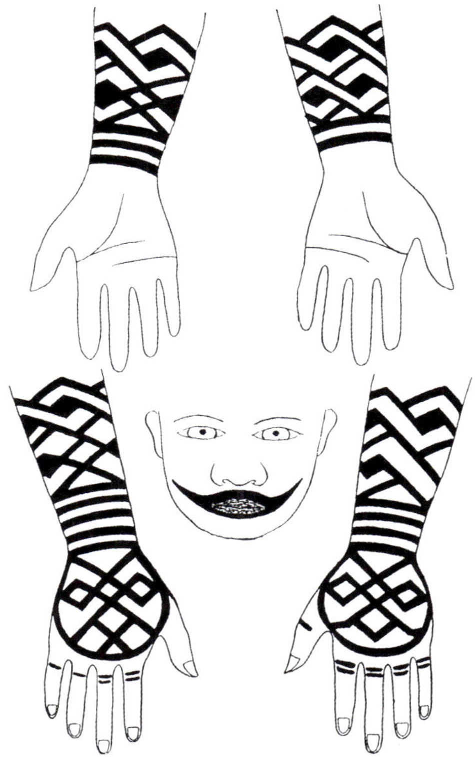

FIGURE 1.28
Ainu woman's tattooing, Piratori village, West Hidaka District, Hokkaido, 1930s. From Kodama 1970:127, fig. 51.

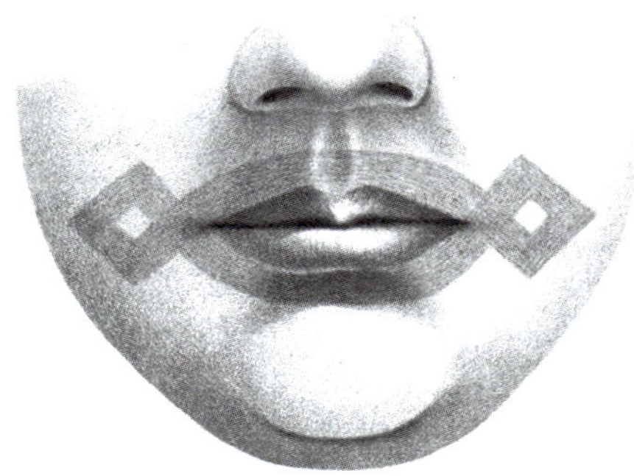

FIGURE 1.29
Ainu woman's facial tattooing, Mooi village, Ishikari District, Hokkaido. From Koganei 1894: pl. X, fig. 3.

FIGURE 1.30
Ainu family, ca. 1920. Although this postcard does not provide the village location, the line tattooed between the eyebrows of the woman was distinctive of the West Iburi District of Hokkaido. Collection of the author.

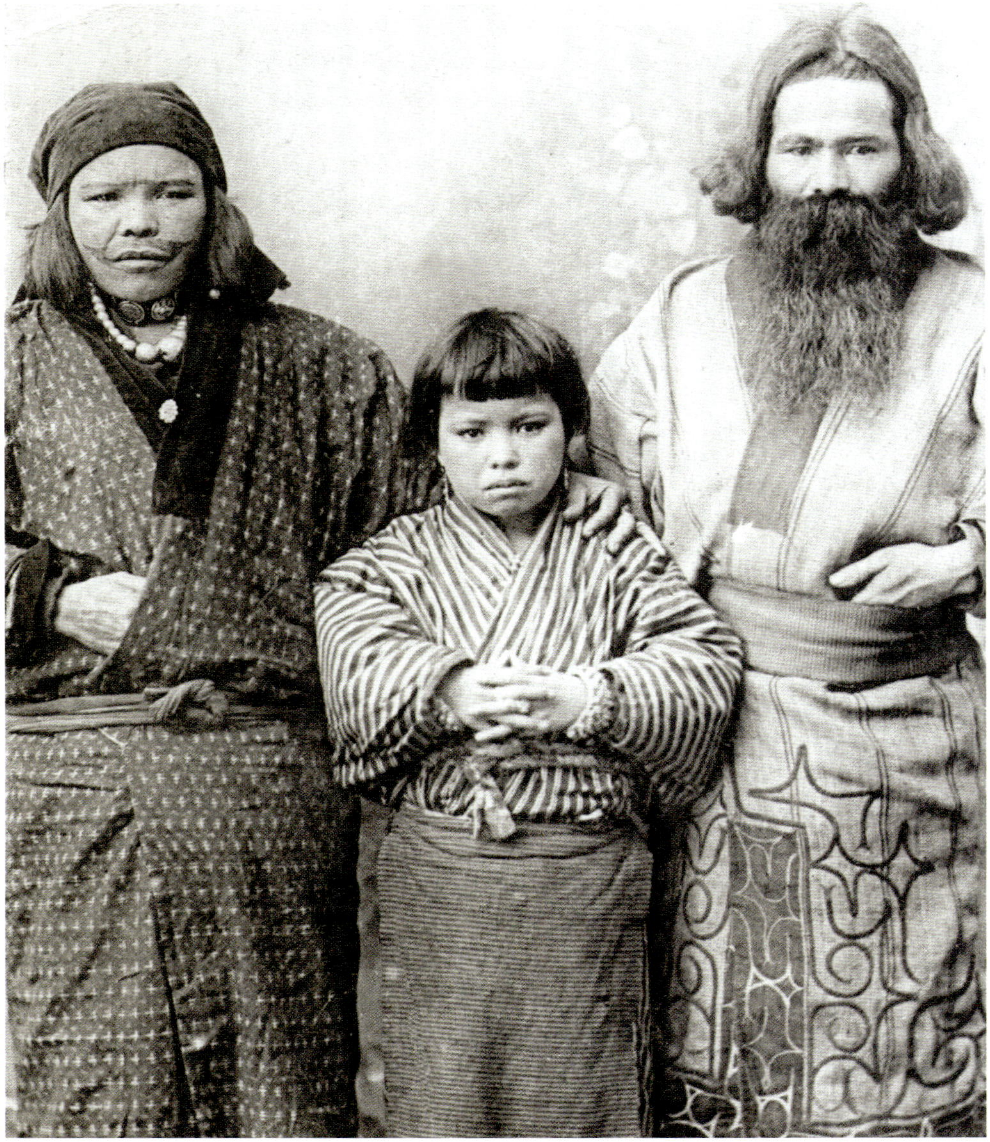

years), the girl would have mastered cooking, thread spinning, and garment weaving skills (Honda 2000:141). Untattooed married women could not participate in feasts, "for to do so would be dishonouring to gods and men alike. Indeed, it would bring down the wrath of heaven upon both them and all the assembled guests" (Batchelor 1901:24). However, a woman's hard-earned tattoos would have assured her of life after death in the place of her deceased ancestors.

Aside from lip tattoos, Ainu women wore bold geometric and curvilinear tattoos on the arms and hands, which also protected them from evil spirits. One motif, the braidform pattern, consisting of two or more interconnected rectilinear lines running diagonally like a net, was often linked to a special design on the back of the hand. The base term for these braided forms is *muriri*, which refers to a kind of tie band used to bind the dead for burial; these ties were thought to embody apotropaic properties (Kodama 1970:121). Two or more wide bands, sometimes connected to the braided patterns above or other patterns below, encircled the wrists of women. These black bands resemble those marking male and female grave posts, which were created with charcoal from the family hearth. Takemitsu Natori (1945:161–162) noted that in some Ainu districts the charcoal was from an elder tree, which was often used as a charm against evil spirits. It was said the soul of the deceased could not go safely to the place of the ancestral spirits without these grave post markings.

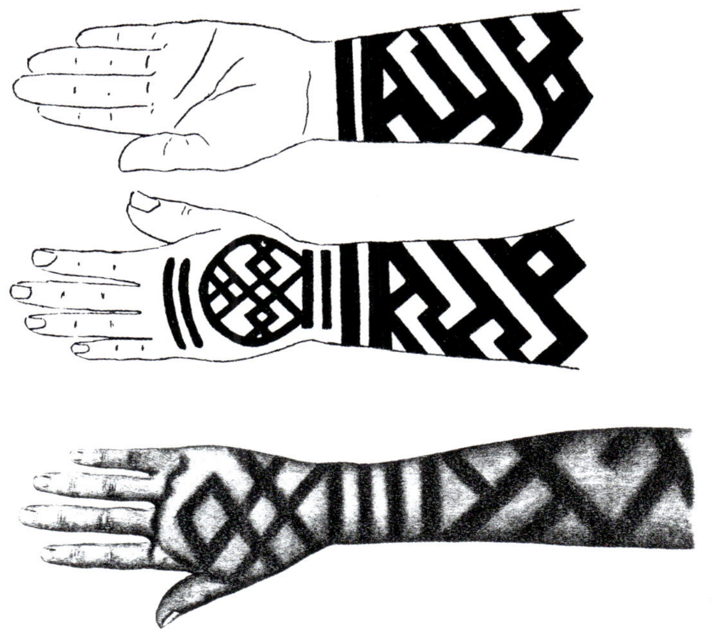

As with burial cords, the braided weave structure of women's *upsor-kut* plaited girdles or "bosom girdles" were also embodied with a powerful supernatural "magic" symbolizing not only a woman's virtue but also her "soul strength" (van Gulik 1982:215). First discussed by Munro (1963), who with his Japanese wife operated a free clinic in Hokkaido in the 1930s, *upsor-kut* were sacred objects worn underneath the woman's *attush* (outer garment) and kept "secret" from Ainu men. They were made of woven flax or native hemp varying in length and width and the number of strands. Composed of either three, five, or seven plaited cords (sometimes alternating with intersecting or overlapping lozenges or chevrons), they closely resemble the tattoo motifs that appear on the arms of Ainu women (Tosabayashi 1948).

Girdles were received on completion of a girl's lip tattooing just before or on the occasion of marriage (van Gulik 1982:216–217). The design specifications of the girdle were passed down by the girl's mother; she instructed her daughter in how to make the girdle and warned that if it was ever exposed to any male, great misfortune would come to her and to the family (Krutak 2007). In Ainu *yukar* (epic poetry and song), the importance of the girdle is emphasized: for a man to see a woman's body, or perhaps her girdle, was tantamount to raping her, and he would have to marry her or kill her (or she kill him). In some epics, when there has been a shipwreck and bodies are washed ashore, other women will run ahead to cover up the bodies of the women who may be lying injured or unconscious so that they will not accidentally be seen by the men (Philippi 1979:50).

FIGURE 1.31
Ainu women's arm tattooing. From Montandon 1937:142 and von Siebold 1881: fig II. Sometimes the abstract geometric hand pattern resembles a degraded anthropomorphic figure.

Tattooed adult women were required to always wear their girdles beneath their clothing to ensure that they could properly interact with Fuchi and not offend her (Lewallen 2016:106). Food preparation, prayer, hunting, and ritual activities directly involved the deity of the hearth. According to Munro (1963:125), all women were compelled to keep a spare girdle ready for their burial, because without one "the soul of the dead woman dare not meet the ancestral spirits." For upon death, a woman was believed to join her matrilineally related female relatives in the afterlife (Ohnuki-Tierney 1976:315).

Munro recorded at least eight types of girdles. Each form was related to a different line of matrilineal pedigree and associated with several animal and spirit deities (*kamuy*), including the fire goddess Fuchi, who originally instructed Ainu women how to make the sacred girdles. There were several magical powers attributed to women wearing girdles: they could calm storms, hold

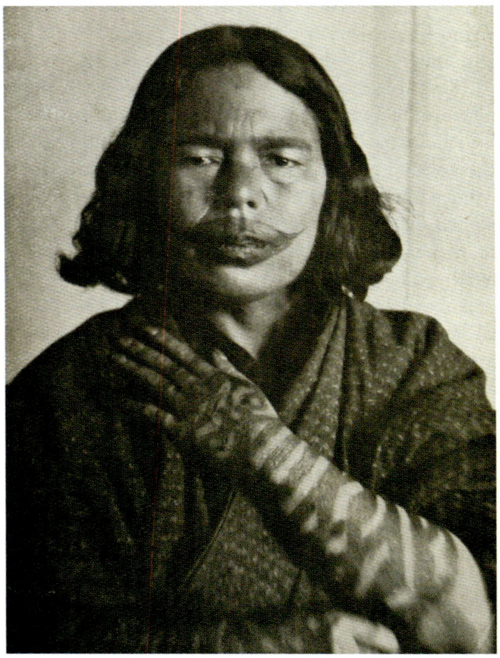

FIGURE 1.32
Ainu woman, ca. 1895. The modern term for tattooing is *nuye*, meaning "to carve," and hence "to tattoo" and "to write" (Shibatani 1990:38, 41, 85), or, more literally, *sinuye*, "to carve oneself" (van Gulik 1982:188). The old term for tattoo was *anchi-piri* (*anchi*, "obsidian"; *piri*, "cut") (Batchelor 1927:49). From Batchelor 1901:21.

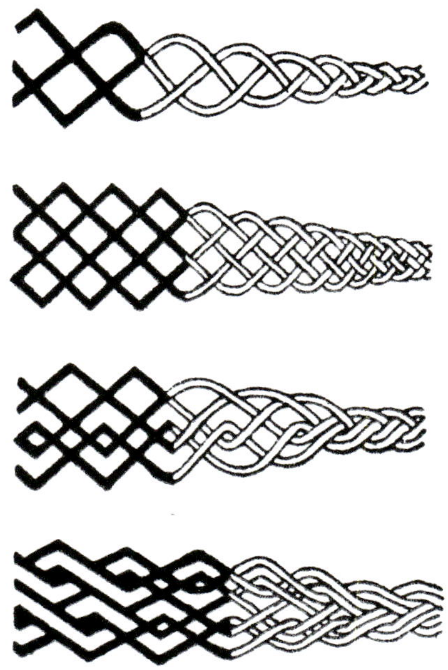

FIGURE 1.33
Weave structure of the three-strand, five-strand, alternating five-strand, and seven-strand *upsor* girdle braid, which closely resemble the braid-form forearm tattoos of Ainu women. From Tosabayashi 1948.

back tidal waves or fires, and repel the spirits of smallpox (Munro 1963:142–143). Similarly, when plagues struck Ainu settlements, untattooed girls were compelled to receive their tattoo marks: "Should contagious disease strike a village, all the women should tattoo one another, to drive the demon [of disease] away. This custom is called *upash-hura-rakkare*, i.e., 'making each other smell of tattoo'" (Batchelor 1901:23).

Aristocratic women, especially the daughters of *kotan* (chiefs), wore more powerfully charged girdles than common women because their ancestry connected them more closely to the gods. Munro (1963:118) observed that the daughters of Ainu chiefs wore more powerful tattoos than others and that they were compelled to complete them before any other women in the village because this action would perhaps "exert a magical influence on the welfare of the village." In this sense, female tattoos and girdles appear to be functionally related.

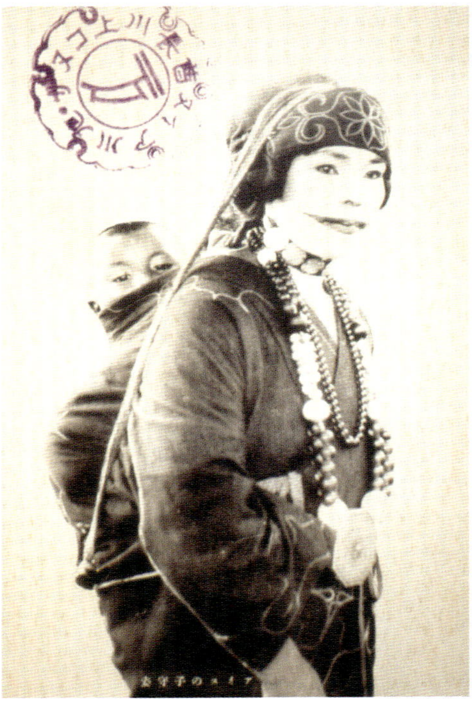

FIGURE 1.34
Postcard portrait of a Chikabumi Ainu woman with child, ca. 1930. The slender form of mouth tattooing was characteristic of this Ainu group. Collection of the author.

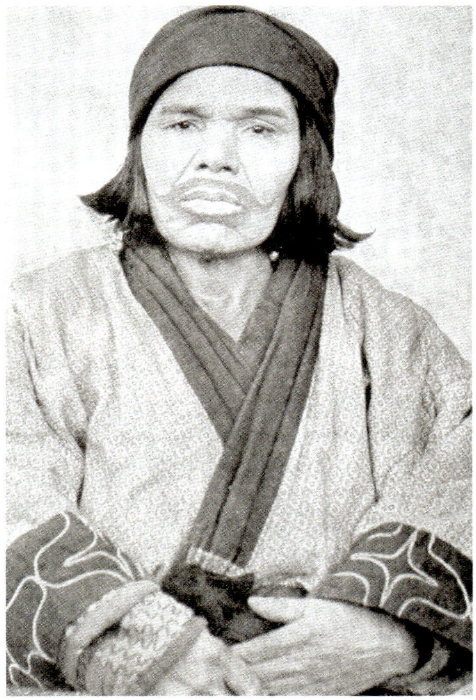

FIGURE 1.35
Ainu woman wearing *attush* garment with magical embroidery, ca. 1895. The embroidery on the sleeves, like tattooing, was believed to keep evil spirits from entering the body. From Starr 1904:69.

As previously noted, Fuchi appears in some oral traditions as the originator of tattooing praxis; she also taught women how to weave their girdles. Moreover, Fuchi was symbolized by the soot used to create tattoo pigment. Because each girdle was associated with a particular deity, or *kamuy*, I would like to suggest that tattooing motifs in the ancient past may also have been associated with specific deities, but these links had been forgotten by the time the last generation of tattooed Ainu elders were interviewed about these timeworn customs. In this connection, Batchelor (1901:23) wrote, "[T]he wives of the heavenly deities are every one of them thus tattooed, so that when the demons [of disease] come, and find that the Ainu women are marked in the same way, they mistake them for goddesses, and forthwith flee away."

Tattooing and girdle making both declined to the point of abandonment in the early twentieth century. Kodama (1970:133) remarked that of the tattooed Ainu women he interviewed in the 1930s and 1950s, most were born before 1892. A few others were tattooed after the tattoo ban, and he stated that the "youngest" tattooed woman he met was born in 1905. Other investigators noted that the tattoo tradition continued in a few locations until about 1920 (Ueno and Yoshii 1955). In the 1930s, Munro observed that young women were no longer skilled in making girdles for themselves, and older women had to perform the task (Seligman 1963:142). One Ainu woman who was tattooed after the ban shared her feelings on the subject with Hilger (1971:150). She said, "I was twenty-one years old before I had this little tattoo put on my lips. After it was done, my mother hid me from the Japanese police for five days. I wish we could have retained at least this one custom!" Another Ainu girl, who was seventeen when she received her mouth tattoo in 1907, was also very afraid of getting her tattoo. She explained that police and local officials patrolled her village, telling the elders, "[I]f you even think about tattooing your daughters we'll tie you up in chains and send you to prison with hard labor, so don't do it" (Lewallen 2016:151).

Despite Japanese colonial pressure to surrender ancient Ainu traditions such as tattooing, the accounts above demonstrate that women refused to abandon the custom completely. Doing so would have forsaken their spiritual connectedness to the ancestors and deities who offered protection and regulated everyday life. Moreover, in Ainu society, tattooing, like girdling, served as a female vehicle for social and spiritual relations, because a woman's identity was closely tied to her female lineage and to Grandmother Hearth. As a material marker of the body, tattooing coexisted with ideas about women's kin networks and generational blood ties that extended into the afterlife.

TRIBAL TATTOO REVIVAL IN JAPAN: TAKU OSHIMA, JAPAN'S BLACKWORK MASTER

Blackwork tattooing, or that which is produced with black pigmentation only, has been a staple of Indigenous tattoo cultures in Japan and elsewhere for thousands of years. Over the millennia, however, blackwork has evolved to become a contemporary art form inspired by ancient tribal and more modern neotribal roots. It has also come to represent other movements in tattoo art such as art brut (raw art), which is characterized by chic noir designs.

As the blackwork scholar Marisa Kakoulas (2013) proclaimed in promotional materials for her groundbreaking book *Black Tattoo Art* 2, "Everything is possible [in blackwork], and everything is allowed." Black lines, spirals, zigzags, dots, and bold geometric zones predominate. The creative scope is unlimited: spiritually infused tribals, sacred geometry, and elaborately stippled patterns with three-dimensional qualities. Today's blackwork is characteristic of completely free, pure, and unconventionally tattooed layouts on the human body. Designs are blacker and bigger than ever before.

The Tokyo-based tattoo artist Taku Oshima has captured the essence of blackwork in his bold and inspirational designs, powerful neotribal works that convey the seemingly endless possibilities of tattoo art that can be created with monochromatic tattoos. And they also ignite the visual senses in deeply profound and spiritual ways.

Oshima has been tattooing for twenty-five years, but before he took the leap to full-time artistry, he studied anthropology at the university. He was first exposed to tattooing in Goa, India, in the midnineties and then traveled the world as an artist nomad for seven years. Because he cultivated his skills and style outside of Japan, he was not heavily influenced by the traditional Japanese *irezumi* school of hand tattooing, featuring colorful realistic portraits of heroes, dragons, and mythological beings enveloping the body. Instead, early on he gravitated to tribal aesthetics, especially Indian *mehndi* (henna) and Indigenous Borneo designs that were graceful, spiritual, and boldly black at the same time. Later, he became inspired by numerous other Indigenous artistic styles, including Polynesian (Marquesan, Māori), Native North American (Northwest Coast), Southeast Asian (Taiwan, Indonesian, Philippines), pre-Columbian (Maya, Aztec), and Indigenous Japanese (Jōmon, Ainu, Ryukyuan), among others.

Over the course of several interviews, Oshima spoke with me about his sources of inspiration. "For me, tattooing is a spiritual act, but I don't mean this in the sense that it is an initiation rite as in tribal societies," he said. "Rather, it's more an act of affirming an already existing identity; it's like deciding to show off the invisible thing which is your soul. I truly believe this. . . . I love any kind of tribal tattoo," he proclaimed. "And ideally the larger the piece, the better. But until recently here in Japan, tribal tattooing was not that popular, and when people decided to get one, these were usually very small pieces. Things are changing now and more Japanese are gravitating to these ancient designs."

But just a few years ago, Oshima was a bit frustrated. "I felt like a Sumo wrestler," he explained. "I was grappling with what clients desired and what I wanted to create for them—big, black, tribally inspired artworks. I wanted entire human canvases or at least large works that could be seen clearly from ten meters away. This is what I love to create!".

In 2016, some of Oshima's dreams came true when he created *The Jōmon Tribe Project* with the writer and photographer Ryoichi "Keroppy" Maeda. For several years before that, Oshima had been pushing his clients to help him revive Indigenous Japanese tattoo traditional patterns—Ryukyuan, Ainu, Jōmon—that were no longer practiced. And some of his first creations were Jōmon-styled tattoos. Oshima told me, "I want people around the world to become aware of these incredibly beautiful tattooing styles that only recently have been rediscovered."

FIGURE 1.36
Taku Oshima at work, 2015. Courtesy of the artist.

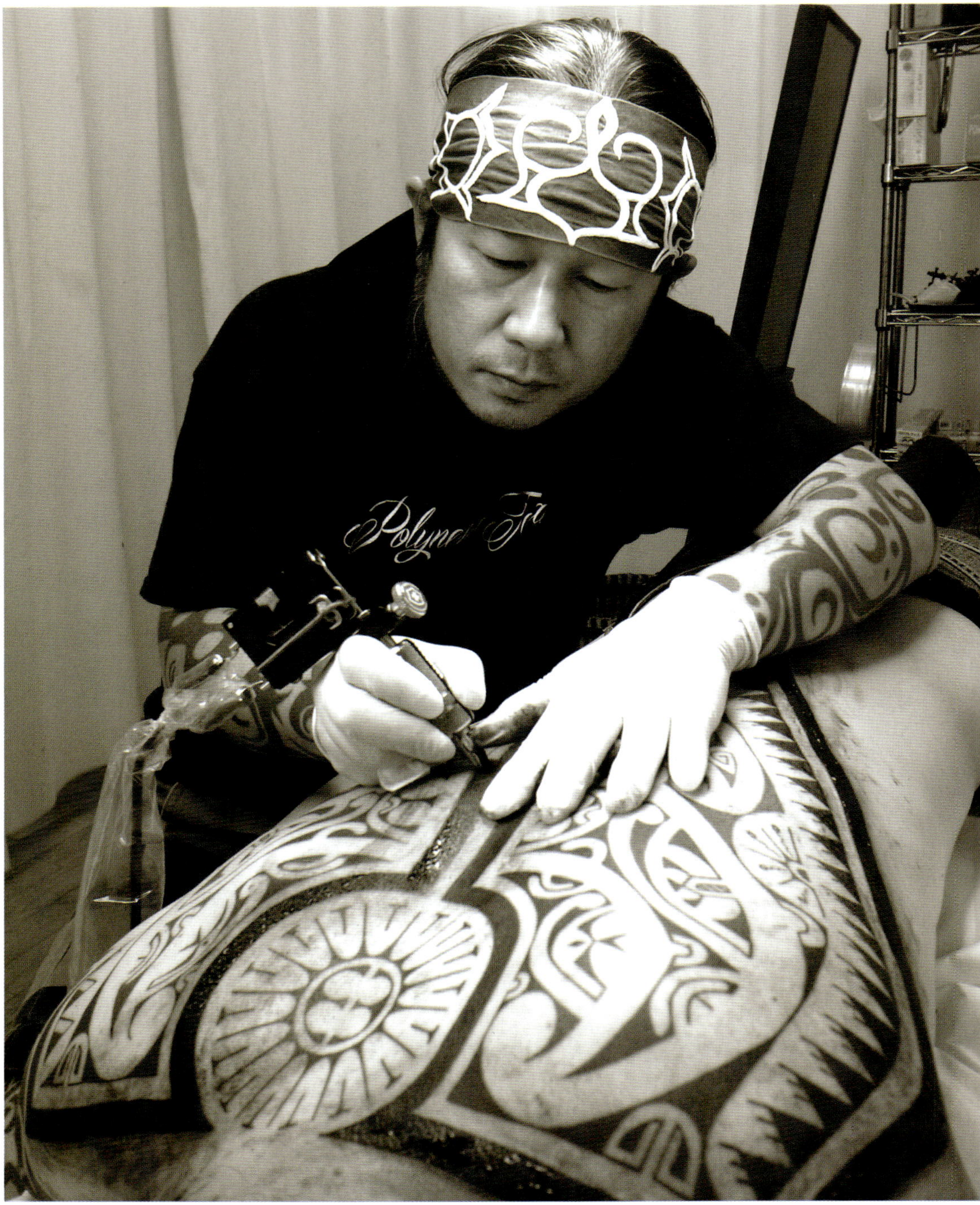

Oshima's clients are drawn to the *Jōmon Tribe Project* for a variety of reasons. The record shop owner Yukako Qudha never thought she would ever receive a tattoo. But she was impressed by Oshima's unique style and by his premise that to participate in the *Project* you accept that your entire body will become tattooed. "I thought it was meaningful that the whole body would become a work of art. I also felt that being able to participate in the project to revive the custom of tattoos that existed in the Jōmon period was significant in itself," she said. She explained, "In order to decipher the social situation of modern Japan, it is very important and meaningful to know what the consciousness and sensations of the ancients were like. I have been researching the ancients to learn more about my own personal history."

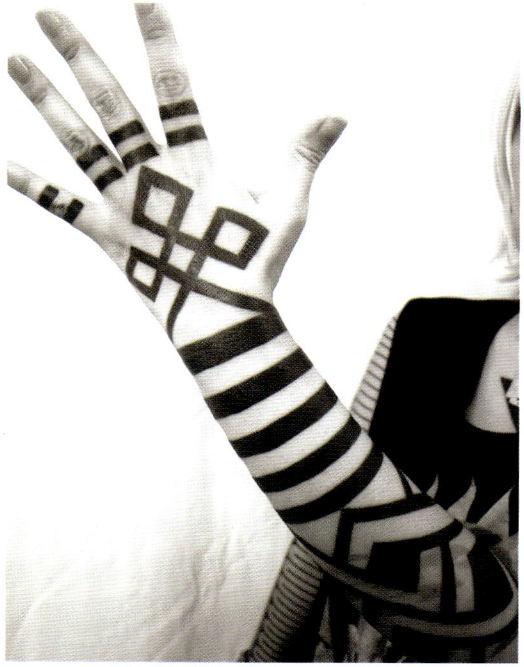

FIGURE 1.37
Ainu inspired sleeve by Taku Oshima, 2016. Courtesy of the artist.

For eight months, Qudha visited Oshima every two weeks for tattooing sessions lasting five to six hours, and then her full-body tattoo was complete. Regarding Oshima's process, she revealed, "The Jōmon tattoo design is created freehand by Taku. The basis of his tribal tattoo is a symmetrical design, but the human body is often not symmetrical. Therefore, he captures the distortions and habits of each model's body and draws the lines that seem most balanced and ideal when viewed as a whole. The enormous and difficult work is truly a mark of craftsmanship, and he aims to create a most beautiful design that can be seen from a distance."

Qudha also told me how her tattoo transformed her: "It's an amazing experience. More than a change in appearance, there was a change in my senses and the inner evolution that accompanied it, which I had never expected before I got a tattoo. I feel less doubtful and anxious about my life, and my senses are more acute. Tattooists were often shamans in ancient times, but they may still have such a role in modern times."

Norihide Ensako is another of Oshima's clients and a practicing psychiatrist. When I asked what compelled him to receive a Jōmon-inspired tattoo versus a more popular Western- or Japanese-style *irezumi* tattoo, he said, "When I thought about my identity, I wanted to connect more deeply with my Japanese identity, both historically and spiritually. It needed to be more archetypal, magical, and spiritual. As a psychiatrist, I know that there is a universal story, a symbol, that is deeper than that of an individual's life story, of a people, of a nation, and that when people lose it, they feel a spiritual emptiness. Taku's Jōmon tattoos had all these things but were also a beautiful form of art embodied with a postmodern cleverness."

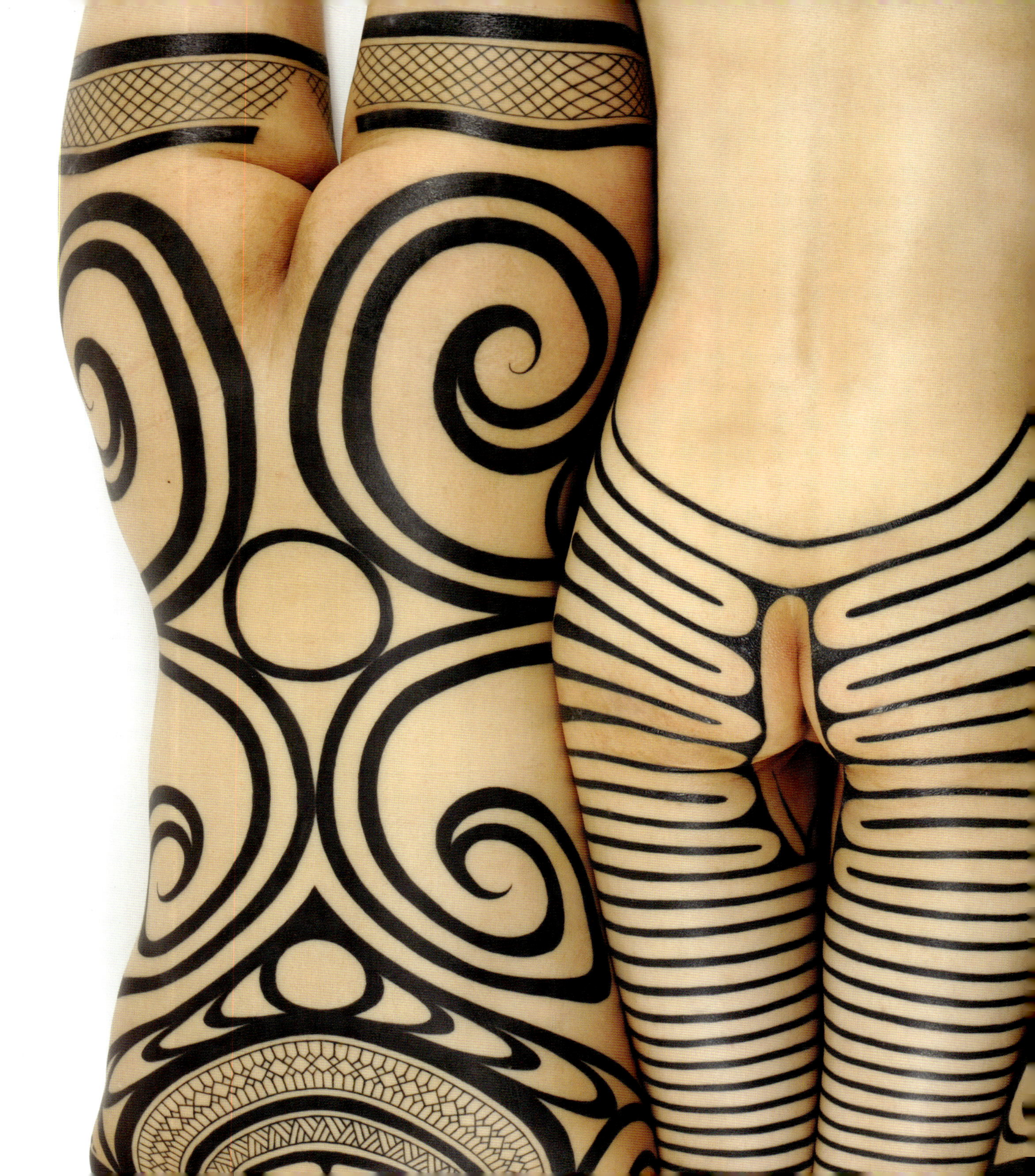

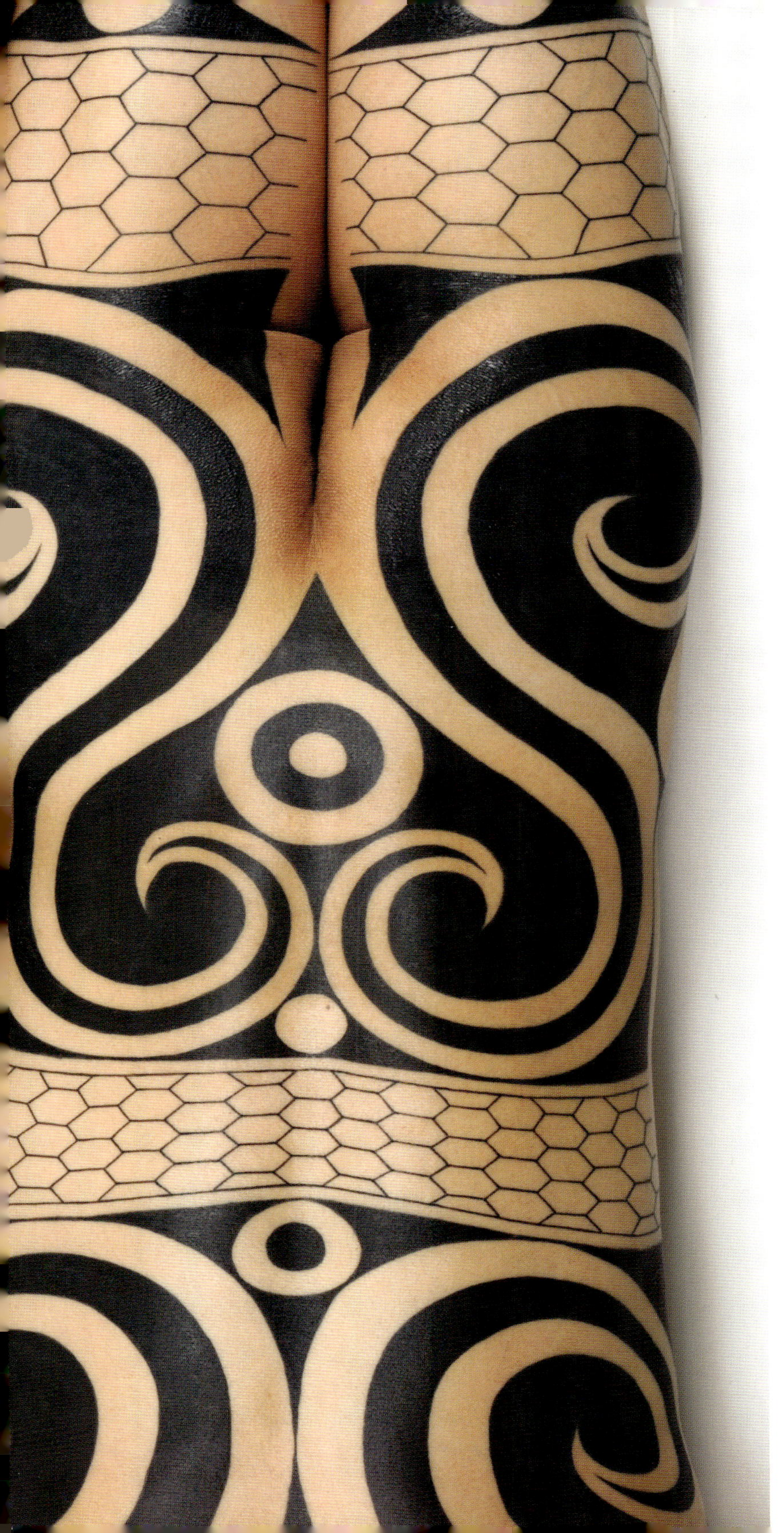

FIGURE 1.38
Jōmon Tribe Project bodysuits by Taku Oshima, 2013. © Ryoichi Keroppy Maeda.

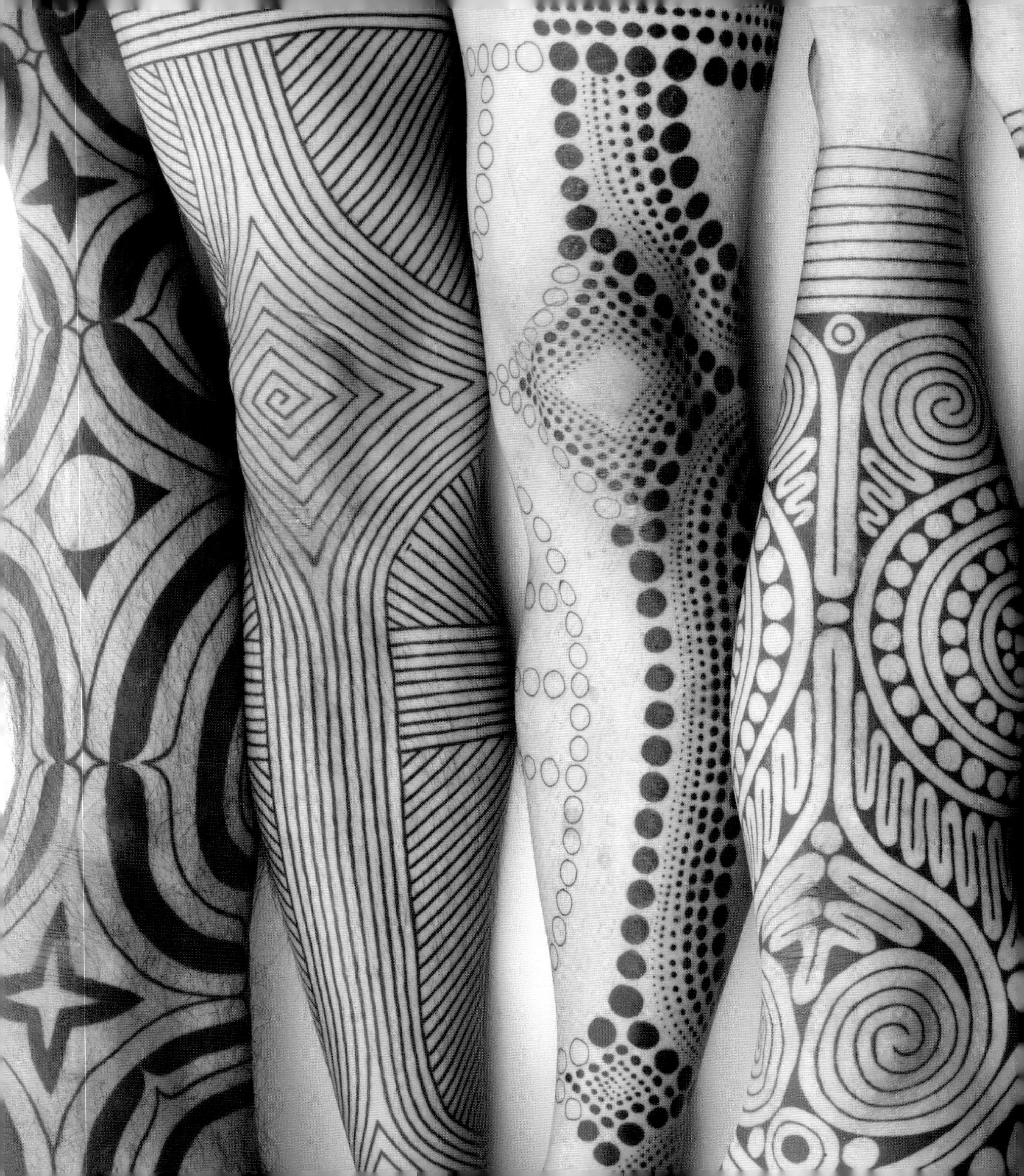

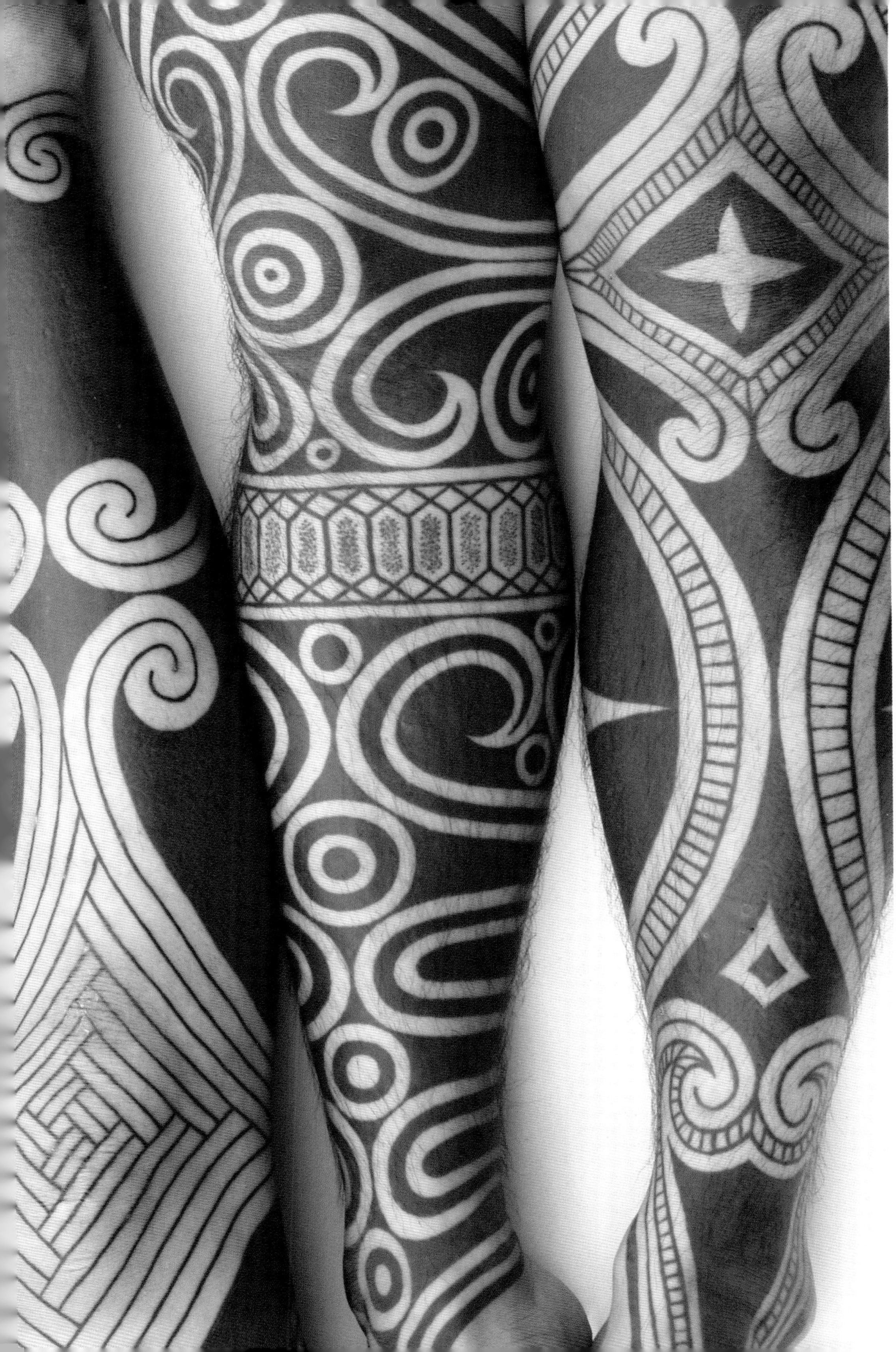

FIGURE 1.39
Jōmon Tribe Project leg pieces by Taku Oshima, 2016.

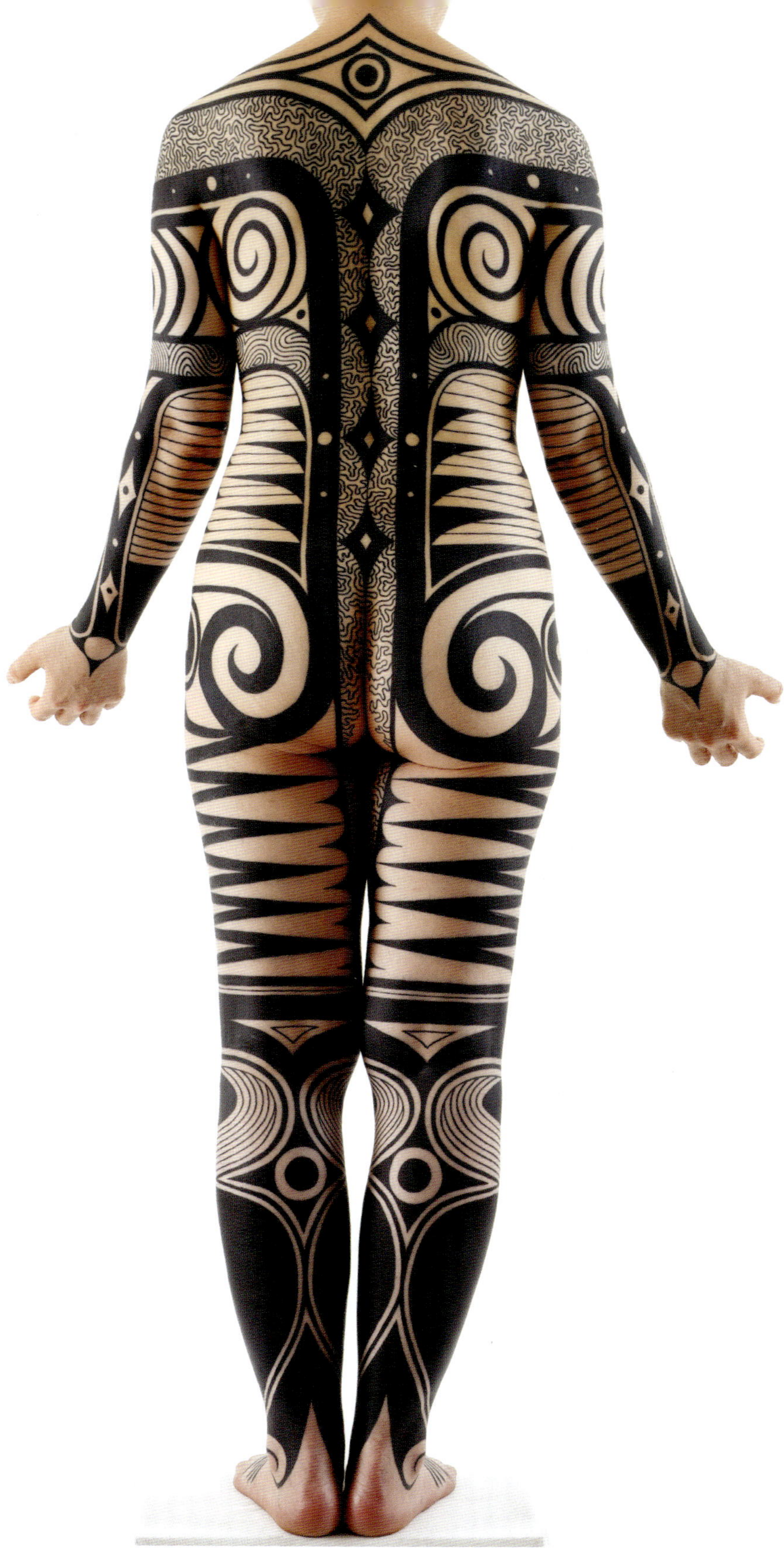

FIGURE 1.40
Jōmon Tribe Project backpiece worn by Yukako Qudha, 2021. Tattooing by Taku Oshima. © Ryoichi Keroppy Maeda.

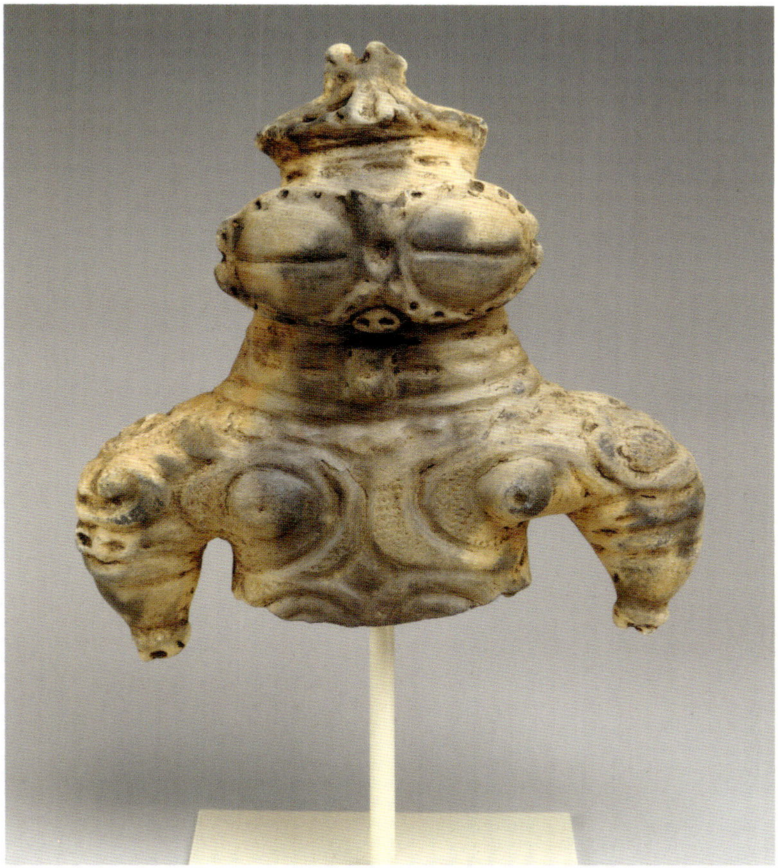

FIGURE 1.41
Prehistoric *dogū* (ceramic figurine) dating to the Final Jōmon period (1000–300 BC). Taku Oshima's *Jōmon Tribe Project* tattoos are influenced by ornamented *dogū*. These objects, which primarily depict the female form, were produced by the Jōmon people for thousands of years (e.g., ca. 12,000–300 BC). This example falls into the category of *shakoki-dogū* that feature goggle-eyed figurines and ornate scrollwork across the surfaces of the body; the treatment of the eyes may indeed represent "snow goggles" that northern peoples used to keep the sun's rays from damaging their eyes. It is not known if the surface decoration of these and other *dogū* represents tattoos, body paint, or scarification, but Oshima captures the spiritual essence of these ancient forms in his bold contemporary blackwork tattoos. Other examples from this era sometimes feature two pairs of lines running downward beneath each eye, a tradition also expressed in ceramic vessels of the Middle Jōmon period (2500–1500 BC) (see Kaner 2009:138–139). Prehistoric ivory carvings from Siberia and the Bering Strait feature similar facial markings resembling tattoos. The Metropolitan Museum of Art, New York (1975.268.193).

Ensako was further inspired to become a member of Oshima's *Jōmon Tribe Project* because it shed light on the somewhat forgotten prehistoric culture of Japan's ancient past, a sentiment that Qudha also shared with me. He explained, "For two thousand years, Japan's history has centered its attention on emperors, but the earlier Indigenous history of the Japanese people has been seemingly relegated to myth and is rarely taught in school. Rituals were administered by emperors in shrines, but in the Jōmon period we were closer to nature and a sense of the transcendent would have existed in daily life. Taku's Jōmon tattoos are messages to the world showing how the culture and worldview of the Jōmon were intertwined on the surfaces of the body and that the practice of tattooing was a form of technoshamanism."

The Jōmon Tribe Project represents Oshima's global desire to restore ancient forms of Japanese tattoo culture and share them with the world. This movement is not only about the reconstruction of ancient tattooing traditions, however; it is also about developing new forms of modern body art and carrying them into the future.

FIGURE 1.42
Jōmon Tribe Project head and backpiece by Taku Ōshima, 2021. © Ryoichi Keroppy Maeda.

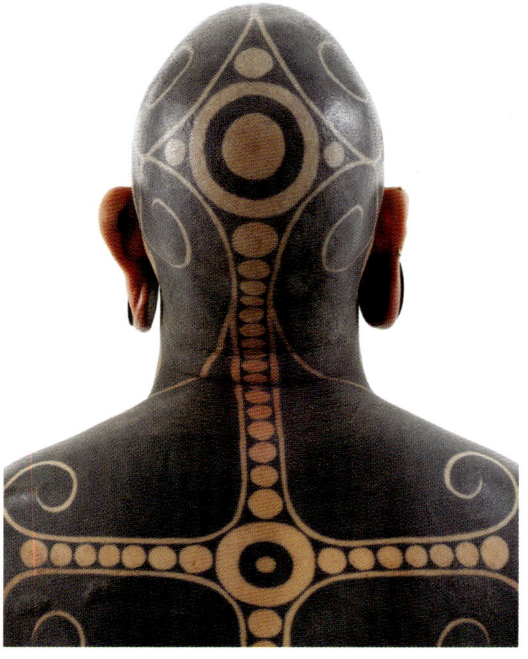

FIGURE 1.43
Ryukyuan-inspired hand tattoos by Taku Oshima, 2018. Courtesy of the artist.

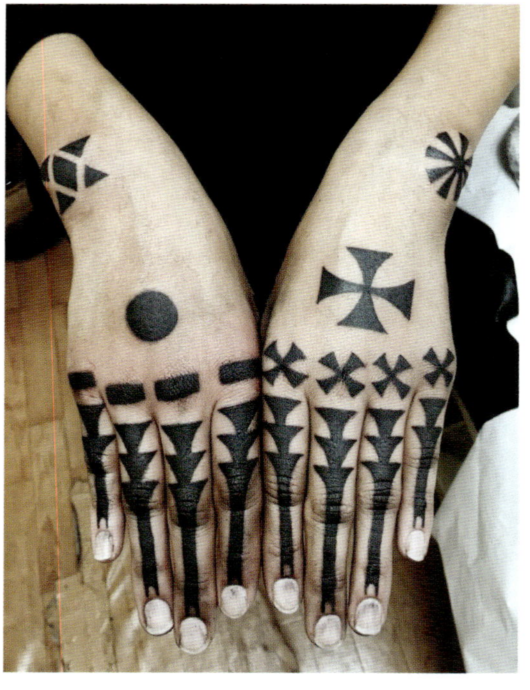

But Oshima is also involved in helping to revive traditional tattoos of the Ryukyus. Several years ago, he was approached to tattoo an Okinawan woman with *hajichi*. Since then he has tattooed more than twenty other women from Okinawa and Amami Ōshima Island with local motifs. "Women are increasingly interested in tracing their ancestral roots through tattooing as a celebration of their cultural identity," he said. "They are not ashamed of this beautiful tradition, and they wear their *hajichi* with great cultural pride."

Morika Yoshiyama, an artist based in Okinawa, wears a full complement of hand and finger tattoos. "I want to make more people aware of the existence of *hajichi*," she told reporter Kazuyuki Ito. "Hajichi symbolized the pride of women," she said, "and I feel proud when I imagine the feelings of my ancestors, and it is my joy to have been born as an Okinawan" (Ito 2019).

In October 2019, the Okinawa Prefectural Museum mounted an exhibition on *hajichi* that compared it to Indigenous tattooing traditions in Taiwan. Oshima was involved in the exhibition and tattooed several women with their first *hajichi*. According to the curator and Ryukyuan tattoo scholar Yoshimi Yamamoto, the comparative approach was used because the Ryukyus and Taiwan both had Indigenous tattooing traditions that were functionally similar. Moreover, Indigenous Taiwanese tattooing was banned by the ruling colonial Japanese government, and today a tattoo revival is currently underway there, a cultural movement explored in the next chapter.

2

TATTOOS OF TAIWAN AND HAINAN

To Honor the Ancestors

We are those who have truly lived by the Atayal traditions. The younger generations who can write must record this tradition, do not forget. . . . Once we are gone, there will be no one else with [traditional] facial tattoos.

—**Lawa Toyu,** tattooed Atayal elder, 2016

I don't want to see this ancient tradition of tattooing disappear in the future. I want to preserve this aspect of Paiwan culture and not let it slip through our fingers.

—**Cudjuy Patjidres,** Paiwan tattoo artist, 2016

Taiwan, formerly known as Formosa, is a mountainous island lying approximately one hundred miles southeast of Mainland China. Indigenous Peoples speaking Austronesian languages have inhabited the island since 4000 BC (Blust 1999; Hung and Carson 2014), and during the Neolithic period segments of these societies journeyed to Island Southeast Asia and beyond, carrying traditions like tattooing with them. Today, less than 5 percent of the total population of the country is Indigenous, consisting of sixteen officially recognized tribes.

Although the island was briefly occupied by the Dutch (1624–1662) before the mass in-migration of Han Chinese during the Qing dynasty (1662–1895), the First Peoples of Taiwan inhabited the entirety of the country. Over the ensuing period of Chinese colonial rule, however, many aboriginal populations living on the plains were assimilated, while other groups retreated to or remained in the fastnesses of the central and southern mountains of the country. This trend toward self-isolation continued into the early years of Japanese colonial rule, which began in 1895. By the turn of the twentieth century, however, the Japanese Empire's commercial interests in heavily forested mountain tracts of camphor trees brought them into confrontation with several local tribes, such as the tattooed Atayal and the Saisiyat, which were known for their aggressive military exploits, including headhunting.

FIGURE 2.1
Pazzeh Watan (Pazzeh Nahee), daughter of Watan Yura, the Atayal headman of Wulai village, 1903. Collection of the author.

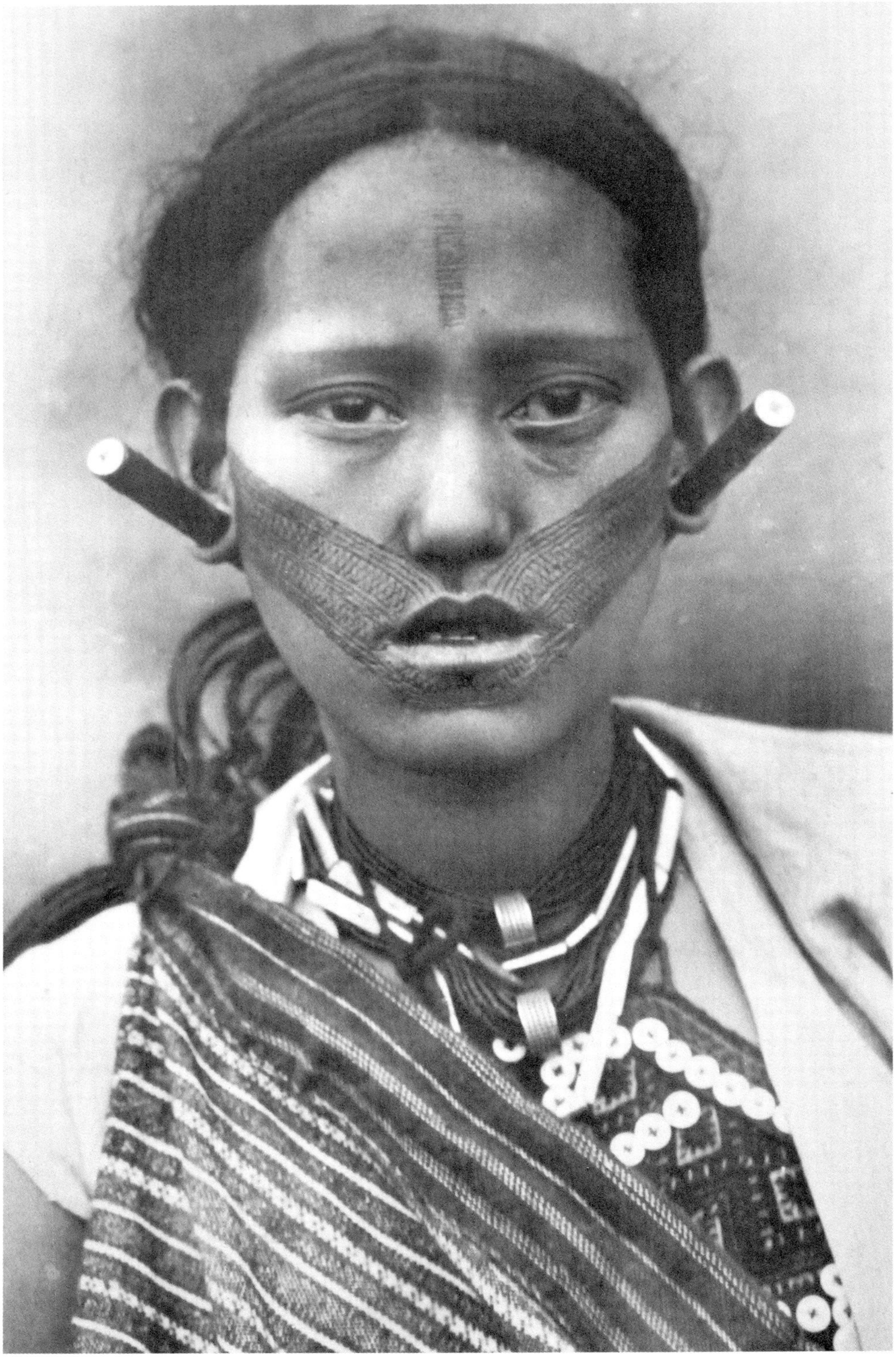

Camphor was an extremely valuable economic resource, and during Chinese rule over Taiwan, it was the second leading export after tea. Growing in immense stands in the Central Mountains of Taiwan, slow-growing camphor trees were used in the early twentieth century for shipbuilding and in the manufacture of mothballs, perfumes, and, more importantly, celluloid, a material that could be used to manufacture drugs, smokeless gunpowder, photographic film, combs, tobacco pouches, and billiard balls (Franck 1924; Hsieh 1964). Before the acquisition of Taiwan, Japan was the leading exporter of camphor. After 1893, Taiwan became the largest exporter, and once the empire exacted its rule over the island two years later, it essentially possessed a global camphor monopoly (Ma 1998). Since the method of collecting camphor necessitated the clear-cutting of the forest, contact and conflicts with Indigenous Peoples inhabiting the regions in and around camphor groves increased, forcing the Japanese government to take up defensive measures to protect their economic interests (Krutak 2007).

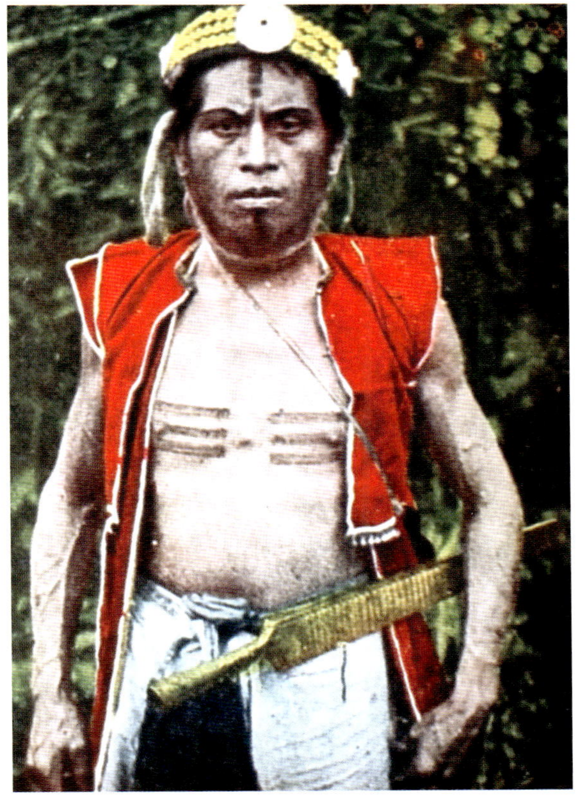

FIGURE 2.2
Colorized postcard titled "Saiset barbarins," ca. 1930, from a 1912 black-and-white photo. Saisiyat (SaySiyat) warrior/leader Zhao Ming-Zheng was descended from the priestly Tawtawasay family that oversaw the *tinato* (enemy head ceremony) (Zining and Bailu 2015:95). He was a revered combatant and it is said he captured fifteen heads over his career. His chest tattoos confirm his prowess, since according to Saisiyat custom each bar represents two heads taken. Collection of the author.

During the Qing dynasty, the Chinese sought to protect its camphor interests by building a defensive system called the *aiyu-sen* (guard line) to protect the valuable tree groves and timber workers. The guard line dated back to the reign of Emperor Qianlong in the mid-eighteenth century, when the Chinese paid Indigenous Peoples under their control to protect them from the bloodthirsty "savages," whom the Japanese later called *seiban*, or "raw barbarians." The Japanese greatly expanded this system, and eventually the line encompassed several hundred miles, encircling Indigenous territories with military outposts connected to battle fences that were constantly advanced as the Japanese conquered new camphor groves (Formosa Bureau of Aboriginal Affairs 1911). Utilizing these policing measures, the Japanese were able to divide up traditional hunting grounds, arable lands, and tribal boundaries while also cutting off communication between the various local ethnic and tribal groups (Lin and Wang 2007). In turn, local populations were displaced if they stood in the way, and in some cases, entire villages, especially those that were rebellious, were relocated to new settlements that were closely monitored by Japanese authorities, including the military and police force. The American travel writer Harry Franck (1924:216–217, 222) visited the guard line in the 1920s and described the *aiyu-sen* as follows:

> The *aiyu-sen*, or guard-line, is a cleared space from fifty to a hundred feet wide, climbing over hill and dale completely around the uncontrolled territory. It started by cutting a road along the crest of a mountain, then destroying the vegetation on either side of this far back so that the guards can see attacking savages in time to defend themselves.
>
> The Japanese have constructed bullet-proof, loopholed forts, barbed-wire entanglements, mines, and wire fences, the latter in some places locally electrified by harnessing mountain streams; hand-grenades, sometimes mountain—and field—guns, are used; on the east coast war-ships have occasionally been called upon to subdue belligerent villages. . . . To-day the guard-line is about three hundred miles long.

Several gruesome accounts of the effectiveness of the electrified sections of the guard line made their way to the American press. In the issue of *Popular Mechanics* from May 1909 a brief article titled "Electricity Used to Capture Head Hunters" was graphically illustrated with the severed heads of two headhunting victims, presumably men who were disabled by the electric fencing and later decapitated. More specifically, one of the photographs depicts two Indigenous men allied to the Japanese seated at a table serving tea over the head of a deposed enemy. The other photograph portrays four captured headhunters, a trophy head, and two Japanese police officers "guarding four head hunters" (*Popular Mechanics* 1909:444). In 1912, an article titled "Surprising the Barbarians of Formosa" was published in the magazine *Popular Electricity*. Therein, the testimony of a Japanese professor visiting Washington, DC, was provided, whereupon he recounted the effectiveness of the guard line during a visit to Taiwan in the late 1890s.

> [A]long the line between them and the savages, a simple wire fence [was laid]; that was all. There was a barbed wire on top and a barbed wire on the bottom, and right between ran an innocent looking smooth wire of the telephone type.
>
> Pretty soon the savage natives, having found that the Japanese soldiers had gone, started to make one of their customary raids upon the crops [planted by Japanese immigrants] lying so temptingly beyond the fence. They got together with their . . . grisly weapons and, starting on their bloody excursion, reached the harmless looking fence and commenced to clamber through—when the Japanese engineers . . . turned on several thousands, or a million volts it was, maybe, along that innocent middle wire. . . . I am told that our people at the electric plants never stirred when they heard the wild shrieks that arose, but merely shoveled in more coal and turned on more "juice." The next day when a party went up to investigate they found the savages strung along the fence like so many dead cattle. (Young 1912:218–219)

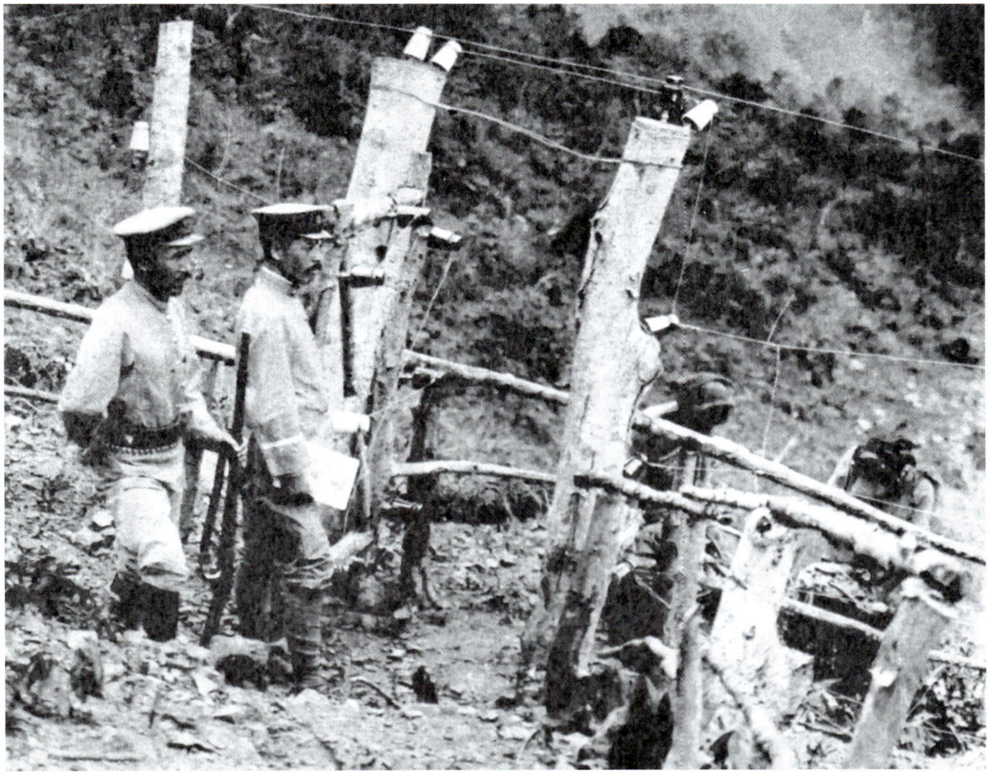

FIGURE 2.3
Japanese soldiers inspect the electrified *aiyu-sen*, or "guard-line," ca. 1915. Postcard collection of the author.

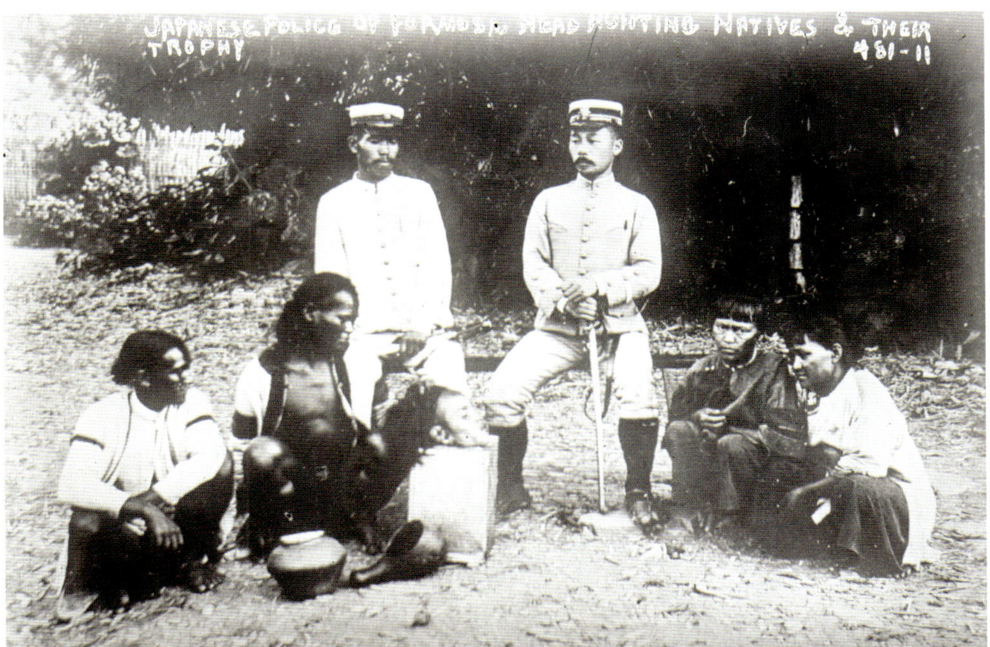

FIGURE 2.4
Japanese police "guarding" captured Atayal headhunters, ca. 1905. Their trophy head is on display. Courtesy Library of Congress, George Grantham Bain Collection (LC-B2-481–8).

FIGURE 2.5
Tattooed Atayal warrior, ca. 1900. His tribal forehead markings consist of a single band of tattooing "braced" by lines on either side. From Ryūzō 1990: pl. 68. Courtesy University Museum, The University of Tokyo.

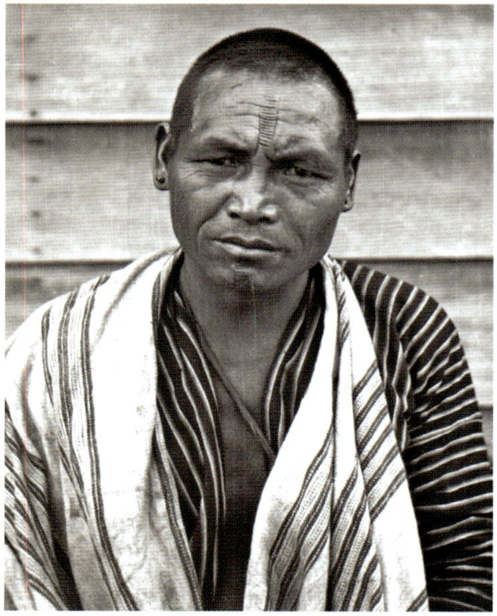

Between 1903 and 1908, the Japanese pushed forward the guard line as an offensive maneuvering tactic. But this grand-scale military campaign did not entirely suspend Indigenous raids into Japanese territory. Rather, Indigenous warriors in search of human heads often came over or under the *aiyu-sen* and its electrified line at nightfall to lay waiting in ambush for unsuspecting victims. For the Atayal, the Seediq, the Truku, the Saisiyat, and the various tribes that comprised these northern aboriginal groups, headhunting was an ancient custom intimately related to becoming an ideal man in the eyes of the ancestors.[1] Furthermore, once a man had proven his success in the human hunt, he was permanently marked with facial tattoos to signify this revered status. "When they tattooed, one became a true Atayal, an adult man," an elder explained to the Danish linguist Søren Egerod (1969:303). "The time had come when this man could do everything. Whatever matter it is [he knows how to do it], whether [killing], or working the field; he also knows how to stab a boar. He is no coward, he is a true Atayal." The Atayal elder Bushi Hayun explained the significance of a man's facial markings to the journalist Tengyue Ma (1998:13): "Facial tattoo represents the essence of Atayal traditional culture [and] non-Atayal people did not understand the significance of facial tattooing [because] they saw it as a barbarous act," he said. "We should never forget th[e] bloody history [with the Japanese], in which our ancestors sacrificed their lives for maintaining the culture of the facial tattoo."

CUSTOMARY LAW AND ANCESTRAL HEADHUNTING PRACTICES IN NORTHERN TAIWAN

Drawing on the oral traditions of Indigenous elders as well as accounts of government agents, anthropologists, and other writers who were active in the twentieth century, it is clear that headhunting and tattooing were two traditional customs considered indispensable to human existence prior to their eventual abandonment at the hands of governmental officials. According to Seediq elder Masau Mona, *ptasan* (tattoos) "represented the teaching of the ancestors and was unchangeable as Ga-ga" because "facial tattooing is key [to our] culture" (Ma 1998:9). In traditional Atayal, Seediq, and Truku culture, the term "Ga-ga" (also Ga-ya) refers to a set of guiding customary laws and protocols by which a person should live their life. It is a kind of "supreme rule and concept" of the tribe that once guaranteed discipline and solidarity, and it encompassed spiritual beliefs, social systems, power structures, ancestry, the clan system, etiquette, naming, learning, hunting, weaving,

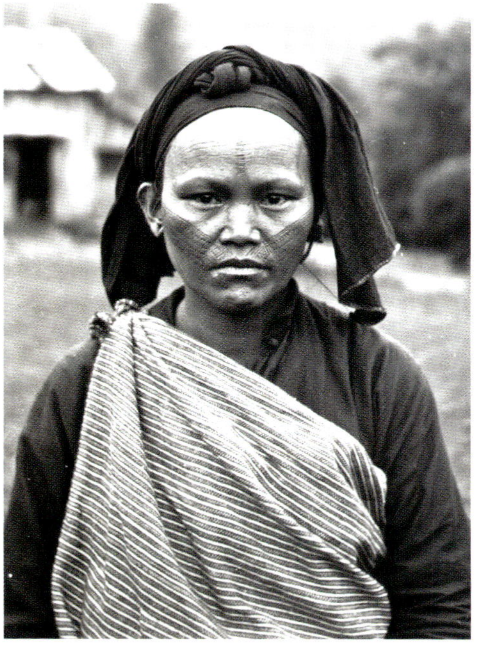

FIGURE 2.6
Atayal woman with facial tattooing, ca. 1900. From Ryūzō 1990: pl. 50. Courtesy University Museum, The University of Tokyo.

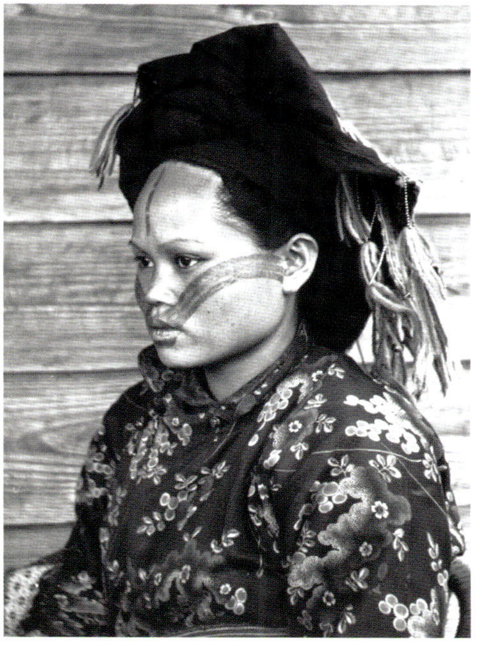

FIGURE 2.7
Atayal woman with facial tattooing, ca. 1900. From Ryūzō 1990: pl. 83. Courtesy University Museum, The University of Tokyo.

marriage, childbirth, death, tribal alliances, tattooing, and sacrificial offerings to the spirits and deities, among other things (Ma 1998:41). Breaching any of the traditional rules as set forth through Ga-ga could result in personal or collective misfortune brought about by the *utux* (also *lyutux*), or ancestral spirits.

Headhunting communities enjoyed enhanced status and could assert their territorial claims to land by challenging rival villages through armed conflict (Krutak 2007). Headhunting also served to maintain several religious functions, including agricultural and community fertility through blood sacrifices that propitiated deities, spirits, and ancestors (McGovern 1922). One Atayal elder recounted in the 1940s that headhunting was believed to induce rapid growth in children, which was desirable:

> After our young men return from killing, they tattoo their foreheads and chins. Even when they went to kill someone our ancestors took many people, even their children, with them. Then, from the head taken, they distributed one hair to each of their children. After they returned, these people who went out to kill were all tattooed. As a result of this, the children grew with the speed of the wind. According

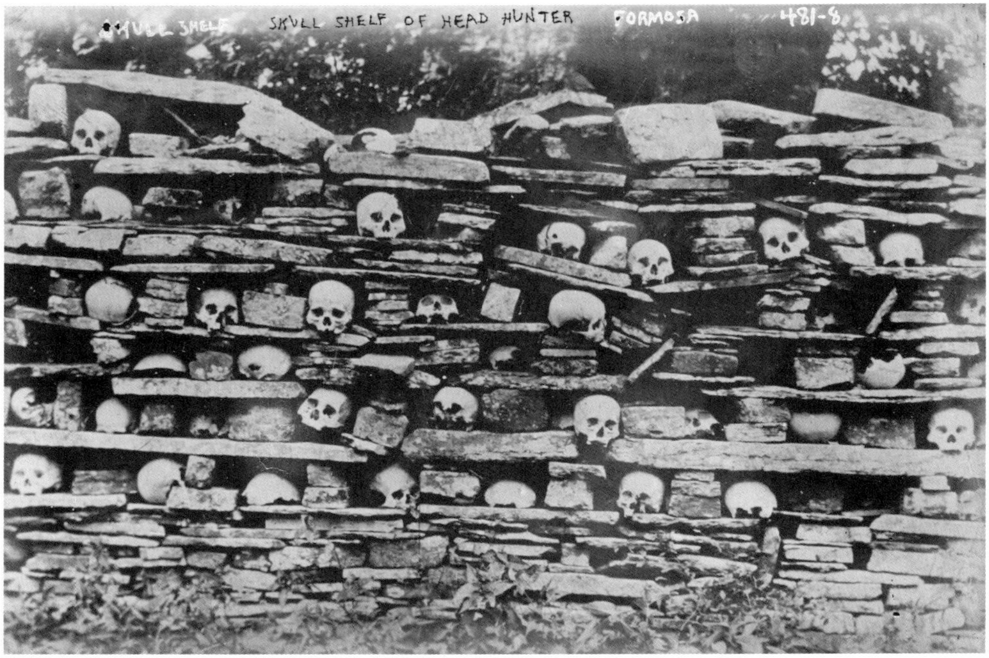

FIGURE 2.8
"Skull Shelf of the Headhunter," ca. 1905. Courtesy Library of Congress, George Grantham Bain Collection (LC-B2-481–11).

> to the Atayal custom, a man who has killed many men tattoos his chest. A man who has killed only a few does not tattoo his chest.
>
> When we return from killing, we return with our voices raised in the war cry along the road. When we get home we all go to the place for the heads [a shelf or rack] and sing. On the following day we assemble and dance, and put the heads in the head stockade. We always place rice flour cakes, which our wives have pounded, into the mouths of the heads. Taking them out again, we let the children of those of us who have returned from head-hunting eat them. We make *owao* [millet wine] in celebration, and also go hunting. When our *owao* is mature, we always invite everyone in the whole village. Then everyone comes and drinks our *owao*. (Norbeck 1950:41–42)

The action of feeding the spirit of the dead with rice cakes was important since this ritual was aimed at convincing them to become one of the tribe's ancestral spirits (cf. Rudolph 2008). In some areas, millet wine was also offered to the head, and the excess liquid was collected in a container underneath the head from which the ritual participants drank (Egerod 1969:303).

Rice cakes were also used as offerings during the *maho*, or annual Atayal agriculture ritual (also called *pslkotas*), to harness the power of their ancestral spirits for the benefit of the community. The ancestral spirits were "called back" with various offerings, consisting of wild game, rice cakes, and rice wine made from grains of the previous year's harvest (I-chun Wang 2015:76).

The more spirits a community possessed, the better, since if these agrarian rituals were performed correctly according to Ga-ga protocols, the *utux* blessed the village with a good harvest and peace, and protected it from malevolent entities like disease-bearing spirits. These rituals were a kind of "contract" with the ancestral spirits, as the following prayer made by an Atayal elder illustrates: "Our ancestors made a contract with you (*lyutux*), and today we present you with the harvest. Please bless our people to have an abundant year with no sickness, and we wish to share our joyfulness with you again at the same time next year" (I-chun Wang 2015:80).

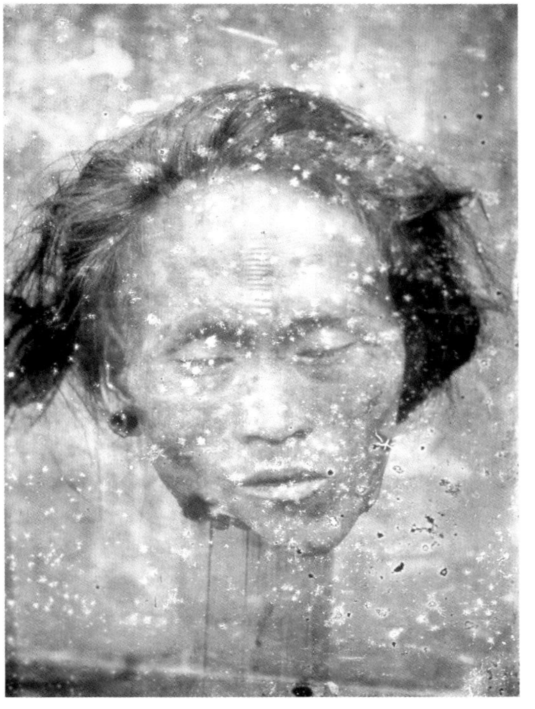

FIGURE 2.9
Atayal war dead with facial tattooing, ca. 1900. From Ryūzō 1990: pl. 30. Courtesy University Museum, The University of Tokyo.

Before a headhunting raid, various rituals were performed to help prognosticate success or failure. The Truku called them *megay bari*, "to feed the spirits," and perhaps the central element was the blood sacrifice before the raid. The throat of a chicken was cut and its flowing blood was collected in a bowl. Then the ritual leader spilled some of this blood, which contained supernatural power, on the weapons and the soil. This act ensured victory and success (Rudolph 2008:108).

Bird omens were also very important. The efficacy of a bird omen lay in the fact that particular birds, especially the *siliq* (Atayal language), or grey-cheeked fulvetta, communicated with the spirits of ancestors who guided the pursuits of their descendants. The *siliq*'s movements and calls were closely monitored. If the bird sang on both sides of a trail, this was a good omen. If the bird sang above the trail and cried "Siq!" as it crossed above, this was a bad omen and the war party should halt; otherwise, there would be accidents, injuries, or worse things to come (Rau 1992:225–227).

The anthropologist and English teacher Janet McGovern,[2] who spent two years in Taiwan during 1916 and 1918, noted other customs related to Atayal headhunting. She observed that war parties typically set off with an odd number of men because their chances to secure an enemy head increased; the idea here is that the enemy would comprise the "'lucky even number' with which they hope[d] to return to the village" (McGovern 1922:112–113). She also noted that specific taboos were to be observed back in the village while the warriors were seeking their enemy. These included the following: women were compelled to abstain from weaving or even handling the raw materials needed to make clothing, and the household fire was never to be extinguished—this action would portend an evil omen (McGovern 1922:113).

MALE TATTOOS IN NORTHERN TAIWAN

The anthropologist Dr. John Ting-Jui Ho (1924–2015), a longtime professor at Florida State University, pioneered the study of Indigenous tattooing in Taiwan. I corresponded with him by letter in 2005, seeking permission to reproduce photographs he took of various forms of tattooing in the 1950s that were later republished in my book *The Tattooing Arts of Tribal Women* (2007). Between 1952 and 1959, Ho visited every tattoo tribe in Taiwan, and the results of this monumental study were published in 1960. He wrote that tattooing traditions would soon vanish, however, since in the northern mountainous region only those Saisiyat men and women above sixty years of age and Atayal over fifty years bore tattoos. In the southern mountains, tattoo bearers among the Paiwan and Rukai were at least or older than forty-five years of age, and tattooed women of the Bunun were all above fifty-five years of age. Ho interviewed hundreds of tattooed men and women during his study, and many of his findings, among others, will be presented in this chapter for the first time in English.[3]

There was no set age for an individual's first tattoo, but Atayal boys of six to seven years of age sometimes received a *hlyangang* (also *liyang*), or forehead tattoo (Vadan, Dao, and Dada 2008:87), although the typical age was eleven or twelve. There were no conditions that an individual had to meet to receive the forehead tattoo (Ho 1960), and depending on its aesthetics it could be read as a kind of tribal or ethnic marker. More specifically, depending on the tribe (e.g., Atayal, Seediq, Truku, or Saisiyat) and subtribe(s) that comprised its respective ethnic unit, there were slight variations in the width and spacing of the horizontal lines tattooed on the forehead. In some groups, the lines were framed with one or more vertical lines along the edges and the patterning resembled a ladder with rungs. In others, the forehead tattoo might consist of one, two, or three interspersed sections or segments of tattooing.

The conditions for receiving a *tabayang* (also *tbayang*), or chin tattoo, were an altogether different matter because it signified adulthood and warrior status and it had to be earned through passing a series of life-threatening tests (Vadan, Dao, and Dada 2008:87). The boy had to master various skills, including self-sufficiency as a hunter. More specifically, he had to prove that he could enter the wilderness alone and successfully capture large animals such as mountain goats or wild boar. Furthermore, he had to demonstrate his abilities as a farmer and the capacity to care for and protect his parents and family, and most importantly he had to participate in a successful war party that captured one or more heads (Vadan, Dao, and Dada 2008:10). Only then could he become an Atayal *tayan*, a "true" or "real" man in society. In turn, men bearing a full complement of facial tattoos were then allowed to marry (Ma 1998:61).

Great warriors who had taken numerous heads with their machete-like beheading knife might also have their chests tattooed. These Atayal short swords, and their handles and scabbards, were adorned with the hair of beheaded enemies, and it was *pasani* (taboo) for anyone other than the owner to touch them. That is because the souls of the enemy were attached to the sword and its scabbard, and if a person, such as a child, handled these "holy" objects, it was believed sores would develop across their bodies (Vadan, Dao, and Dada 2008:86). Tseole Atayal elders employed the word *maotox* for war heroes, meaning "they were afraid of nothing and were good in a fight"

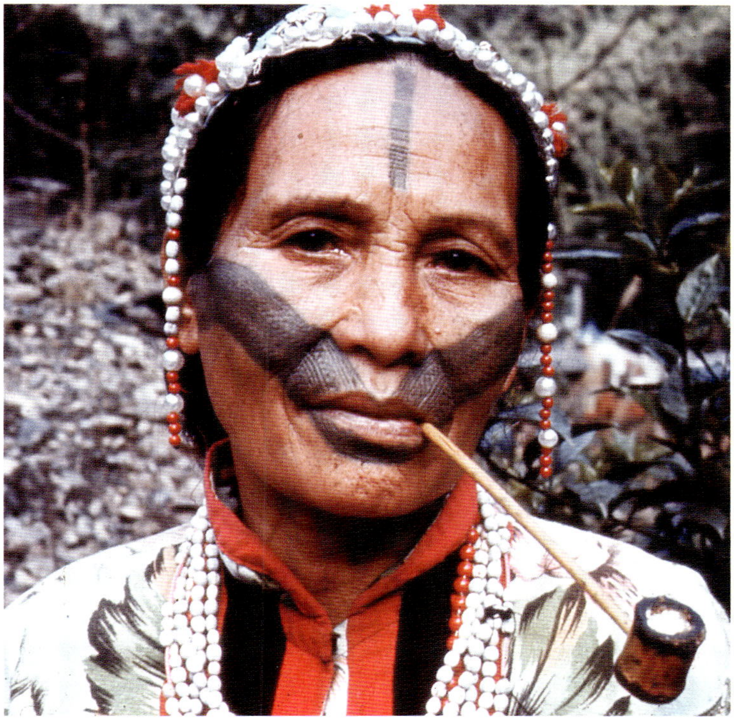

FIGURE 2.10
Tattooed Atayal elder smoking her pipe, ca. 1960. Collection of the author.

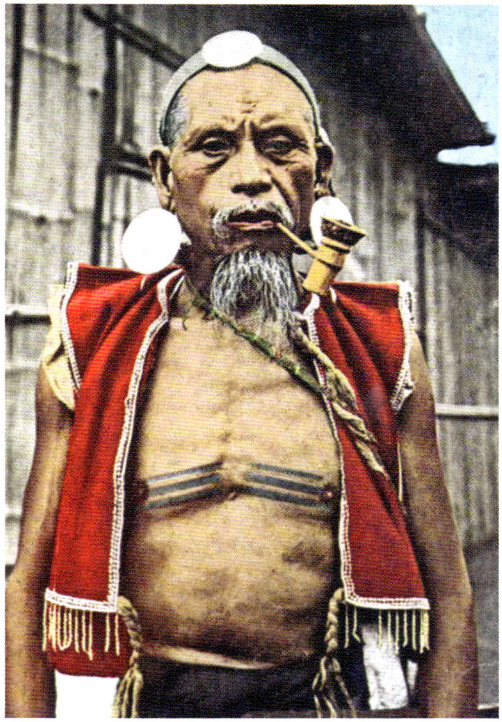

FIGURE 2.11
Saisayat leader Taro Yuuma (b. 1880?) of Sairaks village (see Ho 1960:43), ca. 1935. His chest tattoos and shell ornaments confirm his status as a warrior of the highest rank. Postcard collection of the author.

or "fearless fighter" (I-chun Wang 2015:141, 143). According to the Tseole Atayal elder Ykichi Sayama of the Tubus District, men who took twenty heads were entitled to *pintagaboan* (short horizontal lines) under the right and left nipples on the chest; once completed they resembled six bars or bands of tattooing on the chest—three bars on the left side and three on the right (Ho 1960:10). Men who took thirty or more heads might be called *luax na tsokoliag*, a "real man," or *kazahou na tsokoliag*, a "person who is brave and flawless in morality" (I-chun Wang 2015:141). One such fearless fighter was the late nineteenth-century chief warrior of the P'qwalic Atayal tribe, Maay Gahu, who claimed to have beheaded thirty men and wore two bands of tattooing on his chest intersected with *patihoan*, or three bars of vertical tattoos at the center (Ma 1998:61; I-chun Wang 2015:141, fig. 15; cf. Xuexin Wang 2003). Among other Atayal groups, the chest tattoos of great warriors did not feature horizontal bands. Instead, only the aforementioned vertical bands of short tattooed lines marking the center of the chest were given, with each line symbolizing one head taken.

Among the Saisiyat, only men who had taken heads were allowed to receive a *pintasan* (patterns), or forehead tattoo (Ho 1960:16). This tattoo usually consisted of a single row of tattooing like that of the Atayal. However, some Saisiyat tribes divided the tattoo into segments, while others tattooed vertical lines on each side of the short lines. Ho (1960:17) observed that in "the Garawan community of Penglaicun village of south Saisiyat, both men and women had three sections for tattooing on the forehead." Inveterate warriors who took many heads were also eligible to have their chest tattooed. According to elders interviewed by Ho in the 1950s, a man who hunted two heads could have the *hinokaraʔan* chest tattoo of horizontal stripes; a man who hunted three heads could add *pinairi*, or vertical lines, to the horizontal stripes (Ho 1960:16). In one Saisiyat community, Ho noted a variation of the warrior's chest tattoo. He wrote, "[In the] Shiliying community of Penglaicun village of south Saisiat, [men] had a special tattoo design on the chest—on each breast there were three horizontal sections that looked like a brick wall; on the top there were three vertical lines connecting three small circles" (Ho 1960:17, fig. 4.5). Whether or not these circular elements represented beheaded enemies was not recorded.

The Japanese administration placed a ban on headhunting during the early Taishō period (1912–1925) to help quell unrest in the "savage districts," advance their economic interests in forest products, and further break down the social and religious systems of the Indigenous Peoples who practiced it. From the empire's perspective, "[t]he measure of suppression of such a barbarous habit of head-hunting is a most important duty from the point of view of the administration of the island" (Formosa Bureau of Aboriginal Affairs 1911:109). But men young and old continued to headhunt, or they employed monkey skulls in rituals in place of human heads (Formosa Bureau of Aboriginal Affairs 1911:86).

From the standpoint of tattooing praxis, tribes adapted to the headhunting ban by relaxing the traditional rules that governed how a man could earn the right to be tattooed. Among the Saisiyat, men who succeeded in hunting large game animals could now earn a warrior's tattoo. Moreover, if a father or elder brother killed one of these wild animals, they could transfer this achievement to their son or younger brother so that they could be tattooed (Ho 1960:17). Among the Atayal, warriors were allowed by their tribal leader to transfer any new headhunting credits to other tribal members if the latter succeeded in wounding the enemy. Also, if the tribal head approved, men who carried a trophy head home after a combat mission were allowed to receive a warrior's tattoo. If a father or an elder brother of a family member participated in headhunting, they could pass the tattoo opportunity on to their son or younger brother. Men who damaged a Japanese military outpost or stole and carried military equipment back home could also be eligible for a tattoo (Ho 1960:10). Finally, when headhunting was almost completely abolished by the Japanese, Atayal men, like their Saisiyat counterparts, could receive warrior tattoos for their hunting exploits, especially if a large game animal (boar, bear, or leopard) was taken.

FEMALE TATTOOS IN NORTHERN TAIWAN

Generally speaking, tattoos were inked on the foreheads of Atayal, Seediq, and Truku teenage girls before they were married. Tribes adhered to set norms regarding the aesthetics of forehead tattoos;

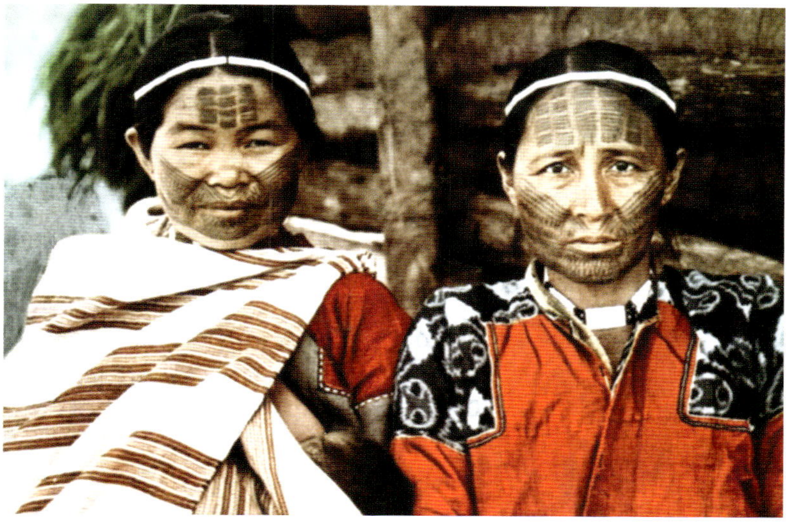

FIGURE 2.12
Tattooed Atayal women of the Tgdaya (Seediq) tribe, Wushe group, ca. 1935. Postcard collection of the author.

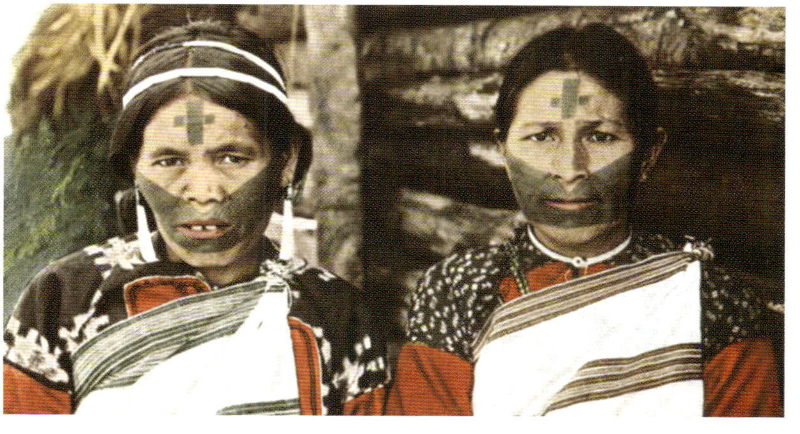

FIGURE 2.13
Tattooed Atayal women of the Michisawa group of Seediq, Nantou County, ca. 1935. Postcard collection of the author.

some groups wore one or more segments of tattooing in the center of their forehead, while Tgdaya (Seediq) tribes of the Wushe group might have three to seven bands of similar tattoos across the entirety of their forehead. The Michisawa group of Seediq wore a cross-like tattoo on their foreheads composed of one band of tattooing from the hairline to the upper bridge of the nose flanked by two small segments on either side. As with their male counterparts, a woman's forehead tattoo could be read as a tribal identity marker.

Girls who had mastered weaving could receive elaborate tattoos on their cheeks because a "real woman was the one who knew how to weave" (Rau 1992:224). Weaving itself was an arduous task because of the labor involved, but a woman also had to perfect cultivating the raw material needed for her family's garments. This material was ramie, a flowering plant in the nettle family.

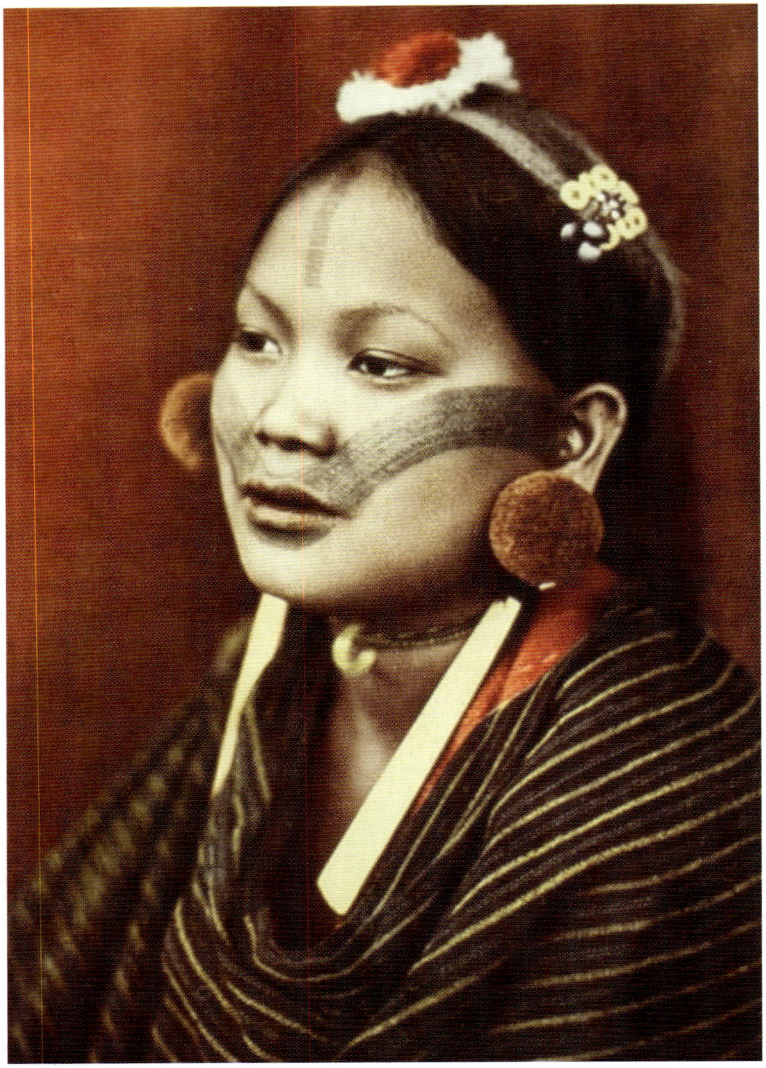

FIGURE 2.14
Atayal woman in festival attire, ca. 1930. Postcard collection of the author.

First, it had to propagated, then harvested by peeling away the outer bark and separating the raw fibers within into threads before they were bleached and dyed (Robbins 2009). One of the most popular weaving patterns was spiritually significant: a series of small rhombi placed inside a larger rhombus representing the protective "eyes of the ancestors."

Master weavers and those women who invented new patterns could also earn the right to be tattooed on their chest, hands, and legs (Ho 1960:10). These chest tattoos resembled those worn by great warriors. Among the Austronesian-speaking Iban of Borneo, master weavers who were female were tattooed with marks on their hands that complemented those worn by the greatest headhunters. In fact, Iban weaving was known colloquially as "women's war" (see chapter 4, this volume).[4]

Fragmentary evidence survives to outline the iconographic elements of the woman's symmetrical *patas*, or Atayal cheek tattooing. The graceful, parallel sloping lines filled with X-like motifs moved down from the ears toward the mouth to form an overall V-shaped pattern. Depending on the tribe, there were variations in the width and shape of the cheek tattoos, which were recognizable as an ethnic marker. Atayal elders interviewed in the 1980s also noted that the width of their facial tattoos was narrower across the subtribes than those of previous generations (Ma 1998).

According to one legend of the Perugawan Atayal, the intersecting X-like patterns of a woman's facial tattoo originated from a weaving pattern that imitated a snake's skin. In the distant past, a mother and her daughter went to work in the mountains and saw a very beautiful serpent. They decided to weave that beautiful pattern on a *lukus lumoan* (garment or gown). After a long period of intense study, they finally worked out how to weave it. Later, women tattooed the pattern on their faces (Ho 1960:15).

Other research reports that the diamond-shaped pattern formed by the intersecting X-like tattoos on a woman's cheek is the "eyes of *utux*," or the eyes of the ancestors (I-chun Wang 2015:94), which, as noted, was a common weaving pattern. The function of this motif was one of protection because the ancestors would always "watch over" the woman if she adhered to Ga-ga.

Throughout his fifty years as a Catholic missionary in the Takekan Atayal region, Father Alberto Papa worked with elders and weavers to discern the primary elements of weaving patterns that were based on *biru* (ideograms). Most Atayals had forgotten this ideographic system, which Papa believed served as the inspiration for the primary elements of a woman's intricate cheek tattoos. The Atayal weavers he interviewed stated that the word *biru* translated to "letters," "scripts," "books," or, more specifically, *biru mian*—"our writing" (Papa 2013:33, 38). The Atayal are believed to have never created a writing system, so this research is interesting from the standpoint of paleography and linguistics.

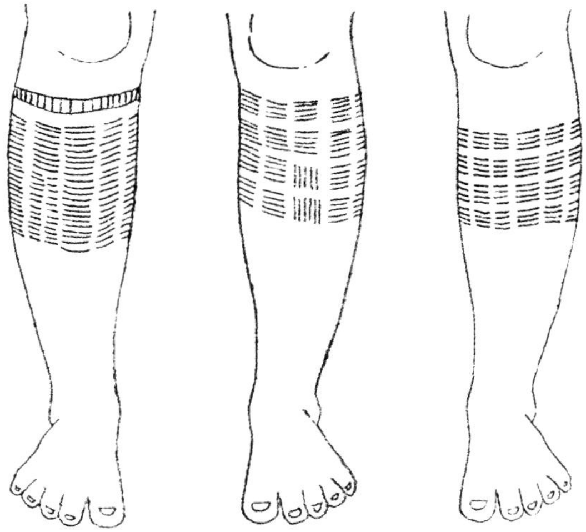

FIGURE 2.15
Atayal women's leg tattooing. From Ho 1960: pl. VI.

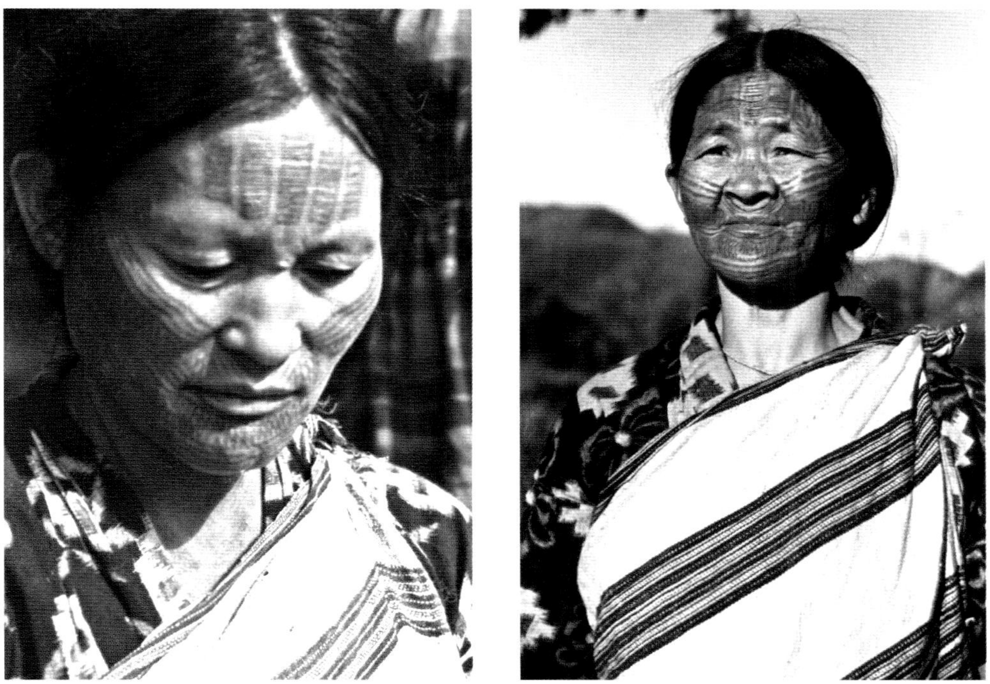

FIGURE 2.16
Atayal women of the Tgdaya (Seediq) tribe (*left–right*), Wushe group, displaying "eyes of ancestors" motif on cheeks, ca. 1950. Collection of the author.

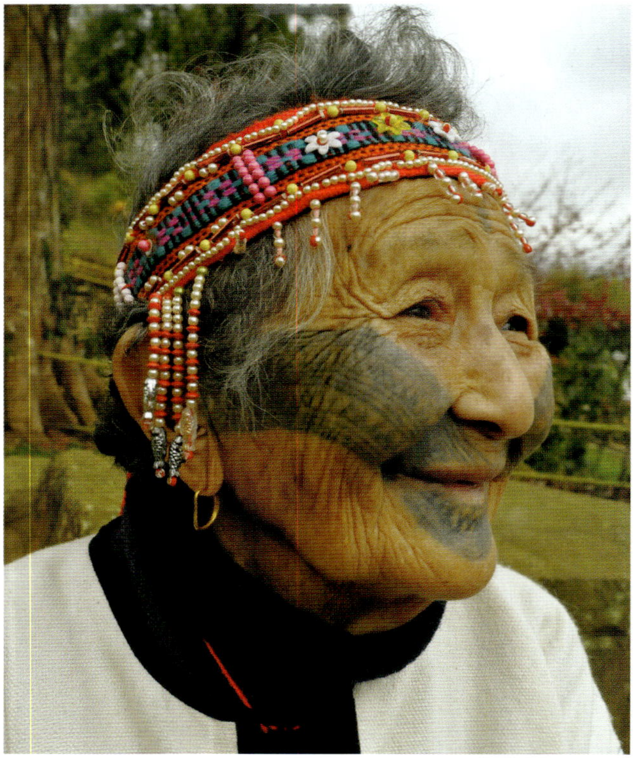

FIGURE 2.17
Atayal elder Iwan Kainu (1916–2018) of Dasing village, Miaoli County, 2016. The facial tattoos of Atayal women were composed of ideograms that represented fundamental beliefs also embodied in weaving traditions. © Lars Krutak.

As early as the age of seven, girls were taught the fundamental ideograms of the weaving patterns they would eventually master. Particular symbols such as the *qutux*, or forward-slash (/), stood for the number one, "indefinite reality," and "man." The *sajiŋ*, or backslash (\), stood for number two, "a location in profundity with a structure of life," and "woman" (Papa 2013:33). When these symbols met as /\, this ideogram stood for the number three, but it also represented a relationship of integration, namely, that man and woman combined metaphysically "to be one with their integrated minds and thoughts" (Papa 2013:34). When these symbols were inverted to form a \/ this ideogram represented that woman and man combined to become one physically. In turn, when the symbols /\ \/ were conjoined to make a diamond ◊, a new meaning emerged: the "Atayal family structure" wherein /\ represents children and \/ signifies authority (Papa 2013:34). This motif (*tiju'* or *ciju'*) also indicated a kind of Atayal garment used to cover one's private parts.

Papa documented many other weaving ideograms, but I will focus only on two more here. The number eight was represented by two conjoined diamonds and backslashes. This ideogram was a primary pattern of Atayal women's facial tattoos and was repeated numerous times depending on the girl's facial dimensions and (sub)tribal traditions. Papa (2013:35) noted that the "woman who has this tattoo means that she is mature enough and has the ability to manage a household, and most importantly, she is ready to get married." Indeed, as a rule of Ga-ga a girl was compelled to receive her tattooing before marriage, and without it, elders stated she would be banished from the community or, during the colonial period, married off to a non-Indigenous person, never to return (Ma 1998:58; Vadan, Dao, and Dada 2008:103). The ideogram for the number ten was called *mpū*, or the X motif formed by the basic patterns of / (man) and \ (woman). When joined as an X, this basic ideogram, which was another primary motif of women's facial tattoo, signified a spousal relationship that would result in new life (i.e., human reproduction) (Papa 2013:37).

Among the Atayal, the Seediq, and the Truku, men's and women's tattoos were very important from the standpoint of the afterlife, because only these "true" or "ideal" people were afforded safe passage to meet their ancestors. One of the earliest accounts of this belief is found in the seventeenth-century writings of the Dutch missionary Georgius Candidius, the first missionary of Taiwan, who spent sixteen months among the Indigenous Austronesian Siraya people of the southwestern plains who once practiced tattooing.[5] Although Candidius does not mention tattooing in this passage, it is known that Siraya men had to earn the right to be tattooed as a result of their martial or hunting exploits; less is known about women's tattooing. Nevertheless, among Austronesian peoples tattooing was typically part of those customary traditions and organizing principles, such as Atayal Ga-ga, that marked one's passage through life. "According to their [Sirayan] belief, an exceedingly narrow bridge, made of bamboo, leads across [the] river [of death], over which the souls of deceased must pass before they can reach the *Campum Eliseum*, or Land of Promise. Moreover, those who have led a bad life, and who attempt to cross the bridge, will find it suddenly turning round; and, instead of entering the Land of Promise, they will fall into the filthy stream [below], there to suffer great torment and pain" (Campbell 1967:23).

Atayal oral histories closely parallel this description, wherein the *utuxan* (the world of the dead) is the afterlife. According to elders interviewed by the American anthropologist Edward Norbeck, only "true women" and "true men" could safely pass the "Bridge of Gods," which was monitored by a watchman who judged all of the visitors at his station (Norbeck 1950:28–29).

Some individuals who did not pass judgment were led to a lower path lined with thorny trees and large numbers of leeches, whereupon they died before reaching paradise. Other "evil" doers were falsely led across the bridge by the guardian, but when they came to the center, he pushed them into the chasm below, where their souls were eaten by serpents and fish. The Austrian archaeologist Erika Kaneko (1960:35) described this land as follows:

> The end of the journey to the land of the ancestors is marked by a bridge spanning a yawning abyss. Sometimes the rainbow is identified with it. On crossing this bridge, every man has to display his hands which ought to be stained with the blood of his head-hunting victims.[6] Only if these stains prove irremovable in spite of vigorous scrubbing, is he admitted and joyously received by his ancestors. A successful head-hunter's tattoo is the condition according to an other [*sic*] version. Women are only admitted, if they have been skillful and diligent weavers [and thus tattooed]. People without the necessary skills are thrown from the bridge and perish.

Today, this bridge is popularly called the Rainbow Bridge or, among the Atayal *hongu utux* or *hawngu-lyutux*, the "ancestral bridge" (Vadan, Dao, and Dada 2008:7; I-chun Wang 2015:75). Some elders suggest that the Rainbow Bridge is mimicked in the V-shaped cheek tattoos of women. This structure serves as an Atayal metaphor for the universe because it supports the belief that there is life after death and that the deceased can live with their ancestors forever (Vadan, Dao, and Dada 2008:9).

Remarkably, a very similar story is told among the Toraja and neighboring peoples of the Celebes (Kruyt 1906:359–361); the Māori of New Zealand (Best 1905:232; Taylor 1870:231); the Kayan (Hose and McDougall 1912:41, 44; Tillema 1989:163); the Punan and the Murut (Rutter 1929:119) of Borneo; and the Chang Naga of Northwest India (Kauffman 1940:329), among other Indigenous Peoples who tattooed (Ngadi 1998:95, 105; Richards 1997:393).

In closing this section, it should be noted that many elders have recounted that during the Japanese occupation of Indigenous lands in northern Taiwan (1895–1945), the reason the Atayal, the Seediq, and other related groups rebelled so violently against the empire was that they did not

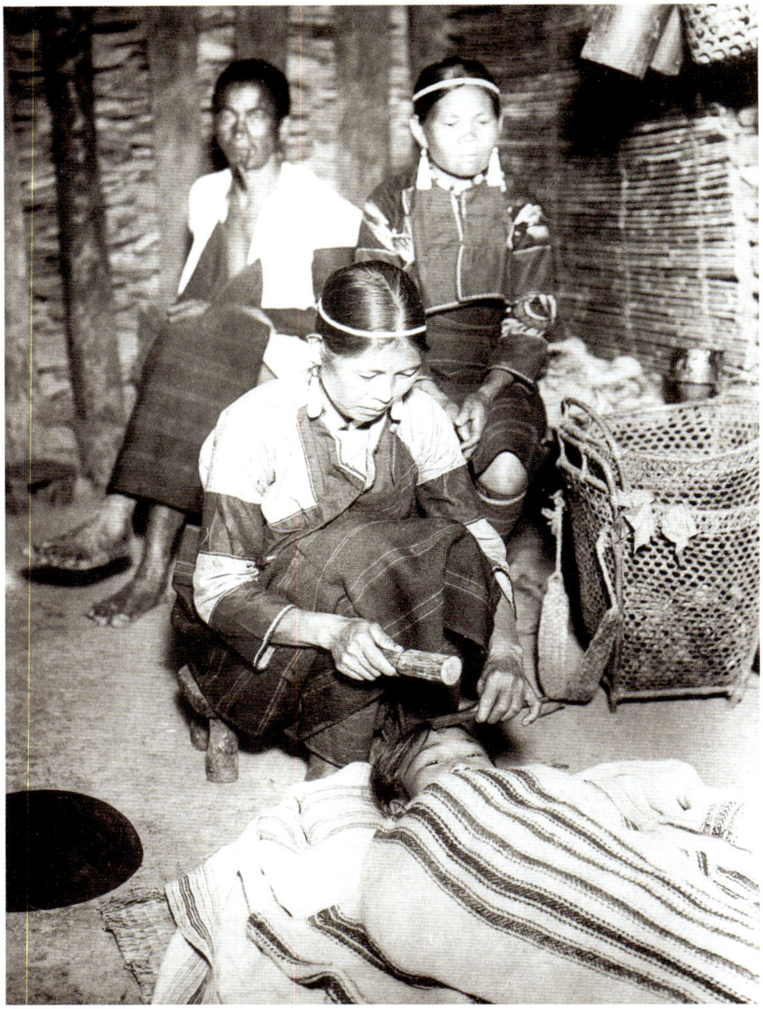

FIGURE 2.18
Atayal tattooist at work, ca. 1935. Postcard collection of the author.

fear death since they believed they would cross the Rainbow Bridge to "return home" and be reunited with their kin (Vadan, Dao, and Dada 2008:12). Living their lives under Ga-ga and Ga-ya, this road to paradise was paved by the heroic deeds of true men and the accomplishments of true women who wore the tattoos of their beloved ancestors.

ATAYAL TATTOO ARTISTS

Atayal *patasan*, or tattoo artists, were women (Chi-Lu 1968). They had to be of high virtue and most of them inherited their profession from their mothers or aunts, although some learned the skill by apprenticeship. The German ethnologist Otto Weidfeldt (1914:23–24) observed that there were approximately two tattooers per Atayal clan, and these women were also knowledgeable about medicinal plants and prognosticating certain events, such as pregnancy and whether sickly people would die.

Usually, there were not many tattooists in any one region, so if one did not reside in a village, one was invited from the outside. Elders interviewed in the 1980s recalled the names of several well-known Atayal tattooists who worked in the Miaoli region, including Yayut Ciwas (Smahan tribe), Lawai Kainu (Smahan tribe), Hagin Ali (Sele tribe), and Duyu Dalau (Sitovang tribe). In 1915, Ciwas moved from her home in Taikang village, Hsinchu County, along the Snow mountain range (Hsueshan), passing through several villages toward Mount Tapachien (J. Chen 1997). Even though the Japanese tattoo ban was in effect, she moved about with her entire family, and tattooed clients along the way. Eventually, she settled in Miaoli County, where she tattooed many individuals from Tai'an Rural Township. Until the passing of the last two tattooed Atayal women in 2018 (Iwan Kainu) and 2019 (Lawa Toyu), there were more tattooed Atayal elders in Miaoli than anywhere else in Taiwan. Although each region she passed through had slightly different female facial tattoo patterns, Ciwas respected these traditions of local identity and clan custom, and she carefully tattooed her clients with their respective ethnic patterns (J. Chen 1997).

Tattooists were well-paid and highly respected in their home communities and local regions. According to historical sources, for the first tattoo (on the forehead) a typical charge for a boy was one piece of *pada* (plain cloth) or two *sinubukan* (beaded necklaces), whereas a girl's parents were charged a *lukus lumoan* (woven blouse with delicate patterns) and one overcoat made of *teyupaipai* (patterned cloth) (Ho 1960:11). However, a male informant told Norbeck (1950:41) that before the adoption of Japanese currency (yen), a "low fee" was equivalent to seven *banun*—that is, five sickles and hatchets wrapped in a bundle equal to the value of seven Japanese yen.

Recently, Atayal elders recalled that the expense of women's facial tattooing, including the cheeks, which were often marked two or three times to make the color bold and beautiful, was sometimes more than a girl's wedding dowry. In 2008, the then ninety-year-old Atayal elder Toyu explained, "Oh! . . . The cost is more expensive than a marriage proposal, and at first, you must bring *rnging* (rice cakes), wild game from the mountains, and rice [or millet] wine to visit the tattoo master. Then, when the tattoo master begins the first tattoo, you must send a few complete sets of Atayal traditional clothing, full-body garments. These costumes will be given to the tattoo master after the pattern is completed. After the wound is completely healed, you must once again formally thank the tattoo master, and prepare a lot of *rnging*, rice wine, more wild game, and give a strong cow!" (Vadan, Dao, and Dada 2008:81). Some families could not afford the expense, and their daughters were married off to Han Chinese men on the plains (Vadan, Dao, and Dada 2008:22).

If the boy or girl had premarital sexual relations or they had been secretly married before the tattooing commenced, the price might double or triple because this was *pasani* (taboo) and not in accordance with Ga-ga. Thus, it was important for the tattooist to know if her client was moral and faithful to Ga-ga, and before she began her work, she quizzed the client about their sexual mores and marital status. In some cases, however, a tattooist already knew there was a breach of taboo from the revelations of a dream or bird omen (Vadan, Dao, and Dada 2008:77, 90). If the tattooist learned that her client had committed a sin, she performed a *tamabalay* ("defilement" or "atonement" ritual) to divine the thoughts of the ancestral spirits and acquire their blessing. Otherwise, if the client lied about their conduct, this breach of taboo would greatly anger the ancestors and misguide the *atuk* or *atok* (tattooing tool), which was the repository of supernatural power and a tabooed object. For these reasons, tattooists used different sets of tattoos depending on the status of their client. Ho (1960:12) interviewed a Seqoleq Atayal tattooist of the Maliqoan District who used three sets of tools: *atok makarakis* for unmarried clients, *atok manaui* for those who had sexual relations or were secretly married before receiving their tattoos, and *atok banakesi* for the married.

If spiritual blessings were not acquired after the atonement ritual, the results could be disastrous for the client: they might experience a high fever, the tattoos could become ulcerated or distorted, the skin might prematurely wrinkle, or the client might die after the operation (Vadan, Dao, and Dada 2008). If the affront was too great and the spirits did not bestow their blessing, the person was not tattooed and they might be cast out of the community, or, in the case of girls, married off to a non-Indigenous family in the lowlands.

During the atonement ritual, incantations were made to the *lyutux* (ancestors) and a blood sacrifice was offered (a chicken) to quell the spirits. The tattooist might then say, "We offer sacrifices to you for this child. I hope *lyutux* will listen to my prayer and accept the offering. When

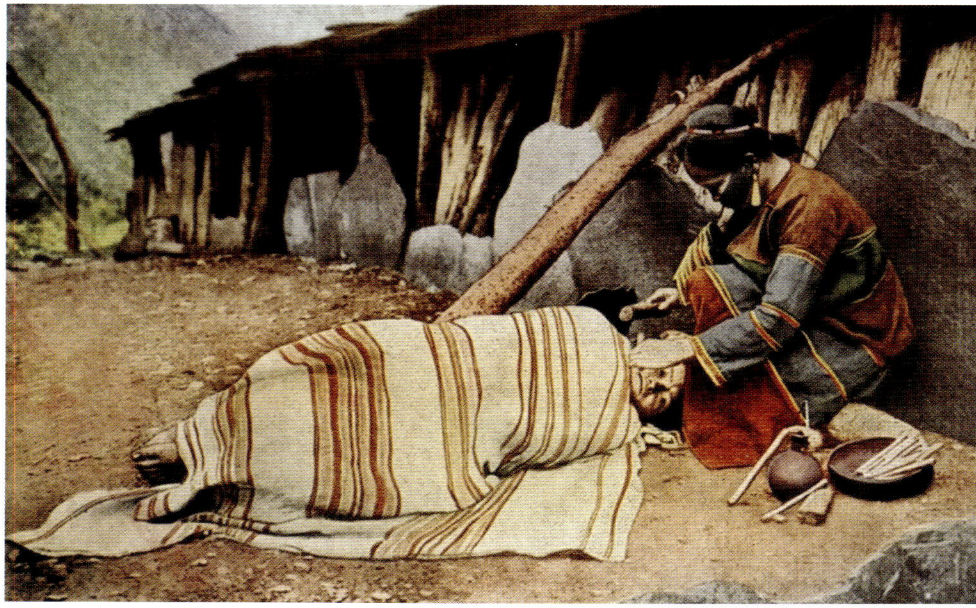

FIGURE 2.19
Truku tattooist at work in Tarowan village, 1915. The Truku were formerly classified as a subtribe of the Atayal, but in 2004 they were officially recognized as a separate people. Postcard collection of the author.

the child is tattooed, please guide the tattooist and her tools so that she can make the pattern, please hear me *lyutux!*" (Vadan, Dao, and Dada 2008:90).

Before the tattooing session, the parents of the child chose a favorable day for the tattooing by dream divination or through the observation of various bird omens in the forest. If the omen was bad, the tattooing was delayed. The "fortunetelling" also informed the parents if the tattooing should take place at their home or at the home of the tattooist (Ho 1960:13). The night before the tattooing, the client and the tattooist slept in the same bed to seek additional omens through dreaming. If the sign was good, the tattooing took place on the following morning; if not, it was further delayed. The tattoo client had to comply with several restrictions before or during the operation: menstruating girls could not be tattooed; male or female clients should not have recently imbibed any animal blood or eaten the internal organs of animals, nor should they wear red clothing during the operation, since these actions would result in their blood flowing unabated (Chi-Lu 1968:250). Furthermore, if someone had recently died in the village or if members of the community were out trapping animals, the tattooing had to be postponed (Ho 1960:13).

A blood sacrifice was offered before tattooing operations began. The parents provided the tattooist with a rooster, whose red comb was cut into four pieces and skewered on a bamboo stick held in the right hand. The tattooist then uttered a prayer: "I offer you, Ancestors, a chicken as sacrifice. Please let my patient be free from pain and give them strength during the operation" (Ho 1960:13).

Tattooing operations were almost always performed in a small hut or in the shadow of a barnlike structure located away from the living quarters. Most tattooing took place in winter because the cold weather was believed to facilitate the healing of the tattoos and prevent scabbing. The Atayal linked suppuration to the lack of virtue of the client (Chi-Lu 1968:249).

Atayal tattoo artists created the *nlsai,* or "foundation," of the cheek design by stenciling it on the skin with a linen thread thoroughly soaked in a small bowl containing *iluh* (soot) mixed with water (Ho 1960). The pigment was made of *ilox* (charred pine wood) scraped from the bottom of a cooking pot. The main framework consisted of *inlesay* (three sloping lines), which were marked first; the bottom line ran from the corner of the mouth to the lower ear opening, and the top line traveled from the lip just below the nostril and eye to the top of the ear opening. The midline was stenciled after these two lines were completed. Once the framework appeared symmetrical, diagonal lines forming a *syux* (latticework of diamond shapes) were inked, then *inlubong* (very fine lines) running parallel to the *inlesay* were set upon the skin (Vadan, Dao, and Dada 2007:86–88). As noted, some Atayal groups called *syux* the "eyes of *utux*" or the "eyes of the ancestors." When the *syux* were designed, the tattooist paid very close attention to the symmetry of these lines.

After the pattern was laid out on the face, it was punctured with different tools struck with a mallet-like "hammer" depending on the line work needed. Before the advent of steel needles, locally available citrus thorns (orange or tangerine) were bound to a tool resembling a toothbrush composed of four to sixteen needles arranged in rows and fastened to a wooden baton about 1.5 centimeters in diameter and 15 centimeters in length (Chi-Lu 1968:247). The *totsin,* or hammer, that pounded the tattoo instrument into the skin was constructed of a single piece of wood varying in diameter and length, although 17 centimeters was typical. Blood that flowed from the wounds was removed with a *quwar* (scraper) made from a rattan or bamboo splint that was bent and bound at either end with linen thread.

The tattoo client lay down with a folded cloth under her head. The tattooist usually sat on a low stool behind her or stood hunched over the patient with her tool. She took the needled instrument and expertly knocked it home with successive hammer blows.

The tattoo instrument for *inlesay* work contained a wider configuration of needles to quickly produce these thicker baselines. The hammers used for these tools were also relatively thick (four centimeters in diameter) compared to the smaller ones used to strike the fine *syux* and *inlubong* lines (two centimeters in diameter) that required a different configuration of very thin and short needles (Vadan, Dao, and Dada 2008). As the tattooist worked and the blood flowed, a process emerged until the tattoo was completed: tap the skin → scrape the blood → insert more pigment into the skin → wipe excess pigment → and repeat two more times per section until the blackwork pattern emerged.

A skilled tattooist could complete the cheek tattoos in one day. However, if the tattoo client struggled during the operation, this would slow down the process. For this reason, the girl was usually held down (head, hands, and feet) by attending female relatives. Men and children were expressly forbidden from observing the tattooing, as were pregnant or menstruating women. If a pregnant woman observed, it was believed the tattoo client would experience great pain like delivering a baby (Ho 1960:13). Some accounts report that a thorny tree branch was placed under the head of the girl to dissuade her from moving her head side to side while the tattooist worked (Vadan, Dao, and Dada 2008:120).

FIGURE 2.20
Atayal tattooing tools, some tipped with thirteen, seven, or five needles. From Chi-Lu 1968:248, fig. 87.

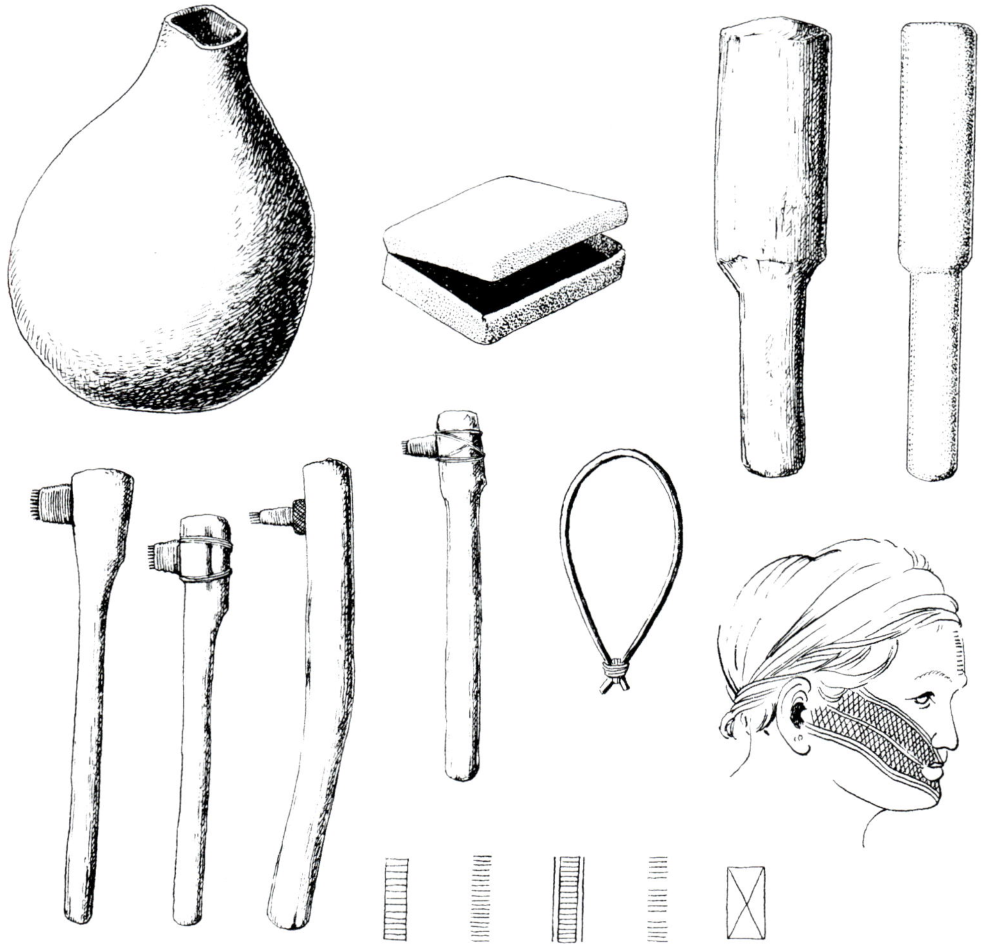

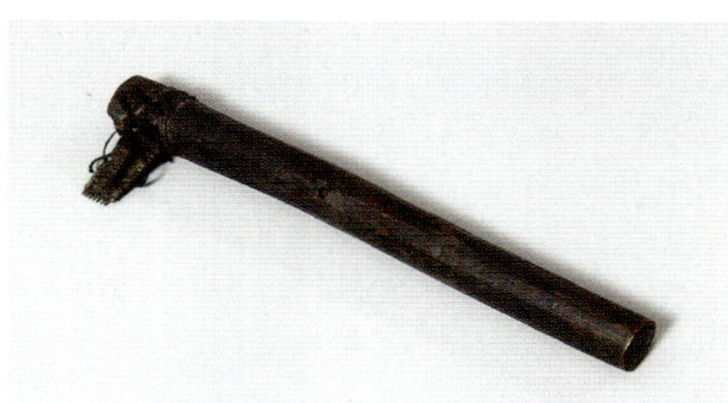

FIGURE 2.21
Atayal tattooing implement containing seven needles, ca. 1930. Courtesy National Taiwan University, Department of Anthropology (1520-6).

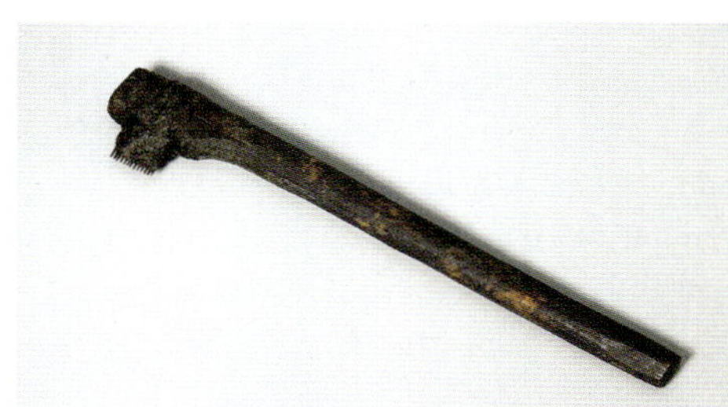

FIGURE 2.22
Atayal tattooing implement containing thirteen needles, ca. 1930. Courtesy National Taiwan University, Department of Anthropology (1520-9).

The Atayal elder Tawyu Nawraw noted that the areas closest to the mouth and under the eyes were the most painful locations for tattooing. She said, "[T]he tattoo master tattooed my face for a whole day, from morning to dark, to advance the pattern's surface. I was struggling to scream during this time, but I remained obedient and did not move so that the pattern was completed faster. After the tattoo, my entire face was painful and swollen. The only place where the pain was lighter was the area under my cheek because there was more meat [flesh] there" (Vadan, Dao, and Dada 2008:100).

Once the tattooing was complete, the girl was taken to the home of a *yaki* (grandmother), an old woman who was skilled in caring for recently tattooed girls—boys were not secluded after their tattooing. Here, the girl stayed in a dark room, usually for one week, until her wounds had partially healed. Her darkened but well-ventilated abode was cordoned off to limit any visitation, except for the caregiver who fed her rice gruel and served her water through a spoon or sipping tube. The girl was told to lie flat on her back when she slept, and her head rested on a pillow of rolled bamboo leaves or cloth.

The tattoo client observed various taboos during the seclusion period. For the first week, she was not to be exposed to light, look at red things, or eat any foods that were red—especially cooked meat or any variety of red rice—since light and red objects might cause her tattoos to fade or become distorted (Vadan, Dao, and Dada 2008:92). She was tabooed from looking at her tattooed face in a mirror or pool of water; if she did her tattoo pattern would "collapse" or disappear (Vadan, Dao, and Dada 2008:42). Salty, bitter, or spicy foods were forbidden, and only vegetable products were consumed. Smoking was not allowed, and oranges were not consumed because it was believed the girl's tattoos might turn orange. It was of the utmost importance to keep the tattoo wounds moist, so the caregiver would regularly apply water to the client's facial tattoos with a black bird feather from a crow or a chicken (Vadan, Dao, and Dada 2008:42, 79).

During the seclusion period, the girl's parents regularly brought food and water for their daughter and "grandma," and always thanked her for her efforts. When her job was done, the girl's parents invited the *yaki* to the feast held in honor of the tattoo artist.

After the Japanese cracked down on tattooing around 1913, many Atayal parents continued to pay tattoo artists to mark their sons and daughters with their ancestral markings, because without them they would not be able to cross the Rainbow Bridge. Tattooing had to be performed in secret, usually in a remote location in the mountains away from Japanese witnesses, and some girls recovered from the rite with their *yaki* in caves (Vadan, Dao, and Dada 2008). The Japanese were intent on dismantling tattoo practices because they were deeply enmeshed within the Ga-ga system, which they sought to destroy. Moreover, tattoos were proudly worn as marks of tribal identity and were seen as signs of resistance to Japanese rule. If the empire could eradicate tattooing, this would enable the colonial regime to more rapidly assimilate the "backward" Atayal and other rebellious groups into the fold of the modern Japanese state (Ma 1998:85).

Between 1918 and 1919, a severe drought combined with the global Spanish influenza resulted in a significant loss of life for Indigenous People inhabiting the northern mountains. Elders attributed these events to ancestral punishment for not continuing the tattooing tradition per Ga-ga (Ho 1960:6). Thus, many parents allowed their children to be tattooed, and

FIGURE 2.23
Atayal elder Lawa Toyu (~1918–2019) of Tai'an Township, Miaoli County, 2016. Due to the tattooing bans of the early twentieth century, Toyu was able to receive only one layer of facial tattooing. Thus, her facial tattoos are very faint. © Lars Krutak.

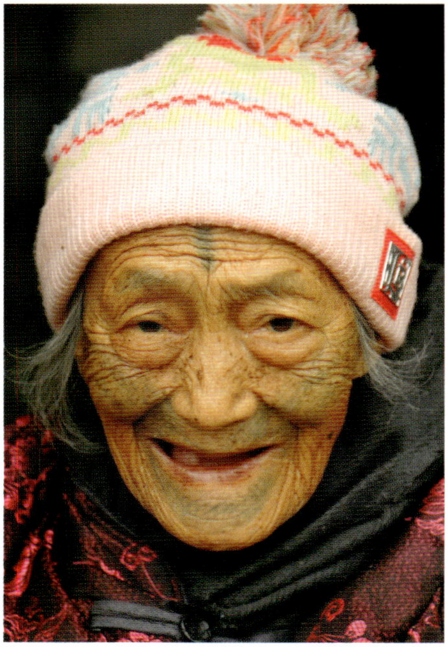

some communities recorded one hundred or more children receiving tattoos. Japanese authorities immediately took strict measures to stop these activities, and they threatened tattoo artists and parents with fines, lashings, servitude (i.e., hard labor), confiscation of tattooing tools,[7] or imprisonment if they allowed tattooing to continue (Ho 1960:6; Ma 1998:86). Once a newly tattooed boy or girl returned home from their secret tattooing session in the mountains, they were immediately admonished by Japanese school teachers, policemen, and other local government agents, and punishments were imposed on the guilty subjects. Several female Atayal elders noted that the reason their facial tattoos were not dark was because they were not able to receive a second or third session with a tattooist because their tools had been confiscated (Vadan, Dao, and Dada 2008). It should be noted here that women who did not have clear and bold cheek tattoos received a smaller dowry than those possessing the greatly valued dark facial markings (Ho 1960:10). In some cases, women with lighter-colored tattoos might have difficulty finding a husband.

Eventually, around 1935, the Atayal and other northern tribes were forced to give up these ancient practices for good (Ma 1998). Some men and women (i.e., those with forehead tattoos) were made to feel ashamed of their tattoos and had them surgically removed.[8] Many men were also forced to join the Japanese Army during World War II, and their tattoos were removed to make them "look more like Japanese" (J. Chen 1997). The method did not involve anesthesia and entailed clamping the tattooed skin with tweezers, then cutting out the tattoo marks with a scalpel and stitching up the wound (Ma 1998:88).

TATTOO TRADITIONS OF SOUTHERN TAIWAN (1895–2016)

In comparison to Taiwan's northern Indigenous groups, less has been published on the tattooing traditions of those groups (e.g., Paiwan, Rukai, Puyuma, and Bunun) inhabiting the southern part of the country. Notwithstanding, most of the extant historical documentation on tattooing culture here focuses on the tattooing traditions of the Paiwan and the Rukai as they existed in the late nineteenth century through the time of the Japanese occupation of their territories in the early twentieth century, and for this reason, this section largely focuses on their tattooing practices.

In 2016, I was invited by the Paiwan cultural tattoo practitioner Cudjuy Patjidres to conduct field research among the last generation of female Paiwan tattoo bearers. Among the Paiwan, tattooing was intimately associated with social status and leadership, and specific motifs could be worn only by ruling chiefs and their family members. Warriors might also receive tattoos, but they had to seek permission from village chiefs before they could bear the intricate body tattooing characteristic of the tribe. Commoners, or those individuals not of aristocratic or high social status, might also bear tattoo motifs associated with their social stratum, but this right had to be purchased from the ruling family of the community. By local standards, the cost of tattooing was very expensive, thus very few commoners could afford it.

The Paiwan are the only southern tribe that retains the tradition of tattooing today, which has been extinct for decades among the neighboring Rukai, Puyuma, and Bunun. At the time of my field investigations, less than forty hand-tattooed *vuvus* (grandmothers), or elderly Paiwan women, remained. Each one was more than eighty years of age. The last generation of heavily tattooed Paiwan chiefs and warriors departed our world in the 1990s. Today, only a few historical photographs exist of the very intricate and incredible tattoo patterns men wore that were infused with spiritual meanings and symbolism.

As with the northern tribes, the decline in traditional Paiwan tattooing customs began during the Japanese occupation of Taiwan (1895–1945). They forbid the practice, although I was told stories of young Paiwan women meeting tribal tattooists secretly in the mountains to be tattooed. The tattooed Paiwan elder Ukani Tjavung (b. 1932), whose mother was a tattooist, spoke about the Japanese attitude toward tattooing. She noted the Japanese tried to dissuade the Paiwan from tattooing because if they continued the practice they would be discriminated against. "They told us, 'If you tattoo, people will know you are Indigenous. Moreover, tattoos look dirty on the back of your hands, like stains that cannot be washed away,'" she explained (Ming-Chieh [Taligu] 2013:138).

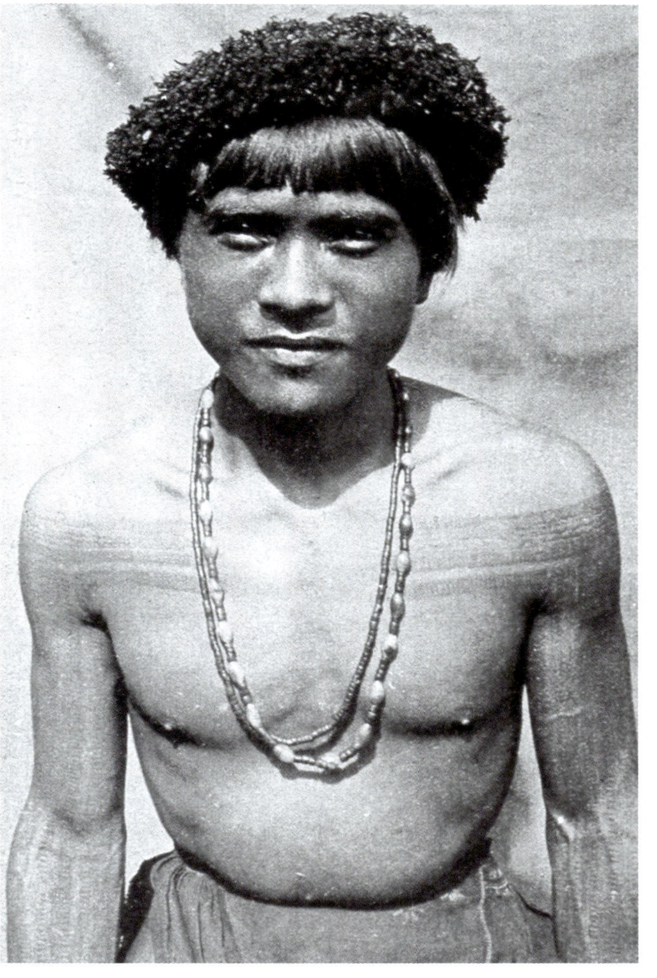

FIGURE 2.24
Paiwan warrior, 1905. From Formosa Bureau of Aboriginal Affairs 1911.

Even the Chinese Nationalist government who took control over Taiwan from the Japanese after 1945 prohibited Paiwan tattooing. "However, it was just at the time that the Japanese were handing over to the Nationalists that our elders were encouraging us to be tattooed for a two-year period," says tattooed elder Ho Yu-mei of Laiyi Township. "After that, the tattooing stopped forever."

Indeed, all of the tattooed *vuvus* I interviewed were tattooed during this short window. Traditional tribal authorities took the opportunity to encourage tattooists and family heads to mark young women in an attempt to resurrect the custom. Ho (1960:18), who conducted field

FIGURE 2.25
Chief of Kulalao village, Butsul group of Paiwan, ca. 1938. Courtesy National Taiwan University, Department of Anthropology (1638–1).

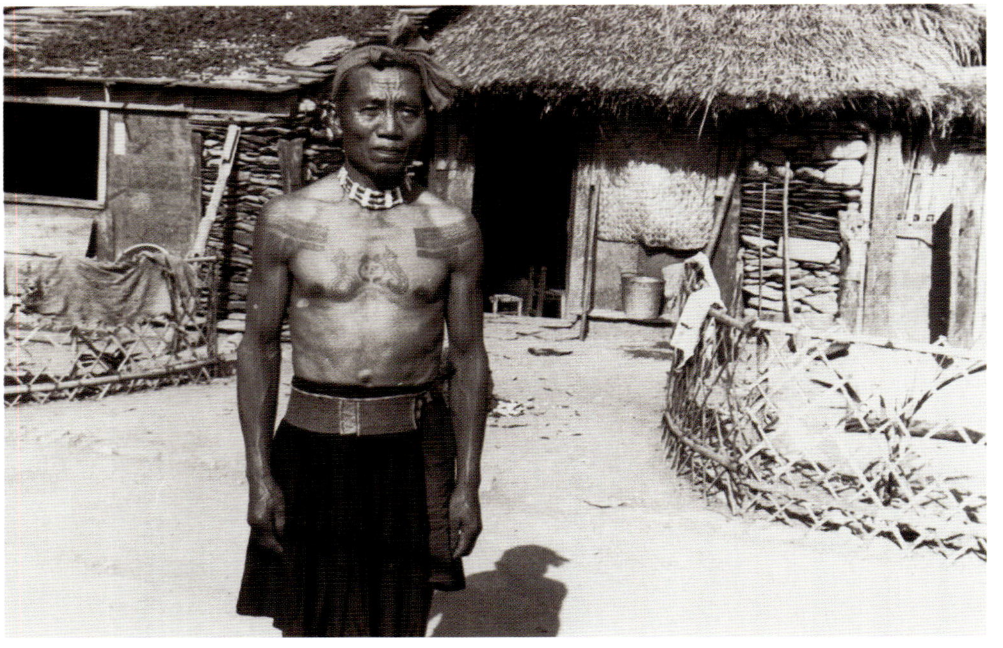

research among the Paiwan, the Rukai, and neighboring groups in the 1950s, wrote that during this time only Paiwan aristocratic men and women above the age of forty-five possessed tattoos. The Japanese tattooing bans that began around 1913 in the north were equally effective in the southern regions.

PAIWAN TATTOOS

The most important and detailed published literature on Paiwan tattooing comes from Ho's (1960) Chinese-language report, and for this reason, it will be cited throughout this section. I will also draw on my field research in Laiyi and Puljetji villages, the exquisite yet scarce Paiwan-produced bilingual (English and Chinese) book *Vecik Izua ta Lima: Writings on the Hand* (Ming-Chieh [Taligu] 2013) focusing on the hand tattoos of the last generation of tattooed Puljetji women, and the largely unpublished fieldwork of the Paiwan researcher and photographer Angusan Palivulj (Chen Wen-Shan, Chinese name), who works as the exhibition curator at the Pingtung County Laiyi Indigenous Museum. Wen-Shan, as he is called locally, was one of my gracious house hosts during my stay in Pingtung County. He has spent several years recording the traditions surrounding the tattooing customs of his people, and this important research has culminated in several museum exhibitions, including the first show on the ancestral tradition of Paiwan hand tattooing at the National Taiwan Museum in Taipei City in 2015. Wen-Shan said he felt a responsibility to record the custom because at the time he initiated his project with a volunteer team in 2012, twenty-one of the surviving thirty-four tattooed *vuvus* resided in Laiyi Township, where he lives today.[9] The stories of these twenty-one Laiyi women were featured in the museum exhibition *Engraving Prestige: The Tattoo Tradition of the Paiwan*. Thankfully, the exhibition director, Chao-Ling Kuo, with the permission of Wen-Shan, shared with me the raw transcripts from those interviews so that I could feature aspects of them here (see Palivulj 2012–2015), translated into English, for the first time.

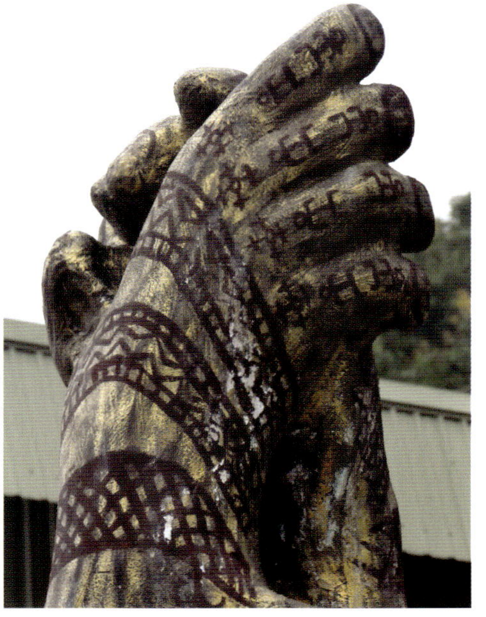

FIGURE 2.26
Monumental sculpture in Puljetji village celebrating Paiwan hand tattooing, 2016. © Lars Krutak.

In the Paiwan language, *iveci'e* (pronounced *i-vu-dʒi*) refers to both hand and body tattoos. Ho (1960:18) called them *vuntsik*, meaning "patterns," and in Puljetji village the term *vecik* (writing) is used (Ming-Chieh [Taligu] 2013). Ho noted that this word also referred to embroidery, carving, painting, and, more importantly, "written language." Some elders have recalled that the Paiwan formerly tattooed the face, namely a "sun" motif placed on one temple, but I can find no pictorial or photographic evidence. However, one oral account collected by Ho (1960:18) noted that the woman who was responsible for birthing the first Paiwan people was facially tattooed, but the pattern was not described. Another story collected by Ho spoke about the origins of the tattooing custom. A male tribal head of the Butsul tribe of Paiwan stated that his tribe's head family was born from the eggs of an unidentified snake or the sun, so to honor them serpentine and solar patterns were tattooed on their bodies to memorialize their ancestors (Ho 1960:18). Oral histories collected in Puljetji reveal yet another tattoo origin story related to the hundred-pace viper (*Deinagkistrodon acutus*),[10] which is considered to be the spirit of life, the greatest of all spirits, because it represents the guardian spirit of the Paiwan people (Krutak 2016a). Paraphrasing Chou Ming-Chieh (Lulji Taligu) (2013:7), the story relates a large hundred-pace viper sitting on a large rock, its home, in the middle of a waterfall above the rapid river currents. It gave birth to a girl, and when she became of age a Paiwan hunter met her in the forest. He liked her very much and wanted to marry her back in his village. However, his mother was very suspicious of the girl, whom she thought was a forest fairy, and she believed the girl might bring harm to the village because she was not human. The girl was powerless to stop the hunter's mother, and she began cleaning her besmirched body until a solar motif appeared on her right shoulder and a mortar and pestle engraved with a snake design on the left. The woman realized she had offended the girl, so she consented to the marriage, which followed. Thereafter, the Puljetji villagers began tattooing their bodies with designs related to their personal stories and family lineages so that other communities could immediately recognize these important individuals.

This story and other Paiwan tales provide direct evidence regarding the early origins of the hundred-pace viper, solar, and mortar and pestle tattoo motifs. Over time, all three came to occupy primary positions in the corpus of Paiwan tattoo iconography: the viper forms the baseline for male body tattoos and is also worn on the hands of women; the sun appears on the knuckles of female aristocrats; and the mortar and pestle, on the digits of lower-class noblewomen.

Originally, tattooing could be worn only by individuals born into noble families. This included the top tribal head, the second head, and the third head, together with their family members (Ho 1960). Depending on one's family background, ancestry, and social rank, different tattoo patterns and motif configurations were placed on different parts of the body. In Laiyi village, there were five *putja vuluvulung* (social ranks or classes), with each one using specific tattoo patterns, such as a family crest, reserved for their stratum; in other villages, there were only three or four classes of hand-tattoo patterns; and in Puljetji up to eight "ranks" of tattoos were observed (Ming-Chieh [Taligu] 2013:31, 105), and these could be worn only by members of four specific families: Taljialep, Sadjiljapan, Vavikiyan, and Sikataqaljan.[11] If a person accepted a tattoo pattern that was above their social position, which was an affront to the *audanan* (ancestral tribal rules) that governed Paiwan society, the tattooist would be severely punished (Palivulj 2012–2015:15).

Paiwan *vuvu* Ipunue 'Edre'edr, who was of the *djaljedjalje* (second class), spoke in detail about some of the hand-tattoo motifs of the various classes in Laiyi. The motifs she refers to appeared on a woman's fingers and knuckles. Some motifs could appear in one or more classes, but they were configured with other motifs that only specific classes could wear. In sum, a woman's hand tattoos performed as a visual language of the skin, communicating one's social status, ancestry, and tribal identity to other community members.

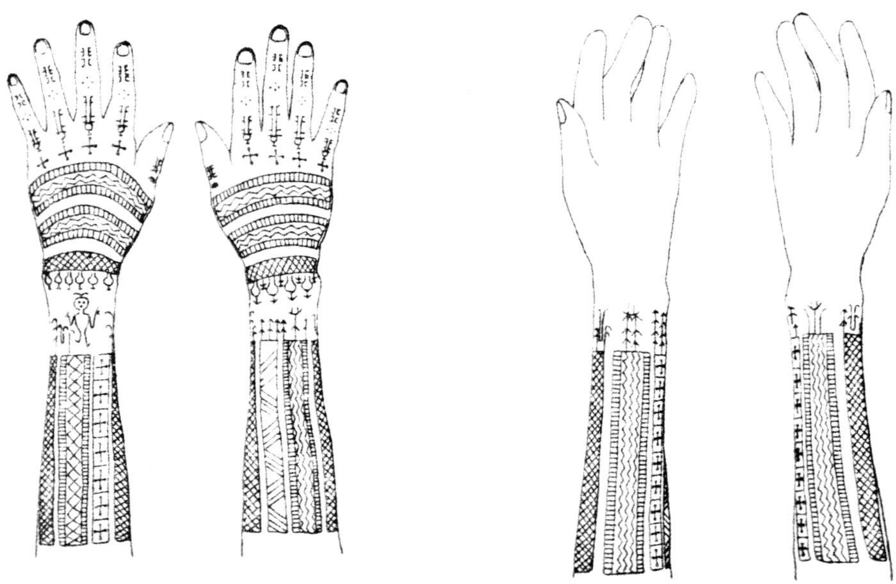

FIGURE 2.27
Forearm tattooing of Rukai women, Taromak village, ca. 1955. The long, rectangular center design (*right*) on the inside forearm represents a "chopping board." From Ho 1960: pl. IV.

The tattoo patterns of the highest class include *kakelayan* (fishing hook) and *tilju* (plate). The second class is *maru qadaw* (sun's rays)[12] and *maru caucaw* ([anthropomorphic] human beings). . . . When we had meetings, we could recognize the *putja vuluvulung* or social classes through the tattoo patterns on our hands. The tattoo patterns of the third class are called *maru qadaw* (sun's rays), or *adjunangan* (land symbol), or *maru caucaw* (human shape) or *maru cacakare* (figure-8 shape [or mortar and pestle]). The tattoo patterns of the fourth class include *maru caucaw* (human shape), or *hakuhaku* (square shape), or *lukuluku*. The tattoo patterns of the fifth class include *maru caucaw* (human shape), or *maru vilji*. (Palivulj 2012–2015:15)

During my field investigations, I learned more information regarding these specific patterns. Perhaps the most important or powerful design was an anthropomorph with rounded legs that was reserved for women of the highest noble class.[13] This could be worn on the thumb or on the side of the wrist. Gatju Ljmljman (b. 1932) from Puljetji village, whose inhabitants speak a different dialect of Paiwan from the people of Laiyi, possessed this very rare tattoo on her thumbs and was considered to be a "princess" of that village. She stated that only female members of the chief's family could bear this tattoo, and no one else would "dare to get it" if they were from a lower social class.[14]

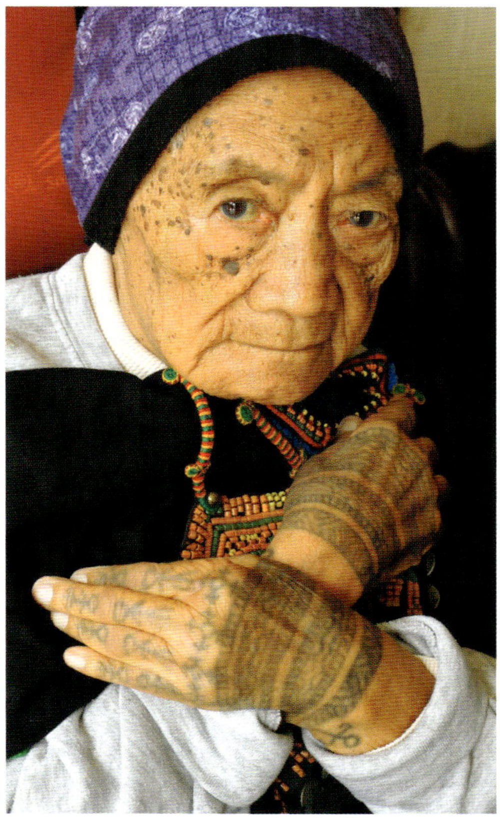

FIGURE 2.28
Ljalep Qamuljilj (1927–2016), a Paiwan elder and aristocrat, 2016. She was tattooed by a female artist and born into a long line of Paiwan shamans. "When the tattoo operation was completed, there must be a ceremony to cool the temperature of the hands," she said. "We also prayed to the Ancestral Spirit so that the wounds would not become infected and that the patterns would be clear and bright." © Lars Krutak.

The Paiwan linguist and researcher Idis Sadjiljapan has recorded more detailed information concerning the tattooed *vuvus* around Taiwu Township. In 2008, she initiated field studies with the eleven remaining female elders of the Jiaxing tribe of Paiwan, including *vuvu* Ljmljman. By 2014, only four of these tattooed elders were alive. The patterning on *vuvu* Ljmljman's hands (from the wrist down to the digits) was as follows: the netlike *pinaruqunecu*, representing the pattern on the neck of the hundred-pace viper (symbolizing Ljmljman's high social position); several thin bands of *pinarualjialjis* (*sinangatj*), or "dentate pattern," that symbolize the management rights of the land, mountains, and villages; two zigzagging bands placed between the dentate pattern, called *pinarukalavikav*, which are "wave" or "river" motifs; on the knuckles appears the *pinarualjialjis* (sun or sun's rays pattern), which stands for the tribal chieftain who is

FIGURE 2.29
Body tattooing of a Paiwan warrior, ca. 1910. A necklace of agate and heirloom beads hangs around his neck. From Ushinosuke 1918.

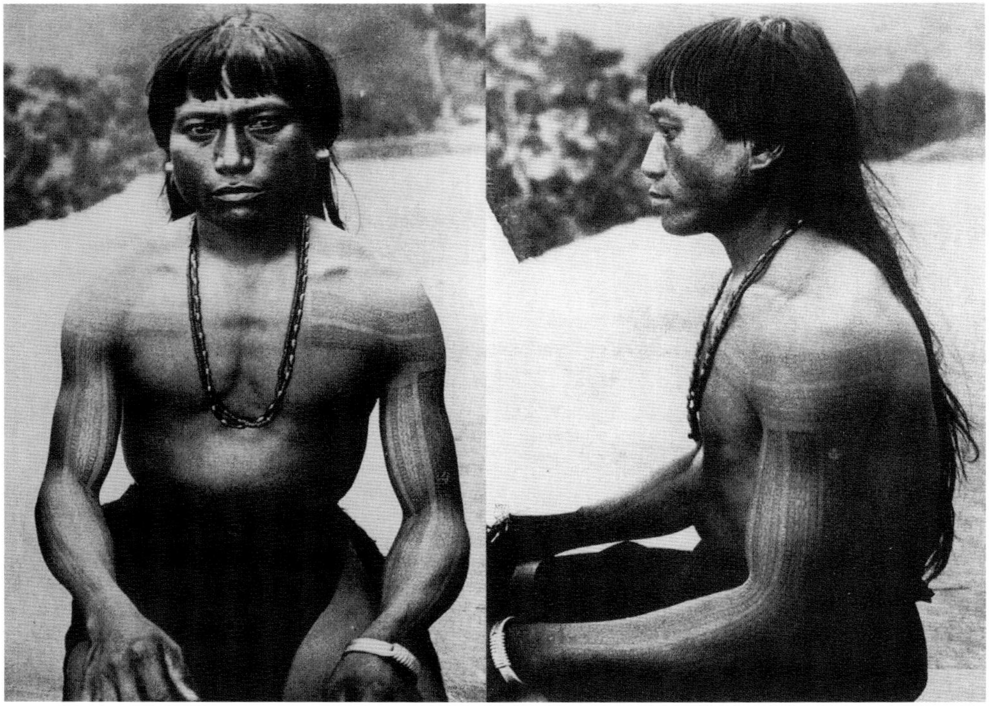

considered a child of the sun who rules from a lofty position, since the sun stands high in the heavens; and finally an inverted and upright *pinarucaucau* (anthropomorph), representing tribal leadership over the people because the chiefly family manages local society, community resources (fishing and hunting grounds, agricultural fields), religious customs (sacrifices), and social order (*Smile Taiwan* 2019a).

In the exhibition space of the Laiyi Museum, the inverted anthropomorph connotes the incarnation of the Ancestral Spirit. This entity is a kind of guardian or protector spirit of the village. Every five years, it is honored during the Maleveq Festival, a major Paiwan ceremonial event that petitions the Ancestral Spirit for protection, rain, fertility for crops, and fertility for women.

Puljetji village elder *vuvu* Ukani Tjavung bore nearly identical tattoo motifs on her hands, except for the thumb motif. She also possessed a tattoo on her inner arm called a *sinan tilju*, or "chopping board," which only third-class nobles could possess. Her family was entitled to a special *puqarut* (livestock tax) when pigs were killed, and the chopping board represents the right to collect this tax (*Smile Taiwan* 2019a).

Other elders, such as Ljalep Qamuljilj (b. 1927) from Laiyi, had the *sina kakelayan* (hanging hook) pattern on their wrists, a motif reserved for the highest social class. Possession of this tattoo motif meant that the woman belonged to a family who owned a hunting ground, and its head was entitled to a *kemakan ta sinipavadis* (game or prey tax) (*Smile Taiwan* 2019a). *Vuvu* Ljalep was also born into a long line of Paiwan shamans, and she possessed a great deal of knowledge surrounding the tattooing rite, which will be discussed below.

Notwithstanding, men and women of commoner status were also granted the honor of receiving tattoos from the village head in certain communities. However, in very conservative Paiwan communities this right might have been granted only for one generation and could not be passed down (Ho 1960). The individuals who could earn the honor of tattooing were warriors; skillful and talented people, such as great hunters, foot messengers, and the housekeepers of tribal heads; wealthy people; and productive farmers. The latter two classes had to pay the tribal head for the right to be tattooed, and feast their village to publicly inform them that they had paid for and been given permission to receive the prestigious markings (Ho 1960). If a wealthy man purchased the right for his daughter when she came of age, this enhanced her dowry and social status, and these traits were greatly valued by potential in-laws. If a warrior or talented individual was physically infirm, they could transfer the right of tattooing to a family member.

PAIWAN TATTOO CULTURE

Paiwan tattoo artists could be male or female, but they were usually women who inherited the occupation through the family line. Each village had one or more artists, and most came from noble families, although commoners could purchase the right to become tattooers (Ho 1960). The technique was a form of hand-tapping, but the tools did not resemble those of groups living in northern Taiwan. Tattoo needles were made by binding a pair of steel needles with linen thread on a bamboo stick about forty centimeters in length. Before the introduction of steel needles, the Paiwan used two or three thorns of the mountain orange or pomelo for tattooing. A small knife with a wooden handle was used to tap the needled tool with sooty pigment into the skin.

The tattoo pattern was first stenciled on the skin with grass or bamboo stems or the back of the knife blade (Krutak 2016a). The stenciling slurry consisted of crushed slate mixed with water applied to the skin. The actual tattoo pigment was composed of charred millet stalks mixed with *qidung* (soot) taken from the underside of a cooking pot.[15] As the tattooing progressed, the knife blade was used to scrape away the flowing blood so the artist could see their work. The tattooist sometimes spat betel nut juice on the wounds to stop excessive bleeding. When all tattooing was completed, the tattoo master applied the ashes of "chestnut grass" on the wounds, then washed them off with cold water (Ho 1960).

Men and women could not request to be tattooed themselves. The ruling chief made these and other decisions, and when an individual approached the appropriate age or had earned the right to be tattooed due to exploits, the chief sent an envoy to the family asking if their son or daughter would like to be marked. The envoy did not speak with the father or mother directly; instead, he communicated with the family representative, who among the nobility was usually the *vusam* (firstborn) of the family (Ming-Chieh [Taligu] 2013:25). Before the tattooing commenced, the ruling chief was offered a ceremonial beverage of millet wine or a spirit made of distilled chestnuts, and through his messenger, he decided which body parts were to be marked and the appropriate day for the tattooing itself. However, if an individual was not deemed worthy, they were not

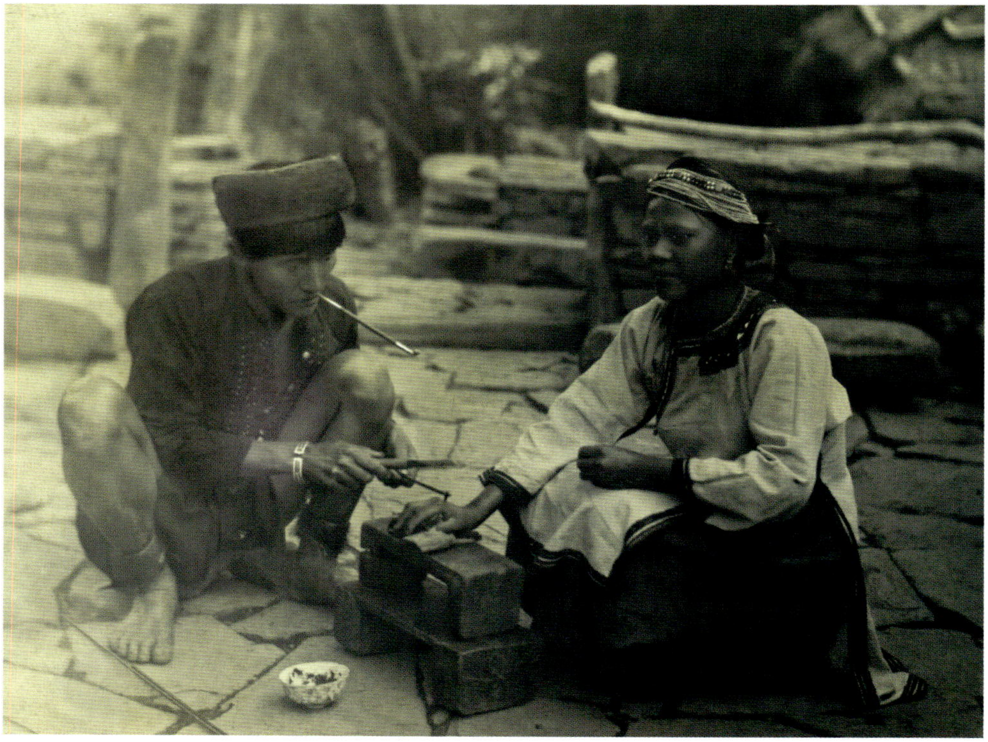

FIGURE 2.30
Male Paiwan tattooist at work, ca. 1910. Courtesy of Tzi-Ning Li.

tattooed. For a girl, the *vusam* asked the chief which class of tattoo pattern she could receive. "We could not decide it ourselves," said the tattooed octogenarian Saivig Vuruvur. "The patterns on my fingers are associated with my social class. And at that time, the tribal rule was that only one child—the eldest one—in one family could have tattoos."

Tattooed Puljetji elder Selep Qaqatiyan said that a chief could not be a proper ruler without a tattoo nor could an untattooed noble person properly represent their family. "My mother always tried to persuade me [to get tattooed] by saying, 'how can a chief be without [a] tattoo[?]. It's a must. Tattoo is our name (*ngadan*), our power (*picul*) and our custom (*kakudaan*)'" (Ming-Chieh [Taligu] 2013:31). "And the villagers of Puljetji know exactly which designs belong to which family," explained tattooed *vuvu* Galaigai (Ljamac) Caqeljip (Ming-Chieh [Taligu] 2013:31).

On the tattooing day, the tattooist prayed at the gate of the house of the person who would be tattooed. A sample Paiwan prayer is as follows: "We ask your help, ancestors, before the operation. Please let the patterns be tattooed like a wild cat's skin, black and straight" (Ho 1960:22).[16] Bit offerings of meat were made to the Ancestral Spirit of the village since it protected the tattooist from evil spirits that were attracted to the flowing blood released during the tattoo operation (Krutak 2016a).[17] Various taboos were observed. For example, tattooing could not take place if a pregnant family member was living in the same house as the tattoo client or if the client herself was pregnant. One Paiwan elder Tju'u Tjuvarevare of Laiyi said she was pregnant when she received her hand tattoos during a two-day tattooing session. She remembered what occurred after breaking the *iciluq*, or tattoo taboo: "Something strange happened. At that time, I was pregnant and expecting to have my first child. Without any reason, the tattoo pigment (*qidung*) would not fix," and to this day her tattoos are very faint (Palivulj 2012–2015:7–8). If the tattoo client was "secretly" married, tattooing was forbidden. If there had been a recent death in the village, the tattooing was postponed. Girls who were having their period could not be tattooed. Also, a person could not be tattooed on the first day of a new lunar month; otherwise, the tattoos might become suppurated (Ho 1960:22). Moreover, tattooing could not take place during the Maleveq Festival.

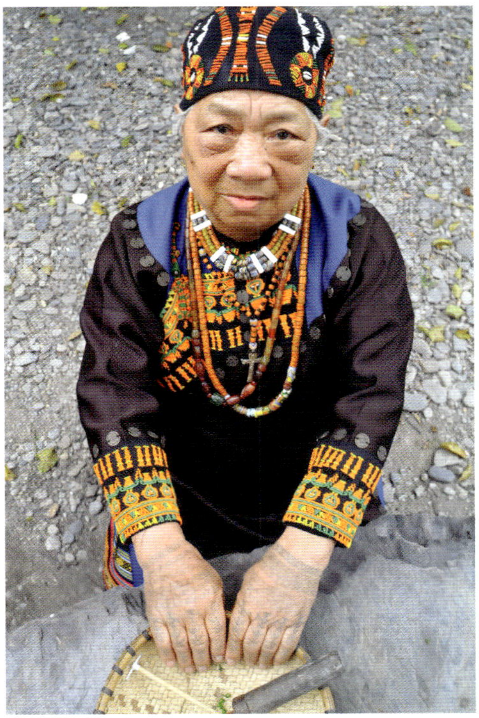

FIGURE 2.31
Vuvu Ukani (b. 1932) of Puljetji village holds a basket with the tools of the Paiwan tattooist, 2016. Her mother was a tattooist and marked her hands at the age of fifteen. © Lars Krutak.

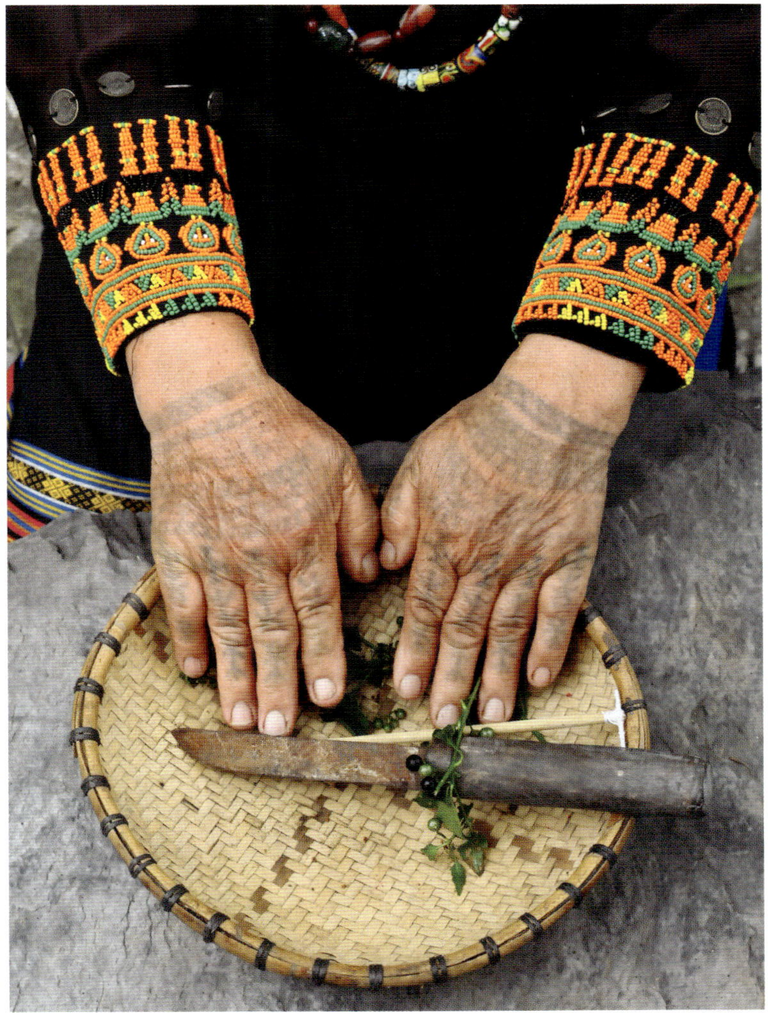

FIGURE 2.32
The basket holds the knife used as the mallet to hand-tap the tattoo needles, stalks of millet (*hidden from view*) used to make tattoo pigment, and a local medicinal plant used to heal the wounds, 2016. © Lars Krutak.

FIGURE 2.33 (RIGHT)
Hand tattoo of the Paiwan elder Muwakai Qeludu of Laiyi village, 2016. Betel nut juice stains her thumb. © Lars Krutak.

FIGURE 2.34 (BELOW)
Female Paiwan tattooist demonstrating her former profession, ca. 1955. From Ho 1960: pl. 7.

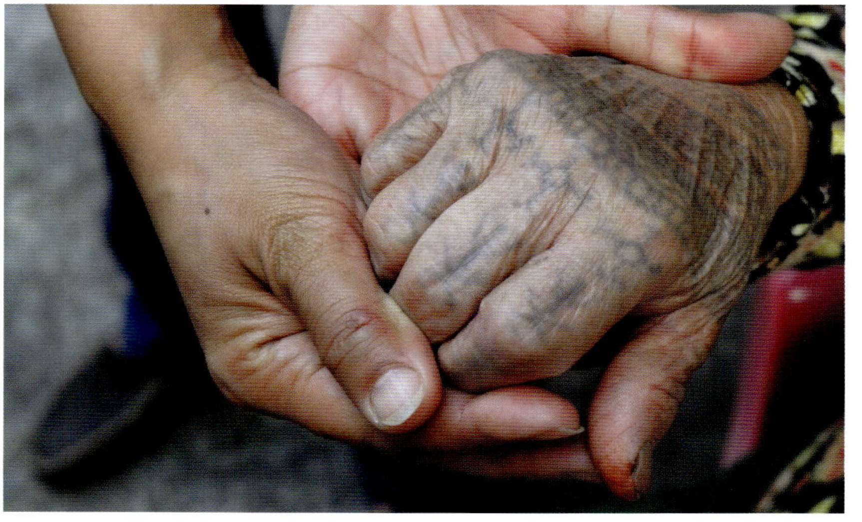

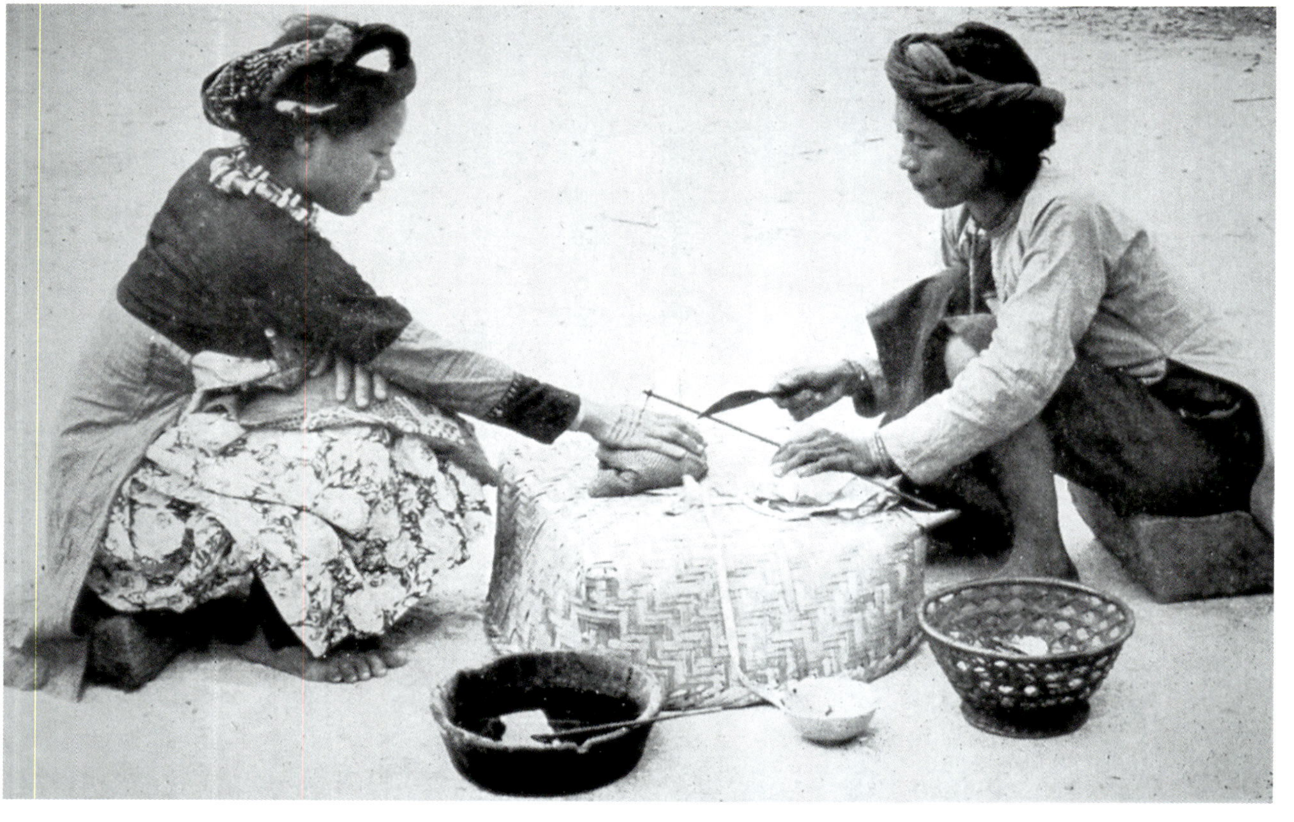

Tattooing was usually performed in winter because the drier air was believed to aid in healing. A small hut or fence of bamboo, straw mats, or blankets was constructed in a semi-isolated area for the tattooing to take place. To prevent intruders from watching, especially pregnant women, a bamboo stick was erected in front of the hut to serve notice. If a pregnant woman saw the tattooing, it was believed that the tattoo client's hands would swell and become septic or their tattoos would fade and eventually disappear (Krutak 2016a). If someone sneezed or farted during the tattooing, the operation was postponed immediately; otherwise, the soul of the person being tattooed "would be taken away" (Ho 1960:22). Another purpose of the small hut or fencing was to keep evil spirits at bay (Ming-Chieh [Taligu] 2013:75).

If the tattooist was the parent of the tattoo recipient, someone else had to make the first puncture. *Vuvu* Ukani's mother was her tattoo artist, but to uphold the taboo her girlfriend made the first incision (Ming-Chieh [Taligu] 2013:35).

Saivig Vuruvur recalls the day she was tattooed:

> An elder in my tribe performed the tattoo operation on my hands. His name was Lageili. He was my father's younger brother. The tattoo operation took two days, that is, one day for each hand. The tattoo operation was very painful. I cried and had tears during the operation. I was 16 years old and during the tattoo operation . . . my hands were placed on a folded cloth (*sawuzayan*) atop a large bamboo basket (*dradrauyan*). My hands were bleeding and I felt great pain. After the tattoo operation, banana leaves [*masu'elilij*] were placed on my hands to cool them down. For healing, we used plants such as sweet potato leaves (*djawdjaw*) or *sini* (leaves of chili pepper).[18] The leaves were crushed and squeezed into a juice, and then put on the hands. Another function of the juice was to make the tattoo patterns clear and bright. (Palivulj 2012–2015:10)

Vuvu Djupelang Tjaraqidis spoke about the healing process of her hand tattoos: "We placed our hands on the slate plates, that formed the house roof, in the morning so the hands could cool; this helped alleviate the pains. The young men were attracted by the hand tattoos, and they attempted to woo us. They picked healing herbs [black nightshade (*sameci*)] for us, and even squeezed the herbs to make a juice which was placed on a cloth, wrung, and the healing fluid dripped on our hands" (Palivulj 2012–2015:13). Babai Qeludu of Puljetji village said she kept her hands raised as they healed, "because as soon as you lay them down, you feel the pain. So, you always remember to keep them high and never dare to lower them. You even need assistance to go to the toilet" (Ming-Chieh [Taligu] 2013:167).

During the tattooing operation, *vuvu* Ukani recalled, relatives, friends, and boys would visit the girl to provide comfort and cheer her. They also attempted to divert the tattooee's attention away from the significant pain that was inflicted on their hands. "But the needle pokes to the joints of the hand and the bony parts of the wrist were almost unbearable," she remembered. "It was useless for them to try and get my attention, it hurt so much!" (*Smile Taiwan* 2019b).

FIGURE 2.35
Patterns of Paiwan hand tattooing: *top row, left to right*: Parirayan village (*a*); Tokubul village (*b–d*); *bottom row*, Timor village (*a*); Kabianan village (*b–c*); Chalaabus village (*d*). From Ho 1960: pl. IV.

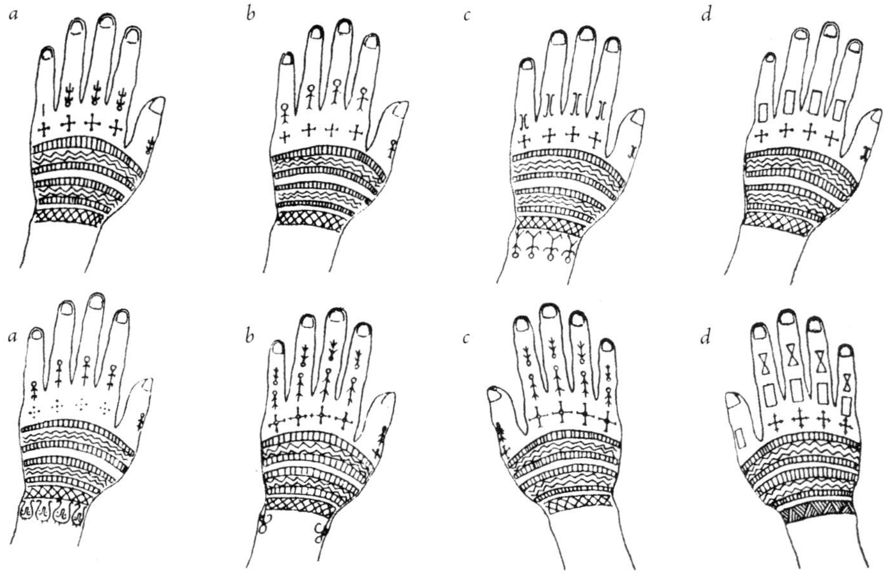

FIGURE 2.36
Patterns of Paiwan hand tattooing: *top row, left to right*, (*a–b*) Kulalao village; (c) Maraji village; (*d*) Chaobobol village; *bottom row*, (*a*) Malipa village; (*b–c*) Pacaval village; (*d*) Carapi village. From Ho 1960: pl. IV.

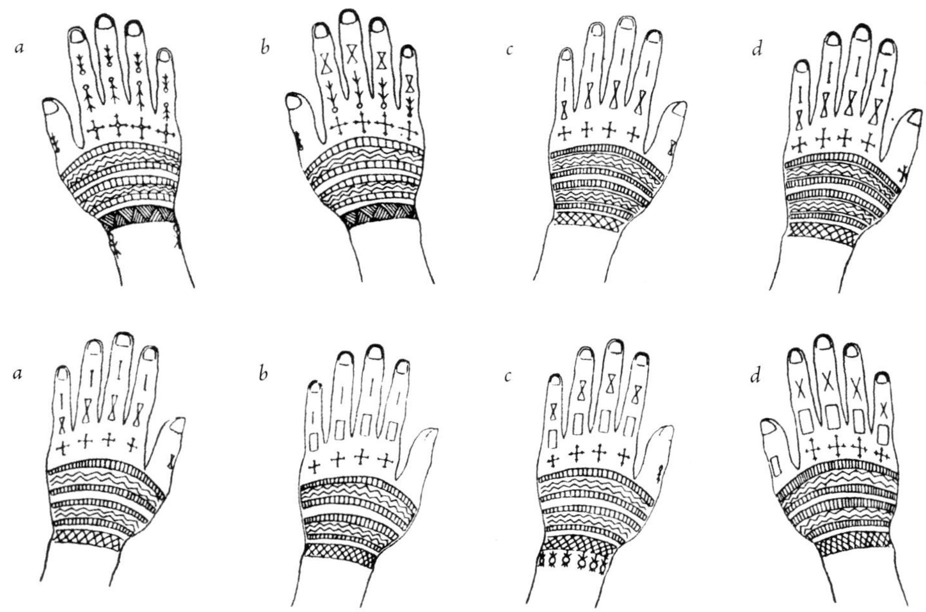

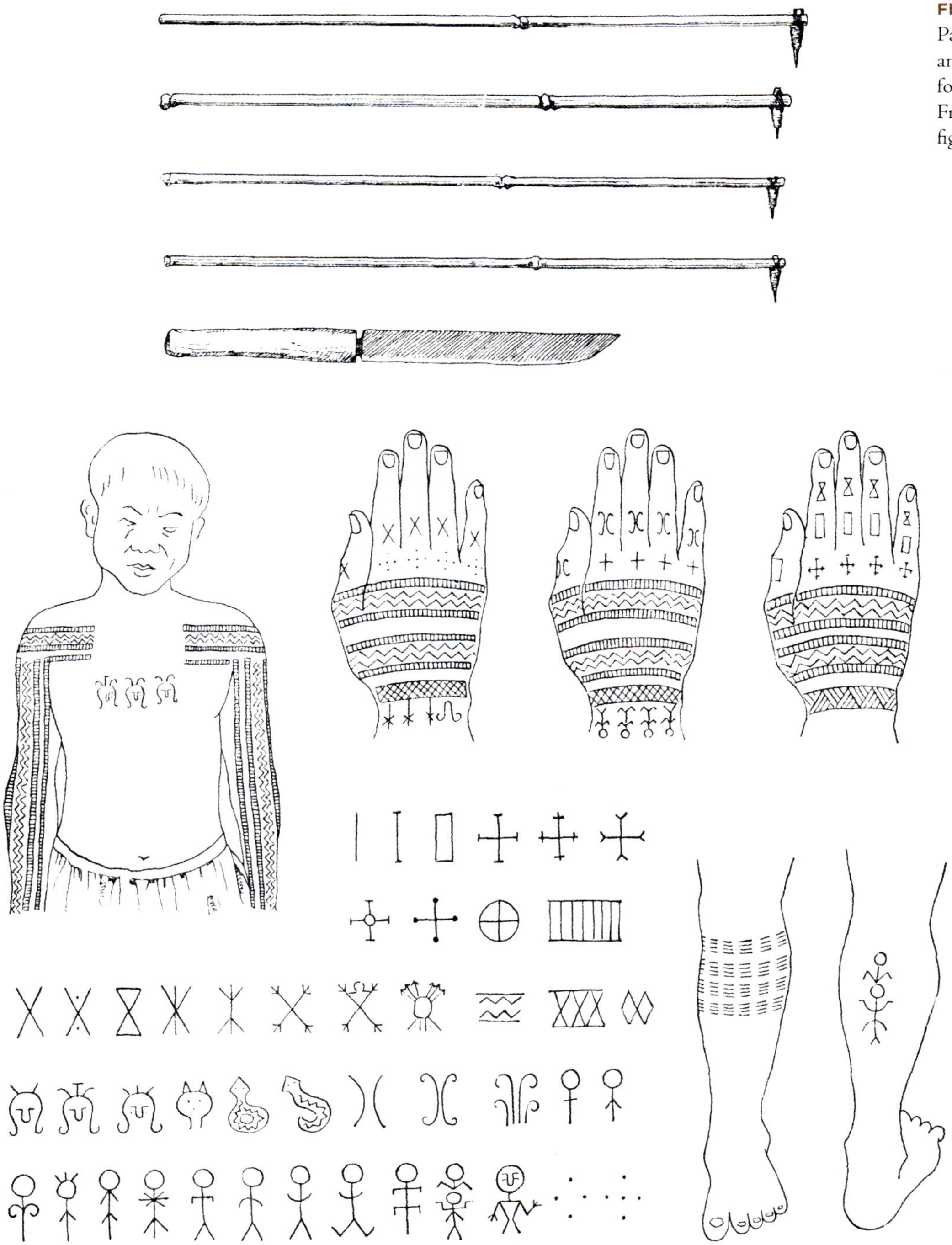

FIGURE 2.37
Paiwan tattooing tools and various patterns for men and women. From Chi-Lu 1968:253, fig. 88.

The shaman *vuvu* Ljalep Qamuljilj noted that there was a formal ritual held once the hand tattooing was completed. This ceremony was called *ijemaljeqel* (cooling and reducing temperature). A prayer was offered to the Ancestral Spirit asking for the tattoo patterns to be clear and bright, and not become infected. Another ceremony called *pasedjaljep* (praying for happiness) was held to give thanks to the tattoo master whereupon one or more pigs were sacrificed, and the pork was shared with the tattoo master and the people who assisted with the girl's tattooing and aftercare (Palivulj 2012–2015:11–12). However, the tattoo client was tabooed from eating this pork or rice. To mark this rite of passage, the girl wore a glass bead bracelet for the first time, symbolizing her adult status (Ho 1960:21). This bracelet was worn until she was married, and it was said that having a tattoo and wearing the bracelet would drive away evil spirits and protect the bearer from bad luck (Ho 1960).[19]

Payments varied according to the complexity of the design given and the social rank of the tattoo recipient (e.g., high-ranking designs cost more than lower-ranking ones), but members of the chief's family did not have to pay for their tattoos. For example, the cost of tattooing a man's chest, back, and both arms was high: one pig, two iron rakes, four knives, an ax, one roll of cloth, one porcelain bowl, and a bottle of millet wine (Ho 1960). Other sources report that payment was akin to the costs of a dowry and included four guns, good-quality clothes, a large pitchfork, a pot, a large iron cooking wok, a reaping sickle, porcelain bowls, alcoholic drinks, and a pig (Ming-Chieh [Taligu] 2013:37; Palivulj 2012–2015:23). This payment had a symbolic component because the four guns represented the location of the tattooing (i.e., a small room with four posts), the clothing was linked to the roof of the tattooing place, and the porcelain bowls symbolized the eyes of the tattoo master (Palivulj 2012–2015:23).

Tattoo artists accepted other forms of payment. "The tattoo masters understood our economic status," said 85-year-old tattooed elder Balu Ratja. "I am from a noble family, but I lost my parents when I was young. After that time, I lived in poverty and I didn't have money to pay for the tattoos. So, I went to the tattoo master's field and did some farming work for him. The number of days that the master needed for the hand tattoo operation was the number of days I worked on his farm," she recalled (Palivulj 2012–2015:7).

PAIWAN AND RUKAI MEN'S TATTOOS

Traditionally, Paiwan tattoos were exceedingly important for one's journey through life and into death. Tattooed *vuvus* told me their hand patterns protected them from evil spirits, and once they passed into the afterlife the Ancestral Spirit would recognize their social standing by the tattoos they wore. Men's tattooing communicated these beliefs as well.

Tattooing for Paiwan and Rukai men was extremely complex, and the iconography depended on the individual's social status, life accomplishments (e.g., warrior), and community, since pattern configurations differed from tribe to tribe and district to district (Ho 1960). Male tattoos were applied to the body in a specific order: hands first, the lower arm, the upper arm, the shoulder, the upper chest, the back, and finally the center of the chest. Each portion of the body was tattooed three or four times, and generally speaking, it took the tattooist one to two months to

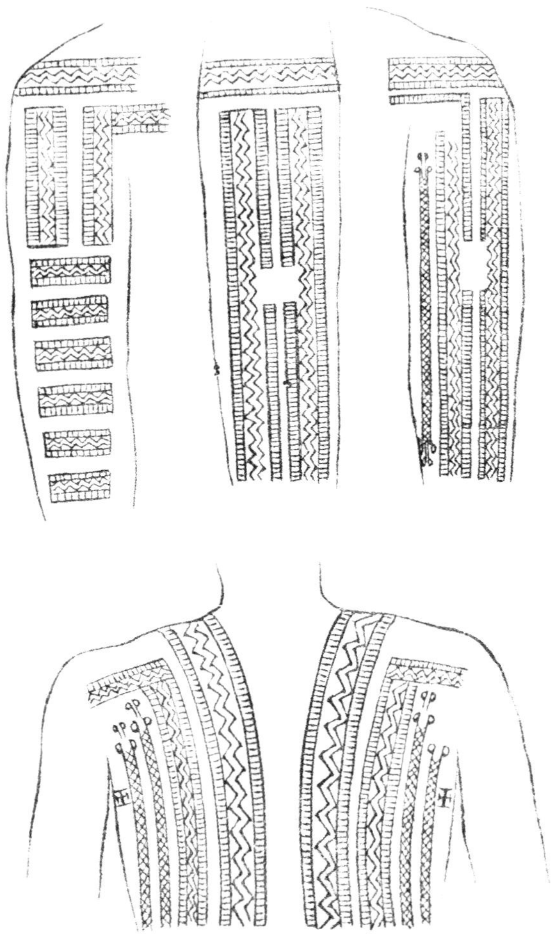

FIGURE 2.38
Rukai warrior chief's headhunter tattoos. From Inō 1910. Like the Paiwan, Rukai tattooists were usually female. Before the marks were placed on the skin, prayers and offerings, consisting of glass beads and betel nuts, were given to the guardian spirits in order to protect the tattoo client from evil spirits attracted by the bloodletting. Other ceremonial taboos tied to the tattooing included no sexual relations immediately before the operation, no tattooing while a corpse lay in the village or when a woman was menstruating, no ingestion of animal blood before the tattooing, and no use of red-colored clothing during the operation (Ho 1960:46). From Inō 1910.

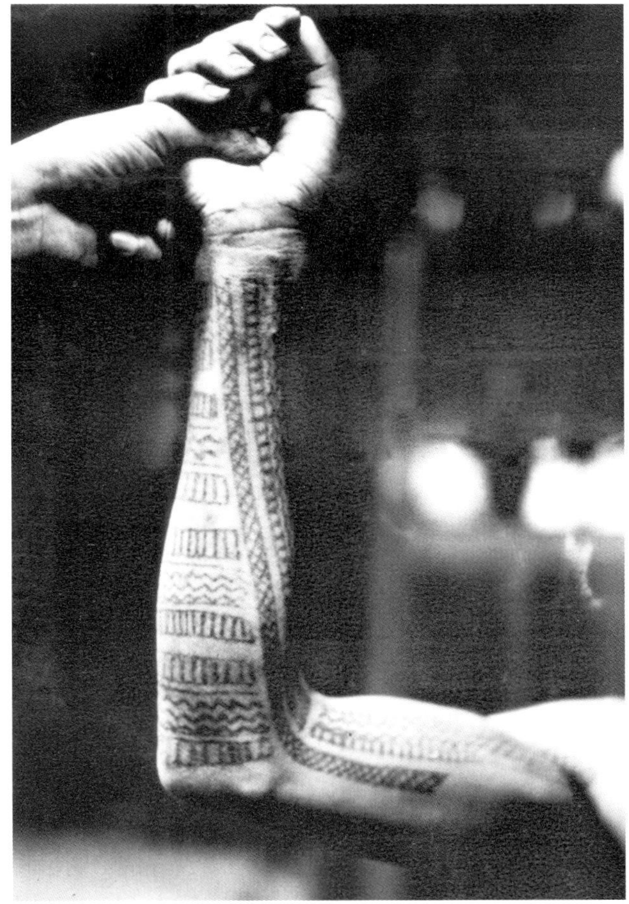

FIGURE 2.39
Paiwan warrior's arm tattooing, ca. 1930. Courtesy National Taiwan University, Department of Anthropology (A292–1).

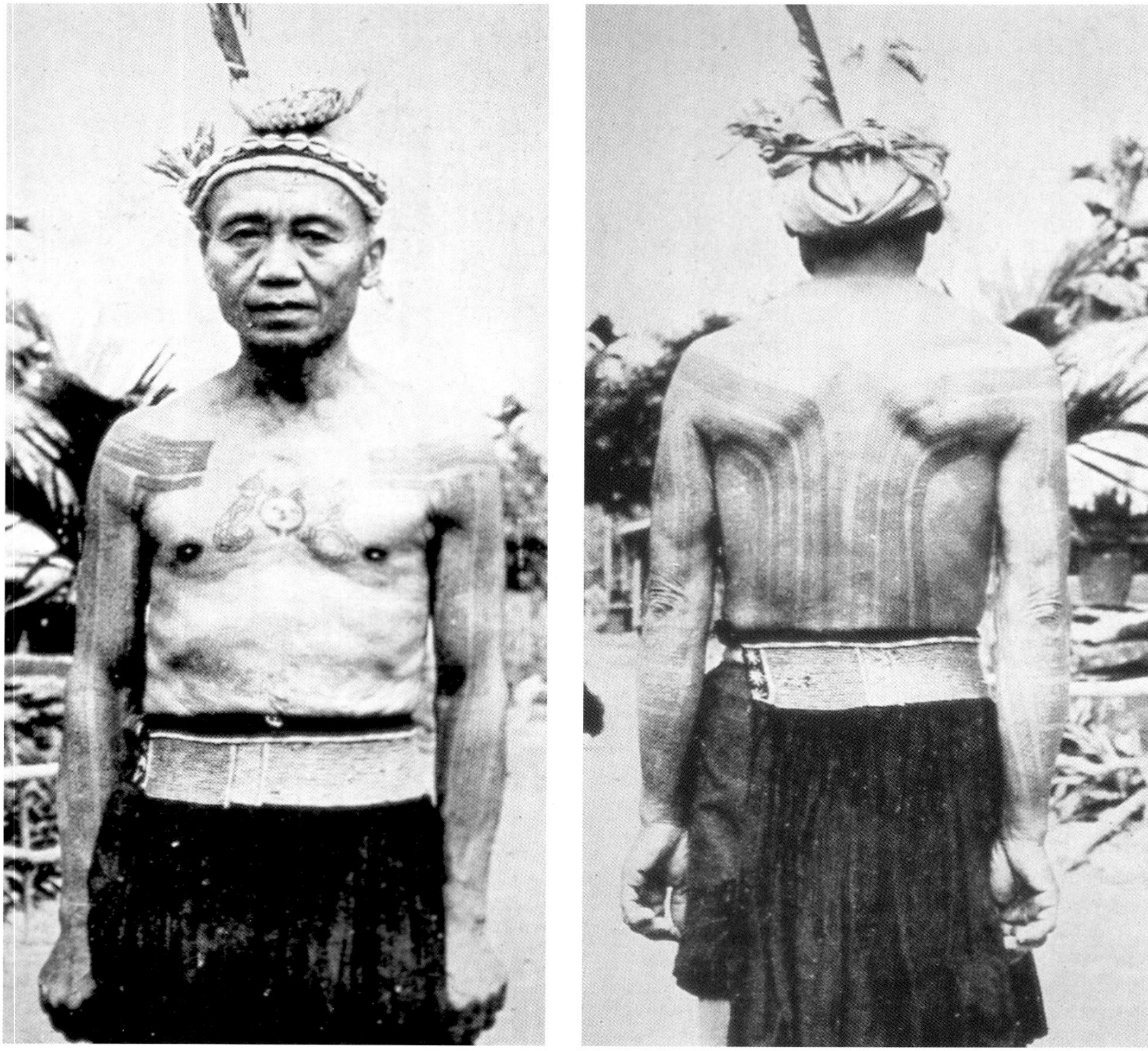

FIGURE 2.40

Chief of Timor village, Butsul group of the Paiwan, ca. 1955. The hundred-pace viper motif flanks the anthropomorphic head at the center of his chest (*left*) and other designs appear on his back (*right*). From Ho 1960: pl. 10.

complete the full complement of body tattooing. The male tattoo client rested in bed near a window to aid the healing process. After the scabs fell off the skin, red chili or bean leaves were ground and applied to the wounds to accentuate the color of the tattoos (Ho 1960).

Ho (1960:22–27) outlined the names and meanings of men's tattooing motifs. For the sake of convenience, I will refer here only to the main baseline motifs. As in the iconography of female tattooing, ladderlike motifs (i.e., dentate or "tooth" patterns) were a primary motif. These tattoos ran in parallel bands down the arms to the wrists, down the back, or across the upper chest. Pairs of zigzagging tattoos /\/\/\/\ and conjoined XXXX motifs on the chest, arms, or back represented the hundred-pace viper. Human heads and/or anthropomorphic tattoos might adorn the chests of warriors among the Paiwan and Rukai, but only tribal headmen among the Paiwan could possess a human head flanked by figural motifs of the hundred-pace viper (Ho 1960).

Between the upper and lower arm, two rectangular spaces were not tattooed. This region was called "the ceiling window," and it was believed this space enabled "the blood vessels to breathe" (Ho 1960:24). A space beside the elbow was said to be the source of a man's strength and for this reason was not tattooed.

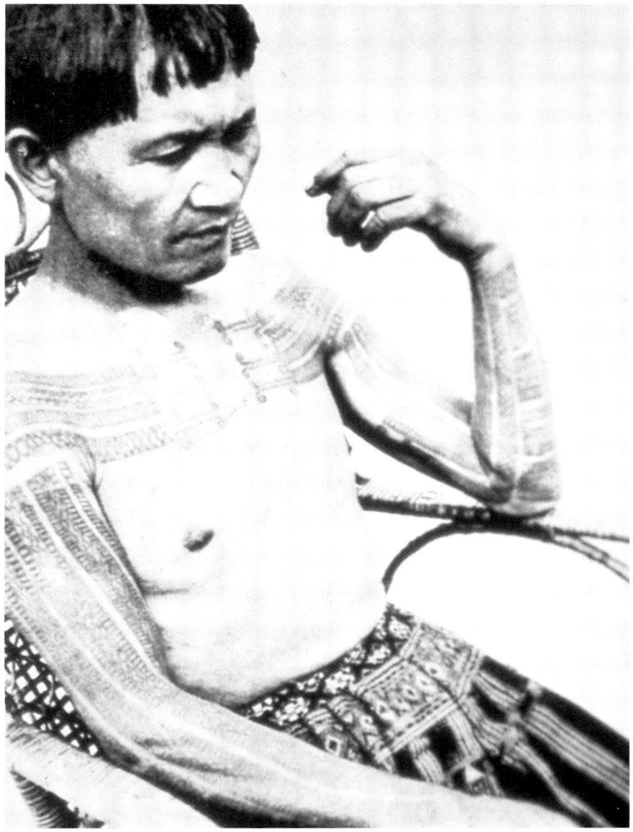

FIGURE 2.41
Warrior of Chalaabus village, Butsul group of the Paiwan, ca. 1955. The intricate line work on his chest ends in tendril-like motifs that have been said to represent the tongue of the hundred-pace viper, the guardian spirit of the Paiwan. From Ho 1960: pl. 10.

In some Paiwan communities, the top headmen had five bands or rows of horizontal tattooing on the upper chest. Second-tier headmen could possess four rows of tattoo elements on each breast. Ho (1960:23) observed that the "seedling-shaped" pattern of each breast, resembling a curlicue or tendril-like motif, was a "special tattoo" worn in only a handful of communities. The groups that possessed this tattoo form did not receive anthropomorphic or figural tattoos, and I was told this motif symbolizes the tongue of the hundred-pace viper.

In some Rukai tribes, only men who captured an enemy head were eligible to receive a tattoo.[20] After the warrior succeeded in bringing his first head home, he was tattooed on the right side of his chest. After his second success, his left breast was tattooed (Ho 1960). Ho also observed that among the Rukai men typically worked as the tattooists and several taboos were observed before and after the operation. No visitors could meet with the tattoo client on the day of their tattooing: otherwise, their tattoos would not be clear in design. After the tattooing was completed, the client could not "eat rice, pork, salt, beans or roasted sweet potatoes" (Ho 1960:26). The wounds were cleansed with the juice of the morning glory (*Ipomoea nil*) to prevent the client from becoming feverish.

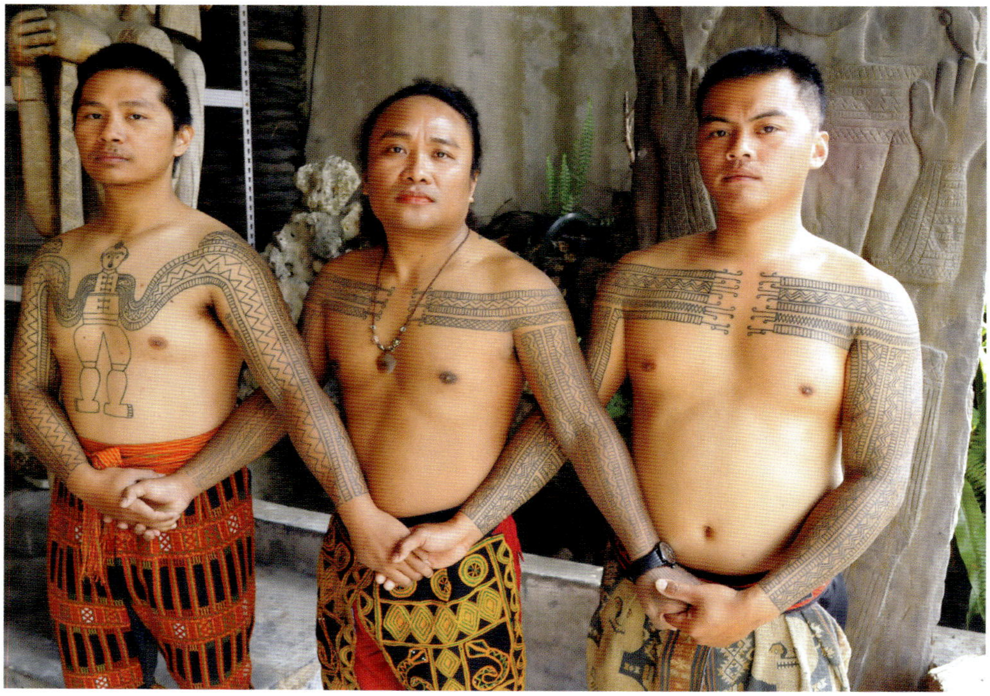

FIGURE 2.42
Tattoo bearers of the Paiwan tribe, Pingtung County, Taiwan, 2016. Pictured here are nobleman Kuljelje Kalivuan, tattoo artist Cudjuy Patjidres (*center*), and future chief Cangal. The central figure comprising Kalivuan's tattoo is based on an old folktale that belongs to his family. Tattoos by Cudjuy Patjidres. © Lars Krutak.

INDIGENOUS TATTOO REVIVAL: CUDJUY PATJIDRES

Nearly ten years ago, the Paiwan artist Cudjuy Patjidres began reviving tattooing for the men and women of his tribe. Thus far, he has created bodysuits for men from noble families and about two dozen hand tattoos for aristocratic women. The designs he uses are traditional; for women's hand tattoos, he uses various combinations of "sun," "door," "millet pounder/mortar and pestle," "human figure," and "hundred-pace viper" designs, among others. For men, the primary patterns are associated with the movements and body parts of the hundred-pace viper, as well as with mythical ancestors.

Cudjuy has been drawing his entire life and began tattooing himself and his friends when he was in high school. His body is wrapped in traditional Paiwan tattoos that were given to him by a friend, who is a sculptor and part-time tattoo artist in Taipei.

Originally from Taitung County in southeastern Taiwan, Cudjuy respects the ancient rituals of Paiwan tattoo. And before he begins a new tattoo, he offers a ceremonial drink to the Ancestral Spirit of his village. "I face the direction of our sacred mountain and offer the Spirit this drink of alcohol," he said.

Cudjuy originally tattooed by machine, but now he is skilled in making and using traditional Paiwan hand-tapping tools. He uses these implements to demonstrate traditional tattoo techniques at cultural events, museums, and international tattoo conventions and employs them for interested clients.

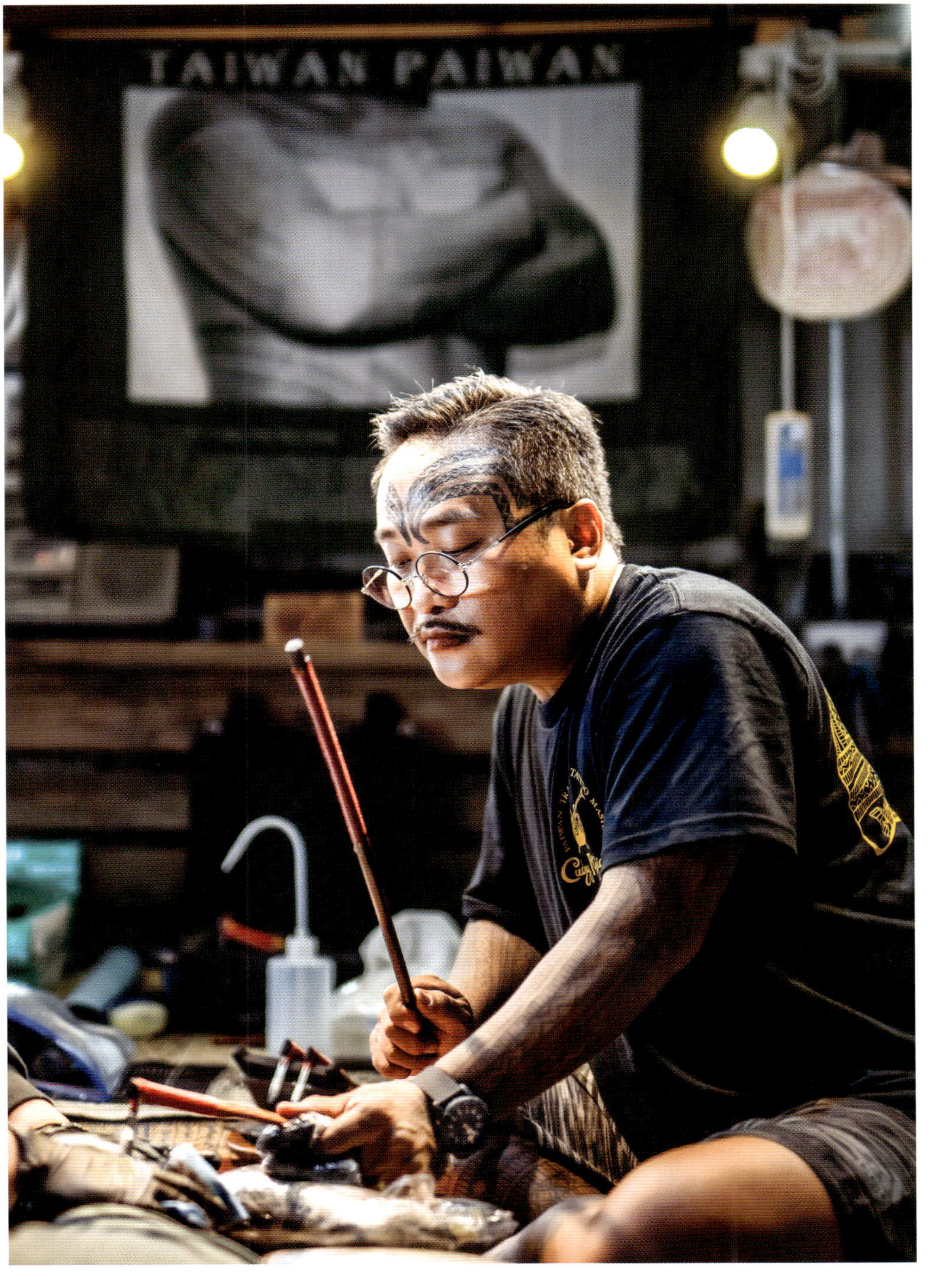

FIGURE 2.43
Cudjuy at work hand-tapping, 2022. Photography by Lin Min-hsuan. Courtesy of Taiwan Panorama.

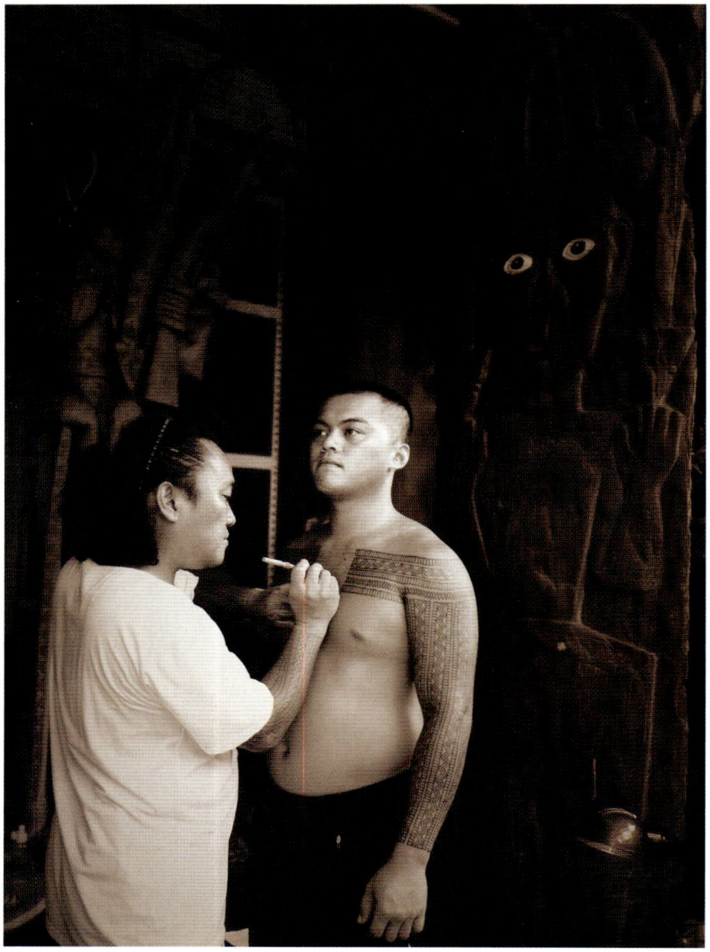

When I first met Cudjuy in Taiwan in 2016, I asked him if he knew of other Paiwan tattoo artists. "There are other artists from my tribe working in Western-style shops in the cities," he observed. "Sometimes they do create tattoos based on Paiwan designs, but they make mistakes regarding the traditional patterns because they haven't done the research and they also don't know the rituals."

I also asked Cudjuy why the Paiwan tattoo revival was important to him. "I don't want to see this ancient tradition disappear in the future," he explained. "I want to preserve this aspect of Paiwan culture and not let it slip through our fingers. I feel a responsibility to bring it back since my grandfather Jiaxuban was tattooed and he encouraged people to have tattoos. I also have the support of the elders and that is very important for me."

In 2014, Cudjuy completed a full-body tattoo for Cangayljan, a future chief of the Gulou Paiwan tribe, whose family is considered royalty. Before the operation, he had to discuss with the head of the tribe what tattoo patterns he could make. After a final drawing of the bodysuit was created, Cudjuy returned to the tribal head to receive his approval before he could begin tattooing. Because Cangayljan's social status is so high, a special offering to the Ancestral Spirit was made. A pig was dedicated to the spirit and sacrificed. Then its meat was distributed to the people in Cangayljan's village.

FIGURE 2.44
Cudjuy stenciling a tattoo design on the chest of Cangal, 2014. Courtesy of Angusan/Laiyi Indigenous Museum.

Kuljelje Kalivuan is another Paiwan nobleman and client of Cudjuy. The center motif of his bodysuit is related to a legendary family ancestor. Kalivuan told me, "The central figure is from an old story that belongs to my family. There was a powerful man. He took two huge pieces of slate from the mountaintop and jumped down into the valley below. Here, he created the chiefly lineage of my family. He is our ancestral hero and that is why he is tattooed on my body."

In 2018, the National Taiwan Museum produced a minidocumentary on Cudjuy's life titled *Images from My Dreams* and directed by Huang Huang-ju. Featured in the film was the story of Amby Lindaw of the Xinxing Paiwan Community. Lindaw is not from a noble family but he greatly desired a contemporary version of a traditional Paiwan tattoo placed on his leg to honor his father. "This was tattooed in memory of my father," he said. "Due to a car accident, his left leg had to be amputated. He was a hunter, and having his leg amputated did not cause him to

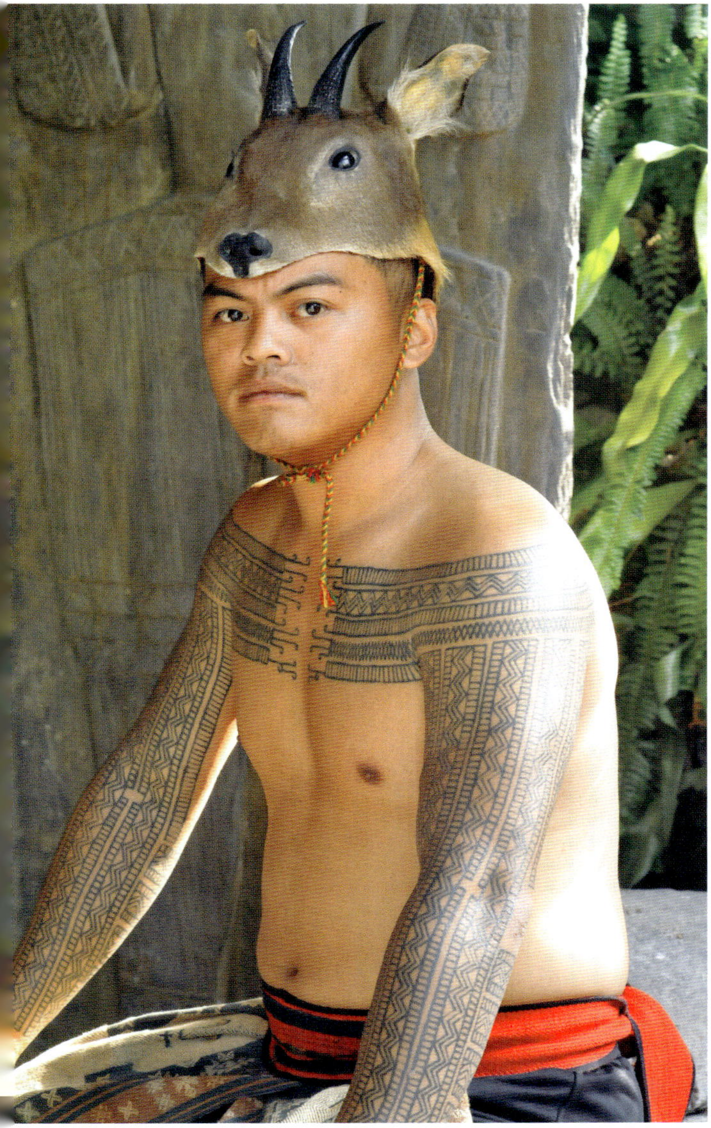

FIGURE 2.45
Cangal, a future chief of the Paiwan Gulou tribe, 2016. "I am aware that I am a member of a high-class family, an important family," he said. "I want to show that I am responsible, so I experienced the pain to get these traditional marks." Tattoos by Cudjuy Patjidres. © Lars Krutak.

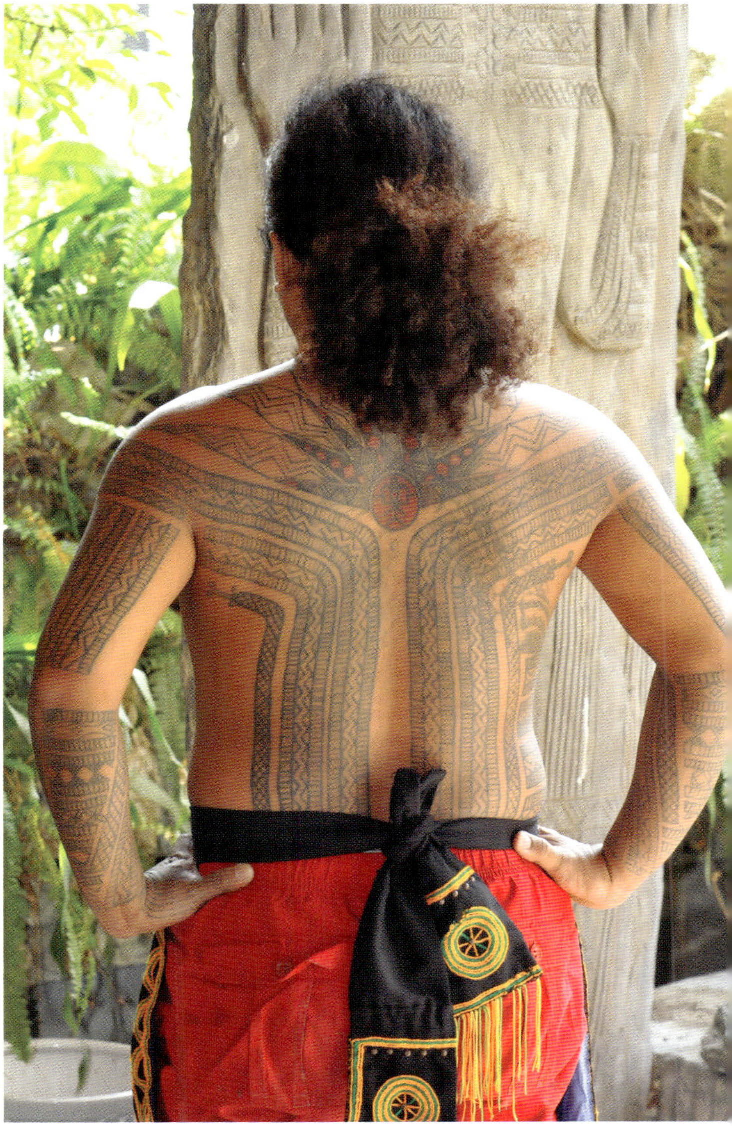

FIGURE 2.46
Back tattoos of Cudjuy Patjidres, 2016. The hundred-pace pit viper dominates the overall composition. © Lars Krutak.

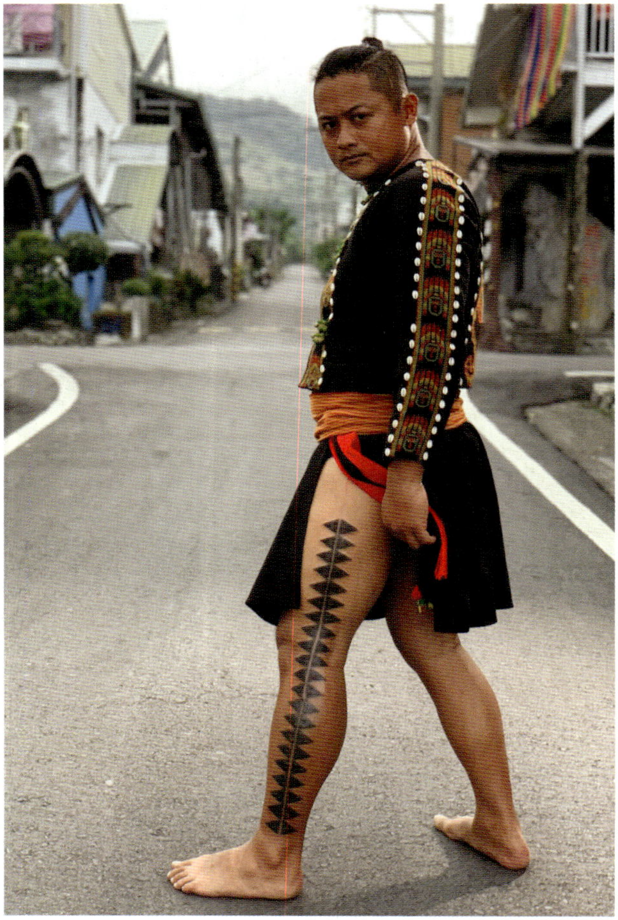

FIGURE 2.47
Amby Lindaw, 2018. Tattoos by Cudjuy Patjidres. Courtesy of Huang Ju-Huang.

become miserable. On the contrary, he continued to live as he did before. He went into the mountains and hunted, [and] this spirit is worth learning from," he explained. For inspiration, Lindaw selected the pattern of the hundred-pace pit viper, the ancestor of the Paiwan people.

In the documentary Cudjuy explained what role innovation plays in today's Paiwan tattoo revival. One hundred years ago, "traditional" Paiwan tattoos were conservative and for a tattooist to create something like Lindaw's tattoo would have been controversial. But that time has passed and so have most of the tattooed elders from that generation. Now Cudjuy strives to combine his client's ideas with his own to create contemporary patterns based on ancient iconography. He views his tattoo work as a responsibility to himself, to his ancestors, and to his clients:

> Those [people] who want to be tattooed must know themselves well. [They must know who they are.] Who are you? The patterns on the body, they represent a kind of responsibility, [and] once these patterns are tattooed, you must be able to carry them well.
>
> The rhythm of striking is like the beating of a heart. Body tattoos have life. You are carrying a life on your body. You introduce them to everyone. You know them well. This is something great! (Huang-ju 2018)

Like Cudjuy, Wen-Shan is also responsible for the current revival of tattooing. His multiyear research study and resulting exhibitions inspired several Paiwan women to resurrect the ancient custom of hand tattooing. For example, his wife, Cutju Malikilikil, and several of her female relatives have been tattooed by Cudjuy. Malikilikil is from a very high-ranking Paiwan family. Initially, she was worried about the pain associated with the tattoos, but she told me that she received a message in a dream from her deceased aunt to get these tattoos. "That gave me the courage I needed," she said, and after several tattooing sessions totaling more than twelve hours of work, her hand tattoos were completed.

One of Malikilikil's female relations, Kmsing, also braved Cudjuy's tattooing needles. She was tattooed publicly in 2015 at the Laiyi Museum during a cultural performance event that extended over a few days. Taboos were observed, and pregnant women were not allowed to watch. She told me that the tattoos she received were appropriate for her social class and that it was an "honorable" act. "I did this to honor my ancestors, my family, and our cultural heritage," she explained. "And I wanted to uphold these beautiful traditions."

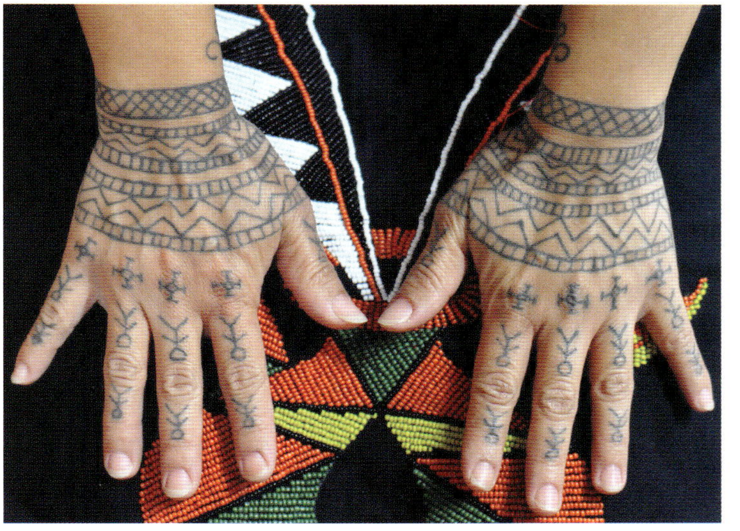

FIGURE 2.48
Hand tattoos of Cutju Malikilikil, Nanhe village, 2016. "I received a message in a dream from my deceased aunt to get these tattoos and that gave me the courage I needed," she said. Tattoos by Cudjuy Patjidres. © Lars Krutak.

Other tribal members in Taiwan have also reclaimed the tattooing traditions of their ancestors. Perhaps the first were Sayun Votu and her husband, Dali Yealo, of Fushing Township, Taoyuan County. Following in the footsteps of her husband, who was facially tattooed in 2001, Votu decided in 2008 to "do something" to help preserve this significant Atayal tradition for future generations because it was disappearing among the elders. She received the full complement of women's forehead and cheek tattoos and was the first woman in nearly one hundred years to obtain these ancestral markings. After receiving her tattoos, she stated it was her hope that her actions would encourage Taiwanese society to have a more open mind about facial tattoos (*Taipei Times* 2008). On a more personal level, however, Votu explained that another purpose of her tattoos was to signal unity as husband and wife (Robbins 2009).

Notwithstanding, the couple have met with criticism by members of their tribe. Some say their patterns are not correct and, more importantly, that they did not seek the guidance of tribal leaders before receiving their tattoos. In the past, tribal leaders performed a "character study" to determine a person's "worthiness" before the receipt of tattoos (Xie 2019). Some tribal historians and culture bearers stated that this was not done in this case, so they are uncertain of the couple's qualifications to carry the tradition into the future. Other elders note that while it was worthy to reclaim Atayal tattooing traditions in this way, perhaps it would have been better to simply remember the "spirit" of ancestral tattooing and not forget it rather than carrying the actual tattoos in physical form on the face (Xie 2019).

Yealo has a different view on the matter and believes Atayal tattoos should be worn again as a symbol of cultural pride. "Twenty years ago, none of us [Indigenous People] dared to wear our traditional costume walking on the street," he said. "No [popular] singers dared to say they were Aboriginals because public opinion was manipulated and the whole of [Taiwanese] society was prejudiced towards believing 'Aboriginals are barbarians,'" he explained (Xie 2019). "So I don't want the world to doubt my Atayal identity anymore, and I will not shrink from being true to myself," he said (WSIC 2008). He went on to explain that "tattooing was part of Ga-ga, the ancient teachings of ethics and morality that our Atayal ancestors abided by until they crossed the Rainbow Bridge" (WSIC 2008).

On the eastern side of Taiwan, the Truku musician I Jyi recently received a full set of facial tattoos to pay homage to his heritage. He ruminated for years before receiving his tattoos and sought the consent of tribal elders. He is comforted by the fact that his ancestors are with him now

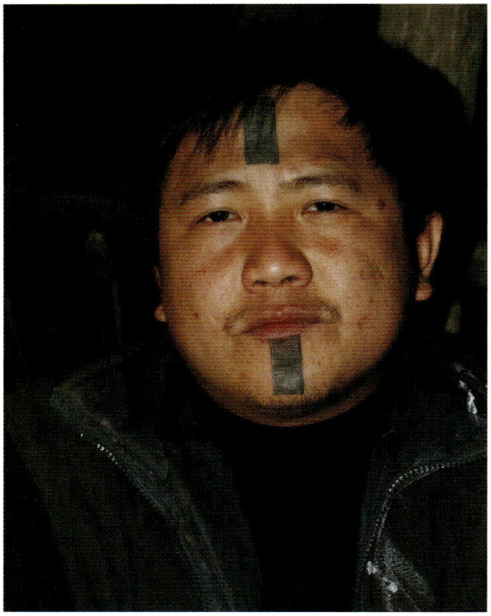

FIGURE 2.49
Wu chun-ying Taureh of the Bailan Atayal tribe, 2016. © Lars Krutak.

everywhere he goes and plays music. "I [have] a deep appreciation of the fact that my ancestors are watching me," he says. "[And] I do not do things that betray my conscience" (*Formosa News* 2019).

In 2016, with the assistance of my friend Rafe Walters and his Atayal wife, Yayun Veihui, I met then thirty-one-year-old Wu chun-ying Taureh of the Bailan Atayal tribe at his remote hunting camp in the northern mountains. In his youth, he said, he felt "lost" because he wasn't connected to his culture. He was very interested in traditional Atayal tattoos, however, because his father-in-law's grandfather was tattooed on the chest and face. When he married in his early twenties, he began thinking about receiving a facial tattoo. He consulted his tribal elders about the prerequisites. They told him that he should go alone into the mountains, make a knife, and kill a pig with it if he could. "In the past, hunting was a very dangerous activity, because you risked losing your head to an enemy tribe," he said. "So this was a good test."

Taureh wanted to prove to his family that he could provide for them, and he was successful in the hunt. After his ordeal, he felt better prepared to receive his facial tattoo. Later, he visited a cultural event where facial tattoo stamps were sold. He purchased one and brought it to a tattooist in Hsinchu City, who then marked his forehead and chin in 2014.

"For me," Taureh said, "I always had a strong desire to get tattooed because of my family history. I also wanted to assert that I was true Atayal," he explained. "Now, I can show this tattoo to my children, because it is a symbol of who we are—Atayal."

AT THE TAIL OF THE DRAGON: TATTOOS OF THE LI PEOPLE (HAINAN ISLAND, CHINA)

The Li are an Indigenous People of Hainan Island, China, composed of five tribes: Qi, Ha, Run, Sai, and Meifu. It is believed they migrated here from the mainland more than two thousand years ago.

Today, the Li are one of fifty-five classified minority peoples of China, and by the fifteenth century Han Chinese immigrants began driving the Li into the southern mountains and forests, forcing them to abandon their traditional settlements on the coastal plains of Hainan.

Hainan has approximately the same geographical area as Taiwan and lies at the same latitude as Hawai'i. The American travel writer Bernard Clark (1938:391) noted that the word

"Hainan" means South of the Sea but that the Chinese formerly called their far southern possession the Tail of the Dragon. Two hundred years ago, Hainan was considered to be at the end of the Chinese world, more remote and mysterious than Tibet or Mongolia.

The Li appear in several early Chinese accounts. They were first encountered during the Han dynasty by agents of Emperor Wu (ruling 141–87 BC), who pacified Hainan and officially established prefectures and counties there. In AD 75, the governor of Jiaozhou, an imperial Chinese province encompassing Hainan, learned of the facial tattooing practices of the Li and advised his people not to promulgate these practices (Xianjun Wang 2016:89). He, along with later Han rulers, attempted to implement policies banning tattooing across the Li District, because for hundreds of years in China tattoos had been associated with "barbarism" and criminality (Reed 2000a, 2000b:12). More specifically, within Han China tattooing ran contrary to popular Confucian and Buddhist filial beliefs that generally discouraged any form of cutting, mutilation, or permanent marking of the body. Chinese authorities exploited these beliefs by employing tattooing as an advanced form of corporal punishment, especially forced facial tattooing with characters, a practice that probably originated as early as the Western Zhou dynasty (ca. 770–249 BC) (Ch'en 2000:19–20).

Despite the tattooing bans, Li tattooing persisted. During the Southern Song Period (960–1279), Li tattooing was again described by Chinese poet and politician Fan Chengda (1126–1193), who provided several noteworthy accounts of the Indigenous Peoples under his rule: "[Li] women had the face tattooed and wore a high bun, adding copper rings upon their hairpins, and their eardrops hanging down to the shoulders. Their upper cloths and skirts were all made of colorful *jibei* [kapok], and they wore several skirts but no trousers" (Fusheng 2016:51).

Throughout later periods, Chinese politicians and military leaders continued with their attempts to exterminate the tattooing practices of the Li. Perhaps one of the most famous was the Chinese general and martial artist Yu Dayou (1503–1579). In 1549, a Li peasant uprising broke out and the general was transferred to Hainan to suppress it. In turn, he proposed another ban on tattoos across the Li District (Xianjun Wang 2016:89), but due to the geographical isolation of Li communities in the mountainous interior of Hainan and to continued resistance, it did not meet with success.

With the formation of the Republic of China in 1912, government authorities soon ramped up their efforts to develop the rural interior areas of Hainan through infrastructure projects (e.g., roads and schools) and other measures aimed at "changing customs," bringing them into conflict with the Li people. In 1924 and 1928, notices were issued prohibiting tattoos and imposed fines (e.g., a cow) on those who sought to acquire them (Xianjun Wang 2016:90–91). In 1933, Chen Hanguang, an army commander, deployed to the interior districts of Hainan with his troops in search of Communist rebels, who were recruiting Li men to join their cause. In efforts to curb the influence of the revolutionaries, provisional regulations were established to punish Li offenders as well as to assimilate the Li into the fold of the Chinese nation. In article seven of this edict, it was stated that if a young woman received facial tattoos her parents would be sentenced to two years in prison (Xianjun Wang 2016:91). The mandatory tattoo ban had an immediate impact, because in 1934 a government-sponsored scientific expedition to the interior noted that very few young women bore newly created tattoos. The majority of the tattoos that were observed appeared

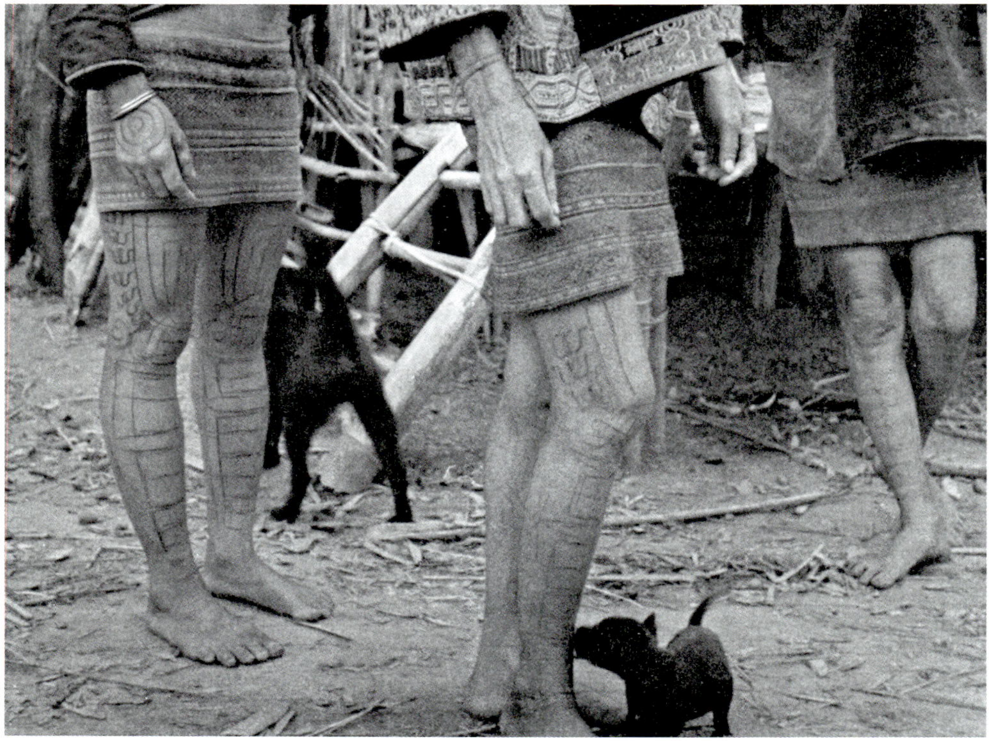

FIGURE 2.50
Tattooed Li women of the Run group, 1937. From B. Clark 1938:405.

on the faces and bodies of women over forty years of age, who comprised about two-thirds of the population at that time.

With the establishment of the People's Republic of China in 1949, the Communist government—adhering to an atheistic ideology—implemented policies of *pochu mixin* (eradicating superstitions) and *yifengyisu* (change prevailing customs and transform social traditions) that began to alter the animistic religion of the Li, one that was based on ancestor worship and shamanism, as well as other salient cultural institutions, including tattooing, which began to gradually disappear (Mu 1996:109–110).

Notwithstanding these historical details, to date there are very few English- or foreign-language monographs on the culture of the Li, let alone on their tattooing practices. In fact, the German anthropologist Hans Stübel (1885–1963), who worked as a professor of physiology at the National Tung Chi University (Shanghai), was one of the first Western scientists to traverse the island north to south in 1931, studying the practices and traditions of the Li. Most of his records and ethnological collections, however, were destroyed by the Japanese during the Shanghai War of 1932 (C. H. Liu 1938). He did return to Hainan shortly after the conflict and compiled a very informative book that was perhaps the first widely accessible study to offer insights into the Li's tattooing practices (Stübel 1937).

Prior to the release of Stübel's book, however, the Chinese anthropologist Chungshee Liu (also known as Xian Liu and Hans Liu), who received his graduate training at Oxford University, conducted additional studies among the Li in 1934. This work led to perhaps the first dedicated study on the tattooing customs of the Li that was later published as a short journal article (C. H. Liu 1936). However, this study was limited in scope because many Run and Meifu communities were not visited, resulting in an incomplete survey (Xianjun Wang 2016:82). Long out of print and extremely scarce outside of China, this resource was not available, although aspects of it have since been reproduced in recent works (Jie and Changfu 2012; Tian Fu 2010; Xianjun Wang 2016) that I have used, among others.

It should be noted that another early and brief source of information on Li tattoos was produced by Kenji Okada and Kunio Odaka during the Japanese occupation of Hainan (Odaka 1950; Shaogong 2016). During a two-month period in 1942, they worked as members of the Special Affairs Department of the navy tasked with investigating the social and economic organization of the Li people living in Ledong County.

LI RELIGION

The Hainan-based photographer Hu Yaling has traveled across Li country for more than twenty years. Apart from capturing imagery of Li architecture, festivals, traditional dress, and other aspects of local Indigenous culture, she has also focused her lens on tattooed Li elders. Yaling's archive includes hundreds of portraits of tattooed Li, but still she believes there is much more that can be done to document and learn from these ancient traditions of body marking. Although she has interviewed dozens of elders about their hard-earned tattoos, she says, "[t]hey have not been completely deciphered, and their meanings have not been clarified." She explained, "There are dozens and dozens of tattoo motifs and we still do not understand what they all mean. More research needs to be performed in order to record these living tattoo symbols in as much detail as possible, because Li tattooing has not been practiced in decades and is gradually fading away. Thousands of years of ancient culture have left behind their memories on human skin, and this is what inspired me to photograph as many elders as possible."[21]

Hundreds of Yaling's Li photographs are featured in her book *The Li and Miao Villages in Hainan* (2012). In this work, Yaling expresses that Li religious beliefs once permeated nearly every aspect of society and reflected interpersonal relationships between humans, spirits, the ancestors, and Mother Earth. Every object within the natural realm—rocks, the wind, water, fire, trees, mountains, thunder, and so on—was believed to be animated by its own spiritual essence (Yaling 2012:216).

Anthropomorphic (ancestral), animal, and plant totems/omen creatures were worshipped, and included dragons, various species of fish and birds, dogs, and frogs, among other creatures. Many of these entities continue to be reproduced in Li brocade, and appear as tattoos on the bodies of Li elders.

Traditionally, the Li were guided in their spiritual affairs by *palu* (shamans). Li shamans, through their communications with spirits, deities, and ancestors, functioned as mediators between

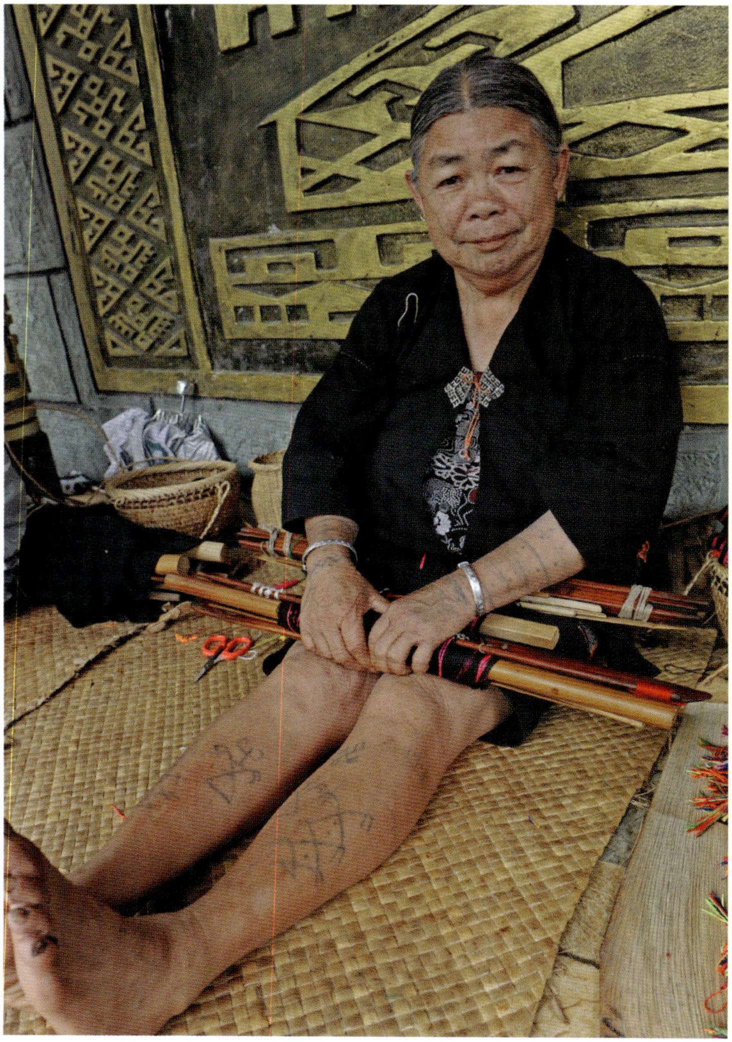

FIGURE 2.51
Ha Li weaver Xing Lian-Guan (Fu Yakai) of Baowan village with tattooed anthropomorphs on her legs and other markings, 2010. © Hu Yaling.

the physical and supernatural realms. The Tokyo University sociologist Kunio Odaka (1950:55), who as previously noted conducted fieldwork in Li territory during the Japanese occupation of Hainan, observed that Li shamans could harness supernatural power to assure victory in war, hunting, curing the sick, and retrieving a person's soul that had been lost. However, these spiritual favors were granted to successful mediators only through the proper channels: various spirits, including those of the ancestral dead, had to be properly "fed" by the shaman and his assistants with sacrifices to gain their favor or repel them. If, however, the spirits were not properly propitiated, they often turned aggressive and malevolent toward humans and brought sickness or misfortune to the village (Odaka 1950:82).

The Li concept of sickness was not, as in the West, attributable to bad health; it was a form of punishment, or a disruption of the social order, caused by not fulfilling social duties correctly (Odaka 1950:86). Sometimes sacrifices to the spirits were made in blood and were connected to the former Li practice of headhunting.[22] Shamans not only captured human blood for use in ritual; they also prepared the severed heads of slain enemies for burial near the entrance to the village, which was supposed to transform the spirits of the "war-dead" into guardians of the community (Odaka 1950:83). Moreover, it was believed that an enemy village was weakened when the heads of its dead members were buried in a location where people walked over them (Okada 1962:126).

Although Li shamans were highly respected, their economic position in society was similar to the layperson because they regularly worked the agricultural fields just as others did. Prior to the People's Republic of China's prohibition of Li slash-and-burn rice cultivation (which was replaced with paddy agriculture) in the 1950s and 1960s, Li families worked together to transplant, weed, and harvest this essential crop. Oftentimes relatives from other villages provided additional labor and this collective agency not only established expansive socioeconomic networks linking households and villages for great distances across the Li landscape but also provided a spiritual platform from which to petition the deities who controlled it.

According to the musicologist Yang Mu (1996:106), women working the mountain slopes sang various propitiatory "mountain-slashing songs" while working the soil. During these performances, mountain and tree spirits were invoked to beg their pardon for being disturbed as the soil was prepared for planting. In the eyes of the Li, all musical expression, including vocal performances and those with musical instruments, was a powerful medium that assisted humans in communicating with the spirits who protected the crops, ensured favorable weather, and provided the people with abundant harvests (Mu 1997:103). More importantly, skillful performances such as these also pleased the ancestral spirits.

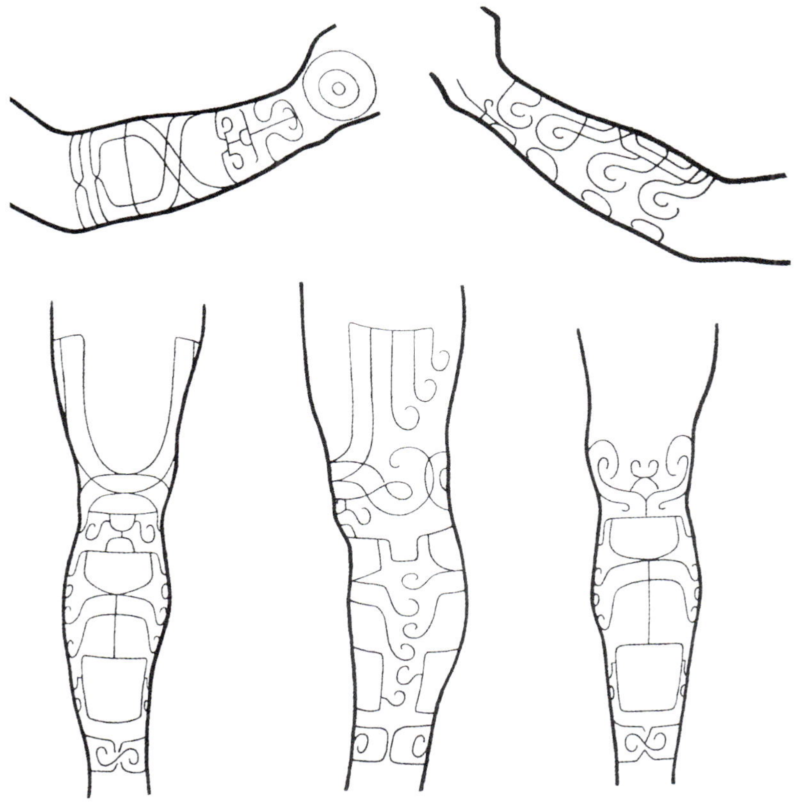

FIGURE 2.52
Illustrations of Run women's tattooing, ca. 1932. From Stübel 1937.

LI TATTOOING

Li culture and cosmology, however, were not only embodied in musical traditions—they were also inscribed on the surfaces of the body as tattoo. All Li groups tattooed,[23] and the practice was more common among women, although men received therapeutic tattoos (e.g., three blue rings around their wrists, small crosses on the hands or body) and other markings for sprains and joint pain (Odaka 1950:24; Xianjun Wang 2016:41).[24] Additional male tattoos have been documented for the Run and Meifu, with the majority of these worn by Meifu men. Although many specific details were not provided, the meanings and motifs included tattoos depicting agricultural tools, tattoos for longevity, sympathetic magic tattoos, and tattoos that enabled the ancestors to identify the bearer in the afterlife.[25]

Tattoo designs and motifs differed among each Li tribe, and sometimes they differed among families. Bernard Clark (1938:407), who penned an article for *National Geographic* magazine in the 1930s, said you could "read the village, social standing, and identity" through a woman's tattoos; her woven textiles supposedly imparted similar information. Li women interviewed in the 1940s said their tattoos not only made them beautiful but also allowed them to be recognized by their ancestors after death (Odaka 1950:24).[26]

Li tattoos signified that a woman had become eligible to be married, namely because all her tattoos were to be completed before she was betrothed. Traditionally, the tattooing rite was accompanied by an elaborate puberty ceremony in the village center. The actual tattooing took place in the cooler weather of the fall season (October–December) within the confines of the family

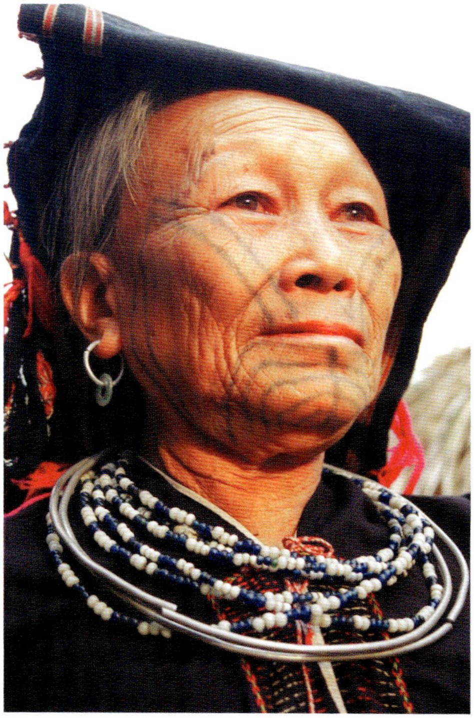

FIGURE 2.53
Tattooed Li woman of the Qi group, Jiaxi village, 2001. From Yaling 2012:183. © Hu Yaling.

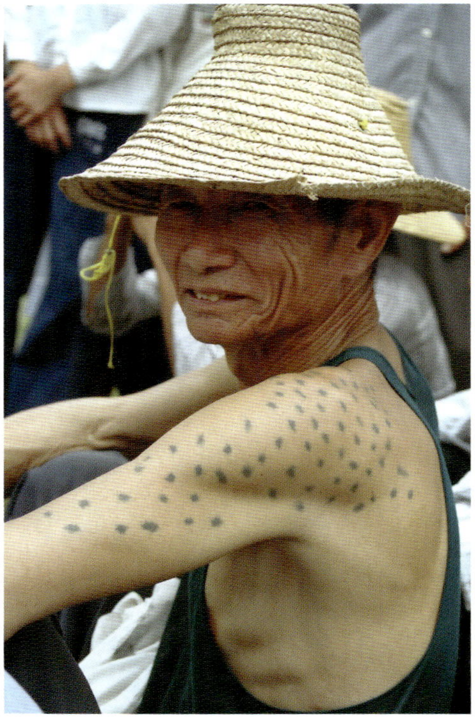

FIGURE 2.54
Meifu man of Jiangbian village displaying medicinal tattooing on his upper arm and shoulder, 2004. © Hu Yaling.

home and men were strictly prohibited from viewing. Young women could not be tattooed during their menstruation, and after the tattooing session was over certain taboos were observed: the girl remained secluded in her home for a short period and she could not eat papaya or pickled cabbage, otherwise her tattoos might become blurred (i.e., "blown out") or infected (Tian Fu 2010:10).

The Li recorded time according to twelve zodiac signs, differentiating auspicious from inauspicious days. One of three auspicious days (ox, pig, and dragon) during the week was chosen for the actual tattooing, which occurred in the morning hours and before noon, because daylight was "strong" at this time and "the human spirit was at its best" (Tian Fu 2010:8).

Before the actual tattooing took place, the motifs were stenciled on the skin with a feather, twig, grass stem, string, or in some villages a chopstick. Tattoos were hand-tapped into the skin with one or more red or white rattan thorns, depending on the design. The rattan stem that held the thorns was soaked the day before the tattooing; this action prevented the thorns from drying out and becoming dull (Xianjun Wang 2016:179).

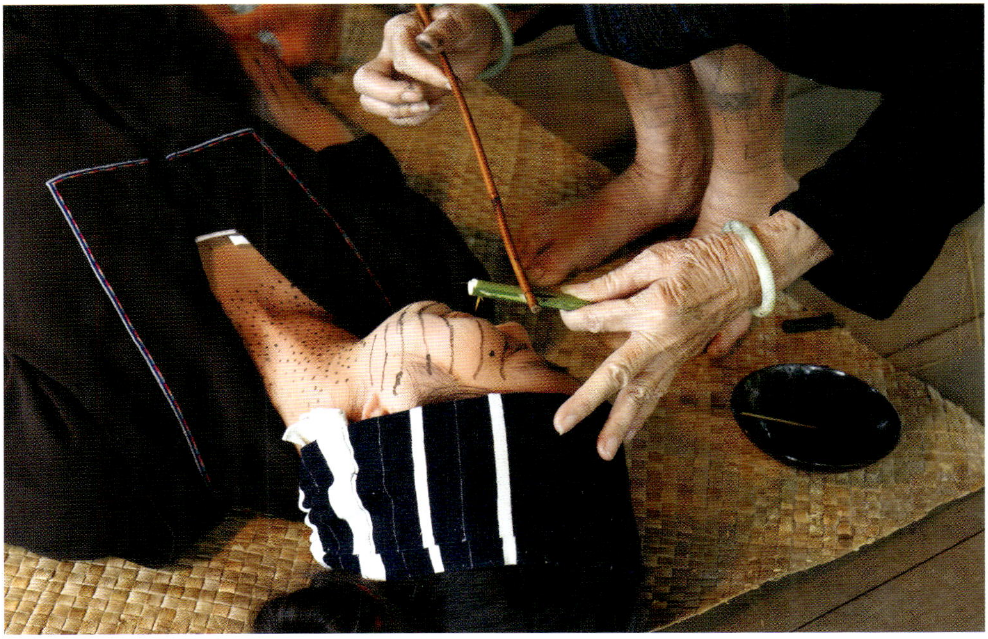

FIGURE 2.55
Meifu tattooist Fu Jinhua demonstrating the tattooing process in Zhongfang village, 2010. From Yaling 2012:171. © Hu Yaling.

Tattoo pigments were derived from a variety of plants. Typically speaking, the charred seeds of the "castor oil plant" (*Jatropha curcus*), castor bean plant (*Ricinus communis*), coconut palm, or charred lentil greens were mixed with water and soot from the bottom of a cooking pot to create tattooing ink (Xianjun Wang 2016:181).

Prior to the tattooing the tattooist uttered a prayer to the ancestors. The name of the tattoo recipient was noted and the operator asked that no harm would come to her client. One such prayer is as follows: "Oh [spirits of the] ancestors! We offer the pig's head; We offer honey wine; We offer rice. Eating and drinking have been arranged, these offerings are delicacies, and please enjoy! Today is an auspicious day, a descendant came to tattoo. Oh [spirits of the] ancestors, we ask you to bless us for success, we ask you to bless us for peace. We ask you to bless us for beauty!" (Tian Fu 2010:9).[27]

When a Li girl of the Run group reached the age of thirteen or fourteen, an old woman who was not necessarily a relative first tattooed her on the nape of the neck and then on the face and throat in the course of four or five days (Odaka 1950:24). Over the next three years, the girl's chest, arms, legs, and thighs were marked, unless somebody in the family died, which interrupted the tattooing.

The Meifu basically adhered to the Run practice while the Ha and Qi applied a facial tattoo consisting of a pair of lines just below or above the corner of each eye that extended down the face to the throat. Slight variations in these facial patterns identified members of specific villages and clans. Among the Qi, Odaka noted that if a woman married a man from another clan and

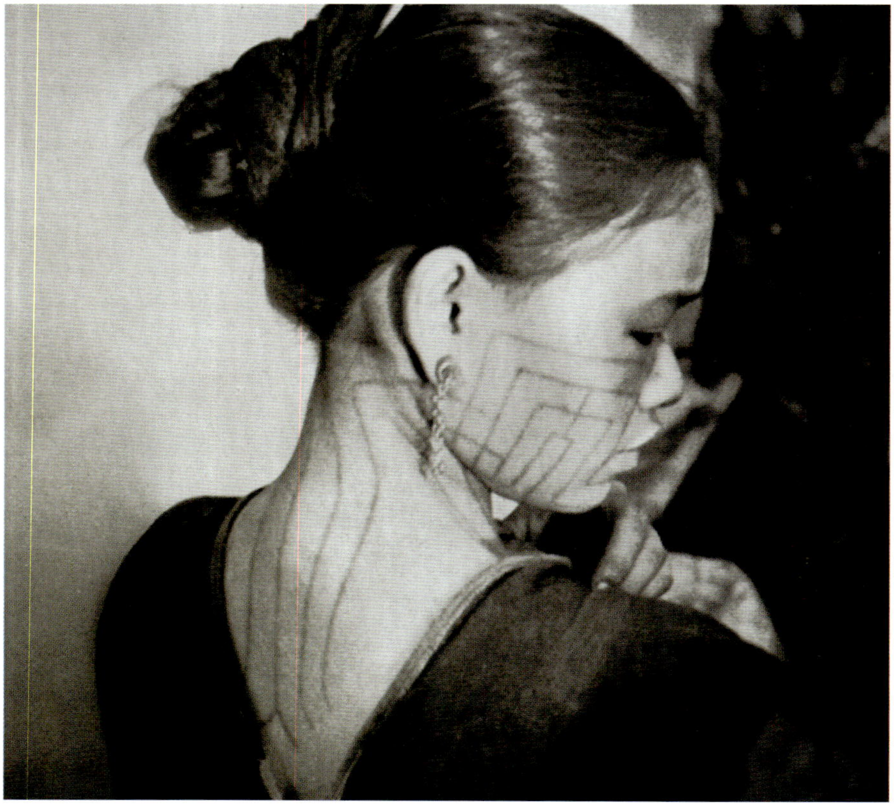

FIGURE 2.56
Run facial and neck tattooing, 1937. From B. Clark 1938:401.

passed away, her soul returned to the home of her mother, and the ancestors of her clan would be able to recognize her based on her identifying marks (Shaogong 2016:41). For the Ha, these pairs of lines continued down the torso and across the breast to outline an oval "gourd" motif surrounding the sternum, with additional lines moving downward to the belly meeting at the navel, which they encircled.[28]

Some Qi women possessed single or double lines on their feet, which are said to possibly have been clan identifiers (Yaling 2012:183). Other Qi women bore branched cruciform-shaped tattoos of "spiders" on their knees, shins, or calves to ward away evil spirits, motifs that some Meifu women also wore (Xianjun Wang 2016:142, fig. 3.17). Meifu and Run women also acquired "frog" tattoos on their arms, legs, and especially on their chests. Frogs played an important role in Li thought concerning agricultural rites and weather prognostication. The chorus of frogs, like thunder, augured rain, and in turn this resulted in a good harvest. Frogs were admired for their reproductive success and ability to move between worlds (from tadpole to amphibian), and the Li believed they were the "transporter of souls" (Chinalai 2004:248). In fact, if a Meifu woman passed away without receiving a frog tattoo, one was traced on her body so she could be recognized by the ancestors (Shunai and Simin 2010:87). Generally speaking, frogs were a fertility symbol and a prayer for many children and other blessings.

Ha women possessed anthropomorphic and figurative tattoos on their shins but today these are nearly extinct. Like the Run, Ha women bear hand tattoos of single, double, or quadruple concentric rings interspersed with dots, circles, or coin-shaped patterns that once served as clan identifiers.

The Shanghai-based filmmaker Emily Shen has shed additional light on Li tattooing patterns. She began visiting Hainan in 2021 to produce a documentary on Li tattoos. At present, her work has focused on Meifu communities, including interviews with one of the last tattoo artists

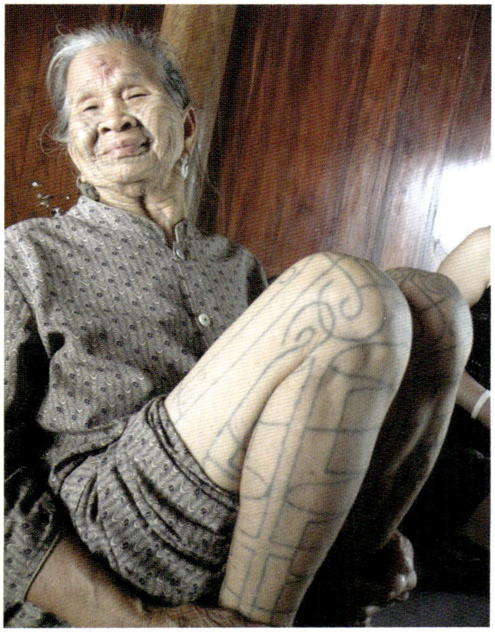

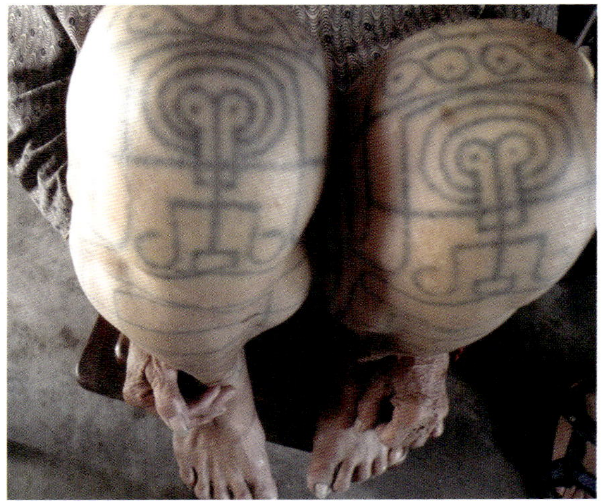

FIGURE 2.57
Tattooed Run elder of Baisha County (*left*) and close-up of her knee tattooing (*above*), 2008. © Thomas Murray and Wenhua Liu.

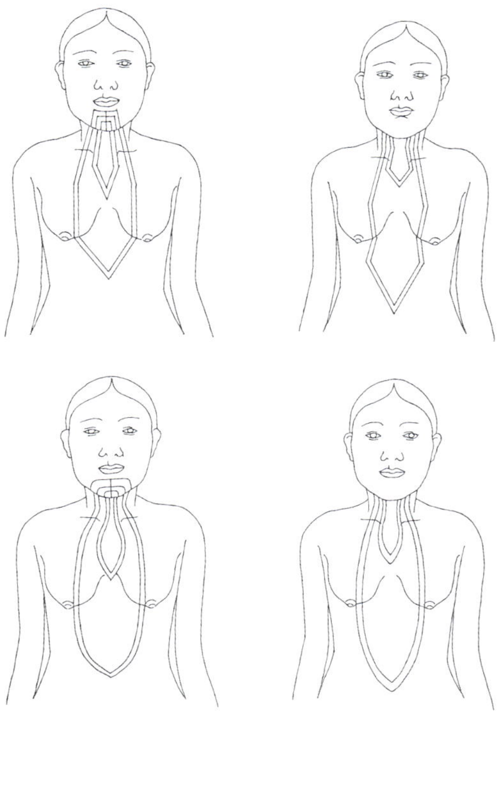

FIGURE 2.58
Tattooed Ha elders of Changjiang County with "gourd" outline tattooed on their chests, ca. 1950. From Tian Fu 2010:177.

FIGURE 2.59
Tattooed Meifu elder of Tumei village with frog motifs on shins and kneecaps among hundreds of dotted marks, 2001. From Yaling 2012:176. © Hu Yaling.

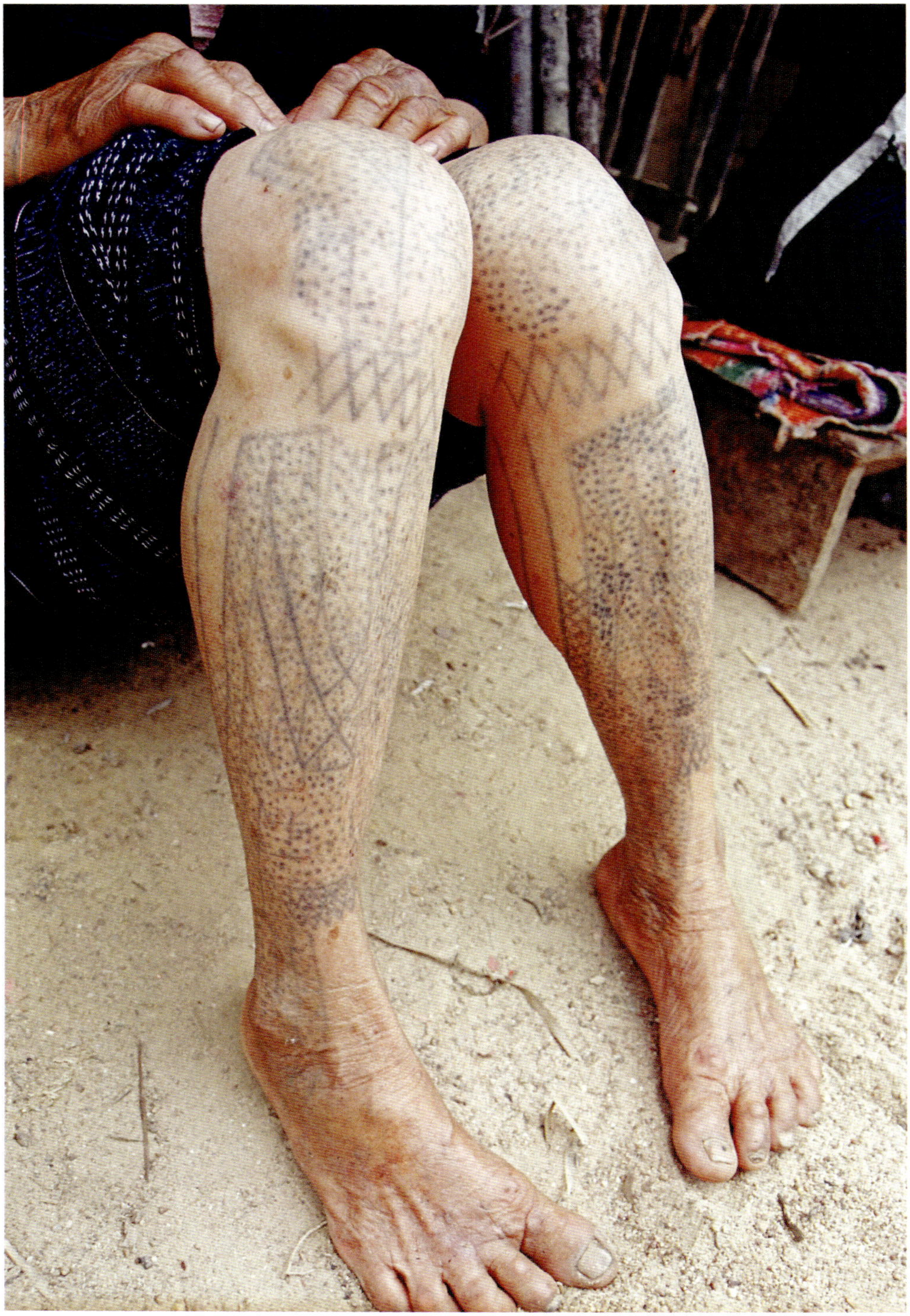

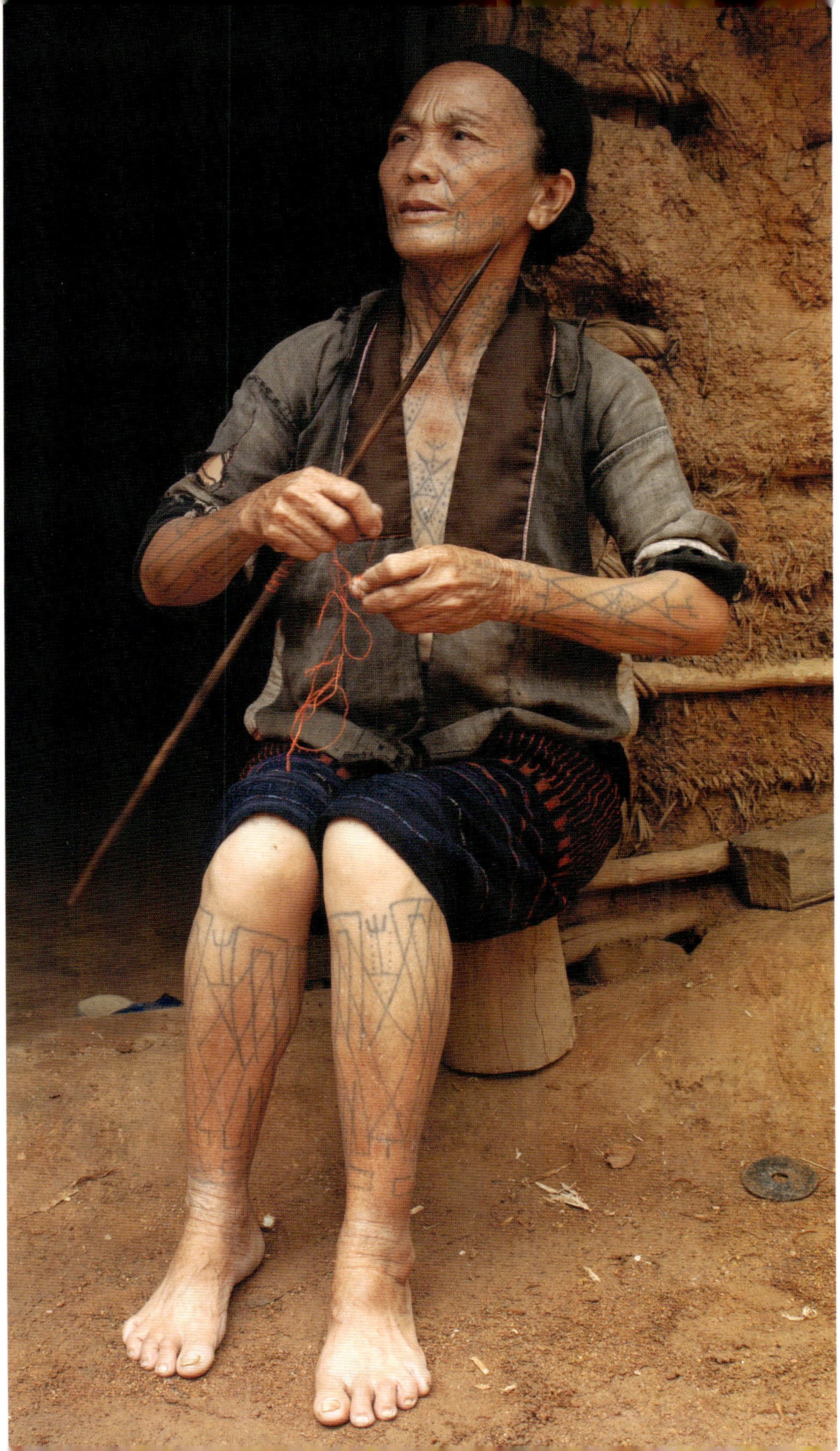

FIGURE 2.60
Tattooed Meifu elder Paya of Jishi village with frog motifs on shins, forearms, and chest, 2007. From Yaling 2012:174. © Hu Yaling.

FIGURE 2.61 (LEFT)
Tattooed Run elder of Yacha town with frog motif on chest and forearms, 2010. From Yaling 2012:189. © Hu Yaling.

FIGURE 2.62 (RIGHT)
Tattooed Meifu elder of Echa village with frog motifs on calves, 2002. From Yaling 2012:176. © Hu Yaling.

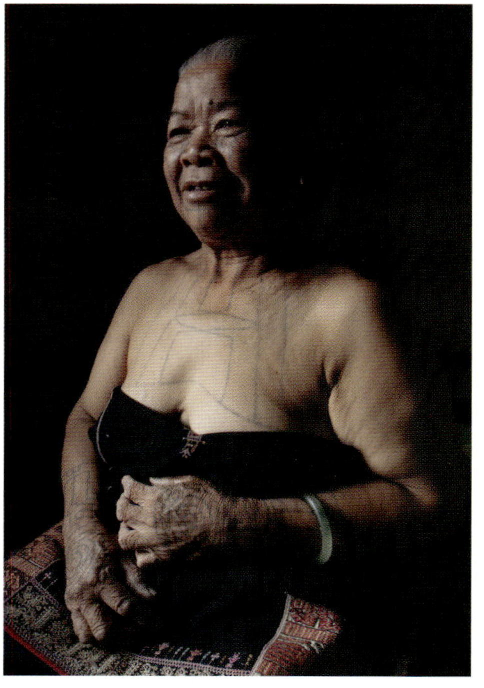

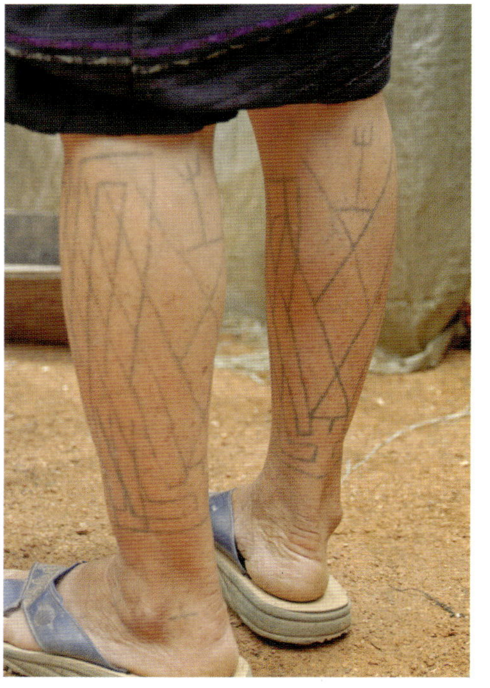

FIGURE 2.63 (LEFT)
Meifu Li tattoo artist Fu LianMei of Baobai village tattooing documentary filmmaker Emily Shen, 2022. © Emily Shen.

FIGURE 2.64 (RIGHT)
Meifu Li tattoo artist Fu LianMei demonstrating the proper technique of hand-tapping, 2022. © Emily Shen.

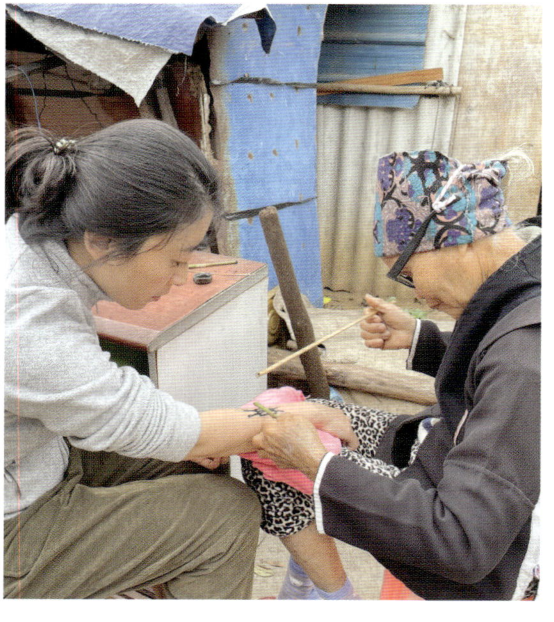

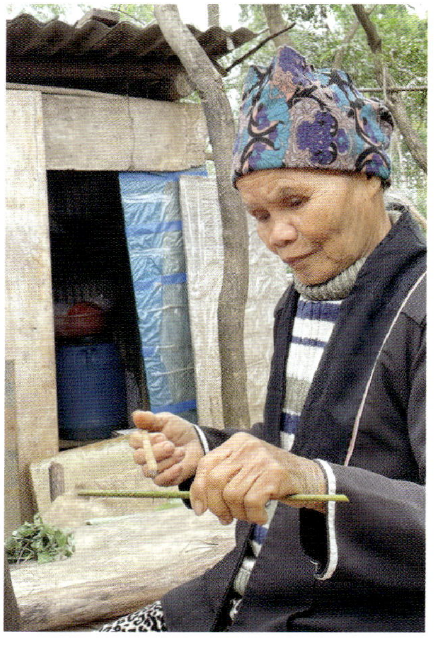

of the group, a ninety-one-year-old woman named Fu LianMei of Baobai village. Several Meifu women noted to Shen that the animal tattoos on their chests and limbs did not represent frogs; rather they signified "turtles."[29] One Meifu woman remarked that she carried a female turtle tattoo on her chest and a male turtle on her leg. The predominance of turtle tattoos in certain Meifu villages has been attributed to geography, since a species of "golden turtle" resided near a local mountain. Shen also documented medicinal tattoos among the Meifu, including a pair of dotted tattoos just below the knee of one elder and another with tattooed dots placed near the wrist. These treatments were aimed to relieve joint pain and sprains.[30]

According to the German ethnologist Hans Stübel (1937:36), the origin of Li tattooing lay in legend: "The progenitor of the Li had a daughter, whose mother died shortly after the birth of this child. Whereupon a hoopoe (*Upupa epops*) fed the child with grains. In remembrance, the Li women still tattoo themselves in order to appear to be as colorful as birds. Perhaps, the tattoos should represent the pattern on the wings of the hoopoes."

Other Li Indigenous histories recorded in the 1930s noted that this female progenitor was the "Li Mother," the first female ancestor of the Li people. She was born from an egg and her father was the Spirit of Thunder who carried this egg into the Li Mother Mountain from which she emerged (H. Liu 1939:309). As noted previously, Run women bear concentric circle tattoos on the backs of their hands. A few Run elders interviewed in 2010 noted that this was the "Thunder God" pattern, the concentric circles representing the movement and propagation of sound waves through the air (Xianjun Wang 2016:148).

3

TATTOOS OF THE PHILIPPINES

Defining Marks of Culture

> The [Visayans] are so-called because all the male Pintados tattooed their entire bodies with so excellent and well-designed symmetry, that the best artist in España could learn from them.
>
> —**Fray Juan de Medina,** Order of Saint Augustine, 1630

> If Kalinga tattooing will stop, we will lose an important part of our culture and tradition that has been handed down from generation to generation. It is our ancestors' legacy to us and it defines who we are as a people. So I believe that Kalinga tattooing must forever live among us because without it we will lose our identity.
>
> —**Apo Whang-Od Oggay,** Kalinga tattoo artist, 2016

The Philippine archipelago is located southeast of Mainland China and composed of more than seven thousand islands stretching from Luzon in the north to Tawi-Tawi in the south. Nearly every island is mountainous, and several active volcanoes dot the lush and rugged landscape.

Although Indigenous tattoo practices were once widespread across the islands, for the sake of convenience I will divide the Indigenous tattooing regions of the country into three main island groups. These groupings follow the principal geographical divisions of the Philippines, which include Luzon in the north, Visayas in the central area, and Mindanao in the south.

TATTOOS OF NORTHERN LUZON: IBALOY AND KANKANAEY

The oldest possible evidence of tattooing practice in the Philippines was uncovered archaeologically in the 1980s. At Arku Cave in the Cagayan Valley of northeastern Luzon, comblike instruments

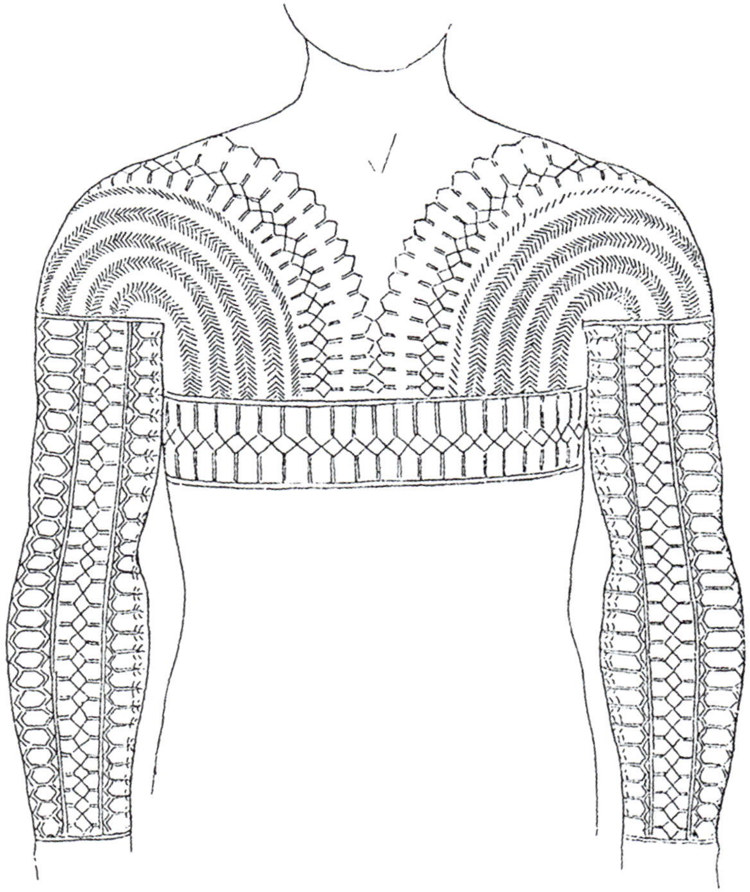

FIGURE 3.1
Kalinga warrior tattoos of Guinaang village, 1882. From Meyer 1885:301.

and two horn chisels dating from 370 BC to AD 220 were unearthed in a grave, and these tools may have functioned as tattoo instruments (Ambrose 2012:12; Salvador-Amores 2017:43; Thiel 1988:248, 262).

To the west of the Cagayan rift valley stands the rugged Cordillera Central mountain range. This region once featured numerous tattooing cultures, and the tradition of permanent body marking here survived longer than in other regions of the country. This fact was due in large part to the relative geographical isolation of the area and inveterate warrior tribes who defended their ancestral homelands from foreign invaders such as the colonial Spanish.

For four centuries of foreign occupation—first by Spain (1521–1898), followed by the United States (1898–1946), and then briefly Japan (1942–1945)—the Cordillera came to represent many things for the many foreign peoples who visited here. This vast expanse of peaks ranging from 3,000 to 9,500 feet in height lured Spanish conquistadors and various denominations of missionaries, explorers, adventurers, ethnologists, mining and timber magnates, and other travelers

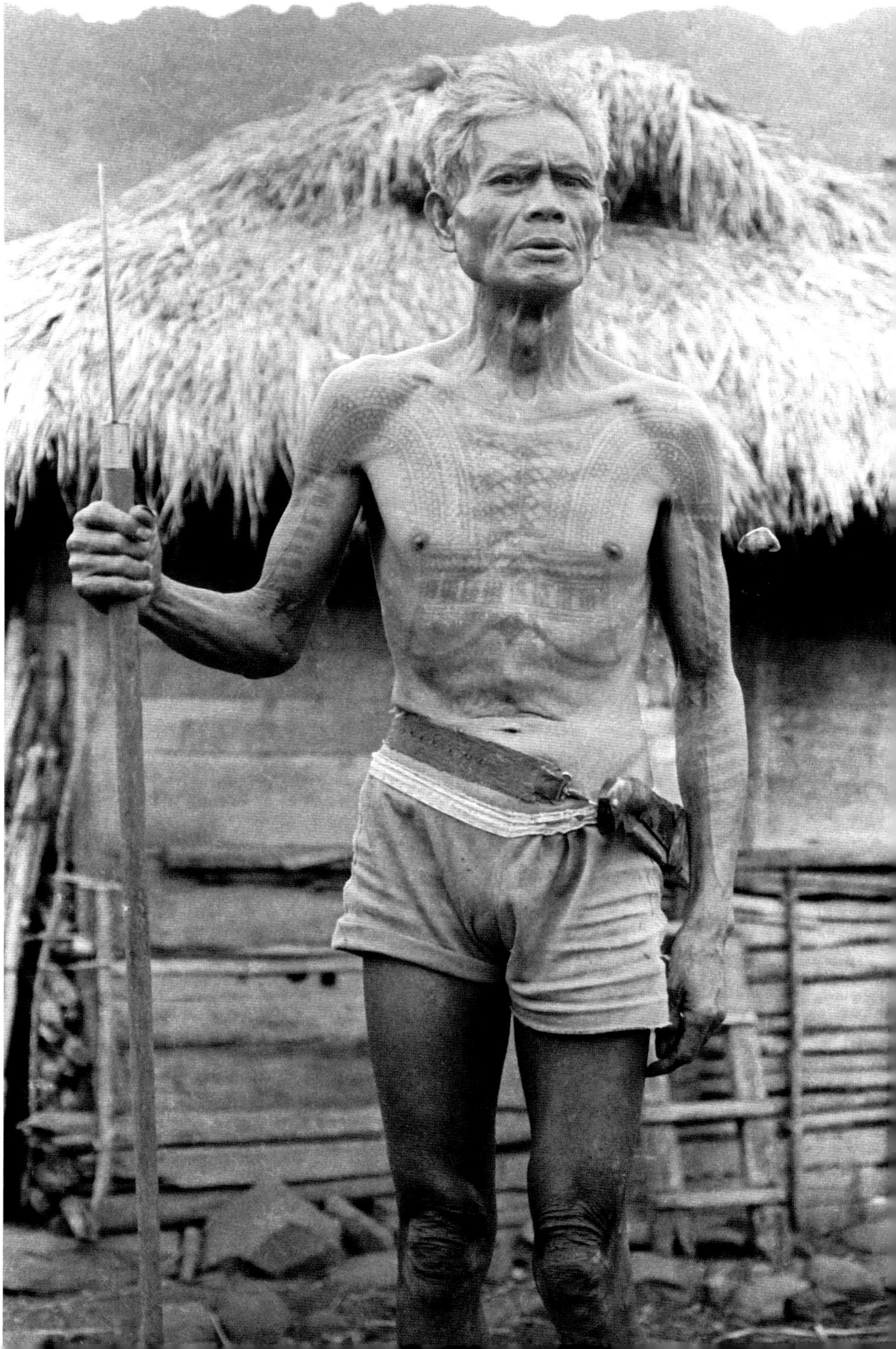

FIGURE 3.2
Tattooed Kalinga warrior of the Tanudan Valley, 1979. © Charles LeNoir.

who sought some sort of treasure or utopia, real or imagined, including lost souls, lost mines, and exotic peoples lost to time (Krutak 2010a).

Indeed, a century ago parts of the Cordillera were considered more remote to Western explorers than Tibet or Siberia. Daniel Folkmar ([1905–1906] 1962:2), an American anthropologist and colonial governmental official who lived in Tinglayan (Kalinga Province), wrote in 1905 that "this culture area is one of the least known" and that there are villages "into which the natives said no white man had entered [before]."

One of the most distinctive and "curious" customs recorded by nineteenth-century travelers to the Cordillera was traditional tattooing. Among the Bontok, Kalinga, Ifugao, Ibaloy, Isneg, Kankanaey, and other Cordilleran peoples who speak Austronesian languages, the practice was widespread and intimately related to ethnic identity, social status, medicinal therapy, rites of passage, and Indigenous spirituality. Although it is not known at what time the custom originated, folktales recorded by anthropologists in the twentieth century recounting the origins of the practice are quite similar, and some of these stories share common themes and patterns found among the Indigenous Peoples of Taiwan. For example, the Taiwanese anthropologist and pioneering tattoo scholar John Ting-Jui Ho compared Indigenous animal marking and tattoo origin stories among Austronesian peoples of Taiwan, Borneo, and the Philippines for his PhD dissertation at Indiana University. Remarkably, a pattern emerged wherein despite the differences in the main actors (usually animals) and the means of decoration (i.e., painting, dying, or tattooing), three subthemes emerged, with the central idea being that two friends agree to decorate each other and because one does a superb job and the other a poor job, enmities arise, and these actions gave rise to the current color patterning of particular animals. Ho (1971:104) concludes, "From a structural point of view, it is hard to deny a close resemblance among [the] variants. It seems unlikely that such similarities can be explained by independent invention. . . . [T]he cluster of subthemes of <u>The Origin of Animal Markings</u> mentioned above almost certainly comprise a specifically Southeast Asiatic theme. Probably the Formosan [Taiwanese], as well as the Philippine versions are the result of diffusion: they were brought by migration from some part of the Southeast Asian mainland in early times." This finding also coincides, I believe, with similarities in tattoo aesthetics, placement, and orthography between southern Taiwan, northern Luzon, and parts of Borneo.[1] I provide a few of these origin stories via paraphrase below.[2]

Rukai (Taiwan)

"Brother, what shall we do? There's no work to do. Let's draw pictures on our bodies," spoke the leopard and the bear. Then the leopard said, "Draw some on me. Make them good." And so the bear drew. When he had finished drawing, the bear said, "This time draw on me." And so the leopard drew on both sides of his shoulders and asked, "Is this all right?" The bear said, "Yes, that's fine." The leopard held the ink in his mouth and blew it on the bear, and the bear turned pitch black. The bear became angry and said, "Why did you do such a thing to me?" They were about to quarrel when the leopard said, "Wait, when I go hunting, I'll share my game with you." So the two became good friends (Ho 1971:308–309; from Ogawa and Asai 1935:361–362).

Isneg (Luzon)

There were, they say, two friends; their names were iguana and crow. The iguana said, "Help me in preparing materials for tattooing, so that we can meet at the cave tomorrow." "Yes," said the crow; they prepared the [m]aterials for tattooing. In the morning they met at the cave. The iguana said, "I shall be the first whom you tattoo, and then you." "Yes," said the crow. The crow started tattooing the iguana; it tattooed very carefully. It began at its mouth; it reached its tail; it was finished. "Now I," said the crow. The iguana started tattooing the crow; the iguana tattooed lazily, as it was hard to do the drawing. It used its wisdom; it said, "Some are barking at me, friend; let us do it like this so that it be quick." It spilled the materials on the body of the crow. That is why the crows are black since then; the iguana is speckled, because the crow did it carefully (Vanoverbergh 1955a:11).

Bontok (Luzon)

There were two young men who were the very greatest of friends. One tattooed the other beautifully. He tattooed his arms and his legs, his breast and his belly, and also his back and face. He marked him beautifully all over, and he rubbed soot from the bottom of an *olla* into the marks, and he was then very beautiful. When the tattooer finished his work he turned to his friend, and said, "Now you tattoo me beautifully, too." So the young men scraped together a great pile of black, greasy soot from pitch-pine wood. Before the other knew what the tattooed one was doing, he rubbed soot over him from finger tip to finger tip. Then the black one asked, "Why do you tattoo me so badly?"

Without waiting for an answer they began a terrible combat. Suddenly, the tattooed one was a large lizard, fanias [*fa-ni'as*], an iguana, and he ran away and hid in the tall grass; the sooty black one was gayan [*gay-yang*], the crow, and he flew away and up over Bontoc, because he was ashamed to enter the pueblo after quarreling with his old friend (Jenks 1905:224–225).

Kayan (Borneo)

Of the origin of tatu [*sic*] the Kayans related the following story: Long ago when the plumage of birds was dull and sober, the coucal and the argus pheasant agreed to tatu each other; the coucal began on the pheasant first, and succeeded admirably as the plumage of the pheasant bears witness at the present day; the pheasant then tried his hand on the coucal, but being a stupid bird he was soon in difficulties, and, observing that he would fail miserably to complete the task, he took the black dye and, having smeared it all over his friend, told him to sit in a bowl of *samak* tan, and, when the coucal did as he was told, flew off remarking that the country was full of enemies, and, therefore, he could not stop; and that is why the coucal to this day has a black head and neck with a tan-colored body (Hose and Shelford 1906:65).

Aside from folklore, the antiquity of the tattooing practice in the northern Philippines can also be traced to elaborately tattooed and purposefully mummified human remains aged seven hundred to nine hundred years from upland rock shelters and caves located in Benguet Province, primarily within the municipality of Kabayan (Beckett et al. 2017; Picpican 2003; Salvador-Amores 2017). These tattooed male and female mummies are preserved within pinewood coffins, some of which are carved with motifs closely resembling the tattoos of the dead, and the mummies are mainly associated with the Indigenous Ibaloy people, who also practiced *bátek* (tattooing) during the historic period. These "fire mummies" were created by smoking them under a low fire to enhance tissue dehydration, inhibit the decay of fats, and form an antimicrobial barrier preventing bacterial growth as well as a physical barrier against insect infestation (Beckett, Lohmann, and Bernstein 2011; Beckett et al. 2017). After this stage, an embalming "juice" was prepared from the leaves of local plants, including guava (*Psidium guajava*), *diwdiw* (*Ficus septica*), *patani* (*Phaseolus lunatus*), *duming* (*Dolichos lablab*), and *besodak/sopedak* (*Embelia philippinensis*) (Piombino-Mascali et al. 2017:63). Finally, tobacco smoke was blown into the mouth of the deceased to assist in the mummification of the internal organs. Once the mummification process was complete, the body and its coffin were carried to their final resting place on the mountain, which the Ibaloy say is the abode of the *kaapuan* (ancestral spirits) (Beckett et al. 2017:27).

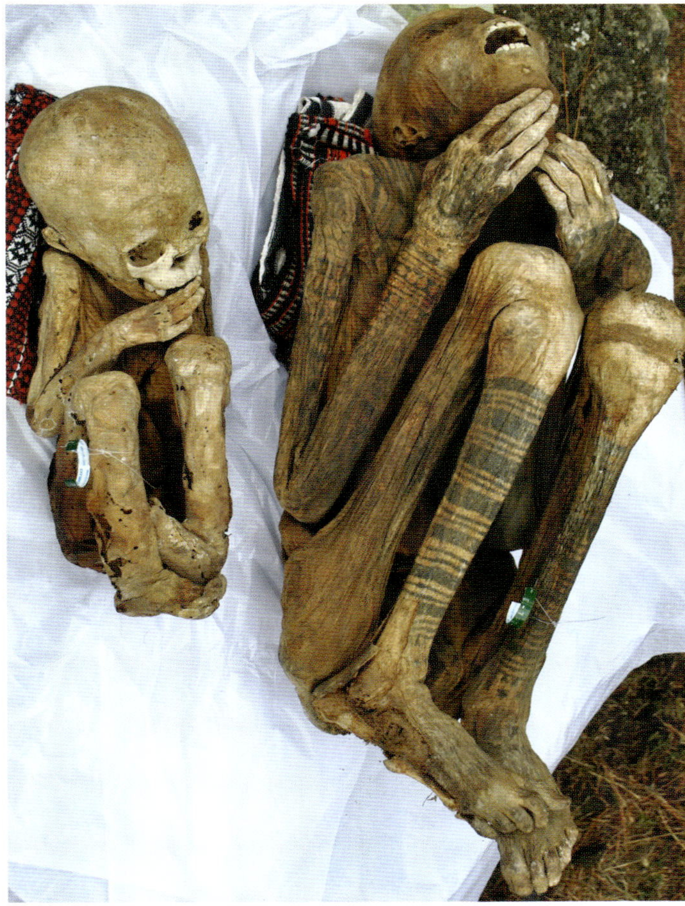

FIGURE 3.3
Male mummies from the Timbac rock shelters, Benguet Province, 2012. The adult mummy on the right bears full-body tattoos and faint "sun-wheels" on his hands, while the child on the left has no traces of tattooing, indicating he did not participate in rite-of-passage ceremonies. © Analyn Salvador-Amores.

One burial site, Mount Timbac, which rests at 8,907 feet above sea level, is oriented toward the northeast, facing the sun. This celestial body is where the Ibaloy believe the *kalaching* (soul) "awakens" to be greeted by the ancestors in the afterlife, where it will become one with the deities beyond the *duvong* (earth-world) (Salvador-Amores 2017:46). According to the American anthropologist Claude Russell Moss (1920a:281), who lived among the Ibaloy and the neighboring Kankanaey for more than a decade in the early twentieth century, "the sun was regarded as the most powerful of all deities, and the fact that he was always appealed to in ordeals [and rituals] seems to indicate that he was the god of justice and the supreme ruler" of all.

Not surprisingly, solar tattoo motifs figured prominently in prehistoric Ibaloy as well as in historic Ibaloy tattooing traditions. Sun motifs have been observed marking the backs of the hands of ancient male mummies from the Kabayan rock shelters, including that of the revered demigod Apo Anno (1100–1300 CE) (see fig. I.8, p. 11), and in the early twentieth century, several writers continued to observe these tattoos on men and women. Frederic Sawyer, a British

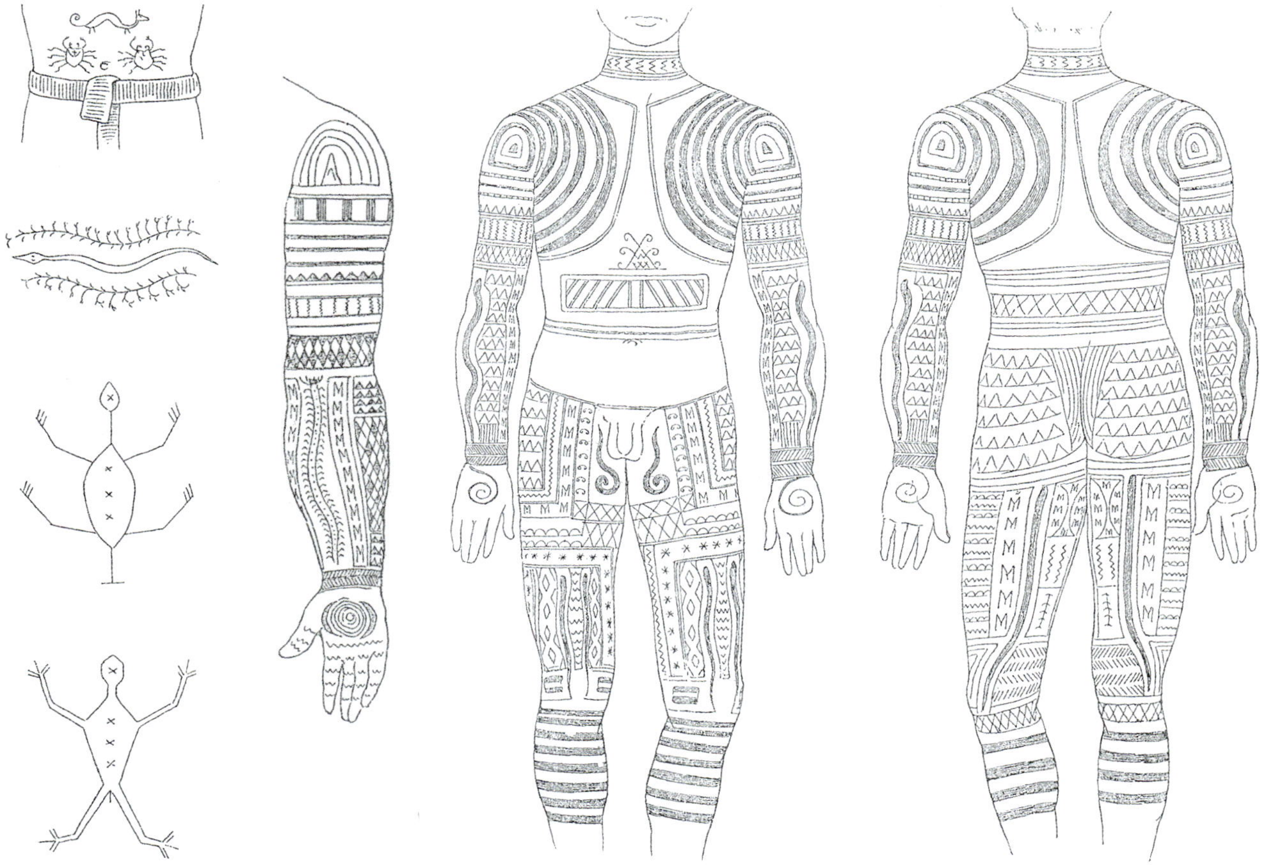

FIGURE 3.4

Hans Meyer's detailed illustration of *burik* (tattoos) in the northern Philippines, 1882. *Burik* is also the name of a tattoo design found on the body and translated as "spotted." The tattoos are composed of figurative (man, lizard, snake, and scorpion) and geometric (lines, circles, stripes, and zigzags) designs. Similar figurative patterns are found on the thighs and buttocks, while the chest, back, and legs display parallel stripes, making the body look like a sailor's striped jacket and the legs like Tyrolean stockings. From Meyer 1885:512–514.

engineer who lived in Luzon in the late nineteenth century, visited many tribal peoples inhabiting the Cordillera Central, including the Ibaloy and the Kankanaey, among others. He wrote, "Tattooing is very general among them. In some districts you can hardly find a man or woman who has not a figure of the sun tattooed in blue on the back of the hand, for in Central Benguet they worship the sun. Some of them tattoo the breast and arms in patterns of straight and curved lines pricking in with a needle in indigo blue" (Sawyer 1900:255).

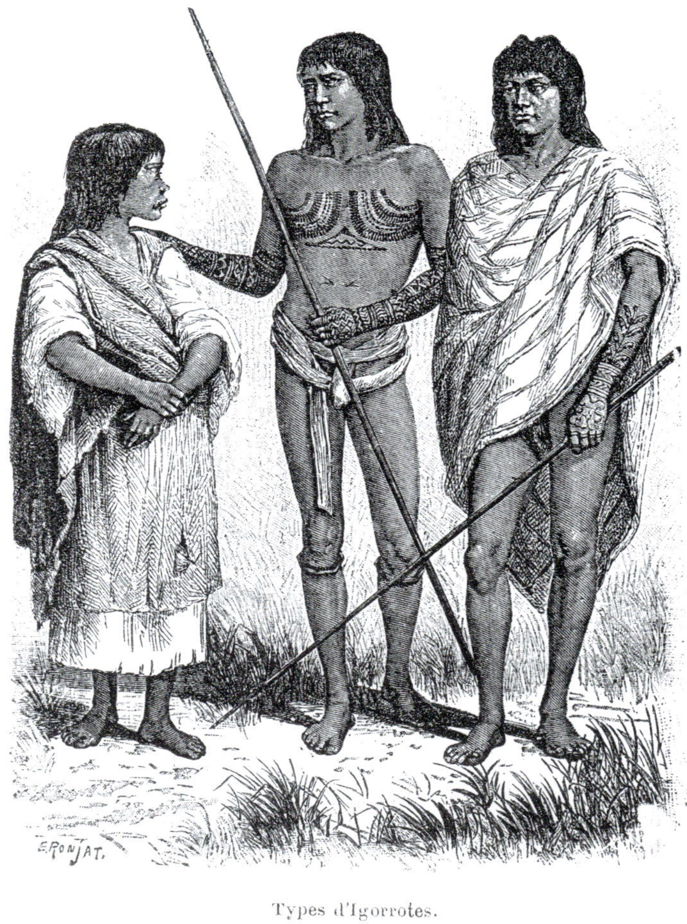

FIGURE 3.5
"Igorrote Types" of Benguet Province with chest, arm, and hand tattoos, ca. 1882. From Marche [1887] 1970:153.

Some twenty years before Sawyer's publication, the German traveler Hans Meyer illustrated the full-body tattooing of an Ibaloy warrior as well as the full-arm tattooing of a Kankanaey man from Banaao village near Mount Data. Among both groups he encountered the familiar solar disc tattooed on the backs of men's hands. The intricate body tattoos were composed of geometric patterns (lines, bands, zigzags, chevrons, triangles) and figurative motifs, including centipedes, serpents, scorpions, lizards, deer, dogs, and anthropomorphs; entities that often served as omen creatures (Moss 1920a:243, 288; 1920b:351; Vanoverbergh 1972a:123) or perhaps were the earthly manifestations of particular deities (cf. Krutak 2010a:116). Meyer noted in Banaao village that only older men possessed full-body tattooing, whereas "the majority of younger men satisfied themselves with a little arm tattooing, a spiral or circular sun-image on the back of the hand, and a series of parallel rings about the calves" (Meyer 1885:514). Regarding the latter, the incomplete tattooing could perhaps be attributed to the fact that these men had not yet proved themselves in battle by taking another human life, which among the Kalinga, the Bontok, and other Cordilleran groups was the general prerequisite for receiving the chest tattoos of the warrior class (cf. Krutak 2010a).[3] Meyer also noted that some of the Kankanaey villages had been "pacified" by the Spanish, and for this reason, tattooing was already in decline. Indeed, by the time Moss was living in the area in the early twentieth century, full-body male tattooing was a practice of the past and in some villages no tattooing had occurred in more than a decade (Moss 1920a).

While the Ibaloy and the Kankanaey wore very similar tattoos, they also shared many cultural traits and beliefs. On closer inspection of these cultural components, particularly mythology, I believe we can unravel some of the meanings behind the tattoo iconography of both groups.

This is an important exercise, because to date the repertoire of Ibaloy and Kankanaey tattooing motifs is not well understood. This fact can be attributed to the paucity of recorded information on tattooing practices, which are largely descriptive (cf. Picpican 2003), and their gradual abandonment at the turn of the twentieth century.

On inspection of Meyer's drawing of the Ibaloy warrior, whom he called a "Burik-Igorrotte,"[4] serpentine forms appear on the forearms, the legs, and perhaps in the genital area (i.e., a coiled snake). However, very few writers have explained why serpents would have been used as a tattoo motif from the standpoint of Ibaloy and/or Kankanaey ideology. Analyn Salvador-Amores (2017:46; cf. Casal 1998) explains that snakes are the spirits of ancestors, and that people bearing them as tattoos were offered their protection. On a brief review of the historical sources, however, the Ibaloy and the Kankanaey believed that *oleg* (snakes) possessed suprahuman powers with which to assist or afflict humankind (Lua 1989:148). In one Kankanaey oral account, a snake who could speak called himself "a god" and taught the greatest Ibaloy and Kankanaey culture hero-cum-deity, Lumawig (Chief of Spirits, Preserver of Life), how to cure wounds through the *sibisib/sabusab* rite (Moss 1920b:371–372). Furthermore, during war expeditions, the movements of particular snakes were closely observed for the omens they delivered, which could make or break a campaign. Serpent reverence is further attested by the observation that any snake entering a Kankanaey village was offered a sacrifice to appease its spirit and ensure its goodwill toward humankind (Vanoverbergh 1972a:113).

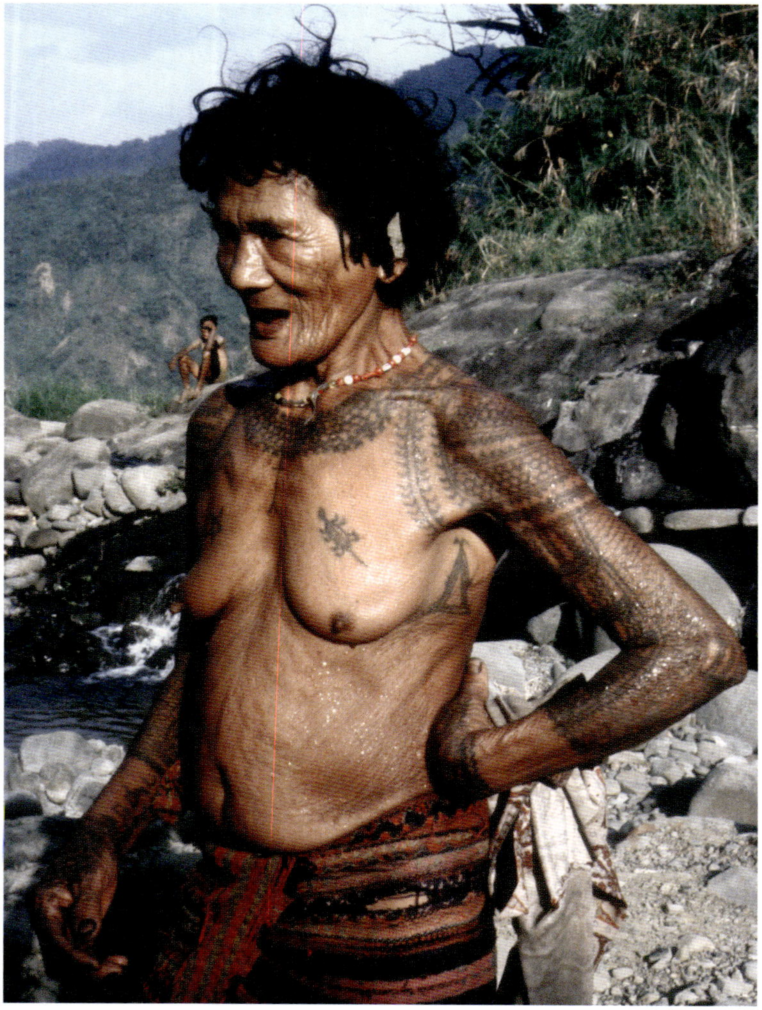

FIGURE 3.6
Tanudan Valley Kalinga woman with tattoos related to omen creatures (lizard, centipede) and celestial events (crescent moon "capturing" a star) related to headhunting, 1979. © Charles LeNoir.

Ideologically, then, possession of a snake tattoo perhaps reinforced the bearer's perception that he would receive protection and good fortune by wearing the motif on his skin, since it may have acted as a kind of spiritual companion or guardian. Among the Kalinga, abstract designs of the *urog* (snake), *irurti-it* (lizard), and *ginay'gayaman* (centipede) appeared as tattoos on the bodies of warriors, as they did among the Ibaloy and the Kankanaey. These reptiles and insects

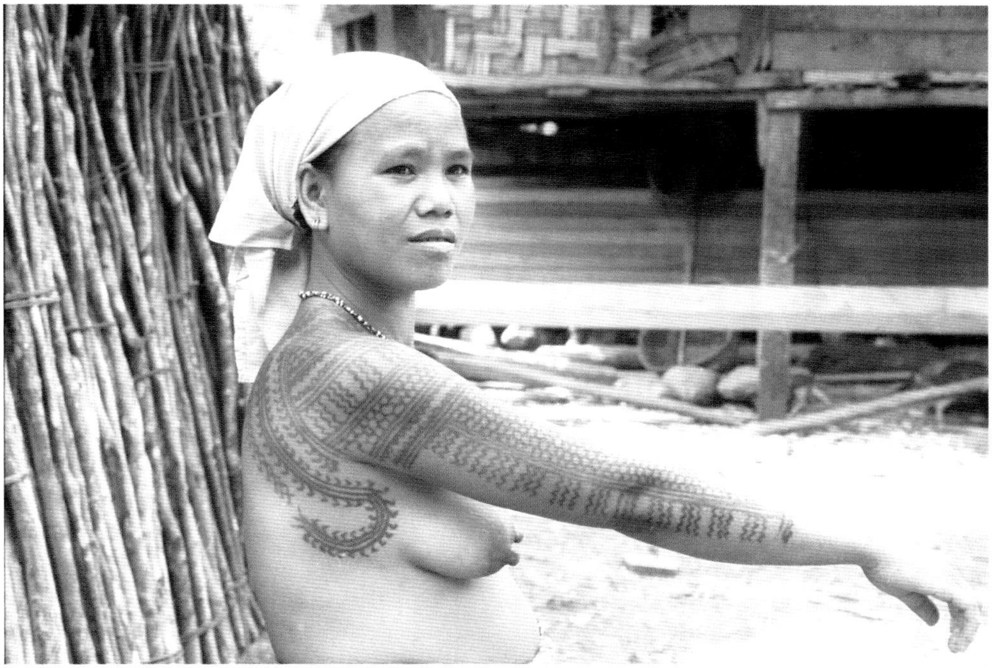

FIGURE 3.7
Kalinga woman of the Tanudan Valley bearing a large centipede tattoo on her back, 1979. © Charles LeNoir.

were considered to be a Kalinga warrior's *furfurun/fufurun* (S. Kalinga) or *bulbulun/bubulun* (N. Kalinga)—that is their "companions" or "friends" and/or spiritual guides, because of the omens they delivered on the warpath (Krutak 2010a:183). These creatures were honored for their aggressive tendencies and were believed to be messengers of particular spirits and gods who provided forecasts portending success, failure, life, or death during times of war. The Bontok relate similar beliefs. The *owug*, or snake, was formerly a man and became a "friend and companion" of the Bontok. In 1903, old Bontok men recounted, "We never kill *o-wûg'*; he is our friend. If he crosses our path on a journey, we stop and talk. If he crosses our path three or four times, we return home, because, if we continue our journey then, some of us will die. *O-wûg'* thus comes to tell us not to proceed; he knows the bad *anito* [spirits] on every trail" (Jenks 1905:225).

The culture hero Lumawig formerly played an important role in the *bindayan*, or headhunting ritual, of the Ibaloy, when new heads were welcomed into the village and his name was recited (Moss 1920a). Lumawig's name was invoked during many Ibaloy and Kankanaey ceremonies, namely because he was the originator of most of them. In oral tradition, this former human was a great hunter who was sometimes assisted by his hunting dogs. *Aso* (canids) once figured as an important tattooing motif. Dog tattoos also play a prominent part in the Indigenous tattooing traditions of Borneo. For the Kayan and the Kenyah, who speak languages in the Austronesian group, the *aso'* or *asu* (dog) was revered for its awareness, speed, agility, and loyalty, traits the Ibaloy and Kankanaey most certainly valued.[5] The *aso'* was carved into numerous implements, including sword handles and scabbards, and architectural features, and was tattooed on the bodies of warriors and aristocratic men and women (Conley 1976; Hose and Shelford 1906; Krutak 2007; Rousseau 1998). *Aso'* were considered supernatural guardians, protecting against a range of malevolent spiritual entities (Alpert 2016:130).

As noted, the sun figured prominently in Ibaloy and Kankanaey tattooing traditions; it was also featured in many oral histories and ceremonies. According to the missionary and scholar Maurice Vanoverbergh, who lived for decades among the Isneg and the Kankanaey of the Cordillera, it was "the most important" celestial body invoked during Kankanaey rituals, and Ni Apo Agew (Mr. Sun) was often substituted for Lumawig in stories because both entities played very similar roles (Vanoverbergh 1972a:90); this same pattern held for the Bontok. Among the neighboring Bontok, two folk tales, one variation featuring the sun and the other Lumawig, demonstrate that these entities were responsible for the origins of headhunting (Jenks 1905:221–222, 225–226).

The sun also appeared in Kankanaey carving traditions. A very rare wooden bowl (cat. number CE1971) dating to the eighteenth or nineteenth century was acquired by the Museo Nacional de Antropologia in Spain after the General Exhibition of the Philippines Islands in Madrid in 1887. It was most likely used in agricultural ceremonies related to the harvest, and rice wine or water was placed in the receptacle as an offering or for ritual libations.[6] The seated figure, with inset eyes and a tuft of human hair, displays incised fingers and wrists and a sun wheel flanked by two serpents on both hands; these motifs are consistent with traditional Kankanaey tattoo patterns. At the exhibition, Bontok, Kankanaey, and other Cordilleran people were put on display as part of the event. One historical account describes the tattoos of the Kankanaey leader and battle-scarred warrior Lao-lao, who was born in the village of Pingad, and specifically mentions the sun disc tattoos on his hands: "[He] was perhaps the fiercest of all of his companions; he has a kind of cogwheel, which must represent the sun, on the back of the right hand, and another with a cross in the center on the left, a kind of dog figure in the hollow of the chest, a figure of a frog with another dog on his left arm, and two other dogs on his right arm; on the chest, belly, arms and legs, [he bears] a multitude of scars" (Peréz 1902:185).

Most references to Ibaloy and Kankanaey tattooing rarely refer to the tattooing traditions of women or the actual process involved in creating tattoos. Additionally, only a few historic photographs exist depicting the full-arm tattooing of women. By 1900, missionization and the adoption of foreign clothing that covered once-tattooed bodies contributed to the decline of tattooing among women. Sawyer (1900:252) observed, "[Tattooing was] now becoming obsolete, for at least those of the Igorrotes who live near the Christian natives are gradually adopting their dress and customs."

However, Salvador-Amores' (2017:47) interviews with Benguet elders demonstrate that female tattoos were once associated with social status, affluence, and spiritual protection, and allowed women to be recognized by their ancestors in the afterlife. Her collaborators have identified some of the important motifs comprising the iconography of women's tattooing: *talaw* (stars), *carabao* (water buffalo), *pinat-pattu* (rice mortar), *inak-akbu* (basket weave), *tiniktiku* or *batikua* (zigzag lines), *pinak-paksey* (seeds), and a *balenay* or curved oxbow design representing a river (Salvador-Amores 2017:48).

The Augustinian priest Fray Angel Peréz described the process he witnessed in the Kankanaey village of Pandayan, located near Banaao. Because it is perhaps the most detailed firsthand account of the practice, I provide it in full below:

> The inhabitants of Pandayan are the most fond of painting or tattooing their legs, arms, chest and back. The form they usually take is a series of squares of alternating points and lines; one side of the square parallel to the vertebrae and the other perpendicular, leaving the sternum and vertebral column free. This same combination of lines and dots, but forming circles, serves as the basis for painting the legs and arms.

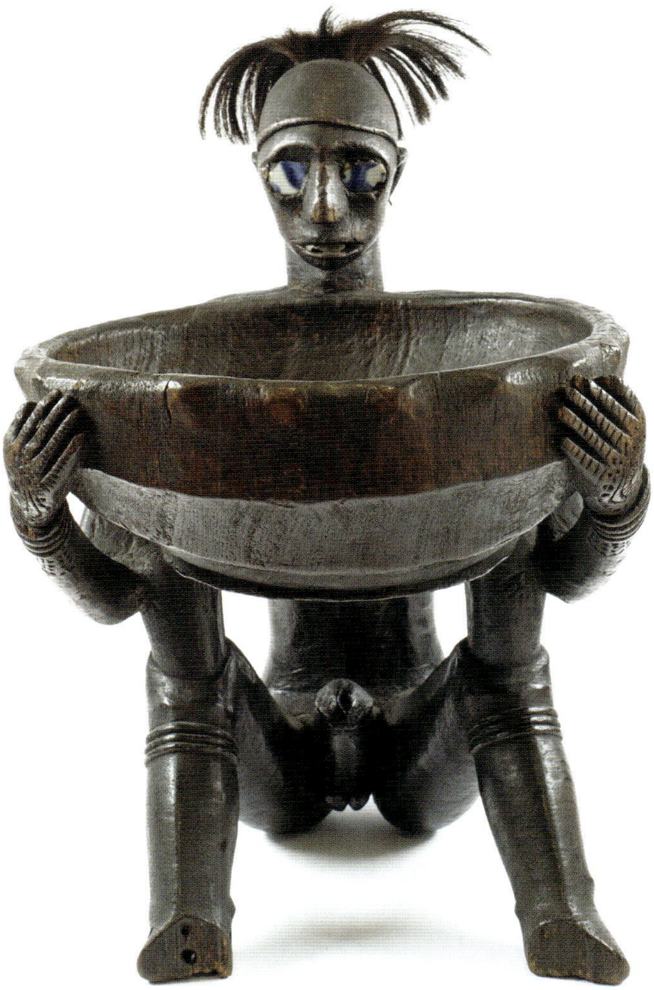

FIGURE 3.8
Kankanaey ceremonial cup likely used in ceremonies related to the rice harvest, eighteenth to nineteenth century (*left*). The male figure displays incised tattoos on the lower arms and wrist, and a solar motif on the back of the hand (*below*), and perhaps represents an ancestral or nature spirit (*anito*). These entities, who could be the harbingers of sickness, health, and/or communal prosperity, were appeased through numerous offerings in connection to agricultural, war, birth, and death rites. Collection of Museo Nacional de Antropología, Madrid (CE1971). Photographer: Javier Rodríguez Barrera.

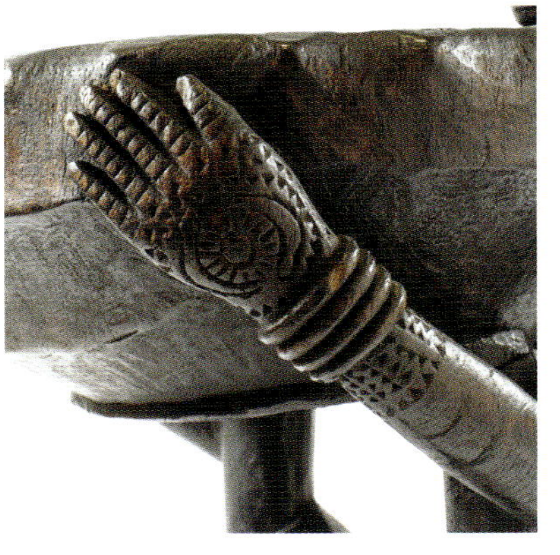

FIGURE 3.9
Tattooed Ibaloy woman, southern Benguet Province, 1904. Photograph taken at the Louisiana Purchase Exposition, St. Louis World's Fair. Collection of Elle Festin.

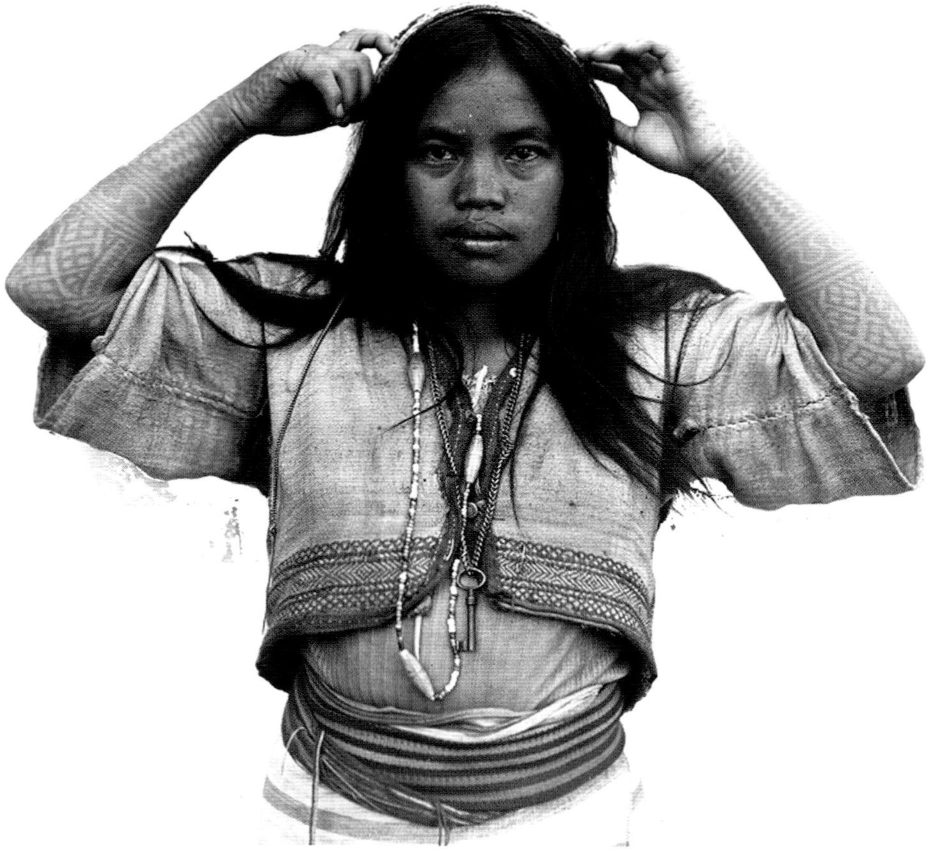

> This marking operation, called in some parts *puñgot*, is carried out with three joined needles, the tips of which are separated from each other by a millimeter in the form of a ladder, and dipped in a liquid similar to ink, made of pig gall and soot, whose mixture[,] called *guisit*, they introduce into the skin in the same way that the vaccine does among us, and it produces such a large inflammation that it prevents them from being able to work for a few days, whose inflammation is always accompanied by strong fever.
>
> Among the drawings of animals, the figure of the lizard predominates in all of them. . . . [When I] asked about its meaning, they always answer that it is an *anito* [or spirit of the deceased].[7] (Peréz 1902:146)

Vanoverbergh (1929:190) was keenly interested in Cordilleran tattooing traditions and he wrote that Kankanaey and Ibaloy tattooists were usually men. Before tapping in the tattoo design, the operator smeared the skin with a sooty pigment derived primarily of pitch pine mixed with sugarcane, lard, gall, or chicken droppings. He added that the Ifugao added juice from the *latong* (black bean plant) to the mixture; the black bean plant was a female Bontok tattoo motif for the arms (Krutak 2010a). The late Kankanaey leader and three-time mayor of Kabayan town Florentino Merino recounted other tattooing implements used by his ancestors. It is thought that his great-grandmother was the last individual of the region to be mummified around 1901. Merino (1989:27) observed that thorns of the maguey cactus were sometimes used for tattooing, and pigment was composed of the "pounded leaves of a native tomato [plant] mixed with soot and water until a consistent and oily ink-like liquid is produced," resulting in a blue to greenish-black coloration. Other writers have described the use of lemon or orange thorns to apply the tattoos (Perez 1979:27), while the pigment might also have been manufactured from a local plant, the Luzon viburnum (*Viburnum luzonicum*) (Igualdo 1989:222).

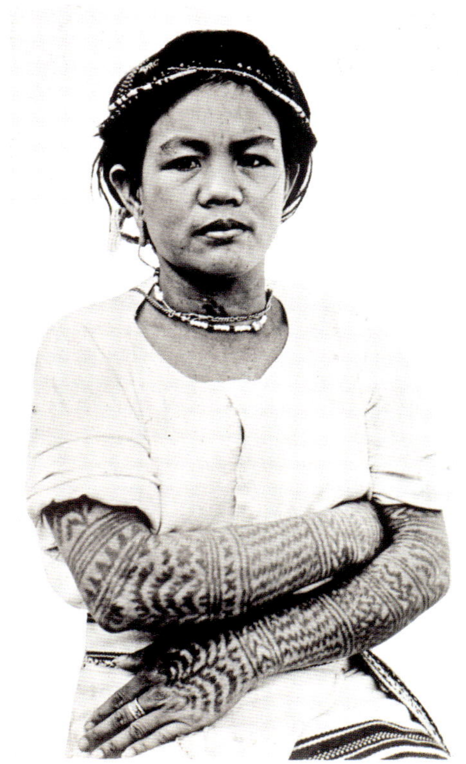

FIGURE 3.10
Tattooed Kankanaey woman, Suyoc region, northern Benguet, ca. 1910. Collection of Elle Festin.

WARFARE AND TATTOOS IN THE CORDILLERA: BONTOK, KALINGA, AND THEIR NEIGHBORS (1890–1945)

To the northeast of Kankanaey territory, the Bontok used similar tattoo implements. Although the *fatek* (tattooing tradition) among these people is no longer an active one, today elders still bear vestiges of the ancestral practice.

Generally speaking, the Bontok recognized several kinds of tattoos, and very often the number of designs worn by men was directly related to the number of human heads he had taken in combat. The *chaklag* chest tattoo, which ran upward from each nipple, curving outward across the shoulders and down the arms, indicated that a man had taken a head, or as the American governmental official Alfred Jenks (1905:172) wrote, "[T]he indelible tattoo emblem . . . proclaims them takers of human heads. Nine-tenths of the men in the pueblos of Bontoc and Samoki wear them." Women received arm tattoos (*pongo*) extending down to their hands to mark their passage from adolescence to adulthood and enhance their beauty, while other tattoos, which were also worn by men, were believed to have medicinal value to remedy varicose veins, goiter, and painful swellings (Jenks 1905:189). However, young boys and girls were also tattooed if a male relative was successful in acquiring a trophy head during combat. Boys generally received facial tattooing before the

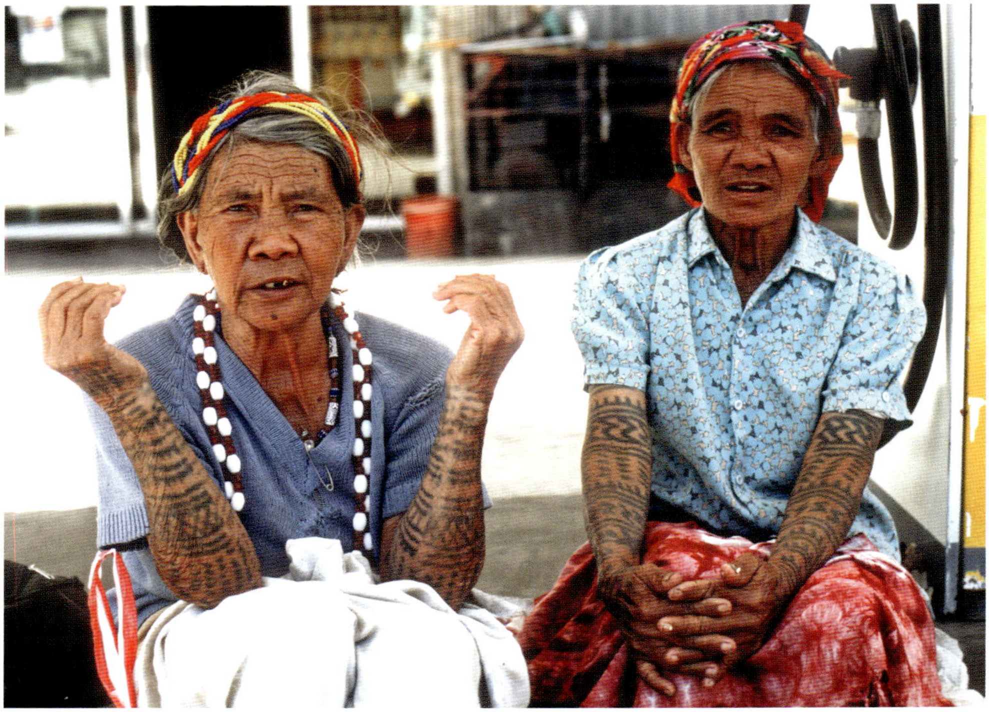

FIGURE 3.11
Two Bontok women sitting at a gas station, Bontoc, Mountain Province, 2007. © Lars Krutak.

age of ten. These first marks were usually a small half-inch cross on either cheek or a line or small cross on the nose. One young adolescent boy witnessed by Jenks bore an elaborate facial tattoo usually reserved for a warrior who earned the chest tattoo: "[He] has a tattoo encircling the lower jaw and chin, a wavy line across the forehead, a straight line down the nose, and crosses on the cheeks" (Jenks 1905:188). It must be assumed that this child received these marks for the martial exploits of his father or another male family member. According to Jenks (1905:181), the people of Bontoc town maintained "that tattooing may not occur at any other time, and that no person . . . [can receive a tattoo] unless [they are] a [headhunting] member of the successful *ato*."

The term *ato* refers to a sociopolitical unit of a Bontok village. It has been glossed as a kind of independent "precinct," or "ward," within a community, and the American anthropologist Felix Keesing wrote that each *ato* had a name and clearly defined boundaries based on historical events and local geography (Keesing 1949:581). The American linguist Lawrence Reid (1972:540), who lived in the Bontok village of Guinaang for several years, stated that the "ward" provided "cohesion within the village across descent groups and specific family lines." The epicenter of each *ato* was formed by a paved stone platform surrounded on three sides with a row of large stones for sitting and leaning, a firepit, and one or more posts that displayed the heads of slain enemies. On the fourth side stood a thatched hut or longhouse, forming a male "clubhouse" of sorts, where older males instructed the youth about customs and the Bontok way of life. In Guinaang,

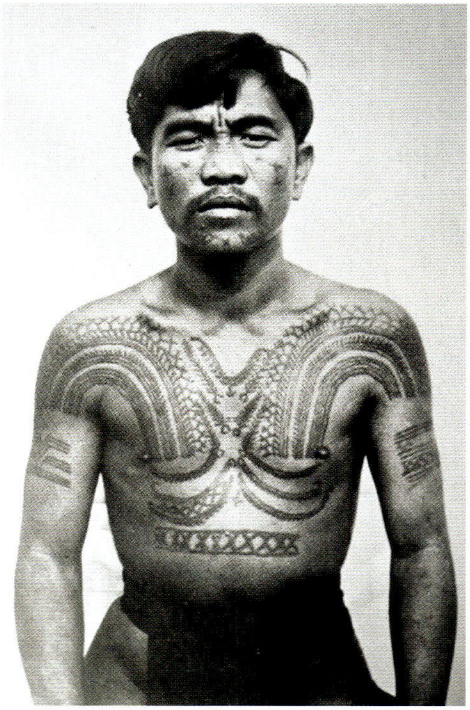

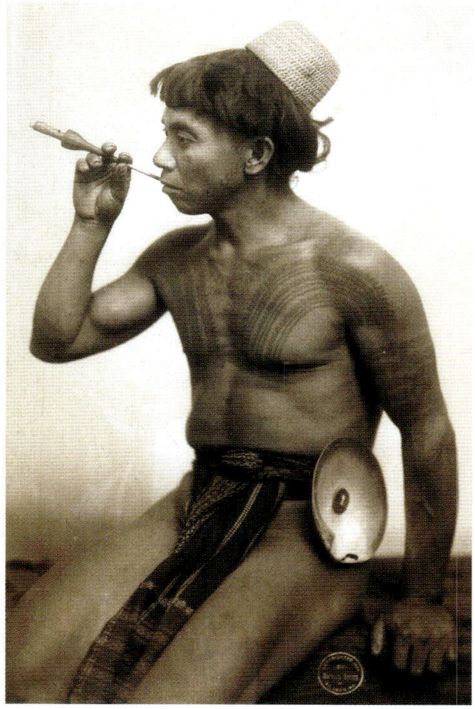

FIGURE 3.12 (LEFT)
Bontok warrior, ca. 1900. From Jenks 1905: pl. CXLV.

FIGURE 3.13 (RIGHT)
Bontok warrior photographed at the St. Louis World's Fair, 1904. Courtesy of the Missouri Historical Society, St. Louis (N28107).

the *qabqabóngan* (from *qábong*, "house"), or ward house, contained sleeping platforms for male children, unmarried young men, and widowers; married men sometimes slept here during ceremonial events or other occasions (Reid 1972:540). Women were generally tabooed from visiting this structure, and here male leaders held council, gossiped about the events of the day, or made important decisions regarding ceremonies, warfare, and economic pursuits, which bound all the residents of the *ato* (Keesing 1949:582). Elders interviewed by Keesing (1949:582) in the 1930s stated that the Bontok culture hero and deity Lumawig was responsible for the *ato*'s creation: "The origin is that Lumawig gave his approval to headhunting, and the *ato* was established as the proper place for carrying it on. It is necessary to have an *ato* in order to have the proper ceremonies." Bontok warriors, children, and women were marked by *bumafatek* (village tattooists) with designs derived from nature. In every sizeable Bontok village there were at least one or more men who operated as a tattooist. Jenks (1905:187) wrote, "[T]here are two such in Bontoc [town]—Toki, of Lowingan, and Finumti, of Longfoy—and each has practiced his art on the other. Finumti has his back and legs tattooed, and the designs were simple. A large double scallop extends from the hip to the knee on the outside of each of Finumti's legs."

When I visited Bontoc town in 2007, I met three heavily tattooed female elders. All of these women were extremely proud of their *fatek* (tattoos) and eager to display them to me. One of the Bontok women, named Pachakeg, said she was eight or nine years old when she began to

FIGURE 3.14
Bontok tattooing tools made of bamboo, cotton thread, and steel needles, 1898. Collection of Museum Volkenkunde, Leiden (RV-1183–622), National Museum of World Cultures.

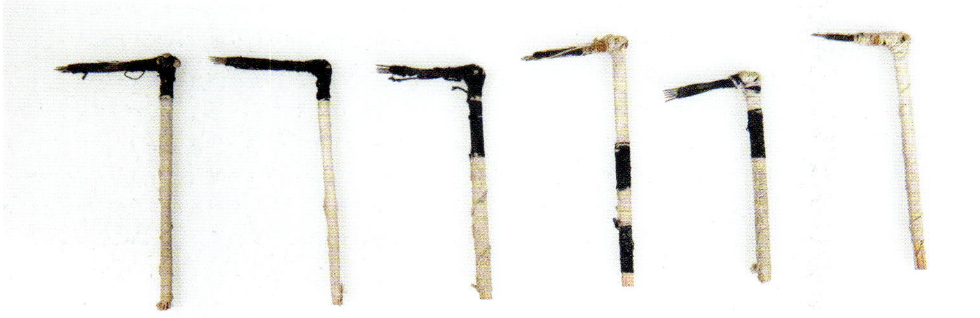

receive her tattoos. In just seven days she received all of her arm tattoos, and she was tattooed by two different artists. Historic photographs taken just after female sessions display heavily swollen arms and welted tattoo designs, which appear to take on a whitish hue. Sometimes these wounds became infected, but I was told that a girl's work in the rice fields never stopped and newly tattooed girls were expected to continue their chores (Krutak 2010a). Some of the Bontok designs for men and women included *kilat* (lightning), *agchan* (steps), *alad* (fence/wall), *teytey* (ladder), *tokwifi* (little stars), *gayyaman* (centipede), *tik-tiko* (zigzags), *falatong* (X-like black bean motifs), *khalu* (fruits of the *Sindora inermis* tree), and *anam-an* (bracken fern) designs (Krutak 2010a:112; Lawrence Reid, personal communications, February 11 and 17, 2010).

Gisi (or *kisi*),[8] Bontok tattooing instruments that resembled one form employed by the Kalinga, were made from a piece of wood or *carabao* (water buffalo) horn bent through heating (Krutak 2010a:114). These tools were approximately ten centimeters long and two centimeters thick, and a set of four to ten needles were inserted in a straight line in the angled tip (Jenks 1905:188).[9] The needled implement was struck with a wooden mallet at the approximate rate of 90 to 120 taps per minute. Before the tattooing began, however, the tattoo design was first stenciled on the skin; soot from resinous woods, such as spruce or pine, mixed with water was used for stenciling and pigment. The sooty residue was usually collected from the bottom of a ceramic vessel that was positioned over a flame (Jenks 1905:188). After the tool began to strike the skin, more soot was pressed into the wounds.

Some southern Kalinga tattooists, such as Apo Whang-Od Oggay from Buscalan, traveled to the Bontok region and tattooed men and women living there.[10] Kalinga tattoo artistry was highly prized by the Bontok because of its fine detail, its composition, and its overall symmetry compared to the less refined work produced by the Bontok themselves (Krutak 2010a:112). Twentieth-century photographs taken of Bontok men attest to these traditions of intercultural borrowing, and often you can see the very fine line work on the chest that is of Kalinga origin interspersed with blockier Bontok tattooing on other parts of the body. This pattern of Indigenous artistic exchange in Cordilleran tattooing has rarely been recognized before (cf. Krutak 2010a), but it does seem that these traditions continued at least until the end of World War II, according to the following story recorded around 1970 by Lawrence Reid in the northern Bontok village of Guinaang:

> We went hunting for Japanese, because it was war. We came upon (them). They were many, and only one was guarding, then we captured him, we took his gun. He did not cry out, because we struck him with a piece of heavy wood. So then we cut off his head, pierced his ears with a vine, and took it home. They said, "Go and perform the *seldak* ceremony, so that the spirit of the person you killed will be pacified, so that it will not come back to (afflict) you."
>
> Now the old men said, "Have yourself tattooed, because you have killed someone." We got his jaw, and attached it on a gong (as a handle). We called a Kalinga man to do the tattooing. We paid him ten (pesos). There were four of us who got that (Japanese soldier) (Reid 1992a: n.p.).

In a previous publication, Reid (1972) provided a description of *ato* activities following the taking of an enemy head as well as other details concerning omen forecasting.[11] He spent numerous years living in the Bontok community of Guinaang, acquiring fluency in the local language and a highly detailed record of ceremonies, rituals, dances, songs, and many other aspects of regional culture.

With regard to head-taking and its attendant ceremonies, the last instance whereupon both activities were performed in Guinaang was during World War II when Japanese victims were slain. In 1945, two Bontok men were also dispatched as a result of a lingering feud between Guinaang and the village of Sadanga (Reid 1961:62). Because Reid's observations surrounding Bontok headhunting in Guinaang are unequaled in the literature and have not appeared in print for decades, I will reference them below at some length.

Before a group of men set forth from their *ato* to locate their enemy, it was of primary concern to conduct a *káyew* (omen ceremony) in the early morning at one of four locations in the bush outside of the village (Reid 1972:544–545). This rite was conducted by several *mamanngel* (hearers) or leading men of the *ato* who set out to interpret the calls of the small reddish *qídew* bird;[12] a bird, called *idao* by the Kalinga, was also their chief omen bird (Krutak 2010a:115). The "hearers" were accompanied by armed *ato* members bearing their shields and spears, since during times of war enemies could ambush the omen seekers at the omen locations. Upon arrival, fires were lit, everyone crouched, armaments were held fast, men remained silent, and everyone remained vigilant in case a surprise attack was mounted from the rear (Reid 1972:544). Once the fires were lit, some of the young men of the *ato* collected two freshwater crabs at a nearby spring; they were then roasted on the fire and speared with sticks thrust into the ground. The crustaceans were offerings made to the *qaníto*, or spirits of men formerly slain in that area (Reid 1972:544).

After this ritual, the *mamanngel*, accompanied by an armed escort, moved into a nearby wooded area to listen for more bird calls. If the omen was good, the men gathered fish and crabs from the river (or mudfish from the rice fields) and returned to the *ato*, where the game was cooked and eaten that evening (Reid 1972:544). Then they began preparations for locating the enemy.

Bontoc and its "sister" village, Samoki, observed omens at a *ko'mis*, a structure that was constructed along all war trails in the forest. It resembled a kind of fence supported by several posts on which sometimes sat carved human heads representing ancestral spirits (Jenks 1905:177,

FIGURE 3.15
Photo postcard of Lubo village Kalinga warriors visiting the Baguio Carnival, 1949. *Left to right: Lakays* (respected elders) Ollasic, Guiwanas, Balinte, and Guyao. Collection of the author.

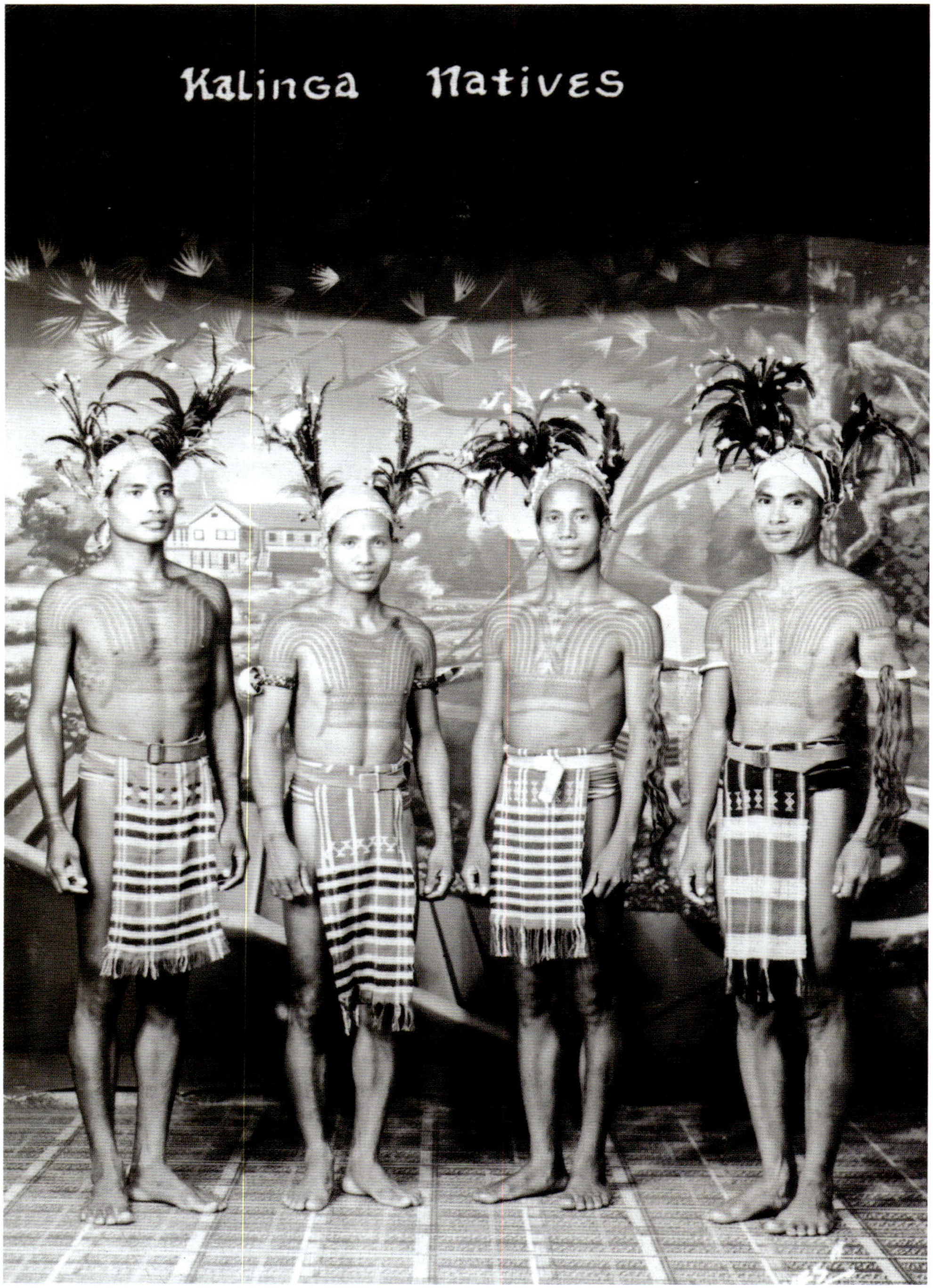

see pl. 128). These heads possessed inlaid eyes and teeth of stone, and baskets containing chickens and small pigs for ceremonial feasting were hung on or near the posts. Before the warriors of Bontoc and Samoki attacked an enemy's village, they spent one or more nights, sometimes up to ten, at one of these structures searching for positive omens for the military expedition. If no omens portending success were observed, the warriors returned to their respective *ato* and held a ceremony whereby a previously captured enemy skull was buried under the paved courtyard of their ward (Jenks 1905:178).

In southern Kalinga villages, military campaigns were organized and undertaken on the advice of one or more elderly war leaders who consulted omens to determine if the time was auspicious for an invasion (Krutak 2010a:115). They often searched for celestial signs in the skies before the war party headed out, including the movements of shooting stars. If a meteor crossed the path of the war party and headed toward their destination, that was a bad omen. But if one meteor was followed by another that seemingly originated at their destination and shot back toward them, this was good sign (Krutak 2010a:115). Moreover, when a star appeared close to a crescent moon, so close as if it were "its captive," this omen meant that an invasion would be successful (Magannon 1972:13). This phenomenon was commemorated as a tattoo among the Kalinga (Krutak 2010a:103) as well as among the Lahanan of Borneo (see chapter 4, p. 217). Kalinga elders told me that the best time to go on a headhunting raid was during the last quarter moon.

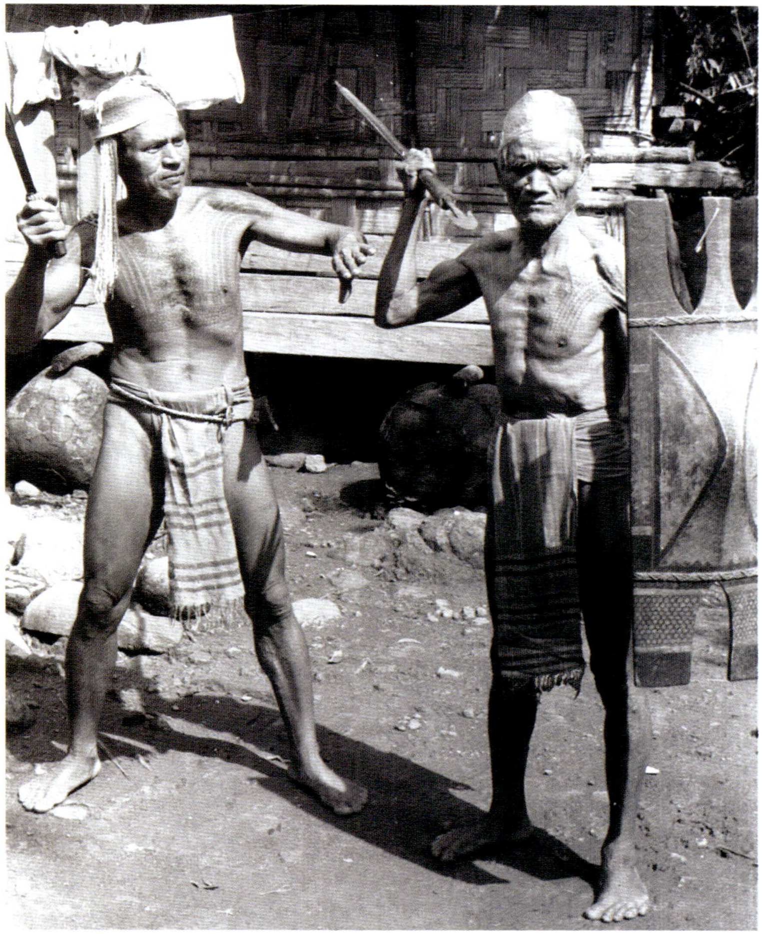

FIGURE 3.16
Kalinga warriors of the Tanudan Valley demonstrating battle tactics, 1979. © Charles LeNoir.

Almost invariably, however, the Kalinga oracle men paid particularly close attention to the flight patterns and calls of the *idao*, a small sparrow-like bird that forecasted future happenings and possibilities. To properly identify the bird's messages, the seers observed its movements and sounds at seven distinct stations when traveling to meet their enemy. Frequently the oracle men did not meet with success and were compelled to repeat their observations for weeks or even months at a time until a favorable forecast was detected (Krutak 2010a:115).

More detailed omen forecasting information exists for the northern Kalinga. It was documented by the pioneering missionary-cum-anthropologist and professor Father Jules de Raedt,

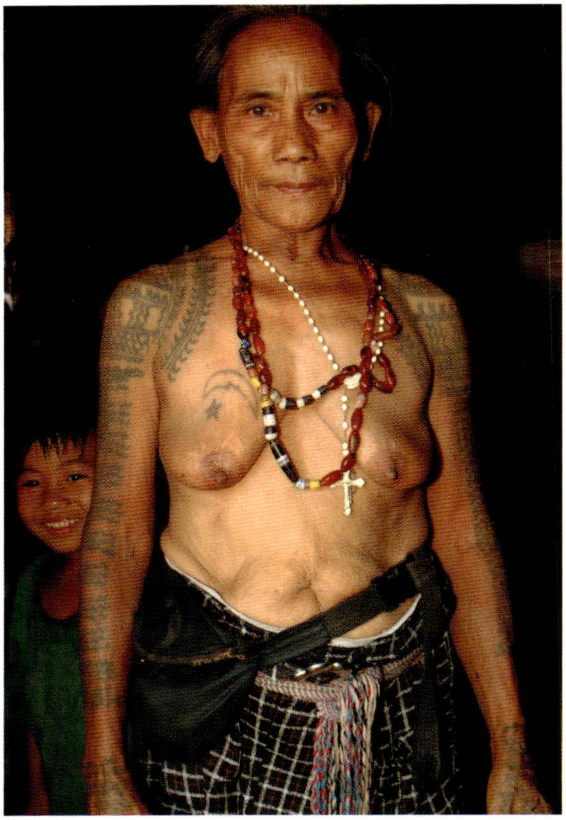

FIGURE 3.17
Kalinga elder of the Tanudan Valley displaying crescent moon and star tattoo on chest, 2004. © Andy Maluche.

who lived for several years in the village of Buaya and mastered the local Kalinga dialect. Here, military campaigns were organized and undertaken on the advice of a female *mandadawak* (spirit medium) who began her prognosticating with the blood sacrifice of a chicken or other animal to divine how each member of a war party would fare (de Raedt 1969). If the medium was in a personal relationship with one of the warriors, she used her powers to insert a *batubatu* (secret stone or agate bead) into his body that was believed to make him as "hard as stone" against the weapons of the enemy (de Raedt 1969:310). She then became possessed by her *maman* (spirit helpers) in the form of *bulbulun di mangayaw* (friends of the headhunters) or "dwarves" who guided the men on their human quest (Krutak 2010a:116). Warriors sought signs that their *bulun* (friends) were coming to meet, direct, or offer favorable omens (or ones of impending danger) to them through earthly messengers, such as snakes, centipedes, large lizards, or even wild roosters. One former Kalinga warrior of Sumadel village told me that if a python crossed your path this was a bad omen because it symbolized *bulig*, the litter used to carry dead people off the battlefield. Moreover, if the hoots of an owl originated in front of a war party that was another bad sign, but if it came from the rear it foretold of good fortune (Krutak 2010a:121n18).

Sometimes particular *maman* were believed to accompany the men and offer their protective services. Madepdeplaw (or Stray) was the name of one of these spirits, and the Buaya Kalinga reported that he caught stray spears that may have bounced off trees and rocks and hit his human friends (de Raedt 1969:312). He also watched over the men during their retreat from the battle zone.

In addition to the *mandadawak*'s friends, warriors might also be accompanied into war by their personal, ancestral, and/or village spirits (Krutak 2010a:121n22). Although each of these entities was powerful in their own right, the Kalinga word *asing* (guardian) was employed as a catchphrase to describe them all. For example, if during a battle the opposing side inflicted the first wounds, the warriors may have remarked that "their *asing* are stronger" (de Raedt 1969:243).

While Kalinga men were on the warpath, relatives back in the village observed several sets of *paniyaw* or *ngilin* (taboos). In the southern Kalinga region, women were forbidden from chewing betel nuts and drinking *basi* (sugarcane wine) if their husbands or boyfriends were away (Krutak 2010a:116). Any breach of these and other taboos was believed to hinder the success of the raid and even cause loss of life in enemy territory.

War parties in north Kalinga traveled along secret *anyang* (paths) through the jungle, hoping to avoid detection by the settlements between their region and that of the enemy. The attack was always intended to be a surprise unless prearrangements had been made for a pitched battle (see below) to occur at a particular location. When Buaya warriors reached the boundary of their enemy's territory from which they launched their raid, they constructed a *sagubay*, or shrine for their spirit "friends" (de Raedt 1969:715). This altar was composed of two sets of *taggitag* or bamboo flutes that were placed on one another to form an X. Around each instrument was deposited a handful of ritual items, including pebbles, quids of betel nut, and rolls of chewing tobacco, among other things. Two reeds were then planted on either side of the shrine and knotted together over it. Strips of red and yellow cloth were tied into the knot because these were the *maman*'s colors as well as those of the headhunter. Yellow symbolized glory, and red, strength, aggression, and superiority (de Raedt 1996:180). Red is also the color of fire, which consumes everything that it meets, and in north Kalinga there was a saying that the headhunter "tasted" his victims. What is meant by this metaphor is that killing a man was likened to "consuming" him (de Raedt 1969:245).

The knotted reeds, together with the ritual chews and pebbles, operated as a kind of blockade or no trespassing sign against the invisible guardian spirits of the enemy's shrine. As de Raedt (1969:716) explained, "When these [enemy spirits] chew the ritual [quid] together with the pebbles, they will say: 'Oh, they are strong. We will be defeated,' and [they] do not attempt to attack the party." The decorated betel nut packets and rolls of tobacco were offerings for the invading party's *maman*, who resided in the shrine from the moment of its construction until the battle was over.

The *sagubay* was always built at a location that was believed to be safe from the approach of the enemy because it was a protective shield for the invading war party itself. It was guarded at all costs and no one would let the enemy overrun it, for once their amulets were wiped out "the *maman* would leave and the party would become utterly defenseless" (de Raedt 1969:716).

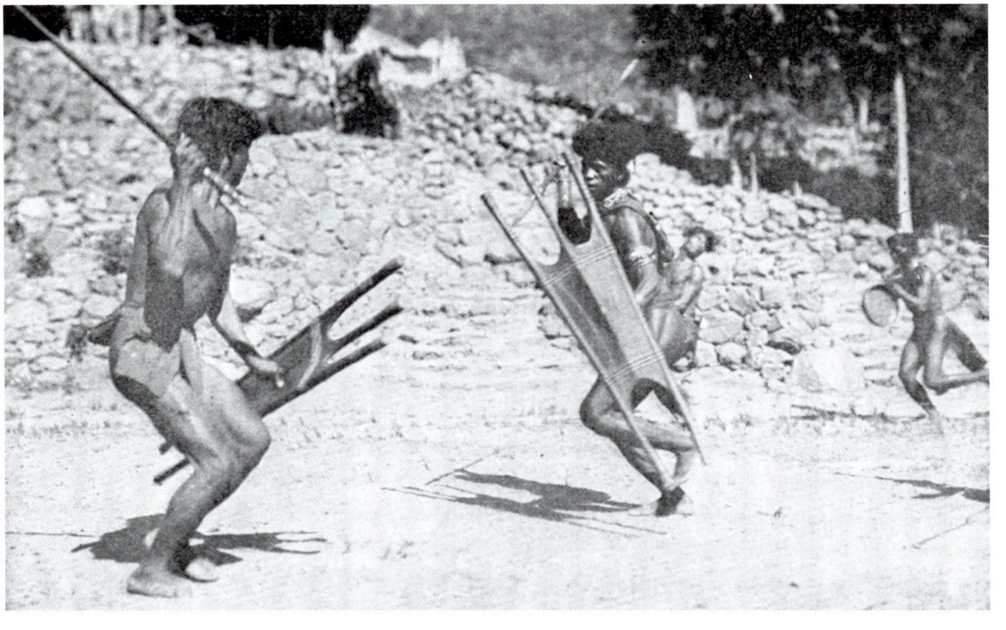

FIGURE 3.18
Kalinga men demonstrating the "war dance," 1905. From Worchester 1912:875.

Isneg headhunters, who lived to the north of Kalinga territory, would never think of going to war without the proper amulets. Vanoverbergh (1954:258–259) provided descriptions of more than a dozen, and I will paraphrase a few of the more interesting ones below:

1. *oldiyítan*, small, round, hard and glossy piece of wood resembling a pebble. This amulet is supposed to be a spirit hiding under this shape, and it prevents men from seeing a species of red snake with round spots that cause the death of whoever happens to see them.
2. *anipán*, a common creeping herb with white flowers that keeps headhunters from becoming sleepy.
3. *básag*, an herbaceous vine that grows in forests and brings success to the individual who wears it.
4. *paddúxăy*, a small herb that helps a man to defeat his enemy.
5. *ápal*, a common creeping herb that enables a pursuer to overtake his fleeing enemy with the utmost ease.
6. *taxalinád*, a low herb from the forest that makes the bearer invisible to his enemies while lying in ambush.
7. *liwliwānān*, a common small cryptogam that makes the bearer invisible to his enemies while lying in ambush.

Like the Kalinga, Isneg warriors were accompanied by *Ilánit* (helper spirits) who also possessed their amulets. Vanoverbergh (1954:259) described them as follows: "[T]he *salāyan* herb, [is used by] one who is wounded in a head-hunting expedition. . . . The *sikaláwan* herb . . . [all they have to do is] sit down when they spy the enemy and let their spear and head-ax do all the work by themselves."

As noted, serious planning, amulet gathering, and omen forecasting were characteristic of Cordilleran warfare. However, there were several kinds of warfare, and the invasion of an enemy village at dawn, nightfall, or even in broad daylight was just one type. Another form of warfare was the pitched battle. In these kinds of engagements, one village would send a messenger to the adversary's village and challenge them to a hand-to-hand clash in an open space (Jenks 1905:176–177; Krutak 2010a:121n29). The final form of combat, which was the most popular, was of the hit-and-run variety. Two or three men kept watch near an enemy village and waited in the shadows for a victim. When someone appeared, he or she was beheaded or simply killed.

A Bontok warrior carried a wooden shield, battle-ax, and one to three spears into combat. His agility and skill kept him from losing his head to the blade of his enemy, and Jenks (1905:178–179) described the necessary acuity for veteran combatants as follows: "Their battles are full of quick, incessant springing motion. There are sudden rushes and retreats, sneaking flank movements to cut an enemy off. The body is always in hand, always in motion, [so] that it may respond instantly to every necessity. Spears are thrown with greatest accuracy and fatality up to 30 feet, and after the spears are discharged[,] the contest, if continued, is at arms' length with the battle-axes. In such warfare no attitude or position can safely be maintained except for the shortest possible time."

Jenks (1905:179) wrote that there was "little formality" to head-taking; most were cut off with a battle-ax before the wounded man was dead. He also outlined who possessed ownership of the enemy head and other body parts taken in battle:

> Not infrequently, two or more men would have thrown their spears into the victim, who was already disabled.[13] If one of the Bontoc warriors at the scene had never taken a head, he would generally be allowed to cut this one from the body, and thus be entitled to the head taker's distinct tattoo [*chaklag*]. However, the head belonged to the man who threw the first disabling spear, and it found its resting place in his *ato*. If there was time, men of other *ato* may cut off the victim's hands and feet to be displayed in their *ato*. Sometimes succeeding sections of the arms and legs were cut and taken away, so only the torso was left upon the field [of battle]. (Jenks 1905:179)

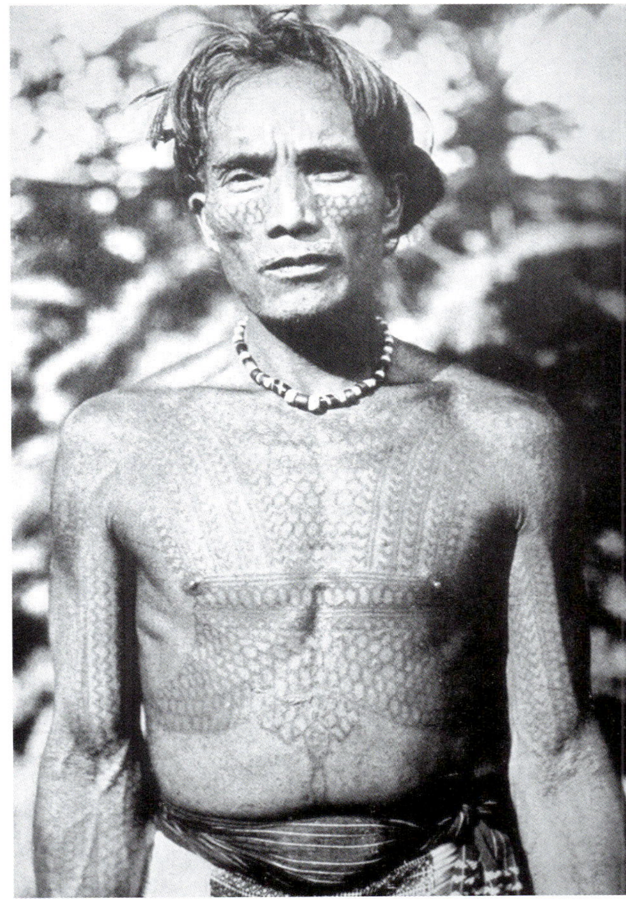

FIGURE 3.19
Veteran Kalinga chieftain of Balatok village displaying facial markings and other motifs associated with *mengor* (warrior) status, 1905. From Worchester 1912:859.

Possession of a freshly severed head did not always guarantee good fortune because the spirit of the killed person had to be pacified first. For this reason, the Bontok performed the aforementioned *séldak* ceremony. Jenks provided details about this and other associated rituals in Bontoc village around 1900.

Jenks observed that after a head was taken, the victor carried it to his *ato* and placed it in a funnel-shaped basket tied to a post in the courtyard. The entire *ato* then gathered for the *séldak* rite, whereupon a dog or pig was killed and eaten and the men danced to the beats of their *gangsa* gongs that featured human mandible grips (Jenks 1905:180).

Early the next morning, the old men of the *ato* took the head to the Chico River. There they built a fire and placed the head beside it, while the other men of the *ato* danced around it. Then everyone sat facing the river and, as each threw a small pebble into the water, he said the name of the village from which the head was taken (Jenks 1905:180). This action was to divert the battle-ax of their enemy from meeting their necks. The head was washed in the river by holding it by its hair and dunking it. Afterward, the assembly returned to the *ato* courtyard, where the lower jaw was cut from the head, boiled to remove the flesh, and became a handle for the victor's *gangsa* gong. In the evening, the head was buried in the courtyard, where it remained for up to three years. Then it was dug up and, after being thoroughly washed, the skull was placed in the funnel-shaped head basket with other enemy skulls (Jenks 1905:180).

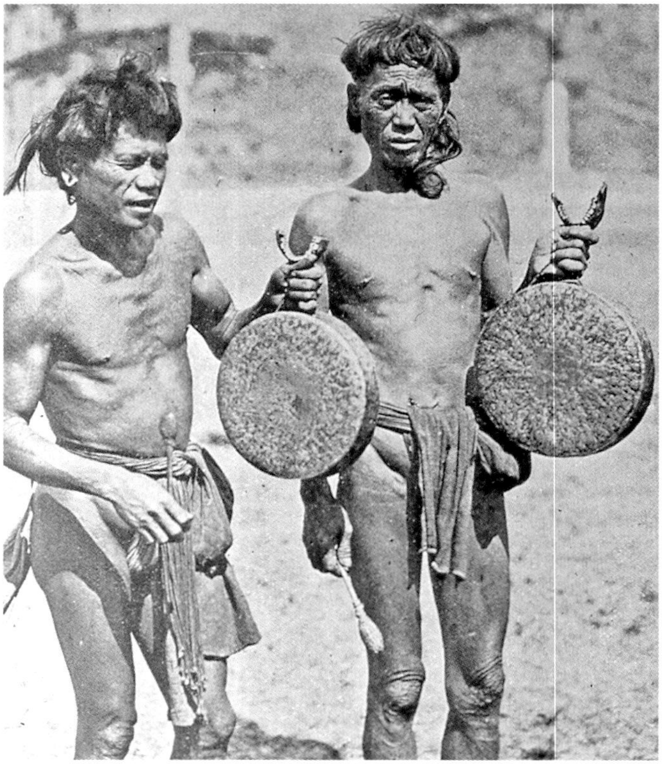

FIGURE 3.20
Bontok warriors holding their *gangsa* gongs with human mandible handles, ca. 1900. From Jenks 1905: pl. CL.

Reid (1972:559–560) described a series of other rituals performed in Guinaang. The morning after the *séldak* ceremony, the head was taken to the edge of the village for the *tóiling* sacrifice, which is also performed for accidental deaths or death at childbirth. Men danced around the head and victory songs were performed. Afterward, the head was returned to the ward house and a pig or dog was sacrificed (*dawqes* rite). Later that day, the *tomo* rite (a pig sacrifice) was held at the home of the head-taker for his spiritual protection.[14] Other rituals were performed, then a wood or stone post was erected at the *ato* to represent the victim. As in Jenks' account, the head was buried, the jaw was prepared to become a gong handle, and after three years the head was exhumed to join others in the skull basket, which hung on the inside back wall of the men's ward house (Reid 1972:560).

Vanoverbergh (1954:257) recounted the ceremonies surrounding the head-taking rite among the Isneg, which were "always performed in honor of Anlabbān, tutelary spirit of head-hunters."[15] Depending on the number of heads taken, the rite might have included several ceremonies extending over several days,[16] but for the sake of brevity, I will focus here on only a couple of attendant rites.

As soon as an enemy fell, everyone in the war party *maxaroróy* (shouted),[17] and the trophy was collected as fast as possible. The Isneg did not take the entire head; rather they lopped it off just above the eyebrows, an action likened to the "splitting of coconuts," a general metaphor for headhunting uttered in rituals, song, and folklore.[18] The trophies were deposited in a split bamboo tube receptacle resembling a funnel staked into the ground. One head, or a piece of this skull if only one head was taken during a raid, was set aside for the *săy-yám* (headhunting rite) and brought to a large *amadínān* (or *pinádin*)[19]—a "sacred tree" that was inhabited by Sinitān, the spirit-helper of the village (Vanoverbergh 1953:76; 1954:261).

On the last morning of the *săy-yám*, the warriors took center stage during the "splitting of the coconuts" rite. One of the *mēnal* (veteran braves) entered the ceremony with an extraordinary form of headgear and string of beads tied around his headband. A quantity of ripe, dry coconuts was brought forth to be split by all the warriors in attendance; this activity directly honored their tutelary spirit, Anlabbān. Now each one of the braves placed a bunch of feathers into his headband and grabbed his head-ax. One by one, they loudly boasted their former deeds on the battlefield, including how many people they had killed, the location of the killing, and the names of their victims—these are fictitious names or animal substitutes. A few short examples of these *pakkáw* (boasts) are as follows:[20]

1. We went to trade to Ilocos; like thunder (the) guns; but I was not dead, sorry; because I continue only cutting heads; I cut [them] on the hearth [stone].
2. I entered Anayan [village]; I caught a wild boar [man]; but I did not catch it with a spear; but I caught it with a head-ax.
3. A couple I cut over the eyebrows; four I cut off their head; one I wound; two I pursue.[21] (Vanoverbergh 1955b:223, 228–229, 231)

After uttering their deeds, each man expertly split his respective coconut with a single stroke, just like the enemies he slew. The warriors then rushed the split coconuts and scrambled to possess its meat, while the women in attendance began trilling *ayay*, lending to the festive atmosphere of the scene.[22]

Although Vanoverbergh (1954:253) himself did not witness an actual *săy-yám* ceremony, because Isneg headhunting was a thing of the past, elders recounted that one of the warriors usually became "possessed" or "mounted" by the spirit Anlabbān; he turned red, began to tremble, and behaved "exactly like a shaman in trance."

Trophy heads were valued on an individual level because a successful head-taker enjoyed special privileges and heightened social status and standing within and outside of his community. Successful warriors were bestowed with the title of *mēnal* (Isneg; *mengor* or *mengol* in Kalinga), or "braves," and they enjoyed the rights of receiving tattoos, handling of important paraphernalia during rituals, and boasting about their military deeds during certain occasions and they also secured the admiration of women. Jenks (1905:174), writing about the Ibaloy, stated that a man could not hope to marry unless he had taken a head first. Trophy heads were also believed to benefit the community at large because they were the repositories of supernatural power.

Across the Cordillera, various historical accounts from different tribes speak about these magical benefits, including the acquisition of abundant harvests of cultivated products or wild game and fish as well as securing general health, well-being, and community fertility. Some of the primary motivations for headhunting were related to these factors and their ties to the spiritual realm. For example, Vanoverbergh (1972a:126–127) wrote that the last headhunting raid in the Kankanaey village of Gensádan occurred around 1914. The male elders "decided to appease the recalcitrant spirits" who they believed were directly responsible for poor rice harvests for several consecutive years, and subsequently, they beheaded two Ifugao men from an enemy village. In an earlier article, Vanoverbergh (1929:189) provided additional details regarding this raid and its spiritual ramifications: "[T]he old men had been spreading the report that Kabunian (the Supreme Being) clamored for a head and that the only means of obtaining a rich harvest was to kill some enemy, [even] though the Kankanaey had abandoned headhunting for many years."

The American governmental official Daniel Folkmar ([1905–1906] 1962), who had numerous conversations with the Kalinga warrior and leader Agpad of Tinglayan, recounted one occasion when Agpad proclaimed his desire for one or two heads "to secure a good harvest." These patterns of belief were widespread (e.g., from Luzon to Borneo, and from Indonesia to the Naga regions of Northeast India and northwest Myanmar) (Davidson and Sutlive 1991:212–213; Hoskins 1996:23), whereby trophy heads were likened to containers of seed that, on germination,

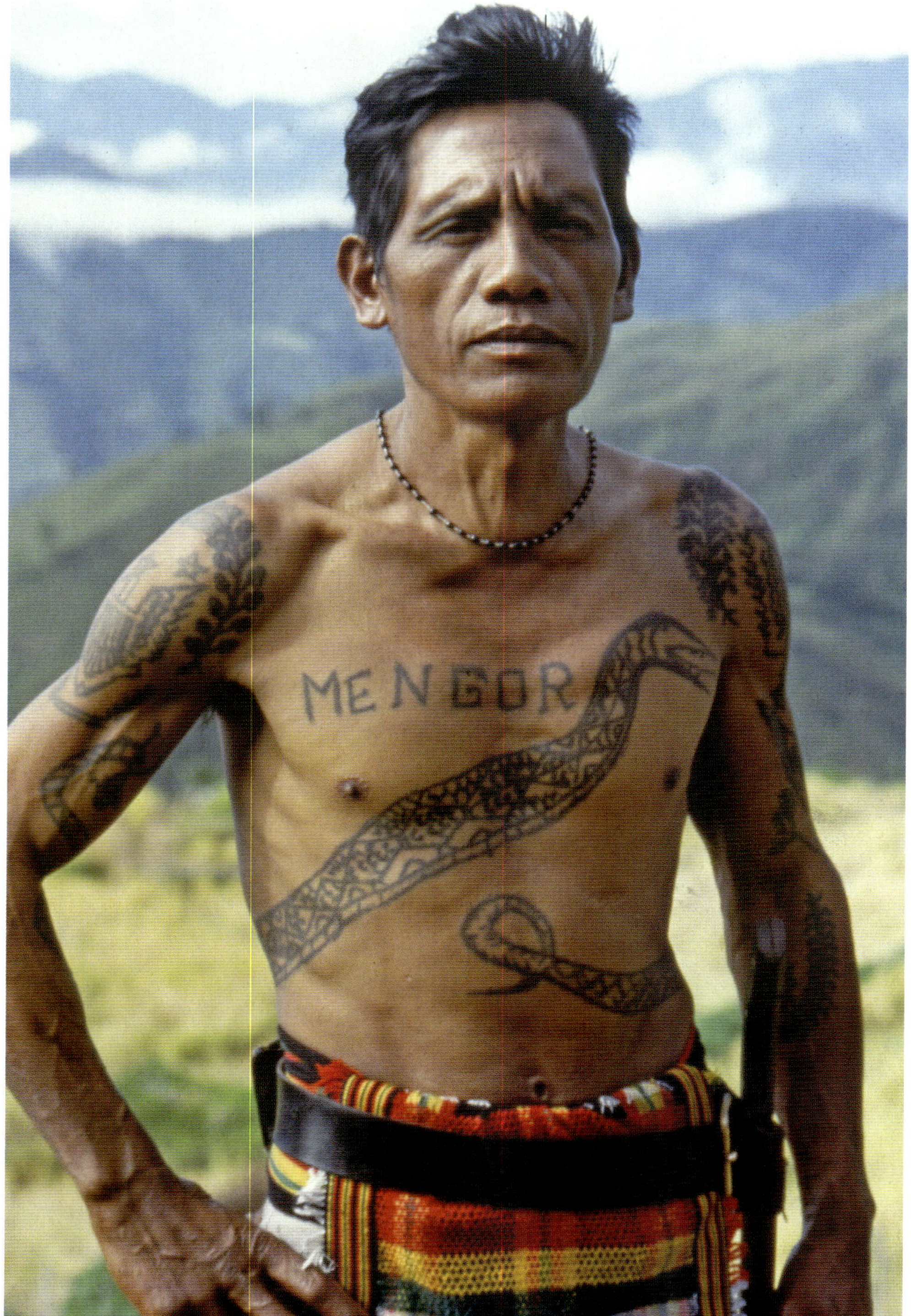

FIGURE 3.21
Kalinga *mengor* (warrior) and leader Ganggang of Nasbalutan village, 1990. © Ben Neild.

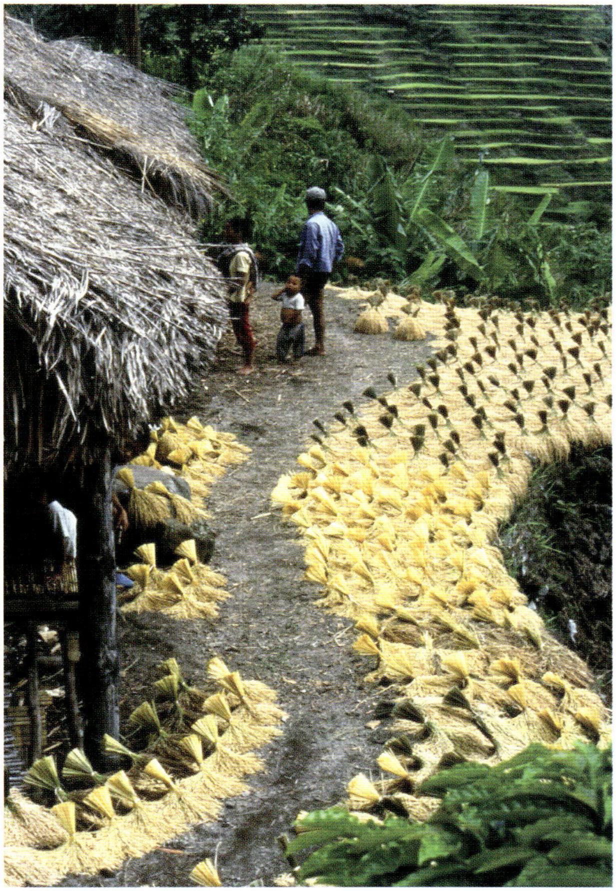

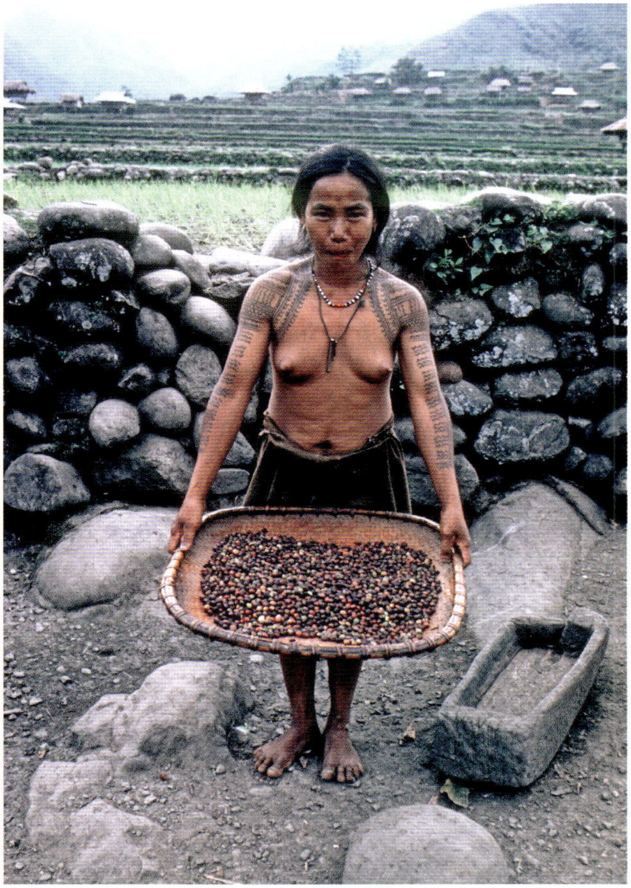

had the magical potential to increase the yield of crops, the number of newborn children in the village, and a man's virility (cf. Krutak 2020:193).

Headhunting across the Cordillera was also spurred by a variety of other circumstances. Perhaps the most common was to avenge the killing of a community or family member. The Bontok of Guinaang called it *bákal* (revenge killing) (Reid 1972:559). However, trophy head-taking could also arise from resolving intertribal disputes over regional or village boundaries; unfulfilled penalties for the breaking of peace pacts; the acquisition of agricultural, fishing, or hunting territories; and to end ceremonial periods of mourning the dead that could last for weeks if not months at a time (cf. Krutak 2010a:47). Women also compelled young men to head to war. Kalinga elders told me, "He is sometimes taunted as being a woman" if he did not go. At other times, women deliberately challenged men to head to war during gatherings held for the sick (*pusipus,* Kalinga) by providing them with sharpened *suga* (stakes) that were used in deadfalls or traps to slow down pursuing enemies after an attack (Krutak 2010a:47). Among the Isneg, one of the bravest warriors

FIGURE 3.22 (LEFT)
Bundles of rice after the harvest, 1990. Rice bundles are a common Kalinga tattooing motif for women. © Ben Neild.

FIGURE 3.23 (RIGHT)
Processing coffee beans in the Tanudan Valley, 1979. © Charles LeNoir.

FIGURE 3.24
Kalinga *mengor* and war captain Jaime Alos of Dananao village, 2008. © Lars Krutak.

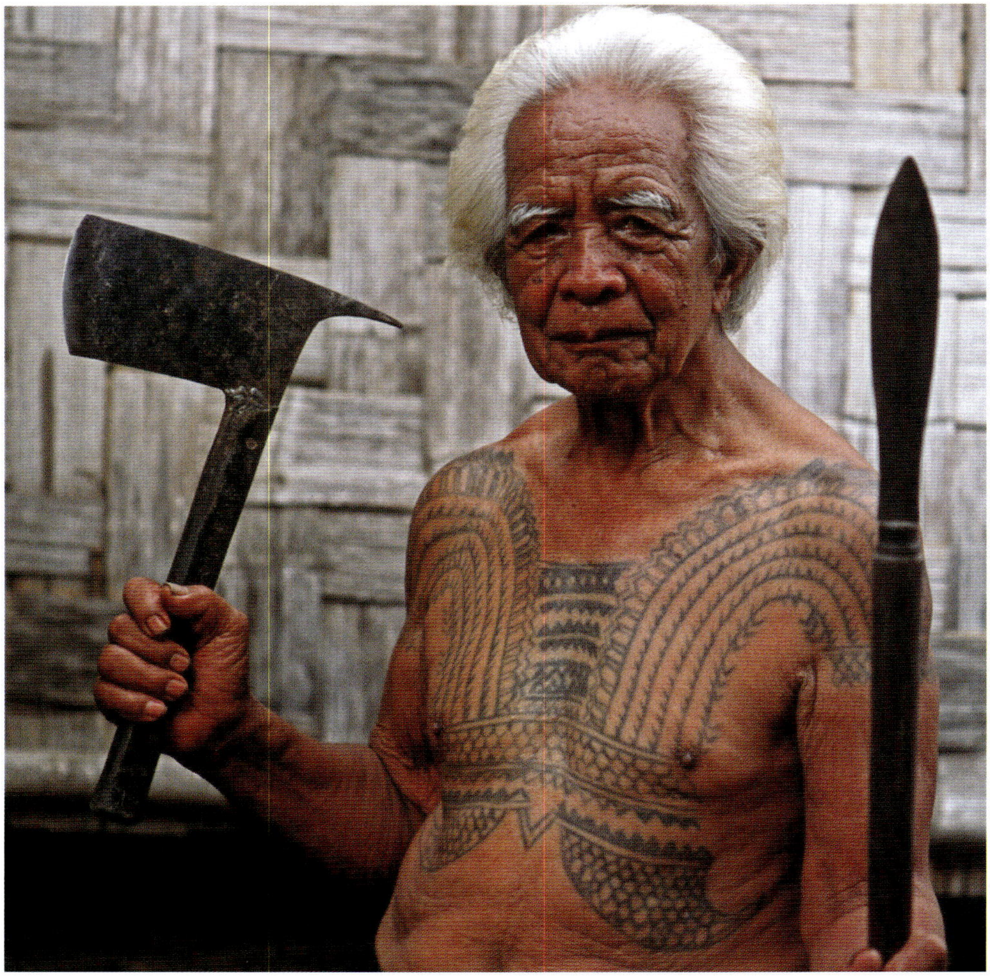

was the *maggalowid;* he covered the rear during retreats from an enemy's village and planted *túxa* (stakes) along the pathway in which pursuing forces must come (Vanoverbergh 1954:260). He was aided in his endeavors with an *xallowid,* an amulet derived from a small shrub tucked into his headband (Vanoverbergh 1954:258).

Headhunting also served religious functions of the highest order. In Cordilleran oral accounts and practice, it was seen as a human sacrifice to the most powerful of spirits (e.g., village guardians and ancestors) and gods, such as Kabuniyan, the Kalingas' Creator deity, and Lumawig, the Kankanaey, Ibaloy, and Bontok hero spirit. These entities influenced human destiny, the local environment, and the surrounding world.[23] The Kalinga historian Miguel Sugguiyao (1998:216) talked about this delicate balance when he described how the land and gods are interwoven into a complex system of religious belief: "This land is the single and most precious legacy the great Kabuniyan has given us. It is the main source of livelihood, as well as that of our children's children. Money is easily spent and does not last. Our land will always be here before our eyes. The land will make us remember the eternal love Kabuniyan has for all of us. This land is the monumental reminder of our ancestors who sacrificed so much that we might live to take their places."

Other writers observed that it was a good thing to have a distinguished headhunter living in a village because it was less likely to become the target of a military attack. Moreover, the spirits of disease and misfortune likewise feared the *mengor* (S. Kalinga; *mengol*, N. Kalinga) or "valiant warriors" because they had "tasted human blood" (e.g., they had killed) and the spirits respected "their equals" (de Raedt 1969:285–286).

Of course, headhunting did not occur as regularly as many writers would like us to believe. As noted, warfare was a highly ritualized institution and was regulated by a series of taboos and omens that were necessary to observe if an expedition was to be successful in its military objectives.[24] Even when these ritual mandates were followed, war parties were often discovered by their enemies before they could act or they were simply outnumbered by their adversaries or repelled by superior combatants. During my fieldwork, I was told that Kalinga villages may have attempted several raids a year, but many of these forays into enemy territory did not meet with positive results and it may have taken a year or more of repeated trials before a war party gained a head (Krutak 2010a:47).

When an Isneg man had killed one or more enemies, he was allowed to receive an *andóri* (warrior tattoo), placed on the inside of one or both of his forearms.[25] If a man had killed several foes, the tattoo was extended to the shoulder, whereupon above the elbow the motif curved to the outer side of the arm (Vanoverbergh 1955c:182).[26] One story also recounts that warriors once possessed the *andóri* on their backs (Vanoverbergh 1953:89). The Isneg tattooist was generally an old woman, who first drew a stencil on the skin with a sooty pigment derived from burning pitch pine or a *litáo* tree (perhaps *Casuarina equisetfolia*) mixed with sugarcane juice (Vanoverbergh 1955c:181).[27] She hand-tapped the design with a unique S-shaped *igixísi* tattooing tool of rattan containing four or five needles connected at both ends with a string.[28] The tattooist "repeatedly beats the curve next to the [needles], on its convex side, to drive them into the skin" (Vanoverbergh 1955c:181). Men were also marked with *xísi* (hand tattoos) and linear elements on the fingers, not to mention the *babalákay* (spider) motif on one or both thighs, in front; women might also receive a full complement of these tattoos,[29] although the spider tattoo could appear on the throat or inside forearm.

Among the neighboring Kalinga to the south, successful warriors who killed one or more men had elaborate *batok* (tattoos) applied to their arms and faces composed of centipede or snake scales,[30] and *bikking* chest designs, representing in abstract form the outstretched wings of the predatorial eagle (Krutak 2012:142). In some cases, the curving baselines of the *bikking* recorded the number of enemies the man had killed. Kalinga men who had performed extreme feats of bravery on the battlefield were also tattooed with *dakag*, or linear markings on their backs; anthropomorphic and geometric designs on their ribcage; and other tattoos behind their ears. War captains displayed *sinaksak'od*, or horn-like motifs, projecting outward above their navels. Sometimes a "shield

FIGURE 3.25

Isneg women's tattoos. The *andóri* pattern was worn on the forearms with additional motifs placed on the hands. These tattoos could be worn only if the father of the girl had killed one or more enemies. The cruciform or rayed "spider" tattoo (#48) was worn on the throat, on one or both thighs (in front), and/or on the forearm. From Vanoverbergh 1929:229, figs. 45–51.

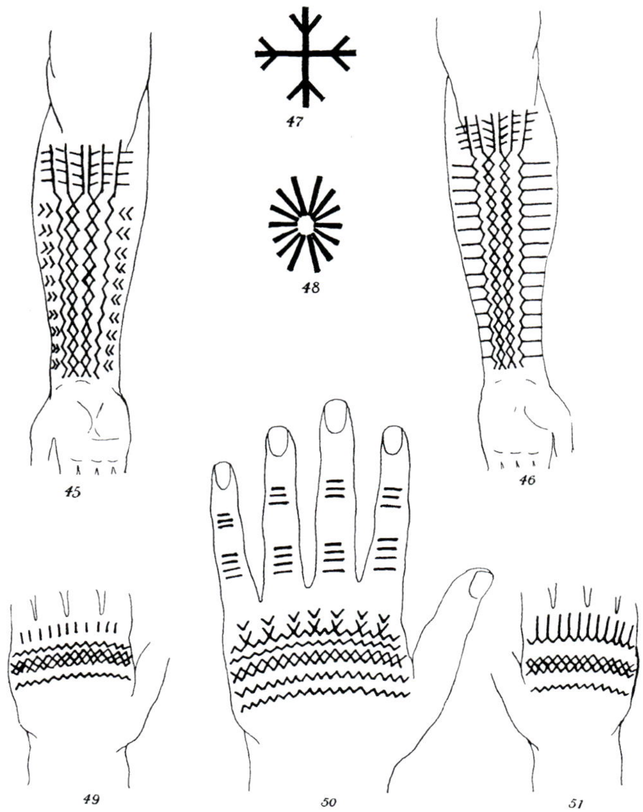

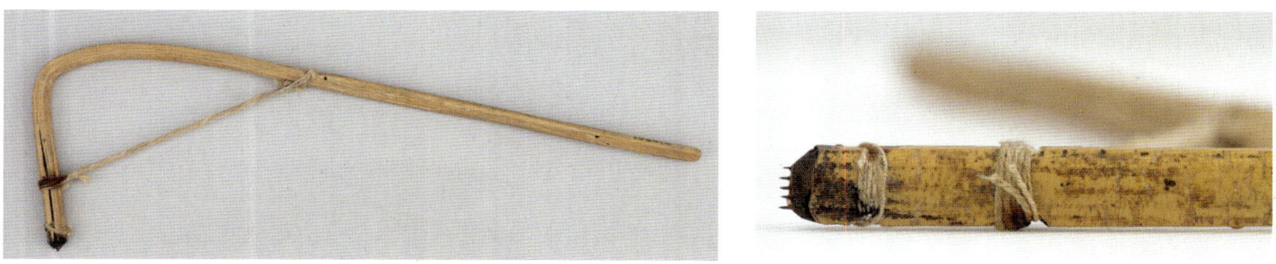

FIGURE 3.26

Itneg *gí-gí-sí* (hand-tapping tool) (*left*) and close-up of needled tip (*right*), Abra Province, 1907–1908. Collection of Field Museum, Chicago (10.9010).

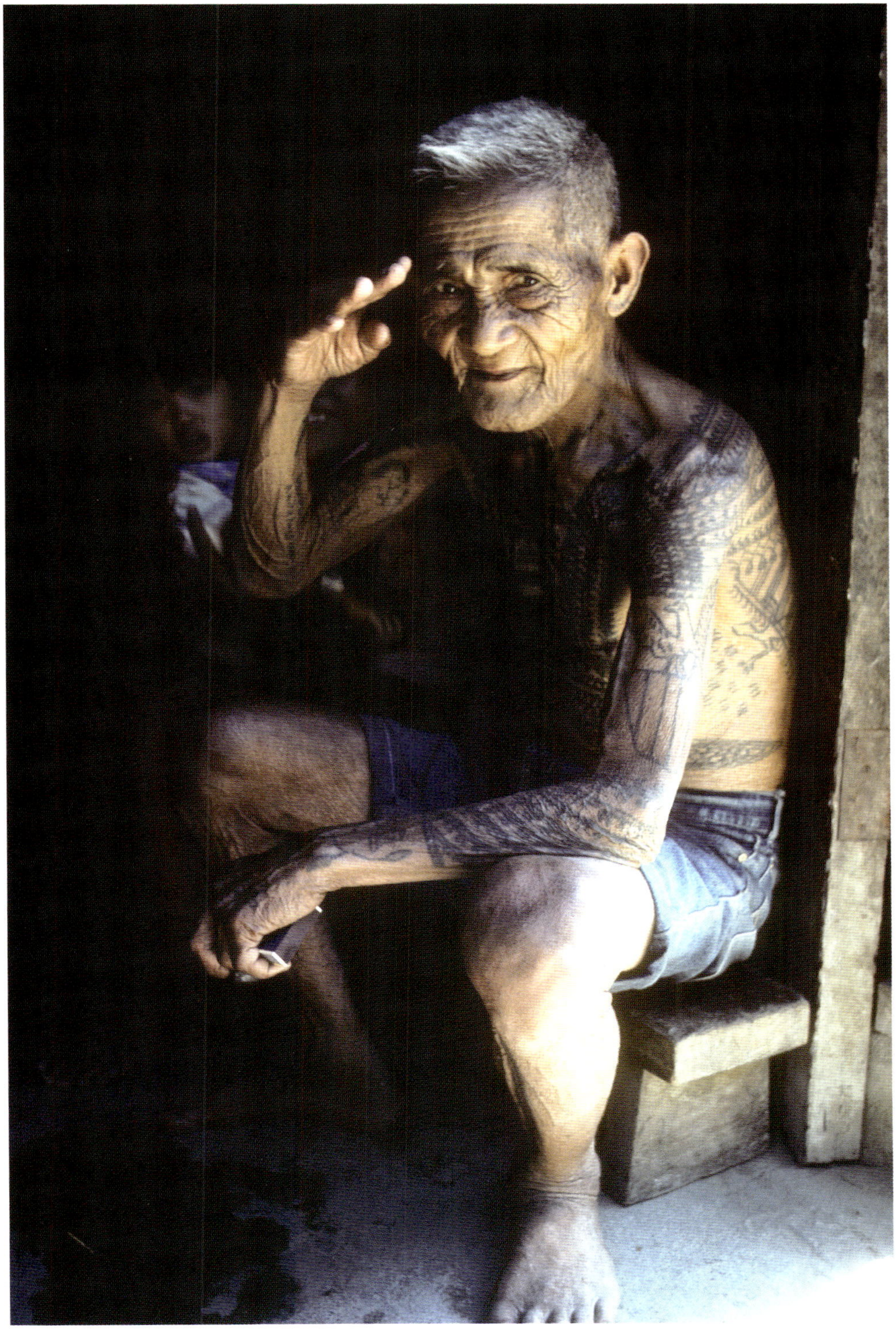

FIGURE 3.27
Veteran Kalinga warrior of the Tanudan Valley with extensive tattooing on his back, arms, and torso that combines Western and traditional tattooing motifs, 1980. © Charles LeNoir.

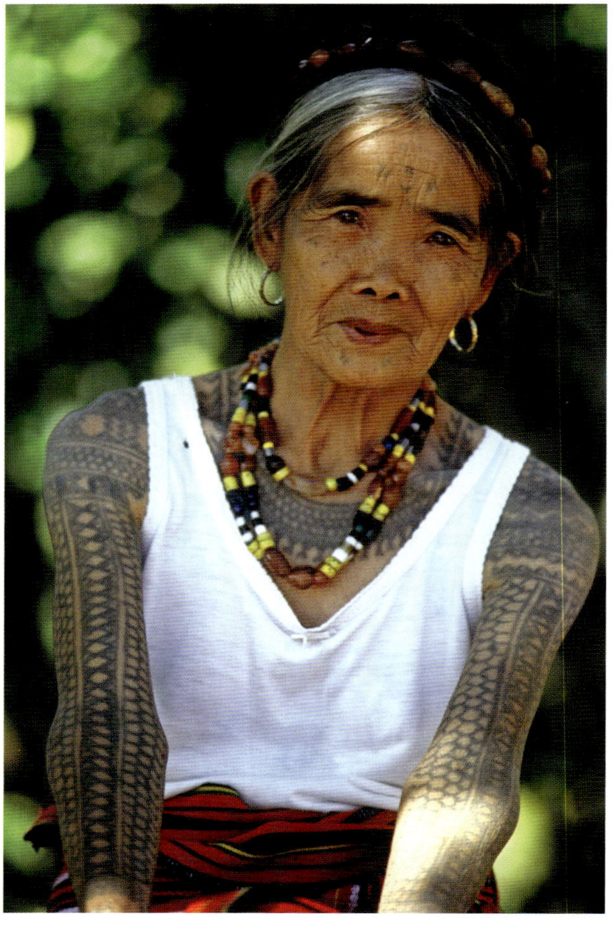

FIGURE 3.28
Kalinga *mambabatok* (tattoo master) Apo Whang-Od Oggay of Buscalan village, 2007. © Lars Krutak.

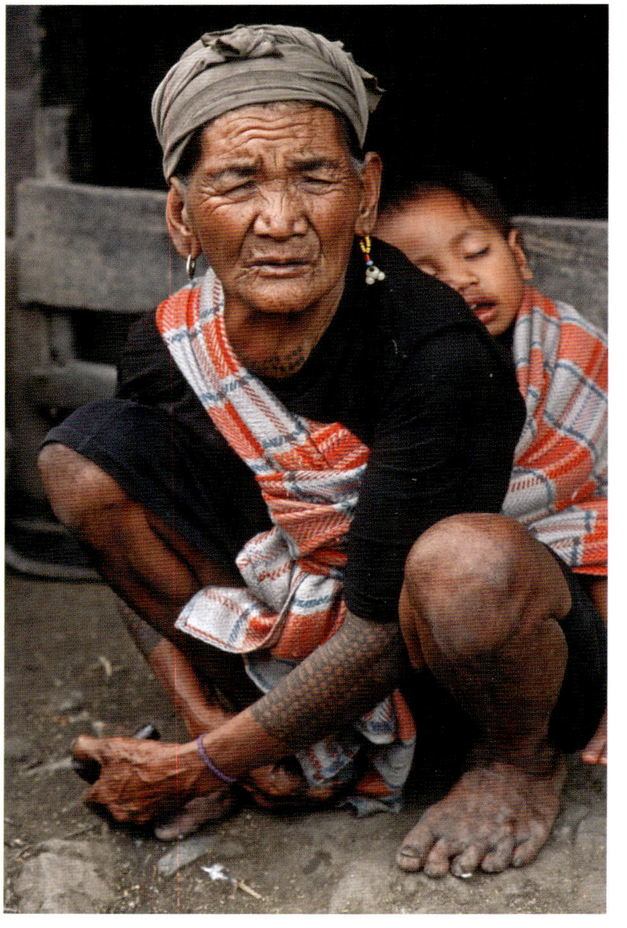

FIGURE 3.29
Apo Machao of Tulgao village bears medicinal tattoos on her neck as a remedy against goiter, 2008. © Lars Krutak.

and spear" pattern was also placed on a man's chest, because as one former warrior said, "[The shield] blocked the pathway of [my] enemies" (Krutak 2010a:105).[31] Nineteenth-century accounts also describe Kalinga warrior tattoos on the calves, thighs, and especially around wound scars that were surrounded with radiating lines (Meyer [1890] 1975:90).

Mambabatok (Kalinga tattooists) who were paid for their services also transformed girls into women through the beautiful and intricate designs they created.[32] These patterns were produced with hand-tapping tools tipped with lemon, orange, and other varieties of local citrus thorns such as pomelo. The oldest practicing Kalinga tattoo artist, Apo Whang-Od Oggay, told me in 2007 an old Indigenous story stating that women should be tattooed to increase their fertility.[33]

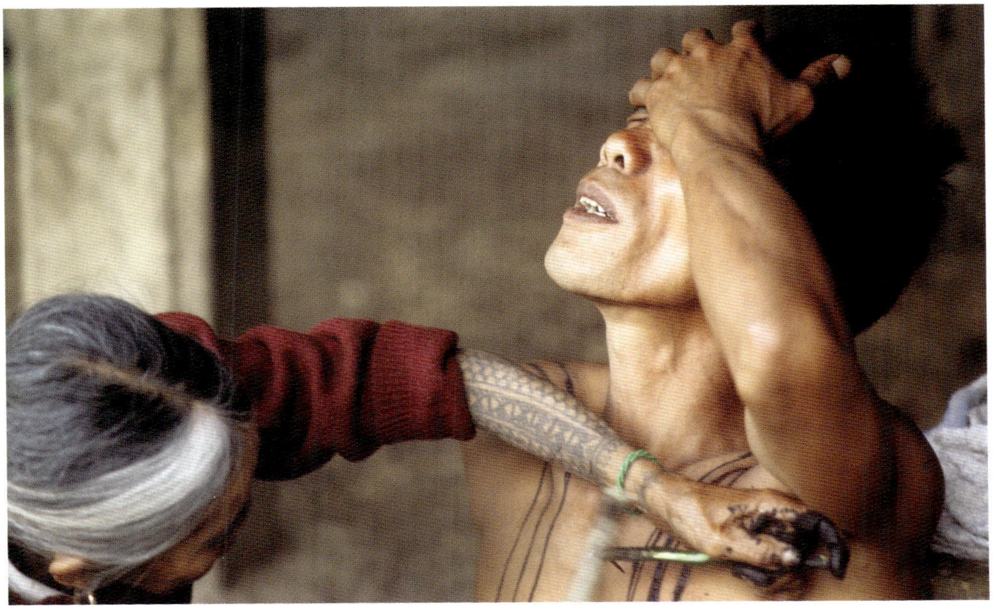

FIGURE 3.30
Apo Whang-Od Oggay hand-tapping a painful tattoo into the chest of a Kalinga warrior who avenged the killing of three men from his village, 2007. Each sloping line serves as a tally mark of his victims. © Lars Krutak.

Although she is globally famous today, in her prime she was highly sought after by childless couples across the southern Kalinga region for her fertility-inducing tattoos. In 2016, she told me that many childless women in her home village of Buscalan had borne healthy children after receiving her tattoos.

Whang-Od also noted that some women could receive additional tattoos if their male relatives were successful in battle. Invariably, female Kalinga tattoo patterns were inspired by nature and everyday objects: rice bundles, rice terrace steps, bamboo shelves, woven grass mats, ferns, rattan fruit, a star or moon, and snake or centipede scales predominated.

Other simpler markings had therapeutic value and were placed over neck goiters, tumors, and varicose veins. Among the Kalinga particular arrangements of centipede scales were believed to ward off cholera. Whang-Od also explained to me that she had on occasion tattooed circles around ringworm to halt its spread in the skin. In Luplupa village, I had heard of a similar treatment whereby people with skin disorders (e.g., psoriasis) were tattooed with a line above and/or below the problem spot to stop it from spreading.

Whang-Od noted that there were ceremonial procedures associated with her profession. Before I received my Kalinga tattoo in 2007, Whang-Od tapped some pigment into the top of my right hand to see if I would "live a long life" (Krutak 2010a:185n5). I asked her what she meant by this and how she would come to interpret the sign. First, she told me this was a custom she had learned from her mentor, and that there were two possible outcomes. If your blood flowed quickly out of the wound, like water, you would have a short life. If your blood flowed slowly and was more drop-like in form, then you would live a long life and could be tattooed.

Moreover, while I observed her tattooing a man who had recently participated in a revenge killing of three men, she said, "Before I drew first blood, I repeated an *ullalim* [chant] so that no spiritual harm would come to [him].[34] I also observed a taboo last evening and did not drink any alcohol. If I did, the tattoos I am creating today may become infected and [he] could even die. And if you or I or [he] sneezed before the tattooing began, this would be a very bad omen and I would have to stop my work. It is believed that a lurking spirit makes someone sneeze because it is jealous or has deemed it wise to postpone the tattooing for a future time" (Krutak 2010a:115).

The American educator-turned-anthropologist Roy Franklin Barton, who worked briefly in the Lubuagan region of Kalinga during 1916 and again before World War II in 1941, noted that there was a somewhat formalized order to the "stages" of warrior tattooing. As a man built up his name and reputation, he acquired additional tattoos that enhanced his status and visibility. Barton observed that only those men who had killed five or more victims could receive designs associated with the highest stations:

> If in killing or disposing of an enemy, a warrior fell into either of the following categories, he was entitled to one or any succeeding stage of the tattoo. After having obtained the first five tattoos, he could have any or all the rest without any further "killings": (1) wounder of the living enemy, *gimaiyang;* (2) giver of the coup de grace, *manela;* (3) taker of the lower jaw—it is taken before the head is severed, *sami;* (4) taker of the head, *maniwat;* (5) wounder of the torso, *dumangin.*
>
> The latter category lets the bar down to all members of the expedition who do not fall into a former one. Some men (they are mighty few, I suspect) are said to disdain taking advantage of it. Women have the right to be tattooed whenever a male relative is. The stages of tattoo are: (1) back of the hand and wrist: men, *pinupungol;* women, *ilulunus;* (2) arms and forearms: men, *sinungdel;* women, *tinali;* (3) shoulders and breast (men only), *biking [bikking];* (4) back (men only), *kinalkalpaiyan;* (5) stomach (men only), *pinipingao;* (6) a "belt" across the juncture of chest and belly (men only), *nilusok;* (7) a band across the throat, *manawat;* (8) cheeks, *aiyang.* (R. F. Barton 1949:238, fn8)

In the northern Kalinga village of Buaya, there were fewer stages according to de Raedt (1993:64). After the first enemy was dispatched, a man was tattooed on the wrist with a *botbotok* (tie band) design.[35] Men with two victories received the *kokolong* pattern on the backs of their hands. Those warriors who achieved more victories had their entire hand tattooed with the elaborate *kulkullipa* pattern. Those men who killed ten or more men were allowed to wear chest and full arm tattoos.[36]

During my field research, I heard tales that just after World War II entire war parties of Kalinga men who had killed Japanese soldiers were tattooed by their village tattooists during extravaganzas lasting two or three days. These activities not only served to pay homage to ancestral customs but also represented a dying era of Kalinga history. These warriors would later become the last generation of men to be tattooed for "lawfully" killing other men and not face prosecution or imprisonment by the government (Krutak 2010a:120).

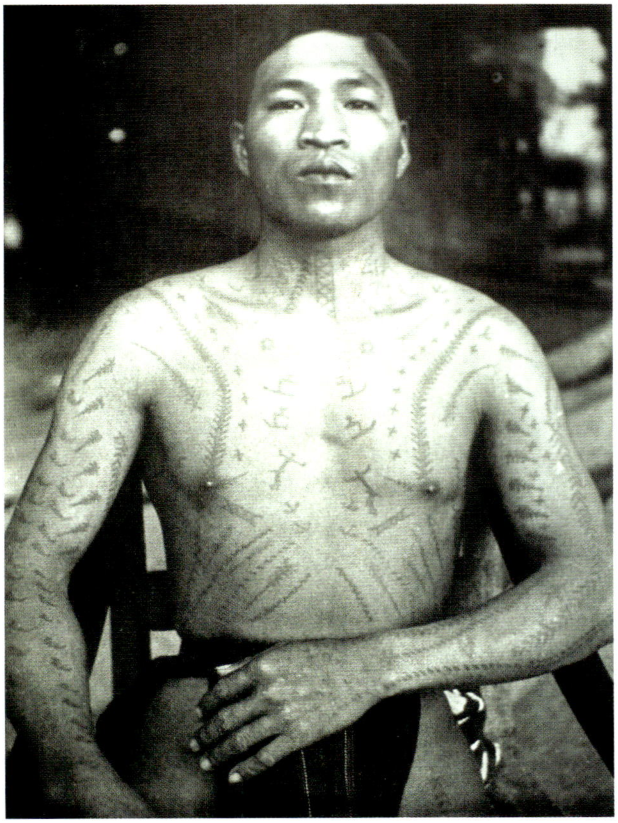

FIGURE 3.31 (LEFT)
Tattooed Ifugao warrior, Mountain Province, ca. 1915. Collection of the author.

FIGURE 3.32 (BELOW, LEFT)
Ifugao hand-poking tools with bamboo handles, twined needles, and a bundle of soot pigment, Mountain Province, 1909. Collection of Field Museum, Chicago (113747).

FIGURE 3.33 (BELOW, RIGHT)
Ifugao tattooing motifs, some of which resemble those on the "fire mummies" of Kabayan and Apo Anno. *Tinágu* (man) on chest (*a*); *kináhu* (dog) on chest and cheeks (*b*); *ginávang* (eagle) on chest and shoulders (*c*); *ginayáman* (centipede) anywhere (*d–e*); *kinílat* (lightning) (*f*); ladder on throat (*n*). From Vanoverbergh 1929:202, 206, fig. 22.

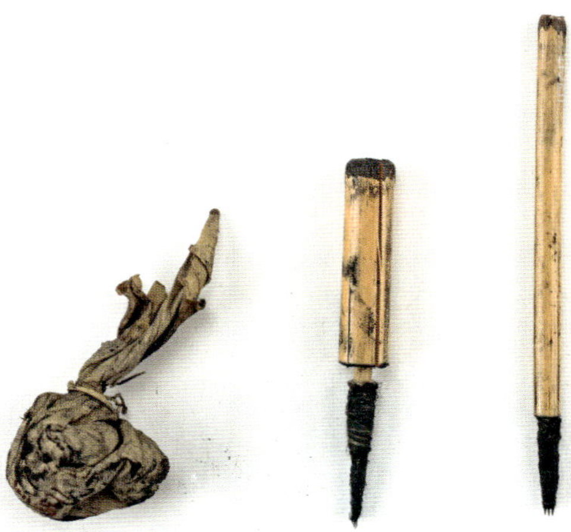

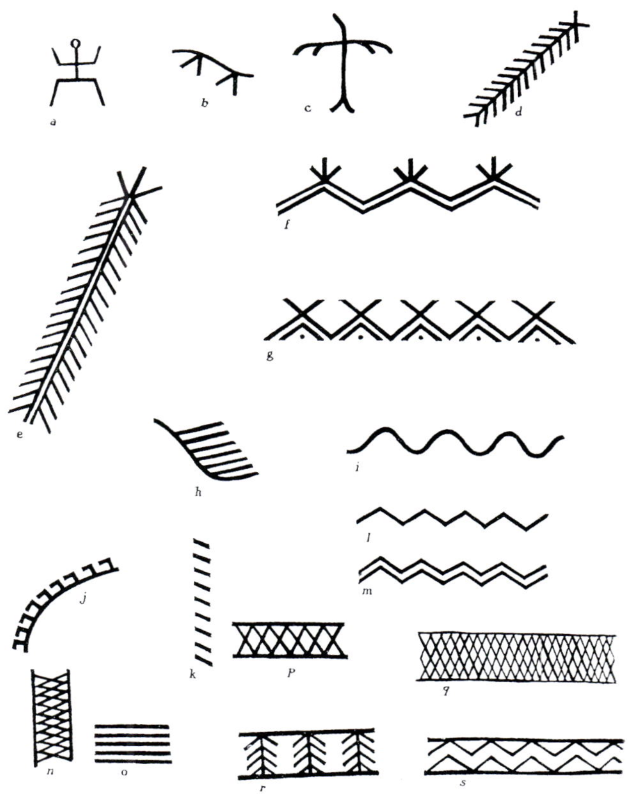

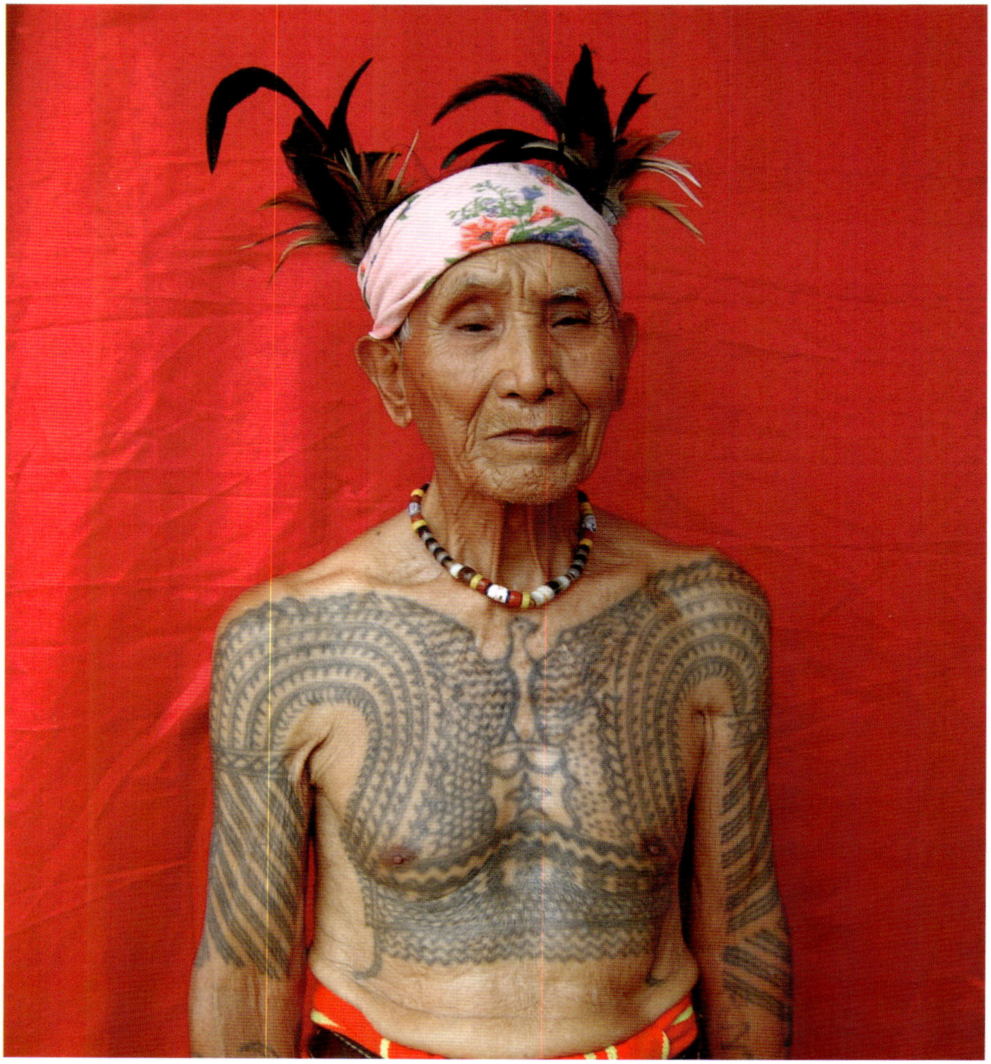

FIGURE 3.34

Kalinga warrior Lakay Dilag at the Batok "Tattoo" Festival, 2004. The overall composition of a Kalinga man's *bikking* (chest tattoo) represents the outstretched wings of the predatorial eagle, or "King of Birds." The Kalinga tattooist Apo Whang-Od Oggay told me the eagle was an oracle bird and messenger of the Creator Kabuniyan. By wearing this potent design, men like Dilag attempted to harness the eagle's power and become birdlike as they swooped down on their human prey with great speed and agility before making a kill. Dilag and other World War II veterans incorporated Western iconography of the eagle into their hard-earned body tattoos, the source of which was coinage minted during the American period featuring the eagle standing on a shield with the stars and stripes of the American flag (Krutak 2010a:101). © Andy Maluche.

As Barton noted, there was a traditional ranking system that dictated who could receive a tattoo and who could not. However, these customs seem to have been relaxed after World War II. For example, some of the tattooed Kalinga World War II veterans I interviewed in 2007 and 2008 wore a belt of tattoos on their belly, yet none of them claimed more than five victories in combat. Also, several of these men told me they were first tattooed on the chest and once that was completed then their arms were decorated later.

Obviously, these and other transformations in Kalinga tattoo culture were largely due to the historical shift that was taking place at that time; the social and religious imperative to take heads had ended in Kalinga. Great men no longer needed human heads to establish their status and position in their respective communities because less violent avenues for leadership emerged in the form of education, politics, government service, and wealth in such forms as rice fields and livestock (Krutak 2010a:120).

Notwithstanding, those Kalinga men who possessed tattoos continued to play an important role in village life. As a warrior grew older, he became a respected *lakay* (elder) and acted as a consultant in *budongs* (peace pacts) between other villages and tribal groups. Because of his distinguished record, he was looked on as an aggressive personality and persuasive arbiter skilled in the art of negotiation. His hard-won tattoos were a permanent record of his victories, and just as people were afraid of such men, they were equally proud to be identified with them. This was because a regional population enjoyed high status and security if it could count among its people men of warrior rank who were the "soul-force" of the community (Krutak 2010a:121).

THE PINTADOS OF VISAYAS: BRIEF RELATIONS (1595–1668)

Little information survives regarding the tattooing practices and associated beliefs regarding traditional tattooing of the Philippines' central islands (i.e., Leyte, Samar, Panay, Negros, Bohol, Bantayan, etc.). Here, Spanish colonial occupation began in the late sixteenth century when conquistadors and clergy used military strength and Christian worship to compel the Indigenous Peoples to assimilate Spanish cultural values. By the mid-1700s, Indigenous tattooing had nearly vanished from this vast insular domain.[37]

The earliest recorded historical accounts related to tattooing in the central islands were written in the sixteenth century.[38] These Spanish chronicles focused on the tattooed Visayans (also Bisayan) whom they called the Pintados (the Painted Ones), after the permanent markings they carried on their bodies. Writers were fascinated by these local customs and numerous brief reports describe these traditions. Writing about 1595, the Jesuit priest Pedro Chirino (1969:253) was "astonished" by the beauty of these indelible traditions, writing: "If they brought it to Europe a great deal of money could be made by displaying it." In 1691, the English buccaneer William Dampier did just that; he purchased a "Painted Prince" named Jeoly from the former Philippine island of Miangis and displayed him for profit in London. Sadly, this heavily tattooed man, whose markings were more similar in form to those of Micronesia, and more specifically to the Palauan Island of Merir (see Kotondo 1928) and other isles in the Sonsorol group (Krutak 2013d), died shortly after he arrived from smallpox.

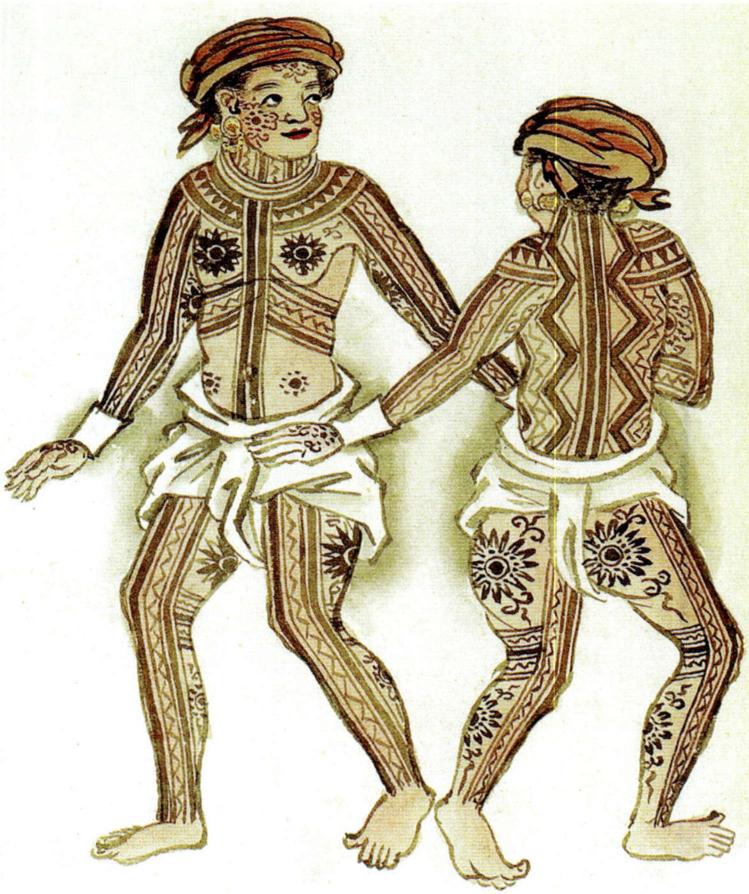

FIGURE 3.35
Tattooed Pintados or Visayans as illustrated in the Boxer Codex, ca. 1590.

Visayan men, who were great warriors and headhunters, endured painful *batuk* or *patik* (tattooing) because each mark related to some brave deed (W. H. Scott 1994:20; cf. Sánchez 1711:71, 402). According to Jesuit priest Francisco Alcina, who lived for more than forty years in Samar and Leyte (1632–1674), men were first marked around the age of twenty and the most renowned warriors displayed cheek tattooing "up to the eyelids" with other marks extending to the forehead and temples (Alcina [1668] 1960:58–59). He noted that Visayan tattooists were male and allowed leeway to display their unique skills. Designs were first stenciled on the skin before they were tattooed with a variety of perpendicularly hafted comblike instruments featuring needles bound at right angles; they were "snapped" or rather hand-tapped by the operator. After the wounds were inflicted, a sooty and odorous pitch derived from tree resin of the *lawá'an* tree (genuses *Shorea* and *Pentacme*) was rubbed into the wounds to create bold and permanent tattoos (Mintz 2011).

Alcina noted tattooists were well-paid for their services, especially those who were very skilled at producing "exquisite" and well-proportioned designs, linework, circular elements, and other motifs. In sum, a completed body suit resembled a form of "armor" covering the back, chest, abdomen, arms, and legs (Alcina [1668] 1960:60).

The Jesuit priest Father Matheo Sánchez (1711:402), who was active in the Philippines in the early 1600s, recorded the Bisayan word *mamatatic* [*mamapatik*] for tattooist. He recorded various other tattooing terms, including *labid* (straight or zigzagging linework of the legs); *ablay* (shoulder markings) or "Sun band"; *dubdub* (chest markings); *dayadaya* (arm tattoos); and *bangut*, referring to a man's facial tattoos placed "up to his eyes" that resembled the beak of a bird of prey or the "gaping" jaws of a crocodile (Sánchez 1711:61, 110, 163, 179).

Alcina [1668] 1960:58) and others mentioned if a man did not receive tattooing, he would be considered a coward by his peers: "He would suffer badly from enemy spears if he didn't have the spirit to suffer the needles of the tattooist." Moreover, if a man received warrior tattooing but had not first proved himself in battle by defeating an enemy, it was believed he would become *sibóng* or ill and perhaps he might die (Mintz 2011).

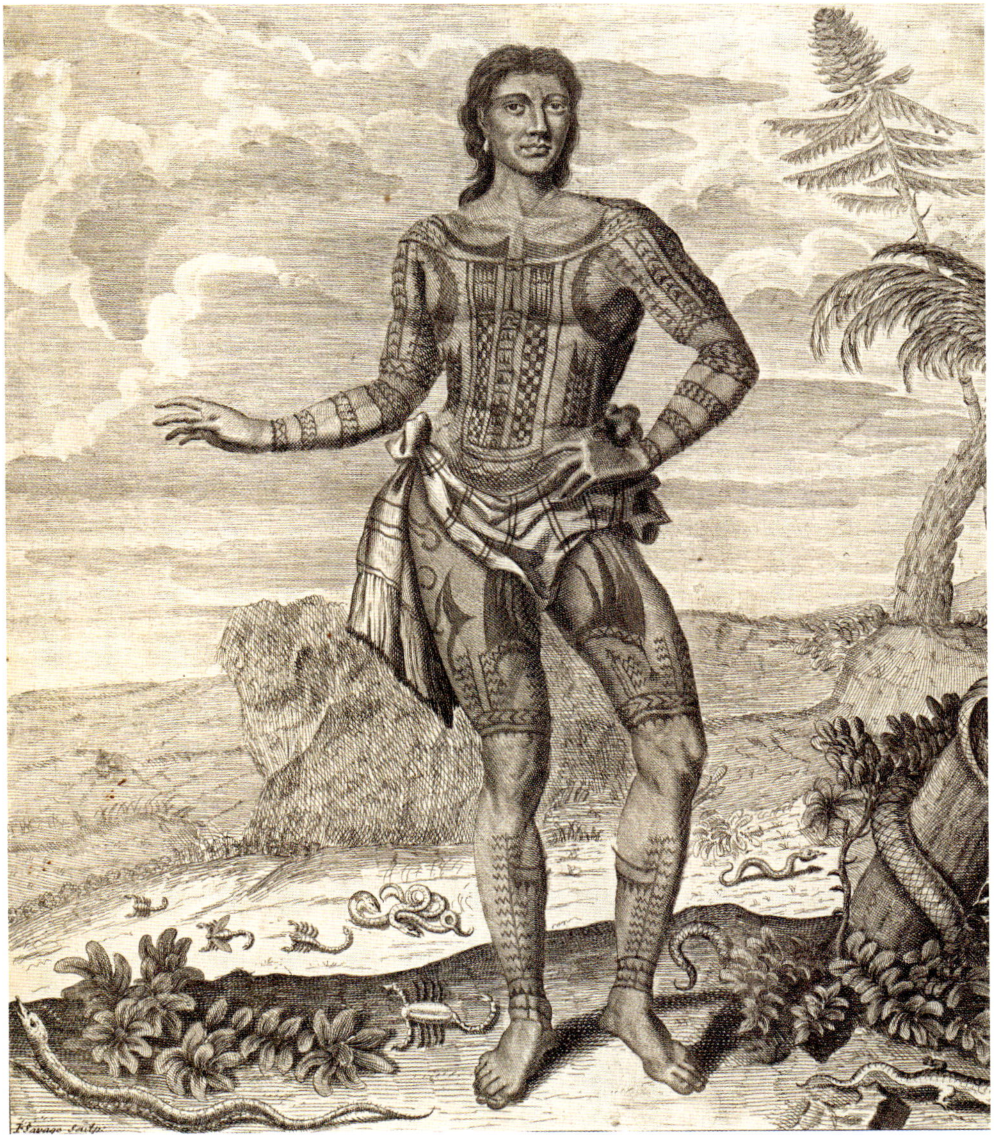

FIGURE 3.36

The "Painted Prince" Jeoly, 1692. Jeoly was born on Miangis Island, which lies some seventy kilometers southeast of Mindanao. He was later purchased as a slave by the English buccaneer William Dampier and eventually brought to England in 1691 as a sideshow attraction in a moneymaking scheme. Three months after his arrival, however, he died of smallpox. A portion of his tattooed skin was preserved and hung in Oxford University's Bodleian Library for centuries until it was lost. Collection of State Library of New South Wales, Australia.

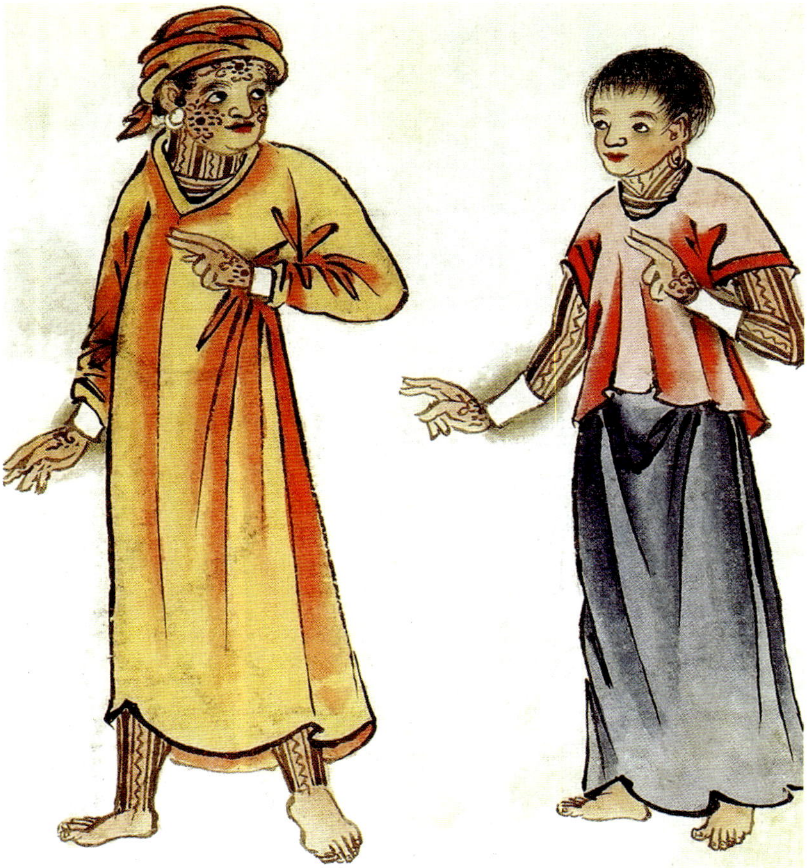

FIGURE 3.37
Tattooed male and female Pintados or Visayans as illustrated in the Boxer Codex, ca. 1590.

I have not discovered any direct proof of taboos associated with the act of tattooing or the seclusion period. However, omen forecasting was practiced by the Visayans before military engagements and other activities.[39] The Spanish soldier Miguel de Loarca recorded in 1582–1583 that the Pintados believed sneezing on leaving one's house was considered a "bad omen," and men heading to war, or those about to begin any important undertaking, immediately turned back in such cases (Blair and Robertson 1903:165). As noted among the Cordilleran people of Luzon, sneezing during the tattooing rite was a bad omen. Thus, it is possible this belief also held for the Pintados.

Due to the breadth of male tattooing, Alcina noted that male tattoo clients recuperated in seclusion for a period of "nine or ten days" (Alcina [1668] 1960:60). Sometimes infections, which were believed to be caused by malevolent spirits of the wind, would result in inflammation and fevers from which some men died (Mintz 2011; cf. Alcina [1668] 2002:145).

According to Alcina and others, women were lightly marked in comparison, receiving delicate tattoos resembling fine embroidery only on their hands up to the wrist. However, an illustration from the Boxer Codex displays a woman with full arm tattoos and others around the neck, and she may have possessed additional tattoos on her torso.

The linguist Malcolm Mintz has provided several Visayan tattooing terms and associated concepts concerning his study of Father Marcos de Lisboa's *Vocabulario de la Lengua Bicol* (1754). This work was based on Father Lisboa's nine-year residence (1602–1611) with the Pintados in the Bikol region of southernmost Luzon. Lisboa noted that tattooing was initiated on the ankle or instep and continued up the leg to the groin. He recorded the term *tiláng-tiláng* as the starting point for tattooing that resulted in *labíd:* full leg and thigh tattoos (Mintz 2011). In Bikol, *túrob* referred to a person tattooed from the waist down, including his thighs and buttocks. Other tattooing terms included *binanóg* (chest tattoos), *tadtád* (the word for "tattoo"), and two words, *lípong* and *táwo-táwo,* that were used in general reference to fully tattooed men.

A prominent male motif seen in illustrations from the anonymously authored Boxer Codex (ca. 1595) depicts rosettes worn about the aureoles that have been described as "floral" designs but may also have been heliolatrous (see comment above and below regarding the *ablay* shoulder motif). Today, similar tattoos continue to adorn the nipples of Talaandig, Pantaron, and Talaingod Manobo elders in Mindanao and live on as *panubok*, or embroidery, among the Panay Bukidnon (Muyco 2016). *Panubok* is featured on men's and women's garments and points to an earlier tradition of Visayan or Pintado body tattooing, although Panay Bukidnon elders also carry tattoo markings today.

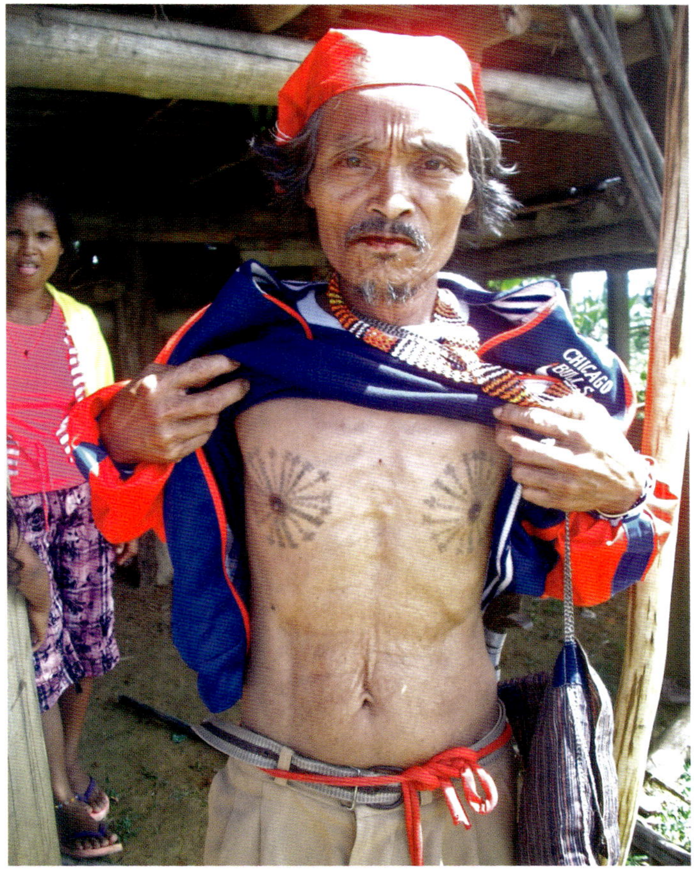

FIGURE 3.38
Talaandig Manobo man displaying elaborate nipple tattoos, 2012. Courtesy of James Mascariñas.

The ethnomusicologist and composer Maria Christine Muyco (2016:71) observes that both forms of personal ornamentation, which seemingly overlap, should be linked to local perceptions of cosmology. For the Panay Bukidnon, the iconography of embroidery maintains a role in the balance and function of their universe and activities. In *panubok*, triangular *girgiti* (teethlike) patterns embroidered below the neckline of women's garments are likened to the sun or upper cosmos, similar to Father Sánchez's findings regarding the *ablay* or "Sun band" tattoo pattern adorning the collars and upper chests of Pintado men. Muyco explains that below this realm dwell the creatures of the air or those that have wings like the bee and *banog* (hawk-eagle), which are sometimes embroidered into the cloth. Remarkably, and on review of Father Lisboa's tattoo vocabulary, the word *binanóg* refers to the chest tattoos of the Pintado warrior, whereas in the Panay Bukidnon (Visayan) language *binanog* refers to the hawk-eagle dance tradition. With this correlation, I would like to suggest that the composite chest tattoo of the Pintado warrior represented *in toto* the outstretched wings of this avian predator, an etiology comparable to the *bikking* of the Kalinga warriors of northern Luzon.

Floral tattoo motifs surrounding the nipples of Pintado men and oblique "stripes" running above the waistline are also mimicked in the embroidered floraform patterns of the Panay Bukidnon; these represent the "middle space" of the cosmos. The bottom sections of embroidered cloth represent the lower realms of the universe, places where creatures of the sea, land, and underground dwell. Here, zigzagging serpent or reptilian designs (i.e., the crocodile's pointed teeth) form the *panubok*'s baseline motifs (Muyco 2016:72), which can be likened to the leg tattoo patterns of the Pintado warrior seen in the Boxer Codex.

ORACION TATTOOS

Unfortunately, we do not know for certain if any magical or religious significance was attached to the tattoos of the Pintados. Did they possess tattoos related to spirit guardians, or to promote fertility, or were they required for safe passage into the afterlife? We may never receive answers to these and other questions, but today there are forms of supernatural tattoos that continue to be made in some areas of the central Philippines; these are called *oracion* or *anting-anting* marks and are derived from Latin prayers of the Catholic liturgy. It is not known how or when this liturgical language of the early missionaries became permanently attached to human skin via tattoo, but the practice itself seemingly points to an underlying system of pre-Christian Indigenous belief whereby in antiquity tattoos offered some form of personal power to those individuals who possessed them. Indeed, the Philippine writer Dennis Villegas (2017:viii) recently observed that this belief stems from an ancient Indigenous spiritual tradition. "Our ancestors endowed nature with supernatural powers and developed a comprehensive belief system that bound all phenomena in the human, natural, and spiritual realms in a causal relationship," he wrote. "So strong is this originary [Indigenous] worldview that it resisted the forced inculcation of foreign religious concepts."

The Roman Catholic priests Daniel Scheans and Karl Hutterer (1970:29) and Richard Arens (1957) were some of the earliest scholars to have explored these traditions, relating that *oracion* tattoos are magical formulas tattooed on the skin that compel the supernatural to act on the human world in specific ways. In essence, they are tattooed amulets (*pancontra, sumpa, hapin sa lawas*) that either shield the body from harm or provide magical protection (Scheans and Hutterer 1970:29). In short, the *oracion* tattooed amulet "protect[s] one from all sort of dangers, accidents and [the] bad intentions of others" (Arens 1957:116).

Traditionally, *oracion* tattoos are applied by a *tambalan*, a kind of shamanic medicinal practitioner of the Samar-Letye area. The *tambalan* who provided Scheans and Hutterer (1970:31) with their primary information noted that the *oracion* tattoo must be completed on a Friday; this was accompanied by prayers that were offered on consecutive Fridays. Tattoo ink was derived from an inkstone and the tool was a simple configuration of two needles bound together with wound thread. The desired *oracion* text was stenciled on the skin with a matchstick dipped into the ink. Typically, the first and last word of the *oracion* was tattooed in full, but the other words appeared in abbreviated form (i.e., two letters only). The *tambalan* pricked over each letter twice with his implement, and the tattoos might be placed on the upper arms, lower legs, upper back, hands, and breast (Arens 1957:116).

Scheans and Hutterer (1970:35) provided a listing of the various powers attributed to the *oraciones*. I provide these via paraphrased format as follows: *oraciones* for protection in fighting; for safe walking (in the forest, etc.); for general protection; for healing wounds; for protection against poison; for easy delivery of newborns; for protection against snakes; to cure a child "sick" of fright; for winning a fight in court; for winning a woman's heart; for protection against witchcraft, sorcery, and/or *barang* (black magic); and those magical tattoos for *encantados*, or harmful spirits, who appear in the guise of a handsome man or woman. More recent studies have added to this list: tattoos that deflect bullets, paralyze an attacker, exorcise an evil spirit from the body, or protect one against blades that cut (Villegas 2017:75).

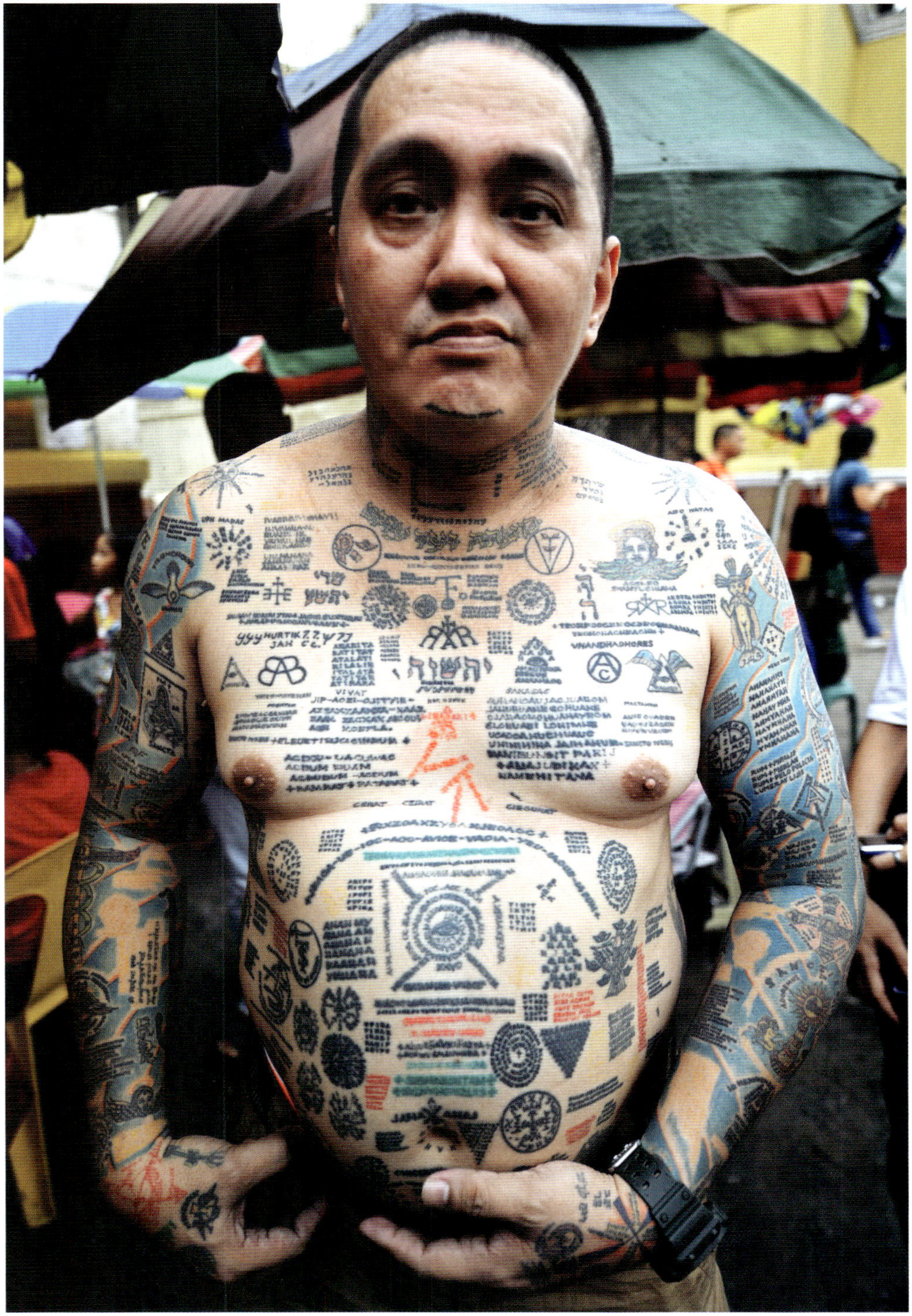

FIGURE 3.39
Oracion tattoos, 2013.
© Sidney Snoeck.

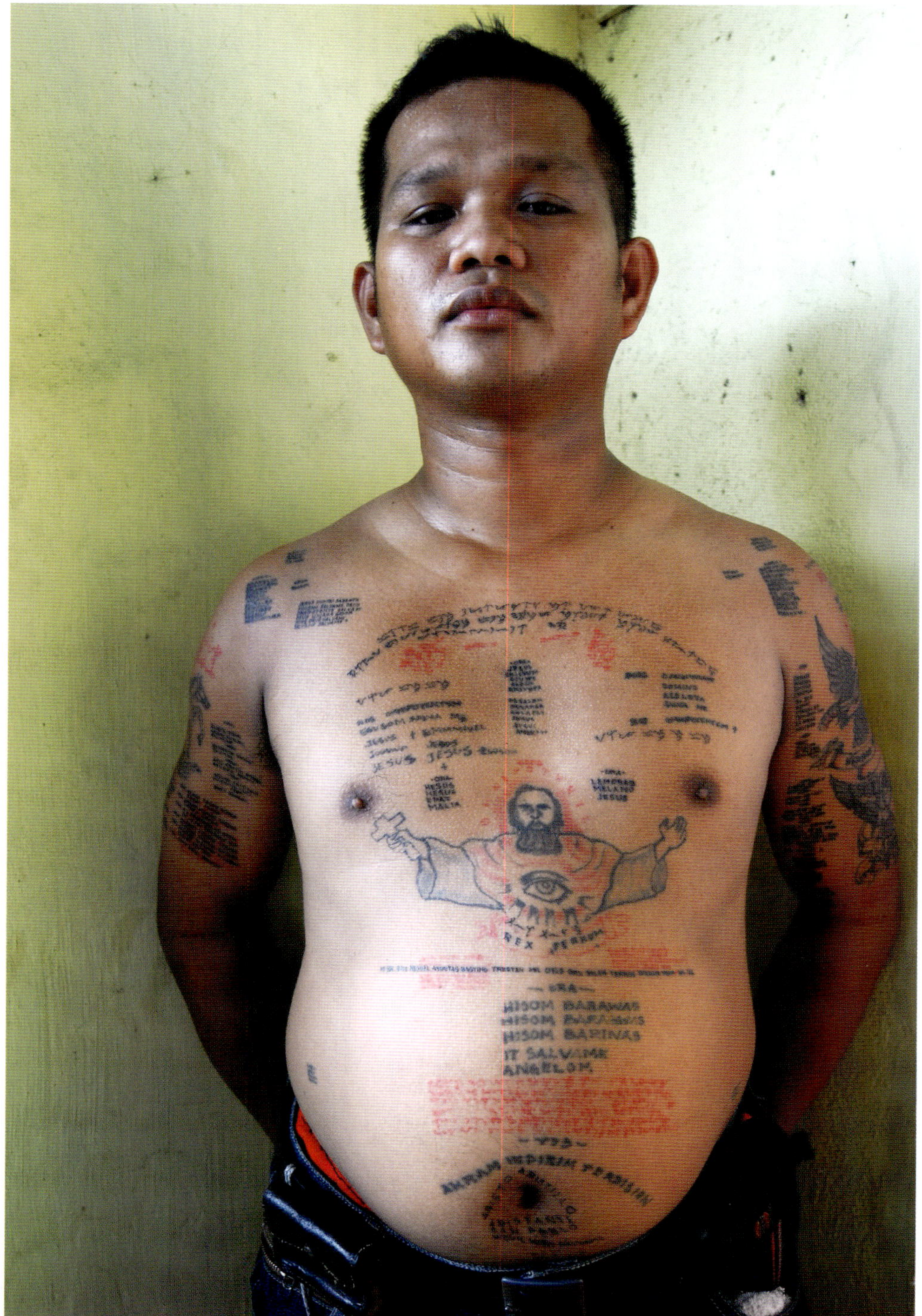

FIGURE 3.40
Oracion tattoos, 2013.
© Sidney Snoeck.

The question as to why *oraciones* came to find a home on people's skin is not perfectly understood. However, individuals who believe in the power of these amulets usually carry them first on a piece of paper in their pocket, but if the paper becomes lost, so too does the power of the *oracion*. Thus, and to not lose it, people began tattooing the prayers on their bodies, making them part of their person forever.[40] This tradition reminds me of a similar practice in Borneo, whereby Indigenous Peoples such as the Kayan, Kenyah, and others once wore a *lukut* (antique bead) around their wrist to keep their soul "close" to the body. Since the bead could become lost, it became a tattooing motif instead.[41]

Father John Rich (1968) also described a similar tattooing tradition among a sect of the Catholic Apostolic Church of the Holy Spirit in Mati, Davao Oriental, in southeastern Mindanao. Known as the *Pinatikan* because of the importance attached to *patik*, religious tattoos, sect members derive their marks from five books containing 360 prayers. Like *oracion* tattoos, the primary powers attributed to the markings are personal protection from harm and curing afflictions, provided that the bearer leads a somewhat ascetic life free of vices (Rich 1968:196). More specifically, the tattoos can be broken down into nine general categories: (1) physical sickness; (2) mental sickness; (3) preventive medicine; (4) self-defense; (5) defense against nature and natural phenomena; (6) defense against animals and insects; (7) supernatural; (8) moral; and (9) miscellaneous.

According to Father Rich, the motifs represent saints, religious symbols, and abbreviated prayers placed across the body. Each tattoo is associated with a particular Latin or pseudo-Latin phrase that must be memorized and recited daily (Rich 1968:196).[42]

MINDANAO

Apart from the pseudo-Christian tattooing rites of the *Pinatikan*, widespread Indigenous tattooing traditions survive today in the southern island of Mindanao. Unfortunately, the documentation of body marking practices here among the T'boli, Banwaon, Manobo, Talaandig, and other groups is limited, and this result is due in large part to the inaccessibility of the local terrain, general disinterest in the topic by early ethnographers, and more recently to Communist (New People's Army) and Islamic insurgents (Moro Islamic Revolutionary Front) who have been active across Mindanao's tribal areas for several decades. In turn, the Philippine Army has restricted visitation to certain tribal areas where tattooing persists, making it nearly impossible to record and document detailed information related to traditional tattooing practices that are on the verge of disappearing.

I would like to note here that some of the information and imagery presented below is derived from preliminary research and documentary photography performed by collaborators who have had some access to these highly restricted areas. Although their work raises more questions than it answers, I feel it is important to include this very cursory research and imagery to share with you the great diversity and beauty of the Indigenous tattooing traditions of Mindanao, which are not widely known outside of the Philippines themselves. Hopefully, more fieldwork can soon be conducted to shed light on these important traditions that are part of our world's (in)tangible cultural heritage and human history.

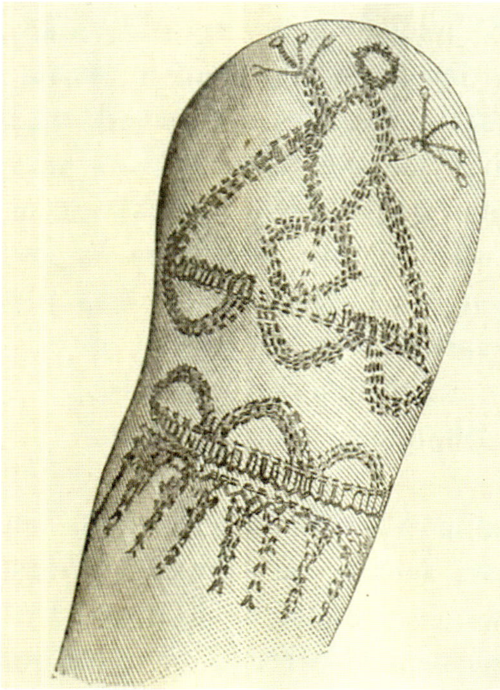

FIGURE 3.41
Bagobo upper arm tattoo applied by a traveling Pantaron Manobo artist via the incision technique. From Schadenberg 1885: 10, fig. 1.

Perhaps the best-documented tattooing culture of Mindanao is that of various Manobo groups, who inhabit lowland areas of Agusan Province and more mountainous areas toward the southwest. One of the earliest sources to mention Manobo tattooing did so inadvertently. Before his journeys across the Philippine Cordillera of Luzon, the German traveler Alexander Schadenberg visited Mindanao between December 1881 and May 1882, during which time he observed the tattooing of Indigenous Bagobo youth near Mount Apo, Davao del Sur Province. The Bagobo were tattooed by traveling "Ata" Manobo tattooists. The term "Ata" or "Atas" has been deployed in the ethnographic literature to broadly refer to the Pantaron Manobo, whereas the Bagobo are a separate ethnolinguistic group (Ragragio and Paluga 2019:263). Schadenberg (1885:10) related that tattooing was associated with the onset of puberty among boys and girls and that the technique used to create the permanent markings was a form of skin cut or scarification tattooing: "With a small, semicircular knife, which they call *Sagni*, they make rather deep incisions in the stretched skin, and rub soot from charred bamboo into the wounds after one hundred cuts have been made." The resulting design, which Schadenberg illustrated in his brief account, includes semicircles, cascading lines, and an anthropomorphic or animal figure (monitor lizard?) with arms and hands outstretched. Schadenburg did not record any further information, apart from aftercare that is unrevealing, although many later sources record the word *pangottob* (Manuel 1962:163) for Bagobo tattooing, one that is very similar to that employed by the Pantaron Manobo, *pangotoeb* (Ragragio and Paluga 2019).

Other early sources focus on the Manobo of Agusan Province, wherein these writers emphasize that body marking was practiced largely for decorative purposes or "ornamentation" (Garvan 1931:56; van Odijk 1925:990). However, in my research with more than fifty Indigenous tattooing societies worldwide, I have learned that it was altogether rare that these peoples tattooed for simple aesthetic purposes. Tattoos were far more important than mere decoration because they related significant information concerning tribal identity, social achievements, and rites of passage ceremonies, as well as spiritual beliefs, among other things.

Notwithstanding, the American anthropologist John Garvan and Dutch missionary Father Antonius van Odijk both related that men and women were tattooed at the time of puberty, but they did not specifically correlate tattooing itself to rites of passage. Each author described two distinct techniques for creating the tattoos: hand-poking and skin-cut tattooing. More specifically, Garvan (1931:56) related that artists were transgendered "women" who had also acquired skills in embroidery. To manufacture the required pigment, the tattooist held a plate or *olla* over a burning torch of tree resin derived from *sai-yung* (*Canarium villosum*). No stencil was laid on the skin and the operator proceeded to puncture the skin with small cuts from an unidentified implement, although it must be assumed it was bladed. The flowing blood was wiped away with a bunch of

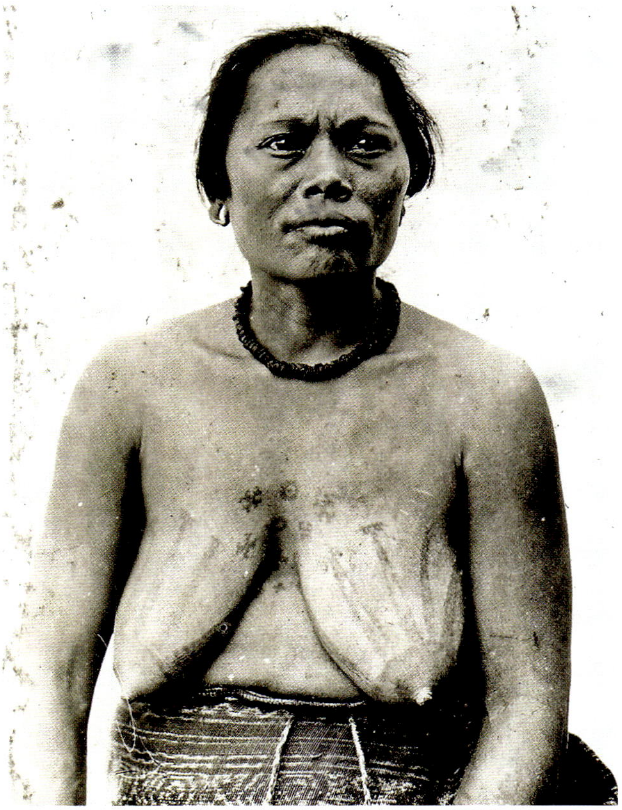

FIGURE 3.42
Agusan Manobo women's tattooing, ca. 1910. From Garvan 1931: pl. 1.

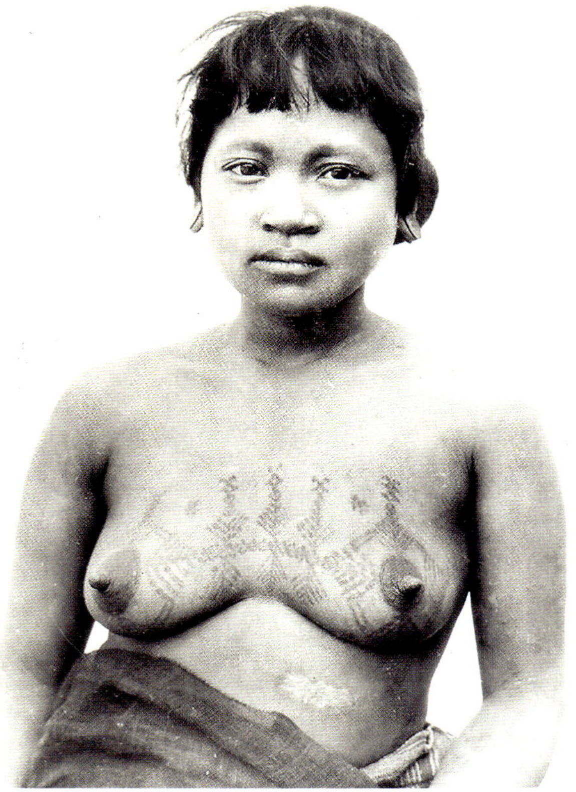

FIGURE 3.43
Agusan Manobo women's tattooing, ca. 1910. From Garvan 1931: pl. 1.

leaves, then soot was vigorously rubbed into the wounds, resulting in a pigmented *pang-o-túb* tattoo (Garvan 1931:56). Van Odijk described a tattoo "bundle" consisting of three needles bound together to form a tool. A thread was wound about the needles up to their tips to control the depth of the punctures. The tattooist worked from memory and did not use a stencil. After the skin was pierced, a sooty tattoo pigment derived from the resin of the *dongon-dongon* tree was rubbed into the wound (van Odijk 1925:992). Van Odijk also mentioned that tattoo patterns could be removed if they were vigorously rubbed with mother's milk.

Agusan Manobo men and women were marked on the chest, upper arms, forearms, and fingers, whereas the latter gender might also receive tattoos on the calves and legs. Garvan described a seemingly "endless" plethora of designs, whereas van Odijk (1925:992) noted that the patterns resembled embroidery motifs consisting of "diamonds," "squares," and "asterisks." Garvan featured photographs of two tattooed women and van Odijk provided illustrations of various unnamed

FIGURE 3.44
Agusan Manobo men's chest tattooing and calf marks worn by women, ca. 1900. From van Odijk 1925: figs. 6–8.

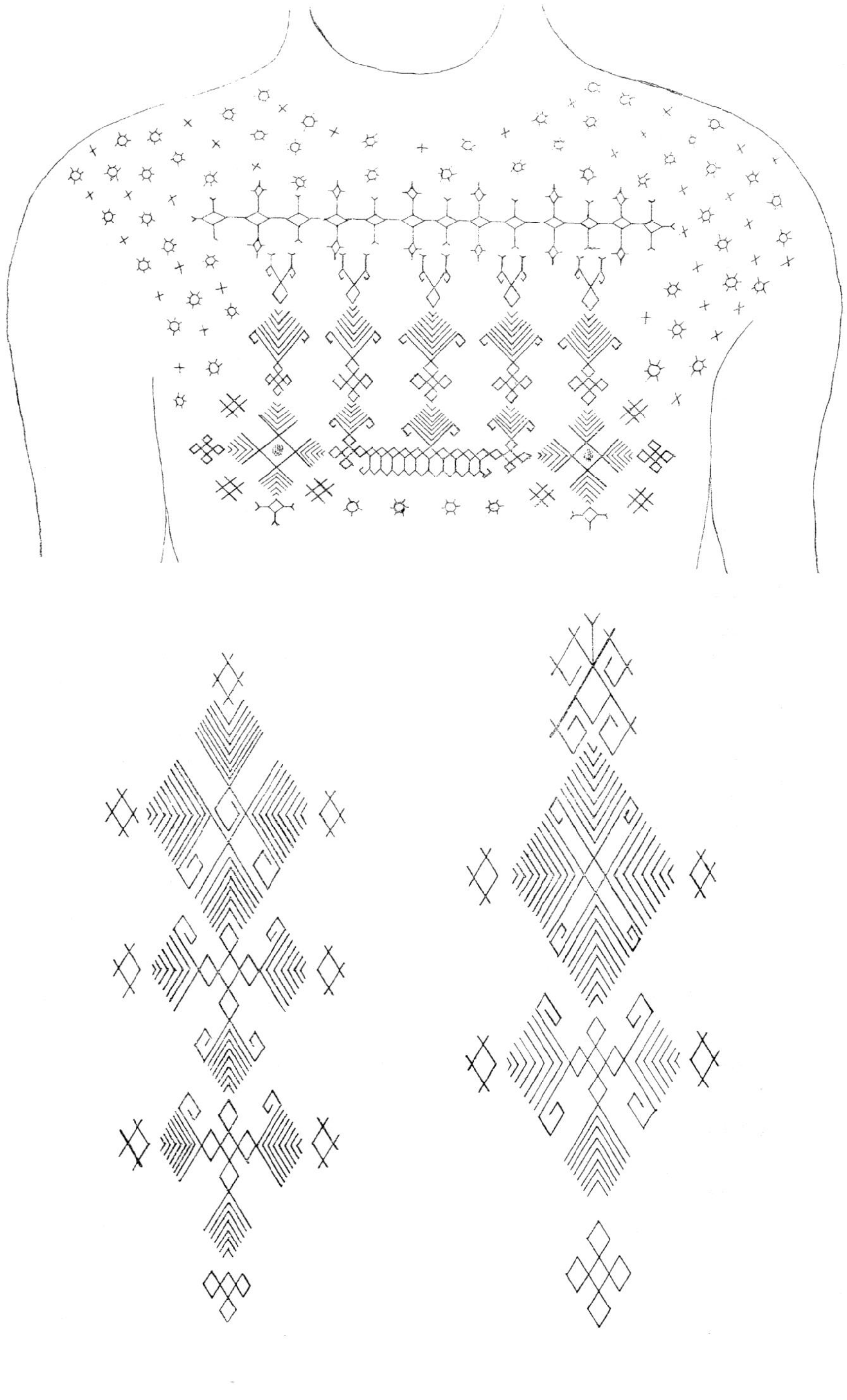

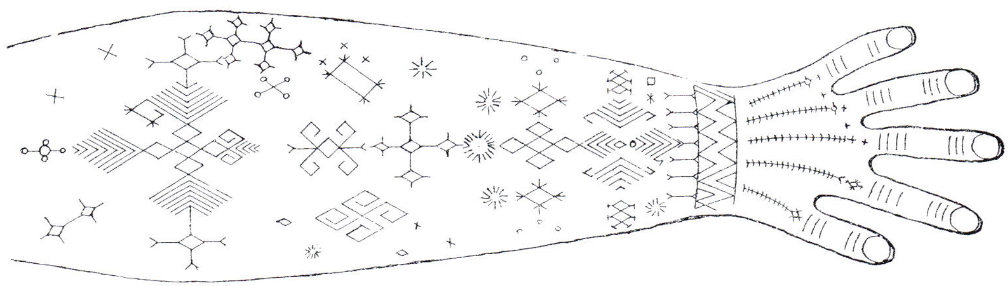

FIGURE 3.45
Agusan Manobo women's arm tattooing, ca. 1900. From van Odijk 1925:992, fig. 9.

tattoos worn by men and women. Although Garvan (1931:57) named a few of the motifs (i.e., *bin-u-á-ja* [from *bu-wá-ja*, crocodile], *gin-í-bang* [from *gí-bang*, iguana], and *bin-ú-yo* [from *bú-jo*, the betel leaf]), he did not specify or illustrate where they were placed on the body.

Another early source (Johnson 1913) briefly mentions and illustrates Agusan Manobo tattoos and relates that certain motifs were associated with heavenly bodies: stars, planets, and the sun. The illustrations are not attributed to a primary source, and the passage abruptly ends as follows, stating that "all" of the tattoos pictured here "have some religious significance."

Garvan hinted that particular "localities" employed specific patterns that differed from other areas. To me, this implies that the Manobo tattoos documented by Garvan were distinctive tribal identity markers that could be read by others. Garvan (1931:57) was impressed by the artistry of the Manobo tattooist, commenting that their "durability . . . can not be surpassed." When he compared tattooing marks on young men with those on the bodies of elders he proclaimed: "I could not discern any difference in the brightness nor in the preservation of the design[s]."

In 2012, one of my colleagues, James Mascariñas, photographed several tattooed Banwaon and Talaandig elders in Agusan Province. Although he was not able to record any patterns or associated meanings, the tattoos were cut in with a bladed tool and their coloration was very clear and bright. One Banwaon man displayed tattooed rosettes around his nipples very similar in style to those worn by Pintado men recorded in the circa 1595 Boxer Codex. The photographer Vincent Go also captured similarly oriented tattoos on the chest of an elderly Talaingod Manobo Datu of Davao del Norte Province. These rosette tattoos "reflect his accomplishments and status in the community" (Go 2014).

The filmmaker Alyx Ayn Arumpac's photodocumentary *Burdado: The Manobos of Arakan* (2012) questions the accuracy of Garvan's ethnographic reportage through the words and images of tattooed Manobo elders and tribal leaders. In this documentary, Datu Antayan Baguio, the leader of the Tinananon Manobo of Tumanding, stated that the origins of tattoo, or *pang-o-túb*, are related to a mythological tale concerning the founder of the tribe, Apo Tulalang: "This ancestor, before he traveled to the heavens, told us that we should tattoo so that we would not forget him, and also to reaffirm our Manobo identities while we wait for him to return to earth. These tattoos are also believed to illuminate our path into the afterlife," a belief that is shared by other Manobo

FIGURE 3.46
Talaingod Manobo elder whose nipple tattoos resemble those of Visayan Pintados illustrated in the sixteenth century, 2014. Davao del Norte Province, Mindanao. © Vincent Go.

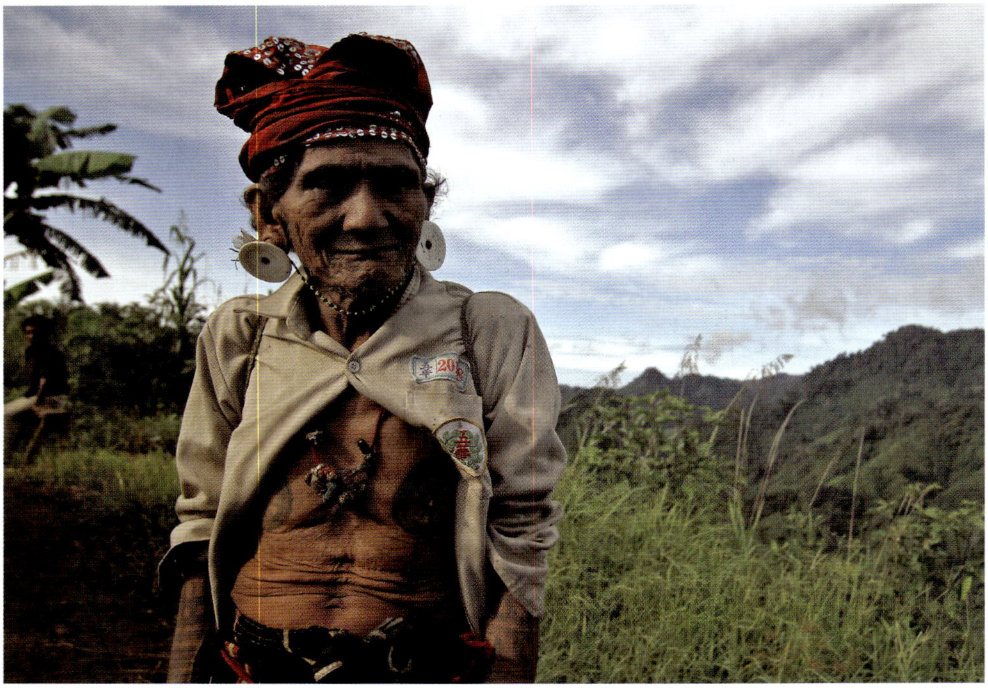

FIGURE 3.47
Belly tattooing of a Pantaron Manobo female elder, 2015. © Andrea Malaya M. Ragragio.

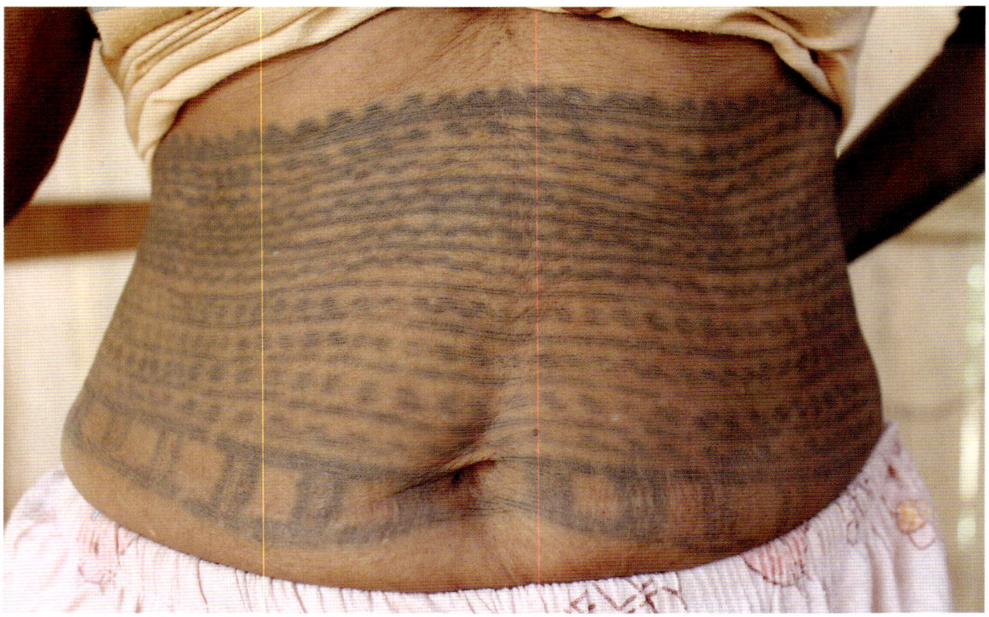

tribes, such as the Pantaron and the Tigwahonon Manobo (Bajo 2004:42; Lagsa 2014), as well as the T'boli (Casal 1978). "When you die, everything is dark. But the tattoo is like a light that will take you to where your ancestors are," Datu Baguio explained. He also reaffirmed that tattoos were identity markers: "When you have a tattoo, it means that you *really* are a Native" (Arumpac 2012).

Before a tattoo was given, a prayer was offered to Manama, the God of the Tinananon Manobo. Tattoos were then cut into the skin with a sharp *burong* (knife), and charred bark from the *lawaan* (lauan) tree was pounded into a powder and then mixed with water to create pigment (Arumpac 2012). After the incisions were made, the ink was vigorously rubbed into the skin cuts and worn for one week before it was washed away. As previously noted, early Spanish chroniclers in Visayas recorded that soot derived from the *lawá'an* tree (genuses *Shorea* and *Pentacme*) was used by the Pintados for tattooing pigment.

Manobo elders interviewed by Arumpac explained that tattoos provided Manobo individuals with strength: "They say a tattooed Manobo does not tire easily, even after a whole day's work in the fields" (Arumpac 2012). Other Manobo groups of Agusan have stated that the various patterns tattooed on their bodies helped to repel evil spirits and bad luck.[43]

The apotropaic aspects of local tattooing customs seem plausible, especially when considered with weaving practices. Among the tattooed Bagobo and B'laan people, whose tattoos closely resemble those of the Banwaon and Agusan Manobo groups, heavily embroidered garments containing patterns that are also seen in their tattoos are adorned with protective motifs. Surface embellishments and evil-averting designs are worn as close to human skin as possible because these garments are believed to embody individual spirits that offer protective power to the wearer (Dhamija 2004:327). Since tattoos are worn *within* the skin and are permanent, I presume one of the reasons they continue to exist today in remote regions is due to their amuletic potency. Moreover, Laura Watson Benedict's (1916:206) study of Bagobo ritual attire and ceremonialism revealed that numerous amulets, including any type of closed circle (bracelet, leglet, waistband, textile pattern, and, by extension, circular tattoo patterns), were employed by the people to form a protective barrier against evil influences. She also noted that representations of crocodiles (in weavings, carvings, paintings, etc.), which Garvan noted was a primary tattoo symbol for the Agusan Manobo, would "fill the demons with fear" (Benedict 1916:209).

Other Manobo groups possessed intricate incised tattoos. Matigsalug Manobo women wear such markings on their abdomens that were received during their first pregnancy. One elder, Vilma Mandanuay, explained to Arumpac (2012), "The flesh is more taut while you are pregnant, so it hurts less. Tattooing is a ritual passed down from our ancestors and this identifies us as members of the tribe. You aren't fully a woman unless you have these tattoos." A related tattooing tradition was practiced by the Tigwahonon Manobo of Bukidnon.

According to the photojournalist Bobby Lagsa (2014), Bae Norita Gabao is perhaps the last actively practicing *pangotoeb* maker of her tribe. She learned the art from her grandmother, Bae Kulotan, who marked her belly in youth with a kind of map that records "the seasons, stars and moons and even the road leading to their mountains." Norita added that *pangotoeb* is a holy mark because Magbabaya, the Creator, "will accept you in the afterlife if you bear the mark of the tribe" (Lagsa 2014).

FIGURE 3.48
Banwaon Manobo woman displaying extensive arm and hand tattooing, 2012. Courtesy of James Mascariñas.

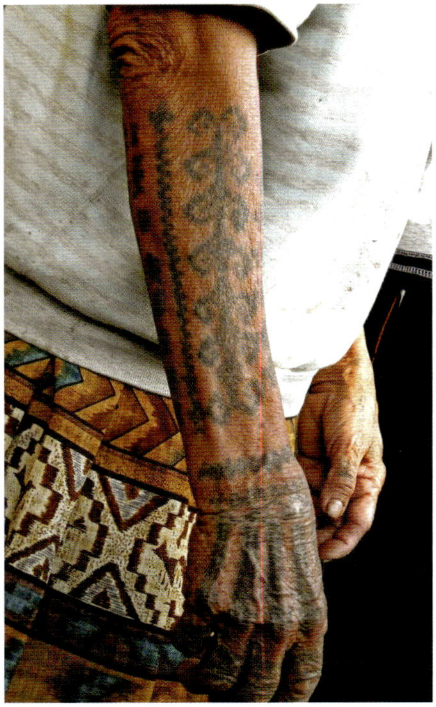

Like Matigsalug women, Tigwahonon women received the painful cuts on their abdomen, but others also received *pangotoeb* on their breasts—a *bulan*, or moon, pattern that was a sign of fertility (Lagsa 2014). Norita noted that prayers and a chicken are offered to Magbabaya before the tattooing to ensure a successful procedure. Her repertoire of motifs is inspired by the surrounding environment. "Planting season, the stars to guide us, the *Kaingin*,[44] the rivers, the houses, and landmarks are prominent in my works," the *pangotoeb* artist said (Lagsa 2014).

Researchers have recently interviewed other living Manobo tattooists. Perhaps the most detailed and systematic study on Mindanao's Indigenous tattooing traditions was published by the researchers Andrea Ragragio and Myfel Paluga (2019). This work brings together the ethnographic literature on Mindanao tattooing and is based on the authors' intermittent fieldwork among the little-studied Pantaron Manobo between 2013 and 2015.

Among the Pantaron Manobo, *mangotoeb* (tattooists) could be male or female, although Ragragio and Paluga encountered only female practitioners in their study. However, male tattooers could tattoo only other males, because it was inappropriate for them to touch unrelated women. Future tattooists were cultivated in their youth by older relatives who were skilled in the practice. They closely observed how the *mangotoeb* worked, and eventually they began incising cassava peels or their age-mates to gain practice (Ragragio and Paluga 2019:270–271).

As a *mangotoeb*'s reputation spread by word of mouth, their skills were greatly desired by the communities they served. One Pantaron Manobo tattooer recalled the workload of her aunt, who mentored her in the profession: "So many people would come . . . sometimes as much as 10 [in a day]. And sometimes, she would do nothing else for two days but to tattoo" (Ragragio and Paluga 2019:271). Boys and girls typically received their first marks between the ages of eight and ten.

Payment usually consisted of beads, fiber leglets, and foodstuffs. If these tokens were not given to the tattooist, it was believed the *mangotoeb*'s eyesight would eventually fail. The Pantaron Manobo calls this preventative action "removing the blood from the *mangotoeb*'s eyes." As Ragragio and Paluga (2019:272) rightly observe, a similar tradition existed for the Kayan of Borneo whereby a *lasat mata* (small gift) was offered to the tattooist to "wipe the eyes clean" (Hose and McDougal 1912:253–254; Hose and Shelford 1906:69; Southwell 1990:127, 153), since it was against custom to draw the blood of a friend, relative, or community member without first offering a small gift to the tattooist. If the gift was not supplied, it was believed the Kayan practitioner would become blind, "and some misfortune would happen to the parents and relations of the girl undergoing the operation of tatu" (Hose and McDougal 1912:254).

This custom also reminds me of the Kalinga *sipat* tradition. After the Kalinga tattooist Apo Whang-Od asked me to tattoo her heavily veined hand with a *ginay-gayaman* (centipede) design, I made a *sipat* gesture to remove any taboos associated with inadvertently drawing blood in the village (Krutak 2010a:184). The *sipat* is like an exchange of peace tokens and begins with the sacrifice of a chicken, whose blood is rubbed near the injured body part. A brief chant is given to ward off any evil spirits, and then I placed an *arugo* (red carnelian bead) on a string around her wrist. This bead is also a protective device against malevolent spirits because it "pays off" any spirit in the vicinity.

I would also like to quickly draw the reader's attention back to the Kayan for a comparative footnote. The American traveler, writer, and ethnographer William H. Furness, who was tattooed by a Kayan woman, described preliminary tattoo rituals around the turn of the twentieth century, whereby beads were broadcast to spiritual entities to keep them at bay (Krutak 2007:88). He wrote:

> As an indispensable preliminary, before the skin is touched, several beads must be given the operator, who may not keep them all, but must hand over some to the 'Toh"—the demons who are always lurking about to see that the rules of the house are obeyed. It is *lali*[45] [taboo] to draw human blood in a house unless the Toh be previously informed that it is for a lawful purpose. Some of the beads are, therefore, flung broadcast out of doors, for the Toh to gather. (Furness 1902a:151–152)

Another tattoo taboo among the Pantaron and the Matigsalug Manobo focused on touching. Regarding the former, the tattoo client was forbidden from touching the tattoo operator, whereas among the latter it was not allowed for the tattooist to touch her client. "If you get a tattoo, you cannot grab on to me even if it is very painful," a tattooist explained to Ragragio and Paluga (2019:273). "If you grab [me, my] life is placed in danger [especially] if there is a[n enemy] raid, [I] will be the one taken, or killed," she said.

As previously described for other Manobo groups, Pantaron tattooers used a small curved *goppos* or *ilab* (knife) to incise the skin. Tattoo pigment was derived from the resin of the Manila copal tree (*Agathis philippinensis*), which is a large coniferous evergreen. It was ignited under a pot and the resulting soot was collected and mixed with water. Once the cuts were made, the pigment was rubbed into the wounds. As part of the healing process, an unidentified species of *kagopkop* (local epiphyte) was heated and applied to the tattooed skin to reduce itching and increase the intensity of the tattoos' coloration (Ragragio and Paluga 2019:277).

Tattoos marked the wrists, arms (up to the elbow), lower legs, breasts, abdomens, and backs of Pantaron Manobo women. Men usually wore patterns on their arms or chests (i.e., rosettes around the nipples) that resembled those of the Tigwahanon Manobo. Ragragio and Paluga (2019:280–281, figs. 8–10) provide an extensive repertoire of named patterns, and each one is derived from nature (a monitor lizard, a fern, and a medicinal grass) or objects made by

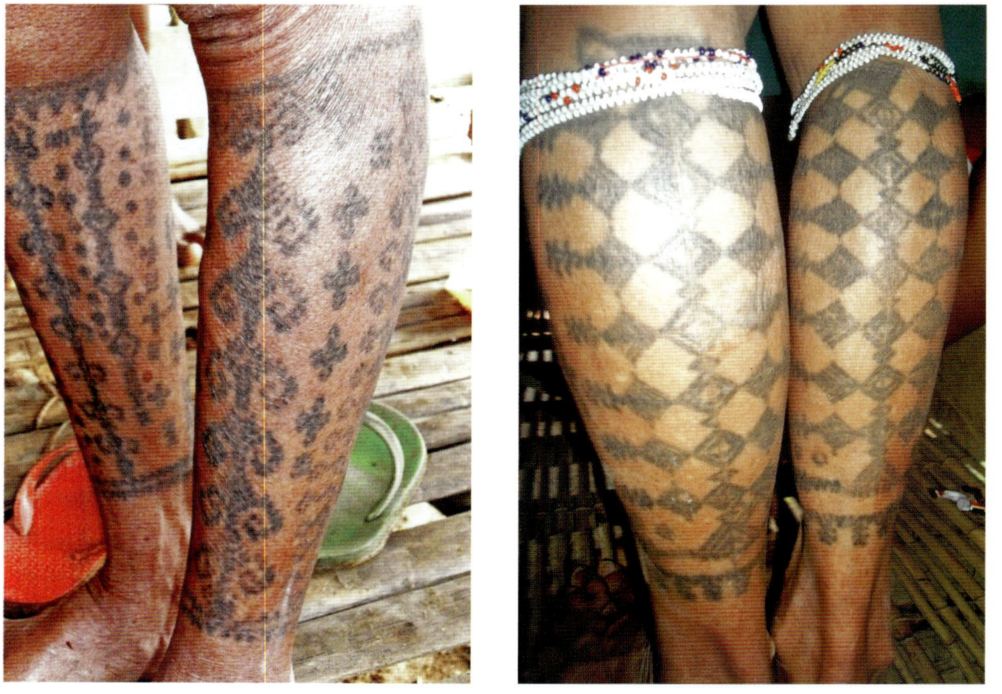

FIGURE 3.49
Banwaon Manobo women displaying different styles of leg tattooing (*left*), including diamond-shaped lozenges on the back of the calf (*right*), 2012. Courtesy of James Mascariñas.

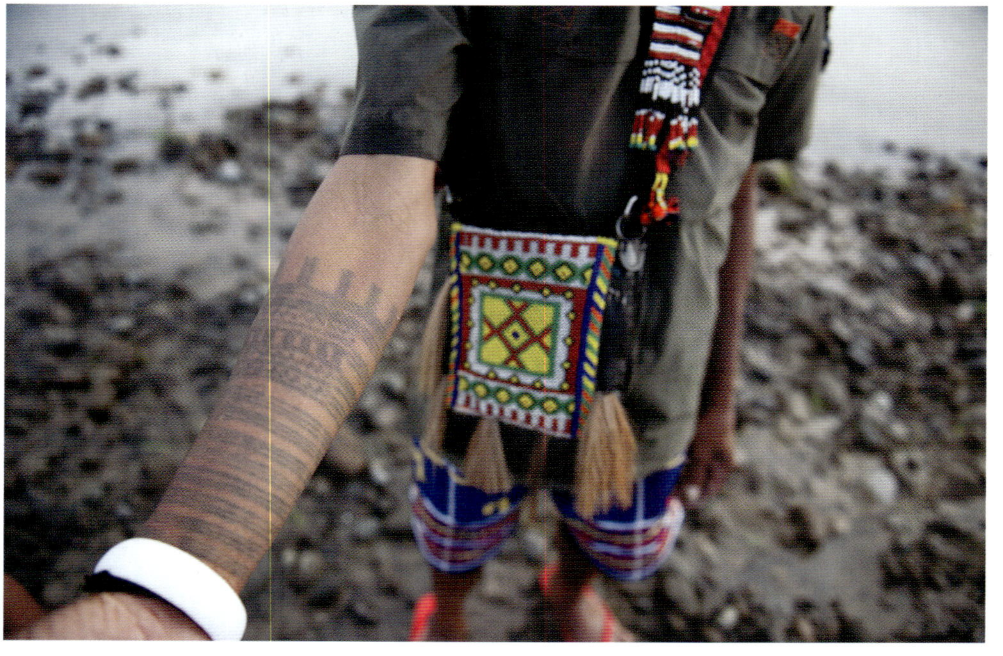

FIGURE 3.50
Bukidnon Manobo man displaying forearm tattooing, 2012. © Jacob Maentz.

humans, such as a house ladder, a *liliongan* (ridge-pole motif of the Manobo house) above the navel, and a knotted rattan time-keeping instrument. Like previously discussed Manobo groups, the Pantaron believe their tattoos serve as a "light" after death to help guide their soul into the afterlife (Ragragio and Paluga 2019:283). Women bearing abdomen tattoos stated that they eased childbirth. Matigsalug Manobo women told Arumpac (2012) that a woman without abdomen tattoos was not "complete" and that the tattoos symbolized "strength," because not all women could withstand the painful cutting and complete their tattoos.

Folklore provides additional information on the antiquity of the Indigenous tattooing traditions of Mindanao. The monitor lizard features prominently in a Bagobo story (see Benedict 1913:57) that is related to the cross-cultural theme set out earlier in this chapter regarding the Austronesian origins of animal marking and tattoo. The Pantaron Manobo employ the monitor lizard as a tattoo motif, and on review, the monitor lizard may be, in fact, the figurative tattoo illustrated in Schadenberg's (1885) account of Bagobo tattooing, which was performed by Pantaron practitioners.[46]

Perhaps more importantly, the Pantaron Manobo state that the primary reason they receive *pangotoeb* is to please Ologasi, a giant or ogre who is the guardian to the afterlife. He is said "to eat" untattooed people on their journey to meet the ancestors (Ragragio and Paluga 2019:282). As noted in chapter 2 of this volume, this folkloric theme, wherein a guardian of the land of the dead inspects individuals for their tattoos, is widespread across the Austronesian world. In turn, it provides further evidence linking various Southeast Asian and other Indigenous traditions of tattooing to an ancient and shared cultural base of religious belief and practice.

MARK OF THE FOUR WAVES TRIBE: THE REBIRTH OF PHILIPPINE TRIBAL TATTOOING (1997–2024)

In 2002, I began corresponding with the Filipino American tattoo researcher-turned-tattoo artist Elle Festin. Five years later, Festin had cofounded the Mark of the Four Waves Tribe (Tatak Ng Apat Na Alon), which at that time was a small group of diasporic men and women of Filipino heritage who were inspired to revitalize the Indigenous tattooing traditions of the Philippines in Orange County, California. "Mark of the Four Waves" refers to multiple waves of immigrants who traveled to the Philippines over the millennia to settle and eventually create the country's rich and diversified culture (Krutak 2010a). These voyagers included the First People, the Afro-Asiatic Aeta; the second wave of Malayo-Polynesians; the third wave of Indians and Arabs; and finally, the Spanish.

Over the ensuing decade, the tribe grew in number and strength and counted hundreds of members across various countries and American urban centers. Members come from all walks of life (e.g., professors, doctors, nurses, chefs, police, musicians, soldiers, firefighters, and IT professionals) and what they share is a profound sense of camaraderie that is expressed through their boldly patterned tattoos (see Krutak 2017c). Many of these tattoos are designed and tattooed by Festin and his fellow tattoo artists at Spiritual Journey Tattoo in Stanton, California, which was founded in 2011.

FIGURE 3.51
(FACING PAGE)
Elle Festin, tattoo artist and cofounder of the Mark of the Four Waves Tribe, 2014. The tribe is a worldwide contemporary group dedicated to preserving Indigenous Filipino tattooing.
© Joe Ash.

Longtime tribe member Tina Astudillo-Ash confided to me that she has met some truly remarkable people since joining the group. "They have become a part of my extended family. These are people who I respect, admire, and strive to make proud through my contributions to the group," she says. In 2018 her son Joseph began apprenticing with Festin, and today he is a practicing tattoo artist at Spiritual Journey, inking the next generation of tribe members.

Although tattoo artists back in the Philippines are resurrecting various Indigenous tattooing aesthetics, iconography, and practices in a number of cities (see Salvador-Amores 2012, 2017), the tribe jump-started this global tattoo revival movement. In turn, they are largely responsible for the current resurgence of traditional Philippine tattoo practices, and their bold, black, and beautiful tattoo artistry is inspired by Indigenous Peoples such as the Kalinga, the Bontok, the Visayans, the Ibaloy, the Manobo, and the Ifugao, among others, from which many members trace their ancestry.

The historian, writer, and Filipino martial arts instructor Mel Orpilla, who is a national trustee for the Filipino American National Historical Society, pays homage to his Ifugao heritage through the tattoos he wears on his body, which were inked by Festin. He told me, "The Orpilla roots come from the Cordillera Mountains and my ancestors were warriors, tribal leaders, hunters, and farmers until the Spanish came and tried to steal their lands. The Ifugao trailhead that was traveled to meet the Spanish is located at the birthplace of my father and his ancestors. And my tattoos are just one way of honoring them and my heritage by retracing their roots" (Krutak 2010a:295).

Tribe member Ryan Mallari's ancestry travels back to Benguet Province, home of the Ibaloy mummies. His grandmother was a traditional healer there, performing curing rituals for family members and her community. "The Ibaloy-inspired tattoos that I wear are an affirmation of that connection and link me to those traditions [that are now] long lost, lost because of cultural assimilation and the colonization of our traditions and heritage by outsiders," he said. "The breaking of skin and imprinting the culture of my ancestors is my own personal revolt against time, forgetfulness, assimilation, and irreverence that would have those traditions disappear. Without a doubt, these tattoos are for my children and those yet to come" (Krutak 2017c:59).

Today, new and old-school tribe members visit Festin and Spiritual Journey for ink, but they also come to learn about Philippine cultural heritage and history. Festin has invested in old and rare reference materials, including books, photographs, and objects of material culture, which his clients and artists draw inspiration from to develop their customized tattoo designs.

Festin, who was born on the Philippine island of Mindoro, is an accomplished traditional tattoo artist who works with hand-poking and hand-tapping tools. He feels that the handcrafted tattoos he creates pay homage to the Indigenous Peoples who created tattooing, because "each tap or poke is like a whisper from another time or place. We want to pay our deepest respects to those tribal artists who came before us, and that is why we give it proper ceremony and ritual when using these kinds of implements. Otherwise, the practice of tattooing will be like an empty vessel, hollow and without meaning, and I will never let that happen now that the Philippine tattoo revival is underway" (Krutak 2014c:195).

One of the oldest members of the tribe is seventy-two-year-old Leandro Cosme Laigo of Hawai'i. His family has deep Ilocano roots, and Laigo is a Vietnam veteran who served in the

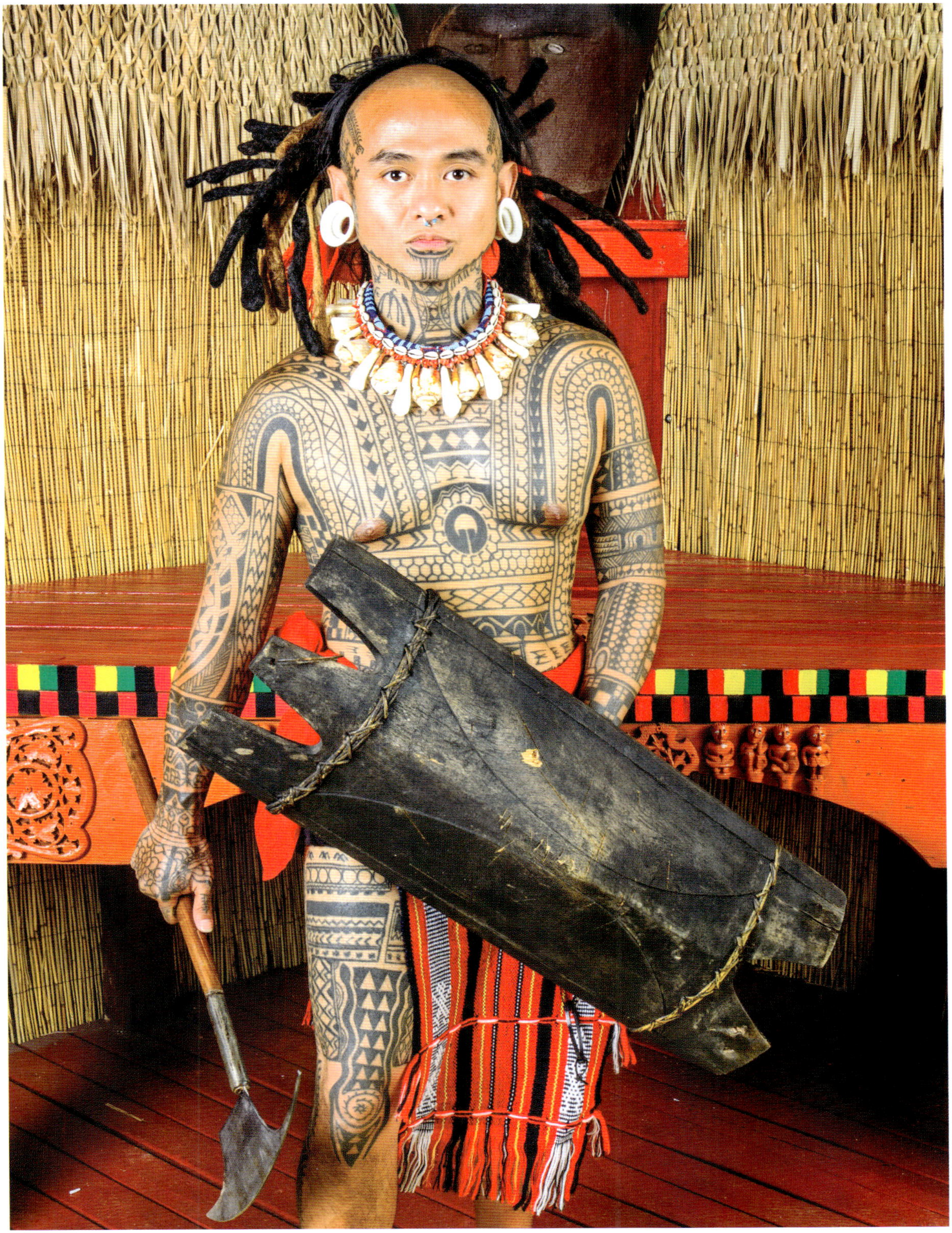

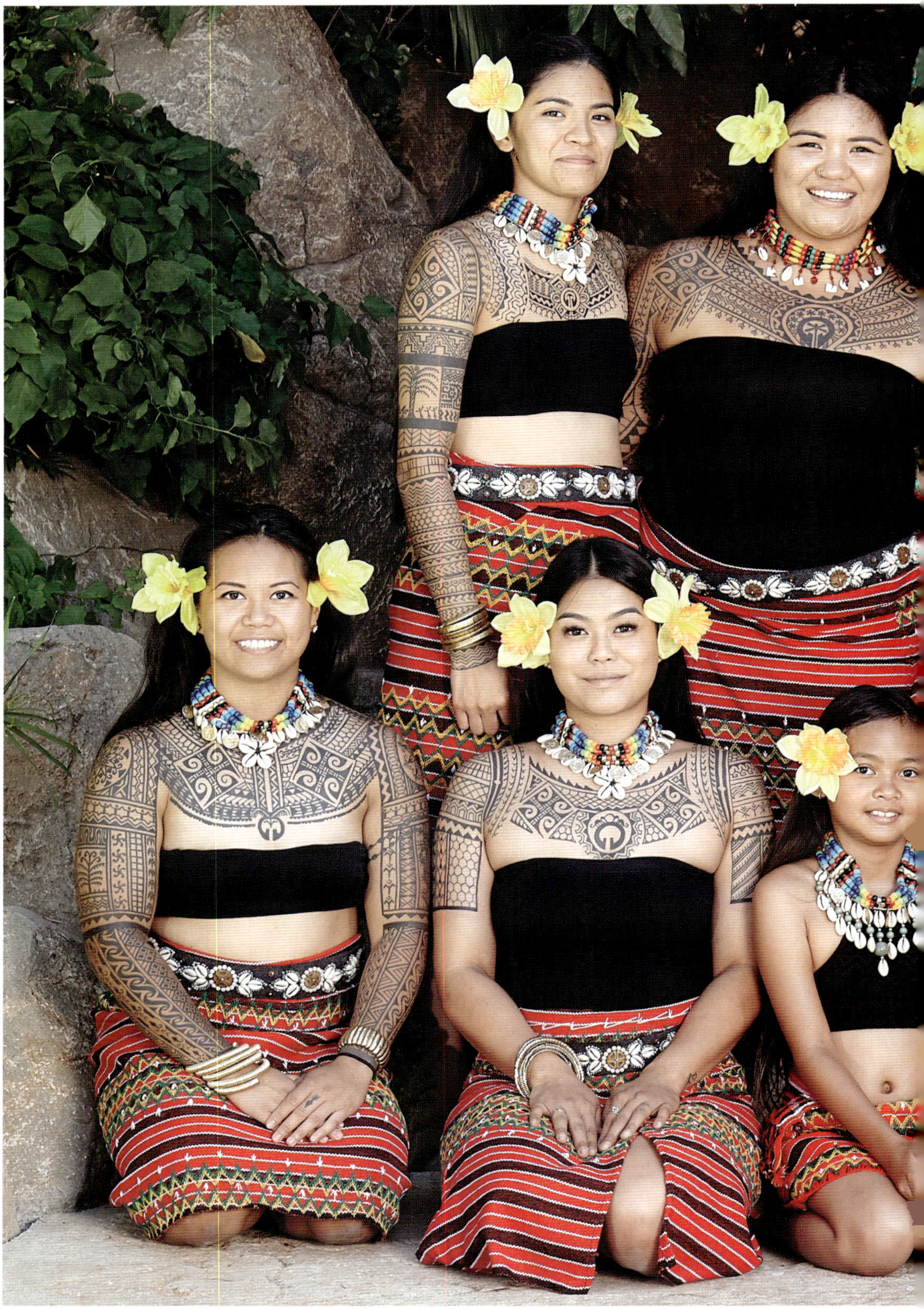

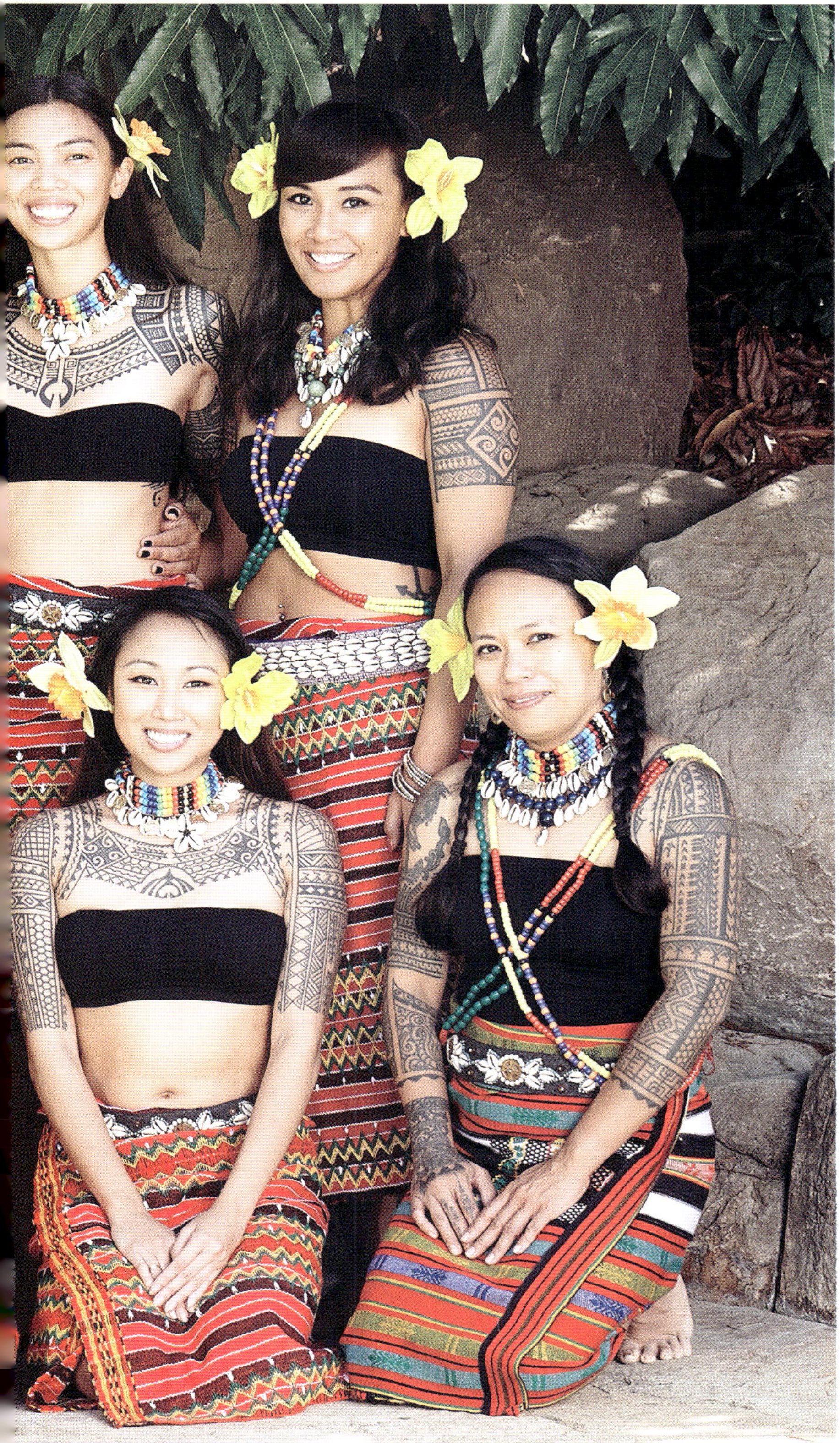

FIGURE 3.52
Mark of the Four Waves Tribe members, 2017. *Top row,* Stacy Romero, Hannah Perez, Kat Atienza, and Katrin Gabriel; *bottom row,* Alyssa Sablaon, Tricia Franco, Kaya Festin, Irene Joyce Magnon, and Jazmine Atienza. © Joe Ash.

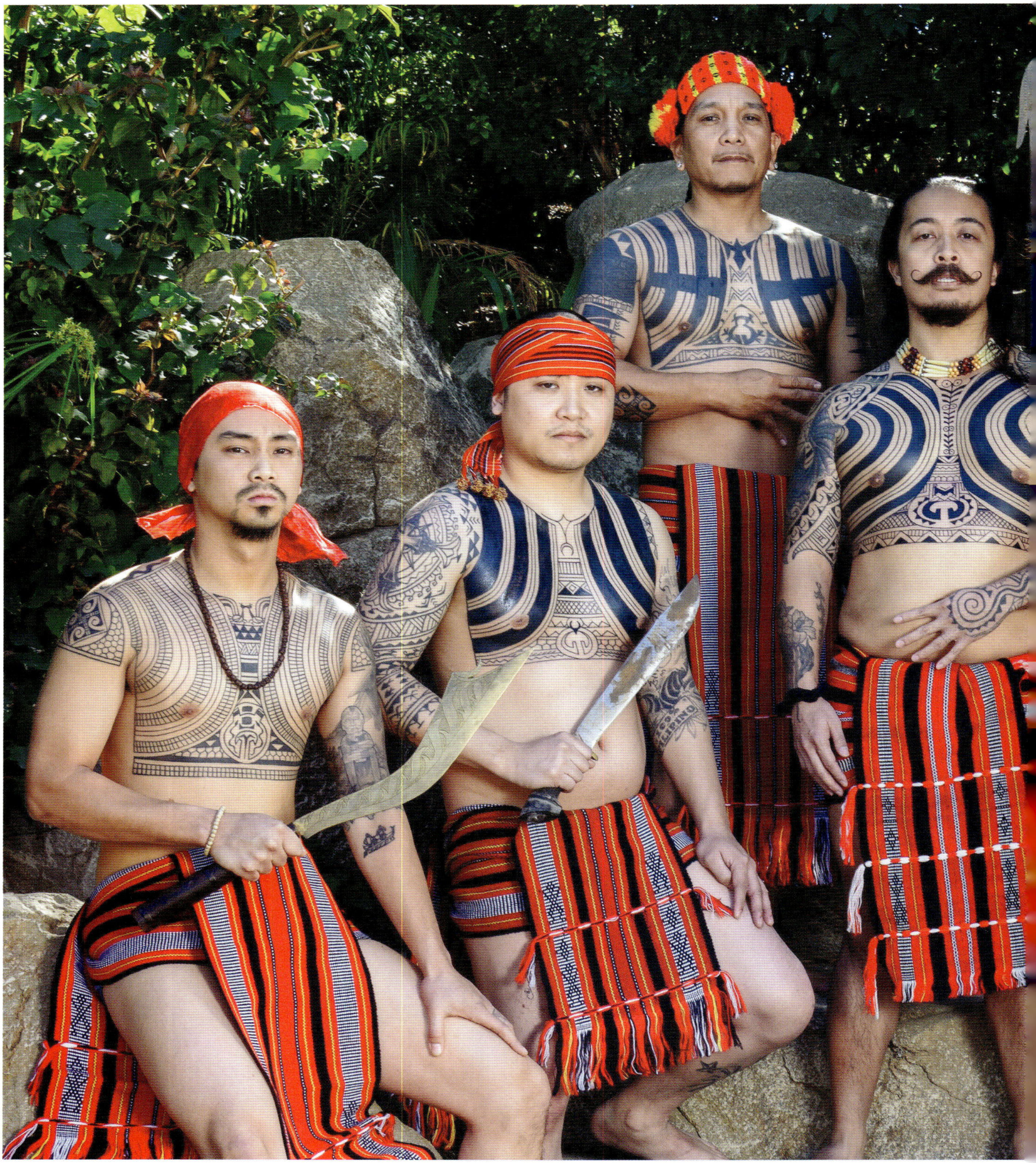

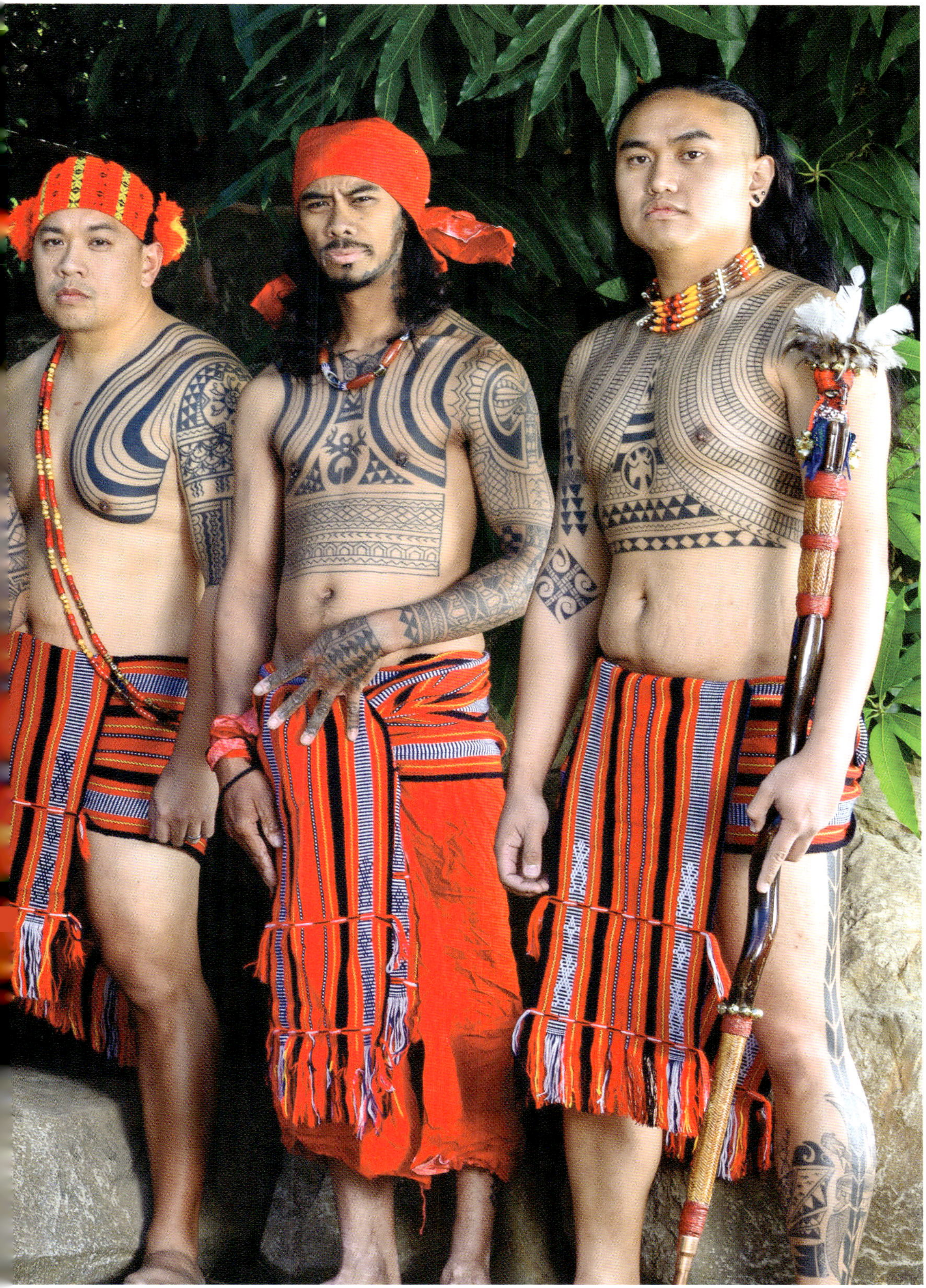

FIGURE 3.53
Mark of the Four Waves Tribe members, 2014. *Left to right*: Timothy Cross, Iam Ordaz, Vince Bantilles, Jordan Lumaquin, Ryan Mallari, Bub Enay, and Kimo Demingoy, each wearing Ibaloy-inspired tattoo designs. © Joe Ash.

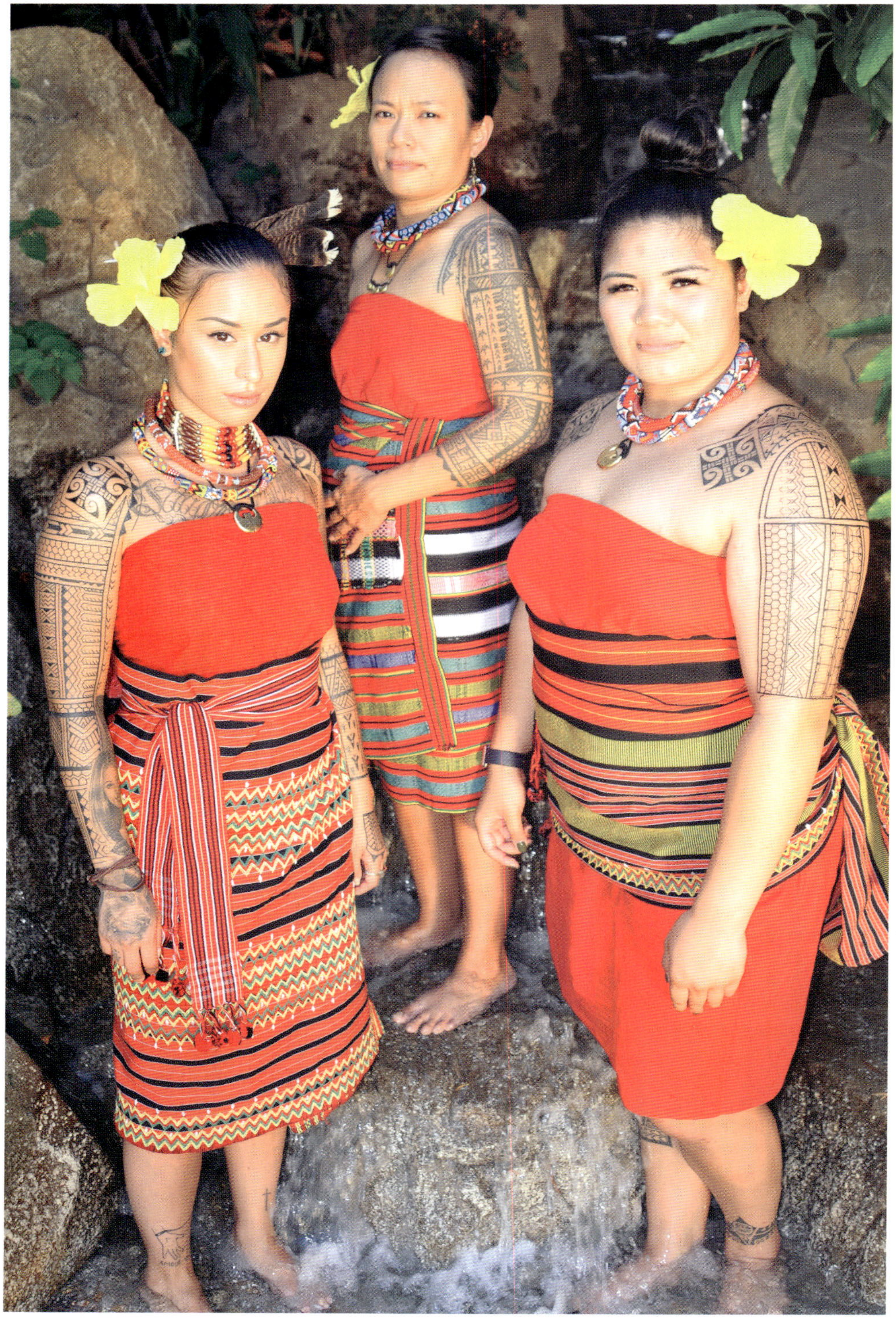

FIGURE 3.54
Mark of the Four Waves Tribe members Sampaguita Jay, Jazmine Atienza, and Hannah Perez, 2017. Jay and Atienza also tattoo for the tribe. © Lars Krutak.

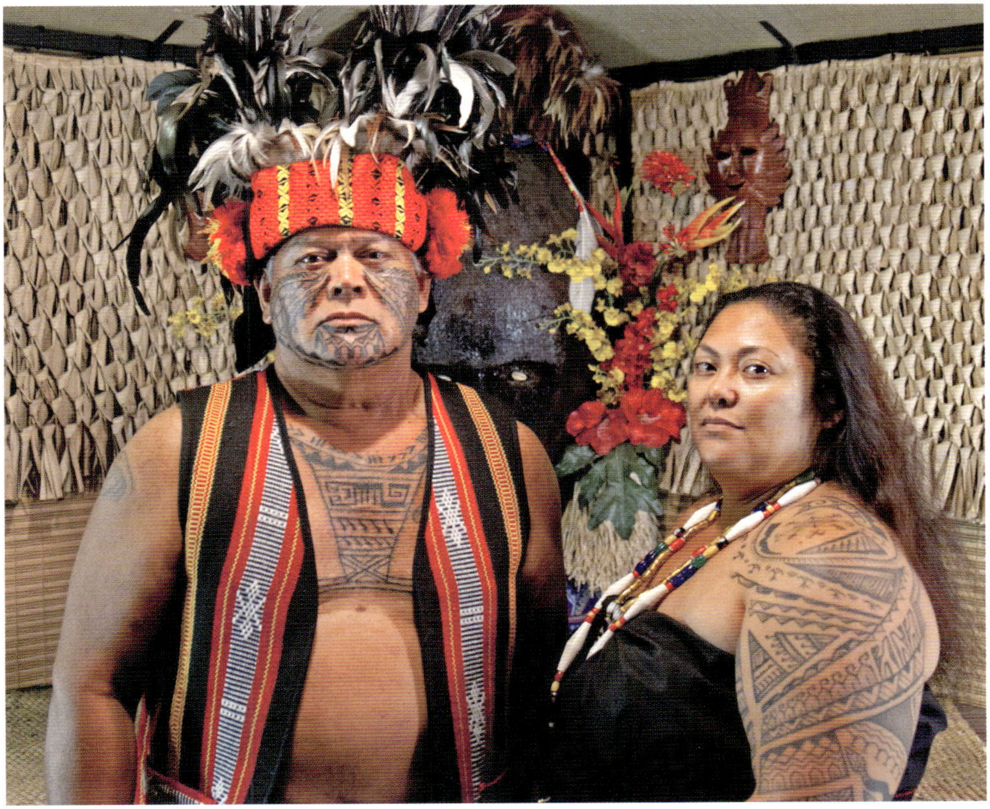

FIGURE 3.55
Mark of the Four Waves Tribe members Leandro Cosme Laigo and Tina Astudillo-Ash, 2014. © Joe Ash.

marines as a helicopter machine gunner during the war. Living in Hawai'i for many years, he admired the many Polynesian tattoos people proudly wore on their bodies and faces. But because he was not Māori, Tongan, or Native Hawaiian, he knew it would be inappropriate for him to wear someone else's culture on his body. Over time, he became aware of Indigenous Filipino tattooing, and this inspired him to contact the tribe because he wanted to permanently honor his ancestors and especially his father with tattoos that were rooted in his culture. In an extended interview, he explained to me the personal factors that led to his decision to become tattooed:

> [A]fter working with the Tribe, I learned that people like the Kalinga helped the Americans during WWII and that their tattoos were earned for bravery in combat. These men were very proud of their marks, and it gave me a certain sense of pride in myself that there was something traditional that I would wear—like a badge or like the medals that I earned in Vietnam—permanently on my body. And because I am half Filipino and a combat veteran, I feel that a tribal warrior tattoo would be certainly fitting, especially one placed on my face for all to see. (Krutak 2010a:297)

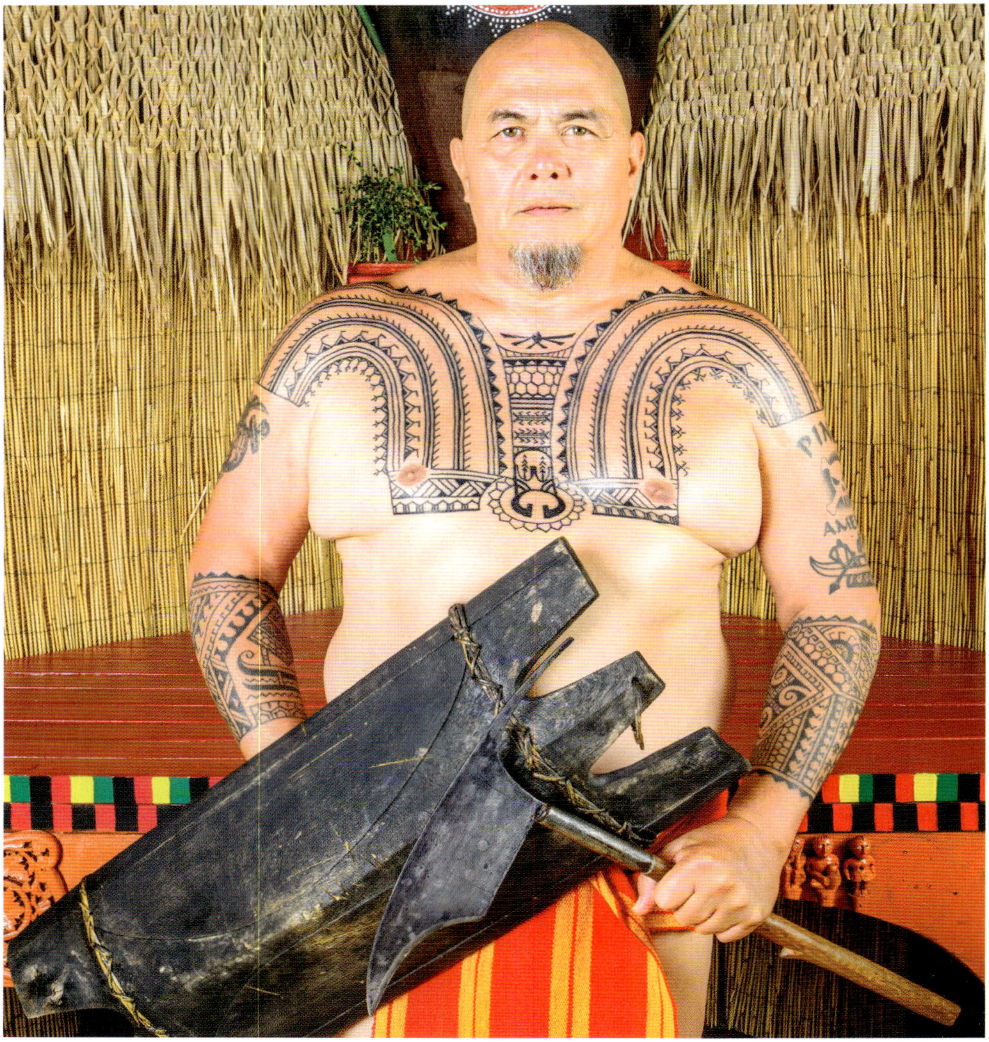

FIGURE 3.56

Larry Alcantra, 2015. Raised in Seattle, Washington, the late Alcantra (1947–2023) was a Filipino American Vietnam veteran who served with the US Marines, 3rd Marine Division, in 1967–1968. For decades, he was actively involved in the US military community, serving as commandant of the Puget Sound Marine Corps League Detachment 336, outreach committee member of the Marine Corps Scholarship Foundation, and Governor's Council member of the Marine Corp Heritage Foundation. Alcantra was very active in Seattle's Filipino community. Since 1990, he served as the organizing committee chair and as advisory board member of Seafair Pista Sa Nayon, a Seattle-area organization and annual community festival dedicated to sharing and celebrating Filipino cultural heritage. Alcantra's tattoos paid homage to his Filipino roots and honor his military service and accomplishments. © Joe Ash.

Tattoos worn by tribe members are deeply personal, as they are embodied with ancestral and individual meanings. They are certainly not meant to be the latest fashion statement. Thus, it would be disrespectful for anyone to copy another person's design because their tattoos are personally sacred. Tattoos should never be worn lightly, because, after all, they define who you are and remain with you throughout your life. And as Laigo told me, "If you forget where you came from, then you *really* don't know where you are going" (Krutak 2010a:297).

BUSCALAN TATTOO REVIVAL (2010–2024)

Since my early visits to Kalinga Province and Buscalan village (2007 and 2008), centenarian Kalinga tattoo practitioner Apo Whang-Od Oggay has gained international recognition. Over the ensuing decade, she has apprenticed several female tattooists in her bloodline—Grace Palicas, Ilyan Wigan, and others—and nearly all of them, including the master, are working today. What was once a sleepy farming village that rarely entertained visitors has now become an international tattoo pilgrimage destination covered in international travel guides. In 2009, Buscalan and Whang-Od were featured in the Discovery Channel series *Tattoo Hunter*, which catapulted the community and its endearing master tattoo artist to worldwide fame (Almendral 2017). The popularity of Buscalan as an international tattoo and travel destination resulted in what locals call "tattoo mania," which has no end in sight. Legions of domestic and international backpackers, tattoo tourists and ecotourists, and members of the media descend on the rural village each year to take home a treasured tattoo from perhaps the oldest practicing tattoo artist in the world or from one of her disciples. During peak season, upward of one thousand visitors a weekend visit Buscalan and are serviced by more than ninety female tattoo artists now working in the village.[47]

With so much outside interest in the village, change has been rapid, especially from the viewpoint of the village's infrastructure. In March 2016, a new billboard by Kalinga Tourism featuring Whang-Od, and a sign reading "Buscalan Tattoo Village" was posted at the foot of a newly constructed paved road (the first ever) from the main highway to the trailhead leading to the village. In 2015 a tramline for tourists' baggage was installed at the trailhead to help facilitate access to the village; today four additional trams are operating. Buscalan sits atop a mountain and is accessible only via a sometimes slick and treacherous trail that ends in more than one thousand concrete steps that must be scaled to reach the lower village. At the tram sites, several small buildings house shops and local tourist guides who were previously trained in a municipality-funded project by the UP Mountaineers, a student organization of the University of the Philippines–Diliman.

Beginning in 2015, Buscalan village began implementing a guiding fee. These monies sustain local employment and help with sanitation and garbage removal and other infrastructural improvements in the community. Although tourist guides visiting Buscalan might come from afar, under a municipal ordinance they must reside in the municipality of Tinglayan, and no foreign or local tourists are allowed to visit the village without the support of a tourist guide. The guiding fee was set depending on the size of the visiting party: one thousand pesos per day for one guide serving one to five tourists, two thousand for one or two guides serving six to ten tourists, three

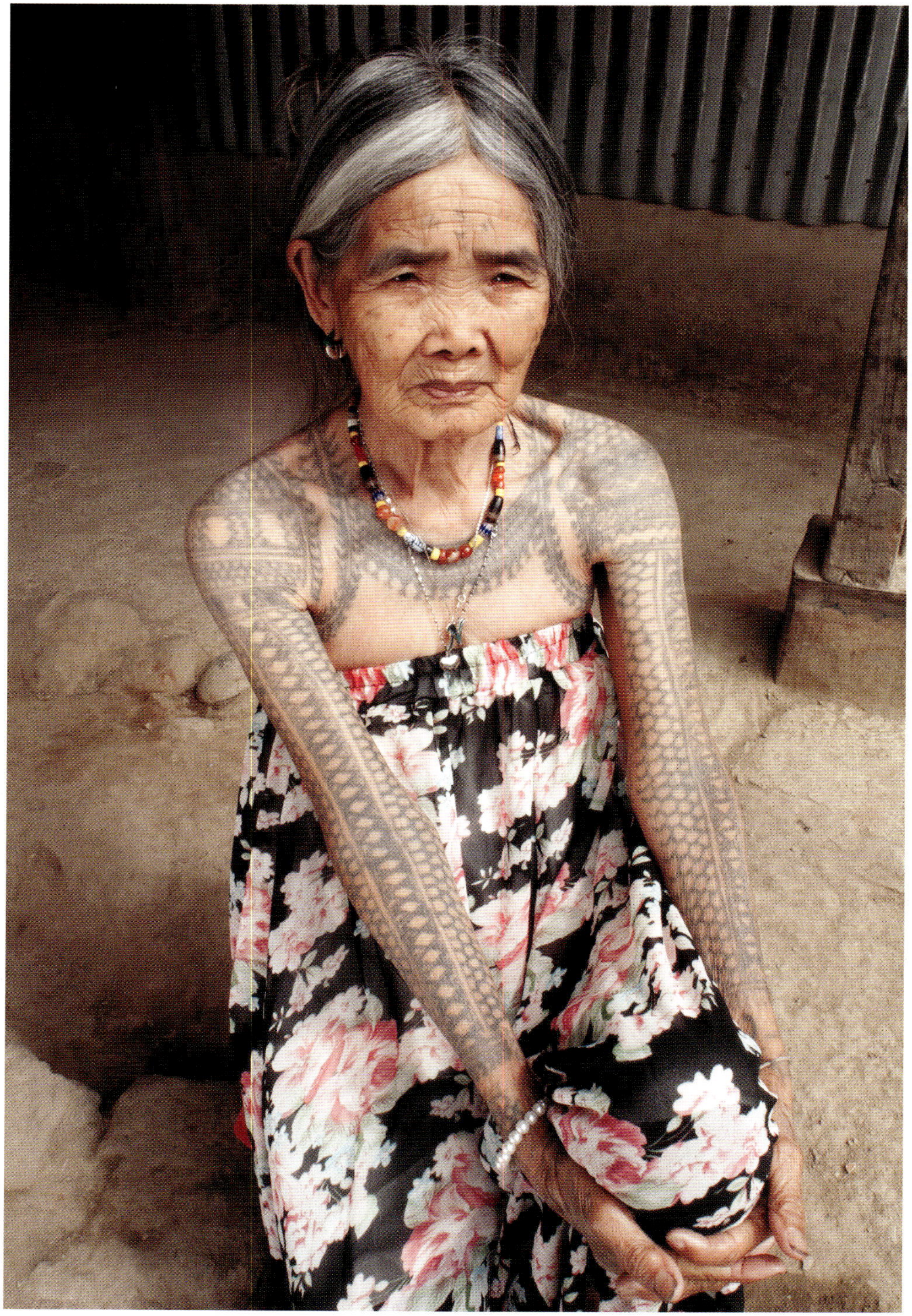

FIGURE 3.57
Kalinga elder and *mambabatok* (tattoo artist) Apo Whang-Od Oggay of Buscalan village, 2016. © Lars Krutak.

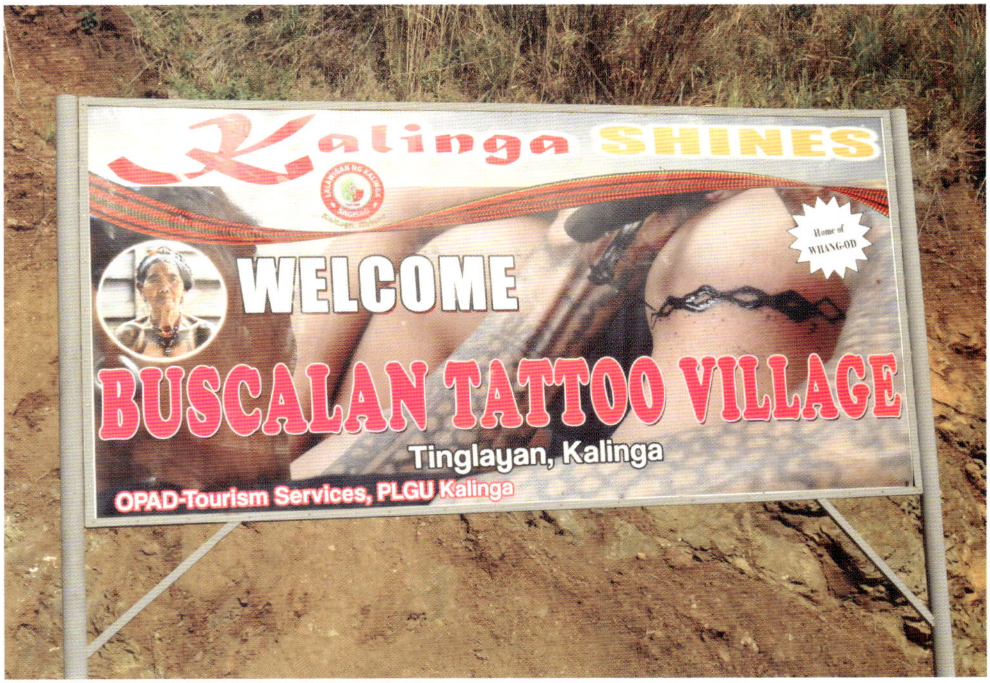

FIGURE 3.58
Tourist sign welcoming "tattoo pilgrims" to the newly paved road leading to the Buscalan village trailhead, 2016. © Lars Krutak.

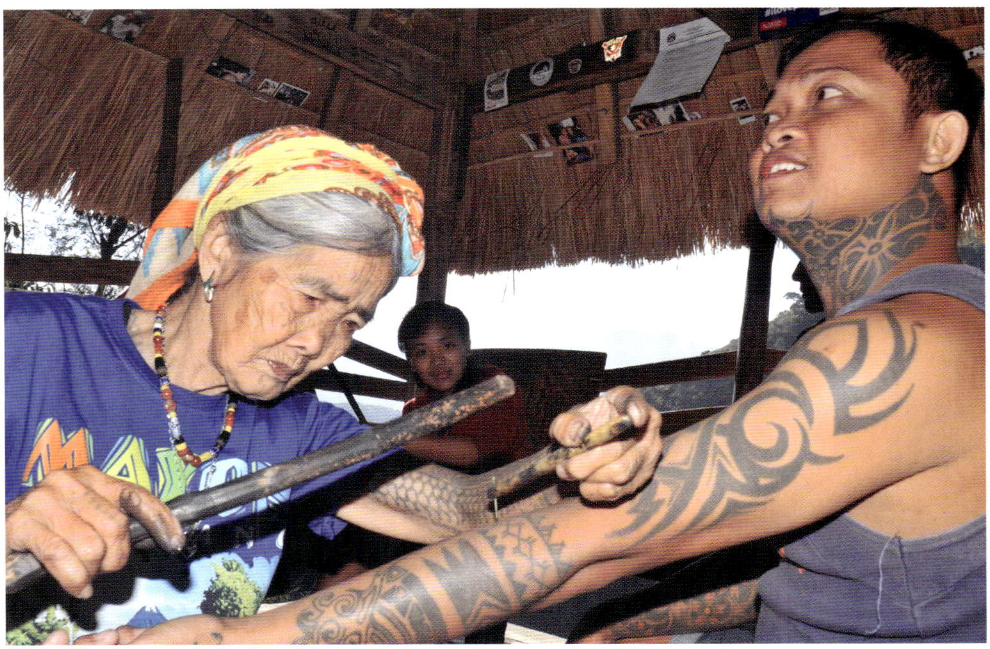

FIGURE 3.59
Apo Whang-Od Oggay tattooing fellow tattoo artist Felix Dixon of Miri, Sarawak, Malaysia, 2016. Oggay's tattooing mentee and great niece, Grace Palicas, appears in the background. Dixon journeyed to Buscalan to meet the master and take home a memento of his experiences there. © Lars Krutak.

thousand for one to three guides serving eleven to fifteen tourists, and four thousand for one to four guides serving sixteen to twenty tourists. With the dramatic increase in tourism and since 2015, these fees have changed. Today, each visitor to Buscalan must pay a one-hundred peso registration fee, an additional fee for using one of the trams (unless they transport their own luggage up the trail to the village), and for overnight guests, groups of one to five tourists pay fifteen hundred pesos per guide, and groups of six to ten tourists pay twenty-five hundred pesos. Homestay costs typically run four hundred pesos per night per person, and guests are provided with unlimited coffee and rice from the host; additional provisions cost extra.

Of course, many Buscalan Kalinga who had previously out-migrated from the community in search of work and other opportunities have returned, because now they can make a living in the village by guiding or by operating homestays, small stores, souvenir shops, and restaurants that cater to the influx of tourists. As a result, however, Buscalan has reached its maximum capacity for new housing, and a satellite community has sprung up across the valley.

Other villages have become "envious" and "jealous" of Buscalan's socioeconomic position, but the popularity of the Kalinga tattoo has inspired Indigenous youth from other villages to teach themselves how to tattoo. In turn, what has resulted is an Indigenous tattoo revitalization movement that will continue into the foreseeable future.

4

TATTOOS OF INDONESIA

Spirits, Souls, Taboo, and Tattoo

> The entire cosmos is filled by the fame of the perfect [tattooed] man. When he is spoken of the animals listen, when his fortune is mentioned, the trees bend their branches low, and when his name is spoken the fishes and boulders leap from the river.
>
> —**Hans Schärer (1963:79),** Protestant missionary to the Ngaju, Kalimantan

Indonesia is the fourth-largest country in the world, and this vast archipelago is home to over seventeen thousand islands, containing over 250 million people and five hundred languages and dialects. Although it is the largest Muslim country in the world today, there are substantial populations of Hindus, Christians, and especially Indigenous Peoples whose cultural traditions of tattooing are the focus of this chapter.

For thousands of years, astonishingly rich and diverse forms of tattooing have been produced by Indonesia's First Peoples. United by a common Austronesian linguistic heritage, *adat* (customary laws), taboos, and religious beliefs focused on the propitiation of spirits and deities, the tribal peoples of Indonesia expressed these and other cosmological relationships visually through tattooing. Body marking here was also worn as a marker of identity, as well as an emblem of personal achievement. In other instances, the bold blackwork tattoos of this vast insular region embodied magical power that was deployed to confront unseen forces to ensure the perpetuation of human life in an always uncertain world. Taken together the Indigenous tattooing traditions of Indonesia have always been, and for many people continue to be, one of the most important elements of religious belief and ritual practice. That is because tattoos were carried through life and onward into the afterlife as Indigenous markers of experience, identity, spirituality, and being that could never be taken away.

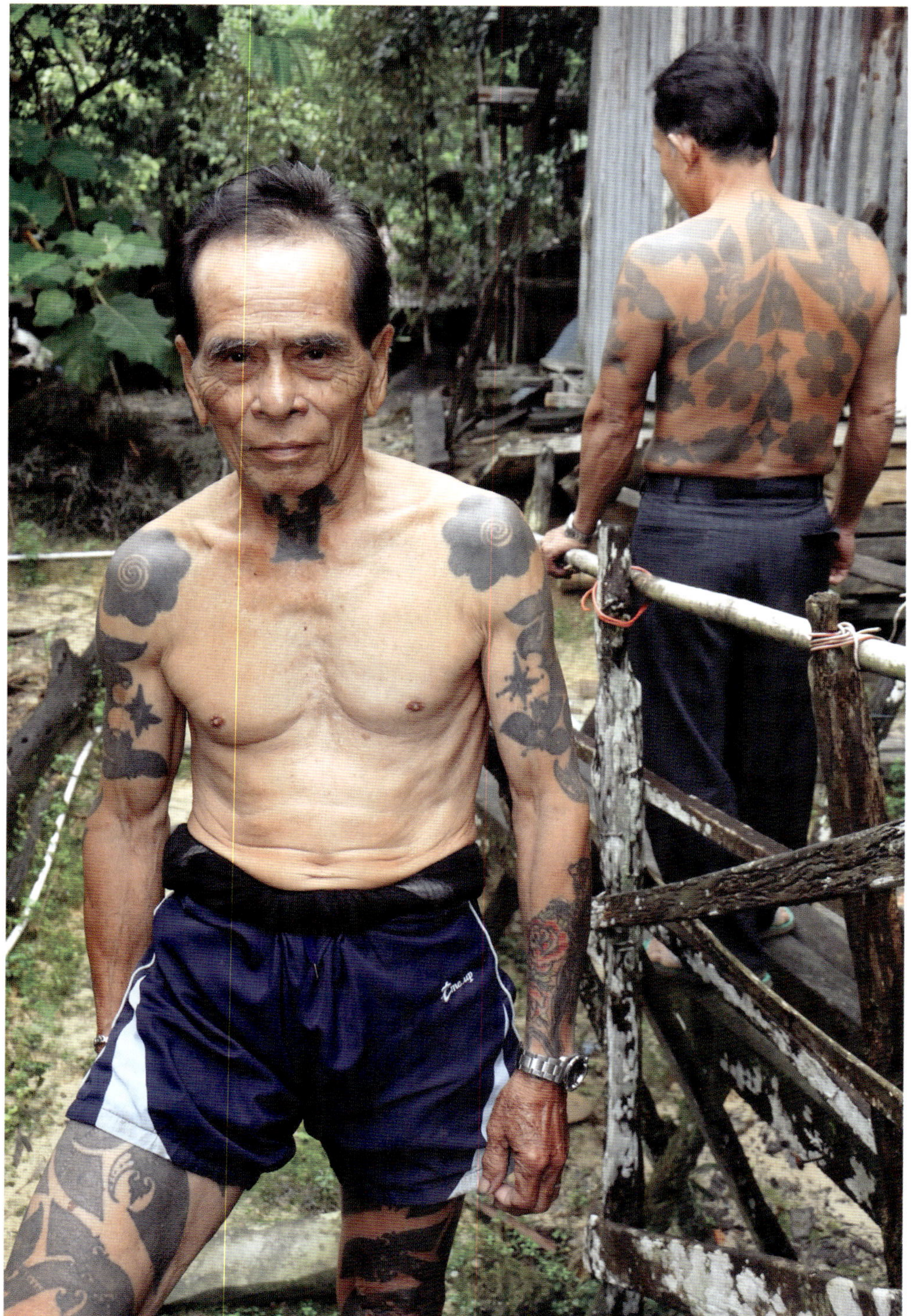

FIGURE 4.1
Ubu and Jalin of Entalau, Skrang River, Sarawak, 2011. © Lars Krutak.

THE ISLAND OF BORNEO: IBAN TATTOOS

On the island of Borneo,[1] tribal tattooing forms may have reached their apex, especially among the Dayak and Orang Ulu. Dayak, meaning "interior" or "inland" person, and Orang Ulu, or "upriver people," are terms used to describe a variety of Indigenous Peoples Native to Borneo: Iban, Kayan, Kenyah, Lahanan, Kejaman, Punan Bah, Punan Busang, Ngaju, Ot Danum, Penan, Baketan (Bakatan), Ukit, Kelabit, Siang, and Sa'ban, among other groups not mentioned in this text.

The Iban are probably the best known of Borneo's tattooed Dayak tribes in the western tattooing milieu, and this is largely due to Filipino American tattoo artist Leo Zulueta, who brought to the world's attention the various tribal blackwork styles of Borneo in the early 1980s (Hardy 1988). Fusing these traditional patterns with those of Polynesia, a "new tribalism" in tattooing circles emerged, gaining global popularity, and sparking a tattoo revival that continues to this day (see Bernstein 2023).

The tattooing iconography of the Iban has itself evolved over the centuries. Indeed, various authors have suggested that Indigenous Iban tattoo designs were slowly replaced long ago by non-Ibanic tattoo forms as the Iban began to migrate across Borneo from their ancestral territory in Kalimantan (Franken and Torfin 1998:139; Haddon 1901:326; Hose and McDougall 1912:273–275; Hose and Shelford 1906:85–87). Yet Iban tattooing has become transformed in other ways. Over the last century, for example, traditional designs have become greatly magnified in scale and are much larger than those seen in the 1920s and 1930s.

Iban tattooists were always male and they often worked under the tutelage of an *antu nulong* (spirit helper) who guided their activities. Tutelary spirits also provided Iban tattooists with *pengaroh* (magical charms) to enhance their tattooing skills and the power of the designs they created. Typically speaking, spirit helpers would communicate with their human counterparts in dreams to provide the locations of charms (Krutak 2012).

Iban tattooing is closely related to the concept of *bejalai*, or journey abroad. Iban customary law prescribed that men could be tattooed only on *bejalai*, or while away from their longhouse community (Freeman 1967:335). Throughout history, Iban men traveled far and wide through the jungle in search of products for trade or to meet their enemies, to visit relatives or unmarried women in other longhouse communities or to seek new locations for a longhouse itself. To commemorate these trips, they often acquired *pantang* (body tattoos) to mark these memorable occasions. But if a man was a warrior, he could also acquire special *tegulun* tattoos on his fingers and hands to signal that he had been successful in taking one or more enemy heads during a war raid (Hose and Shelford 1906:66–67; Richards 1997:375). Among the Iban of the Batang Lupar, the Dutch physician and ethnologist Hendrik Tillema (1878–1952) stated that warriors who had taken more than two heads could be tattooed on their right hand. If a man had captured seven or more, he could tattoo both hands. However, if a man had received hand tattoos but had not taken the required number of heads he risked "the vengeance of the gods" (Tillema 1930:203). Native Iban scholar Benedict Sandin (1980:90) observed, "If [you] tattoo the back of your hand before you have killed an enemy in war . . . you shall become *layu*, gradually ill, and may eventually die before your time."

FIGURE 4.2
Iban warrior *tegulun* (hand tattoos) that in former times denoted successes in the head-hunt, ca. 1955. From Morrison 1966:195.

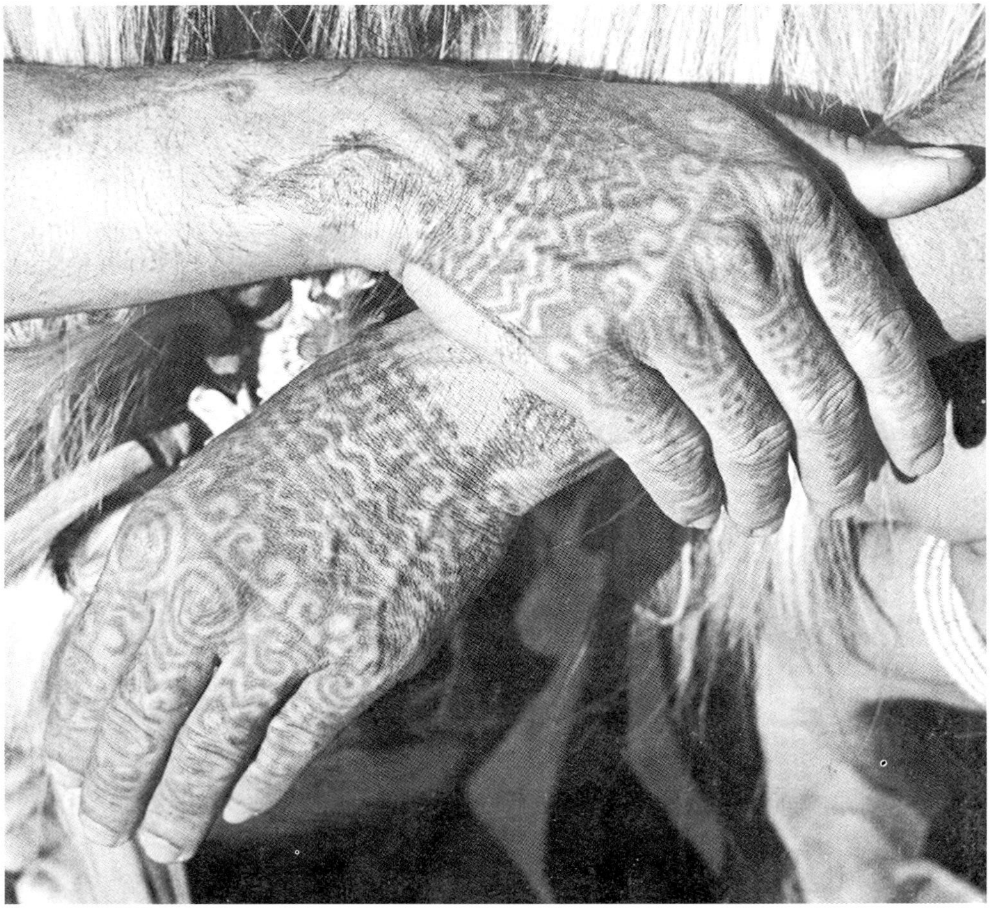

As an Iban man built up his name through various exploits performed abroad, his skin became enhanced with bold tattoos that covered nearly every surface of his body. These tattoos not only accentuated his muscularity and masculinity but also acted as a résumé by establishing his reputation through a language of symbols that were readable by all—symbols that deceased ancestors could see in Sebayan, the Land of the Dead.

Men were rarely tattooed in the longhouse because the flowing blood attracted *antu* (spirits) that were potential sources of misfortune. Instead, they were hand-tapped outside in a kind of portable shrine formed by walls of sacred and apotropaic *pua kumbu'* textiles to guard against any supernatural presence entering through the wounds (Heppell 2005:16).[2]

Like the neighboring Kayan, Iban tattoo motifs were first carved by men into wooden blocks or bone stencils and then stamped onto human skin. The patterns were derived from nature (e.g., eggplant flower, prawn, scorpion, dragon-dog, crab, frog, centipede, etc.). Early chroniclers of

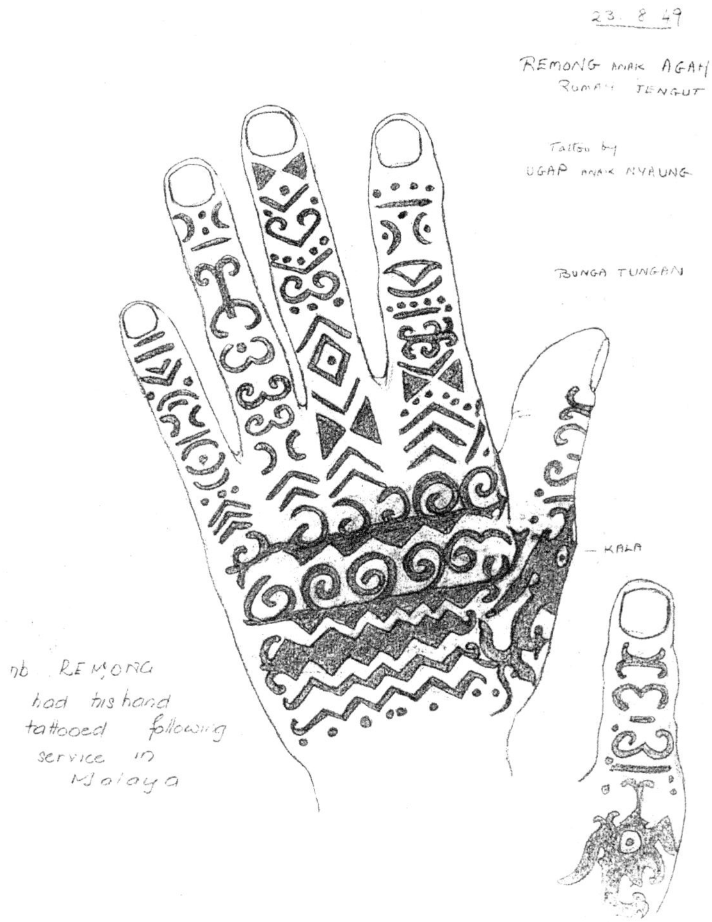

FIGURE 4.3
Iban warrior *tegulun* (hand tattoos) belonging to Remong of Rumah Jenggut, lower Baleh River, Sarawak. These intricate markings are also called *bunga tungan* or "flowers of the hand." A *kala* (scorpion) motif marks the base of his thumb, 1949. Drawing by Monica Freeman. Courtesy National Library of Australia (Ms. Acc12.055).

Borneo tattoo art have argued that the Iban originally borrowed many of their tattooing motifs from other peoples, including the Kayan and nomadic Baketan, Punan Busang, Ukit, and Penan, before making them their own. However, the Iban scholar Benedict Sandin (1980:90) related that the Iban developed their own tattooing traditions as early as the late seventeenth century, since it was an important practice borrowed from *orang panggau,* mythological culture heroes-cum-deities. Perhaps the most famous of these superhuman entities was Keling, who taught the Iban how to tattoo and find charms so they would be successful in hunting, warfare, and other pursuits (Kurzman 1993:70). The concept of *bejalai* was also modeled after this male entity who was on a perpetual quest seeking adventures.

Generally speaking, Iban men acquired their tattoos in a set order. For example, in the Sungai Sut region near Kapit, Sarawak, the American anthropologist Steve Kurzman noted that the first tattoo placed on young men was the *ginti,* or fishhook on the calf. This motif might resemble a simple J or double hook. Kurzman recorded that this motif prepared boys for the more elaborate and painful tattooing to come in the future, especially after each *bejalai* excursion. On the Skrang River, this tattoo was also called a *pantang betis* (calf tattoo). It was tattooed at late puberty for those reasons mentioned above, but it also served as a "charm for successful fishing" (Franken and Torfinn 1998:142); in other areas this tattoo allowed the possessor "to catch good things" (Freeman Papers 1948–1958). In former times, this mark might also have indicated that the bearer was fitted with a *palang*, or penis pen, which aroused the curiosity and interest of longhouse maidens. Other tattoos might also indicate a *palang* bearer, including rosettes on the lower back and one near the groin, and ribcage tattoos called a *suit*, or "crosspiece" (Franken and Torfinn 1998:158–159; Tillema 1930:203).

A young man's second tattoo was oftentimes the *buah terong* (also *bunga terong*) derived from the eggplant flower, although men might also acquire their *ukir dedok* (neck tattoos) at the same time or even before (see below). This tattoo was composed of a pair of rosettes placed on the deltoids of the shoulder, and was received after circumcision (Franken and Torfinn 1998). The petals composing this bold pattern might vary, and I was told by Skrang elders that each one

FIGURE 4.4
Iban *cuan telingai*, or tattoo stencil blocks, ca. 1895. *Left, top row, aso'* (dragon-dog) and *kala* (scorpion); *middle row, kala* (scorpion) variation; *bottom row*, two *aso'* (dragon-dog) variations. © Sarawak Museum Department, Kuching (1054.67, 1054.69. 1054.99, 1054.70, 1054.109).

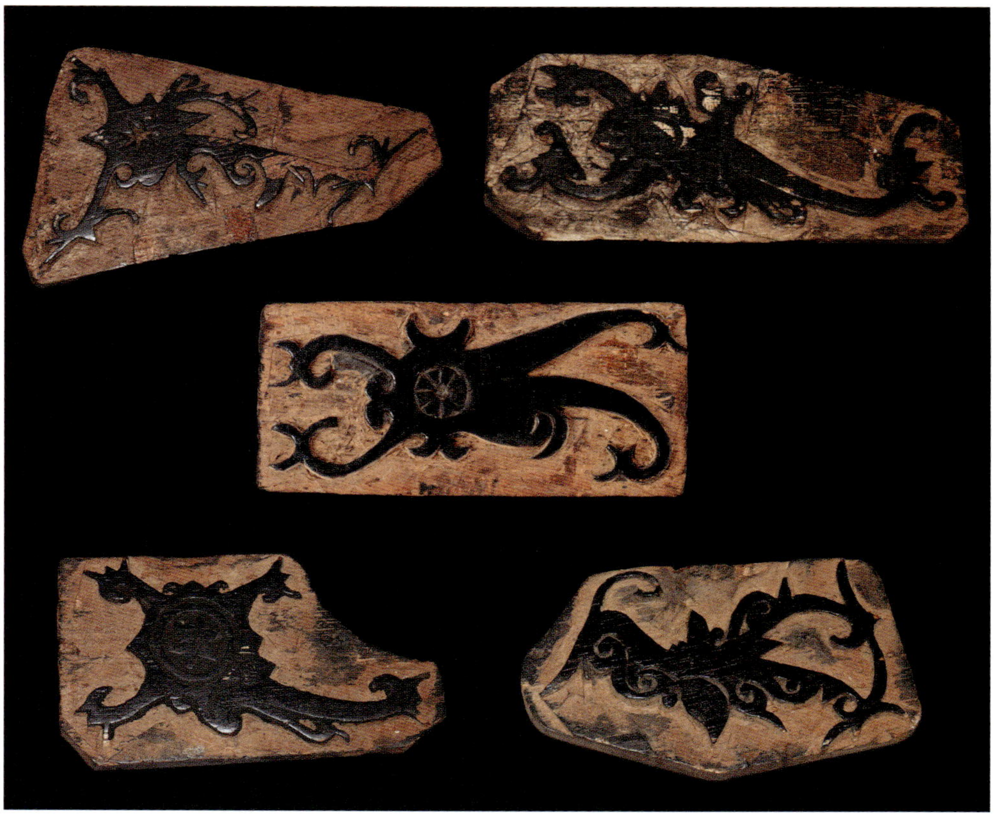

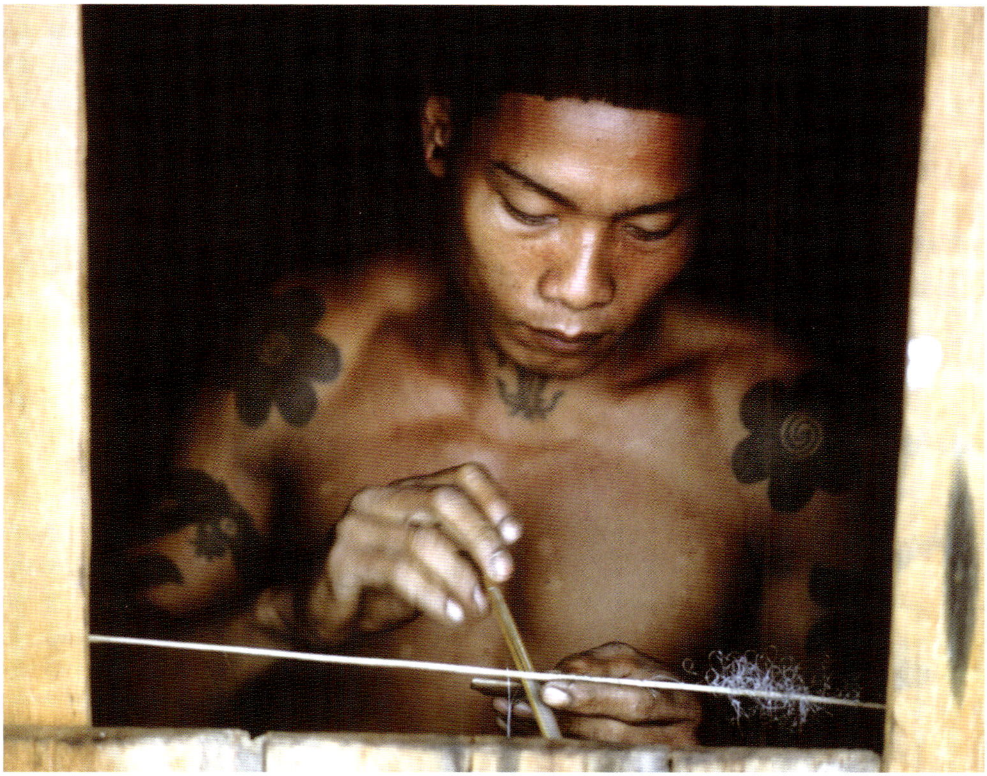

FIGURE 4.5
Tattooed Iban man crafting a tool, 1966. © Sonia Solmssen.

represents the degrees of patience a man should carry with him throughout his lifetime. The spiral in the center of the tattoo symbolizes a tadpole, which represents initiation to manhood.

The unpublished fieldnotes of anthropologists Derek and Monica Freeman from circa 1950 reveal that men of the Sungai Sut region sometimes acquired their throat tattoos prior to or at the same time as their shoulder rosettes (Freeman Papers 1948–1958). According to the testimonies of their tattooed Iban informants, whom Monica sketched in great detail, all of these tattoos were invariably acquired during a young man's first or second *bejalai*. For example, the heavily marked U'Bong of Rumah Nyala longhouse was born in 1906. In 1920, at the age of fourteen, he received his throat tattoos from a distant relative, Kenawang, at Rumah Ikok on the Sungai Dia during a three-month *bejalai* hunting for hornbill products on the Rajang River. In 1921, U'Bong returned to the Rajang in search of hornbill products and received his shoulder rosettes at Rumah Ikok from a different tattooist named Lasah. Buda (b. 1929), also of Rumah Nyala, was tattooed during his first *bejalai* while doing five months of logging work on the Rajang River in 1945. Seventy other Iban men accompanied him on this journey. His throat tattoos were hand-tapped by an artist from Rumah Santing on the Sungai Tiau River, and the rosettes were marked afterward by a fellow member of his longhouse, Jabang, who was a tattooist.

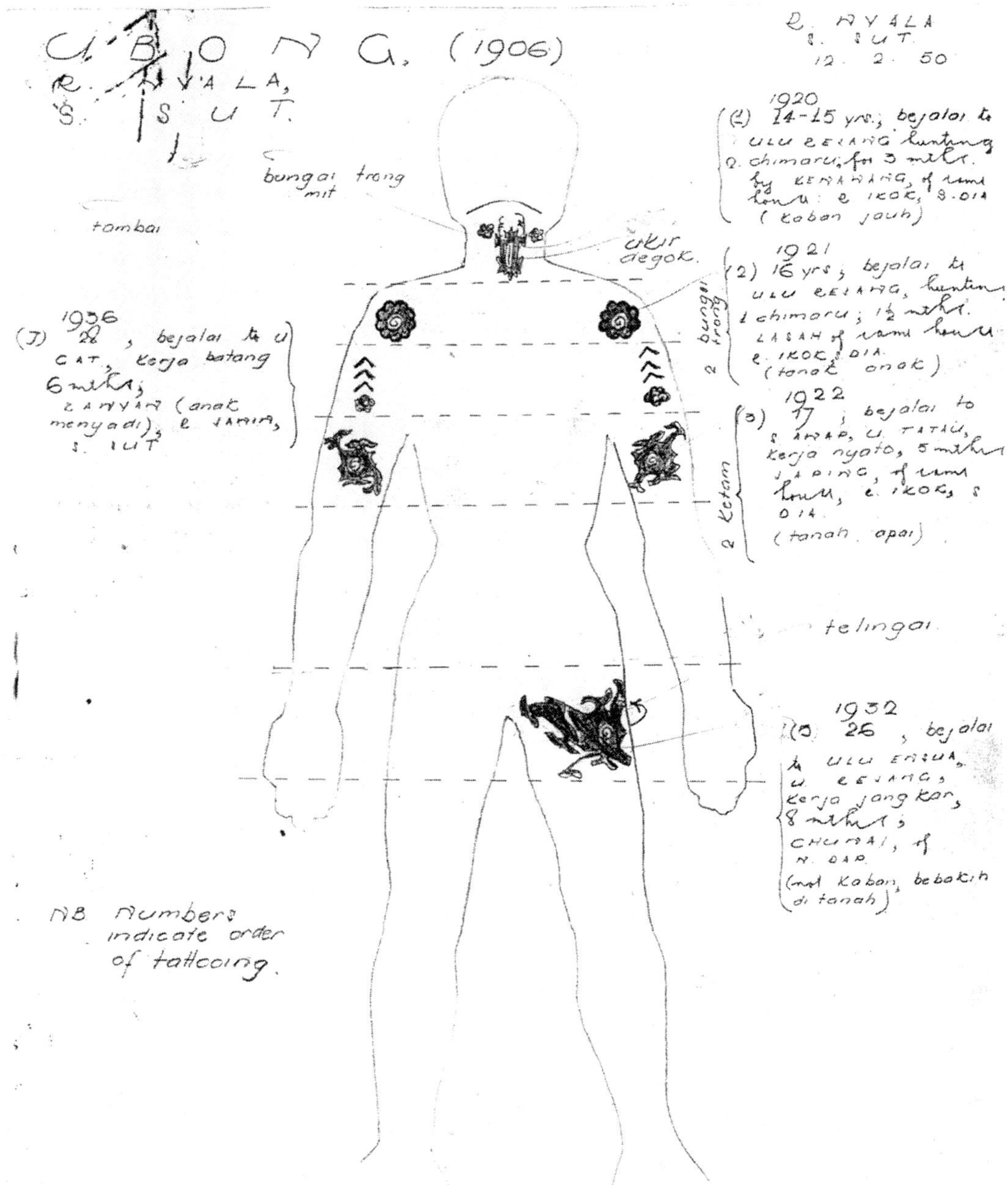

FIGURE 4.6

Body tattoos of U'Bong with a chronology of when they were received, Rumah Nyala, Sungai Sut River, Sarawak, 1950. Drawing by Monica Freeman. Courtesy National Library of Australia (Ms. Acc12.055).

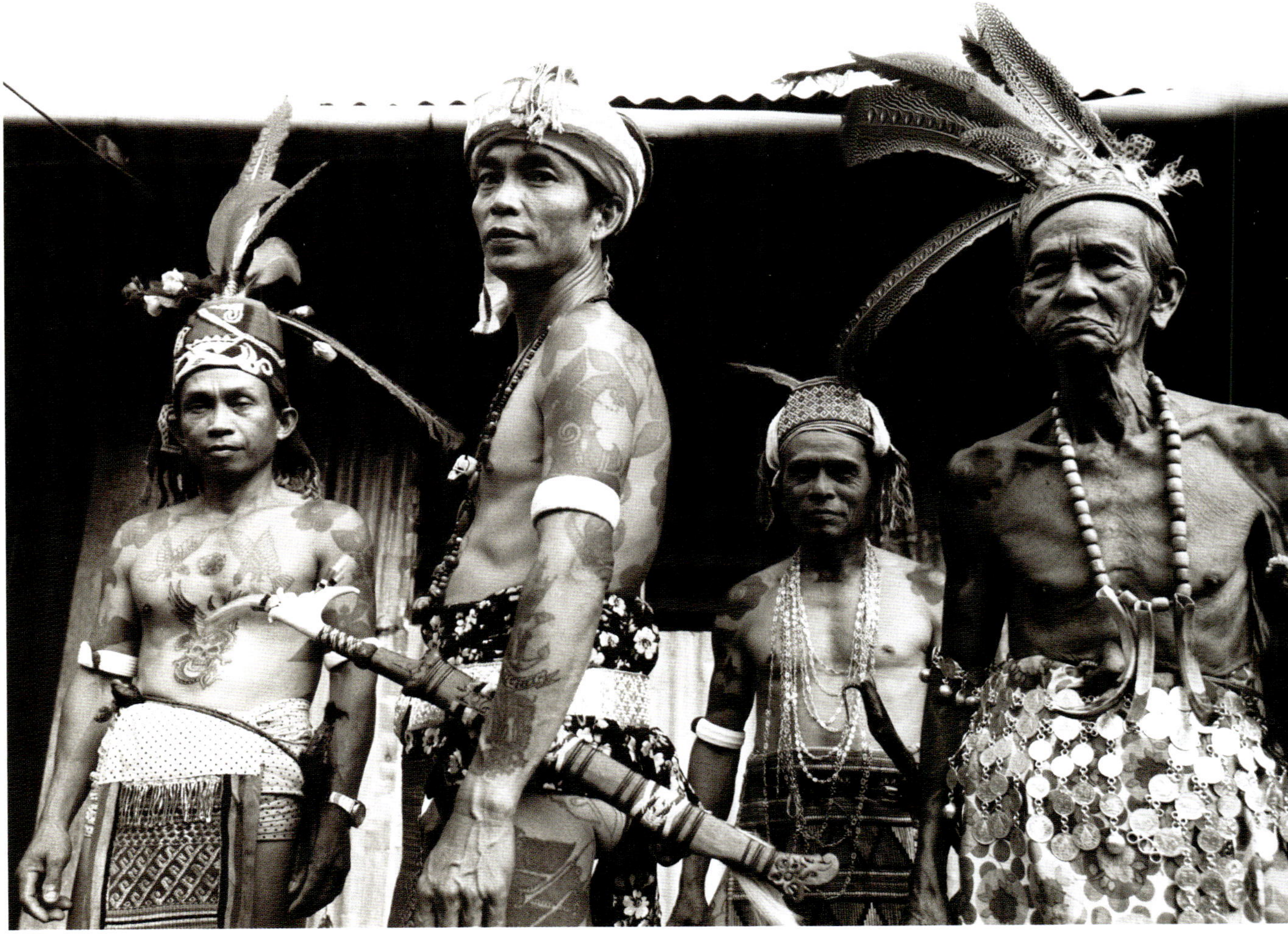

FIGURE 4.7

Jalin, Legan, Ubu, and Mang anak Jilap of Rumah Entalau, Skrang River, Sarawak, 1996. Mang was the last master tattooist and designer of the Skrang River Iban. When he was a young man and learning to tattoo, he was contacted by a tutelary and protector spirit in a dream. This entity instructed him to seek out a special tree in the forest within which he would find a charmed amulet that would offer protection to the men he tattooed. Mang was also part of an elite World War II fighting force known as the Iban Rangers. He and his Iban comrades bravely fought heavily armed Japanese soldiers with their *mandau* swords, blowguns, and spears. The rangers he tattooed were never injured, because the bullets "just went around us and no one was wounded." On the night of Mang's passing in 2002, I interviewed him about these and other experiences. He revealed that his tattooing charm was a meteorite. Because of his great ability as an artist, Mang possessed a pair of the special *buah klauh* (creeper fruit) tattoos resembling stars on either side of his throat tattoo. This tattoo is worn by Iban men who have magical skills in carving, tattooing, or designing, and perhaps in war, since the motif also appears in the *tegulun* (hand tattoos) of successful headhunters. © Sven Torfinn.

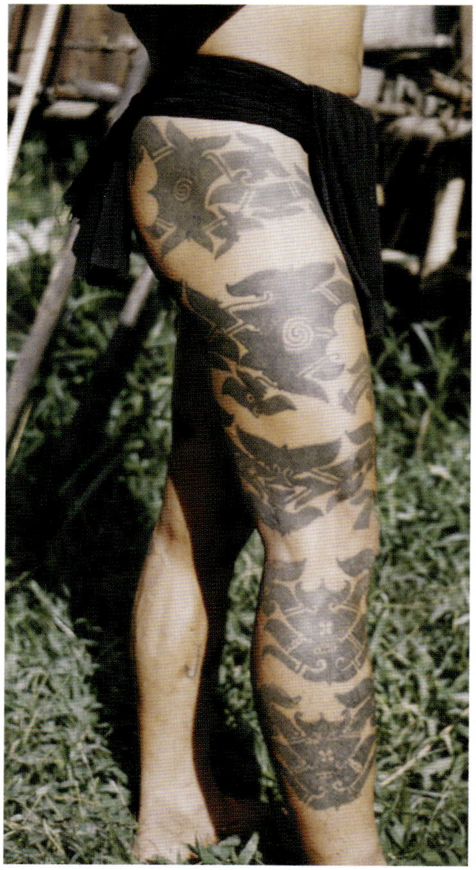

FIGURE 4.8
Kala pah (thigh scorpion) tattoos and other Iban leg designs, Lower Baleh River, Sarawak, ca. 1950. Courtesy of Monica Freeman.

After these tattoos, it was important for men to acquire another set of paired tattoos on the lower forearms and/or back during *bejalai*. These were usually *ketam*, or crab designs, and are depicted in several of Monica Freeman's illustrations of tattooed men. The next major pattern was the *kala pah*, or "thigh scorpion." The scorpion is widely employed in the decorative arts of the Iban because it is an apotropaic motif. According to the Freemans (Freeman Papers 1948–1958: n.p.) and Kurzman (1993:71), the *kala pah* had to be tattooed after the shoulder rosettes and crab tattoos because they needed "food" to eat and the latter provided that. If the scorpion(s) did not have this food, they might "eat" the tattoo bearer for lack of food, thus he might become ill or plagued by misfortune.

There are many other markings that comprise the Iban men's tattoo lexicon, and a few more with magical qualities from the Skrang River will be mentioned here. I draw heavily on the informative book *Pantang Iban* (Franken and Torfinn 1998:155–156), which provides an excellent illustrated index to Skrang Iban tattooing motifs and their meanings. The authors, one of whom (Franken) is a professional tattoo artist, based his findings on field interviews with Iban tattoo artists and tattooed elders on the Skrang and Bangkit Rivers in 1996.

A major motif often placed on the neck and upper shoulders below the back of the head is the *kara jangkam*, or strangling parasitic fig. As it grows on a tree, it eventually suffocates and kills its host. The hollow trunk is never felled because it is believed to be the home of spirits and malevolent entities that can harm or kill any person who might offend them. This tattoo is a form of protection, since a man bearing it is believed to have attained a certain level of invincibility from enemy warriors who seek human heads to enhance their prestige and status.

The *buah andu*, or fruit of the parasitic fig, is another back tattoo. It is placed on the spinal column and sometimes on the sides of the ribcage and other empty spaces. If the fig is trimmed or cut back, it quickly regenerates and spreads rapidly across the forest floor. Some Iban men have claimed that individuals with these tattoos are capable of invisible and rapid jungle-running.

Another back tattoo motif derived from nature is the *embayar*, or centipede. Several species of centipedes inhabiting Iban territory are phosphorescent and emit light in the darkness of the jungle. Centipedes also figure prominently in Iban women's tattooing (see below). On men these tattoos resemble a wavy line flanked by rows of dots that are connected to other motifs on the back.[3] Skrang elders observed that men who possess these tattoos know how to find their way through the jungle and along waterways in darkness.

As noted, *tegulun* (hand tattoos) were worn only by men who had taken several lives (and their heads) on the battlefield. It has also been recorded that those men who were greatly skilled in carving ritual objects might also bear these exquisite markings (Franken and Torfinn 1998).[4] Sometimes glossed as the *bunga tungan* (flowers of the hand), several motifs, many of which have not been defined, composed the overall patterning of the *tegulun* and included the *kala*, or scorpion (base of the thumb); *antu pala*, or trophy heads (back of the hand); *buah klauh*, or creeper fruit (back of the hand); and anthropomorphs (mid-digits) (Appell-Warren 2009:86, fig. 28; Freeman Papers 1948–1958). Some of the aforementioned motifs were certainly apotropaic, and I was told by the Skrang combat veteran Itan of Rumah Entalau that a scorpion on the thumb signified that a captive had been taken during an enemy battle.

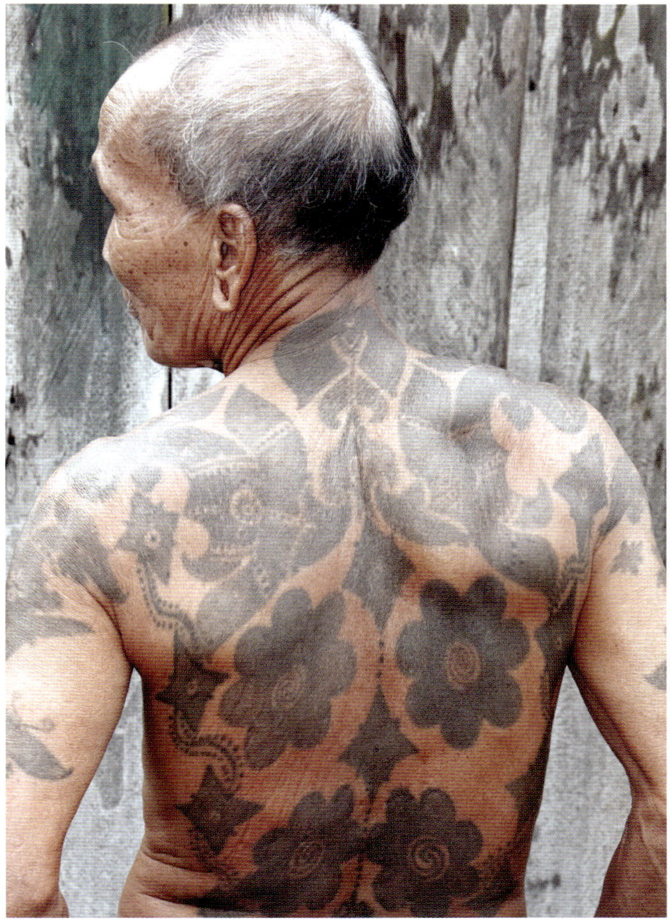

FIGURE 4.9
Back tattoos of Long Anak Jimbak, Rumah Emperan, Skrang River, Sarawak, 2011. The predominate motifs include *kara jangkam* (strangling parasitic fig creeper), *buah andu* (crawling parasitic fig creeper), *embayar* (centipede), and *bunga terong* (brinjal flower). © Lars Krutak.

Tillema recorded a similar mark of honor among the Batang Lupar Iban. *Tali sabit pantang* was a traditional chest design resembling a zigzagging double line of diamond patterns, with each line terminating in circular designs that are rayed (Tillema 1930:204). The motif was derived from a piece of an old garment that was used as a sling to hold children. Although Tillema noted that this tattoo denoted the owner had captured a child during a headhunting raid, it is likely that this important mark signified that the warrior had captured the head of an *anak umbung*. These individuals were usually young girls that were secluded in the loft of a high-ranking family's longhouse *bilik* (apartment). They were trained to become master weavers, among other things, and eventually they learned how to weave the most powerful textiles used in various Iban ceremonies, including rites wherein these objects received enemy heads. The girls were secluded until a preferable marriage was arranged, usually to a similarly high-ranking individual who was also an accomplished warrior. The feat of bringing home the head of an *anak umbung* was a nearly impossible task because such children were "always protected by the last line of defense of the fiercest of the [longhouse] leader's warriors" (Kedit 2017:224). Therefore, this exceptional tattoo was worn only by men of the highest warrior class.

Returning to Itan's testimony, he also noted that a particular unnamed hand pattern signified that the owner had tasted enemy flesh. This comment caught me by surprise when I heard it because I had not yet encountered similar information in published accounts. Two years later, I shared this information with the Iban scholar and anthropologist Dr. Mike Heppell, and he confirmed this activity was customary. "I certainly was told that a victorious warrior would eat bits of flesh," he noted.[5] Heppell then paraphrased some of Derek Freeman's fieldnotes about head-taking, which I provide below at some length.[6] This scene revolves around the taking of a Japanese head during World War II:

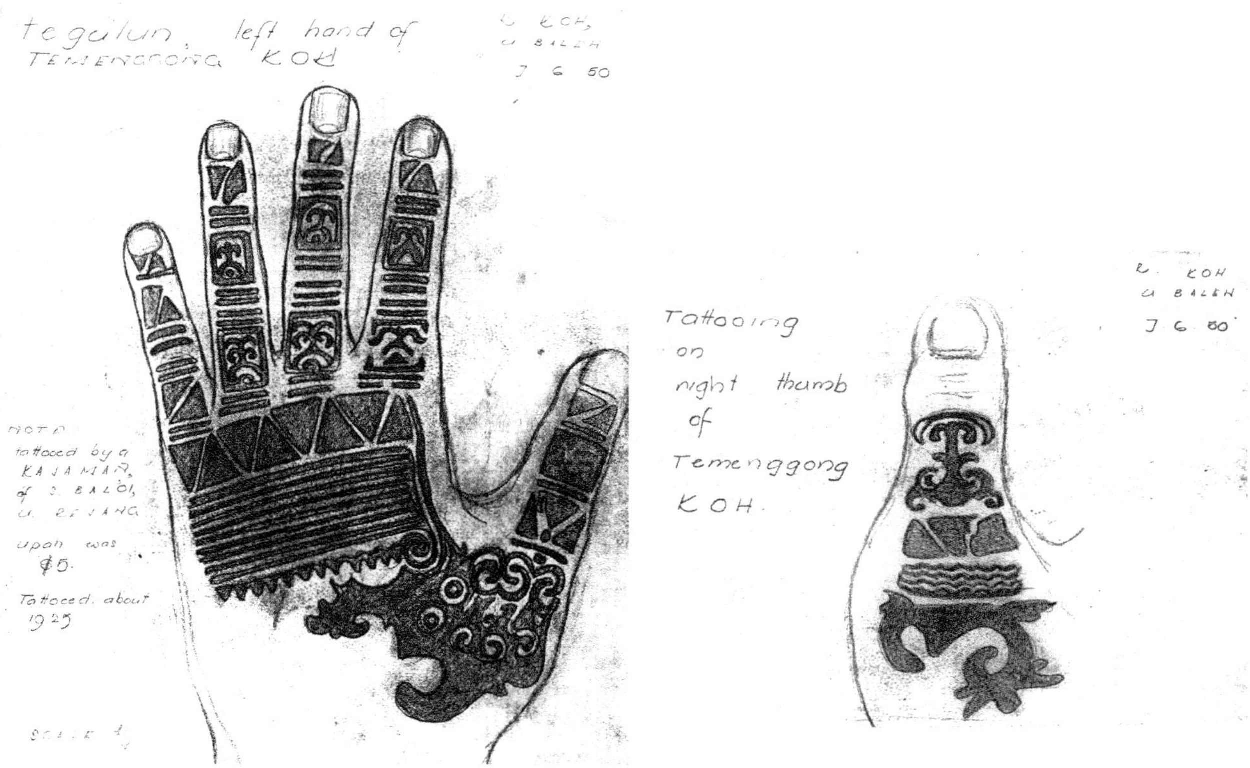

FIGURE 4.10

Hand (*left*) and thumb (*right*) tattoos of the Iban leader and veteran warrior Temenggong Koh, Baleh River, Sarawak, 1950. Koh was the *penghulu* (high-ranking chief) of the Ibans of the Kapit region of Sarawak in the early to mid-twentieth century. He was a great *pun ngayau* (war leader) and assisted by a *tua'* (guardian spirit), the "Remaing (Tiger Cat) war demon," that appeared to him again and again in visions and dreams with instructions or advice (Richards 1972:81). Other writers noted that he was empowered by other entities, including the Nabau (King of Serpents) and "twenty of the culture heroes of the Iban and twenty tiger spirits" (Freeman 1981:60n48). It is said he took more than one hundred heads in hand-to-hand combat. Both hands were completely marked from the wrists to the fingernails. When an Iban man took a head, he earned the right to have one joint of one finger tattooed. With each additional head to his credit another joint was hand-tapped. When the number of slain enemies could no longer be counted on all the joints of the fingers and two thumbs of both hands, the pattern was continued down the back of the hands. The depicted tattoos were made by an unnamed Kejaman tattooist in 1925 for the price of five Sarawak dollars. Drawings by Monica Freeman. Courtesy National Library of Australia (Ms. Acc12.055).

Makai darah—when a head is newly taken all those who are *berani* [brave] take some of the blood on their fingers and swallow it. This is to prevent *menawa ngayau* when *ngayau* [going on a war raid] (*menawa ngayau* is described as a kind of blackout—giddiness and blindness which overtake a person when faced with an enemy). [*Menawa usually means some serious illness, and in the case of the head, I would suppose taking the blood would act as some kind of prophylactic against a vengeful spirit of the victim working on the same principle as most traditional vaccines.*]

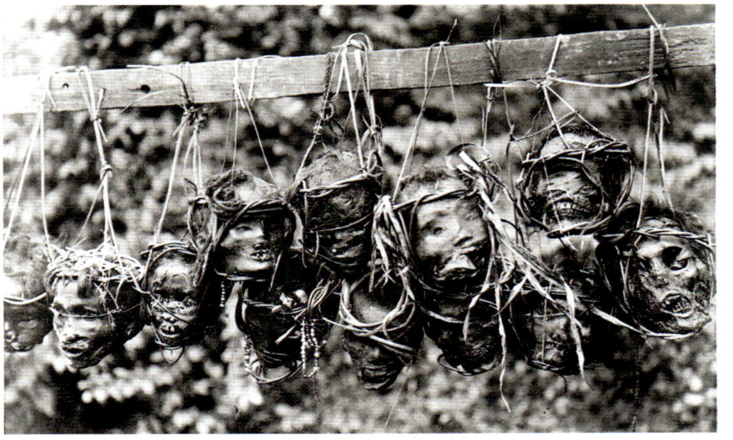

FIGURE 4.11
Enemy heads taken by the Iban, ca. 1905. Wellcome Library Collection (31448i).

When the *pala Jipun* [Japanese head] arrived at R[umah] Nyala [longhouse on the Sungai Sut River] it was received by Gayar and Bunsia. Gayar bit into the flesh of the head and Bunsia bit off some of the flesh and swallowed it. This was to *malas*, an expression of hatred for Japanese who had killed Iban in an attack on Kapit.

The first opportunity is taken to remove [the] brains of [the] head to make it lighter to carry. This is usually on [the] night after [the] attack. Camp is made in jungle. *Ngeb[u]k antu* [removing the brain from the skull]—the process is commenced with a *lungga* [small knife], then a piece of twisted rattan is used to scoop out the brains from [the] foramen. [*Ngebuk, while it is not a ritual, it is a very spiritually dangerous operation, hence an experienced man with some very power[ful] charms to be able to resist the vengeful spiritual power of the victim would always be sought. The charms would have to be present and I would imagine the lungga would be washed in water together with the charms, so that it does not make a mess of the operation.*]

On head hunting each man takes a *lungga*—this *lungga* is the *upah* [payment] of [the] man who does *ngeb[u]k*; often it is someone who did not take part in the attack[,] especially an older man. When doing *ngeb[u]k*, the operator must not *mutah* [vomit]; sanction *takut alah semengat ari munsoh* [*because the person performing the action would be overcome by the soul of the dead person*]. End *enda gayu* [*and their life would be cut short*]. *Lubang untak* is the foramen.

Then at succeeding camps the head is dried. The process takes about 5 nights; the operator stays up the whole night through (only dozing) keeping the fire burning. The skin is not cut off, but allowed to dry onto skull.

[The] last Japanese to be killed at Kapit [was] bayoneted [by] *Penghulu* Ngangau. [He] was smoked out of [a] dug out. Ganing says that part of the body was *tunu* [cooked/burned] and eaten on the spot. He says this was mainly because the Iban were *pedis [h]ati* [angry] at [the] death of *P[enghulu]* Ngangau. People said the meat was *nyamai baka babi* [tasty and like pork].

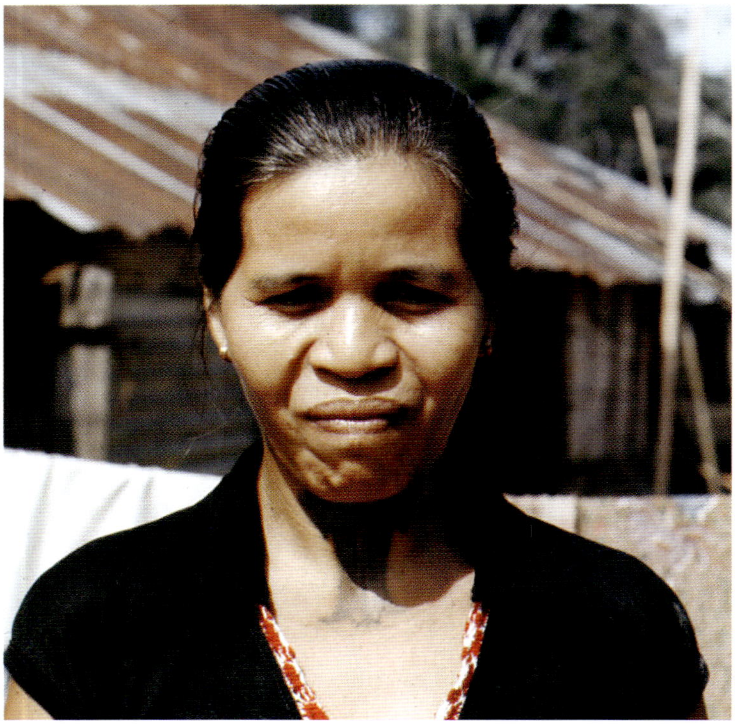

FIGURE 4.12
Ilam bini Penghulu Ngali, an Ulu Ai' Iban woman with a Brahminy kite throat tattoo, Nanga Delok, Sarawak, 1972. The photographer of this image noted that all of the women he met with the throat tattoo were childless. © Michael Heppell.

IBAN WOMEN'S TATTOOS

Although across their vast home territory many Iban tattooing motifs resembled one another and many generalizations have been, and continue to be, made in the literature that they are derived from the same source, the more accurate assessment is that each river system had its own variations regarding the meaning and source of origin of nearly every tattoo design. For example, the neck tattoo of Batang Ai Iban men, as well as of women,[7] living in Sarawak represented the Brahminy kite (Heppell 2005:114), whereas among the Skrang Iban the neck tattoo, which was never worn by women, was derived from the scorpion or frog (Franken and Torfinn 1998:144; Krutak 2007:82).[8]

Nevertheless, just as great Iban men were tattooed to mark their personal achievements, Iban women were tattooed as proof of their accomplishments in weaving *pua kumbu'* ceremonial fabrics. Although many Iban women were accomplished weavers, gaining prestige and enhanced status through their labor-intensive work, only a few were truly "experts" able to produce the most powerful and intricate patterns (Gavin 1995; Krutak 2007). It was these highly skilled women who were the preferred marriage partners of powerful, capable, and heavily tattooed Iban men (Heppell 2005; Howell 1912:63), a fact that was expressed to me in 2011 by Iban elders of Entalau on the Skrang.

More specifically, the highest-ranking Skrang Iban weavers attained their status through following strict protocols over the course of their lifetimes. They were *anak umbong* (secluded) from puberty in the *meligai* (attic) of their *bilik* (living quarters) in the longhouse. It was here in the attic or loft that they conducted their weaving. They were protected and served by the family's slaves, who brought them food, as well as water to bathe in. Technically speaking, they rarely left this confined space until marriage, all the while they honed their weaving skills through practice, charms (some of which were handed down), and inherent abilities—a practice that continued into married life. These women were also "trained" to receive *naka pala* (trophy heads, see below), and *raja brani* (great warriors) sought them out because of their high status, hand tattoos, abilities, and weaving achievements. It was believed that the union of a gifted weaver and a great warrior resulted in "greatness" that would carry into the next generation of the family line.

Notwithstanding, *pua kumbu'* had several functions, with the most powerful cloths, called *lebur apis* ("white hot" or "white heat"), being employed by distinguished women (i.e., expert or senior weavers who were often the wives of war leaders) to receive freshly severed human heads captured by Iban warriors in combat (Kedit 2017). When the Iban still practiced headhunting, the *lebur apis* were woven only while warriors were on the warpath; all other *puas* currently in progress were stopped. For if a woman tied a knot on *pua kumbu*, she risked "tying the legs" of her longhouse's warriors and they "would trip and fall" during their raid (Kedit 2017:211). Conversely, there was positive sympathetic magic associated with weaving *lebur apis* when a headhunt was underway. Lifting supplementary weft threads with a bodkin was "akin to stabbing the eyes of enemies and blinding them" (Kedit 2017:211). The *lebur apis* thus created featured only the most powerful "rank" of designs, and as the women prepared for the ritual reception of the heads, the longhouse's warriors were compelled to remain outside of it for a period of days until, as noted, the enemy heads had been prepared.

An Iban informant, Leo Nyuak (1906:406–408), described this *encabau arong* (Richards 1997:80) or *enchabuh arung* (Kedit 2017:214) ceremony in detail to the English missionary Reverend Edmund Dunn circa 1900, highlights of which are paraphrased below. I also provide a few excerpts of a "head-song" that was performed at the rite, as well as other details concerning these rituals among the Saribas Iban (cf. Kedit 2017).

On the return of a successful war expedition, men were compelled to wait in their boats until the following morning, otherwise sickness would break out in the longhouse. A *kelingkang* (receptacle) was then made for each head, which was created from a five-foot-long bamboo pole split and spread out at one end. This area was woven to create a basketlike container that was adorned with the young yellow leaves of the *isang* (areca palm), which signified victory.[9]

In the morning the warriors carried the trophy heads to the foot of the longhouse ladder, and the *kelingkang*, each holding a head, were planted in the ground in a line. A large plaited mat was laid on the ground on which the men sat. Here, they awaited the arrival of the women who fetched the trophies and transported them into the longhouse. The women descended the ladder, each swathed in a *lebur apis* and bearing an offering plate. An elaborate exchange ensued between the leading woman of the longhouse, often the wife of the war leader and most experienced and spiritually mature weaver, and the leader of the war party. Using archaic and stylized metaphoric language, she asked about the war expedition and then asked to see what "fruits" had been "plucked" so that they could be secured within the *lebur apis*, which "called out to be filled" (Kedit 2017:215). The smoked heads were then revealed, and the women cried out in a *minjung tampak* (high pitched shrill) and rushed the trophies, each grabbing one in her hands and biting its cheeks as a signal of authority over the head.

One by one, the heads were then placed on the plates. The women covered each head with the ends of their *lebur apis* shawls, or, if not enough of these were available, a *pua belantan* (special cloth) was used (Kedit 2017:215), then a processional was formed and the women ascended the ladder and entered the open veranda of the longhouse. They crossed this space, which ran the entirety of the longhouse, three times, all the while chanting the head-song. This tune, which has several variations depending on the locale, is called the *naku antu pala* and was deployed to incite young Iban men to go out and obtain more heads. One version of this song is as follows:

Aih! Get more!
Get for me one more!
Aih! Some more!
I feel very ashamed praising
this old head trophy,
Not seeing it bloody!
I am ashamed, my love,
Praising this dried-up old head trophy,
I have been keeping these warp threads
Covered with cobwebs[.]
Aih! Get more!
Get for me one more!
I am ashamed, my love, praising
[This] dried-up head trophy! (Tun Jugah Foundation 1992:100)

After these invocations, the *naku*, or head dance, was performed by four women and kept up during the greater part of the day. They faced each other two by two, swinging the heads in their right hands. They advanced and receded with a slow swinging step, partly forward, partly sideways, with each step accompanied with the cry of *Ha Hai!*, the head being swayed to and fro.

In the accompanying chants the heads were asked how they came by their deaths. What was the bad dream that foretold their fates? The head answered—how it dreamed, it had been bitten by a snake, or carried off by a crocodile. It was told, "That was a lucky dream for it directed the spear that struck you, it rendered keen the edge of the sword that struck you from your body."

Meanwhile, a vessel containing water and a flat stone was placed near the head of the longhouse ladder, and as each warrior stepped into the longhouse, he placed his foot on the stone and his back was rubbed with oil. A coil of wire was placed around the neck of the young men who participated in their first headhunting foray. These ceremonies were supposed to ward off any evil that might befall the warrior or the village from the curses of their enemies.

Apart from the ritual occasions surrounding a successful headhunting foray, *puas* of a lesser power were used by Iban *manang* (shamans), tattoo artists, and warriors to create sacred enclosures. They sat under these ceremonial fabrics to await the arrival of their spirit helpers for guidance and success (Ong 1999: 9; Taylor and Aragon 1991:168). Sometimes men were covered with a *pua* on the night before a major undertaking, hoping for a special dream or visitation by a protective spirit or deity (Appell-Warren 2009:xxxiii). Tattooists and shamans also deployed these spiritually charged fabrics as protective devices. In tattooing, *puas* shielded the operator and their client from malevolent spirits attracted to flowing human blood. In healing ceremonies,[10] shamans hung *puas* to create defensive "walls of stone" to keep evil spirits at bay (Freeman 1967:321).

Like Iban tattoo artists and warriors,[11] weavers employed the use of many protective charms in their work, usually small sacred stones, unusual snail shells, deer horns, and porcupine quills (Gavin 1995). Sometimes these charms were discovered during unusual events (i.e., a charm imbedded in a banana stem or a root used to create textile dyes) or in a dream wherein a helping spirit or deity revealed them. Such objects embodied various properties and could be deployed to increase a weaver's skill or memory so that she could execute and remember complex patterns, or they might enhance her ability to acquire knowledge quickly or boost her confidence level regarding the tedious work at hand (Gavin 1995; Masing 1981).

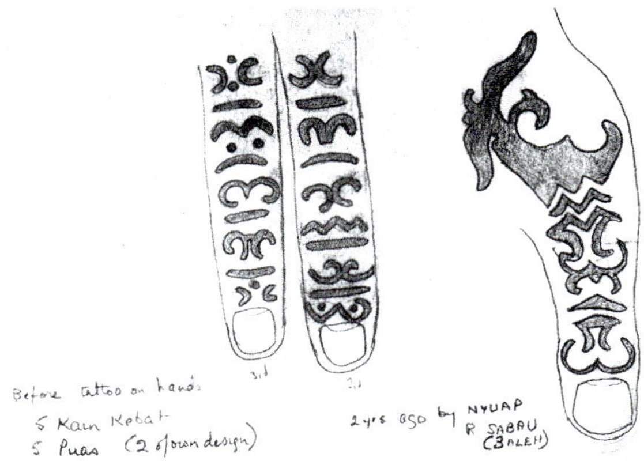

FIGURE 4.13
Illustrations of Iban woman's finger tattoos communicating prowess in weaving, Rumah Pedang, Baleh River, Sarawak, 1949. A notation delineates the necessary accomplishments needed for obtaining these prestigious marks and the tattooist's name. Drawings by Monica Freeman. Courtesy National Library of Australia (Ms. Acc12.055).

Other charms were important because they offered protection by shielding the weaver's body and ensuring her physical well-being from malevolent energies. Still more charms protected a weaver from "madness" or people who might cast evil spells, whereas the most effective charm prevented the weaver from being "consumed by the task at hand" (Gavin 1995:67). This *penyeliah jamah* (a kind of special charm) allowed the weaver to proceed directly to the most complicated patterns without having to first master others of a lower order.[12] In order to "activate" these weaving charms, they were tied to the weaver's loom and/or threads, placed in her hair (i.e., quills), or dipped into tattoo pigment so that their powers could be transferred to the weaver through her skin.

The woven patterns Iban women created were vested with great meaning and spiritual energy, and powerful designs brought the weaver into sometimes dangerous contact with spirits and deities—entities that could "break loose" from the pattern and cause disharmony and misfortune in the longhouse community (Krutak 2007:76).[13] Thus, a weaver's communications with her *antu nulong* (spirit helpers) or guides were of paramount importance, especially since spirits were attracted to the *engkudu* (deep-red dye) used in *pua* blankets that, from a symbolic standpoint, was nearly equivalent to human blood (Howell 1912:63).

The *ngar* procedure or ritual of mixing the blood-red dye to the proper color was difficult to achieve, and around 1900 it has been said that perhaps only one in fifty women knew how to do it (Howell 1912:63). But the technical preparation of the pigment was only one part of the ritual. A weaver had to receive permission from her spirit helper(s) or a deity to initiate the dyeing ritual in order to create or invent her own unique designs, a spiritual invitation that did not come to all women (Vogelsanger 1980:117).[14] This "commanding" entity showed the weaver what pattern to weave in a dream and supplied the proper charms necessary for success, but if it was disobeyed it could bring on illness, madness, or even the death of the woman (Gavin 1991:4).

Obviously, *pua* weaving was a hazardous spiritual undertaking. And for this reason, it was recognized by the Iban as *kayau indu'* (women's war) or the "warpath of women"[15] (Howell 1912:63), a cultural tradition considered complementary to headhunting.[16] In turn, expert weavers who could weave original designs with the most powerful motifs, some of which were believed to incite men to go on the warpath, received *entegelun* (hand tattoos) on one or more of their fingers, the back of the thumb, or across the back of their hand similar to those worn by headhunting

FIGURE 4.14
Enyan anak Usen, a highly respected Ulu Ai' Iban weaver, with hand and forearm tattoos, 1984. She is preparing threads for *pilih* (supplementary weft) weaving. © Anthony Howarth.

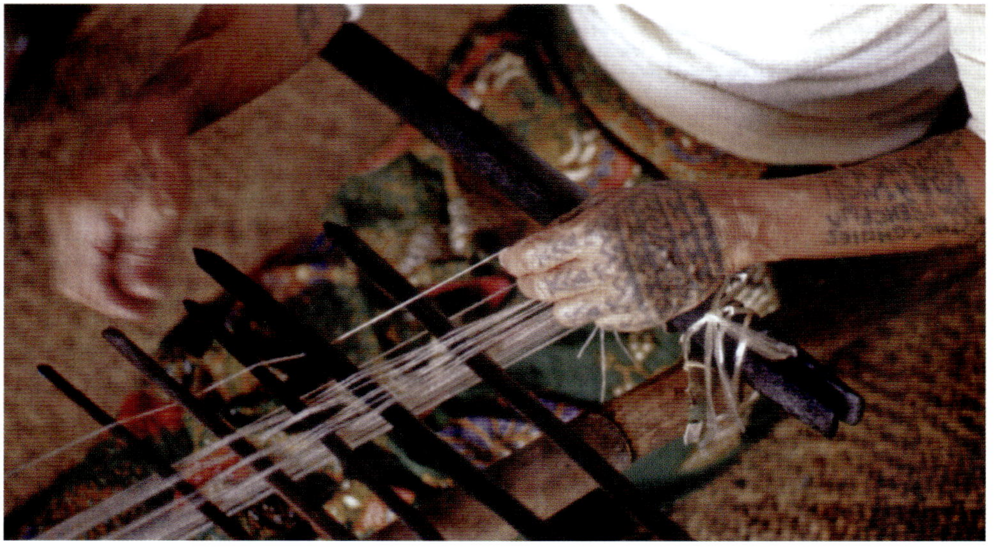

FIGURE 4.15
Skrang River Iban weaver displaying *pala tumpa'*, or "head of bracelets," tattoo composed of pincer-like *kala* (scorpion) motif and *kemebai* (centipede) band, 2002. Both are protective symbols widely used in Iban art. © Lars Krutak.

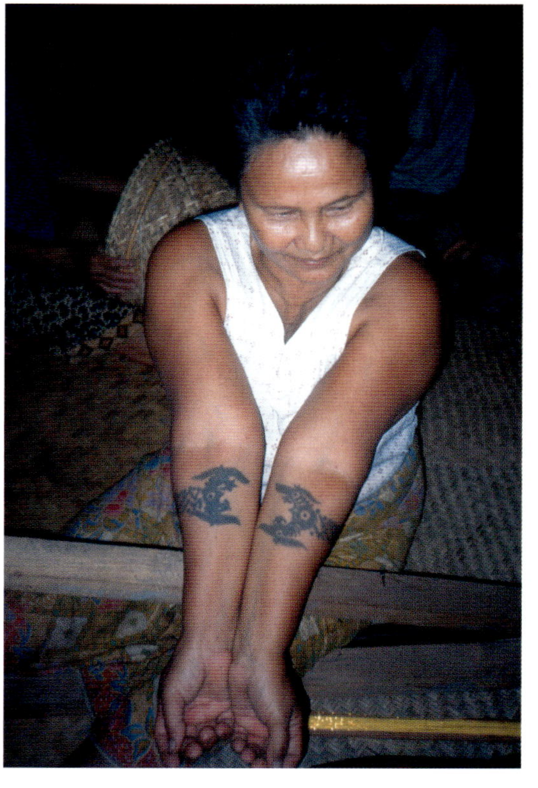

men. High status weavers decided to be tattooed at the time of the *ngar* ritual because Meni and Kumang, the deities that presided over dyeing and weaving, were believed to be present to witness the weaver's newly elevated status and bestow their blessings (Gavin 1991:25). Among the Baleh Iban of Sarawak, a woman could receive a hand tattoo only if she had woven five *ikat* patterned *kain kebat* (skirts) and five *puas*, of which two must have been original designs (Appell-Warren 2009:111). Women who had not quite achieved this level of renown but who displayed skill and ability in the production of *puas* and other handicrafts (cf. Franken and Torfinn 1988:140) could receive the *pala tumpa'* (head of bracelets) tattoo on their upper forearms (Krutak 2007:80).[17] The name of this tattoo refers to its position on the woman's upper forearm, because it sat atop rows of bangle bracelets worn from the wrists to the elbows. This composite tattoo was usually formed by two apotropaic creatures,[18] namely the *kala* (scorpion) with its pincers and a zigzagging band around the arm depicting the *kemebai* (centipede). Both motifs are widely used in Iban arts, including weaving.

ORANG ULU: KAYAN, KENYAH, AND THEIR NEIGHBORS

The Indigenous Orang Ulu (Upriver People) inhabit the interior areas of Borneo, especially along the Upper Rajang and its tributaries, and the Middle and Upper Baram River and its branches in Sarawak. In Kalimantan, their major settlement areas occur along the middle and upper courses of the Kayan, Mendalam, Barito, Mahakam, Melawi, and Kapuas Rivers and their many tributaries.

The Kayan and Kenyah are two of the largest Orang Ulu groups and share particular cultural and social characteristics, including rigidly stratified societies of a hierarchical order and attendant tattooing traditions that demarcate an individual's rank. These social strata consist of the ruling elite or aristocrats (two tiers, a high and low order), commoners or ordinary villagers, and the former "slave" class.[19]

In contrast to the Iban, Kayan and Kenyah tattooists were always female, and women were more heavily marked than Kayan men.[20] Typical male patterns included rosettes on the shoulders and chest, and prawn, crab, or centipede motifs on the thighs and arms (Hose and Shelford 1906); some of these motifs were inspired by the Iban and other groups, such as the once nomadic Penan and Punan Busang and longhouse-dwelling Lahanan of the Upper Rajang River region.

According to the ethnographic record, the Kayan *tedek* (tattoo) procedure for men was treated with little to no ceremony, namely because they acquired most of their tattooing while on adventurous journeys abroad. As the Dutch explorer and physician Anton Willem Nieuwenhuis (1904:456, 459) wrote long ago, "[T]he shoulder rosette is given to the young man before he has taken part in a large trading expedition or in a headhunt. . . . [And] an initiate can tell by the tattoos of the [Kayan] men which tribe they have visited." Thus, well-traveled individuals might carry the markings of several Borneo tribes.

In turn, little information has been recorded detailing the activity of Kayan male tattooing or its ceremonial significance. However, it is known that great warriors were tattooed on their hands and thighs to demonstrate their accomplishments in headhunting. If the warrior did not take a head in his lifetime but participated in a successful raid, generally speaking only his left thumb

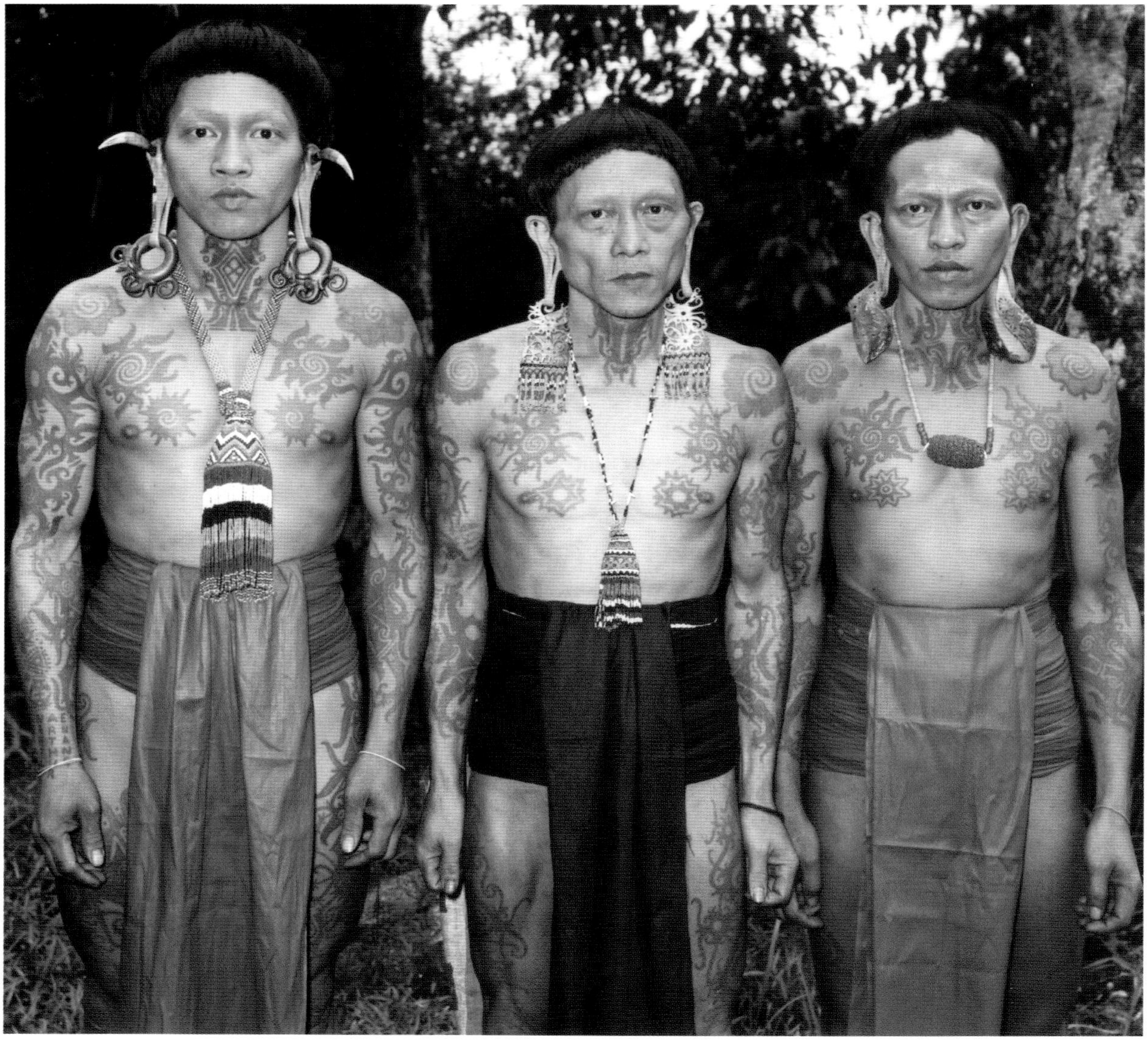

FIGURE 4.16

Pictured here, *left to right*, are Ninyang Inang, Nanyap Inang, and Raee Tingon, ca. 1965. Little information has been recorded about the meanings behind the tattoo iconography of Borneo's formerly nomadic people, including patterns of the Punan Busang illustrated here. Also known as the Punan Vuhang, both men and women tattooed but the practice was forbidden by household members while a woman was pregnant; otherwise, it was believed she would endure difficulties during childbirth (Chan 2007:252). Powerful *otu kunyuling* (spirits), who lived far beneath the earth's surface, were also believed to be tattooed. They had red bodies and were amenable to humans. Some became the "patron" spirits of Punan Busang shamans (Chan 2007:182). Photograph by Tom Harrison. © Sarawak Museum Department, Kuching.

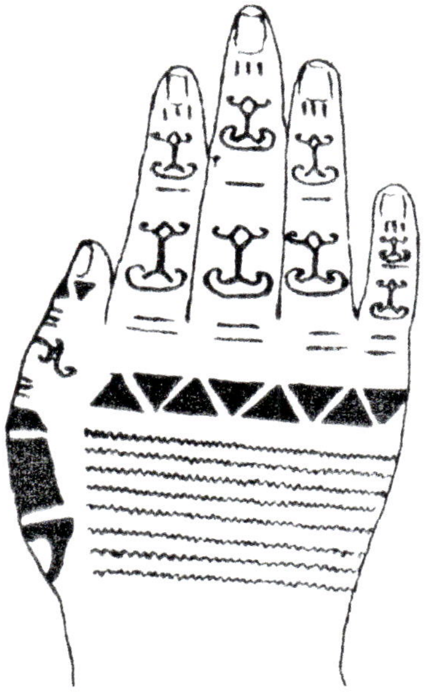

FIGURE 4.17
This illustration depicts the hand tattoos of a Sekapan warrior in the Kayan style. In the Kayan language, the *tegulun*, or anthropomorphic figures on the phalanges, are known by the same word as the word for the hand tattooing of Iban warriors. In ancient times, when a Kayan or Kenyah chief built a new house, the first post driven into the ground was decorated with human and other figures. Within the post hole was placed a slave, whose body was pierced by the monumental timber. This human sacrifice was offered to the *bali akang* (Kenyah), or protective spirits, of the local community so that their benevolence toward the people was secured (cf. Galvin 1974). Among the Kayan, the term *tegulun* also referred to this totem-like pole (Hose and Shelford 1906:67; Southwell 1990:400). From Hose and Shelford 1906: pl. XI.

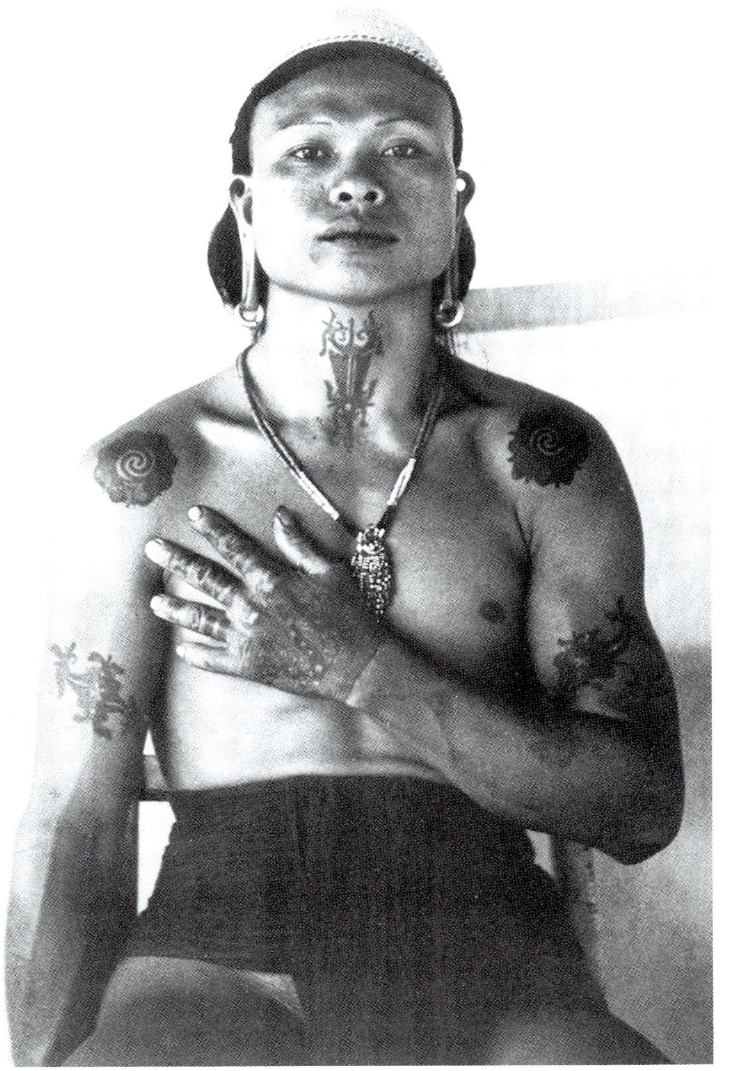

FIGURE 4.18
Kenyah warrior tattooed in the Iban style, 1932. His left hand is heavily marked with a motif that looks like an *aso'*, or dragon-dog. Photograph by Hendrik Tillema. From Tillema 1989:165, fig. 146.

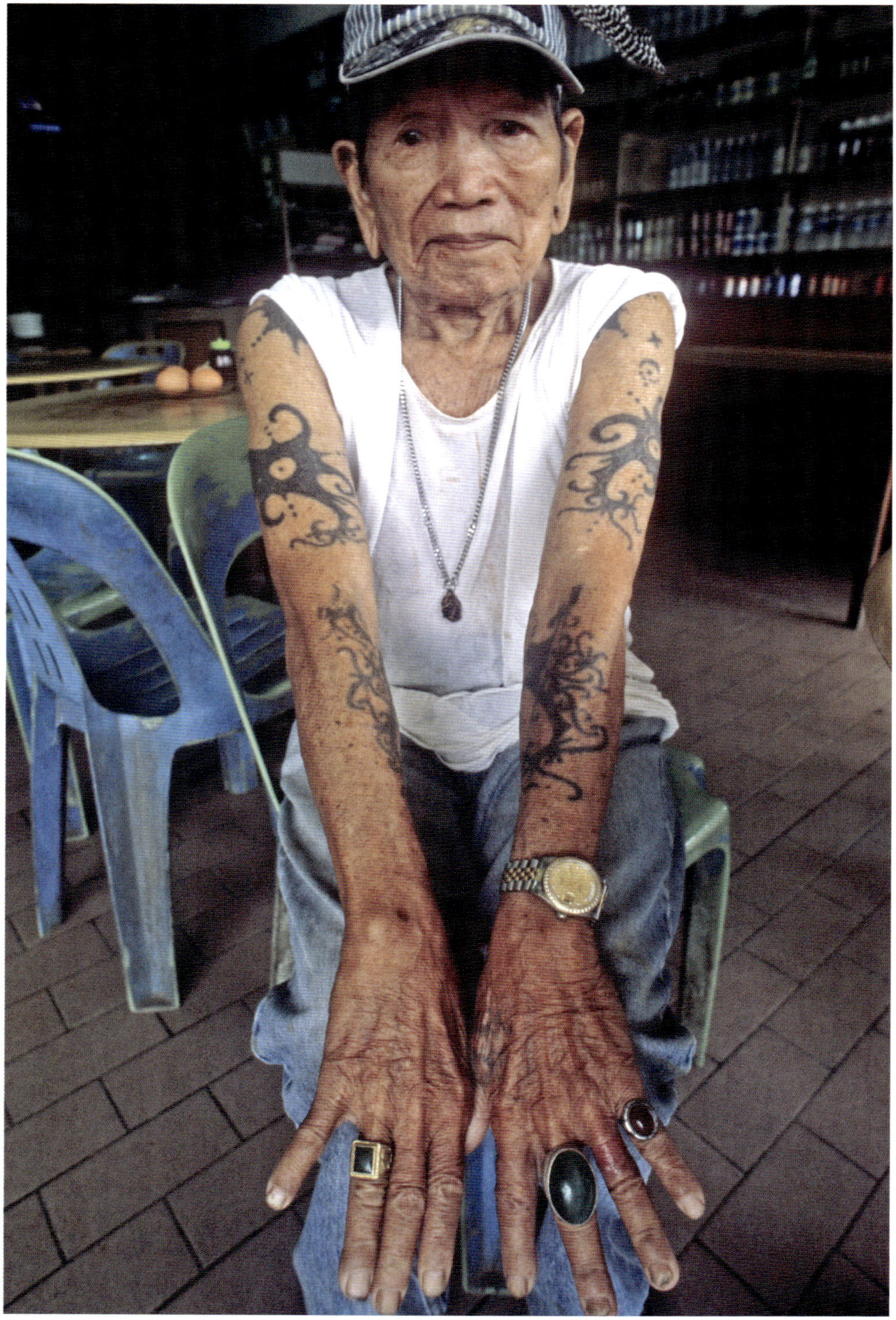

FIGURE 4.19
Former warrior and Lahanan elder Lake' Kulleh Emang, 2002. © Lars Krutak.

could be marked. More specifically, if a Kayan man captured the head of an enemy, he earned the right to have the backs of his hands and fingers tattooed with anthropomorphs on the digits, and with *song irang* (bamboo shoots), *ikor* (lines), and other designs that have not been described (Hose and Shelford 1906:67). There are only a few illustrated examples of these Kayan hand tattoos, and each of them closely resembles those of the Iban.

In 2011, I met a former Lahanan elder named Lake' Kulleh Emang with a warrior tattoo on his left thumb. He was approximately ninety-four years old at that time and a former war captain who was responsible for taking the heads of three enemies. Lahanan men of this distinction were allowed to wear a special tattoo on the bridge of their thumb and index finger that displayed a flowing *aso'* (dragon-dog) motif for all to see. Other small markings were also tattooed on his body for good omens, including a small crescent moon and star pattern (upper left shoulder) that was related to combat. For example, the Lahanan, like the Kalinga of the Philippines who share similar beliefs related to this type of tattoo (see chapter 3, p. 145), looked for favorable signs in the sky before heading to war. When a star appeared close to a crescent moon, this was a good signal that a Lahanan war party should begin their excursion into enemy territory. Eventually this celestial event came to be incorporated into a tattoo placed on Lake' Kulleh Emang's body, and in some sense, it was a good luck symbol. Lake' Emang was also assisted in his martial endeavors by amulets, including a stone worn about his neck for bodily protection.

Another important Kayan men's tattoo was the *lukut*, or "antique bead," pattern. I have documented this motif on the knuckles, wrists, legs, and forearms of Kayan and Kenyah women, whereas others have noted its presence among the nomadic Punan Busang (Hose and Shelford 1906:65). This tattoo, which may consist of two or more sunburst or starlike motifs, was believed to keep the soul from wandering away from its human host.

The origin of this tattoo motif among the Kayan is the stuff of legends. Long ago, when a man fell ill, it was supposed that his soul had escaped from his body, and his recovery was attributed to the return of his lost soul. To prevent the soul's departure in the future, the man tied it in by fastening around his wrist a piece of string threaded with a *lukut* bead, where magic was considered to reside. Because the string could break and the bead could become lost, the Kayan replaced them with a tattooed bead motif that has come to be regarded as a charm to ward off all disease (Hose and Shelford 1906:65; Krutak 2016b:73).

There are very few tattooed Kayan and Kenyah men living today, and I have met only two in my travels: the Kayan elder Tlie Ngo and the Kenyah elder Ibon Chau. However, Mr. Ngo's unique style of chest tattooing was not Kayan. He told me he was tattooed by a female Punan Busang artist while traveling abroad in his youth.

Kenyah men's tattooing aesthetically resembles that of the Iban. Ibon Chau, who was tattooed by his mother-in-law, wears arm and throat tattoos, but the meanings and source of origin behind these tattoos are uniquely Kenyah. As noted among the Iban, neck tattoos usually symbolize a kite, a scorpion, or a frog. Ibon Chau told me his throat tattoo symbolized the swiftlet, a bird that was revered by Kenyah warriors because once it took flight it rarely landed. For the Kenyah, this characteristic was a sign of great endurance and strength, characteristics every warrior wished to possess. The wings of the bird, which appear in Mr. Chau's tattoo, were believed to harness other

FIGURE 4.20
Kayan elder Tlie Ngo who was tattooed by and in the style of the nomadic Punan Busang, 2011. © Lars Krutak.

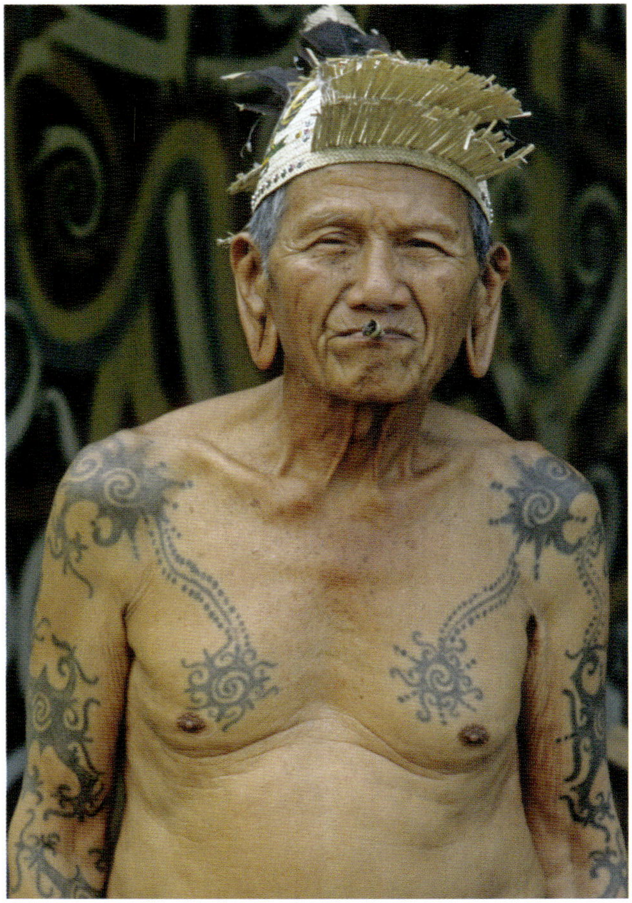

FIGURE 4.21
Kenyah elder Iban Chau possesses a swiftlet tattoo on his throat that was revered for its endurance, hornbills on his arms, and rosettes on his shoulders, 2011. He noted he was inspired to receive these tattoos in order to preserve ancestral traditions that were being forgotten. © Lars Krutak.

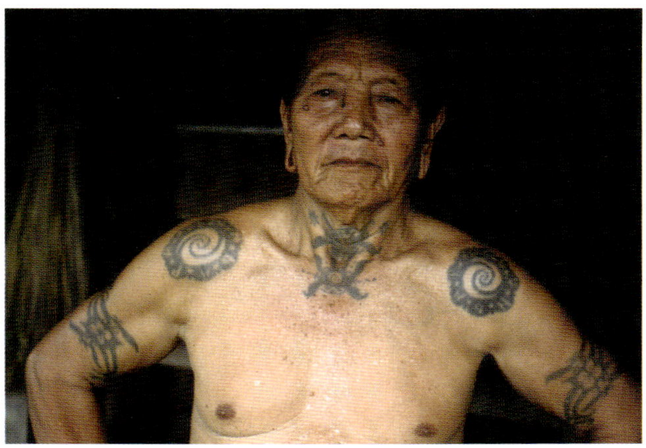

powers. "The wings of the bird offered shelter to the men who wore this warrior class tattoo, and in that sense, it was protective as well," he explained. Apart from his shoulder rosettes, Mr. Chau's arm tattoos were composed of the heads of the *ulu temengang* (rhinoceros hornbill). The beak of the bird was particularly auspicious and believed to bring the person who wore it "good luck." For this reason, a hornbill beak often decorated the toggle worn on a Kenyah warrior's sword belt (Conley 1976:127).

THE TIME FOR TATTOO

In former times, for young Kayan girls tattooing was initiated during certain cosmological events. When a girl was around ten years of age,[21] she would have had her fingers and the upper part of her feet tattooed around the ninth day after a new moon, the *butit halap* lunar phase (Hose and Shelford 1906:70). A year later, the girl might have her forearms completed, followed by her thigh markings. In short, all the tattooing was completed some three to four years after the first tattooing session.

These tattoos not only functioned as tribal identifiers but also marked important life stages. For example, the intricate forearm tattoos were usually made when a girl acquired domestic skills, such as cooking and weaving. Moreover, young Kayan women endeavored to have their tattoos completed before they were married and especially before they bore their first child, since it was considered "immodest" to be tattooed after having become a mother (Hose and Shelford 1906:67).

Kayan tattoo artists and their clients were subjected to numerous taboos before and after a tattooing session. Girls and young women were prohibited from being tattooed during rice seeding time or if a dead person was lying unburied in the longhouse, because it was taboo to let blood during these times (Nieuwenhuis 1904:453). The anthropologist Sharon Thomas (1968:219) added if a female friend of the girl to be tattooed had recently died, the tattoo client must postpone her tattooing for a year. Additionally, women could not be tattooed during their menses, because it was believed that the flowing blood attracted evil spirits. Bad dreams, such as those of floods or fires, metaphorically foretold of much bloodletting during the forthcoming tattoo rite and in such cases the tattooist would postpone her work, sometimes for one year (Krutak 2007:85; S. Thomas 1968:219). Tattooists were forbidden from eating certain foods, such as raw and bloody meat or fish. It was believed that if an artist disregarded any of these prohibitions, the designs that she tattooed would not appear clearly, and she herself would sicken and die.[22]

While I was conducting fieldwork on the Upper Rajang in 2011, I was very fortunate to meet a *dayong* (male or female Kayan priest) named Hunyang Lisang of Uma Bawang who shared detailed knowledge of the Kayan tattooing ritual. She noted that Kayan tattoo artists worked under the tutelage and protection of two goddesses, Bua Kalung and her daughter Laleng Lahay Bua, who were invoked before any new tattoo pattern was initiated for a female client (Krutak 2014c). However, the invocation differed depending on the social status of the tattoo client, because she was restricted to wearing specific tattoo designs appropriate for her social position. For example, if the client belonged to the *maren* or *hipuy*,[23] the two aristocratic Kayan social classes, a Kayan *dayong*

FIGURE 4.22
Kayan tattooist and her assistants at work, Long Jegan, Sarawak, 1956. © Sarawak Museum Department, Kuching.

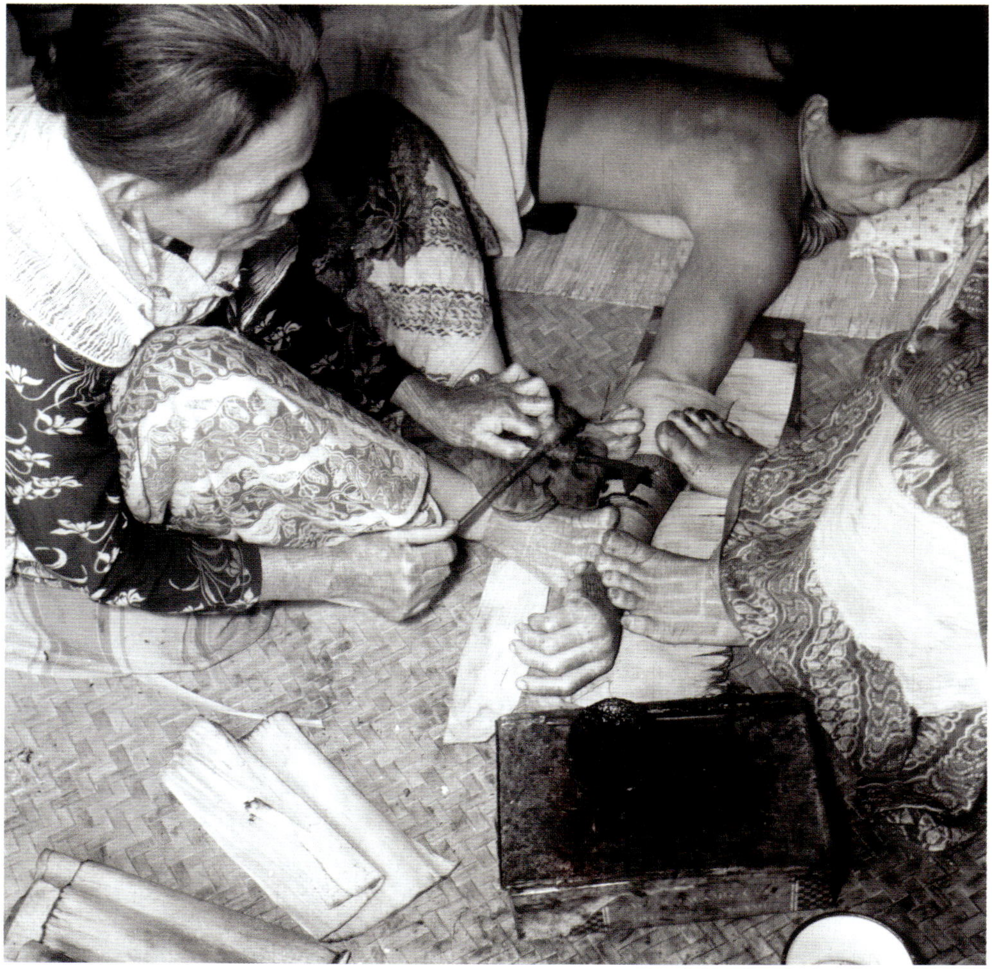

was present and prayed to Bua Kalung because she "owned" *aso'* (dragon-dog), *tingang* (hornbill), *kalong kelunan* (ancestral design), and other patterns reserved for nobility.[24] The prayer announced to the deity the design that was to be applied and asked for the client to feel little pain and for the tattooist to make beautiful designs. A gong was also used during the tattoo rite. It was invoked by the *dayong* to serve as a "shield" of "solid protection" to prevent the client from becoming sick or experiencing misfortune.

If the client was a *panyin* (commoner) then the *dayong* prayed to Lahay Bua, because she owned *kalong tushun tuva* (tuba root design), *kalong pako'* (fern design), and other tattoo patterns associated with that class. Of course, there were many other patterns that could be worn by members of the aristocracy and commoners alike, such as *song irong* (bamboo shoots) on the

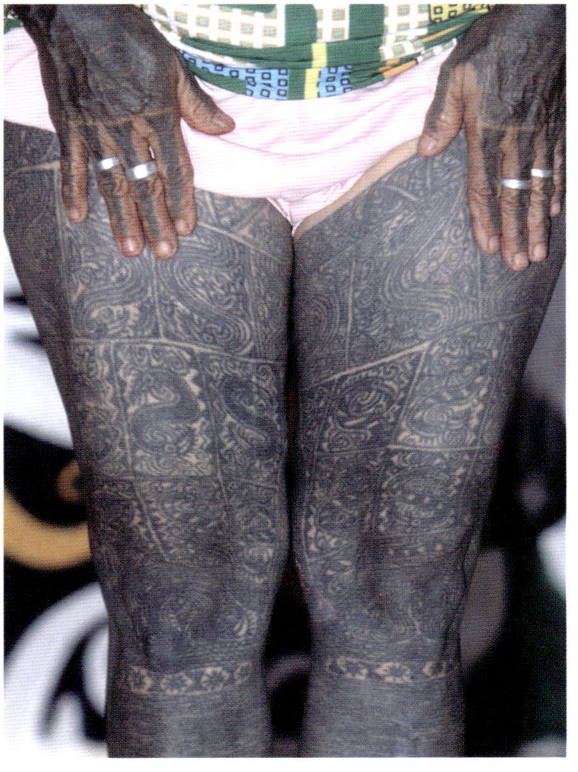

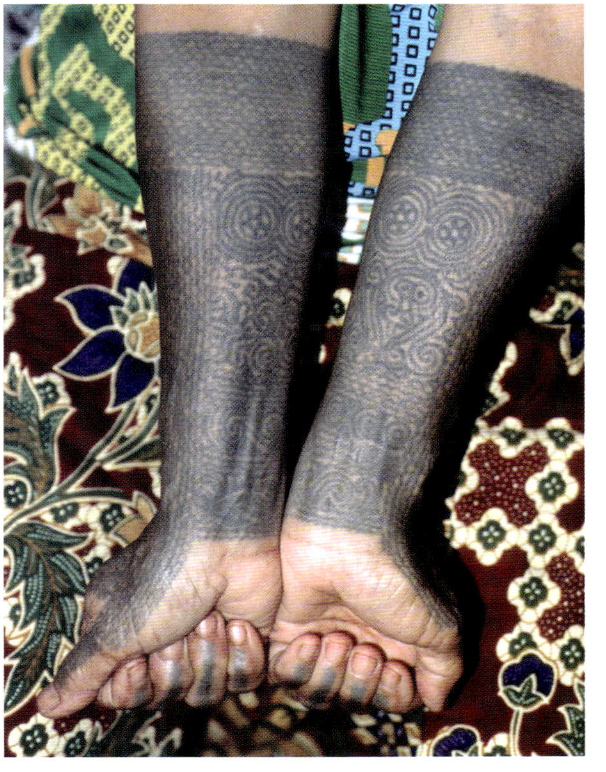

FIGURE 4.23
Kayan elder and aristocrat Avok Avun with tattooed thighs (*left*) and arms (*right*), 2011. Kayan, Kenyah, and several Orang Ulu groups believed that a woman's body tattoos played an important role after death. Avun explained, "My grandparents told me that tattoos were equipment for the afterlife, so that our ancestors could distinguish our social class and identity." According to early ethnographic accounts, on death a woman's bold body tattoo transformed into torches that enabled her to travel through the murky afterworld to find the longhouses of her beloved ancestors (Hose and Shelford 1906:67). Those women who possessed the appropriate full-body tattoos were also allowed to bathe in the heavenly river, Telang Julan, where they collected exquisite pearls from the river's bed (Hose and McDougall 1912:263). © Lars Krutak.

knuckles and fingers, *beliling bulan* (full moon[s]) on the forearm, *dulang harok* (bow of a boat), *ji'am manuk* (bird's beak), *manok wak* (eyes of the scops owl), and *selungan* (band of rattan), among several other designs.

During the tattooing ritual, which mighthave extended over several days, food was offered to the deity and presiding *dayong*. These meals had to be served on a *talem* or bronze tray. Other "gifts" were offered to the tattoo deity. For example, women of the *maren* and *hipuy* class offered specific types of valuable *inu septin* and/or *inu puun* (heirloom beads) so that the tattooist would have "clear eyesight." *Avalanay*, another bead variety, provided protection from lurking spirits attracted

FIGURE 4.24
Kayan elder Ado Ngo displays her bold hand tattoos, 2011. *Song irang*, the black spikes along her fingers, represent bamboo shoots, a fertility symbol. Other motifs are believed to protect the bearer from evil spirits encountered in the jungle. © Lars Krutak.

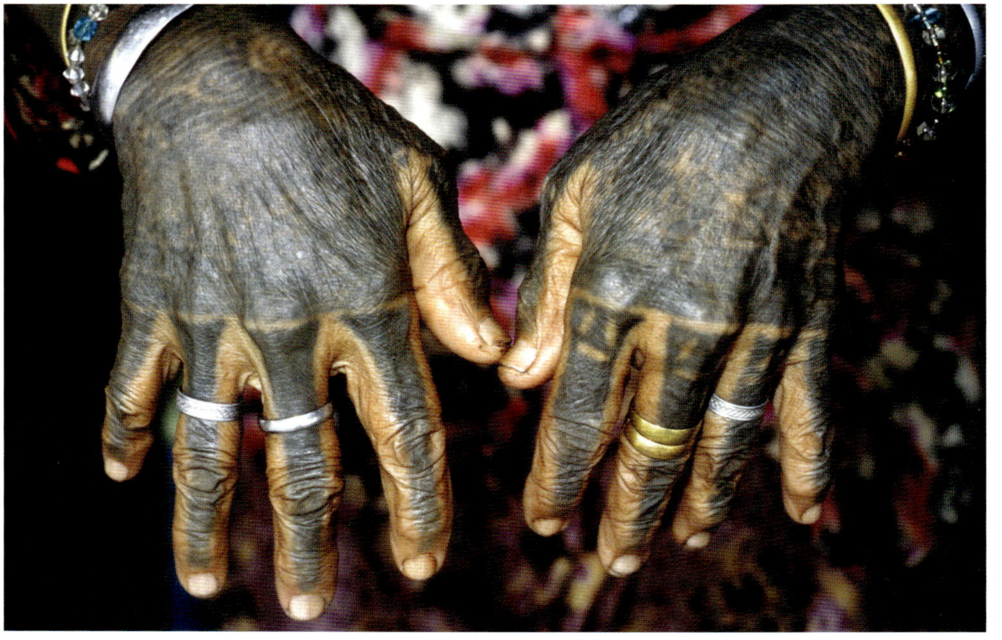

by the flowing blood. These beads eventually became the property of the tattooist on completion of the tattooing.

At the conclusion of the tattooing session, the *dayong* recited a ritual prayer to the tattoo spirit. "This invocation is uttered so that no harm would come to the tattoo client, since her bloody wounds could perhaps attract a lurking spirit," Hunyang Lisang explained.[25]

The tattooist also called on the tattoo deity to return to its world and placed a *malat* (sword) across both knees of the tattoo client, the kneecap being the last location to be tattooed. The sword metaphorically illustrated a *palang* (bridge) or *alan* (path) along which the tattoo deity could return home.

The tattooist was then paid for her services; namely, most of the items used in the ritual: the heirloom beads, the gong, the sword, the food tray, and other items. The *dayong* was also paid for her work, a gong, a sword, or a quantity of heirloom beads being the usual sum (Krutak 2011).

Like the Iban, tattoo patterns were carved by men into *klingé*, or stencil blocks. The tattoo artist worked with one or more assistants, especially as it was necessary to have a skin stretcher before the intricate designs were tapped into the skin. The assistant also soaked up the excess blood with a piece of fibrous palm bark or a cloth (Hiller 1896).

Although tattoo artists of the *pinyin* class could tattoo aristocrats, an elderly Kayan tattoo artist named Ping Saram told me that they could not touch, own, or use *aso'* (dragon-dog) or *tingang* (hornbill) tattoo blocks. If they did, they risked becoming sick or meeting with future misfortune (Krutak 2011). Therefore, only high-class tattooists could apply these sacred designs.[26]

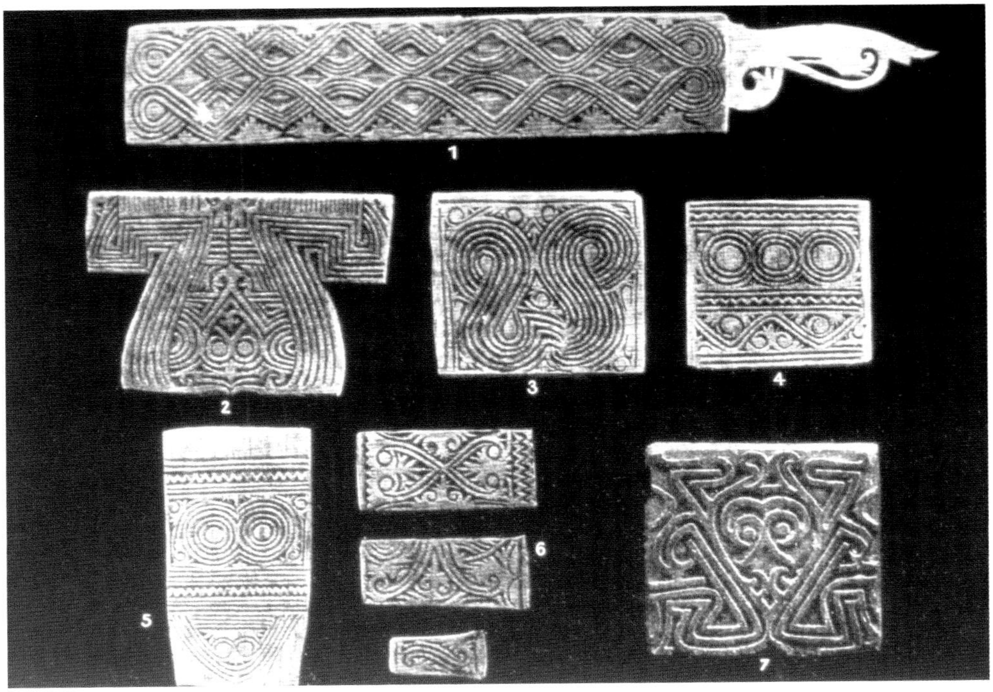

FIGURE 4.25
Kayan *klingé* (tattoo stencil blocks), ca. 1898. From Nieuwenhuis 1900: pl. XXVIII.

Kenyah women also possessed very intricate and spiritually powerful tattooing that was related to their social position in society. Many of the motifs used in tattooing were also employed by the Kayan, and Kenyah tattooists similarly worked under the guidance of a tattoo deity or spirit, "invoking the entity to enter her basket of tattooing tools with offerings of old pearls and *kawit* [charms]" (Nieuwenhuis 1904:452). As with the Kayan, Kenyah tattooing was never conducted inside the longhouse community but rather small specially built huts were constructed for the purpose.

Prior to the operation, the tattooist uttered a prayer to her spirit guide. This was to ensure that the artist would produce only good work, that her client would feel little pain, and that atmospheric conditions would be suitable for a comfortable tattooing session (i.e., plenty of light, not too hot, etc.) (S. Thomas 1968:219).

If a man of the household was away on travel, the tattooing of the woman was not allowed to begin until he returned. Among some Kenyah groups, such as the Leppo' Tau of Long Nawang (Kalimantan), the daughter of a chief had to be tattooed before any other women, but if she died beforehand, the other girls in her community were then allowed to be marked (Hose and Shelford 1906:77).

Nineteenth-century writers observed that Kenyah men of the tattoo client's family were compelled to dress in bark cloth during the operation and remain confined to the longhouse until the tattooing was completed (Nieuwenhuis 1904:453). Bark cloth, made from the paper mulberry

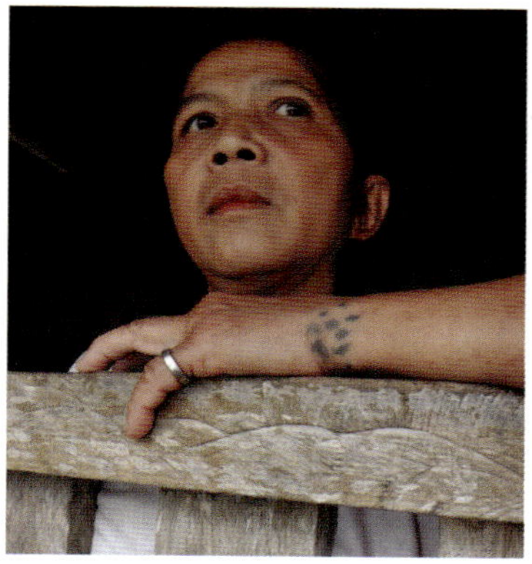

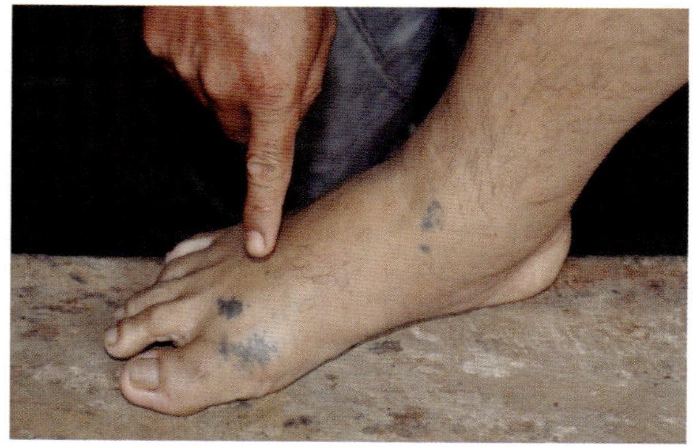

FIGURE 4.26
Kayan tribal members with medicinal tattoos, 2011. Several Kayan families I met have therapeutic tattoos akin to pigmented acupuncture applied to their injured joints and sprains. These tattoos often marked their primary limb joints: wrist, elbow, and knee (*left*), and ankle and toe (*right*). In some cases, the therapeutic markings resembled a tattooed band or bracelet encircling the wrist. Such tattoos are reminiscent of those worn by the 5,200-year-old European "Iceman" dubbed Ötzi, who was tattooed with sixty-one marks across his body for purported medicinal purposes (Krutak 2013a). The Kayan told me that this form of tattooed medicine was extremely effective in the treatment of sprains. After the tattoo was applied, swelling decreased and full mobility was restored to the injured area within one week. If a joint was injured more than once, tattooing treatment was repeated at the same location. Researchers also believe that several of the Iceman's joint tattoos are the result of multiple applications, because today they appear to be very dark. Like many Indigenous Peoples around the world, the Kayan employed carbon (i.e., charred wood) as the primary tattoo pigment for these therapeutic markings. Carbon is sterile by nature and possesses bacteria-absorbing and anti-inflammatory properties. The use of carbon tattoos as a remedy for joint sprains, muscle pains, rheumatism, and lumbago has been documented ethnographically with a near global distribution (see Krutak 2019; Piombino-Mascali and Krutak 2020). © Lars Krutak.

tree, was normally worn during coming-of-age rituals and mourning rites, when widowers set aside their normal clothes until the mortuary feast had been held.

Tattooing, like other initiation rites, symbolized a transition from an old life, a death of sorts, to a new beginning, or a new life. Thus, after the tattoo client had been transformed, recast, and reborn via tattooing, her male kin set aside their bark cloth garments and new clothes were worn.

As described by Dutch physician J. M. Elshout (1926), one of the largest Kenyah tattoo gatherings once occurred at the massive longhouse complex of Long Nawang on the upper Kayan River of Kalimantan. Here, female tattooing was associated with headhunting and the nine-day Mamat Festival, where the *bali akang* (spirits of courage) were called on to help protect the community from illness and danger. In order to gain their favor male attendees performed various purification rites (e.g., *melewa* ceremony), and numerous sacrifices and offerings were made, especially the heads of recently slain enemies.[27] Human heads possessed a spiritual essence that had "a cleansing

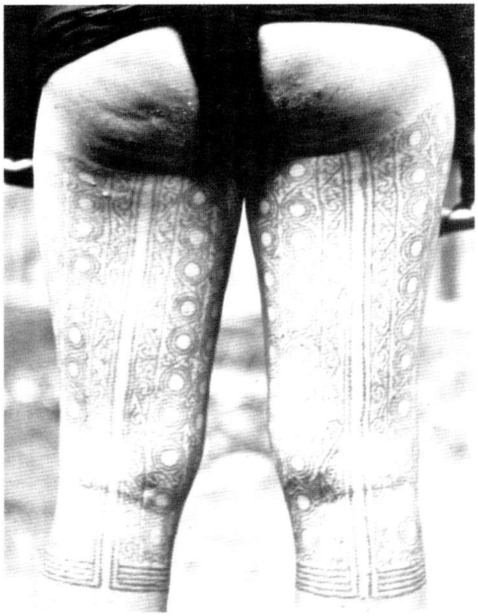

FIGURE 4.27
Woman of the Segah River, Kalimantan, with scrollwork leg tattoos featuring circular moon and other motifs, probably Modang, 1928. Photography by Hendrik Tillema. From Tillema 1936a:216.

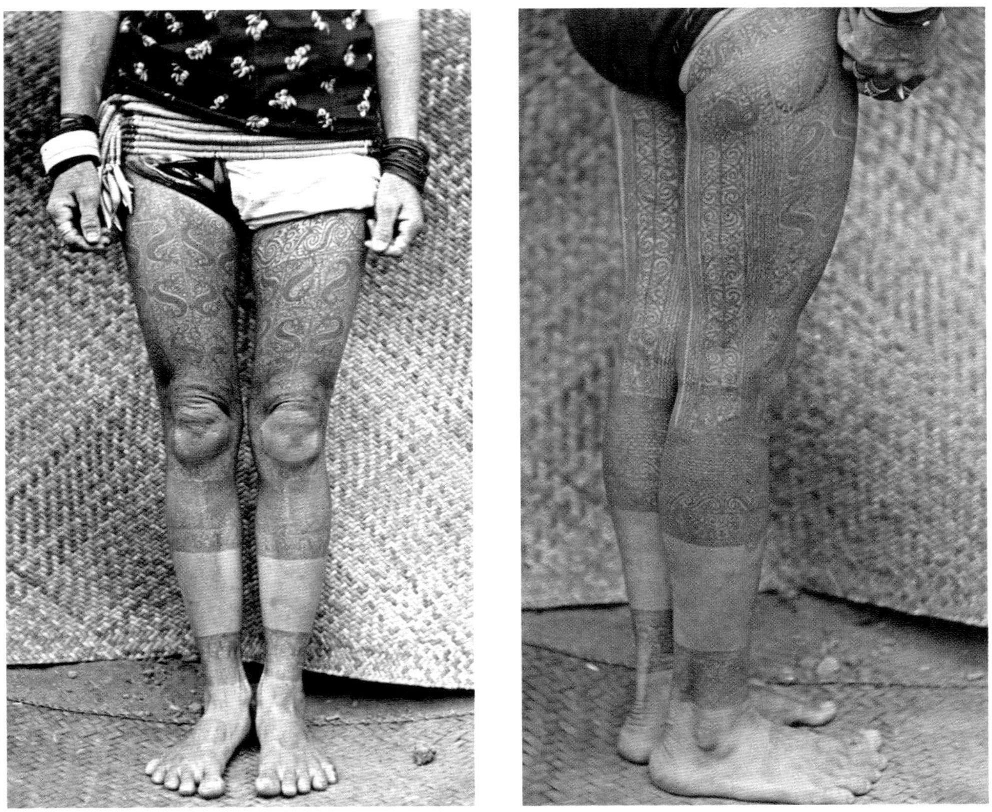

FIGURE 4.28
Front (*left*) and profile (*right*) views of high-ranking Kenyah woman of Long Nawang, Kalimantan, with *aso'* motifs and other designs reserved for her status, 1932. Photograph by Hendrik Tillema. From Tillema 1936b:197. Collection of Leiden University Library (KITLV 173835–36).

FIGURE 4.29
Back view of high-ranking Kenyah woman of Long Nawang, Kalimantan, with rows of apotropaic "tiger's faces," singular ancestral faces (both legs), and curlicue *tuba* (root) designs on her calves, 1932. It was believed if the undecorated V-shaped area was marked a woman's legs would become inflicted by gangrene and the bearer would be denied passage into the afterlife. Photograph by Hendrik Tillema. From Tillema 1936c:191, pl. 4.

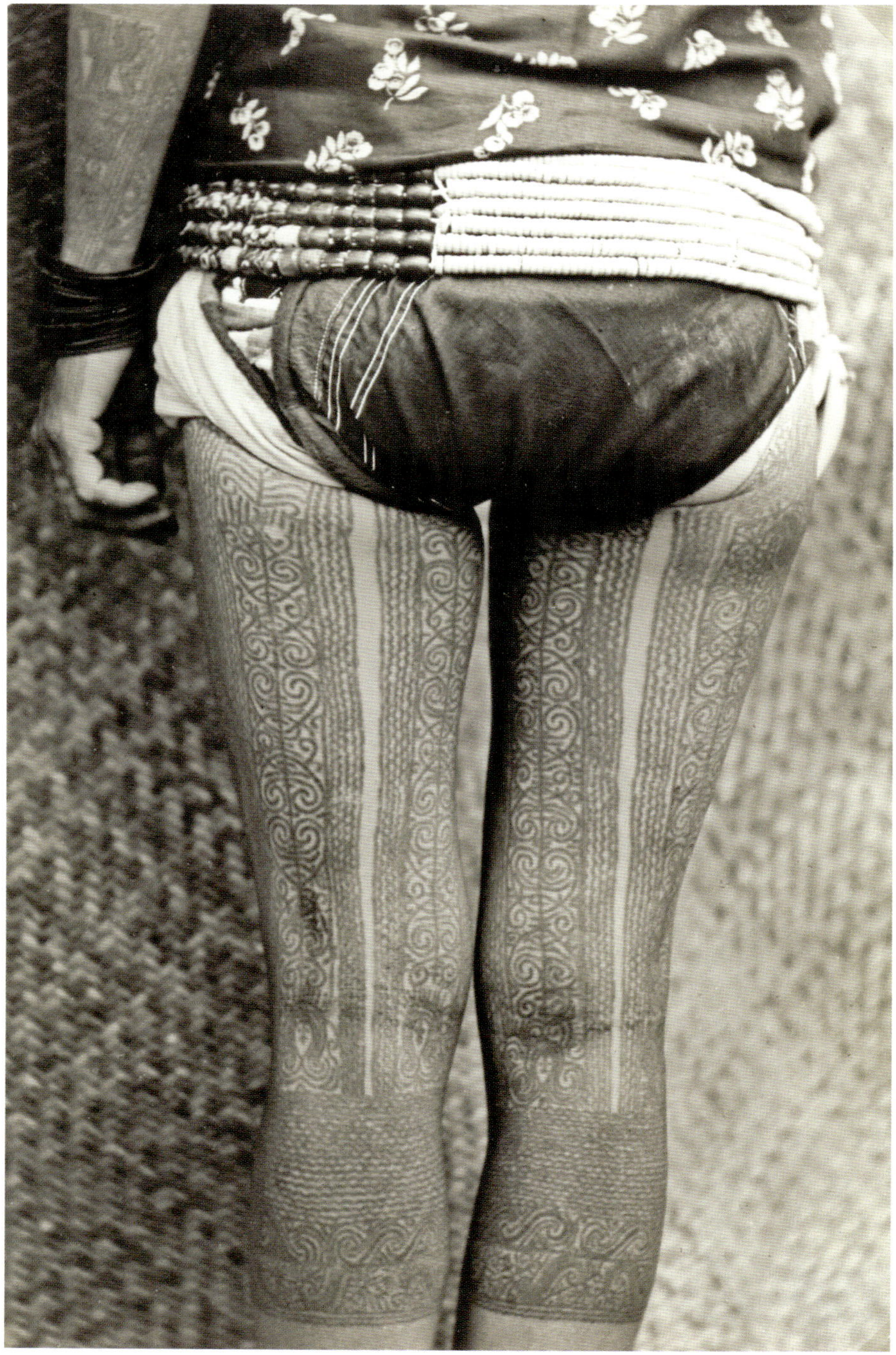

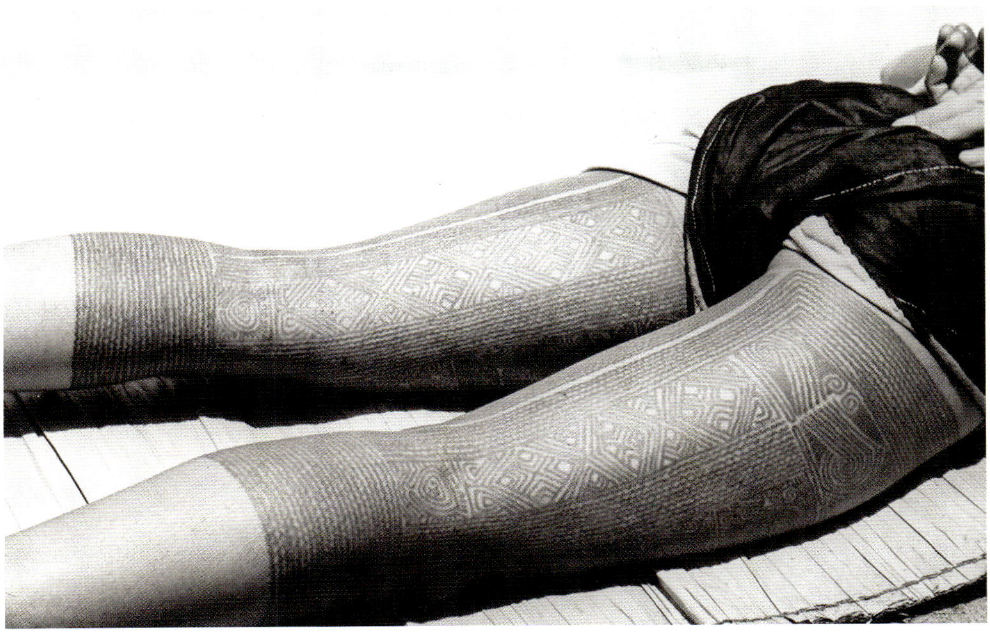

FIGURE 4.30
High-ranking Kenyah woman, Kalimantan, with apotropaic ancestral face (back of knee) and assorted geometric motifs, 1932. Photograph by Hendrik Tillema. Collection of Leiden University Library (KITLV 173508).

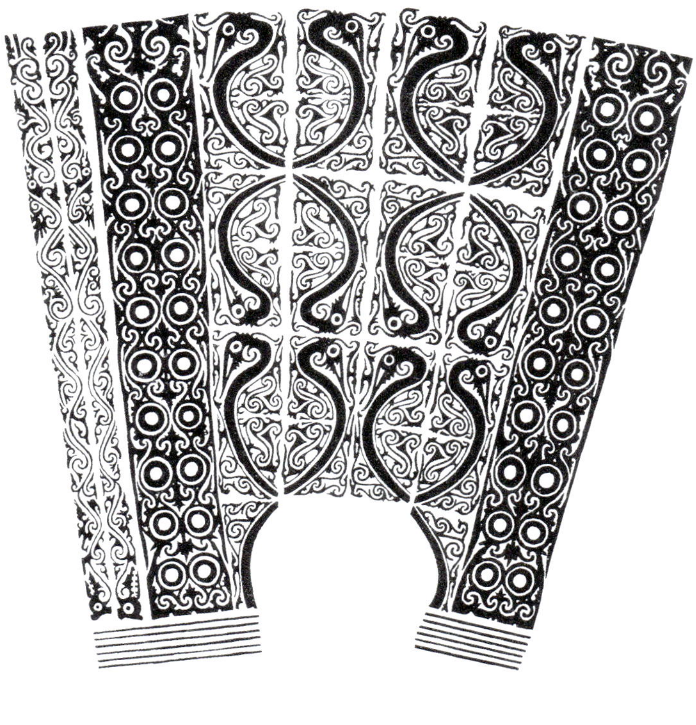

FIGURE 4.31
Thigh tattoo pattern for a Long Glat noblewoman composed of hornbill heads, *lukut* (bead) motifs, argus pheasant, and other motifs, Kalimantan, ca. 1898. From Nieuwenhuis 1904: pl. 86.

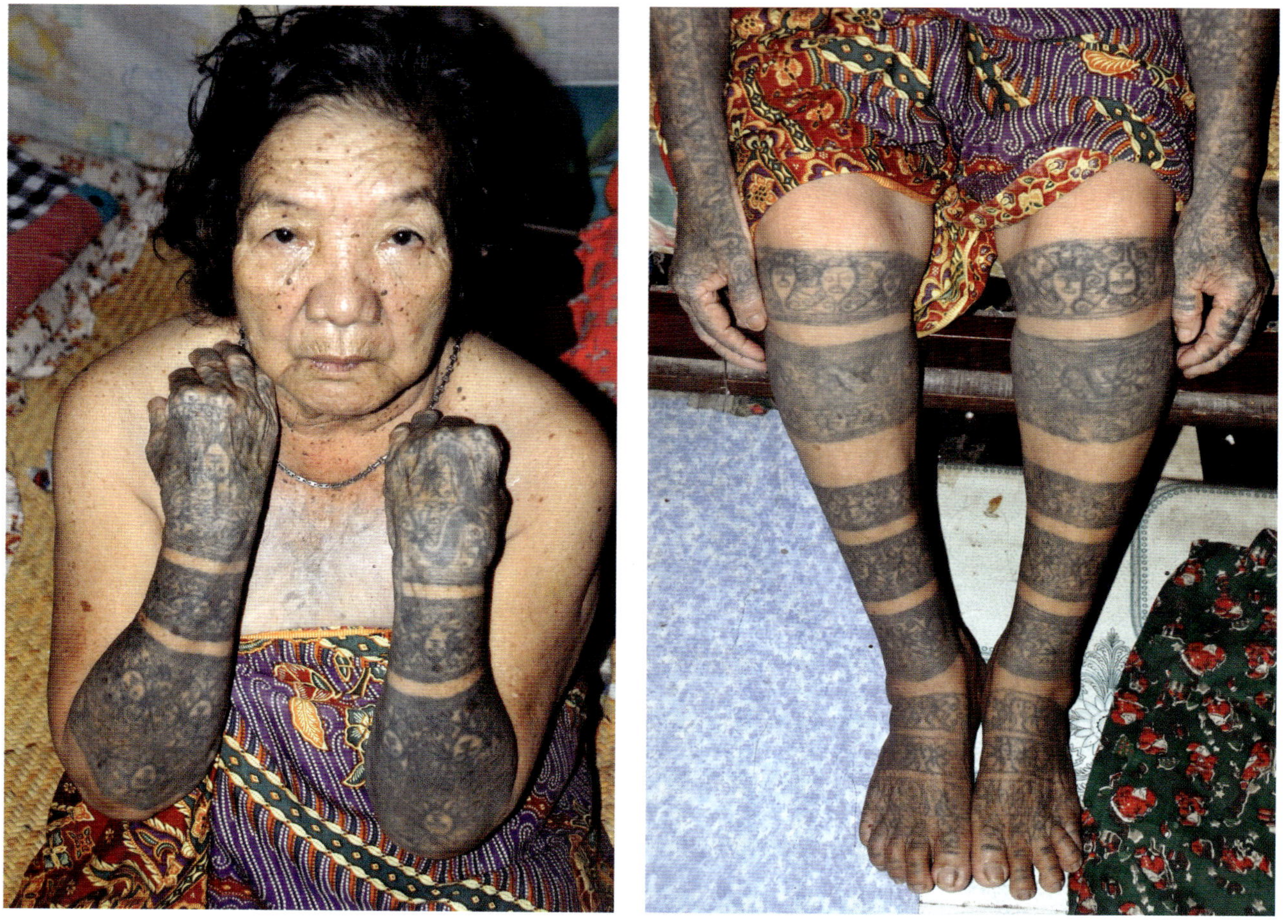

FIGURE 4.32
The late Poi Mirang Pai (*left*), a Kenyah aristocrat and one of the last fully tattooed members of the royal family of the Uma Bakah clans, Sarawak, 2011. She bears various tattooing motifs (arms, hands, legs, feet) reserved for her lofty social status, including the face of Bungan Malan, the Goddess of Creation (*right*). © Lars Krutak.

effect on mankind" (Galvin 1974:21), and their blood, along with that of the multitudes of pigs and chickens that were sacrificed, "flattered" the *bali akang* to the point that they transferred courage to the male attendees (Tillema 1937:96).

Women were excluded from the Mamat activities because the spirits of courage were not attracted to them. In fact, women were associated with *bali leang bali kadjang* (spirits) that caused fear and a decline in physical activity (Elshout 1926:284). For this reason, the ruling chiefs of Long Nawang permitted women's tattooing only once every six to ten years, the performance taking place at the conclusion of a major Mamat. That is because the numerous blood sacrifices and other purificatory rituals conducted at the Mamat counteracted the *bali leang* and "magic spells" surrounding female tattooing that could threaten the men of the community (Tillema 1989:168).

Due to these circumstances, tattooing could not take place in the longhouse during the Mamat, because it might weaken the spirits of courage (Elshout 1926:282). Instead, the operation was performed in small huts away from the festival activities. Tattooed women remained in a tabooed state and as they healed, they could not feed themselves; their bosom friends did this work.

Sometimes the women of Long Nawang obtained their tattoos outside of the Mamat. In such cases, they traveled to a neighboring tribe, the Ma Koelit, who were skilled tattooers. Here, they remained for a month or more until their wounds healed. On their return to Long Nawang, however, they had to help "cool down" the ruling chiefs by offering them a pig and sword, the latter being a strong magical defense (Elshout 1926:403).[28] A feast was then given that was intended to ritually cleanse all the men and the longhouses from the "harmful magic of the women" (Tillema 1989:168).

As with the Kayan, a Kenyah woman's social status could be read based on the patterning of her tattoos. Poi Mirang Pai, a *paren* class noblewoman and one of the last fully tattooed members of the royal family of the Uma Bakah clans, told me that only women of her status could wear anthropomorphic tattoos that represented the face and body of Bungan Malan, the Kenyah Goddess of Creation; these motifs adorned her legs, arms, and hands. Commoners and slaves could never wear these designs, and they risked severe injury and even death if they attempted to bear them. That is because only women of high rank possessed the power to resist any negative magic associated with the designs, since aristocrats were closer to the spirit world (Mashman 1989:218).

Kenyah leg tattooing is unlike other tribal tattoos in Sarawak because among women it is applied in progressive bands. Royal family members like Mirang Pai owned five such bands of tattooing, with lesser nobles receiving four to two bands depending on their social status (S. Thomas 1968).

Kenyah leg tattooing extends up the thighs to the pubis. The overall composition is extremely delicate and symmetrically balanced, and composed of tendril-like elements that represent the teeming plant, animal, and mythic life of the jungle, such as the hornbill, *aso'* (dragon-dog), and other motifs representing the Tree of Life.

NGAJU, OT DANUM, AND "TREE OF LIFE" TATTOOS

The Batang Garing (Tree of Life) finds prominence in the tattooing of Kalimantan's Indigenous Peoples. Although no longer found today, traces of Tree of Life full-body tattooing of Ngaju and Ot Danum men could still be seen in the early twentieth century.

The Ngaju (often written as "Biadjoe" and "Ngadjoe" in early Dutch literature), meaning "upriver," is an ethnic denomination covering numerous peoples of Central Kalimantan who inhabit several parallel river basins (Kapuas, Katingan, Kahayan, and Mentaya) (Sellato 2012:349). The cultures and languages of these groups were akin to the neighboring Ot Danum (also Uut Danum), who lived to the north along the Melawi River.

For these and other Dayaks the Tree of Life embodied deep cosmological beliefs about the origins of the universe, the creation of the first people, the gods, the tripartite division of the world (heaven, earth, underworld), and the teeming plant and animal life that inhabited it. In turn, men's tattooing among the Ngaju and Ot Danum could be understood only in connection with the Tree of Life and local concepts of divinity.

For the Ngaju, the upper world, which is the source of all life, is located at the top of the sacred tree and is the home of higher divinities, heroes (i.e., tattooed men), and the aristocracy. According to oral traditions, the symbols of this realm include the sun, hornbills, trophy heads, and objects associated with riches. Virility, maleness, and heat also belong to this domain. The middle levels embody the human world, and the lower regions the underworld—a shadowy layer

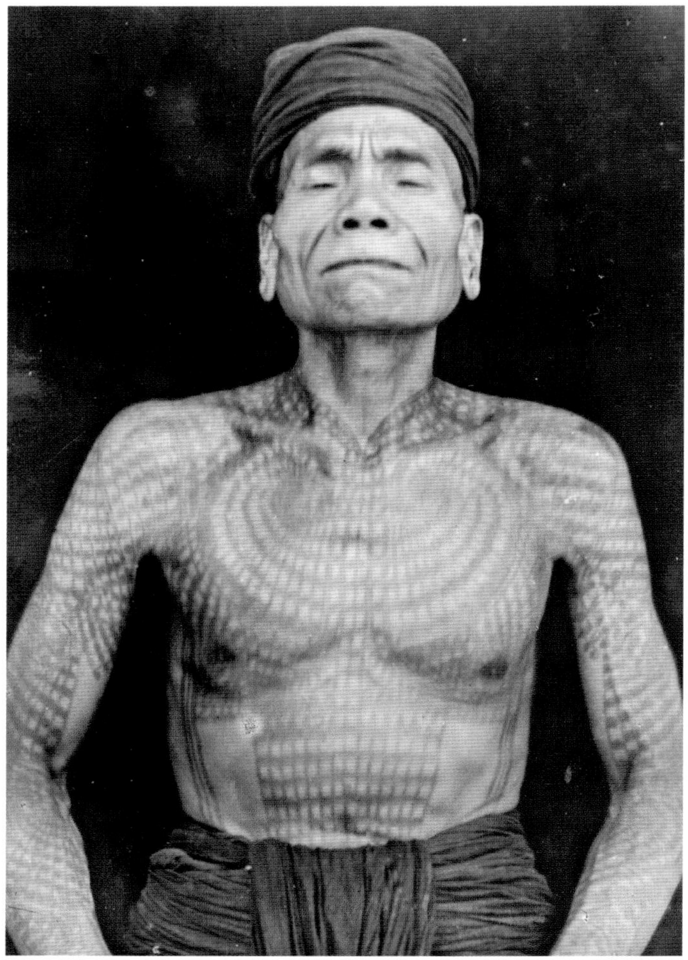

FIGURE 4.33
Damang Batu, an Ot Danum elder of Tumbang Anoi village, Kahajan River, Kalimantan, ca. 1898. He is tattooed with the Tree of Life on his torso. Photograph by Jean Demmeni. From Nieuwenhuis 1904: pl. 81.

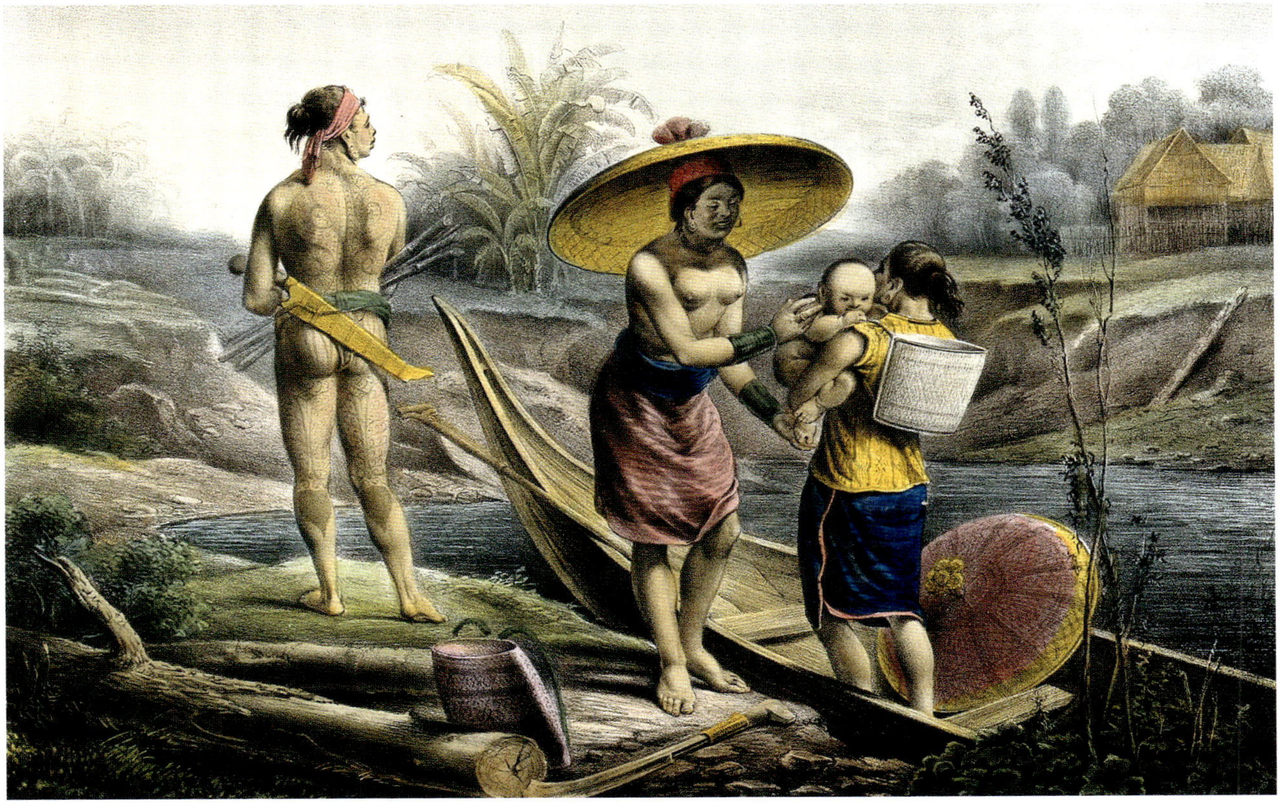

where water serpents, crocodiles, and other powerful beasts dwell (Alpert 2016:118). Fecundity, femaleness, and coolness characterize this domain. As each level is an individual branch bound to the trunk of the Tree of Life; each tier is interconnected and therefore unified in its cosmic totality.

FIGURE 4.34
Ngaju family of Kalimantan, ca. 1839. The man is tattooed with elements of the Tree of Life. Color lithograph by H. A. Henrici and W. J. Gordon. Wellcome Library Collection (569536i).

Among the Ngaju and Ot Danum, men's tattooing was done in stages over many years. The first tattoos, a full moon on each calf and a water serpent to the side of it as well as on each upper thigh, were given when a young Ngaju man began wearing his loincloth—a sign of puberty. The tattoo operator, who was male, used a hand-tapping tool. The highly detailed patterns to be executed were first stenciled on the skin with dammar soot mixed with coconut oil and gold dust (Den Hamer 1885:453; Mallinckrodt 1924).[29] The needles were continuously dipped into the pigment and flowing blood wiped away with tree bark bast. The swollen and inflamed wounds were then rubbed with salt and assumed a whitish color. A heated banana or caladium leaf was then applied to the markings, which reduced the swelling.

After a Ngaju man had acquired some wealth and established a reputation through trading expeditions abroad and other exploits, his shoulders were adorned with a star and his arms decorated with what have variously been described as "bird" or "hawk" wings, although I believe

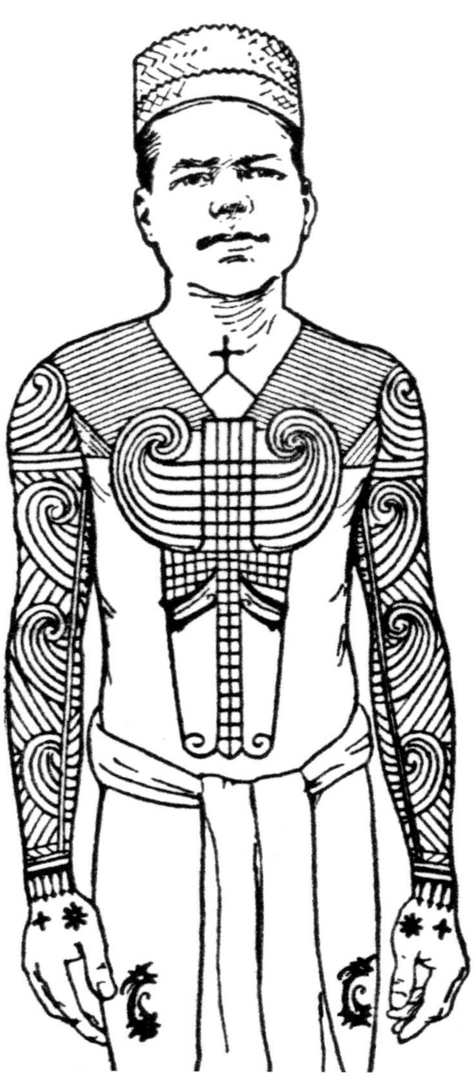

FIGURE 4.35
Man of the Lower Katingan River, Kalimantan, tattooed with elements of the Tree of Life, "bird wings" on his arms, and the beak and eyes of the hornbill on his hands, ca. 1915. From Lumholtz 1921.

these were derived from the hornbill and the branches of the Tree of Life (Lumholtz 1921; Mallinckrodt 1924:71; Schärer 1963:90; Den Hamer 1885:454).[30]

However, the major stage of tattooing occurred later in life, around the age of forty. Only "perfect" men were allowed to receive this complete form of Ngaju tattoo, which took many days to create. This composite tattoo was placed on the man's torso and at other locations. Men who bore these markings had distinguished themselves by living their lives according to *adat* (ceremonial law), acquiring wealth, participating in headhunting expeditions, and offering a human sacrifice during their lifetime (Schärer 1963:90).

There were various elements of this tattoo, but writ large it represented the Tree of Life, which was an everlasting symbol of strength and divinity that protected the man from his flesh-and-blood enemies. The trunk of the tree was tattooed vertically on the abdomen. Above it was placed the outstretched wings (curling upward) of the hornbill; its tail curled upward just above the navel below the trunk of the Tree of Life. Circles with four rays, representing the sun, marked the cheeks. On each hand were tattooed a small cross and starlike motif; these represented the beak and eyes of the hornbill. In essence, fully tattooed men were considered semidivine, perfect, and sacred, because they emerged out of the Tree of Life and were godlike. It was believed that in the afterlife they would receive a golden body.

According to Hans Schärer (1963:79), a Protestant missionary who lived with the Ngaju-speaking people of the Katingan and Barito Rivers for more than seven years, the true and perfect man was *basewut*—renowned: "He stands in the community like a tall tree in the village square, in the sunlight, like a

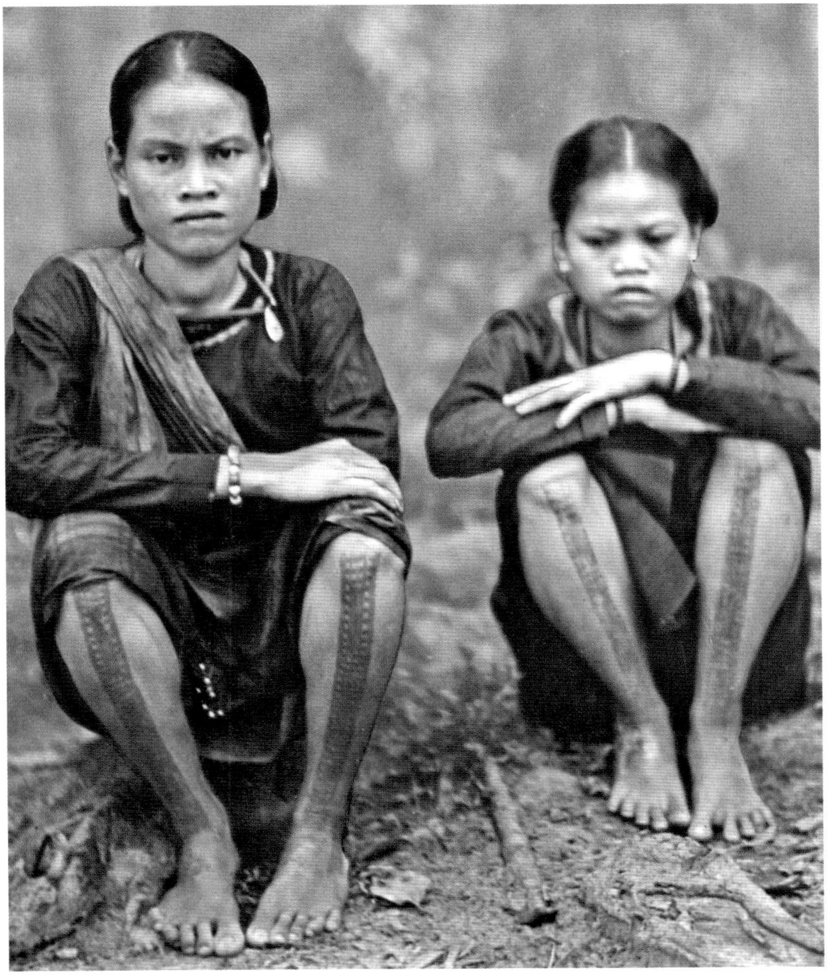

FIGURE 4.36
Two Siang women displaying their leg designs, 1928. When Hiram H. Hiller (1898) visited the tribe, he was told the motif was intended to represent a consecutive series of *naga*, or "dragons," but the linework was so blown-out that the pattern was virtually indistinguishable. A recent traveler to the Siang region told me that women believed these marks became torches in the afterlife and helped guide them to their ancestors (Bonfilio Yosafat, personal communication, August 21, 2020). Photograph by Hendrik Tillema. From Tillema 1936c:192, pl. 5.

magnificent house, not veiled in the mists of misfortune." The description continued, "His fame spreads from village to village and from river to river. He is blessed by God, and people speak about this blessing. . . . Through him the deities address the community and the entire cosmos, and they bless these also with sacred gifts that they have bestowed upon him. What a man possesses in the form of material and spiritual wealth he possesses for the community and the entire cosmos, to which he bears common responsibility as a member for both." Schärer (1963:79) concluded his philosophical observations with the following statement: "The entire cosmos is filled by the fame of the perfect [tattooed] man. When he is spoken of the animals listen, when his fortune is mentioned[,] the trees bend their branches low, and when his name is spoken the fishes and boulders leap from the river."

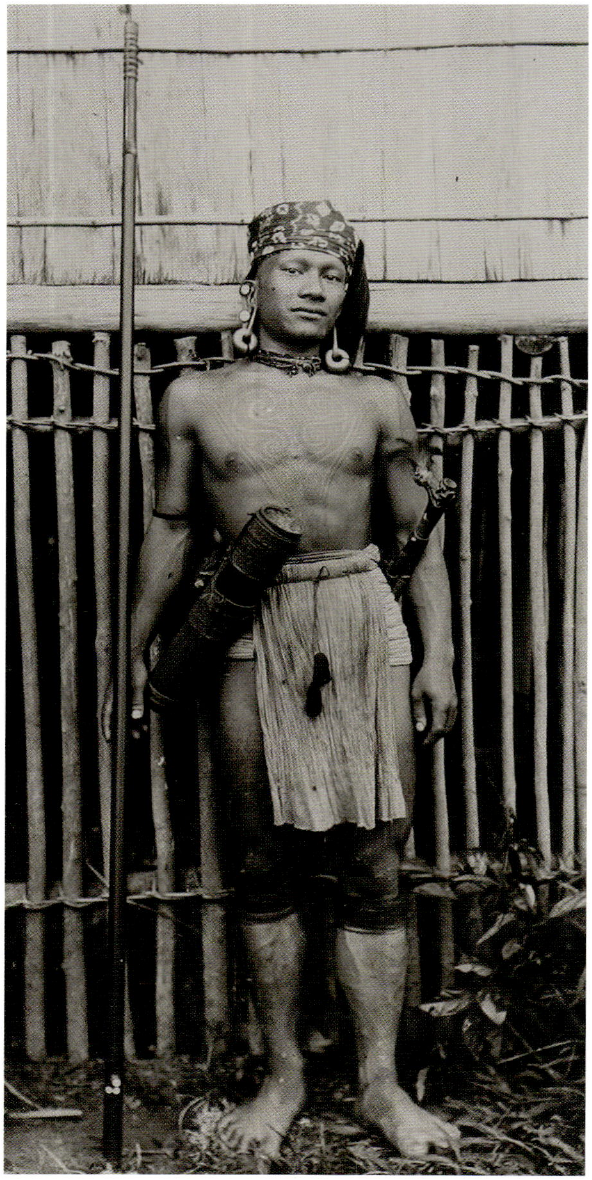

FIGURE 4.37
Baketan warrior with elaborate *gerowit* (hooks) chest tattoos holding a blowpipe and sword lashed to his waist belt, ca. 1898. Photograph by Jean Demmeni. After Nieuwenhuis 1904: pl. 80.

NOMADS OF THE RAINFOREST: BAKETAN AND UKIT TATTOOS (1898–1968)

The floraformesque and scrolling chest tattoos of the formerly nomadic Baketan (also Bakatan, Bukitan) and Ukit (also Bukit, Bukat) peoples are also reminiscent of the Tree of Life. However, little information is available about the meanings behind these exquisite tattoos, and only a handful of historic photographs and illustrations of these tattooing traditions exist. Baketan tattooing became extinct in the early twentieth century, and partial forms of Ukit tattooing, which were by then heavily influenced by the Kayan style of tattooing (S. Thomas 1968), could still be seen among the elderly in the 1980s.

The disappearance of these tattooing traditions was recognized as early as the 1890s, when the English ethnographers Charles Hose and Robert Shelford (1906:82) wrote, "Of these people, as of so many others, the melancholy tale of [the] tatu [*sic*] amongst the present generation and replacement of indigenous [marks] by Kayan designs was told, and it seems only too likely that within the next decade or two none will be left to illustrate a once flourishing and beautiful art."

Hose and Shelford (1906:83) noted that Baketan tattooing was forbidden from taking place in the house and could be performed only on the "warpath"; consequently, men worked as the tattooists. Sharon Thomas (1968) met a living Ukit tattooist who was female.

One hundred years ago, Baketan and Ukit nomads, who were masters of the blowgun, roamed the jungle domain as hunters and gatherers collecting forest products (beeswax, resins, hornbill "ivory," rhinoceros horn, bird feathers, etc.) for trade. In the headhunting era, Indigenous nomads collaborated with larger ethnic groups such as the Kenyah and Kayan to help scout and take down the latter's enemies. Their intimate knowledge of jungle paths and expertise with the deathly silent blowgun, which was often equipped with poisoned darts, was in great demand (Tillema 1989:125). If a man distinguished himself in war, his first tattoo was an intricately designed triangular chest piece, after which the shoulders, neck, arms, back, and lower jaw were marked. After further heroic deeds, the calves were tattooed and the only surface not marked was the insides of the legs (Nieuwenhuis 1904:451–452).

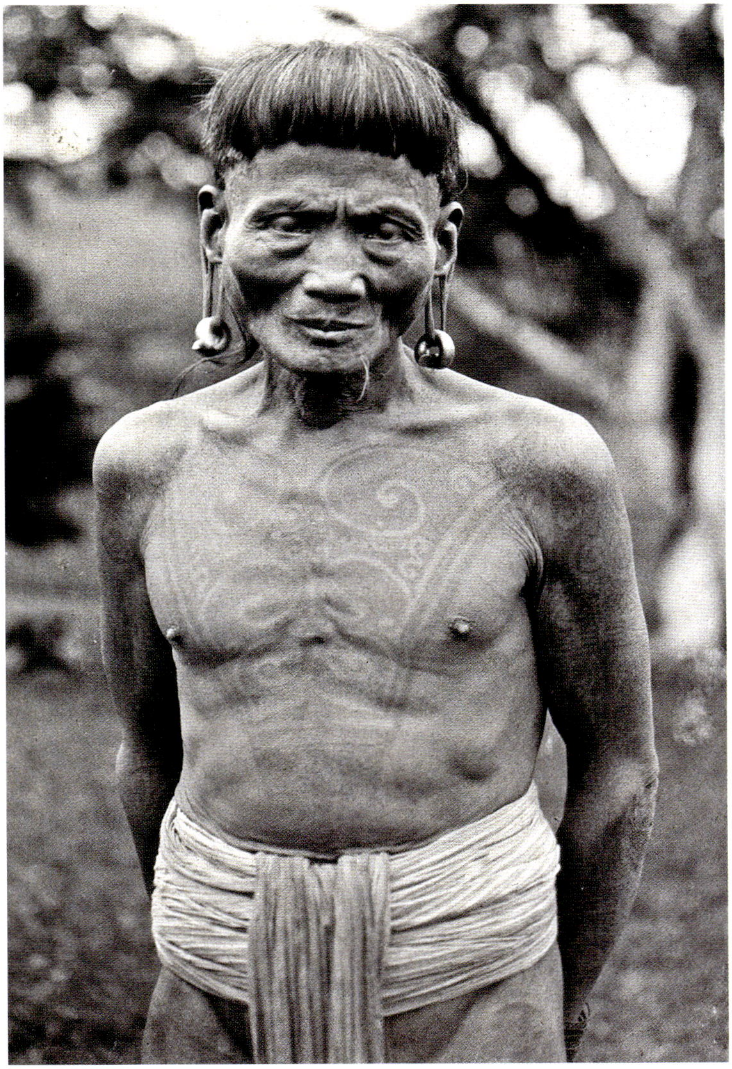

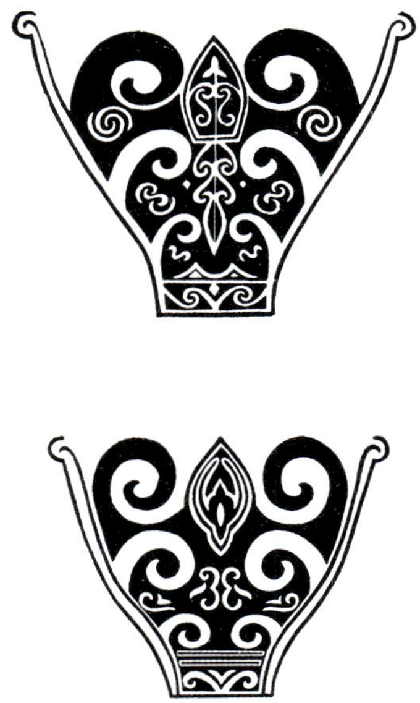

FIGURE 4.38 (LEFT)
Tattooed Ukit elder, Sarawak, ca. 1910. Wellcome Library Collection (30635i).

FIGURE 4.39 (ABOVE)
Ukit chest tattoos for men, Sarawak, ca. 1898. From Hose and McDougall 1912: pl. 143.

The tendril-like curves were called *gerowit*, or hooks, and marked the chest, throat, and neck. The shoulder was tattooed with the *akih*, a gecko lizard (*Ptychozzon homalocephalum*) used in haruspication, and the *selong bowang*, or "horse-mango" pattern, marked the calves. The lines (*ja*) on the jaw were also called *kilang*, or sword pattern. Men's *kukum* (hand tattoos) were similar in fashion to those of Kayan warriors, and the feet were marked with *iwu* (broad black bars), similar to those of Kayan women. *Jango*, or lines, encircled the ankles and were reserved for veteran warriors only (Hose and Shelford 1906:83–84).

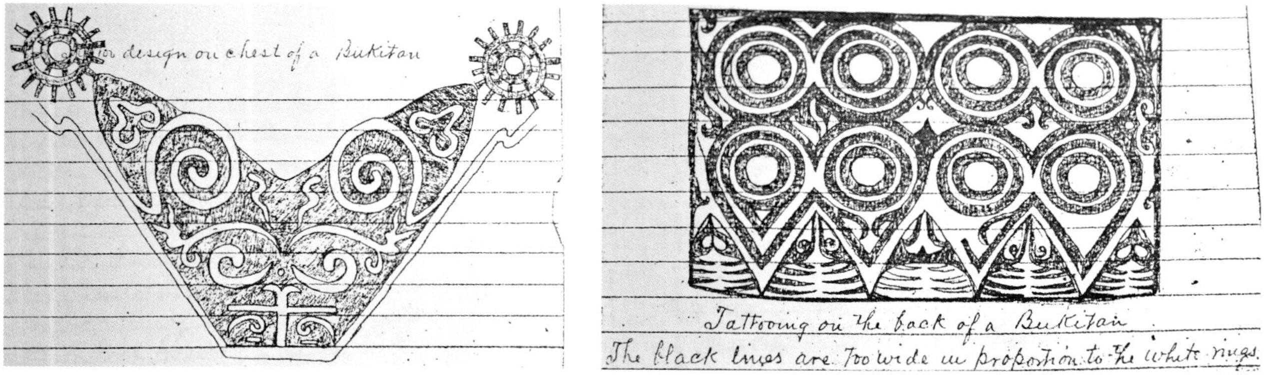

FIGURE 4.40
Chest (*left*) and back (*right*) tattoos of a Baketan warrior illustrated in the journals of Hiram Hiller, 1896. Courtesy Penn Museum Archives (PU-Mu. 1060).

Some Baketan warriors were seen wearing forehead tattoos of a rosette pattern or star called *lukut* (Hose and Shelford 1906:83). As previously noted, this "antique bead" design had spiritual significance for the Kayan and Kenyah because it kept the human soul close to the body.

Additional notes concerning Baketan tattooing occur in the unpublished fieldnotes of the Philadelphia-born Hiram M. Hiller. Along with the travel writer William H. Furness and his traveling companion, the financier Alfred Harrison, Jr., Hiller traveled extensively across Borneo in 1896–1898, making zoological and ethnographic collections for the University of Pennsylvania. Although each of the men kept diaries and journals of their experiences, including the receipt of tattoos from a Kayan female practitioner, only Hiller's illustrated journals survive to this day. Most of his observations regarding Baketan tattooing were published by Hose and Shelford (1906), including the metatarsus tattooing, but a few important details and drawings did not appear in that pioneering work.

Hiller described meeting an old Baketan warrior with full-body tattooing in 1896. Although he attempted to photograph the warrior's tattoos, he was unsuccessful, but he created a series of schematic drawings that accompany his notes; some of these illustrations are provided here for the first time. Hiller (1896:12) noted that this man in almost every way resembled a Kayan, and he even resided in a Kayan community on the Mendalam River, but his tattooing was "entirely unique." Some of the most interesting tattoos Hiller observed on this elder were those on his chin, neck, and back. "He was the first man I ever saw tattooed on the face, parallel lines running from the angles of the jaw meeting in the mid-line, while the neck was covered first beneath the lower jaw with a different design, but continuous with the other," he wrote. "[On the back,] a series of rings, eight in number across the upper half. Each ring [he] claimed, represented a head taken" (Hiller 1896:12). Hiller also met with two tattooed Ukit men, both of whom were successfully photographed by Harrison after Chinese ink was overpainted on their chest tattoos.[31] Hiller reported that their chest pieces and upper arm tattoos (i.e., deltoid) were different from those of the Baketan elder. Hiller (1896:53a) later met an Ukit woman, who noted that tattooists among her people could be male or female.

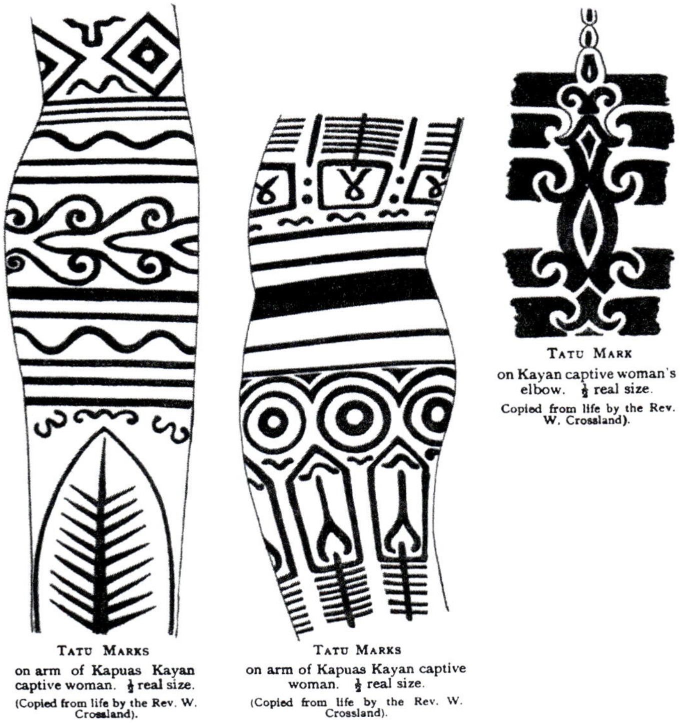

FIGURE 4.41
Arm tattoos of an unidentified "slave" woman seen in Kalimantan, ca. 1898. Based on the iconography, she was likely Ukit or Baketan. Illustrations by Rev. W. Crossland. From Roth 1896:87.

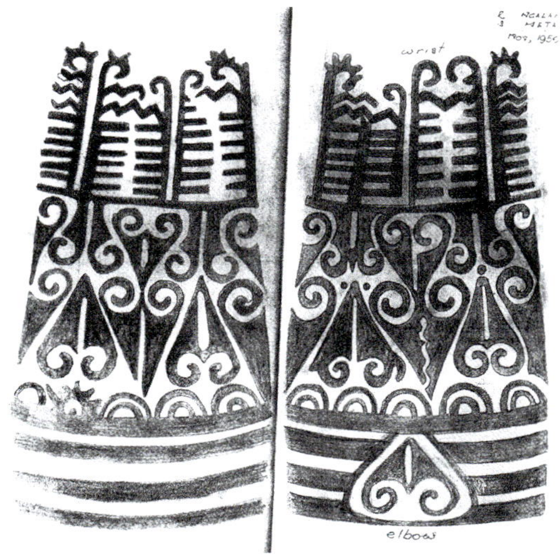

FIGURE 4.42
Arm tattoos of an unidentified woman of Rumah Ngalang, Sungai Meta, Sarawak, 1950. This unique iconography resembles that of the Ukit or Baketan. Illustrations by Monica Freeman. Courtesy National Library of Australia (Ms. Acc12.055).

Women's tattooing among the Baketan and Ukit was less complex by comparison. Small designs were inked on the forearms, and black bars on the metacarpals (Hose and Shelford 1906:84). Two *lukut*, or starlike, motifs linked by a line were tattooed on the wrist, and it is possible that these markings had spiritual significance.

A series of three drawings that resemble the tattooing style of the Baketan and the Ukit were drawn by Reverend W. Crossland in the late nineteenth century (Roth 1896:87). These boldly patterned tattoos were copied from the arms of a "captive woman" seen in Kalimantan on the Kapuas River. The tribal identity of the lady was not recorded, and the motifs look unlike any found in this region. Therefore, it is possible the woman was from a nomadic tribe straddling the Sarawak-Kalimantan border. Similar drawings of a tattooed woman were made by Monica Freeman circa 1950 on the Upper Balui River but the tribe of the owner was not identified.

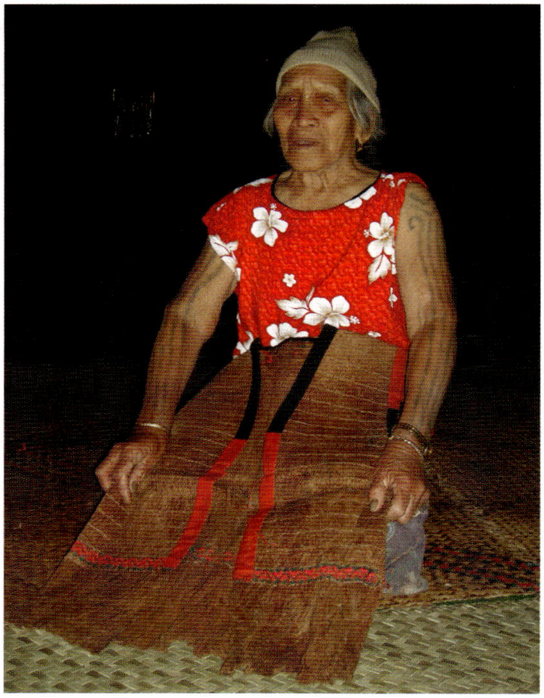

FIGURE 4.43
Tattooed woman from Kalimantan photographed near Bario, Sarawak, 2005. Her tribe is yet to be identified. Collection of the author.

KELABIT, SA'BAN, AND OTHER TATTOOS

After conducting tattoo research among the Kelabit of the Sarawak highlands in 2011, an individual emailed me with a photograph of a tattooed women he met in a longhouse near Bario. He wanted to identify the ethnicity of this woman because her unique arm tattooing did not resemble that of the Kelabit. Since that time, I have contacted several anthropologists and other local researchers who work along the Sarawak-Kalimantan borderlands, and to date no one has been able to confirm the tribal origins of this elder. I have not encountered this form of tattooing in the ethnographic record nor in archival sources, and it is a mystery that hopefully someone will solve in the future after reading my brief account here.

Back in 2011, I was presented with another mystery of sorts. While interviewing tattooed Kenyah men and women on the Upper Baram River of Sarawak, they mentioned that their traditional enemies, a tribe some three hour's drive away on a logging road, possessed unique tattoos unlike any other. I had never heard of this Orang Ulu group, the Sa'ban, and at that time approximately one thousand members of the tribe lived in three villages. Their language is distantly related to Kelabit, but many of its linguistic elements are quite distinct.

Sa'ban tattoo patterns are simply named after the part of the body on which they are placed: "leg design," "arm design," and so on. Sa'ban tattooists were female, and I was told that men formerly wore tattoos on their shoulders to signify bravery and status among their peers. In the village of Long Banga', I photographed two tattooed women, but only one tattooed man was still living. At the time of my brief visit, which lasted four hours, he was out of the village working on his farm up in the mountains.

The following year, while skimming ethnographic records at the Tropenmuseum in Amsterdam, I located illustrations of Sa'ban men's shoulder (rosette), upper, and lower forearm tattooing in an obscure publication by the Dutch civil-servant Jan Jongejans (1922:68, figs. 75–76), along with drawings of women's tattooing. Jongejans (1922) also depicted the tattooing of a neighboring people he called the Sesajap. Based on the motifs, these markings closely align with those of Lun Bawang women who inhabit several highland villages on the Sarawak, Sabah, and Kalimantan border.

Linguistically related to the Kelabit and the Sa'ban, these former warrior people practiced *batik* (tattooing), with men hand-tapping the designs. The pigment was derived from the charred resin of the *Agathis* tree mixed with water. Elders of Long Tanid village, located in the rural Lawas District of Sarawak, explained that a woman's forearm tattoos (*arit belipid*, "twining lines"), which parallel those appearing in Jongejan's drawings, glowed on death, guiding the tattoo bearer to the afterlife (Yap 2014).

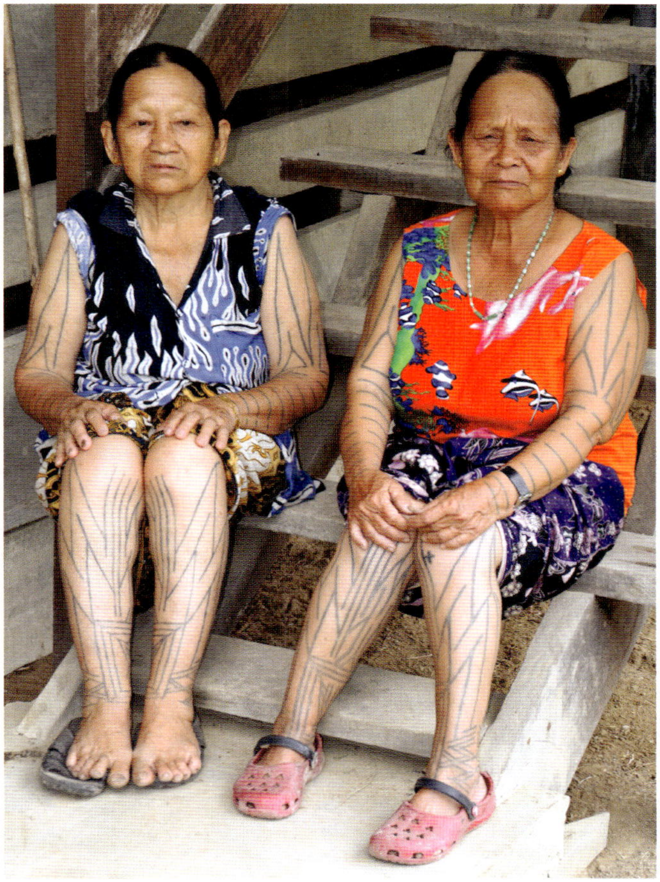

FIGURE 4.44
Tattooed elders Bulan Wa and Seung Irang of Long Banga, Sarawak, 2011. Sa'ban tattooists were female, but the practice stopped with the influx of missionaries around 1960. A woman's extensive tattooing occurred in stages: legs first (four days) followed by arms (four days). A woman received her tattoos around the time of marriage and before she bore her first child. The designs were stenciled on the skin before they were hand-tapped, and payment usually consisted of heirloom beads. I was told that there were no accompanying rituals. Note the cruciform tattoo near Ms. Wa's left knee, which was applied for joint pain. This tattoo appears in nearly the same position as one of the 5,200-year-old Iceman's therapeutic tattoos, a cruciform near his right knee. © Lars Krutak.

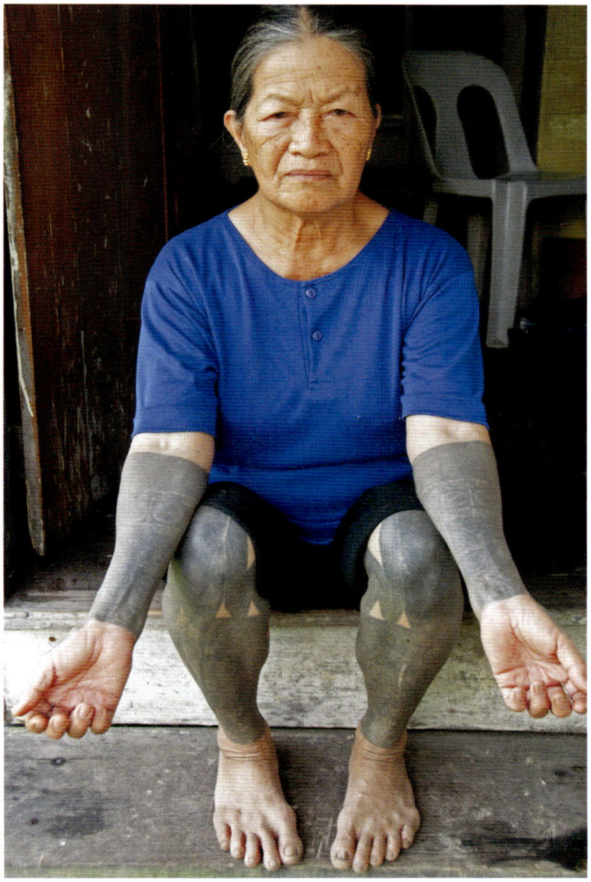

FIGURE 4.45
A Kelabit elder at her home in Bario with a hybrid form of tattooing, 2011. In the 1950s, her husband worked in the lowlands in a Kayan settlement on the Baram River. Because she thought Kayan tattoos were beautiful, she had her arms tattooed in this regional Kayan style. One of the important Kayan motifs on her forearms is the starlike *lukut* (bead) pattern. As noted, this motif was believed to help "tie in" the soul and keep it close to the body. Her leg tattoos were hand-tapped in the traditional Kelabit style. © Lars Krutak.

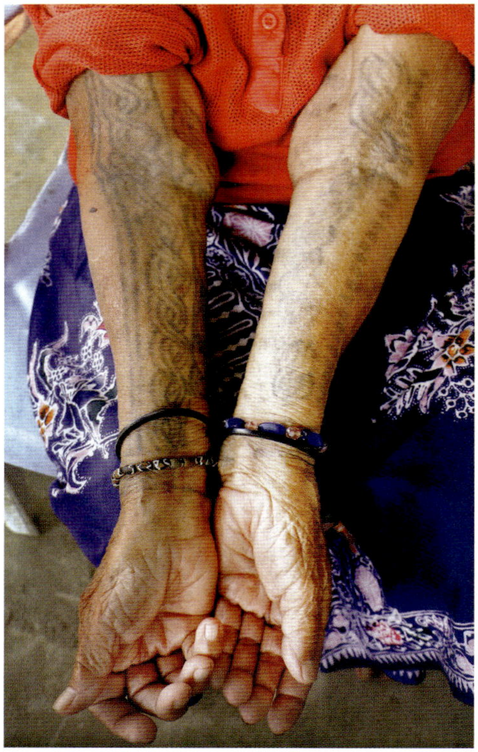

FIGURE 4.46
Lun Bawang elder Pu Udang Ukab displaying *arit belipad* (twining lines), forearm tattoos that will help guide her into the afterlife, Long Tanid village, Sarawak, ca. 2014. From Ng 2015:44.

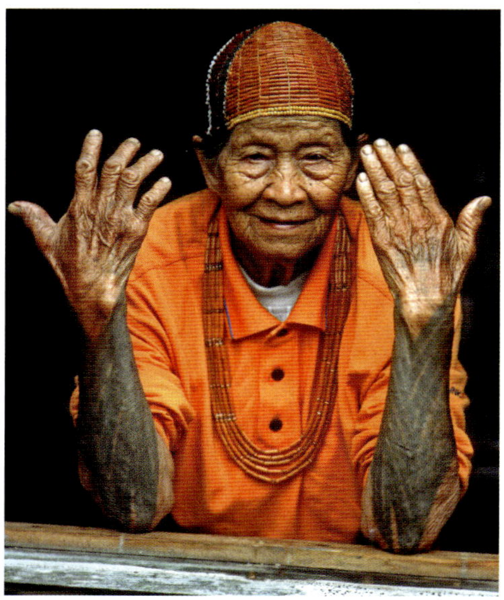

FIGURE 4.47
Sina Ngalinu Karuh, a tattooed Kelabit elder, Bario, Sarawak, 2011. The faint tattoos on her hands were a "test," and if a young woman could withstand the pain of the tattooist's needles, then her arms and legs were tattooed. The arm tattoos' outlines were completed while the girl remained unmarried; once she was wed these bands were filled in. © Lars Krutak.

One of the last owners of this tattoo, Udang Ukab, explained that the cost of the tattoo was high: "It would normally cost one *tajau* (a large [ceramic] jar prized by Sarawakian communities) to get the tattoo artist to come [and] tattoo both arms," while others noted a *rubih,* or heirloom Chinese dragon jar, would suffice. Tattooed elder Kapit Barok (b. 1916) explained that her tattoos served an additional function—young girls who possessed these striking tattoos commanded higher marriage dowries (Yap 2014). She continued, "I followed in the traditions of my mother and grandmother who also had these tattoos. My mother's were different though with more straight lines while my grandmother was more heavily tattooed than both of us," she said (Yap 2014).

Although Lun Bawang tattoos are certainly unique in form, the geometric tattoos of the neighboring Sa'ban somewhat resemble those of the Kelabit. Today, a handful of elderly Kelabit women continue to wear these bold blackwork designs on their arms and legs that were applied in stages over a lifetime. Each *betik* (tattoo pattern) indicated that a woman had reached an important life event: puberty, marriage, or childbirth.

Kelabit women's body tattoos were applied by female tattooists via the hand-tapping technique. As with the Sa'ban, *Agathis* tree resin was burned, then the tattooist held a cooking wok over the flame, whereupon soot collected on the surface of the vessel.[32] The soot was scraped and mixed with water to create the pigment. The tattooing process began after the onset of puberty and around the age of fifteen with approximately one year between each stage: back of the leg, around the knee, then the shin. Two layers of ink were applied to create the desired hue. Eight bold zigzagging

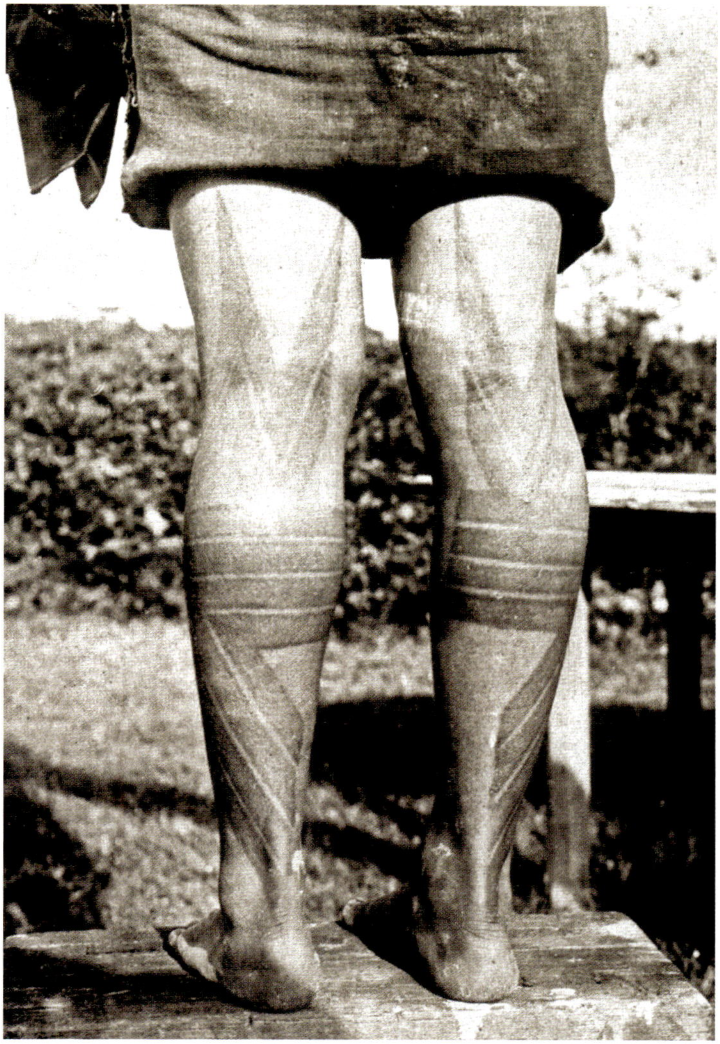

FIGURE 4.48
Tattooed Kelabit woman, Bario, Sarawak, ca. 1910. With historic drawings, photographs, and ethnographic accounts on Kelabit tattooing in hand (cf. Hose and McDougall 1912:266), in 2011 I interviewed several tattooed Kelabit elders and local Bario historians to cross-check the information recorded therein. For the most part these records were accurate, however I provide additional details below. The zigzagging bands on the back of the leg of the Kelabit woman are termed *betik buah*, "fruit pattern." The ninety-degree angular shin bands that carry over to the back of the leg are *betik lawa*, or "trunk pattern." The tattoos on the shin, *betik lulud* (shin pattern), are named after that body location. The tips of the vertical bands on the shins are called *ujat batu*, "hill tops," and the horizontal bands of tattooing on the upper shin that carry over to the back of the leg are *betik kalang*, derived from a Kelabit basketry term for a "design that wraps around." From Hose and McDougall 1912: pl. 135.

betik tidú (hand pattern) bands that did not completely encircle the arm were applied to unmarried girls; when the client married these bands were filled in with black pigment. I was told that unmarked girls would not find a marriage partner.

Several Kelabit women described to me the tattoo ceremony in some detail. What is interesting is that it always occurred at night by the light of candles or flammable *Agathis* tree resin, and not during the day, which is the preferred time to tattoo among other Indigenous Peoples of Borneo. Men were usually not allowed to witness the tattooing because visiting spirits might cause the client's tattoo to become infected.

Tattooing sessions were lengthy, and over the course of these painful occasions the tattooist would often recite a *sadirir*, or folk story, related to ancestral personages. The purpose of such narratives was to instill courage into the tattoo client and reinforce the importance of the tattooing tradition. An extract from one of these tales is as follows:

Detsur ribid urit betik binodong	I am a beautifully tattooed woman.
Betik uih papo lam detsin layun	With tattoo patterns laid out in the shadowy darkness.
Pépik kuh ngan élo' nateng senotong	I was tattooed by the light of the flame from burning dammar resin.
Na'um taan senotong tonang perayan	It was hard to bear the pain. (Janowski 2014)

Very little information exists concerning Kelabit men's tattooing. Hose and Shelford (1906:266) simply noted "men tatu [*sic*] but rarely, and then with stripes down the arms." By the time of my visit to the Bario highlands in 2011, I could find no visible traces of such traditions, but on inspection of family portraits I did see what was described to me as a *baye* (crocodile) motif on the outside of a man's upper arm. Crocodiles do not exist in the highlands, but they are said to reside there as spirits. The term *baye* is used in male grandparental names among the Kelabit and implies "power." One elder told me that the motif might have been deployed as a tattoo pattern because crocodiles were great hunters and hard to kill, just like the Kelabit warrior.

Other elders noted that successful Kelabit headhunters had small lines or marks called *tada idah* placed on the digits of their fingers to tally the number of their victims, a custom practiced by the Iban, the Kayan, the Kenyah, and others. The wives of these men might also have a few marks tattooed on their fingers to communicate their husband's status.

Because Kelabit tattooing involved the processing of something (i.e., pigment) derived from a natural substance to create a new object (i.e., tattoo), the Kelabit believed that *lalud*, an inherent power, was thereby harnessed and activated (cf. Janowski 2003). This spiritual life force was potentially dangerous, but if it was managed correctly, it could help empower individuals.

Initiation rites, like tattooing, were associated with *lalud*. Prior to World War II, these coming-of-age ceremonies, where "new" humans were created, were usually conducted immediately after a successful headhunting expedition because human heads were embodied with high levels of *lalud*. This association between headhunting, life force, and fertility (for crops and humans) has and will continue to be emphasized throughout this book.

OUTER ISLANDS OF INDONESIA: SPIRITUAL TATTOOS OF THE MENTAWAI

Twelve hundred miles to the southwest of Kelabit territory lies isolated Siberut Island. Part of the Mentawai archipelago, it is home to the Mentawai people, one of the most profusely tattooed Indigenous People living today. Although Siberut is famous the world over as the "last frontier of surfing," it is difficult to reach and requires an open sea voyage from Padang in West Sumatra.

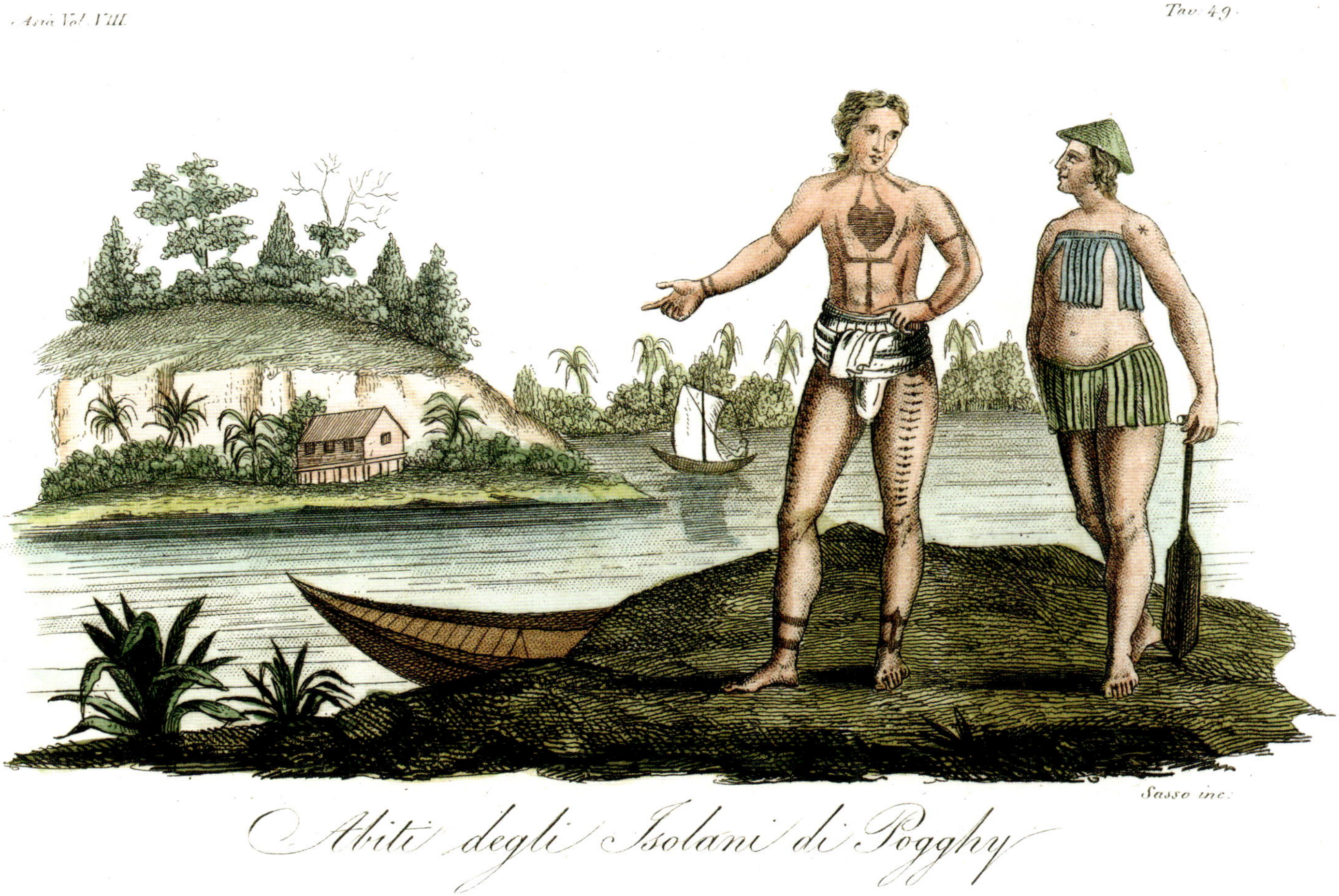

FIGURE 4.49

Copperplate engraving from Crisp titled "Dress of the Poggy [Pagai] Islanders," ca. 1800. Perhaps the oldest drawing of the Mentawaian people was published in 1799 in an essay by the Englishman John Crisp, who visited the Strait of Sikakap on North Pagai in 1792. In his account, the tattooing practice was described and the tools accurately illustrated. A "Mr. Best" accompanied Crisp on this voyage and submitted to the operation on his leg. He is perhaps the first visitor ever to be tattooed by the Mentawai (Wagner 2003:200). Over the ensuing centuries, other European travelers returned home with a permanent souvenir, including the Italian anthropologist and explorer Elio Modigliani (1910:454), who was hand-tapped by a Sipora Island tattooist on his right hand. Modigliani also collected a set of Mentawaian tattooing tools that today are housed at the Ethnographic Museum of Florence. From Ferrario 1826: pl. 49. Collection of the author.

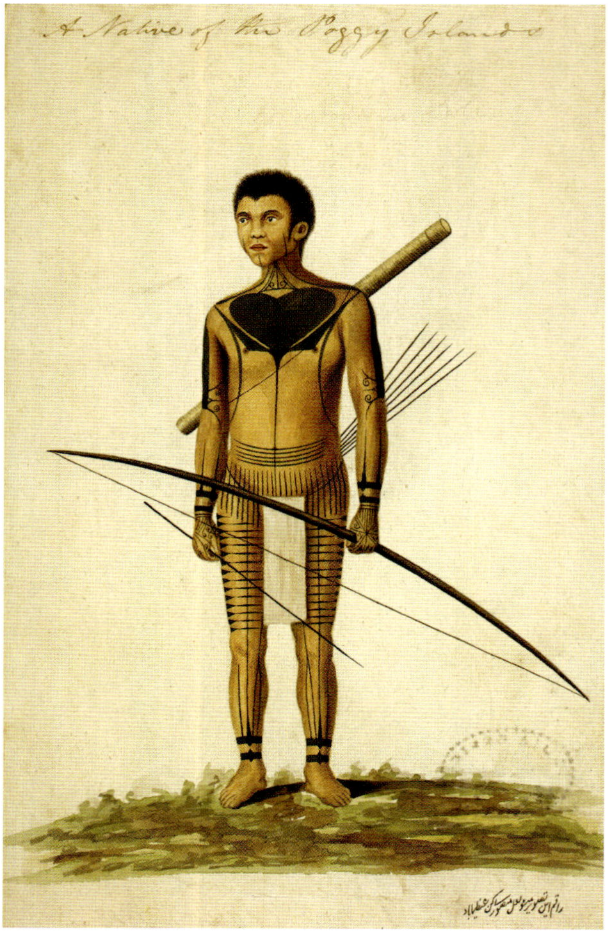

FIGURE 4.50
In this portrait of a Pagai islander with bow and quiver, the subject's tattoos are extremely detailed in comparison to Ferrario's portrayal, but the bold chest tattoos are quite similar in both renditions, 1810. The watercolor, housed in the India Office Library of the British Library, may represent the second-oldest known illustration of a Mentawaian individual. The artist who created this beautiful work was named Manu Lala and was of Persian descent (Wagner 2003:201). A longtime resident of Calcutta (1798–1812), he accompanied Richard Parry of the East India Company to Sumatra. Collection of British Library (490).

The Mentawai are an ancient people that have probably lived in the Mentawai archipelago for more than two thousand years (Burman-Hall 2017; Schefold 1989). Although early nineteenth-century Christian missionaries converted most of the Mentawai living on the southern islands of Sipora and North and South Pagai (which are relatively flat), the traditional culture of the Mentawai living on rugged (and somewhat mountainous) Siberut remained relatively intact, albeit just barely.

With Indonesian independence in 1950, an aggressive government campaign was soon launched to modernize the Mentawaians and especially those inhabiting Siberut. Here traditional religious practices based on animistic beliefs held firm in interior regions, whereas in the southern islands the activities of missionaries led to a relinquishing of traditional customs, such as tattooing, decades before.[33]

Traditional cultural practices such as *titi* (tattooing), tooth filing, and the wearing of loincloths were forbidden because they were considered "heathen" and savage, in stark contrast to the modern and progressive Indonesian state (Schefold 1992:113). These and other Mentawaian cultural practices were intimately linked to *arat sabulungan*, a complex cultural belief system that gives reverence to the spirits of the ancestors, the sky, the land, the ocean, the rivers, and everything that composes the natural world through continual offerings (Tulius 2012:69–70).

Thus, in order to assimilate the Mentawaian people among contemporary Indonesians, the government believed it was necessary to break down local Indigenous religious practices, and every individual was forced to join either the Christian or the Muslim faith.

In the 1990s, cultural oppression against the Mentawai took on more brutal forms of forced relocation from jungle villages to resettlement sites in government-created villages. Mentawai religion, which was led by charismatic and fully tattooed *sikerei*, or shamans,[34] was outlawed, and for the most part police stripped practicing shamans of their medicine bundles, sacred objects, loincloths, and long hair (Henley 2001:140). Mentawai shamans, the keepers of the rain forest (cf. Lindsay 1992), were denied their basic human rights.

Thankfully, several Mentawai clans living in the remote interior of Siberut succeeded in escaping the disruptions and dislocations of the government. One such group, the Sarereiket, in an attempt to retain their original culture made a courageous decision to leave their ancestral village of Ugai—a place where mosques, Catholic missions, and Western clothing were becoming a thing of the present—and move deeper into the jungle.

For the Mentawai, the jungle has always been a place where everything—plants, rocks, animals, and man—has a *kina* (spirit). Spirits are believed to live everywhere and in everything—under the earth, in the sky, in the water, in the treetops, in bamboo, in a dugout canoe—and they are spoken too because they speak and act as human beings do (Krutak 2008a:41; Loeb 1928:414). Some spirits offer protection and help to humankind. But others are evil and hand out punishment in the form of sickness and disease.

In the malaria-infested jungles of Siberut, there is no doubt that human existence is constantly threatened by disease. For this reason, the population density has always been low. The Mentawaians attempt to explain the onslaught of illness as not living in harmony with oneself and the environment. To maintain this harmony, religious and everyday codes of conduct must be always followed because acting recklessly or breaking taboo will anger the spirits of disease that live in the jungle.

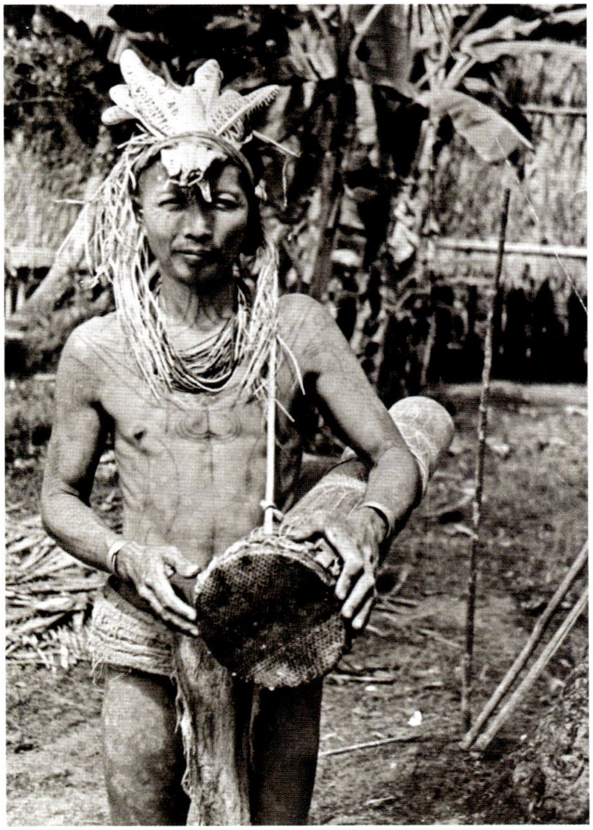

FIGURE 4.51
Tattooed Mentawai man holding a *kajeuman*, or lizard skin and palm wood drum, 1948. He is wearing a *kabit* (barkcloth loincloth), and palm leaves are tucked underneath his headband. The location was not recorded but his tattooing is done in the Sipora style. Collection of Tropenmuseum (TM-10005504), National Museum of World Cultures.

For these reasons alone, the Mentawai have developed an elaborate system of taboos that govern everything they do. For example, they live in harmony with nature by taking only what they need; they eat fruit only when it is in season, and they eat meat only during ceremonial occasions. At all other times of the year, they eat their staple food, sago, which comes from the sago palm, as well as various types of greens, and rice.

But taboos extend far beyond breakfast, lunch, and dinner. In the traditional *uma*, or longhouse, of the Mentawai people, sex is taboo.[35] Before a hunt, men cannot wash their hair or they will shoot their arrows poorly or will become sick. When making arrow poison, men are forbidden to sleep or bathe that night.[36] If they do, the monkeys they hunt will die high in the trees, or the poison will become diluted and ineffective. During the hunt itself, hunters cannot strike their dogs, because if they do, it is believed that they will not catch any game.

The religious beliefs of the Mentawai are centered on the importance of coexisting with the invisible spirits that inhabit the world and all the animate and inanimate objects within it. Health is seen as a state of balance or harmony, and for the Mentawaians it is something holy and beautiful. But if the balance is broken, the only way to restore it is by placating the spirits that have been offended or accidentally distressed.

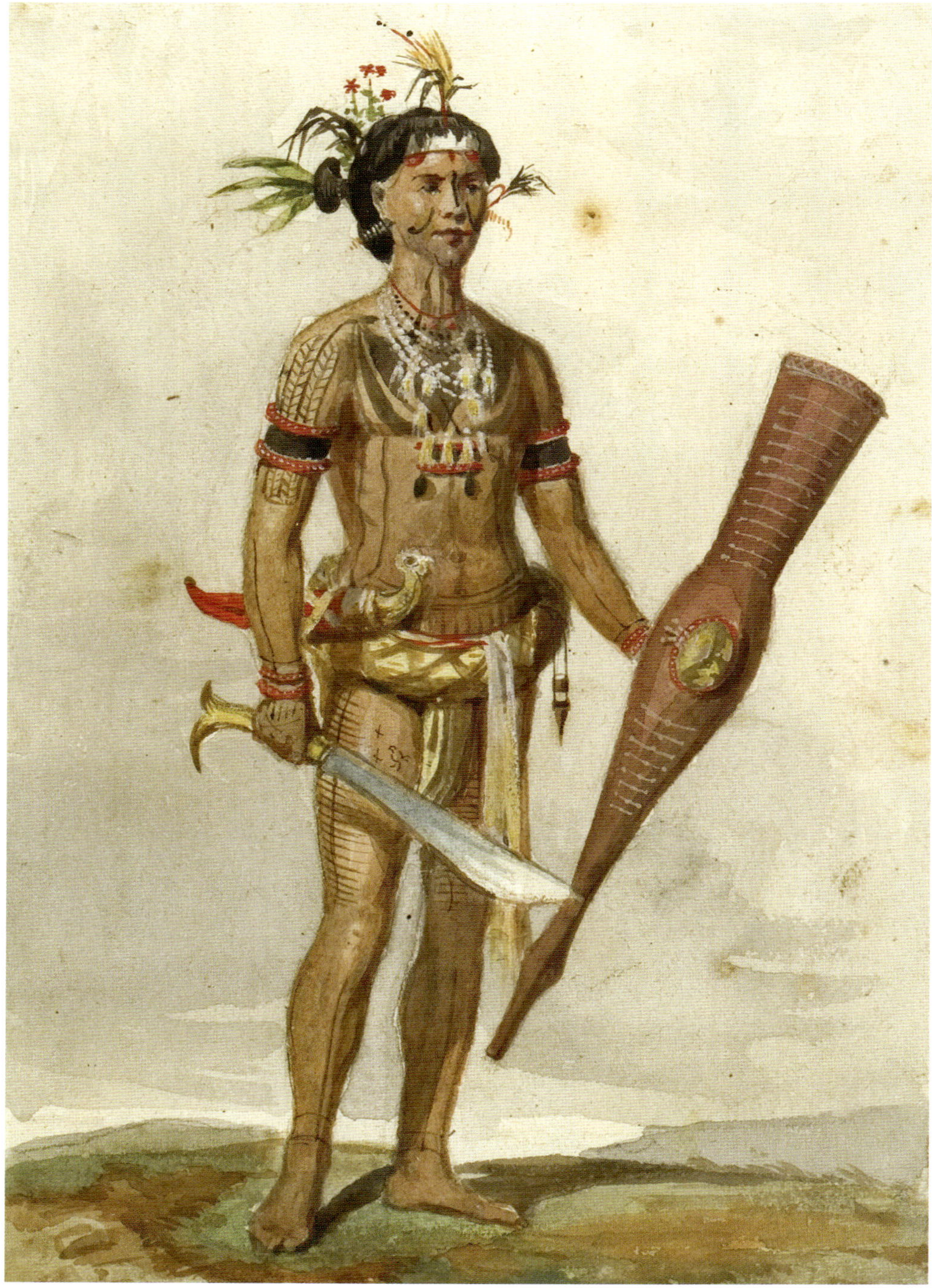

FIGURE 4.52
Mentawai warrior in full dress, ca. 1850. Watercolor by Carl von Rosenberg. Collection of Leiden University Library (36A113).

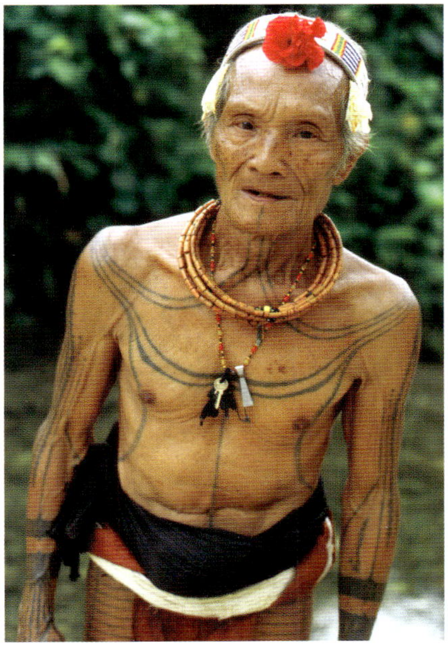

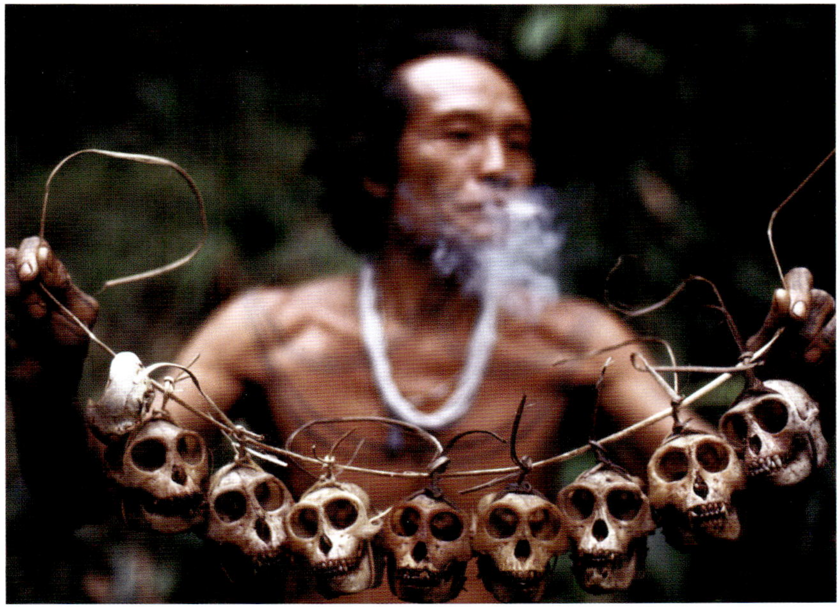

FIGURE 4.53
Mentawai shaman Aman Toshi in later years, 2007 (*left*) and as a younger man (*right*) holding a string of monkey skulls, 1988. These will come to rest in his *uma* (house) to retain their spirits. Buttui, Siberut Island. © Lars Krutak. © Charles Lindsay.

With the help of medicinal plants, these malevolent spirits can be "cooled down" by magical means, and then they are appeased with sacrifices (Schefold 1992:110). The intermediary in these contacts is always the *sikerei*, or Mentawai shaman, because only he can communicate with the spirits.

Aman Lau Lau Manai (d. 2023) is a Mentawai *sikerei*, literally "one who has magic power" (Loeb 1929a:66). But he is not just a doctor. He is also a leader, priest, herbalist, physician, psychologist, dancer, family, and community man. Although Mentawaian society is egalitarian, shamans are considered to be the leaders of their people. They are the tribe's connection to the spiritual world, and to the outside world as well. Sometimes they travel to distant cities to meet with government officials to fight for their human and environmental rights.

Because the Mentawaian belief system is animistic and has many taboos limiting it, it is the responsibility of shamans like Aman Lau Lau to maintain his people's balance with the natural and spirit worlds. For Aman Lau Lau and the other Mentawai shamans of Buttui village, nature is both religion and survival, and they must know the forest inside and out to successfully maintain the balance between these complex worlds.

Sickness may be treated with medicinal plants, but it is the intervention of the shaman on the spiritual plane that ultimately determines a patient's fate. For this reason, the *sikerei* must fly away on the wings of trance to work his deeds of magic rescue.

FIGURE 4.54
Mentawai shaman Aman Lau Lau adorning himself with turmeric and facial paint, Buttui, Siberut Island, 2011. © Tomasz Madej.

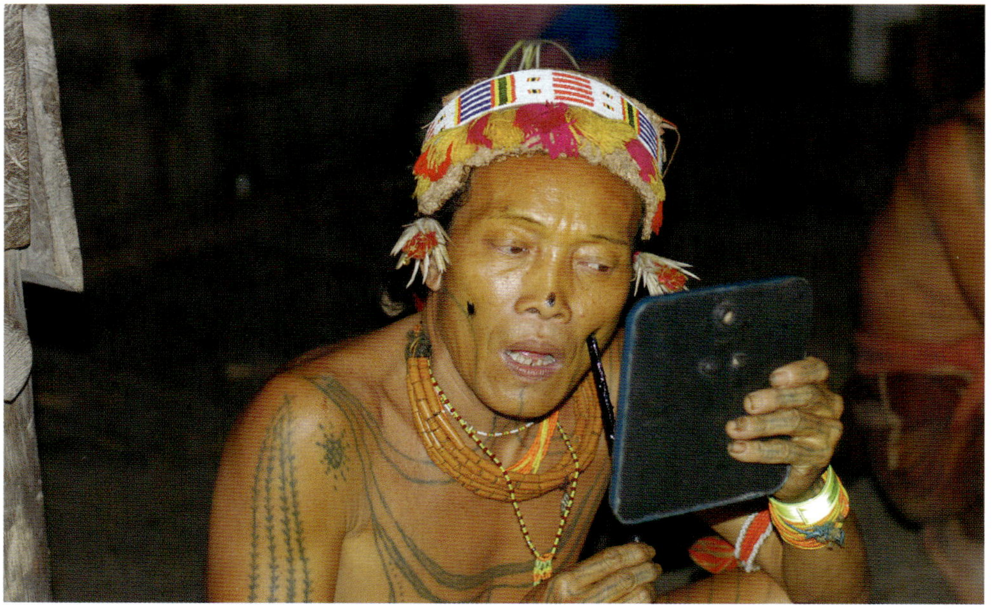

FIGURE 4.55
Mentawai shaman Aman Lau Lau and his wife, Bai Lau Lau, enjoy a moment during a festival, Buttui, Siberut Island, 1988. © Charles Lindsay.

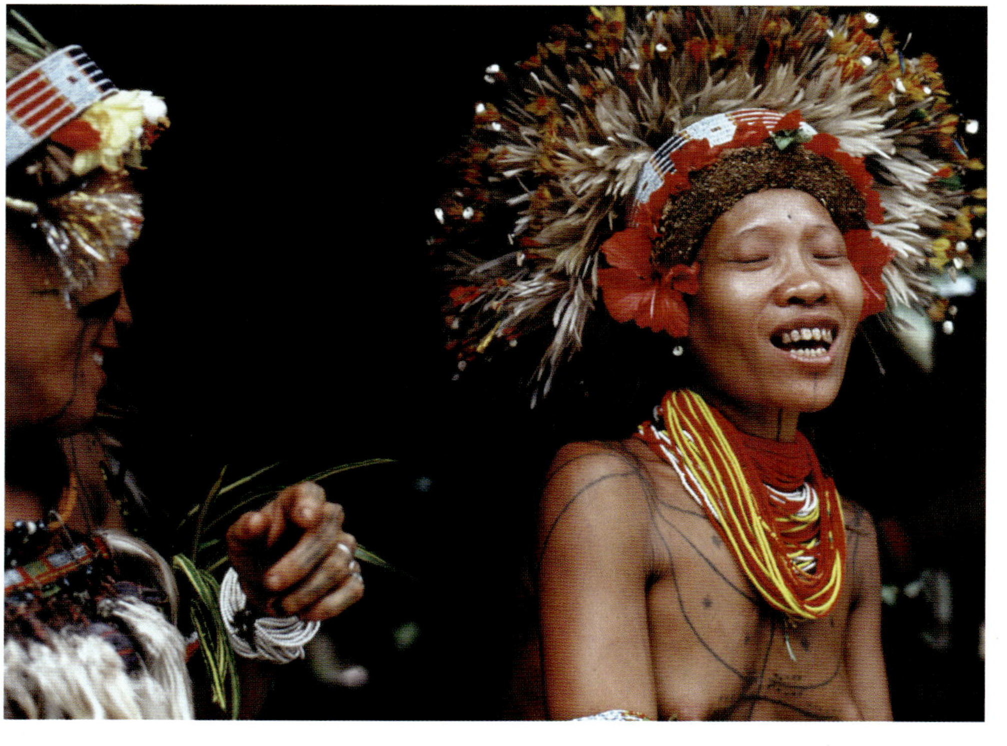

As in other Indigenous cultures, the Mentawai believe that all disease is nothing but the loss of the *simagere* (soul), and if the soul abandons the body, sickness or death will be the result (Loeb 1928:413; Schefold 1992:114). Soul loss is usually attributed to the spirits of disease or of *sanitu* (ancestral ghosts), and numerous ceremonies are carried out to appease them if taboos have been broken.

Mentawai shamans habitually perform *pasaksak* rituals to mend broken taboos. Once they begin, all work is taboo except for activities related to the performance. Though Mentawaians observe numerous rites such as these—for the cutting of trees, the building of canoes and longhouses, and for weddings, funerals, hunting expeditions, initiations, visiting strangers, healing rituals, and tattooing—all of them are conducted to make amends to the spirits of the jungle and of the ancestors for the breaking of any number of taboos.

However, another way the Mentawaians please their ancestors and keep their souls "close" is by beautifying the body. Individuals, be they male or female, who neglect their bodies by not keeping them beautiful with beads, flowers, sharpened teeth, and especially tattoos will cease to be attractive to their souls (Schefold 1992:111). In such cases, the soul may decide to leave its human host and roam about the body free. If the soul does not return to its home, it may decide to withdraw to the ancestral world, at which point that person will die.

Shamans such as Aman Lau Lau, Aman Toshi, and Aman Berita are experts at beautifying themselves. And almost every day flowers adorn their hair, beads their necks and wrists, and facial paint accents their rigid faces or their strong bodies are smeared with fragrant ground turmeric.

Continual care for one's soul is one of the guiding principles in the life of the Mentawai people. And permanent decoration of the body through tattooing keeps it near at hand. So does good food, music, and dance, because each is a religious means of benefiting the members of the community and *uma* (longhouse) by pleasing their souls as well as Teteu, their "Grandfather," the deity Pagete Sabbau.[37]

Today as well as in the past, tattooing was performed as both a rite-of-passage ceremony, signifying a new life stage of a male or female individual, and an activity that "dignified" the body, thereby pleasing one's soul. However, men and other community members formerly acquired additional motifs after a successful headhunt,[38] at which time a *punen lepa* (North Pagai) or *mulepa* (Siberut) purification ceremony was held (Loeb 1928:411n3).[39] This rite, which was remembered by elders and documented by the American anthropologist Edwin M. Loeb on North Pagai in the early twentieth century, was performed to wipe out the evil influences surrounding human blood spilled in the community, especially that of headhunting victim(s) whose souls were potential sources of danger. It also served to reintegrate the members of the *uma* into the protective sphere of the group's own ancestors (Schefold 2007:485),[40] because without their favor future success in warfare and other endeavors might fail.[41]

Prior to the tattooing and *mulepa* rite, a special porch was constructed for the procedure in front of the *uma*, so that no blood would fall to the ground (Loeb 1929b:233). On North Pagai, this prohibition was linked to Teteu because spilling blood on the ground was a method of summoning him, the result being an earthquake (Loeb 1929b:210). *Biti*, or cuff-like rings, were tattooed around the calves and *pumumurat* (forearms), then the backs of the hands and the sides of

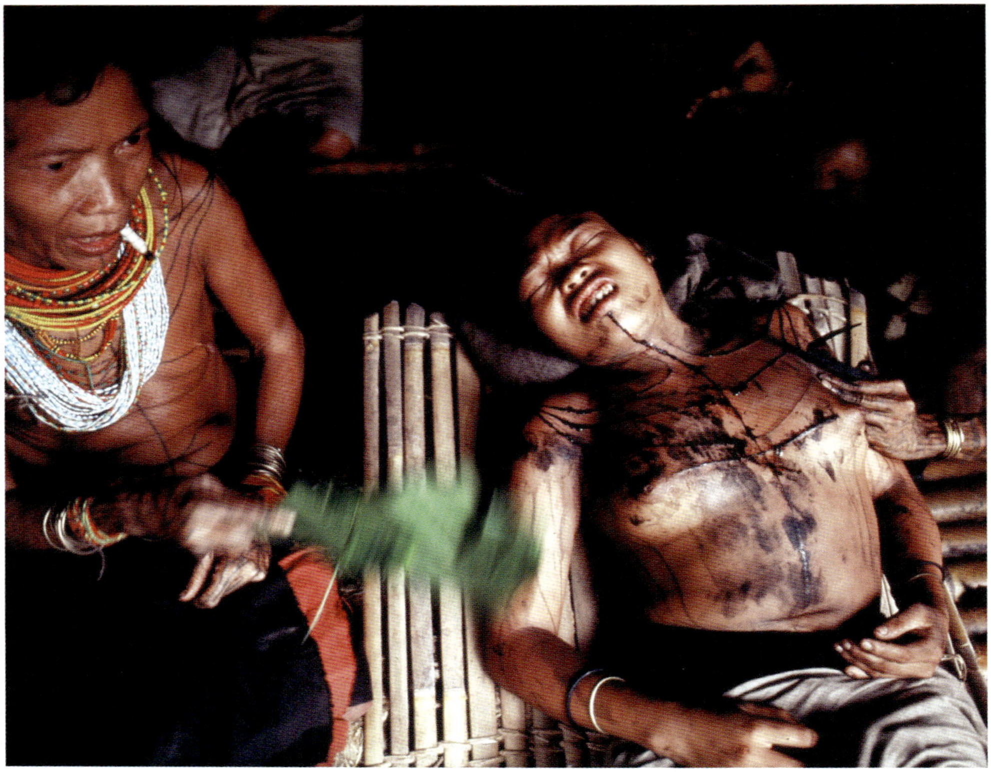

FIGURE 4.56
Aman Lau Lau's sister Leiai is fanned by her mother while being tattooed, Buttui, Siberut Island, 1988. © Charles Lindsay.

the body were marked. This tattooing was said to "complete" the individual, but only those individuals who were fully grown (i.e., reached puberty) were thus marked; otherwise, the linework might lose its shape over time.

Some scholars have implied that these locations were tattooed because, apart from the head, successful warriors often returned home with the arms and legs of the enemy (Schefold 2007:484). Notwithstanding, the ceremony concluded after every tattoo recipient was magically treated with a black chicken to ensure their tattoo pigments would always remain clearly visible (Schefold 2007:485).

Afterward the attendees killed as many pigs (or chickens) as there were people tattooed; these gifts were offered to the spirits of the *uma*. The attendees then entered the *uma*, and the leading *sikerei* or *rimata* (clan leader) spoke: "Here is your food, spirits of the *uma*. Here are livers of pigs for the tattooing of the children of the *uma*. If the children have lost blood in being tattooed, do not make them sick. Bless us, guard us, drive off all that is evil" (Loeb 1929b:233).

According to oral traditions, Pagete Sabbau (or "Grandfather") was the first Mentawai shaman. Through his son Maligai, he taught the Mentawai how to construct the *uma*, (head) hunting, healing with medicinal plants, tattooing, and everything else they know today. Through

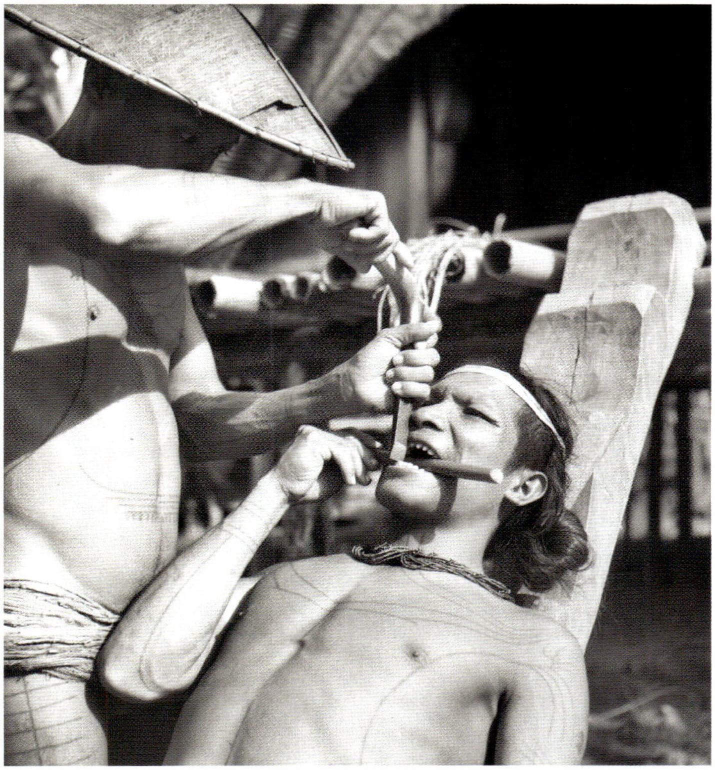

FIGURE 4.57
Mentawai man undergoing a teeth modification procedure, Sipora Island, 1938. Apart from tattooing, one of the hallmarks of Mentawaian beauty was the former custom of tooth filing. When a child reached puberty, an adult family member sharpened their upper and lower incisors using a chisel, axe blade, or small machete hammered with a heavy object; skilled practitioners completed the painful process in less than an hour (Schefold 1980a:82). Once the filing was completed, the corners of the teeth were rounded off with a knife. This activity was not associated with rituals or taboos. Collection of Tropenmuseum (TM-10002931), National Museum of World Cultures.

Maligai, Pagete Sabbau also created all of the animals and trees of the forest, including the sago palm, which is the Mentawai Tree of Life. But the people became jealous of Maligai because of his magical abilities and determined to kill him. When they built their first *uma*, they sent Maligai down to dig under the center post. Then they let the post down on his head, imprisoning him in the ground. In revenge, Maligai knocked the *uma* down with an earthquake.[42]

To make amends for this disaster, the Mentawai people began to offer human sacrifices to the Grandfather. These individuals were captured during headhunting raids into enemy territory. Traditionally, these offerings were made under the center pole of a new *uma* on its construction.[43] Although these types of sacrifices have not been practiced in living memory, today the prohibition against spilling blood on the ground continues. Thus, when chickens or pigs are offered to various spirits, their necks are wrung or their bodies are speared so that they bleed to death internally.

Pagete Sabbau is so revered today that it is taboo to mention his name unless in the most serious of conversations. Aman Lau Lau is very hesitant to speak about him, because his power is so great. And the only time Teteu is summoned these days is when a new *uma* is built, because he is pleased by the beautiful dancing that takes place in his honor.

TITI TODAY: TATTOOS OF THE MENTAWAI SHAMAN

Because the soul is pleased by beautiful and complete body tattoos, the Mentawai believe that it allows them to bring their material wealth into the afterlife. The Mentawai also say that their *titi* (tattoos) allow their ancestors to recognize them after death. More importantly, however, many forms of tattooing are specifically believed to protect their owners from evil spirits lurking in the jungle.

After the cessation of headhunting in the early twentieth century, tattooing was focused on marking life stages. Prior to those tattooing sessions I observed at Buttui, *kera*, or fetish poles, were planted in the ground at the entrances of the *uma* and hung with magical plants. The *kina* (spirits) of the poles kept away potentially malevolent *sanitu* (ghosts) that could bring misfortune or illness if any taboos were broken during the tattooing. Tattoos were applied by a designated hand-tapping *sipaniti* (tattoo artist) or "man who makes the needle."

Once a boy or girl reached puberty, they received back tattoos, which, according to some contemporary tattoo bearers, symbolize the Tree of Life (Schefold 2021). In various Mentawaian stories, this cosmic tree divides the world into three parts: an upper world (tree branches), a middle world inhabited by humans (tree trunk), and the underworld (roots) (cf. Schefold 2016:24, 2021). For others, such as Esmat Wandra Sakulok of the Saibi Samukop clan of Siberut, the back tattoo represents a kind of scale that is related to balancing the forces of the cosmos. "The [tattooed] lines on my back symbolize a scale," he explained. "It refers to the balance between humanity and nature [inherent in the cosmic order]. This balance is very important" (Patterns of Life 2021). For Sakulok, however, this balancing act is related to sailing. "This tattoo represents the balance of the boat," he said. "The purpose of balancing a boat is to prevent it from tipping over. Thus, one's actions must be in balance with nature. We must not destroy the forest, we must not violate ancestral rules so that nature can take care of us."[44]

FIGURE 4.58 Mentawai shaman Aman Alangi Kunen from Matotonan, Siberut Island, 2009. © Aman Durga Sipatiti.

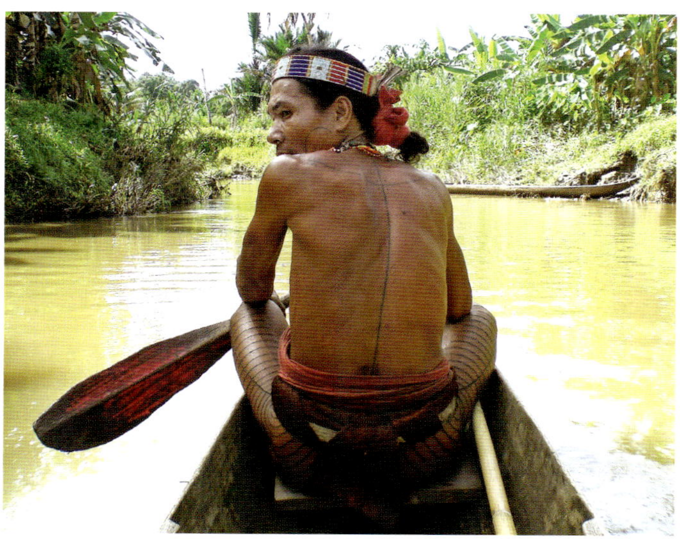

After one or two years had elapsed after the back tattoos, the upper arms and backs of the hands were tattooed. Next, the tattooing of the upper thighs and legs was executed (note: traditionally these marks were made just before marriage), followed by the intricate tattoos of the chest and neck. The final stage of tattooing, which usually commenced after the individual reached forty years of age, was completed when the calves, shins, and the forearms were tattooed (Krutak 2008a:45–46).

Of course, different Mentawai clans observed their own customs when it came to the different stages of tattooing. Bai Lau Lau, Aman Lau Lau's wife, who is from a different region of Siberut, told me that her hands were tattooed first (all in one day), then she waited one year and her chest and back were tattooed (all in one day).

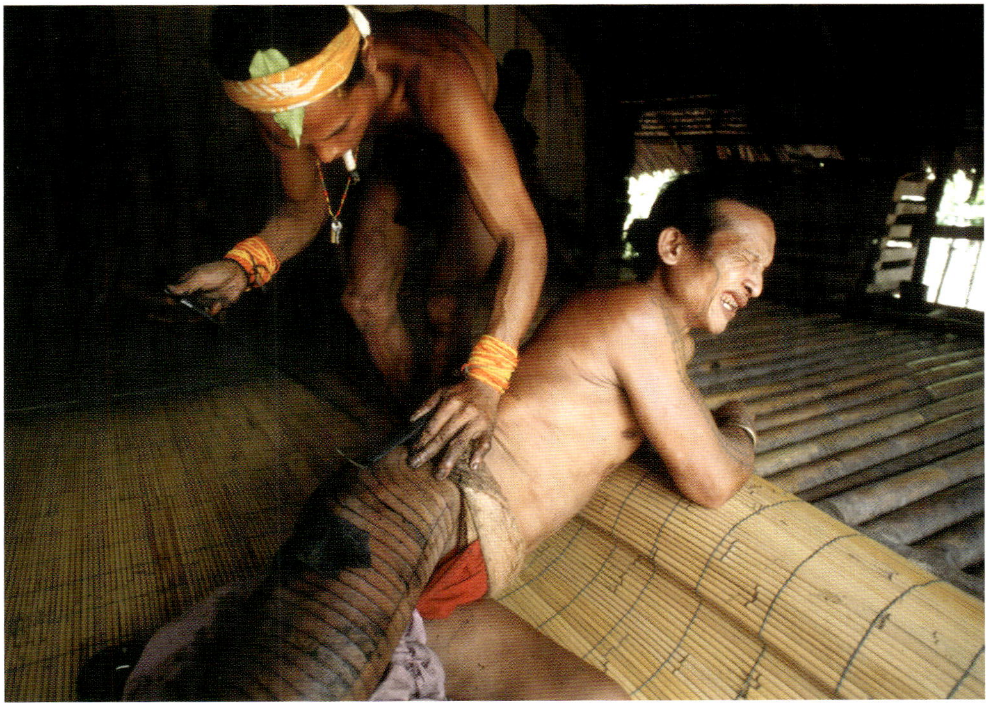

FIGURE 4.59
Mentawai shaman Aman Bereta tattooing Aman Ipai, Buttui, Siberut Island, 2007. © Lars Krutak.

Traditionally, Mentawai tattoo artists sometimes used a sharpened piece of bark taken from the Karai tree as their skin-plying tool. Others used a lemon thorn set into a small bamboo stick or deer horn, which was hand-tapped into the skin with a wooden mallet. Among the Indigenous Atayal and Paiwan of Taiwan, and the Kalinga of the Philippines, thorns of the mountain orange or pomelo tree were used in this capacity (Krutak 2007, 2010a; see chapters 2 and 3 in this volume). However, several coastal peoples of Papua New Guinea, who like the Mentawai also belong to the Austronesian language family, also used a lemon or orange thorn in their hand-tapping tools (Krutak 2014b).

Anyone in the Mentawai community could become a tattoo artist, but only those people with sufficient skills and talent found work. Tattoo pigment was manufactured from the sticky juice squeezed from a variety of red sugarcane mixed with soot in a coconut bowl.

According to the Dutch medical doctor J. A. van Beukering, who worked on Siberut, and the German ethnologist and explorer Alfred Maass, formerly soot was mixed with charred tree resin and sugarcane juice to make tattoo pigment (van Beukering 1941:324; Maass 1906:438).[45] Aman Bereta, who tattooed me and two Mentawai men living in Buttui with an old brass nail, learned the art from his father, who was a renowned artist. Unfortunately, there are not many practicing tattoo artists working on Siberut today, and the reason Aman Bereta is not fully tattooed is because there is no one in his community who can properly tattoo him.

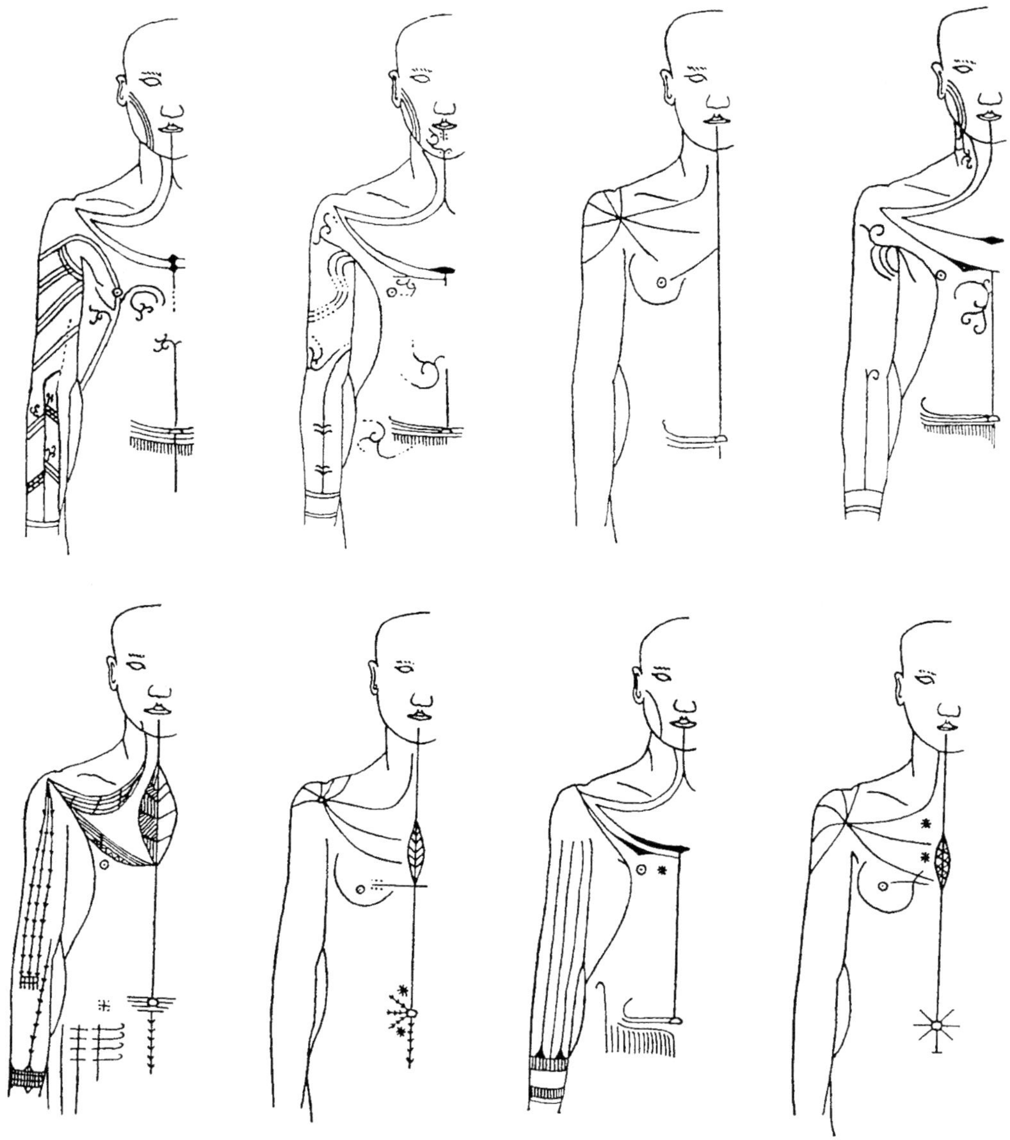

FIGURE 4.60

Mentawai tattooing styles: *top row,* Sipora and Pagai Islands; *bottom row,* Paipadjet and Silaoinen region, Siberut Island, ca. 1940. From van Beukering 1941:326–327.

Moreover, tattoo artists like Aman Bereta cannot find apprentices who have the talent or the patience to learn the traditional techniques. And, of course, some Mentawai people who wish to get tattooed cannot afford these expensive markings. For example, the cost of a full suite of tattoos in Buttui, which may take almost a lifetime to receive, is high by Mentawaian standards: 1 medium size pig; 1 durian tree; 4 sago palm trees; 1 coconut palm tree; and 1 chicken basket with several chicks![46] But if you want to become a "real" Mentawai man, woman, or shaman, tattooing is the necessary vehicle because it is the apex of everything that comprises Mentawaian identity. As he was being tattooed with linework on his kneecap, the Buttui community member Aman Ipai told me, "A needle to the bone is hard to take. But this is our tradition. I cannot accept the reality of losing our Mentawai tradition. I will bear the pain like a true Mentawaian. This is Mentawai culture, a symbol of our prosperity. We must not forget it" (Discovery Channel 2009).

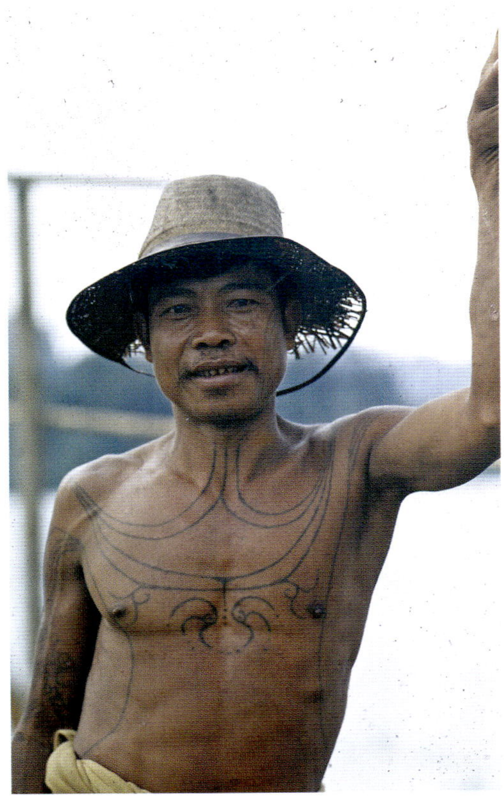

FIGURE 4.61
Tattooed Mentawai man with filed teeth, Sipora or Pagai Islands, ca. 1960s. The swirling center motif varies depending on the clan of the bearer. Photograph by Dorothy West Peltzer. Courtesy National Anthropological Archives.

Tattoos can distinguish people regionally, and I was amazed that the Mentawai with whom I visited could tell me which community a man or woman was from by the style of their tattooing. In the past, great headhunters were easily distinguished by their markings, including tattoos of frogs on their torsos or shoulders.[47] These motifs somewhat resemble headless anthropomorphs, and Maass (1906:438) observed on Sipora that such figures were also placed on the forehead. According to Sakuddei elders living on Siberut, spiral patterns on the forehead and shoulders distinguished the warrior (Schefold 2007:485).

Sakuddei and other Mentawai men sometimes possessed tattooed figures of deer, monkeys, roosters, turtles, and other animals on their bellies. These marks were applied when hostilities arose with a neighboring group. Through these figures, which functioned as a kind of hunting tally, they "shamed" their rivals through expressing their superiority in the hunt (Schefold 1980a:126).

Over the last century and a half, various explorers and writers recorded details concerning the tattooing motifs of the Mentawai inhabiting the islands of their archipelago. Most of these obscure publications have been overlooked by contemporary students of Indigenous tattooing praxis, perhaps because they are not available in the English language. That being said, a few important traditional patterns are as follows.

FIGURE 4.62
Tattooed Mentawai man of Sioban region, Sipora Island, ca. 1905. From Volz 1906:102.

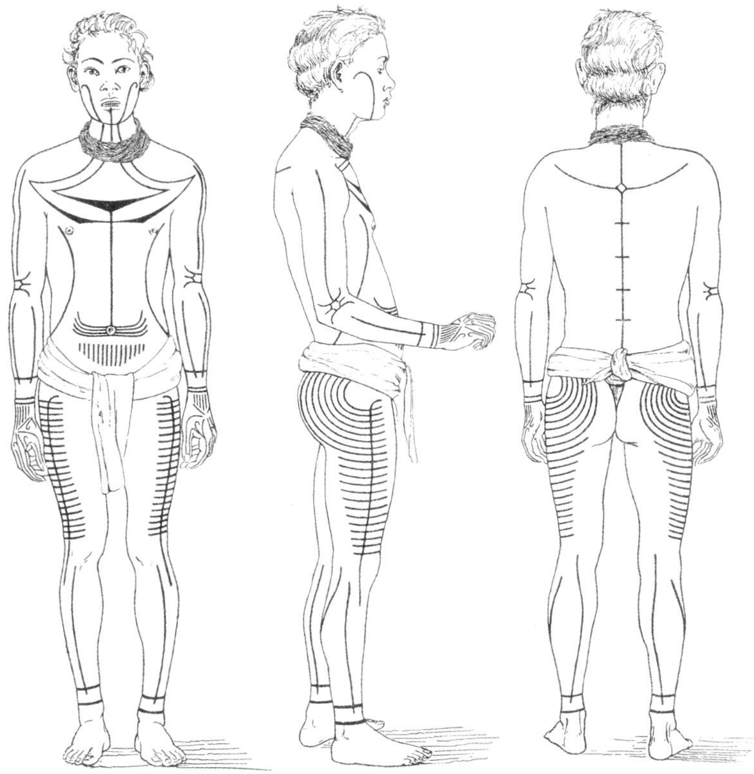

FIGURE 4.63
Tattooed Mentawai women of Katorei and Tabekat region, Siberut Island, ca. 1905. From Volz 1906:105.

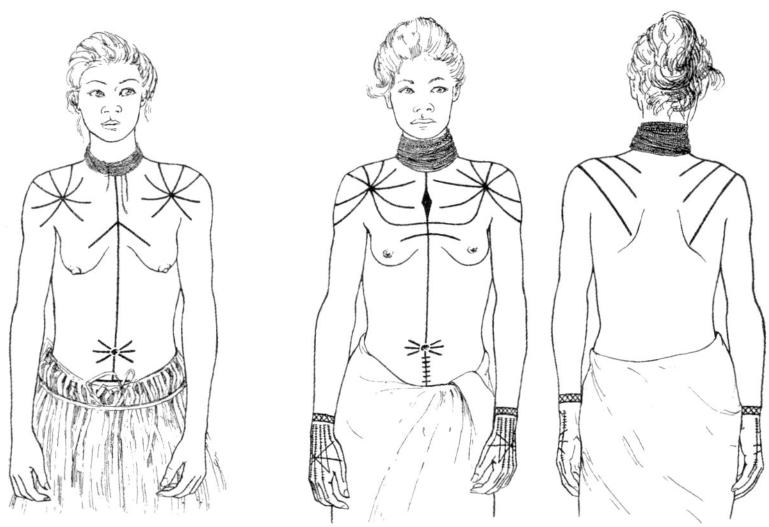

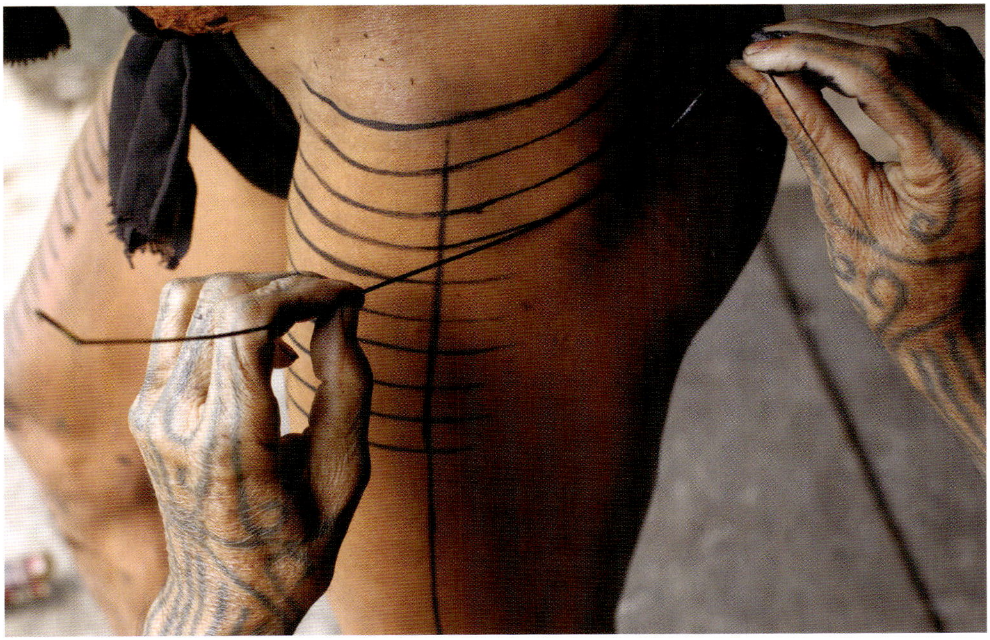

FIGURE 4.64
Mentawai tattooist Aman Pauja of Ugai village stenciling a line on his client's leg in Buttui village, Siberut Island, 2011. © Tomasz Madej.

Early visitors to the Mentawais were intrigued by the bold triangular-shaped upper chest design. Variations in this pattern could be read by other Mentawaians as a regional and perhaps even as a clan indicator. Most early observers who described this pattern noted that it was simply an element formed of curved lines but little else. However, the Italian anthropologist and explorer Elio Modigliani (1910:452), who was tattooed by a local North Pagai Island artist, recorded the name *titi duducat* for the chest piece. On Siberut, the *tudukat* is a small type of log drum placed in the rafters of the *uma*. It is struck with a variety of beats during major and minor ceremonies and to announce a birth, a death, a hunting success, and, in former times, victory in headhunting. In profile, its shape does resemble the chest motif.

Modigliani (1910:450) and Maass (1906:439) recorded the terms *suga sugania* and *suga suga*, respectively, for the fringe-like vertical lines that ran downward from a horizontally tattooed line below the navel. Variations of this linework existed among groups inhabiting Siberut, Sipora, and the Pagais. The German ethnologist and surgeon Augustin Krämer, who was very interested in Indigenous tattooing and authored several works on these traditions in Polynesia (e.g., Krämer 1903, 1904, 1906), also inquired about these motifs during a short visit to North Pagai in 1906. In the village of Seai, he first recorded that the outer lines curving upward to the neck from the chest piece (i.e., *duducat*) were called *lambinan*, or "carrying straps," on which a basket or decorations are hung (Krämer 1907:37). Then he inquired about the *suga suga* motifs, which he wrote were related to the "ground." More specifically, he stated that *suga suga* referred to sharpened bamboo stakes that were placed upright, just like these vertically oriented tattoo lines, in pitfalls or "man traps"

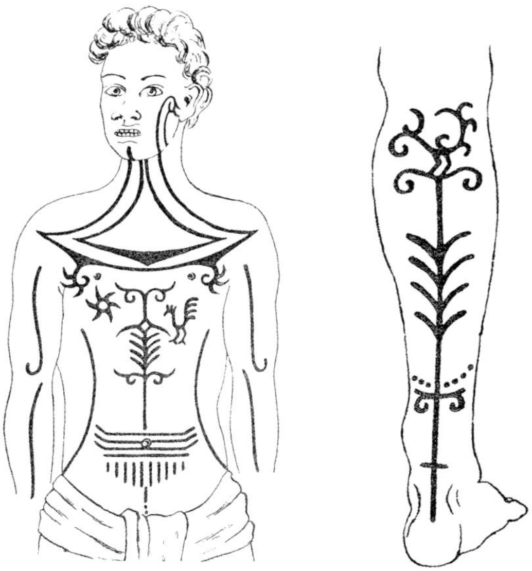

FIGURE 4.65
Seai village man of North Pagai Island with Tree of Life and rooster tattoos on his torso and leg, 1906. From Krämer 1907: 38–39, figs. 1, 5.

to protect a community from marauding headhunters. As noted in chapter 3, the Kalinga of the northern Philippines also positioned *suga* (bamboo stakes) in dead falls or pits to slow down headhunting enemies. These spikes could produce wounds that punctured deep into the feet, legs, thighs, and even abdomens of anyone unfortunate enough to make contact with these devices.

As noted, some Siberut tattoo bearers have indicated that specific body tattoos represent the cosmic Tree of Life. Some groups specifically mention that this tree is the sago palm: the stripes on the upper thighs represent the veins and trunk of the sago; long dotted lines running down the arms symbolize the prickly fronds of its branches; patterns on the hands and ankles may mirror the bark or roots; and the curved lines on the chest represent the sago flower (Henley 2001:93). Some Mentawai elders say that this Tree of Life must be tattooed on every shaman, because there can be no death when one is part of a Tree of Life. Of course, the sago palm is the staple food of the Mentawai people, and all of their domestic animals eat it too.

This observation might also be connected to former tattooing traditions on Sipora and North Pagai, since some writers recorded that the primary torso tattoo line, upper thigh markings, and midline on the back of the calf were related to the "trunk" of a tree (Krämer 1907:38–39; Maass 1906:439). In the tripartite division of the Mentawai cosmos, the trunk of the Tree of Life symbolizes the human realm. Furthermore, Krämer (1907:38–39, figs. 1 and 5) illustrated a Seai village man from North Pagai with a rooster tattooed on his chest and the back of his leg.[48]

Both birds were sitting in the upper branches of a tree. Chickens and roosters are held in high esteem by the Mentawai since they are animals frequently used in offerings to the spirits. Both birds also fly "straight" and know when morning has come, and generally speaking they are "wise bird[s]" (Loeb 1928:429).

But the Mentawai of Buttui told me that their tattoos do not necessarily depict the Tree of Life for them. For example, the barbed tattoos running down their arms represent the thorny fronds of the rattan palm. Small marks tattooed on the inner thighs and tops of the feet of men (that resemble chicken's feet) are dog's paws, a kind of sympathetic magic that enables the men to run as fast as their hunting companions (Krutak 2008a:47). The intricate *ngalou* (this word also means "talisman") tattoos that appear on the chest and wrists are tattooed beads that "tie in" the soul and keep it close to the body. The hooklike tattoos on the backs of the hands have a similar function, but Aman Lau Lau also told me that they help you catch fish and game animals more easily by making your fingers and hands more dexterous. The *sepippurat* rosettes tattooed on the shoulders of men and the bold *gaylan* starburst patterns inked on the shoulders and backs of women symbolize that evil should bounce off their bodies like raindrops from a flower (Lindsay 1992:61). Of course, no evil will find someone marked in this way, because it is the protective shield of the Mentawai.

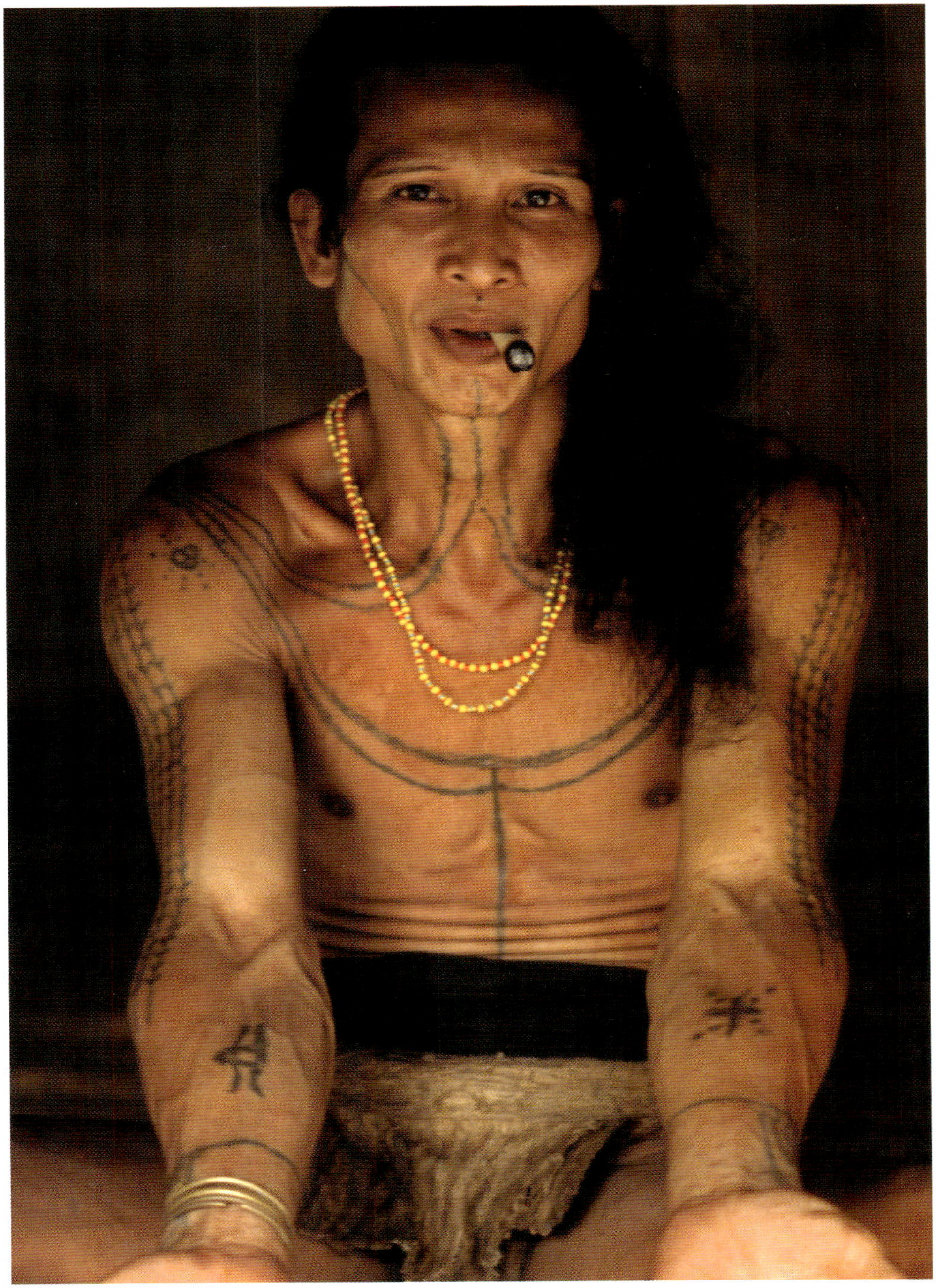

FIGURE 4.66
Aman Ipai possesses many tattoos, including a crucifix-like crab on his forearm, Buttui village, Siberut Island, 2007. Although he is not a shaman, crabs are invoked by Mentawai shamans during healing and other rites because they are believed to never die (e.g., they can discard their old bodies and obtain new ones or regenerate severed limbs). Like Aman Lau Lau, Aman Ipai bears two rosettes on his shoulders symbolizing that evil will bounce off his body like raindrops from a flower. © Lars Krutak.

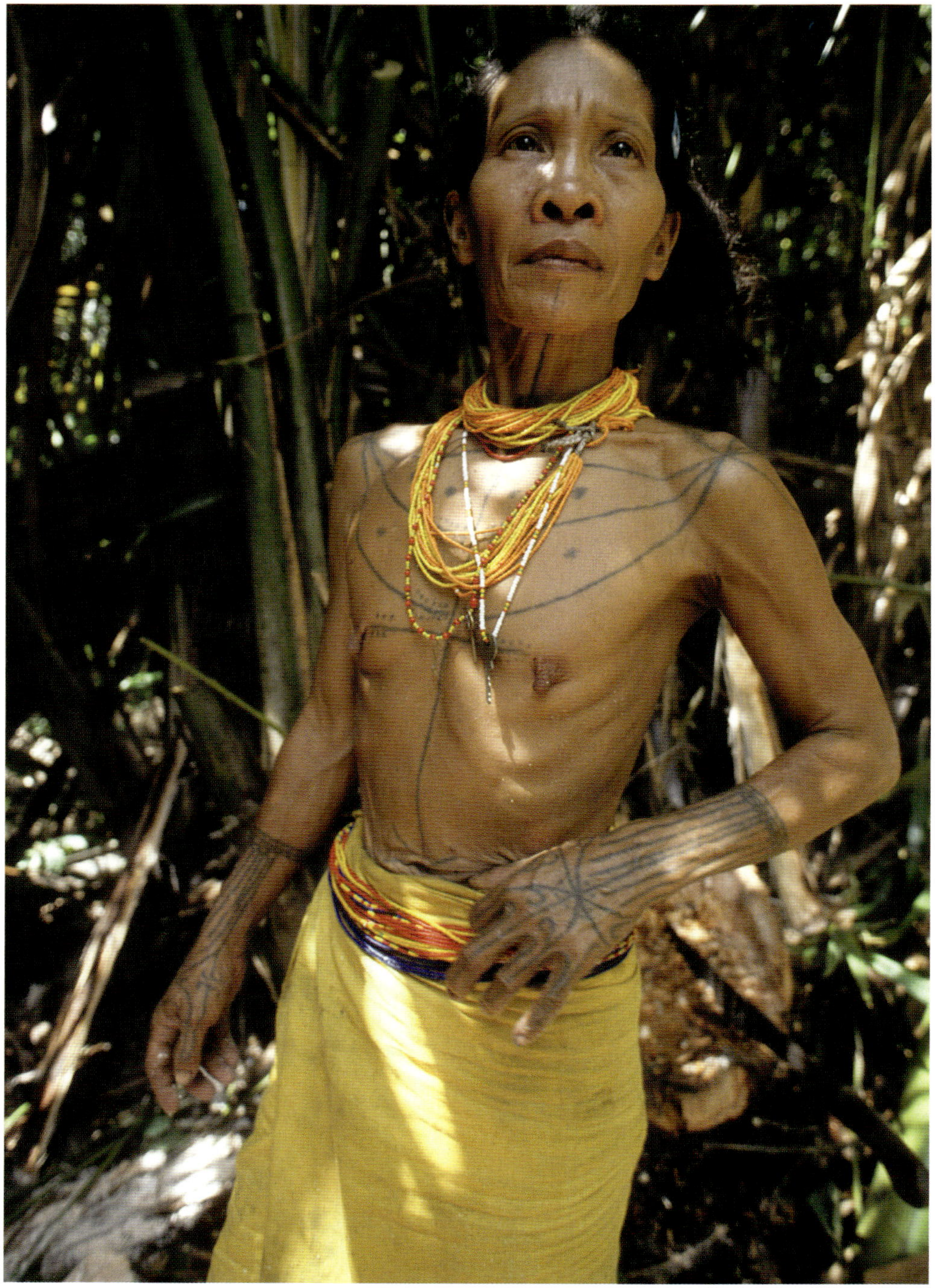

FIGURE 4.67
The late Bai Lau Lau of Buttui, Siberut Island, 2007. © Lars Krutak.

SOUTHERN ISLANDS: SUMBA, TIMOR, SULAWESI, AND SERAM: LABOYA TATTOOS

On the island of Sumba, tattooing was formerly associated with rite-of-passage ceremonies for women and a distinguishing mark for headhunting warriors. The Dutch anthropologist Danielle Geirnaert-Martin (1992:121), who worked with the Laboya of West Sumba, observed that girls received thigh tattoos after their first menstruation and the onset of the first life-giving rains of the season. The patterns consisted of floral motifs (lianas) or iconography inspired by the agricultural fields (cassava creepers). After a woman married and bore her first and second child, her leg tattoos (i.e., shins, calves) were completed in a two-step process. Following the delivery of her first newborn, a local male or female tattooist was called on to visit her once she had recovered from childbirth. The artist applied a water buffalo head or body to her shins. After her second child was born, the calves were tattooed with a pair of *kaduna kamadila* (buffalo horns) (Geirnaert-Martin 1992:185).

For the Laboya, the water buffalo is synonymous with the landscape, since landmarks, territories, megalithic tombs, and villages are associated with it through names and metaphors. In Laboya, the *uma* (house), the village, and the cultivated fields surrounding it are essentially considered to be "buffalos," because this animal, which has been domesticated, symbolizes social unity, in contrast to the uninhabited and unprotected wild areas outside of the village (Geirnaert-Martin 1992:56). In the cosmology of the Laboya, the village of Kadengara is considered the *lede* (navel, umbilical cord, bridge) of the Buffalo Land, which binds Laboya and the island of Sumba to the sky and the rest of the world. As Geirnaert-Martin (56) writes, "This animal implies a strong sense of identity . . . similar to other human groups [on Sumba] and yet different just as one individual is never identical to another. The buffalo is a living functioning being with bodily functions that are metaphors for specific social processes," including tattooing that performed as a socializing process.

Although Geirnaert-Martin did not describe the actual tattooing process in her published account, in other regions of Sumba hand-tapping was the preferred technique. Among the Kodi people who inhabit the southwestern portion of the island, prior to the tattooing a chicken was offered to the spirit of the woman's maternal village to ensure its consent (Hoskins 1989:162). Several lemon thorns were then affixed to a perpendicularly hafted wooden tool, then struck into the skin with a mallet or other heavy object (A. C. Kruyt 1921a:544). Kodi tattoo pigment, as it was among the Rindi and other Indigenous Peoples of Sumba, was derived from charred, pulverized *kemiri* (candlenuts) mixed with soot and sugarcane juice; the liquid substance was rubbed into the open wounds (Forth 1981; Hoskins 1989; A. C. Kruyt 1921a).[49]

Laboya *kamadila* (tattooing) was believed to enhance the status of the woman, and traditionally men would not marry "white-legged" individuals because they were associated with "animality," in contrast to humans (Geirnaert-Martin 1992:181).[50] The floraform tattoos represented the tattoo bearer's ability to give life, and it was at this time that the girl was taught how to weave, a skill she would carry with her for the remainder of her life.

On receipt of her first tattoos, the maternal grandmother of the girl gifted her a black cock, an animal also used by the Mentawai to consecrate a new tattoo. Unlike the latter, its function was not to ensure that the tattoo pigments would always remain in the skin. Instead, the black fowl was perhaps employed to *maringi* (ritually "cool down") the girl, since her newly tattooed skin felt like it was on fire (cf. Geirnaert-Martin 1992:120–121). The color black was also related to Laboya concepts of moisture and procreativity, in contrast to white, which was indicative of dryness and heat. For the Laboya, individuals who remained in a state of heat and "hotness," like headhunters returning from a successful raid and newly circumcised boys, had to be ritually cooled down before entering the village and its respective *umas*. Being "hot" was considered dangerous, because this condition could pose threats to the agricultural crops (i.e., drought) and endanger the village and its inhabitants.

Notwithstanding, a girl's first and second set of tattoos also enhanced her spiritual foundation. The painful first markings attested that she could control the flow of *mawo* (shadow), an aspect of a person's soul that also resides in all living things, from the ancestors of her kin house (Geirnaert-Martin 1992:59). On marriage, the fully tattooed woman also brought another spiritual component of her being into her husband's *uma;* her *dewa* (spirit or vital force), which was inherited from her ancestral house.

Dewa was the counterpart to one's *mawo*, and a *tau* (living body) was composed of these two spiritual components that were fused together during one's lifetime. At death, one's *mawo* and *dewa* became separated from one's living body and followed separate paths into the afterlife (Geirnaert-Martin 1992:59).

Although women's tattoos were a token of her increased *dewa* as a fertile woman, an important aspect of the *dewa* concept was that it also embodied a protective function, since ancestors looked after their kin. But as a woman became integrated into her husband's *uma*, she also gained the *dewa* of her spouse's ancestors. Through offerings made to her husband's ancestors, their *dewa* helped ensure her success in childbirth and offered protection from potentially evil spirits of the dead (Geirnaert-Martin 1992:185).

Men's tattooing among the Laboya was associated with the former practice of headhunting, which could be undertaken only by circumcised men. Men were compelled to take heads in order to avenge the loss of an *uma* or community member and to gain notoriety and build up one's name. Successful warriors were entitled to bear a *madu* (star) on their chests. This symbol was a sign that the man was a feared war leader or, more appropriately, a *mori bani*, "war master" (Geirnaert-Martin 1992:187). The descendants of these renowned men were entitled to bear the star tattoo, and when a war master died, his name was often given to a male child in his lineage. The Laboya believed that war masters had the greatest concentration of *dewa*, and after their death these esteemed men continued to protect the wealth, name, and flow of *mawo* into their respective *uma* (Geirnaert-Martin 1992:187).

Warriors possessed higher levels of *dewa* because of their association with trophy heads captured in battle. Each enemy head was embodied with some level of *dewa* depending on the renown of the slain. This life force could be harnessed and was added to the *dewa* of the victor.

Communities also benefitted from the accumulation of enemy *dewa*. After the heads were ritually prepared and cooked to remove the flesh, they came to rest in the *katoda* (skull tree), which often sat at the highest point of the village and was associated with hotness (Geirnaert-Martin

1992:162). The skull tree was said to "bring luck," because it helped protect the settlement. Numerous skulls bleaching in the sun was a frightening sight, warning enemies that the nearby village was not to be trifled with, especially since it was inhabited by men infused with the power of ancestral and enemy *dewa*.

KODI AND OTHER INDIGENOUS TATTOOS

Among the Kodi of westernmost Sumba, enemy raids were usually undertaken to avenge the death of a noble or other important personage. Sometimes a message sent by an "unhappy" ancestral ghost was divined, leading to such a conflict (Hoskins 1993:312). Like the Laboya, skull trees were associated with hotness, and in the Kodi ritual language used in divinations before a raid, the trophy tree was said to "boil with heat," and the stone circle surrounding it "steam[ed] with anger" (Hoskins 1993:312). If an ancestor decreed a raid but the dead remained unavenged, the entire community might be adversely affected. Fevers, fires, and other misfortunes might soon follow until a head was secured.

Men and women were tattooed by female practitioners who often worked as herbalists and midwives (Hoskins 1989:162). Warriors were tattooed with stars or horns on their chests denoting their status. Kodi women were tattooed to demarcate life stages, but the process began only after the first child had been born. These marks consisted of geometric designs placed on the forearms. After several children had been born, a woman was then allowed to have her legs and thighs tattooed, the latter having a strong erotic allure (Hoskins 1989:162).

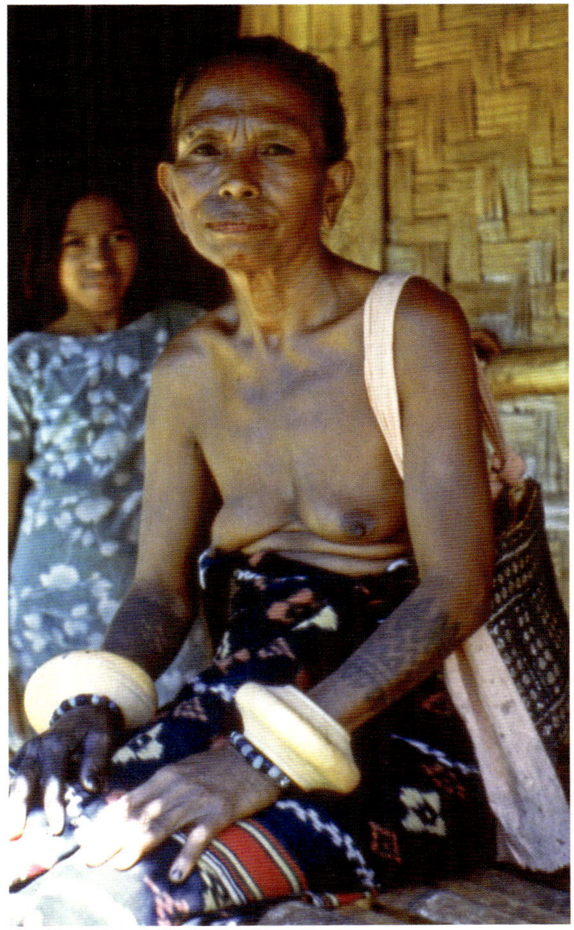

FIGURE 4.68
Tattooed Kodi elder Gheru Wallu, Sumba Island, 1980. © Janet Hoskins.

Kodi women's tattoos, like those of the Laboya and male circumcision, were associated with the concepts of "heat" and purity. Women who willingly submitted to the tattooist's painfully sharp needles and the dangerous heat that resulted from the soot-stained wounds became "clean" enough to marry, because the tattoos established their virtue as wives and mothers and they were incorporated into their husband's patrilineage (cf. Hoskins 1993:163). For the Laboya and Kodi, tattoos transformed girls into adults and they became "ideal" women. They were "completed" by the tattoos worn on their new skins (cf. Saul 2011).

During his tour of Sumba in 1920, the Dutch missionary-ethnographer Albert Christian Kruyt recorded other tattooing traditions across the island. In Central Sumba he witnessed black sheets of tattooing across the shins, knees, and calves of Weyewa women, which are still worn by very elderly women today. These bold markings were given at the onset of puberty or as soon as possible after marriage (A. C. Kruyt 1921a:544). The motifs were hand-tapped by female practitioners at the onset of the first rains of the season. The tattooist was given one spear, a knife, a ring,

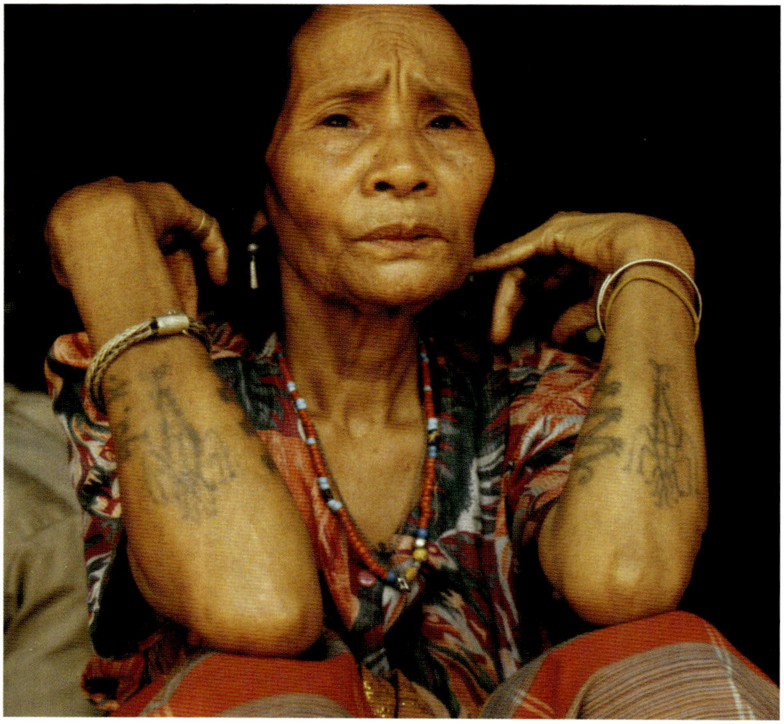

FIGURE 4.69
Tattooed Rindi elder, Sumba Island, 1989. Photograph by Michael Barak. Collection of Tropenmuseum (TM-20018330), National Museum of World Cultures.

and boiled rice and pork or chicken for payment. If a young girl passed away before she received her tattoos, she was buried with a tattooing kit: a bundle of lemon thorns and *kemiri* (candlenut) for pigment.

To the north of Weyewa territory, the Laura people also believed that tattoos were necessary for the afterlife, a belief widely held across nearby Timor. Among the Laura, where a Jesuit mission was founded as early as 1866 but local animist beliefs continued to hold sway into the twentieth century, tattoos were viewed as necessary equipment for the afterlife because they could be exchanged for fire after death (A. C. Kruyt 1921a:544). Variations of this tradition were also part of tattooing culture on East Sumba, especially among the Rindi and the Mamboru. Among the latter, a woman exchanged her tattoos in the afterworld to pay for materials to make her cooking fire (Saul 2011). The Rindi believed the request for such materials would be denied if the person was untattooed (Forth 1981:165). However, some writers have added that unmarked individuals were refused entrance to the afterlife itself (Kapita 1976).

Early travelers to East Sumba recorded a variety of tattooing motifs for men and women, especially figurative tattoos placed around the forearms, but their functions were not recorded. These motifs included "stars, lizards, snakes, dragons, birds, houses, and people" (A. C. Kruyt 1921a:544) as well as the rooster. Kruyt also observed a rooster tattoo placed on both sides of one man's chest. The Dutch anthropologist Herman F. C. ten Kate (1894:245), who illustrated the tattooed cock motif on the forearm of an East Sumbanese man, wrote that the rooster was chosen as a *katátu* (tattoo) motif due to its usage as an oracular and protective totemic animal.[51] In the Dawan (also known as Atoni) village of Haulasi on the island of Timor, the rooster's head was tattooed on the chests of valiant warriors or *meo* (war heroes) (Gual et al. 2019:173). Its local importance was also tied to its role in haruspicy.

TIMOR

The tradition of tattooing totem animals on the body has been widely documented for the Indigenous Peoples of Timor. These markers—which included animals, floraform designs, and objects of everyday use—performed several functions. In West Timor, the Dutch civil servant Dr. Johann

Gerard Friedrich Riedel commented that many of the indelible tattoos he found among the Dawan were also used as property marks or "brands" to demarcate territorial boundaries, family lands, natural resources (specific trees), animals, and textiles (Riedel 1907:181). Female tattooing, which marked the arms, hands, legs, and thighs and included a design stretching from the chin to the navel, incorporated some of these patterns (i.e., sun, fire, fire-making tool). Combined together, these motifs worked apotropaically to repel *nitu* (evil spirits) from harming women during pregnancies—presumably because they were related to "heat," which evil spirits abhorred, and Usi-Neno, the Lord Sun, who was guardian of the hereafter. From his union with Usi-Afu, Lady Earth, the world and everything in it was thought to have originated. And it is this union that continues to impart fertility and growth to every living thing.

The association between heat and tattooing extended into the afterlife. The Indonesian author Fransisco Jacob (2021:59), who recently studied the vanishing *lunat* (tattooing) traditions of the Dawan, wrote that tattoos were exchanged for fire in the afterworld. The Dawan believe that when a person dies, their *smanaf* (soul) will return to the world of the *pah nitu* (ancestors) via a local mountain, Mount Mutis. The path is very dark, thus the soul needs fire to illuminate its journey, and it can be obtained only by exchanging it for one's body tattoos.[52] The soul also needs fire to cook its food and keep itself warm.

Albert Kruyt (1923:385), who interviewed tattooed Timorese elders during his tour of the island in 1920, learned more details about the fire exchange. In the account he provided, a tattooed woman was led to Usi-Neno, the Heavenly Lord, who decided whether the individual could stay in the murky afterworld. The human soul carried a piece of wood, and Usi-Neno asked the person to close their eyes. With a piece of iron in his hands, he kindled the flame on the soul's piece of wood. The woman's forearm tattoos were exchanged for fire, but she continued to possess her other bodily markings for future use.

Because the fear of being untattooed before passing away was so great, young children between the ages of three and four received small dotted tattoos on their forearms resembling a simple cross.[53] Albert Kruyt (1923:385) noted that one dot was sufficient for a child to purchase fire in the afterlife, and the remaining dots could be used on future occasions if the original fire went out. However, if a soul was not tattooed and could not purchase fire, that individual remained a "servant" for the soul who possessed it.

On the neighboring island of Rote, *balatete* (tattooing) was also associated with the afterlife. Female *manbalatetes* (tattooists) hand-tapped local patterns (stars, animals, cruciforms with dots, and floraform and geometric designs) with tree thorns to the arms, legs, and sometimes the chests of men and women (A. C. Kruyt 1921b:292).[54] According to the Dutch missionary F. H. van de Wetering (1924:23), tattoos were used as a form of currency for exchanges of food, not fire, in the afterlife with the Lord of the Ground (Mani Daè or Bei Daè). Traditional tattoos were more commonly seen on women, and girls received their first marks around the onset of puberty. The latter were hand-tapped on their thighs (*poek*, thigh tattoo), then after a period had elapsed their shins and calves were marked. Tattoos were not given during the rainy season, and pregnant women were prohibited from receiving tattoos, otherwise they risked blinding their infant child. To help heal the wounds, leaves of the thorn apple (*Datura metel* L.) were applied to the tattooed area.[55]

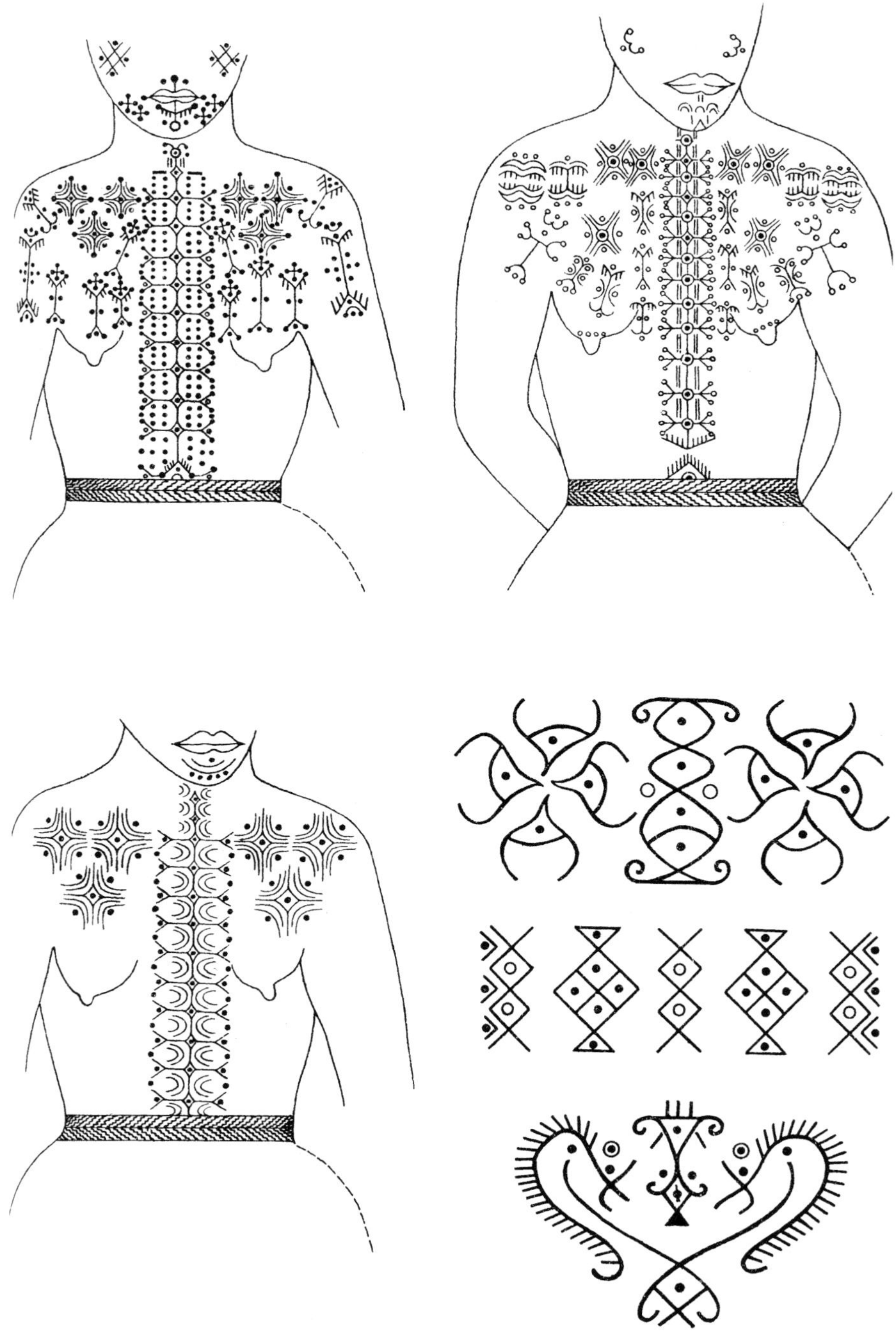

FIGURE 4.70
Female body tattooing patterns, Timor Leste, ca. 1900. The Dutch civil servant Johann Riedel illustrated complex tattooing patterns of Timorese women spanning the chin downward toward the navel. The "fire-making tool" was a primary tattoo motif placed on either breast. This tool consisted of a fire-board, a stick that was rapidly spun on it, and tinder that was set aflame from the resulting friction of the stick on the board. Riedel suggested that the four open areas on each side of the tool probably represented smoke from the tool. The cavity, or "gutter," created by the rapidly spinning stick was associated with the productive force, the fire, from which life radiates (Riedel 1907:185). In turn, Riedel believed the motif was a fertility emblem. From Riedel 1907.

Local informants stated, "[A]s the body become larger [with age], more tattoo marks are needed to buy food for the big body later on [in the afterworld]" (van de Wetering 1924:24).

Returning to West Timor, a local proverb recorded by Riedel (1907:182–183) noted that female tattooing and tooth filing were related to "making" women in the eyes of the ancestors and community. In sum, through the painful tattooing of the cheeks, chin, breast, and abdomen down to the navel a woman became holy, vigilant, and a "wife" of the tribe. By enduring the agonizing process, she demonstrated her power and strength to all and proved she could endure the challenges of life for her family, clan, and community.

In West Timor tattooing was performed by skilled women. The tattoo pattern to be marked was first stenciled on the skin with a liquid pigment of charred leaves and tree resin. In some regions, tattoo ink was derived from soot mixed with sugarcane juice and even honey (A. C. Kruyt 1923:386). A thorn from the kaffir lime tree was attached at a right angle to a wooden baton that was hand-tapped into the skin.

The timing of the tattooing event varied across the region. Apart from the aforementioned "fire marks" applied to young children, girls received more substantial tattooing around the onset of puberty. Girls or women were not tattooed during their menses, since it was believed the blood from the resulting wounds might flow unabated. After a woman had borne children, typically speaking she did not receive additional tattoos since she had become "old" (A. C. Kruyt 1923:386).

In the North Amanatun District, the day for tattooing was related to the agricultural calendar, more precisely the day before the corn harvest and rainy season arrived (Jacob 2021:59). If tattooing was applied outside of this time, it was believed the tattoo client's wounds would not heal properly. In South Amanatun, Dawan elders interviewed by Jacob (2021:58) stated that tattooing was performed in summer while a deceased community member lay in state in the village. This testimony contradicts that provided by Albert Kruyt (1923:387), who wrote that it was forbidden to tattoo if a dead person's body had not been buried, because its soul would become "angry."

In Timor Leste, it has been documented that Tetun men and women of Suai Loro village received tattoos during funerals. During these events, entire families gathered and the spirits of ancestors were called up by the *lia nain*, a traditional leader and spokesperson who carried intimate knowledge of the law and history of the village, not to mention the names of the dead. Paraphrasing the journalist Fareed Kaviani (2015), the scene was set as follows. Beside the body the family members sang the deceased's history in a rhythm accompanied by their tears. Clusters of cousins drank and gambled in little pockets of light about the village, all the while the ancestors began arriving one by one from their graves to receive the spirit of the dead. At this time, a few individuals received tattoos; namely, one or more recently betrothed women. The brides-to-be were marked on the hands and forearms with motifs derived from the husband's family.

In the Suai region and other parts of Central Timor, a woman's arm and leg tattoos were derived from symbols of her *uma lulik*, or "sacred house." These lineage houses belong to a specific family, but they also stand for all other descendant groups that have formed a bond with them through marriages. Ultimately, the *uma lulik*, which was carved or painted with totemic iconography and was the repository for ancestral sacra, embodied the spirit of the family, its network, its history, its traditions, and, inevitably, its essence.

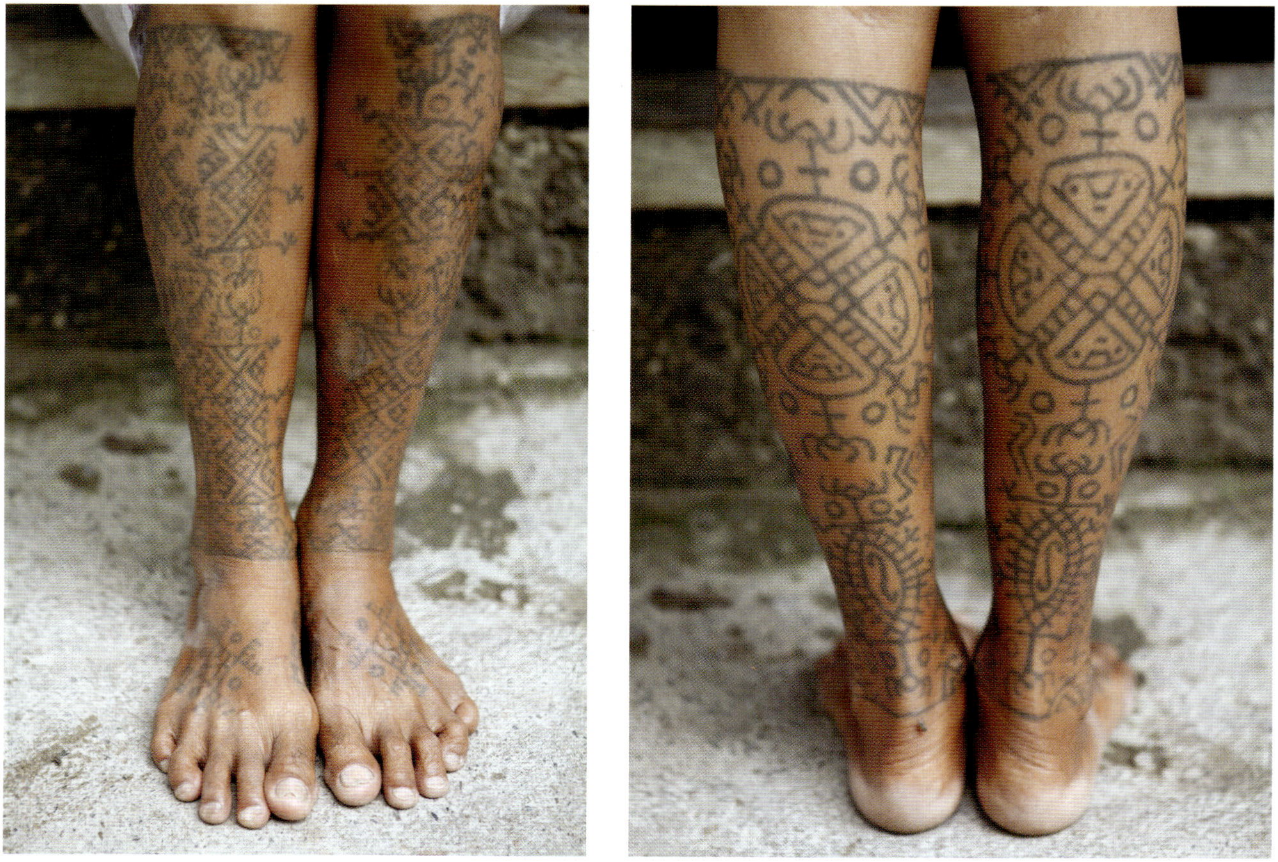

FIGURE 4.71
Tattooed Wehali elder Meliana Luruk Kauk with symbols on her shins (*left*) and calves (*right*) representing her family's *uma lulik* or "sacred house," Timor Leste, ca. 2002. © Bernadino Soares.

Although the precise functions of these tattoos have largely been forgotten, I believe they worked as mnemonic devices to help recall the history of one's *uma lulik*. Drawing on fragmentary research recorded among "Southern Tetun" peoples such as the Wehali and aforementioned Suai (cf. Francillon 1967), the primary motifs contain numerous referents to important mythological animals or others (totems) likened to family and/or clan crests.

The anthropologist Andrea Molnar, who worked with the Atsabe Kemak people of north central Timor Leste, observed that pictographs are often drawn to help illustrate significant oral traditions. To her, these drawings resembled local tattoo motifs, textile patterns,[56] and carvings featured on *uma lulik*. After mentioning these possible relationships, one of her primary informants, who was in the process of recounting an origin story, pulled up his sleeve and with a gentle smile revealed a tattoo that looked like the drawing he had just made while explaining the pictographs featured in his account (Molnar 2011:99n20).

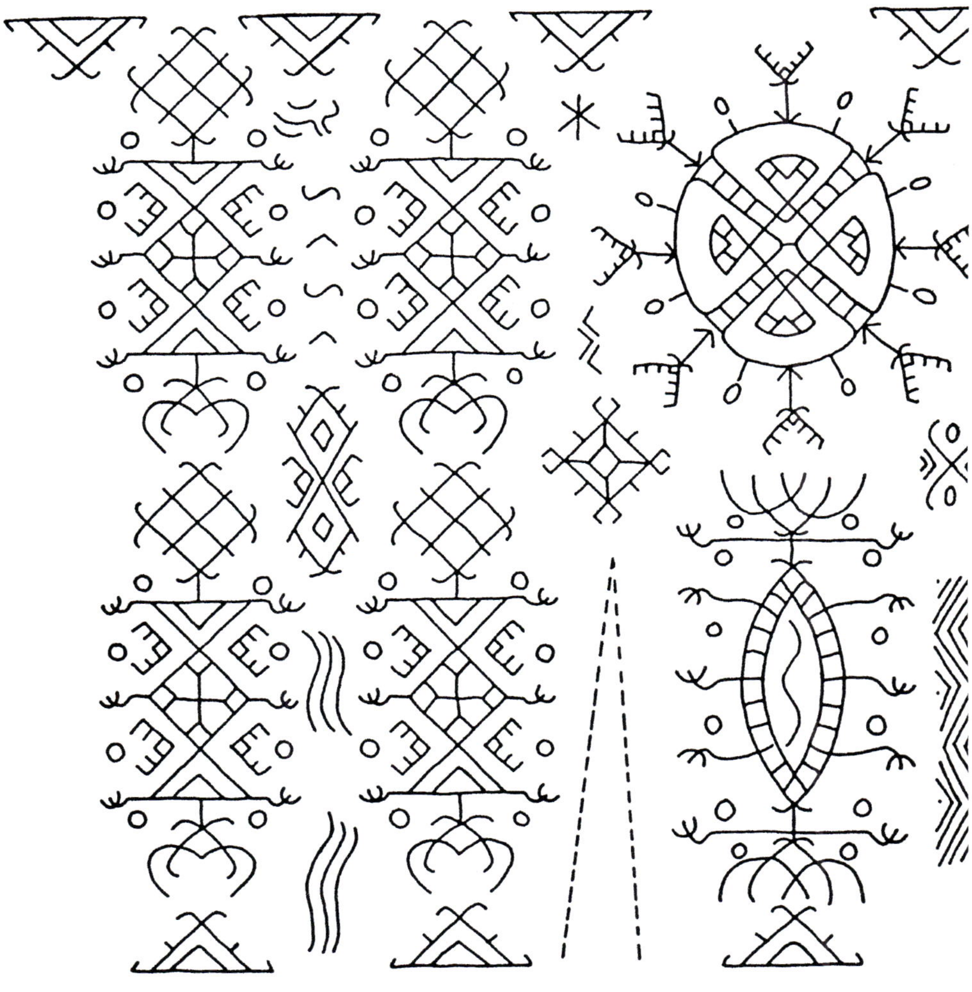

FIGURE 4.72

Illustrations of Wehali shin and calf tattoos for women, Timor Leste, ca. 1963. Four triangular-shaped "half-moons" appear at the top just below the knee. Underneath, four six-legged lizards are tattooed on both sides of the shin. Three undulating lines represent water, whereas two S and ∧ motifs are "dog tracks." A large oval pattern on the shin signifies an eight-clawed turtle and underneath it appears a ten-legged "water-lizard." Three half-moons encircle the ankle. From Francillon 1967:309.

TIMORESE TATTOO PATTERNS AND ICONOGRAPHY TODAY

Even at the time of Riedel's visit to West Timor in 1878, he noted that knowledge concerning the meaning and origins of most of the tattoo motifs had been lost. Similarly, Albert Kruyt (1923) mentioned that the oral traditions he recorded focusing on tattoos and the afterlife were largely forgotten by the time of his visit. What little information he obtained came from two ninety-something-year-old elders. On Rote, van de Wetering (1924) observed that elders retained little information concerning the meanings behind their tattoos.

Notwithstanding, in the past there were literally hundreds of tattooing motifs employed by certain groups across this region of Indonesia. A tattoo pattern book collected around 1862 contains 388 individual motifs. This unique and rare document once belonged to the female tattooist Raboe of the Tetun (also known as Belunese) people of what today is Timor Leste.

Although tattooing was once a widespread practice on Timor, Jacob (2021) reminds us that fragments of the tradition remain. Among the Dawan, tattoos continue to appear on the bodies of men and women that are more than fifty years of age. These tattoos are no longer composed, as Riedel illustrated long ago, of carefully crafted composite elements spanning multiple regions of the body. Instead, they now appear as singular almost randomly placed motifs that mark isolated body parts. As eighty-one-year-old Zacharias Koebanu noted, "My grandmother was heavily tattooed, she had tattoos on her hands, feet, and thighs. Others had marks on their chins that ran down to the chest and stomach" (Jacob 2021:57).

The meanings behind Dawan tattooing motifs have also been largely forgotten, apart from a few primary patterns. The most common tattoos encountered by Jacob were crocodiles and lizards. Elders recounted that the island of Timor was formed from the back of the crocodile: "They live, work, forage, and die on the backs of the crocodile [and] they are considered sacred animals" (Jacob 2021:58). Ten Kate (1895:3) similarly recorded the mythological position of the crocodile; it was an important tattoo motif on Timor due to its "protective" or apotropaic properties. In some Dawan villages, very large crocodiles, who lived in known habitation sites (i.e., large pools), were offered sacrifices by village priests because they were believed to be "ancestors" (Middelkoop 1958:386).

FIGURE 4.73

Two tattoo motifs from the 388-page pattern book of female Tetun tattooist Raboe, West Timor, before 1862. National Museum of Ethnology, Leiden (inv. 26–37).

Among the Dawan of Haulasi village (West Miomaffo District), the crocodile was a sacred animal and appeared as a tattoo on the legs and arms of men and women of specific clans. Researchers from the Widya Mandira Catholic University observed that it was a "totem animal" and was regularly provided with offerings in order to ensure bountiful harvests, among other positive outcomes (Gual et al. 2019:163). The tattoo motif also provided a form of protection against illnesses and was worn by warriors in former times.

Every clan in Haulasi village possessed at least one "sacred, totemic" plant or animal that served as a "protector, giver of strength, and a source of life's fortune" (Gual et al. 2019:164). Offerings to these entities were made at stone altars constructed near water sources, because they were associated with "life-giving" powers. These gifts were necessary to ensure the continued favor of the respective totem being and were made according to events surrounding the agricultural calendar (i.e., preparing the fields, harvest, etc.) and "life" calendar (i.e., births, deaths, wars, disasters).

For the Nahas clan, their primary totem was the *be'e* (crocodile) because their primordial ancestors were crocodiles. Due to this intimate relationship, many taboos were associated with this reptile, including prohibitions against eating certain colored foods and wearing specific colors of clothing. Every year, the Nahas clan ceremonially "feeds" crocodiles in their local place of worship, which is a specific water source (Gual et al. 2019:164). Clan members are not allowed to wear traditional clothing that is "too red," nor can they consume red sugarcane, red bananas, red corn, palm sugar, red papaya, civets, or *bi kase* (horses), which was a secondary totem and former tattoo motif of the clan.[57] If a clan member disregarded any of these taboos, it was believed that their family members would become ill or disabled (Gual et al. 2019:164).

Other animals that served as tattoo motifs were important because of the omens they delivered. In the Dawan village of Baus in South Amanatun, *bik lusu* (lizard) motifs adorn the arms of men and women; the motif also appears in textiles and house carvings (Leokoy 2018:16). Depending on the "cries" of the reptile, these audio cues can signal impending danger, among other things. The *lunat* (tattoo) of a *kolo*, an unspecific black-and-white bird, might appear on a woman's thigh. When the bird appears and begins to sing, it is a signal to plant and fence the gardens. Another important omen creature was the *teke* (gecko), which appears as a tattooing pattern on women's calves. When the reptile is heard crying from a hole in a tree this signals that the old moon will appear and a new month is coming (Leokoy 2018:17).

SULAWESI

Little documentation survives regarding the former practice of tattooing on Sulawesi. The Swedish ethnographer Walter Kaudern explored the island over the course of four years (1917–1920), and he encountered no "true" tattooing in the northern regions. However, he did observe a tradition of body painting with *nompi*, a local dyeing substance, which other writers confused with permanent tattooing. Kaudern, who traveled to every corner of Sulawesi, eventually witnessed "true" tattooing, but only in one region.

More specifically, in the highland village of Kantewu, in central Sulawesi, he met two female "slaves" who "were tattooed from the tips of their fingers all over their hands, arms, and shoulders with a variety of dark blue scroll work. From the shoulders the tattoo extended to the back as well as to the chest where two buffalo horns were the single ornaments" (Kaudern 1944:167). These women were not natives of Kantewu, wrote Kaudern, and he was led to believe they were members of the Sa'dan Toraja from the village of Pada.

Based on the motifs thus described, these women were more likely members of the Seko Toraja, who lived in villages some thirty-five miles to the south of Kantewu. Johannes Kruyt, the son of the Dutch Calvinist missionary-ethnographer Albert Kruyt, visited the Seko region in 1919 and vividly described and illustrated the *marronno* (tattooing) traditions there. The younger Kruyt wrote that only vestiges of the tradition survived, as it was completely "dying out" due to the advancements of Islamic and Christian missionaries. In other Toraja regions (i.e., Sa'dan Toraja of the Makale District), Kruyt (J. Kruyt 1920:254) noted that tattooing once existed there, but it had not been practiced for "several generations."

Kruyt's research demonstrated that tattooing was closely related to the most important religious festival of the Seko Toraja, which he called the "*Ma'Boea* Feast."[58] This costly event, which was hosted by noble families, was celebrated every decade or so and was held "to strengthen the life forces [fertility] of man, buffalo and rice," especially after agricultural calamities, livestock losses, or illnesses affected the local area (J. Kruyt 1920:236–237). The lengthy ceremony, which might have spanned one or more years, culminated in the human sacrifice of a slave and the tattooing of *baliangs*,[59] or unmarried women of the festival hosts' family. Kruyt (253) noted that the first *ma'bua* feast was given to humans by a "water spirit," but the tattooing itself originated from a giant named Talamia.

Nowadays, this Toraja rite (sans human sacrifice and tattooing) is rarely practiced in Sulawesi, and when it does occur it is performed under the guise of a "harvest" festival. Among the Seko Toraja, the performance of the *ma'bua'* entertained and pleased the *deata* (spirits of life) while simultaneously placing them in debt to humankind through offerings of chickens, pigs, and buffalo (cf. Crystal 1989:10; Waterson 2009:339). The unfolding of this festival is a kind of prayer, or in Toraja terms, *pelambean,* meaning there was great "hope" or "expectation" that the *deata* would reward them with a bountiful harvest and increased community fertility (cf. Waterson 2016:178).

THE SEKO *MA'BUA'* (CA. 1900)

Due to the length and complexity of the Seko *ma'bua'* as described by Johannes Kruyt (1920:238–255) more than one hundred years ago, I will summarize important aspects of it below. Additional details from other researchers will accompany his account.

When the time arrived for obtaining a *tandasang* (sacrificial slave) for the *ma'bua',* a group of men traveled to a "far away land" to purchase a man or woman with a number of water buffalo. The individual had to be a "stranger," and one who had never visited the Seko region before (J. Kruyt 1920:238).

After the long journey abroad, the village eventually received word that the procession was almost home. Every household then prepared one chicken and a quantity of rice, which they brought to the returning party on the outskirts of the village. At this time, the *tobara* (head) of the village or tribe, who was a nobleman, selected three unmarried young women from his family to serve as *baliang,* or temporary caretakers of the *tandasang.*

On the following days, numerous offerings (buffalos, pigs, chickens) were made to the *deata*. Most of these occurred at or near the *tobara*'s house, especially at a stone altar located in the house yard that was considered a sacred location. During these activities, the *haliangs*, who observed various taboos,[60] remain cloistered in the *tobara*'s house with the *tandasang* and refrained from participating in any rituals.

On the fourth day, in the villages of Pewaneang and Ambalong, the *haliangs* were carried out of the *tobara*'s house and "bathed" with water from bamboo tubes. All ritual prohibitions were now expunged and they walked to the *tobara*'s rice barn, where they were tattooed along with anyone else who wished to submit to the needles of the *poronno* (male tattooist). In the village of Wono, however, the *haliang*s remained in their position for a period of two or more years. After each annual harvest, Wono women received segments of tattooing on their bodies (order: hands, forearms, upper arms, shoulder blades, back, chest),[61] whereas Pewaneang and Ambalong *haliang*s were tattooed over a period of consecutive days until it was completed.

On the seventh day, the festival temporarily ended and normal agricultural activities were resumed by the villagers. In the meantime, however, the *tandasang* continued to live in the *tobara*'s house for a period of two to three years; s/he was looked after, well fed, treated kindly, and performed light work for the *tobara*. The residential period ended according to the well-being of the rice crop, health of the village inhabitants, and healthiness of the buffalos. If the local situation began to deteriorate after two years, the ceremony concluded and the slave was put to death.

Once the decision was made to "close" the *ma'bua'*, several days of sacrifices and offerings to the *deata* spirits ensued. Before the sunrise on the fourth morning, the *tandasang* was bound, richly adorned, and brought outside of the house. A large feast was prepared primarily consisting of meat from sacrificial buffalos. After the meal was consumed, the *tandasang*'s head was first hit on the *tapa* cloth beating board below the *tobara*'s house, then the feast attendees transported the *tandasang* to their respective houses, banging their head on their rice mortars while also placing rice grains in their mouth.

The *tandasang* was returned to the *tobara*'s house and then appeared at the top of the steps leading into it. The feast attendees waited below armed with sticks. The *tobara* spoke, "Don't blame me because I killed you. I am also a human like you, but I have bought you with my buffalo." After this, the *tandasang* was beaten to death.

After the *tandasang* was killed, their head was detached from the body and roasted over a fire to remove the hair and flesh. Afterward, the skull was hung along with the horns of the slaughtered buffalo on the *petuho'* (central pillar) of the *tobara*'s house; the *petuho'* was the "cosmic navel" of the house that anchored it to the heavens by way of the *lalan deata* (path of spirits) that ran from the front to the rear of the house (cf. Crystal 1989:13). This pathway enabled the spirits of life, who were the guarantors of the harvest and human fertility, to flow through the dwelling when offerings were made.

The next day, the *tandasang*'s skull, along with those from previous *ma'bua'*, was taken to a sacred mountain near the village. Here, the skulls were placed on the ground and additional offerings were made to the *deata*. Once these rituals were completed, the skulls were returned to the *tobara*'s house and the *ma'bua'* ritual was closed.

TATTOOING IN SEKO

Johannes Kruyt (1920:248) believed the position of tattooist was a hereditary profession because it seemed that specific families produced these individuals who were invariably men. Seko tattooists did have assistants, and they could be male or female.

Prior to the tattooing of the *haliangs* and other community members, a buffalo was slaughtered. The tattooist then took small bits of its meat and other body parts and provided offerings to the spirits of the earth and mountains, calling on them for assistance to create the tattoo (J. Kruyt 1920:248). Afterward, the meat and other items were cooked and eaten by the tattooist, his helpers, and the tattoo clients.

Tattooing pigment was derived from the soot of dammar resin mixed with python bile and a bit of water. The desired motif was stenciled on the skin, and a hand-tapping tool tipped with two needles was struck to sink the ink into the epidermis. If the required motif was not bold enough, a second layer of tattooing was added; elders recalled that the dye permeated so deeply that "even the bones become black" (J. Kruyt 1920:249).

In the village of Lodang, elders interviewed by Johannes Kruyt (1920:252) noted that only members of the noble and commoner class could receive tattoos. In Wono village, all members of society, including the slave class, could receive marks. However, certain motifs were reserved for each social class except for the nobility, who could carry any tattooing motif.

Individuals who submitted to the tattooing process, not to mention the tattooist and his assistants, were also bound to several taboos. In Wono, these individuals could not eat anything that was "sour," including a local fern and taro. If they did, the tattoos "would not hold" and soon thereafter would "disappear" (J. Kruyt 1920:250). If the new markings were seen by another person while still swollen, it was believed the swelling would increase and the marks would vanish. Moreover, the newly tattooed could not visit the rice fields or they might fail. During the first day of tattooing, if it began to rain, thunder clapped, a rainbow appeared, or someone died in the village, the tattooist immediately ceased working. Otherwise, it was believed the tattooed limbs would swell and the marks would disappear. The tattooist's payment typically included a quantity of cooked rice, a chicken, copper bracelets, and woven goods.

The tattooing motifs placed on women included the *sila-sila* (face pattern), *seriria sipu'* (handle of the betel nut bag), *aripang* (scorpion), water buffalo and buffalo horns, *kapa-kapa* (cotton), *takale* (small and large bracelets), *papupapu* (a type of inedible fern), *salungang* (handle of a machete tied with rattan), and *tabang* (a sacred medicinal plant), among other patterns (J. Kruyt 1920:251–252; Ngelouw 2008:223–224). For men, common patterns included a *manuk* (bird or rooster motif), a rosette placed on the sternum derived from a local grass, and multiple small elements (hanging hook, banana stem, knot) that composed large chest pieces.

Although Kruyt could not decipher the underlying significance of these tattooing motifs, studies of Toraja material culture perhaps indicate a few cosmic dimensions. In Toraja wood carving and painting traditions, the water buffalo holds a prominent position as a protective animal. For example, the doors, shutters, and other openings of the Toraja house are often adorned with

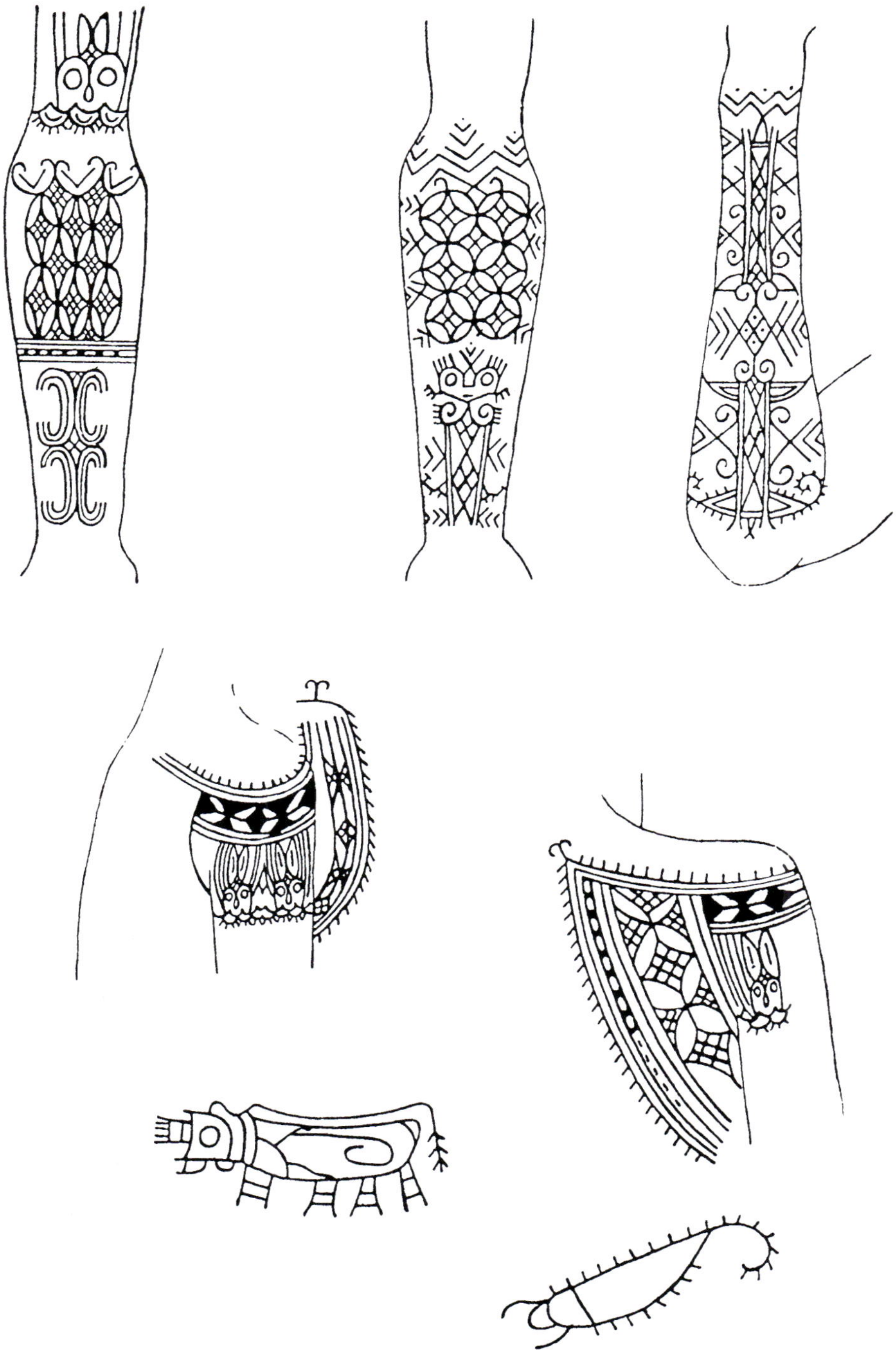

FIGURE 4.74
Seko Toraja women's tattooing for arms and shoulders, Sulawesi, 1919. *Top from left to right*, tattoo elements include *sila-sila* (face), fern, betel nut bag, cotton pods, small bracelet, and double C-shaped "inedible fern" patterns; *bottom*, a *baloelang* (buffalo) and *aripang* (scorpion) figure are illustrated. From Kruyt 1920: pl. 1.

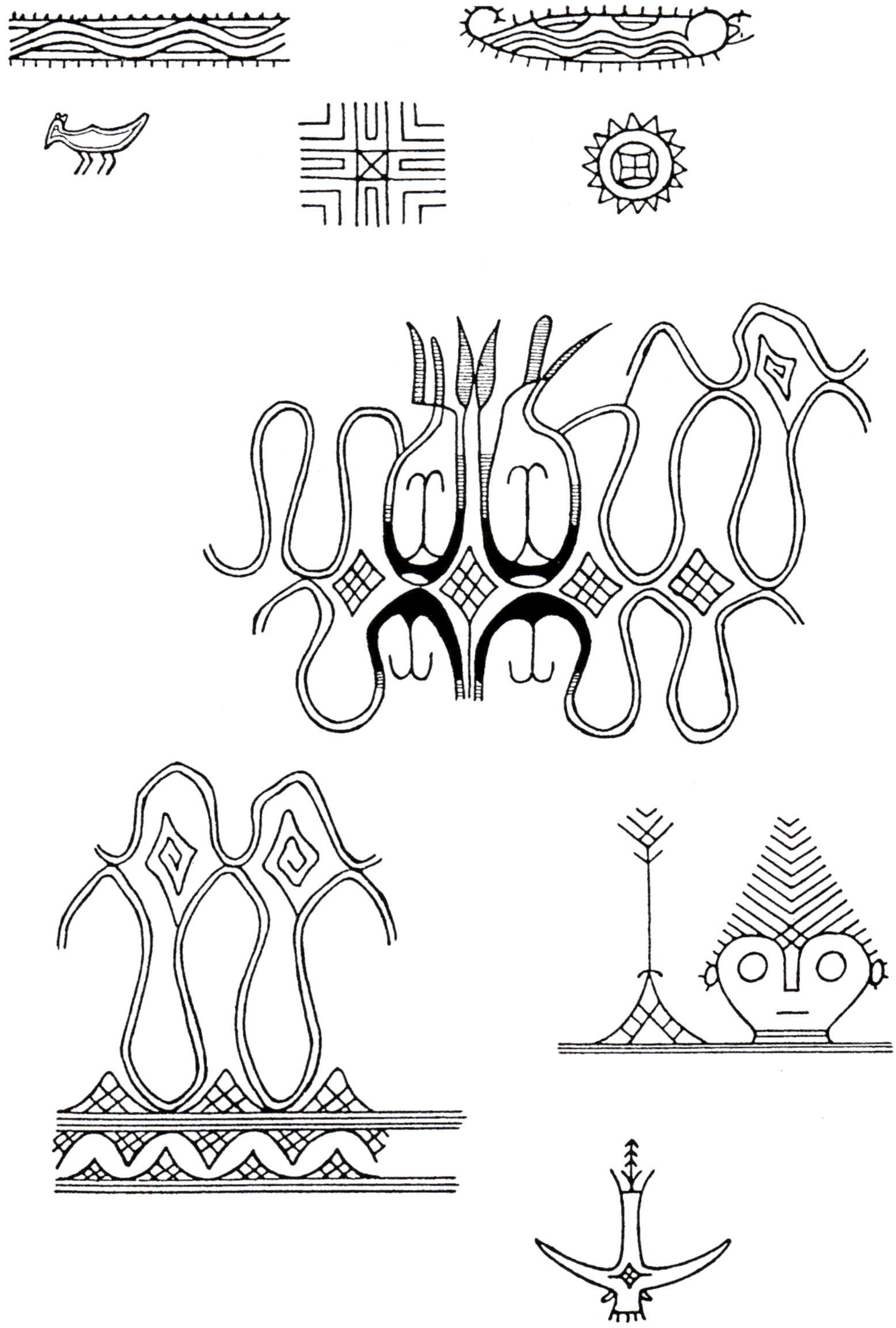

FIGURE 4.75
Seko Toraja tattoos, Sulawesi, 1919. *Top left, takale* (armbands) and a bird seen on women; *top right,* the *soerede* (rosette motif) might appear on the sternum of men; and large undulating patterns (*center and bottom left*) appeared on the chest of an elderly man from Pewaneang village. The *tannoek* (horns) motif (*bottom right*) was likely derived from the buffalo and was seen on the forearms of men and chests of elderly women. A *sila-sila* (face) pattern is also illustrated. From Kruyt 1920: pl. 2.

stylized *pa'tedong* (buffalo heads) because these "vulnerable" passageways are susceptible to the advances of evil spirits (Nooy-Palm 1999:97).

The *manuk* (rooster) also holds an important position in Toraja thought, symbolism, and architecture. Because the bird greets each day, it is associated with the sun, light, maleness, bravery, and vitality. Carvings of the cock standing on a *barre allo* (sun disc) sometimes appeared on the façade of a warrior's home, denoting to all the boldness and bravery of its resident and his descendants (Waterson 1989:66).

SERAM

Seram (also known as Ceram) is the largest island of the Maluku province of Indonesia. It is traversed by a rugged central mountain range inhabited by several ethnic groups, two of which will be featured here: the Wemale and the Alune (also called Makahala) of West Seram.[62] Both peoples, whose languages belong to the Malayo-Polynesian family, originated from a common ancestral group called the Patasiwa, but they were usually not allowed to intermarry (Duyvendak 1926:43–44).

During the Dutch colonial period, all of the inhabitants of Seram were known as Alfoeren (also Alifuru, Alfur), a pejorative term meaning "barbarians" or "wild savages" (van Baarda 1895; Vion 1999:140). While this term referred to all non-Muslim and non-Christian peoples inhabiting the island, it was especially linked to mountain-dwelling groups such as the Wemale and Alune, who often conducted headhunting raids in Central Seram, among themselves, and on the coast where some of their villages were located. Since time immemorial, headhunting played an important role in the religious and social life of the "mountain people," and was intimately connected to male initiation rituals known as Kakean that culminated in the receipt of tattoos.

By the time historians and ethnographers became interested in these and other rites in the early twentieth century, they had already begun to fade due to the advances of Protestant and other missionaries who arrived as early as the 1880s. Headhunting was summarily outlawed and the Dutch colonial government banned the Kakean around 1915. This action did not permanently stop the rite, and compelled communities to take it underground and perform it in secret.

Generally speaking, the Kakean was held annually or sometimes biennially, but the timing depended on gathering the requisite number of adolescent initiates from one or more villages. According to the German ethnologist Adolf E. Jensen (1948:89), who worked among the Wemale, a *mauwen* (high-ranking "priest") decided exactly when the ritual would take place. Prior to the actual ceremony, however, the *tutué* (Kakean house) had to be constructed.

Traditionally, a freshly hunted human head was needed to consecrate the structure, which was placed under the center supporting post. If none was available an old human skull was used, and the post was erected while ritual songs were performed (Riedel 1886:109).

After the Kakean house had been constructed and the required rituals had been performed, each *masau* (initiate) received two male *maselu* (Wemale for "godparents") who belonged to their clan (Jensen 1948:89). These *maselu* possessed tattoos from participating in

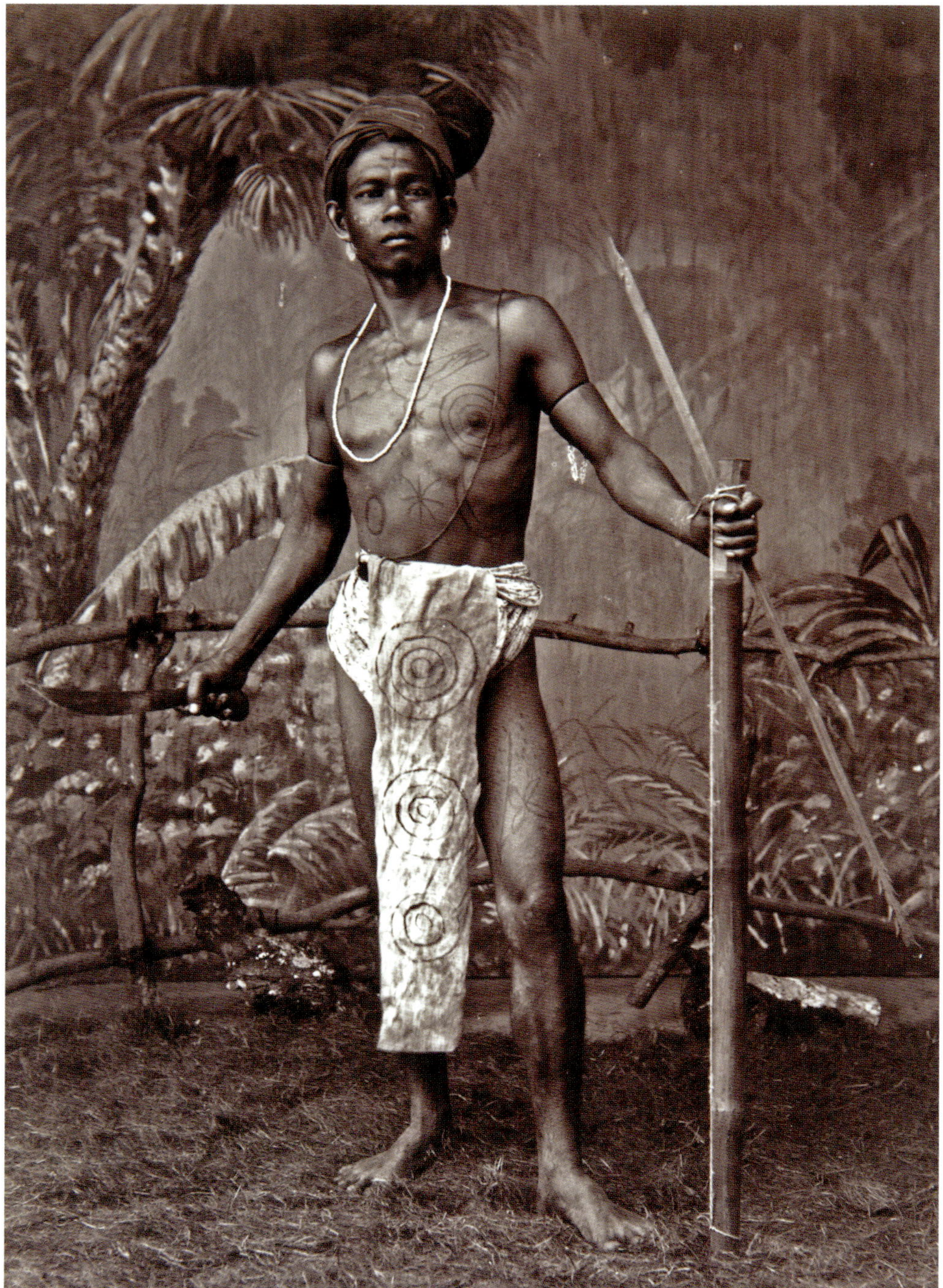

FIGURE 4.76
Studio portrait of a tattooed Alfuru warrior of West Seram, 1910. Collection of Leiden University Library (KITLV 28592).

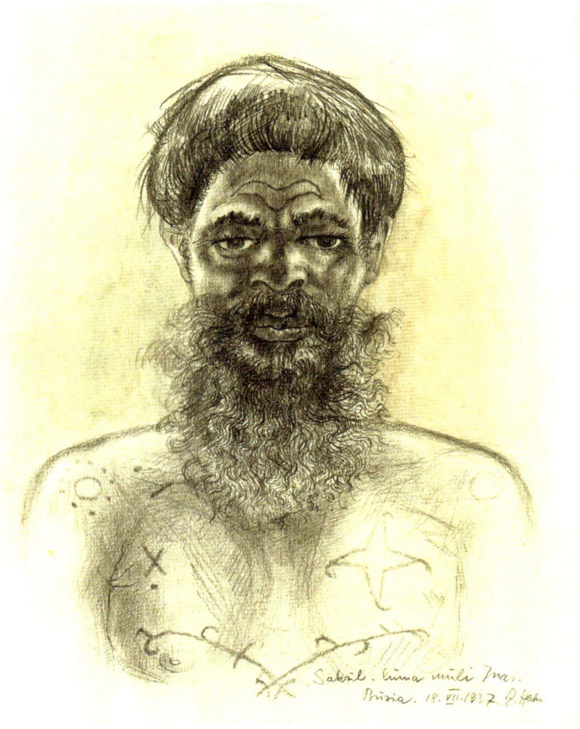

FIGURE 4.77
Tattooed Alune man, Buria village, West Seram, 1937. Illustration by Albert Hahn. Frobenius-Institut, Frankfurt am Main (EBA-B 02868).

previous initiations and perhaps others gained from success in the headhunt.[63] The mothers of the initiates stood by and watched the *maselu* blindfold their sons. The priests in charge of the ceremony told these women that they might never see their sons again, for their "spirits" or souls would be removed from their bodies during the rite, only to be restored after the priests offered lengthy prayers and supplications to Nitu Elake—the great spirit of the Kakean house (Jensen 1948:88). Each boy was then led by the hand to the entrance of the *tutué*, a structure that was prohibited to women, with entry punishable by death. Once assembled at the entrance, which resembled a toothy crocodile or serpentlike figure, the high priest of the village called on Nitu Elake and *iola* (ancestral spirits) to witness the gathering. Nitu Elake was a giant serpent believed to be the group ancestor of the clan and all other *nitu* (spirits), including those of the human dead who were his progeny or descendants (Deacon 1925:344; Riedel 1886:111). The Kakean house was Nitu Elake's residence and suddenly a calamitous groaning sound was heard from the interior of the *tutué*, which the attending women believed was the voice of Nitu Elake himself; this rumble was produced by men inside the *tutué* playing the sacred bamboo pipes. As the initiates entered the Kakean house, they were believed to have been "devoured" by Nitu Elake. Shortly thereafter, blood-stained spears and swords began to protrude from the house roof and its walls and the horrified mothers began to wail and weep because Nitu Elake had "killed" the neophytes in their midst.

Once inside the *tutué*, the blindfolds were taken off and a *kaki* (tattoo) was pricked with tree thorns on the foreheads or other body parts of the initiates by a priest, and an indelible pigment of charred dammar was rubbed into the wounds.[64] The tattooing was said to have been pricked on them by Nitu Elake in order to make the *masau* "worthy to be presented" to him (Riedel 1886:109; Stresemann 1923:394, 423).

The German naturalist and ornithologist Erwin Stresemann, who visited Seram in 1910–1912 and took detailed anthropological notes, recorded the names *tanela* (Uli region) and *pa'atei* (Eti and Tala regions) for the initiation marks (Stresemann 1923:419). However, there were a great diversity of motifs,[65] because each tattoo, even though it may have closely resembled others,

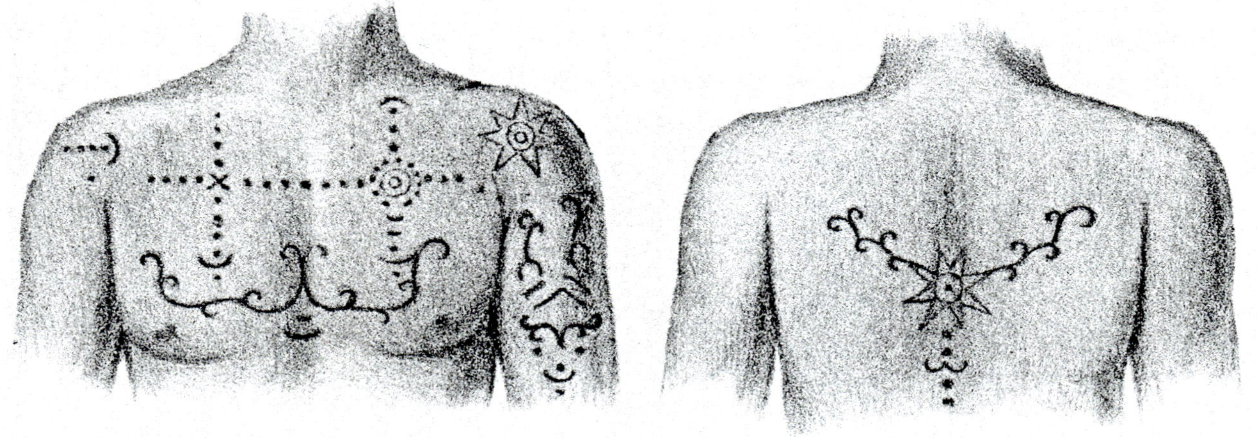

FIGURE 4.78
Kakean and other tattoo markings as seen in Hatusua village, Southwest Seram. From Martin 1894: pl. XXVI.

contained slight variations (e.g., extra lines or dots, different end lines, etc.) that identified the clan of the respective *masau* (Jensen 1948:97). Other tattoos (*pela-pela* or *pelen*), which were also applied in the Kakean house (i.e., Eti, Tala, and Sapalewa groups), were "insignia of rank" and given to men who performed *maselu* and other duties in subsequent rites; each of these tattoos was different from those previously marked on the body. In the Tala area of Wemale territory the forehead mark resembled the spread wings of a bird whose tail terminated on the bridge of the nose. In the Uwin area, the same mark might also appear on other parts of the body (Jensen 1948:93).

Once the tattooing was completed, the *maselu* coated the boys with turmeric and compelled them to sit crosslegged and keep their hands open as if they were to receive something. Each godfather then placed a sacred bamboo pipe in his respective godson's hand. At the same time, the *maselu* threatened them with the death penalty if they did not fulfill their Kakean duties in full or shared the secrets of the house with others, especially women and the uninitiated (Duyvendak 1926:97). In short, the initiates were instructed on the customs of their tribe and how to become proper men. They were encouraged to treat their kinsmen well, not quarrel with them, and not to commit adultery (Riedel 1886:111). They were compelled, however, to take the heads of nonrelatives and even their fellow Kakean-mates, if necessary.

When the instruction period ended, the initiates began their journey to the realm of the dead. The Kakean house, which sat on stilts, contained an opening in the floor leading down to the dark recesses of the "basement," which was completely devoid of light. The initiates were compelled to jump through the floor opening where the spirits of the *iola* (deceased) awaited; these were groups of initiated men belonging to several clans who were armed with bamboo lances (Jensen 1948:99). A wild fight ensued in which the *masau* and their accompanying *maselu* were inflicted with wounds in the great commotion.

Even though it was very dark in this space, the initiated men who acted as the *iola* attempted to discern which clan each *masau* belonged to based on the tattoo that had just been

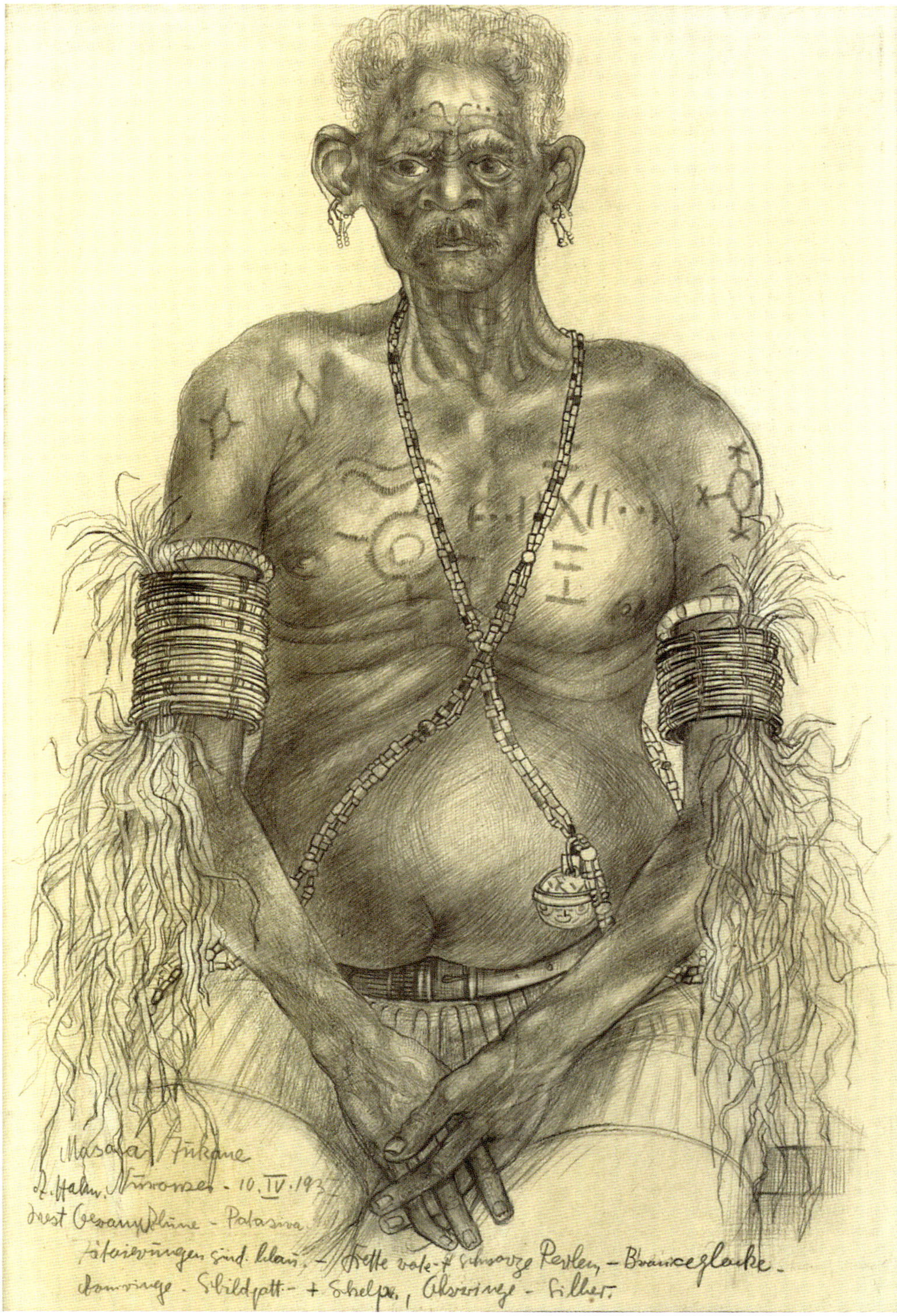

FIGURE 4.79
Elderly Alune man of Nurwe village in festive attire, West Seram, 1937. Illustration by Albert Hahn. Frobenius-Institut, Frankfurt am Main (EBA-B 02849).

applied. The "deceased" members of a foreign clan attempted to "seize" *masau* belonging to other cohorts in an attempt to change their tattoo and make them a member of their own clan (Jensen 1948:99). The *iola* who actually belonged to the clan of the *maselu* drew near them and together they valiantly defended the initiate against the attacks of other *iola*. After the initiates were saved by their ancestral clan spirits, they were kidnapped through a secret hole in the wall of the Kakean house. It was at this time that they disappeared into the bush with their *iola* for a period of one or more months to commune with the deceased. Here, they were taught how to hunt animals, among other manly pursuits.[66]

Eventually, the initiates, whose bodies had been physically recast with tattoos, reemerged in the village "reborn" as men (Duyvendak 1926:101). Each man received an engraved staff or bamboo tube adorned at each end with cassowary feathers. These items were supposed to have been given to them by Nitu Elake, and they represented that the young men had traveled to the spirit lands of the hereafter and been restored to life (Deacon 1925:347).

Scholars have long noted that the Kakean ritual resembles those male initiation rites performed in nearby New Guinea. I myself have participated in the initiation and scarification rite among the Kaningara people of Papua New Guinea (Krutak 2012:280–289). Here, young men are secluded in the *haus tambaran* or "spirit house" of the village for a two-month period, where they are utterly divorced from their mothers and female relatives. The initiates, or "house boys" as they are called, enter the spirit house through the gaping mouth of their ancestral crocodile spirit Marsivo, who taught the Kaningara almost everything they know. The elaborate and painful scarification that completes the rite, which ultimately compels the initiates to face their own death through much blood loss, aims to remove any residual traces of the initiate's mother's postpartum blood from his body. Symbolically speaking, this act is necessary to permanently divorce young men from the world of womenfolk, and to fill them with the power of the crocodile spirit, who ultimately recasts them as men through a process of "rebirth."

During the initiates' seclusion in the spirit house, they will be told of the significance of every Kaningara ceremony; they are instructed how to hunt and be a proper man; and they also learn the origins and functions of every image and object in the spirit house. The wisdom thus imparted will inevitably earn for them an elevated social position, since a man's personal power depends on being adept at manipulating various series of words designating real and mythical names, places, and special objects, among other things. In turn, the young men gain a profound knowledge of their ancestral beliefs and Indigenous histories that speak of the origin of all things and of their magic. Among the Kaningara, knowledge is power, and once endowed with this spiritually significant information, "boys" become "men." Of course, if any of this secret information is imparted to women or children, I was told, "you could die," and indeed elders recounted to me that men have met their fate because of these breaches of taboo (Krutak 2012). Another important aspect of the initiation rite is that it also builds bonds of male kinship and friendship that span the generations as well as the region, because young men from surrounding communities, even enemy settlements, come to Kaningara village to be initiated and cut. In this way, intervillage conflicts are oftentimes mediated through male bonds of association formed through the ritual, a process that Kakean members must have also participated in.

Apart from the Kakean marks, men who met with success in the headhunt were, as noted, entitled to special tattoos demarcating this status. The ethnographers of Alfurese tattooing were at great pains to learn the origins behind these and the Kakean tattoos, and only a few "secrets" were shared with them. In fact, Jensen (1948:108) observed, "the natives in almost all the villages refused to have the ornamental signs drawn on their bodies and told the same story several times as a reason for this: A man had the Kakihan symbol on his forehead. While he slept, his son had drawn the ornament on a piece of wood and showed it to his father when he woke up. As soon as the father looked at the wood, he fell dead. If a stranger points to the tattoo and asks for it, you must kill him immediately, otherwise you will die yourself."

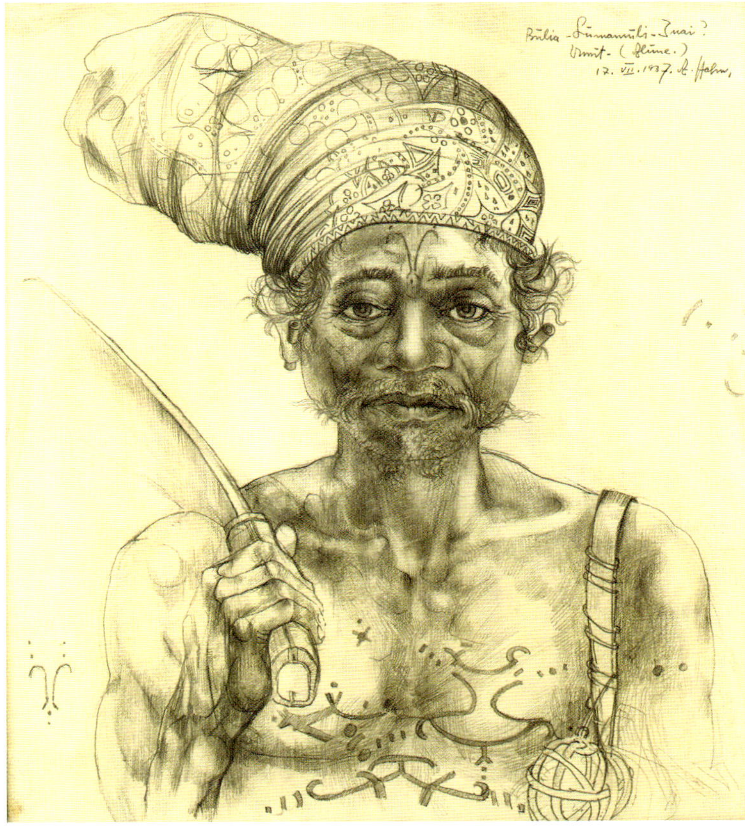

FIGURE 4.80
Tattooed Alune man of Uwit village with headscarf and *parang* sword, West Seram, 1937. Illustration by Albert Hahn. Frobenius-Institut, Frankfurt am Main (EBA-B 02867).

The time for applying the headhunter's mark occurred during a ceremony called *matunu manua* (Wemale). This name applied to several general festivals that were celebrated by an entire village or several villages together (Jensen 1948:186). The hallmark of the rite involved affixing the signs associated with the headhunt on the warrior's *tjidako* (tapa cloth girdle) and on his body via tattoo; these symbols overlapped to some degree. The primary motif adorning the *tjidako* and a man's body was the *oiale*, a circular disclike design, sometimes composed of concentric lines, representing one or more captured heads (Stresemann 1923:423). Jensen (1948:243) called the motif *manue matai*, or "eye of the bird." Adjoining this mark, at the cardinal points, was an M-shaped "bird" motif with a forked tail. This motif was tattooed on the thigh of the warrior underneath his *tjidako*. Stresemann, who was a noted ornithologist, learned that the bird represented was the frigate bird. In Papua New Guinea and on several islands situated in Oceania, including southeasternmost Rapa Nui (Easter Island), the frigate bird was a common tattooing motif (F. R. Barton 1918:27, 77; Krutak 2007:144, 2014b:23; Métraux 1940:243; Pendergrast 2000:41–42, 75; Tichelman 1939:232; Tickle 1975:4–5, 9). Among some of the peoples inhabiting these insular territories, the frigate bird was characterized in folk belief as a rapacious, ravenous, and voracious seagoing predator (Tichelman 1939),[67] acquiring "a special mystique as a symbol of invasion, aggression . . . and the warrior class" (Lee 1992:20).

Unlike the *masau*, warriors were not tattooed by priests. Instead, a male or female tattooist of the village applied these tattoos. While I was not able to find an eyewitness account of

FIGURE 4.81
Wemale tattoo marks for men and women, Seram, 1911–1912. FromTauern 1918: pl. 3.

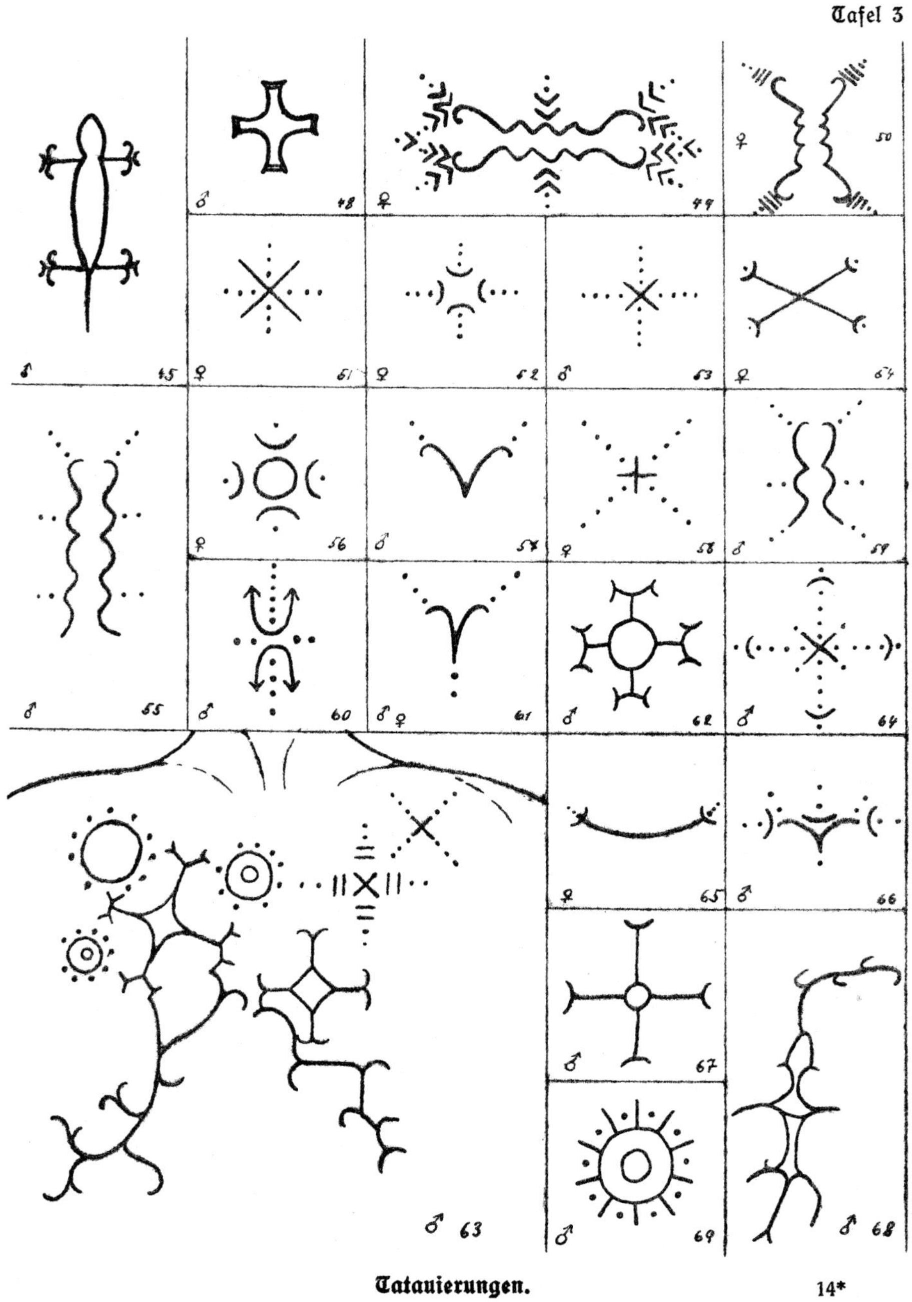

warrior tattooing, perhaps the most detailed account of a tattooing session was provided by Stresemann, who along with expedition mate, Karl Deniger, was tattooed on his forearm by a female Wemale artist in the coastal village of Hatunuru around 1912. The old lady stirred a batch of indigo secured from traders into a thin paste. She stenciled the design with the thin stalk of a local herb, then pierced the skin with "numerous stitches of a sewing needle" (Stresemann 1923:423). She wiped away the oozing blood, then applied the liquidy tissue of a freshly split banana tree, and then pressed the wounded area several times with the heated stem of a banana leaf. Then she applied an oily pasty pigment of charred candlenut into the punctures.

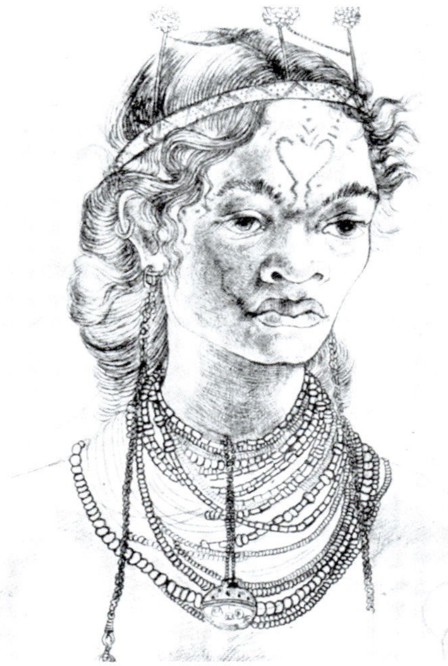

FIGURE 4.82
Tattooed Wemale woman of Waraloin village, West Seram, 1937. Illustration by Albert Hahn. From Jensen 1948:112, fig. 14.

Prior to the adoption of sewing needles, citrus thorns plied human skin and the leaves of crushed coleus (*Coleus scutellarioides*) were used for producing pigment (Stresemann 1923:424). Writing around 1860, the Dutch physician E. W. A. Ludeking (1868:75) recorded that tattooing ink was prepared from the juice of leaves from the bottle gourd (*Lagenaria vulgaris ser.*). Due to the adoption of indigo as the pigment source, Stresemann reported that the tattoos he saw were no longer black but dark blue.

In comparison to male tattooing traditions, the ethnographic record is rather silent concerning women's tattooing, although Stresemann (1923:421) observed it was primarily practiced for "decorative" or "ornamental" purposes. In some areas in the early twentieth century, however, women appeared to be more profusely tattooed than men, but the chroniclers of these traditions did not link these practices to a female initiation rite. Instead, it seemed that a young woman's primary tattoo, which was placed on her forehead and a prerequisite for marriage (Jensen 1948:109), was applied at the time just before young male initiates entered the Kakean house. The Dutch ethnologist Johan Duyvendak (1926:110) reported that, as a rule, these women were the sisters of the initiates. Depending on the region or village, male or female tattooists applied these markings, although old women were the typical practitioners.

Jensen (1948:110), however, noted that adolescent "marriageable" girls performed a function during the Kakean rite; namely, these *maloine* women, as they were titled, were paired with an initiate, whereupon "she entered into a steady relationship" with him. After the rite had concluded, each *maloine* presented her *masau* with a series of gifts: a mat, a rain cover, a shell bracelet, a necklace, and a headdress that was an important badge for the newly initiated youth. *Maloine* who participated in subsequent Kakean initiations could add to their collection of tattoos, and elderly men interviewed by Jensen (1948:101) could immediately remember the name of "their" *maloine*.

FIGURE 4.83
Herpianto Hendra at work, Sungai Utik, Kapuas Hulu, West Kalimantan, 2012. © Herpianto Hendra.

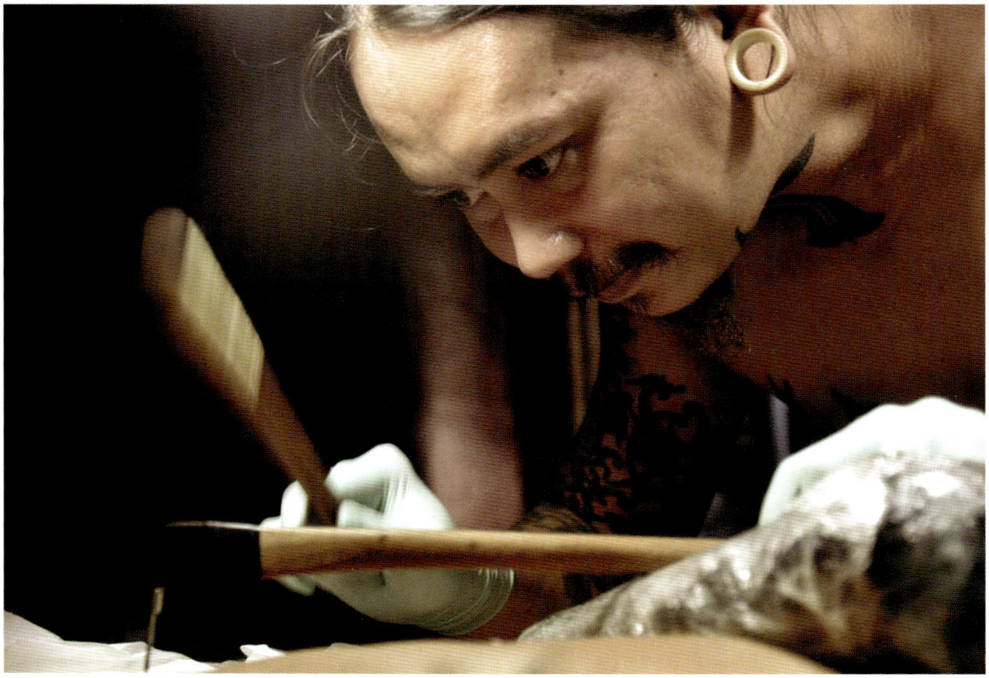

INDONESIAN TATTOO REVIVALS TODAY: HERPIANTO HENDRA: IBAN TATTOO REVIVAL (2009–2024)

Herpianto Hendra was born and raised in the Iban region of the upper Kapuas River on the Indonesian side of Borneo, West Kalimantan. He has been a tattooist for more than a decade, and his bold blackwork tattoos give expression to a wide variety of Iban iconography as well as other Indigenous tattooing styles from Borneo.

Hendra is a graduate of the Indonesian Institute of the Arts in Yogyakarta. As a self-taught tattoo artist, in 2009 he created Folk Space Tattoo studio in Yogyakarta that specializes in Indonesian tribal tattoos. Hendra regularly travels to West Kalimantan to visit his extended family and conduct research on Dayak tattoos and associated customs. During his trips he creates new tattoos for Iban men and women based on traditional designs, and retouches old tattoos to make them bold once again. Hendra's work is very important because there are only a very few elderly Dayak tattooists still living in West Kalimantan but most of them are no longer practicing their artform.

Hendra's creative scope is seemingly unlimited: swirling zoomorphic and floraform patterns of *aso'* (dragon-dogs), *ketam* (crabs), *kala* (throat and thigh scorpions), *bunga terong* (eggplant flowers), and other ornamental designs based on natural motifs inspired by the teeming life existing within Borneo's vast jungle domain.

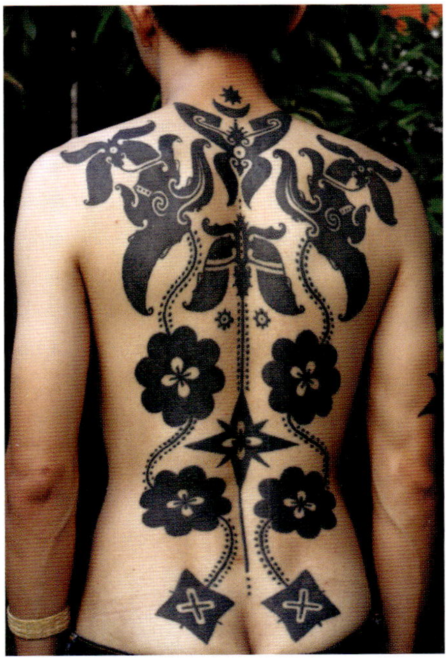

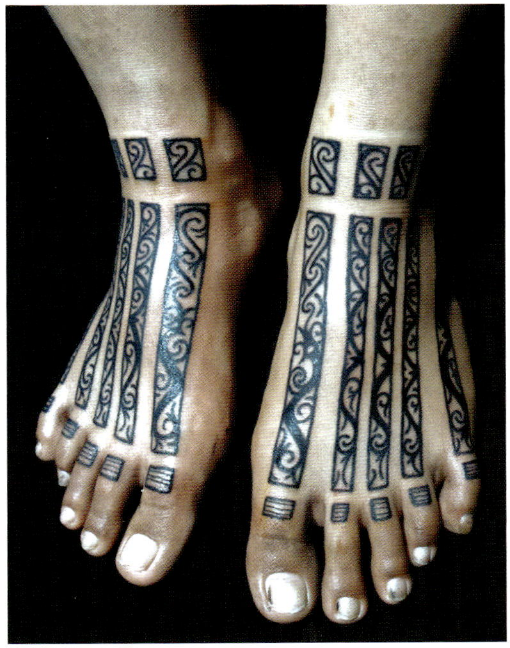

FIGURE 4.84 (LEFT)
Iban style tattoos, Yogyakarta, Indonesia, 2012.
© Herpianto Hendra.

FIGURE 4.85 (RIGHT)
Custom Kayan style tattoos, Yogyakarta, Indonesia, 2012.
© Herpianto Hendra.

In a recent interview, I asked Hendra about the various meanings that Dayak tattoos (*pantang*, Iban) have carried over the generations. "Traditionally, Dayak tattoos were infused with very important religious values because they were an important part of our *adat* or customary laws," he said. "These laws have been handed down over the millennia by our forefathers, and by living in accordance with these basic values all parts of the universe will remain healthy and in balance." He went on to explain, "One hundred years ago, Iban tattoos adorning the skin of men and women could be read like a text and they told the reader much about that person's accomplishments; these stories can still be seen on the bodies of elders, and herein lies the wealth of tattoo art."

"Tattooing can tell you so much about any given person's biography," he continued. "For example, an Iban woman with tattoos on her hands or thumbs told all comers that she was an expert weaver and able to create the most spiritually powerful designs on *ikat* textiles called *pua kumbu'*. Moreover, if a woman was particularly skillful in more domestic concerns, she would receive a band of zigzagging tattoos around her upper forearms signaling her status. As you can imagine, young men in the community were particularly keen to marry women marked in this way."[68]

Through moving his ancestral Iban tattooing culture forward, Hendra aims to pass it on to the next generation of artists after he is gone. "Tattooing is one of the most important activities to keep a culture alive," he said. "It also plays a role in reviving it. Because once you create a tattoo, you are permanently recording that moment in time, which makes it a part of history."

FIGURE 4.86
Iban style *pala tumpa'* (head of bracelets) tattoos, Sungai Utik, Kapuas Hulu, West Kalimantan, 2011. © Herpianto Hendra.

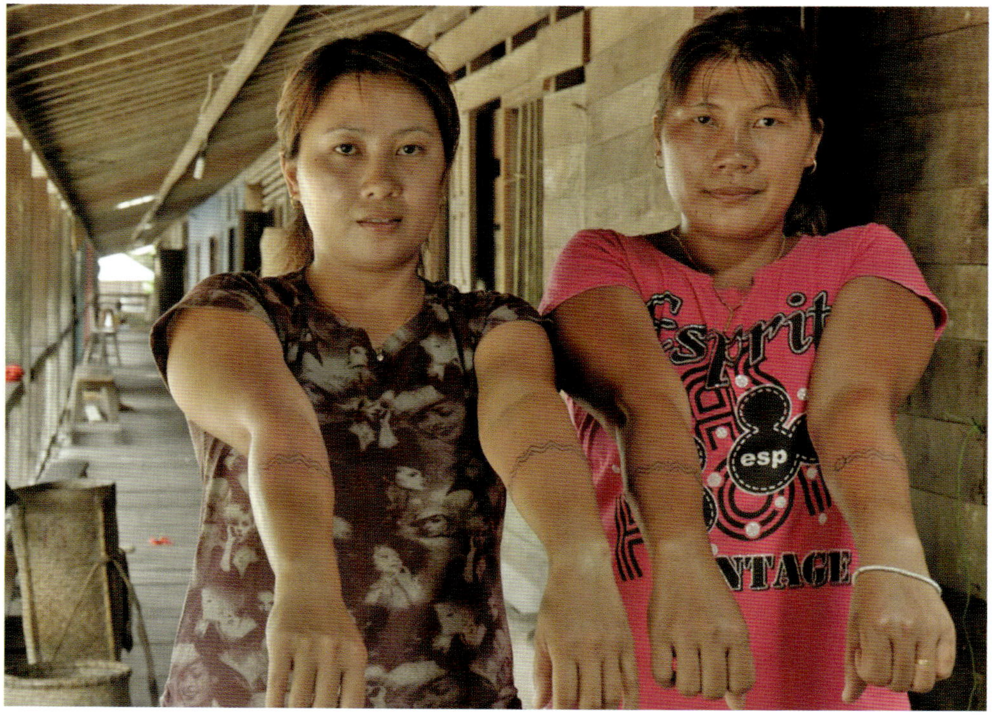

FIGURE 4.87
Hendra hand-tapping a new *bunga terong* (brinjal flower) tattoo on an Iban elder's shoulder, Sungai Utik, Kapuas Hulu, West Kalimantan, 2011. © Herpianto Hendra.

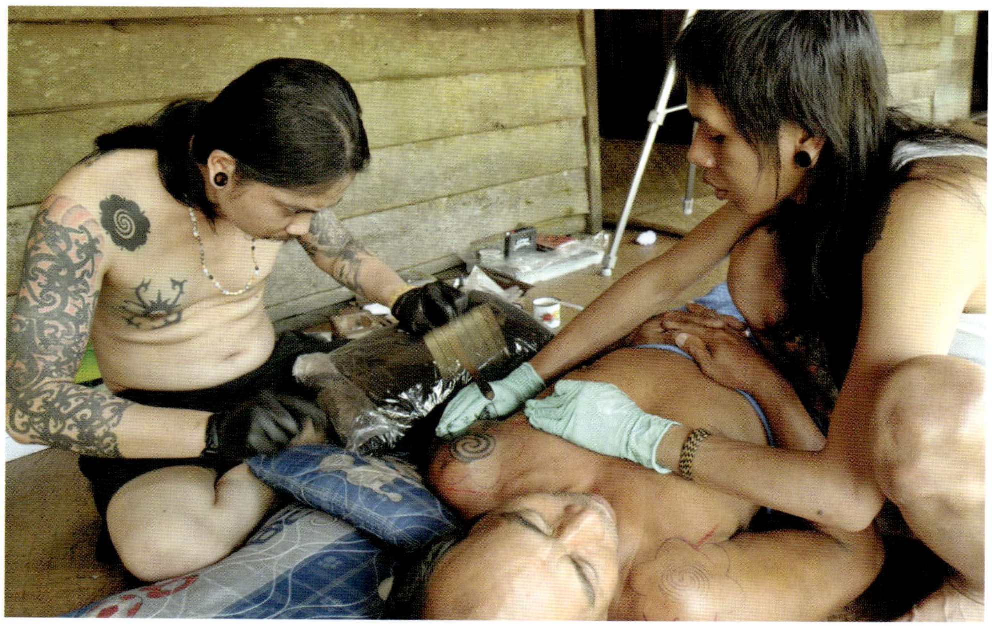

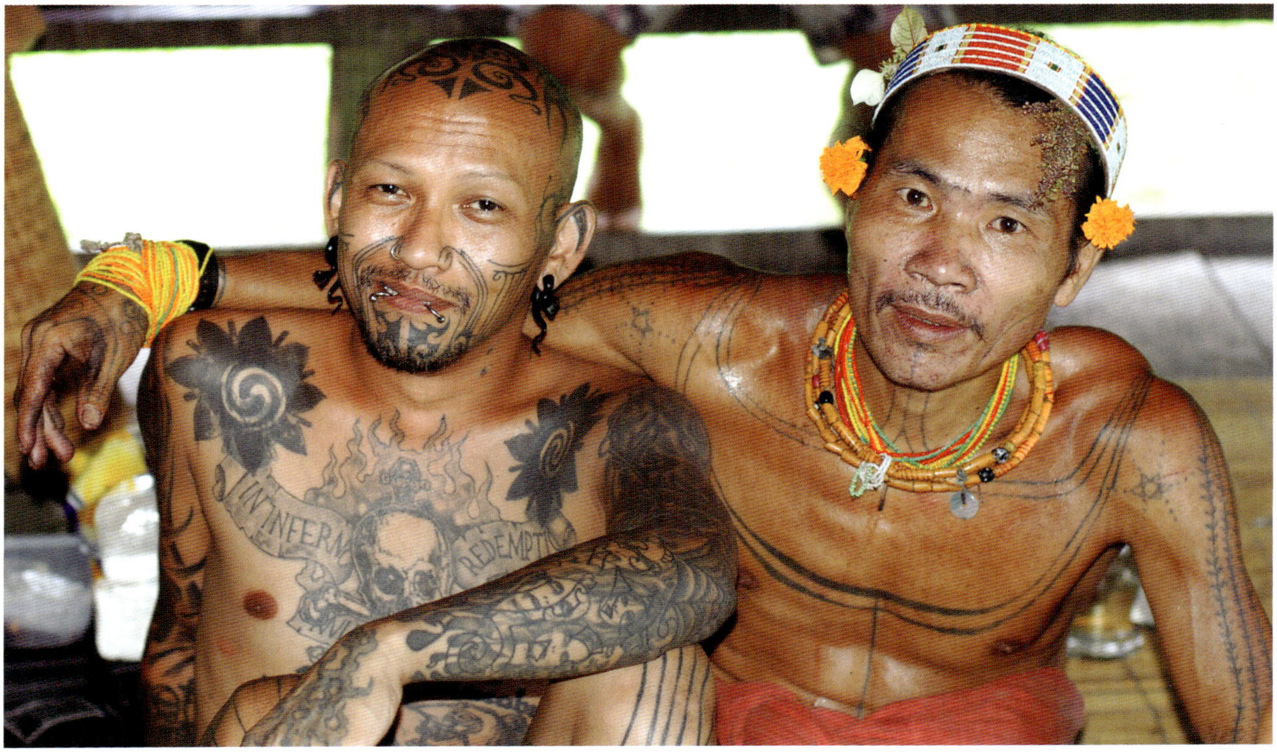

AMAN "SIPATITI" DURGA: MENTAWAI TATTOO REVIVAL (2006–2024)

FIGURE 4.88
Aman Durga Sipatiti with Mentawai shaman Aman Alangi Kunen from Matotonan, Siberut Island, 2011. © Tomasz Madej.

Yogyakarta-born tattooist Aman Durga, who works out of his studio Durga Tattoo, has visited Siberut Island nearly a dozen times. Along the way he has spearheaded a Mentawai tattoo revival project, which has led to the revitalization of tattooing among many clans there.

Like Hendra, Durga graduated from the prestigious Indonesian Institute of the Arts with a degree in graphic design. Ever the nomad, in the early 2000s he took his skills and talents to the United States, where he apprenticed as a tattoo artist under Sua Sulu'ape Freewind at Black Wave Tattoo in Los Angeles. It was here that he became inspired by tribal and traditional tattoos.

Animism and polytheism, the original religions of Indonesia, greatly influence Durga's tattoo art and design, but his artistic works are also infused with Hindu, Buddhist, and shamanic elements.

After finding traditional tattoos, Durga dedicated all his energy to studying every tattooing culture of Indonesia, including those of the Lesser Sunda archipelago (Sumba, Rote, Timor), Seram Island in the Malukus, Kalimantan (Borneo), and that which continues to exist on Siberut Island (Mentawai archipelago).

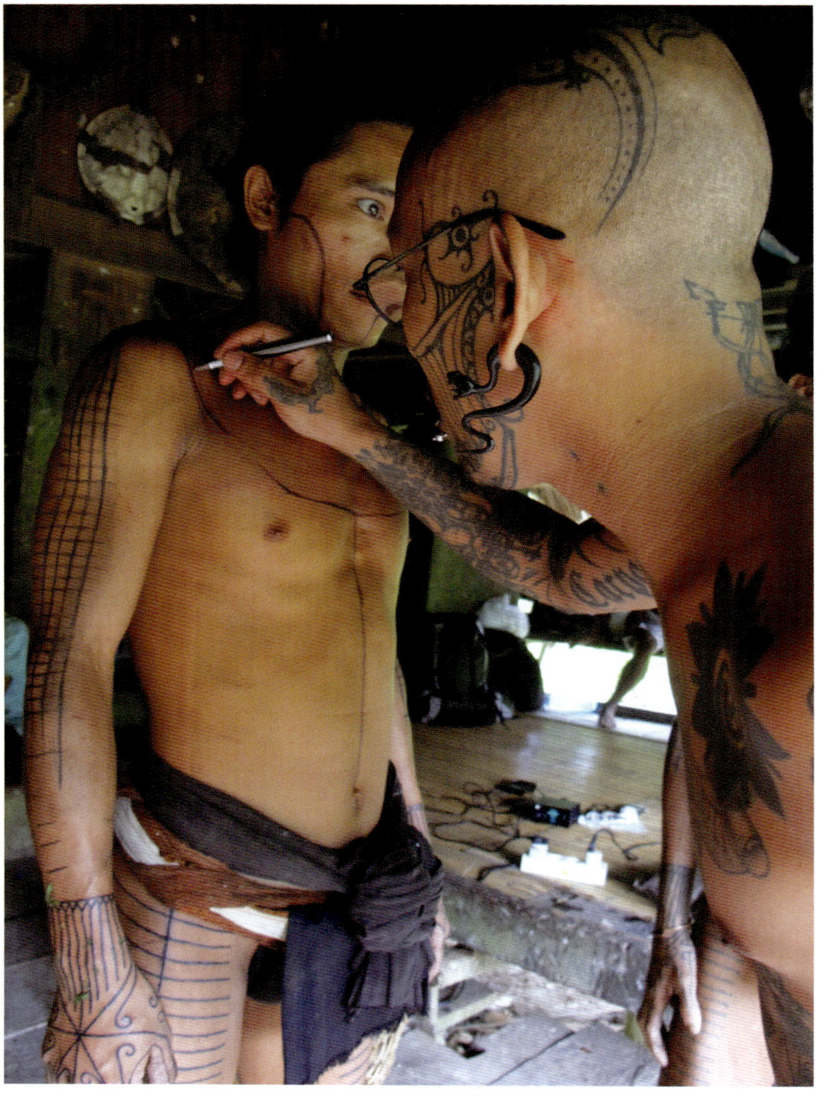

In 2009, he made his first journey to Siberut. At that time, only a few remaining tattoo artists were living and practicing their ancestral art. Many Mentawaian youth no longer wished to be tattooed because of the negative connotations it brought in Indonesian towns, especially since tattooing is widely believed to be associated with criminality.

Because traditional Mentawaian tattooing was gradually fading away, Durga jumpstarted Mentawai Tattoo Revival, which has helped sustain the culture and tradition of *titi* (tattooing) from disappearing. The project features tattoo workshops directly in the middle of the Siberut jungle, where Durga works together with several *sikerei* (Mentawai shamans), who were the tattoo artists among their tribe, to further enhance and preserve their tattoo culture and related traditions.

Over the course of his expeditions, Durga has completed the tattooing of many *sikerei* and other community members, and become a *sipatiti* (a professional tattoo artist in the Mentawai language) in his own right. He continues to spread awareness of Mentawai tattooing at cultural events, in publications, and through carefully crafted and produced video documentaries. Durga is a widely sought-after artist on the international tattooing circuit, and you can often find him at the most prestigious conventions (London, Amsterdam, Frankfurt, Florence) and other venues hand-tapping or creating machined tattoos in the Mentawaian or other Indonesian tribal styles.

FIGURE 4.89
Aman Durga Sipatiti stenciling a chest design for Mentawai shaman Aman Telepon, Buttui village, Siberut Island, 2011. © Tomasz Madej.

Durga recently expressed his thoughts to me, and his career mantra is simple: "Tattoos are the Indonesian culture, and if these tribal designs and everything they are connected to disappeared we would lose an important part of our country's very unique cultural heritage." He explained, "For the Mentawai, *titi* symbolizes their identity and ancestral beliefs, their *arat sabulungan*. This is one system of values that organizes the social and spiritual life of the Mentawai tribe. Each tattoo motif

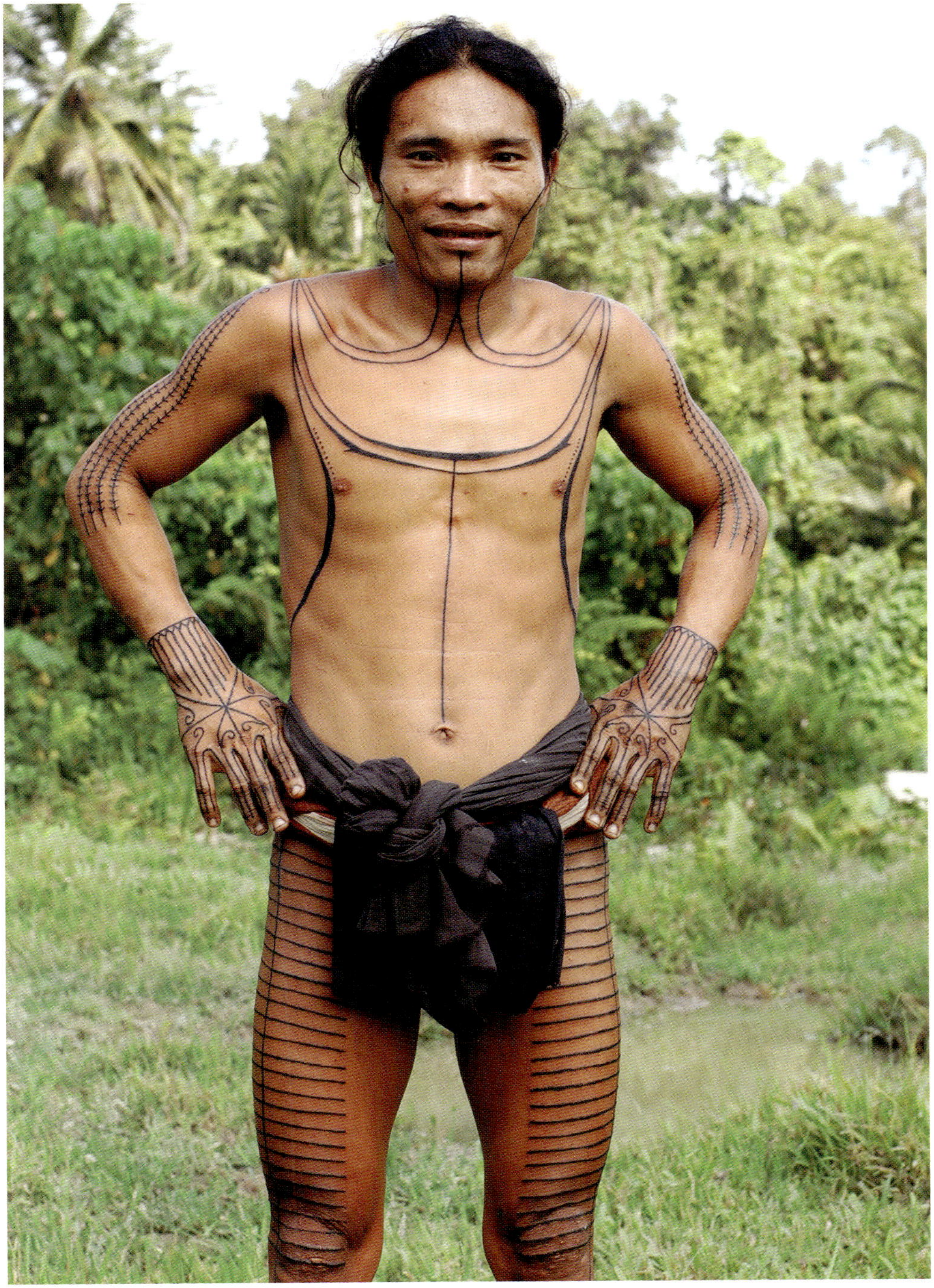

FIGURE 4.90
Mentawai shaman Aman Telepon displays his new tattoos, Buttui village, Siberut Island, 2011. Tattooing by Aman Durga Sipatiti. © Tomasz Madej.

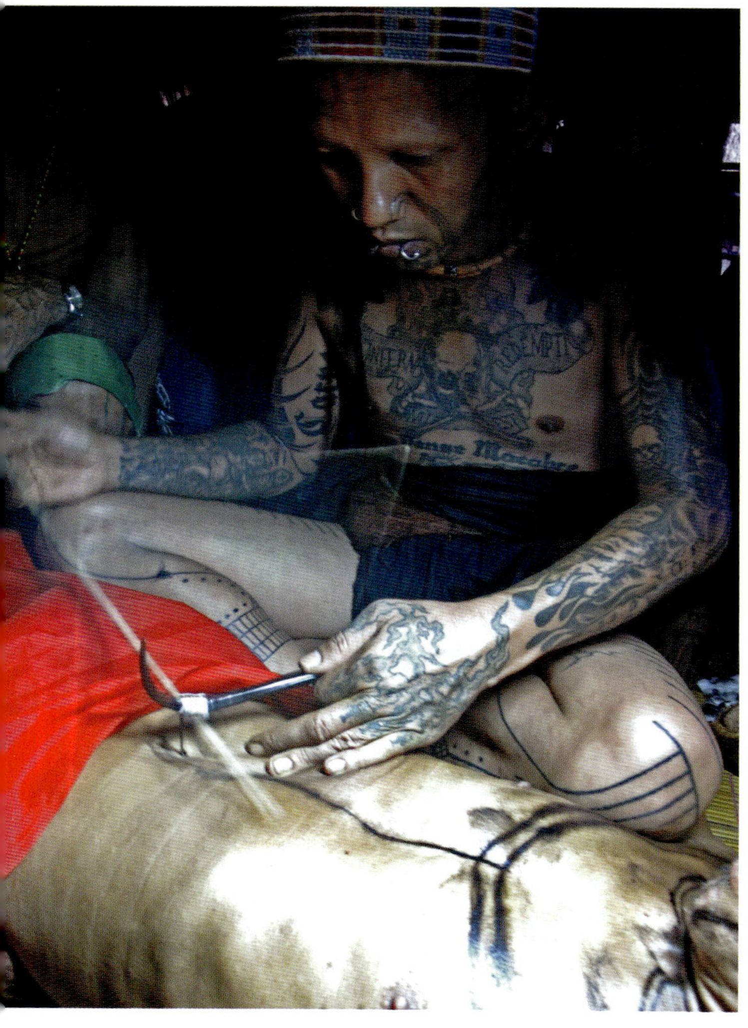

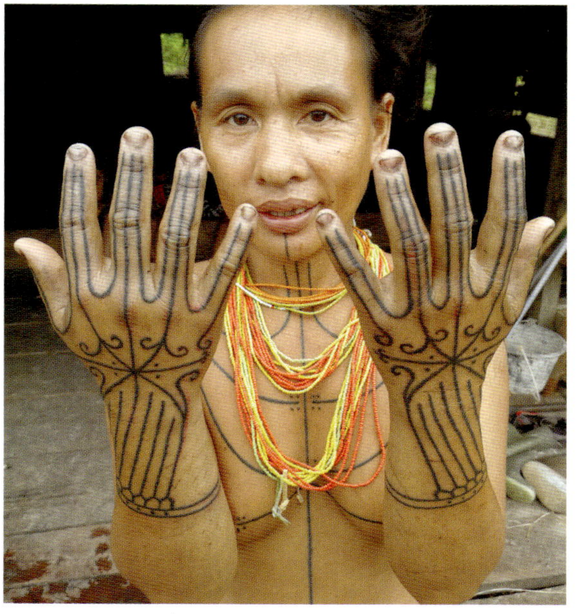

FIGURE 4.91 (LEFT)
Aman Durga Sipatiti hand-tapping a chest piece for a Mentawai client, Siberut Island, 2010. © Aman Durga Sipatiti.

FIGURE 4.92 (ABOVE)
Bai Telepon displaying her new Mentawai tattoos, Buttui, Siberut Island, 2018. Tattooing by Aman Durga Sipatiti. © Nadja Ritter.

FIGURE 4.93 (FACING PAGE)
Esmat Wondra Sakulok of the Saibi Samukop clan displaying his tattooed Mentawai body suit, Siberut Island, 2021. Artwork by Aman Durga Sipatiti. © Fajar Dhika Vandra.

represents something spiritual and meaningful. And from the tattoos found on their bodies we can recognize their original subclans, as well as their professions."[69]

"Additionally," he said, "tattooing is a kind of spiritual makeup because it makes the human body beautiful in the eyes of the spirits that control human destiny and the surrounding world. Tattoos furthermore make one more recognizable to their ancestors whom they meet in the afterlife."

Durga also supports the living tattoo traditions of the Dayak peoples of Kalimantan in collaboration with the Dayak Youth Community in Jakarta, as well as with Herpianto Hendra, who has dedicated his life to documenting, preserving, and promoting the Indigenous tattoo art of his Iban ancestors.

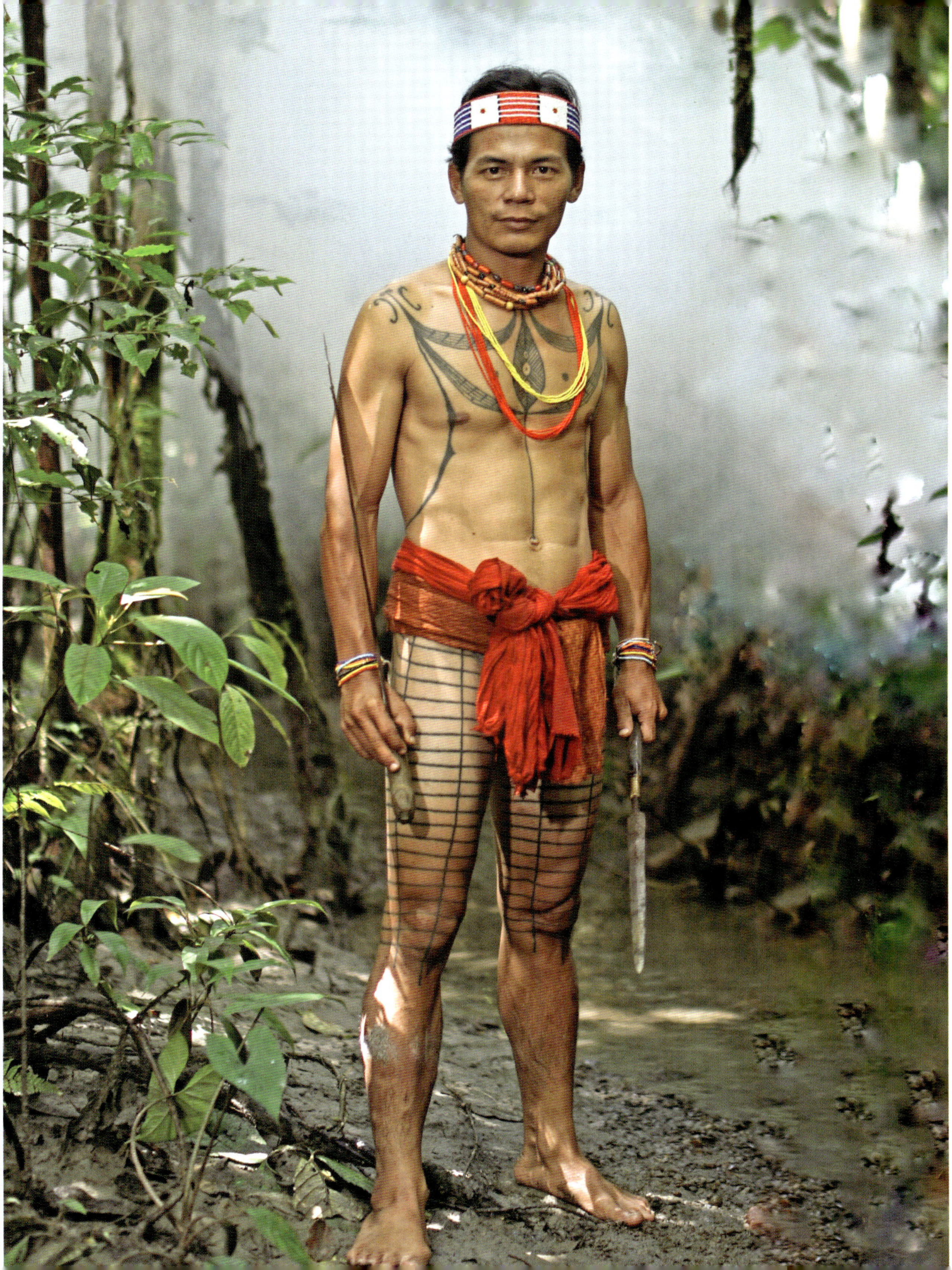

FIGURE 4.94
(FACING PAGE)
Portrait of Joe Patty-Sabandar, Amsterdam, Netherlands, 2020. © Stacii Samidin.

JOE PATTY-SABANDAR: MALUKU TATTOO REVIVAL (2008–2024)

Joe Patty-Sabandar, a tattooist of Alifuru descent, was born in Rotterdam, the Netherlands, in 1989. He speaks the ancient Sou Allane language of his ancestors and is a practitioner of their tattoo tradition.

Patty-Sabandar grew up with friends and family who had tattoos and eventually he began tattooing in 2008. In 2011, he met a Māori tattooist from the Tuhaka family (Ngāti Porou) who became his teacher. His mentor realized that traditional tattooing in Maluku had been lost during the colonial period, and encouraged Patty-Sabandar to explore creating traditional Moluccan-style tattoos, especially with the hand tools that he began to use in 2012.

"He wanted me to give something back to my people," Patty-Sabandar told me in a recent conversation. "At that time, however, I was not really into the Moluccan culture because I am Dutch, but also Moluccan, and I was caught somewhere in between. I was tattooing my client base with an electric machine, but my teacher compelled me to start using traditional hand-tapping tools and conduct research, which helped me grow as an artist and person."[70]

Around the same time, Patty-Sabandar tattooed an ancestral clan symbol on one of his cousins. His mother, who has the ability to see the deceased, was visited by an Alifuru ancestor who gave him permission to continue with this work. "From that moment forward, symbols began to appear in my thoughts and dreams with their meanings in the old language," Patty-Sabandar said. "This ability grew stronger with time, and I felt I was given an important responsibility to rebirth our tattooing culture and to mark our people again."

Eventually, Patty-Sabandar created the Patasiwa Allane Tatu Family, a name that he works under today out of his studio in Hoorn, the Netherlands. "I work from this namesake because Patasiwa Allane is the clan of my village in Maluku. Patasiwa is a clan that comes from the birthplace of our first ancestor on Nunusaku Mountain," Patty-Sabandar explained. "As you know, in the past the Patasiwa tattooed during the Kakean, a secret society of the Alifuru. Our ancestors were very protective of our culture and tattooing during the Dutch regime, and that is why, even after studying all of the old published accounts, it is difficult to gain knowledge of these nearly forgotten traditions."

Patty-Sabandar does not see himself as a tattoo artist. Rather, he is a cultural practitioner, a cultural person. "People from the Moluccan community have shared with me secret clan and family information which is not meant to be known by outsiders," he revealed. "And the tattoos I create mean many things to the many people I tattoo. For me, these symbols are an educational tool to help other Malukan people better understand their ancient culture," he said. "But these markings also speak about the origins and histories of clans and villages and families. They embody information about social constructs, protocols, and statuses, as well as their connection to nature and the universe and much more. Our tattoos tell who someone is, who someone was, and who someone will be. And I always say these symbols are our ancestors and our ancestors are these symbols."

Although the traditional Alifuru tattooing tradition disappeared by the mid-twentieth century, glimpses of that indelible past can still be gleaned when Patty-Sabandar initiates a new

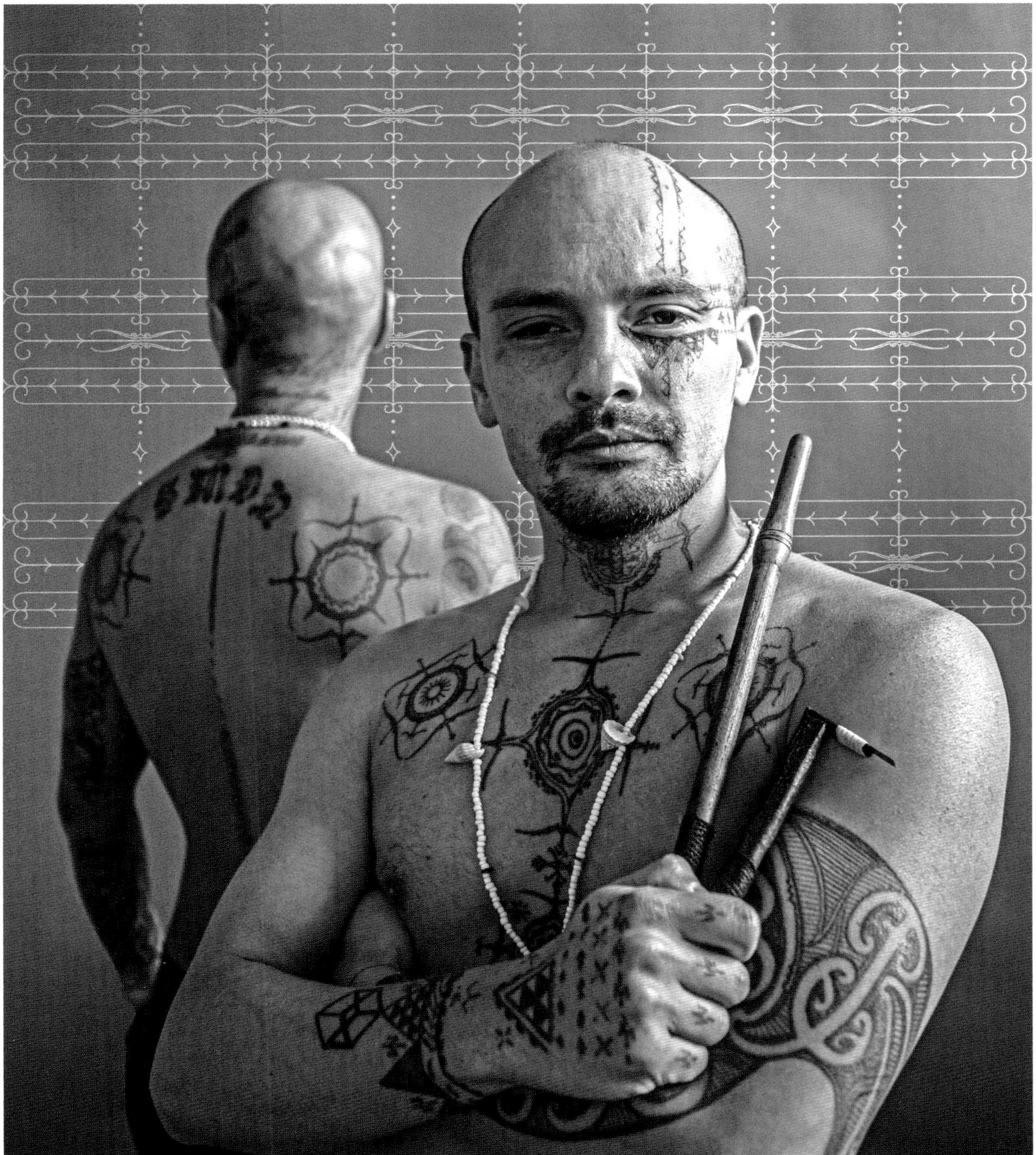

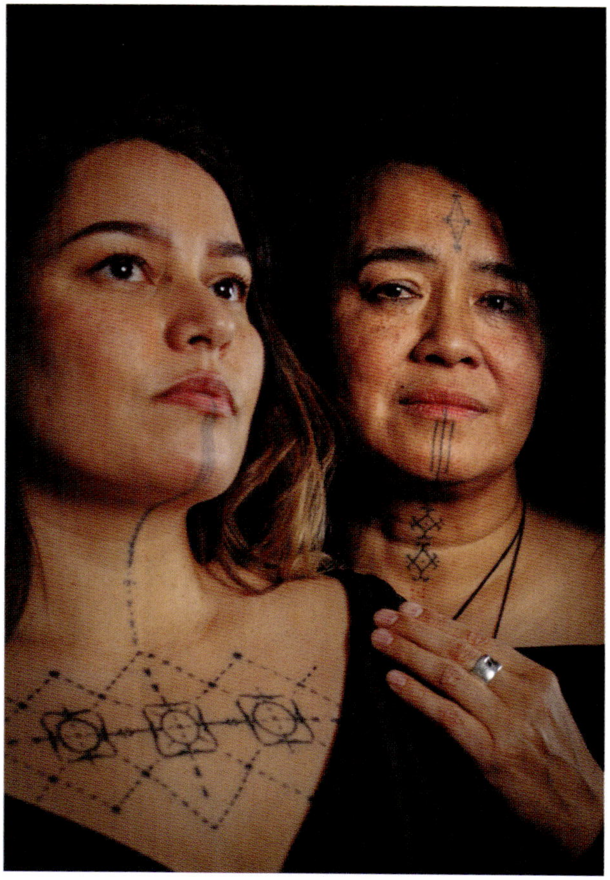

FIGURE 4.95
Portrait of Charlotte Hol Souhuwat and elder Chériette Lemaire Wattimena, Utrecht, Netherlands, 2020. Souhuwat is Patty-Sabandar's wife, and she recounted the moment just after receiving her chin markings: "When I first got my chin tattoo (*alalihunu metata*, "black chin"), it was very emotional because my parents did not want me to do it," she revealed. "'You are so beautiful,' they said, but I tried to explain that it was not a tattoo, it is like a jewel you wear with pride. When Joe finished and I looked into the mirror, there was so much emotion . . . and a weight came off me. Now I am complete, and I can be the woman I want to be, and I truly feel this here [pointing to her heart]." © Rachèl Luttikhuisen Tauran.

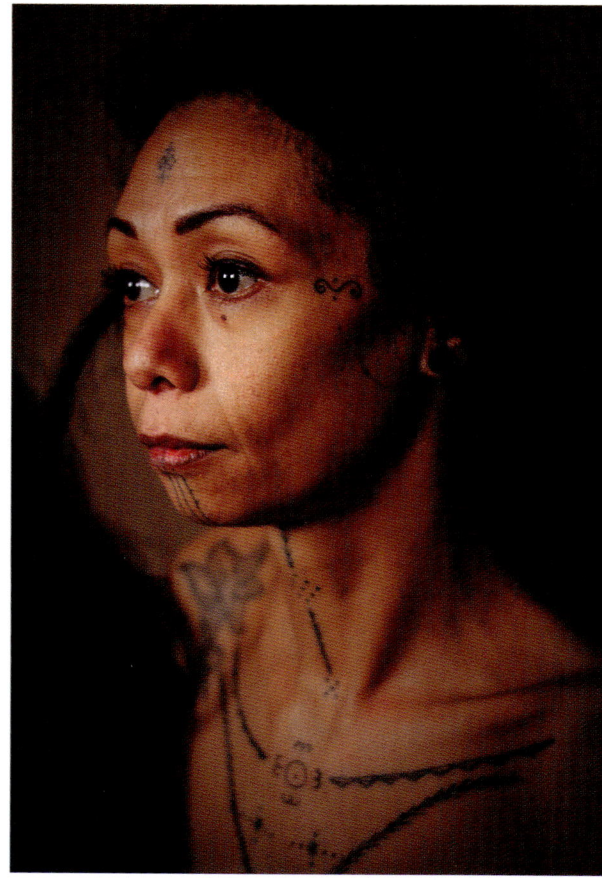

FIGURE 4.96
Portrait of Juressa Ipsen, Utrecht, Netherlands, 2020. © Rachèl Luttikhuisen Tauran.

FIGURE 4.97 (FACING PAGE)
Portrait of Alec Kakisina, Sascha Huliselan, and elder Phaidra Johannis, Rotterdam, Netherlands, 2020. © Rachèl Luttikhuisen Tauran.

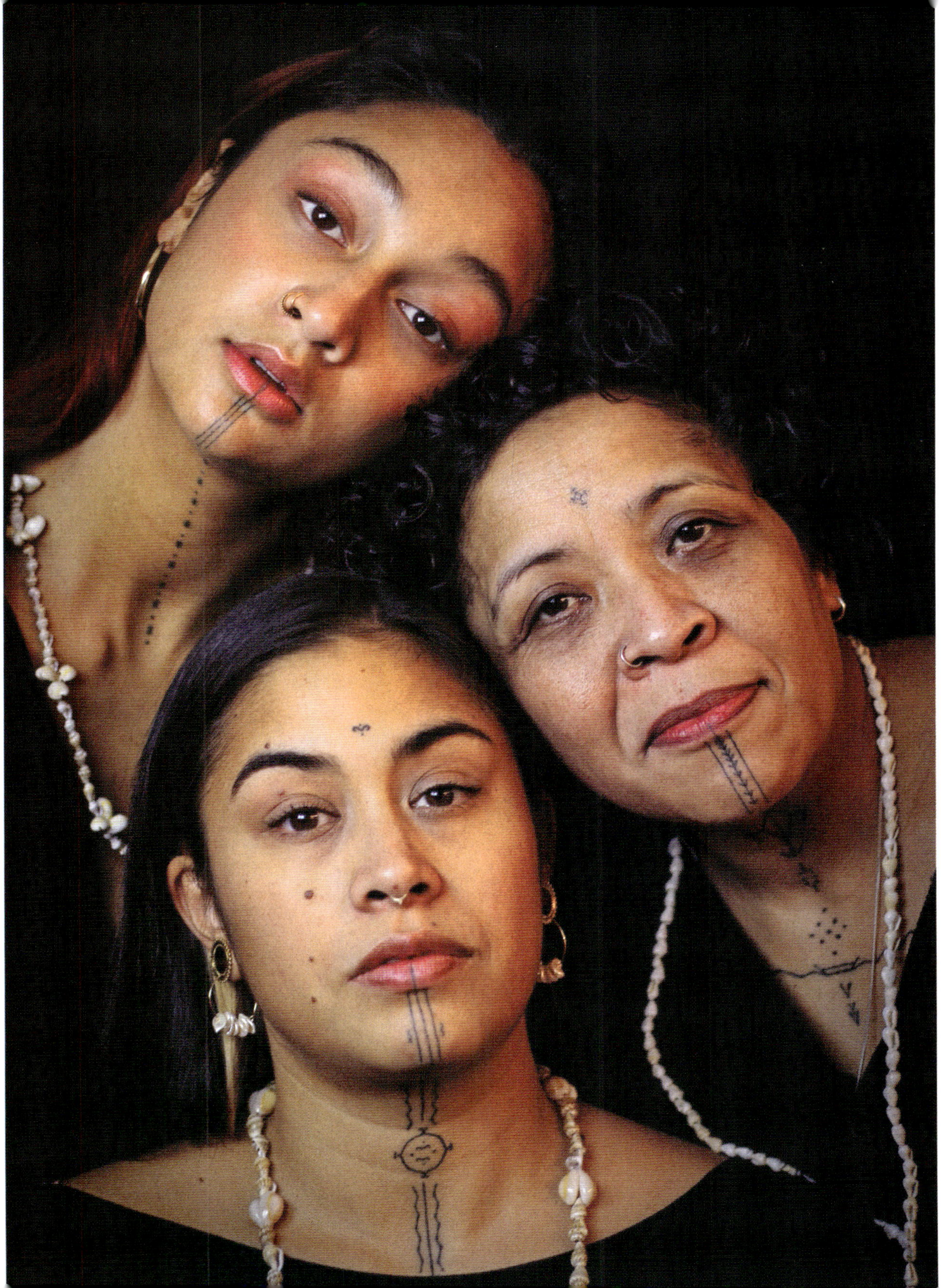

tattoo. He treats tattooing with the utmost ceremony and respect, and offers prayers that help to activate the tattoos' meanings:

> Hearing the rhythm of the hand tools and feeling the skin punctured by thorns or boar tusk needles is a significant part of the ceremonial engagement. Our tattoos are once again gaining popularity with men, women, and teenagers from the Moluccan diaspora. Although they all grew up with a Dutch worldview, the younger generations see the markings as a form of identity and embrace it. Even the older generations have gravitated to our tattooing, and they are beginning to wear ancestral markings even though they were always taboo due to their belief in Christ. The colonizers tried to erase all of our spiritual traditions but they never completely disappeared. And thanks to the Internet, old books, and archives, we have been able to slowly reclaim many of our cultural traditions that were formerly lost. What is important, however, is that the world knows we still exist and that we are still fighting for our continued existence. And tattooing certainly has an important role to play in the revival of our people's shared spiritual traditions, cultural heritage, and history.
>
> The Maluku tattooing revival means reclaiming Indigenous beauty, embracing our Indigenous heritage, and the survival of our ancestral ways. And it will continue into the future. When my daughter was five years old, she asked me if I wanted to teach her the ways of *Tupuisinu* (*tupu* means to "stab" or "insert," and *isinu* means "knowledge"). I began teaching her, and her confidence and spirituality is growing. She would be the first female tattooist to work since the 1930s, and this waterdrop made a wrinkle which I hope will roll into a wave and spread across the diaspora. I see this wave as cultural transmission in the form of *Tupuisinu*, *Pa'atei* (marking skin with Kakean protocols), and *Ha'apita* (marking skin without the Kakean protocols). Hopefully, my grandchildren will follow in their ancestors' footsteps and pass these traditions down to their own children.

5

TATTOOS OF MAINLAND SOUTHEAST ASIA

Magical Mysteries in Ink

> After sundry ceremonies, the figure of a cat or a demon or "beloo" was tattooed on the patient's breast with the medicine [pigment] prepared, he all the while biting and chewing the piece of raw human flesh. The supposed effect of this wonderful and disgusting operation is to enable the man to leap like a cat prodigious heights and lengths—a hundred feet would be nothing; or else to endow him with the strength, ferocity, and power of a demon.
>
> —**Charles J. Forbes (1878:240),** British official, Burma

For over a thousand years, tattooing has been a significant part of religious life among several peoples of mainland Southeast Asia. For the purposes of this book, this continental portion of Southeast Asia includes the countries of Thailand, Myanmar, Cambodia, Laos, and Vietnam. Integrated into a system of belief encompassing Theravada Buddhism, Hinduism, animism, and ancestor worship, tattooing evolved into a kind of magical text that adherents used to navigate through an uncertain, unpredictable, and imperfect world dominated by human enemies, deities, nature spirits, and the dead.

In Thailand and in parts of Cambodia, Laos, Vietnam, and Myanmar, tattoos were largely administered by holy monks, former holy men, and laymen who apprenticed under one of the former individuals. Today, the esoteric art is believed to provide its wearers with not only indelible protection from a variety of misfortunes but also the mystical power to influence other peoples' behavior, carry the deceased safely into the afterlife, or simply increase a person's "luck" (Krutak 2016b:66).

Whatever the personal motivation may be for receiving these sacred and lasting symbols, tattooing in contemporary Myanmar, Thailand, Laos, Cambodia, and Vietnam continues to firmly anchor the religious faith of its devotees on human skin for all to see. Although many traditional motifs have disappeared or have been replaced with modern versions of ancient designs, the desire

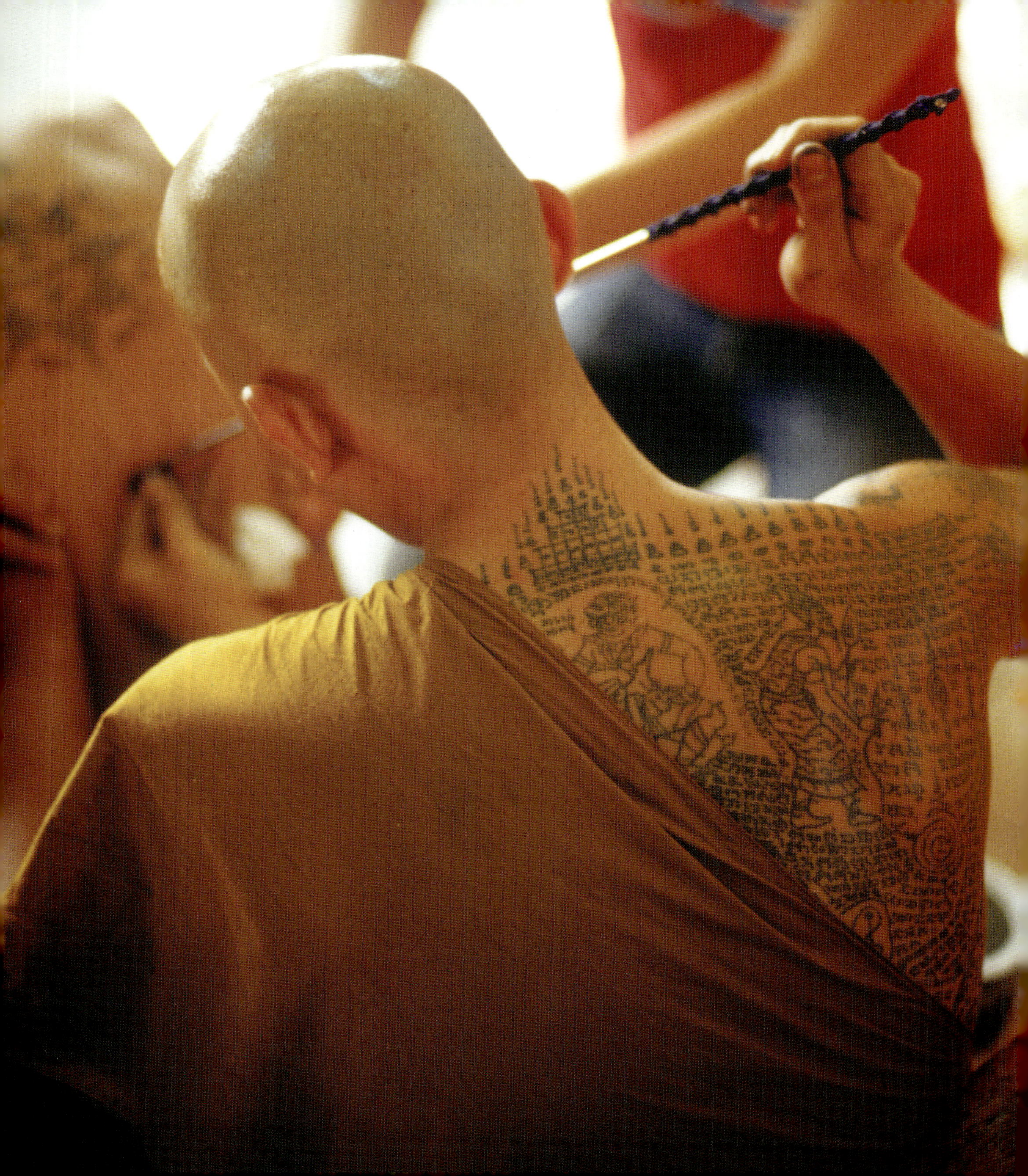

to be marked with powerful amulets remains. Why, you ask? Because tattoos are seen as magical mediators between this world and the next that are capable of channeling powerful cosmic forces that transcend nature, the mind, the body, and the soul.

FIGURE 5.1 (FACING PAGE) Monk of Wat Bang Phra monastery, Thailand, transferring his spiritual energy into a magical tattoo, 2007. © Lars Krutak.

TATTOOING MONKS OF MAINLAND SOUTHEAST ASIA (1875–2024)

Most tattooed people in Mainland Southeast Asia will tell you that the real magic of their tattooing probably comes from the monk who created it. Therefore, it should come as no surprise that even the smallest and poorest towns and villages throughout Thailand, Laos, Cambodia, and Myanmar maintain temples and *ajarn*,[1] or tattooing monks. Animal figures such as the tiger, tortoise, and others from the Hindu pantheon (e.g., Hanuman, Garuda, etc.) are part of the magic of some tattoos, but many other human skins are also inked with holy *katha*, or magic spells, and diagrams (called *ang* by Shans in Myanmar) written in Khom (Thailand, Laos, Cambodia), the sacred calligraphy of the ancient Khmer language, Pali (Myanmar), the sacred canonical text of Indian origin (Krutak 2012), or other scripts (Cummings 2014). Sometimes spells and prayers are tattooed in Sanskrit.

Katha are taken from verses of the Buddha's teachings and are either written out on the flesh or encoded in cryptic diagrams that only master monks know (Tannenbaum 1987:695). *Katha* and diagrams are used in every category of Theravada Buddhist tattooing and particular verses depend on the function of the tattoo itself. Although there are various levels of *katha* magic, the power of the inscription ultimately depends on the level of power embodied in the monk or former holy man who gives it.

As with all magical tattoos of this sort, the monk making them recites *katha* just before, during, or after his tattooing session. These verses may be voiced in a whisper or mumble barely discernable to the client. Regardless of the method of delivery, the power of the tattoo will not work for the tattoo recipient unless he continually obeys at least one of the five Buddhist precepts during his life. Therefore, and in their attempts to maintain the magic of the tattoo, men are careful to observe one or more of the following fundamental doctrines: refraining from killing, stealing, lying, intoxication, and/or the pursuit of improper sexual behavior (Tannenbaum 1987:696). (I use the pronoun "he" since it is men, not women, who typically wear these powerful pigmented tattoos, although some monks will tattoo women with invisible oil tattoos in Thailand or with pigmented tattoos in Myanmar, Thailand, or Laos.)

Older and more devout people may choose to follow eight precepts: the aforementioned five plus abstaining from meals at noon, entertainments, and sleeping on a high and wide bed (Tannenbaum 1987:696). Not surprisingly, the more precepts a person is able to keep, the greater the strength of their tattoos.

It has also been recorded that specific human actions can "dissolve" the power found in their tattoos. A medical officer in Myanmar wrote that men wearing magical tattoos may not enter a laboring room within one week after a baby was delivered there; "[i]f they do they may lose their potency or 'glory of manhood'" (Foll 1959:55).

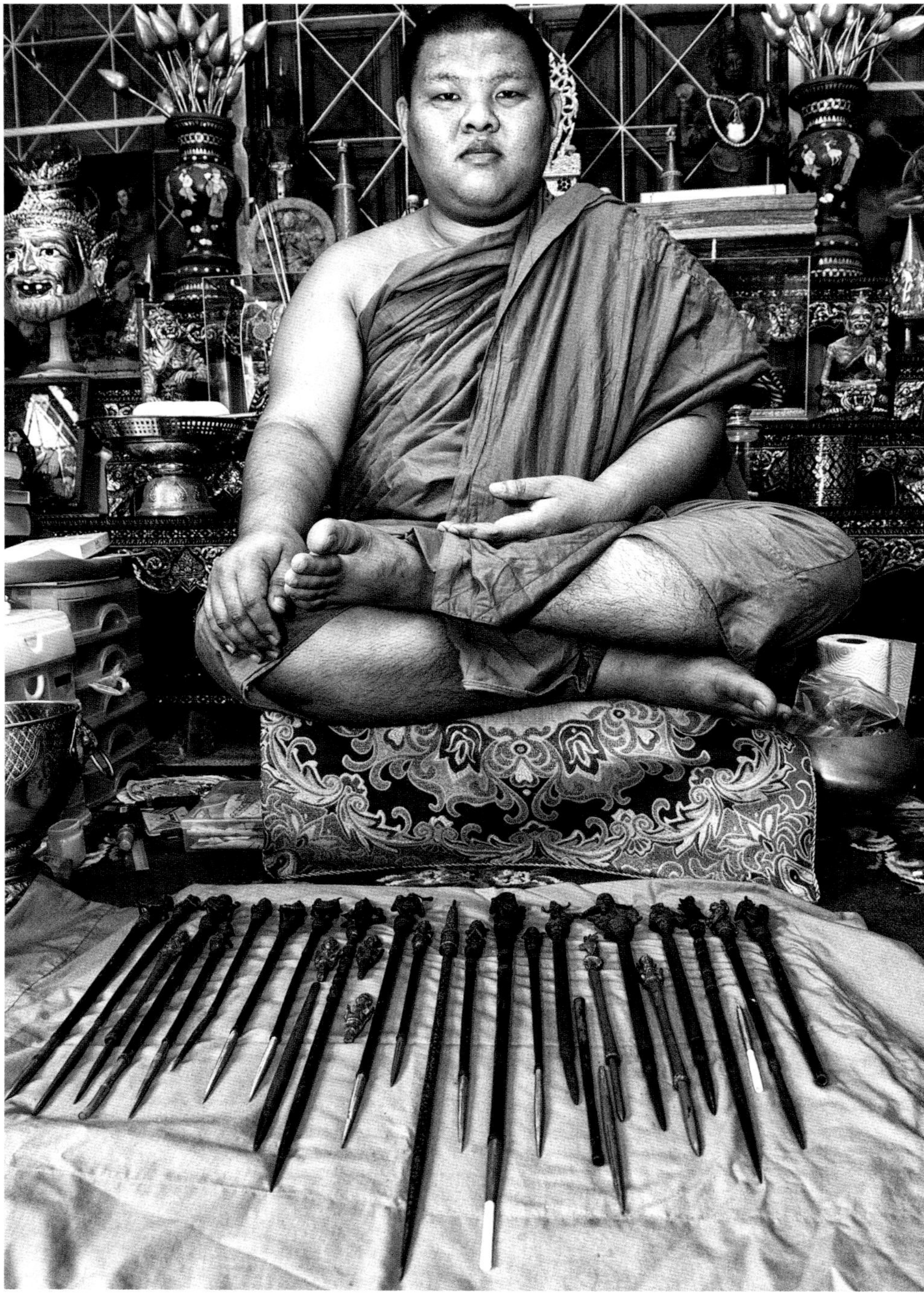

FIGURE 5.2
Ajarn Luang Pi Man in his temple with a collection of *mai sak*, or tattooing needles, Thailand, 2012. © Matthieu Duquenois.

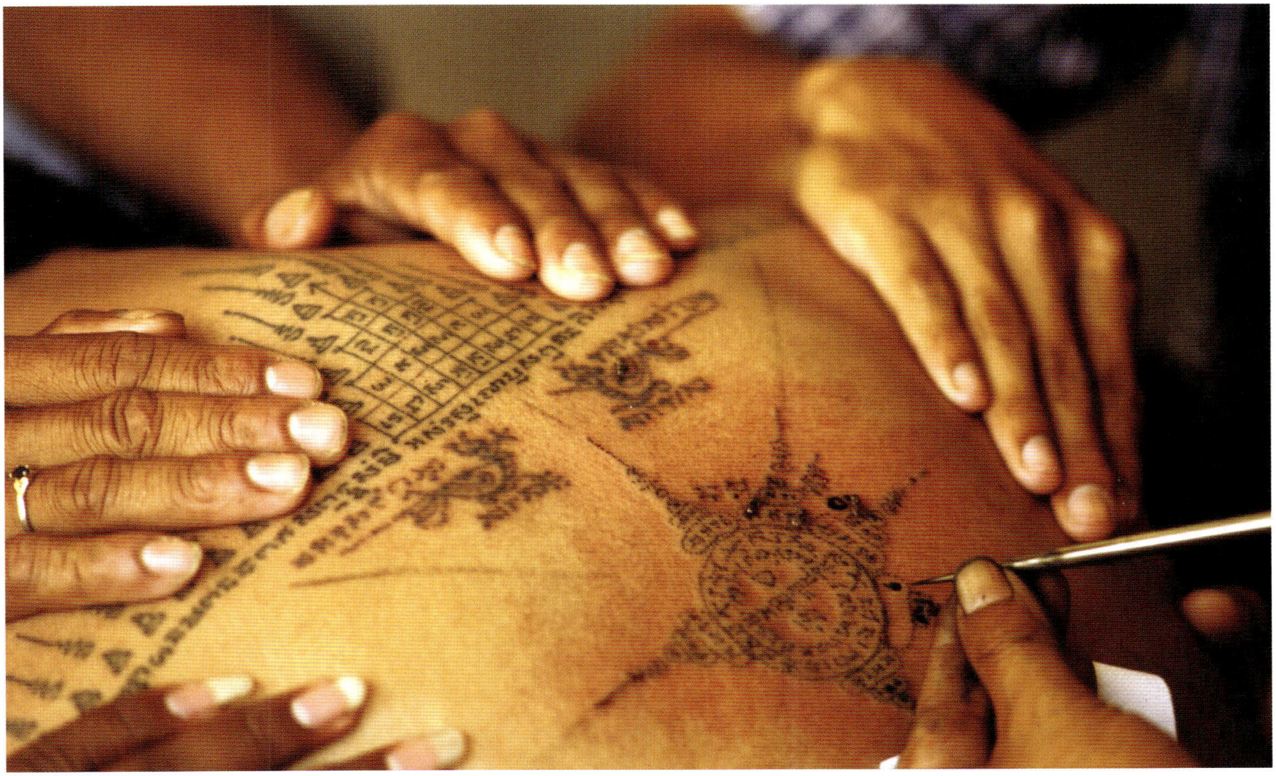

FIGURE 5.3
Thai man receiving a *sak yan* tattoo, 2007. Before a Thai *ajarn* (tattoo master) applies a magical tattoo, he must first read your aura to determine what design you need. The ancient eight-pointed compass tattoo is highly sought after because it is empowered with protective magic. Wat Bang Phra monastery is the only temple in Thailand that offers this tattoo. © Lars Krutak.

Tattooed men were also dissuaded from simply visiting the house where a baby was recently born, and if they did "[t]hey must cleanse themselves with water into which a gold or silver coin has been placed [while stating] a special prayer at the same time. This is almost certainly based on Hinduism where the uncleanliness of a woman who is menstruating or post-partum is much stressed" (Foll 1959:55).

Regardless of these and other taboos, scholars argue that *katha* (tattoo spells) have power because the sacred words have power. But others suggest it is not the words themselves that have power but rather their source and the circumstances under which they were learned (Tannenbaum 1987:701). For example, one cannot simply memorize a *katha* and expect it to be efficacious. One must learn the *katha* from a pious teacher or monk with whom one has established a proper ritual relationship because these individuals have a kind of power that not only relates to the physical components of the body but also to kindness, beneficence, or a favor for which the recipient should show gratitude and respect (Tannenbaum 1987:701). Beings like Buddhist monks are powerful, and if people enter the proper relationship with them then they have access to that power. Thus, by keeping precepts and being an honorable person, monks can create power for themselves that can be passed on to their students and clients through tattooing (Krutak 2012:14).

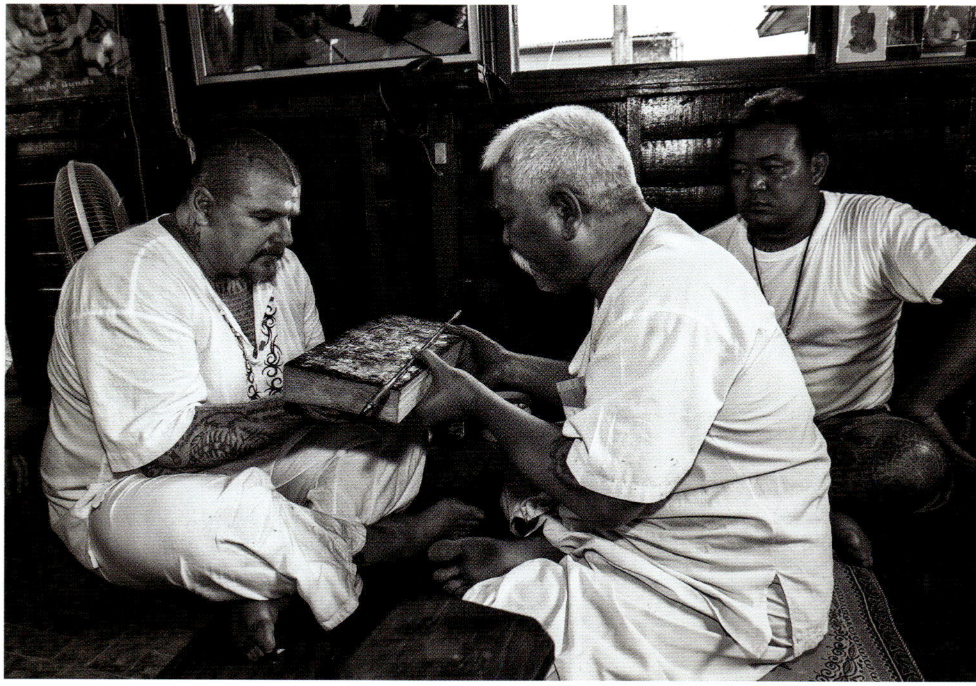

FIGURE 5.4
French-born Ajarn Matthieu Duquenois receiving the Krop Khem blessing from his mentor, the late Ajarn Thong, Thailand, 2013. This ceremony conferred the title of *ajarn* (tattoo master) on him. Thong presented Duquenois with a *mai sak* (tattooing tool) and a *tamla yan* (book) of *sak yan* (tattoo) designs and secret formulas he had learned from his master. Shortly thereafter, Duquenois became a monk in order to purify himself and prepare for the tattooing that was to come. © Matthieu Duquenois.

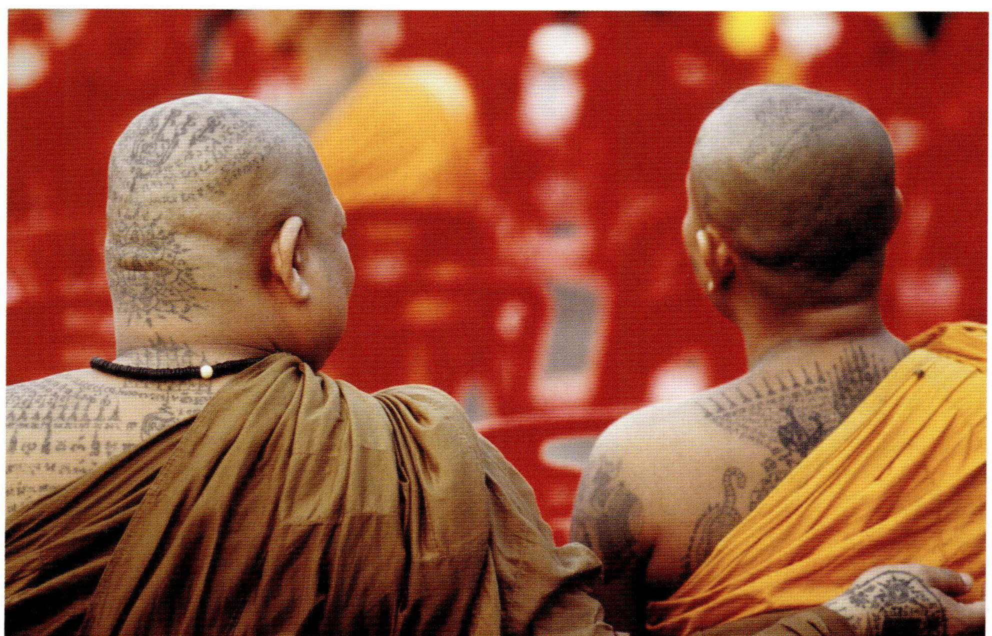

FIGURE 5.5
Chatting monks at Wat Bang Phra monastery, Thailand, 2007. © Lars Krutak.

Aside from these efficacious chants men in monkhood have access to other kinds of powerful knowledge that can be used to increase their power. This type of power accrues to them by following the Buddha's precepts but also through the practice of personal discipline, and through the teachings of elder monks who represent the lineage of every monk that came before them, including the Buddha and the objects associated with him (Tannenbaum 1987). All these powers augment those of a tattooing monk whenever he undertakes a new tattoo.

Tattooing monks must also practice restraint. Without this, they do not have power of their own or access to the power of their teachers and the Buddha. Practicing restraint means keeping precepts and being honorable. In turn, monks should always keep the five basic precepts, and this level of restraint and withdrawal from the world provides sufficient power to give protection to others through blessings embodied via *sak yan*,[2] or magical tattoos in Thai.

Most importantly, however, and assuming a monk has the interest and the necessary dexterity to become a tattooist, he must acquire the knowledge and power required to make effective tattoos. This necessary knowledge takes the form of *katha* used in making tattoo "medicine" and reciting these spells while tattooing. Because all *katha* are recited from memory, master tattooists must have an extensive repertoire of them or else their tattoo magic will be, for the most part, ineffective (Krutak 2012:14).

A learned monk of Wat Bang Phra in Thailand told me, "You can't take getting or giving a tattoo lightly. You have to be physically and mentally prepared every time you do it. It took me ten years to master the art and science of tattooing, including the memorization of the sacred scripts [*katha*] that I tattoo onto my patron's bodies. All great tattoo masters must do this" (Krutak 2012:14).

That being said, tattoos have power because they draw not only on the power of the tattooist but also on his monk mentors, and the Buddha and his teachings. These are all sources of power (Tannenbaum 1987:703).

A MONK'S TATTOOING KIT AND OTHER MAGICAL DEVICES

The *mai sak* (also *mae sak, khem sak*), or tattooing tools, I have seen in Thailand resemble a sharp two-foot-long metal skewer split at one end about two inches to form a needle-sharp pronged tip. Similar devices are also used in Myanmar but they are heavier and shorter, the pronged tip is stouter, and the tool is capped off with a tattoo "weight" that takes the form of a deity or other powerful personage (Singer 1988). Gold and silver tools were said to have been made for members of the Burmese royal family but none has survived to this day (Singer 1988:74). Nevertheless, the space created between the two needle tips acts as a reservoir to hold the tattoo pigment. In Thailand, these tools look much like a shish-kebab skewer used to barbeque meat and vegetables on the grill.

Some monks use a pointilinear style, while others achieve fine line work that looks very machinelike. The inks that the monks use are personal recipes; some are thought to have special "protective" qualities due to their unusual and magical ingredients (Krutak 2012:14). For example, some *ajarns* in Thailand use sandalwood steeped in herbs or white sesame oil to impart protection.

FIGURE 5.6
Collection of *sak yan* (tattoo) counterweights, 2014. © Matthieu Duquenois.

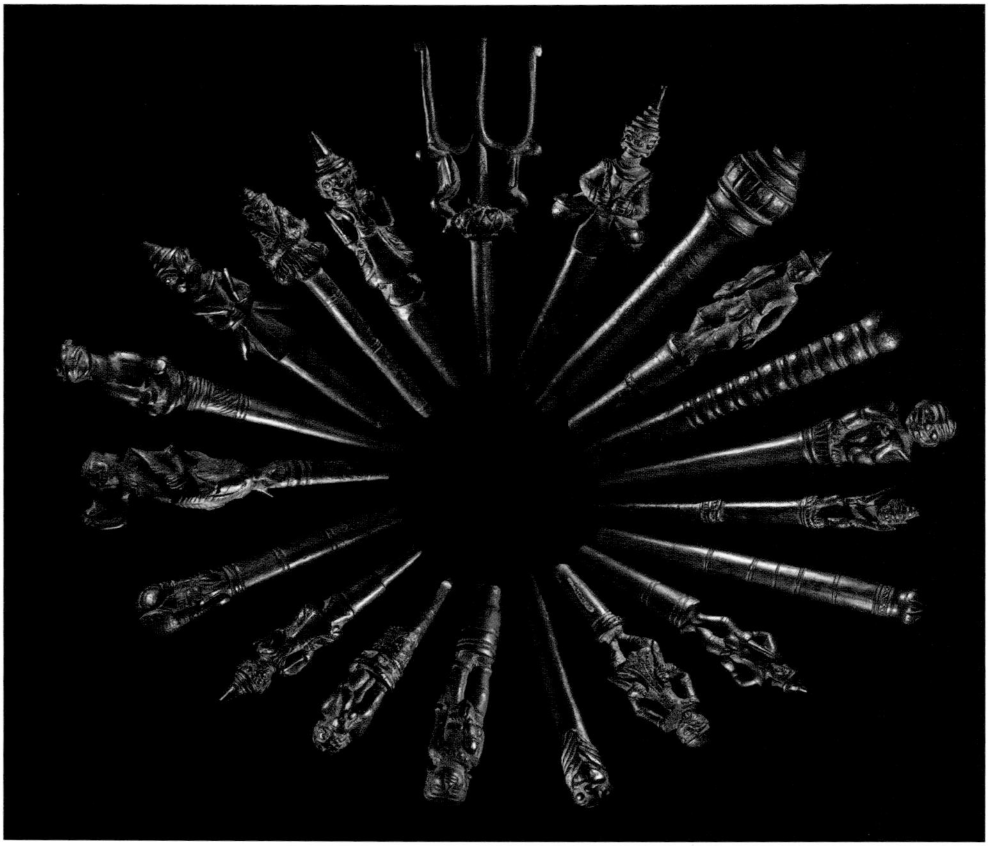

Liquids extracted from wild animals, such as the bile of tigers and bears, and even cobra venom, are mixed into ink for empowerment (Krutak 2016b:69).

One monk mentioned to me that the exfoliated skin of a revered *ajarn* was added to Chinese ink mixed with holy water to make his tattoo pigment. This ink would cause those people who interact with the wearer to behave as if they were in the presence of a monk, because the pigment was imbued with qualities that engendered reverence and respect.[3]

None of the men who enter a monk's working space mumble a word before they are tattooed, and usually two male friends will stretch the client's skin for the tattooist. Some tattoo patrons begin to shake and go into light trances while being tattooed, while others go into deep meditation. Other than the occasional grunt from a semipossessed client, the area in which the monks work remains eerily quiet. Regardless of whether the patron is possessed or not, the monks continue to work the pigment under the skin, stopping only to wipe off the flowing blood. After the tattoo is complete, the monk mumbles a prayer in Pali or Thai/Pali, and blows on the tattoo to activate its potential through a transfer of his *weecha*, or magical power (Krutak 2012:16).

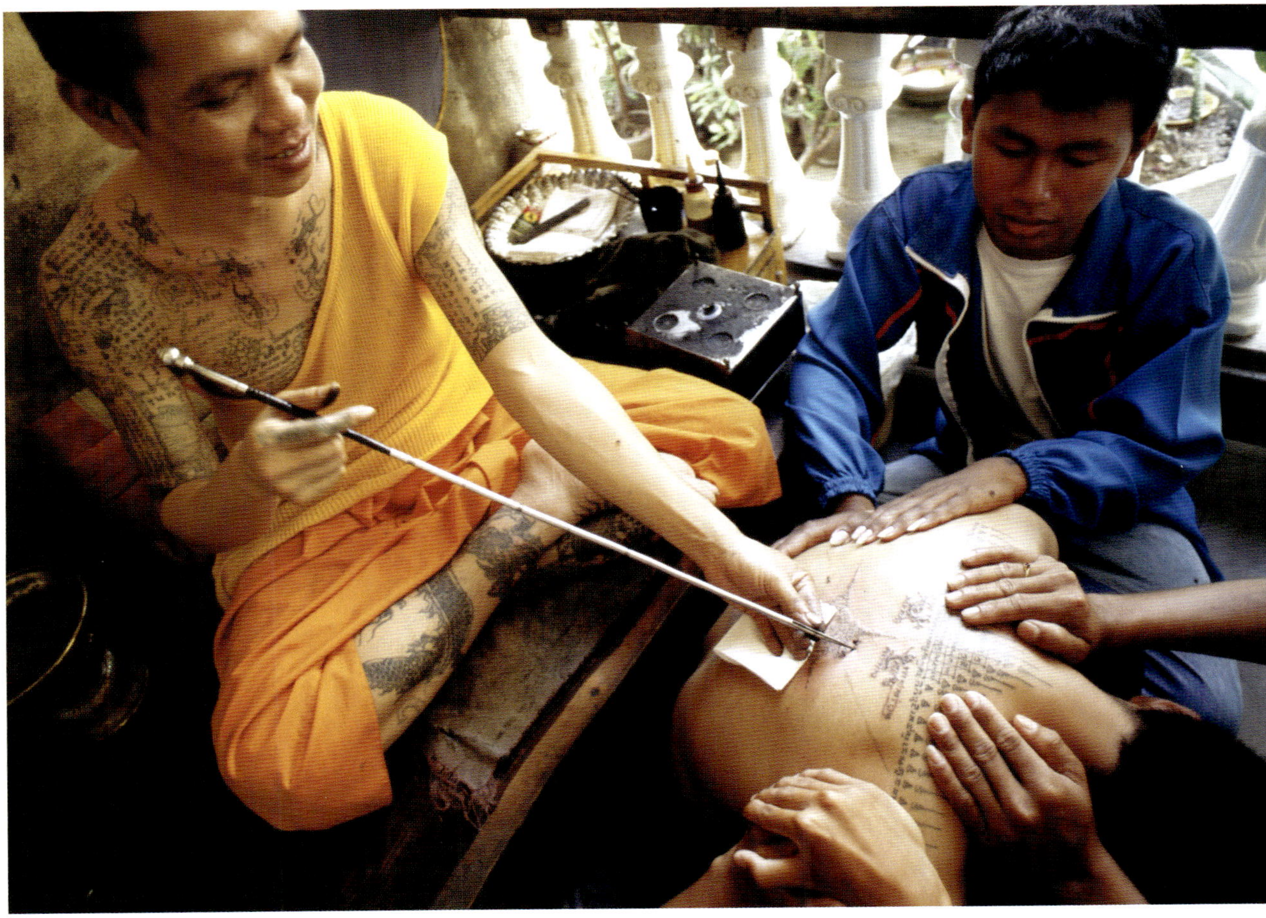

FIGURE 5.7
Buddhist monk Ajarn Luang Pi Paeo applying a tattoo at Wat Bang Phra monastery, Thailand, 2007. *Sak yan* are believed to provide their bearers with good fortune or success in work or business. Other tattoos are thought to add to the personal charisma of the wearer, or to make them more attractive to the opposite sex. In some cases, specific tattoos can turn enemies into friends, while others provide their owners with commanding and attractive speech, which adds to a person's sacred virtue. © Lars Krutak.

This action also fuses the patron with the monk's meditative and transcendental powers, as well as that of the Buddha.

From firsthand experience, I can honestly say that tattooing monks work very quickly. And in the blink of an eye an empowering tiger, holy *katha*, seated buddha, or other magical tattoo comes into being on human flesh. Small tattoos are completed in ten to fifteen minutes, but more complex designs can take twice as long.

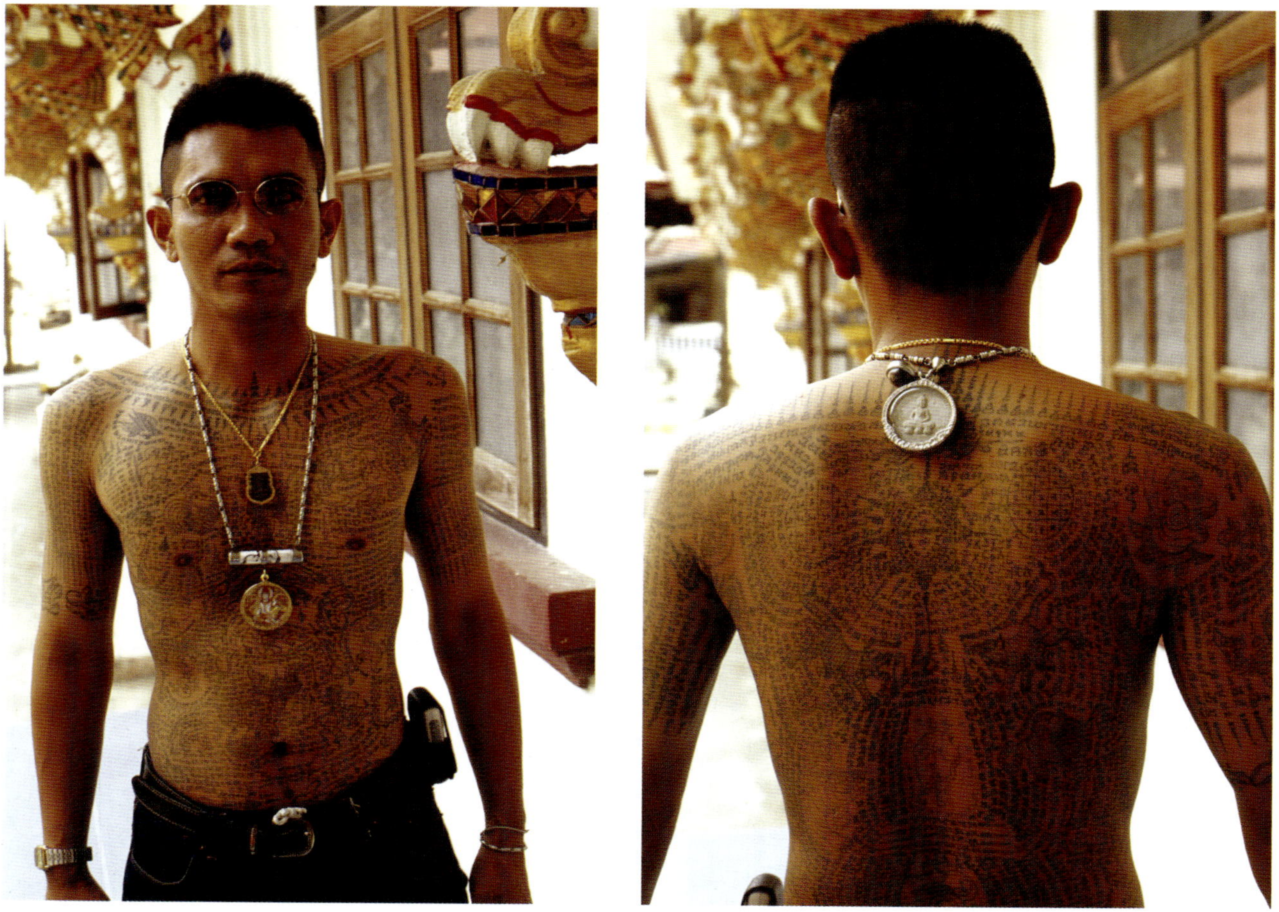

FIGURE 5.8
Tattoo devotee covered in magical tattoos (*left*), Wat Bang Phra monastery, Thailand, 2007. The *unalome*, or "twenty-nine tips," tattoo crosses the top of his shoulders (*right*). Like the carved ivory amulet worn around his neck, each figure beneath the pointed temple spires represents a seated Buddha. This specific tattoo is believed to diffuse any evil thoughts the bearer might possess before he acts on them. © Lars Krutak.

Payment schedules are not fixed, and it is usually up to the client to provide an "offering" to the monk and his temple for their services. These transactions may involve a small amount of cash in addition to a lotus blossom, bundle of incense, and perhaps a couple of packs of regular or mentholated cigarettes.[4] Such gifts are a means to *tham boon* (Thai), or make merit, a Buddhist concept closely akin to (but not identified with) positive karma. Merit seems to grow over time, being augmented by *boon*, karmically positive actions, while at the same time being decayed by *baap*, or sinful action. Merit is often spoken of as the source of good luck, as a religious practice (e.g., praying), and as a kind of moral currency. Any compassionate or wise action is said to create merit, but one of the most powerful ways to make merit is by donating food, money, clothing, or other objects to Buddhist monks. Another way to make merit, outside of becoming a monk, is to fund the construction of a temple or, failing that, to fund the repair or restoration of a temple.

Generally speaking, there are four classes of tattoos that can be received: those that act on others, causing them to like or fear the bearer; those that act on the bearer, increasing his skill with words and causing the listener to do as he asks and instilling him with courage; those that increase his agility; and those that create a protective barrier around the person to prevent animals of all sorts (especially poisonous snakes) from biting, knives from cutting, bullets from entering the body, and fire from burning the body (Krutak 2012:16). These magical tattoos, whether for these or other purposes (e.g., for eternal health), are in a sense like preventive medicine and can be thought of as a kind of vaccination against various diseases and misfortunes.

But there are other tattoos that you cannot see because they are invisible. These are oil tattoos, which are said to be just as powerful as the pigmented variety. Some monks use sesame or coconut oil, which is then mixed with other herbs and sandalwood. Many of the most powerful *ajarns* are covered in these types of tattoos, while others wear a combination of both varieties.

The belief in the potency of these and other forms of magical tattoos is certainly as ineradicable as the indelible designs themselves, but one account from 1881 sheds some negative light on the potency of one particular kind of tattoo. A young Burmese man desired the figure of the great *peguan byeing* bird, or egret, to preserve him from drowning. Once the design was completed, the young man suggested that an experiment be conducted to confirm the power of the tattoo. The British writer J. G. Scott, who authored several works under the pen name Shway Yoe, documented the tale:

> Accordingly, his hands and feet were tied, and he was tossed over the side of a boat into the Rangoon River. The under-currents in the river were very dangerous, and the poor fellow was never seen again. The tattooers, master and assistant, were brought up on a charge of murder [by the ruling British] and convicted of manslaughter, but the great mass of the Burman population thought they were very badly treated and that they were not charlatans because perhaps they made an astrological miscalculation before administering the tattoo. (Yoe [Scott] 1896:47)

Another kind of Burmese tattooing that only highly powerful tattoo masters specialized in was that of *ah kyan say*, or the "violent medicine," which had the power to turn an ordinary person into a *Bawdithada*, or superman—invincible, destructive, and immensely powerful (Singer 1988:75). However, if the ritual that accompanied the tattooing was not properly carried out, the tattoos had the power to unhinge the mind of the client and he would go mad instead. For example, the "deranged" would frequent graveyards, tearing up and trying to devour corpses like ghouls (Yoe [Scott] 1896:44).

The tradition of *ah kyan say* has its origins with the cannibal King Porisada of India, or Bawdithada, as the Burmese call him (Singer 1988:75). His irresistible thirst for flesh, first beef

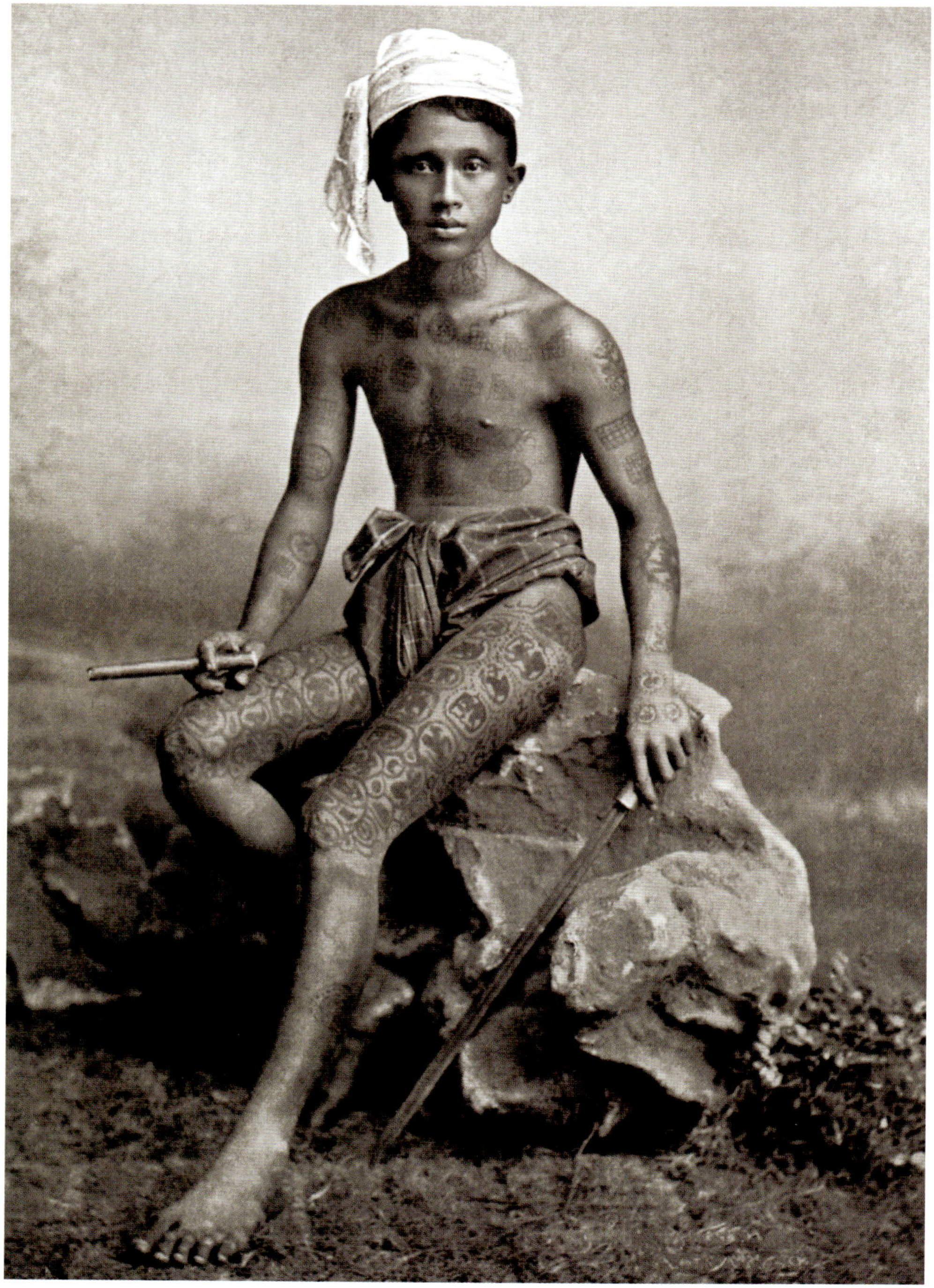

FIGURE 5.9
Burmese youth with extensive body tattooing, ca. 1895. He holds a cheroot in his hand. Collection of the author.

then human, ultimately led to the loss of his kingdom and subsequent banishment to the jungle, where he became a tremendous athlete and was able to "run like a lion," among other incredible feats. Eventually he was "saved" by the incarnate Buddha himself and that is why the *ah kyan say* tattoo is believed to hold so much power if it can be managed by the individual who wears it. Noel Singer (1988) suggested that there are three designs that are associated with him, each depicting an episode in his life, whereas Yoe ([Scott] 1896) explained that still more tattoos embody the power of Bawdithada. A fascinating account of the late nineteenth century describes *ay kyan say* in more detail, and I quote it here at some length:

> One of the most weird and extraordinary superstitions among the Burmans is connected with tattooing, and is called "Bandee-tha" [Bawdithada]. When some credulous Burman wished to become a great warrior, or, more probably, a great thief and robber, he applies to one of these "doctors" [*sayas*], who directs him to procure a piece of flesh about six inches long from a human corpse. The flesh of a man who has been hung, or died on a Saturday is most eagerly sought. Also certain parts of the body, the nose, fingers, and ears especially, having been dried and carefully compounded with various magical drugs, the [tattoo] mixture is then preserved. After sundry ceremonies, the figure of a cat or a demon or "beloo" [*belu*] was tattooed on the patient's breast with the medicine [pigment] prepared, he all the while biting and chewing the piece of raw human flesh. The supposed effect of this wonderful and disgusting operation is to enable the man to leap like a cat prodigious heights and lengths—a hundred feet would be nothing; or else to endow him with the strength, ferocity, and power of a demon.
>
> An instance has been known, where the relatives of a criminal who had been hung sold his body to these "doctors," as they are called, after it had been handed over to them for burial by the authorities. The writer once had a case in which, after, in the performance of his duty, having superintended the execution of a murderer, finding no relatives come forward to claim the body, causing it to be decently interred; but, in consequence of information received, on opening the grave a couple of days afterwards, the body was found mutilated as above described. (Forbes 1878:239–240)

Yoe ([Scott] 1896) added additional details, including the "maddening" effects of such a tattoo on a young Burmese boy he knew. This tattoo was administered by a wandering tattoo master who was not necessarily a monk, although he may have been a disrobed priest, but rather a kind of "doctor" (described by Forbes above) that was likewise called a *saya* in the Buddhist tradition. These men were skilled in both traditional herbal and primary care medicine and channeled the power of the Buddha into the bodies of their clients. They sometimes tutored one or more apprentices and always carried a *parabaik*, or folding book of designs. After the *saya* had painted the desired stencil, he would stretch the skin of the client by placing his feet a few inches from the design and then leaning inward between his parted knees to execute the tattoo. Sometimes the

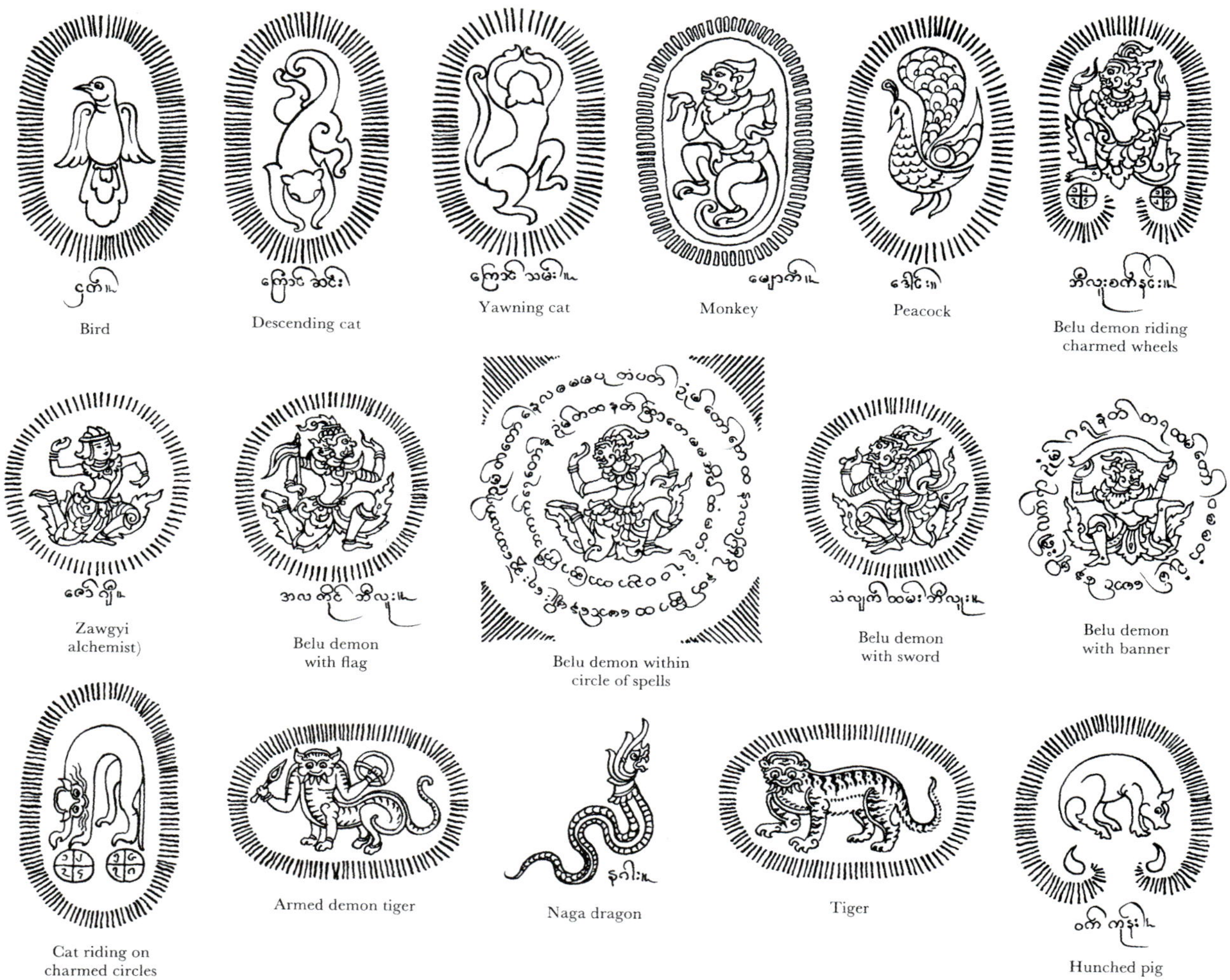

FIGURE 5.10

Various Burmese tattooing motifs. From Singer 1988:79.

client's thighs swelled so badly that he was incapable of walking properly for a week or more. It was recorded that the fatality rate from infection was largely negligible. Perhaps this speaks to the magical power that was believed to embody and emanate from the *saya* himself? Due to the incredible details of the account, I provide it here in full:

> There are but very few sayahs who are acquainted with the necessary drugs and incantations, and fewer people still who have the courage to submit to the operation, for many men are pointed out whose mind has given way under the gruesome process, and who wander about graveyards, gnashing their teeth and fumbling about for human bones to gnaw and mouth. And no wonder, for some tattooers make them chew the raw flesh of a man who has been hanged, while the figure is being tattooed on the breast[!]
>
> Some become Baw-dee-thah-da without knowing it, and without the sickening necessity of mumbling human flesh like a ghoul. I knew an instance in a monastery. The patient was a boarder about fourteen years of age. A Shan tattooer wandering about the country spent a couple of nights there, and the boy, attracted by the fellow's eerie tales, managed to save up a good many tidbits for him from the food going in the monastery. Out of gratitude, and having nothing better to give him, for he was very poor and homeless, the sayah tattooed on the lad a figure with singular drugs, muttering queer phrases the while. Then he went away saying no more than that it would make the boy very strong.
>
> In about a month's time the boy displayed unmistakable signs of being a Baw-dee-thah-da. He leapt enormous heights in the air, jumped about and ran at random, carried with the utmost ease things which no one else could move. The abbot locked him up in a sadeik, the box in which the palm-leaf manuscripts were kept; he got out without injuring the lock in any way, sprang on to the roof of the monastery, forty feet in height, and turned a somersault to the ground without hurting himself in the least. He has been a boy of very soft, easy temper, and now he became fiery and uncertain, and with his vast strength, very dangerous. He only calmed down when a monk preached the law to him.
>
> He was constantly doing marvelous things; one day he walked across the river in front of the monastery, holding a monk's ohk, or food canister, in his hands. The depth of the water was over six fathoms, but it did not reach higher than his waist. On another occasion a tree which was being cut down fell on him. He sank into the ground and came forth quite uninjured. . . . After some years he became a dacoit [brigand], but a holy ascetic came across him, soothed him with the payeht gyee [Pali sermons and forms of worship], and then with a rusty nail and sacred medicines, tattooed out the figure put on with such lamentable results by the Shan sayah. . . . He was fortunate; most Baw-dee-thah-das have to be killed in their sleep. (Yoe ([Scott] 1896:4–45)

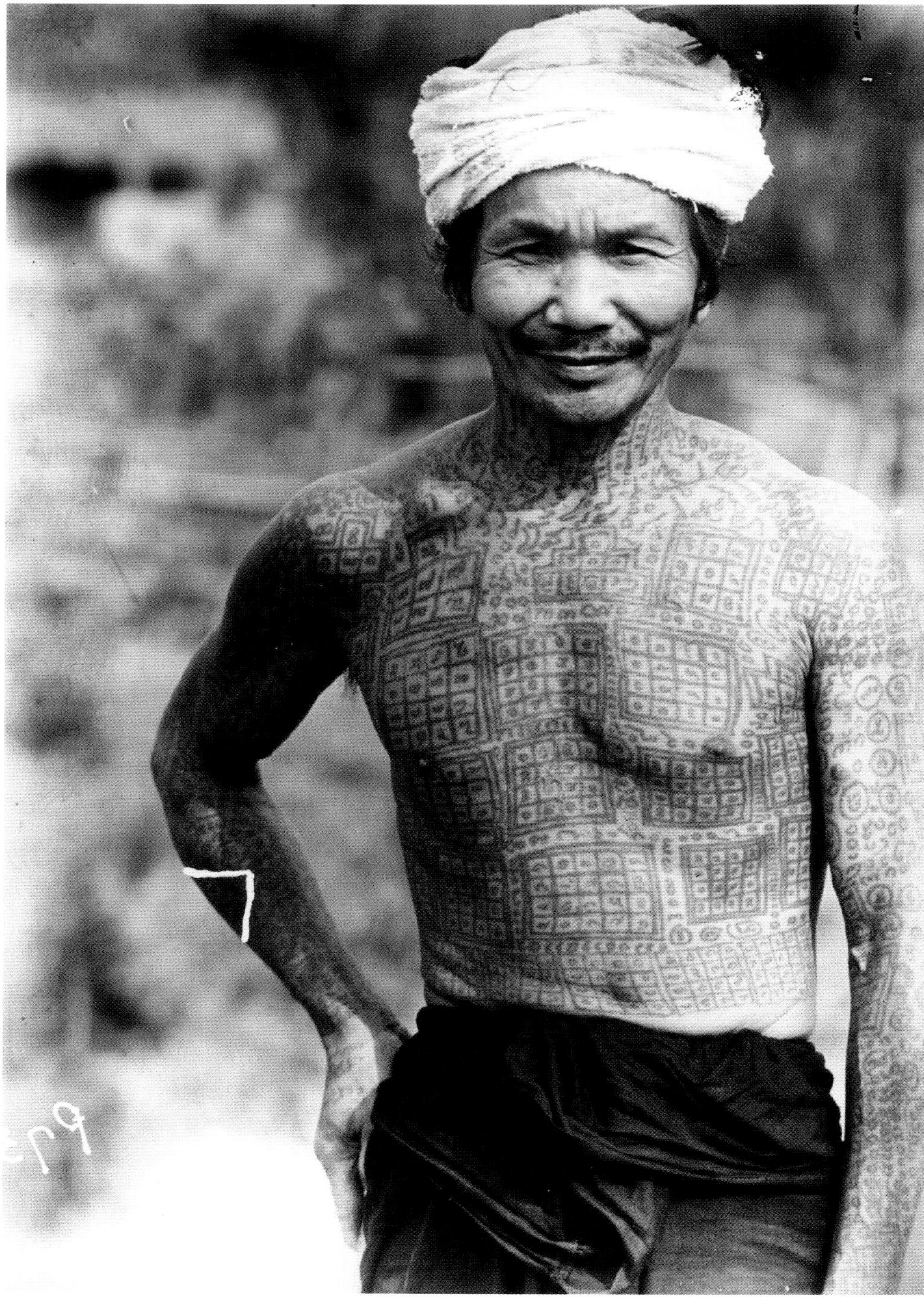

FIGURE 5.11
Tattooed Shan man, Burma, ca. 1940. James Henry Green Charitable Trust Collection. © Brighton & Hove Museums (WAP0073).

Aside from such magical tattoos, other charms were used by men for protective purposes. Sometimes these objects included rubies; balls of mercury; silver, gold, or lead discs; pieces of tortoise shell; and bits of horn that were blessed by a priest and implanted into the skin (Hallett 1890:138). Most of these consecrated objects also contained incantations written on them or mystical animals to enhance their supernatural effect. Engraved fish, monkeys, crabs, or peacocks appearing on these talismans related to the various forms the Buddha assumed in his previous lives before taking his human form (Conway 2006:76). These animals were believed to be imbued with intelligence and wisdom, and wearing them endowed the person with their attributes.

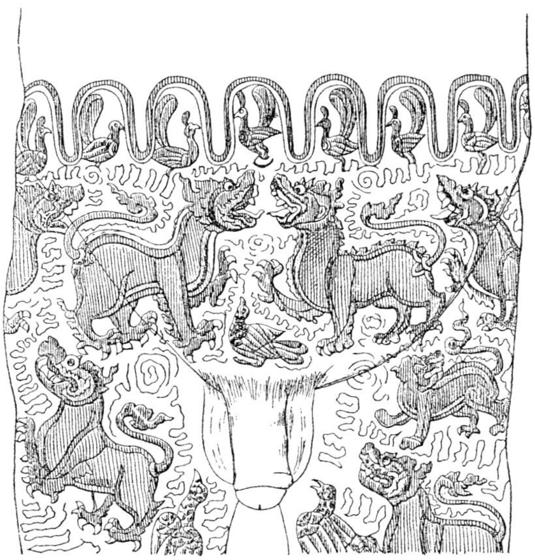

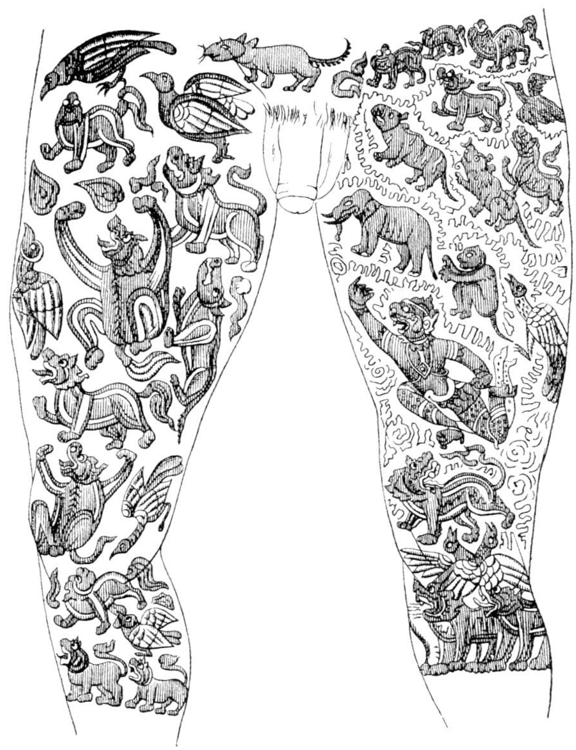

FIGURE 5.12

Heavily tattooed Laotian men with peacock motifs running around the waist (for increased virility and sexual prowess) (*left*), various protective demon and rakshasa figures, a Hanuman motif (*right*), and cats, elephants, lions, rats, and other animals, western Laos, ca. 1880s.

It was said that "every self-respecting Laotian man must get a tattoo" or they "incurred collective moral sanctions" (Bouteiller 1953:521–522). Moreover, untattooed men were not allowed to bathe upstream of the women and no woman would have accepted an unmarked man as a husband. From Bock 1885:260–261, figs. 122–123.

In closing this section, I would like to recount a nearly forgotten story of a very powerful and heavily tattooed nineteenth-century Burmese "sorcerer." His personal tale combines many features concerning my previous discussions of magical tattoos not to mention amuletic implants. Now let me provide some personal background to set the stage.

In 2014, I saw the remains of a heavily tattooed man from Laos at the Musée du quai Branly exhibition *Tattoo* (May 6, 2014–October 18, 2015) in Paris. The preserved skin was from an unidentified man, and it was simply labeled "Piece of Tattooed Skin, Laos, 19th–20th century." I was fascinated by what I witnessed and began searching through archival materials and obscure journal articles in an attempt to identify the man on display, but I was not successful. In turn, I learned about another tattooed man, the Burman warrior-magician Kouabilai, whose skin was removed from his corpse in 1886 and later transported to France. To date, however, it is not known what happened to Kouabilai's tattooed epidermis once it reached Toulouse, since it seems to have disappeared from history shortly after its arrival in Europe.

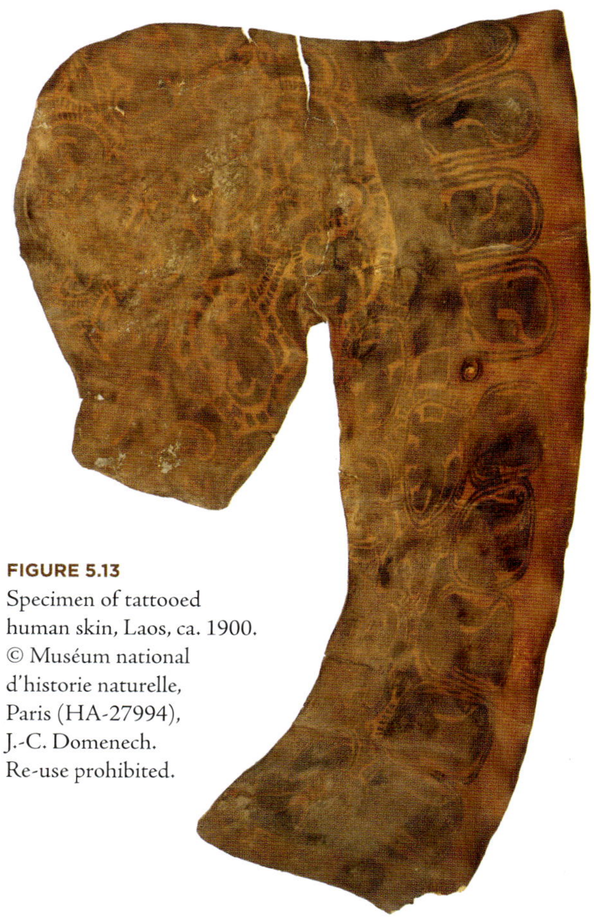

FIGURE 5.13
Specimen of tattooed human skin, Laos, ca. 1900. © Muséum national d'historie naturelle, Paris (HA-27994), J.-C. Domenech. Re-use prohibited.

The extended account of his incredible story, which is presented below, is largely paraphrased from the brief chronicle published by the writer L. Jammes (1900:740) as well as from a communiqué based on the experiences of the medical doctor who performed the flaying (L'Homme 1886).

Kouabilai was a famous wizard hired by rebels in Cambodia during their insurgency against the French in 1885–1886. He stood on the front lines of the rebel troops, exciting them with his gestures and screams. His allies affirmed that he was "the most powerful man on earth and that no human force could terrify him. He possessed sacred objects, *gris-gris* [talismans], and amulets of such virtue that at close range, a rifle bullet was incapable of grazing him" (Jammes 1900:740).

Every warrior respected him, and they solicited a little of his hidden (magical) virtue that made him invulnerable. To all, the Burmese sorcerer gave the warriors who surrounded him a parcel of immunity.

Jammes observed that the rebels were a formidable band, one that, commanded by such a powerful man, held their line for a year against the immense French columns. The French officers affirmed that these warriors could not be Cambodians.

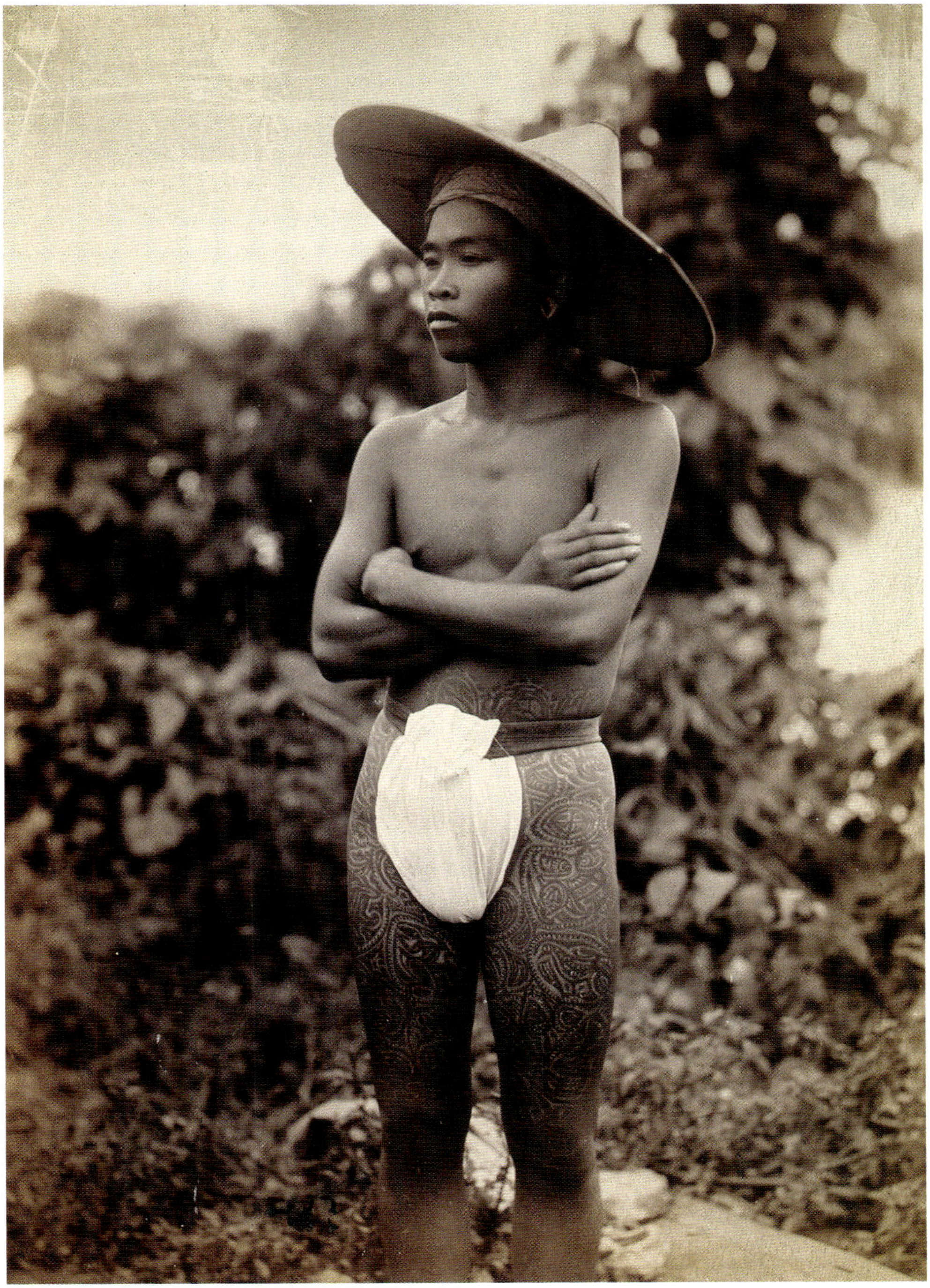

FIGURE 5.14
Young man with elaborate tattoos on his waist and thighs, Burma, ca. 1896. Wellcome Library Collection (645296i).

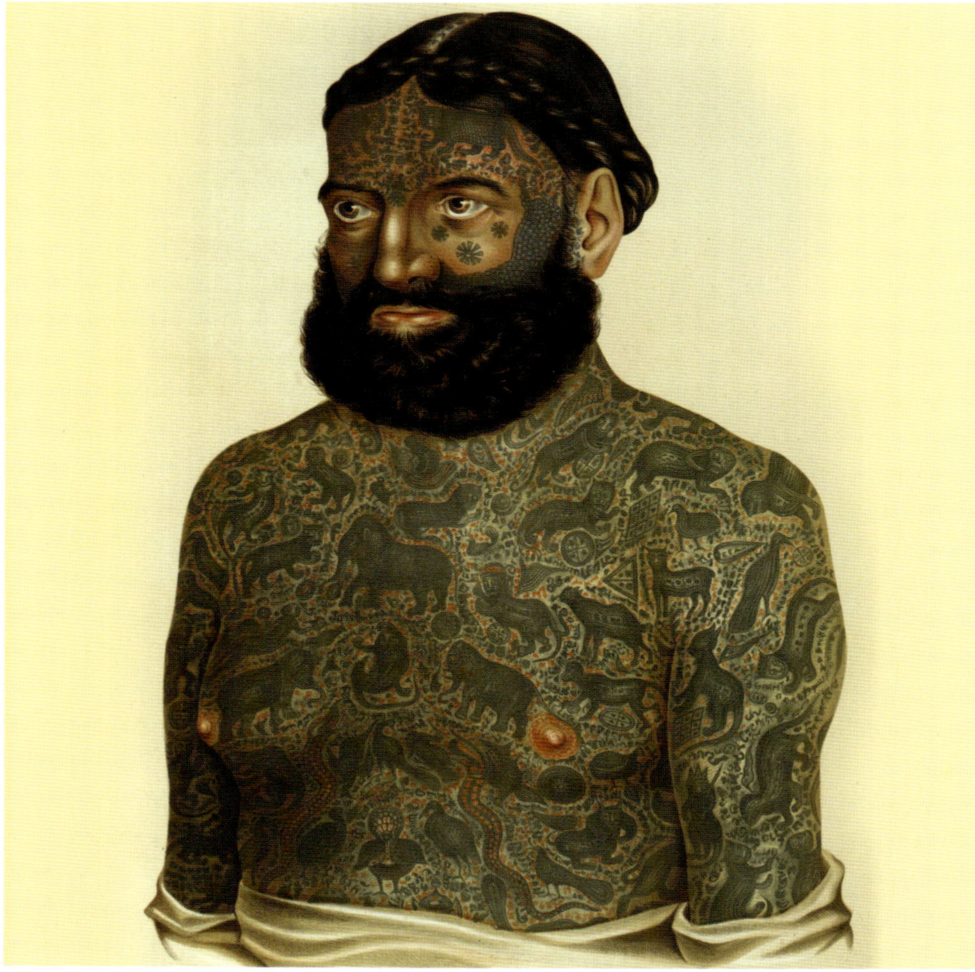

FIGURE 5.15

Portrait of the heavily tattooed circus showman "Prince Constantine," ca. 1874. Of Albanian or Greek descent, Georgius Constantine took part in a French expedition in the early 1870s with the object of penetrating into the interior of India and Burma in quest of gold. During a rebellion, his band was proclaimed hostile on account of their taking up arms against the natives and supplying the rebels with weapons. On the defeat of the insurgents, the prince and eleven of his companions fell into the hands of the (presumably Burmese) government troops. Nine of these were executed; Constantine and two others were spared their lives but condemned to the "tattoo process." This was very severe, for during it one died and the other became blind. In total, the prince came to possess 388 tattoos. The tattooing took three months—the artist working three hours a day—and was so severe that Constantine had to be held down by four men, and submit quietly to the operation on fear of death. After a lengthy imprisonment he escaped, and after four months' tramp through China he was rescued. Eventually, the "Prince" became a circus sideshow attraction. (cf. Gilbert 2000:141–142). Lithograph from Hebra 1875: pl. X.

"They were, in fact, so brave," Jammes wrote (1900:740). And they died in a very brave manner. They were a perpetual threat to the French posts, and the French commander Colonel de Badens resolved to end the fight with this brigade, and eventually sent his best soldiers against Kouabilai's partisans.

After the offensive was launched by the colonel, and despite Kouabilai's miraculous amulets, the sorcerer and his whole band soon fell into the hands of the French. Kouabilai was injured in the thigh and sustained a comminuted fracture of the right femur (L'Homme 1886:670), and fell on a marshy plain. His warriors made every effort to withdraw him from the French forces. Instead of shooting him, as was customary at that time, the extraordinary personage was captured, had his wound dressed, and was sent alive to the resident general of Cambodia (Jammes 1900:740).

Jammes observed that the capture of Kouabilai made enormous "noise" throughout the country. The Cambodians could not believe that a wizard of his power had allowed himself to be injured by the projectiles of the French. Nevertheless, people across the country would speak of his warlike prowess: "[I]n all the huts, in the evening, by torchlight, only the great deeds of Kouabilai were mentioned," Jammes (1900:740) wrote.

Although it had been dressed, the wizard's wound worsened dangerously, despite the care of a naval doctor named Maurel who was deeply interested in the fate of this unfortunate man. Amputation became necessary due to the onset of gangrene but unfortunately was not successful. The warrior-sorcerer died the next day in excruciating pain.

During his illness, Jammes had asked to see this extraordinary man, who filled the capital city of Phnom Penh with news of his name. "He was very tall for an Oriental and surely represented one of the most beautiful specimens of his breed," Jammes (1900:740) proclaimed. "But what was a remarkable rarity about him were the tattoos that covered his body, from the soles of the feet to the beginning of the neck. Kouabilai's body was a marvel worthy of attracting the attention of ethnographers," he wrote. Kouabilai's tattoos, "of incredible finesse," were documented by a French artist and the good doctor Maurel, who resolved to preserve his skin as an ethnographic curiosity "worthy of having its place in a national museum" (Jammes 1900:740).

Jammes was present at the tattoo removal operation. During the surgical procedure, while the men inspected the skin of Kouabilai on the cadaver's slab, they were greatly surprised to find grainy places of extreme hardness on the skin, like the pellets from a shotgun blast (L'Homme 1886:670). Cross cuts were made on the specified parts, which revealed the presence of precious stones, small discs of gold and silver, or rather amulets that the Burmese had introduced under Kouabilai's epidermis to protect him against spirits and other misfortunes. Jammes and Maurel thus discovered a dozen such stones in the fat of Kouabilai's thighs and a few more in the skin of his neck. A superb sapphire, of a splendid blue color like water, was brought to light near the navel. In sum, "at least sixty" of these amulets were distributed across the surfaces of the body, especially within the upper limbs and torso (L'Homme 1886:671).[5]

"The scalp was a real treasure chest," Jammes (1900:670) exclaimed. "A ruby the size of a millet seed appeared under the fingers of the doctor in charge of removing the famous sorcerer's scalp." But alas, "all of these gems did not protect him from being attacked with the terrible weapons that the Whites from the West had flooded into the country," Jammes concluded.

FIGURE 5.16
Tattooed *mahout* (elephant trainer) Mr. Ya displays the *gâo yôt* or "nine peaks temple tattoo" below his neck that repels evil from all directions, 2007. He received the sacred and powerful *chang* (elephant) backpiece from his village monk because he believed he would absorb some of the elephant's power; to this day he has never been injured despite the dangers associated with his profession. Buddhists believe the Buddha himself was an elephant before he assumed his human form. Mr. Ya noted that his tattoos help his elephant companion recognize him—they have poor eyesight—because they are part of his physical identity. © Lars Krutak.

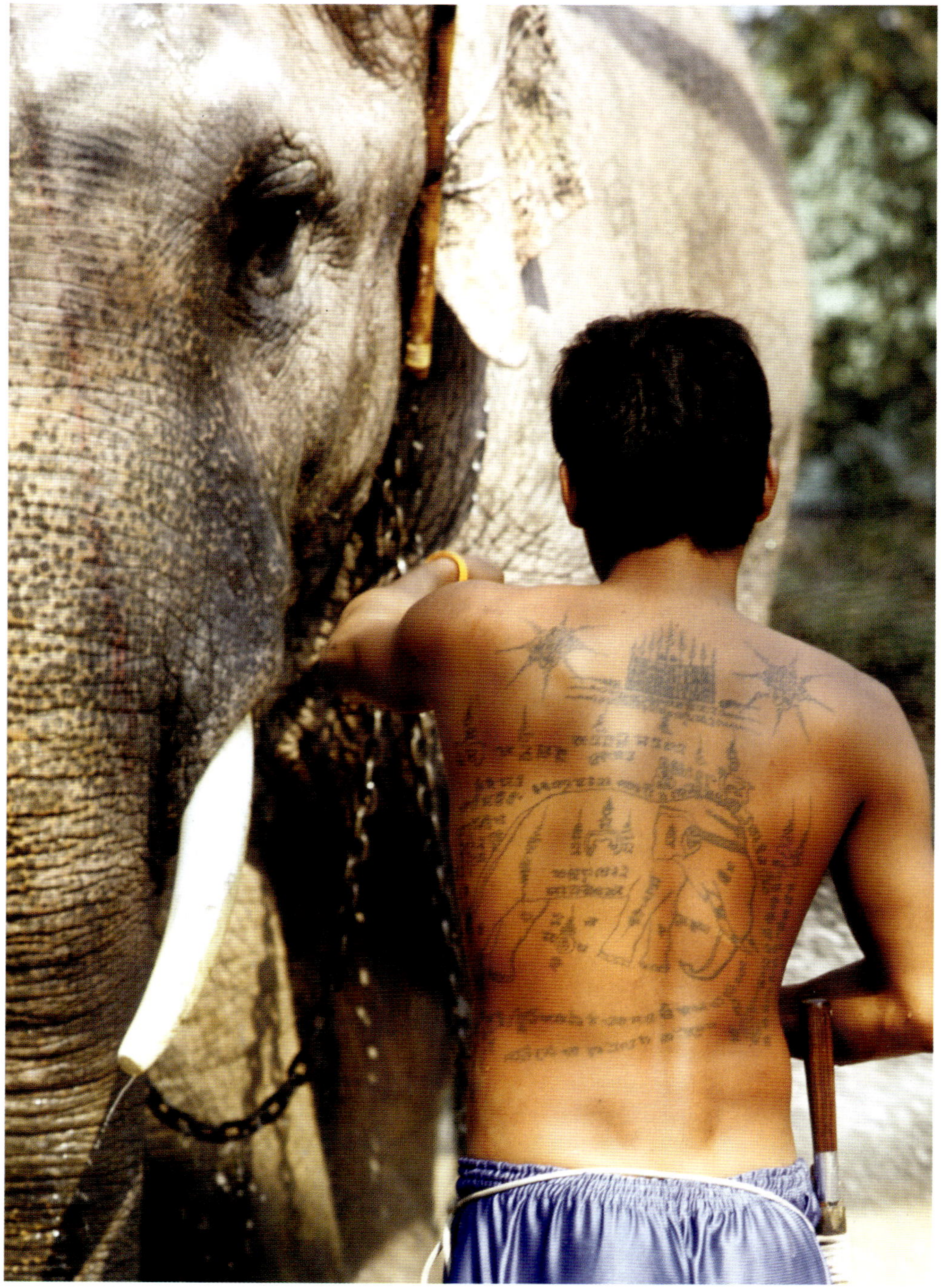

TRIBAL TATTOO TRADITIONS OF VIETNAM AND LAOS

Apart from the magical tattoos of the Hindu-Buddhist tradition, Indigenous tribes inhabiting Mainland Southeast Asia and parts of Yunnan (China) also practiced unique forms of facial and body marking, including the Chin (Myanmar) and Dulong (China), who are discussed in subsections below. Women of the Mang tribe of China and Vietnam also wore tattoos on their faces, but today they have faded to the point where they are nearly indistinguishable. Called *khuoi luong*, these greenish-hued markings were necessary for an easy journey into the afterlife. If a woman was not marked with them before her death, it was believed that her ancestors would burden her with difficult labors. In turn, her tormented soul would cry out to her living relatives on earth to lighten her heavy load (Laukien 2009:30).

Brao and Katu men and women inhabiting the Bolaven Plateau of southern Laos and neighboring Vietnam were also inscribed with facial tattoos and other motifs on the body.[6] These tribes are culturally and linguistically (i.e., Mon-Khmer speakers) related, but not since the 1920s have tribal members had their faces tattooed as a rite of passage into adulthood.

I myself have not visited any of the tattooed tribes of Laos or Vietnam, but two of my friends have: the Croatian tattoo artist Sasha Aleksandar and the tattoo journalist Michael Laukien (a.k.a. Travelin' Mick). The former noted that Brao tattooists, who were male, employed rattan thorns to prick the skin,[7] whereas the latter observed that acacia tree thorns were used (Laukien 2004:27). Tattoo pigment was a form of vegetable carbon manufactured from the charred leaves of an unidentified local plant; this soot was combined with charcoal and water and mixed in a coconut shell. After the skin pokes were made, the pigment was vigorously rubbed into the open wounds to effect a permanent mark.

Due to linguistic barriers, however, the nomenclature of the Indigenous tattoo patterns of the Brao were not recorded by my colleagues. Another recent traveler to the Brao, the photographer Dylan Goldby, made one additional ethnographic note. His tattooed elderly informants were emphatic that their facial tattoos repelled the attacks of tigers.

For the Katu, specific tigers could be the manifestation of a dead spirit that could become malevolent toward humans (Le Pichon 1938:385). The Katu referred to the tiger as *abhuy*, or spirit (Århem 2014:319), and the worst fate that could befall an individual was death by tiger attack, a rare event. If this occurred, the entire village of the deceased was tabooed and abandoned after all the animals living there were killed. After the taboo period was observed (one or more months), the villagers lived in the forest. During this timeframe, they could not eat the flesh of buffalo nor could they rebuild their homes (Le Pichon 1938:396). Moreover, if a tiger was purposefully hunted, another rare occurrence, the entire community participated in ritual ceremonies that were larger than any other. Over the course of these events, the tiger's meat had to be completely consumed, and if the accompanying gong and drum music fell silent at any time during the ceremony, it was believed the tiger's soul could consume the villagers (Århem 2014:319). After the rituals had been completed, the tiger's complete skeleton was interred deep in the forest.

Notwithstanding the above, the facial tattoos of Brao women form a circular band that runs around nearly the entire edge of the face. The primary element of this tattoo appears at the

FIGURE 5.17
Tattooed Brao woman wearing large earplugs, Laos, Sekong Province, 2008. The forehead mark is a probable derivative of the "dancing lady" forehead tattoo with outstretched arms worn by the Katu of Vietnam. © Yves Picq.

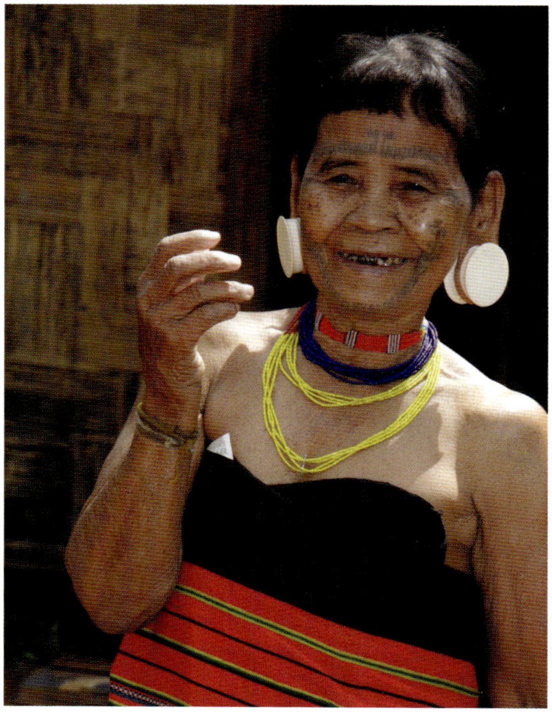

center of the forehead and resembles a small anthropomorph standing upright with arms outstretched. The neighboring Katu once employed a very similar motif, but it was larger in size.

More specifically, the Katu of Vietnam employed a popular motif called the *padil yaya*, or "dancing lady," in their tattooing traditions. The motif was inked in the middle of the forehead or on other parts of the body, and was also incorporated as a decorative element in textiles, the *guöl* (community house) sculptures at the village gate, and gravestones (Le Pichon 1938). But the symbol was also the name of a dance that was performed during major animal sacrifices, agricultural and rain prayer ceremonies, and warfare rituals (e.g., celebrations for the return of successful warriors).

The Katu, like their linguistic relatives the Sedang, wore small dot-like tattoos at the corner of their mouths. The Katu also applied carbon-based cruciform and solar motifs to the center of their foreheads, and these tattoos, as well as others (stars) and the "dancing woman," were worn on the arms and/or chest. Other designs, including a swastika-type motif circumscribed within a rosette, were once worn in pairs above each nipple on the chest.

The French scholar Louis Bezacier (1951) stated that *padil yaya* tattoos were not literal examples of a dancing woman; rather they were physical manifestations of the human soul and offered protection from lurking spirits.[8] In Katu belief, the head was the seat of the soul and might leave the body during sleep, sickness, and/or dreaming. The soul exited the head through the ear and traveled to a "second world," where it could be harmed or captured by spiritual entities (cf. Guilleminet 1952:400). The tattoo acted as a type of "sentry" in the present world, since through its physical manifestation on the body any malevolent spirit visiting the present or "first world" would be led to believe that the individual's soul was close at hand and that the individual was in a wakeful and healthy state rather than disembodied in the second world, where it was susceptible to danger (Bezacier 1951:40). Other writers have suggested the tattoo marked the way home for the soul after it traveled to the spirit world. Bezacier (1951) added that the *padil yaya* tattoo also activated the possessor's intelligence, will, and wisdom, so that the person would embark only on successful enterprises. Generally speaking, village leaders and warriors, not women, were the recipients of the *padil yaya* tattoo.

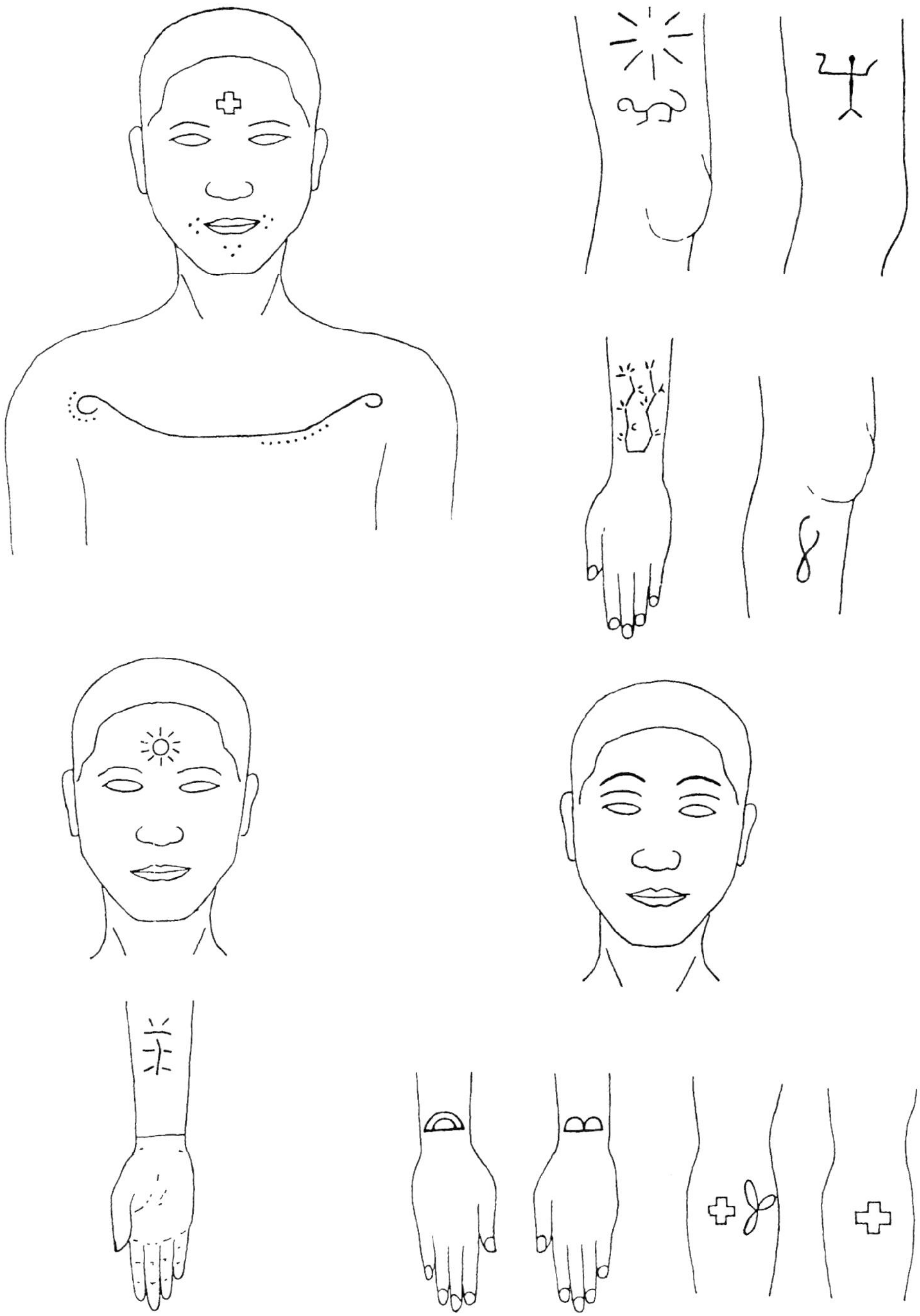

FIGURE 5.18
Types of tattoo motifs that are believed to have acted as a form of prayer to the agricultural deity Grandmother Rice, ca. 1940. Katu elders recently interviewed in Vietnam said that tattoo motifs related to the "dancing lady" varied greatly from one individual to another, including a round spot, three spots, the sun, and so on (Tuan 2004). From Bezacier 1943: fig. 5, 7–8.

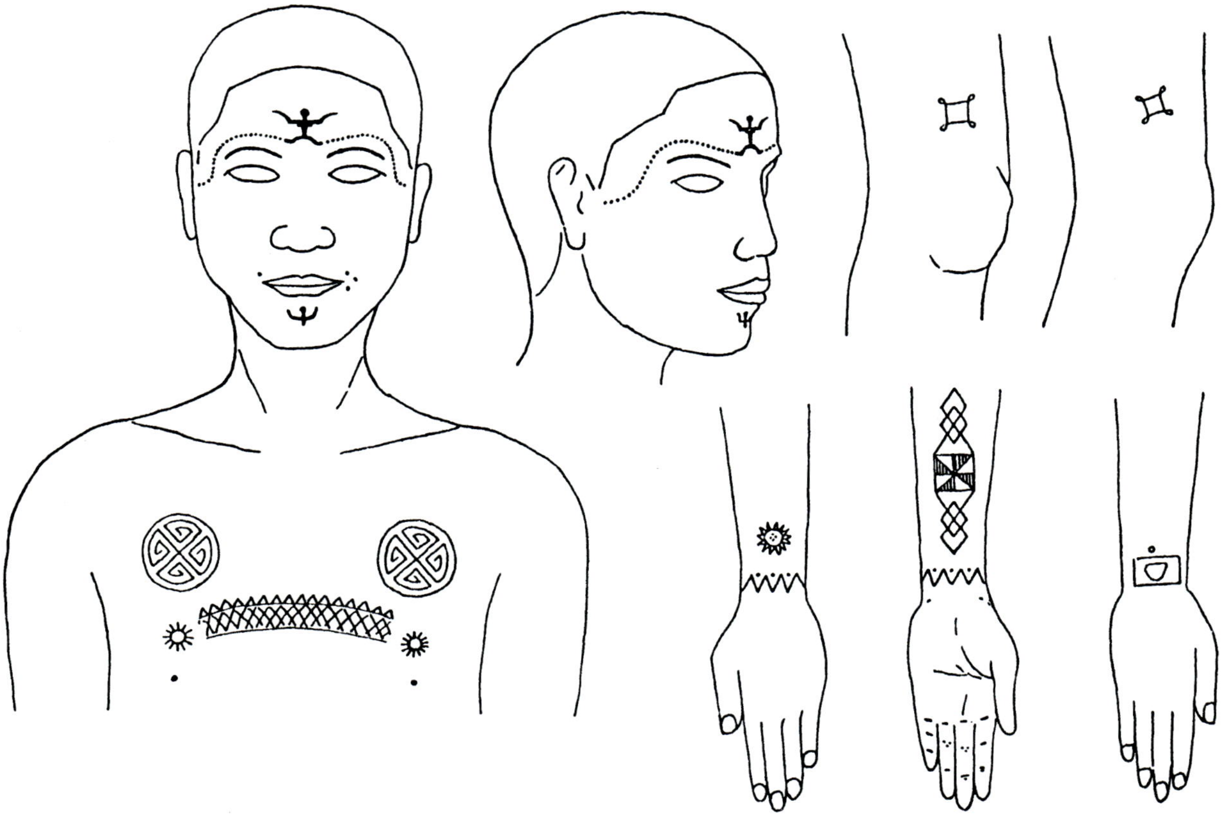

FIGURE 5.19
Illustration of the Katu *padil yaya* tattoo motif (forehead) and other tattoo designs, ca. 1940. From Bezacier 1943: fig. 4.

Other researchers now suggest that the "dancing lady" has a deeper significance because it ultimately symbolizes Grandmother Rice, a major agricultural deity in the Katu pantheon (Århem 2014:229; Tuan 2004). When compared to the choreography of the sacred *padil yaya* dance, the characteristic features of the tattoo motif can be deciphered. During the dance, which is held prior to agricultural (i.e., rice) and other significant annual rites,[9] the hands of the female performers face the sky in their attempts to petition the gods of heaven and earth for their favors (Tuan 2004:48).

More specifically, the *padil yaya* was danced during the rice seedling ceremony to implore Grandmother Rice and good spirits for a successful crop and harvest. In the festival of the new rice, rice seeds were placed on the dancer's hands as a direct offering to Grandmother Rice, the goddess of rice.

The neighboring Sedang believe the fertility of their rice fields is directly related to the power of the "rice soul" of the cultivator's house (Schrock 1966:741). The strength of the *mahua phae* (rice soul) can be empowered through specific rituals performed by the *tyin*, or head woman of the household. The rice soul is believed to reside in her cooking hearth (Schrock 1966:741).[10]

Le Anh Tuan (2004) visited several Katu settlements but no elders continued to carry the *padil yaya* tattoo. However, one elderly woman was seen bearing a large tattooed spot on her forehead for protection against "spells" (Tuan 2004:57). Whether this motif was derived from the sun was not recorded, although in many Indigenous tattooing traditions heliolatrous motifs are believed to possess purificatory properties. The neighboring Sedang believed the "spirit of the sun represents fertility" (Schrock 1966:741).

A song collected by Jean Le Pichon (1938:384) reveals the Katu association between the sun's rays and fertility, as well as the connection between rice and the spiritual realm:

—Rice, good rice cooked in the pot!
I will carry a bowl of it to my fathers' tomb,
Because the spirits love rice,
The good rice that grows in the *ray* [swidden fields].
    —The spirits make it ripen,

Spreading rain and warm sun
Because they love rice,
The good rice that grows in the *ray* [swidden fields].
    —At the harvest festival,

We will kill a buffalo:
All the spirits will come to rejoice
Around the *guöl* [community house].
    —Because this year the rice is beautiful,

And the spikes are heavy,
And they bow their heads to the ground:
Each woman will fill a hundred baskets!
    —Rice gives strength and courage!

This year our granaries will be full;
We will eat rice every day,
The good rice that grows in the *ray* [swidden field]!

Facial Tattoos of the Southern Chin of Myanmar

JENS UWE PARKITNY

Myanmar is home to the largest group of traditionally face-tattooed women in Asia: the women of the Southern Chin. The Chin, who are of Tibeto-Burmese descent, are one of over 130 distinct ethnic groups living in the country. What might sound like a homogenous group of people is actually a very diverse one. In the nationwide censuses of 1983 and 2014, the Myanmar government grouped the Chin into fifty-three subgroups speaking over forty different languages and dialects. The closest linguistic relatives to the Chin are the Naga of Northwest Myanmar and Northeast India.

It is not known when the Chin first settled in their current territory of Western Myanmar. Scholars suggest that their ancestors were descended in part from groups immigrating into Burma from the north, starting about the beginning of the Christian era. Some of the groups, however, might have been in Burma already or "in the remote past, long before a date indicated by any present historical evidence" (Lehman 1963:22).

Chin ethnic groups enjoy some similarities in material culture and customs; however, only the "Southern Chin" practiced female facial tattooing. Southern Chin groups dwell predominantly in Mindat, Kanpelet, Matupi, and Paletwa Townships in Southern Chin State. Their villages are also situated along the banks of the upper Kaladan and Lemro Rivers in western Rakhine State, as well as in a few villages and towns in the adjacent Magway region, an administrative division in central Myanmar.

Whereas the Naga of India and Myanmar practiced male and female facial tattooing, the Southern Chin tattooed the faces only of young women. Chin groups that settled in Northern Chin State as well as in India and Bangladesh did not practice facial tattooing.

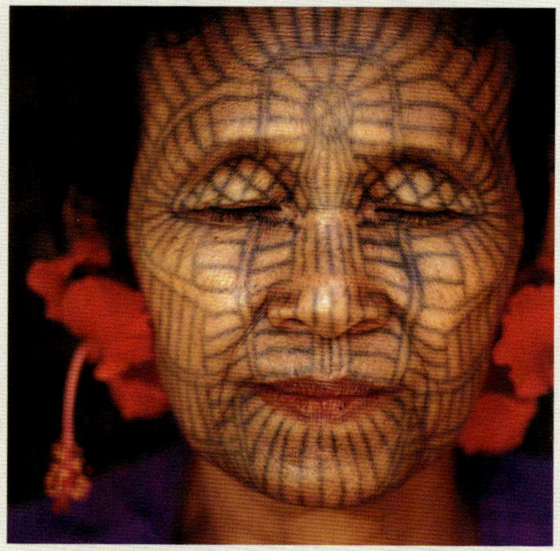

FIGURE 5.20
Laytu Chin elder Daw Ma Hla Oo, Northern Rakhine State, 2004. © Jens Uwe Parkitny.

The last confirmed traditional facial tattooing session of a Chin girl took place twenty years ago in a remote village in Myebone Township, Rakhine State. This Laytu Chin girl, Khin Htay, was twelve years old when the intricate tattoo patterns of her group were applied to her forehead, cheeks, nose, chin, and eyelids. This is quite remarkable considering that facial tattooing in Myanmar was banned because of "health concerns" by the Union Revolutionary Council, the supreme governing body of Burma from 1962 to 1974. This ban continues to this day. In remote areas, however, tattooing continued to be practiced in Chin communities, because here even the long arm of the government was not able to reach these far-flung settlements.

For this reason, Myanmar maintains the largest population of heavily face tattooed women in Asia today. Incredibly, the practice stopped only two decades ago, whereas among other Indigenous Peoples in other Southeast Asian countries it ceased much earlier.

After the tattooing ban, Chin tattooists who were caught performing their occupation were forced to serve time in prison.[11] Eventually, the practice was discontinued because of governmental oversight and the influence of Buddhist and Christian missionaries (Htwe 2013). These cultural outsiders established a permanent presence in the farthest corners of Chin and Rakhine State, and strongly discouraged what they perceived to be a "heathen" practice.

Although it is known today why tattooing is no longer practiced, little is known about how the custom began or what the different patterns and symbols mean. Furthermore, it remains a mystery why only some Chin groups living in a relatively small and geographically confined region practiced facial tattooing vis-à-vis other Chin populations who did not.

Perhaps the earliest historical account of the facial tattooing tradition was provided by the British diplomat Michal Symes in 1795. The illustrated account depicted "Kayn," or Chin, tattooing and briefly described it as follows: "[B]ut the most remarkable part was her face, which was tattowed all over in lines mostly describing segments of circles." As an "unaccustomed beholder," Symes believed the effect was "truly hideous" (Symes 1800:446).

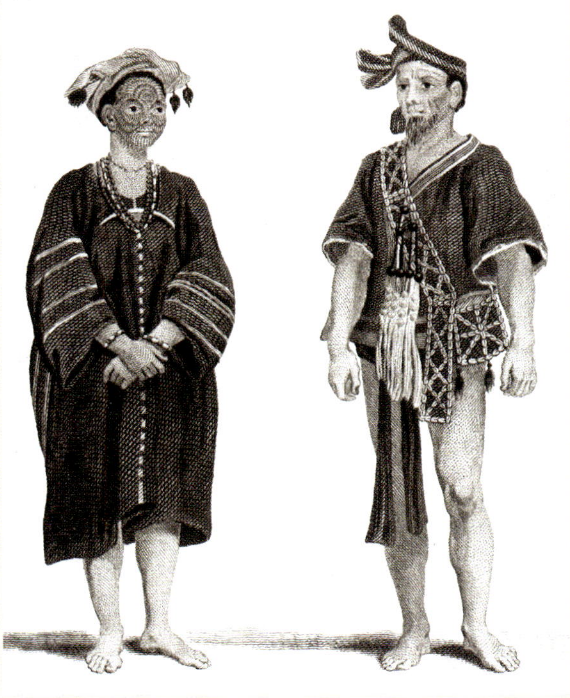

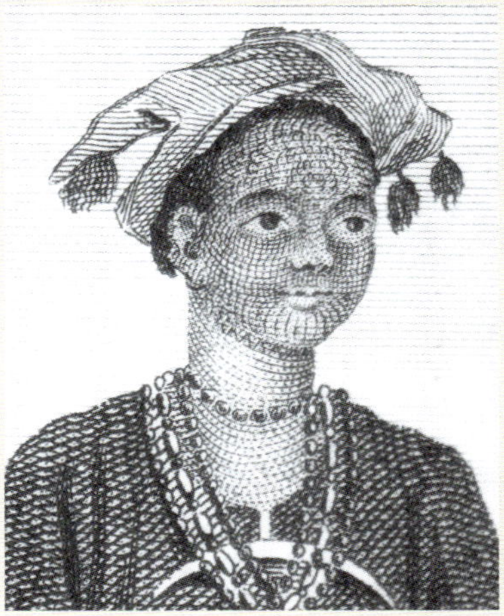

FIGURE 5.21
The oldest published depiction of a tattooed Chin woman (*left*), and a close-up of her face (*above*), ca. 1795. From Symes 1800.

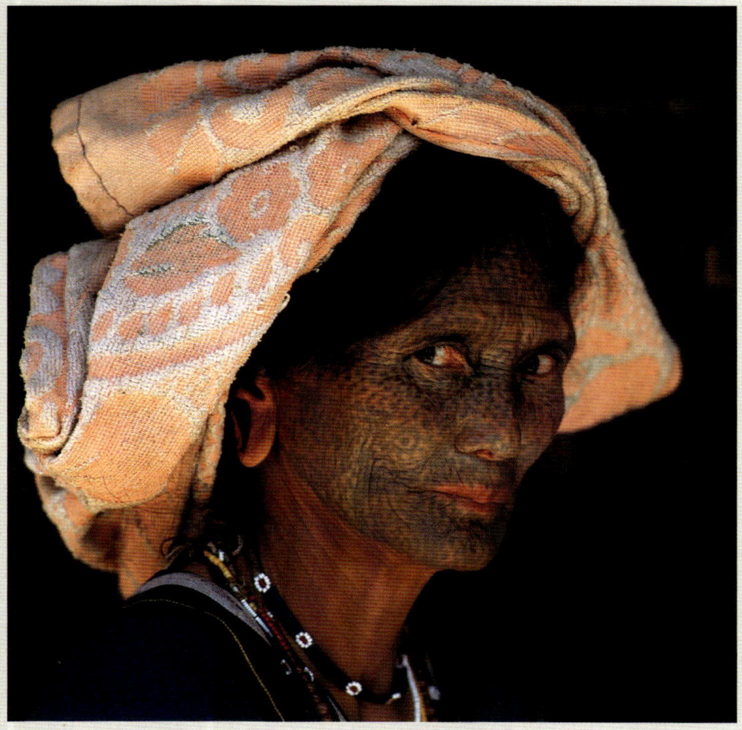

FIGURE 5.22
M'khan Chin tattoo bearer Daw Mna Thi, 2004. © Jens Uwe Parkitny.

Other officials of the British administration who encountered "Kayn" "Khengs," and "Khyens" tribes in the Chin Mountains and the Arakan Hills during colonial rule (1824–1948) shared a similar deprecatory view on these "tribal" women with facial tattoos. They were perceived as "disfigured" (Dalton [1872] 2007) and of being "lamentably conspicuous" in lacking female beauty altogether (Hughes 1881).

It might well be that over time this colonial viewpoint gave birth to the tale that the Chin disfigured the faces of their beautiful young girls with tattoos so that "the dominant race" would not carry them off "in lieu of tribute" (Dalton [1872] 2007:114). Nowadays, the prevalent story still being told to visitors in Myanmar is that the Chin started to tattoo the faces of their young girls to prevent the Burmese kings from raiding Chin villages and enslaving the young women living there.

Historically, there is no evidence that any of the kings who ruled in the current territory of Myanmar ordered frequent raids of Chin villages to kidnap women. British administrators during the colonial occupation as well as scholars doubt that this is the root cause for introducing the facial tattoo practice (Hughes 1881; Lehman 1963). However, there is historical evidence that groups in the Chin and Arakanese Hills were fierce raiders that frequently came down from the mountains to ransack Burmese villages on the plains and abduct women and children (Dalton [1872] 2007; Hart 1897; Hughes 1881).[12]

The only comprehensive anthropological field study on the Chin and their social structure, material culture, and customs was conducted in 1957–1958 by the anthropologist Frederick Lehman (1963). This study briefly mentions the practice of facial tattooing among Southern Chin groups, describing it as "part of the local sociocultural symbolism," and noting that each "tribe has its own designs" (Lehmann 1963:37). Not much additional information on the subject is presented, except that the Matu Chin "tattoo their women's faces with a very different, much less closely spotted design" than the M'Khan and that "while M'Kang [M'Khan] tattooing is heavier than Ng'Men [Mün], that of Southern Kanpelet is denser still" (Lehman 1963:85–86).

Until recently, the specific patterns of each group that practiced facial tattooing were neither researched nor documented (Parkitny 2007, 2010, 2017), and the question concerning how many different facial tattoo patterns existed among the Southern Chin cannot be satisfactorily answered. No written or verbal accounts exist that would deliver any clues. What can be said for certain is that the intricate tattoo design that Michael Symes (1800) saw on the face of the Chin woman he met in November 1795 was not a pattern that continues to exist on the faces of Chin women living today.

Having traveled the Southern Chin Hills and upper Kaladan and Lemro Rivers and some of their tributaries between 2001 and 2014, I can state that the patterns vary geographically. Altogether, I was able to document thirteen different group and subgroup patterns (e.g., three different main patterns among the Laytu). Subtle variations within the base patterns distinguish clan members from one another and thereby establish socio-kinship identities. These baseline marks were not copied by other clans and functioned as a kind of "hallmark." One Sunghtu Chin woman told me that if another clan had copied such motifs, "that would have meant war" (Parkitny 2010:19). I should also note here that within each Chin group or subgroup, every design is unique in the sense that the tattoo is "customized" to the individual features of a woman's face (Parkitny 2010:12).

Southern Chin montane groups, such as the M'Khan (M'Kan), Mün (Ng'men, Muun), Yindu Dai (Zindu), N'Gha (Ya), Hmoye (Nghmoye), Matu, and Ubtu (Uppu, Ubun), use rather simple designs, consisting mainly of dots (M'Khan, Matu, Hmoye), interrupted vertical lines with dots (Yindu Dai and N'Gha), half-circles and vertical lines, dots, and a Y-post-shaped rune on the forehead (Mün), or no pattern at all but a completely blackened face (Ubtu). The designs of the Southern Chin hill groups ("Highland Chin") are relatively simple and lack complexity as compared to the designs used as tribal identity markers among the various groups living along the Lemro River, such as the Laytu, Sunghtu and the Sutu (Sone-glai).

One group that has settled on the banks of the upper Lemro River in Southern Chin State is the Magan; they are not to be confused with the M'Khan who dwell in the northeast corner of the region further up in the mountains. The tattoos that adorn the faces of Magan women are composed of a grid with squares filled with dots. A flowerlike design ornaments the left and right corners of the forehead. The dominating design elements, such as dots and vertical and horizontal lines, are typically used by the Highland Chin groups and not by groups living along the Lemro further downstream. The Magan design is more elaborate than that of other groups living higher up in the mountains. The design of the Hmoye Chin looks very similar but lacks certain features. In its sophistication the Magan pattern appears almost like a link between the rather less complex patterns of the Highland Chin, and the sophisticated patterns of the Lemro River Chin groups. What can be said as a rule is that the further one moves down the mountains and downstream along the Lemro River, the more intricate the facial tattoo patterns become.

Nicknamed "spider women" because their tattoo resembles the design of a spider web spanning the entire face, the tattooed Laytu Chin women stand apart. Their facial tattoo is a visual testimony to superb craftsmanship, considering that only rattan thorns served as the tattoo implement. Three or four thorns were bound together to create two different implements used for the tattooing: one for the forehead (four thorns) and the other for the rest of the face (three thorns). The ink was created by mixing soot with water and the sap of the leaves of a particular vine. Apart from other Burmese tattooists who added juices derived from animal gall bladders (e.g., from a python, a fish, or an old bull) to create a blackish-green hue (Singer 1988), Chin tattooists seemed to have used no ingredients other than the aforementioned substances for ink production.

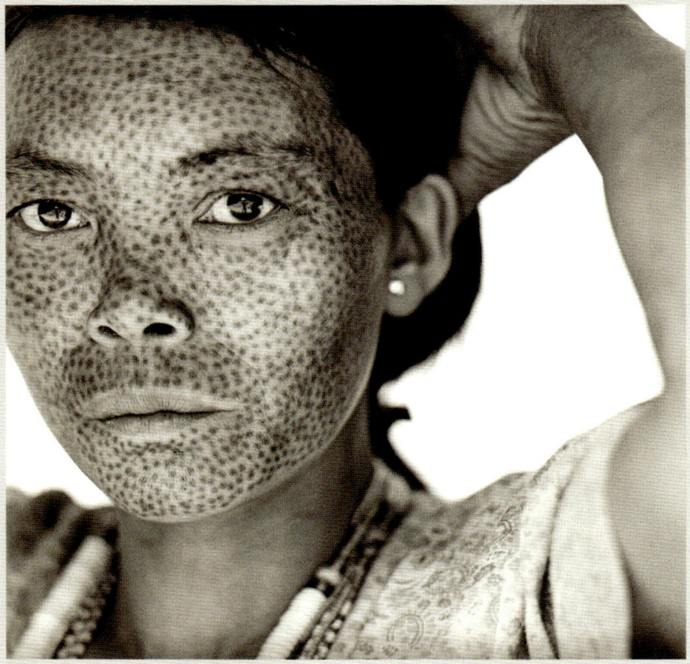

FIGURE 5.23
Matu Chin tattoo bearer Ma Shen Tang, Southern Chin Hills, 2005. © Jens Uwe Parkitny.

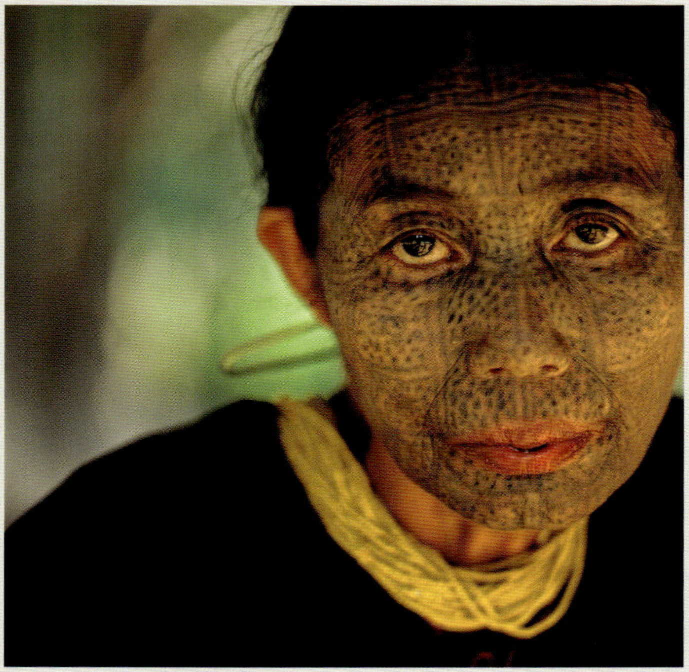

FIGURE 5.24
Magan Chin tattoo bearer Daw Ham Bu, Upper Lemro River, 2004. © Jens Uwe Parkitny.

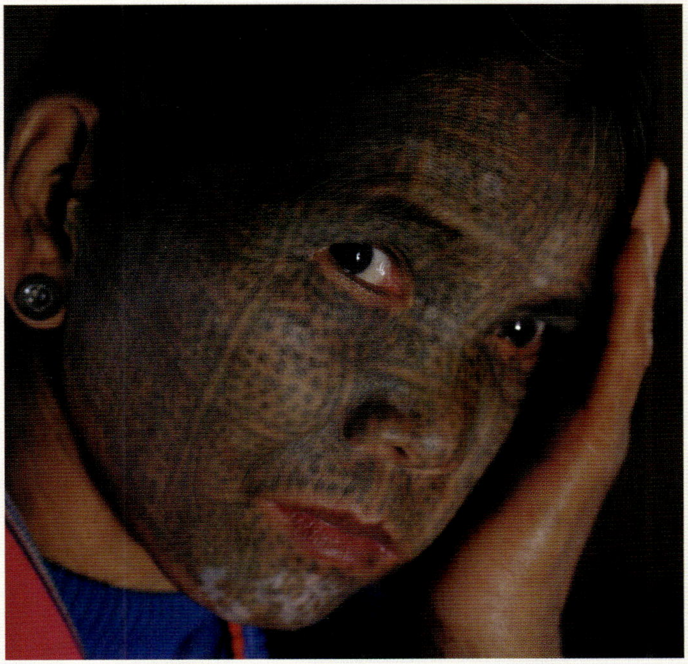

FIGURE 5.25
Hmoye tattoo bearer of Hkangnam, Kanpelet Township, 2014. © Jens Uwe Parkitny.

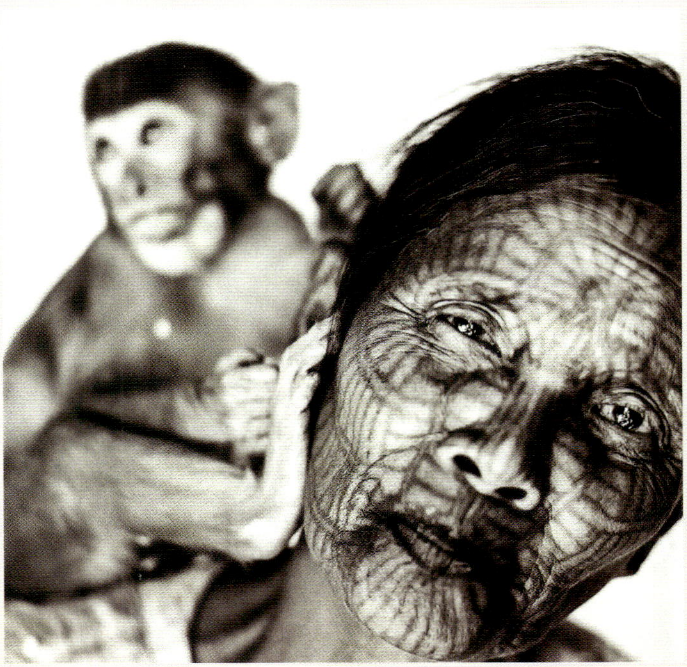

FIGURE 5.26
Laytu elder Daw Ma Htwe of Kaung Chaung village, Upper Lemro River, 2003. © Jens Uwe Parkitny.

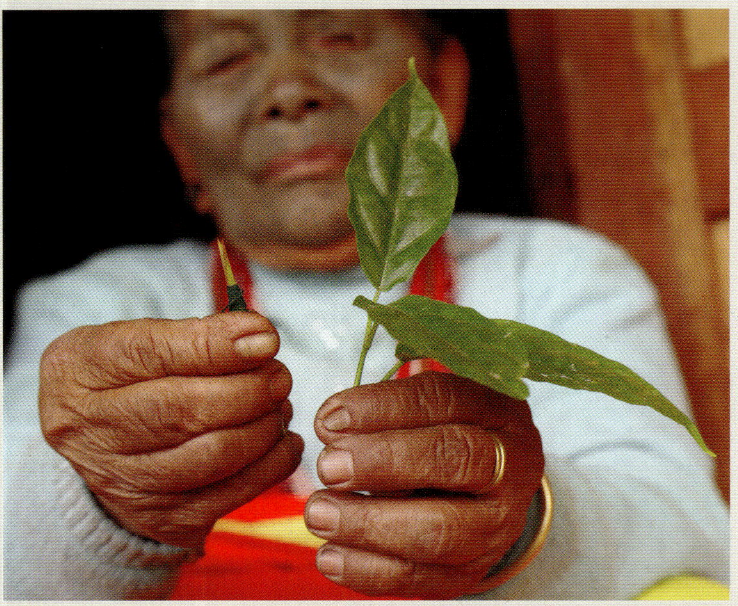

FIGURE 5.27
Yindu Dai elder of Hlaing Doh village displaying items used to make tattooing tools and pigment, 2014. © Jens Uwe Parkitny.

Chin tattoo masters enjoyed status and were well compensated for their sessions. According to U Bhutaung of Hlaing Doh village (Southern Chin State), for a full facial tattoo Yindu masters, who could be male or female, received as payment "five arrows, one cotton blanket, one glass beads necklace, one basket of raw cotton and one cotton ball" (Parkitny 2017:30). Ubtu tattooers living in the plains of what today forms the Magway Division were paid in currency.[13] Yindu and Hmoye women could participate in several tattoo sessions with a male or female tattooist over a period of years before their facial tattooing was completed (Sherman and Sherman 1922). Some Yindu and Hmoye women therefore display pattern breaks and irregularities, such as slight differences in tattoo coloration, which demonstrates that their tattoos were done in stages, and perhaps by multiple artists, rather than in a single session. In 2014, I met Yindu women that had their faces tattooed in a single session. It was up to each woman to decide on single or multiple sessions, depending on her pain threshold.[14]

The perfect symmetry and fine linework of Laytu facial tattoo, which was created by female practitioners, suggests that these markings were always completed in a single session. Indeed, my female informants confirmed this was the case. The same seems to hold true for the application of the patterns among the Sunghtu and the Sutu. The Ubtu, who were tattooed by male or female professionals, also completed their patternless tattoo in one session, with several helpers stretching the skin and assisting the master, who used four or five rattan thorns bound together to form the tattoo implement. Girls were tattooed before or at the age of puberty, typically between the ages of seven and fifteen.[15]

To date, the meaning of the different patterns and symbols that adorn the faces of the Southern Chin women have not been deciphered. None of the Chin tattoo masters nor any of the women I have interviewed were able to provide an adequate explanation (Parkitny 2001–2014). On every occasion I queried my Chin collaborators, I received a similar answer, one that Michael Symes (1800:446) also recorded two hundred years ago: "We don't know. The practice existed since time immemorial."

What is known from other Indigenous People that have practiced facial tattooing in Asia, such as the Naga (Myanmar, India), Atayal (Taiwan), Brao (Vietnam), Ainu (Japan), Li (China), and Dulong (China), among others, is that the custom worked as an apotropaic device, served as a group identity marker in life and supposedly in the afterlife, and possessed therapeutic properties (cf. Krutak 2007, 2012, 2019; Piombino-Mascali and Krutak 2020). Indeed, this pattern seemingly holds true for some Chin, since the Mün elder Daw Gei Sein recently noted that only women

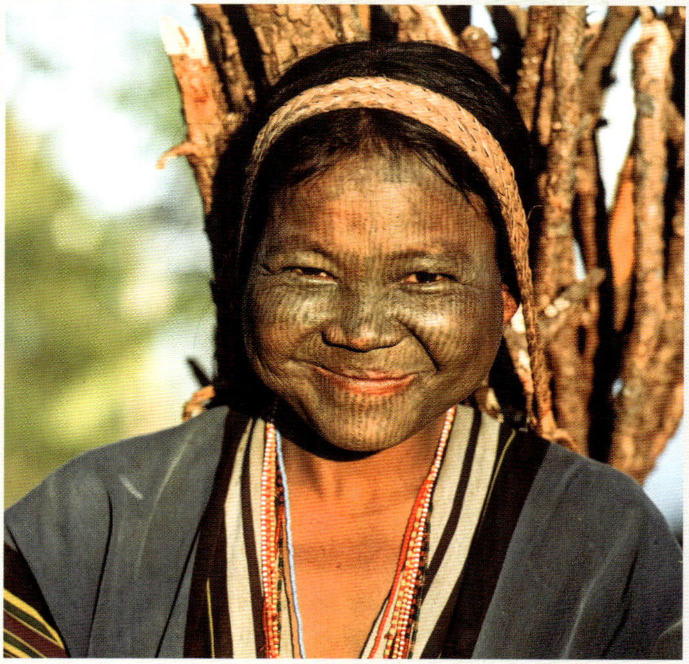

FIGURE 5.28
Yindu Dai tattoo bearer of Kanpelet, 2001. © Jens Uwe Parkitny.

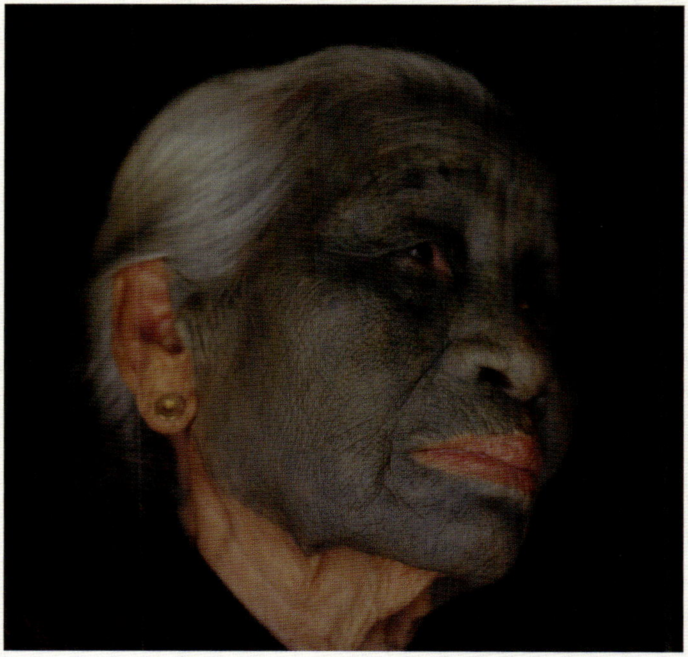

FIGURE 5.29
Ubtu Chin elder Daw Zee of Sedotaya Township, Myanmar, 2014. © Jens Uwe Parkitny.

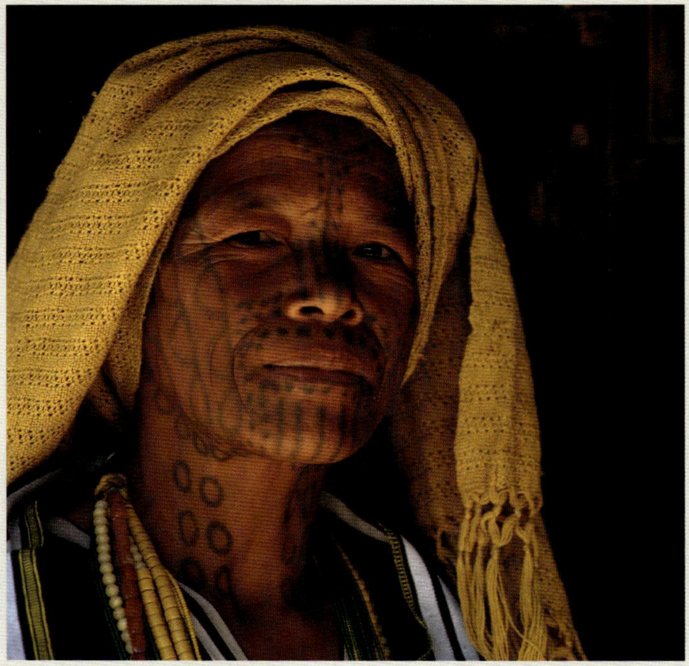

FIGURE 5.30
Mün Chin tattoo bearer Daw Leang, Mindat, 2003. © Jens Uwe Parkitny.

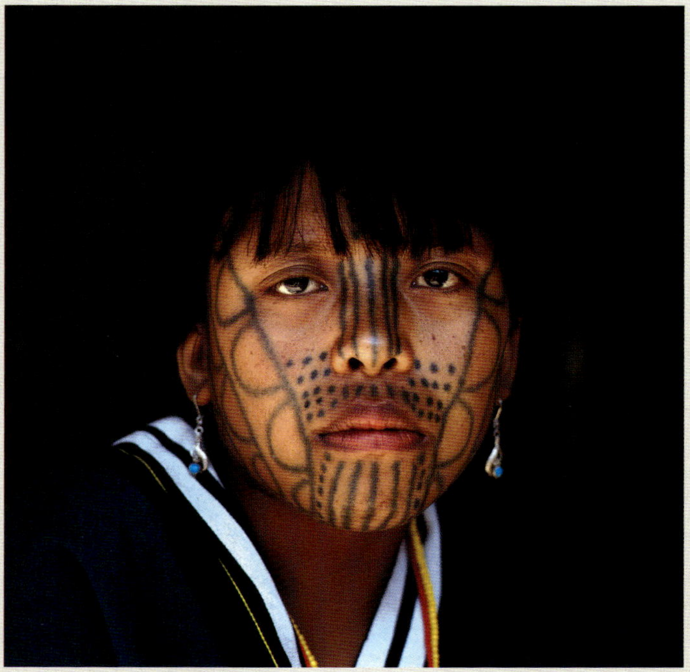

FIGURE 5.31
Mün Chin tattoo bearer Ma Ning Li, Chador village, 2003. © Jens Uwe Parkitny.

with tattooed faces are shown "goodness" in the afterlife, while those without are destined for purgatory (Htwe 2013). One Laytu woman I met in 2011 was tattooed by a male healer with a large circle enclosing a cross to cure a neck goiter, which she believed would have "killed" her without this treatment. In 2005, I met a Sunghtu elder with a series of four small geometric tattoos on the top of her spine, which were placed there to help alleviate her "strong back pain."

Moreover, facial tattooing functions as a visual expression that the bearer has traveled across important life stages, such as the transition from adolescence to adulthood, and she has achieved status within the community. Traditionally, facial tattoos were also like a permanent mask applied by masters who charged it with protective spells through ceremonial offerings to nonhuman entities. The Yindu elder U Bhutaung explained elements of the rite: "It all begins with welcoming the tattoo master at home early in the morning, at sunrise, and presenting to him a white chicken . . . to get him into the right mood. Freshly cut rice paddy and a chicken egg are placed by his side to please the spirits. If too much blood is dripping down the face of the girl that is being tattooed, the egg is rolled over the intense bleeding section to stop it" (Parkitny 2017:30). Of course, in the Chin universe the facial tattoo is a hallmark of female beauty, and expresses the essence of what an ideal woman should look like.

It is possible to further decipher and delineate the tattoo symbols and patterns of the respective Chin groups, but this effort would require a dedicated anthropological study. The window of opportunity still exists, but it is closing fast, since among some Chin groups less than a dozen elderly women still bear the ancient facial marks of their tattooed ancestors.

Drung Female Tattooing in Southwest China

STÉPHANE GROS

Today, less than twenty Drung (*bǎktüq*) women possess a facial tattoo.[16] Their homeland, the secluded Dulong Valley located in the southwestern Chinese province of Yunnan, is often depicted as at once mysterious and "lost to time." Journalistic depictions convey a sense of the atemporal primitiveness of the people living there. Even today, little is known about Indigenous Drung culture beyond the fact that the women used to tattoo their faces.

DISFIGUREMENT OR BEAUTIFICATION?

A common and long-standing interpretation found in the literature holds that the practice of female tattooing among the Drung was a form of "disfigurement" that originated as an adaptive response to abductions perpetrated by predatory neighbors before the 1950s. Following their political integration into the newly founded People's Republic of China, the Drung became recognized as one of the country's official *minzu* (minority nationalities) under the Chinese name of Dulongzu. In turn, they were compelled to achieve a "direct transition" to socialism and were encouraged to abandon cultural practices such as tattooing, which were deemed "superstitious" or "primitive."

Viewed from a larger regional perspective, numerous travelers and writers over the centuries have similarly characterized other female tattooing practices (e.g., Chin of Myanmar, Apatani of the Indian Himalayas) as devices created for the sole purpose of "protecting" women from enemy raiders through disfiguring them (Hughes 1881:13; Nawani 2006; J. G. Scott 1880:164–165). This interpretation implies that facial tattooing made local women repulsive enough to prevent them from being taken away from their communities to be possibly traded as slaves.

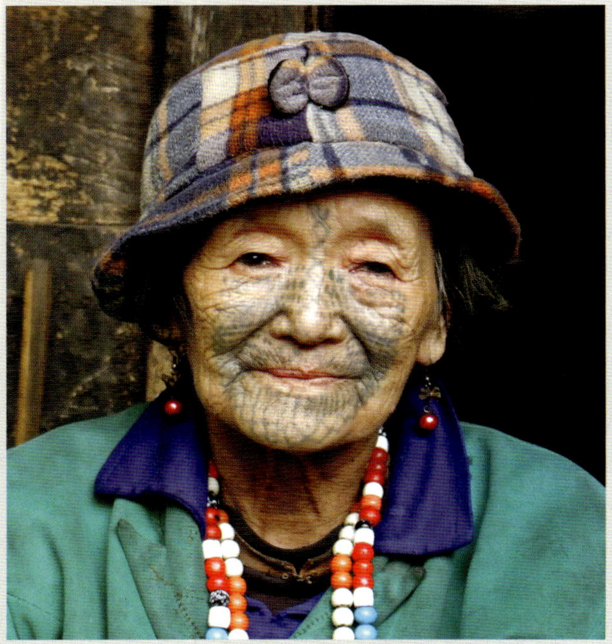

FIGURE 5.32
Drung elder Ji Didai photographed in Dizhengdang village, Dulongjiang Township, 2002. Photograph © Wang Qingyuan.

The logic of the tattoo as a protective form of facial disfigurement often remains unquestioned in scholarly works. The emergence of this practice has generally been interpreted in relation to forms of abduction and servitude historically attested in Southeastern Tibet (e.g., Cai 1983; Chen, Luo, and Yang 2004; Li 1994; D. Liu 1981; Luo 1995a, 1995b). Or, as the anthropologist Huashan Zhou (2004) more recently concluded, it was a means of protecting women from the transgressions of the neighboring Lisu people, who, compelled by long-standing disputes and vendettas, conducted retaliatory expeditions sometimes leading to the kidnapping of Drung women.[17] Both interpretations are based on justifications that are sometimes put forth by the Drung themselves: facial tattooing originated, so some of them say, to prevent women from being captured and enslaved. However, these justifications are not agreed on and are difficult to disentangle from dominant discourses and the experience—widespread in China—of retelling the past as a history of (class) oppression. Furthermore, it is assumed that the tattoo played this protective role for women simply because it was considered ugly and repulsive to these cultural outsiders. However, there is no evidence that the tattoo was effective in preventing women from being captured.[18]

To offer a different interpretation of the existence of this purely feminine practice, it is necessary to consider the evolving construction of knowledge about the tattoos worn by Drung women. In fact, and for several decades now, tattooed women have been regularly photographed, scrutinized, and interviewed by several outsiders for travel, tourism, and other popular publications.

As tattooed women have routinely been portrayed as "cultural curiosities" inhabiting an exotic mountainous world, public opinions concerning the dominant motivations and justifications for why the Drung originally practiced facial tattooing have been transformed.[19] These outsiders' interpretations are often overdetermined by their own personal interests in the subject. This external gaze and discourse about tattooing has greatly influenced local views, from cadres to villagers, deeply affecting tattooed women's perception and presentation of themselves.

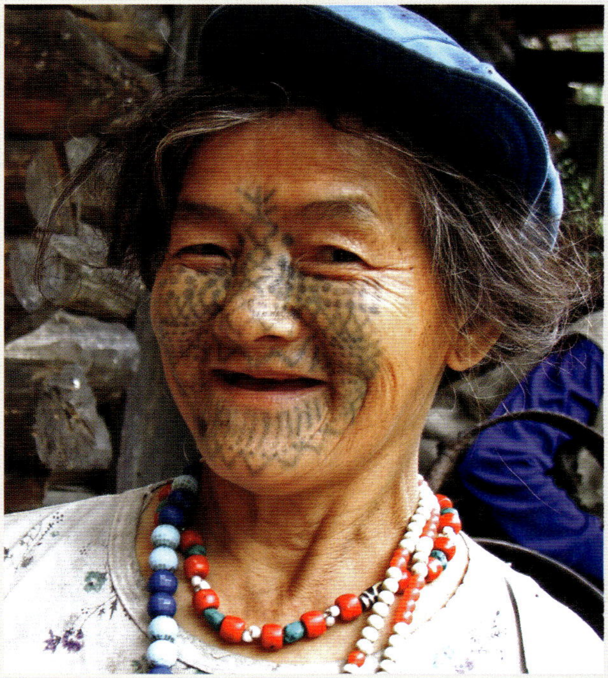

FIGURE 5.33
Drung elder Li Wensi of Xiongdang village, Dulongjiang Township, 2002. Photograph © Wang Qingyuan.

Few alternative analyses have been put forth. Whereas the Indigenous Drung ethnologist Jingming Li (1994) reiterates the several conventional interpretations, Rongfen Luo (1995a, 1995b) investigated the practice in more depth in her search for her own cultural roots and suggested that the motif of the facial tattoo might perhaps be a representation of a butterfly, which, according to Drung people's conceptions, is the form the human soul takes at the end of its sojourn in the afterlife, before its final disappearance. This interpretation has been somewhat popularized and reiterated in other writings (e.g., Gao 2010, 2015; Zheng 2001:181). Other authors have emphasized the need to address tattooing as a form of beautification or an expression of a kind of totemic worship (R. Chen 1992; Duan 1999; Shen 2005). These interpretations fall short both methodologically and in terms of factual evidence. Thus, the existing emic and etic interpretations of the meanings of tattooing need to be addressed in their changing historical context.

While the idea that women's facial tattoos were a form of beautification seems on the surface to be a positive valorization of this practice, it is a rather simplistic formulation and is not in itself a convincing argument. Instead, what is needed here is a more thorough discussion concerning the Drung's concept of "beauty." For sure, older tattooed women today often declare that they dislike their *angmvr naq* (black faces), while younger women carry a negative attitude toward the practice itself. Whereas both reactions attest to the tattoos' actual devaluation, we should not isolate the tattoo from the process of its inscription on the female body and the various contextual aspects of its actual valorization in the past. For the Drung tattooing was an intimate cultural performance that transformed the person through the creation of a new identity. Thus, the aesthetic interpretation distorts the value of the tattoo and its connection to the person. As I will endeavor to show, Drung tattoos were part of a larger process of shaping the individual and the body through a series of transformational cumulative actions. If it can be said that the tattoo "makes one beautiful," then beauty must be understood as a vitalist notion anchored in the function that it amplifies, which is to make visible a property of the self, to ensure sexual maturity, reproduction, and the creation of new social bonds.

HISTORICAL EVIDENCE FOR DRUNG TATTOOING (NINETEENTH AND TWENTIETH CENTURIES)

The existence of facial tattooing in the region where Yunnan, Myanmar, and Tibet meet was well attested to in reports from the late nineteenth century and later confirmed by other travelers. The first reliable indications about female facial tattooing among the Drung, then known under the more generic Chinese exonym of Qiuzi, are found in travel accounts.[20] Among the earliest eyewitnesses was the French Prince Henri of Orléans (1898:235), who led an expedition across the southern part of the Dulong Valley to Burma (present-day Myanmar), wherein he mentioned seeing facial tattoos in the shape of a "green grid." A few years later, the Mandarin Xia Hu led his own expedition to the area to gain control over this territory. He provided a more detailed description of the practice, mentioning that "on the upper course of the [Qiu, i.e., Dulong] valley, the entire face of women, nose, cheeks, upper and lower lips, are all tattooed," while "women of the lower reaches of the river only tattoo the upper and lower lips. At the [southern] extremity of the river, Qu [Qiu] and Li [Lisu] live together, and women do not usually tattoo" (Xia [1908] 1994:116, 118). Further westward in upper Burma, women's tattoos consisted, he wrote, "[o]nly in a circle on the nose and a few lines on the lower lip" (Xia [1908] 1994:119). The practice was also to be found in the Adung Valley, where, at this time, the facial tattoo was composed of one or two lines on the lower lip.

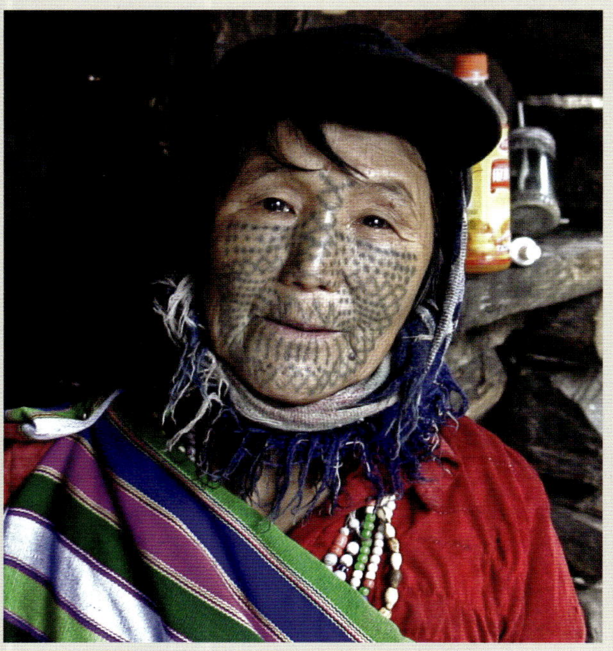

FIGURE 5.34
Drung elder Dang Muxi of Longyuan village, Dulongjiang Township, 2002. The fee for her tattooing included a pot of wine, a large bowl, and a sack of grain. Photograph © Wang Qingyuan.

The intrepid botanist F. Kingdon Ward (1924:196–197), who traveled extensively throughout this region for his plant-hunting activities, described the diverse tattoo designs he came across, from the complete "dots and zigzags" covering the whole face in "Upper Taron" [Dulong] to the few curved lines across the chin to the corners of the mouth and a circle on the tip of the nose in the Tazu and Nam Tamai Valleys (northernmost Myanmar). Ward's numerous writings provide evidence of the practice throughout the region of the eastern Himalayas. He saw the progressive disappearance of tattooing further west as evidence that the practice might indeed be linked to forms of servitude, which were more widespread when the Drung were in contact with the Tibetans (cf. Ward 1923:13, 1924:196). This interpretation of a progressive westward disappearance of the practice would, however, lose its validity if we consider, as mentioned previously, that the Drung people say it was in fact the Lisu who often raided their villages in areas more to the south and west.

There is in any case evidence that various tattoo motifs previously existed among Drung kin groups in upper Myanmar and Yunnan, who were all equally designated by the generic ethnic label Qiuzi in Chinese sources (cf. Siguret 1937:105). Until recently, facial tattoos existed among the Daru (Rawang subgroup) and are said to have been linked to clan membership (Morse and Morse 1966:196). One might add that, according to the French missionary Auguste Desgodins (1872:321–322), the practice may have also existed among the Nung of the upper Salween Valley, where young girls used to have a tattoo that was "a blue moustache, going down at the corners of the mouth to the bone mandible, then back to the front of the ears."

Such scattered and incomplete historical information does not provide solid evidence of the geographical extent of female facial tattooing among or within various groups in the region, and even less so allows for a solid interpretation of the practice. Contemporary ethnography may not shed any light on its origin, but it is the only valid source of knowledge that enables an understanding of the practice faithful to women's own words.

The last women to wear tattoos are now very few. There were only about sixty tattooed women when I started my research in the late 1990s. Given that I was unable to observe the practice of tattooing, as young women no longer have their faces tattooed, what I learned about tattooing was through the narratives of older tattooed women themselves.[21]

TATTOO MOTIFS

The tattooed Drung women I met lived in the center and in the north of the Dulong River Valley, and most had a facial tattoo that covered their entire face. The patterns, or *rvmū* (designs), were essentially the same, with only very minor variations. The stability of the overall tattoo design demonstrates that the few motifs are linked to specific parts of the face. They are often simply designated in a descriptive manner as the *shòn* (straight line[s]) on the *mvkāi* (chin) and what is *dvbàng do rù* (pricked on the cheeks) or *svnā do rù* (pricked on the nose). The dots on the cheeks are, however, distinguished by their size and given a different name: *tùjī* designate the smaller dots tattooed in lines on the lower part of the cheeks, whereas *nēq-rām*, literally "eyes-row," designates the rows of larger dots (in fact small circles) under the eyes (from two to four rows).

Along with these more descriptive terms, two other named patterns can also be identified and are specific to the tattoo. The *mvgōp* is a diamond shape characteristic of the pattern tattooed on the nose and around the cheeks. And the *tvkkā mvlà*, literally "crow/curved line," is the zigzag pattern, such as on the upper lip, under the nose, or on the lower part of the chin and cheeks. This terminology does not seem to carry any particular symbolism and in general people did not have explanations or commentaries to offer about these motifs.

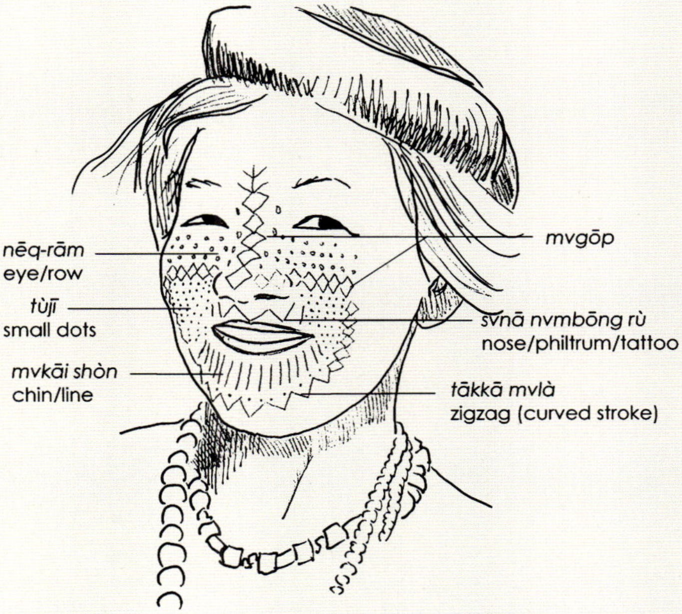

FIGURE 5.35 Drung tattoo terminology. Illustration © Stéphane Gros.

Overall, the graphic repertoire has no figurative meaning and the tattoo designs are made up of repeated simple geometric patterns and are not intended to function as a symbolic system—either that or such knowledge has been lost. What matters most is that the women's tattoos look like those of their elders—that is to say they should conform to tradition. Thus, the meaning of the tattoo is given not by the graphic repertoire but by its properties and the context, practices, and discourses in which it is embedded.

TATTOO TECHNIQUE

On a practical level, it was relatively simple to master the tattooing technique, but the quality of the tattoo itself depended on the skill of the person doing it. There was no formal transmission of this knowledge and women learned on their own through trial runs.

The ink was obtained from *svmà* (soot), which pine wood gives off when it burns, and was scraped from the bottom of the iron pot on the fireplace. Two kinds of conifers were used, one resulting in a more greenish tattoo. The soot was *jìn* (soaked) in water for about a week until it was properly diluted. The tattoo was first drawn using this ink, then the pattern was hand-tapped onto the face so that the ink penetrated under the skin.

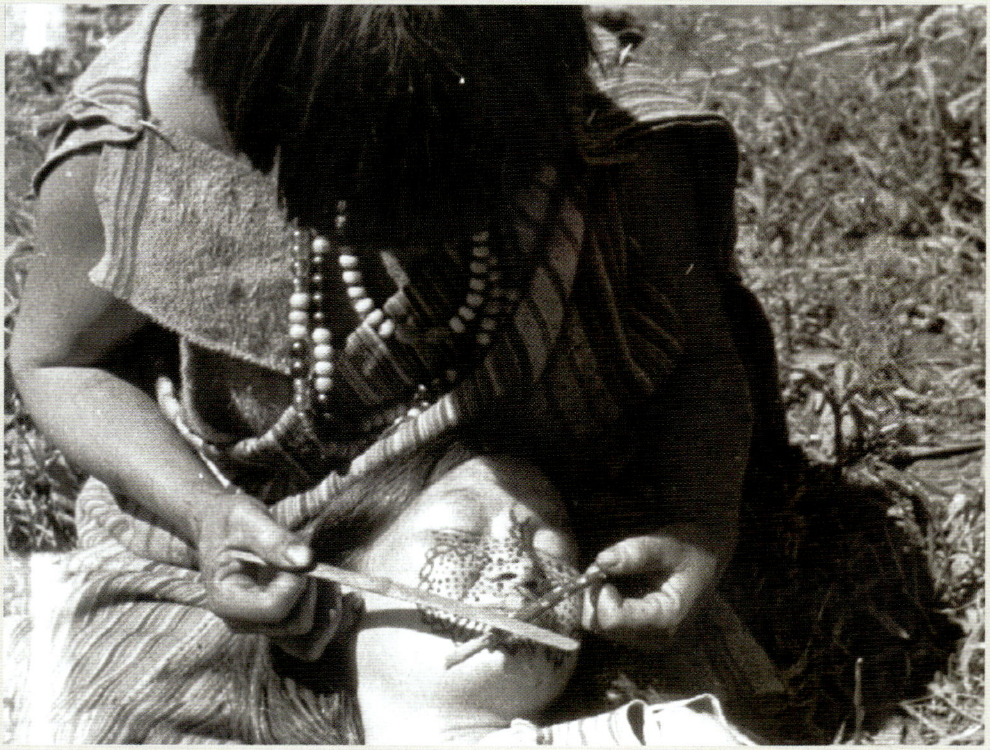

FIGURE 5.36
Tattoo demonstration filmed for a documentary, *The Dulong* (1961). Footage © Yang Guanghai. From Guanghai 1961.

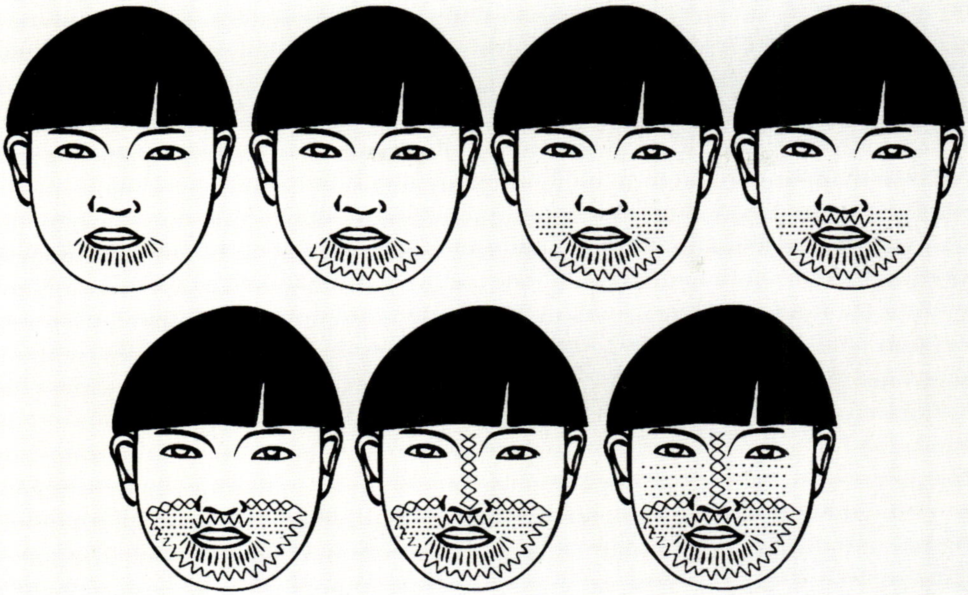

FIGURE 5.37
Drung facial tattoo order. Illustrations © Stéphane Gros.

The pricking instruments were generally constructed from *băkxreŭ*, or thorny brambles. A branch was cut to a length of about six inches, then it was cleared of leaves and thorns, except for a single thorn at one end. The tattooist held this little rod in one hand, the spine against the woman's face, and with the other hand-tapped it with a piece of wood (or bamboo) to prick the skin one dot at a time. Several tools were often used for the same tattoo, because the single thorn tool dulled over time; these were simply discarded with no special precautions. Women used two species of brambles, one containing larger thorns that were more painful. The pain was so intense that the tattooist could not always complete the tattoo in one session.

The tattoo was generally executed in a specific order, starting at the chin and then moving slowly up the face. Generally speaking, the *mvgōp* on the nose was the last pattern to be tattooed. The order in which the different patterns were tattooed reflects the relative importance of the lower part of the face. In the past (prior to the 1950s), one type of tattoo consisted of only the designs on the lower face, what my fully tattooed informants referred to as a *băktùq xuài* (incomplete tattoo). Similarly, it happened that only the vertical lines under the lower lip would be tattooed. A few women were tattooed this way in the late 1950s or early 1960s, at which time tattooing was banned by governmental authorities.[22] The *mvkāi shòn*, or lines on the chin, seem to be the most basic component of the facial tattoo, a possible "elementary form."[23]

Sometimes teenage girls, feeling fully prepared, would go to find a tattooist themselves. But more often than not, a girl's parents took the initiative to schedule their daughter's tattoo marks. In the past, all girls between the age of ten and sixteen would get tattooed. For most girls, the person who created the facial tattoo was a close relative: their own mother, an older cousin, or an aunt, whether paternal or maternal. The realization of a woman's facial tattoo was not the exclusive prerogative of one parent and did not stress a particular line of transmission or the role of in-laws according to prospective matrimonial alliance.

The tattooist was in no way a professional tattooer; as they say in Drung, it is a *rù sō vtsàng* (a person who knows how to prick). As the tattooists learned their skills through experience without receiving any kind of training, any woman could potentially become a tattooer, but there was often only one tattooist for several hamlets.

The tattooist's mastership, an expertise born of experience, is seen as a gradual progression. Those who had successfully performed a tattoo—which was sometimes done over the course of several days—were likely to gain some reputation. A woman had to test her own ability before acquiring this mastery that earned her recognition as an expert tattooer. Women generally attributed the subtle variations in the tattoo patterns to the skills, or lack thereof, of the tattooist. In other words, the tattooist, and not only the woman receiving the tattoo, had to feel ready and be prepared for it.

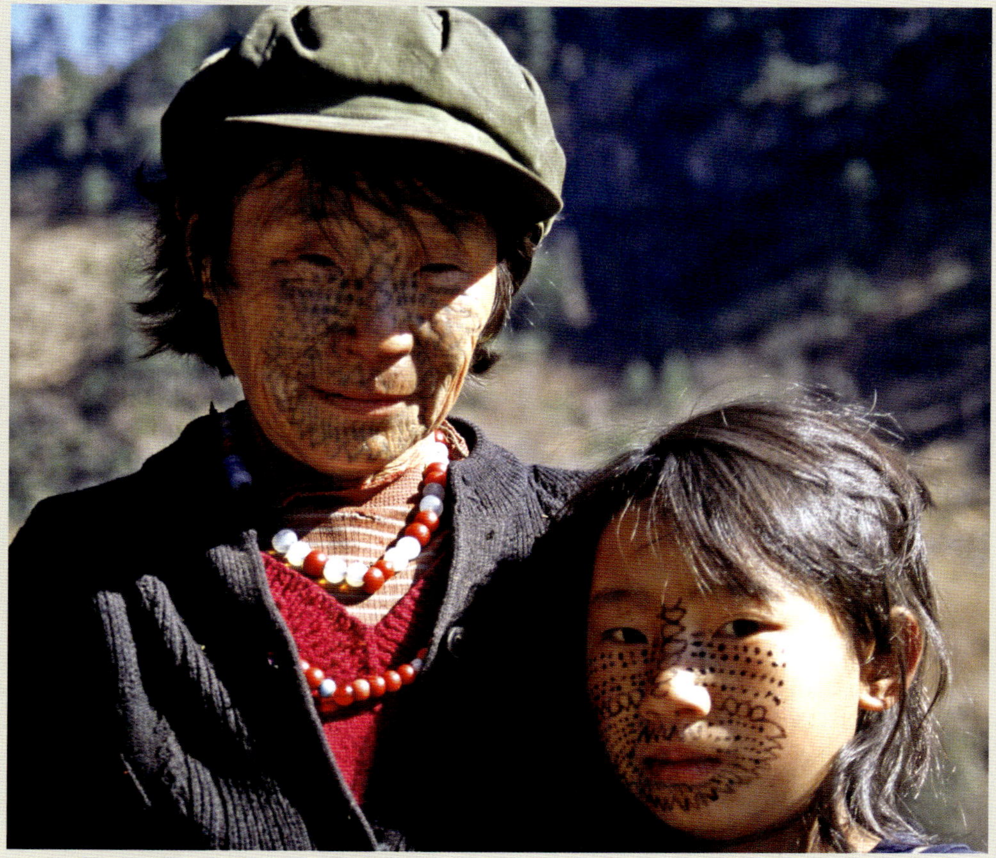

FIGURE 5.38
Drung tattooist Tshineng stands with her granddaughter, Tsemu, who bears a stenciled tattoo pattern on her face, Dizhengdang (Zungdam) village, 2003. Photograph © Stéphane Gros.

THE POWER OF TATTOOS

It goes without saying that the facial tattoo is a particularly painful bodily inscription. The pain of tattooing is real but tolerable. It is part of the process, just like the pain of childbirth, an intrinsic part of the transition to become an ideal woman. For the women I talked to, the tattoo evoked the memory of blood, the pain of the thorn penetrating the skin, and a face that remained swollen for several days. Swelling and a sensation of heat recall the "cooking" metaphor that is often cross-culturally associated with women's tattooing. As the tattoo anthropologist Lars Krutak (2007:111) put it, "[The] tattoo also enabled life, since it was the heat that 'cooked' the woman until she had achieved maturation." In short, the tattoo makes a woman nubile, and in the formality of its execution by a tattooist, the facial tattoo was a key element in the construction of Drung womanhood.

The facial tattoo is not a formalized event or a one-time initiation or ritual of maturity but the continuation of a transformative process, a form of initiation that unfolds over time and is performed in the intimacy of the tattooist-tattooed relationship. As such, it is an identity-bestowing process whose end (the initiated woman) is the very means of its reiteration. In other words, in its cumulative actions, tattooing as a process is comparable to an initiation that prepared women for marriage and their eventual role as a mother.[24]

While never explicitly stated by the people I talked to, many of the references to blood in relation to tattooing seem to point to women's menstruation, which, as an index of fertility, heralds the possibility of life. The responsibility of the tattooists—of the countless stings and what they contribute to bringing about—is to reveal a power that is specific to women.

In this process that results in the tattoo "being on view," there is the potential danger for the tattooist of losing her eyesight, of having her *nēq ma* (eyes affected) in a negative manner. The woman who receives the tattoo manifests a potentiality, a power that threatens the eyesight of the other woman, the tattooist, who enabled the transformation.[25] The one who receives the tattoo has to provide an *akpeù* (retribution) or *tvpeù* (compensation) in kind (various typically feminine goods). In a similar vein, these exchanges can be likened to those at childbirth. More specifically, Drung women who act as midwives face the same risk of having their eyes and vision affected after the birthing event. Midwives too receive compensation for "washing [their] eyes." Witnessing the child-bearer exposes the midwife to the risk of "no longer seeing."

In Drung language, the notion of vision is associated with potency, and, because of their physiology, the eyes of women specifically are invested with formidable power. Vision and the eyes are the obvious symbols of a channel of mutual influence and exchanges of forces: the *nēq kù* (envious eye) speaks of jealousy or the *nēq mvdàm* (full eye) of satisfaction. These expressions locate human desire in the focal gaze but they also allude to the belief that such sight may harbor potentially harmful effects on a household's fertility.

For the Drung, key moments of transformation such as tattooing or childbirth carry a potential danger. In both cases, the woman who helps tattoo a young woman or delivers a baby is in contact with what, in the other woman, is an exteriorization of an inner vitality perhaps first manifested by blood: the blood that drips down the face of the tattooed young woman, the blood that is lost by the woman giving birth. This evocation of the woman's blood also refers to her menstruation, which the tattoo came to anticipate or validate. Though menstrual blood is always a danger to Drung men (i.e., it is likely to defile them, to diminish their strength, to ruin their luck at hunting, etc.),[26] and is commonly interpreted as being linked to a form of pollution, the risk of a woman being affected highlights a more subtle ambivalence.[27] There is a positive side to this feminine power, symbolized by the blood but not limited to it, once its normal flow has been restored. If these transformative events in a woman's body can, under certain conditions, affect another woman's eyesight, it is because of what constitutes an "overflow": the blood from a tattoo or delivery accompanies a "birth"; it denotes a life force, or what we can simply call "fertility." The potential danger that the act of tattooing could represent for the tattooist lies in this relating through fertility with the woman who receives the tattoo. Therefore the "problem," so to speak, is not with women's blood itself; rather, it lies in how the two women, equally characterized by their blood and generative power, are temporarily transitively related.

AN IMPOSSIBLE REVIVAL?

Drung women's tattooing has increasingly become an artifact for public consumption, and the special attention it has attracted has transformed it into a cultural emblem. After having been forbidden during the period of high socialism, the recent focus on intangible heritage has triggered a growing concern by state authorities because safeguarding Drung women's facial tattoos for the future is impossible—they will soon disappear with the last generation of traditionally tattooed women. A recent article published in the newspaper *Zhongguo funü* 中国妇女 (Chinese Women) reports that twenty-six tattooed women were still living in 2015 and were to be "safeguarded" as "living fossils" of traditional Drung culture—a conventional designation derived from social evolutionist orthodoxy. According to the article, the local police station in the Dulong Valley keeps health records of these "last tattooed women" and their health is now closely monitored via monthly checkups (Yulin Zhou 2015).

The disappearance of the tattooing practice today primarily raises the question of the redefinition of personal identity in the changing sociocultural and political context, and how it affects the values associated with tattooing. None of the young women I have met throughout the years since the late 1990s expressed a wish to have their faces tattooed. Instead, through experience of schooling outside of the valley, generalized access to television broadcasting, and the influence of pop music and fashion other and more modern models of femininity are now widely available, influencing clothing habits or the use of makeup, for example. It is also likely that, following tremendous changes affecting local livelihoods and agricultural practices, a drastic decline in traditional religious practices, and a surge in the number of Christian converts, Indigenous conceptions of gender roles and social reproduction are being fundamentally reshaped. In the context of changing values and the imminent disappearance of the tattoo practice, it is critical to give proper attention to women's voices and their experiences in order to understand aspects of this once vibrant tradition.

Icons of Courage: Leg Tattoos of the Kayin of Myanmar

JENS UWE PARKITNY

Among the Kayin of Myanmar, there is a largely untold story of an Indigenous tattooing tradition that is on the verge of disappearing. Based on research and interviews conducted in 2014 with tattooed Kayin men and the tattoo master U Sein Lin of Hpa An, these elders represent the last generation of tattooed Kayin men in Myanmar, and their bold black designs commemorate a commitment to cultural values and spiritual beliefs that were once rooted to local traditions of body modification. The Kayin, the Bama, and other ethnic groups that have settled in the territory that forms the Union of Myanmar have kept tattooing traditions alive over many centuries until quite recently. The origins of these practices are not well known. When or why the Kayin men started tattooing remains a mystery and one can only assume that the practice was adopted from the Bama to imitate their visual expression of manhood and belief. Since so little is known about Kayin tattooing, it is of paramount importance to document the ancient patterns and symbols that still adorn the skins of the Kayin elders and create a cultural record. After all, it is an untold story of identity and belief that deserves to be shared and be added to all the other stories that form the global tattoo heritage.

TATTOOS IN MYANMAR

Before the British colonialized the territory that today forms the Union of Myanmar, it was unthinkable for men of the Kayin, Bama, or Shan not to permanently adorn their skin from the waist to below their knees with mythical or animal figures. In Burmese literature, over sixty different figures are mentioned, such as the *belu* (demon ogre), the Kinnari birds, Garuda, the black cat, the peacock, the turtle, the gecko, and the monkey (Thein 2014). Each of these entities possessed specific powers (e.g., empowerment, agility, longevity, sexual prowess, etc.) that could be transmitted to the tattoo bearer.

A completed tattoo on both legs and the waist served as a visual expression of manhood and courage and also signaled that the bearer possessed almost supernatural strength and capabilities. In the early seventeenth and eighteenth centuries, the tattooed image was usually surrounded by magical numbers and *sar yan* (zodiac symbols) that formed either an oval or a rounded frame.

Moreover, tattoos expressed devotion to Buddhism, and the permanent religious scripture on skin served as a protective device against evil forces. As this tradition evolved over time, the writing around the images was replaced by single or double lines—which merely symbolized the magical scripture—and square frames also emerged.

Men of all classes, including laymen and aristocrats, adopted the practice of leg tattooing. A young man without a tattoo was not considered to be attractive to the opposite sex, and

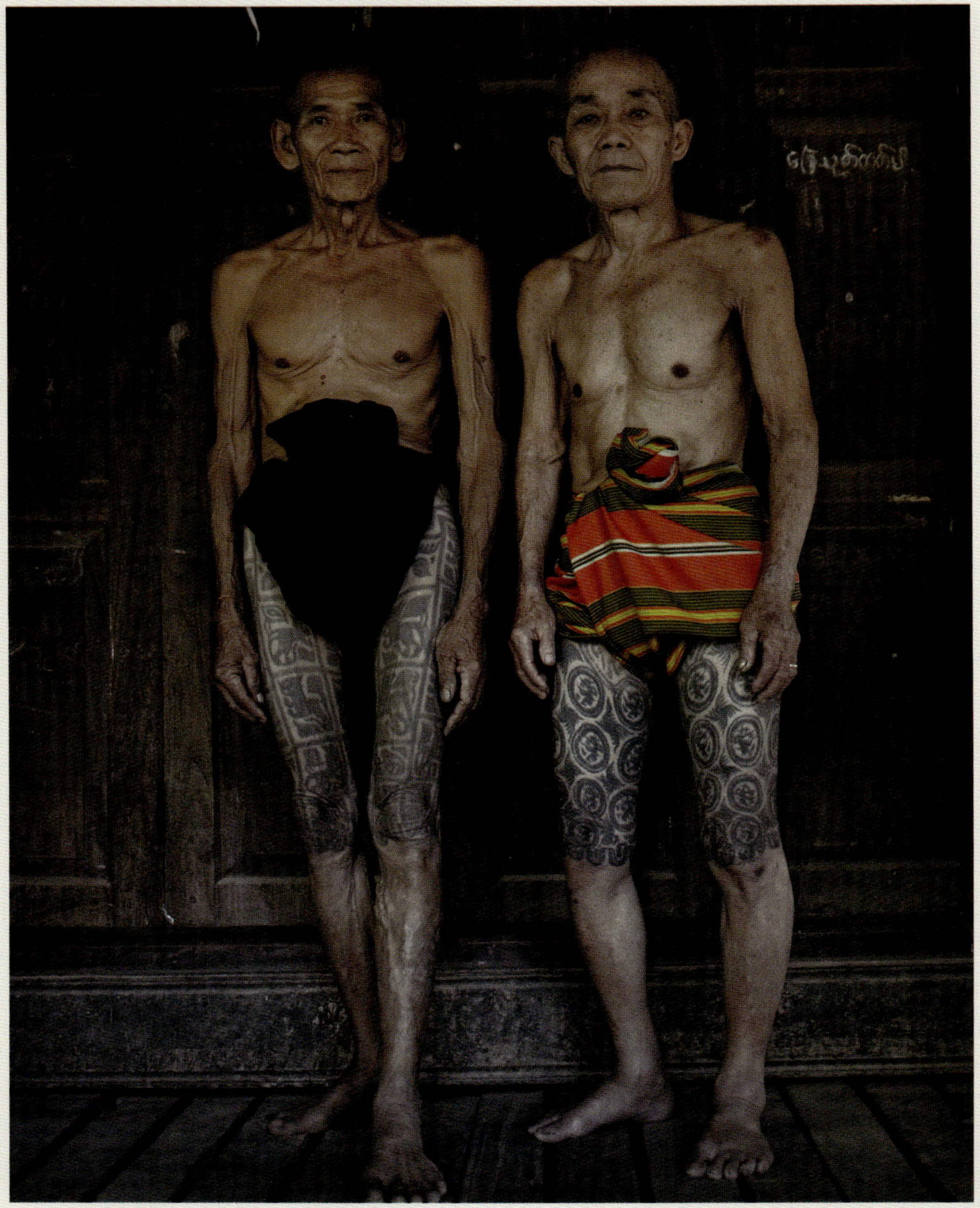

FIGURE 5.39

Eighty-year-old U Nen Nya (*right*) and sixty-eight-year-old U Myat Thein Shwe (*left*), both of Hpa-An, 2015. Before the British colonialized Burma in the nineteenth century, men of the Kayin, Bama, or Shan were permanently marked from waist to below their knees with mythical or animal figures. In Burmese literature, over sixty different figurines are mentioned. A completed tattoo on both legs served as a visual expression of manhood and courage as well as the bearer's devotion to Buddhism. © Jens Uwe Parkitny.

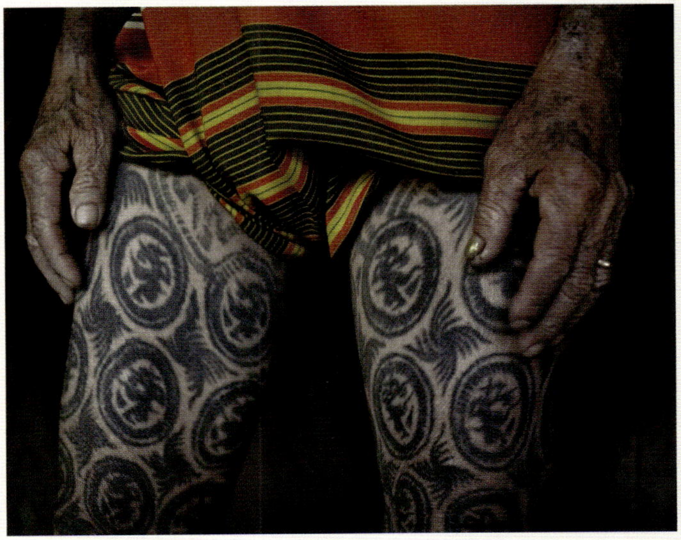

FIGURE 5.40
Close-up of U Nen Nya's thighs, 2015. The swirling motif represents a peacock, a symbol of virility and sexual prowess. U Nen Nya recalled, "I can't remember at what age I was tattooed. But I recall the name of the master: U Aung Myat Yin. I approached the master myself. He tattooed my right leg first; the left one was done by him ten days later. Before the sessions, he gave me a little opium to chew so I could stand the pain." © Jens Uwe Parkitny.

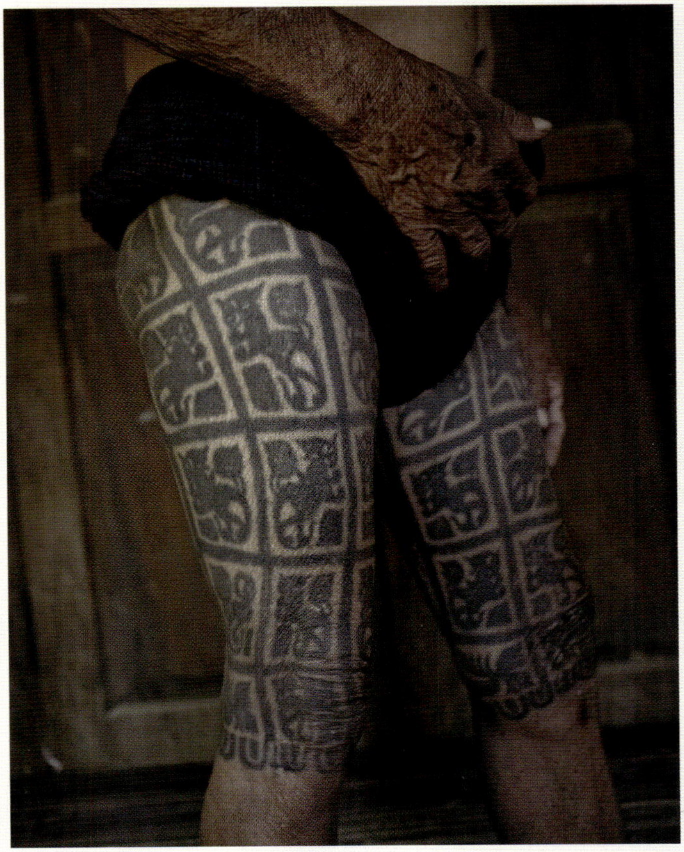

FIGURE 5.41
Thigh tattoos of seventy-eight-year-old U Sein Myat Naw of Sabunnoun village, 2015. U Sein Myat Naw stated, "I was tattooed by master U Aung Myat Win when I was a novice [monk] at the age of twelve. It was the lunar year of 1317 and I have this number tattooed on my right thigh. The master gave me a little opium to chew and started tattooing my left leg. He chose the figures and the pattern. Seven days later, he also tattooed my right leg and my waist. Once the tattoo was completed, the monk asked me to fight with the other boys." He added, "My tattoo made an impression on girls and I eventually got married. I have five children and made a living as a paddy and vegetable farmer." © Jens Uwe Parkitny.

FIGURE 5.42
Honorable Dhamawathi Sayadaw (*left*), eighty-one years old, head monk of Kayin State, and fellow monk Sayadaw U Adainsa (*right*), seventy-five years old, proudly show their leg tattoos depicting giants, black cats, and other figures, 2015. "I was tattooed in the lunar year of 1311," Sayadaw explained. "At the time I was a novice [monk] and fourteen years old. The reason I got the tattoos? I wanted to impress the girls. In those times, a girl sent you packing when you approached her without tattoos. 'Please get a tattoo first,' the girl would say." He went on, "My right leg was tattooed by master U Aung Myat Yin from Pauk Sein village. My left leg was tattooed by another master a year later. I forgot his name but I recall that he was singing to distract my mind during the session." © Jens Uwe Parkitny.

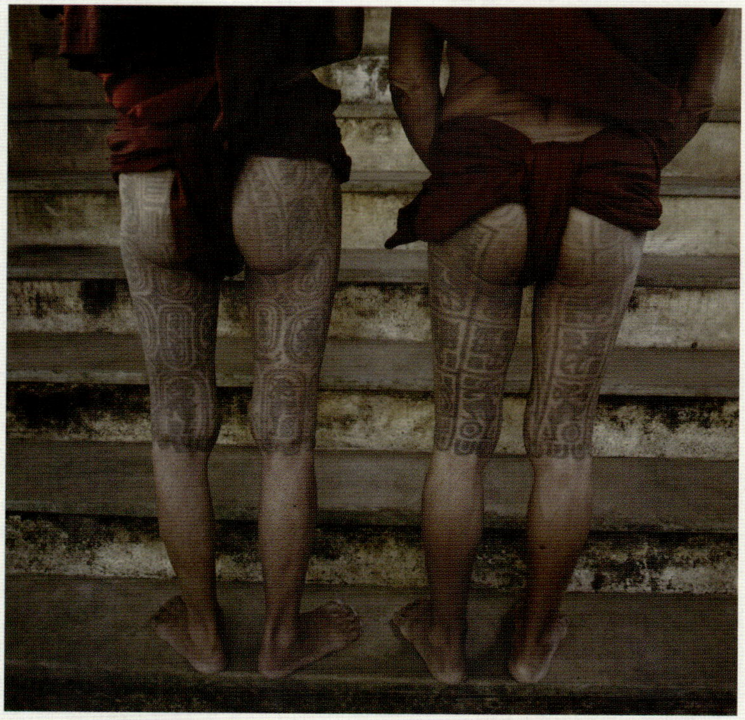

FIGURE 5.43
U Nay Mida, an eighty-three-year-old monk from Ka Kauk Thann village, 2015. The black cat climbing upward is a popular tattoo motif and dominates the thighs of U Nay Mida. It represents stealth, agility, and the ability to jump great distances. © Jens Uwe Parkitny.

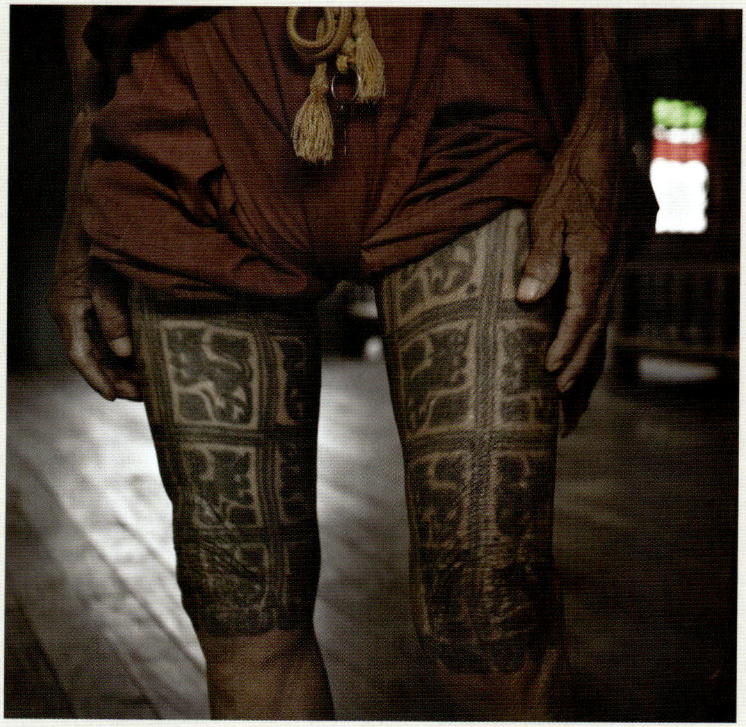

parents made sure that their future son-in-law would bear the ancestral symbols of courage and devotion on his legs and thighs (Yoe [Scott] 1896). The famous early seventeenth-century court poetess Yaway Shin Dway immortalized the attraction she felt when seeing the waist tattoo of her lover, Prince Nat Shin Naung, by describing it in one of her verses as "a band of emerald green" (Thanegi 2014).

In Buddhist thought, the temporary ordination of young men into monkhood and subsequent entry into monastic life was considered as important as getting the thighs tattooed. Monks often sent their novices to local tattoo masters in an attempt to transform the young, timid boys into courageous men. For these novices, the painful tattoo session that stretched over many hours became their rite of passage into manhood.

It took skilled tattoo masters up to seven hours to ink the patterns onto one leg, from the waist to below the kneecaps. The masters started the procedure early in the morning, around 3 a.m. Their tattooing implements were *hnitkwasok* (long brass rods) about two feet long (about sixty centimeters in length) that consisted of three different segments that were mantled together: a pointed double-pronged end piece with two-inch slits that formed a reservoir able to hold and transfer tattooing ink under the skin, a cylindrical middle section, and a brass headpiece that was attached to the midsection and served as a counterweight for balancing the tool.

Saya (tattoo masters) fasted a day before performing the tattoo session. They took pride in their tattoo utensils. The headpiece usually took the form of an elaborately cast mythical or animal figurine, such as an ogre, giant, monkey, or snake. Some counterweights added extra qualities to the tattoo mark. For example, a tattoo featuring a serpent was believed to protect the wearer from snakebites. Some masters even gilded their headpiece to show how sacred it was to them.

Tattoo masters tried to distract their young clients from feeling pain by telling them stories or singing; however, the sensation was excruciating, particularly when perforating the tender inner parts of the thigh and the skin at the joints of the knee. It was therefore common to give the boys a little opium to chew, which not only calmed them down but also helped to control the bleeding of the fresh wounds. Only one leg at the time was tattooed, and the other one followed, usually within a span of a seven days.

To obtain the typical greenish-blue hue of the tattoo, masters mixed the dried and pulverized gall bladders of fish, cattle, chickens, monkeys, or pythons with black soot collected from lamps or pots in which sesame oil, crude oil, or lard was burned. These ingredients were then mixed with water and cooked until they thickened into a paste. This substance was collected and placed into a bamboo container, which was sealed and buried. After a year or so the container was unearthed. The tattoo pigment now resembled a dried paste and was cut into blocks for ease of transport and storage (Singer 1988). Once mixed with water, the resinous mass became suitable for tattooing.

When Burma officially became a British colony in 1886, the leg tattooing tradition began to fade. Eventually, the custom was suppressed by the colonial administration. By the time the country gained its independence in 1948, the practice of leg tattooing had ceased to exist. Today, the "youngest" Kayin men still bearing the traditional marks are well over seventy years of age. They are icons of courage and the last "true men" still standing.

MAGIC TATTOO MASTER OF THAILAND: AJARN MATTHIEU DUQUENOIS (2009–2024)

The tattoo master Ajarn Matthieu Duquenois sits beside an elaborate altar in his hometown of Hua Hin composed of numerous buddha statues, charmed amulets, and masks of the sage Pho Kae (Old Father), the wise hermit who is believed to have begun the tradition of *sak yan*, or magical tattooing, in Thailand more than one thousand years ago. His client soon approaches on his knees and provides an offering and donation of money placed on a platter. Raising the tray above their head, the disciple now presents it to the master, who blesses it. An incense bundle is lit to summon the spirits of past tattoo masters in Duquenois' lineage and then he blesses his elongated tattooing needle before plunging it into his client's skin.

For nearly a decade, French-born Duquenois has studied the magicoreligious culture of *sak yan* and the *yantra*s that complete it. Visiting private sanctuaries where these hallowed tattoo rituals take place, he has learned the rituals of Thailand's most esteemed tattoo masters by apprenticing under many while also becoming the second European to bear the title of *ajarn* himself. He documented his journey with incredible photography—images that appear throughout this chapter.

A MAGICAL TATTOO ADVENTURE

Duquenois' magical tattoo adventure began in 2009 when he received his first *sak yan* at the age of thirty-seven. "I was facing a difficult time in my life and needed something spiritually to move forward so that I could progress," he said. "I became a Buddhist monk for a time, then I began visiting several *ajarns* across Thailand, and I participated in different magical rituals. Eventually, I was tattooed by twenty-five of the two hundred masters I met and suddenly *sak yan* became my passion, my obsession."[28]

The intimate scenes captured by Duquenois' camera convey a profound landscape of spiritual faith. From the sacred tattoo rooms of *ajarns* and Buddhist temples to the bloodied and newly consecrated skins of *sak yan* disciples, these mystical realms offer a metaphysical statement on the meaning of human belief and life itself.

"I became a Thai tattoo master, an *ajarn*, in different steps," Duquenois says. "At first, my wife Rung and I joined three other Thais to become students of the renowned tattooist Luang Pi Man. We participated in a ceremony called 'Yoke Pan Khru' in which we made a special offering to the master who accepted us into his lineage and started to teach us the Khom script—the sacred calligraphy of *sak yan*—and basic tattoo techniques. At this point, I still was not thinking about tattooing people but on the second day of my apprenticeship my master compelled me to give a Hanuman tattoo to a devotee.

"Every year while I was apprenticing, I would attend the Wai Khru or Master's Day of the late Ajarn Thong, one of the greatest and most respected tattoo masters of this century who started tattooing me four years earlier," he explained. "During Wai Khru, devotees come to have the power of their tattoos 'reactivated' or tested for efficacy and power. Thong was told that I had started to learn the sacred art of *sak yan*, but instead of the standard blessing he gave to his disciples

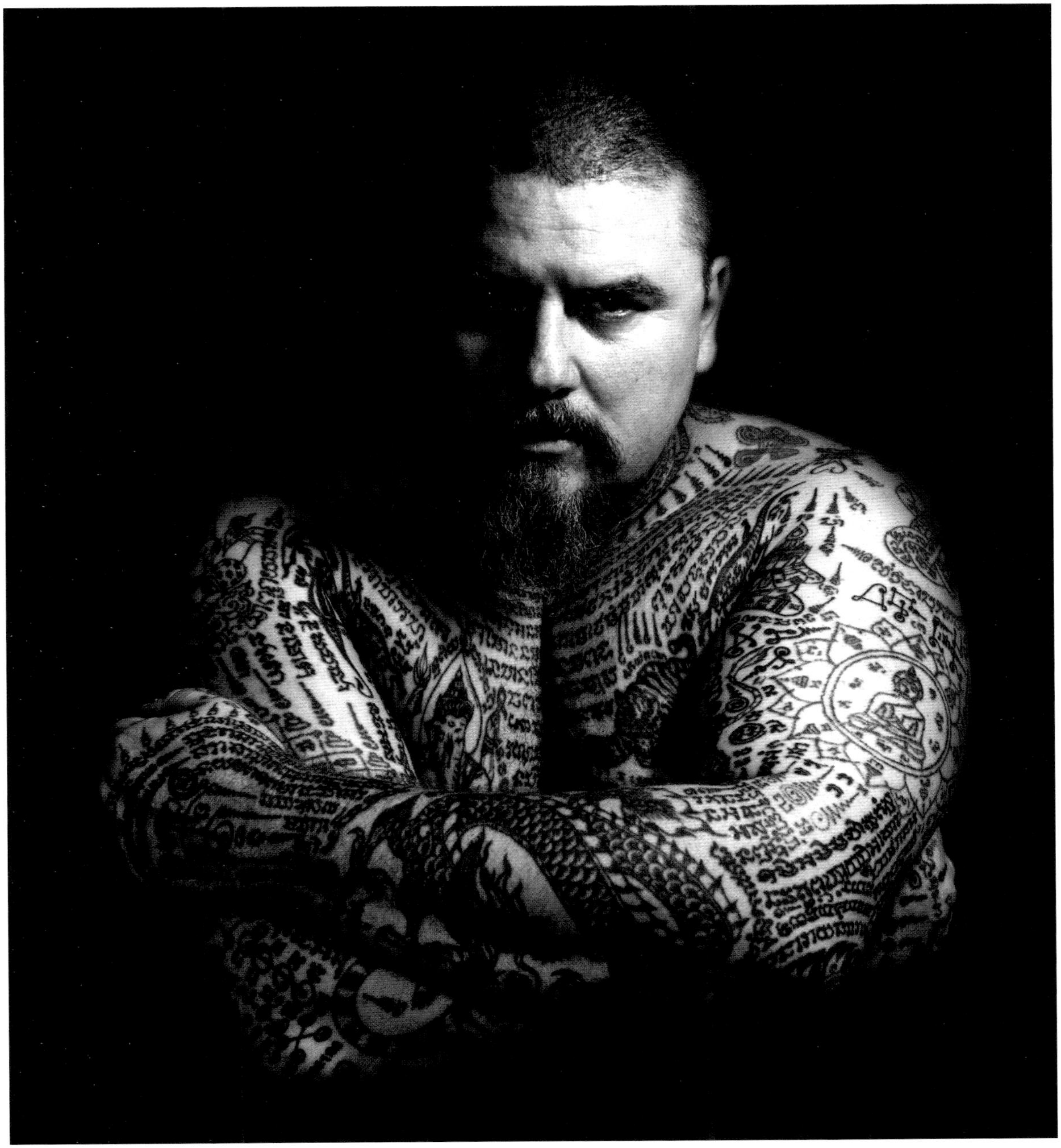

FIGURE 5.44
Ajarn Matthieu Duquenois, 2014. © Matthieu Duquenois.

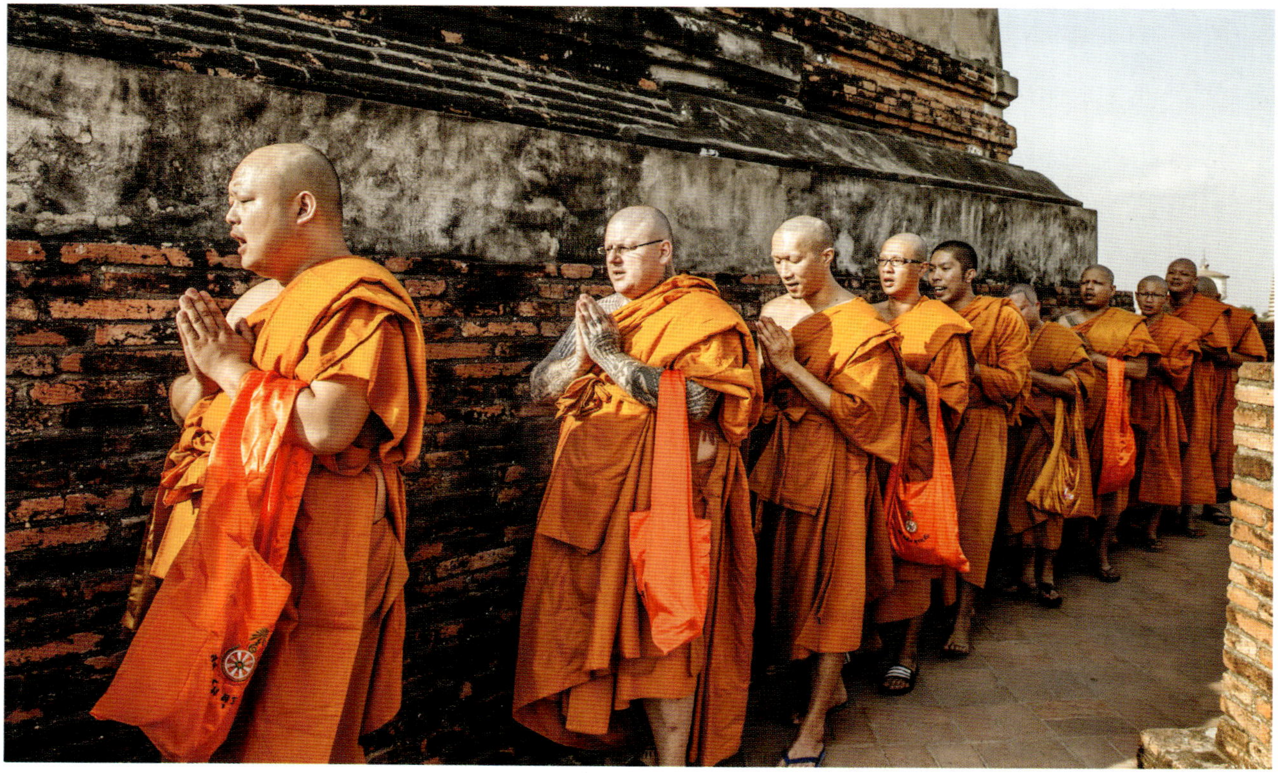

FIGURE 5.45
To prepare himself for the world of *sak yan*, Duquenois devoted himself to Buddhism and became a monk for a short time, Thailand, 2013. © Matthieu Duquenois.

he blessed me with a very special one, called Krop Khem, that conferred the title of tattoo master upon me. He presented me with a *mai sak* (tattooing tool) and a *tamla yan* (book) of *sak yan* designs and secret formulas he had learned from his master," he said. "According to the other masters of Ajarn Thong's lineage, he gave me this honor because he sensed something in me. He then told me that I would now continue in his path and become a full-time tattoo master. That same year, I became a Buddhist monk for a short time in order to purify myself and prepare for the tattooing that was to come."

MASTERING MYSTICAL KNOWLEDGE

I myself have a few *sak yan* and they are very pointilinear, but some monks I met in Thailand are so precise that their tattoos look almost machinelike, with beautiful line work. I asked Duquenois what was the hardest part of making Thai-style tattoos.

"As a foreigner, making genuine *sak yan* nowadays is a real challenge in many ways," he said. "Many people think it is easy to tattoo a *sak yan* design because they often see monks or others using stencils. But the meaning of these designs stem from a combination of many complex factors."

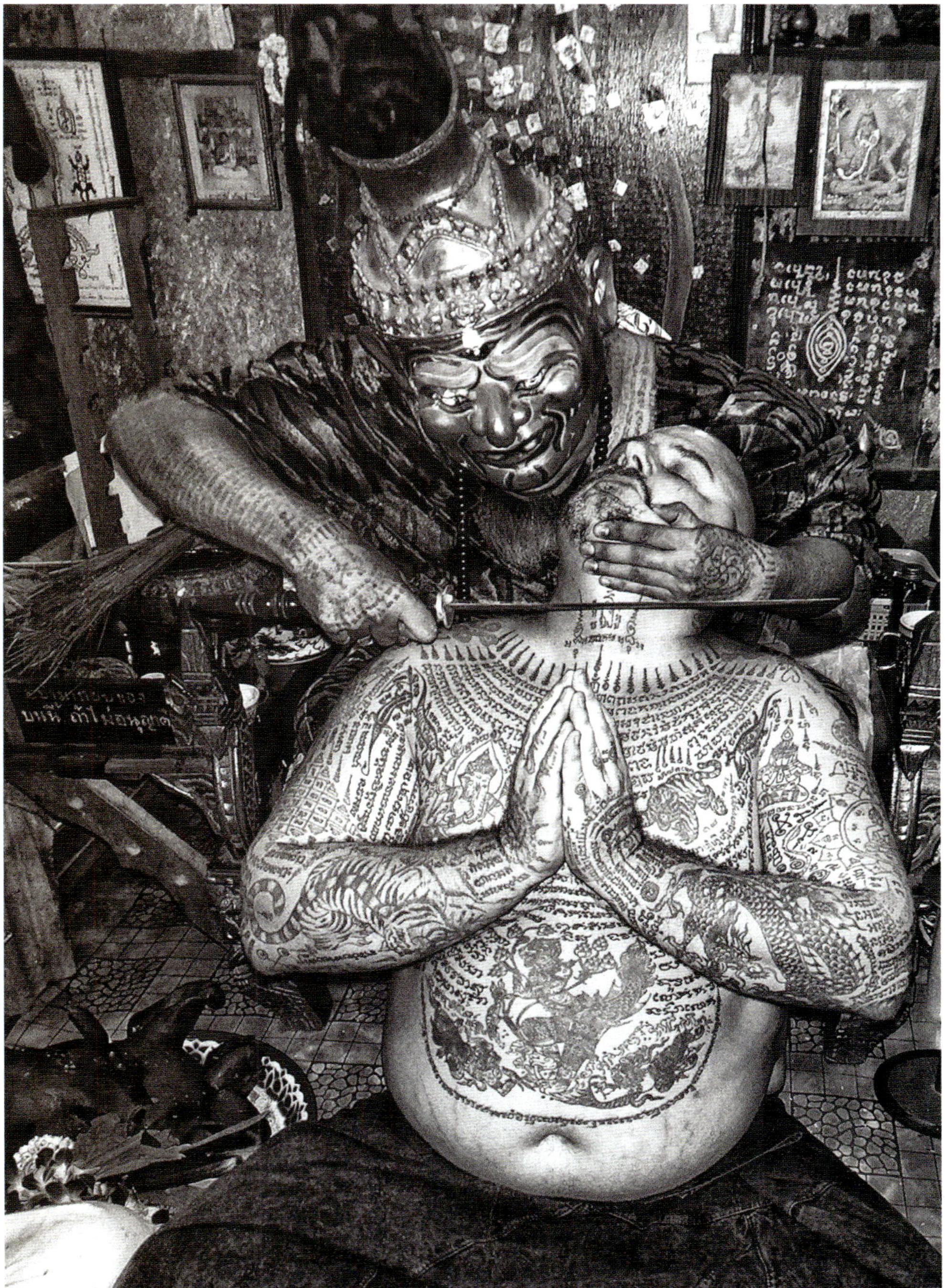

FIGURE 5.46
The famous Ajarn Toy of Bangkok is masked with Pho Kae, the hermit monk, and attempts to cut Duquenois' skin, 2012. The ritual of *Long Kong* is performed by tattoo masters on special occasions such as the Wai Khru to test the power of the tattoos in front of an assembly in the tattoo sanctuary. © Matthieu Duquenois.

FIGURE 5.47
Ajarn Matthieu completing a design to empower the tattoo thus created, 2012. © Matthieu Duquenois.

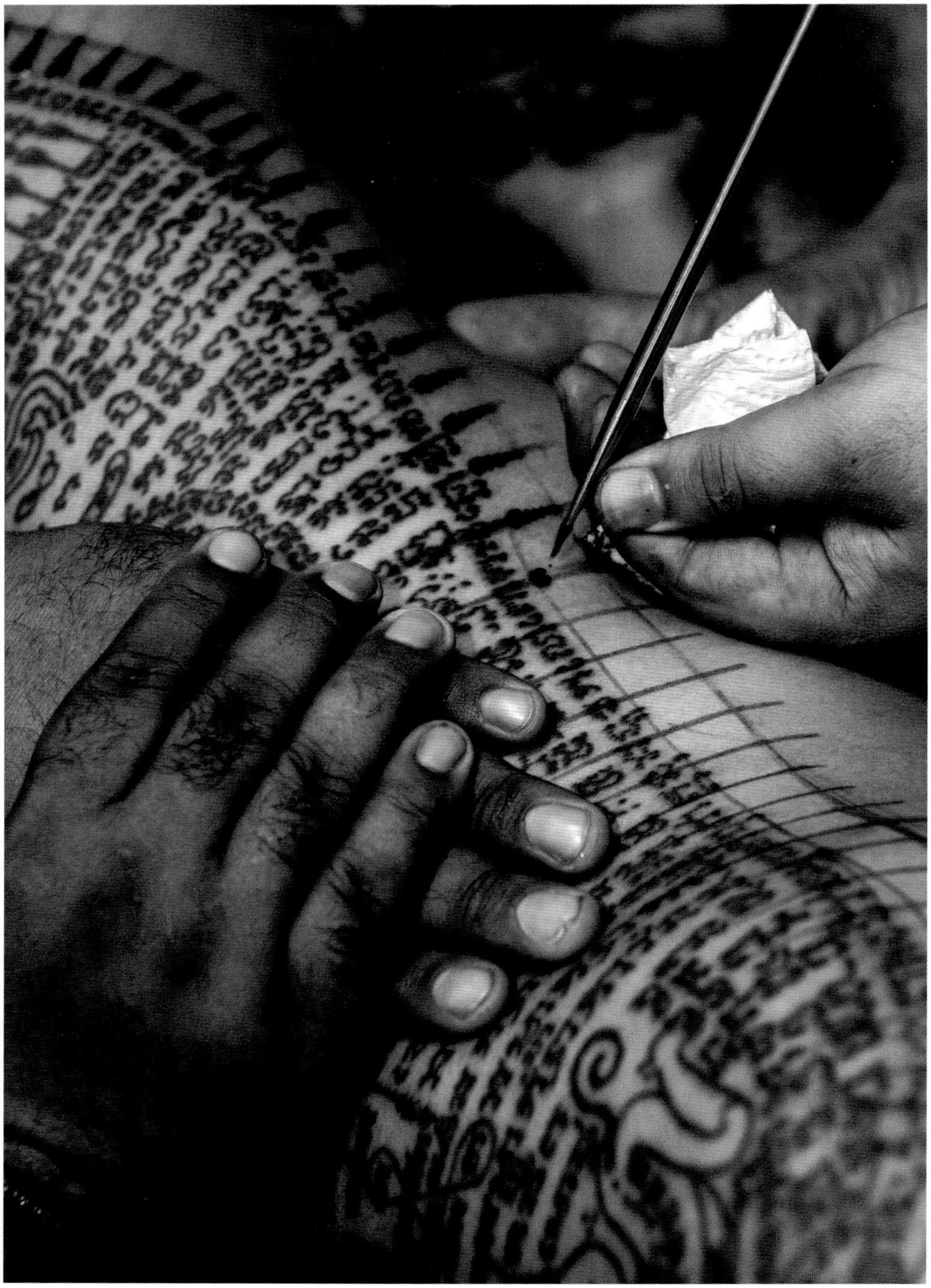

"First, the master tattooist must be part of a lineage of masters. The more powerful the lineage, the more powerful are the master's tattoos. We also must respect a certain number of rules of conduct and respect the lineage and the Buddhist precepts. The most difficult is the apprenticeship where we must learn and memorize scripts in a variety of ancient languages like Khom, Pali, Lanna, Tai Yai, Môn, and Burmese, not to mention countless *mantra* chants," he observed. "We chant these *mantras* loudly or silently to pay respect and call the spirits of our masters, to bless the body of the devotee before starting tattooing. During the tattooing ritual we keep chanting specific *mantra* for each design, each curve, or each script we ink. It is a very complicated and secret process. Each tattoo master keeps his own secret spells and they are different from one lineage to the other. That is why only a tattoo master can bless his own tattoos. Once the physical tattoo has been completed, it needs to be activated or empowered with more *mantra* chanting and blessings. My wife and I are still learning from our *ajarns* and it will take us years to become accomplished *sak yan* masters."

PRESERVING *SAK YAN* HERITAGE

For centuries, *ajarns* have marked human skin with powerful animals (tigers, centipedes, turtles, lions), deities (Garuda, Ganesh, Hanuman), *ruesi* (hermit sages), and sacrosanct symbols in their quest to render the body everlasting and invincible. Drawing on knowledge of astronomy, sacred

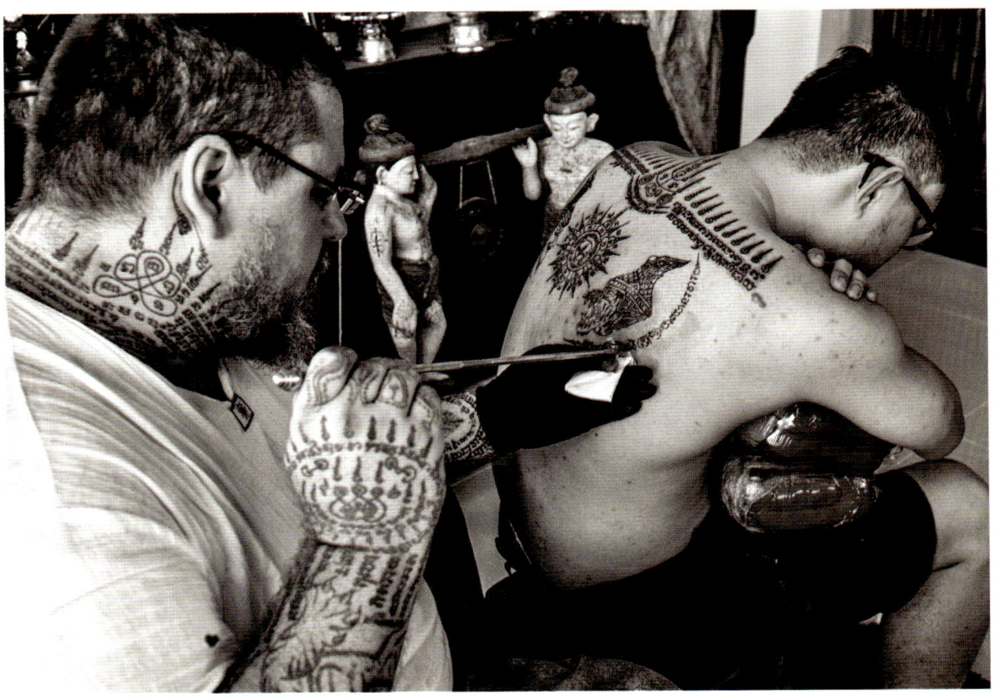

FIGURE 5.48
Ajarn Matthieu completing a line of Khom script to empower the Ruesi Pho Kae and Ruesi Na Sua designs that convey knowledge, healing, and protection, 2015. © Matthieu Duquenois.

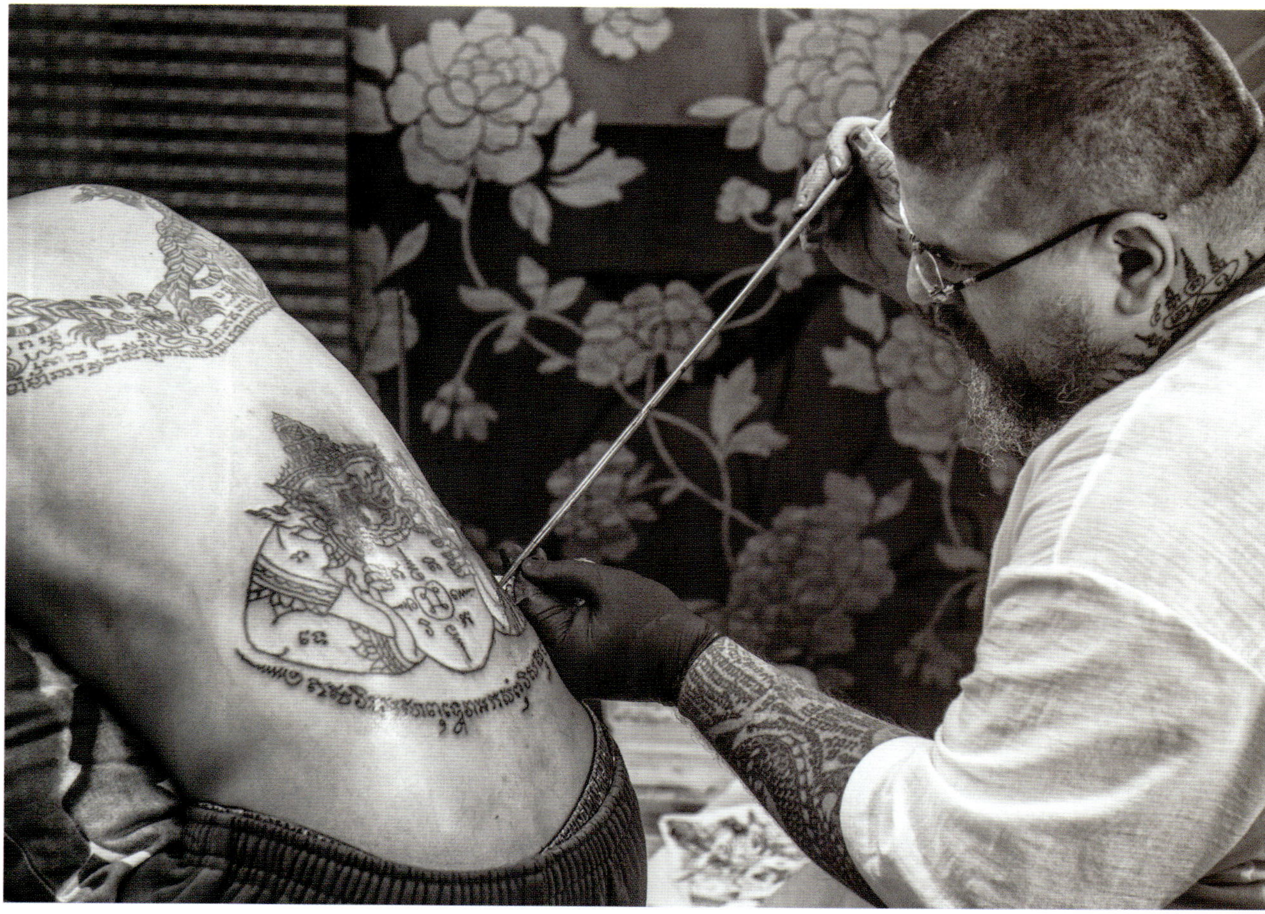

FIGURE 5.49
With tattooing tool in hand Duquenois inks the "Rahu eating the moon" *yantra,* which symbolizes that all evil will be eaten by this demon deity, 2015. © Matthieu Duquenois.

geometry, holy texts, and incantations, the tattooist plunges his large tattooing needles into the flesh to render a rich visual mosaic of tattoo iconography that is at once a blessing of protection and a personal sacrifice to the supernatural.

But according to Duquenois, these incredible traditions are in danger of vanishing. "Indeed, *sak yan* is gaining in popularity and can easily be machined at a rapid rate," he said. "But genuine Thai magical tattooing with full traditional ritual is slowly disappearing as the elder masters pass away. Although there are new tattoo artists practicing now, very few of them totally dedicate themselves to the tradition, learn the requirements, and respect the lineage" (Krutak 2016b:66).

Duquenois continued, "Although I just used the term 'tattoo artists,' my wife and I do not really consider ourselves to be among them. For us, the tattooing ritual is the medium to instill the required magic into the devotee's body. Our credo is to listen to people's needs, sometimes their distresses, and try to temper or balance them with the proper *yantra* and *mantra*s to complete them."

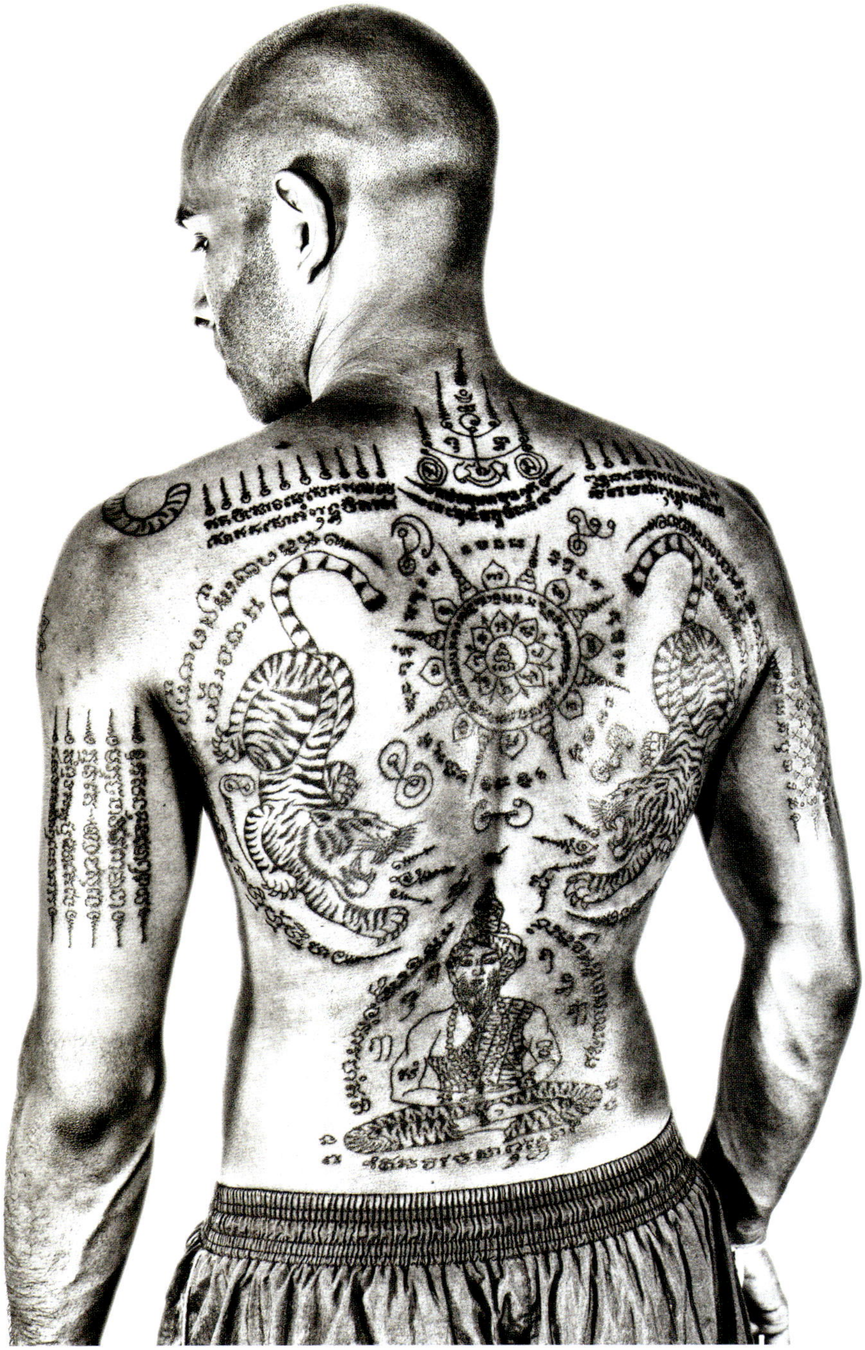

FIGURE 5.50
Backpiece tattooed by Ajarn Matthieu on a *luksit* (disciple) depicting *yantras* for strength and courage (tigers), universal protection (neck), and knowledge, healing, and protection (sage Pho Kae on lower back), 2014. © Matthieu Duquenois.

"In our view, the meaning of *sak yan* is to try to help devotees to reach their goals through the power of their tattoos. *Sak yan* often takes people down paths they never even suspected or expected. The animist roots of *sak yan* really attract me and I can feel a deep and ancient force in these tattoos, so you can see why they are not art to me" (Krutak 2016b:66).

In order to keep the spirit of *sak yan* alive, Duquenois and his wife are building the first tattoo museum in Thailand in their hometown of Hua Hin. Their goal is to help preserve the rich cultural and religious heritage of *sak yan* for future generations of students and disciples.

"Soon the collection will hold up to seven hundred different pieces. Bronze tattoo weights, different types of ancient needle tips, wooden stamp blocks, ink pots, magical ingredients, books of spells, and lots of other accessories used by tattoo masters will be displayed," he said. "Eighty-percent of the proceeds we receive for our *sak yan* will be used to purchase as many of these objects as possible before they vanish completely. We are also reaching out to private collectors to acquire more objects to complete the collection" (Krutak 2016b:66).

"The museum project came about as an urgent necessity to save and protect vanishing tools and objects related to Thai sacred tattoos, but also those from Burma, Laos and Cambodia because all of these tattooing traditions share the same roots," Duquenois explained.

6

TATTOOS OF THE NAGA OF INDIA AND MYANMAR

Marks for the Afterlife

All tattoos travel with you into the afterlife, so that they can be shared with the ancestors.

—**Nganhai,** a tattooed Khiamniungan warrior of Pangsha village, Nagaland, 2008

Why are you acting like a woman? Honor your ancestors, be brave and strong [during your tattooing].

—**Leithong Phom,** son of tattooist Mrs. Hongnyu of Younphong village, Nagaland, 2010

It is early April 2010 on the Indo-Burmese border and the Konyak Aoleang festival is in full swing. Here in the village of Longwa, volleys of musket fire explode—*Pop! Pop! Pop!*—and clouds of heavy smoke interrupt the blue sky. Throngs of plumed, tattooed, and traditionally garbed Konyak warriors jump, chant, and reenact their former exploits on the battlefield in a concerted attempt to honor and attract the attention of Wangwan, their divine spirit of blessing.

Aoleang is a New Year celebration of sorts, marking the end of winter and the coming of the new agricultural year. The millet, rice, and other fields have been sowed by now and the Konyak eagerly await the arrival of the rejuvenating rains. Through elaborate feasting they give thanks to those friends and relatives who provided them with assistance in the previous year, including the spirits of the ancestors. But above all, they celebrate and give praise to Wangwan until the six-day festival ends.

In bygone days, Aoleang was also the time for tattooing boys and girls who reached adulthood. These ethnic markers were applied to various parts of the body by skilled tattooists, who were usually female. Men who had participated in combat and who had taken a human life were also entitled to unique tattoos, usually on the neck or face, which proclaimed their status in Naga society. Warriors could receive tattoos at any time during the year, especially after a successful military campaign.

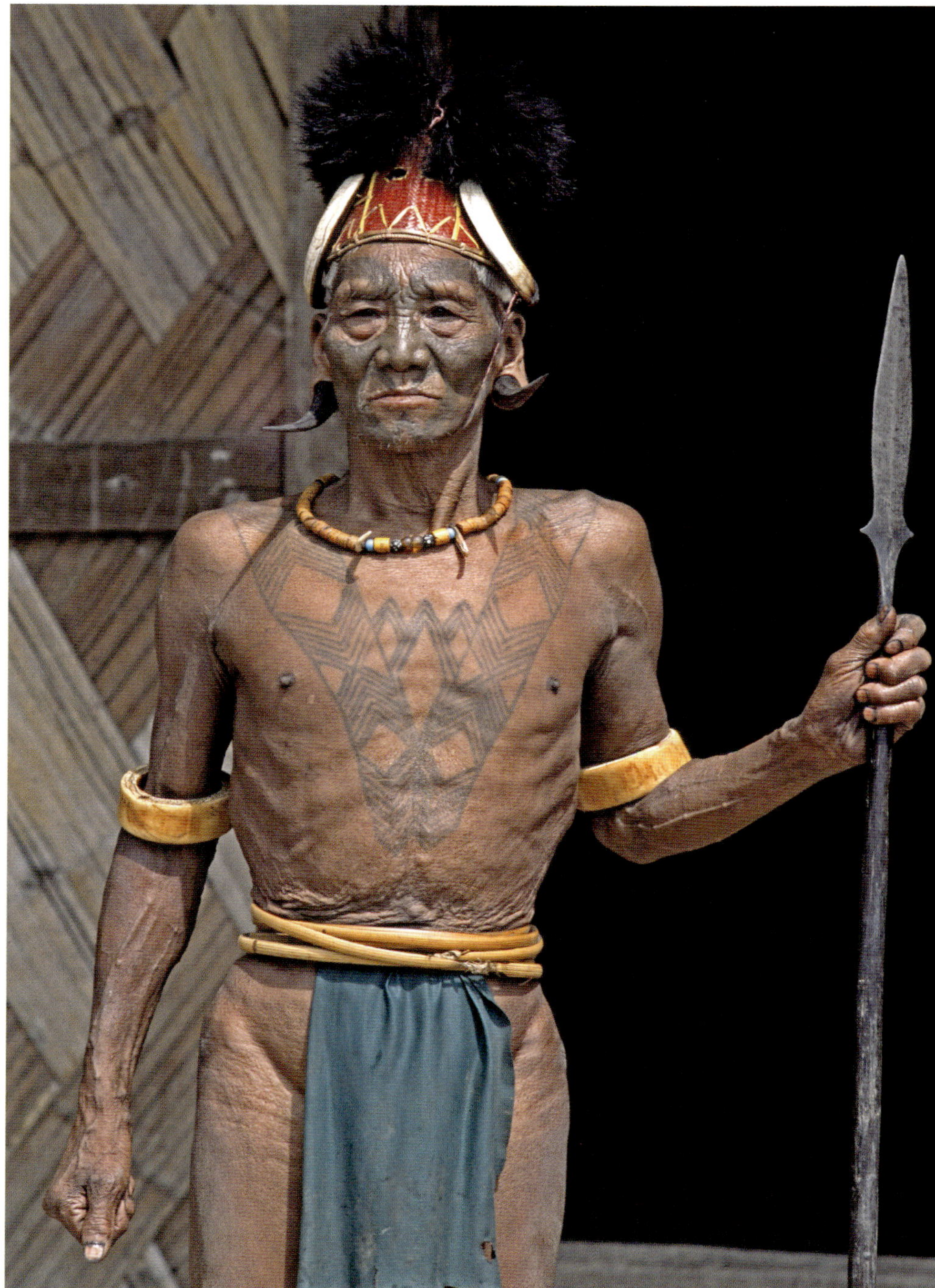

FIGURE 6.1
The late Upper Konyak warrior Lanang of Longwa village, which straddles the Myanmar border, Nagaland, Northeast India, 2010. His goggle-like facial markings denote his participation in hand-to-hand combat, and the V-shaped chest tattoos were earned for dispatching enemies. © Lars Krutak.

One of these men was the late Lanang (d. 2012), a striking Konyak elder who was blind. When I met him in 2010, he told me he was uncertain how old he was, but I presumed he was around ninety years old. Despite his advanced age, he sprung into combat mode with ease: crouching, tracking, circling, then thrusting his spear into the chest of his make-believe enemy. Once injured, his imagined victim was beheaded with a swift blow of his razor-sharp *dao*, a machete-like sword—a weapon he had used for this purpose three times before the Naga stopped headhunting in the mid-twentieth century.

Indeed, the last headhunting raid carried out by Longwa warriors was around 1968. According to the charismatic Baptist deacon Honggo Wangshu, who participated in the battle, the enemy village was in Myanmar. Although Honggo himself did not take an enemy head, his war party was nevertheless successful, and each of the Longwa warriors earned the right to the thick and dark spectacle-like *shen tu* (facial tattoo) that is one of the hallmarks of Konyak manhood.

"We measured the time to get the tattoo by the position of the sun in the sky," Honggo said. "From 7:30 a.m. to 2 p.m., the tattooist worked on my face. It was done by the *anghya* (wife of the chief), only she could do it. Young girls and female family members gathered around and held my arms tight to prevent me from moving. Some of them had to stretch my face to keep the skin tight, while others wiped away the blood. That is how it was done," he explained.

"During those times, everyone was considered an enemy—there was no peace," Honggo continued. "And in the times of our forefathers, everyone was in conflict. *Fighting, fighting, ambush, ambush*, it kept on going for a long time. There was no love for the enemy villages," he proclaimed. "And if we had not converted to Christianity, you would not be sitting here today and talking to me! Your head would have been taken as an enemy because you entered our territory. But today you are safe, because we believe in Christ and he preaches friendship. We are all one today!"

In the early 1970s, Honggo and other Longwa villagers had heard about neighboring villages converting to Christianity and embracing the changes it brought, including education, development, medical care, and improved living standards. Honggo was attracted by the idea of peace and brotherhood too, because since time immemorial the Konyak world had been marked by violence and war. He and others were tired of the constant fighting over land disputes, blood feuds, and other calamities, and on February 24, 1978, he made a pledge to walk in the path of Christ.

"I am one of the first persons to be baptized in this village," he told me. "And that was a stepping stone, because other members of my clan, my family, and household were also ready to convert. Eventually seventy-four members of my clan were baptized in 1978. Today, my children have graduated from high school, and my youngest son is in law college. Some of my grandchildren are also attending college, and because of this I am very happy and at peace now."

But with the adoption of a Christian way of life, local tattooing practices were soon to fade. Long considered a "degrading and repulsive" custom (see M. M. Clark 1907:54) by local Baptist missionaries, tattooing had to be eradicated because it was linked to shamanic rites and traditional religious practices that the Church sought to replace with its ideology.

I queried the tattooed deacon about the days following the receipt of his tattoo, mainly about whether he observed a special diet after what must have been a very painful experience. Honggo revealed that his face was badly swollen and that he could only eat soft and tender foods

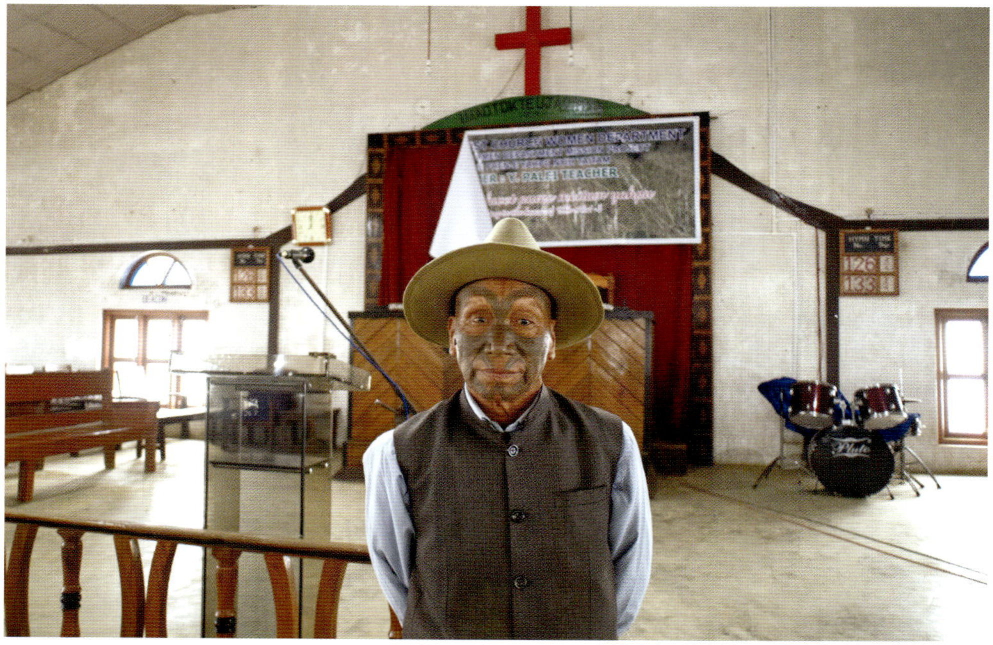

FIGURE 6.2
The Konyak Baptist deacon Honggo Wangshu, one of the first men of his village to convert to Christianity, Longwa village, Nagaland, Northeast India, 2019. Prior to his conversion, Honggo participated in the last headhunting raid conducted by his community in the late 1960s. For his exploits, he received a warrior's facial tattoo. © Lars Krutak.

with a bamboo spoon. Then he pointed to his tattoo. "Can you see the tattoo on my face?" he exclaimed. "In my personal opinion, the tattooing tradition should have continued, because it is the custom of the Konyak. Because it is the Konyak identity card—the identity card of the Konyak! The Longwa identity card! This tattooing should not have been stopped, because without these tattooed marks everyone looks plain and simple. . . . This was the way of the Konyak!"

NAGA WARFARE AND WARRIOR TATTOOS

Across the Naga region, April was a month for war. Able-bodied men were compelled to take human heads for a variety of reasons, ranging from long-standing blood feuds, territorial disputes, revenge killings, the appeasement of debt, and other reasons outlined below. Human heads were considered sacrosanct by the Naga because they were believed to be a source of future prosperity. More specifically, enemy heads or even human sacrifices were deployed to please various spirits (of the mountains, the earth, the afterlife), the sun and moon,[1] and the Supreme Being who controlled the Naga universe, and were used to effectuate a variety of significant rituals (cf. Dewar 1931). The tattooed Naga chief of Pounyo Naukkon village in Burma, which sits just across the border of Nagaland, told the British military commander H. J. Mitchell (1929:17) that "we take the heads of human beings because they are the only fit morsels for the Nat [Great Spirit]." Trophy heads obtained in war concluded men's initiation ceremonies into their respective *paan* (also *morung*), or "clan house," or they might be used to consummate the manufacture of large log drums, each of which contained a male or female forest spirit, for the *paan* itself. Heads also helped end periods of mourning or to forestall epidemics, or were deployed to propitiate spirits prior to or after agricultural harvests (Joshi 2004; Sardeshpande 1987; Saul 2005).[2]

Among some Naga groups, slave sacrifices were believed to help end periods of agricultural blight, famine, and disease through the propitiation of the spirits held responsible for such calamities, or they accompanied the building of a new house for a chieftain or wealthy man, or helped purify a home wherein a woman died in childbirth (Dewar 1931; von Fürer-Haimendorf 1962). For these occasions, the magical soul substance of the sacrificial being, or its body parts, assured prosperity, wealth, and happiness for the occupants of the home, and helped ward off evil spirits from attacking the members of its household, including its domesticated animals (cf. Dewar 1927).[3]

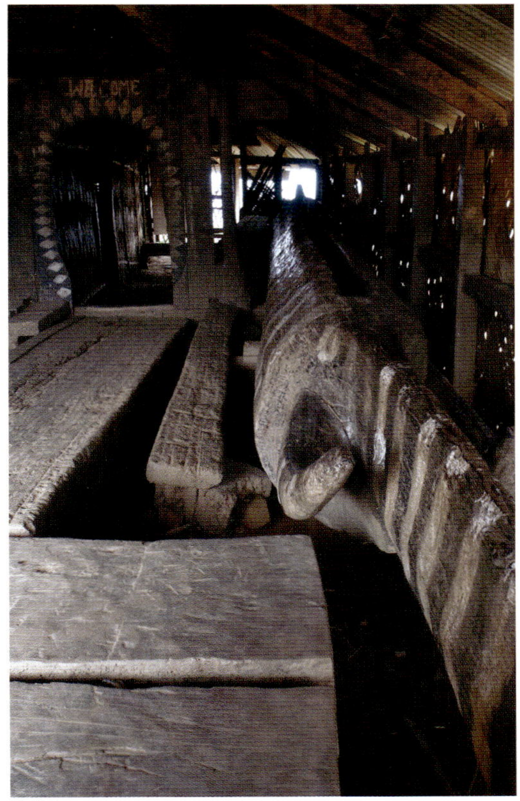

FIGURE 6.3
Phom Naga log drum in the shape of an elephant, Longleng village, Nagaland, 2010. © Lars Krutak.

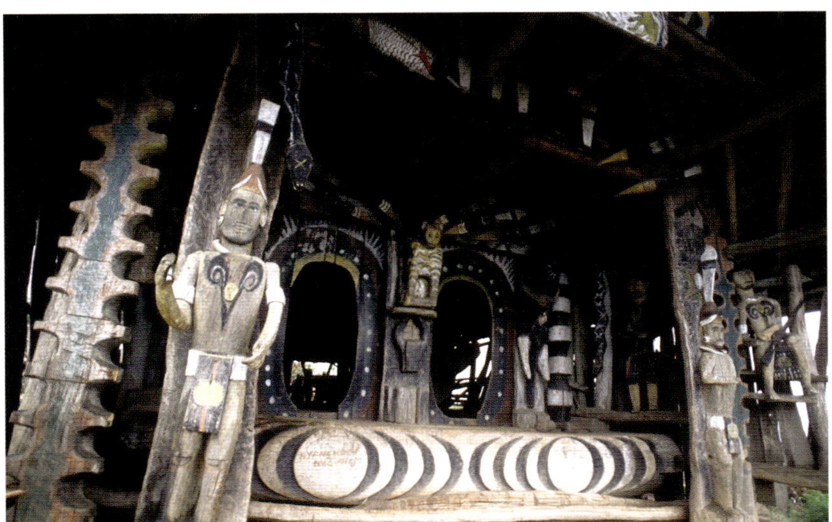

FIGURE 6.4
Mangthong *paan* (men's clan house) of Yongshei village, Nagaland, 2010. The façade displays tattooed Phom warriors and animals related to desired virtues: *mithun* (bovine) for wealth; tigers for strength; elephants for power; hornbills for beauty and their feathers for success in headhunting; and the python for negating evil influences. The rayed oval doors represent the vagina, since when young men are initiated into the men's house, they are reborn as warriors (cf. van Ham and Saul 2008:58). © Lars Krutak.

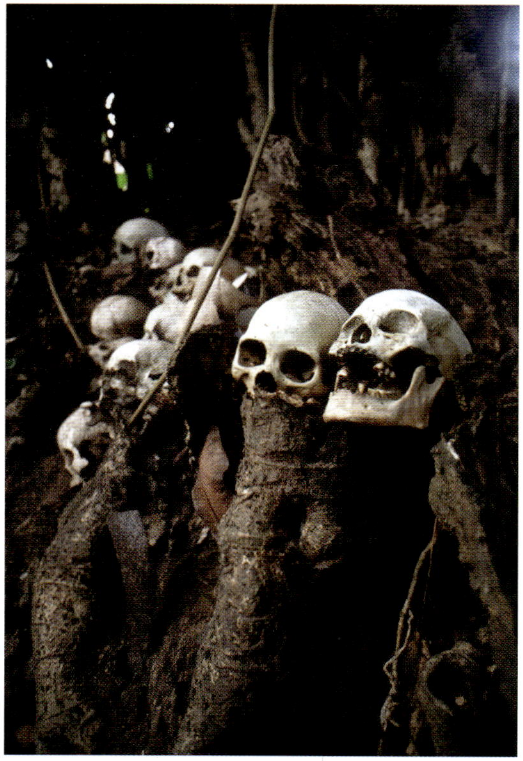

FIGURE 6.5
Skull shrine of Shangnyu village, Konyak Naga, Nagaland, 2010. In the Naga universe, human heads were believed to contain the spiritual essence of the deceased. In order to activate this beneficial power, village shamans performed rituals throughout the year to "please" the heads. These rituals were closely linked to the agricultural cycle, especially the cultivation and harvesting of hill rice, when heads were ceremonially fed with rice cakes and given drinks of potent rice beer to keep their favor close to the living. The skulls of decapitated enemies and even revered ancestors were traditionally kept in *paan* (also *morung*) men's clan houses, or sacred banyan tree groves that today can sometimes still be seen in Naga villages. © Lars Krutak.

The origins of human sacrifice lay in legends. At the Rangpan Naga village of Mitai in Burma, just south of the Arunachal Pradesh border, Mitchell (1929:19) recorded the following tale in the 1920s: "To ensure good crops and freedom from disease, the Nats [Spirits] decreed the usual sacrifice of cattle and poultry. Later on these sacrifices lost their potency and the sacrifice of monkeys was ordained. Monkeys grew wily and the Nats then decided that before the harvest festival raids should be carried out and heads obtained in these raids would suffice. Even this became difficult as villagers began to devise schemes for their security and so the Nats decreed that as men could not be obtained in battle, they should be bought and then sacrificed."

For the Naga, human heads were like containers of seed that, on germination, could increase the fertility of the crops, of livestock, and of the men and women in the village community. In order to receive this life-giving power, village shamans performed rituals throughout the year to "please" the heads, which eventually came to rest on or in log drums, in men's houses, in the earth, or in the houses of chiefs or warriors. The skulls of revered ancestors or family members were also curated in this way, and came to rest in rock shelters, stone cysts placed in cemeteries, or sacred banyan tree groves that can sometimes still be seen in remote villages.

Far above Longwa, along a lonely stretch of dirt road, lies a cluster of villages inhabited by the Chen Naga. They also celebrate the coming of spring in April, soon after the first sowing of the millet and maize crop, and in times of war the rites associated with headhunting. These ceremonials included the worship and installation of recently acquired enemy heads from the previous year in the various men's clan houses locally called *paan*. The Chen are a subtribe of the Konyak Naga who live along both sides of the mountainous and heavily forested international border of India and Myanmar in the Patkai Range. Although they speak a dialect of Konyak, the common term for "tattooing" used across the region is *tu*, or "marking" (Konyak and Bos 2017:74). Among the Chen can be found some of the rarest tattoos on earth: the *shahnyu yaya*, or tiger familiar spirit tattoo, and the *ring tu pu*, or warrior's neck tattoo. These tattoos could be made by only male tattooists, whereas among the Wancho and some Naga tribes inhabiting Myanmar, male neck tattoos were applied by women.

The Chen have inhabited this area of Nagaland for hundreds of years. One of the leaders of Chenwetnyu village, the subchief Chen-o Khuzuthrupa of Hoyang (d. 2023),[4] told me that his ancestor Khuzu, a Chen chieftain, migrated to the present Chen areas twenty generations ago. His family title, Khuzuthrupa, is conferred to the firstborn male child of Khuzu's direct bloodline.

Traditionally, as with other Naga groups, male tattooing among the Chen was primarily associated with militaristic culture and the former practice of headhunting. Although some young men might inherit the right to bear specific forms of warrior tattooing from their fathers if they were members of the *angh* (ruling class) or sons of *lowang* (rich men), typically speaking only combat veterans who had proved themselves on the battlefield could earn the right to be tattooed on their faces and bodies. There were, of course, different grades of Chen warrior status and specific tattoos associated with each station, as I will discuss below. All of these tattoos were placed on visually prominent areas of the body and could be read by friend and foe like military insignia. But before I go into further detail, I will discuss the various tactics of warfare practiced by the Naga.

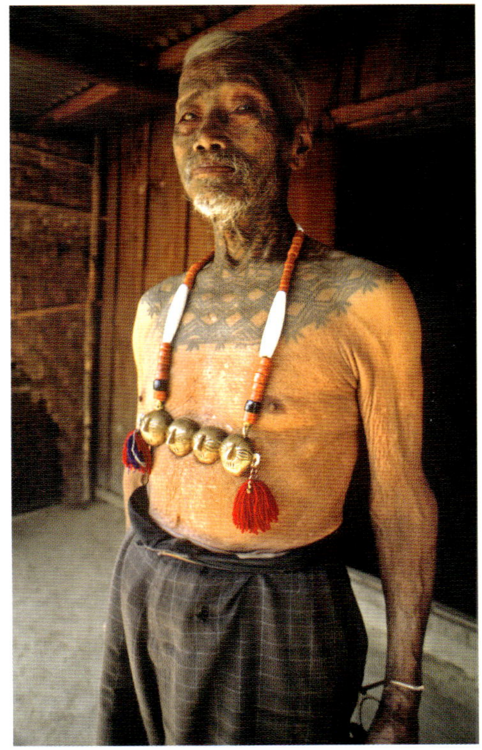

FIGURE 6.6
The late tattooed Chen elder Eno Nockshom of Chenmoho village, Nagaland, bears the *ring tu pu* (neck tattoos) of a veteran *naomei* (warrior), 2010. The lozenge pattern is derived from woven bamboo, which is a symbol of strength. In former times, the number of brass heads appearing on a man's necklace communicated how many men he had beheaded on the battlefield. © Lars Krutak.

As Honggo previously noted, warfare and raiding were part and parcel of everyday life in the ancestral past. Describing the situation along the Indo-Burmese borderlands of the 1920s, the British military commander T. P. Dewar (1931:159) of the Burma Frontier Service wrote of the stressful experience village inhabitants encountered daily:

> The tribesmen lived in constant terror of attack from their enemies. . . . All the village pigs, cattle, etc., enter and sleep within the [palisaded village] defenses at night. A watch is kept, the fighting men sleeping with their arms by their sides ready for immediate action. Travelling after sundown is rarely undertaken and then only in a large party. No one leaves the village defenses in the morning until the sun is well in the heavens; there is always fear of a lurking foe. The cultivation of the land and hewing of wood is performed by parties sufficiently large for some members to detect an enemy in the vicinity. On the least alarm being raised such parties return to the village defenses with as great haste and little delay as possible. It must be remembered that the [enemies] were a head-hunting race, who made no discrimination and killed men, women, children and even infants, taking the head, arms and legs of their victims to offer to the communal Nats [Spirits] . . . for the welfare of the crops, health of the community, etc., etc.

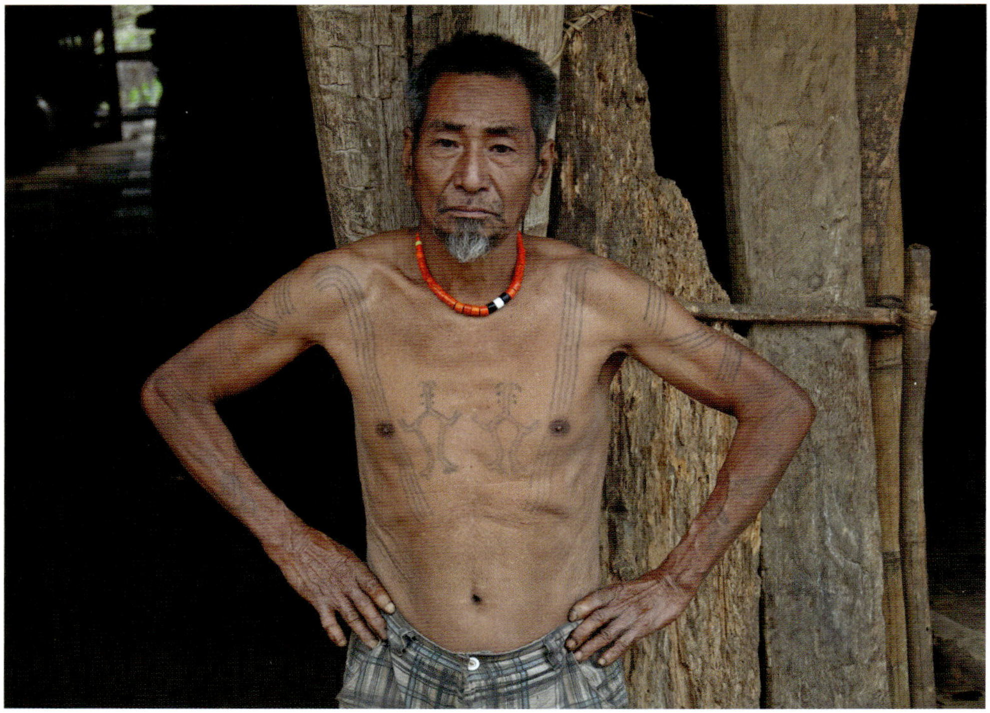

FIGURE 6.7
U Ngòm Pok, a Lainong elder, tribal historian, and author living in Lahe, Myanmar, wears chest tattoos to honor his tribal traditions, 2014. Traditionally, Lainong chest tattoos were a mark of a warrior. "Braces"—parallel lines down either side of the chest—were worn by warriors to indicate they had been part of a war party. Tattooed human figures were also an important part of these warrior traditions. For the Lainong, these icons were supposed to protect the wearer from the spirit of the enemy (Saul 2005). Mr. Pok has long been troubled by the vanishing customs of his tribe, including tattoo. He recently said, "The [entire] Lainong tribe should be concerned about losing these traditions" (Win and Macnamara 2016). © Lars Krutak.

Before a raid, however, various omens were observed to determine the best time for a successful attack. I was told by Phom warriors that the fifth day after a new moon was an auspicious time, especially if a star appeared near the celestial body.[5] Moreover, a chicken was sacrificed, and if its head fell in the direction of the raiding war party, the group would be successful. If its head fell in the direction of the enemy, that was an inauspicious sign (Krutak 2010b: n.p.). The chicken's intestines were also examined for signals of success or failure, as were cooked egg yolks; if they appeared entire, this was a good sign, but if broken this was inauspicious (Dutta 1978). While on the warpath, various animal omens were observed, including the movements of the civet; if one crossed the warrior's path, the party would return homeward because "it is a sign of bad luck" (Krutak 2010b: n.p.).

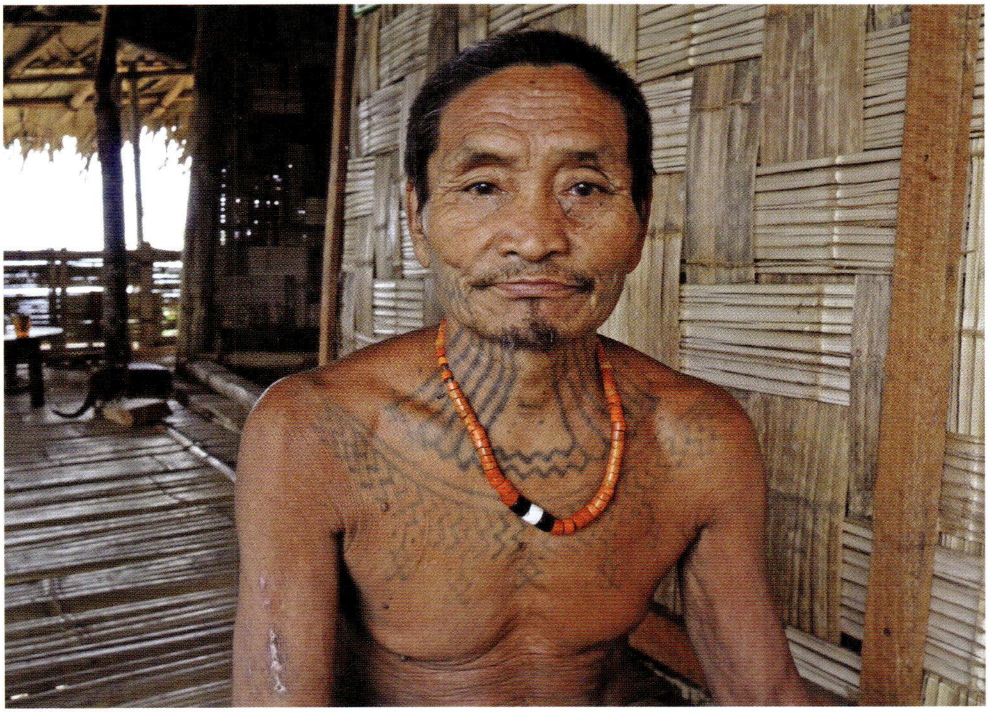

FIGURE 6.8
Macham Naga elder U Shel Maw, 2014. During my travels documenting Naga tattoos in Northwest Myanmar, I met several men bearing tattoos that in the past signified warrior status. However, none of these men had participated in combat and they acquired these ancestral marks to honor the tattooing traditions of their tribes and/or family. I had seen a photo of the Macham Naga elder U Shel Maw published in the book *The Naga of Burma* (Saul 2005). There, he was described as a "headhunter" because of his neck tattoos. After interviewing him, I learned that this was not the truth. He noted, "My father and grandfather were great Macham headhunters and warriors. Because of this I was given the honor to carry on his prestige through the same tattoo patterns they once wore." © Lars Krutak.

Prior to combat, warriors and the village community observed various taboos. Among the Konyak of Wakching village, "[w]hen a head-hunting party has gone to war, their women may not pound rice [nor] go to the fields—they only fetch wood and firewood, and they don't allow strangers to come into their houses. The night before a man goes to war, he does not sleep with his wife but in the *morung* [*paan*]" (von Fürer-Haimendorf 1936a:191, n.b. 3). I was told by Phom elders that the wives of warriors must remain "pure" at all times, and they could not visit their agricultural fields or their neighbors' homes, or touch another person's possessions, otherwise their husbands might not return (Krutak 2010b: n.p.).

Certain rituals might also be performed to assist the warriors in their endeavors.[6] Konyak warriors of Chi village carried an egg onto enemy soil. It was blown on, with the breath directed toward the location of the enemy village, in the hopes that its inhabitants would become blind (von Fürer-Haimendorf 1936b:115, n.b. 6). Christoph von Fürer-Haimendorf (1936c:59, n.b. 7) recorded other instances of Konyak "war magic" with eggs. While visiting Kongan village, he observed, "When a head-hunting party reached the land of the enemies, they mixed some bad eggs with mud and smeared the mixture on their *dao* and spear blades and on their bodies to make the enemies sleepy and half blind." In Arunachal Pradesh, a Lazu Naga priest prepared a concoction of egg yolks mixed with egg whites; this liquid was placed in a bamboo tube. The contents were poured onto the boundary of the enemy village and the priest uttered an incantation to make the people living there fall fast asleep (Dutta 1978).

In my interviews with Khiamniungan warriors in Myanmar, I was told that the village shaman or a powerful warrior made a magical powder that was blown in the direction of an enemy village to make its residents easier to kill. The concoction consisted of infertile chicken eggs and charcoal, mixed with *opai* (a special leaf) that was pulverized. Their crossbow bolts were also coated with another magical substance manufactured from a *sepai* fruit mixed with the resin of an unidentified tree: "If we hit an enemy, this 'poison' makes the victim sleepy and easier to kill" (Krutak 2016c:54). Another kind of poison had the effect of making wounds more septic.

Naga warfare took several forms (pitched battle, ambush, etc.) but one common thread united them: the element of surprise that usually resulted in success. A common tactic was for a small party of warriors to attack a group of people traveling to or from their agricultural fields or water sources. Conversely, large groups who were headed by two or three veteran *naomei* ("commanders" in Konyak) might attack in massed formation coming boldly, albeit silently, toward an enemy village in darkness or at dawn. The main party awaited some short distance from its target while a few scouts crept toward the village gates to assess the number of sentries and surrounding defenses. The defenses might include tripwires attached to improvised devices firing poisoned arrows or deadfalls covered with leaves and brush and studded with four- to five-foot-long *panjis* (bamboo spikes) that were sometimes poisoned. While the *panjis* might not kill an individual, a man who was unfortunate enough to make contact with them might be lamed for the rest of his life.

If possible, the sentries at the village gates were dispatched and these fortified entrances were stormed. Intruders let out blood-curdling war cries and the village was then lit by fire, throwing its sleeping inhabitants into a frenzy. As the villagers began streaming out of their homes, the enemy warriors cast their spears at them in attempts to hit their mark. The wounded were rushed by their attackers and the enemy warriors unsheathed their *daos,* machete-like short swords, and with expert blows quickly removed the heads and limbs (hands, feet) of their quarry. While several men may have pounced on the same enemy at once, the man who threw the first disabling spear usually claimed the right to the head trophy itself; the limbs were shared among the other warriors on their return home.

According to the unpublished notes of the anthropologist and Indian governmental advisor Verrier Elwin, the Konyak usually followed a specific technique while severing the head: "It is considered very bad to cut off a man's head from the back so that the *dao* comes out through the mouth. This means people of your own group will lose their heads. The correct method is to cut from [the] left to right side. [Moreover,] a youth should not actually decapitate on his first foray.

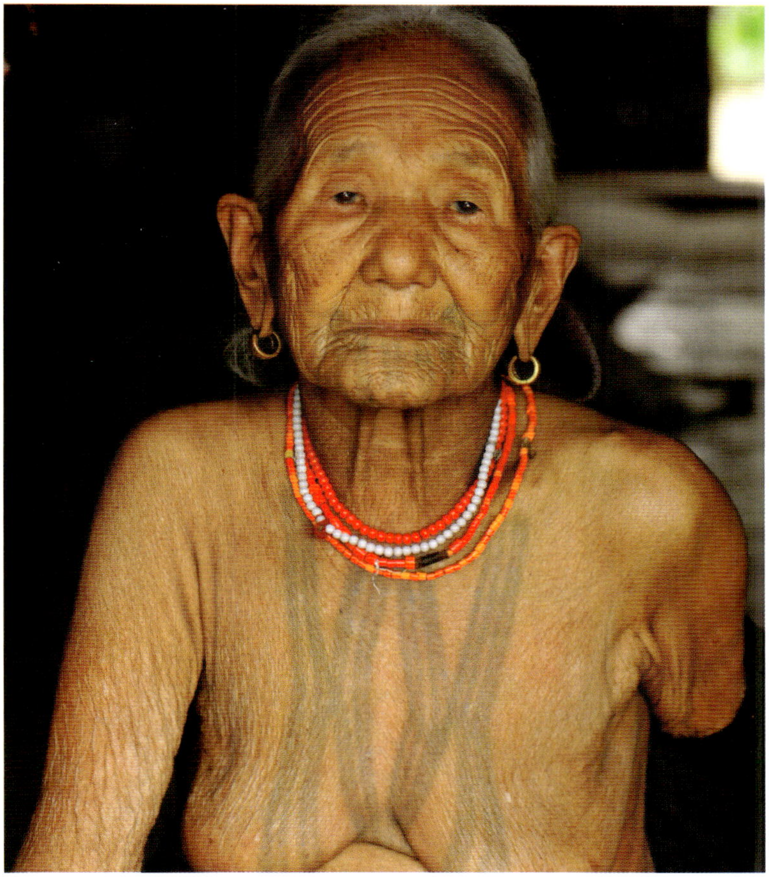

FIGURE 6.9
Konyak elder Echi Wangnyu, Ukha village, 2018. While traveling near the Indo-Myanmar border, I met one of the Konyak women who escaped the Ukha battle in her youth. Wangnyu is the last bearer of a unique chest tattoo, a large double X design that she received due to her father's prowess as a head-taker. This tattoo conferred honor and prestige on her family and was publicly visible since it was placed above her traditional outer garment. This incredible tattoo was illustrated schematically by Hutton (1929:13), but its function was not recorded. © Lars Krutak.

He should begin by cutting off hands and feet. Then once blood[i]ed, he may go on to the supreme achievement of the head" (Elwin 1953/1954: n.p.).

The trophies were immediately secured in a woven cane head basket suspended over the shoulder. In the ensuing chaos, the warriors tapped their knees against their war shields and began to hop and dance, all the while shouting insults at the villagers to further distract them. These brazen attacks ended almost as quickly as they started, and once the requisite number of trophies had been taken and substantial damage inflicted, the attackers fled the scene. Those in the rear of the column planted razor-sharp *panjis*, or bamboo spikes, in the ground to slow down any likely pursuers.

One of the bloodiest mass attacks on a Naga village occurred in the fall of 1948, and it has been recorded that more than six hundred people lost their lives and/or heads (Ganguli 1984). This gruesome event involved the once indomitable Konyak village of Ukha, which had long subjugated numerous other neighboring villages and tribes in the region. In fact, approximately twenty villages from four Naga tribes (Chang, Phom, Yimchungru, and Khiamniungan) participated in the destruction of Ukha, and nearly every inhabitant, except for a small number of young men and women who luckily escaped through a secret passage, was killed.

The last straw that led to the village's invasion occurred when the Ukha Konyaks beheaded a notable Chang warrior named Chingmak who was fishing alone at a river that formed the boundary between his home village of Tobu and Ukha. Because the military strength of Ukha was so great, the warriors of Tobu sought the assistance of other tribes and villages who also sought vengeance in their own long-standing blood feuds with this mutual enemy. After deliberations were made among the numerous communities, Tobu messengers were sent to every headman of the united force indicating when the attack would take place. Because the operation was so great it was nearly impossible to keep it a secret, and the Ukha war leaders soon learned of the ensuing attack and began to prepare their fortifications. According to the revered Chang warrior Sakchiba, who took ten heads in the attack, the Ukha villagers studded the entire several-kilometers-long path toward their settlement with sharp *panjis*. They also dug a ditch around the village, which they filled with thorny plants and other obstacles, and placed sentries at the four village gates (Ganguli 1984).

At midnight before the day of the attack, the invading force sent scouts to remove as many of the *panjis* as possible, since this pathway was the only access point to Ukha itself. Before the attack commenced at dawn, the men tied palm leaves around their heads and ankles so that their fellow warriors would not mistake them for the enemy in the heat of battle.

At 4 a.m., the Ukha village sentries informed the villagers that the war party was advancing. Soon thereafter, the boom of war drums commenced, frantically beaten by the Ukha women to encourage their husbands to engage the invading force with increased effort. Sakchiba recounted his memories of the event:

> From the gates one could hear the maddening war cries of the sentries, who stood there with raised weapons. We rushed towards them firmly determined to finish them off to the last man. A combat ensued, a long and cruel one, but in the early stages at the gates and outside the fortified village on the hill slopes. Spears flew and shining *daos* flashed all around the adversaries[,] who fell to the ground. The sun rose high in the sky when we brought down the last of the defenders. Four of our men lost their lives and many of them were injured. Our clansmen made stretchers and hurried them home.
>
> Over the dead bodies of the sentries the attackers rushed into the village. At all entrances they posted guards to prevent the villagers from escaping. The invaders waved their *daos* above their heads yelling: "We have come to settle with you, now you can't run away!" In wild enthusiasm they attacked the enemies and with violent strokes thrust down everybody within their reach.
>
> Soon the village was filled with a huge crowd of attackers. It did not take too long, and of the Ukha inhabitants not a single one remained alive. In all my life I had never seen so much blood, so many severed heads—there must have been well over one thousand. (Ganguli 1984:203)

After a war party was victorious, they returned home. En route they sang victory songs and pinned some of the hands and feet of their victims to trees to deter pursuers and also to denote to others their prowess in war (Mitchell 1929). On arrival in the village, they participated in several days of ceremonies related to their successful conquest. Although there is not enough space to describe these rituals in detail here,[7] one of the most important was the consecration of the trophy head(s). These objects were imbued with great supernatural power, both positive and negative, and it was of paramount concern to neutralize the latter through rituals of sympathetic magic or other means. Among the Naga, some of these methods included one or more of the following:[8] removing the ears, nose, and tongue then sacrificing a chicken, whereby a spell was pronounced by which the relatives of the victim were called on to share a similar fate;[9] thrusting bamboo spikes into the eye sockets and/or mouth, so that the enemy may not open them again in the afterlife;[10] attaching *mithun* (buffalo) or wooden horns to the skull to prevent the dead man from hearing the call of his friends who were searching for him, since his spiritual essence or soul might lure them toward his location;[11] placing the captured head(s) on the log drum of the respective *paan* or *morung*, which was vigorously struck with the victory tune, rendering the skulls deaf so that their souls could not hear their relatives calling; placing chili powder, spittle, and rice beer on the head—and in the mouth—to scare away the spirit of the dead, which could become malevolent, and to blind it in the afterlife; or smashing a chicken egg over the head,[12] which was supposed to blind the relatives of the dead and render them powerless in the event they sought revenge (Hutton 1922a; Ganguli 1984; Krutak 2010b; Saul 2005; von Fürer-Haimendorf 1938a).

Sometimes these associated rituals took place months after the actual head-taking event. Among the Wancho, fresh heads were first cleaned of their flesh, then stored in a clan's *morung* until the festival of Gantang, which was performed after the rice harvest. At this time, the *gampa*, or ritual expert in charge of headhunting ceremonials, offered the heads ginger and rice beer,[13] then addressed them: "Call your father, your mother, your brothers and your sisters. You were a thief, a bad man, and so you are killed. You spoke ill of us and so you are killed. Take this rice beer" (Dutta 1990:238). A similar ritual and chant, albeit one that was performed after fresh heads entered the village, has been documented for the Konyak of Wakching village, whereupon these words were "believed to compel the souls of the dead to call their relatives" so that more enemy heads could be taken (von Fürer-Haimendorf 1962:189).

Other Naga groups observed annual rites to propitiate the trophy heads in order to keep their favor close to the living. These major ceremonies usually occurred during the annual spring festivals (e.g., Aoeleng [Konyak]; Monyu [Phom]). In the Phom village of Ponyo, I was told the skulls were fed sticky rice then greased with pig fat to please the spirits of the deceased from bringing sickness to the community (Krutak 2010b).[14]

Some enemy heads, especially those of *anghs* (ruling chiefs), were believed to be embodied with dangerous power themselves. For this reason, they were tabooed from being taken by commoners, although accidents did happen. Among the Wancho, if this occurred the beheader was "abused and henceforth to the end of his life he could not eat goat's flesh, beef or fowl and certain kinds of fish. If he broke the rule, he would become a leper" (Elwin 1955:77). The Konyak held a similar belief, since "leprosy may be the consequence" of killing a great *angh*, like those who ruled over Mon and Chi (von Fürer-Haimendorf 1936d:129, n.b. 8). Lepers who sought to become cured of their ailments often participated in combat because it was believed that enemy blood smeared on their skin would treat their condition.[15] Moreover, lepers were "always" taken on Wancho headhunting expeditions because it was held to be extremely risky to take a leper's head: "[I]f even a drop of his blood fell on you, you would be infected" (Elwin 1958:268n5).[16]

Chen Naga boys who participated in their first headhunting raid, like their Konyak and Wancho Naga counterparts, earned the right to a goggle-like facial tattoo. This bold tattoo was significant, because this badge of courage conferred initiation into their respective clan's *paan*, or men's house.[17] Forming a male "clubhouse" and dormitory of sorts, it was within the *paan* that male elders instructed the youth about Chen customs and the proper way of life. Herein, male leaders held council, gossiped about the events of the day, or made important decisions regarding ceremonies, warfare, and economic pursuits, which bound all the members of the *paan*.

Men who sought to separate themselves from their peers and who succeeded in beheading an enemy could have their facial tattoos amended to include a series of *goa-wat* (latticework-like tattoos) on their cheeks derived from bamboo weave patterns, which were a symbol of strength. Great *naomei*, or warriors who acquired several heads, were entitled to elaborate *ring tu pu* (neck tattoos) that were also inspired from the bamboo weave.

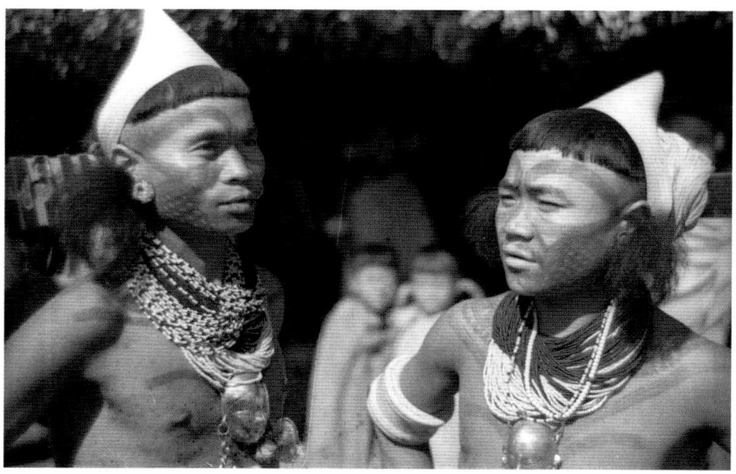

FIGURE 6.10
Two young Konyak Naga men with fresh tattoo marks that traditionally indicated headhunter status, 1937. Although the original catalog record is not precise, these men were either from Hungphoi or Longkhai village, Nagaland. Contrary to other accounts (Jacobs 1990), they themselves did not take a head, and their tattoos were earned for participation in headhunting rituals. Photograph by Christoph von Fürer-Haimendorf. Courtesy of Nicholas Haimendorf. University of London, Special Collections, SOAS Library (PP MS 19/6/ NAGA/1982).

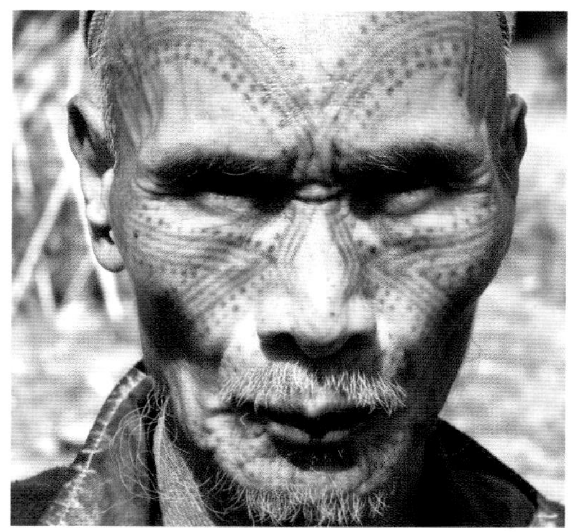

FIGURE 6.11
Infrared photograph of Wancho warrior facial tattooing, Tirap District, Arunachal Pradesh, 2007. © Jonathan Derksen.

The tattooed Chen elders Chingkei Sokompa and Chingham Chatrahpa (d. 2023), whose fathers were *lowang* (wealthy men), greatly desired to earn the right to be tattooed as teenagers in the early 1950s. With the passage of the Government of India Act in 1935, however, headhunting was officially prohibited by the then ruling British in "administered areas" of the southern and western Naga hills. In the "unadministered" eastern regions of Naga territory, which encompassed Konyak, Chen, and other Indigenous lands, headhunting persisted well into the 1960s,[18] but by the time Chingkei and Chingham came of age, Indian military and governmental agents began forcefully imposing the old headhunting bans in their district. Notwithstanding, Chingkei, Chingham, and their mates, like other neophyte Naga warriors of this time (see Krutak 2020:201), devised new forms of warfare that could be rewarded with the receipt of a headhunter's tattoo.

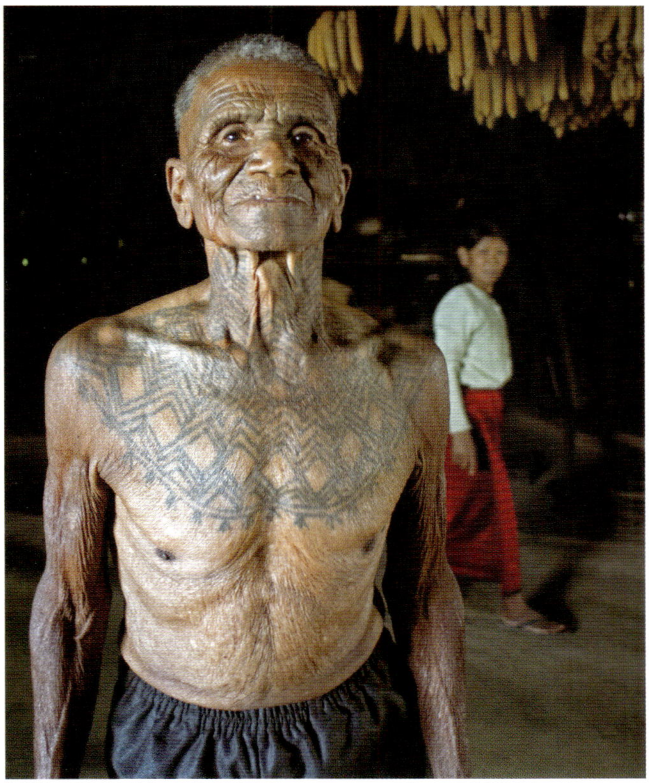

FIGURE 6.12
Chingkei Sokompa of Chen Loisho village, Nagaland, 2019. Due to headhunting bans in the 1950s, he was allowed to earn the right to a warrior's neck tattoo for beheading a wooden effigy placed behind enemy territory. Today, he is the last Chen elder to bear these tattoos. © Lars Krutak.

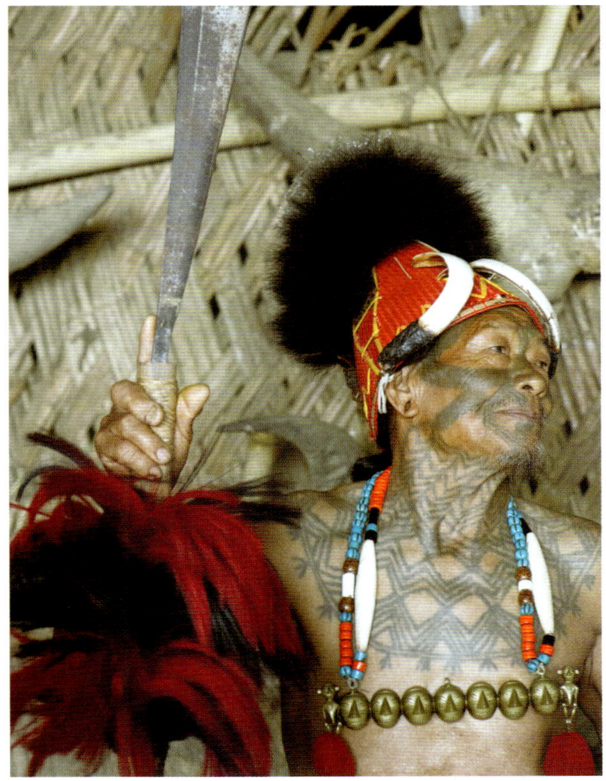

FIGURE 6.13
Chen Naga elder Chingham Chatrahpa (d. 2023) of Chen Loisho village, Nagaland, was one of only two men with the neck tattoos of his ancestors at the time of this photograph, 2019. "Both my father and grandfather had these neck tattoos—the same patterns," he said. © Lars Krutak.

In November 2019, I conducted interviews with these heavily tattooed elders in Chen Loisho village.[19] They spoke with me about their motivations to earn facial and neck tattoos as well as about the circumstances surrounding the acquisition of these permanent markings. Both men were, at the time, the last Chen Naga to bear the elaborate neck tattoos of their ancestors, and they began their conversations speaking about how their neck tattoos were genealogical markers. Chingkei noted, "My father and grandfather had the same neck patterns; they have been in my family for generations. It was somewhat compulsory that I had to get them, otherwise it would be like I was not a member of my own family and I would have been ridiculed. So, when I came of age, I decided I should get these tattoos" (Krutak 2022:95).

Since headhunting was prohibited by the Indian government at this time, Chen tribal elders reconfigured traditional protocols in order to allow their young men to receive warrior markings. Anthropomorphic effigies made of wood were carved and transported behind the boundary of an enemy's territory. Chingkei recounted that day:

> The raid had to be sanctioned by the village council or *angh* [village chief] since the time for tattooing was coming to an end. Because our desire was so great, they said *yes* because the headhunting ban had not yet been totally enforced in our area and Christianity was coming; missionaries looked down at these practices.
>
> Around ten to twelve young men went down together to the Tehok River towards Aboi village to kill the effigy. When we reached our *paan*, we placed the wooden head on the ancestral stones [that commemorate great events of the past], and the celebrations began. The head was treated as if it were human, and later it was placed with the skulls of enemies housed in the *paan*. (Krutak 2022:95–96)

Chingham related similar motivations for obtaining warrior tattoos: "Both my father and grandfather had these neck tattoos—the *same* patterns. When we were young, we weren't wearing any clothes at all. But after you received the tattoos you not only come of age, but you are allowed to start wearing clothes and ornaments as well. We could also get married afterwards" (Krutak 2022:96).[20] Indeed, for young Naga men who had not taken a head, or even a token part of it, obtaining a spouse would be difficult. Women and young girls egged on their menfolk so much so that the hapless males had little choice in the matter, and they were compelled to take a head in order to consummate a marriage proposal (cf. Elwin 1955:75; Sardeshpande 1987:50). Relatedly, Khiamniungan warriors of Pangsha village on the Myanmar border told me, "[O]nce you have a tattoo, you can proclaim yourself to be a man. If you don't have it, you are a nobody" (Krutak 2008b). Konyak elders related similar stories, and one of the administrators of Jakphang village bluntly stated that "people would laugh at you if you didn't take a head" (Krutak 2008b). Although the wooden effigy that Chingham hunted was placed at a different location than Chingkei's, the result was the same: it came to rest with the human heads in his *paan*. Chingham added a few details about his journey home from the mock headhunting event, including one of the celebratory songs they sang on their way home: "We took its head, then on our way home we came back singing: 'Your father has given you away; your mother has given you away; and we happily take you back to our village!'" (Krutak 2022:97).

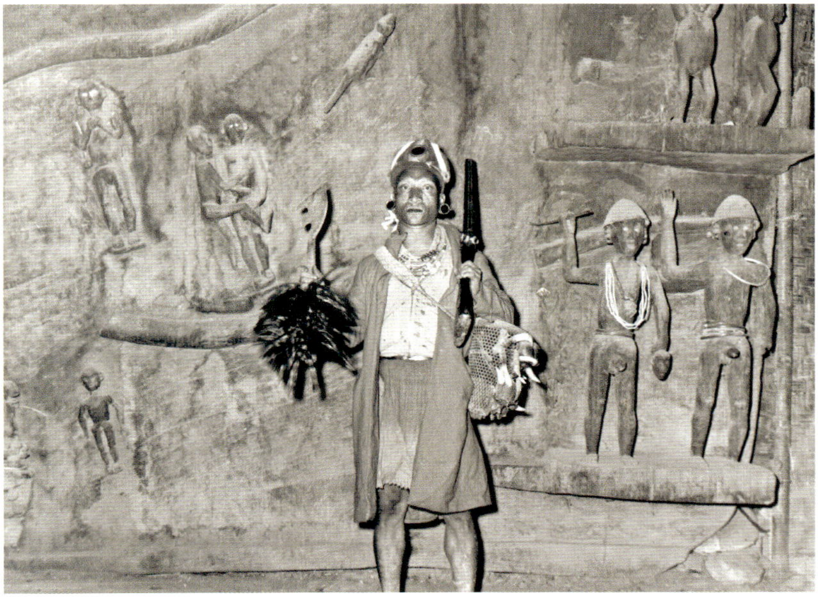

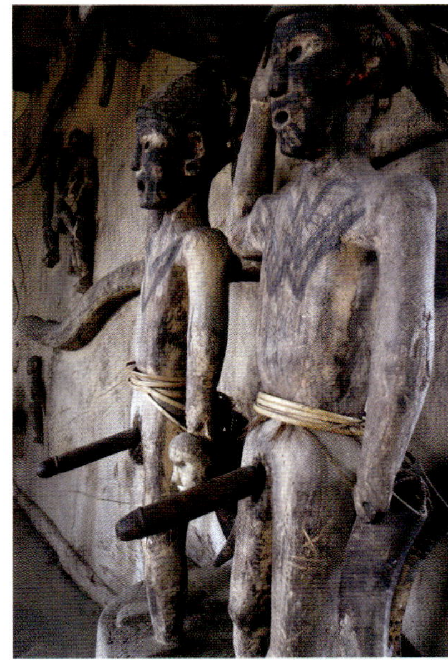

FIGURE 6.14
A massive wooden sculpture (*left*), perhaps the largest surviving example of its kind in Nagaland, once rested in the home of the *angh* of Shangnyu village (pictured here), 2010. Under the guidance of spirits, it was carved by a supernatural figure named Honu, who later became an official of the Shangnyu court (cf. Longkumer 2017). Some of the most prominent portrayals revolve around human fertility, and especially the association between severed heads, tattoos, and male virility (*right*). Historic photograph by Verrier Elwin, ca. 1954. Courtesy of Ashok Elwin. National Anthropological Archives, Smithsonian Institution (04457500). © Lars Krutak.

Shortly after the victory celebrations concluded, Chingkei, Chingham, and their "brothers" received facial tattoos from the tattooist of their village. Among the Konyak and Chen Naga, this position was held by the *anghya*, the wife of the ruling *angh* of their village. After their wounds had healed, both men received their neck tattoos, but these were applied by a male tattooist whose name was Phochai.

Of the men who accompanied Chingkei on the mock headhunt, he was the only individual who received the neck tattoos. The reason being is that the occasion necessitated a Feast of Merit, which was an expensive undertaking but one that his family could afford. Among the Chen and other Naga groups, Feasts of Merit enhanced the status of the host's family and household through the display and redistribution of wealth in the village, namely the meat of large bovines called *mithun*, or buffalo, which were slaughtered during such events. However, these feasts also operated on a spiritual level, since meat was offered ritualistically to ancestral and village spirits. These actions ensured the favor of these entities, and were also believed to contribute to the communal fertility of the household and village. Human heads taken in combat provided

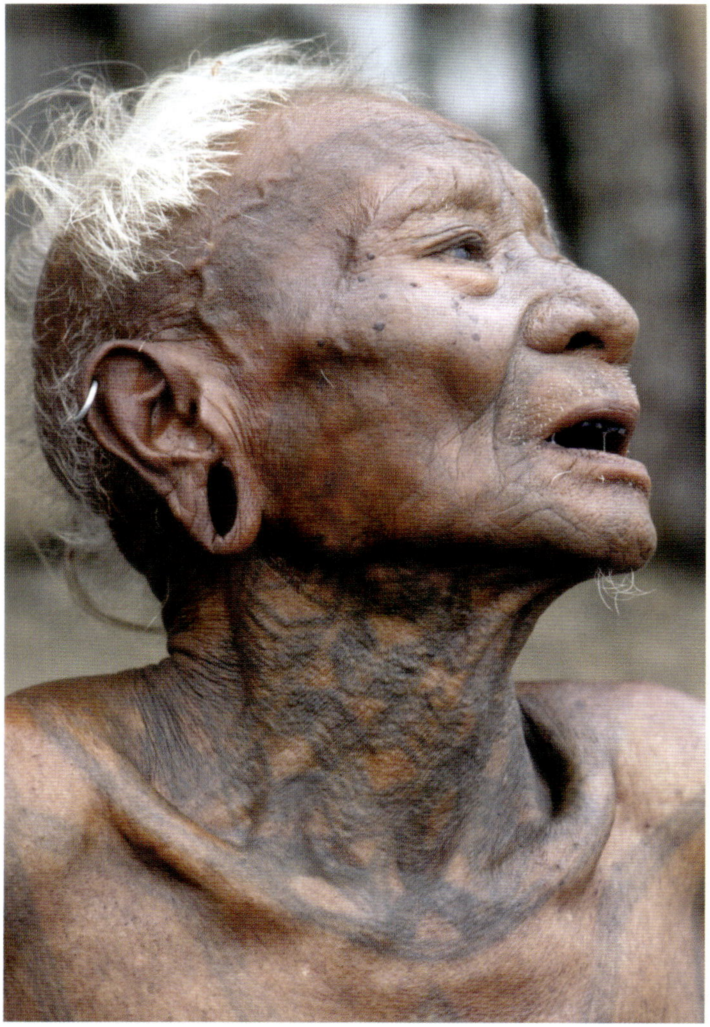

FIGURE 6.15
The former Konyak warrior and *gaonbura* (village headman) Nokngam of Shangnyu village, Nagaland, 2010. His *ding hu* (neck tattoos) were earned for head-taking in his youth and established his identity as a great *naomei* (warrior). Stylistically, neck tattoos were composed of subtle yet distinctive design elements that varied across Konyak villages; they could be read by others and identified the man thus marked (cf. Konyak and Bos 2017). When this photograph was taken, Nokngam was the only tattooed man of the *naomei* class still living in Shangnyu. © Lars Krutak.

similar benefits, because they were believed to contain life-giving powers that, when properly harnessed, could increase the yield of agricultural crops, the number of newborn children in the village, and a man's virility (Krutak 2020).

Notwithstanding, Chingkei's *paan* was punished by governmental authorities for his participation in mock headhunting and his resulting tattoos; a fine of two cows was levied.

From a spiritual standpoint, facial tattoos were compulsory after a war party had taken an enemy head. In 2018, I interviewed the nearly one-hundred-year-old tattooed veteran Konyak warrior Beyau Waisha of Monyakshu village. Pointing first to his faded facial tattoos, then to the thorns of an aloe plant growing beneath his back porch, he explained, "If you don't get tattooed and spill your own blood after killing an enemy, then after you die your soul will be constantly tortured by spirits with thorns like this and your soul will not rest in peace. You must spill your own blood as a form of purification" (Krutak 2020:194). I recorded similar information related to V-shaped chest tattoos of Phom warriors. Eno Henham Buchemhü of Yongshei village told me, "[W]hen you kill, the enemy's blood is polluting and so when you are tattooed its residue is released" (Krutak 2010b: n.p.).

Naga warrior tattoos had other performative functions in the afterlife. The Sangtam warrior Pusutsu Thongru, who bears the warrior chest tattoos of his tribe, observed, "The Naga people believe that if we die and are not marked with these tattoos, our souls do not get food and drink in the afterlife" (BBC 2016). The female Lazu Naga elder Posen Mangyut, who bears the incredible bold facial tattoos of her tribe, told me, "My ancestors will only recognize me after I die because of my tattoos" (Krutak 2009:59).

When I asked Chingkei and Chingham about life after death, they both offered the same answer. "When you die, I believe you take along

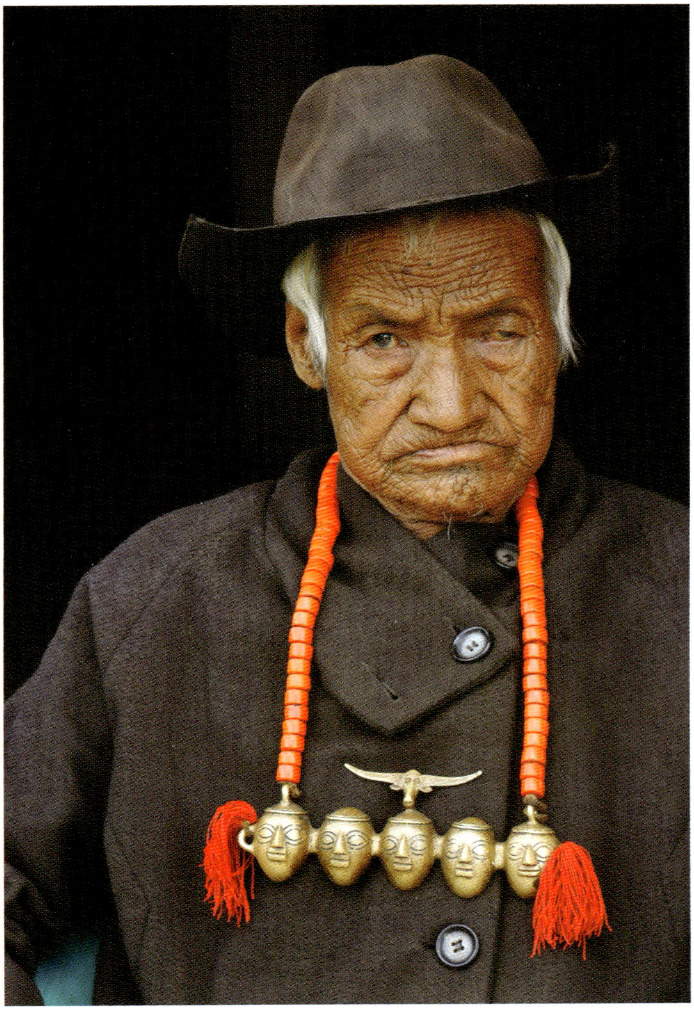

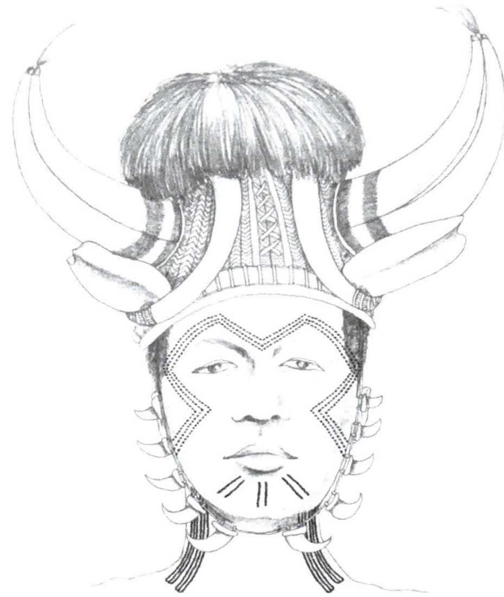

FIGURE 6.16
The former combat participant and nonagenarian Beyau Waisha of Monyakshu village, Nagaland, 2018. He noted that tattooing was a prerequisite after taking the life of an enemy because it was a form of purification. His facial and neck tattoos are faded now (*left*), but an illustration clearly depicts the unique tattoo patterns of his village (*above*). Drawing by Sonal Dhama, D4Design. From Konyak and Bos 2017:160. Courtesy of the authors. Photograph © Lars Krutak.

your tattoos to the afterlife." Throughout the Konyak, Phom, Chang, and other Naga tribal regions, the tattoo markings of great warriors often adorn their gravestones. These memorial markers forever communicate their honorable deeds, accomplishments, and life force across the planes of the living and dead.

Notwithstanding, the recalibration of headhunting practices in response to government bans speaks of a process of retraditionalization, whereby a cultural practice is renewed through its remaking in response to an identifiable set of external forces implicated in its past erasure (Krutak 2020). Tradition is mobilized but the new cultural configuration that results is not meant to entirely supplant the established beliefs and practices that gave rise to these new traditions. Instead, in this case, neo-Naga headhunting practices speak about the creative imagination and agency of individuals to modify and reclaim their history through new patterns and performances of warfare.

These modifications of inherited beliefs and practices were also adopted by other Naga communities outside of the region. After Indian governmental agents began forcefully imposing headhunting bans on the remote eastern territories of the Naga in the 1950s, traditional headhunting and associated tattooing practices were reconfigured by local Konyak and Wancho Naga. In the unpublished diaries and papers of Verrier Elwin, he describes how Naga warriors adapted to the government's ban on headhunting through the creation of new forms of warfare that could be rewarded with the receipt of a headhunter's tattoo. In the Konyak Naga region around Mon, Elwin

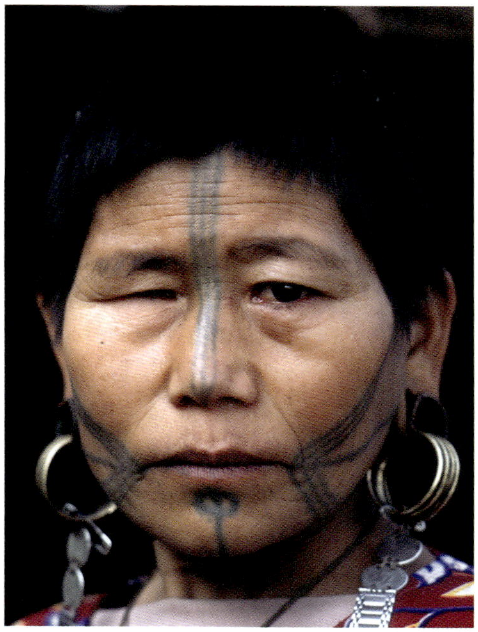

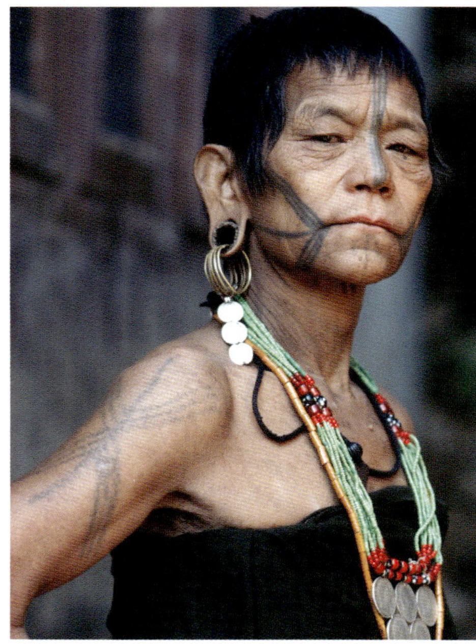

FIGURE 6.17

Posen Mangyut (*right*), a Lazu Naga woman, adorned with a necklace of silver coins, Khonsa, Arunachal Pradesh, India, 2008. Mangyut told me, "My ancestors will only recognize me after I die because of my tattoos." A full complement of tattoos was necessary for the afterlife. The Lazu Naga live on opposite sides of the Arunachal Pradesh and Myanmar border near the town of Khonsa. Women bear distinctive facial tattoos that are tribal identifiers. When a girl was about five years old, her chin was marked with a circle and line through it, as seen in this portrait (*left*). After puberty the cheeks and nose were tattooed, and later the upper arms. The latter tattoos were called "the baby's pillow" because this is where an infant's head often rested. These geometric motifs were derived from bamboo stems. Lazu *binu* (tattooists) were female and they stenciled the designs on the skin. The tattoos were pricked into the skin with cane thorns and soot smeared into the open wounds. The young shoots of a local tree were pounded then smeared over the punctures to promote healing (Dutta 1978:64–65). Due to pressure from local student organizations, the last Lazu tattoos were given in the 1980s. © Lars Krutak.

was told circa 1950 that a youth could not receive a tattoo unless he captured or was a member of an expedition that had taken a human head. Since headhunting was prohibited by the Indian government at this time, anthropomorphic wooden effigies, like those described by the Chen warriors Chingkei and Chingham, were also carved and transported behind the boundary of an enemy's territory. Later, a group of youths tracked down the effigy, cut off its head, and returned to their home village, where they were subsequently tattooed. Elwin (1955:75) wrote, "The old rituals are performed with the [wooden] head, some of which may be found hung as trophies in the *morungs* [men's dormitory]."

Similarly, I interviewed the last group of tattooed Konyak warriors from the village of Hungphoi, near Mon, Nagaland, in May 2018. Because their desire to receive a warrior tattoo was so great (it meant, for example, enhanced social status and interest from village maidens), they devised a new military tactic that enabled them to subvert the headhunting ban while also earning them the right to be tattooed by the village's tattoo artist. For many years, they had a dispute with a distant Konyak village, but in the 1950s, it was illegal for them to travel there and take a head. Instead, they secretly traveled behind the territorial boundary of their sworn enemy and fired their shotguns and muzzle loaders in the direction of their adversaries' village. This feat, they said, was equivalent to taking an enemy's head, and on their return home, three days of feasting and dancing commenced as if it had been a real headhunt. They were tattooed shortly thereafter.

The Konyak of Oting village, which fell into the "administered areas" of British control, also invented similar practices but at a much earlier date. In the unpublished notes of von Fürer-Haimendorf (1936d:66, n.b. 8), Oting men traveled to their enemy's land and thrust a spear into the soil or a tree, proclaiming "I have killed him, I took one young man's head."

CHEN TIGER-SPIRIT TATTOOS

Apart from the aforementioned warrior tattoos, there are other markings that were embodied with great supernatural power. During field interviews conducted in the Chen Naga villages of Chenwetnyu, Chen Loisho, and Chen Moho in 2010 and 2019, as well as reviews of the existing ethnographic literature, I learned that these *shahnyu yaha*, or "tiger-spirit" tattoos, which were worn only on the backs of Chen men of the *angh* (chiefly) lineage, are related to their spirit companion and guide—the tiger. Today (i.e., 2024), only one Chen elder bears these incredibly rare and culturally significant designs, which form a significant part of our world's unrecognized (in)tangible cultural heritage.

The origins of tiger-spirit tattoos derive from legendary tales. In Konyak oral traditions, man and tiger were originally *hu* (brothers) and born from the same mother. Although there are several variations of this story across the Konyak and Naga universe (Ao 1999; Dutta 1990; Heneise 2019; Hutton 1921; Sutter 2008), these siblings, who shared the same spirit or soul, had a disagreement that compelled them to live separate lives thereafter. The man became the progenitor of the chiefly clan that gave rise to the *angh* (ruling class), and the tiger was banished to the forest. In Konyak and Chen belief, when a new *angh* was born, his tiger familiar spirit was also born in the forest (cf. Konyak and Bos 2017). This inextricable relationship of spiritual coessence gave rise to

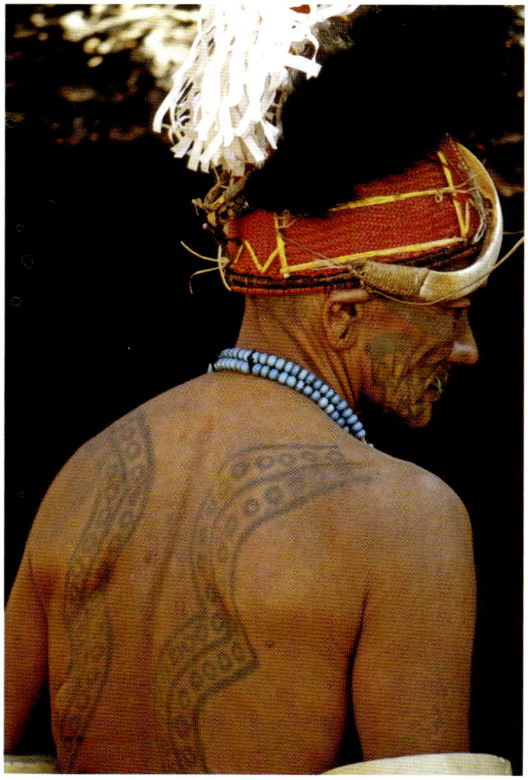

FIGURE 6.18
Winkhang Wingkhangpa, the former tiger-man of Chen Loisho village, Nagaland, 2010. He is the last *shahnyu yaha* (tiger-spirit) tattoo bearer living today. © Lars Krutak.

an ancient tattooing tradition whereby men of the Chen ruling class acquired patterns on their backs derived from the limbs, legs, stripes, and spirit of "their brother," the tiger.

Apart from acquiring the physical characteristics of the tiger on their body via tattoo, the tiger-spirit also inhabited his human companion and vice versa. This mutual type of soul transfer usually manifested itself when a human bearer of the tiger-spirit tattoo entered a deep dream state while sleeping (Heneise 2019; Hutton 1920), although according to my Chen informants the tiger-spirit can also manifest itself during waking life through visions. In turn, the man's soul traveled out of his body and into that of his tiger familiar, where it became fully engaged with the surrounding environment.

The late tiger-spirit tattoo bearer Tolei Angh of Chenwetnyu village, who passed in January 2023, told me that a tiger-man can see through the eyes of his feline friend and hear and smell what his animal kin encounters on the trail, and that in the headhunting era warrior chiefs could employ the help of their "protector" to track the movements of their enemies (Krutak 2020:194). Men who possessed these spiritual assistants would become tigerlike in their actions as well as perform superhuman feats (e.g., manifest extraordinary strength, travel great distances in the blink of an eye), and were rarely defeated in battle.

But Tolei Angh noted that there were risks associated with having an animal counterpart. If one's tiger familiar was wounded or killed, then the human linked with it would experience a similar fate, and sometimes cuts, scars, lethargy, physical ailments, or sickness accompanied a tiger-man thus affected. Moreover, if your animal companion had a very powerful spirit and you could not control it, Tolei Angh noted it was very likely that you would become insane and die.

However, none of the Chen tiger-spirit tattoo bearers I interviewed became "possessed" by their spirits (cf. Hutton 1920:43) in the sense that they lost their own volition while inhabited by their familiar. Furthermore, they did not imply that they could not communicate intelligibly with other persons while they were visited by the tiger-spirit. In fact, the tiger-men I interviewed noted they were always in perfect harmony with their alter ego, including during the daytime.

These findings contrast markedly with those made by John H. Hutton (1920:43–44) and others (W. G. Archer, cited in Jacobs 1990:85–86) who, in uncertain terms, stated that tiger-men were subservient to their familiars. In turn, these writers downplayed the human agency of tiger-men during their waking lives. But the tiger-spirit men I spoke with were firmly in control of their familiar spirits, and I attribute this to the mythical and genealogical ties that bound Chen noblemen to their consanguineal feline relations. Chen-o Khuzuthrupa of Hoyang (d. 2023), the tattooed *lowang-naomei* of Chenwetnyu village, said, "Although it is powerful, I never felt threatened by the tiger-spirit, including those of other men who possess it."[21]

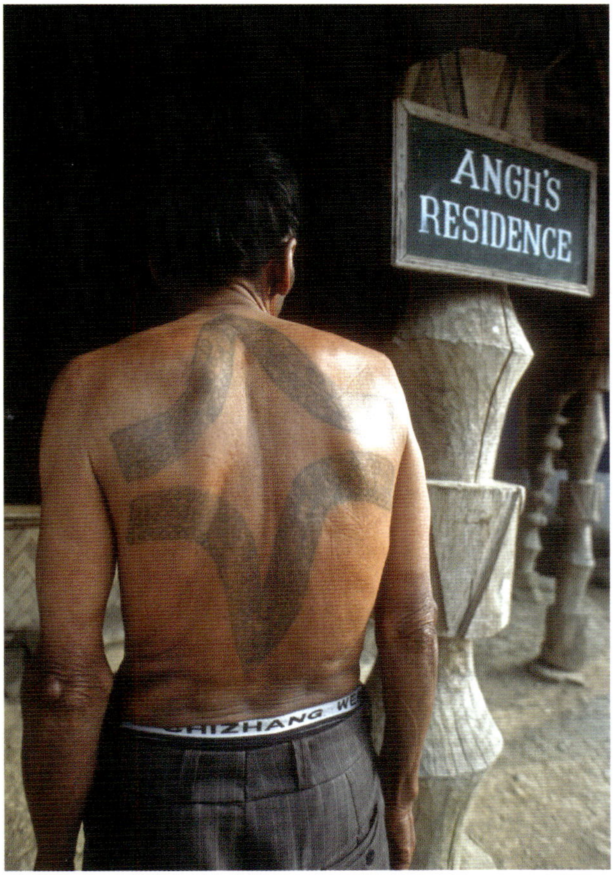

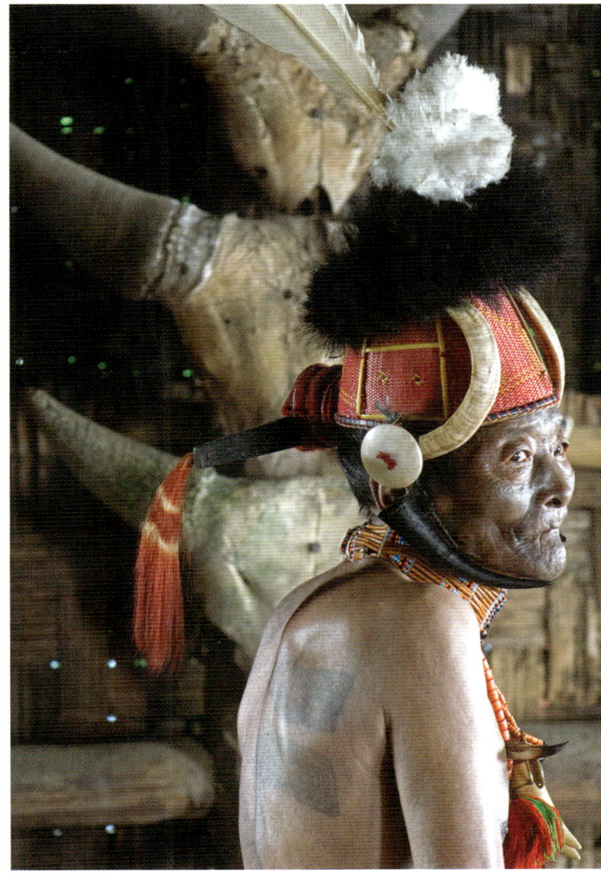

FIGURE 6.19
Tolei Angh, a tiger-spirit tattoo bearer of Chenwetnyu village, Nagaland, 2010 and 2019. He bears faded goggle-like tattoos on his face (*left*) and the *shahnyu yaha* (tiger familiar spirit) pattern on his back (*right*). © Lars Krutak.

In those Naga areas where belief in tiger-spirits was once prevalent, descriptions relate that the tiger-spirit world is ordered in ways that resemble human communities and their attendant social structures (Heneise 2019). Felines of this realm organize themselves through a stratified system of ranks, rules and laws, and other sociopolitical structures that guided the duties of the cohort, all of which was presided over by a "Council of Tigers" (Sutter 2008:284–285). The laws of this world also prescribed a specific diet that was to be maintained throughout one's lifetime. Tolei Angh stated he could not eat "anything that comes from beneath the earth," especially tubers (e.g., cassava, yams), and a variety of red rice.

Chen-o Khuzuthrupa agreed with Tolei Angh's assessment, but he added more details: "Apart from tubers, I could not consume vegetables from creepers, and certainly no meat from the cat family: no civet, leopard, or tiger flesh. If I ate tiger meat it would kill me! Pork and *mithun* meat are okay to eat. Moreover, I can only eat out of special baskets and leaves, and cannot share my utensils with anyone; that is tabooed. Although I would be offered the lion's, *ahem* tiger's, share

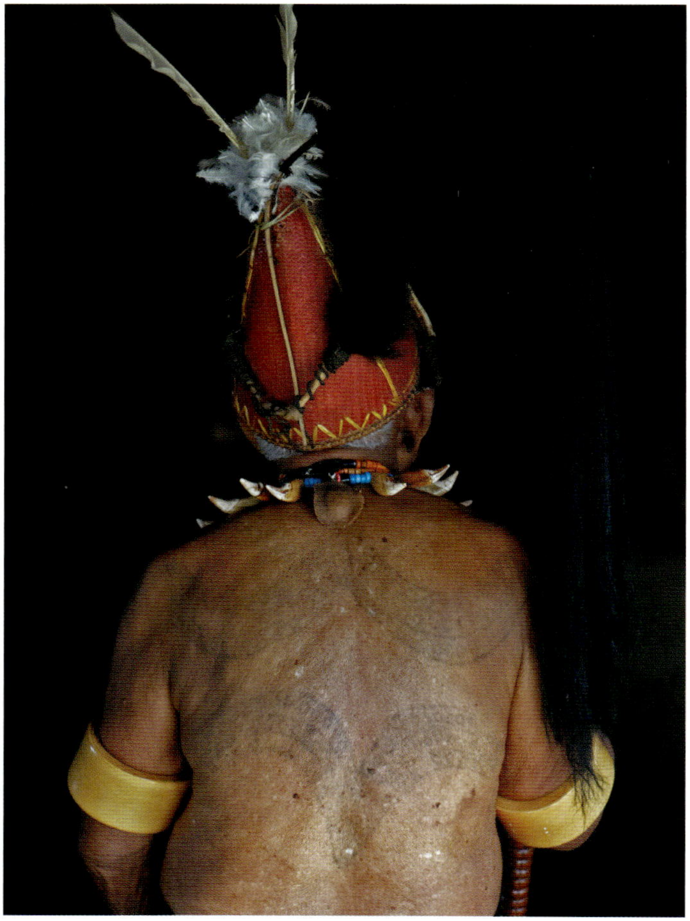

FIGURE 6.20
Centenarian and *shahnyu yaha* tattoo bearer Chen-o Khuzuthrupa of Hoy-ang, Chenwetnyu village, Nagaland, 2019. © Lars Krutak.

of any kill, I would wait for all others to eat and would not consume everything on my plate. That was considered unbecoming of a tiger-spirit bearer. Whatever food I left untouched would go to others who were in need. And even when I eat, I must sit in a special position too."

What Chen-o Khuzuthrupa meant by the latter statement is that he sat on an elevated pedestal during any social gathering or community celebration. After acquiring the tiger-spirit tattoo, his persona was elevated to that of a "caretaker" of his people, and during important community discussions, he maintained the final word, especially in matters involving warfare, land disputes, or annulling local alliances with other villages.

Unlike Tolei Angh, who was not a warrior chief, Chen-o Khuzuthrupa was an inveterate combatant and took seven heads in his prime. Under his military leadership, hundreds of enemy heads came to rest in the various *paans* of Chenwetnyu village. According to Chen-o Khuzuthrupa, his *shahnyu yaha* (tiger familiar spirit tattoo) was a hereditary mark passed down for hundreds of years along his family line. Although some Chen and Konyak leaders may have inherited a leopard spirit (cf. Hutton 1920), Chen-o Khuzuthrupa inherited the spirit of the tiger, which his father and grandfather also possessed.

Chen-o Khuzuthrupa related to me that men from only three Chen dynastic families could bear the tiger familiar spirit tattoo: his, Tolei Angh's, and a third, that of Wingkang Wingkhangpa of Chen Loisho village. After his father passed away, Chen-o Khuzuthrupa was next in line to receive the powerful tattoo of his ancestors, but he could not receive it until he had taken a human head and partaken in certain ceremonies. Once embodied with the tiger-spirit, Chen-o Khuzuthrupa's personality changed. He recalled this spiritual transformation to the Ao Naga musician and writer Anungla Longkumer (2017:56): "There was a time when I was full of energy. At sunrise, my spirit would come alive, and I had only one thought: how many animals I could kill, how many heads could I take.[22] . . . It was a bravery that I had in me, just to be alone anywhere, not to fear anything. That perhaps is the tiger-spirit."

Chen-o Khuzuthrupa provided me with additional information concerning his tiger-spirit powers. He also described a time when he faced severe illness but recovered due to his connection with his feline spirit:

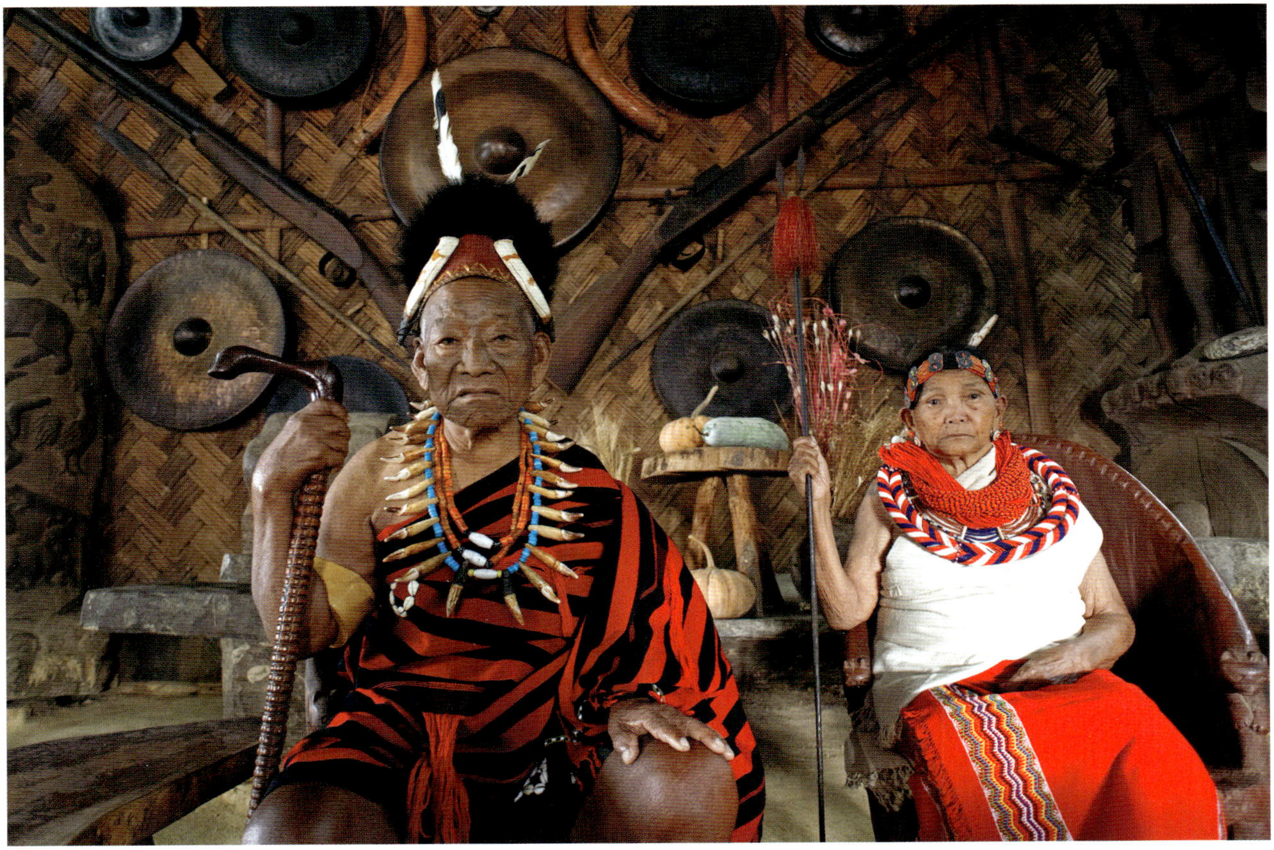

FIGURE 6.21
The former "tiger-man" Chen-o Khuzuthrupa of Hoyang seated with his wife, Pongkhao Khuzuthrulymn, of Hoyang, Chenwetnyu village, Nagaland, 2019. © Lars Krutak.

When someone is causing ill will against you, the tiger-spirit will attack or bite them. Then, it provides you with protection. However, at one time in my life someone placed black magic on me through an effigy figure placed in a graveyard. They were jealous of my power and skills, and I was sick for a very long time. Because of my tiger-spirit, which was very strong, I did not die.

When my tiger-spirit is injured, I would also feel its pain. To heal both our spirits, my family and the *Voompa* (high priest) of the village would make sacrifices. They would carve a wooden effigy of the animal and make offerings to it.

More specifically, if the bearer of the spirit is taken seriously ill, an investigation is carried out to find out if any tiger was captured or killed in the far reaches of Konyakland or beyond [through a kind of tribal Interpol]. If an injured or captured tiger is indeed discovered, the *Voompa* is immediately called upon to offer penance for the salvation of the animal. At his behest, animal sacrifices are carried out by the designated priest.

FIGURE 6.22
The façade of the Hoyang *paan* in Chenwetnyu village (*a*) depicts the history of Chen warfare and its evolution through the teachings of Christianity, a religion of peace, 2019. The enemy skull racks of this *paan* were some of the largest during the headhunting era. Although warfare is a thing of the past, former combatants such as Eno Chinglong and Eno Chennyem demonstrate timeworn Chen battle rhythms and other messages transmitted via the log drum (*b*). © Lars Krutak.

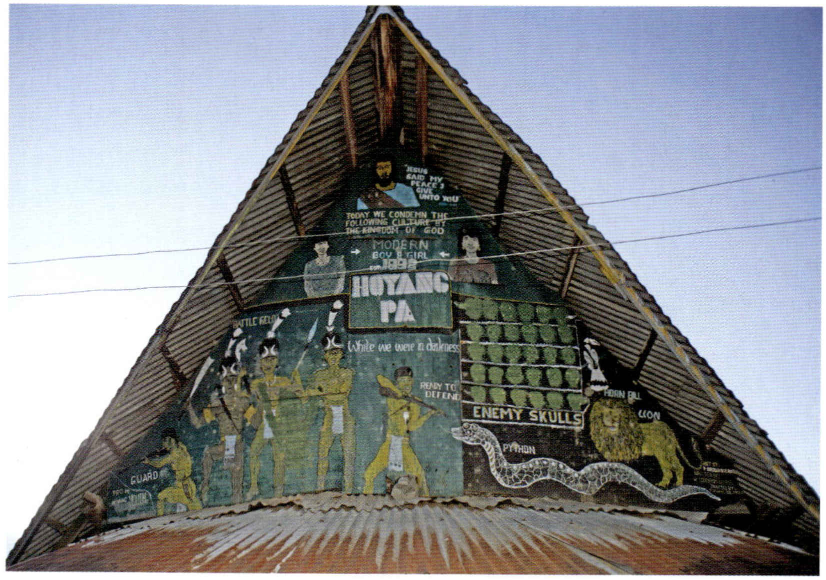

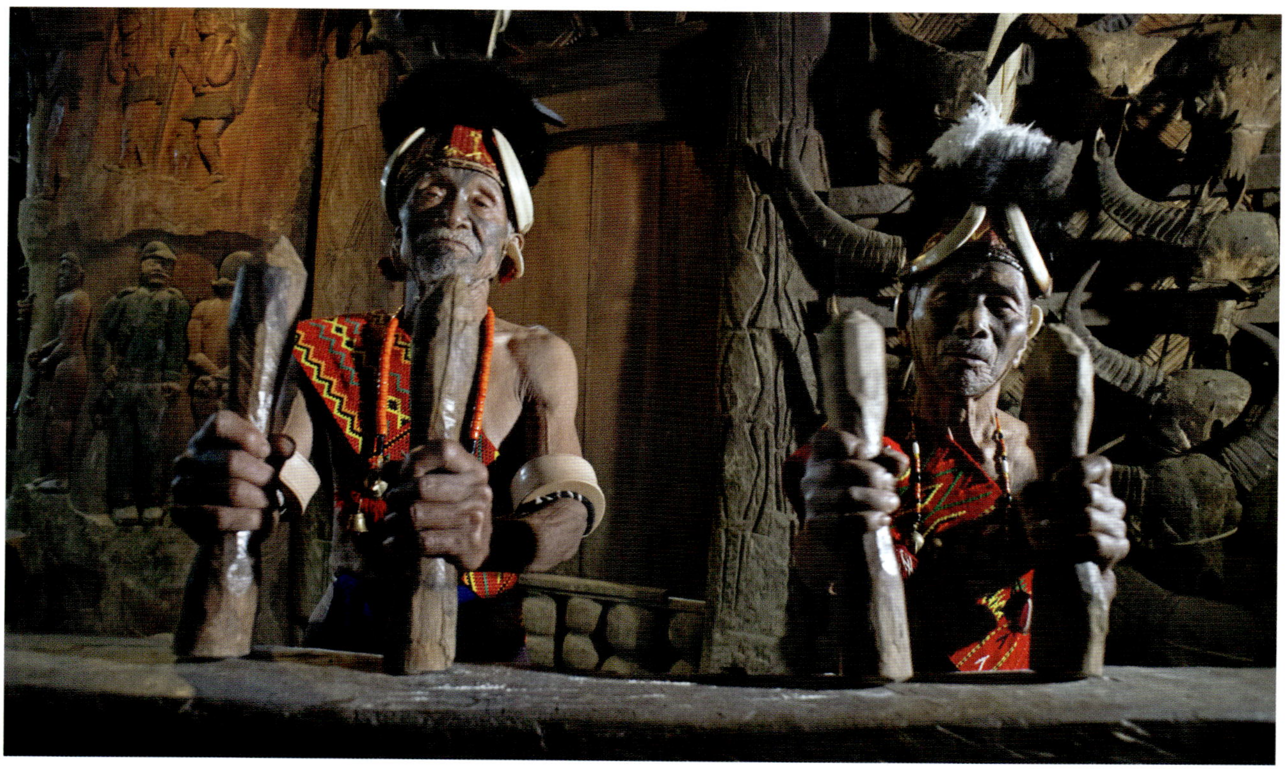

> If the host animal is unfortunately killed, elaborate prayers and community prayers are offered to the Almighty *Yowan* [the good spirit], and the dreadful *Maanthra* [the bad spirit]. In this case, high priests from neighboring villages were also called upon. An effigy of the host animal is ceremoniously sent off to the afterlife and a new host is appointed, in which case, the bearer is conferred a new spirit. Of course, no new tiger-spirit tattoo needs to be given, but a feast is organized to sanctify the new host animal. The appointment of a new animal is more spiritual and symbolic than actual, since no "real" tiger is assigned. (Krutak 2022:104)

Furthermore, Chen-o Khuzuthrupa explained to Longkumer (2017:56) the meanings behind his tattoos, which highlight his kinship with the powerful familiar spirit. His testimony also reveals that his tattoos possess the agency to make immaterial spirit matter real.

The curved lines in the tiger-spirit tattoo signify the legs and hands of the animal, so the spirit is protecting your back. The lines are the limbs of the tiger, and the dotted lines are the stripes, but it is the circle that signifies the spirit. The circle in the center signifies the essence, the spirit (Longkumer 2017:56).

WOMEN'S TATTOOS AND INITIATION MARKS

Some thirty miles south of Chen territory along the rugged Patkai Range live the Khiamniungan Naga. Once feared as the most indomitable of headhunting groups living in the Indo-Burmese region, their tattoo traditions are also associated with tigers but in a different way. During field interviews conducted in the Khiamniungan villages of Nokyen, Noklak, Pangsha, and Yakhao in 2008 and 2010, I learned that warriors who brought back enemy heads were permitted to have their chest tattooed with a V-shaped pattern that the Khiamniungan call "tiger-chest," in reference to the belief they become "tiger-like" when killing their enemy (Krutak 2010b, 2013c:67). The design is presumed to derive from a similar pattern seen on the back of a tiger's head (Saul 2005). After additional victories, tattoos of human figures could also be added to the chest.

Anthropomorphic designs also figured prominently in the tattooing traditions of the Wancho, Konyak, Chang, Phom, Yimchungru, and Myanmar Naga groups. However, warriors who wanted to "build up" their name with additional victories earned the right to bear additional anthropomorphic tattoos that marked the arms, shoulders, calves, eyelids, cheeks, and back, and other marks that in some instances blackened the penis (Konyak and Bos 2017:60–61; Saul 2005:36). Thus, and as a whole, there was no particular tattooed emblem that completed the ritual of Naga warrior tattooing. Any man who sought greatness could continue to have his body marked after successive victories in combat until he no longer had space to fill (Krutak 2020).

Naga villages also sought to promote their renown and reputation through tattooing. More specifically, in some Konyak communities (e.g., Sowa, Mohung, Aboi villages), if a head was taken by anyone in the village, it was compulsory for the entire age group of unmarked young men to receive a *kong tu pu* (forehead-to-nose tattoo), resembling an exclamation mark without its circular base, running along the bridge of the nose upward between the eyes (Krutak 2010b). In other

FIGURE 6.23 (LEFT)
Khiamniungan Naga warrior Thangming, 2010. Thangming was described to me as the last great tattooed "war hero" of Yakhao village, Nagaland, and bears the "tiger-chest" tattoo as well as crossbow motifs on his shoulders. © Lars Krutak.

FIGURE 6.24 (RIGHT)
Chellia, a great Khiamniungan warrior of Noklak village, Nagaland, who tallied eight human kills during his military career, 2010. The tattooed anthropomorphs symbolize some of his victims, and his arm tattoos represent "the path of the tiger." © Lars Krutak

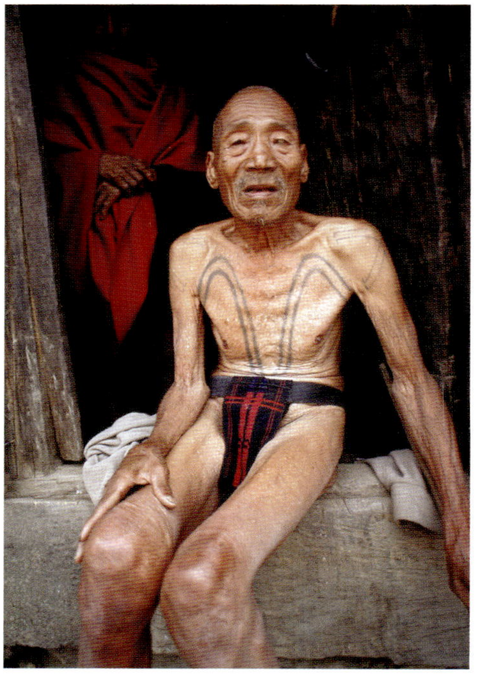

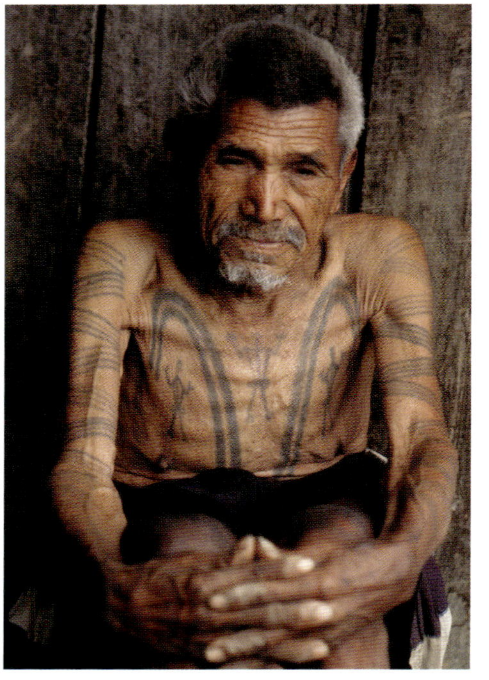

Konyak villages, such as Jakphang, three elders reported to me that this mark was acquired after a young man participated in his first combat mission. The tattoo also conferred a man's initiation into his *paan*, and when any of his male relatives took another head, he received one or more lines on his chin (Konyak and Bos 2017). Konyak girls of this region acquired clan markings on their chins and cheeks when an enemy head entered the village. The village headman called for the proper time for the tattooing to commence, which happened over a course of one to three days until it was completed (Krutak 2010b).

Families and clans also competed against one another for heads. As the late great Konyak Wangkau Angh of Chi told me in 2008, "If your family didn't get a head, they would make fun of you and call you a woman. There was definitely a kind of competition between families and clans for heads." In turn, young girls or women might acquire tattoos signifying that a male family member or husband had taken human life. Mrs. Nyamshan, a more-than-ninety-years-old Konyak elder from Sowa village,[23] told me that when the husband of a young woman or male relative took their first head, the girl received—apart from her chin and cheek tattoos—one small black box tattooed below her eye. If a woman's husband or a male relative took a second head, then an additional set of black boxes were tattooed below the first. Mrs. Nyamshan said she was forcibly tattooed with these designs when she was fifteen to sixteen years of age because it was compulsory, "because having more facially tattooed women in the family proclaimed to all villagers and visitors that great heroes resided in the family" (Krutak 2010b).

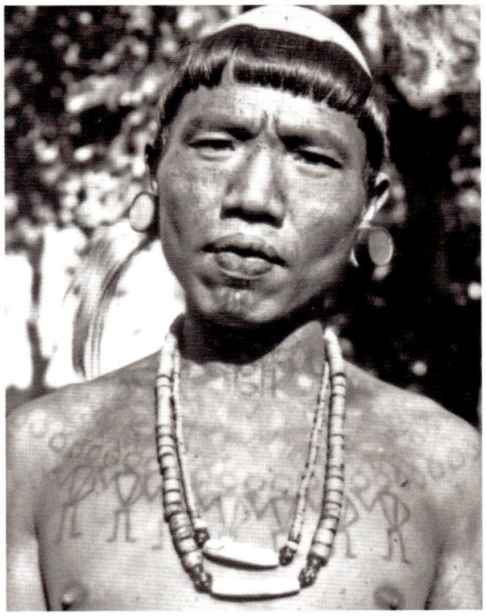

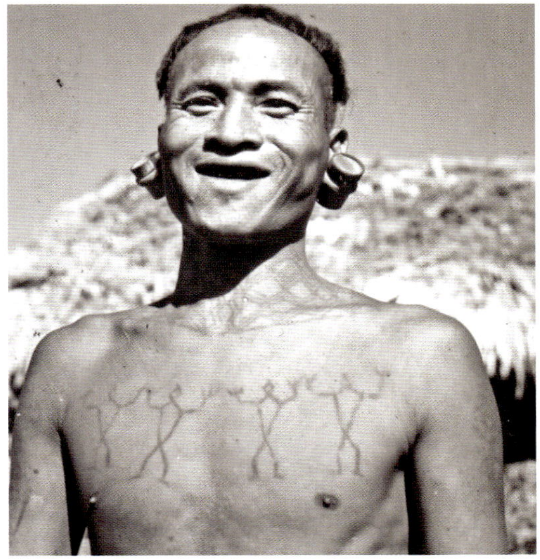

FIGURE 6.25
Two Wancho headhunters displaying neck tattoos and human figures that tallied their victories on the battlefield (*left–right*), ca. 1954. Photographs by Verrier Elwin. From Elwin 1959:33.

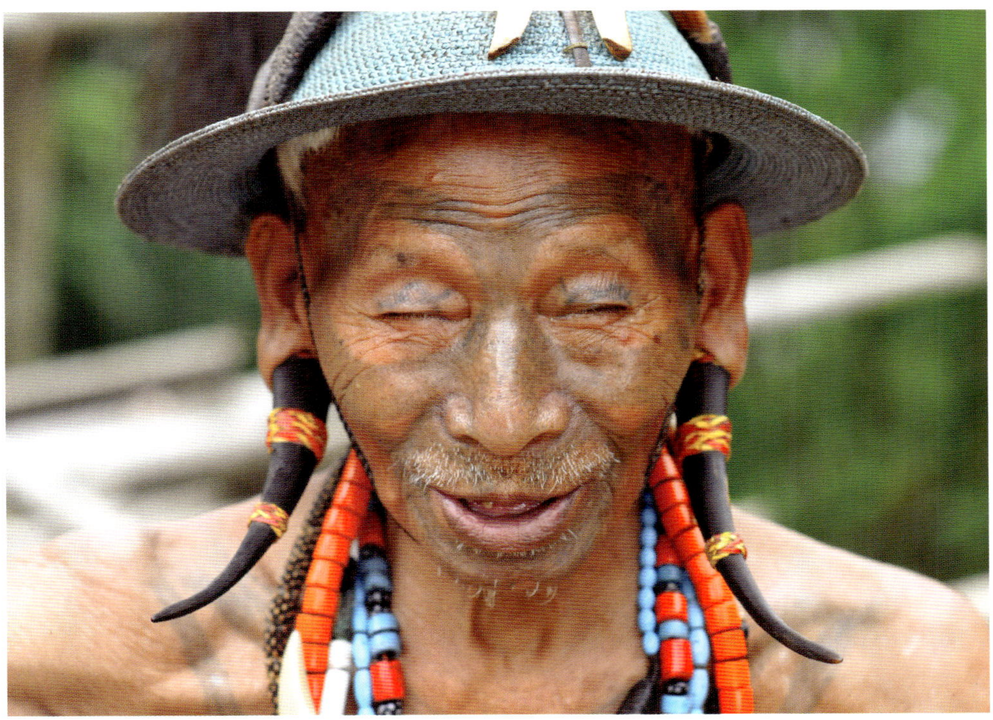

FIGURE 6.26
Wanghon Wangshu of Phuktong village, Nagaland, 2018. Wangshu is a skilled basket maker, artist, former warrior, and family man who bears rare eyelid tattoos that designate his relation to the blue-blood Konyak *anghs* of eastern Nagaland. Eyelid tattoos could also be worn by veteran warriors. His turquoise beads further designate his aristocratic status. © Lars Krutak.

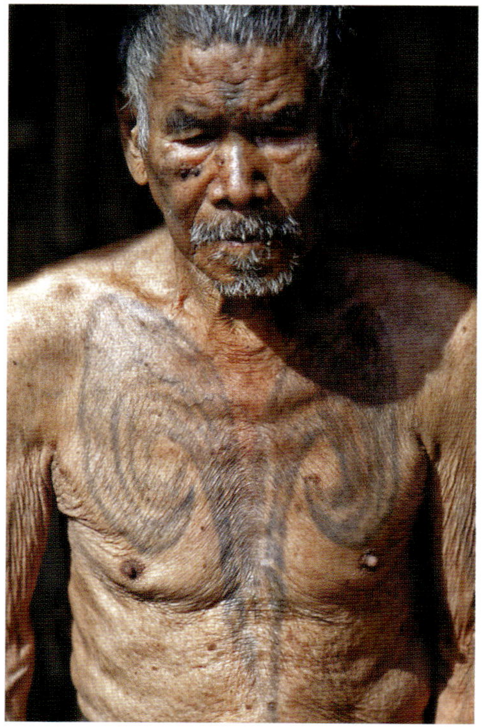

FIGURE 6.27
Phuting, a Konyak warrior of Tobu village, Nagaland, 2010. Phuting noted that his faded forehead tattoo was received after initiation into his *paan*, and the chest tattoo could be received for participation in a successful combat mission. He added that only men who had taken heads could add to their markings with a series of lines on their upper arms. © Lars Krutak.

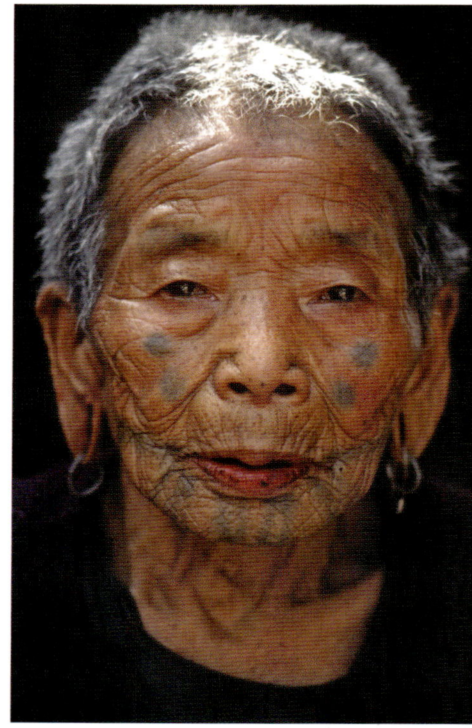

FIGURE 6.28
Mrs. Nyamshan, a Konyak elder of Sowa village, Nagaland, displaying a set of boxlike cheek tattoos proclaiming the military prowess of her family, 2010. © Lars Krutak.

Among the Konyak, there were many other types of tattoos denoting that headhunters resided in a woman's family. In Tobu village, small flag-like tattoos were applied on a girl's cheeks. In Jakphang, I met women with a crescent and + motif appearing on the right forearm, while in other villages this pattern might consist of two X's, one atop the other, separated by horizontal lines. In Nganching village, an elderly Konyak woman displayed a + mark with two parallel lines and an ^ above it on her left forearm.[24] In this village as well as in neighboring Mohung, two sets of small circular tattoos on the cheeks below the eyes signaled that the woman belonged to a family of warriors.

Perhaps the most common Naga female tattoos, however, were those related to life stages. These rite-of-passage tattoos took various forms across the Naga universe and, generally speaking,

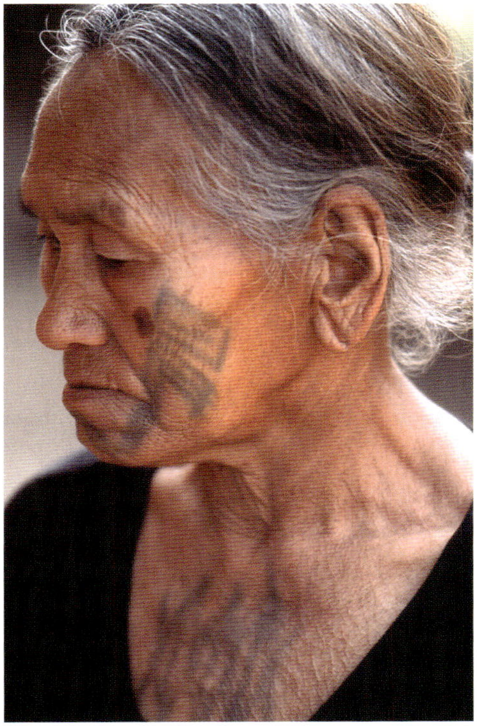

FIGURE 6.29
Konyak elder Monyu of Tobu village, Nagaland, displays flag tattoos on her cheeks, 2010. She noted that girls received these facial tattoos when an enemy head was brought into the village. Her chest tattoos were received before her marriage to her husband. © Lars Krutak.

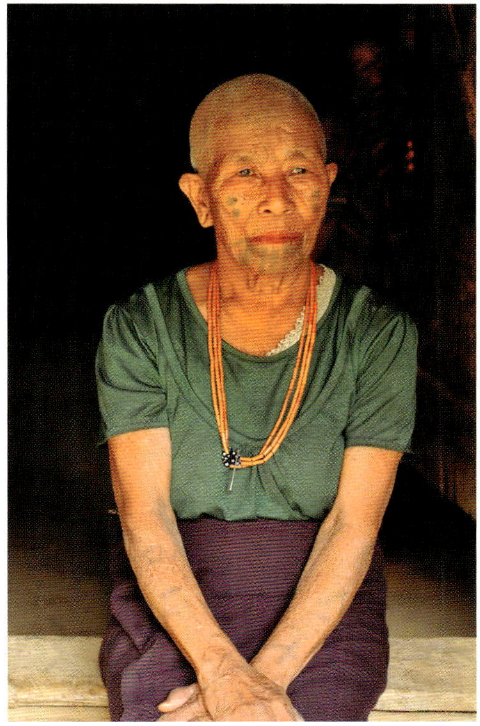

FIGURE 6.30
Konyak elder Pongnyu with a faded crescent and + on her arm and two sets of circle tattoos on her cheeks denoting her male relatives were headhunters, Nganching village, Nagaland, 2018. © Lars Krutak.

conformed to the following pattern documented for several Naga tribes, especially the Konyak. However, it should be noted that in some Naga and even Konyak tribes there was no female facial tattooing. Thus, whereas facial tattoos were usually the first marks placed on an individual or their entire "age set" between six and ten years of age, in those groups (e.g., Wancho) that did not practice facial marking the first area of the body to be tattooed might have been the navel and/or the calves. Notwithstanding, facial tattoos, especially those placed on the forehead, were extremely important from the standpoint of the afterlife, since if a Lainong, Khiamniungan, Makuri, Chang, or Pounyu Naga girl died without receiving them, they were stenciled on the skin so she could meet and/or be recognized by her ancestors (Mills 1926; Saul 2005).[25] Moreover, it was believed that these tattoos could also be exchanged for provisions in the afterworld.

Naga women wore a diversity of chin and calf tattoos, and sometimes these marks displayed very subtle variations within a village or village group. The reason being is that these permanent markings typically identified the bearer's particular clan and/or Naga subtribe. Other variations, especially in the linework or design of navel and calf tattoos, might also identify the social class of the wearer.

For the Wancho and some Konyak groups, tattooed lines ending in /\/\/\ or XXX denoted aristocratic status. Among the Chen, diamond shapes applied to calf tattoos denoted a woman's noble pedigree. Other forms of Naga tattooing could be worn only by members of the Naga ruling class itself, such as the special leg patterns worn by female Konyak and Wancho

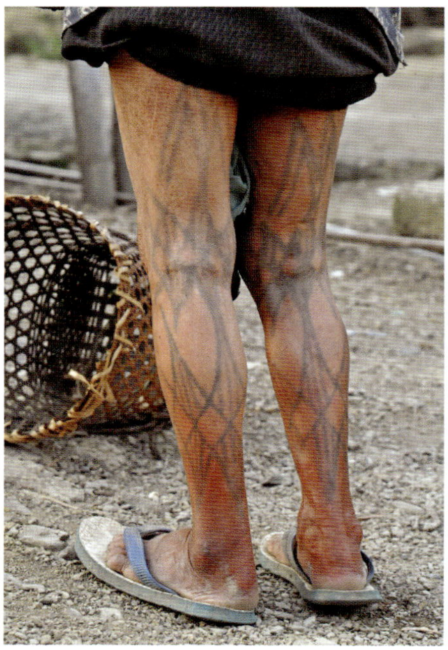

FIGURE 6.31
Leg tattoos of Konyak elder Monyu from Jakphang village, 2018. These markings are regional indicators and worn only by women from a specific group of neighboring villages in Nagaland. Across the Naga universe, there are a variety of leg tattooing styles that serve various functions. Some worked as regional, tribal, or clan identifiers, while others marked one's social status. For example, Konyak, Chen, and Wancho noblewomen possessed design elements denoting their elevated status. © Lars Krutak.

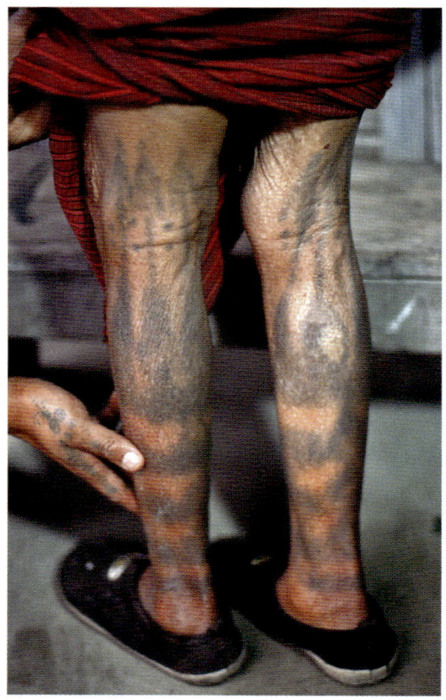

FIGURE 6.32
An Ao elder of the Chungli group, Nagaland, 2010. Women's leg tattooing identifies the linguistic group of the bearer. These tattoos differentiated those individuals of the Chungli, Mongsen, and Changki divisions. © Lars Krutak.

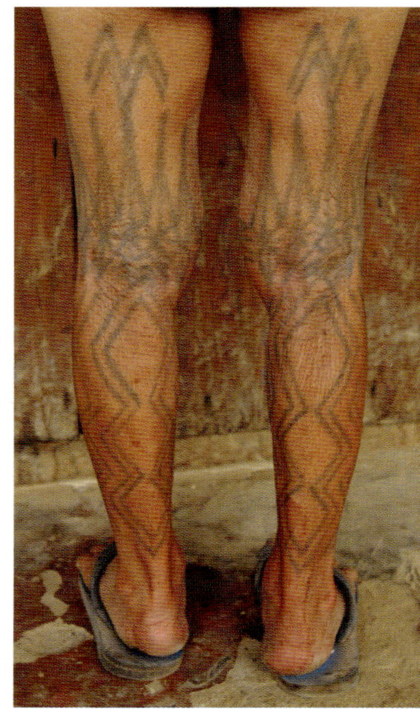

FIGURE 6.33
Leg tattoos of Konyak elder Eho-Pongnyu of Angphang village, Nagaland, 2018. © Lars Krutak.

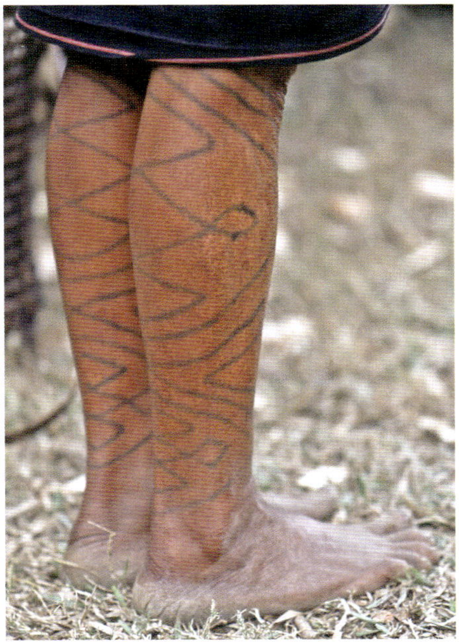

FIGURE 6.34
Khiamniungan leg tattoos, Noklak village, Nagaland, 2008. © Lars Krutak.

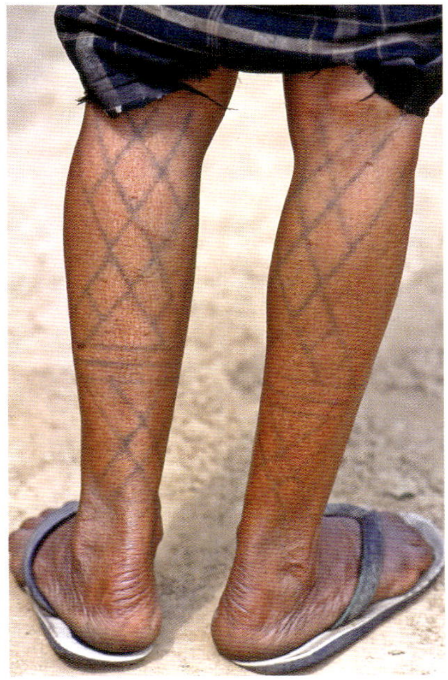

FIGURE 6.35
Tikhir Naga leg tattoos, Shamator village, Nagaland, 2008. © Lars Krutak.

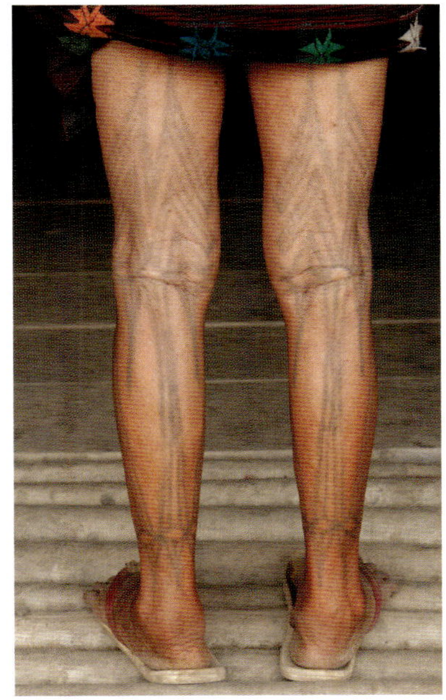

FIGURE 6.36
Konyak leg tattoos, Changlangshu village, Nagaland, 2018. © Lars Krutak.

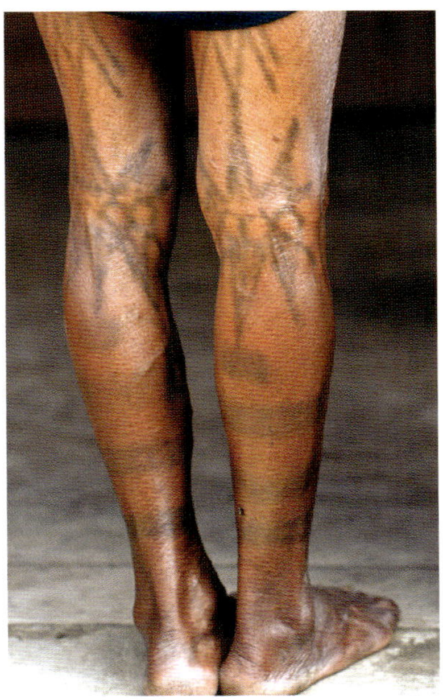

FIGURE 6.37
Phom Naga leg tattooing, Pongo village, Nagaland, 2010. © Lars Krutak.

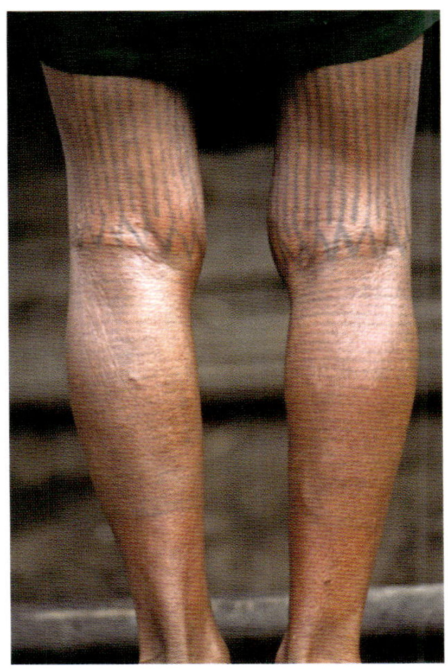

FIGURE 6.38
Wancho leg tattooing for a woman of the commoner class, Nianu village, Arunachal Pradesh, 2008. © Lars Krutak.

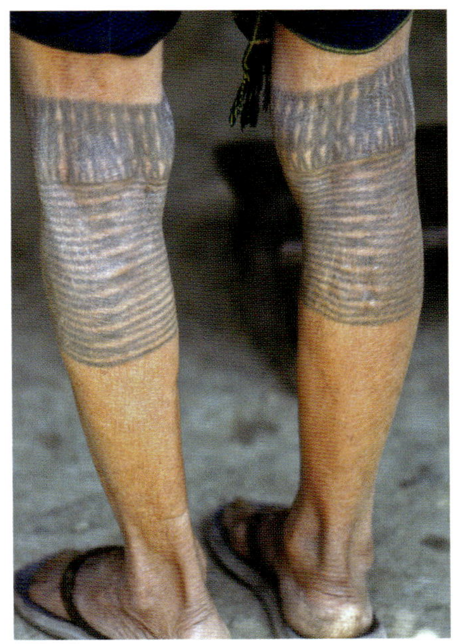

FIGURE 6.39
Konyak leg tattooing for a woman of the aristocratic class, Wanching village, Nagaland, 2008. © Lars Krutak.

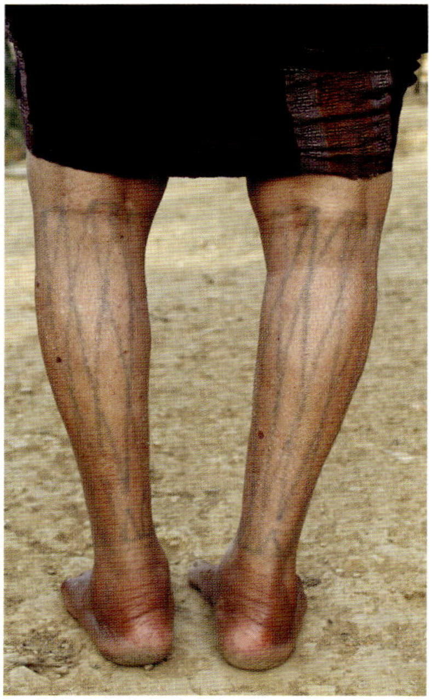

FIGURE 6.40
Pochury Naga leg tattooing, Hutsü village, Nagaland, 2015. © Ruokuonuo Yhome.

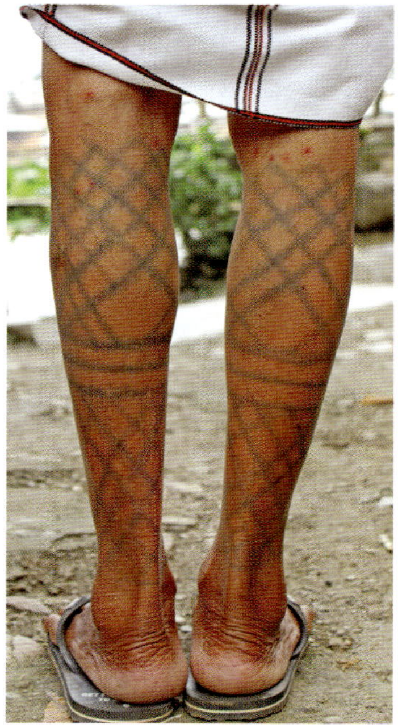

FIGURE 6.41
Leg tattooing of Sangtam elder Mrs. Pusutsu Thongru, Phelungre village, Nagaland, 2013. © Mo Naga.

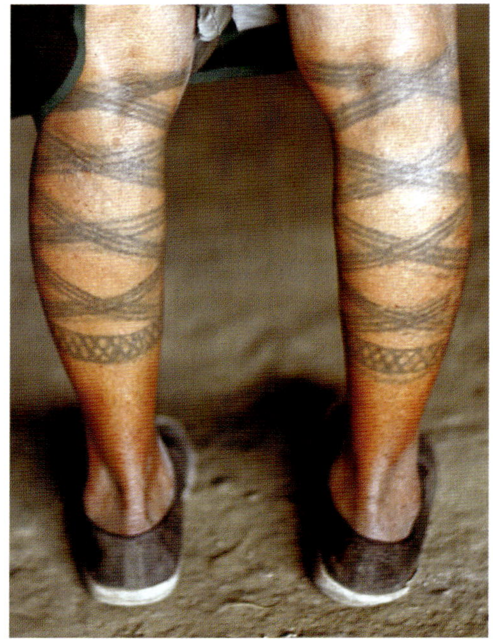

FIGURE 6.42
Leg tattooing of Chen elder Yathron, Chen Loisho village, Nagaland, 2010. © Lars Krutak.

members of the ruling chief's family. These designs resembled diamond or lozenge designs placed over their tibias or shins. These women also bore special designs atop their shoulders and hands composed of checkered patterns of diamonds, lozenges, and X-marks. A Wancho chief's daughter may have also possessed eight small dots arranged in two rows atop the lines tattooed on her thighs (Dutta 1990: fig. 4).

Male rulers might also bear special tattoos signifying their high rank, such as the "necklace" tattoo worn by Wangkau Angh of Chi, who was the last bearer of this tattoo (see fig. 6.47). Small diamond patterns were featured in the facial tattooing of great Konyak *anghs* (see Konyak and Bos 2017:107). Macham chiefs in Myanmar were marked with various small anthropomorphs on their bodies (e.g., arms, back, legs). And as a man built up his name and reputation through mediating conflicts and resolving other disputes, he might acquire many of these *mothin'kyun* (human figures), which were a sign of his leadership abilities and status.

Once an unmarried girl had received her clan marks and reached the onset of puberty (at fifteen to seventeen years of age), her shoulders were tattooed if that was a customary practice of her people. For those Naga tribes that practiced forearm and back-of-the-hand tattooing, these areas of the body were also tattooed at this time. Once a Konyak or Wancho girl was engaged to be

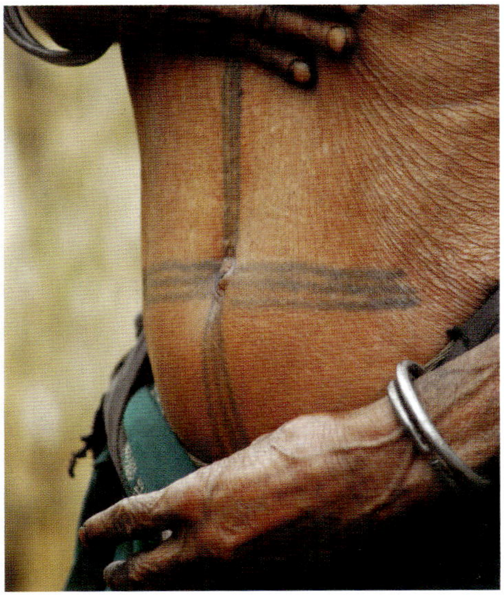

FIGURE 6.43
Wancho elder Apu Wangsni, with navel tattooing illustrating her social status, Nianu village, Arunachal Pradesh, 2008. Queens possessed /\/\/\ marks at the terminus of each tattooed line. Common women such as Apu Wangsni do not have such lines. © Jonathan Derksen.

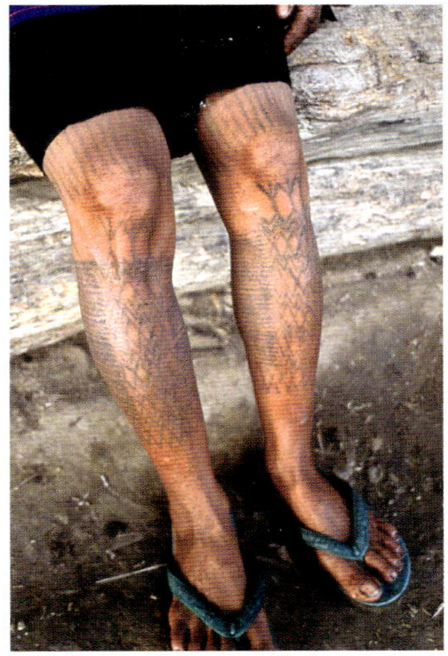

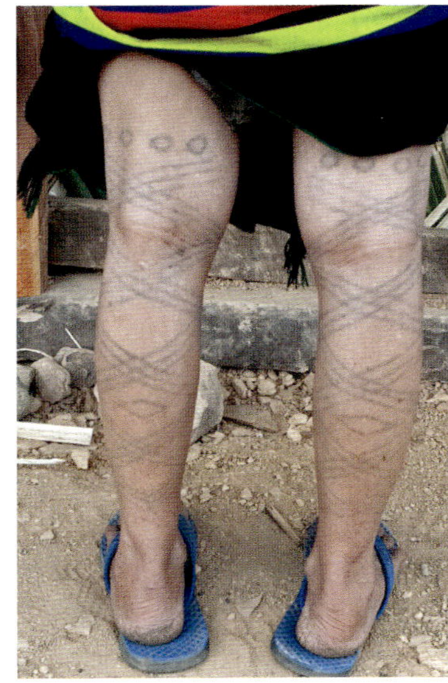

FIGURE 6.44
Phekhaw Wangcha (*left*), a Wancho queen and former tattooist of Nianu village, Arunachal Pradesh, 2008. She wears special tattoo leg motifs consisting of various XXX, diamond, and Y-form patterns that only women of her social status can own. Chen Naga aristocrats also bear special tattoos on each of their calves (i.e., a single diamond motif), like this noble woman of Yan Khone village (*right*), Myanmar, 2014. © Lars Krutak.

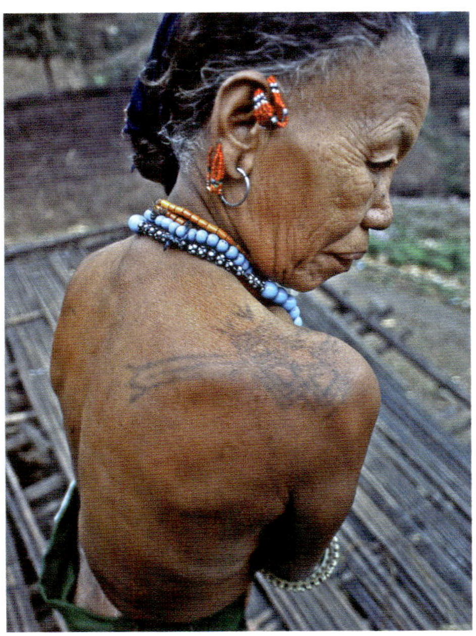

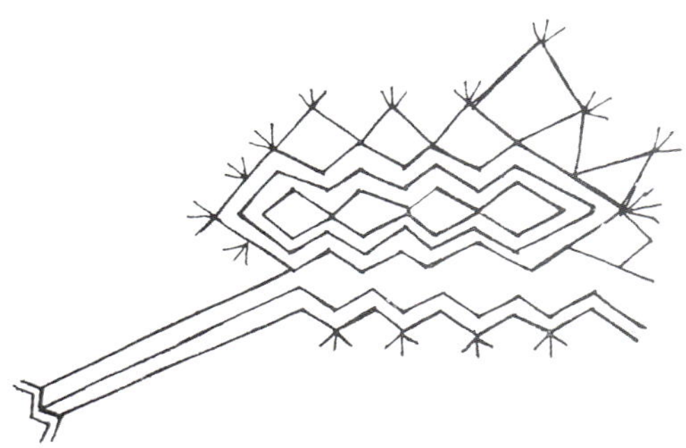

FIGURE 6.45 (LEFT)
Phebo Joham, a Wancho aristocrat of Nianu village, Arunachal Pradesh, displays *saku hu* (shoulder tattoos) denoting her high status, 2008. © Lars Krutak.

FIGURE 6.46 (ABOVE)
Illustration of Wancho shoulder tattooing showing a slight variation in the patterning. From Dutta 1990: fig. 10.

FIGURE 6.47
Wangkau Angh, the late chieftain of Chi village, Nagaland, displays a necklace-like tattoo reserved for Konyak leaders, 2010. © Lars Krutak.

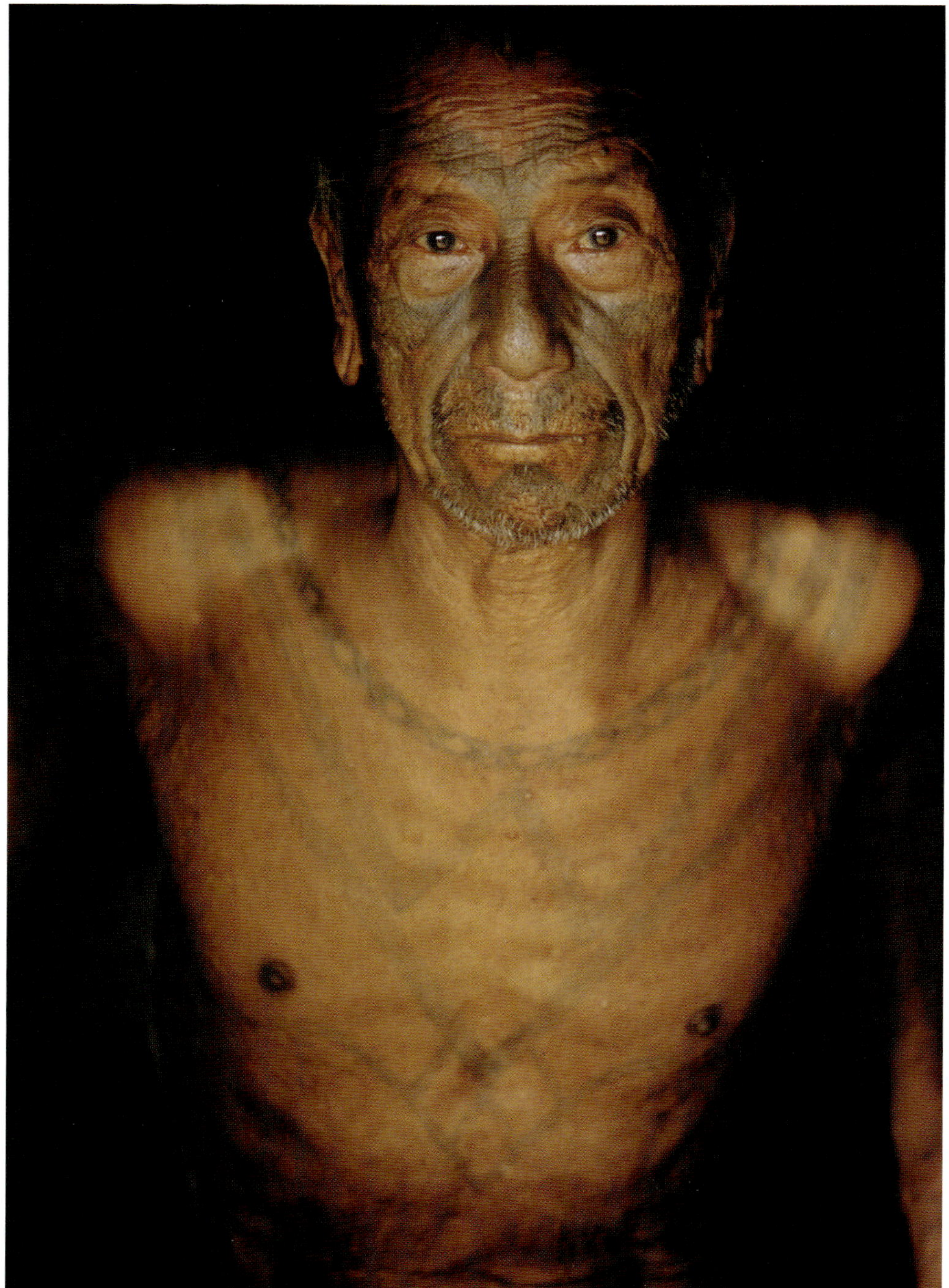

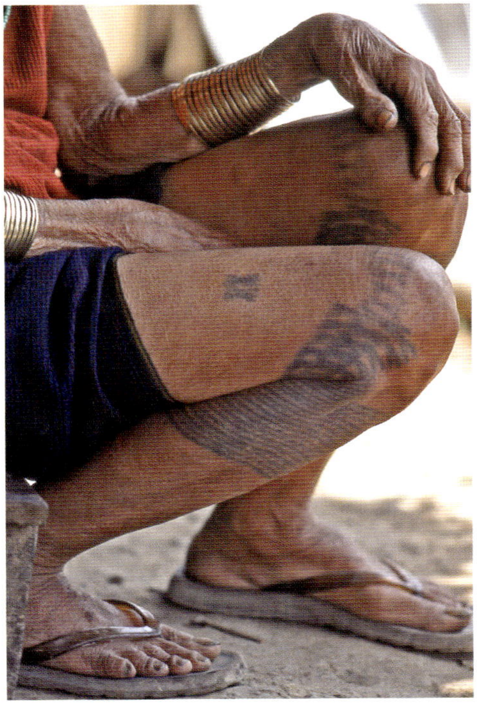

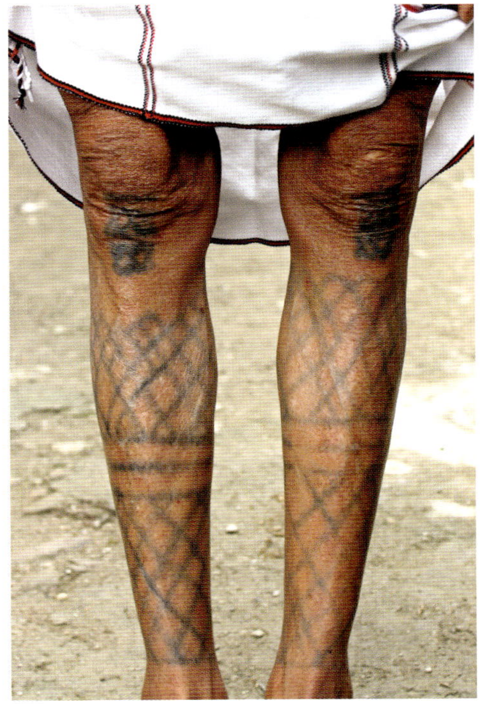

FIGURE 6.48 (LEFT)
The Konyak *anghya* of Wanching village, Nagaland, showing the *naopai*, or "cradling the baby" XX tattoo on her upper thigh, 2010. © Lars Krutak.

FIGURE 6.49 (RIGHT)
Mrs. Tsakiuchi Thongru, a Sangtam Naga aristocrat of Phelungre village, Nagaland, displaying knee tattoos related to her social status, 2013. © Mo Naga.

married, her knees were tattooed with customary patterns, then her upper chest was hand-tapped after betrothal and subsequent resettlement into her husband's home.

After the birth of a Konyak or Wancho woman's first child, two small Xs were placed on her right thigh. Konyak elder Ngipen of Totok Chingnyu village told me this was done "to ensure fertility" (Krutak 2018). The local colloquialism for this tattoo was *naopai,* or "cradling the baby," since a newborn's head often rested on this mark (Konyak and Bos 2017:137).

Among the Ao, the life stages of tattooing closely paralleled those of the neighboring Konyak, but there were slight differences. According to James P. Mills (1926:30), a twentieth-century British civil servant–turned-anthropologist, "When a girl is about ten or eleven years old her legs are tattooed up to the bottom of the calf; the next year her chin, chest and the fronts of her shoulders are completed; in the third year the pattern on the calf is [completed], and in the fourth year her knees are tattooed; in the final year her wrists and stomach are ornamented."

Some female tattoos were embodied with supernatural power. While Chang women possessed chin tattoos that denoted their clan membership, large forehead designs served to protect them from tigers. The most popular pattern was a lozenge placed near the hairline when a girl was about ten years of age (Krutak 2017b:17). Chang women told me that they wore such a tattoo because it would frighten any tigers that crossed their path. Obviously, the tactic worked, because there are no memories of tattooed women being attacked by tigers.

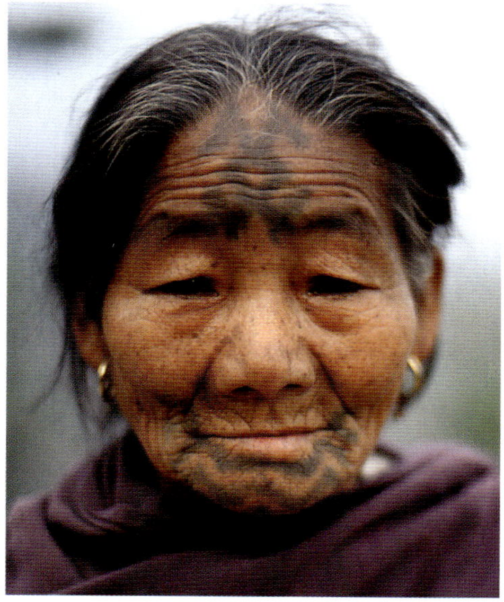

FIGURE 6.50
Antikungtang, a Chang elder of Hakchang village, Nagaland, showing the forehead lozenge specific to her village, 2010. Her chin patterns provide her clan affiliation. © Lars Krutak.

Chang women of Hakchang village have shared a different tale related to the origins of their forehead tattoos. Here, the pattern is associated with a maiden named Molola who sacrificed her own life to save the village from a great flood brought about by a breach of taboo. The deity responsible for the incident promised that the water would recede if the women of Hakchang began tattooing this symbol on their faces (see Hutton 1922b; Krutak 2010b).

Various food prohibitions were observed in relation to Naga tattooing, and some elders told me that these customs were based on clan protocols. Although what follows is not an exhaustive list, some of the restrictions I have recorded include garlic, ginger, and vegetables and beans with strong odors, because they might cause the tattoos to become septic (Chang Naga, Yimpang village); the tattoo recipient could not consume fresh foods or fruits, only dried fish and rice to help heal the wounds (Phom Naga, Nian village); the tattooist could eat only rice and bamboo shoots on the tattooing day, otherwise the recipient's tattoo would swell, become septic, and she would die, and the tattoo recipient also had to follow this diet until her tattoos healed (Phom Naga, Younphong village); garlic, ginger, corn, and creeper plants (e.g., gourds and pumpkin family products) were not eaten for six days, otherwise the tattoo punctures would become septic (Khiamniungan Naga, Noklak village);[26] fermented soybeans, meat, and curries were strictly forbidden and only plain rice could be eaten until the third day after the tattooing (Khiamniungan Naga, Yakhao village); pork, chilies, and fresh meat were forbidden until the tattoos healed (Wancho Naga, Kamhua Noknu village); no chicken could be consumed for two days or the tattoos would become septic (Yonkon Naga, Kar Chan village); and scaleless fish (especially catfish)[27] could not be eaten for the remainder of one's lifetime (Ao Naga, Ungma village) (Krutak 2010b).

Tattoo payments also varied widely, and poor families could provide labor in the tattooist's fields if they had no other forms of compensation. According to the tattooed elders I have interviewed over the years, other fees were as follows: a sum or rice and five to six pieces of meat to book the initial tattoo session, then coin currency to complete each successive stage of leg and forearm tattooing (Ao, Ungma village; female); coin currency, meat, and rice beer for leg and forearm tattooing (Ao, Yisemyong village; female); a spear or four rupees (ca. 1950) for a large V-shaped chest tattoo (Phom, Yongshei village; male); a quantity of rice and meat for leg tattoos (Konyak, Wanching village; female); a quantity of vegetables, pork, and rice wine for facial and leg tattoos (Konyak, Jakphang village; female); raw and cooked meat, and Naga beans for various anthropomorphs on the limbs (Chang, Chang village; male); a pig's leg and rice beer for the XXXX band on the upper chest (Wancho, Nianu village; male); a pig's leg, one basket of cooked rice, four bamboo tubes of rice beer, and one metal armlet (Wancho, Nianu village; female commoner); and one King George coin for lower jaw and chin tattoos (Yonkon, Kar Chan village; male).

Among the Wancho and Konyak, however, the more a female commoner's family could pay to the tattooing queen (*huhtu wangchanyu*, Wancho; *anghya*, Konyak) of the village, the more prestige the family gained. The Wancho queen of Nianu village, Phekhaw Wangcha, told me that a "high payment" for a commoner family might be a *mithun* or water buffalo thigh, accompanied by labor in her agricultural fields (Krutak 2008b). When a Wancho or Konyak noblewoman was tattooed, a village feast was held wherein many animals were sacrificed and their meat was shared with the entire community.

Great warriors, who had already acquired baseline motifs, might receive additional tattoos for free, since having many such men in the community bolstered the warlike reputation of the village far and wide. One such village hero was the Khiamniungan warrior Shing Ling (Ling = "Braveheart") of Noklak village (Longkumer 2017:398). The heavily tattooed warrior Chellia (see fig. 6.24), who took eight enemy heads in his youth and bears anthropomorphic tattoos across the surfaces of his skin representing *eisoe* (enemies) slain, told me in 2008 that Shing, who passed away circa 1992, claimed thirty trophy heads during his lifetime. "He was *nyeplao* (hand-tap tattooed) by a female artist with a *nyaptsao* (thorned tool) from his ankles to his waist, everywhere but his back. He didn't pay for his tattoos, because they were a free service for the greatest headhunters," he said.

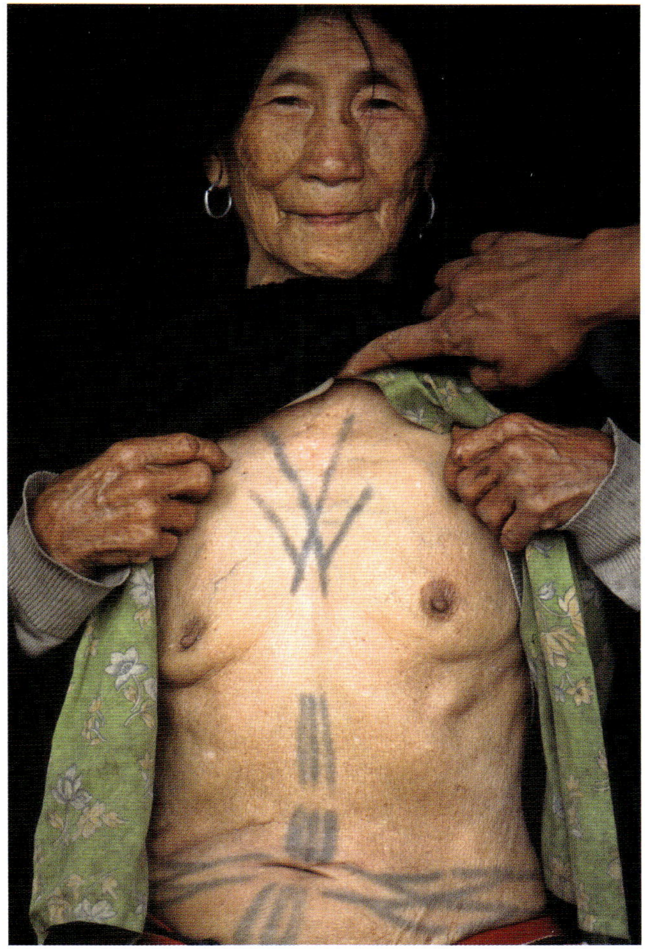

FIGURE 6.51

Tattooed Phom woman with torso markings, Nian village, Nagaland, 2010. It is difficult to encapsulate the great range and diversity of female tattooing among the Naga, which was often associated with permanently marking specific life stages. While Konyak and Wancho women living in certain villages might receive chest tattoos to commemorate their marriage, tattooed Phom women of Nian village told me that their unique chest and navel tattoos signified that they were eligible to be married. These tattoos embodied other functions too. Surrounding Phom villages did not possess this form of tattooing, so it differentiated Nian women and therefore was a distinguishing mark of local identity. Moreover, in the past women did not wear shirts, so the design enhanced a girl's beauty. © Lars Krutak.

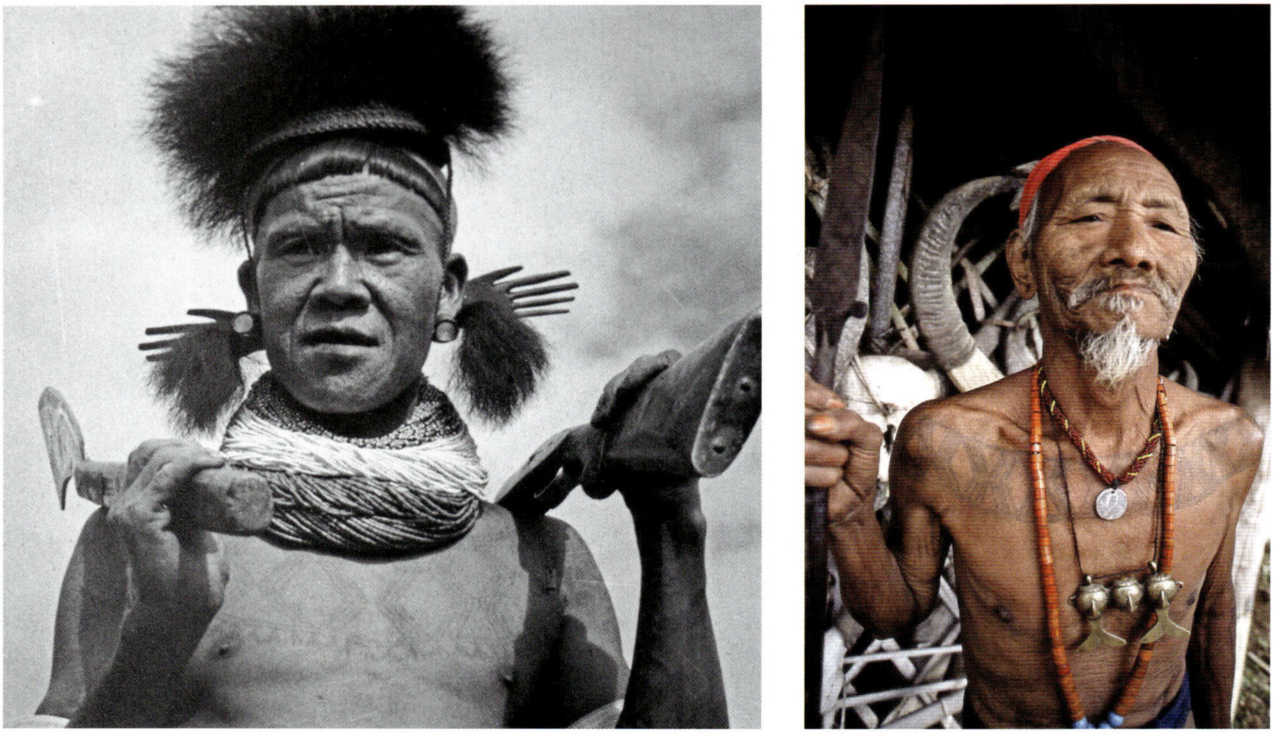

FIGURE 6.52
The Wancho chieftain of Khanu village, Arunachal Pradesh. Tattooing was an expensive undertaking among the Wancho Naga, unless you were a member of the royal family like the chieftain of Khanu (*left*). His wife was the tattooist, and he paid no fee. However, the former warrior Langtun Lukham of Nianu village (*right*) paid a pig's leg and a quantity of *zu* (rice beer). He received his tattoo for participating in a successful head-hunting raid, and his chest tattoo was completed in one day. Black-and-white image by Verrier Elwin, ca. 1954. Courtesy of Ashok Elwin. National Anthropological Archives, Smithsonian Institution (04452900). Color photograph 2008 © Lars Krutak.

Additional details concerning Khiamniungan tattooing will also be stated here. The Indian military officer S. C. Sardeshpande (1987:183) documented Khiamniungan tattoo aftercare protocols, whereby the leaves of a *shangteesho* (local bush) were crushed and applied to the wounds; this holistic remedy reduced bleeding and promoted healing. The Khiamniungan of Wui village applied therapeutic tattoos to injured joints. The Ao Naga author Anungla Longkumer[28] met a female tattooist named Neyoung in 2017 who formerly tattooed X-marks on leg and arm joints to help people suffering from *jiu*.[29] This ailment was explained as "where bad blood gathers" or "where the nerves are all jumbled up." After a client received these medicinal tattoos, which were created with a thorned tool derived from the *sangkhang* plant, full mobility was restored to the limb and/or joint.

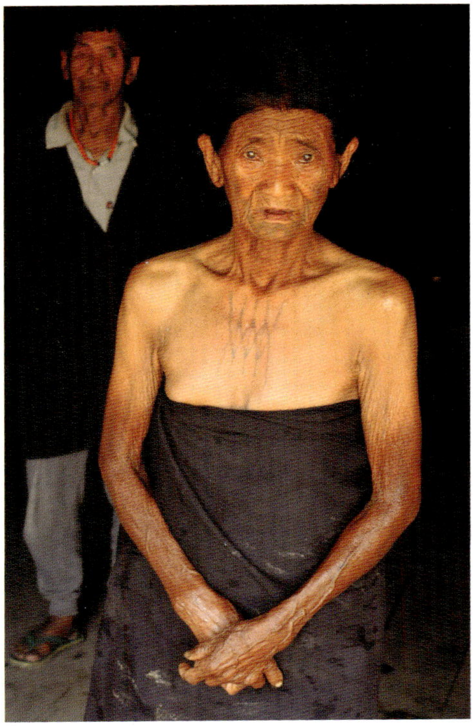

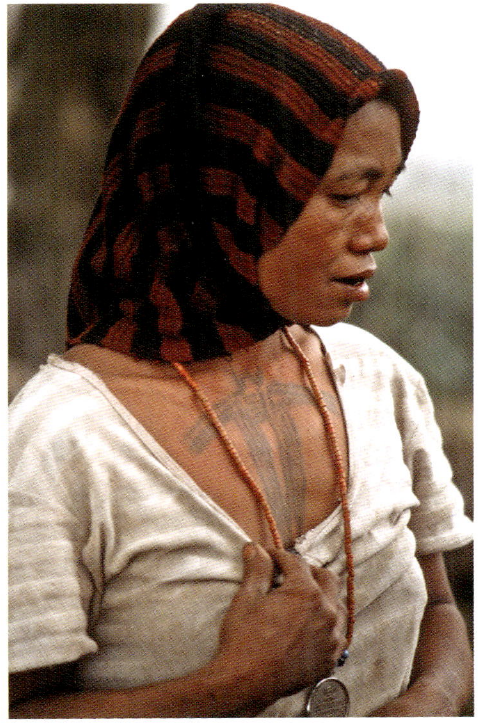

FIGURE 6.53 (LEFT)
Konyak elder Shejiang Eanglam's facial tattoos have faded, but her sternum tattoo is still clear, Changlangshu village, Nagaland, 2018. This tattoo was received before marriage to her husband, who stands in the background. © Lars Krutak.

FIGURE 6.54 (RIGHT)
Wancho woman of Nianu village displaying the chest tattoo that is given after a girl has wed, Arunachal Pradesh, 2008. The queen of the village bears a slightly different style, which is more V-shaped in form. I was told the motif represents an anthropomorphic being but no further information was given regarding its origin or meaning. © Lars Krutak.

THE TATTOOIST: TOOLS, TECHNIQUES, AND PIGMENTS (1900–2019)

While most Naga men might be tattooed at any time of the year after a successful war campaign, women were usually marked in the winter months (i.e., October–February) since the drier cold air was believed to promote healing. Generally speaking, most Naga tattooing was performed by women via the technique of hand-tapping.[30] However, Yonkon Naga *rewbon* (tattooists) in Myanmar employed a hand-poking method.

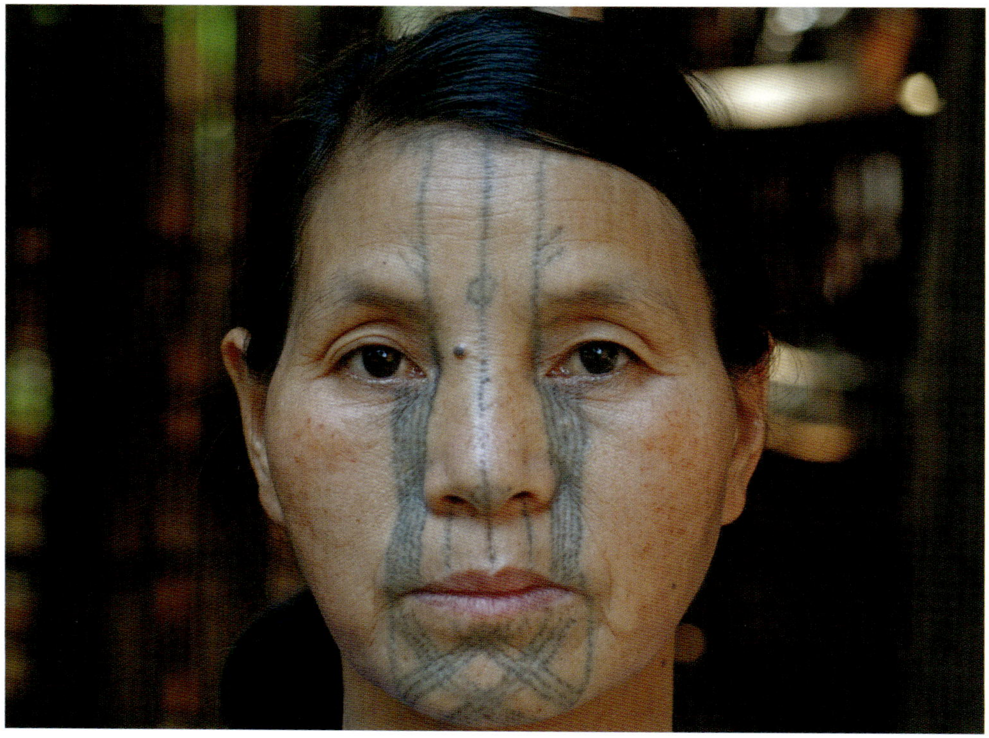

FIGURE 6.55
Ta'kong, a tattooed Yonkon Naga woman, Hkamti town, Sagaing Region, Northwest Myanmar, 2014. Yonkon women wear some of the most distinctive tattoos among the Naga. Described as "tears," they stretch down from the eyes toward the corners of the mouth. Before any Yonkon man or woman could be tattooed, prayers were offered to the shrine of the guardian spirit of the village for good health, long life, and for the tattoos not to become infected. Yonkon tattoos were hand-tapped into the skin with local bush thorns by female tattooists. Tattoo pigment was produced from the juice of the lacquer tree. Ta'Kong told me that this pattern protected women from evil spirits, and that her ancestors would recognize her in the afterlife. © Lars Krutak.

It should be quickly noted here that it was, for the most part, taboo for any man to witness a female tattooing session. Among the Konyak and Wancho, for example, a man could be plagued with bad luck in hunting and/or fishing for the rest of his life if he witnessed this performance (Krutak 2008b). In the Lower Konyak village of Tamlu, William H. Furness (1902b) wrote that the tattooing room was barred from entry, and if any man or stranger watched the tattooing session the color would fade.[31]

Sometimes a kind of prayer was offered prior to the actual tattooing. On visiting the Naga region of Myanmar in 2014, I learned that among the Yonkon of Kar Chan village the female tattooist called on the *yawan*, or local guardian spirit of the village, to bless the tattoo recipient with good health and long life;[32] she also petitioned the deity asking that no infections would arise from the painful marking. Ma Apham, a Wancho noblewoman from Kamhua Noknu village in Arunachal Pradesh who relocated to Lahe, Myanmar, remembered a tattoo prayer uttered by the "tattooing queen" of her community: "The color of your tattoo will be bright and will not fade. You will finish your tattoo and become a beautiful woman."

During an extended trip across Nagaland in 2010, I learned more details about tattooing. In the case of young men receiving their first tattoo, sometimes the pain was so great they were held down by relatives. Or the tattooist would shout words of encouragement. The son of the last Phom tattooist of Youngphong village, a woman named Mrs. Hongnyu, who was quite famous and traveled outside of her village to mark others,[33] told me his mother would proclaim: "Why are you acting like a woman? Honor your ancestors, be brave and strong!"

In Khiamniungan villages, male tattoo clients were hand-tapped by a young female tattooist who could not be of the same clan.[34] An older woman, referred to as an "architect," first stenciled the designs on the body, but she would not perform the actual tattooing, which was reserved for her younger counterpart.[35] In Yakhao village (Nagaland), I was told that if the architect was not paid, it was believed she would go blind. In the Phom village of Yongshei, tattooed warriors told me the tattooist was assisted by the wife of the tattoo recipient or, if he was not married, by his female relatives. These women stretched the skin for the tattooist and/or wiped away any excess blood from the hand-tapped wounds, which were created by a tattooing comb holding twenty-five to thirty cane thorns secured from the rattan palm.

In 2008, I witnessed a Wancho Naga tattooing session in Nianu village, Arunachal Pradesh. By this time, tattooing had not been regularly practiced in the area since the early 1980s, when Baptist missionaries forbade the practice. Since I was a cultural outsider and this was perhaps the last tattooing session to be held in the village, Queen Phekhaw Wangcha allowed me to observe it, although normally it would have been taboo for any male to watch. The technique involved is what I call "hand-hammering," because a large adze-like tool made direct contact with the skin; it was not struck with a mallet. The tool that held the needles was made from the stem of a palm frond containing one row of five to seven *siit* (cane needles) attached to the head of the tool with cotton thread. Traditionally, the day for tattooing was arranged through a divination ritual and a feast was given to mark the occasion. Prior to the arrival of Baptist missionaries in the Wancho area, the tattooist observed a food restriction and ate only rice and pickled bamboo shoots. She also wore the leaves of a *chunian* (wild plant) in the ear (cf. Dutta 1990), which "cooled down" any spiritual activity in the immediate vicinity since spirits were attracted to flowing blood.[36] Patterns were stenciled on the body part to be tattooed with dried stems of grass, and the pigment was prepared from soot obtained from charred wood mixed with water and *jing* (a resin) from the *kong*, or red cedar tree (*Toona ciliate*). While the skin was lightly "hammered" with the tattooing implement, it was also stretched by an assistant. The blood that oozed out was smeared with a bluish juice made from the charred and pulverized remains of leaves from the Jamun tree (*Syzygium cumini*) to enhance the blue-black coloration and help heal the punctures. Excess blood was wiped away with *tapo* (unidentified local leaf);[37] the underside of these leaves possesses small hairy white fibers like cotton. After a few blows to the shin of the client, the Wancho tattooist comforted the young

FIGURE 6.56

Phekhaw Wangcha preparing tattooing tools with her assistants, Nianu village, Arunachal Pradesh, 2008. The first step in making a Wancho tattoo is collecting local bush thorns that are woven together along a piece of stiff bush grass with cotton string to form a single line of needles (*right*). This comblike head is attached to the end of a bamboo shaft that is fastened at a right angle to a palm frond stem (*below, left*). The tattooist (*below, middle*), who is a queen of the village, has two or more assistants that help her prepare the ink (i.e., soot scraped from a ceramic vessel), and medicinal plants that are pulverized and later applied to the fresh wounds to promote healing. These substances are held in individual bamboo containers. The overall tool resembles a hand adze that is hammered into the skin (*below, right*), in this case the shins of the client. © Jonathan Derksen and Lars Krutak.

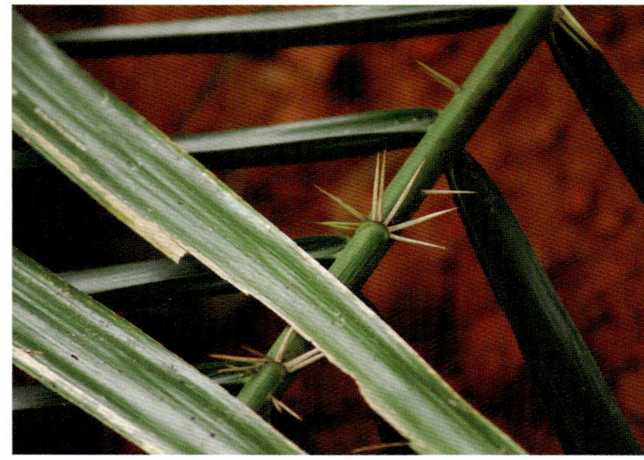

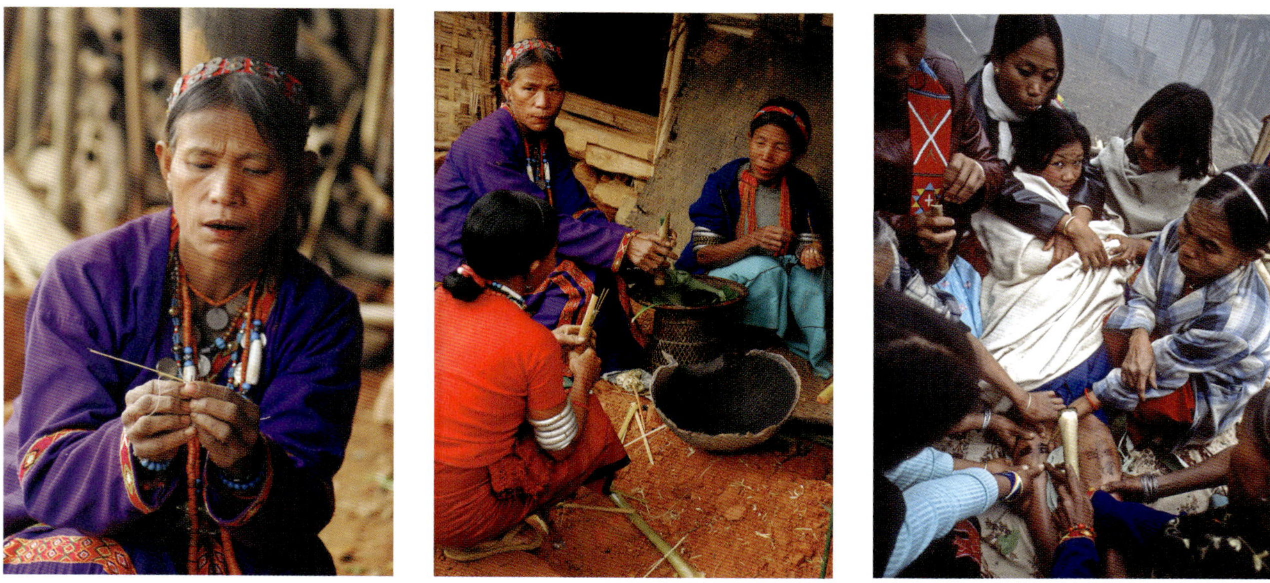

woman with words of encouragement: "This is going to make you beautiful. . . . You will have many children and your family will prosper. So don't worry about the pain!"

After the tattooing concluded, I interviewed the tattooing queen about her profession and the required training involved. "It is my obligation to give tattooing so that girls can become women and that is why I have practiced for so many years," she said. "I gave my first tattoo when I was a little girl. That's how we practiced because all of the old women told me that is how they did it. We used to have contests with the other noble girls who wanted to be a tattooist, but I practiced the most and that is why I became the tattoo queen. I would have been ashamed if I didn't know how to tattoo because I was the daughter of the queen," she proclaimed.

James P. Mills (1926:30–33) documented the Ao Naga female tattoo (noun, *teptsü;* verb, *atepsa*) process in some detail, and I paraphrase his account at some length below.[38] Roughly speaking, Ao tattooing can be subdivided into three "styles" that are derived from the three major linguistic groupings of the tribe: Chungli, Mongsen, and Changki. Variations in these baseline patterns worked as clan identifiers. By the early twentieth century, however, Ao tattooing was beginning to fade due to missionary activity that had begun several decades earlier. More specifically, in 1872 the American Baptist mission to the Naga Hills was founded on Ao lands and sought to "plant the banner of the Cross among the savage tribes" and eradicate "degrading and repulsive" customs, like tattooing (M. M. Clark 1907:54). The Baptist mission was established by two Americans, Edwin W. Clark and his wife, Mary. Headquartered in an Ao village for more than three decades, the Clarks opened a mission school and trained numerous Naga preachers, predominantly Ao, to bring the Gospel to remote areas where the "pagan" religion was still practiced. By 1960, more than half of the Naga population had converted to Christianity, lured by a religion that espoused peace and promoted education and Western medicine. It was also at this time that Ao preachers arrived in the remote villages of the eastern Naga Hills, and as they spread the new faith, tattooing and other traditions (polygamy, shamanism, warfare, working on the Sabbath, etc.) were condemned (cf. J. Thomas 2016:52–54).

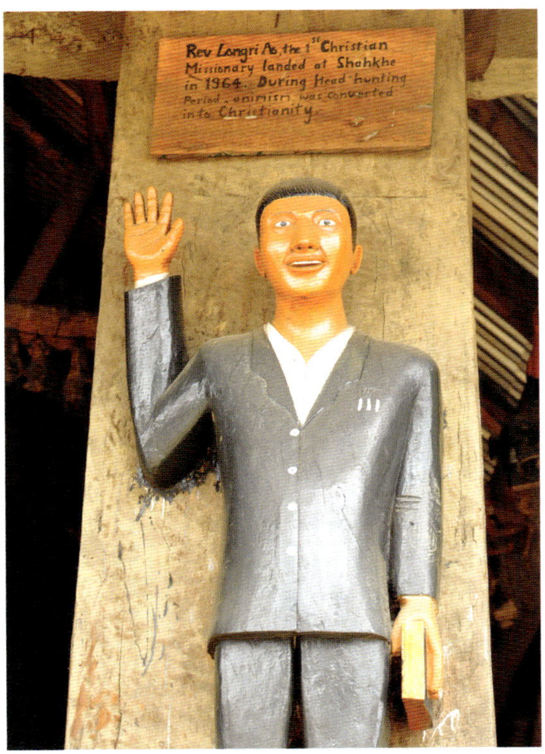

FIGURE 6.57
Carved sign in the Konyak Naga village of Monyakshu, Nagaland, depicting the Baptist reverend Longri Ao (1906–1981), the first Ao Naga missionary to arrive here in 1964. Ao was recognized for spearheading the gospel mission among the Konyaks of the eastern Naga Hills. The carving hangs on the Shahkhe *paan*, 2018. © Lars Krutak.

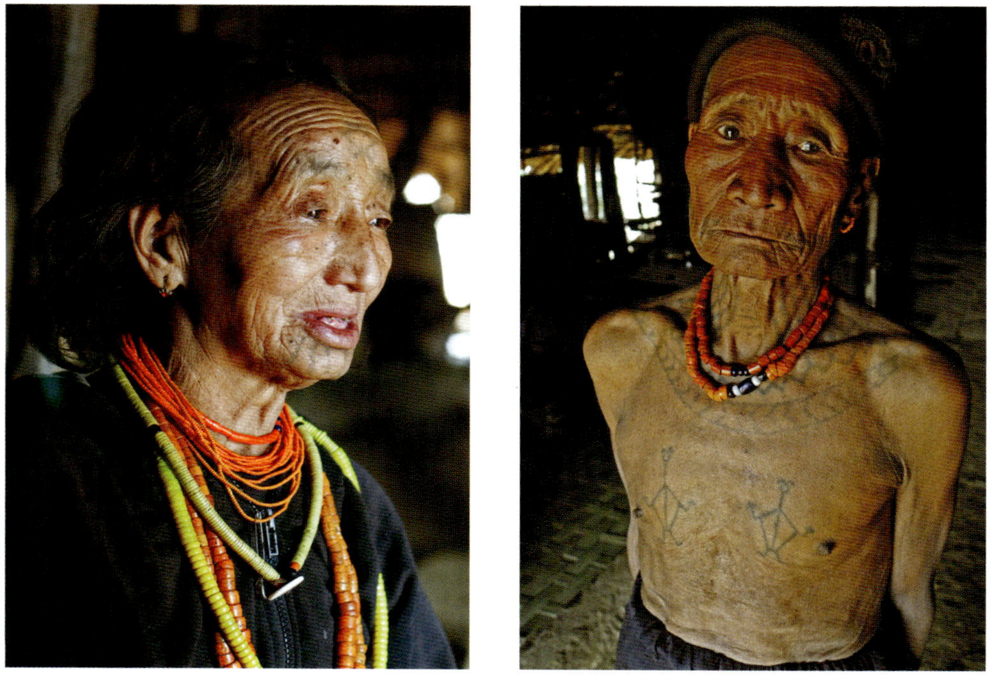

FIGURE 6.58
Ma Taw Pa (*left*), the last living Macham Naga tattooist of Kar Lay village, Myanmar, 2014. She possesses a faded forehead lozenge and the chin tattoos of her tribe. When I met her in 2014, she was nearly blind. She lamented that the Burmese government forbid hand-tapping over forty years ago. Then Christian priests came in the 1980s, followed by Buddhist monks who also discouraged the ancient custom. For these reasons, only those Macham tribespeople over sixty years of age wear tattoos today, including her husband, U'Wan'Nuu (*right*), who wears tattoos earned for tiger hunting. © Lars Krutak.

Mills noted that Ao Naga tattoo artists were always old women who performed the rite in the jungle near their village. It was strictly forbidden in many villages for any male to be present when a woman was being marked. The old women with the necessary knowledge to tattoo were found only in a comparatively few villages, and they toured the country in December and January. These months were usually chosen for the operation on the grounds that the colder it was, the more quickly the tattoo punctures healed. The knowledge of the art was hereditary in the female line, the operators teaching it to their daughters, who in turn taught it to their daughters. In some villages, it was more or less obligatory for a daughter of a tattooist to follow her mother's profession. It was believed that if she didn't, her life would be filled with illness and she would eventually waste away.

Girls were generally tattooed before puberty, when they were from ten to fourteen years old, with leg, calf, chest, shoulder, knee, and chin markings over successive sessions that delineated her Ao subgroup. Later, and prior to marriage, her stomach, wrists, and forearms were tattooed. Elders in Chungli village told me that only women who were wives of warriors and who had given

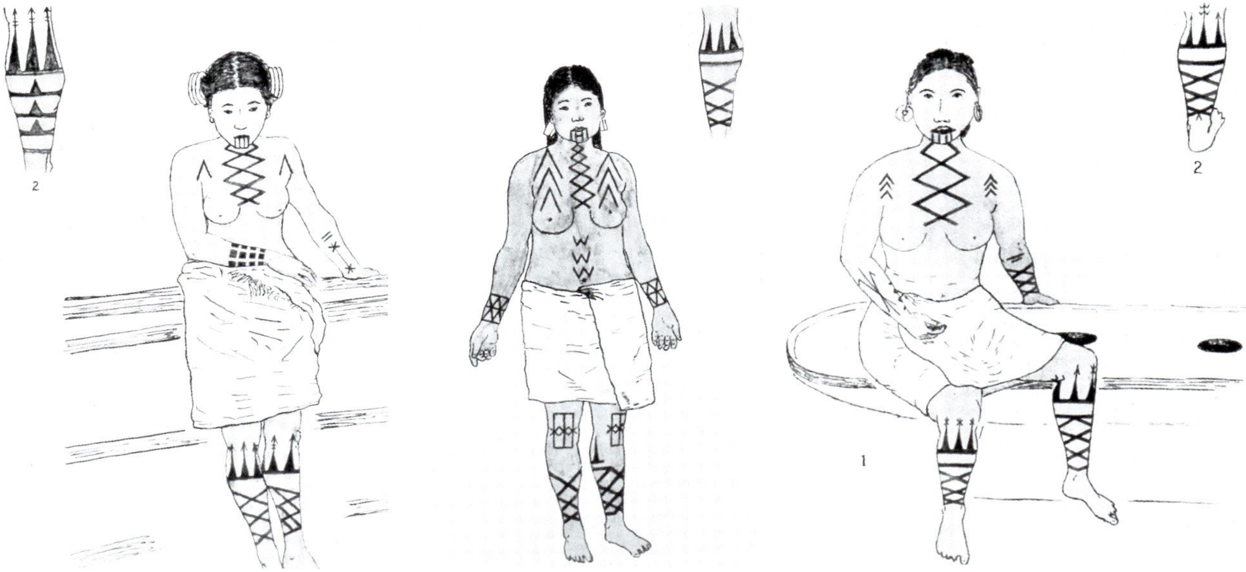

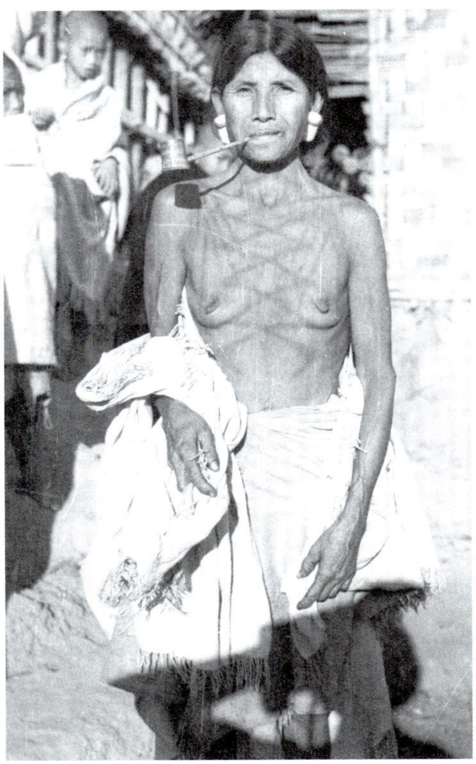

FIGURE 6.59
Tattoo styles of the Ao Naga subgroups, 1937: Chungli (*above, left*) and Changki (*above, middle*) with rectangular "bamboo mat" motif above knees; Mongsen (*above, right*). From Mills 1926. A Phom woman of Mirinokpo village (*left*), Nagaland, who adopted the chest tattooing practices of the neighboring Ao. Photograph by Hans-Eberhard Kauffmann. © Kauffmann Nachlass, Institut für Ethnologie, University of Munich. From Mills 1926.

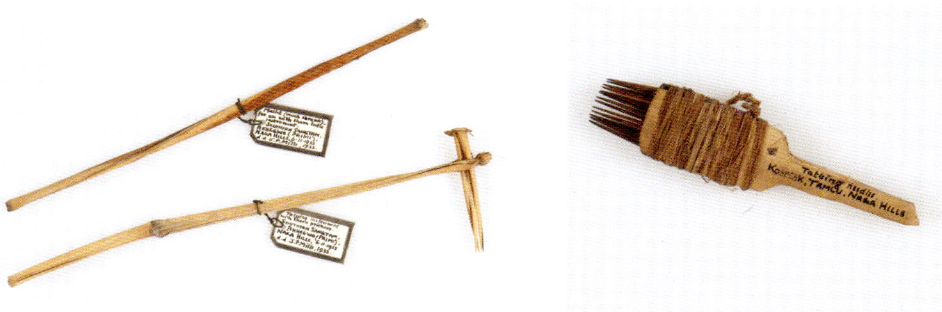

FIGURE 6.60
Sangtam (*left*) and Konyak Naga (*right*) tattooing tools from Tamlu village, Nagaland. Female tattooists of Tamlu and other Konyak villages created tattoo pigment by mixing the soot from charred resin procured from the *kong* tree with rice beer (Furness 1900:13). The *ying tee* (pigment) was kept in a bamboo container from which it could be removed and applied to the skin with flattened palette-like stencil sticks. Thorn bundles of various widths were used to create the desired pattern (linework, circles/dots, etc.) and these "combs" were inserted into a hand-tapping tool that was struck with a wooden mallet. The liquid pigment was vigorously rubbed into the resulting wound. The American traveler writer and ethnologist William H. Furness, with some difficulty, acquired a pigment container and small bundle of tattooing needles in 1900 from an elderly Tamlu practitioner. In unpublished fieldnotes he wrote, "The next day [after my purchase] they had to make a sacrifice of a fowl in order to avert the evil of having shown these instruments to strangers, let alone having sold them (Lon Kamni is the god to whom they sacrifice, and the house is . . . properly tabooed)." Today, Furness' tools are housed in the collections of the Penn Museum, Philadelphia (A 184); Pitt Rivers Museum (1928.69.1659, 1936.4.14).

a Feast of Merit were allowed to have both inner and outer arm designs, whereas less fortunate women could bear tattoos only on their inner forearms. Most of the Ao names for women's tattoos refer to the body parts on which they were applied (e.g., neck tattoo, kneecap tattoo, etc.), although a few symbols are derived from objects, such as the inner arm tattoos called *mekhum yak* (stool) and *khala* (lit., "bamboo or branch spreading or splitting outward at a fork").[39]

Takarenla and Chubalemla, two elderly Ao Naga informants I interviewed in Ungma village in 2008, stated that it was of the utmost importance for a girl to be tattooed, otherwise she would not marry well and might be chased out of the village. One Ao man from Yisemyong village told me that a woman was not acceptable for marriage if she was not tattooed. Furthermore, I was told if you did not carry tattoos on your body, you would not pass into the afterlife and see your ancestors.[40]

When an Ao girl was about to be tattooed, a bamboo mat was placed on the ground and she reclined on it. One of the primary tattoo motifs of the Changki Ao group was the rectangular bamboo mat, which was tattooed above both knees (see fig. 6.59). Two or more women held the tattoo client down while the operator plied her instruments; another woman stretched the skin and a second wiped away the excess blood and/or helped with applying pigment. The tool used for puncturing the skin consisted of a little bunch of cane thorns bound on a wooden wand that was inserted into an adze-like head made from the stalk of a plant. The pattern to be tattooed was marked by the old woman on the girl's skin with a piece of wood dipped in the coloring matter. If a girl struggled and screamed during the tattooing, a fowl was hastily sacrificed close by to appease any evil spirit that might be increasing the pain. Chubalemla mentioned that if a girl was crying or complaining, the tattooist would tell her to be quiet or she would threaten to throw her off a local cliff near Ungma and onto the rocks below!

The puncturing was done by hammering the instrument into the skin with a *tatapba* (mallet) of *kamri*, a particularly heavy, sappy plant with an onion-shaped root. After the blood was washed off the black coloring matter was then applied once more, and the tattoo client was left to bemoan her sores until they healed. Apparently, Mills observed several tattooing sessions despite local prohibitions concerning males, noting that some girls remained perfectly still while undergoing the operation, speaking only occasionally or asking a friend to spit on the wounds because they felt like they were "burning" (Mills 1926:33).

Apart from the previous lists of taboos associated with Naga tattooing, Mills (1926:33) recorded others. "A girl who has been tattooed may not eat cane berries or *kamri* berries till 'the new rain has washed the world clean,'" which was in April, and if a stem of the *yaribi* root was used as a mallet, berries from the plant were tabooed. Until their sores healed, tattoo clients were compelled to eat only rice, pickled bamboo shoots, and fowl.

Usually, the pigment was made from the sap of the bark of the *napthi* tree, although Mills noted that lumps of gum found under certain trees were burnt and the ash mixed with rice beer. Notwithstanding, the *napthi* resin was collected and burned in a pot on the fire. A leaf or a bit of broken pottery was placed over the receptacle in which the sap was burning, and the soot that accumulated was collected and placed in a *nap* (bamboo tube receptacle). When used for tattooing, it was mixed with rice beer. One very elderly Ao woman named Akangtola from Chuchuyimlang village shared another local tattoo pigment recipe with me. Pigment was obtained from the *mezünglashi* tree. A section of bark was cut away then incisions were made into the tree to release its resin. After two days, the sap hardened and could be scraped off the trunk. The sap was burned to create charcoal, which was mixed with rice beer.

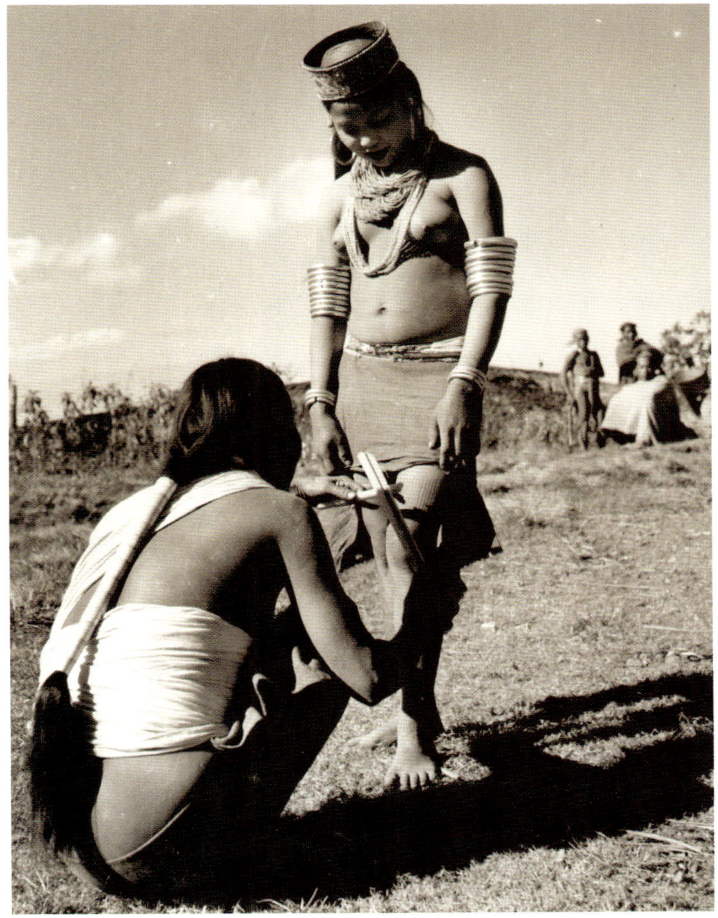

FIGURE 6.61
Wancho tattooist demonstrating the hand-tapping tattoo technique on the daughter of the chieftain of Niausa village, Arunachal Pradesh, ca. 1954. Photograph by Verrier Elwin. Courtesy of Ashok Elwin. National Anthropological Archives, Smithsonian Institution (04454700).

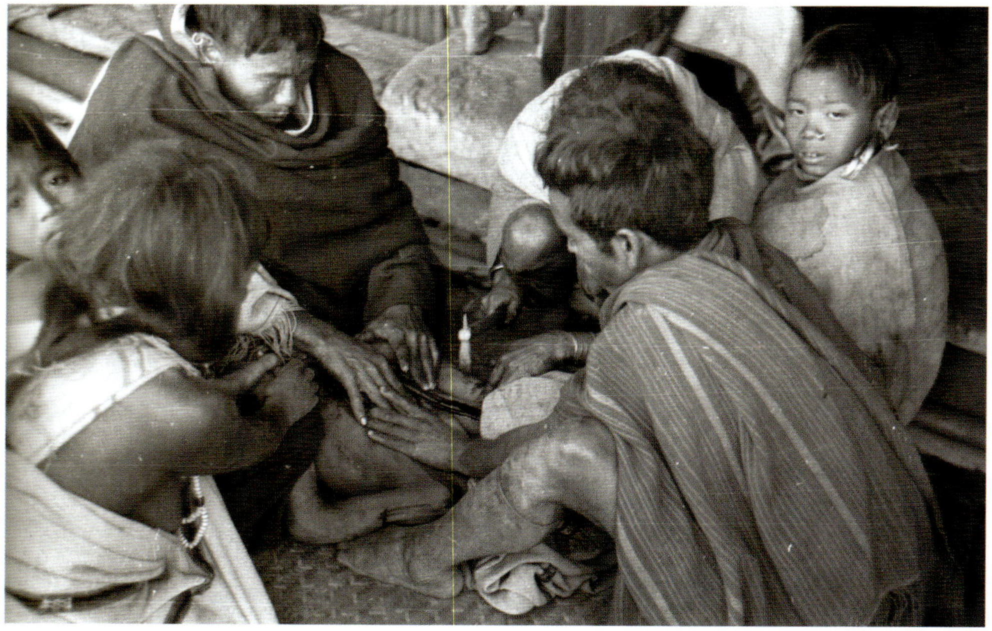

FIGURE 6.62
Konyak tattooist of Wakching village using an adze-like tool to tattoo a young man's chest, 1937. Fürer-Haimendorf's diaries reveal that two sisters of the *angh*'s clan, Liniu and Nangpha, are featured in this photograph, and both created tattoos: one is tattooing and the other, who stenciled the design on the skin, is helping to hold down the client. An example of the comblike needled tip of this tool is presented in figure 6.60, which was collected in neighboring Tamlu village. Photograph by Christoph von Fürer-Haimendorf. Courtesy of Nicholas Haimendorf. University of London, Special Collections, SOAS Library (PP MS 19/6/NAGA/1875).

Across the Naga tattooing world, many other natural substances were used to create tattooing pigment. I have often attempted to identify specific plants, shrubs, and trees that were harnessed for their resins, juices, and aftercare products but usually they have no known English, Hindi, or Burmese equivalent, so they remain for the most part unknown outside of local Naga dialects.

One of the most exotic ingredients was prepared for Pounyo warriors in Myanmar, who were some of the most aggressive and hence heavily tattooed of all Naga. According to a report of the colonial British military commander and administrator H. J. Mitchell (1929:17), who was based in Lahe, he observed that headhunting for the Pounyo Nagas "is undoubtedly a pastime—a pastime which they consider is the means of making men of their Race. . . . I saw [warriors] who had taken so many heads in raids that the [anthropomorphic] figures of men had to be tattooed on the forehead, cheek, and calves of [their] legs."[41] Regarding the latter, these "little men" were tattooed with a pigment that included pieces of an enemy's heart mashed up in its own blood.

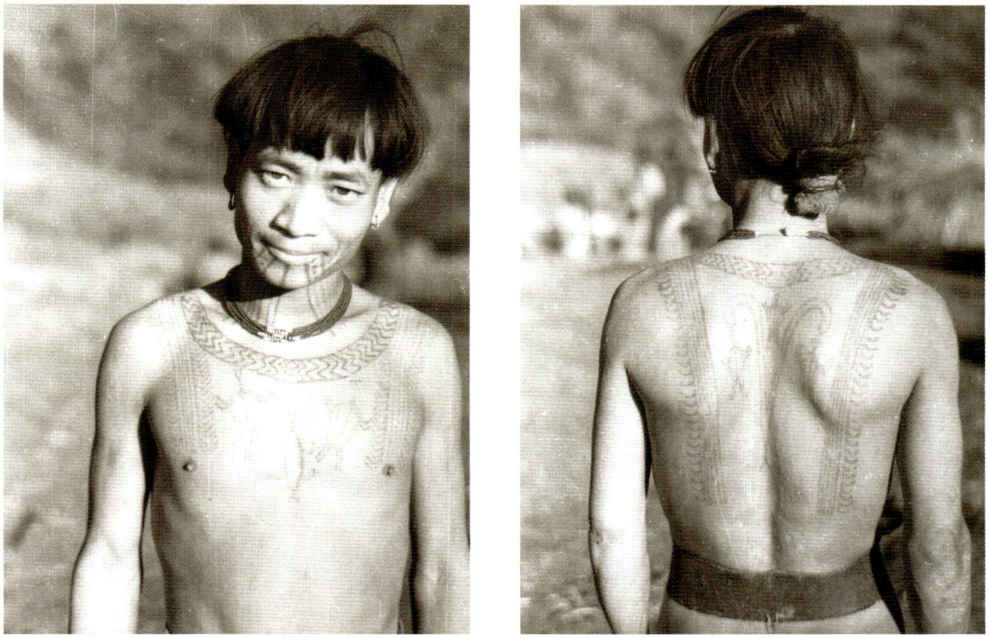

FIGURE 6.63
Pounyo Naga warrior of Ponyo village, Myanmar, displaying "buffalo necklace" tattoo and anthropomorphs on his chest (*left*) and back (*right*) representing human victims, 1936. Photograph by Christoph von Fürer-Haimendorf. Courtesy of Nicholas Haimendorf. University of London, Special Collections, SOAS Library (PP MS 19/6/NAGA/1251–1252).

The organ was then mixed with a sooty pigment of charred pine wood and the juices of a pulverized *kyin za re mat* (local leaf) to create the human figures tattooed on the chest (Krutak 2014d; Mitchell 1929). These anthropomorphs represented the "enemy,"[42] and Pounyo warriors told me that such tattoos helped "strengthen" them.

In 1936, the Austrian ethnologist Christoph von Fürer-Haimendorf (1938a) accompanied the colonial British administrator J. P. Mills to the Indo-Burmese border to pacify the bellicose Khiamniungan village of Pangsha, which had long terrorized numerous communities across this "unmapped" and largely "unknown" area of the world. During this trip, both men met heavily tattooed Pounyo Naga warriors, who were allied with Pangsha, and von Fürer-Haimendorf wisely took a series of photos depicting these tattooed warriors. The expeditionary force also collected numerous skull trophies from Pangsha and other villages, such as Yimpang, to discourage headhunting activities in the "unadministered" Naga territory. Several of these trophies were later gifted to "administered" Konyak villagers in Wakching, where von Fürer-Haimendorf was based. Since headhunting was banned in this region by the British, the heads were put into ceremonial use and headhunting festivities and tattooing soon commenced, since the opportunity to conduct these important activities would perhaps never again be possible in their traditional context.

With a special permit from the Myanmar government, I visited the Pounyo homeland in 2014 via motorcycle from Lahe. I was told that I was perhaps the first outsider to come in more than fifty years. The once richly tattooed warriors of Ponyo village were long gone, and only one man named Muang bore traces of the warrior tattoo tradition on his neck and cheeks. I was able

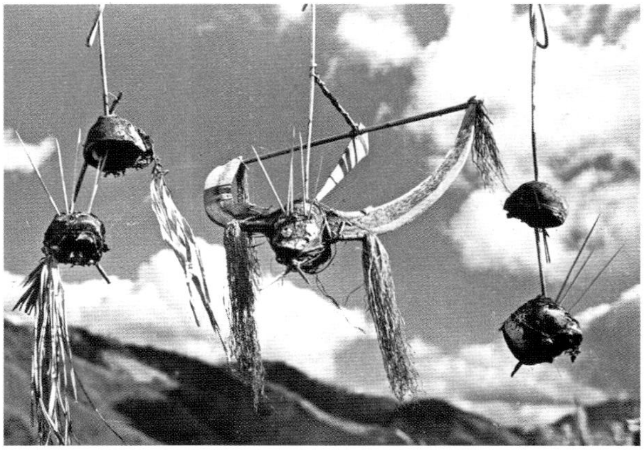

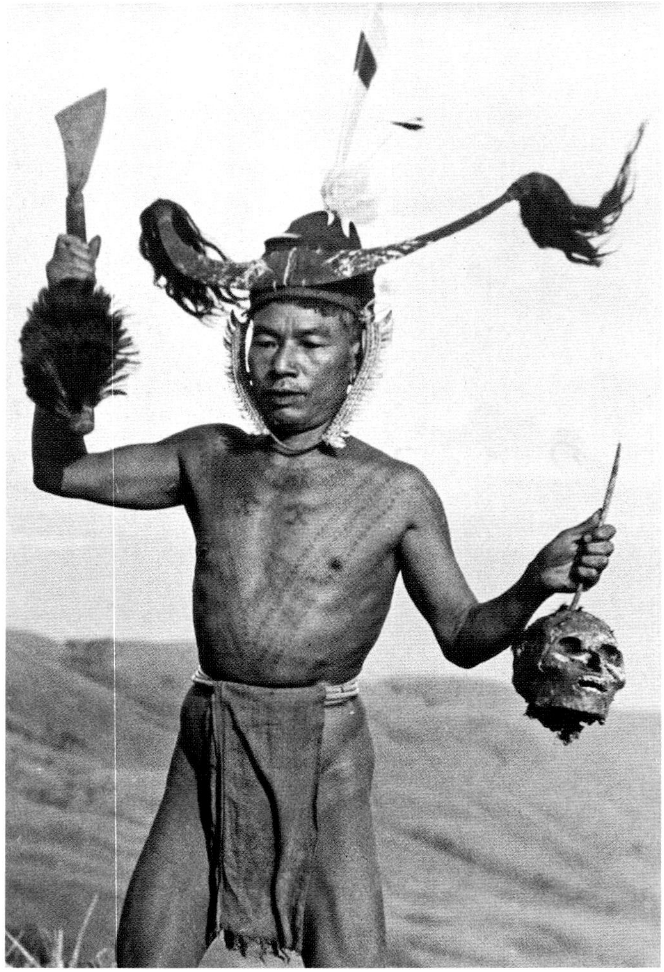

FIGURE 6.64 (ABOVE)
Skull trophies hanging at the mixed Khiamniungan and Chang village of Yimpang, 1936. Photograph by Christoph von Fürer-Haimendorf. Wellcome Library Collection (663250i).

FIGURE 6.65 (RIGHT)
Tattooed Konyak warrior of Wakching village holding trophy head retrieved by a British Expeditionary Force to the Khiamniungan village of Pangsha, which lies on the Nagaland and Myanmar border, 1937. During this era, the region surrounding Pangsha had not been mapped and was terra incognita. The two human figures on his chest denote two victims slain in the past. Photograph by Christoph von Fürer-Haimendorf. Courtesy of Nicholas Haimendorf. Wellcome Library Collection (663208i).

to record several Pounyo tattooing terms, including the words *phakam dao* (arm tattoos), *zak thong dao* (chest tattoos), *bok hei dao* (neck tattoos), and *san pi dao* (V-shaped back tattoos); the general word *hean khong dao* for back tattoo; and the word *san pi dao* for the "buffalo necklace" tattoo.[43] Muang noted that one or more women might stencil complex tattoo designs on the body, but only one of them applied the tattoos through hand-tapping. He said that chili was tabooed until the tattoos had healed.

A few days after visiting Ponyo village, I traveled to the village of Lon Khin, where I met several heavily tattooed former headhunters, including U Pha Kyaw and Vom. These men possessed particularly elaborate chest tattooing, and the former also wore arm tattoos similar to the one seen in von Fürer-Haimendorf's images. I learned that U Pha Kyaw was a war captain due to

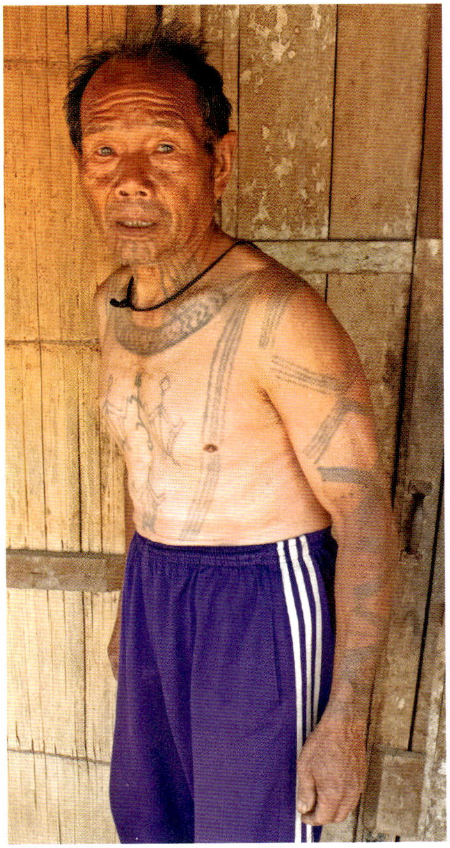

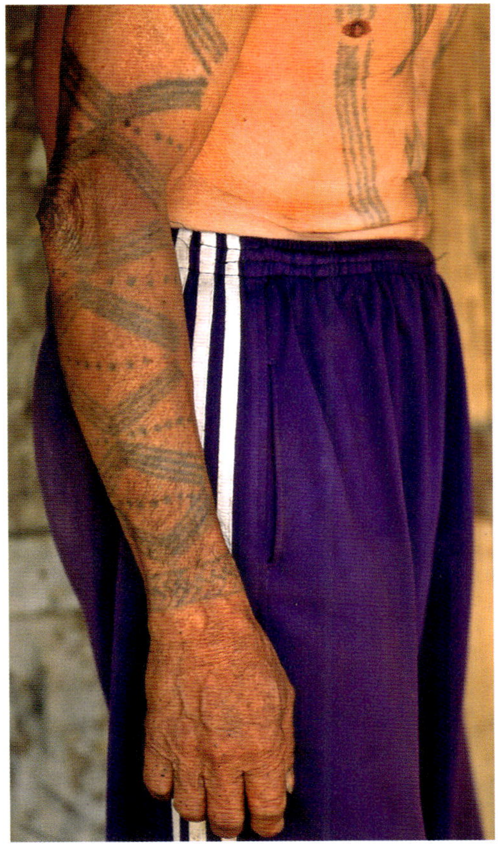

FIGURE 6.66 (LEFT) Former warrior U Pha Kyaw of Lon Khin village, Myanmar, 2014. The dotted patterns on his forearms verify his status as a war captain and headtaker. © Lars Krutak.

FIGURE 6.67 (RIGHT) Close-up of Pounyo Naga war captain's tattooed arm, 2014.

the dotted motifs running in between the interspersed double << ●● >> designs. Lainong, Khiamniungan, Konyak, and Chang warriors bear similar arm designs, and star motifs, round circles, or small V-shaped designs placed between the scalloped lines also denoted war captain status (Krutak 2008b, 2010b, 2014d).

In my interviews with other Pounyo men bearing these chest tattoos, however, I was given different answers concerning the legged zoomorphic image placed on the center of the chest. One man, who had killed a tiger, said it represented this animal and that everyone in the village would know him as a "tiger hunter." Another man said it was a kind of lizard, and yet another elder stated it was a bat. For the Pounyo, bats are powerful animals because they are related to ghosts. In Pounyo oral traditions, lizards were associated with headhunting, as they were in headhunting societies of the Philippines.[44] The tattooed bars along the sides of a man's chest denoted he had participated in combat, and were often the first markings to declare this achievement. Furthermore, these bars, which extended over the shoulders, were believed to provide their owners with spiritual protection from enemy weapons, in essence rendering them "bullet proof" (Saul 2005:36).

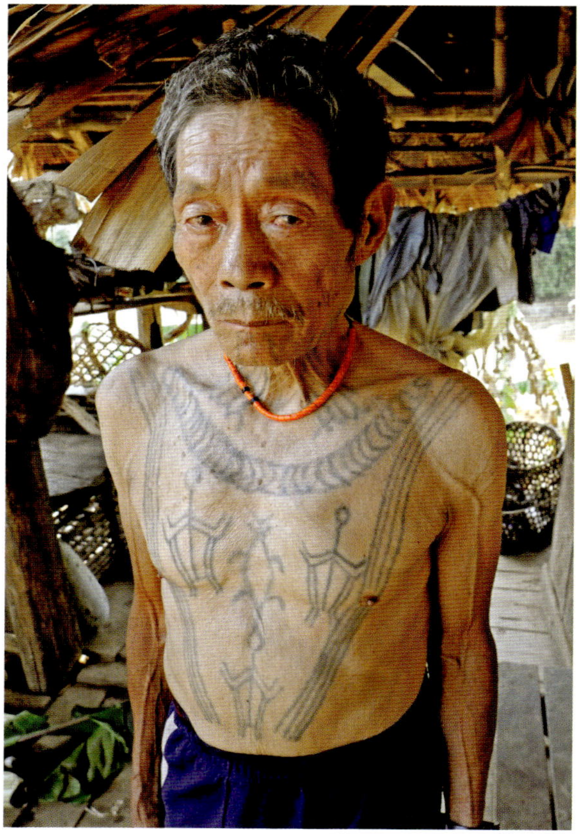

FIGURE 6.68

Pounyo Naga warrior Vom of Lon Khin village, Myanmar, 2014. A common feature of men's tattooing along the Nagaland/Myanmar borderlands is the "buffalo necklace," which was a sign of a warrior or head-taker. Pounyo tattoo pigment consisted of charred pine wood soot and water. However, it was sometimes "strengthened" with pieces of a human heart taken from an enemy. © Lars Krutak.

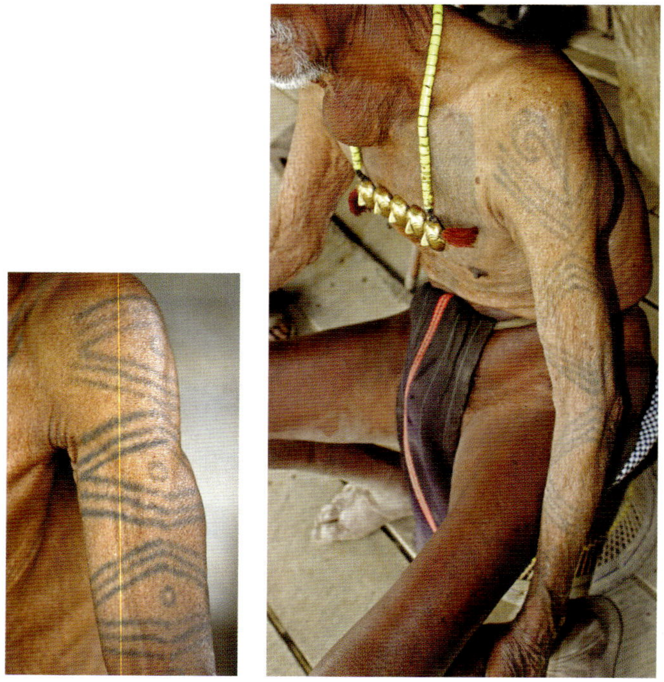

FIGURE 6.69

Arm tattooing (*left*) of the Khiamniungan warrior Khon of Noklak village, Nagaland, 2008. The circles tattooed between the diamond lozenges signify war captain status. © Lars Krutak. The V-shaped *mithun* (bovine) horns (*right*) on the arm of this former Konyak warrior of Monyakshu village, Nagaland, communicate the same information, 2013. © Mo Naga.

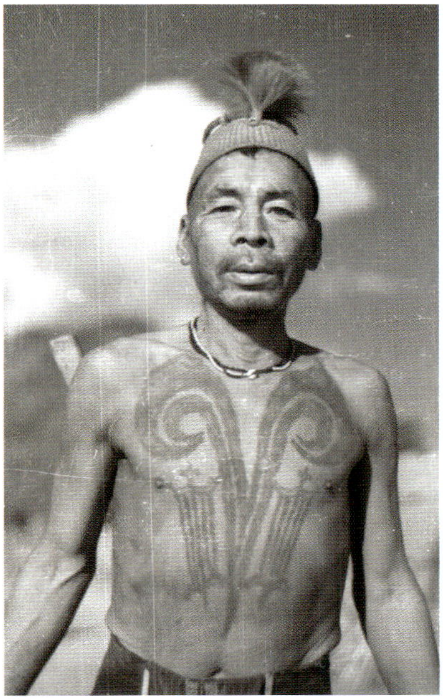
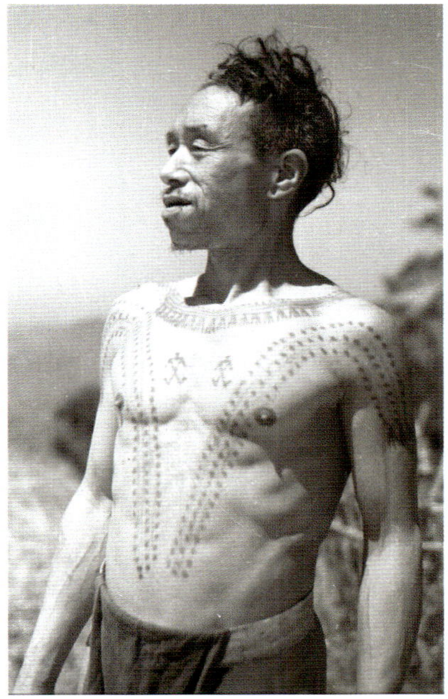
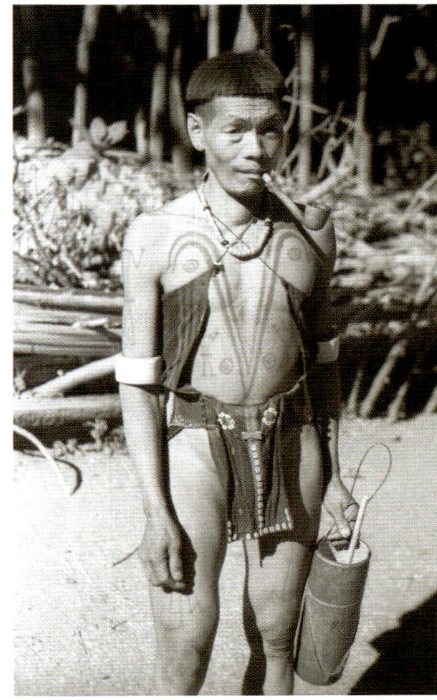
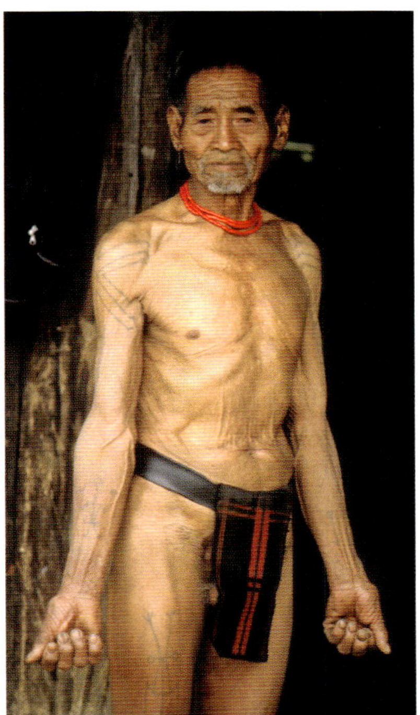

FIGURE 6.70

Chang (*above, left*) and Konyak warriors (*above, middle*), 1937; Khiamniungan headhunter smoking a pipe (*above, right*), 1937. Photographs by Christoph von Fürer-Haimendorf. Courtesy of Nicholas Haimendorf. University of London, Special Collection, SOAS Library (PP MS 19/6/ NAGA/1354; 2359; 1250). Fürer-Haimendorf photographed several Naga warriors in the 1930s during his time in the "unadministered" areas of what today is known as Nagaland. Chang warriors, along with the Phom, Konyak, Khiamniungan, and other Naga groups, possessed a very distinctive V-shaped chest tattoo whose origins have perplexed ethnographers, anthropologists, and other travelers to the region over the last 150 years; sometimes high-ranking Chang warriors added two "lizard" motifs on either side of the center design, whereas other Naga applied small circles, which may have represented the number of heads taken. In my mind, the V-shaped chest marking is the Naga tattoo par excellence for men and formerly it spoke volumes about Naga identity and personal achievement relative to other tribes and the surrounding world.

Variously described by early writers as a "fountain of fertility," "Ostrich plumes," "*mithun* [bovine] horns," or "*mithun* nose and eyes," the Khiamniungan warrior Lonshei (*left*) of Yakhao village explained to me that it was an essential hallmark of humanity. Over tea at his hearth, Lonshei, who on his legs and arms bears anthropomorphic tattoos that tallied his victims, reflected, "Khiamniungan warriors were heavily tattooed—like other Naga—with emblems of the greatest and most powerful animals. Our headgear contains hornbills, the teeth of wild boar, fur from bears, tiger teeth, and we wear ivory armbands from the elephant. But humans are greater than these creatures and superior, so we devised a permanent design to show that we are more powerful, and that is the meaning of the Naga chest tattoo," 2010. © Lars Krutak.

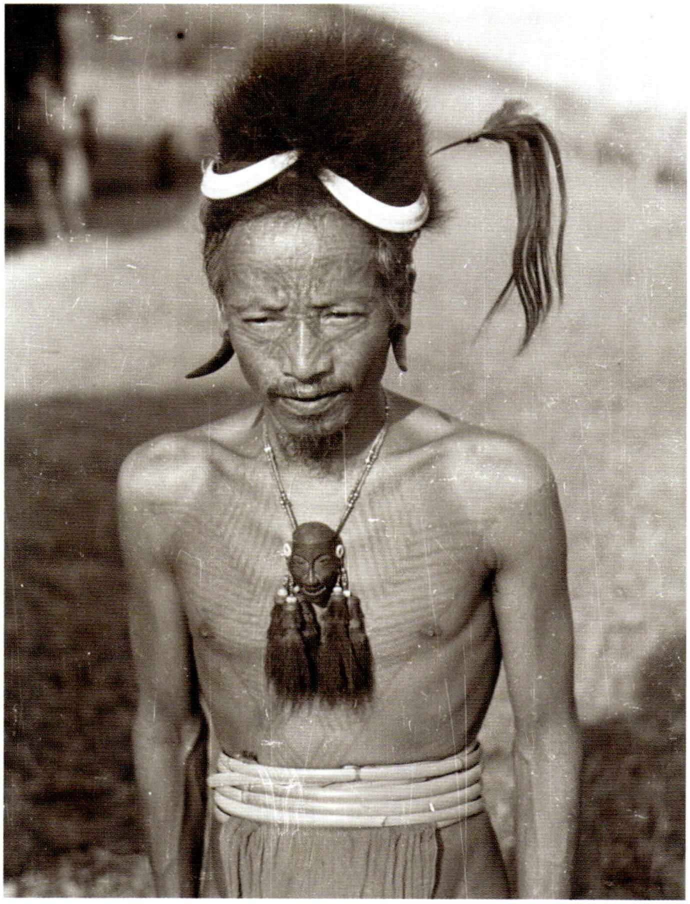

FIGURE 6.71
Konyak warrior of Zu-nyu village bearing the distinctive chest and facial tattooing of his village, 1936. Photograph by Christoph von Fürer-Haimendorf. Courtesy of Nicholas Haimendorf. University of London, Special Collection, SOAS Library (PP MS 19/6/ NAGA/0490).

TIGER TACTICS AND TATTOOS

In 2008, I traveled to the Indo-Burmese border for the first time. Inspired by the photographs of the German author and photographer Peter van Ham (cf. Stirn and van Ham 2003), I was on the hunt for fully tattooed Khiamniungan warriors in Noklak and Pangsha villages who were known for possessing "little men" tattoos representing *eisoe* (the enemy), and was fortunate to meet a few of these distinguished men. Two years later, I traveled to a different and more remote valley searching for additional tattooed "heroes." Here, I managed to interview one tattooed Khiamniungan elder named Lonshei of Yakhao village (see fig. 6.70d) who was an incredible repository of traditional knowledge. He himself had killed two enemies around 1960, and two anthropomorphs tattooed on his legs accounted for his victories. His chest was not tattooed with the traditional V-shaped motif of war heroes because he said it was too painful. Nevertheless, I was curious to learn about the geometric tattoos on his upper arms and shoulders because I had not encountered much information about them in old books and articles.

Lonshei described a fascinating phenomenon. His village sits at the border of the territory of the Khiamniungan Naga (to the east) and the Yimchungru Naga (to the west).[45] If a man killed an enemy from the villages to the west he was tattooed on his right arm. If he killed an enemy from villages to the east he was tattooed on the left. Of course, if he killed men on either side of his village, he was tattooed on both sides of his body. The motif appearing at the top of his arm represents the crossbow, a deadly weapon that was used in combat by the Khiamniungan, Chang, Tikhir, Pounyo, Yimchungru, and other Naga—the bolts were often poisoned.

After my stay in Yakhao, I journeyed to the large Yimchungru village of Sangpurre. Here I met the last war hero, named Lakiumong, who had twenty kills to his credit. Lakiumong had very intense eyes and told me he had not received any tattoos until after his tenth kill, at which time he was over thirty-five years of age. To mark this achievement, he received the characteristic V-shaped chest marking of high-ranking warriors as well as an anthropomorph symbolizing his enemies. His ear ornaments and brass necklace also indicated that he was a proven headhunter. The necklace, especially the circular elements, reinforced his valorous status because, as he told me, "I circled the enemy like a tiger and killed it."

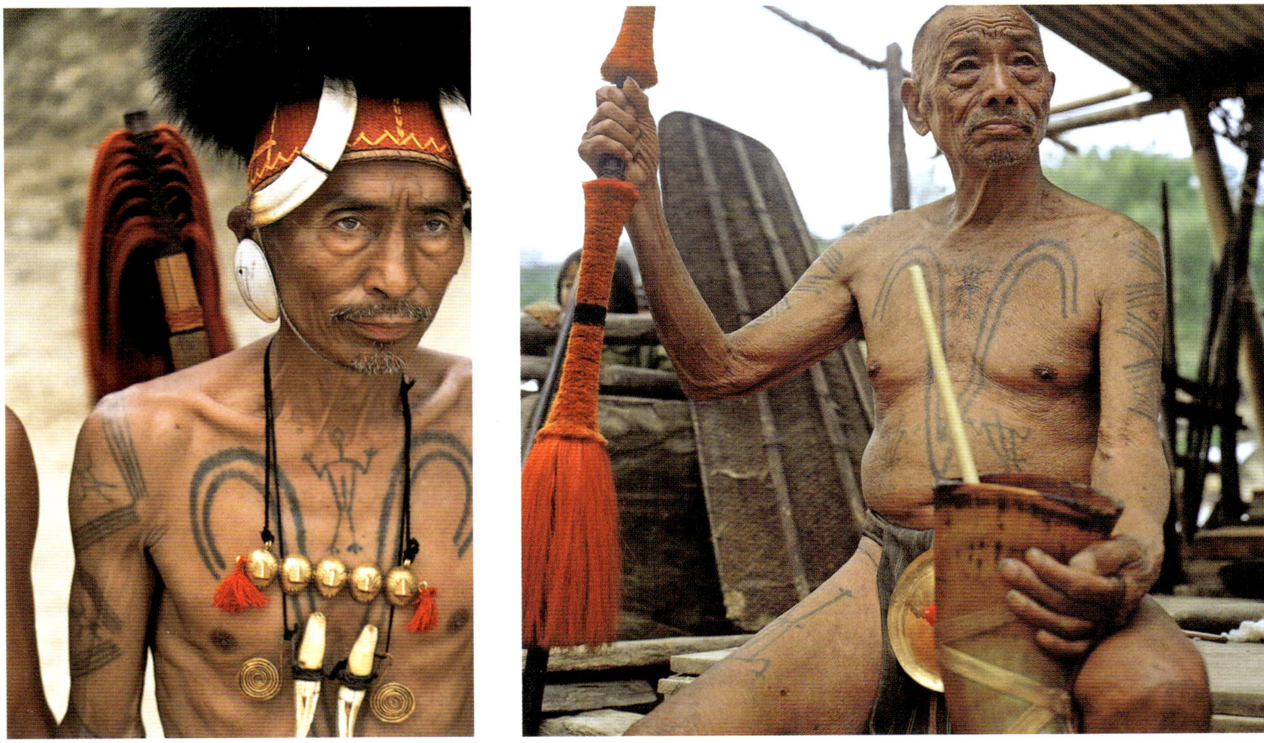

FIGURE 6.72
Tattooed Khiamniungan warriors of Noklak and Nokyen villages (*b*), Nagaland, 2001. At the time of writing, Chenko (*a*), bearing festival attire, was still living and more than one hundred years of age. I visited his home village of Noklak on two occasions (2008, 2010), but he was abroad each time. In his prime, he secured the heads of five enemies, four on one day. Chenko recounted to the Ao Naga writer Anungla Longkumer (2017:398–401) that he was tattooed by two female tattooists, Thongkoi and San, over the course of five days. He did not observe any taboos and his marks healed one month after his painful tattooing session. When he married his wife, she received three short vertical lines on her chest to signify she was marrying an important person in the community, and that she herself was a good and dignified woman. Images from Stirn and van Ham 2003:88, 165. © Peter van Ham.

Indeed, many Naga warriors inhabiting the Indo-Burmese border have described their military exploits as a form of combat likened to the method a tiger uses to kill its prey—circling then moving in for the kill. Nuchichung, a veteran warrior and headhunter from the mixed Chang-Khiamniungan village of Yimpang near the Myanmar border, possessed tattoos related to his "tiger tactics." In his prime, he took five heads and was hand-tap tattooed on his arms and chest in one day by a female tattooist of his village; two layers of tattooing were applied and he paid one gong for her services. He said that his tattooed collar signified *khukpahbou* (military tactics) because it demonstrated to all that "you don't confront your enemy face to face, rather you circle around him

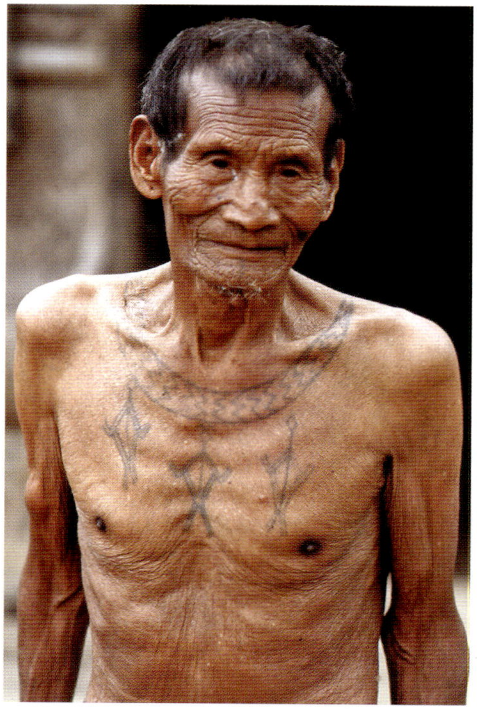

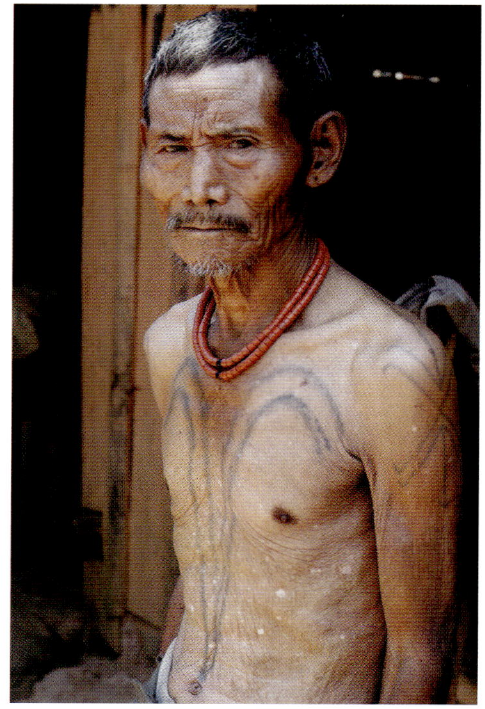

FIGURE 6.73 (LEFT)
Tattooed Khiamniungan warrior Hangkom of Pangsha village, 2008. Pangsha was once infamous for its reputation as perhaps the greatest headhunting village in the Myanmar/Nagaland borderlands. Pangsha took heads from neighboring Khiamniungan villages, not to mention Pounyo, Lainong, and other tribal settlements in Myanmar. Former Khiamniungan warrior Chenko of nearby Noklak village stated that Pangsha men might take two hundred or more heads in one year (Longkumer 2017:400). Hangkom took three heads around 1947 from a village in Myanmar. He explained that enemy heads were always brought to a sacred tree in the village called Klabai. This tree possessed a malevolent spirit, and if it was not routinely appeased with gifts (i.e., human heads, chicken eggs, and/or sacrifices, etc.), the spirit would cause epidemics or famines. Moreover, if you collected wood or leaves from the tree, sickness or some other misfortune would befall you.

Hangkom, who bears a single faded tattoo line on his chin, told me if you didn't have a tattoo here when you died, one was stenciled on the chin with tree resin to guarantee passage to the afterlife. "All tattoos travel with you into the afterlife, so they can be shared with the ancestors," he explained. "And once you have a tattoo, you can proclaim yourself to be a man. If you don't have any, you are a nobody." © Lars Krutak.

FIGURE 6.74 (RIGHT)
Tikhir warrior Shuven of Shamator village, Nagaland, who took three heads in his prime, 2010. The crossbow was a customary tattoo pattern of Naga warriors living in villages inhabited by the Khiamniungan and Tikhir. While great warriors who took the heads of enemies earned the right to wear V-shaped chest tattoos, men who carried crossbows into combat and severed the hands, feet, and/or legs of their foe were allowed to receive the crossbow mark on their upper arms. © Lars Krutak.

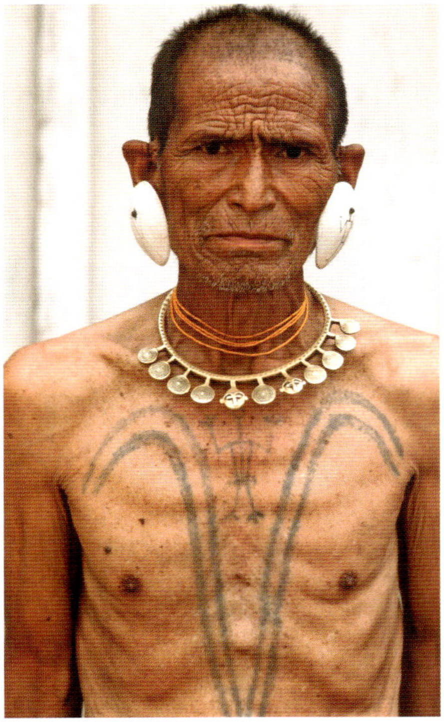

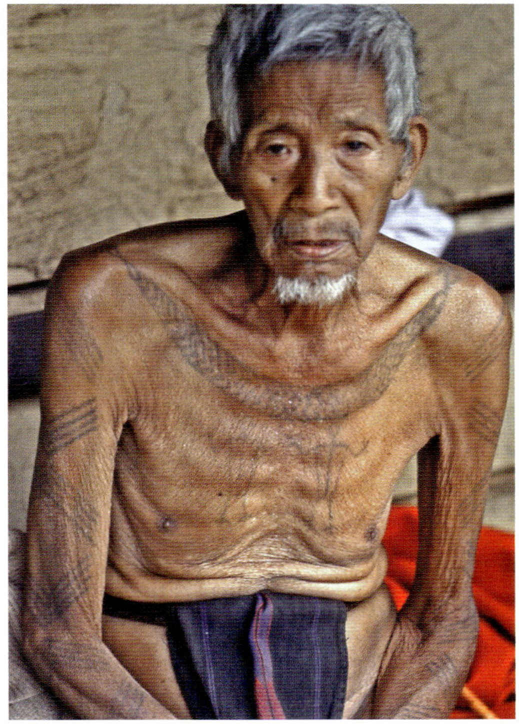

FIGURE 6.75 (LEFT)
The late Yimchungru war hero Lakiumong (d. 2016) of Sangpurre village, Nagaland, 2010. He was credited with twenty combat victims over his career. © Lars Krutak.

FIGURE 6.76 (RIGHT)
Nuchichung, a former Chang warrior of Yimpang village, bearing the tattoos of a veteran warrior, Tuensang, Nagaland, 2008. A common feature of Naga warrior tattooing along the Indo-Burmese border is the "buffalo necklace," which was a sign of a warrior or head-taker. This motif has been documented for the Chang, Pounyu, Konyak, and Khiamniungan, and for several Naga groups in Myanmar. It brings up an interesting phenomenon I have repeatedly observed when visiting Naga villages that sit at the boundary between other Naga tribes. In these communities, I have often documented hybrid forms of tattooing, whereby warriors might possess styles of tattooing from other Naga groups. For example, in the border villages of Yimpang (Nagaland, Chang-Khiamniungan), Tamkong (Nagaland, Konyak), Yakhao (Nagaland, Khiamniungan), and Tsawplaw (Myanmar, Gongvan), among others, men wear tattoo patterns that are shared with other Naga tribes whose territories are adjacent to theirs. However, in other villages that do not have a tribal boundary with another Naga group, warrior tattooing retains its characteristic patterning and can be used to clearly differentiate the tribal identity of the bearer. © Lars Krutak.

and come from behind and take their head like a tiger." "Through these tattoos, everyone can see you are brave because you have performed this skillful maneuver!"[46]

However, brave men could also earn the right to receive a chest tattoo if they had killed a tiger in hand-to-hand combat. In essence, a tiger was equated to a human kill, and as with human prey was hunted with a crossbow. The Indian general S. C. Sardeshpande, who lived among the Khiamniungan for several years, wrote that the *sanyulibu* (tiger killers) were entitled to tattoo themselves like head-takers. "The tiger . . . is considered as dangerous and deadly an opponent as a head-hunting enemy . . . and conferred the same honor as a head-taker," he observed. "*Sanyulibu* must discard all clothes worn during the hunt. Tiger flesh is not eaten, it is buried with all the ceremony due for a dead villager. . . . Tiger killers have to offer the correct sacrifices, failing which they might come to grief," because as noted previously in this chapter, some tigers are in communion with *sheepu* or "tiger-spirit" men (Sardeshpande 1987:151–152).

In his fieldnotes von Fürer-Haimendorf (1937:171–173, n.b. 14) described Konyak beliefs associated with tiger hunting in the village of Wakching. If a man had killed a tiger, he would never state it openly, for the "relations of the tiger might revenge him and eat the hunter or his children." Moreover, for a few days after killing a tiger, the hunter changed his clothing and *dao* daily in order to deceive the tiger's spirit or its relatives. If a tiger was hunted and killed by a large village party, other rituals were held and some of these resembled those performed after a human head trophy had been taken. Small pieces of the tiger's meat were impaled on many bamboo stakes placed near the paths leading to all of the village's *paan*s. This action was thought to mislead the deceased tiger's relatives from learning where it had gone. The corpse was carried into the village and the men danced as if they had taken an enemy head. The ceremonial attendants attempted to mislead the tiger's relatives again by loudly uttering the following chant, wherein the name of another village is inserted: "We have not killed the tiger, [name of another village] killed it!"

Over the international borderline in Myanmar, Mitchell interviewed the Lainong chief of Lahe in the 1920s about tigers. The chief told the British military commander quite seriously, "[T]igers are bad, dangerous and shifty. They are the reincarnation of our deadliest enemies. The whole village has to turn out to kill them after we have had much feasting and praying. When killed he must be skinned and his skin stretched over a cane frame and the whole [body] placed on the village sacrificial posts, above the heads of the victims taken by us in raids" (Mitchell 1929:21). I have seen similar taxidermy tigers in the spacious homes of Konyak *anghs*, including one that hung from the rafters of Wangnau Angh's home, the late great leader of Chi.

Numerous religious beliefs and ceremonies were also associated with the tiger.[47] Mitchell (1929:16) noted that when Lainong Naga made an oath, especially when *kah yang* (exacting revenge) for a killing, it "is usually taken by biting a tiger's tooth and repeating [the] oath to the effect that if the wearer is lying, he should be eaten by a tiger. As tigers are rather scarce the parties are usually safe. I [myself] usually make them take the same oath but substitute a rifle bullet or cartridge for the tiger' tooth." William H. Furness (1902b:464) observed similar practices for the Naga he met in the Lower Konyak region. Here, he observed that men bit down on a tiger's tooth and consumed earth taken from a grave while uttering "The gods will see me, and if I am lying, they will send a tiger to eat me, or they will turn my head to earth like this grave."

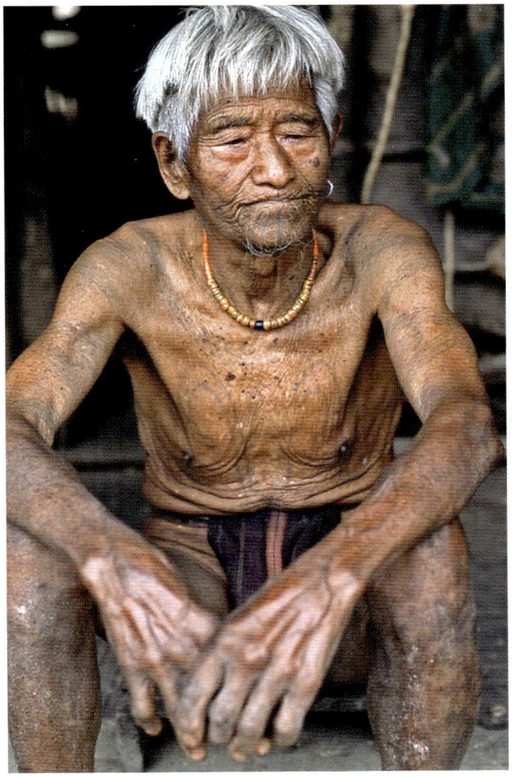

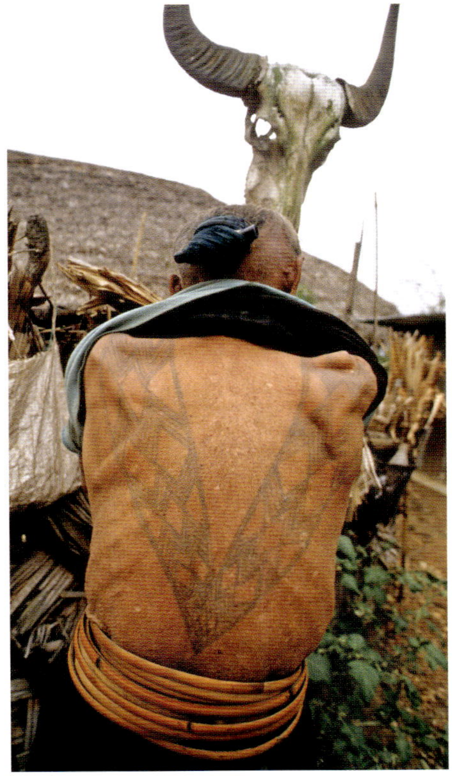

FIGURE 6.77 (LEFT)
U'Alan, one of the last tattooed Gongvan elders, 2014. While skirting the Indo-Burmese borderlands via motorcycle, I traveled to the Gongvan Naga village of Tsawplaw, which early British colonial writers described as one of the most formidable and warlike communities in the region. Here I met the last fully tattooed man of the village, an approximately one-hundred-year-old elder named U'Alan, who bore a nearly complete set of very faded tattoos on his arms, the *sa daung*, or V-shaped chest emblem, and *sit daung*, markings on his back consisting of parallel lines or "bars" running down the sides. U'Alan had not beheaded any enemies, however, and his tattoos were earned for killing two tigers; he was a master hunter of all living things and widely respected for his skills. His tattoos were hand-tapped by a woman and all his markings were received prior to marriage. For payment, he feasted the tattooist. © Lars Krutak.

FIGURE 6.78 (RIGHT)
Former warrior Tangyen of Tang village, Nagaland, 2008. Among most Naga tattooing tribes back tattoos were reserved for high-status warriors who had taken large numbers of heads. However, in the Konyak villages of Tang and Yuching a uniquely patterned *tang tok tu pu* (back tattoo) was received after an individual participated in their first combat; the goggle-like facial tattoos were given at the same time (Bos and Konyak 2017:104). This distinctive V-shaped tattoo pattern was originally created so that men from these two villages could easily recognize one another as allies as opposed to enemy combatants in the heat of battle. © Lars Krutak.

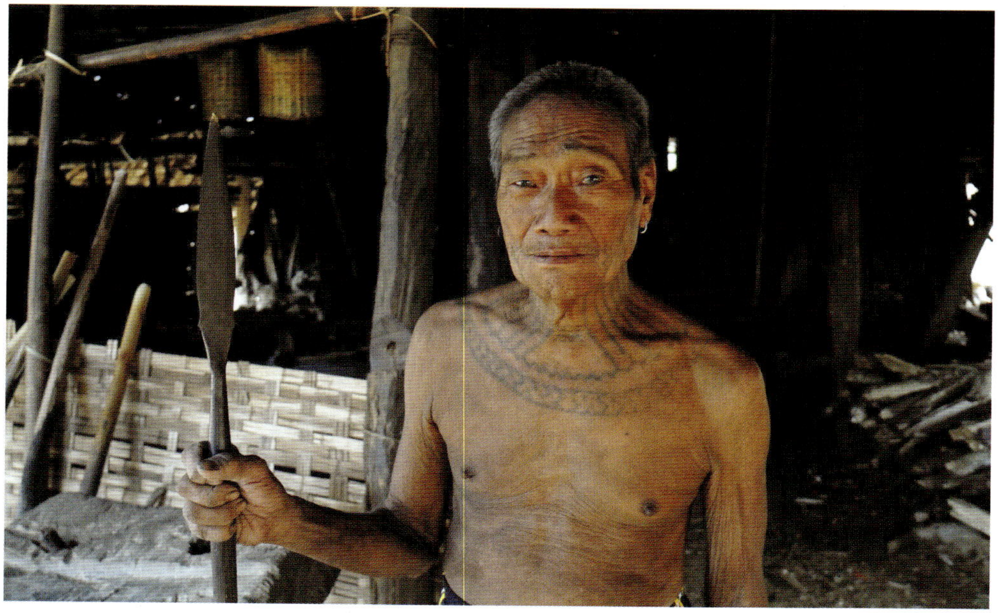

FIGURE 6.79
U'lum, a Macham tiger hunter of Lon Khin village, Myanmar, 2014. © Lars Krutak.

The Khiamniungan, like other Naga, hunted tigers with crossbows and poisoned bolts. This was not done for sport nor was it common. Only when a tiger repeatedly entered a village to kill livestock was it then hunted. One elder in Myanmar told me that *sel* is the name for "tiger poison,"[48] and when the bolt makes its mark it is very painful for the tigers because "they cry," which enabled trackers to easily follow them. A Macham tiger-hunter named U Wan Nuu stated that tiger poison was manufactured from *kaw'wa* (a tuber) mixed with *u'tel*, a kind of fruit.

After a tiger was struck with a poisoned bolt and cornered, it was "finished off" with a spear. The Macham tiger hunter U'lum of Lon Khin village, who has two tiger kills to his credit, was tattooed for his exploits in dispatching the dangerous feline. He told me that in Macham culture, killing a human enemy was equated to killing a tiger. And so great warriors and great hunters could wear the same tattoos. On his first tiger foray, U'lum was the first man to strike the tiger with his spear, so he earned the right to his neck tattoo.

Other tattoos reserved for warriors might also come to find a home on the arms of tiger hunters. A Wancho family told me that the main tiger "disabler" who makes the first strike with a spear or gun can receive a warrior tattoo on his chest. But if you are the first man to go up to the kill and cut off a paw, you earn the right to a warrior's tattoo on the same arm as the paw; if you sever both paws then you can receive honor markings on both arms. Traditionally, Wancho arm tattoos were given to warriors who severed the arm of the enemy and returned home with the trophy. Here, a ceremony was held prior to the arm tattooing. The warrior set free two chickens and uttered prayers for health and fertility. If he failed to do this, it was believed that bad luck would befall him (M. K. Oo 2003).

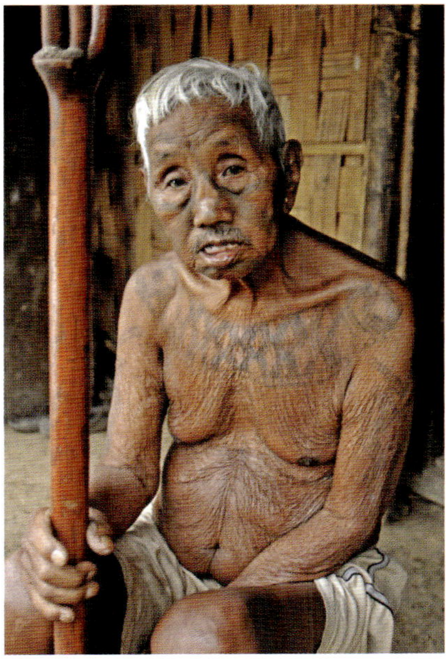
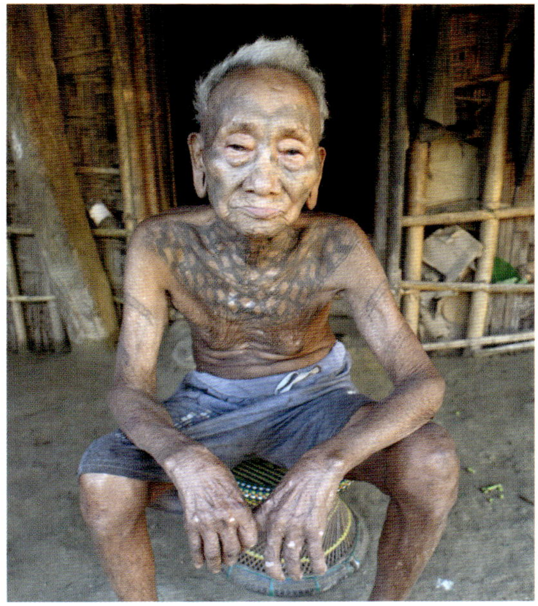

FIGURE 6.80 (LEFT)
The late Leichat Wangnao, a Konyak warrior of Joboka village, Nagaland, 2018. At the time of this photo Wangnao was one of only two tattooed Konyak warriors living in his village—the other was 103-year-old Ashen. He took his first head at the age of fourteen, and acquired three more over the course of his career. The faded zigzagging lines tattooed on his wrinkled arm tally the total number of military campaigns he participated in: four. The symmetry of his facial tattooing created a perfectly clear diamond on his nose. All the tattooing was performed by a female artist, an *anghya* (queen) of the village. © Lars Krutak.

FIGURE 6.81 (RIGHT)
The late centenarian Ashen (d. 2021) of Joboka village, Nagaland, 2019. He was the last major Konyak *naomei* (warrior) of his village and first went to war at the age of fourteen. He took four heads over his career, earning the right to bear neck and arm tattoos for extraordinary feats on the battlefield. © Lars Krutak.

It should be noted here that a warrior's arm tattoos might impart other information. In 2018 and 2019, I interviewed and photographed the last two tattooed Konyak warriors of Joboka village, which sits near the border with Arunachal Pradesh, the home of their traditional enemy the Wancho Naga. Ninety-one-plus-year-old Leichat Wangnao (d. 2018), who took his first head at the age of fourteen, noted that the four zigzagging motifs on his upper arms were tally marks, each representing the number of combat missions wherein he took an enemy head. Such tattoos were reserved for great Konyak *naomei*, or warriors. His near neighbor, the hundred-plus-year-old Ashen (d. 2022), noted that one of the first tattoos he received was on his upper arm. This honor marking was received for setting fire to and destroying an enemy Wancho village during his first combat mission as a youth. This tattoo was also given to other young men who were part of that foray and marked their initiation into their respective *paan*.

In the Lower Konyak region, elaborate ceremonies accompanied a young man's initiation into his *paan*, which culminated in the receipt of a chest tattoo. In the village of Wakching, von Fürer-Haimendorf (1938b:358–361) painstakingly described this multiday event for members of the Aokeang *paan*. For the sake of convenience, I will now paraphrase his account focusing on the *shao paan pu*, or initiation ceremony. The ceremony was usually performed annually during the month of October, but only when there were enough boys (aged six to ten) ready to enter their *morung* or *paan*. In other villages, the induction ceremony was held when boys have reached adolescence. Wealthy fathers of the inductees provided pigs for ritual sacrifice, whereas those less fortunate offered chickens. These items and other foodstuffs gathered from the jungle (wild herbs and plants) were the proper foods for the initiation feast. The live animals were slain by the oldest man of the boys' clan, who uttered this prayer, "May grandsons and sons all remain well, may they become tall."

On the morning of the eighth day after the new moon, the fathers of the initiates feasted their entire clan with huge quantities of food and rice beer: in this case three clans were feasted since this was the number of clans comprising this *paan*. Three of the men who offered pigs for the feast took their heads and leaf cups of rice beer to the house of the *niengba* (ceremonial leader) of

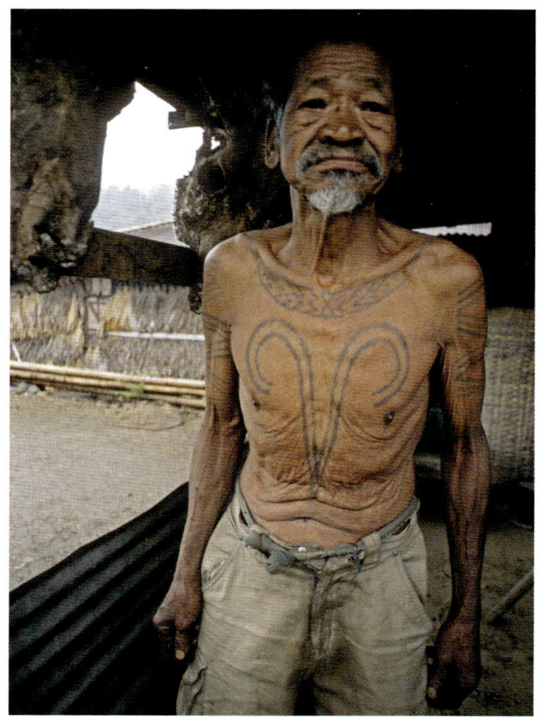

FIGURE 6.82
Former Khiamniungan warrior Khon, Noklak village, Nagaland, 2008. The arm tattoos of Naga warriors imparted various forms of information. Some of these markings told others that the person had severed the limb of a human enemy or tiger, or they served as the first tattoo placed on the body to commemorate one's membership and initiation into their respective *paan* or *morung*. However, great war leaders who had taken several heads were tattooed up and down the outsides of their arms with various scalloped, elliptical, or geomorphic patterns. Early ethnographers rarely recorded the origins, meanings, and/or names of such tattoos, but several Khiamniungan warriors, like Khon, told me his arm tattoos represented "the path of the tiger," or the path from which you attack the enemy. Khon took five human trophy heads in his prime, and he was also a war leader. As noted previously, war captains could be identified by small tattoo motifs placed between "tiger tracks" on their arms; Khon bears small circles in these areas. Khon noted that you could receive the V-shaped tattoo marking only if you had taken trophy heads from another village, not for killing a tiger. This statement demonstrates that certain Khiamniungan villages did not place the same emphasis on tiger hunting as on the human hunt and/or warrior status. © Lars Krutak.

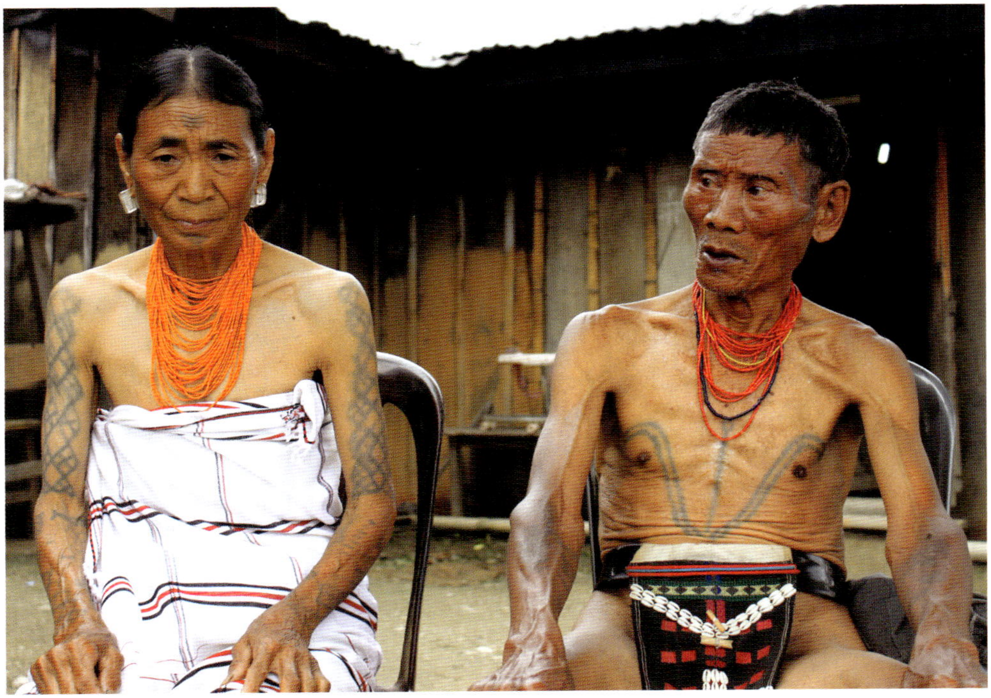

FIGURE 6.83
Sitting with his wife Tsakiuchi, veteran Sangtam warrior Pusutsu Thongru of Phelungre village, Nagaland, counts three headhunting victims to his credit, 2013. Speaking of that era, he said, "In the old days, it was a time when the word of Christ had not reached here. It was a time when we went to war. We brought back heads, and we brought back feet. And warriors were worshipped like gods. Here, the tattoos on my chest, they are not tattooed easily. Only those who have taken heads, only the brave warriors can have these tattoos on the chest." (BBC 2016). © Mo Naga.

their *paan*. Here, the *niengba*'s mother greeted the three men, asked them to empty their rice beer into a bamboo container, and then refilled their cups with water. The men turned to one another, swinging their leaf cups, then said, "May my rice beer increase, may my rice become plentiful; may all enemies, all head-takers, all Ang[s] eat my rice." This statement was a form of sympathetic magic, with the idea being that enemies' heads should be fed with rice and rice beer, as was done after a successful headhunting raid.

After several other ritual performances that spanned the entire day, eventually the boys were compelled to run off shouting and swinging small pointed bamboo sticks toward a large tree just outside the village. They "speared" the tree then returned to their *paan*, whereupon they began to beat the enormous log drum inside with a rhythm announcing that an enemy's head had been taken. That night the newly initiated boys slept in the *paan* for the first time and were eventually tattooed on their chests.

FIGURE 6.84
Konyak elder Eno Wang Yao of Chingpoi village, Nagaland, 2010. © Lars Krutak.

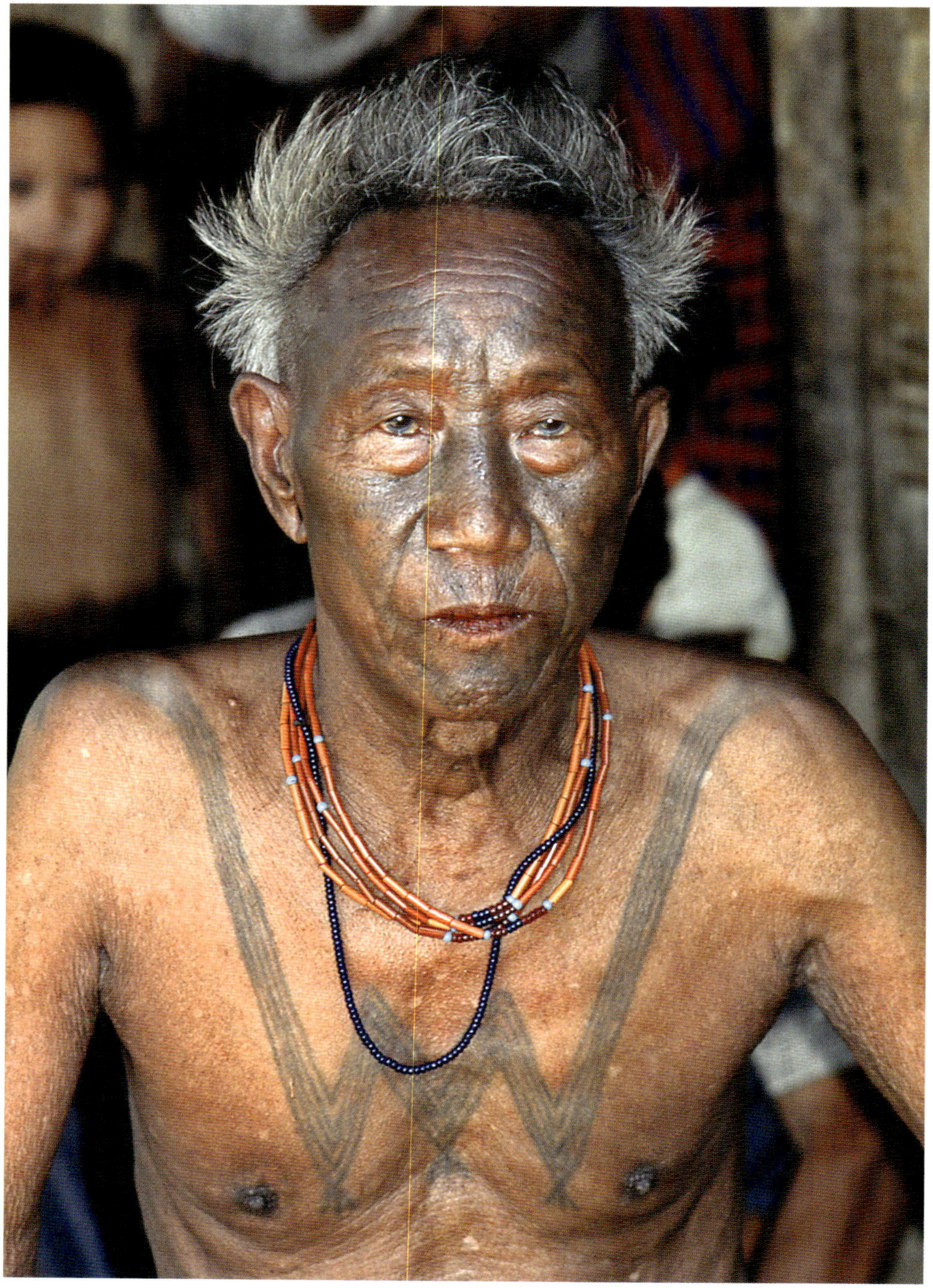

In the Konyak village of Chingpoi, I interviewed elderly warriors who described their motivations for becoming *paan* members and men. Here, boys were initiated at an older age than at Wakching, and the tattooed men I met said they became *paan* members between the ages of twelve and fifteen. Eno Wang Yao, who bears the characteristic W-shaped *mongjang tu pu* (initiation chest tattoo) of his village (which by the way differs from that of neighboring Wakching), told me, "Before becoming a *morung* member people encouraged you to prove yourself in combat and take a head. You were chided by your peers like, 'Oh, look at that woman, he is unmanly!'" (Krutak 2008b).

Eno Yao eventually received facial tattoos for participating in combat. He continued, "We had long hair and it had to be brushed down in front of your face in shame, because we were not yet considered to be men. But once you completed a combat mission, you shaved the sides of your head and were allowed to tie back your hair and pin it in a bun like all the other warriors!" he said proudly.

MO NAGA: THE NAGA TATTOO REVIVAL (2004–2024)

Moranngam Khaling (known as Mo Naga) is an ethnic Uipo Naga tattoo artist. His bold, modern, and geometric tattoo designs, whether they are created for Naga or non-Naga, are derived from traditional Naga tattoo patterns, and also from textile designs, beadwork, sculpture, and objects of material and ritual culture, such as painted human skulls and *mithun* (bovine) horns (Krutak 2015c).

For more than fifteen years, Mo Naga has attempted to reclaim the Naga tattoo that was nearly eradicated by the locally powerful Baptist Church and then largely forgotten by younger generations of Naga in the twentieth and twenty-first centuries. Originally from the northeastern Indian state of Manipur, he trained as a fashion designer at the prestigious National Institute of Fashion Technology in Hyderabad, where he started tattooing in 2004. In 2008, Mo Naga opened his first tattoo studio in Delhi, and in the same year he became the brand ambassador for Lee Jeans, a transnational US company established in 1889. Over the course of his career, he has become recognized as one of India's most prominent tattoo artists. Mo Naga was one of only three India-based artists featured in *The World Atlas of Tattoo* (Krutak 2015d), which chronicles the work of one hundred leading global tattooists, and his artistic accomplishments have been featured in dozens of media features. In 2010, Lee Jeans promoted him as India's best tattooist in a national campaign, and in 2011, the *Hindustan Times* rated him among the top tattooists in the country (Sharma 2012).

Although he had a very successful career as a professional tattoo artist in New Delhi and achieved national status, Mo Naga left the capital in 2012 and moved to Guwahati, Assam, to open Headhunters' Ink, the first tattoo studio and tattoo school in India's northeast.[49] Armed with social capital and inspired by the desire to resurrect traditional Naga tattooing through training the next

FIGURE 6.85
Uipo Naga tattoo artist Mo Naga hand-tapping a client at the annual Hornbill Festival, Nagaland, 2016. © Mo Naga.

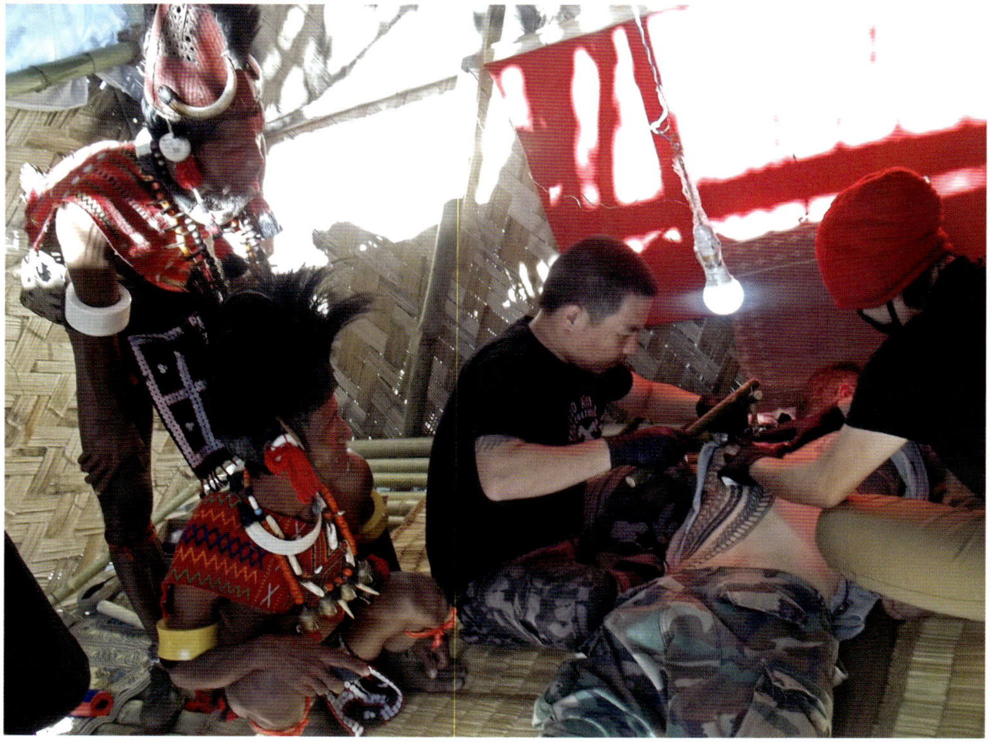

FIGURE 6.86
Two "neo-Naga" tattoo flash sheets (*left–right*). The neo-Naga tattoo style is based on traditional iconography derived from Naga motifs employed in carving, basketry, textiles, tattooing, and other visual arts. © Mo Naga.

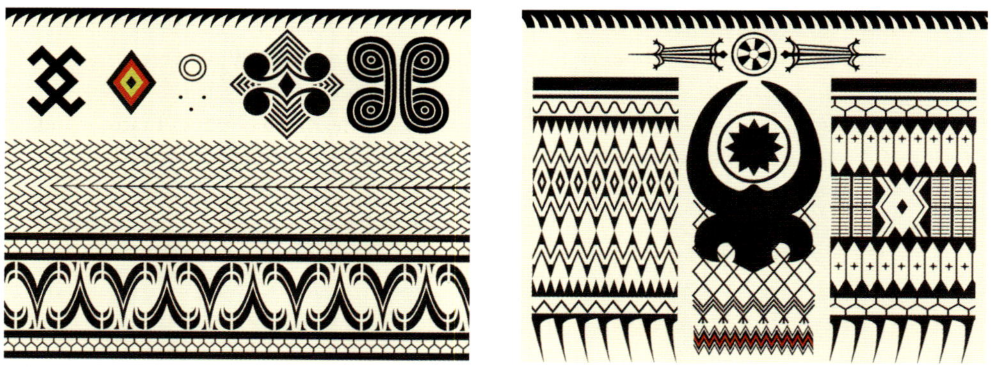

generation of artists, Mo Naga in his eight-hundred-square-foot space provided two courses that taught basic design, tattoo machine mechanics, clinical hygiene, and sterilization practices, among other offerings. Subsequently, his base of tattoo operations moved to Dimapur, the capital of Nagaland state, then back to his home village of Tengnoupal, Manipur, where Headhunters' Ink now operates as a seasonal enterprise under the aegis of The Tattoo Village. In order to sustain the tattoo school financially, however, Mo Naga opened a new tattoo studio called Godna Gram in Delhi, where he and his team of tattoo artists were dedicated to promoting Naga tattoo art and culture through contemporary renditions of traditional patterns and responsible tattooing. The Delhi studio closed in September 2020.

Just after Headhunters' Ink opened in Assam, Mo Naga spoke to me about his inspiration to help local artists develop their skills and transform them into professional tattoo artists. In a 2013 interview, he said, "With our experience in design and art, through safe and hygienic tattooing, and through our understanding of the industry, we can offer the best in tattoo art education. In turn, the region would become a force and source of inspiration in the global world and culture of tattooing. . . . After all, if Americans, Japanese or Polynesians can boast of an ancient culture and heritage in tattooing, why shouldn't we do the same?" he exclaimed (Krutak 2015c:54).

Mo Naga decided to establish the tattoo school in Northeast India because it was the gateway to the Naga homeland and had not been part of the country's "booming" tattoo industry. Moreover, the region had skilled artists and he wanted to cultivate their talents. According to Mo Naga and other Delhi-based tattoo artists I interviewed in May 2018, tattooing has certainly exploded across the subcontinent. In 2004, there were perhaps three or four professional tattoo studios in India. By 2013, there were approximately two hundred to three hundred. Today, in Delhi alone, there are roughly one hundred studios, employing five hundred to six hundred artists (Krutak 2020). Hardy Mitra, owner of Delhi's oldest tattoo studio, Funky Monkey, believes that there are fifty thousand tattoo artists working in India now, up from an estimated figure of twenty-five thousand three or four years ago. Everyone agrees that television programs such as *Miami Ink* and *LA Ink* ignited the explosion in tattooing interest, which has only been catapulted by tattooed Bollywood celebrities such as Priyanka Chopra, Hrithik Roshan, and Saif Ali Khan.

During these conversations in Delhi, I was curious to learn what types of tattoos Indian celebrities received and if there was an "Indian tattoo style." Mo Naga replied to me that if there was one, it was a very recent phenomenon in India, and that only a handful of artists regularly employ designs inspired by Hindu mythology and particular deities. He added that there are only a small number of "tattoo collectors" of this style in India, meaning that there are very few clients who are willing to spend top dollar to receive large pieces (e.g., backpieces, sleeves, etc.) from established artists or follow them to international tattoo conventions. In fact, most of the tattoos given in India today are small to medium in size and consist of designs typically related to family, such as names or portraits, or Western motifs (e.g., stars, angels, butterflies) that are seen as fashionable. Lokesh Verna, one of the pioneers of tattooing in Delhi and owner of Devilz Tattooz (established 2005), has stated that most of his tattoo clientele "repeatedly plagiarize" designs seen on A-list Bollywood actors or on TV shows like *Miami Ink*. He said, "I try to tell them to be more original . . . but they think it's in fashion," so they get it (Riat 2016).

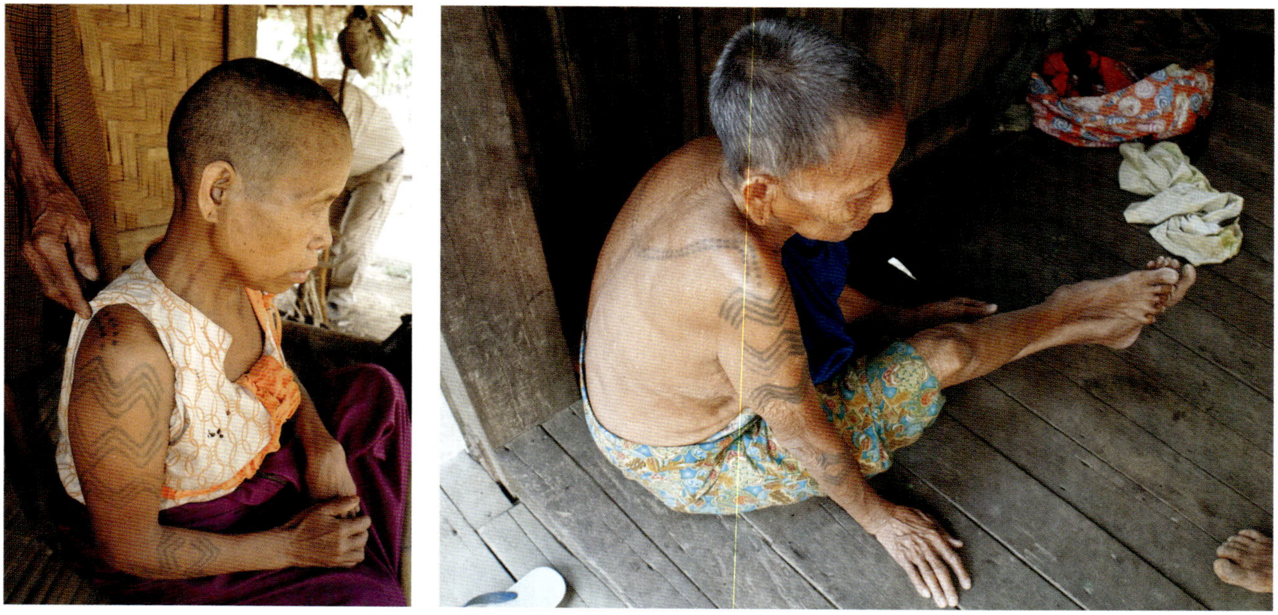

FIGURE 6.87
Daw Thom Kar (*a*) and Daw Sin Be (*b*), two Heimi Naga women from Myanmar, 2014. The hair of elderly Naga women was sometimes closely cropped to their head and almost appears to have been shaved. In some cases, this is an old clan custom, whereas in others it has been documented that this tradition is related to headhunting activity. Warriors anxiously sought the heads of women for their long tresses, which were used to adorn their *daos* (machetes) and other headhunting gear. Heimi Naga elders Daw Thom Kar and Daw Sin Be possess trimmed hair and unique arm and dotted back tattoos. They were tattooed with these markings to signal that they had reached adulthood and were ready to be married. A third Heimi elder I met bore faded facial tattoos consisting of an exclamation-like mark above the nose and running down the bridge, four lines running down the cheeks below the eyes, three lines at each corner of the mouth, and a single line down the chin; these were specific to her village. I was told there were many tattoo variations across Heimi territory and individual villages. To my knowledge, these are the only published photographs depicting the tattoo traditions of Heimi women. © Lars Krutak.

I was also curious about what kind of iconography Mo Naga typically tattoos on his clients, especially those with Naga heritage. He explained that he largely avoided Western tattoo designs in his work: "Tattoos' global popularity has emerged in India as a fashion craze among our young people. Today, the Western tattoo designs that Naga youth see and receive are completely foreign to their culture. But if we can develop tattoo designs inspired by our local Indigenous art and heritage, tattooing will become more meaningful and more acceptable to them and in this way, it can be reclaimed and revived" (Krutak 2015d:301).

Furthermore, I queried the tattoo artist about how he differentiated between Western and Naga tattoos. He explained that both Western and Naga tattoos come from the same core,

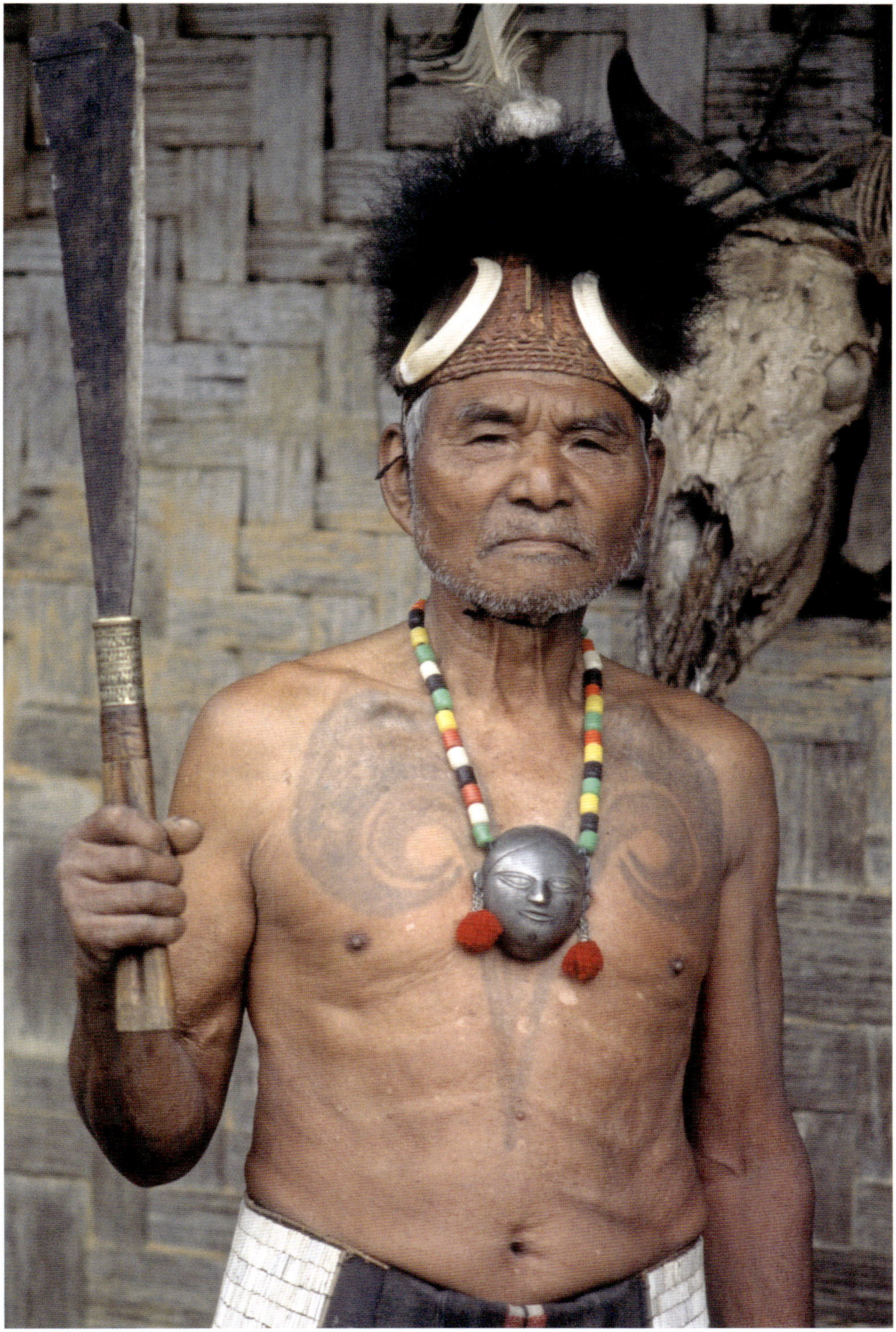

FIGURE 6.88
Former Phom Naga warrior Eno Henham Buchemhü of Yongshei village, Nagaland, 2010. Over the past century, writers have described the broad V-shape style chest tattooing of Phom, Chang, and some neighboring Konyak villages as "ostrich feathers" or a "fertility fountain." Neither of these explanations is correct, and Phom warriors have told me that they symbolize the horns of a *mithun*, a sacred semidomesticated bovine. © Lars Krutak.

because they tell stories about the person or community they come from: "They are a language, an expression, and they talk about the people, their journey, their beliefs, and their community and way of life. They are based on aesthetics that developed over a period of time, so I do not differentiate between them. But of course, and if we look at them from a design standpoint, there are differences and similarities. Naga tattoos are prominently inspired by nature, and the aesthetics of the designs are built around that. Just as Western tattoos are built around an environment that is an expression of that community" (Krutak 2020:200).

Traditionally, Naga tattoos were meaningful marks earned as a result of particular life achievements and were not worn as local fashion statements. But Mo Naga believes that creating "a new line" of contemporary neo-Naga tattoos for Naga people to wear will help preserve this disappearing ancestral practice. He said, "Naga warriors may not be headhunting anymore and receiving tattoos for valor, but the relevance of those designs should not be lost. Even now a Naga person can still get a tattoo in accordance with their achievements, just like their ancestors did. In this way, we can preserve our [tattoo] culture and ensure that the noble way of our Naga forefathers does not fade from memory" (Krutak 2015d:303).

This retraditionalization of the Naga tattoo speaks about a process whereby a cultural practice (i.e., Naga tattooing) is recalibrated and renewed through its remaking in response to an identifiable set of external forces implicated in its past erasure (Krutak 2020). Tradition is mobilized but the new cultural configuration that results is not meant to entirely supplant the established beliefs and practices that gave rise to these new traditions. Instead, in this case, neo-Naga tattoo traditions speak about the creative imagination and agency of individuals to modify and reclaim their history through new tattoo patterns and performances.

The neo-Naga tattoo revival that is currently underway is certainly in its nascent form. Most of Mo Naga's clients who desire a neo-Naga tattoo are foreigners, not other Naga. Recently, he explained to me that approximately 75 to 80 percent of his clientele are non-Naga, 15 percent are Naga, and 5 percent are from other parts of India. The non-Naga clients are usually cultural tourists who respect and value local cultures. He said, "They don't come to me to get tattoos just because they look good, or for fashion, or because they are unique. They come to me to learn about the Naga, their way of life, and our tattooing culture because very little has been written on the subject. They do not want to offend anyone or misappropriate culture, so they learn what tattoos they can and cannot get. What I do for them is combine elements of traditional Naga tattoo patterns with other art forms that tell a story of our ancestors as well as some aspect of their personal journey" (Krutak 2020:202).

The tattoo artist's non-Naga clientele also want to support the tattoo revival, a process that is ongoing in Delhi but not so back in the Naga heartland. Mo Naga explains that most Naga are very reluctant to get an ethnically inspired tattoo, and to come forward and support it in the public sphere. Those who do are typically important figures such as Naga youth leaders, professional or government workers, cultural performers, or Naga working abroad. "For them, coming to me and getting a tattoo becomes very special," he said. "They are proudly carrying the tattoo all the time as part of their cultural identity" (Krutak 2020:202).

There are other factors that have limited Indigenous interest in the neo-Naga tattoo. Although Christianity continues to be a deterrent, there are many contemporary Naga with tattoos,

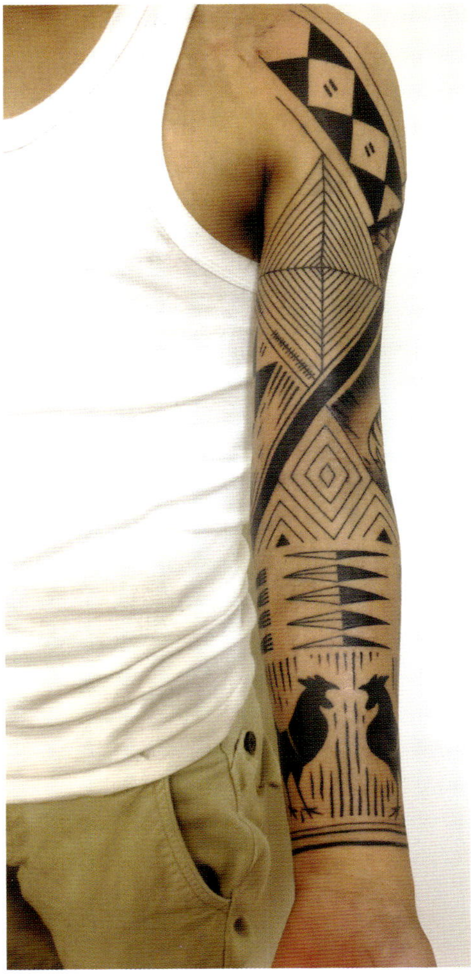

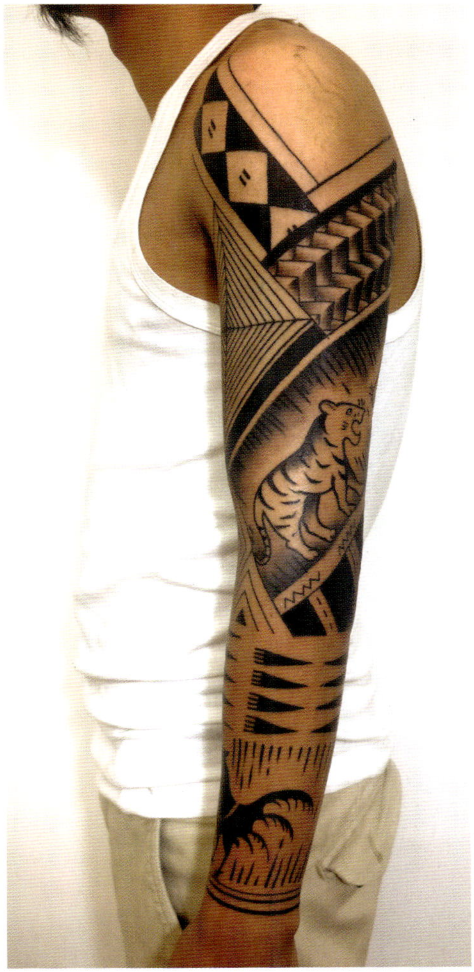

FIGURE 6.89
Customized tattoo designs by Mo Naga, 2017. Ao Naga warriors were not tattooed but earned the right to wear *tsunkotepsü* or special shawls denoting their head-taker status. Inspired by these shawl designs, an Ao client displays forearm (*left*) and outer arm (*right*) tattoos created by Mo Naga. Tattooed at Godna Gram, Delhi. © Mo Naga.

but they bear Western-styled tattoos because they are perceived to be "modern" or "fashionable." Mo Naga suggested that even if he offered free Naga-styled tattoos to Naga youth, tattoos that are part of their cultural history and identity, they would probably not choose them right now because they are perceived as being somehow backward. "They have only read what has been written about tattoos in old books or newspapers by outsiders, where tattoos have constantly been associated with headhunting and negative activities like that," he said. "They have been made to believe that our tattoos are something that was barbaric and uncivilized and should be discarded" (Krutak 2020:202).

Understandably, Mo Naga has yet to accomplish his mission, which is to carry Naga tattooing into the future through a revival movement that is fully embraced by the Naga people, and especially the youth. He said,

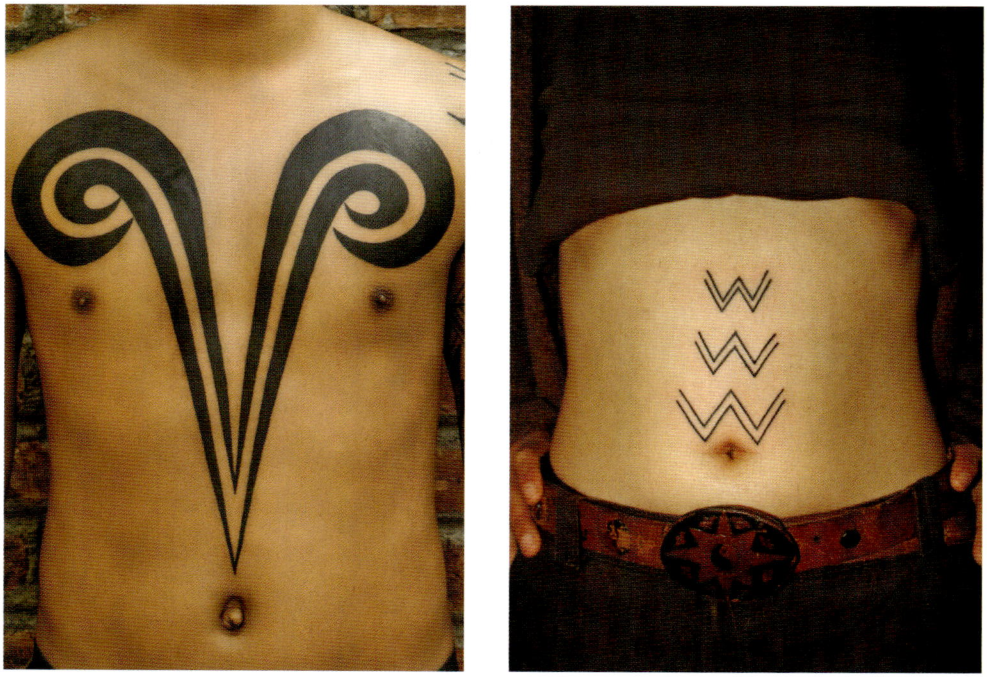

FIGURE 6.90
Neo-Naga style tattoos inspired by a Chang headhunter's tattoo (*left*) and Ao woman's abdomen tattoo (*right*), 2020, 2015. © Mo Naga.

> The Naga people as a whole do not consider this to be a significant thing *yet*. It needs a lot more time, but now we are in a better place than a few years ago. The movement is a reclamation of Naga tattoo culture, moving it forward. But I don't look at it yet as a form of decolonization *per se* or as a form of cultural healing, like the Native North Americans and other ethnic groups such as the Māori, who have embraced and reclaimed their tattoo cultures for several decades. I have not had time to think about the movement in this way, but perhaps in the future it will hold these meanings as more people join the movement. (Krutak 2020:203)

That being said, the Naga tattoo revival does involve a transformational and historical process of (re)indigenization. For Naga individuals who grapple with issues of identity loss and selfhood, the act of receiving a neo-Naga tattoo not only represents culture but also recreates it through artful, innovative, and emergent new traditions that (re)affirm and (re)legitimate Naga culture, traditions that may become conventional customs in future generations (cf. Tambiah 1979).

In our interview, Mo Naga reiterated that the Naga tattoo revival is about preserving an art form and cultural expression that is rapidly vanishing. In essence, time is his enemy. Thus, as part of his desire to understand the legacy of Naga tattooing, he regularly travels to remote tribal villages in Nagaland and his home state of Manipur to learn about the meaning of tattoos from the

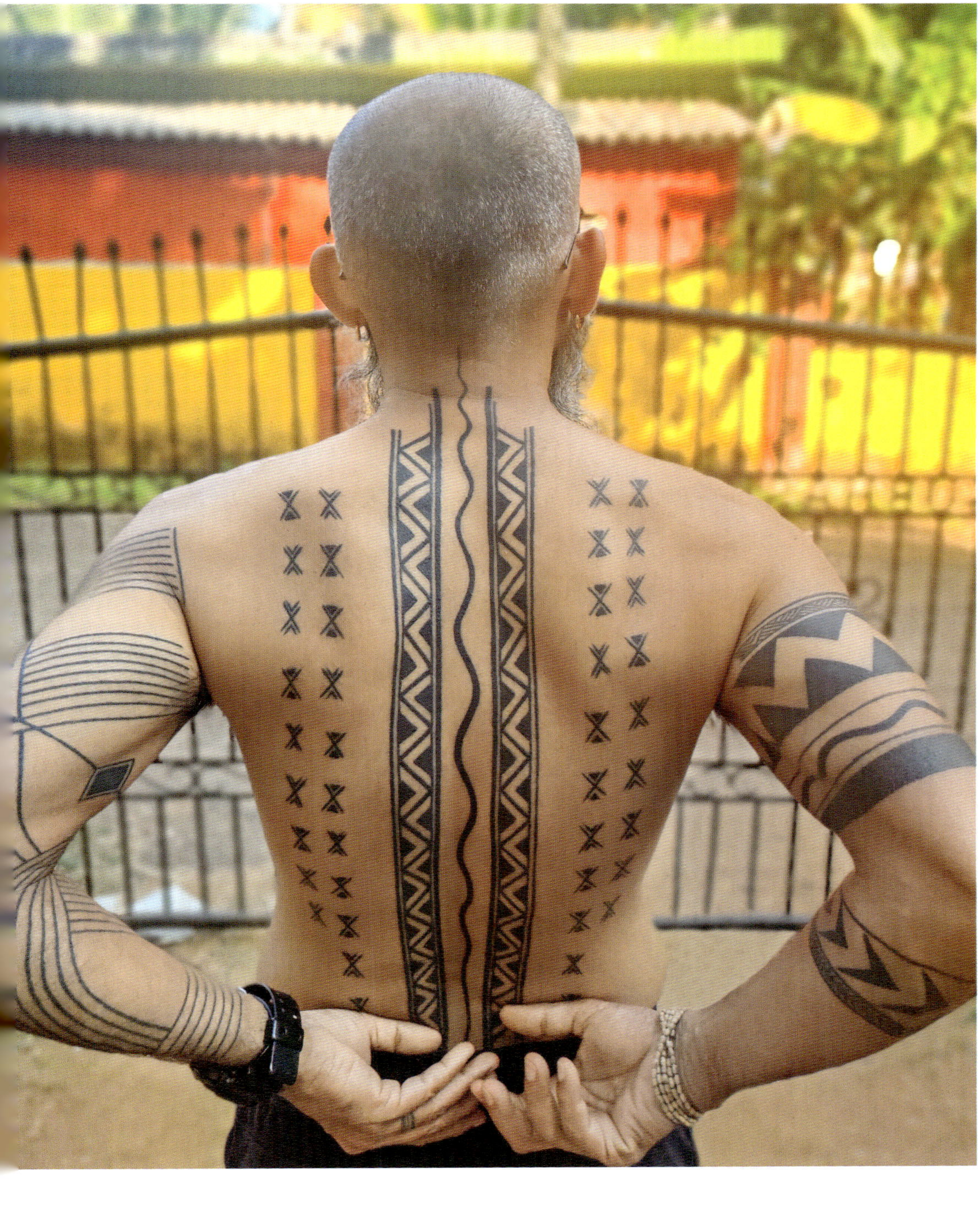

FIGURE 6.91
Neo-Naga backpiece, 2021. © Mo Naga.

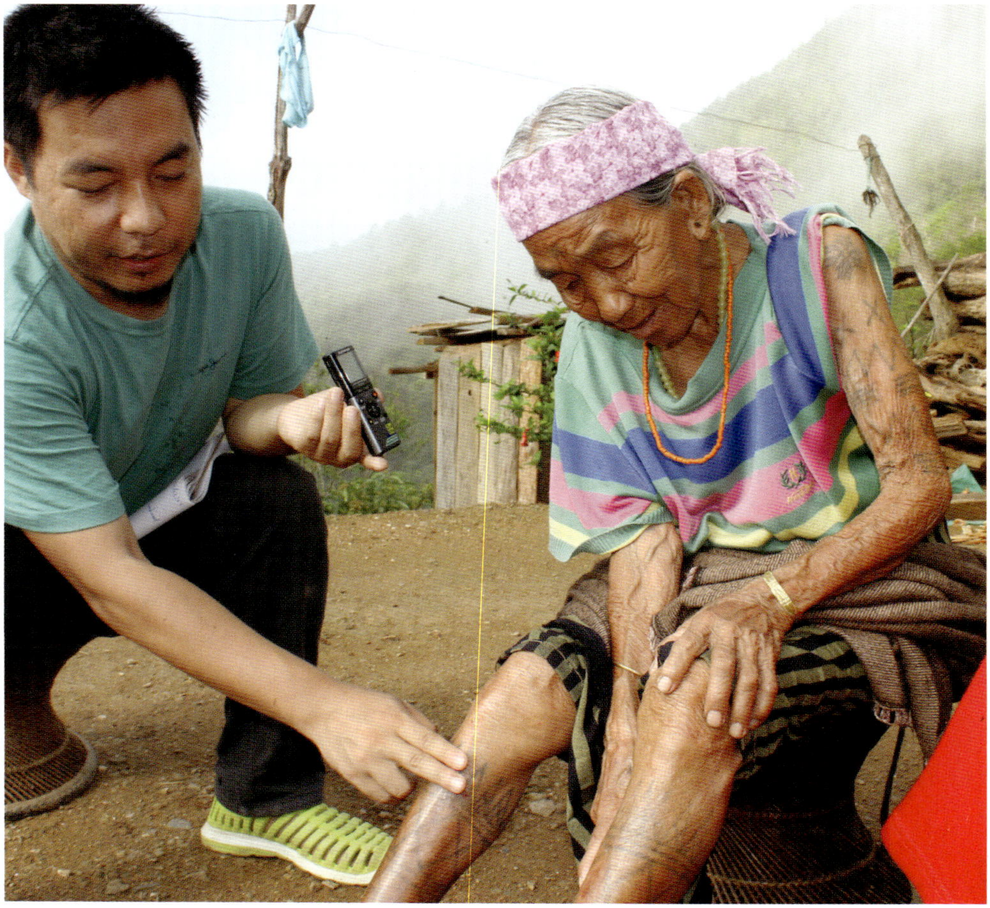

FIGURE 6.92
Mo Naga interviewing a tattooed Pochury Naga elder in Laruri village, Nagaland, 2013. © Mo Naga.

last generation of tattoo bearers. He also interviews surviving tattoo artists about traditional tattoo techniques and rituals. I asked him why it is important that Naga researchers like himself conduct this fieldwork to help reclaim the meanings and stories of tattooing, as opposed to outsiders who have left an enduring legacy of reports, ethnographies, and travel narratives. He replied, "Reclaiming is the right word. But if there is nothing left to reclaim, then we will not be in position to do anything about this culture loss. I feel that whoever can contribute should do so, because this is a dying tattoo culture" (Krutak 2020:204).

For Mo Naga, another important experience documenting the tattooing heritage of his people occurred when he, together with two of his Naga friends, Phejin Konyak and Anungla Longkumer, who also bear neo-Naga tattoos, met one of the last traditional Konyak tattoo artists. The elderly Ngon-Am Anghya of Sheanghah Chingnyu village, who has since passed, had not performed a tattoo in more than fifty years. But she agreed to demonstrate the technique as well as

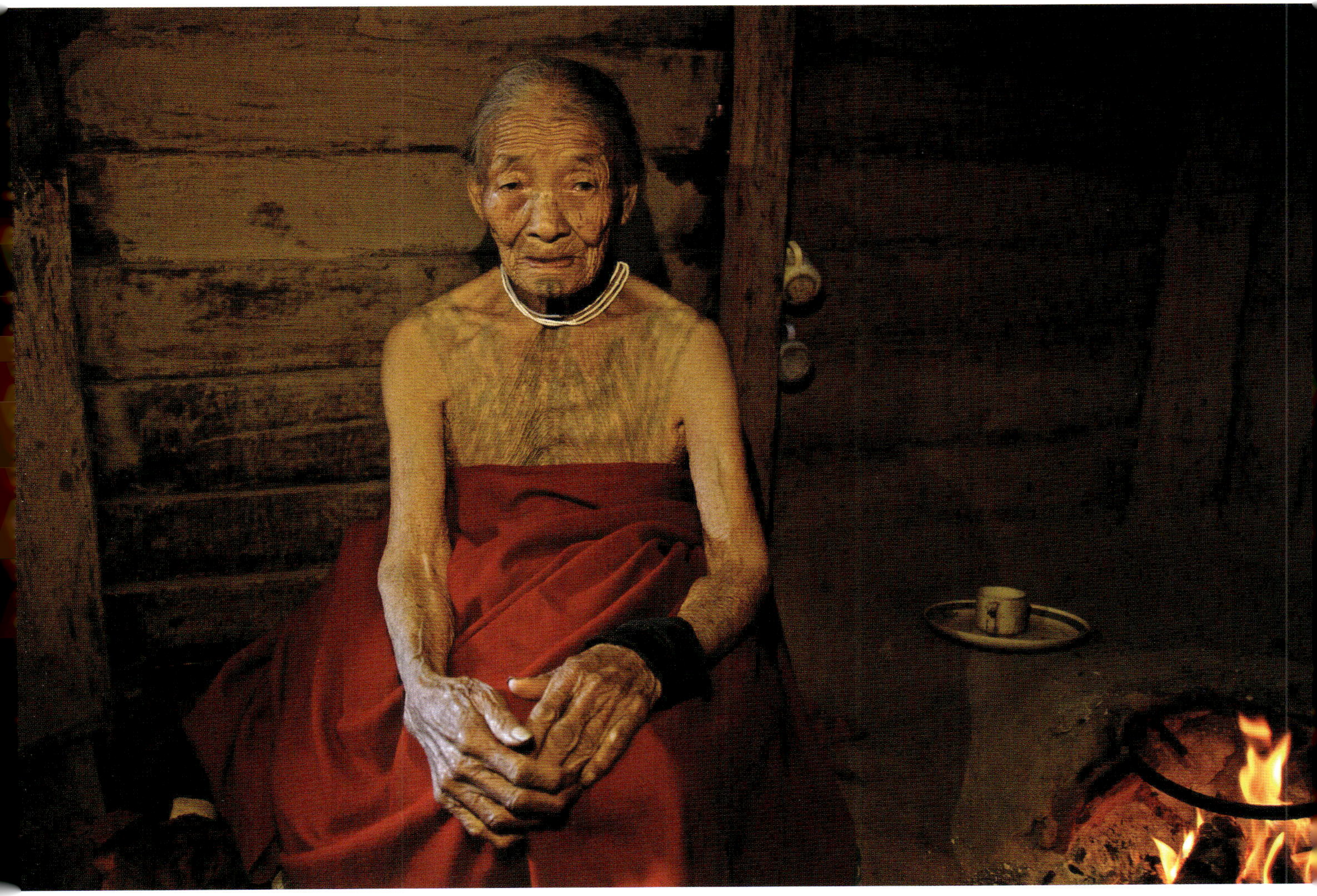

FIGURE 6.93
Ayi Shimtherla, Khamasom village, Manipur, 2018. Prior to her death in December 2022, 109-year-old Shimtherla was perhaps the last fully tattooed Tangkhul woman of her generation. Originally tattooed as a young woman in her home village of Huisu, she pointed to her heavily tattooed chest, stating, "This tattoo signifies the mark of womanhood, implying that I am a complete woman." Her other tattoos consisted of three lines running downward from the chin that connect to the overall chest pattern. Soot from the hearth was the primary pigment and the tattoos were hand-tapped into the skin by a female practitioner with thorns of local citrus trees. Tattoos of this type were given outside the confines of the village at specific sites; if this taboo was broken it was believed a tiger would appear inside the village—a bad omen. According to local oral histories, the *kameo* (spirits) of the field and forest would not harm women who bore tattoos. © Mo Naga.

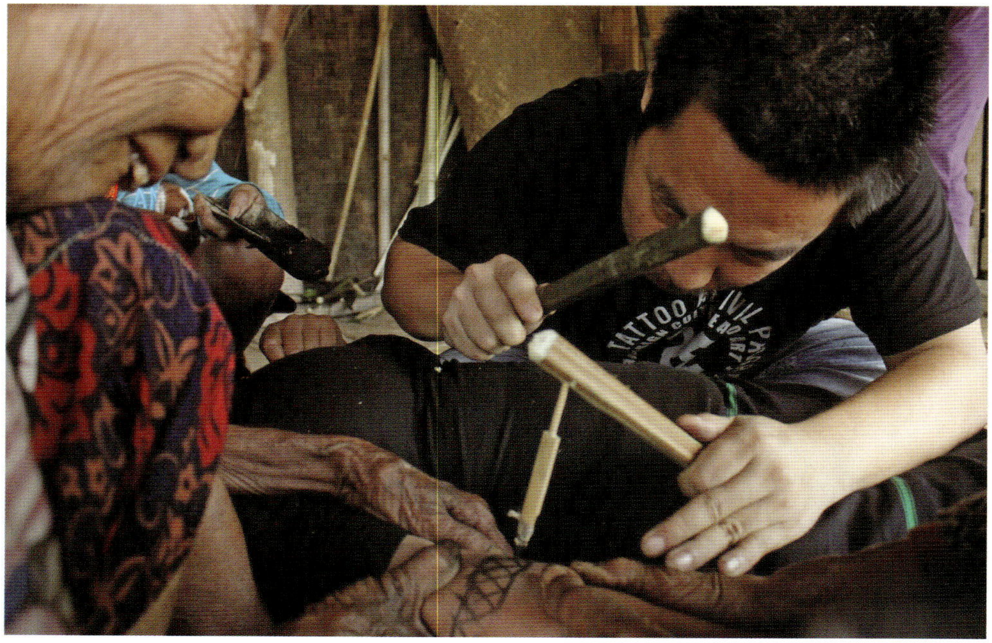

FIGURE 6.94
Mo Naga hand-tapping under the watchful eye of former Konyak tattoo artist Ngon-Am Anghya, of Sheanghah Chingnyu village, Nagaland, 2016. Courtesy of the artist. © Mo Naga.

provide information on the functions and meanings of the Konyak tattoo. Mo Naga described to me his thoughts about that very special day.

"It was my dream to learn the techniques, but getting tattooed by [her] was overwhelmingly surreal," he said. "The experience left me stronger, more rooted[,] and it humbled me. She was heartbroken when the tattooing was banned [by local missionaries]. And she even wrote song[s] in protest,"[50] he explained. "It was an emotional moment for her too, because she was tattooing for the first time in almost sixty years! She was very happy to pick up the tools and tattoo me and Phejin. But she assured us that she was doing it to pass down the knowledge and that it was for the very last time" (Krutak 2020:212–213).

Notes

INTRODUCTION

1. I base these generalizations on interviews of "tattoo pilgrims" I met in 2016 while (re)visiting Apo Whang-Od's village of Buscalan.

CHAPTER 1: TATTOOS OF JAPAN

1. According to Criminal Code number 428, article 9, which was published in newspapers in 1899, fines ranged from ten sen to one yen (Ryūkyū News Report 1899, cited in Nakijin Village Board of Education 1983:42).
2. Perhaps the earliest written record of tattooing in Japan dates to AD 400. It speaks about an individual who attempted to overthrow Emperor Richū (van Gulik 1982). Instead of receiving the death penalty, he was given a punitive tattoo near his eye. For the next thousand years, records continue to describe various forms of *irezumi* (the insertion of ink) tattooing for criminal offenses, such as theft, fraud, dealing in fake goods, etc.
3. "Austronesian" refers to a language family widely spoken across insular Southeast Asia, mainland Asia, Oceania, and Madagascar.
4. Very few English-language sources focus on Ryukyuan tattooing traditions, and the survey provided in this chapter brings most of them together for the first time. Moreover, this chapter also includes several important Japanese sources on the Ryukyuan tattoo, which have been translated here into English for the first time.
5. It should be noted that among the Indigenous groups mentioned here (i.e., the Indigenous People of California, the Drung of China, the Chin of Myanmar, and Ryukuans), female tattoos were considered a form of beautification, not disfigurement, among other things.
6. A similar term, *hajicji-ayaa,* or "aunt that makes tattoos," was used in the Nakijin village area of Okinawa (Nakijin Village Board of Education 1983:19n16). This word is a term of respect or endearment for elder females who may not necessarily be a blood relative of the tattoo client.
7. Among the Ainu, the receipt of a tattoo was a prerequisite for marriage (Hilger 1971:150). The linkage between Ryukyuan tattooing and marriage is captured in a tattoo song recorded in Nakijin village in the 1980s: "Two months until the wedding, still two more months. Will it be postponed again? Let's get pajichi." This tune was sung by a woman before her marriage in the hopes that becoming tattooed would lead to the promise of marriage. It also indicated that if the bride had not yet received her

tattoos before the time of her betrothal, the wedding could be postponed (Nakijin Village Board of Education 1983:33).

8. Depending on the preparation, this plant was also used in traditional Ryukyuan medicine to heal boils and skin ulcers, and to reduce pain and swelling in the limb joints, especially in relation to rheumatism.
9. On Ishigaki Island, an informant said the "arrow" motif meant the tattooed woman would be shot, like an arrow, from her family home to that of her in-laws and never return (Yamamoto 1995:7–8). Hibbett (2011:48) recorded similar testimony from Okinawa: "On the backs of her fingers and thumbs was a design of arrows shooting out toward her fingernails. The arrows signified that she had been shot away from her home to be married and, like an arrow, shot once and for all, never to return."
10. Among the Ainu, when a baby met the goddess of the hearth for the first time, its parents asked her for protection in raising it (Fujimura 1999:270).
11. Some Ainu women wore an *eka eka*, or amulet, that was activated by partially burning it in the hearth, which was the abode of the fire goddess Fuchi. This action gave it a "soul" (Fujimura 1999:270). These amulets—whether carried on the body, worn as a necklace, or attached to other objects—were believed to ward off illness and cure disease.
12. The sex of the particular ceramic object illustrated by McCallum was not identified.
13. Other folktales recount that a pit-dwelling people called the Koro-pok-kuru, who preceded the Ainu, were the originators of the tattooing custom. The custom was greatly envied by Ainu women and later adopted (Hilger 1971:151; Landor 1893:251–252). However, Ryūzō's (1919:150) Ainu informants on the Kurile Islands told him that the custom of tattooing "existed with them, from the highest antiquity, without ever having received it from anyone."
14. Batchelor recorded the woman's name as Okikurumi Turesh Machi.
15. As noted, Koganei (1894) observed that the tattooed lines he saw on a woman's forehead in Ishikari Province, western Hokkaido, were a form of medicinal treatment. However, Kodama (1970) illustrated similarly tattooed women he met in the 1930s, not to mention others with small tattoos between the eyes. These women resided in Iburi Province of southwestern Hokkaido. Kodama did not state that these types of forehead tattooing were medicinal; rather, he implied they were tribal or regional markers. Thus, it is possible that these tattoos were identity markers or medicinal treatments or perhaps both.

CHAPTER 2: TATTOOS OF TAIWAN AND HAINAN

Epigraphs: Lawa Toyu (born circa 1918–2019), interview with the author, February 21, 2016; Cudjuy Patjidres, Paiwan tattoo artist, interview with the author, February 20, 2016.

1. Indigenous groups inhabiting southern Taiwan (Paiwan, Rukai, and Puyuma) also practiced headhunting and tattooing, but the faces of men were not tattooed. Instead, complex forms of tattooing covered the torsos and backs of warriors. These traditions are discussed later in this chapter.
2. McGovern's son, the professor and adventurer William Montgomery McGovern, is believed to be the likely inspiration for the character of Indiana Jones.
3. Other Chinese-language sources that have been translated into English for the purposes of this chapter include Youbas Vadan, Wei Dao, and Yuma Dada (2008), Tengyue Ma (1998), and the unpublished research of anthropologist I-chun Wang (2015).
4. In addition to the beautiful textiles and garments they wove on the loom, Atayal weavers who were married manufactured net bags that their headhunting husbands used to carry their trophy heads

home. Next to his beheading knife, which was sometimes adorned with the hair of slain enemies, these bags were a warrior's most prized possession (McGovern 1922:180).

5. The word "Taiwan" originated from the Siraya word *Taiouwang*, which was the name of one of their villages.
6. The American anthropologist Edward Norbeck (1950:28–29) collected a variation of this story among the Atayal.
7. The Japanese also banned weavers from their work, confiscating their tools and/or burning their treasured looms, which in some cases were family heirlooms.
8. Records indicate that the surgical removal of facial tattoos began as early as 1917. Ho (1960:7) observed that during the period between 1917 and 1940, approximately seventy Atayal men, twenty Atayal women (i.e., forehead markings), and two men of the Saisiyat tribe had their facial tattoos removed.
9. Wen-Shan was elected mayor of Laiyi Township in 2019.
10. It is believed that if an individual is bitten by this venomous creature, s/he would be able to walk only one hundred paces before they collapsed and died.
11. The latter family were commoners and had to fulfill two preconditions before its members could receive a tattoo: they had to demonstrate that they came from a pure bloodline originating in Puljetji and prove there was no cross-village marriage within the family. The latter action would show disloyalty to Puljetji village, and its members would not be tattooed (Ming-Chieh [Taligu] 2013:32–33).
12. Ho (1960:22) conducted tattoo research in many Paiwan villages. He was told that this motif, which had many variations, could represent the following: spider web, sunshine, or eyes.
13. Ho (1960:24) elaborated on female hand patterns and social classes: "Generally speaking, the direct relatives of the top tribe head had the intermediate and proximal parts of the finger tattooed with human figures. Some of them even tattooed two human heads on the intermediate and proximal parts, respectively, in the opposite direction so that the two heads could face one another. The second tribal heads and their families had the intermediate finger part tattooed with human figures and the proximal part tattooed with the X-shape pattern [or a rectangular shape he called a "door"]. The third tribal heads had the intermediate finger part tattooed with human figures, and nothing was tattooed on the proximal part. . . . The common people could only have the rectangular ["door"] or double curve lives tattooed on the intermediate finger. There was no tattoo on the proximal part."
14. Another rare tattoo was the *pinaruqungcu* (shape of snake), which I did not see during my fieldwork. Before she passed away, only one Puljetji elder, Paules Kaciljeqan (1918–2012), possessed this tattoo on her middigits and thumbs, along with other motifs reserved for commoner status (i.e., a figure-eight shape) (Ming-Chieh [Taligu] 2013:188).
15. Ming-Chieh [Taligu] (2013:81) notes that charred millet helps to "fix" the color of the tattoo pigment. Millet stalks are commonly used in ceremonies to summon the ancestral spirits, especially during the Maleveq Festival.
16. Ho (1960:29–20) recorded another opening prayer among the Puyuma, which was accompanied by offerings. The offerings were composed of three to five areca (betel) nuts, which were cut in the middle, and a glass bead was inserted into the opening. The prayer focused on asking the deities not to cause harm during the operation and to offer their protection: "'We are here tattooing. Please don't ask who we are. We offer you food. Please leave us alone. Please do not give us trouble.' After the prayer, the operator placed one extra bead at each corner of the [tattooing] hut and three on a nearby chair. Five more were placed in the hands, on the head, and on the shoulders of the person being tattooed. This ritual symbolized praying to the gods to give them strength and offer protection."

17. This entity is not gender-specific.
18. Among the Puyuma, the juice of wild tomato leaves was applied to the hand tattoos to support healing (Ho 1960:29).
19. See chapter 4, this volume, for similar beliefs among the Kayan and Kenyah (e.g, *lukut*, or bead tattoo).
20. An obscure Japanese government report stated that one Paiwan tribal group applied tattooing to the thighs of men and women. "This kind of tattoo is for identification purposes in the event of being beheaded or another unusual death. The pattern for this kind of tattoo is taken from a snake called '*googoo*'" (Taiwan Governor's Office 1921:201).
21. Hu Yaling, personal communication, December 23, 2022.
22. Odaka (1950:82–83) listed the names of various spirits (ancestral and others), whom he called "devils," that were regularly propitiated with sacrifices to keep their favor close to the living. Some of these included the malaria spirit (ancestor), the spirit of eye diseases and boils (nonancestral), the spirit of stomach pain (nonancestral), the spirit of bodily paralysis (a snake), the spirit of headaches and heart disease (ancestral), the spirit of smallpox (nonancestral), and the spirit protector of children.
23. The Sai formerly tattooed but by the mid-twentieth century these practices became extinct (Tian Fu 2010:7).
24. Formerly, Meifu boys who were the only male child in their respective families sometimes wore figurative tattoos on their chest. The motifs consisted of a tiger head and a moon below it. Two Chinese characters 求安 ("seeking peace") were placed between them. A *daoishi*, or Taoist monk, stenciled the symbols on the body, which were then hand-tapped by a female tattooist. Bearers of such tattoos were believed to seek peace in all their endeavors (Hu Yaling, personal communication, December 12, 2021).
25. Among these, the "fishtail" pattern is particularly worth mentioning. One Meifu male elder who possessed it said that it enabled him to catch fish and swim better in the water (Xianjun Wang 2016:205).
26. It has been documented that if a Li woman was not accepted by her ancestors, she would become a "homeless and wild ghost" (Xueping 2001:199).
27. I would like to thank Dr. Stéphane Gros for helping me translate the finer points of this passage.
28. In Daoist traditions, the bottle gourd has long held profound importance in China. In folktales and symbolic depictions, gourds were used as charms for longevity and healing, among other things (Reed 2000a:35n88).
29. Emily Shen, personal communication, January 31, 2021.
30. Shen, personal communication.

CHAPTER 3: TATTOOS OF THE PHILIPPINES

Epigraphs: Blair and Robertson (1905:163); Apo Whang-Od Oggay, interview with the author, February 15, 2016.

1. *Iveci'e* (pronounced *i-vet-chik*) is the word for "tattoo" among the Paiwan of southern Taiwan. Ho (1960:18) employed the Paiwan word *vuntsik*, meaning "patterns." The neighboring Puyuma used the word *tiktik* and the Rukai *tsikitsiki*, both words translating to "patterns" (Ho 1960:25,28). The Austronesian roots *-tik*, *-tak*, *-tuk*, *-tek*, *-dek* and the word *tok* all refer to noises, such as "ticking," "clicking," "knocking," or "beating" (Blust and Trussel 2012), as in a hand-tapping tool being struck with a mallet. The words used for "tattoo" across the Cordillera and elsewhere (i.e., *bátek*, Ibaloy and Itneg; *batok*, Kalinga; *fatek*, Ifugao; *bátak*, Kankanaey; *batuk/patik*, Visayans; and *tedek*, Kayan of Borneo) are onomatopoeic and ultimately derived from the same linguistic source.

2. Another folktale following this theme (i.e., how the monitor lizard and the chameleon received their coloration) comes from the southern Philippines, specifically among the Bagobo of Mindanao (see Benedict 1913:57).
3. Scott (in Meyer [1890] 1975:67n11) observed that the calf tattoos and incomplete tattooing perhaps demarcated that these young men had participated in battle. The French scientist Antoine-Alfred Marche, who visited the Kankanaey area in the late eighteenth century, encountered serpentine and floraform tattoos on the bodies of men (see fig. 3.5, p. 133). He also noted: "As one becomes richer and more powerful, the designs increase" (Marche [1887] 1970:115).
4. The words "Igorrotte" and "Ygolotes" (var. Igorot) derive from Spanish terminology used to describe the highlanders of Luzon. The root *golot* means "hill" or "mountain range" in Tagalog, and the prefix "I" translates to "dweller in" or "people of." Combined, these form the term "mountaineer" (Scheerer 1904:98). The term *burik* was used to describe local Indigenous People who were tattooed in a certain manner (Craig and Benitez 1916:110).
5. In the Indigenous arts of Borneo, the *aso'* motif possessed more ambiguous associations. Sometimes it was referred to as a deer, a lizard, a scorpion, a dragon, a crocodile, or a water spirit (Mashman 1989:219).
6. Vanoverbergh (1972a:106) notes that ritual libations of water were associated with preparations for constructing a new Kankanaey rice field. A chicken is sacrificed and a prayer is offered relating to a *bakná* (venomous yellow snake), who originally provided the instructions for the ritual itself.
7. Such anitos perform mediating roles for the living, such as providing omens.
8. The German explorer Alexander Schadenberg ([1887] 1975:134) visited the Kalinga village of Guinaang in 1886. He provided one of the earliest descriptions of a Kalinga tattooing tool, a thin piece of *carabao* horn bent at a right angle furnished with sharp needles. He described the hand-tapping method and observed that pigment was manufactured "by burning resinous wood, a pot being held over the flames to collect the soot."
9. Schadenberg ([1887] 1975:142) observed the *carabao* tattooing tool of the Bontok. He noted that "all of the adjacent mountain tribes as far down as the Tinguians use tattooing instruments of the same design."
10. In south Kalinga orthography, her name would be spelled "Whang-ud." However, when asked what spelling I should use for publications and other projects (i.e., exhibition texts), she asked me to use "Whang-Od." In 2016, the tourism department placed a flashy sign at the foot of a new paved road to Buscalan village that displays her name as "Whang-Od." A hand-painted sign above her home also reads "Whang-Od: Tattoo Artist."
11. The missionary Jules de Raedt (1977, 1996) has provided the most extensive and detailed account of these ceremonies among the Kalinga.
12. For more information on the calls of the *qídew* bird, see Reid (1972:544n13).
13. Rocks were not infrequently used during combat to knock an enemy senseless or break his leg or other limbs (Jenks 1905:179).
14. Among the Ifugao, funerals for high-ranking men who lost their heads usually took place after a search party had located the decapitated body. During the search party's absence, religious ceremonies were performed by members of the man's clan. Shamans invoked the souls of all of their clan ancestors to ensure success for the search party. According to the American educators turned anthropologists Otley Beyer and Roy Barton (1911:232), "Thousands of the ancestral souls were called upon by name with particular attention being paid to famous warriors and brave fighters of the past. These were counselled

to aid those who had gone out to get the head and body, and to prevent [the ancestral souls of the enemy] from injuring them or placing obstacles on their path."

Ifugao shamans also called on their "tormentor" spirits. The tormentors were urged to strike the enemy warriors with "blindness and dizziness and to fill them with fear, so that they would not attack the rescue party" (Beyer and Barton 1911:232). Shamans propitiated these spirits with small chickens, rice wine, betel nuts, and betel leaves. Larger gifts of pigs and other things were also promised to the spirits if the expedition proved successful.

One of my Kalinga informants told me if a man lost his head in battle but his fellow warriors were able to retrieve the body, it was brought home. A *mandadawak* (priestess) would chant, then drive wooden stakes into the ground and call on ancestral and other village spirits to "fly back" to the enemy community to weaken its inhabitants (Krutak 2010a:122n40). Through these actions, the priestess ultimately asked the spiritual guardians of her village for revenge on the next headhunting foray.

15. Although it has never been explicitly stated in the literature, I believe major deities (i.e., Lumawig, Anlabbān, etc.) and other powerful spirits that could assume human form were probably tattooed like humans. Reid (1992b) related one Guinaang Bontok tale that identified a "tattooed man" who was a visiting spirit.
16. For a full description of the ceremonies, see Vanoverbergh (1954:241–257).
17. There was a specific amulet, called *aroróy* (a type of herb), carried by Isneg warriors so they would not become hoarse before the shouting (Vanoverbergh 1954:258).
18. The Isneg explained that a trophy head resembled a coconut in that the hair corresponded to the outer fibers of the husk and the nutmeat the brain (Vanoverbergh 1954:269).
19. Vanoverbergh (1954:241) believed the tree was a species of ficus because of its large, protruding roots. Villagers placed various offerings here over the year, including dog heads, dog livers, and fermented *basi* (sugarcane alcohol), among other things. The remains of these offerings and other items (earthenware vessels) were scattered among the roots of the tree, and if anyone removed one of these items it was believed they would become ill. If a person threw a stone toward the tree, that person was "certain to become sick."

    Although I have never visited Isneg country, this description reminds me of similarly sacred offering trees of the ficus family used by the Naga of Northeast India, whereupon gifts of rice, alcoholic beverages contained within earthenware pots, and the skulls of ancestors are placed (see chapter 6, this volume). I learned that the ancestral dead inhabiting this realm were provided with seasonal offerings during the spring Aoleang Festival to enhance the fertility of the nearby village and its people (see Krutak 2020).
20. For Kalinga examples, which are called *dinnayan* or *assay-du*, see Krutak (2010a:30, 117, 119, 184).
21. This *pakkáw* describes the "complete catalogue of bravery" because it includes the four kinds of attack: "cutting off the calvarium, cutting off the head, wounding and pursuing" the enemy (Vanoverbergh 1955a:223).
22. Kalinga women greeted headhunters returning home from a successful raid with the *ayay*, an eerie staccato sound made by quick movements of the tongue against the upper teeth (see Krutak 2010a:117–118).
23. Anthropomorphs were once a very common tattooing motif seen on the bodies of Cordilleran warriors. Resembling a man with outstretched arms and legs, the motif is seen on the back of the ancient mummy Apo Anno (Salvador-Amores 2017:43, fig. 2.5) and in early twentieth-century photography and illustrations of Kalinga and Ifugao warriors (Krutak 2010a:137; Vanoverbergh 1929:203, figs. 9–10;

Worchester 1912:859, 880), and is described as a tattooing motif for Bontok warriors (Jenks 1905:189; Schadenberg [1887] 1975:142). It is doubtful that this tattoo served as a tally mark for enemies killed because it usually appears as a singular tattoo placed on the body. Moreover, it is not known if this tattoo represents a culture hero, a deity (e.g., Lumawig), or another personage from antiquity.

24. On warfare as a highly ritualized institution, see Krutak (2010a:112–122) for an extended discussion among the Kalinga.
25. Isneg warriors may have had their daughter's forearms, instead of their own, tattooed with these designs (see Vanoverbergh 1929: 229, figs. 45–46). Vanoverbergh (1955b:182) noted that this tattoo "was bound to disappear" since headhunting practice had been "practically abandoned" in the early twentieth century.
26. The four border areas of the forearm tattoo (i.e., on either end, above and below) were called *dalidít*. This term might derive from the word *dalidítān*, a small forest herb with linear leaves used by Isneg shamans to communicate with spirits (Vanoverbergh 1972b:200).
27. Soot from the hearth or bottom of a cooking pot was used by the Isneg as a medicinal treatment for headache. It was applied directly to the forehead (Vanoverbergh 1972b:272).
28. The Itneg (also called Tinggian in older literature) used a *gí-gí-sí*, or L-shaped tool composed of one piece of bent bamboo featuring a string fastened above the needled tip connected to the arm of the implement. The arm was struck with a mallet. Two of these tools reside at the Field Museum (catalog numbers 10.9010 and 10.9011) and were collected in 1907–1908 in Manabo, Abra Province (see fig. 3.26, p. 156). The accompanying catalog notes state that pigment was created with charcoal mixed with water. Very little documentary or photographic evidence exists concerning the functions and meaning of Itneg tattooing, although it is known that men received markings on their thighs, hands, or forearms (Cole 1908:201). Women bore full arm tattoos that resembled those of the Kalinga, but they are often obscured in photography by a sleevelike beaded ornament covering the length of the arm from wrist to elbow.
29. Vanoverbergh (1955b:183) noted that the word *tutunrāt* was used for women's hand tattoos and *bo-botó* were the small lines appearing on their digits, which could also be dotted. He observed that the aesthetics of the women's hand tattoos might differ between communities.
30. In the southern Kalinga region, male and female elders are likely to say that they are profusely tattooed with python scales, whereas in other regions further north the same designs are said to be centipede scales. These two tattooing symbols seem to dominate the Kalingas' designs.
31. There are many more Kalinga tattoo designs for warriors, but due to space constraints, I cannot reference them here. See Krutak (2010a:100–109) for a complete glossary.
32. For a range of payment options, see Krutak (2010a:182).
33. Across the Cordillera, except for the Isneg, the profession of tattooist was usually one practiced by men. Whang-Od is an obvious exception to this rule (see Krutak 2010a:182–185). It should be noted that Whang-Od began apprenticing other women to tattoo around 2006, and today several of her much younger female relatives are practicing tattooists.
34. Traditionally, there were a series of ceremonies held before a neophyte Kalinga warrior was tattooed (see Krutak 2010a:118–121). The festive mood continued even after the man was permanently marked. In the account provided here, a young married man with children had just died in the same village where the tattooing took place. It was thus taboo to conduct any festivities or play celebratory gong music during the mourning period, which may have lasted one month or longer. Therefore, the mood in the community was quite subdued and I traveled to another village.

35. For more information on this and other patterns, please refer to my photoglossary of Kalinga tattooing motifs (Krutak 2010a:100–108).
36. Schadenberg ([1887] 1975:134) described the chest and arm tattoos of those Kalinga warriors he met, noting, "I learned that the right to wear the tattoos . . . is acquired only by a man who has slain at least five human beings."
37. The Indigenous tattoo has survived in some areas. Elders of the Panay Bukidnon people, who live in the central mountains of Panay Island, continue to bear tattoos today but the practice is fading. Both men and women received *batuk* (tattoos) that were pricked into the skin with a native ink made from the juice of ripe *langi-ngi* fruits (*Cayratia trifolia*) and powdered charcoal (Jocano 1958:407). One very old female tattoo bearer recently stated that *batong-batong* was the word for "full-body tattoos" (Muyco 2016:65).
38. A Chinese text dating to the thirteenth century describes maritime raiders called the "P'i-she-ya," presumably a transliteration of "Visaya" or "Bisaya," who were "tattooed up to the neck" (W. H. Scott 1984:73–74). The Visayans were known for their voyaging, piracy, and slave raiding. The "Pi- sia-ye" may have also been responsible for a series of twelfth-century attacks on the Chinese coast (Laufer 1907:253).
39. Writing in about 1640, the Jesuit Father Diego de Bobadilla observed that the Pintados were in tune with several creatures that delivered messages about one's fate: "If they saw a snake or a lizard, or if they heard a bird that they called corocoro [fishing gannett, *Sula piscatrix*] sneeze or sing, they took it as a bad sign, and did not go farther" (Blair and Robertson 1905:285).
40. Villegas (2017:89) added to these details that "by permanently inscribing images and sacred words on their bodies, *antingeros* [or *oracion* practitioners] believe that the gods can finally become permanent parts of their bodies. *Oracion* tattoos require complete faith in the [markings] because of their permanence."
41. See chapter 4, pp. 217, fig. 4.31, 236-237, fig. 4.45 .
42. The information provided here comes from a published abstract on Father Rich's research into the *pinatikan* tradition of southern Mindanao. It is derived from a much larger work, an unpublished master's thesis that I was not able to access.
43. James Mascariñas, personal communication, December 18, 2012.
44. *Kaingin* is a type of agricultural activity whereby forest land is cleared and burned for planting. It is also known as slash-and-burn farming.
45. The Pantaron Manobo terms *pamaleye* and *liliyan* are equivalent to "taboo" (Ragragio and Paluga 2019:272).
46. Benedict (1916:265) also noted that the Bagobo tattoos she observed were produced by a traveling "Ata" man.
47. Dan EDan, personal communication, July 10, 2020.

CHAPTER 4: TATTOOS OF INDONESIA

This chapter is based, in part, on my field research conducted in Sarawak (2002, 2011) among the Iban, Kayan, Kenyah, Lahanan, Kelabit, Sa'ban, Kejaman, Punan Bah, and Sihan. In 2007, I had the privilege to live and work with the Mentawai of Buttui. Due to editorial considerations, this chapter does not cover the tattoo traditions of Papua (also known as Western New Guinea), which are related to the tattooing traditions of Papua New Guinea and Melanesia (see Hermkens 2004; Krutak 2007, 2013b, 2014b, 2017d).

Aspects of the section titled "Orang Ulu: Kayan, Kenyah, and Their Neighbors" are excerpted from Krutak (2007:83–90), with additional information based on fieldwork conducted in 2002 and 2011.

Due to space constraints, the section titled "Southern Islands: Sumba, Timor, Sulawesi, and Seram: Laboya Tattoo" will focus only on tattooing traditions of Sumba, Timor, and Rote. Other islands in the Lesser Sunda chain will not be covered, but for additional information, please see ten Kate (1895:3–4, figs. 5–6); van Suchtelen (1921:153–155); Vatter (1932); and Weber (1890:9, figs. 1–7).

Again, due to spatial constraints, the section titled "Seram" will focus only on tattooing traditions of Seram and not on the adjacent islands of Maluku Province. For information on tattooing traditions outside of Seram proper, see Bassett-Smith (1894), Campen (1884), and Riedel (1886).

1. Borneo is the largest island in Asia and the third-largest in the world. Geopolitically speaking, the island is split between the Malaysian-governed states of Sarawak and Sabah in the north, the sovereign state of Brunei, and Indonesian-governed Kalimantan in the south. This chapter focuses solely on the Indigenous tattooing practices of Sarawak and Kalimantan.
2. Some men were also blanketed by the *pua* while being tattooed.
3. Kayan and Penan men also possessed a very similar tattoo but it was worn on the upper chest as a design that connected their shoulder rosettes to patterns on the pectoral muscle (see fig. 4.20, p. 218).
4. If desired, *tegulun* could also be placed on the feet (cf. Franken and Torfin 1998).
5. Michael Heppell, personal communication, May 28, 2013.
6. Here I provide English translations for certain Iban terms in brackets. I was assisted in this endeavor by referencing Anthony Richards' encyclopedic *Iban-English Dictionary* (1997), which contains a wealth of linguistic and cultural material on the Iban. Additional comments provided by Heppell in a separate personal communication on June 3, 2021, have been set in italics in brackets.
7. This tradition is unique among the Ulu Ai'. Iban women from other river systems did not possess neck tattoos. Heppell noted to me that all of the neck-tattooed women he lived and worked with on the Ulu Ai' during his field studies were childless (Michael Heppell, personal communication, April 18, 2018). Whether or not this fact contributed to their becoming tattooed, however, was not documented.
8. It should be noted that each of these creatures has a prominent place in other Iban art forms (e.g., carving, weaving) as well as in augury and oral traditions.
9. *Mayang* (areca palm blossoms) were used by Iban *manang* (shamans) in exorcism rites (Richards 1997:210). In short, they were effective "weapons" that repelled interfering *antu* (malevolent spirits) (Graham 1987:82).
10. It is important to note here that tattoos sometimes played an important role in Iban healing rites. When *pelian* (normal rites) failed, a more intensive ceremony termed *saut* was held by the shaman. At the conclusion of this ritual, the patient's name was changed and their recovery marked by a new *pantang* (tattoo) (Richards 1997:326), the form of which has not been described. It has been suggested that this rite was performed to confuse and dissuade any marauding spirit(s) from continuing their pursuit of the sick individual: "When they come to take the [person's] soul away, they do not hear [their] old name uttered any more, and so they conclude [they] no longer exist, and return without [them]!" (Gomes 1911:103). In short, the shaman conceals the identity of the afflicted via the name change, and the tattoo recasts their physical appearance.
11. A warrior's charms were typically held in a small pouch tied to the handle of his *mandau*, or short sword, to a cord about the waist or bicep, or attached to a shoulder cord that hung under the arm.

Some *pengaroh* (charms) might include stone charms for invulnerability, which were oftentimes provided by a shaman. Others included charms for invisibility, making the possessor strong to pursue the enemy, success in scouting the enemy, tripping up the enemy, striking fear into the heart of the enemy, breaking the ranks of the enemy, blinding the enemy, turning aside enemy spears, and overall protection (Harrison 1965:49; Nyuak 1906:416; Richards 1997:271; Sandin 1966:94).

12. Similar charms of the same name were employed by warriors because they assisted them in "avoiding" and "evading" the blows of enemy swords and spears (Masing 1981:341).
13. Weavers also fortified themselves against evil spirits by biting on pieces of steel to strengthen their souls (Howell 1912:63).
14. "For a woman, completing a *pua kumbu'* with her own design is the equivalent of taking a head" (Vogelsanger 1980:121).
15. During the *ngar* ritual, the red dye is heated and placed in a trough. The *pua* threads are immersed in the dye and the head weaver, or "war leader," treads through this scalding liquid three times to mirror "walking the warpath" (Gavin 1991:5).
16. After a woman had completed several *ngar* rituals, weavers of less accomplishment would ask her to be their "leader." Like Iban war leaders, expert weavers were highly skilled and guided by helping spirits that assisted them in attaining the highest levels of Iban social achievement. Iban women have said, "Men brave the dangers of headhunting. We women brave the dangers of *ngar*. It is the same" (Gavin 1991:5).
17. Some Skrang Iban women told the author that today this design is simply decorative and has no function.
18. Monica Freeman noted that the *ketam* (crab) motif, with its *sipit* (pincer), could also appear as a primary motif. In such cases, the crab took the place of the scorpion. She illustrated other variations of the "head of bracelets" tattoo in the Baleh region, wherein the *bunga terong* motif might also appear (see Freeman Papers 1948–1958, box 8, file 52, n.p.).
19. The slave class was composed of war captives and hostages "given by an enemy village under siege, or surrendered to a war party which threatened attack" (Conley 1976:189). Generally speaking, they became the possession of aristocrats or families with notable warriors. They led comfortable lives and could marry only among themselves. On special occasions, however, they might be used in human sacrifices, especially at the funeral of a chief or when a new longhouse was erected. Such offerings were made to the *bali akang*, protector spirits, of a community and noted individuals (i.e., warriors) so that future prosperity would be ensured.
20. The Kayan men I met in Sarawak were sometimes tattooed by nomadic Punan Busang artists in that tribal style. Among this tribe, women worked as the tattooists.
21. The anthropologist Sharon Thomas (1968:217–218) visited numerous Kayan and Kenyah longhouses and tattooists along the Rajang and Balui Rivers of Sarawak. She noted that the tattoo procedure had become "simplified" by this time and that many of the "old beliefs" surrounding tattooing had "died out" as the local religions had changed. She interviewed several living tattooists, some of whom had converted to Christianity and Islam. Some stated that young girls could be tattooed "at any [age]," whereas others explained that they "had to be" tattooed after their first menstruation and not before. Thomas observed live tattooing sessions, noting that these occurred "at all different phases of the moon."
22. Sometimes Kayan women became tattoo artists in order to become cured of illnesses, since the tutelary spirits of tattoo artists protected them from disease-bearing spirits.

23. There are four Kayan social classes, with the *maren* and *hipuy* composing the *kelunan jia*, or "refined people," and the *pinyin* and *dipen* (slaves), the *kelunan ji'ek*, or "inferior people" (Rousseau 1979:218). Even though the *maren* and *hipuy* form one category, *hipuy* and *pinyin* are considered commoners. However, *hipuy* women could bear certain tattoo patterns that were also worn by *maren* ladies because as "refined people" they had "greater spiritual powers and the ability to come into more intimate contact with the supernatural," not to mention *tulan maren* (aristocratic animals) like the hornbill, which inferior people could not touch (Rousseau 1979:218).
24. The Maloh of north-central Kalimantan employed several of these motifs in their material culture, and each one embodied apotropaic or important agentive properties. For example, the *ulu asu* (dog head) barked at evil spirits, thus repelling them. The *ulu naga*, or "dragon head," frightened away evil spirits and devoured others, while the *ulu burong* (head of the hornbill) flew about calling on amiable spirits (Harrison 1966:150).
25. Hunyang Lisang, personal communication, May 13, 2015.
26. *Maren* and *hipuy* tattooists were qualified to apply these designs.
27. In his discussion of Kenyah headhunting, Rodney Needham (1976:75) states that trophy heads were a sign that the *bali akang* favored the victors, otherwise they would not have been successful in their headhunting endeavors. Moreover, he writes, "Men in particular are dependent on these spirits, and it is thanks to this spiritual support that they are able to protect themselves, their womenfolk, and their children from possible attacks by other longhouses or tribes." Writing of the power of trophy heads, J. M. Elshout (1926:216) observed, "A fresh head is the best means for the strengthening of the sick and the old people and indeed of everyone's soul in the village. Everybody benefits from it and hence the Kenyah says: 'We become stronger through it.'"
28. Coolness is associated with good health.
29. Mallinckrodt (1924:70) also observed other colored tattoos among the Ngaju, writing, "[S]mall colored motifs are applied in yellow or red; for that purpose, dragon's blood [*Daemomorops draco*] or *kungit* [turmeric] has been used." I presume gold dust somehow enabled the tattooed individual to successfully cross over into the next world.
30. In the Ngaju creation story, a male and female hornbill play a significant role. Through a series of transformational events that resulted in the deaths of the hornbills, the upper, lower, and middle worlds and the first ancestors are created. The bones of the bird are used to construct another Tree of Life where departed human souls enjoy eternal happiness in the afterlife (cf. Alpert 2016:118).
31. Hiller (1898:58) encountered a third tattooed Ukit man that he wished to photograph: "He said he could not consent because his wife was pregnant and if he was photoed [*sic*] his wife would miscarry."
32. One elder noted that a dried squash might be used to collect the soot on its surface.
33. For example, a recent survey reported that only three Mentawaian elders from the southern islands possessed traditional tattoos, and perhaps less than one hundred from Siberut (Bachyuljb 2018).
34. In Mentawaian dialects, a *kerei* is a shaman. *Si-* is an honorific prefix. Some clans and villages use *sikerei* to refer to their traditional healers and shamans, whereas others prefer *kerei* (Burman-Hall 2017:122n14). For the purposes of this book, I employ *sikerei* throughout.
35. Across Indonesia, the word *uma* refers both to the physical house structure and to the group of people related to it by blood ties and/or affinal relations.
36. During the headhunting era, Mentawai warriors tipped their arrows with this potent poison that has no cure. The main ingredient is processed from the *Antiaris toxicaria*, a tree in the mulberry and fig family (Loeb 1928:411).

37. Albert C. Kruyt (1923:146), who worked on Siberut among the Mentawai of Katorei, recorded the name as Teteu. Other Mentawai groups, such as the Sakaliou and the Sakuddei of Siberut, employ the names Pagetta Sabbau or Si Gegeugeu (The Shaker) for this deity (Hammons 2010:39; Schefold 1980b:92). However, I employ the Sarereiket moniker Pagete Sabbau in this text.
38. Headhunting was not a common occurrence across the Mentawai archipelago. Sakuddei elders on Siberut Island recalled that such raids might occur no more than four to five times in one's lifetime (Schefold 2007:486).
39. Loeb's sources of information concerning tattooing were recorded from informants living on North Pagai. In areas of Siberut, this ritual is called *mulepa* (Hammons 2010:83).
40. After a series of rituals in the *uma*, the headhunting trophies eventually came to rest in the branches of a designated tree on a riverbank near the *uma*. Here, heads from previous expeditions hung and all passersby could clearly see that great warriors resided nearby.
41. Unlike other headhunting societies of Asia, it seems that through the Mentawaian example success in future endeavors was not directly associated with magical powers embodied in the trophy heads themselves. Instead, any beneficial influences that were connected to the activity of headhunting were the direct result of pleasing the spirits who governed the world and everything within it.
42. Today, when an earthquake occurs some Mentawai groups on Siberut shout "*Moili moili!*" (Slowly slowly). This supplication is in reference to the earthquake deity, asking him to roll over slowly underground so he does not destroy one's *uma* (Hammons 2010:8).
43. See this elsewhere in this chapter for similar practices among the Iban, Kenyah, and Kayan of Borneo.
44. Esmat Wandra Sakulok, personal communication, September 26, 2021.
45. Schefold (1980a:83) recorded the Sakuddei term *muno* for the tree resin used in tattooing. Maass (1906:439) received a Mentawai tattoo in the Sipora Island village of Sioban. His tattooist was named Simaila.
46. For one stage of tattooing, rather than a full suite, a pig or chicken might suffice for payment.
47. Successful warriors also painted scenes from the headhunt, sometimes including the death stroke, on the rear wall of their *uma*'s verandah. Among the Sarereiket, effigies of human victims were carved in relief on wooden planks that were placed in a prominent location of their *uma*, namely, the main interior crossbeam that was surrounded by the skulls of animals hunted and other carvings. These effigies were painted with the body tattoos of the deceased, which identified their place of origin (Schefold 2007:486). The paintings and effigies were proof of the *uma*'s courage and vigor.
48. Van Beukering (1941:332, fig. 23a–23b) provided additional illustrations of Pagai and Sipora men tattooed with avian forms that appear to be roosting in trees.
49. For the Rindi, *tibu* (sugarcane) is associated with fertility, rapid growth, vitality, and "coolness" (i.e., it is conducive to prosperity and beyond the reach of harmful influences) (Forth 1981:163).
50. The Rindi associate blackness and blackening with a "civilized, moral condition" from which children, witches, and wild spirits are excluded (Forth 1981:164).
51. *Katàtu* is the Rindi word for tattoo. It is possible the man was from this ethnic group (Forth 1981:165).
52. Among the Dawan of Haulasi village, after a person dies a fire is lit under their bed for a period of four days. The flame is a light for the souls of the dead to use in order to cross over into the afterlife. After four days has elapsed, the soul can use its body tattoos in an exchange with the Creator, the Giver of Life, for fire (Gual et al. 2019:165).
53. In East Sumba, Rindi children also received a "simple cross" on their forearms. As noted, Forth (1981)

wrote that Rindi tattoos were exchanged for fire in the afterlife, but he did not make explicit whether a child's first marks (i.e., cruciform) were related to this belief.

54. Tattoo payment on Rote might consist of rice, betel nuts, tobacco, dried fish, or meat, whereas wealthy individuals might offer a pig, sheep, or goat (van de Wetering 1924:24–25).
55. The raw materials for preparing *kadek* (tattooing pigment) were described in detail by van de Wetering (1924:25). The tattooist scrapes a small amount of soot residue from the exterior of the rice cooking pot and mixes it with the juice of the fruit of the thorn apple plant. To this mixture is added lontar palm sugar. The resulting matrix is thoroughly stirred and left to sit for two days before it is used. If one's rice pot is new, then a fruit of the Java olive (*Sterculia foetida*) tree (locally known as the Nitas tree) is charred and the smoky soot is captured on a hanging rice pot.
56. In Dawan communities of North and South Amanatun, tattoos serve as a medium for storing knowledge about weaving patterns. Numerous women interviewed by Jacob (2021:60) stated that they look to their bodies and those of friends before they execute textile iconography.
57. In former times, the Nahas clan comprised the military class of the village. Their primary mode of transportation during the headhunting era was the horse, and due to this association, it became a clan tattoo motif (Gual et al. 2019:164). This tattoo motif, however, no longer exists in the community.
58. This major festival was practiced by other Toraja groups and is known as the *bua'* (Nooy-Palm 1975:83, 1979:61).
59. In the Sa'dan Toraja region, these women were called *to tubang*. The word is derived from the goddess of medicine and protective female spirit Indo' Belo Tumbang. She presides over the medicine used in rituals to heal the sick (Nooy-Palm 1979:120, 289).
60. *Haliangs* could not be seen by strangers or by members of the public, nor could they be touched by rain or luminated by the sun's rays. Bathing was forbidden and only light work (e.g., rice pounding, basket weaving, etc.) was performed during the time of their restriction. For a listing of these and other restrictions (i.e., food), see J. Kruyt (1920:243, 254).
61. Kruyt did not describe back and/or chest tattooing for women, but he did note that men could be tattooed all over their bodies. More specifically, he was only able to locate two tattooed women, both very elderly, from the villages of Lodang and Wono. The women witnessed by Kaudern who were tattooed on the back and chest almost certainly must have been from the Seko region. The motifs thus described probably resembled the *tannoek* or buffalo "horn" motifs illustrated by Johannes Kruyt (1920: pl. II, fig. 9) appearing as singular motifs on each side of men's chests.
62. The Wemale inhabited the Tala River valley, and the Alune, the Sapalewa and Eti River basins. In early accounts, the combined population was described as the people of "the three rivers" (Duyvendak 1926:16).
63. The German anthropologist Adolf Jensen (1948:93) observed that some Wemale men bore several tattoos that were acquired after repeated participation in the Kakean festival. Other writers suggested that some of these tattoos were associated with a "ranking" system within the Kakean itself. *Tipane* were individuals who completed the initiation ceremony, and *pamanawa* (*manawa* = "man") were those men who participated in more than one festival.
64. The initiation mark was applied to the forehead in the Sapalewa and Tala River valley areas, but in the Eti region it was usually worn on the chest. In the Uli region, initiation marks were seen on the chest, at the corners of the eye, on the bridge of the nose, and sometimes on the thigh or back (Stresemann 1923:420–421). To hide the initiate marks from missionaries, governmental officials, and school teachers, tattoos were often placed under the armpits so as to not attract notice.

65. Tauern (1918) recorded more than 230 tattooing motifs for men and women but did not specify which of these were tied to the Kakean rite, to headhunting, or worn for solely "decorative purposes."
66. Several writers have suggested that in former times initiates might have participated in their first headhunt during this extended period in the bush (e.g., Sachse 1907:94).
67. Frigates are magnificent flyers with large wingspans and prey on fish and display the habit of forcing other birds to disgorge their prey for their benefit (Tichelman 1939:233).
68. Herpianto Hendra, personal communication, October 21, 2021.
69. Aman Durga, personal communication, November 14, 2021.
70. Joe-Patty Sabandar, personal communication, January 14, 2021.

CHAPTER 5: TATTOOS OF MAINLAND SOUTHEAST ASIA

Parts of the introductory section have been excerpted from Krutak (2012).

1. *Ajarn* is the common Thai term, but *khru sak* is also employed. In neighboring Myanmar, *saya* is used.
2. Following Cummings (2014:204n1), *yan* is the Thai pronunciation of the Pali-Sanskrit word *yantra,* meaning "sacred or magical design."
3. I have also heard that the chin fat of a deceased monk could be mixed with ink to imbue it with similar qualities.
4. Offerings of betel nut or alcohol are said to appease any mischievous spirits in the vicinity (Cummings 2012:30).
5. This tradition in Asia is certainly ancient. Marco Polo recounted in 1269 that two Mongol chiefs were set to behead several prisoners from an unidentified culture. Their skins were impervious to the cuts of steel weaponry due to the sacred stones or amulets inserted under their epidermis. Instead, these men were clubbed to death and the precious stones were removed from their bodies (Jones 1880:163).
6. Some Brao women were also tattooed with protective Sanskrit letters encased in diagrams to protect them from bullets, biting animals, and other dangers from all directions.
7. Sasha Aleksandar, personal communication, January 7, 2012.
8. Le Pichon (1938:377) observed the apotropaic properties of Katu *padil yaya* sculptures, which were placed on or near footpaths in the forest to scare away evil spirits.
9. After a successful war campaign, the *padil yaya* was performed to give thanks to the gods who ensured that the Katu warriors met with no injuries or casualties during their military campaign (Tuan 2004:57).
10. I have not found detailed documentation concerning how Katu tattoos were made or what materials were used to create tattoo pigments. Although their tattoos were carbon-based, I would not be surprised if soot from the hearth was used to make them. If so, it has not been documented if hearth soot carried religious import for the Katu as it did for the Ainu and Ryukyuan people (see chapter 1).
11. According to the Christian Chin pastor Shweykey Hoipang, one of the last female tattoo masters was sentenced to six months in prison after the authorities in Mindat, Southern Chin State, learned that she had tattooed eight "Dai" girls. "Dai" (or Daai) is a collective term used to characterize Chin groups (Yindu, Hmoye, M'Khan, and Matu) that speak Dai, a Kuki-Chin-Mizo language, and predominantly use dots in their facial tattoo signatures.
12. Men were killed during these raids and not enslaved.
13. Most Ubtu groups lived on the plains and in closer proximity to Burmese populations and therefore adopted coin and paper currencies at an early date.

14. One Laytu woman told me that girls were sometimes wrapped in a braided mat so they could not move during the tattoo procedure (Parkitny 2010).
15. I interviewed more than one hundred women, and these figures represent the average age range.
16. The Drung (also known as the Trung) population is estimated to number approximately five thousand individuals.
17. The Lisu are a numerically large and important group whose population is scattered over Yunnan, Myanmar, and Thailand. While trade relations and intermarriage between Lisu and Drung people were common in the past, there are also stories of blood feuds and vendettas, or what is sometimes referred to by the Drung as "plunder" expeditions, during which bands of lawless Lisu would capture women or men. For a discussion, see Gros (2001:31–34, 2012:177–180). For a regional overview of forms of servitude, see Lazcano Nebreda (1999).
18. One could add that any custom that is highly visible and distinctive (facial tattooing, tooth blackening, the neck rings of the Padaung/Kayan, the leg rings of the Kayah, etc.) serves mainly as a visible symbol of a claim to distinctive ethnicity. Regarding Drung tattooing, McCabe (2008) also argues that the social custom of female facial tattooing enhanced a woman's tribal identity and discouraged women from leaving their community, since they might feel ostracized outside of their ethnic group.
19. For a discussion of this picturesque portrayal of the Drung, please see Gros (2001). Academic or popular publications are quite numerous in China; Chu (2007), J. Liu (2007), Yunshui Zhou (2009), and Gao (2010) discuss methodological problems with various interpretations of Drung female tattooing in Chinese language scholarship. Among recent examples of press coverage, see Yuan (2019).
20. Many Chinese historians assert that the Drung practice of tattooing probably dates to the Tang dynasty (618–907) because of references to an "Embroidered Faces" tribe (Xiumian) in the *Manshu* (Book of Barbarians). However, this argument cannot be substantiated. For a detailed discussion of early Chinese tattoos and tattooed "barbarian" tribes, see Reed (2000b).
21. For a more contextualized analysis of Drung female tattooing, see Gros (2012:203–228, 2017; 2021). During my anthropological fieldwork (conducted chiefly between 1998 and 2010), I focused on women's oral narratives and seldom took photographs to document their facial tattoos. I felt at the time that tattooed women were too often objectified by such demands from journalists or photographers just passing through and hoping for a close-up portrait.
22. According to my interlocutors during fieldwork, the first interdiction of tattooing dates to the 1930s, when the Dulong Valley started to be more directly administered by central Guomindang authorities, although the reasons for the interdiction are unclear. Starting in the 1950s after the Communist takeover, the interdiction to tattoo women's faces was variously justified by the generalized fight against "old" and "primitive" customs and by the idea that female tattooing was a form of patriarchal oppression and devalorizing of women.
23. Comparatively speaking, it is interesting to note that the lines on the chin were the most common tattoo motif for Indigenous women worldwide (see Krutak 2007). In some Indigenous Asian societies, such as the Chin of Myanmar and the Konyak and Chang Naga of Northeast India, subtle variations in the facial or chin tattoo patterns of women signify the clan identity of the bearer (Krutak 2020; Parkitny 2017). In the Bering Strait, at the crossroads of Asia and North America, facial tattooing was "part of the ritual of social maturity, a signal to men that a woman had reached puberty. Chin patterns also served to protect women during enemy raids. [T]heir chin patterns made them more recognizable as females and their lives would be spared. Once captured, however, they were bartered off as slaves" (Krutak 2007:160).

24. See Turner's (1985:28) classic description of a woman's initiation rite in a different ethnographic context.
25. See chapters 3 (p. 178) and 4 (p. 221) for a discussion of similar beliefs among the Pantaron Manobo of the Philippines and the Kayan of Borneo.
26. Among the Wancho Naga of Arunachal Pradesh, India, men must abstain from viewing the female tattooing rite for fear of ill luck in hunting and/or fishing.
27. This is of course not all there is to the symbolism of blood, or of menstruation in particular. See, for example, Buckley and Gottlieb (1988) and Knight (1995) for some of the earliest anthropological reconsiderations.
28. Much of the interview material presented here was published in Krutak (2015b) unless noted otherwise.

CHAPTER 6: TATTOOS OF THE NAGA OF INDIA AND MYANMAR

This chapter is based on multi-sited ethnographic fieldwork and interviews conducted in the Indian states of Arunachal Pradesh, Nagaland, Assam, and Meghalaya; the National Capital Territory of Delhi; and the Naga region of Northwest Myanmar in 2008, 2010, 2013, 2014, 2017, 2018, and 2019, respectively.

The section titled "Mo Naga: The Naga Tattoo Revival (2004–2023)" has been excerpted in part from Krutak (2020).

Epigraphs: Nganhai, interview with the author, February 6, 2008; Leithong Phom, interview with the author, April 1, 2010.

1. According to Dewar (1931:14), in some Pounyo Naga villages in Burma the trophy head was offered to the sun and moon by the victor: "These two luminaries are requested to always shine for the tribesmen of the village which has secured the offering and to be obscured in cloud and fog when enemy raiders come to revenge the death of the deceased."
2. Formerly, on the fourth day of the Aoleang festival in the Upper Konyak village of Wakching near the border of Assam, every enemy skull taken during military campaigns in the previous year was transported to the house of each clan head. This man then sacrificed a rooster and sprinkled its blood on the head of each skull to propitiate the spirits of the deceased. After this rite, the trophy heads were installed into the respective *paan* of the clan.

   Warriors of the village lamented the end of the headhunting era: "When we captured heads, then we had good harvests, then we had many children, and the people were healthy and strong. But now we are no longer allowed to go to war, and many die of illness" (von Fürer-Haimendorf 1962:65).
3. It has been documented that the Konyak formerly purchased slaves for the purpose of beheading them for trophies, but the Supreme Being "is supposed to disapprove of such killings and to punish the killer either by shortening his span of life or by denying him male issue" (von Fürer-Haimendorf 1967:95).
4. "Hoyang" refers to the Khuzuthrupa's centuries-old territory in Chenwetnyu village.
5. See chapter 3 and chapter 4 for similar beliefs among the Kalinga of the Philippines and the Lahanan of Borneo.
6. While raiding parties were abroad, the women, children, and old men left behind often devoted their time to praying and offering sacrifices to various spirits (Mitchell 1929).
7. Elwin (1953/1954: n.p.) noted that if the Konyak captured an enemy during a raid, he was treated

with great brutality: "Chili was rubbed into his eyes, his ears and nose were pierced, a cord put through them[,] and he was led weeping through the village. His organs were then removed and his head cut off. If anyone refused to join a raiding party, then if an enemy was captured and brought in, he had to 'purchase' him with the *mithun* [large bovine]. It was then his duty to decapitate."

Mitchell (1929:17–18) observed firsthand that the Pounyo Naga of Burma "tries to cut out the hearts of as many victims as possible, [since by removing] the heart the victim or enemy cannot retain any feelings of hatred."

8. Saul (2005:180), writing about the Khiamniungan, observed, "The Khiamniungan would take more drastic steps. . . . The eyes and mouth were pierced with spikes, and wooden horns fixed over the ears, while the warriors chanted, 'You did not listen to us so we close your ears, you did not see us so we blind you, you did not talk to us so we stop your mouth. You were against us, now we kill you twice.'" I interviewed a Khiamniungan chief and warrior in Myanmar, who similarly noted that *panjis* (bamboo spikes) were hammered through the mouth and eyes of the man he killed to keep them permanently shut. Then he and his fellow victorious companions shouted, "It was your mistake to open them in order to insult us!"

9. The German photographer and writer Peter van Ham visited the Phom village of Yongnyah in 2002 for the Spring Festival, or Monyu. During the festivities, he witnessed the annual clan shaman's blessing of enemy skulls, which were stored on outdoor shelving beside the Phamjong clan's *morung*. The dignified elder recalled the names and village of origin of each of the sixty-five enemy skulls, which were revered and respected. Startled by this feat of memory, van Ham asked the shaman how he could recall all of these details, since many of the trophies had been acquired decades ago. He replied, "It was customary among us Naga to name the next-born child of our clan after the enemy we had beheaded—provided there was enough time to get that information from him before his death" (van Ham and Saul 2008:48).

   I met a Konyak warrior in 2019 who had beheaded a woman in his youth, which conferred the right to his chest tattoo. He noted that the women announced her name before she was beheaded, as this action was important "for her to prepare herself for the afterlife."

   I visited Yongnyah in 2010, but I was told the skulls had been buried "because it was not honorable to have tourists photograph them, since that was not respectful."

10. Piercing the eye sockets also prevented "their souls [from] seeking out and avenging their murderers" (von Fürer-Haimendorf 1962:141).

11. Von Fürer-Haimendorf (1962:136) visited the Chang Naga village of Chingmei in 1935. He noted that the human trophy heads were attached with horns to increase "their magical power and further the 'virtue' of the whole village."

12. Writing of the Nocte of Arunachal Pradesh, Dutta (1978:187) observed, "After a successful raid . . . one of the old men then took powdered rice and an egg and threw it on the heads in order to drive out the hostile spirits of the dead."

13. Ao Naga men who were about to travel typically carried a lump of ginger because it was believed to offer "great protection against evil influences" (Mills 1926:291).

14. In unpublished fieldnotes, Elwin (1953/1954: n.p.) observed that in some Chen villages a few trophy heads were bound and fed with slices of pork: "Where the jaws of a head is [*sic*] missing, it means that two men were engaged in the killing—the actual killer gets the head."

15. Tiger meat was consumed as a cure among the Konyak of Wakching village (von Fürer-Haimendorf 1937:172, notebook 14).

16. A clan ritual specialist of the Khiamniungan wrote of washing the hands of "head-choppers" returning from combat, since "they may be struck with leprosy" if they were not purified (Sardeshpande 1987:126).
17. In the ethnographic literature, the term *morung* is more commonly used to refer to these pan-Naga institutions, but I refer to the local term *paan*.
18. Scattered reports of head-taking activity have been documented for the eastern Naga regions along the Indo-Burmese borderlands well into the 1980s (Shimray 2005:159). While conducting tattoo research in the Sagaing District of Myanmar in 2014, I heard rumors of head-taking occurring in remote areas into the early 1990s.
19. I briefly met both men in 2010, but due to time constraints I was not able to properly interview them.
20. There were a host of clothing items and ornaments that signified warrior status. For example, Khiamniungan boys could only wear white loincloths or shawls until they brought back a head, after which time they could don the black versions for men (Longkumer 2017). More specifically, the shawls were patterned with black and red squares. U Pa Soe, a Khiamniungan chief of Myanmar, told me the red squares represent "blood spots." Sometimes these textiles also contain circles of cowrie shells, symbolizing that the wearer "encircled the enemy."
21. Chen-o Khuzuthrupa is not the *angh* (ceremonial head) of the village but rather his status perhaps eclipses this rank. He is a kind of "kingmaker," whose influence carries more weight across Chen territories in Nagaland and neighboring Myanmar. His ancestor Khuzu, a Chen chieftain, migrated to the present Chen area of Nagaland twenty generations ago. Khuzu's descendants shaped the history of the Chen regions of India and Myanmar, and the title "Khuzuthrupa" is conferred on the firstborn male child of Khuzu's direct bloodline. Chen-o is the eighteenth generational descendant of Khuzu to bear his namesake.
22. Hutton (1920:44) was perhaps the first researcher to document therianthropy in relation to the Naga. He noted that men who possessed spiritual familiars displayed great prowess in warfare: "Of men, those who have taken heads are the most dangerous, and are believed to kill as many men as leopards or tigers as they have done as warriors."
23. Girls from neighboring Mohung village might also wear these black box tattoos.
24. The wife of the revered Khiamniungan warrior Chenko of Noklak village received a special tattoo after she married him. She received three short vertical lines on her upper chest to signal she was wedding a "dignitary, and that she was a good and dignified woman herself" (Longkumer 2017:401).
25. Tattooed Khiamniungan warriors of Pangsha village told me if a young man died before receiving his first tattoos, or those appearing on the chin, one line was drawn on the skin with tree resin to guarantee passage into the afterlife. "All tattoos travel with you into the afterlife, so that they can be shared with the ancestors," they said (Krutak 2008b: n.p.).
26. Chellia, the heavily tattooed warrior who provided this information, stated that he recalled a man in his grandfather's clan who stopped eating these foods for the rest of his life.
27. The origins of this taboo are related in oral histories. Long ago, three women traveled into the jungle in search of bamboo shoots to pickle. One was swept away by river water, and her friends later found her in a fish trap. Her body had half transformed into a catfish, and that "is why catfish carry tattoo marks to this day and are not eaten by women" (Mills 1926:313).
28. Anungla Longkumer, personal communication, January 1, 2021.
29. Longkumer's informants noted that in the past *jiu* was believed to be contracted by people who visited locations with negative energies or where "bad winds blew" (e.g., trees that had been struck by lightning and died, places where *mithun* had sickened and died, etc.).

30. Exceptions to this rule can be found among the Phom, where men could tattoo other men and women could tattoo members of both sexes. Nocte tattooists could be male or female (Dutta 1978). As previously noted, male tattooists existed among some Konyak groups and the Chen, whereby they created neck tattoos for great warriors. Male tattooers also applied the tiger-spirit tattoos of Chen aristocrats.
31. Furness' (1900) unpublished fieldnotes, which are deposited in the Penn Museum Archives (Philadelphia, PA), relay the village name, which is not provided in his published account. Regarding the latter, when Furness speaks about the "Miri" Naga he is referring to the Konyak of Tamlu. When he describes the tattoos of the "Sema" Naga, he is incorrect. Based on the drawings in his fieldnotes, these tattoos are Lower Konyak and perhaps from the village of Chingpoi, or a neighboring village, because the chest tattoos depict the distinctive W-shaped motif of these communities (see fig. 6.84, p. 424, for an example of this tattooing).
32. I have seen Yonkon village shrines dedicated to the guardian spirit of the community. However, there are other shrines dedicated to the Nats (Spirits) of the household. In times of illness, the Yonkon, the Lainong, and other Naga tribes of Myanmar make offerings to these spirits. The British colonial administrator H. J. Mitchell (1929:20) wrote about these practices for the Lainong living in and around Lahe: "Outside of the home, a shrine is built whereupon various sacrifices are given. First some rice and a few chicken's feathers are placed on a leaf outside the house, and the patient prays, 'If you make me well, I will offer this fowl to you.' If the Nats accept this the patient recovers. If he does not recover, the hair of a pig is pulled out and the patient repeats the same prayer. This has to be continued till everything imaginable . . . up to several mythun [*mithun*] . . . has been offered, till the patient is cured. If he dies, well he has died through the unappeasable anger of the Nats. If he recovers, he has to sacrifice just what he has promised to sacrifice. The Hiamye [Heimi] Nagas ascend the scale of sacrifices till they reach the sacrifice of a human being."
33. Mrs. Hongnyu, who passed away circa 1978 and was over one hundred years old, had a very good regional reputation, and her Ahponghü clan was famous for producing tattooists. She often traveled by herself across Phom country to work, and her son said she did not worry about losing her head because of her celebrity. I met several elderly Phom men who were tattooed by her in the 1950s, and none of them lived in her village.
34. In the Sangtam village of Chare, I was told that virgin girls worked as the tattooists.
35. In the Phom village of Nian (Nagaland), I was told that some female tattooists had inscribed the various female leg patterns of each clan on stalks of bamboo. These were kept in their houses for future reference.
36. See chapter 4 for similar beliefs among the Mentawai of Indonesia.
37. In the Konyak village of Shiyong, *tapo* is also the name of this leaf (Phejin Konyak, personal communication, February 1, 2021).
38. Even in Mills' time, only a few individuals could recall any tattooing traditions associated with Ao men. He wrote, "Tradition has it that formerly Ao warriors who had taken heads had circles tattooed on their backs, and the conventional [V-shaped] curved design on their chests, but the practice has been given up, it is said because of the irksome food restrictions imposed on men so decorated" (Mills 1926:30).
39. The American travel writer William H. Furness recorded the Ao word "Ying An Shu" for the resinous tree that produced tattoo pigment, which is the *kong* tree (Konyak and Bos 2017). The local Konyak word *ying tee* is used for tattoo pigment. The Wancho employ the term *jing*.

40. Ao elder Ms. Senyangerla Longkong of Yisemyong village noted, "It was compulsory for a woman to get all of her tattoos; these tattoos prevented women from contracting diseases, especially those that were brought by evil spirits[,] and these markings kept these spirits away" (Krutak 2010b). Ms. Longkong told me that she did not personally hold this belief herself, but she did say that she believed that her tattoos "have given me a long life."
41. Mitchell (1929:17) continued to describe the warrior prowess of the Pounyo: "When I spoke to Wunapay the biggest Chief of Ponnyo about their occupations he told me quite candidly, 'we are not traders. We grow sufficient crops for ourselves and while waiting for crops to mature or between the time of reaping and sowing, we carry out as many raids as possible.'"
42. Saul (2005:36) wrote that Lainong warriors told him these anthropomorphs would "protect them from the spirit of the enemy."
43. On review of von Fürer-Haimendorf's photograph of the Pounyo warrior with back tattoos, I asked Ponyo village men if *lang kem vun* (centipedes) were a tattooing motif. Muang could not recall if this was true, but elderly Pangsha warriors I interviewed in 2008 confirmed that centipedes were applied as tattooing motifs among the Pounyu Naga.
44. See chapter 3 for more details (e.g., fig. 3.6).
45. I visited other Khiamniungan villages in Myanmar as well as those in Nagaland (Noklak, Nokyen, etc.) but the crossbow tattoo of the upper arm is not part of their tattooing traditions. Instead, other motifs might appear here.
46. Von Fürer-Haimendorf's colleague the German anthropologist Hans-Eberhard Kauffmann (1940:333) wrote about Chang Naga warrior tattoos in the late 1930s. He observed, "In Chingmei [village], a man who avenged his father's murderer, or who brought in more than ten heads, is allowed to have a stylized human figure on the upper arm and a series of concentric ellipses on the forearm, in addition to the wide 'ostrich feather' pattern on the chest, which is characteristic of Chang warriors." Although Nuchichung is Chang from Yimpang, due to his village's proximity to the Myanmar border, where other regional tattoo styles proliferated and were partially shared among several Naga tribes, his chest tattoos are unlike those of the Chang who inhabit villages to the west (i.e., the broad V-shaped pattern) and are unique.
47. Mitchell also observed that the Lainong believed eclipses were due to the actions of tigers. He wrote, "Even in the Nat [Spirit] world beyond the skies there are tigers. They are few but have voracious appetites. Sometimes a tiger commences to eat the sun or the moon and this is observed when an eclipse takes place. It is then the duty of the people living in this world to drive off the tiger by making as much noise as possible. This noise must continue till the tiger releases his victim and the eclipse ends" (Mitchell 1929:20).
48. All Khiamniungan "poisons" go by this name.
49. Mo Naga selected the business name Headhunter's Ink not as an attempt to conjure up exoticized images of Naga people. Rather, the moniker is a literal translation that should not be perceived in a negative light. "If you look at it on its face," Mo Naga said, "it speaks about the stories of my brave tattooed ancestors, who were headhunters and warriors. Their stories were told in ink. So, this name reflects positivity, and was certainly not meant to appropriate some Western visage or concept."
50. The *anghya*'s biography and songs are published in Konyak and Bos (2017).

Bibliography

Alcina, Francisco. (1668) 1960. *The Muñoz Text of Alzina's History of the Bisayan Island (1668), Part 1.* Translated by V. Baltazar. Chicago: Philippine Studies Program, University of Chicago.

———. (1668). 2002. *History of the Bisayan People in the Philippines Islands.* Vol. 1. Translated by O. P. Cantius, J. Kobak, and L. Gutierrez. Manila: UST.

Almendral, Aurora. 2017. "Buscalan Journal: At 100 or So, She Keeps a Philippine Tattoo Tradition Alive." *New York Times,* May 15, 2017. www.nytimes.com/2017/05/15/world/asia/tattoo-artist-kalinga-buscalan.html. Accessed May 16, 2017.

Alpert, Stephen G. 2016. "Borneo: The Island—Its Peoples." In *Eyes of the Ancestors: The Arts of Island Southeast Asia at the Dallas Museum of Art,* edited by R. Schefold and S. G. Alpert, 117–172. Tokyo: Tuttle.

Ambrose, Wal. 2012. "Oceanic Tattooing and the Implied Lapita Ceramic Connection." *Journal of Pacific Archaeology* 3 (1): 1–21.

Ao, Temsula. 1999. *Ao-Naga Oral Tradition.* Baroda: Bhasha Publications.

Appell-Warren, Laura P. 2009. *The Iban Diaries of Monica Freeman, 1949–1951.* Borneo Research Council Monograph Series 11. Phillips, ME: Borneo Research Council.

Arens, Richard. 1957. "The Use of Amulets and Talismans in Leyte and Samar." *Journal of East Asiatic Studies* 6:115–126.

Århem, Nikolas. 2014. *Forests, Spirits, and High Modernist Development: A Study of Cosmology and Change among the Katuic Peoples in the Uplands of Laos and Vietnam.* Uppsala: Uppsala Universitet.

Arumpac, Alyx Ayn. 2012. "Pan-go-tub: The Tattooing Tradition of the Manobo." *GMA News Online,* August 28, 2012. www.gmanetwork.com/news/newstv/reeltime/271561/pang-o-tub-the-tattooing-tradition-of-the-manobo/story. Accessed June 1, 2020.

Arutiunov, Sergei A. 1999. "Ainu Origin Theories." In *Ainu: Spirit of a Northern People,* edited by W. W. Fitzhugh and C. O. Dubreuil, 29–31. Washington, DC: Arctic Studies Center, National Museum of Natural History/Seattle: University of Washington Press.

Bachner, Andrea. 2014. *Beyond Sinology: Chinese Writing and the Scripts of Culture.* New York: Columbia University Press.

Bachyuljb, Syofiardi. 2018. "The Last Mentawai Tattoo Bearers." *Jakarta Post*, October 2. https://www.thejakartapost.com/life/2018/10/02/the-last-mentawai-tattoo-bearers.html. Accessed September 3, 2021.

Bacus, Elisabeth. 2002. "The Archaeology of the Philippine Archipelago." In *Southeast Asia: From Prehistory to History*, edited by I. Glover and P. Bellwood, 257–281. London: Routledge-Curzon.

Bajo, Rolando O. 2004. *The Ata-Manobo: At the Crossroads of Tradition and Modernization*. Kapalong: CARD-Davao.

Barske, Valerie H. 2013. "Visualizing Priestesses or Performing Prostitutes? Ifa Fuyū's Depictions of Okinawan Women, 1913–1943." *Studies on Asia* 3 (1): 65–91.

Barton, Francis R. 1918. "Tattooing in South Eastern New Guinea." *Journal of the Royal Anthropological Institute of Great Britain and Ireland* 48:22–79.

Barton, Roy F. 1949. *The Kalingas: Their Institutions and Custom Law*. Chicago: University of Chicago Press.

Bassett-Smith, Peter W. 1894. "Damma Island and Its Natives." *Journal of the Anthropological Institute of Great Britain and Ireland* 23:134–141.

Batchelor, John. 1882. "Notes on the Ainu." *Transactions of the Asiatic Society of Japan* 10 (2): 206–219.

———. 1901. *The Ainu and Their Folk-Lore*. London: The Religious Tract Society.

———. 1927. *Ainu Life and Lore: Echoes of a Departing Race*. Tokyo: Kyobunkan.

Beckett, Ronald G., Ulla Lohmann, and Josh Bernstein. 2011. "A Field Report on the Mummification Practices of the Anga of Koke Village, Central Highlands, Papua New Guinea." *Yearbook of Mummy Studies* 1:11–17.

Beckett, Ronald G., Gerald J. Conlogue, Orlando V. Abinion, Analyn Salvador-Amores, and Dario Piombino-Mascali. 2017. "Human Mummification Practices among the Ibaloy of Kabayan, North Luzon, the Philippines." *Papers on Anthropology* 25 (2): 24–37.

Benedict, Laura Watson. 1913. "Bagobo Myths." *Journal of American Folklore* 26:13–63.

———. 1916. *A Study of Bagobo Ceremonial, Magic, and Myth*. Annals of the New York Academy of Sciences. Vol. 25. New York: New York Academy of Sciences.

Bernstein, Joseph. 2023. "Cool Tribal Tattoo. Is It from the '90s?" *New York Times*, May 19, 2023. www.nytimes.com/2023/05/19/style/tribal-tattoo-90s.html. Accessed May 20, 2023.

Best, Elsdon. 1905. "Maori Eschatology." *Transactions of the New Zealand Institute*, no. 38: 147–239.

Beyer, H. Otley, and Roy F. Barton. 1911. "An Ifugao Burial Ceremony." *Philippine Journal of Science* 6 (5): 227–252.

Bezacier, Louis. 1943. "Note sur quelques tatouages des Moï 'Ka-tu'" [Some Notes on Moï "Ka-tu" Tattoos]. *Institut Indochinois pour l'Étude de L'Homme Bulletins et Travaux* 5 (2): 117–124.

———. 1951. "Interprétation du tatouage frontal des Moi Ka-tu" [Interpretation of the Moi Ka-tu Forehead Tattoo]. *Bulletin de la société de Études Indochinoise* 26:39–51.

Blair, E. H., and J. A. Robertson, eds. 1903. *The Philippine Islands, 1493–1803*. Vol. 3. Cleveland: Arthur H. Clark.

———. 1905. *The Philippine Islands, 1493–1803*. Vol. 23. Cleveland: Arthur H. Clark.

Blust, Robert. 1999. "Subgrouping, Circularity and Extinction: Some Issues in Austronesian Comparative Linguistics." In *Selected Papers from the 8th International Conference on Austronesian Linguistics*, edited by E. Zeitoun and P. J.-K Li, 31–94. Taipei: Academia Sinica.

Blust, Robert, and Stephen Trussel. 2012. *The Austronesian Comparative Dictionary* (web edition). https://www.trussel2.com/acd. Accessed June 11, 2020.

Bock, Carl. 1885. "Le tatouage au Laos Occidental" [Tattooing in Western Laos]. *Revue D'Ethnographie* 3:259–261.
Bouteiller, Marcelle. 1953. "Le tatouage: Technique et valeur sociale ou magico-religieuse, dans quelques sociétés d'Indochine (Laos, Siam, Birmanie et Cambodge)" [Tattooing: Technique and Social or Magico-Religious Value in Some Indochina Societies (Laos, Siam, Burma and Cambodia)]. *Bulletins et Mémoires de la Société d'anthropologie de Paris* 4 (5–6): 515–534.
BBC (British Broadcasting Corporation). 2016. *The Dying Art of Headhunter Tattoos* (online). www.bbc.com/news/av/world-asia-india-36206485/the-dyingart-of-headhunting-tattoos. Accessed November 2, 2017.
Buckley, Thomas, and Alma Gottlieb. 1988. "Introduction." In *Blood Magic: The Anthropology of Menstruation*, edited by T. Buckley and A. Gottlieb, 3–50. Berkeley: University of California Press.
Bull, Earl Rankin. 1958. *Okinawa or Ryūkyū: The Floating Dragon*. Newark, OH: self-published.
Burman-Hall, Linda. 2017. "Only in Mentawai: Unique Primate Vocalisations and Songs in an Isolated Indonesian Island Group." *Shima* 11 (2): 120–150.
Cai, Jiaqi. 1983. *Dulongzu shehui lishi zonghe kaocha baogao* [Synthetic Study Report on Dulong Society and History]. Kunming: Zhongguo xinan minzu yanjiu xiehui and Yunnansheng minzu yanjiusuo.
Campbell, Rev. William. 1967. *Formosa under the Dutch: Described from Contemporary Records with Explanatory Notes and a Bibliography of the Island*. Taipei: Ch'eng-wen.
Campen, C. F. H. 1884. "Halémahera." *Tijdschrift voor Nederlandsch-Indie* 13 (2): 1–9.
Caplan, Jane, ed. 2000. *Written on the Body: The Tattoo in European and American History*. Princeton, NJ: Princeton University Press.
Carter, Beth, and Dion Kaszas, eds. 2018. *Body Language: Reawakening Cultural Tattooing of the Northwest*. Vancouver, BC: Bill Reid Gallery of Northwest Coast Art.
Casal, Gabriel. 1978. *T'boli Art in Its Socio-cultural Context*. Makati, Philippines: Ayala Museum.
———. 1998. *Kasaysayan, the Story of the Filipino People: The Earliest Filipinos*. Vol. 2. Manila: Asia Publishing.
Chan, Henry. 2007. "Survival in the Rainforest: Change and Resilience among the Punan Vuhang of Eastern Sarawak, Malaysia." PhD diss., University of Helsinki.
Ch'en, Yüan-p'eng. 2000. "Shenti yu huawen: Tang Song shiqi de wenshen feng-shang chutan" [Body and Design: Preliminary Exploration of Tang and Song Period *Wen-shen* Practices]. *Xin Shixue* [New History] 11 (1): 1–44.
Chen, Jackie. 1997. "The Disappearing Custom of Facial Tattoo." *Taiwan Panorama*, February 2, 1997. www.taiwan-panorama.com/en/print.php?id=199728602040E.TXT&table=3. Accessed February 25, 2016.
Chen, Ruijin. 1992. "Dulongzu funü de wenmian xisu" [The Facial Tattoo Custom among Dulong Women]. *Yunnan Minzu Xueyuan Xuebao* [Journal of Yunnan Minzu Institute] 4:40–41.
Chen, Ruijin, Jinhe Luo, and Fashun Yang. 2004. *Lishi de yinhen: Zuihou de wenmian ren* [Imprints of History: The Last Face Tattooed Women]. Beijing: China Travel and Tourism Press.
Chenciner, Robert, Gabib Ismailov, and Magomedkhan Magomedkhanov. 2006. *Tattooed Mountain Women and Spoon Boxes of Daghestan*. London: Bennett & Bloom.
Chi-Lu, Chen. 1968. *Material Culture of the Formosan Aborigines*. Taipei: The Taiwan Museum.
Chinalai, Lee J. 2004. "Dragon Covers—Mysterious Aberrations of the Li." *Textile Society of America Symposium Proceedings* 454:242–251.

Chirino, Pedro. 1969. "Relación de las Islas Filipinas: The Philippines in 1600." *Historical Conservation Society* 15. Translated by R. Echevarria. Manila: Historical Conservation Society.

Chu, Xiaobai. 2007. "Jiyi, duihua, zhenlixing yiwei: You Dulongzu wenmian xisu yanjiu xianzhuang yinfa de kunhuo yu fansi" [Memory, Dialogue and the Sense of Truth: Confusion and Reflection on Current Study of Face Tattooing Custom of Dulong People]. *Yunnan Shehui Kexue* [Yunnan Social Sciences] 5:37–40.

Clark, Bernard. 1938. "Among the Big Knot Lois of Hainan." *National Geographic Magazine* 74 (3): 391–418.

Clark, E. W. 1911. *Ao-Naga Dictionary*. Calcutta: Baptist Mission Press.

Clark, Geoffrey, and Michelle C. Langley. 2020. "Ancient Tattooing in Polynesia." *Journal of Island and Coastal Archaeology* 15 (3): 1–14.

Clark, Mary M. 1907. *A Corner in India*. Philadelphia: American Baptist Publication Society.

Codrington, R. H. 1891. *The Melanesians: Studies in Their Anthropology and Folk-Lore*. Oxford: Clarendon Press.

Cole, Fay Cooper. 1908. "The Tinggian." *Philippine Journal of Science* 3 (4): 197–214.

Conley, William. 1976. *The Kalimantan Kenyah: A Study of Tribal Conversion in Terms of Dynamic Cultural Themes*. Nutley, NY: Presbyterian and Reformed Publishing.

Conway, Susan. 2006. *The Shan: Culture, Art and Crafts*. Bangkok: River Books.

Craig, Austin, and Conrado Benitez. 1916. *Philippine Progress prior to 1898*. Manila: Philippine Education.

Crisp, John. 1799. "An Account of the Inhabitants of the Poggy [Pagai] Islands Lying off Sumatra." *Asiatick Researches* 6:77–91.

Crystal, Eric. 1989. "Myth, Symbol and Function of the Toraja House." *Traditional Dwellings and Settlements Review* 1 (1): 7–17.

Cummings, Joe. 2012. *Sacred Tattoos of Thailand: Exploring the Magic, Masters, and Mystery of Sak Yan*. Singapore: Marshall Cavendish.

———. 2014. "Thailand's Magico-Religious Tattoos." In *TATTOO*, edited by S. Galliot, P. Bagot, Anne & Julien, 199–206. Arles: Actes Sud and Musée du quai Branly.

Dalton, Edward Tuite. (1872) 2007. *Tribal Worlds of the Eastern Himalaya and Indo-Burma Borderlands*. Bangkok: White Lotus.

Davidson, J., and Vincent H. Sutlive. 1991. "The Children of Nising: Images of Headhunting and Male Sexuality in Iban Ritual and Oral Literature." In *Female and Male in Borneo: Contributions and Challenges to Gender Studies*, edited by V. H. Sutlive, 153–220. Williamsburg, VA: Borneo Research Council.

Deacon, Arthur B. 1925. "The Kakihan Society of Ceram and New Guinea Initiation Cults." *Folklore* 36:332–361.

Den Hamer, C. 1885. "Iets over het Tatoueeren of Toetang bij de Biadjoe-Stammen in de z/o afd- van Borneo" [Notes about Tattooing or *Toetang* among the Biadjoe Tribes in the Southwest Department of Borneo]. *Tijdschrift voor Indische Taal-, Land- en Volkenkunde* 30:451–458.

de Raedt, Jules. 1969. "Myth and Ritual: A Relational Study of Buwaya Mythology, Ritual and Cosmology." PhD diss., University of Chicago.

———. 1977. "The Kalinga Notion of Sacrifice." In *Filipino Heritage: The Making of a Nation*, 337–345. Manila: Lahing Pilipino Publishing.

———. 1993. *Buaya Society*. Baguio, Philippines: Cordillera Studies Center, University of the Philippines Baguio.

———. 1996. "Buaya Headhunting and Its Ritual: Notes from a Headhunting Feast in Northern Luzon." In *Headhunting and the Social Imagination in Southeast Asia*, 167–183. Stanford, CA: Stanford University Press.

Desgodins, C. H. 1872. *La Mission du Tibet, de 1855 à 1870, comprenant l'exposé des affaires religieuses et divers documents sur ce pays, d'après les lettres de l'abbé Desgodins* [The Mission to Tibet, from 1855 to 1870, including the Exposition of Religious Affairs and Various Documents on This Country, from the Letters of Father Desgodins]. Verdun, France: Imprimerie de C. H. Laurent.

Deter-Wolf, Aaron, and Lars Krutak. 2017. "Introduction." In *Ancient Ink: The Archaeology of Tattooing*, edited by L. Krutak and A. Deter-Wolf, 1–8. Seattle: University of Washington Press.

Dewar, T. P. 1927. *The Nagas East of the Namphuk Hka*. Rangoon: Superintendent, Government Printing and Stationery.

———. 1931. *Confidential Report on the Naga Hills (Upper Chindwin) Expedition for the Release of Slaves and the Abolition of Human Sacrifice, 20 December 1930–26 March 1931*. Rangoon: Superintendent, Government Printing and Stationery.

Dhamija, Jasleen, ed. 2004. *Asian Embroidery*. New Delhi: Abhinav Publications.

Dinter, Martin T., and Astrid Khoo. 2020. "'If Skin Were Parchment . . .': Tattoos in Antiquity." In *Tattoo: Transcultural Perspectives on the Narratives, Practices, and Representations of Tattooing*, edited by S. Kloß, 85–102. New York: Routledge.

Discovery Channel. 2009. *Tattoo Hunter: The Mentawai*. Directed by Mike Masland. 44 min.

Duan, Mingming. 1999. "Dulongzu funü wenmian de wenhua neihan" [Cultural Meaning of Dulong Women's Facial Tattoos]. In *Minzu Bowuguan Lunwen Ji* [Selected Writings of Minzu Museums], edited by Gao Zongyu, 256–262. Kunming, China: Yunnan minzu chubanshe.

Dutta, Parul C. 1978. *The Nocte*. Shillong, India: Directorate of Research, Government of Arunachal Pradesh.

———. 1990. *The Wanchos*. Itanagar, India: Directorate of Research, Government of Arunachal Pradesh.

Duyvendak, Johan P. 1926. *Het Kakéan-genootschap van Seran* [The Kakéan Society of Seram]. Almelo, Netherlands: Hilarius.

Eco, Umberto. 1997. *Kant e l'ornitorinco* [Kant and the Platypus]. Translated by A. McEwen. New York: Harcourt.

Edwards, James Rhys. 2014. "Between Two Worlds: A Social History of Okinawan Musical Drama." PhD diss., University of California, Los Angeles.

Egerod, Søren. 1969. "The Origin of Headhunting: An Atayal Text with Vocabulary." *Bulletin of the Institute of History and Philology Academia Sinica* 39 (2): 291–325.

Ellis, Juniper. 2008. *Tattooing the World: Pacific Designs in Print and Skin*. New York: Columbia University Press.

Elshout, J. M. 1926. *De Kenja-Dayaks uit het Apo-Kajan-gebied: Bijdragen tot de Kennis van Centraal-Borneo* [The Kenyah Dayaks of the Apo Kayan Region: Contributions to the Knowledge of Central Borneo]. The Hague: Martinus Nijhoff.

Elwin, Verrier. 1953/1954. Notebook 18, December 1953–July 1954. Manuscript in the possession of Ashok Elwin Shillong, India.

———. 1955. *Studies in N.E.F.A. Folklore*. Vol. 1. Unpublished manuscript, Shillong, India.

———. 1958. *Myths of the North-East Frontier of India*. Shillong, India: North-East Frontier Agency.

———. 1959. *The Art of the North-East Frontier of India*. Shillong, India: North-East Frontier Agency.

Esaka, Teruya. 1967. *Dogū*. Tokyo: Azekura Shobo.

Ferrario, Giulio. 1826. *Il costume antico e moderno . . . di tutti i popoli antichi e moderni* [Ancient and Modern Costumes of All Peoples of the World]. Firenze: Vicenzo Batteli.

Field, Henry. 1958. "Body-Marking in Southwestern Asia." *Papers of the Peabody Museum of Archaeology and Ethnology, Harvard University* 45, no. 1: 1–162.

Fiksa, Radomir. 2019. *Lexicon of Tribal Tattoos: Motifs, Meanings, and Origins*. Atglen, PA: Schiffer.

———. 2021. *Tribal Tattoo Encyclopedia*. Prague: Bodyart Press.

Fitzhugh, William. 1999. "Ainu Ethnicity: A History." In *Ainu: Spirit of a Northern People*, edited by W. Fitzhugh and C. O. Dubreuil, 9–27. Washington, DC: Smithsonian Institution Press.

Folkmar, Daniel K. (1905–1906) 1962. "Social Institutions of the Tinglayan Igorot." *Sagada Social Studies* 12.

Foll, C. V. 1959. "An Account of Some of the Beliefs and Superstitions about Pregnancy, Parturition, and Infant Health in Burma." *Journal of Tropical Pediatrics* 5 (2): 51–59.

Forbes, Charles J. 1878. *British Burma and Its People: Being Sketches of Native Manners, Customs, and Religion*. London: John Murray.

Formosa Bureau of Aboriginal Affairs. 1911. *Report on the Control of the Aborigines in Formosa*. Taihoku: Bureau of Aboriginal Affairs.

Formosa News. 2019. "Two Women Are Taiwan's Link to a Treasured Tradition." *Formosa News*, September 18, 2019. www.englishnews.ftv.com.tw/read.aspx?sno=4D3E06DBC6EC2F8EEEE5C03E066107BA. Accessed May 10, 2020.

Forth, Gregory L. 1981. *Rindi: An Ethnographic Study of a Traditional Domain in Eastern Sumba*. Verhandelingen van het Koninklijk Instituut voor Taal-, Land- en Volkenkunde 93. The Hague: Martinus Nijhoff.

Francillon, Gérard. 1967. "Some Matriarchic Aspects of the Social Structure of the Southern Tetun of Middle Timor." PhD diss., The Australian National University, Canberra.

Franck, Harry A. 1924. *Glimpses of Japan and Formosa*. New York: Century.

Franken, Jeroen, and Sven Torfinn. 1998. *Pantang Iban*. Rotterdam: Typography & Other Serious Matters.

Freeman, Derek. 1967. "Shaman and Incubus." *Psychoanalytic Study of Society* 4:315–344.

———. 1981. *Some Reflections on the Nature of Iban Society*. Department of Anthropology, Research School of Pacific Studies, The Australian National University, Canberra.

Freeman Papers. 1948–1958. Papers of Derek and Monica Freeman. Ms acc12.055, box 6, file 21; box 7, file 34; box 8, file 52, National Library of Australia, Canberra.

Friedman, Anna Felicity. 2015. *The World Atlas of Tattoo*. New Haven, CT: Yale University Press.

Fujimura, Hisakazu. 1999. "Life and Death." In *Ainu: Spirit of a Northern People*, edited by W. W. Fitzhugh and C. O. Dubreuil, 268–273. Washington, DC: Arctic Studies Center, National Museum of Natural History/Seattle: University of Washington Press.

Fukui, Yoshimaro. 1814. *Ezo no shimabumi* [Traversing Ezo Island]. https://www.worldcat.org/title/52072241.

Furey, Louise. 2017. "Archaeological Evidence for Tattooing in Polynesia and Micronesia." In *Ancient Ink: The Archaeology of Tattooing*, edited by L. Krutak and A. Deter-Wolf, 159–184. Seattle: University of Washington Press.

Furness, William H. 1899a. "Life in the Luchu Islands." *Bulletin of the Free Museum of Science and Art* 1 (2): 1–28.

———. 1899b. "Collections and Publications." *Bulletin of the Free Museum of Science and Art* 2 (1): 39–50.

———. 1900. "Fieldnotes." William H. Furness, Alfred C. Harrison, Hiram M. Hiller Collection—Assam, India, 1899–1900, Penn Museum Archives, Philadelphia.
———. 1902a. *The Home-Life of Borneo Head-Hunters: Its Festivals and Folklore.* Philadelphia: J. B. Lippincott.
———. 1902b. "The Ethnography of the Nagas of Eastern Assam." *Journal of the Anthropological Institute of Great Britain and Ireland* 32:445–466.
Furuie, Shinpei. 1994. *Hi to mizu no minzoku bunkashi* [Fire and Water Folk Culture Magazine]. Tokyo: Yoshikawa Kōbunkan.
Fusheng, Liu. 2016. "Apparel and Accessories." In *A Social History of Middle-Period China: The Song, Liao, Western Xia and Jin Dynasties,* edited by Z. Ruixin, Z. Bangwei, L. Fusheng, C. Chongbang, and W. Zengyu and translated by B. Q. Zhu, 1–59. Cambridge: Cambridge University Press.
Galliot, Sébastien. 2018. "On Sāmoan Tattooing." In *Tatau: A History of Sāmoan Tattooing,* edited by S. Mallon and S. Galliot, 27–28. Honolulu: University of Hawai'i Press.
Galliot, Sébastien, Pascal Bagot, and Anne & Julien, eds. 2014. *TATTOO.* Arles: Actes Sud/Paris: Musée du quai Branly.
Galvin, Rev. A. D. 1974. "Headhunting—Fact or Fiction?" *Brunei Museum Journal* 3 (3): 16–142.
Ganguli, Milada. 1984. *A Pilgrimage to the Nagas.* New Delhi: IBH.
Gao, Zhiying. 2010. "Dulong nü wenmian de wenhua chanshi" [The Cultural Interpretation of Dulong Women's Facial Tattoo]. *Xinan Minzu Daxue Xuebao* [Journal of Southwest Minzu University] 2:21–27.
———. 2015. "Dulong nü wenmian de tu'an chanshi yu wenhua jiangou" [Interpretation of the Motif of Dulong Women's Facial Tattoo and Its Cultural Construction]. *Minzu Yanjiu* [Ethno-National Studies] 6:68–77.
Garvan, J. M. 1931. *The Manóbos of Mindanáo.* Memoirs of the National Academy of Sciences 22. Washington, DC: US Government Printing Office.
Gavin, Traude. 1991. "Kayau Indu: The Women's Warpath: A Ngar Ritual at Entawau, Baleh in October 1988." *Sarawak Museum Journal* 42 (63): 1–42.
———. 1995. "Iban Ritual Sacrifice Fabrics: Their Patterns and Names (Part 1)." PhD diss., University of Hull.
Geirnaert-Martin, Danielle C. 1992. *The Woven Land of Laboya: Socio-Cosmic Ideas and Values in West Sumba, Eastern Indonesia.* Leiden: Center of Non-Western Studies, Leiden University.
Gell, Alfred. 1993. *Wrapping in Images: Tattooing in Polynesia.* Oxford: Clarendon Press.
Gilbert, Steve. 2000. "The Circus." In *Tattoo History: A Source Book,* edited by S. Gilbert, 134–147. New York: Juno Books.
Glacken, Clarence J. 1955. *The Great Loochoo: A Study of Okinawan Village Life.* Berkeley: University of California Press.
Go, Vincent. 2014. "In Pictures: Filipino Manobos Seek Peace." *Al Jazeera,* May 30, 2014. www.aljazeera.com/indepth/inpictures/2014/05/pictures-filipino-manobos-seek-2014523103758161418.html. Accessed June 12, 2020.
Gomes, E. H. 1911. *Seventeen Years among the Sea Dyaks of Borneo.* London: Seeley.
Graham, Penelope. 1987. *Iban Shamanism: An Analysis of the Ethnographic Literature.* Department of Anthropology, Research School of Pacific and Asia Studies, The Australian National University, Canberra.

Gros, Stéphane. 2001. "Du politique au pittoresque en Chine. À propos des Dulong, nationalité minoritaire du Yunnan" [From Politics to Picturesque in China: About the Dulong, a Minority Nationality of Yunnan]. *Ateliers d'anthropologie* 24:28–68.
———. 2012. *La Part manquante: Échanges et pouvoirs chez les Drung du Yunnan* [The Missing Share: Exchange and Power among the Drung of Yunnan]. Nanterre, France: Société d'ethnologie.
———. 2017. "Quand les femmes font corps: Le tatouage facial féminin chez les Drung du Yunnan" [When Women Become One: Female Facial Tattoo among the Drung of Yunnan]. In *Le Battement de la vie: Le corps naturel et ses représentations en Chine* [The Beat of Life: The Natural Body and Its Representations in China], edited by B. Baptandier, 163–187. Nanterre, France: Société d'ethnologie.
———. 2021. "Fertile Tattoos: Play, Embodiment, and the Transition to Womanhood in Drung Female Facial Tattooing." *Asian Ethnology* 80 (2): 319–341.
Gual, Yoseph A., Fransiska D. Setyaningsih, and Primus P. Bolaer. 2019. "Tattoo Tradisional Masyarakat Dea Haulasi Kecamatan Miomafo Kabupaten Timor Tengah Utara" [Traditional Tattoo of the Dea Haulasi Community, Miomafo District, North Central Timor Regency]. *Jurnal Pendidikan dan Kebudayaan Missio* 11 (1): 160–178.
Guanghai, Yang, dir. 1961. *Dulongzu* [The Dulong]. Historical and Ethnographical Film Series. 52 min.
Guilleminet, Paul P. 1952. "La tribu bahnar du Kontum (plateaux de l'Indochine centrale): Contribution à l'étude de la société montagnarde du Sud indochinois" [The Bahnar Tribe of Kontum (Central Indochina Plateau): Contribution to the Study of Mountain Society in Southern Indochina]. *Bulletin de l'École française d'Extrême-Orient* 45 (2): 393–561.
Haddon, Alfred C. 1901. *Head-Hunters; Black, White, and Brown.* London: Methuen.
Hall, Basil. 1820. *Account of a Voyage of Discovery to the West Coast of Corea and the Great Loo-Choo Island.* London: John Murray.
Hallett, Holt S. 1890. *A Thousand Miles on an Elephant in the Shan States.* Edinburgh/London: William Blackwood and Sons.
Hambly, Wilfrid Dyson. (1925) 2009. *The History of Tattooing.* Mineola, NY: Dover.
Hammons, Christian S. 2010. "Sakailou: Reciprocity, Mimesis, and the Cultural Economy of Tradition in Siberut, Mentawai Islands, Indonesia." PhD diss., University of Southern California, Los Angeles.
Hardy, Don Ed, ed. 1988. *Tattootime: New Tribalism.* Honolulu: Hardy Marks Publications.
Harris, Roy. 1995. *Signs of Writing.* London: Routledge.
Harrison, Tom. 1965. "Borneo Writing." *Bijdragen tot de Taal-, Land- en Volkenkunde* 121 (1): 1–57.
———. 1966. "Maloh Coffin Designs." *Sarawak Museum Journal* 14:146–130.
Hart, Alice M. 1897. *Picturesque Burma, Past and Present.* London: J. M. Dent.
Hata, Awagimaru. 1799. *Ezotō kikan* [Wonders of Ezo Island]. https://www.worldcat.org/title/1340516673.
Hebra, Ferdinand. 1875. *Atlas of Portraits of Diseases of the Skin.* London: W. West.
Heneise, Michael. 2019. *Agency and Knowledge in Northeast India: The Life and Landscapes of Dreams.* London: Routledge.
Henley, Thom. 2001. *The Living Legend of the Mentawai.* Victoria, BC: Baan Thom.
Heppell, Michael. 2005. *Iban Art: Sexual Selection and Severed Heads.* Leiden: C. Zwartenkot/Amsterdam: KIT.
Hermkens, Anna-Karina. 2004. "Marking the Female Body: Tattooing among the Maisin of Papua New Guinea." *Raffia: Journal of the Institute for Gender Studies* 16 (3): 23–26.
Hibbett, Akiko Yamagawa, ed. 2011. *From Okinawa to the Americas: Hana Yamagawa and Her Reminiscences of a Century.* Honolulu: University of Hawai'i Press.

Hilger, M. Inez. 1971. *Together with the Ainu: A Vanishing People.* Norman: University of Oklahoma Press.

Hiller, Hiram M. 1896. Furness, Harrison, and Hiller Expedition Records, PU–Mu, 1060, box 1, H. M. Hiller Journals, Penn Museum Archives, Philadelphia.

———. 1898. Furness, Harrison, and Hiller Expedition Records, PU-Mu, 1060, box 2, H. M. Hiller Journals, Penn Museum Archives, Philadelphia.

Ho, John Ting-Jui. 1960. "A Study on Tattooing Customs among the Formosan Aborigines." *Bulletin of the Department of Archaeology and Anthropology* 15:1–48.

———. 1971. *A Comparative Study of Myths and Legends of Formosan Aborigines.* Asian Folklore and Social Life Monographs. Vol. 18. Taipei: The Orient Cultural Service.

Honda, Katsuichi. 2000. *Harukor: An Ainu Woman's Tale.* Translated by K. Selden. Berkeley: University of California Press.

Horton, Donald. 1948. "The Mundurucú." In *Handbook of South American Indians,* edited by J. H. Steward, 271–282. Washington, DC: US Government Printing Office.

Hose, Charles, and William McDougall. 1912. *The Pagan Tribes of Borneo.* London: Macmillan.

Hose, Charles, and Robert Shelford. 1906. "Materials for a Study of Tatu in Borneo." *Journal of the Anthropological Institute of Great Britain and Ireland* 36:60–91.

Hoskins, Janet. 1989. "Why Do Ladies Sing the Blues? Indigo, Cloth Production, and Gender Symbolism in Kodi." In *Cloth and Human Experience,* edited by A. B. Weiner and J. Schneider, 141–173. Washington, DC: Smithsonian Institution Press.

———. 1993. *The Play of Time: Kodi Perspectives on Calendars, History, and Exchange.* Berkeley: University of California Press.

———. 1996. "Introduction: Headhunting as Practice and as a Trope." In *Headhunting and the Social Imagination in Southeast Asia,* edited by J. Hoskins, 1–49. Stanford, CA: Stanford University Press.

Howell, William. 1912. "The Sea-Dyak Method of Making and Dyeing Thread from Their Home-Grown Cotton." *Sarawak Museum Journal* 1:61–64.

Hsieh, Chiao-min. 1964. *Taiwan-Ilha Formosa: A Geography in Perspective.* Washington, DC: Butterworths.

Htwe, Nyein Ei Ei. 2013. "Chin Tattoos: A Fading Tradition." *Myanmar Times,* November 17, 2013. www.mmtimes.com/lifestyle/8791-tradition-s-fading-marks.html. Accessed October 2, 2020.

Huang-ju, Huang, dir. 2018. *Images from My Dreams: The Story of Tattoo Artist Cudjuy Patjidres.* Taipei: National Taiwan Museum. 8:46 min.

Hughes, W. Gwynne. 1881. *The Hill Tracts of Arakan.* Rangoon: The Government Press.

Hung, Hsiao-chun, and Mike T. Carson. 2014. "Foragers, Fishers and Farmers: Origins of the Taiwanese Neolithic." *Antiquity* 88 (342): 1115–1131.

Hutton, John H. 1920. "Leopard-Men in the Naga Hills." *Journal of the Royal Anthropological Institute* 50:41–51.

———. 1921. *The Sema Nagas.* London: Macmillan.

———. 1922a. "Divided and Decorated Heads as Trophies." *Man* 12 (67): 113–114.

———. 1922b. "Molola: A Chang Naga Folk-Story." *Man in India* 22 (1–2): 84–87.

———. 1929. "Diaries of Two Tours in the Unadministered Area East of the Naga Hills." *Memoirs of the Asiatic Society of Bengal* 11 (1): 1–72.

Ichikawa, Shigeharu. 1983. *Nantō hajichi kikō: Okinawa fujin no irezumi o miru* [Southern Islands Travelogue: Looking at Tattoos of Okinawan Women]. Haebaru-chō, Japan: Naha Shuppansha.

Igualdo, Lolito. 1989. "The Social World of the Kankana-eys." PhD diss., Baguio Central University.

Iha, Fuyū. (1919) 2000. *Okinawa josei-shi* [Okinawa Women's History]. Naha: Ozawa Shoten.

Inō, Y. 1910. "The Marks of the Chiefs among the Tsarisen [Rukai] in Formosa." *Journal of the Anthropological Society of Tokyo* 25:131–140.

Inoue, Naohiko, and Shoko Kochi. 1987. "Ritual Ablation of Anterior Teeth in Recent Ainu." *Journal of the Anthropological Society of Nippon* 95 (3): 305–324.

Irimoto, Takashi. 1997. "Ainu Shamanism." In *Circumpolar Animism and Shamanism*, edited by T. Irimoto and T. Yamada, 21–46. Sapporo: Hokkaido University Press.

Ishida, Hajime. 1999. "Ancient People of the North Pacific Rim: Ainu Biological Relationships with Their Neighbors." In *Ainu: Spirit of a Northern People*, edited by W. W. Fitzhugh and C. O. Dubreuil, 52–56. Washington, DC: Arctic Studies Center, National Museum of Natural History/Seattle: University of Washington Press.

Ito, Kazuyuki. 2019. "Once Outlawed, Okinawa's 'Hajichi' Tattoo Culture Revived." *Asahi Shinbum*, September 20, 2019. www.asahi.com/ajw/articles/AJ201909200005.html. Accessed April 14, 2020.

Jacob, Francisco de Ch. Anugerah. 2021. "Lunat: Tato Tradisional Masyarakat Dawan di Timor Barat Lunat: The Traditional Tattoo of the Dawan Peoples in West Timor." *Anthropos: Jurnal Antropologi Social dan Budaya* 7 (1): 54–66.

Jacobs, Julian. 1990. *The Nagas: Hill Peoples of Northeast India. Society, Culture, and the Colonial Encounter.* London: Thames and Hudson.

Jammes, L. 1900. "Le Tatouage chez les peoples de l'Indo-Chine" [Tattooing among the Peoples of Indo-China]. *Revue Indo-Chinoise* 93:739–740. July 30.

Janowski, Monica. 2003. *The Forest, Source of Life: The Kelabit of Sarawak.* British Museum Occasional Paper 143. British Museum.

———. 2014. *Takad Rini, Cosmic Traveller from the Heart of Borneo.* Copenhagen: Nias Press.

Jenks, Albert E. 1905. *The Bontoc Igorot.* Manila: Philippine Islands Ethnological Survey.

Jensen, Adolf E. 1948. *Die Drei Ströme: Züge aus dem Geistigen und Religiösen Leben der Wemale, einem Primitiv-Volk in den Molukken* [The Three Rivers: Traits from the Spiritual and Religious Life of the Wemale, a Primitive People in the Moluccas]. Leipzig: Otto Harrassowitz.

Jie, Zhang, and Zhang Changfu. 2012. *Xiu mian yu diao shen: Li to wen shen wen product yan jiu* [Embroidered Face and Carved Body: A Study on Tattoo Culture of the Li Nationality]. Shanghai: Shanghai University Press.

Jinam, Timothy, Nao Nishida, Momoki Hirai, Shoji Kawamura, Hiroki Oota, Kazuo Umetsu, Ryosuke Kimura, Jun Ohashi, Atsushi Tajima, Toshimichi Yamamoto, Hideyuki Tanabe, Shuhei Mano, Yumiko Suto, Tadashi Kaname, Kenji Naritomi, Kumiko Yanagi, Norio Niikawa, Keiichi Omoto, Katsushi Tokunaga, and Naruya Saitou. 2012. "The History of Human Populations in the Japanese Archipelago Inferred from Genome-Wide SNP Data with a Special Reference to the Ainu and the Ryukyuan Populations." *Journal of Human Genetics* 57:787–795.

Jinam, Timothy A., Hideaki Kanzawa-Kiriyama, Ituro Inoue, Katsushi Tokunaga, Keiichi Omoto, and Naruya Saitou. 2015. "Unique Characteristics of the Ainu Population in Northern Japan." *Journal of Human Genetics* 60:565–571.

Jocano, F. Landa. 1958. "The Sulod: A Mountain People in Central Panay, Philippines." *Philippine Studies* 6 (4): 401–436.

Johnson, Susan C. 1913. "Historic Ornament with Application to Decorative Design in the Philippines." *Philippine Craftsman* 2 (3): 113–164.

Jones, William. 1880. *Credulities Past and Present.* London: Chatto and Windus.

Jongejans, J. 1922. *Uit Dajakland Kijkjes in het Leven van den Koppensneller en Zijne Omgeving* [From

Dayakland: Glimpses into the Life of the Headhunter and His Surroundings]. Amsterdam: J. M. Meulenhoff.

Joshi, Vibha. 2004. *The Land of the Naga*. Ahmedabad, India: Mapin.

Kakoulas, Marisa. 2009. *Black Tattoo Art: Modern Expressions of the Tribal*. Aschaffenburg, Germany: Edition Reuss.

———. 2010. *Black and Grey Tattoo: From Street Art to Fine Art*. 3 vols. Aschaffenburg, Germany: Edition Reuss.

———. 2013. *Black Tattoo Art 2: Modern Expressions of the Tribal*. Promotional materials. Aschaffenburg, Germany: Edition Reuss.

Kaneko, Erika. 1960. "Some Aspects of Atayal Religion and Their Impact on Atayal Culture." In *Proceedings on the IX International Congress for the History of Religions, 1958*, 33–38. Tokyo: Maruzen.

Kaner, Simon, ed. 2009. *The Power of Dogū: Ceramic Figurines from Ancient Japan*. London: British Museum Press.

Kapita, Oe. H. 1976. *Masyarakat Sumba dan Adat Istiadatnya* [Sumba People and Their Customs]. Waingapu, Indonesia: Gereja Kristen Sumba.

Kaszas, Dion. 2018. "Echoes of the Ancestors: Inherited Knowledge and Responsibilities." In *Body Language: Reawakening Cultural Tattooing of the Northwest*, edited by B. Carter and D. Kaszas, 7–27. Vancouver, BC: Bill Reid Gallery of Northwest Coast Art.

Kaudern, Walter. 1944. *Ethnographical Studies in Celebes: Art in Central Celebes. Results of the Author's Expedition to Celebes, 1917–1920*, edited by T. Kaudern and H. Wassén. The Hague: Martinus Nijhoff.

Kauffmann, Hans-Eberhard. 1940. "Deutsche Naga-Hills Expedition 1936/7 (3. Bericht)" [German Naga-Hills Expedition 1936/7 (3rd Report)]. *Ethnologischer Anzeiger* 4 (6): 318–337.

Kaviani, Fareed. 2015. "Tattooing Timor." *The 4th Wall*. https://www.the4thwall.net/blog/2015/11/19/guest-article-tattooing-timor-by-thomas-henning-dedicated-to-the-dilli-collective. Accessed October 1, 2021.

Kedit, Vernon. 2017. "A Chief's Caveat, a Rajah's Gift, a Museum's Treasure: Journey of a 19th-Century Iban Textile Called a *Lebur Api* from Borneo to the British Museum." *Borneo Research Bulletin* 48:210–235.

Keesing, Felix M. 1949. "Some Notes on Bontok Social Organization, Northern Philippines." *American Anthropologist* 51:578–601.

Keira, Mitsunori, and Tomoko Keira. 1999. "Village Work: Seasons and Gender Roles." In *Ainu: Spirit of a Northern People*, edited by W. W. Fitzhugh and C. O. Dubreuil, 234–239. Washington, DC: Arctic Studies Center, National Museum of Natural History/Seattle: University of Washington Press.

Knight, Chris. 1995. *Blood Relations: Menstruation and the Origins of Culture*. New Haven, CT: Yale University Press.

Kodama, Sakuzaemon. 1970. *Ainu: Historical and Anthropological Studies*. Sapporo: Hokkaido University School of Medicine.

Koganei, Yoshikiyo. 1894. *Beiträge zur physichen Anthropologie der Aino: II: Untersuchungen am Lebended* [Contributions to the Physical Anthropology of the Ainu: 2: Investigations of the Living]. Mittheilungen aus der Medicinischen Facultät der Kaiserlich-Japanischen Universität. Tokyo: Verlag der Kaiserlichen Universität.

Konyak, Phejin, and Peter Bos. 2017. *The Konyaks: Last of the Tattooed Headhunters*. Delhi: Roli Books.

Kotondo, Hasebe. 1928. "Seibu Micronesia-jin no irezumi" [The Tattooing of the Western Micronesians]. *Journal of the Anthropological Society of Tokyo* 43 (3): 120–146.

Krachennikov, Stepan. 1768. *Voyage en Sibérie, contenant la description du Kamtchatka* [A Trip to Siberia, Containing a Description of Kamchatka]. Edited by Jean Chappe d'Auteroche. Paris: Debure.

Krämer, Augustin. 1903. *Die Samoa Inseln: Entwarf einer Monographie mit besonderer berücksichtigung Deutsch-Samoas* [The Samoa Islands: A Draft Monograph with Special Focus on the German Samoas]. Stuttgart: E. Schweizerbart (E. Nägele).

———. 1904. "Die Ornamentik der Kleidmatten un der Tatauierung auf den Marschall-Inseln" [The Ornamentation of the Dress Mats and Tattoos on the Marshall Islands]. *Archive für Anthropologie* 2:1–28.

———. 1906. *Hawaii, Ostmikronesien, und Samoa: Meine zweite Südseereise (1897–1899) zum Studium der Atolle und ihrer Bewohner* [Hawaii, Eastern Micronesia, and Samoa: My Second Trip to the South Seas (1897–1899) to Study the Atolls and Their Inhabitants]. Stuttgart: Strecker & Schröder.

———. 1907. "Zur Tatauierung der Mentawei-Insulaner" [On the Tattooing of the Mentawai Islanders]. *Archiv für Anthropologie* 34:36–41.

Krutak, Lars. 1999. "St. Lawrence Island Joint-Tattooing: Spiritual/Medicinal Functions and Inter-Continental Possibilities." *Études/Inuit/Studies* 23 (1–2): 229–252.

———. 2007. *The Tattooing Arts of Tribal Women.* London: Bennett & Bloom.

———. 2008a. "*Titi:* Spirit Tattoos of the Mentawai Shaman." *Skin and Ink: The Tattoo Magazine* 35:38–49. July.

———. 2008b. Unpublished fieldnotes. Arunachal Pradesh and Nagaland.

———. 2009. "Shamanic Skin: The Art of Magical Tattoos." *Paranormal Magazine* 35:54–59.

———. 2010a. *Kalinga Tattoo: Ancient and Modern Expressions of the Tribal.* Aschaffenburg, Germany: Edition Reuss.

———. 2010b. Unpublished fieldnotes. Nagaland.

———. 2011. Unpublished fieldnotes. Sarawak, Borneo.

———. 2012. *Spiritual Skin: Magical Tattoos and Scarification.* Aschaffenburg, Germany: Edition Reuss.

———. 2013a. "The Power to Cure: A Brief History of Therapeutic Tattooing." In *Tattoos and Body Modifications in Antiquity,* edited by P. Della Casa and C. Witt, 27–34. Proceedings of the Sessions at the EAA Annual Meetings in The Hague and Oslo, 2010–2011. Zurich Studies in Archaeology.

———. 2013b. "Thorn Hit: Managalase Tattoos of Papua New Guinea." *Tattoo Savage* 123:44–51. April.

———. 2013c. "Die tätowierten Tigermenschen Indiens" [The Tattooed Tiger-Men of India]. *Tätowier Magazin,* July, 66–71.

———. 2013d. "Myth Busting Tattoo (Art) History." *Lars Krutak.com,* August 22, 2013. https://www.larskrutak.com/myth-busting-tattoo-art-history/. Accessed October 16, 2021.

———. 2014a. *Tattoo Traditions of Native North America: Ancient and Contemporary Expressions of Identity.* Arnhem, Netherlands: LM Publishers.

———. 2014b. "The Bold and the Beautiful: Women's Tattoos of Coastal Papua New Guinea." *Ink Fashion* 8:16–23.

———. 2014c. "Tribal Tattoos of Indonesia: An Ancestral Art." In TATTOO, edited by A. Gros and translated by S. Pleasance, R.-L. Torti, and P. Varejka, 188–192. Paris: Musée du quai Branly/Arles: Actes Sud.

———. 2014d. Unpublished fieldnotes. Myanmar.

———. 2015a. "The Cultural Heritage of Tattooing: A Brief History." In *Tattooed Skin and Health,* edited by J. Serup, N. Kluger, and W. Baumler, 1–5. Current Problems in Dermatology 48. Basel: Karger.

———. 2015b. "Maître du sak yant: Ajarn Matthieu Duquenois" [Master of Sak Yan: Ajarn Matthieu Duquenois]. *Rise Tattoo Magazine* 60–67. November–December.

———. 2015c. "Neo-Naga." *Tätowier Magazin*, July, 50–54.

———. 2015d. "Mo Naga." In *The World Atlas of Tattoo*, edited by A. F. Friedman, 300–303. New Haven, CT: Yale University Press.

———. 2016a. "Taïwan: Renaissance du Tatouage Paiwan" [Taiwan: Paiwan Tattoo Renaissance]. *Rise Tattoo Magazine* 52–57. August–September.

———. 2016b. "Indelible Grace: In Asia, Tattooing Traditions Abide as Both Prayer and Protection." *El Palacio* 121 (2): 64–73.

———. 2016c. "Naga: Tattoos der Tigerjager und Krieger" [Naga: Tattoos of Tiger Hunters and Warriors in Myanmar]. *TätowierMagazin*, August, 50–54.

———. 2017a. "Sacrificing the Sacred: Tattooed Prehistoric Ivory Figures of St. Lawrence Island, Alaska." In *Ancient Ink: The Archaeology of Tattooing*, edited by L. Krutak and A. Deter-Wolf, 262–285. Seattle: University of Washington Press.

———. 2017b. "The Visual Language of Facial Tattooing." In *Marked for Life: Myanmar's Chin Women and Their Facial Tattoos*, edited by J. U. Parkitny, 14–19. Bielefeld/Berlin: Kerber.

———. 2017c. "Reviving Tribal Tattoo Traditions in the Philippines." In *Ancient Ink: The Archaeology of Tattooing*, edited by L. Krutak and A. Deter-Wolf, 56–61. Seattle: University of Washington Press.

———. 2017d. "Reading between Our Lines: Tattooing in Papua New Guinea." In *Ancient Ink: The Archaeology of Tattooing*, edited by L. Krutak and A. Deter-Wolf, 185–192. Seattle: University of Washington Press.

———. 2018. Unpublished fieldnotes. Nagaland.

———. 2019. "Therapeutic Tattooing in the Arctic: Ethnographic, Archaeological, and Ontological Frameworks of Analysis." *International Journal of Paleopathology* 25:99–109.

———. 2020. "Sacred Skin: Tattooing, Memory, and Identity among the Naga of India." In *Tattoo: Transcultural Perspectives on the Narratives, Practices, and Representations of Tattooing*, edited by S. Kloß, 191–217. New York: Routledge.

———. 2022. "*Hüh tu pu*/To Mark with Tattoo: Chen Naga Tiger-Spirit Tattoos and Indigenous Ontologies in Northeast India." In *Tattooed Bodies: Theorizing Body Inscription across Disciplines and Cultures*, edited by J. Martell and E. Larsen, 91–116. Cham: Palgrave Macmillan.

Krutak, Lars, and Aaron Deter-Wolf, eds. 2017. *Ancient Ink: The Archaeology of Tattooing*. Seattle: University of Washington Press.

Kruyt, Albert C. 1906. *Het Animisme in den Indischen Archipel* [Animism in the Indian Archipelago]. The Hague: Martinus Nijhoff.

———. 1921a. "De Soembaeezan" [The Sumbanese]. *Bijdragen tot de Taal-, Land- en Volkenkunde* 78:466–608.

———. 1921b. "De Roteneezen" [The Rotese]. *Tijdschrift voor Indische Taal-, Land- en Volkenkunde* 40:266–344.

———. 1923. "De Timoreezen" [The Timorese]. *Bijdragen tot de Taal-, Land- en Volkenkunde* 79 (1): 347–490.

Kruyt, Johannes. 1920. "Het Ma'Boea en de Tatouage in Seko (Midden-Celebes)" [The Ma'Boea and Tattooing in Seko (Middle-Celebes)]. *Bijdragen tot de Taal-, Land- en Volkenkunde van Nederlandsche-Indië* 76 (3/4): 235–257.

Kurzman, Steve. 1993. "Pantang Iban: A Description and Analysis of Iban Tattooing." *Sarawak Museum Journal* 65:69–76.

Lagsa, Bobby. 2014. "The Body Art of Bae Norita Gabao." *Rappler*, February 24, 2014. www.rappler.com/life-and-style/arts-and-culture/51363-body-art-bae-norita-gabao-traditional-tattoo-artist. Accessed June 16, 2020.

Landor, Arthur Henry Savage. 1893. *Alone with the Hairy Ainu: Or, 3,800 Miles on a Pack Saddle in Yezo and a Cruise to the Kurile Islands*. London: John Murray.

Laufer, Berthold. 1907. "The Relations of the Chinese to the Philippines Islands." *Smithsonian Miscellaneous Collections* 50 (4): 248–284.

Laukien, Michael. 2004. "Vanishing Facial Tattoos of Laos." *Skin and Ink Magazine* 5:26–28. May.

———. 2009. "Letter from Mang, Vietnam." *Skin and Ink Magazine* 7:28–30. July.

Lazcano Nebreda, Santiago. 1999. "La cuestion de la servidumbre en el sudeste de Tibet y regiones colindantes del Himalaya Oriental hasta la ocupación China de 1950" [The Issue of Serfdom in Southeastern Tibet and Adjoining Regions of the Eastern Himalayas until the Chinese Occupation of 1950]. *Boletin de la Asociacion Española de Orientalistas* 34:221–237.

Lebra, William P. 1966. *Okinawan Religion: Belief, Ritual, and Social Structure*. Honolulu: University of Hawai'i Press.

Lee, Georgia. 1992. *The Rock Art of Easter Island: Symbols of Power, Prayers to the Gods*. Monumenta Archaeologica 17. Institute for Archaeology Los Angeles: UCLA.

Lehman, Frederick K. 1963. *The Structure of Chin Society: A Tribal People of Burma Adapted to a Non-Western Civilization*. Urbana: University of Illinois Press.

Leokoy, Nancy K. 2018. "An Analysis of Traditional Tattoo (*Lunat*) Used by People in Baus Village, Boking District South Central Timor Regency (a Semiotics Study)." *Academic Journal of Education Studies* 1 (1): 23–30.

Le Pichon, Jean. 1938. "Les Chasseurs de sang" [The Blood Hunters]. *Bulletin des Amis du Vieux Hue* 25:357–409.

Lewallen, Ann-Elise. 2016. *The Fabric of Indigeneity: Ainu Identity, Gender, and Settler Colonialism in Japan*. Albuquerque: University of New Mexico Press.

L'Homme. 1886. "Amulettes introduites dans le tissue cellulaire" [Amulets Introduced into the Cell Tissue]. *L'Homme Journal Illustré des Sciences Anthropologiques* 3 (21): 670–671. November 10.

Li, Jinming. 1994. "Dulong wenmian nü" [Dulong Face-Tattooed Women]. *Shancha* [Camelia] 6:1.

Light, Douglas W. 1972. *Tattooing Practices of the Cree Indians*. Calgary, Canada: Glenbow-Alberta Institute Occasional Paper 6.

Lin, Yi-hung, and Huey-jiun Wang. 2007. "From Barrier Defense Lines to Stationary Offices: The Evolution of Managing the Aborigines in the Mt. Li-tung Area during the Japanese Colonial Rule." *Taiwan Historical Research* 14 (1): 71–137.

Lindsay, Charles. 1992. *Mentawai Shaman: Keeper of the Rainforest*. New York: Aperture.

Lisboa, Marcos de. 1754. *Vocabulario de la Lengua Bicol* [Vocabulary of the Bicol Language]. Sampaloc: Convento de Nuestra Señora de Loreto.

Liu, Chungshee H. 1936. "Hainan dao lizu wenshen fengsu yanjiu" [A Study of the Tattooing Custom among the Li of Hainan Island]. *Science Society of China* 1–36.

———. 1938. "Book Review of Hans Stübel's *Die Li-Stämme der Insel Hainan: Ein Beitrag zur Volkskunde Südchinas*." *Man* 38:134–135.

Liu, Dacheng. 1981. "Dulongzu funü de wenmian" [Dulong Women's Tattooing]. *Minzu Wenhua* [Ethno-National Culture] 2:20–21.
Liu, Hans. 1939. "Hainan: The Island and the People." *China Journal* 29 (5–6): 236–246, 302–314.
Liu, Jun. 2007. "Dulongzu wenmian chutan" [Preliminary Discussion of Dulong Facial Tattooing]. *Zhongyang Minzu Daxue Xuebao* [Journal of the Central University for Nationalities] 34 (6): 76–81.
Loeb, Edwin M. 1928. "Mentawei Social Organization." *American Anthropologist* 30:408–433.
———. 1929a. "Shaman and Seer." *American Anthropologist* 31:60–84.
———. 1929b. "Mentawei Religious Cult." *University of California Publications in American Archaeology and Ethnology* 25 (2).
Longkumer, Anungla. 2017. *Folklore of Eastern Nagaland*. Dimapur, India: Department of Underdeveloped Areas, Government of Nagaland, and Heritage Publishing.
Lowenstein, Tom. 1993. *Ancient Land: Sacred Whale, the Inuit Hunt, and Its Rituals*. New York: North Point Press.
Lua, Norma N. 1989. "Myth in Traditional Kankanay Society." *Philippine Studies* 37:145–173.
Ludeking, E. W. A. 1868. *Schets van de residentie Amboina* [Sketch of the Residence Amboina]. Martinus Nijhoff: 's-Gravenhage.
Lumholtz, Carl. 1921. *Through Central Borneo: An Account of Two Years' Travel in the Land of the Head-Hunters between the Years 1913 and 1917*. New York: C. Scribner's Sons.
Luo, Rongfen. 1995a. *Face-Tattooed Women in Nature: The Dulongs*. Kunming: Yunnan jiaoyu chubanshe.
———. 1995b. "Dulongzu wenmian nü" [Dulong Tattooed Women]. *Shancha* [Camelia] 1:16–23.
Ma, Tengyue. 1998. *Tai ya zu wen mian tu pu* [Atayal Facial Tattoo]. Taipei: self-published.
Maass, Alfred. 1906. "Die primitive Kunst der Mentawai-Insulaner" [The Primitive Art of the Mentawai Islanders]. *Zeitschrift für Ethnologie* 38:453–455.
Magannon, Esteban T. 1972. *Religion in a Kalinga Village: Its Implications for Planned Change*. Quezon City, Philippines: Community Development Research Council.
Mallick, Ata. 2020. "The Custom of Marking the Body among the Santals of India." In *Tattoo: Transcultural Perspectives on the Narratives, Practices, and Representations of Tattooing*, edited by S. Kloß, 176–190. New York: Routledge.
Mallinckrodt, J. 1924. "Ethnographische mededeelingen over de Dajaks in de Onderafdeeling Kapoeas." *Bijdragen tot de Taal-, Land- en Volkenkunde van Nederlandsch-Indië* 80:397–446, 521–600; 81:61–115, 165–310.
Mallon, Sean, Peter Brunt, and Nicholas Thomas. 2010. *Tatau: Samoan Tattoo, New Zealand Art, Global Culture*. Wellington: Te Papa Press.
Mallon, Sean, and Sébastien Galliot. 2018. *Tatau: A History of Sāmoan Tattooing*. Wellington: Te Papa Press.
Mangos, Therese, and John Utanga. 2011. *Patterns of the Past: Tattoo Revival in the Cook Islands*. Auckland: Punarua Productions.
Manuel, E. Arsenio. 1962. "Bagobo Riddles." *Folklore Studies* 21:123–185.
Marche, Alfred. (1887) 1970. *Luçon et Palaouan: Six années de voyages aux Philippines* [Luzon and Palawan: Six Years of Journeys in the Philippines]. Paris: Librarie Hachette.
Martin, Karl. 1894. *Reisen in den Molukken, in Ambon, den Uliassern, Seran (Ceram), und Buru* [A Journey through the Moluccas, in Ambon, the Uliasses, Seram, and Buru]. Leiden: E. J. Brill.
Mashman, Valerie. 1989. "Ethnic Arts and Society—an Orang Ulu Study." *Sarawak Museum Journal* 40 (61): 215–230.

Masing, James J. 1981. "The Coming of the Gods: A Study of an Invocatory Chant (*timang gawai amat*) of the Iban of the Baleh Region of Sarawak." PhD diss., The Australian National University, Canberra.

McCabe, Michael. 2002. *Tattoos of Indochina: Magic, Devotion, and Protection*. Atglen, PA: Schiffer.

———. 2008. "Tattooed Women of Yunnan, China." *Skin & Ink Magazine*, no. 39, 64–74. November.

McCallum, Donald. 1988. "Historical and Cultural Dimensions of the Tattoo in Japan." In *Marks of Civilization: Artistic Transformations of the Human Body*, edited by A. Rubin, 109–134. Los Angeles: Museum of Cultural History, University of California, Los Angeles.

McGovern, Janet M. 1922. *Among the Head-Hunters of Formosa*. London: T. Fisher Unwin.

Merino, Florentino S. 1989. *The Kabayan Mummies and the Bendiyan Canao*. Self-published.

Métraux, Alfred. 1940. *Ethnology of Easter Island*. Bulletin 160. Honolulu: Bernice P. Bishop Museum.

Meyer, Hans. 1885. *Eine Weltreise: Plaudereien aus einer zweijährigen Erdumseglung* [A Journey around the World: Stories from Circumnavigating the World for Two Years]. Leipzig: Verlag des Bibliographischen Instituts.

———. (1890) 1975. "A Trip to the Igorots in the Interior." In *German Travelers in the Cordillera, 1860–1890*, translated and annotated by W. H. Scott. Manila: Filipiniana Book Guild.

Middelkoop, Pieter. 1958. "Four Tales with Mythical Features Characteristic of the Timorese People." *Bijdragen tot de Taal-, Land- en Volkenkunde* 114 (4): 384–405.

Mignolo, Walter. 1994. "Signs and Their Transmission: The Question of the Book in the New World." In *Writing without Words: Alternative Literacies in Mesoamerica and the Andes*, edited by E. Boone and W. Mignolo, 220–270. Durham, NC: Duke University Press.

Mills, James P. 1926. *The Ao Nagas*. London: Macmillan.

Ming-Chieh, Chou (Lulji Taligu). 2013. *A Catalogue of Hand Tatoos [sic] at the Puljetji Village of Paiwan: The Writings on the Hand (Vecik Izua ta Lima)*. Majia: Taiwan Indigenous Peoples Culture Park.

Mintz, Malcolm W. 2011. *The Philippines at the Turn of the Sixteenth Century: With Particular Reference to the Bikol Region*. Intersections: Gender and Sexuality in Asia and the Pacific. Monograph 1. www.intersections.anu.edu.au/monograph1/mintz_jewellert.html. Accessed June 13, 2020.

Mitchell, H. J. 1929. *Report on the Naga Hills (Upper Chindwin) Expedition for the Release of Slaves and the Suppression of Human Sacrifice (15th December 1928 to 14th April 1929)*. Maymyo, Myanmar: Government Branch Press.

Mizoguchi, Koji. 2017. "Anthropomorphic Clay Figurines of the Jomon Period of Japan." In *The Oxford Handbook of Prehistoric Figurines*, 521–543. Oxford: Oxford University Press.

Modigliani, Elio. 1910. "Il tatuaggio degli indigeni dell'Is. Sipora, Archipelago Mentavei" [The Tattoo of the Indigenous People of Sipora Island, Mentawai Archipelago]. *Archivio per L'Antropologia e la Etnologia* 40:450–454.

Molnar, Andrea. 2011. "Darlau: Origins and Their Significance in Atsabe Kemak Identity." In *Land and Life in Timor-Leste: Ethnographic Essays*, edited by A. McWilliam and E. G. Traube, 87–115. Canberra: Australian National University Press.

Montandon, George. 1937. *La Civilisation Aïnou et les Cultures Arctiques* [The Ainu Civilization and the Arctic Cultures]. Paris: Payot.

Morrison, Hedda. 1962. *Life in a Longhouse*. Hong Kong: Dai Nippon.

Morse, Robert, and Betty Morse. 1966. "Oral Tradition and Rawang Migration Routes." In *Artibus Asiae: Essays Offered to G. H. Luce by His Colleagues and Friends in Honour of His Seventy-Fifth Birthday*, edited by B. Shin, J. Boisselier, and A. B. Griswold, 195–204. Supplement 23, vol. 1. Ascona, Switzerland: Artibus Asiae.

Moss, Claude R. 1920a. "Nabaloi Law and Ritual." *University of California Publications in American Archaeology and Ethnology* 15 (3): 207–342.

———. 1920b. "Kankanay Ceremonies." *University of California Publications in American Archaeology and Ethnology* 15 (4): 343–384.

Mu, Yang. 1996. "Music Loss among the Ethnic Minorities in China—a Comparison of the Li and Hui Peoples." *Asian Music* 27 (1): 103–130.

———. 1997. "On Musical Instruments of the Li People of Hainan (China)." *World of Music* 39 (3): 91–112.

Munro, Neil Gordon. 1963. *Ainu Creed and Cult*. Edited by B. Z. Seligman. New York: Columbia University Press.

Murikami, Shimanojo. 1799. *Ezo-Shima Kikan* [Curious Sights of Ezo Island]. N.p.

Muyco, Maria C. 2016. *Síbod: Ideology and Expressivity in Binanog Dance, Music, and Folkways of the Panay Bukidnon*. Quezon City, Philippines: Ateneo de Manila University Press.

Nakijin Village Board of Education. 1983. "Nakijin no Haritotsu (Pajichi): Kieyuku Shūzoku" [Nakijin Tattoo (Pajichi): Disappearing Customs]. *Nakijinmura bunkazai chōsa hōkoku-sho dai 7-shū* [Nakijin Village Cultural Property Survey Report, vol. 7.] Okinawa Prefecture, Nakijin, Japan.

Natori, Takemitsu. 1945. *Funka-wan Ainu no hogei* [Whale Hunting among the Funka Bay Ainu]. Sapporo: Hoppō-bunkasha.

Nawani, N. P. 2006. *District Administration: Theory and Practice*. New Delhi: Publications Division, Ministry of Information and Broadcasting, Government of India.

Needham, Rodney. 1976. "Skulls and Causality." *Man* 11 (1): 71–88.

Ng, Alicia K. C. 2015. *Highland Tales in the Heart of Borneo*. Kuching, Malaysia: Ministry of Tourism Sarawak.

Ngadi, Henry G. 1998. *Iban Rites of Passage and Some Related Ritual Acts: A Description of Forms and Functions*. Kuala Lumpur: Dewan Bahasa dan Pustaka, Kementerian Pendidikan.

Ngelouw, Zakaria J. 2008. *Masyarakat Seko Pada Masa DI/TII 1951* [The Seko Community during the DI/TII Period (1951–1965)]. Makassar, Indonesia: Yayasan Ina Seko.

Nieuwenhuis, Anton. W. 1900. *In Centraal Borneo* [In Central Borneo]. Leiden: E. J. Brill.

———. 1904. *Quer durch Borneo* [Across Dutch Borneo]. Leiden: E. J. Brill.

Nisbett, John. 1901. *Burma under British Rule—and Before*. Vol. 2. Westminster: Archibald Constable.

Nooy-Palm, Hetty. 1975. "Introduction to the Sa'dan Toraja People and Their Country." *Archipel* 10:53–91.

———. 1979. *The Sa'dan Toraja: A Study of Their Life and Religion*. Vol. 1, *Organization, Symbols, and Beliefs*. The Hague: Martinus Nijhoff.

———. 1999. "Sulawesi: The Wood Carving of the Sa'dan and Mamasa Toraja." In *Arts of the South Seas: Island Southeast Asia, Melanesia, Polynesia, Micronesia. The Collection of the Musée Barbier-Mueller*, 90–101. Munich: Prestel.

Norbeck, Edward. 1950. *Folklore of the Atayal of Formosa and the Mountain Tribes of Luzon*. Anthropological Papers, Museum of Anthropology, University of Michigan 5. Ann Arbor: University of Michigan Press.

NSJNJH (Naha-shi Sōmubu Joseishitsu Naha Joseishi Henshūiinkai). 1998. *Naha: Josei no ashiato* [Naha: Women's Footprints]. Naha, Japan: Ryūkyū Shimpō.

Nyuak, Leo. 1906. "Religious Rites and Customs of the Iban or Dyaks of Sarawak (Rev. E. Dunn, trans.)." *Anthropos* 1 (1): 11–23, 165–184, 403–425.

Obara, Kazuo. 1962. *Nantō irezumikō* [On Tattoos of the Southern Islands]. Tokyo: Chikuma Shobō.

Odaka, Kunio. 1950. *Economic Organization of the Li Tribes of Hainan Island.* Translated by Mikiso Hane. Southeast Asia Studies, Translation Series. New Haven, CT: Yale University.

Ogawa, Naoyoshi, and Erin Asai. 1935. *Taiwan takasagozuku densets shu* [The Myths and Traditions of the Formosan Native Tribes]. Tokyo: Toko Shoin.

Ogihara, Shinko. 1999. "Mythology and Animal Tales." In *Ainu: Spirit of a Northern People*, edited by W. W. Fitzhugh and C. O. Dubreuil, 274–277. Washington, DC: Arctic Studies Center, National Museum of Natural History/Seattle: University of Washington Press.

Ohnuki-Tierney, Emiko. 1976. "Regional Variations in Ainu Culture." *American Ethnologist* 3 (2): 297–329.

———. 2014. *Illness and Healing among the Sakhalin Ainu: A Symbolic Interpretation.* Cambridge: Cambridge University Press.

Okada, Yuzuru. 1962. "Social Organization of the Li Tribe of Hainan Island." *Sociological Review* 10:115–126.

Okazaki, Manami. 2009. *Tattoo in Japan: Traditional and Modern Styles.* Aschaffenburg, Germany: Edition Reuss.

Ong, Edric. 1999. *Pua: Iban Weavings of Sarawak.* Kuching, Malaysia: Society Atelier Sarawak.

Oo, Maung Kyawt. 2003. "Timeout: Naga Tattoo." *Myanmar Times,* May 2.

Orléans (Prince d'), Henri. 1898. *Du Tonkin aux Indes* [From Tonkin to India]. Paris: Calmann Levy.

Pabst, Maria Anna, Ilse Letofsky-Pabst, Elisabeth Bock, Maximiliam Moser, Leopold Dorfer, Eduard Egarter-Vigl, and Ferdinand Hofer. 2010. "Different Staining Substances Were Used in Decorative and Therapeutic Tattoos in a 1000-Year-Old Peruvian Mummy." *Journal of Archaeological Science* 37:3256–3262.

Palivulj, Angusan. 2012–2015. Unpublished transcripts of interviews, Pintung County, Laiyi Township.

Palmgren, Nils. 1934. "Kansu Mortuary Urns of the Pan Shan and Ma Chang Groups." *Palaeontologica Sinica,* series D, vol. 3, facs. 1.

Papa, Fr. Alberto. 2013. *Picture Writings on Atayal Tattooed Women's Cloths in Taiwan.* Taipei: Gabriel Printing.

Parkitny, Jens Uwe. 2001–2014. Unpublished fieldnotes.

———. 2007. *Bloodfaces. Through the Lens: Chin Women of Myanmar.* Singapore: Flame of the Forest.

———. 2010. *Im Porträt: Gesichtstatauierungen der Chin-Frauen in Birma/Chin Women of Burma and Their Facial Tattoos: A Portrait.* Munich: Staatliches Museum für Völkerkunde.

———. 2017. *Marked for Life: Myanmar's Chin Women and Their Facial Tattoos.* Bielefeld, Germany: Kerber Verlag.

Patterns of Life. 2021. "Patterns of Life." Documentary trailer. 2:46 min. https://www.patternsof.life/.

Pendergrast, Mick. 2000. *Tikopian Tattoo.* Bulletin of the Auckland Museum 18. Auckland: Auckland Museum Publications.

Peréz, Angel. 1902. *Igorrotes: Estudio geografio y etnografico sobre algunos distritos del Norte del Luzon* [Igorots: Geographic and Ethnographic Study of Some Districts of Northern Luzon]. Manila: El Mercantil.

Perez, Ursula G. 1979. "The Ibaloys of Benguet and Their Material Customs." *Mountain State Agricultural College Research Journal* 4–5.

Philippi, Donald L. 1979. *Songs of Gods, Songs of Humans: The Epic Tradition of the Ainu.* Princeton, NJ: Princeton University Press.

Picpican, Isikias. 2003. *The Igorot Mummies: A Socio-Cultural and Historical Treatise.* Quezon City, Philippines: Rex Bookstore.

Piombino-Mascali, Dario, Ronald G. Beckett, Orlando V. Abinion, and Dong Hoon Shin. 2017. "The Mummification Process among the 'Fire Mummies' of Kabayan: A Paleohistological Note." In *Ancient Ink: The Archaeology of Tattooing*, edited by L. Krutak and A. Deter-Wolf, 62–65. Seattle: University of Washington Press.

Piombino-Mascali, Dario, and Lars Krutak. 2020. "Therapeutic Tattoos and Ancient Mummies: The Case of the Iceman." In *Purposeful Pain: The Bioarchaeology of Intentional Suffering*, edited by S. G. Sheridan and L. A. Gregoricka, 119–136. Cham: Springer.

Polonski, Aleksandr S. 1871. *Kurily: Sostavil d͡ieĭstvitel'nyĭ chlen Imperatorskago russkago geograficheskago obshchestva* [The Kurils: Bulletin of the Imperial Russian Geographical Society]. Saint Petersburg: N.p.

Popular Mechanics. 1909. "Electricity Used to Capture Head Hunters." *Popular Mechanics* 11:444. May.

Powers, Stephen. 1877. *Tribes of California*. Contributions to North American Ethnology 3. Washington, DC: US Geographical and Geological Survey of the Rocky Mountain Region.

Priewe, Sascha. 2017. "Prehistoric Figurines in China." In *The Oxford Handbook of Prehistoric Figurines*, edited by Timothy Insoll, 469–492. Oxford: Oxford University Press.

Ragragio, Andrea, and Myfel Paluga. 2019. "An Ethnography of Pantaron Manobo Tattooing (*Pangotoeb*): Towards a Heuristic Schema in Understanding Manobo Indigenous Tattoos." *Southwest Asian Studies* 8 (2): 259–294.

Rau, Der-Hwa Victoria. 1992. "A Grammar of Atayal." PhD diss., Cornell University.

Reed, Carrie E. 2000a. "Early Chinese Tattoo." *Sino-Platonic Papers* 103:1–52.

———. 2000b. "Tattoo in Early China." *Journal of the American Oriental Society* 120 (3): 360–376.

Reid, Lawrence. 1961. "Dancing and Music." *Philippine Sociological Review* 9 (3/4): 55–82.

———. 1972. "Wards and Working Groups in Guinaang, Bontoc, Luzon." *Anthropos* 67:534–563.

———. 1992a. "The Killing of a Japanese Soldier at Fekes." In *Guinaang Bontok Texts*. Tokyo: Institute for the Study of the Languages and Cultures of Asia and Africa. www.aa.tufs.ac.jp/~reid/Bontok/pdf/h08.pdf. Accessed June 10, 2009.

———. 1992b. "When Chay-ot Met a Spirit in the Fields." In *Guinaang Bontok Texts*. Tokyo: Institute for the Study of the Languages and Cultures of Asia and Africa. www.aa.tufs.ac.jp/~reid/Bontok/pdf/h03.pdf. Accessed June 10, 2009.

Riat, Amrita. 2016. "Devilz Tattooz Are Breaking the Tattoo Taboo in New Delhi: An Inky Revolution in India." *Huck* (online). www.huckmagazine.com/perspectives/reportage-2/tattoos-new-delhi/. Accessed June 1, 2018.

Rich, John. 1968. "Pinatikan: Religious Tattoos in a Davao Sect." *Philippine Sociological Review* 16 (1/2): 196.

Richards, Anthony. 1972. "Iban Augury." *Sarawak Museum Journal* 2:63–81.

———. 1997. *An Iban-English Dictionary*. 3rd printing. Kuala Lumpur: Oxford University Press.

Riedel, Johann G. F. 1886. *De Sluik- en kroesharige rassen tusschen Selebes en Papua* [The Straight and Curly Haired Races between Celebes and Papua]. The Hague: Martinus Nijhoff.

———. 1907. "Prohibitieve teekens en Tatuage-vormen op het eiland Timor" [Prohibitive Signs and Tattoo Forms on the Island of Timor]. *Tijdschrift voor Indische Taal-, Land- en Volkenkunde* 49:181–187.

Robbins, Cheryl. 2009. "Atayal Tribe: Recording and Reviving Traditions." *Taiwan News*, February 26, 2009. https://www.taiwannews.com.tw/en/news/876997. Accessed May 16, 2020.

Robitaille, Benoît. 2007. "A Preliminary Typology of Perpendicularly Hafted Bone Tipped Tattooing Instruments: Towards a Technological History of Oceania Tattooing." In *Bones as Tools: Current Methods and Interpretations in Worked Bone Studies*, edited by C. G. St. Pierre and R. B. Walker, 159–174. British Archaeological Reports International Series 1622. Oxford: Archaeopress.

Roth, Henry Ling. 1896. *The Native Races of Sarawak and British North Borneo*. London: Truslove & Hanson.

Rousseau, Jérôme. 1979. "Kayan Stratification." *Man* 14:215–236.

———. 1998. *Kayan Religion: Ritual Life and Religious Reform in Central Borneo*. Leiden: KITLV.

Rudenko, Sergei I. 1929. "Graficheskoye iskusstvo ostyakov i vogulov" [Graphic Art of Ostyaks and Voguls]. *Materialy po etnografii Rossii* [Materials on the Ethnography of Russia] 4 (2): 13–40.

Rudolph, Michael. 2008. *Ritual Performances as Authenticating Practices: Cultural Representations of Taiwan's Aborigines in Times of Political Changes*. Berlin: LIT Verlag.

Rutter, Owen. 1929. *The Pagans of North Borneo*. London: Hutchinson.

Ryūzō, Torii. 1919. "Études archéologiques et ethnologiques: Les Ainous des Illes Kouriles" [Archaeological and Ethnological Studies: The Ainus of the Kurile Islands]. *Journal of the College of Science, Imperial University of Tokyo* 42:1–336.

———. 1990. *The Torii Ryūzō Photographic Record of East Asian Photography*. Vol. 3. Tokyo: University Museum.

Sachse, F. J. P. 1907. *Het Eiland Seran en Zijne Bewoners* [The Island of Seram and Its Inhabitants]. Leiden: E. J. Brill.

Salvador-Amores, Analyn. 2012. "The Recontextualization of *Burik* (Traditional Tattoos) of Kabayan Mummies in Benguet to Contemporary Practices." *Humanities Diliman* 9 (1): 55–94.

———. 2013. *Tapping Ink, Tattooing Identities: Tradition and Modernity in Contemporary Kalinga Society, North Luzon, Philippines*. Baguio: Cordillera Studies Center, University of the Philippines.

———. 2017. "*Burik:* Tattoos of the Ibaloy Mummies of Benguet, North Luzon, Philippines." In *Ancient Ink: The Archaeology of Tattooing*, edited by L. Krutak and A. Deter-Wolf, 37–55. Seattle: University of Washington Press.

Samadelli, Marco, Marcello Melis, Matteo Miccoli, Eduard Egarter Vigl, and Albert R. Zink. 2015. "Complete Mapping of the Tattoos of the 530-Year-Old Tyrolean Iceman." *Journal of Cultural Heritage* 16 (5): 753–758.

Sánchez, Matheo. 1711. *Vocabulario de la lengua Bisaya* [Vocabulary of the Bisaya Language]. Manila: Impresso en el Colegio de la Sagrada Compañía de Jesús, por Gaspar Aquino de Belén.

Sandin, Benedict. 1966. "Iban Hero Dreams and Apparitions." *Sarawak Museum Journal* 14:91–123.

———. 1980. *Iban Adat and Augury*. Pulau Pinang: Universiti Sains Malaysia.

Sardeshpande, S. C. 1987. *The Patkoi Nagas*. Delhi: Daya Publishing.

Saul, Jamie. 2005. *The Naga of Burma: Their Festivals, Customs and Way of Life*. Bangkok: Orchid Press.

———. 2011. "Tattoos of Sumba." *Visit Sumba Island*. http://visitsumba-indonesia.blogspot.com/2011/07/tattoos-of-sumba.html. Accessed July 9, 2021.

Sawyer, Frederic Henry Read. 1900. *The Inhabitants of the Philippines*. New York: Charles Scribner's Sons.

Schadenberg, Alexander. 1885. "Die Bewohner von Süd-Mindanao und der Insel Samal, nach eignen Erfahrungen: 1. Süd-Mindanao" [The Inhabitants of Southern Mindanao and the Island of Samal, according to My Own Experiences: Vol. 1. Southern Mindanao]. *Zeitschrift für Ethnologie* 17:8–37.

———. (1887) 1975. "Berlage zur Kentniss de Banao-Leute und der Guinaanen. Gran Cordillera Central, Insel Luzon, Philippinen" [The Banao People and the Guinaangs, Gran Cordillera Central, Luzon Island, Philippines]. In *German Travelers in the Cordillera (1860–1890)*, translated and annotated by W. H. Scott. Manila: Filipiniana Book Guild.

Schärer, Hans. 1963. *Ngaju Religion: The Conception of God among a South Borneo People*. The Hague: Martinus Nijhoff.

Scheans, Daniel J., and Karl Hutterer. 1970. "Some Oracion Tattoos from Samar." *Leyte-Samar Studies* 4 (1): 29–45.
Scheerer, Otto. 1904. *The Nabaloi Dialect.* Department of the Interior Ethnological Survey Publications 2 (2). Manila: Bureau of Public Printing.
Schefold, Reimar. 1980a. *Spielzeug für die Seelen: Kunst and Kultur der Mentawai-Inseln (Indonesia)* [Toys for the Soul: Art and Culture of the Mentawai Islands (Indonesia)]. Zürich: Museum Rietberg Zürich.
———. 1980b. "The Sacrifices of the Sakuddei (Mentawai Archipelago, Western Indonesia): An Attempt at Classification." In *Man, Meaning and History: Essays in Honour of H. G. Schulte Nordholt,* edited by R. Schefold, J. W. Schoorl, and J. Tennekes, 82–108. Verhandelingen van het Koninklijk Instituut voor Taal-, Land- en Volkenkunde, vol. 89. The Hague: Martinus Nijhoff.
———. 1989. "The Origins of the Woman on the Raft: On the Prehistory of the Mentawaians." In *Mentawai Identitaet und Wandel auf Indonesischen Ausseninseln* [Mentawai Identity and Change on the Indonesian Outer Islands], edited by W. Wagner, 1–26. Geographic Sheets, vol. 5. Bremen, Germany: Veroeffentlichungen aud dem Uebersee-Museum Bremen Reihen C Deutsche.
———. 1992. "Shamans on Siberut: Mediators between the Worlds." In *Mentawai Shaman: Keeper of the Rain Forest,* 105–117. New York: Aperture.
———. 2007. "Ambivalent Blessings: Head-Hunting on Siberut (Mentawai) in a Comparative Southeast Asian Perspective." *Anthropos* 102:479–494.
———. 2016. "General Introduction: Art and Its Themes in Indonesian Tribal Traditions." In *Eyes of the Ancestors: The Arts of Island and Southeast Asia at the Dallas Museum of Art,* edited by R. Schefold and S. G. Alpert, 16–28. Tokyo: Tuttle.
———. 2021. "*Jaraik:* Origin and Uses of an Ancient Mentawaian Design." *Art of the Ancestors.* https://www.artoftheancestors.com/blog/jaraik-mentawaian-design-reimar-schefold. Accessed May 29, 2016.
Schildkrout, Enid. 2001. "Body Art as Visual Language." *AnthroNotes* 22 (2). https://www.researchgate.net/publication/295919657_Body_Art_as_Visual_Language. Accessed June 5, 2017.
Schrock, Joann L., ed. 1966. *Minority Groups in the Republic of Vietnam.* Washington, DC: Department of the US Army.
Scott, James George. 1880. *The Burman: His Life and Notions.* Vol. 2. London: Macmillan.
Scott, William H. 1984. *Prehispanic Source Materials for the Study of Philippine History.* Manila: University of Santo Tomas Press.
———. 1994. *Barangay: Sixteenth-Century Philippine Culture and Society.* Quezon City, Philippines: Ateneo de Manila University Press.
Seligman, B. Z. 1963. "Social Organization." In *Ainu Creed and Cult,* edited by B. Z. Seligman, 141–158. New York: Columbia University Press.
Sellato, Bernard. 2012. "Mats of the Ngaju, Ot Danum, and Related Peoples." In *Plaited Arts from the Borneo Rainforest,* edited by B. Sellato, 349–357. Jakarta: Lontar Foundation/Honolulu: University of Hawai'i Press.
Shaogong, Han, ed. 2016. *Hainan dao lizu de shehui zuzhi he jingji zuzhi* [Social Organization and Economic Organization of the Li Nationality in Hainan Island]. By Kenji Okada and Kunio Odaka. Translated by Jin Shan. Haikou, China: Hainan Publishing.
Sharma, Rooplin. 2012. "Mo Naga (Moranngam Khaling) Profile: One of India's Best Tattoo Artist[s]" (online). http://e-pao.net/epSubPageExtractor.asp?src=features.Profile_of_Manipuri_Personalities.Mo_Naga_ Moranngam_Khaling_Profile_one_of_India_Best_Tattoo_Artist. Accessed June 30, 2018.

Shen, Xingshi. 2005. "Dulongzu wenmian xisu xianzhuang diaocha" [An Investigation into the Current Custom of Facial Tattooing among the Drung People]. *Anhui Shifan Daxue Xuebao* [Journal of Anhui Normal University] 33 (2): 243–246.

Sherman, Lucian, and Christine Sherman. 1922. *Im Stromgebiet des Irrawaddy, Birma und seine Frauenwelt* [In the Irrawaddy River Basin, Burma's Women's World]. Munich: Schloss.

Shibatani, Masayoshi. 1990. *The Languages of Japan*. Cambridge: Cambridge University Press.

Shimray, Atai. 2005. *Let Freedom Ring: Story of Naga Nationalism*. New Delhi: Promilla.

Shunai, Zhang, and Wu Simin. 2010. "Research on Frog Pattern in Li Brocade." *International Journal of Costume Culture* 13 (2): 82–87.

Siguret, J. 1937. *Territoires et populations des confins du Yunnan* [Territories and Populations of the Yunnan Borderlands]. 2 vols. Beijing: H. Vetch.

Simon, Edmund M. H. 1914. *Beiträge zur Kenntnis der Riukiu-Inseln* [Contributions to Knowledge of the Ryukyu Islands]. Leipzig: R. Voitländers.

Singer, Noel F. 1988. "Tattoo Weights from Burma." *Arts of Asia* 18 (2): 70–79.

Skinner, Alanson B. 1926. "Ethnology of the Ioway Indians." *Bulletin of the Public Museum of the City of Milwaukee* 5 (4): 181–351.

Smile Taiwan. 2019a. "Qiu Xiaofeng: The Handprint Is the Thread to Retrieve the Kite, So That the Paiwan People Can Also Find Their Way Home." *Smile Taiwan*, April 1, 2019. www.smiletaiwan.cw.com.tw/article/1862. Accessed May 10, 2020.

———. 2019b. "Handprint Is My ID Card! Paiwan Elder—Vuvu Ukani Tjavung." *Smile Taiwan*, April 1, 2019. www.smiletaiwan.cw.com.tw/article/1861. Accessed May 10, 2020.

Southwell, C. Hudson, comp. 1990. *Kayan-English Dictionary*. 2nd ed. Kuching, Malaysia: Sarawak Literary Society.

Starr, Frederick. 1904. *The Ainu Group at the Saint Louis Exposition*. Chicago: Open Court Company.

Stirn, Aglaja, and Peter van Ham. 2003. *The Hidden World of the Naga: Living Traditions on Northeast India and Burma*. Munich: Prestel.

Stresemann, Erwin. 1923. "Religiöse Gebräuche auf Seran" [Religious Customs on Seram]. *Tijdschrift voor Indische Taal-, Land-, en Volkenkunde* 62:305–424.

Stübel, Hans. 1937. *Die Li Stämme der Insel Hainan: Ein Betrag zur Volkskunde Südchinas* [The Li Tribes of Hainan Island: A Contribution to the Folklore of Southern China]. Berlin: Klinkhardt & Biermann.

Sugguiyao, Miguel. 1998. *The Kalinga Hilltribe of the Philippines*. 2nd ed. Baguio, Philippines: Unique Printing Press.

Sutter, Rebekka. 2008. "Shadows and Tigers: Concepts of Soul and Tiger-Men." In *Naga Identities: Changing Local Cultures in the Northeast of India*, edited by M. Oppitz, T. Kaiser, A. von Stockhausen, and M. Wettstein, 275–292. Ghent, Belgium: Snoeck.

Symes, Michael. 1800. *An Account of an Embassy to the Kingdom of Ava*. London: Nicol.

Taipei Times. 2008. "Atayal Woman Receives Full Facial Tattooing Tradition." *Taiwan News*, January 22, 2008. www.taipeitimes.com/News/taiwan/archives/2008/01/22/2003398275. Accessed February 10, 2016.

Taiwan Governor's Office. 1921. *Banzoku chôsa hôkoku sho: Paiwan zoku, Saiset zoku* [Report of an Investigation of the Savage Tribes: Paiwan Tribe, Saiset Tribe]. Taihoku.

Takayama, Jun. 1969. *Jōmonjin no irezumi: Kodai no shūzoku o saguru* [Tattoo of the Jomon People: Exploring Ancient Customs]. Tokyo: Kōdansha Shōwa.

Takenaka, Masami, Kazuharu Mine, Kazuhiko Tsuchimochi, and Kazuyuki Shimada. 2001. "Tooth Removal during Ritual Tooth Ablation in the Jomon Period." *Indo-Pacific Prehistory Association Bulletin* 21 (5): 49–52.

Tambiah, Stanley T. 1979. "A Performative Approach to Ritual." *Proceedings of the British Academy* 65:113–169.

Tanaka, Sakurako. 2000. "The Ainu of Tsugaru: The Indigenous History and Shamanism of Northern Japan." PhD diss., University of British Columbia.

Tannenbaum, N. 1987. "Tattoos: Invulnerability and Power in Shan Cosmology." *American Ethnologist* 14 (4): 693–711.

Tauern, Odo D. 1918. *Patasiwa und Patalima: Vom Molukkeneiland Seran und seinen Bewohnern* [Patasiwa and Patalima: From the Moluccan Island of Seram and Its Inhabitants]. Leipzig: Voigtländer.

Taylor, Paul M., and Lorraine V. Aragon. 1991. *The Java Sea: Art of Indonesia's Outer Islands.* Washington, DC: National Museum of Natural History, Smithsonian Institution.

Taylor, Rev. Richard. 1870. *Te Ika a Maui: Or, New Zealand and Its Inhabitants. Illustrating the Origin, Manners, Customs, Mythology, Religion . . . of the Maori and Polynesian Races in General; Together with the Geology, Natural History, Productions and Climate of the Country.* London: W. Macintosh and H. I. Jones.

Te Awekotuku, Ngahuia. 2006. "*Mata Ora*: Chiseling the Living Face—Dimensions of Maori Tattoo." In *Sensible Objects: Colonialism, Museums and Material Culture,* edited by E. Edwards, C. Gosden, and R. B. Phillips, 121–140. Oxford: Berg.

———. 2007. *Mau Moko: The World of Māori Tattoo.* Auckland: Penguin Group.

ten Kate, Herman F. C. 1894. "Beiträge zur Ethnographie der Timor-Gruppe I" [A Contribution to the Ethnography of the Timor Group I]. *Internationales Archiv für Ethnographie* 7:242–249.

———. 1895. "Beiträge zur Ethnographie der Timor-Gruppe II" [A Contribution to the Ethnography of the Timor Group II]. *Internationales Archiv für Ethnographie* 8:1–16.

Thanegi, Ma. 2014. "Körperkunst." In *Myanmar: Das Goldene Land* [Myanmar: The Golden Land], edited by I. de Castro and G. Noack, 39–47. Munich: Philipp von Zabern.

Thein, Aung. 2014. *Myanma Kwin Min Kyaung Dalae* [Myanmar Traditional Tattoo]. Yangon, Myanmar: Daw Khaing Khaing Oo/Bagan.

Thiel, Barbara. 1988. "Austronesian Origins and Expansion: The Philippine Archaeological Data." *Asian Perspectives: The Journal of Asia and the Pacific* 26:119–129.

Thomas, John. 2016. *Evangelising the Nation: Religion and the Formation of Naga Political Identity.* Abingdon, UK: Routledge.

Thomas, Nicholas, Anna Cole, and Bronwen Douglas. 2005. *Tattoo: Bodies, Art, and Exchange in the Pacific and the West.* Durham, NC: Duke University Press.

Thomas, Sharon. 1968. "Women's Tattoos of the Upper Rejang." *Sarawak Museum Journal* 16:209–234.

Tian Fu, Cheng, ed. 2010. *Li zu wen shen xin tan* [Discoveries of Li Tattoos]. Beijing: China Federation of Literary and Art.

Tichelman, Gerard L. 1939. "Dr. Carl Schuster on Bird-Designs in the Western Pacific: Indonesia-Melanesia-Polynesia." *Cultureel Indië* 1:232–235.

Tickle, Les. 1975. *Tau Kuka: A Tattooing of the People of Bellona Island.* Cultural Association of the Solomon Islands Special Issue.

Tillema, Hendrik F. 1930. "Tatoeëeren op Borneo" [Tattooing in Borneo]. *Nederlandsch-Indië Oud en Nieuw* 15:193–208.

———. 1936a. "Tatoeëeren bij de Dajaks: Be teekenis en oorsprong" [Tattooing among the Dayaks: Meaning and Origin]. *Natuur en Techniek* 6:214–216.
———. 1936b. "The Subtleties of Tattooing." *Nederlandsch-Indië Oud en Nieuw.* Yearbook 1936, 197–200.
———. 1936c. "Vom Tätowieren" [About Tattooing]. *Die Umschau* 40 (10): 190–192.
———. 1937. "The Kenya Dayak and His Magic." *Nederlandsch-Indië Oud en Nieuw* 22:95–98.
———. 1989. *A Journey among the Peoples of Central Borneo in Word and Picture,* edited by V. T. King. Singapore: Oxford University Press.
Tosabayashi, Yoshio. 1948. "Ainu irezumi moyō no kōsei" [Ainu Tattoo Composition]. *Minzokugaku kenkyū* 13 (4): 72–78.
Trimble, Nakkita. 2018. "The Wahlingigat: The Ancient Nisga'a Ancestors." In *Body Language: Reawakening Cultural Tattooing of the Northwest,* edited by B. Carter and D. Kaszas, 37–46. Vancouver, BC: Bill Reid Gallery of Northwest Coast Art.
Tuan, Le Anh. 2004. "An Investigation into the Changes in Meaning of the *Padil Yaya* Symbols in the Katu Culture." *Viet Nam Social Sciences* 104 (6): 45–60.
Tulius, Juniator. 2012. "Family Stories: Oral Tradition, Memories of the Past, and Contemporary Conflicts over Land in Mentawai—Indonesia." PhD diss., University of Leiden.
Tun Jugah Foundation. 1992. "Iban Oral Literature." *Borneo Research Bulletin* 24:92–111.
Turner, Edith. 1985. "Girl into Woman." *Anthropology and Humanism Quarterly* 10 (2): 27–32.
Ueno, K., and T. Yoshii. 1955. *Hidaka Ainu no irezumi kenkyū e no kōken* [A Contribution to Studies of Tattooing among the Hidaka Ainu]. Hokkaidōdaigaku igakubu kaibō gakka kara no hōkoku. New Series 20.
Ushinosuke, Mori. 1918. *Taiwan banzoku zufu* [Atlas of Taiwan Aboriginal Tribes]. Tokyo: Taiwan Old Habits Survey Association.
Vadan, Youbas, Wei Dao, and Yuma Dada, eds. 2008. *Tai ya au wun mian chi lao kou shu li shih ji ying siang ji lu cheng guo bao gao* [Study on Atayal Tattoo Patterns, Oral History, and History Research Report]. Tai'an Township, Miaoli County, Taiwan: Sheba National Park Administration, Conservation Research Report.
van Baarda, M. J. 1895. *Woordenlijst: Galelareesch-Hollandsche: Met ethnologische aanteekeningen, op de woorden, die daartoe aanleiding gaven* [Word List: Galelareesch-Dutch: With Ethnological Notes, on the Words That Gave Rise to It]. The Hague: Martinus Nijhoff.
van Beukering, J. A. 1941. "Een en ander het tatoueeren bij de Mentaweiers" [Aspects of Tattooing among the Mentawaians]. *Tijdschrift voor Indische Taal-, Land-, en Volkenkunde* 81:319–332.
van de Wetering, F. H. 1924. "Het Tatoueeren op Rote" [Tattooing on Rote]. *Bijdragen tot de Taal-, Land- en Volkenkunde* 80 (1): 23–32.
van Dinter, Maarten Hesselt. 2005. *The World of Tattoo: An Illustrated History.* Amsterdam: KIT.
van Gulik, Willem R. 1982. *Irezumi: The Pattern of Dermography in Japan.* Leiden: E. J. Brill.
van Ham, Peter, and Jamie Saul. 2008. *Expedition Naga: Diaries from the Hills in Northeast India, 1921–1937/2002–2006.* Woodbridge, UK: Antique Collectors' Club.
van Odijk, Antonius. 1925. "Ethnographische Gegevens over de Manobo's van Mindanao, Philippijnen" [Ethnographic Data about the Manobos of Mindanao, Philippines]. *Anthropos* 20 (5/6): 981–1000.
Vanoverbergh, Maurice. 1929. *Dress and Adornment in the Mountain Province of Luzon, Philippine Islands.* Washington, DC: Catholic Anthropological Conference.
———. 1953. "Religion and Magic among the Isneg: Part I: The Spirits." *Anthropos* 48 (1/2): 71–104.

———. 1954. "Religion and Magic among the Isneg: Part III: Public Sacrifices." *Anthropos* 49 (1/2): 233–275.
———. 1955a. "Isneg Tales." *Folklore Studies* 14:1–148.
———. 1955b. "Religion and Magic among the Isneg: Part V: Samples of Pakkáw." *Anthropos* 50 (1/3): 212–240.
———. 1955c. "Isneg Domestic Economy." *Annali Lateranensi* 18:119–256.
———. 1972a. "Kankanay Religion (Northern Luzon, Philippines)." *Anthropos* 67:72–128.
———. 1972b. *Isneg-English Vocabulary.* Honolulu: University of Hawai'i Press.
van Suchtelen, Bertho C. C. M. M. 1921. *Endeh (Flores)* [Ende (Flores)]. Weltevreden, Java: N. V. Uitgev Papyrus.
Vatter, Ernst. 1932. *Ata kiwan: Unbekannte bergvölker im tropischen Holland* [Ata Kiwan: Unknown Mountain Peoples of the Tropical Netherlands]. Leipzig: Bibliographisches Institut A. G.
Villegas, Dennis S. 2017. *You Shall Be as Gods: Anting-Anting and the Filipino Quest for Mystical Power.* Quezon City, Philippines: Vibal Foundation.
Vion, Anne-Marie. 1999. "The Southern Moluccas." In *Arts of the South Seas: Island Southeast Asia, Melanesia, Polynesia, Micronesia: The Collection of the Musée Barbier-Mueller,* 140–145. Munich: Prestel.
Vogelsanger, Cornelia. 1980. "A Sight for the Gods: Notes on the Social and Religious Meaning of Iban Ritual Fabrics." In *Indonesian Textiles,* edited by M. Gittinger, 115–126. Washington, DC: The Textile Museum.
Volz, Wilhelm. 1906. "Beiträge zur Anthropologie und Ethnographie von Indonesien: I. Zur Kenntnis der Mentaweiinseln" [Contributions to the Anthropology and Ethnography of Indonesia: 1. For Knowledge of the Mentawei Islands]. *Archiv für Anthropologie* 4:93–109.
von Fürer-Haimendorf, Christoph. 1936a. Notebook 3, record R70214. *The Nagas: Hill Peoples of Northeast India.* Rivers Videodisc Project, Cambridge University, UK. http://himalaya.socanth.cam.ac.uk/collections/naga/record/r70214.html. Accessed April 11, 2018.
———. 1936b. Notebook 6, record R70403. *The Nagas: Hill Peoples of Northeast India.* Rivers Videodisc Project, Cambridge University, UK. http://himalaya.socanth.cam.ac.uk/collections/naga/record/r70403.html. Accessed April 11, 2018.
———. 1936c. Notebook 7, record R70475. *The Nagas: Hill Peoples of Northeast India.* Rivers Videodisc Project, Cambridge University, UK. http://himalaya.socanth.cam.ac.uk/collections/naga/record/r70475.html. Accessed April 11, 2018.
———. 1936d. Notebook 8, record R70602. *The Nagas: Hill Peoples of Northeast India.* Rivers Videodisc Project, Cambridge University, UK. http://himalaya.socanth.cam.ac.uk/collections/naga/record/r70602.html. Accessed April 11, 2018.
———. 1937. Notebook 14, record R70876. *The Nagas: Hill Peoples of Northeast India.* Rivers Videodisc Project, Cambridge University, UK. http://himalaya.socanth.cam.ac.uk/collections/naga/record/r70876.html. Accessed April 11, 2018.
———. 1938a. "Unexplored Mountains of the Assam-Burma Border." *Geographical Journal* 91 (3): 201–219.
———. 1938b. "The *Morung* System of the Konyak Nagas, Assam." *Journal of the Royal Anthropological Institute of Great Britain and Ireland* 68:349–378.
———. 1962. *The Naked Nagas.* 2nd rev. Indian ed. Calcutta: Nagendra Misra.

———. 1967. *Morals and Merit: A Study of Values and Social Controls in South Asian Societies.* London: Weidenfeld and Nicolson.
von Petzinger, Genevieve. 2016. *The First Signs: Unlocking the Mysteries of the World's Oldest Symbols.* New York: Atria Books.
von Siebold, Heinrich. 1881. *Ethnologische Studien über die Aino auf der Insel Yesso* [Ethnological Studies on the Aino of Yesso Island]. Berlin: Verlag von Paul Parey.
Wagner, Wilfred. 2003. "The Mentawaian Sense of Beauty: Perceived through Western Eyes." *Indonesia and the Malay World* 31 (90): 199–220.
Wang, I-chun. 2015. "The Secularization of Identity in a Religious World: A Case Study of the Atayal Bienjing Village." PhD diss., Durham University.
Wang, Xianjun. 2016. *Li zu wen shen: Hai nan dao li zu de dun huang bi hua* [Li Nationality Tattoo: Dunhuang Murals of Li Nationality on Hainan Island]. Beijing: National Publishing House.
Wang, Xuexin. 2003. *Ri ju shi qi zhu miao di qu yuan zhu min shi liao hui bian yu yan jiu* [Historical Literature and Studies of the Aboriginal Groups in Hsinchu and Miaoli in the Japanese Period]. Vol. 1. Nantou, Taiwan: Taiwan Historica.
Ward, F. Kingdon. 1923. "From the Yangtze to the Irrawaddy." *Geographical Journal* 62 (1): 6–20.
———. 1924. *From China to Hkampti Long.* London: Edward Arnold.
Waterson, Roxana. 1989. "Hornbill, Naga and Cock in Sa'dan and Toraja Woodcarving Motifs." *Archipel* 38:53–73.
———. 2009. *Paths and Rivers: Sa'dan Toraja Society in Transformation.* Leiden: KITLV.
———. 2016. "The Art of Sulawesi." In *Eyes of the Ancestors: The Arts of Island Southeast Asia at the Dallas Museum of Art,* edited by R. Schefold and S. G. Alpert, 173–208. Tokyo: Tuttle.
Weber, Max W. C. 1890. *Ethnographische Notizen über Flores und Celebes* [Ethnographic Notes on Flores and Celebes]. Leiden: P. W. M. Trap.
Weidfeldt, Otto. 1914. *Wirtschaftliche, Rechtliche, und soziale Grundtatsachen und Grundformen der Atayalen auf Formosa* [Economic, Legal, and Social Basic Facts and Original Forms of the Atayal of Formosa]. Berlin: Behrend.
Win, Thin Lei, and Kelly Macnamara. 2016. "Leading the Creation Song." *The Kite Tales* (online). https://kite-tales.org/en/article/leading-creation-song. Accessed June 19, 2018.
Wise, James. 1883. *Notes on the Races, Castes, and Trades of Eastern Bengal.* London: Harrison and Sons.
Woods, Simon. 2012. "Writing on the Body: The Modern Morality of the Tattoo." In *Tattoos: Philosophy for Everyone. I Ink, Therefore I Am,* edited by R. Arp, 206–217. Chichester, UK: John Wiley & Sons.
Worchester, Dean. 1912. "Head-Hunters of Northern Luzon." *National Geographic Magazine* 23 (9): 833–930.
World Summit of Indigenous Cultures (WSIC). 2008. "Dali Yealo and Votu Sayum Votu." www.indigenous.pristine.net/events/2008/wsic/presentations/dali_and_sayum_zh-tw.html. Accessed February 22, 2021.
Wu, Fang-Chin, Chin-Wen Ho, Chang-En Pu, Kuang-Yu Hu, Sascha Willuweit, Lutz Roewer, and David Hwang Liu. 2010. "Y-chromosomal STRs Halotypes in the Taiwanese Population." *International Journal of Legal Medicine* 125 (1): 39–43.
Xia, Hu. (1908) 1994. "Nu Qiu bian'ai xiang qing" [Details on the Qiu and Nu Border]. In *Nujiang wenshi ziliao xuanji (1)* [Selected Cultural and Historical Materials of Nujiang], vol. 1, edited by Zhengxie Nujiangzhou weiyuanhui wenshi ziliao weiyuanhui, 113–134. Dehong, China: Dehong minzu chubanhe.

Xie, Anxie. 2019. *Decadent Atayal Culture of Face Tattoos Withering, Inheriting, or Changing.* Video documentary. 8:30 min. https://www.youtube.com/watch?v=fgNRVjtVncU. Accessed May 18, 2020.

Xueping, Wang, ed. 2001. *Li zu chuan tong wen hua* [Traditional Culture of the Li Group]. Beijing: Xinhua.

Yaling, Hu. 2012. *The Li and Miao Villages in Hainan.* Haikou, China: Hainan Publishing House.

Yamamoto, Yoshimi. 1995. "Yaeyama, Okinawa no irezumi ni tsuite—toku ni kekkon to minkan ryoho ni kanren suru" [On the Tattooing among the Yaeyama, Okinawa—Especially Related to Marriage and Folk Medicine]. *Seiji-gaku kenkyū ronshū* 2:41–63.

———. 1996. "Mon'yō no sekai-kan ichi Okinawashotō no irezumi ni kansuru ichikōsatsu" [A Cosmology of Tattooing: A Study of Tattooing in Okinawan Islands]. *Seiji-gaku kenkyū ronshū* 3:85–118.

Yap, Joanna. 2014. "Hidden Gems of Long Tanid." *Borneo Post Online.* https://www.theborneopost.com/2014/09/21/hidden-gems-of-long-tanid/. Accessed February 26, 2020.

Yoe, Shway (J. G. Scott). 1896. *The Burman: His Life and Notions.* London: Macmillan.

Yomitan-son Kyōiku I'inkai. 1982. *Okinawa no seijo girei: Okinawa hontō hajichi chōsa hōkokusho* [Okinawan Adult Ritual: Report on the Vanishing Tattoos of Okinawa Island]. Yomitan, Japan: Yomitan-son Kyōiku I'inkai.

Young, Henry W., ed. 1912. "Surprising the Barbarians of Formosa." *Popular Electricity* 5 (3): 218–219.

Yuan, Yuan. 2019. "Tattooed Life." *Beijing Review,* May 16, 2019. http://www.bjreview.com/Nation/201905/t20190510_800167529.html. Accessed December 4, 2020.

Zheng, Weichuan, ed. 2001. *Dulongzu: Gongshan Bingzhongluo xiang Xiaochala she* [The Dulong: The Xiaochala Commune, Bongzhonglo Township, Gongshan]. Kunming: Yunnan Daxue chubanshe.

Zhou, Huashan. 2004. *Wenmian nü zhi mi: 58 ge Dulongzu wenmian nü de kousu yanjiu* [The Riddle of the Face-Tattooed Women: An Oral Study of 58 Face-Tattooed Dulong Women]. Hong Kong: Minzu yanjiushe chubanshe.

Zhou, Yulin. 2015. "Wenmian nü: Dulong chuantong wenhua de huohuashi" [Face-Tattooed Women: The Living Fossils of Dulong Traditional Culture]. *Zhongguo Funü* [Chinese Women], November 17. http://paper.fnews.cc/content/2015–11/17/022192.html. Accessed November 21, 2016.

Zhou, Yunshui. 2009. "Wenhua jiaoliu yu dulungzu funü wenmian de yinyu" [Cultural Exchange and the Implicit Language of Dulong Women's Facial Tattoo]. *Sixiang Zhanxian* [Ideological Front] 35 (6): 14–16.

Zining, Li, and Wu Bailu, eds. 2015. *MaSpalaw (hui niangjia): Taiboguan Saixiazu wenwu fanxiang tezhan tulu* [MaSpalaw (Return to Mother's Home): Catalogue of the Saixia Cultural Relics Returning to Hometown Special Exhibit at the National Taiwan Museum]. Taipei: Guoli Taiwan Bowuguan.

Index

Page references in **bold** refer to illustrations.

About the Author

LARS KRUTAK is a research associate at the Museum of International Folk Art in Santa Fe, New Mexico. He is the author of several books on Indigenous tattoo culture and practice, including *Tattoo Traditions of Native North America: Ancient and Contemporary Expressions of Identity* and *Spiritual Skin: Magical Tattoos and Scarification*, and senior editor of *Ancient Ink: The Archaeology of Tattooing*, the first book dedicated to the archaeological study of tattooing. His writing has appeared in scientific journals, edited volumes, and popular magazines and his photography exhibited at the Museum of Modern Art in New York as well as the Pushkin Museum, the Humboldt Forum, Musée du quai Branly–Jacques Chirac, and other international institutions.